Readings in SPEECH RECOGNITION

Readings in SPEECH RECOGNITION

Edited by
Alex Waibel
& Kai-Fu Lee

Morgan Kaufmann Publishers, Inc.
San Mateo, California

Editor *Michael B. Morgan*
Production Manager *Shirley Jowell*
Copy Editor *Paul Medoff*
Cover Designer *Andrea Hendrick*
Typesetter *Technically Speaking Publications*

Library of Congress Cataloging-in-Publication Data

Readings in speech recognition/edited by Alexander Waibel
and Kai-Fu Lee.
p. cm.
ISBN 1-55860-124-4
1. Automatic speech recognition. 2. Speech processing systems.
I. Waibel, Alex. II. Lee, Kai-Fu.
TK7882.S65R42 1990
006.4'54--dc20

89-71329
CIP

MORGAN KAUFMANN PUBLISHERS, INC.
Editorial Office:
2929 Campus Drive
San Mateo, California
Order from:
P.O. Box 50490
Palo Alto, CA 94303-9953

Printed in the United States.

Preface

Despite several decades of research activity, speech recognition still retains its appeal as an exciting and growing field of scientific inquiry. Many advances have been made during these past decades; but every new technique and every solved puzzle opens a host of new questions and points us in new directions. Indeed, speech is such an intimate expression of our humanity—of our thoughts and emotions—that speech recognition is likely to remain an intellectual frontier as long as we search for a deeper understanding of ourselves in general, and intelligent behavior in particular. The recent decade has not rested on the laurels of past achievements; the field has grown substantially. A wealth of new ideas has been proposed, painful and sweet lessons learned and relearned, new ground broken, and victories won.

In the midst of our excitement and eagerness to expand our horizons, we conceived this book to fill a real need. We were motivated in part by the desire to tell the casual observer what speech recognition is all about. More importantly though, we found ourselves much too often at the copier, copying what we felt was important background reading for our colleagues and students, whom we have the good fortune to work with or supervise. To be sure, there are several good textbooks that introduce speech processing in general or describe speech recognition in the context of a particular approach or technique. Yet, because the field has grown so rapidly, none of these books covers the more recent developments and insights.

The present *Readings in Speech Recognition* is intended to fill this need by compiling a collection of seminal papers and key ideas in the field that we feel a serious student of speech recognition should know about. Rather than presenting the material in predigested form, we believe that readers should be exposed to the original papers and learn about the ideas themselves. There is no better way than to learn directly from the field's pioneering efforts—the motivations and inspirations, the points of view and controversies, the partial attempts, difficulties and failures, as well as the victories and breakthroughs. In a field as dynamic as speech recognition, learning about the problems and being exposed to the creative process of solving them is just as important as learning about the current methods themselves. In order to make this book timely, we have purposely included not only classic papers but also a number of important recent developments, thus providing an up-to-date overview of the latest state of the art.

Beyond collecting some key papers, we have attempted to organize the major schools of thought into individual chapters and to give the reader perspective in the form of book and chapter introductions. The introductions highlight for each chapter some of the major insights, points of view, differences, similarities, strengths, and weaknesses of each technique presented. It is our hope that the casual reader will find these introductions useful as a quick guided tour and as an entry for selective reading to satisfy his or her curiosity about aspects of the field. For the serious student or system developer, we hope that the introductions help to pass on some of the hard-learned lessons of research in decades past, provide pointers to important detail, and put any one particular technique into an overall perspective.

In editing this book, we have profited immensely from our colleagues, students and friends. In particular, the detailed comments and suggestions by several known leaders in the field who have reviewed our initial outline have added considerable balance and quality to this book—we gratefully acknowledge their contributions. We would like to thank Fred Jelinek and Erik McDermott for providing us with two original contributions for this volume. We are particularly indebted to Prof. Raj Reddy, one of the founders and pioneers of speech recognition. We were both fortunate to have grown into this field under his supervision during our own student years. Special thanks are also due to Mike Morgan and Shirley Jowell for their persistent reminders to keep moving ahead on draft revisions and organization and their tireless efforts to get this book to press in a timely fashion. We would also like to thank IEEE for giving us permission to reproduce their publications. Last, but not least, we would like to thank our wives, Naomi and Shen-Ling, for their patience during the preparation of this book.

Contents

Chapter 7 Connectionist Approaches

Chapter 8 Language Processing for Speech Recognition

Chapter 1

Why Study Speech Recognition?

1. Introduction

The goal of automatic speech recognition is to develop techniques and systems that enable computers to accept speech input. The problem of speech recognition has been actively studied since the 1950's, and it is natural to ask why one should continue studying speech recognition. Does it have practical utility? Is it interesting in the first place? What lessons will we learn from exploring the questions in speech recognition? In light of past activity, what aspects of the problem have already been solved? What are the challenges for future research? Do the rewards warrant our continued efforts?

We firmly believe that automatic speech recognition is a very rich field for both practical and intellectual reasons. Practically, speech recognition will solve problems, improve productivity, and change the way we run our lives. Intellectually, speech recognition holds considerable promise as well as challenges in the years to come for scientists and product developers alike.

1.1 Practical Utility

The performance of speech recognizers has improved dramatically due to recent advances in speech science and computer technology. With continually improving algorithms and faster computers, it appears that man–machine communication by voice will be a reality within our lifetime.

Even in the short term, many speech recognition applications will be possible. Information retrieval is a major component of these applications. For example, simple inquiries about bank balance, movie schedules, and phone call transfers can already be handled by small-to-medium sized vocabulary, speaker-independent, telephone-speech recognizers. While information retrieval is often telephone based, another application, data entry, has the luxury of using high-quality speech. Voice-activated data entry is particularly useful in applications such as medical and darkroom applications, where hands and eyes are unavailable as normal input medium, or in hands-busy or eyes-busy command-and-control applications. Speech could be used to provide more accessibility for the handicapped (wheelchairs, robotic aids, etc.) and to create high-tech amenities (intelligent houses, cars, etc.).

Whereas these short-term applications will increase productivity and convenience, more evolved prototypes could in the long-run profoundly change our society. A futuristic application is the *dictation machine* that accurately transcribes arbitrary speech. Such a device can further be extended to an *automatic ear* that "hears" for the deaf. An even more ambitious application is the *translating telephone* [Kurematsu88] that allows interlingual communication. The translating telephone requires not only speech *recognition*, but also speech *synthesis*, *language understanding* and *translation*. Finally, the ultimate *conversational computer* has all of these capabilities, as well as the ability of thought. Computers that listen and talk are the ultimate application of speech recognition.

1.2 The Intellectual Challenge and Opportunity

Like many frontiers of artificial intelligence, speech recognition is also still in its infancy. Speech and language are perhaps the most evident expression of human thought and intelligence—the creation of machines that fully emulate this ability poses challenges that reach far beyond the present state of the art.

The study of speech recognition and understanding holds intellectual challenges that branch off into a large spectrum of diverse scientific disciplines. Time and again the field has fruitfully and productively benefited from sciences as diverse as computer science, electrical engineering, biology, psychology, linguistics, statistics, philosophy, physics and mathematics. Among the more influencial activities within these disciplines are work in signal processing, pattern recognition, artificial intelligence, information theory, probability theory, computer algorithms, physiology, phonetics, syntactic theory, and acoustics. Speech-recognition research continues to be influenced and driven by scientists with different backgrounds and training, who have contributed a variety of important intuitions and who, in turn, have motivated aspects of ongoing research in their own fields.

The questions raised range from philosophical questions on the nature of mind to practical design consideration and implementational issues. Motivated by the desire to understand human intelligence, speech recognition can provide a good testing ground for an otherwise introspective and potentially subjective undertaking. Engineering design, in turn, is always evaluated against its progress toward the ultimate goal—unrestricted, free communication between man and machine—in a changing and uncertain world. This interplay between different intellectual concerns, scientific approaches, and models, and its potential impact in society make speech recognition one of the most challenging, stimulating, and exciting fields today.

2. Dimensions of Difficulty in Speech Recognition

Considering the immense amount of research over the last three decades, one may wonder why speech recognition is still considered an unsolved problem. As early as 1950s, simple recognizers have been built, yielding credible performance. But it was soon found that the techniques used in these systems were not easily extensible to more sophisticated systems. In particular, several dimensions emerged that introduce serious design difficulties or significantly degrade recognition performance. Most notably, these dimensions include

- Isolated, connected, and continuous speech
- Vocabulary size
- Task and language constraints
- Speaker dependence or independence
- Acoustic ambiguity, confusability
- Environmental noise.

We will now explain the difficulty involved in each of these areas.

The first question one should ask about a recognizer or a task is: *is the speech connected or spoken one word at a time?* Continuous-speech recognition (CSR) is considerably more difficult than isolated word recognition (IWR). First, word boundaries are typically not detectable in continuous speech. This results in additional confusable words and phrases (for example; "youth in Asia" and "Euthenasia"), as well as an exponentially larger search space. The second problem is that there is much greater variability in continuous speech due to stronger coarticulation (or inter-phoneme effects) and poorer articulation ("did you" becomes "didja").

A second dimension of difficulty is the size of the vocabulary. The vocabulary size varies inversely with the system accuracy and efficiency—more words introduce more confusion and require more time to process. Exhaustive search in very large vocabularies is typically unmanageable. The collection of sufficient training data becomes practically more difficult. Finally, word templates (or models) are untrainable and wasteful. Instead, one must turn to smaller subword units (phonemes, syllables), which may be more ambiguous and harder to detect and recognize. In order to realize a large vocabulary system, research in compact representation, search reduction, and generalizable subword units is essential.

Vocabulary size alone is an inadequate measure of a task's difficulty, because in many applications not all words are legal (or active) at a given time. For example, a sentence like "*Sleep roses dangerously young colorless*" need not be searched because of its illegal syntactic construction. Similarly, a sentence like "*Colorless yellow ideas sleep furiously*" is syntactically sound, but semantically absurd. A system with a semantic component may eliminate such sentences from consideration. Finally, a sentence like *"I look forward to seeing you."* is much more likely to occur than *"Abductive mechanism is used in model generative reasoning,"* although both are meaningful sentences. A system with a probabilistic language model can effectively use this knowledge to rank sentences. All of the above examples require use of higher-level knowledge to constrain or rank acoustic matches. These knowledge sources, or language models can reduce an impossible task to a trivial one, but in so doing, severely limit the input style. The challenge in language modeling is to derive a language model that provides maximum constraint while allowing maximum freedom of input. Like the vocabulary size, the constraining power of a language model can be measured by *perplexity*[1], roughly the average number of words that can occur at any decision point.

In addition to vocabulary and linguistic constraints, there are a number of other constraints that can affect accuracy and robustness. The most prominent issue is that of *speaker dependence* as opposed to *speaker independence*. A speaker-dependent system uses speech from the target speaker to learn its model parameters. This strategy leads to good accuracy, but requires an inconvenient period for each new speaker. On the other hand, a speaker-independent system is trained once and for all, and must model a variety of speakers' voices. Due to their increased variability, speaker-independent systems are typically less accurate than speaker-dependent systems. In practice, some applications can be speaker dependent, while others require speaker independence. Both types of systems have been built and studied extensively.

Speech-recognition-system performance is also significantly affected by the acoustic confusability or ambiguity of the vocabulary to be recognized. While some recognizers may achieve respectable performance over relatively unambiguous words (e.g., "zero," though "nine"), such systems may not necessarily deliver acceptable recognition rates for confusable vocabularies (e.g., the words for the alphabetic letters, B, D, E, P, T, C, Z, V, G). A confusable vocabulary requires detailed high-performance acoustic pattern analysis.

Another source of recognition-system performance degradation can be described as variability and noise. Some examples include environmental noises (e.g., factory floor, cockpit, door slams), crosstalk (several people may be talking simultaneously), differing microphone characteristics (headset microphone, telephone receiver, table microphones), speaker induced noise (lipsmacks, pops, clicks, caughing, sneezing), speaking rate, and speaker stress (emotional, physiological).

With so many dimensions of difficulty, speech recognizers naturally have a wide range of accuracies. For example, for recognition of high-quality, read, legal credit-card numbers, a sentence accuracy of over 99.9% can be reached. On the end of the spectrum, recognition of noisy conversational speech with infinite vocabulary and no grammar far exceeds the capabilities of any system to date. While the ultimate goal of truly unrestricted, spontaneous, speech understanding may require decades of further research, many useful applications are achievable today, since most applications can impose restrictions along some of the dimensions outlined here. Credit-card numbers, telephone numbers, and zip codes, for example, require only a small vocabulary. Similarly, dictation may be limited, in some cases, to a "master's voice;" or follow a typical limited grammar, style, or vocabulary.

3. The Chapters of this Book

This book is intended to cover background material on speech recognition. We try to provide a cross section of today's most promising ideas and follow the evolution of speech recognition research in the past 20 years.

Chapter 2 includes two papers on the *background* of the speech recognition problem. They describe in greater detail the motivation, the difficulty, and the missing science in speech.

Chapter 3 describes the *front end* of speech recognizers, or *speech analysis*. Four papers here describe the most promising and popular digital representations of speech as used in most speech-recognition systems today.

Chapter 4 begins a four-part "schools of thought in speech recognition." This chapter describes the *template-based approach*, where units of speech (usually words) are represented by templates in the same form as the speech input itself. Distance metrics are used to compare templates to find the best match, and dynamic programming is used to resolve the problem of temporal variability. Template-based approaches have been successful, particularly for simple applications requiring minimal overhead.

1. See Paper 8.1 for a precise definition.

One criticism of template-based techniques was that they do not facilitate the use of human speech knowledge. Chapter 5 describes the *knowledge-based approach*, proposed in the 1970s and early 1980s. The pure knowledge-based approach emulates human speech knowledge using expert systems. Rule-based systems have had only limited success. A more successful approach segregates knowledge from algorithms and integrates knowledge into other mathematically sound approaches. The addition of knowledge was found to improve other approaches substantially.

Another weakness of the template-based approach is its limited ability to generalize. Chapter 6 describes the *stochastic approach*, which is somewhat similar to the template-based approach. One major difference is that probabilistic models (typically hidden Markov models, or HMMs) are used. HMMs are based on a sound probabilistic framework, which can model the uncertainty inherent in speech recognition. HMMs have an integrated framework for simultaneously solving the segmentation and the classification problem, which makes them particularly suitable for continuous-speech recognition. Most successful large-scale systems today use a stochastic approach.

One characteristic of HMMs is that they make certain assumptions about the structure of speech recognition, and then estimate system parameters as though the structures were correct. This has the advantage of reducing the learning problem, but the disadvantage of relying on often-incorrect assumptions. Chapter 7 describes the *connectionist approach*, which differs from HMMs in that many of these assumptions need not be made. Connectionist approaches use distributed representations of many simple nodes, whose connections are trained to recognize speech. Connectionist approaches is a most recent development in speech recognition. While no fully integrated large-scale connectionist systems have been demonstrated yet, recent research efforts have shown considerable promise. Some of the problems that remain to be overcome include reducing training time and better modeling of sequential constraints.

Spoken sentences always contain ambiguities that cannot be resolved by pure word-level acoustic-phonetic recognition. Successful sentence recognition must therefore incorporate constraints that transcend this level, including syntactic, semantic, and prosodic constraints. Chapter 8 on language processing reviews papers addressing this concern. Indeed, most of the best current large-scale recognition systems succeed by taking advantage of powerful language models.

Chapter 9, finally, gives a selection of papers that represents some of the seminal speech-recognition systems developed in the past two decades. The papers presented here are by no means a complete list of existing systems. Rather, we attempt to give a sample of some of the more-successful systems that have extended recognition capabilities along the dimensions discussed above while maintaining high recognition accuracy.

4. Further Study

The primary sources of information on speech recognition in the U.S. are *IEEE Transactions on Acoustics, Speech,* and *Signal Processing (ASSP), Computer Speech and Language*, and *Journal of the Acoustical Society of America (ASA)*. *IEEE Transactions on ASSP* is an engineering journal that covers topics beyond speech recognition and has the widest readership. *Computer Speech and Language*, published by Academic Press, is a newer quarterly journal devoted to the processing of speech and language. By comparison, the *Journal of the ASA* contains fewer speech-recognition-system articles and emphasizes human-speech production, perception, and processing papers. The *IEEE ASSP Magazine* and the *Proceedings of the IEEE* also have special issues devoted to speech and speech recognition. Speech articles have also appeared in other IEEE Transactions, such as *Pattern Analysis* and *Machine Intelligence, Computer, Information Theory, Systems, Man, and Cybernetics*, and *Communication*. In Europe, the largest publication is the multinational *Speech Communications* published by the European Association of Signal Processing. Another publication is the journal of the British *IEE*. In Japan, major activity is reported in the *Journal of the Acoustical Society of Japan (ASJ)* and the journal of the *IECE*.

Major conferences which report research in speech recognition include: the IEEE; the International Conference on Acoustics, Speech, and Signal Processing (ICASSP); Acoustical Society of America; Speech Tech.; Eurospeech (in Europe); and International Conference on Spoken Language Processing (in Japan). Numerous other conference organized in Europe and Japan (such as the ASJ and the IECE) are held in their own languages.

Because speech is a relatively young science, most of the recent research is found in the journals and conferences described above. There are a few books that cover all aspects of speech in general, including speech communication, processing, synthesis and coding, such as [Flanagan 72], [Rabiner 78], [Oshaughnessy 87], and [Furui 89]. In addition, there are a number of earlier anthologies similar to this one available for further study. Four of these, edited by Reddy [Reddy 75], Lea [Lea 80], Dixon and Silverman [Dixon 79], and Cole [Cole 80] focus on speech recognition. Another anthology edited by Fallside and Woods [Fallside 83] contains papers that contributed to a speech course. Finally, two books edited by Perkell and Klatt [Perkell 86] and Furui and Sondhi [Furui 90] have somewhat different emphases, but both contain substantial papers on speech recognition.

References

[Cole 80] Cole, R.A. *Perception and Production of Speech.* Lawrence Erlbaum Associates, Hillsdale, N.J., 1980.

[Dixon 79] Dixon, N.R. and Martin, T.B. *Automatic Speech and Speaker Recognition.* IEEE Press, New York, 1979.

[Fallside 83] Fallside, F., Woods, W.A. *Computer Speech Processing.* Prentice-Hall International, Englewood Cliffs, N.J., 1983.

[Flanagan 72] Flanagan, J.L. *Speech Analysis; Synthesis and Perception.* Springer-Verlag, Berlin, 1972.

[Furui 89] Furui, S. *Digital Speech Processing.* Marcel Dekker, Inc., New York, 1989.

[Furui 90] Furui, S., Sondhi, M. *Recent Progress in Speech Signal Processing.* Marcel Dekker, Inc., N.J., 1990.

[Kurematsu 88] Kurematsu, A. A Perspective of Automatic Interpreting Telephony. *Journal of the Inst. of Electronics*, Information and Communication Engineering, August, 1988.

[Lea 80] Lea, W.A. *Trends in Speech Recognition.* Speech Science Publishers, Apple Valley, Minn. 1980.

[Oshaughnessy 87] O'Shaughnessy, D. *Speech Communication; Human and Machine.* Addison Wesley, Reading, Mass., 1987.

[Perkell 86] Perkell, J.S., Klatt, D.M. *Variability and Invariance in Speech Processes.* Lawrence Erlbaum Associates, Hillsdale, N.J., 1986.

[Rabiner 78] Rabiner, L.R., Shafer, R.W. *Digital Processing of Speech Signals.* Prentice-Hall International, London, 1978.

[Reddy 75] Reddy, D. R. (editor). *Speech Recognition.* Academic Press, New York, 1975.

Chapter 2

Problems and Opportunities

Introduction

Why is speech recognition so difficult and still a subject of so much study? Human beings grow up learning to speak with no apparent instruction of programming and communicate with each other via speech with remarkable ease. Fast, efficient, reliable speech is a critical part of intelligent behavior and of human self-expression. So much is speech a central part of our humanity that the complexities of speech understanding have always been vastly underestimated, despite several decades of research. We begin this book with two papers that give a general introduction to the problem of speech recognition, its difficulties, and its potential. *Speech Recognition by Machine: A Review*, by Raj Reddy is a classic that, many years later, still holds fundamental insights and lessons in the field. *The Value of Speech Recognition Systems* by Wayne Lea discusses the value and potential of machines capable of recognizing and conversing with humans by way of speech.

Speech Recognition by Machine: A Review

D. RAJ REDDY

Abstract—**This paper provides a review of recent developments in speech recognition research. The concept of sources of knowledge is introduced and the use of knowledge to generate and verify hypotheses is discussed. The difficulties that arise in the construction of different types of speech recognition systems are discussed and the structure and performance of several such systems is presented. Aspects of component subsystems at the acoustic, phonetic, syntactic, and semantic levels are presented. System organizations that are required for effective interaction and use of various component subsystems in the presence of error and ambiguity are discussed.**

I. Introduction

THE OBJECT of this paper is to review recent developments in speech recognition. The Advanced Research Projects Agency's support of speech understanding research has led to a significantly increased level of activity in this area since 1971. Several connected speech recognition systems have been developed and demonstrated. The role and use of knowledge such as acoustic-phonetics, syntax, semantics, and context are more clearly understood. Computer programs for speech recognition seem to deal with ambiguity, error, and nongrammaticality of input in a graceful and effective manner that is uncommon to most other computer programs. Yet there is still a long way to go. We can handle relatively restricted task domains requiring simple grammatical structure and a few hundred words of vocabulary for single trained speakers in controlled environments, but we are very far from being able to handle relatively unrestricted dialogs from a large population of speakers in uncontrolled environments. Many more years of intensive research seem necessary to achieve such a goal.

Sources of Information: The primary sources of information in this area are the *IEEE Transactions on Acoustics, Speech, and Signal Processing* (pertinent special issues: vol. 21, June 1973; vol. 23, Feb. 1975) and the *Journal of the Acoustical Society of America* (in particular, Semiannual Conference Abstracts which appear with January and July issues each year; recently they have been appearing as spring and fall supplements). Other relevant journals are *IEEE Transactions* (Computer; Information Theory; and Systems, Man, and

Manuscript received September 1, 1975; revised November 19, 1975. This work was supported in part by the Advanced Research Projects Agency and in part by the John Simon Guggenheim Memorial Foundation.

The author is with the Computer Science Department, Carnegie-Mellon University, Pittsburgh, PA 15213.

Originally appeared in IEEE Proceedings 64(4):502–531, April, 1976.

Cybernetics), *Communications of ACM, International Journal of Man–Machine Studies, Artificial Intelligence,* and *Pattern Recognition.*

The books by Flanagan [44], Fant [40], and Lehiste [84] provide extensive coverage of speech, acoustics, and phonetics, and form the necessary background for speech recognition research. Collections of papers, in the books edited by David and Denes [25], Lehiste [83], Reddy [121], and Wathen-Dunn [158], and in conference proceedings edited by Erman [34] and Fant [41], provide a rich source of relevant material. The articles by Lindgren [88], Hyde [66], Fant [39], Zagoruiko [171], Derkach [27], Hill [63], and Otten [113] cover the research progress in speech recognition prior to 1970 and proposals for the future. The papers by Klatt [74] and Wolf [163] provide other points of view of recent advances.

Other useful sources of information are research reports published by various research groups active in this area (and can be obtained by writing to one of the principal researchers given in parentheses): Bell Telephone Laboratories (Denes, Flanagan, Fujimura, Rabiner); Bolt Beranek and Newman, Inc. (Makhoul, Wolf, Woods); Carnegie-Mellon University (Erman, Newell, Reddy); Department of Speech Communication, KTH, Stockholm (Fant); Haskins Laboratories (Cooper, Mermelstein); IBM Research Laboratories (Bahl, Dixon, Jelinek); M.I.T. Lincoln Laboratories (Forgie, Weinstein); Research Laboratory of Electronics, M.I.T. (Klatt); Stanford Research Institute (Walker); Speech Communication Research Laboratory (Broad, Markel, Shoup); System Development Corporation (Barnett, Ritea); Sperry Univac (Lea, Medress); University of California, Berkeley (O'Malley); Xerox Palo Alto Research Center (White); and Threshold Technology (Martin). In addition there are several groups in Japan and Europe who publish reports in national languages and English. Complete addresses for most of these groups can be obtained by referring to author addresses in the *IEEE Trans. Acoust., Speech, Signal Processing*, June 1973 and Feb. 1975. For background and introductory information on various aspects of speech recognition we recommend the tutorial-review papers on "Speech understanding systems" by Newell, "Parametric representations of Speech" by Schafer and Rabiner, "Linear prediction in automatic speech recognition" by Makhoul, "Concepts for Acoustic–Phonetic recognition" by Broad and Shoup, "Syntax, Semantics and Speech" by Woods, and "System organization for speech understanding" by Reddy and Erman, all appearing in *Speech Recognition: Invited Papers of the IEEE Symposium* [121].

Scope of the Paper: This paper is intended as a review and not as an exhaustive survey of all research in speech recognition. It is hoped that, upon reading this paper, the reader will know what a speech recognition system consists of, what makes speech recognition a difficult problem, and what aspects of the problem remain unsolved. To this end we will study the structure and performance of some typical systems, component subsystems that are needed, and system organization that permits effective interaction and use of the components. We do not attempt to give detailed descriptions of systems or mathematical formulations, as these are available in published literature. Rather, we will mainly present distinctive and novel features of selected systems and their relative advantages.

Many of the comments of an editorial nature that appear in this paper represent one point of view and are not necessarily shared by all the researchers in the field. Two other papers appearing in this issue, Jelinek's on statistical approaches and Martin's on applications, augment and complement this paper. Papers by Flanagan and others, also appearing in this issue, look at the total problem of man–machine communication by voice.

A. The Nature of the Speech Recognition Problem

The main goal of this area of research is to develop techniques and systems for speech input to machines. In earlier attempts, it was hoped that learning how to build simple recognition systems would lead in a natural way to more sophisticated systems. Systems were built in the 1950's for vowel recognition and digit recognition, producing creditable performance. But these techniques and results could not be extended and extrapolated toward larger and more sophisticated systems. This had led to the appreciation that linguistic and contextual cues must be brought to bear on the recognition strategy if we are to achieve significant progress. The many dimensions that affect the feasibility and performance of a speech recognition system are clearly stated in Newell [108].

Fig. 1 characterizes several different types of speech recognition systems ordered according to their intrinsic difficulty. There are already several commercially available isolated word recognition systems today. A few research systems have been developed for restricted connected speech recognition and speech understanding. There is hope among some researchers that, in the not too distant future, we may be able to develop interactive systems for taking dictation using a restricted vocabulary. Unlimited vocabulary speech understanding and connected speech recognition systems seem feasible to some, but are likely to require many years of directed research.

The main feature that is used to characterize the complexity of a speech recognition task is whether the speech is connected or is spoken one word at a time. In connected speech, it is difficult to determine where one word ends and another begins, and the characteristic acoustic patterns of words exhibit much greater variability depending on the context. *Isolated word recognition systems* do not have these problems since words are separated by pauses.

The second feature that affects the complexity of system is the vocabulary size. As the size or the confusability of a vocabulary increases, simple brute-force methods of representation and matching become too expensive and unacceptable. Techniques for compact representation of acoustic patterns of words, and techniques for reducing search by constraining the number of possible words that can occur at a given point, assume added importance.

Just as vocabulary is restricted to make a speech recognition problem more tractable, there are several other aspects of the problem which can be used to constrain the speech recognition task so that what might otherwise be an unsolvable problem becomes solvable. The rest of the features in Fig. 1, i.e., task-specific knowledge, language of communication, number and cooperativeness of speakers, and quietness of environment, represent some of the commonly used constraints in speech recognition systems.

One way to reduce the problems of error and ambiguity resulting from the use of connected speech and large vocabularies is to use all the available task-specific information to reduce search. The *restricted speech understanding systems* (Fig. 1, line 3) assume that the speech signal does not have all the necessary information to uniquely decode the message and

	Mode of Speech	Vocabulary Size	Task Specific Information	Language	Speaker	Environment
Word recognition-isolated (WR)	isolated words	10-300	limited use	—	cooperative	—
Connected speech recognition-restricted (CSR)	connected speech	30-500	limited use	restricted command language	cooperative	quiet room
Speech understanding-restricted (SU)	connected speech	100-2000	full use	English-like	not uncooperative	—
Dictation machine-restricted (DM)	connected speech	1000-10000	limited use	English-like	cooperative	quiet room
Unrestricted speech understanding (USU)	connected speech	unlimited	full use	English	not uncooperative	—
Unrestricted connected speech recognition (UCSR)	connected speech	unlimited	none	English	not uncooperative	quiet room

Fig. 1. Different types of speech recognition systems ordered according to their intrinsic difficulty, and the dimensions along which they are usually constrained. Vocabulary sizes given are for some typical systems and can vary from system to system. It is assumed that a cooperative speaker would speak clearly and would be willing to repeat or spell a word. A not uncooperative speaker does not try to confuse the system but does not want to go out of his way to help it either. In particular, the system would have to handle "uhms" and "ahs" and other speech-like noise. The "–" indicates an "unspecified" entry variable from system to system.

that, to be successful, one must use all the available sources of knowledge to infer (or deduce) the intent of the message [107]. The performance criterion is somewhat relaxed in that, as long as the message is understood, it is not important to recognize each and every phoneme and/or word correctly. The requirement of using all the sources of knowledge, and the representation of the *task*, *conversational context*, *understanding*, and *response generation*, all add to the difficulty and overall complexity of speech understanding systems.

The *restricted connected speech recognition systems* (Fig. 1, line 2) keep their program structure simple by using only some task-specific knowledge, such as restricted vocabulary and syntax, and by requiring that the speaker speak clearly and use a quiet room. The simpler program structure of these systems provides an economical solution in a restricted class of connected speech recognition tasks. Further, by not being task-specific, they can be used in a wider variety of applications without modification.

The restricted speech understanding systems have the advantage that by making effective use of all the available knowledge, including semantics, conversational context, and speaker preferences, they can provide a more flexible and hopefully higher performance system. For example, they usually permit an English-like grammatical structure, do not require the speaker to speak clearly, and permit some nongrammaticality (including babble, mumble, and cough). Further, by paying careful attention to the task, many aspects of error detection and correction can be handled naturally, thus providing a graceful interaction with the user.

The *(restricted) dictation machine* problem (Fig. 1, line 4) requires larger vocabularies (1000 to 10 000 words). It is assumed that the user would be willing to spell any word that is unknown to the system. The task requires an English-like syntax, but can assume a cooperative speaker speaking clearly in a quiet room.

The *unrestricted speech understanding* problem requires unlimited vocabulary connected speech recognition, but permits the use of all the available task-specific information. The most difficult of all recognition tasks is the *unrestricted connected speech recognition* problem which requires unlimited vocabulary, but does not assume the availability of any task-specific information.

We do not have anything interesting to say about the last three tasks, except perhaps speculatively. In Section II, we will study the structure and performance of several systems of the first three types (Fig. 1), i.e., isolated word recognition systems, restricted connected speech recognition systems, and restricted speech understanding systems.

In general, for a given system and task, performance depends on the size and speed of the computer and on the accuracy of the algorithm used. Accuracy is often task dependent. (We shall see in Section II that a system which gives 99-percent accuracy on a 200-word vocabulary might give only 89-percent accuracy on a 36-word vocabulary.) Accuracy versus response time tradeoff is also possible, i.e., it is often possible to tune a system and adjust thresholds so as to improve the response time while reducing accuracy and vice versa.

Sources of Knowledge: Many of us are aware that a native speaker uses, subconsciously, his knowledge of the language, the environment, and the context in understanding a sentence. These sources of knowledge (KS's) include the characteristics of speech sounds (*phonetics*), variability in pronunciations (*phonology*), the stress and intonation patterns of speech (*prosodics*), the sound patterns of words (*lexicon*), the grammatical structure of language (*syntax*), the meaning of words and sentences (*semantics*), and the context of conversation (*pragmatics*). Fig. 2 shows the many dimensions of variability of these KS's; it is but a slight reorganization (to correspond to the sections of this paper) of a similar figure appearing in [108].

1. Performance	Nature of input Response time Accuracy	Isolated words? connected speech? Real time? close to real-time? no hurry? Error-free (>99.9%)? almost error-free (>99%)? occasional error (>90%)?
2. Source characteristics (acoustic knowledge)	Acoustic analysis Noise sources Speaker characteristics	Airconditioning noise? computer room? reverberation? Dialect? sex? age? cooperative? High quality microphone? telephone? Spectrum? formants? zerocrossings? LPC?
3. Language characteristics (phonetic knowledge)	Features Phones Phonology Word realization	Voiced? energy? stress? intonation? Number? distinguishability? Phone realization rules? junction rules? Insertion, deletion and change rules? Word hypothesis? word verification?
4. Problem characteristics (task specific knowledge)	Size of vocabulary Confusability of vocabulary Syntactic support Semantic and contextual support	10? 100? 1,000? 10,000? High? what equivalent vocabulary? Artificial language? free English? Constrained task? open semantics?
5. System characteristics	Organization Interaction	Strategy? representation? Graceful interaction with user? graceful error recovery?

Fig. 2. Factors affecting feasibility and performance of speech recognition systems. (Adapted from Newell *et al.* [108].)

To illustrate the effect of some of these KS's, consider the following sentences.

1) Colorless paper packages crackle loudly.
2) Colorless yellow ideas sleep furiously.
3) Sleep roses dangerously young colorless.
4) Ben burada ne yaptigimi bilmiyorum.

The first sentence, though grammatical and meaningful, is pragmatically implausible. The second is syntactically correct but meaningless. The third is both syntactically and semantically unacceptable. The fourth (a sentence in Turkish) is completely unintelligible to most of us. One would expect a listener to have more difficulty in recognizing a sentence if it is inconsistent with one or more KS's. Miller and Isard [101] show that this is indeed the case.

If the knowledge is incomplete or inaccurate, people will tend to make erroneous hypotheses. This can be illustrated by a simple experiment. Subjects were asked to listen to two sentences and write down what they heard. The sentences were "In mud eels are, in clay none are" and "In pine tar is, in oak none is." The responses of four subjects are given below.

In mud eels are,	*In clay none are*
in muddies sar	in clay nanar
in my deals are	en clainanar
in my ders	en clain
in model sar	in claynanar

In pine tar is,	*In oak none is*
in pine tarrar	in oak ? es
in pyntar es	in oak nonnus
in pine tar is	in ocnonin
en pine tar is	in oak is

The responses show that the listener forces his own interpretation of what he hears, and not necessarily what may have been intended by the speaker. Because the subjects do not have the contextual framework to expect the words "mud eels" together, they write more likely sounding combinations such as "my deals" or "models." We find the same problem with words such as "oak none is." Notice that they failed to detect where one word ends and another begins. It is not uncommon for machine recognition systems to have similar problems with word segmentation. To approach human performance, a machine must also use all the available KS's effectively.

Reddy and Newell [124] show that knowledge at various levels can be further decomposed into sublevels (Fig. 3) based on whether it is task-dependent *a priori* knowledge, conversation-dependent knowledge, speaker-dependent knowledge, or analysis-dependent knowledge. One can further decompose each of these sublevels into sets of rules relating to specific topics. Many of the present systems have only a small subset of all the KS's shown in Fig. 3. This is because much of this knowledge is yet to be identified and codified in ways that can be conveniently used in a speech understanding system. Sections III through V review the recent progress in representation and use of various sources of knowledge.

In Section III, we consider aspects of signal processing for speech recognition. There is a great deal of research and many publications in this area, but very few of them are addressed to questions that arise in building speech recognition systems. It is not uncommon for a speech recognition system to show a catastrophic drop in performance when the microphone is changed or moved to a slightly noisy room. Many parametric representations of speech have been proposed but there are few comparative studies. In Section III, we shall review the techniques that are presently used in speech signal and analysis and noise normalization, and examine their limitations.

There are several KS's which are common to most connected speech recognition systems and independent of the task. These can be broadly grouped together as task-independent aspects of a speech recognition system. Topics such as feature extraction, phonetic labeling, phonological rules, (bottom-up) word hypothesis, and word verification fall into this category. In Section IV, we will review the techniques used and the present state of accomplishment in these areas.

Given a task that is to be performed using a speech recognition system, one is usually able to specify the vocabulary, the grammatical structure of sentences, and the semantic and contextual constraints provided by the task. In Section V, we will discuss the nature, representation, and use of these KS's in a recognition (or understanding) system.

Control Structure and System Organization: How is a given source of knowledge used in recognition? The Shannon [140] experiment gives a clue. In this experiment, human subjects demonstrate their ability to predict (and correct) what will appear next, given a portion of a sentence.

Just as in the above experiment, many recognition systems use the KS's to generate hypotheses about what word might

Type of knowledge	Task-dependent knowledge	Conversation-dependent knowledge	Speaker-dependent knowledge	Analysis-dependent knowledge
Pragmatic and Semantic	A priori semantic knowledge about the task domain	Concept subselection based on conversation	Psychological model of the user	Concept subselection based on partial sentence recognition
Syntactic	Grammar for the language	Grammar subselection based on topic	Grammar subselection based on speaker	Grammar subselection based on partial phrase recognition
Lexical	Size and confusability of the vocabulary	Vocabulary sub-selection based on topic	Vocabulary sub-selection and ordering based on speaker preference	Vocabulary subselection based on segmental features
Phonemic and phonetic	Characteristics of phones and phonemes of the language	Contextual variability in phonemic characteristics	Dialectal variations of the speaker	Phonemic subselection based on segmental features
Parametric and acoustic	A priori knowledge about the transducer characteristics	Adaptive noise normalization	Variations resulting from the size and shape of vocal tract	Parameter tracking based on previous parameters

Fig. 3. Sources of knowledge (KS). (From Reddy and Newell [124].)

(1) Speed of Communication	Speech is about 4 times faster than standard manual input for continuous text.
(2) Total System Response Time	Direct data entry from remote source, which avoids relayed entry via intermediate human transducers, speeds up communication substantially.
(3) Total System Reliability	Direct data entry from remote source with immediate feedback, avoiding relayed entry via intermediate human transducers, increases reliability substantially.
(4) Parallel Channel	Provides an independent communication channel in hands-busy operational situations.
(5) Freedom of Movement	Within small physical regions speech can be used while moving about freely doing a task.
(6) Untrained Users	No training in basic physical skill required for use (as opposed to acquisition of typing or keying skills); speech is natural for users at all general skill levels (clerical to executive).
(7) Unplanned Communication	Speech is to be used immediately by users to communicate unplanned information, in a way not true of manual input.
(8) Identification of Speaker	Speakers are recognizable by their voice characteristics.
(9) Long Term Reliability	Performance of speech reception and processing tasks which require monotonous vigilant operation can be done more reliably by computer than by humans.
(10) Low Cost Operation	Speech can provide cost savings where it eliminates substantial numbers of people.

Fig. 4. Task demands providing comparative advantages for speech. (From Newell *et al.* [109].)

appear in a given context, or to reject a guess. When one of these systems makes errors, it is usually because the present state of its knowledge is incomplete and possibly inaccurate. In Section VI, we shall review aspects of system organization such as control strategies, error handling, real-time system design, and knowledge acquisition.

B. The Uses of Speech Recognition

Until recently there has been little experience in the use of speech recognition systems in real applications. Most of the systems developed in the 1960's were laboratory systems, which were expensive and had an unacceptable error rate for real life situations. Recently, however, there have been commercially available systems for isolated word recognition, costing from $10 000 to $100 000, with less than 1-percent error rate in noisy environments. The paper by Martin in this issue illustrates a variety of applications where these systems have been found to be useful and cost-effective.

As long as speech recognition systems continue to cost around $10 000 to $100 000, the range of applications for which they will be used will be limited. As the research under way at present comes to fruition over the next few years, and as connected speech recognition systems costing under $10 000 begin to become available, one can expect a significant increase in the number of applications. Fig. 4, adapted from Newell *et al.* [109], summarizes and extends the views expressed by several authors earlier [63], [78], [87], and [89] on the desirability and usefulness of speech—it provides a list of task situation characteristics that are likely to benefit from speech input. Beek *et al.* [17] provide an assessment of the potential military applications of automatic speech recognition.

As computers get cheaper and more powerful, it is estimated that 60–80 percent of the cost of running a business computer installation will be spent on data collection, preparation, and entry (unpublished proprietary studies; should be considered speculative for the present). Given speech recognition systems that are flexible enough to change speakers or task definitions with a few days of effort, speech will begin to be used as an alternate medium of input to computers. Speech is likely to be used not so much for program entry, but rather primarily in data entry situations [33]. This increased usage should in turn lead to increased versatility and reduced cost in speech input systems.

There was some earlier skepticism as to whether speech input was necessary or even desirable as an input medium for computers [116]. The present attitude among the researchers in the field appears to be just the opposite, i.e., if speech input systems of reasonable cost and reliability were available, they would be the preferred mode of communication even though the relative cost is higher than other types of input [109]. Recent human factors studies in cooperative problem solving [23], [110] seem to support the view that speech is *the* preferred mode of communication. If it is indeed preferred, it seems safe to assume that the user would be willing to pay somewhat higher prices to be able to talk to computers. This prospect of being able to talk to computers is what drives the field, not just the development of a few systems for highly specialized applications.

II. Systems

This section provides an overview of the structure of different types of speech recognition systems. To accomplish this, one needs to answer questions such as: what are the important concepts and principles associated with each of these systems, what are their distinguishing features, how well do they perform, and so on. It is not always possible to answer these questions. Very few comparative results based on common test data are available. In many cases all the returns are not yet in. There are so many possible design choices that most systems are not strictly comparable with each other. Therefore, it will be necessary to restrict our discussion to somewhat superficial comparisons based on accuracy, response time, size of vocabulary, etc.

In this section, we will examine the structure and performance of the first three classes of systems shown in Fig. 1: *isolated word recognition systems, restricted connected speech recognition systems,* and *restricted speech understanding systems.* We will illustrate the principles of design and performance by picking a few systems which are representative of the state of the art in each category. For the sake of brevity, we will leave out the words "isolated" and "restricted" for the rest of this paper. Unless otherwise indicated, it is to be assumed that we are always talking about isolated word recognition systems, restricted connected speech recognition systems, and restricted speech understanding systems.

A. Word Recognition Systems (WRS)

Here we will look at the structure and performance of three systems by Itakura [70], Martin [96], and White [161]. Given a known vocabulary (of about 30 to 200 words) and a known speaker, these systems can recognize a word spoken in isolation with accuracies around 99 percent. The vocabulary and/or speaker can be changed but this usually requires a training session. These systems, though similar in some respects, have several interesting and distinguishing features. Fig. 5 summarizes some of the features of these systems that affect cost and performance. Researchers desirous of working in the field of word recognition would also benefit from studying the structure and features of several earlier (and somewhat lower performance) systems by Gold [51], Shearme and Leach [141], Bobrow and Klatt [18], Vicens [152], Medress [98], Valichiko and Zagoruiko [151], Vysotsky *et al.* [153], Pols [117], Von Keller [154], Itahashi, Makino, and Kido [67], and Sambur and Rabiner [135].

All three systems use the classical pattern recognition paradigm as their recognition strategy. The general paradigm involves comparing the parameter or feature representation of the incoming utterance with the prototype reference patterns of each of the words in the vocabulary. Fig. 6 presents the flow chart of a typical word recognition system. The main decisions to be made in the design of a word recognition system are: how to normalize for variations in speech; what is the parametric representation; how does the system adapt to a new speaker or new vocabulary; how does one measure the similarity of two utterances; and how to speed up the matching process.

Normalization: Even when the speaker and the microphone are not changed, variations in speech occur as a result of free variation from trial to trial, as well as the emotional state of the speaker and the ambient noise level of the environment. These result in changes in amplitude, duration, and signal-to-noise ratio for a given utterance. Before a match with stored templates can take place, some form of normalization is necessary to minimize the variability. Itakura [70] uses a second-order inverse filter based on the entire utterance to achieve noise and amplitude normalization. Martin [96] identifies several types of noise related problems: room noise, breath noise, intraword stop gaps, and operator-originated babble. Some of these result in incorrect detection of beginning and end of the utterance. Most of the noise problems can be overcome by careful attention to detail, such as close-speaking microphones, looking for spectra that are typical of breath noise, rejecting utterances that do not get a close match to any of the words, and so on. White, before measuring distances, normalizes all filter samples by dividing by the total energy.

Parametric Representations: Itakura uses linear predictive coding (LPC) coefficients, Martin uses hardware feature detectors based on bandpass filters, while White uses a 1/3-octave filter bank (see Section III). White [161] has studied the effect of using different parametric representations. Results of this experiment are given in Fig. 7. It shows that the 1/3-octave filter bank and LPC yield about similar results, and using a 6-channel-octave filter bank increases the error rate from 2 to 4 percent while doubling the speed of recognition. Transforming the parametric data into a pseudophonemic label prior to match can lead to significant reduction of storage but the error rate increases sharply to 9 percent. Reference pattern storage requirement is also affected by the choice of parametric representation. Assuming an average duration of 600 ms per word, White requires from 2160 to 7200 bits of storage (depending on parametric representation) per reference pattern and Itakura requires 4480 bits, while Martin requires only 512 bits per pattern.

Training: Change of speaker or vocabulary is accomplished in all three systems by training the system to produce a new set of reference patterns. Both Itakura and White use a single reference pattern per word. A single reference pattern cannot capture all variations in pronunciations for even a single speaker. Thus when a word exhibits higher than acceptable error rate it is desirable to store additional patterns. But this

	ITAKURA	MARTIN	WHITE
1. Transducer	Telephone	Close speaking microphone	Close speaking microphone
2. Noise level	68 dB (A)	90 dB (A)	65 dB (A)
3. Parametric representation	LPC	Hardware feature extractor	1/3 octave filter bank
4. No. of templates per word	Single template	Average of multiple templates	Single template
5. Space required per reference pattern	4480 bits	512 bits	7200 bits
6. Computer system	DDP-516	Nova, PDP/11 or Microcomputers	SIGMA-3

Fig. 5. Distinctive aspects of three word recognition systems. (Compiled from Itakura [70], Martin [95], [96], and White and Neely [161].)

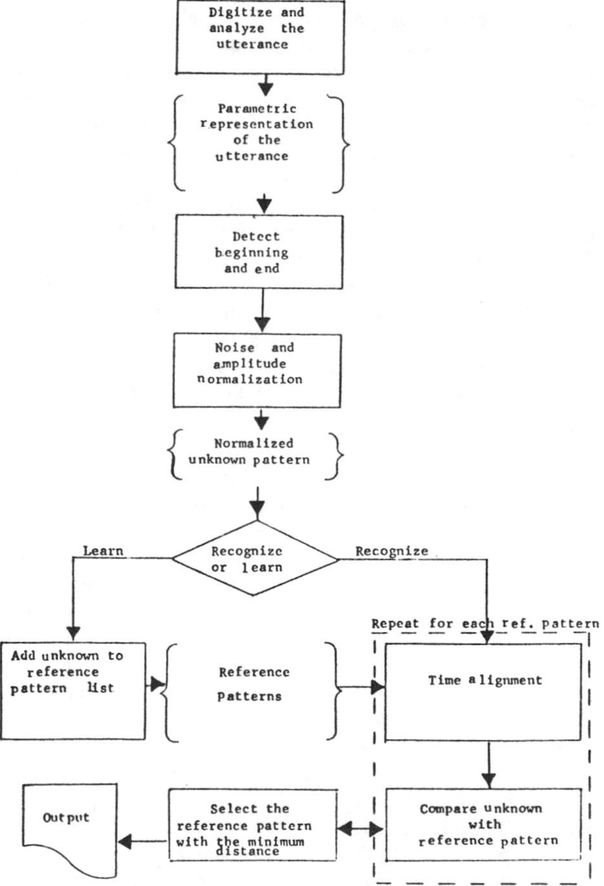

Fig. 6. Flow chart of a typical word recognition system.

Preprocessing method	Alpha-Digit vocabulary % correct	Recognition time per utterance	Data Rate bits per sec approximate
20 channel (1/3 octave filters)	98%	30 sec	12,000
LPC	97%	20 sec	4,200
6 channel (octave filters)	96%	15 sec	3,600
Phone code	91%	2 sec	500

Fig. 7. Effect of parametric representation on accuracy and response time of a system. Preprocessing produces four different parametric representations arranged in order of increasing data compression (lower bit rate). Recognition accuracy goes down as compression goes up. Phone code attempts to give a single pseudophonetic label for each 10-ms unit of speech.

requires additional storage and computation. Martin attempts abstraction of reference patterns by generating an average template from multiple samples.

Matching and Classification: Given an unknown input word, it is compared with every reference pattern to determine which pattern is most similar, i.e., has the minimum distance or maximum correlation to the unknown. This similarity measure is usually established by summing distances (or log probabilities as the case may be) between parameter vectors of the unknown and the reference. There are many design choices that affect the performance at this level, e.g., the choice of the basic time unit of sampling, the choice of the distance metric, differential weighting of parameters, and the choice of the time normalization function.

Itakura and White use dynamic programming for time normalization, while Martin divides the utterance into 16 equal time units. Itakura measures the distance between the unknown and the reference by summing the log probability based on residual prediction error every 15 ms. White measures the distance by summing the absolute values of the differences (Chebyshev norm) between the parameter vectors every 10 ms. Martin uses a weighted correlation metric to measure similarity every 40 ms or so (actually 1/16 of the duration of the utterance).

White shows that the nonlinear time warping based on dynamic programming is better than linear time scaling methods. He also shows Itakura's distance measure based on LPC linear prediction error yields about the same accuracy as other conventional methods. It is generally felt (based on speech bandwidth compression experiments) that significant loss of information results when speech is sampled at intervals exceeding 20 ms. However, note that Martin extracts averaged features based on longer time intervals and is not just sampling the signal parameters.

System	Vocabulary	Size	Noise	Microphone	Number of speakers	Accuracy (includes rejects if any)	Resp. time in times real time
Martin	Digits	10	—	Close speaking microphone (CSM)	10	99.79	Almost real-time
Martin	Aircraft ops.	11x12	—	CSM	10	99.32	Almost real-time
Martin	1 thru 34	34	90dB	CSM	12	98.5	Almost real-time
White	Alpha-digit	36	65	CSM	1	98.0	30
White	North Am. states	91	65	CSM	1	99.6	—
Itakura	Alpha-digit	36	68	Telephone	1	88.6	—
Itakura	Japanese geographical names	200	68	Telephone	1	98.95	22

Fig. 8. Performance characteristics of three word recognition systems. (Compiled from Itakura [70], Martin [95], [96], and White and Neely [161].)

Heuristics for Speedup: If a system compares the unknown with every one of the reference patterns in a brute-force manner, the response time increases linearly with the size of the vocabulary. Given the present speeds of minicomputers which can execute 0.2 to 0.5 million instructions per second (mips), the increase in response time is not noticeable for small vocabularies of 10 to 30. But when the size of vocabulary increases to a few hundred words it becomes essential to use techniques that reduce computation time. Itakura uses a sequential decision technique and rejects a reference pattern if its distance exceeds a variable threshold at any time during the match operation. This results in a speedup of the matching process by a factor of almost 10. White uses the duration, amplitude contour, and partial match distance of the first 200 ms as three independent measurements to eliminate the most unlikely candidates from the search list. Others have used gross segmental features [152] and pronouncing dictionary with phonological rules [67] in reducing search. But these require a more complex program organization.

Performance: Fig. 8 gives the published performance statistics for the three systems. It is important to remember that accuracy and response time are meaningful only when considered in the context of all the variables that affect the performance. Although recognition performance scores have been quoted only for systems ranging from 10 to 34 words, Martin's system has been used with vocabularies as high as 144 words. It is the only system that has been shown to work in very high noise (>90 dB) environments and with multiple speakers (using reference patterns which represent all the speakers). The accuracy of Itakura's system drops to 88.6 percent on the alpha-digit word list (aye, bee, cee, · · · , zero, one, · · · , nine). But note that it is the only system that uses a telephone as the transducer. In addition to restricting the frequency response to about 300 to 3000 Hz, the telephone introduces burst noise, distortion, echo, crosstalk, frequency translation, envelope delay, and clipping to list a few. In addition, the alpha-digit vocabulary is highly ambiguous. The fact that the system achieves about 1-percent error rate (and 1.65-percent rejection rate) on a less ambiguous 200-word vocabulary is indicative of its true power. White's system not only achieves high accuracies but also is notable for its system organization which permits it to use different parameters, different time normalization strategies, and different search reduction heuristics with ease. The important thing to remember is that each of these systems seems capable of working with less than 2-percent error rate in noisy environments given vocabularies in the range of 30 to 200. It seems reasonable to assume that accuracy will not degrade substantially with larger vocabularies. A useful indicator of this is the early system by Vicens [152] which achieved 91.4-percent with a 561-word vocabulary.

Future Directions: As long as the cost/performance requirements do not demand an order of magnitude improvement, the present systems approach will continue to be practical and viable. The improvements in computer technology have already brought the cost of such systems to around $10 000. However, if it becomes necessary to reduce the cost to the $1000 range, significant improvement to the basic algorithms will be necessary. The principal avenues for improvement are in the reference pattern representation and search strategies. Rather than storing a vector of parameters every 10 ms, it may be necessary to go to a segmentation and labeling scheme (see Section IV) as has been attempted by some earlier investigators [67], [152]. Rather than storing multiple reference patterns for multiple speakers, it will be necessary to find techniques for abstraction. It may also be necessary to use mixed search strategies in which a simpler parametric representation is used to eliminate unlikely candidates before using a more expensive matching technique. Since many of these techniques are essential for connected speech recognition, it is reasonable to assume that progress in that area will gradually lead to low-cost/high-performance word recognition systems.

B. Connected Speech Recognition (CSR)

In this section we will look at the structure and performance of four different connected speech recognition (CSR) systems: Hearsay-I and Dragon developed at Carnegie-Mellon University [7], [123]; the Lincoln system developed at M.I.T. Lincoln Laboratories [47], [48], [56], [97], [159], [162]; and the IBM system developed at IBM, T. J. Watson Research Center [10], [30], [31], [71], [72], [149], [150], [172], [173]. Hearsay-I was actually designed as a speech understanding system, but the semantic and task modules can be deactivated so as to permit it to run like a connected speech recognition system. Both the Dragon and Lincoln systems were designed to add task-specific constraints later, but in their present form can be looked upon as connected speech recognition systems. These systems have achieved from 55- to 97-percent word accuracies. Since a sentence is considered to be incorrect even if only one word in the utterance is incorrect, the sentence accuracies tend to be much lower (around 30 to 81 percent). With tuning and algorithm improvement currently in progress, some of these systems are expected to show significant improvement in accuracy. Researchers interested in CSR systems might also wish to look at the papers in [26], [28], [95], [120], [148], and [152].

Why Is Connected Speech Recognition Difficult? When isolated word recognition systems are getting over 99-percent accuracies, why is it that CSR systems are straining to get similar accuracy? The answers are not difficult to find. In connected speech it is difficult to determine where one word ends and another begins. In addition, acoustic characteristics of sounds and words exhibit much greater variability in connected speech, depending on the context, compared with words spoken in isolation.

Any attempt to extend the design philosophy of isolated word recognition systems and recognize the utterance as a whole becomes an exercise in futility. Note that even a 10-word vocabulary of digits requires the storage of 10-million reference patterns if one wanted to recognize all the possible 7-digit sequences. Some way must be found for the recognition of the whole by analysis of the parts. The technique needed becomes one of analysis and description rather than classification (moving away from pattern recognition paradigms toward hierarchical systems, i.e., systems in which component subparts are recognized and grouped together to form larger and larger units).

To analyze and describe a component part, i.e., a word within the sentence, one needs a description of what to expect when that word is spoken. Again, the reference pattern idea of word recognition systems becomes unsatisfactory. As the number of words in the vocabulary and the number of different contextual variations per word get large, the storage required to store all the reference pattern becomes enormous. For a 200-word vocabulary, such as the one used by Itakura [70], a CSR system might need 2000 reference patterns requiring about 8-million bits of memory, not to mention the time and labor associated with speaking them into the machine. What is needed is a more compact representation of the sound patterns of the words such as those used by linguists, i.e., representation of words as a sequence of phones, phonemes, or syllables. This change from signal space representation of the words to a symbol space representation requires segmenting the continuous speech signal into discrete acoustically invariant parts and labeling each segment with phonemic or feature labels. A phonemic dictionary of the words could then be used to match at a symbolic level and determine which word was spoken.

Since CSR systems do not have the advantage of word recognition systems, of knowing the beginning and ending of words, one usually proceeds left-to-right, thereby forcing at least the beginning to be specified prior to the match for a word. Given where the first (left-most) word of the utterance ends, one can begin matching for the second word from about that position. One must still find techniques for terminating the match when an optimal match is found.

However, the exact match cannot be quite determined until the ending context (the word that follows) is also known. For example, in the word sequence "some milk" all of the nasal /m/ might be matched with the end of "some" leaving only the "ilk" part for a subsequent match. This is a special case of the juncture problem (see Section IV). Techniques are needed which will back up somewhat when the word being matched indicates that it might be necessary in this context. (see also Section VIII of Jelinek [72].)

Finally, error and uncertainty in segmentation, labeling, and matching make it necessary that several alternative word matches be considered as alternative paths. If there were 5 words in an utterance and we considered 5 alternative paths after each word, we would have 3125 (5^5) word sequences, out of which we have to pick the one that is most plausible. Selection of the best word sequence requires a tree search algorithm and a carefully constructed similarity measure.

The preceding design choices are what make CSR systems substantially more complex than word recognition systems. We do not yet have good signal-to-symbol transformation techniques nor do we fully understand how to do word matching performance of CSR systems when compared with word recognition systems. However, researchers have been working seriously on CSR techniques only for the past few years, and significant improvements can be expected in the not too distant future. The following discussion reviews the design choices made by each of the four systems (Fig. 9).

Front End Processing: The purpose of the front end in a CSR system is to process the signal and transform it to a symbol string so that matching can take place. The first three design choices in Fig. 9 affect the nature of this signal-to-symbol transformation. The Dragon system uses the simplest front end of all the systems. It uses the 10-ms speech segment as a basic unit and attempts matching at that level. Given a vector of 12 amplitude and zero-crossing parameters every 10 ms, the system computes the probabilities for each of 33 possible phonemic symbols. To account for allophonic variations, it uses multiple reference patterns (vectors) to represent each phonemic symbol.

Hearsay-I uses amplitude and zero-crossing parameters to obtain a multilevel segmentation into syllable-size units and phoneme-size units. Every 10-ms unit is given a phonemic label based on a nearest neighbor classification using a predefined set of cluster centers. Contiguous 10-ms segments with the same label are grouped together to form a phoneme-size segment. A syllable-like segmentation is derived based on local maxima and minima in the overall amplitude function of the utterance. These larger segments are given gross feature labels such as silence, fricative, and voiced.

The Lincoln system is described in detail by Weinstein *et al.* [159]. The fast digital processor (FDP) computes LPC spectra, tracks formant frequencies [97], performs a preliminary segmentation, and labels the segments as one of vowel, dip (intervocalic voiced consonants characterized by a dip in amplitude), fricative, and stop categories. Formant frequencies, formant motions, formant amplitude, and other spectral measurements are used in further classifying the segments into phone-like acoustic–phonetic elements (APEL) labels.

The IBM system front end is based on the approach developed by Dixon and Silverman [31], [32], for pattern

	Hearsay-I	Dragon	Lincoln	IBM
Parametric representation	Amplitude + zero crossings in 5 octave bands	Amplitude and zero crossings in 5 octave bands	LPC Spectra formants	Spectrum
Segmentation	Heuristic multilevel (syllabic + phonetic)	None	Heuristic	Heuristic
Labeling	Two level prot. matching	Prototype matching	Feature based	Prototype matching
Word matching	Heuristic	Stochastic	Heuristic	Stochastic
Phonological rules	Ad Hoc	None (can be added)	Yes	Yes
Word representation	Phonemic base form	Network	Phonemic base form	Network
Syntax	Productions anti-productions	Finite state network	Productions anti-productions	Finite state network
Search	Left to right search best first	Left to right search all paths	Left to right search best first	Left to right search using sequential decoding (similar to best first)

Fig. 9. Design choices of the four connected speech recognition (CSR) systems. (Compiled from Reddy *et al.* [123], Baker [8], Forgie *et al.* [48], Baker and Bahl [10], and other related publications.)

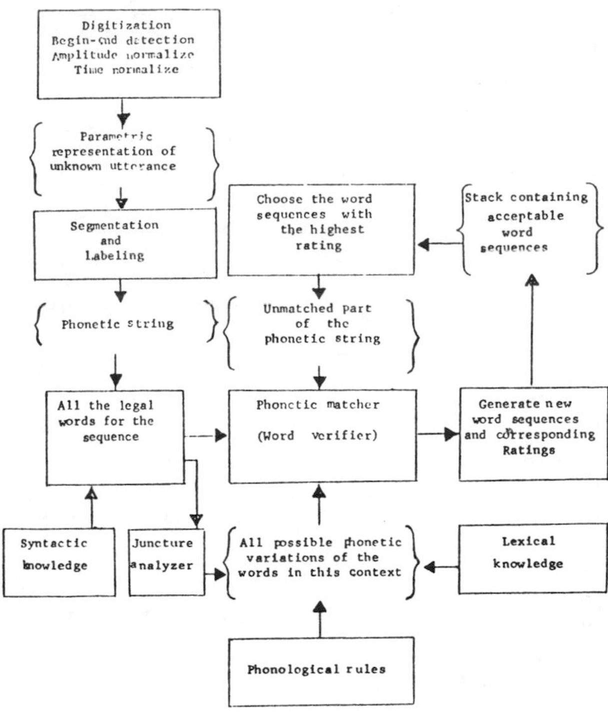

Fig. 10. Flow chart of a typical CSR system.

recognition using complex decision-making rules and dynamic segmentation [148]. The segmentation and labeling procedure uses energy, spectra, spectral change, an ordered list of five "most similar" classes, and their similarity values. The labeling is done by prototype matching as in the case of Hearsay-I and Dragon but using about 62 label classes.

Knowledge Representation: There are three types of knowledge that are usually required in a CSR system: phonological rules, lexicon, and syntax. The Dragon system has the most elegant representation of knowledge of the four systems [7]. All the knowledge is represented as a unified finite-state network representing a hierarchy of probabilistic functions of the Markov processes.

Hearsay-I organizes knowledge into independent and cooperating knowledge processes, which makes it easy to add or remove a knowledge source. The representation of knowledge within each process is somewha arbitrary and depends on the needs of that process. Syntax is represented as a set of productions (generative rewriting rules) and antiproductions (analytic prediction rules). The lexicon contains only the phonemic base forms. Phonological information is embedded in various acoustic analysis procedures.

In the Lincoln system, syntactic constraints are represented by a set of production rules. Phonological and front-end-dependent rules are used to construct a lexicon from a base form dictionary [55], [56]. Other such rules are also applied during a heuristic word and matching process.

The IBM system uses a finite-state grammar and a directed graph representation of each lexical element [24]. Phonological rules are compiled into the lexicon. To account for the rules that do involve word boundaries, the graphs have multiple starting nodes labeled with conditions that must be met by preceding or following words. An important component of the IBM system is the extensive use of statistical information to provide transition probabilities within the finite-state networks representing task-dependent information. (See also Jelinek [72].)

Although both the Dragon and IBM systems use network representations and stochastic matching, they differ in several respects. Dragon uses an integrated representation of all the knowledge, whereas the IBM system has independent representations of the language, phonology, and acoustic components. Dragon evaluates the likelihood of all possible paths, while the IBM system uses sequential decoding to constrain the search to the most likely path.

Matching and Control: Fig. 10 is a flow chart of the recognition process of a typical CSR system. All the systems except Dragon use a stack (or a set) containing a list of alternative word sequences (or state sequences) arranged in descending order of their likelihoods (or scores) to represent the partial sentence analysis so far. Given the word sequence with the highest likelihood, the task-specific knowledge generates all the words that can follow that sequence. Each of these words is matched against the unmatched symbol (phonemic) string to estimate conditional likelihoods of occurrence. These are used to generate a new list of acceptable word sequences and their likelihoods. This process is repeated until the whole utterance is analyzed and an acceptable word sequence is determined. The Dragon system, rather than extending the best word sequence, extends all the sequences in parallel. The Markovian assumption permits it to collapse many alternative sequences into a single state, thus avoiding exponential growth.

The four systems differ significantly in the way in which insertion, deletion, and substitution errors are handled in the matching process, and the way in which likelihoods are estimated. Hearsay-I and Lincoln systems use heuristic techniques, while Dragon and IBM systems use the principles of stochastic modeling [72], [7] to estimate likelihoods. In Section IV, we will discuss techniques for word matching and verification in greater detail.

Performance: Fig. 11 gives some performance statistics for the four systems. The systems are not strictly comparable because of the number of variables involved. However, some

	Hearsay-I	Dragon	Lincoln	IBM
No. of Sentences	102	102	275	363
No. of Word tokens	578	578	-	-
No. of Speakers	4	1	6	1
No. of Tasks	5	5	1	2
Sentence Accuracy	31%	49%	49%	81%
Word Accuracy	55%	83%	-	97%
Response Time (x real-time)	9-44	48-174	15-25	25
Environment	Terminal room	Terminal room	Computer room	Sound booth
Transducer	CSM and telephone	CSM	CSM	HQM
Size of Vocabulary	24-194	24-194	237	250
Live Input	Yes	No	Yes	No
Date Operational	1972	1974	1974	1975
Computer	PDP-10	PDP-10	TX-2/FDP	360/91 and 370/168
Average No. of instructions executed per second of speech in million	3-15	15-60	45-75	30

Fig. 11. Performance statistics for four CSR systems. (From sources given for Fig. 9.)

general comparisons can be made. The IBM system has the best performance of the four, but one should bear in mind the fact that most of their results to date are based on relatively noise-free high-quality data for a single speaker. It is also the only system being improved actively at present. This tuning of the system should lead to even higher accuracies.

Hearsay-I and Dragon were run on the same data sets to permit strict comparison. Dragon yields significantly higher accuracy, though it is slower by a factor of 4 to 5. Hearsay-I yields much higher accuracies on tasks and speakers with which it is carefully trained (see Fig. 15). It was tested on several speakers and several tasks. As the vocabulary increases, its relatively weaker acoustic–phonetic module tends to make more errors in the absence of careful tuning. It was one of the first systems to be built and still is one of the very few that can be demonstrated live.

The Dragon system performance demonstrates that simple and mathematically tractable CSR systems can be built without sacrificing accuracy. Although searching all possible alternative paths becomes unfeasible for very large vocabularies, for restricted tasks with a few hundred word vocabulary, Dragon with its simpler program structure represents an attractive alternative.

The Lincoln system is the only one of the four that works for several speakers without significant tuning for the speaker. The 49-percent sentence accuracy represents the composite accuracy for all the speakers taken together. It was also tested with a 411-percent word vocabulary, yielding about 28-percent sentence accuracy over the same set of six speakers.

Future Directions: How can CSR systems achieve significantly higher performance and cost under $20 000? Better search, better matching, and better segmentation and labeling are all essential if the systems are to achieve higher accuracies. The best-first search strategy used by Hearsay-I and other systems leads to termination of search when it exceeds a given time limit. When this happens, it is usually because errors in evaluation have led to a wrong part of the search space, and the system is exploring a large number of incorrect paths. In most systems, this accounts for 20–30 percent of the sentence errors.

Dragon does not have the problem of thrashing since it searches all the possible extensions of a word (state) sequence. An intermediate strategy in which several promising alternative paths are considered in parallel (best few without backtracking), rather than all or the best-first strategies of the present systems, seems desirable. Lowerre [90] has implemented one such strategy in the Harpy system currently under development at Carnegie-Mellon University and has reduced the computation requirement by about a factor of 5 over Dragon without any loss of accuracy. The number of alternative paths to be considered is usually a function of the goodness of the parametric representation (and accuracy of the segmental labels). Continued research into this class of systems should lead to the development of low-cost CSR.

Accuracies in word matching and verification approaching those of word recognition systems, i.e., greater than 99 percent, are essential for the success of CSR. Since words exhibit greater variability in connected speech, this becomes a much more difficult task. Klatt [75] proposes the use of analysis-by-synthesis techniques as the principal solution to this problem. Near-term solutions include learning the transition probabilities of a word network using training data, as is being done by IBM, or learning the lexical descriptions themselves from examples, as is being attempted at Carnegie-Mellon University. There has been very little work on comparative evaluation of segmentation and labeling schemes. Further studies are needed to determine which techniques work well, especially in environments representative of real life situations.

C. Speech Understanding Systems (SUS)

In this section, we will study approaches to speech understanding systems (SUS's) design by discussing three systems, viz., Hearsay-II [36], [86], SPEECHLIS [166], and VDMS [127], [156], currently being developed, respectively, at Carnegie-Mellon University, Bolt Beranek and Newman, and jointly by System Development Corporation and Stanford Research Institute. We cannot give performance statistics for these systems as they are not working well enough yet. However, at least one earlier system, Hearsay-I, illustrates the potential importance and usefulness of semantic and conversation-dependent knowledge. Experiments on this system show that 25–30-percent improvement in sentence accuracies (e.g., from about 52 to 80 percent on one task) were achieved using chess-dependent semantic knowledge in the voice-chess task. Researchers interested in other attempts at speech understanding systems should look at [13], [20], [35], [47], [64], [123], [134], [152], [157], and [160].

What Makes Speech Understanding Difficult? In addition to the problems of having to recognize connected speech, SUS's tend to have the additional requirement that they must do so even when the utterance is not quite grammatical or well formed, and in the presence of speech-like noise (e.g., babble, mumble, and cough). The requirement is somewhat relaxed by the concession that what matters in the end is not the recognition of each and every word in the utterance but rather the intent of the message. The systems are also required to keep track of the context of the conversation so far and use it to resolve any ambiguities that might arise within the present sentence. Clearly, one can attempt to build CSR systems with all the preceding characteristics and yet not use any task-specific information. Here we will restrict ourselves to the apparent differences in approach between the CSR and the SU systems of the current generation.

How do the above requirements translate into specific problems to be solved? We still have the problem of determining when a word begins and ends in connected speech, and the problem of wide variability in the acoustic characteristics of the words. But the solutions adopted in CSR systems to solve these problems do not quite carry over to SUS. One can no longer proceed left-to-right in the analysis of an utterance because of the possibility of error or unknown babble in the middle of the utterance. Thus the useful technique of keeping an ordered list of word sequences which are extended to the right after each iteration has to be modified significantly.

Another design choice of CSR systems that leads to difficulties is the notion that there is a bottom-up acoustic analyzer (the *front end*) which generates a phonemic (or some such) symbol string, and a top-down language model (the *back end*) predicting possible word candidates at that choice point, which are then compared by a matching procedure. As the vocabularies get larger, often the roles have to be reversed. One cannot afford to match 1000 possible nouns just because the grammar predicts that the next word might be a noun. In such cases, the phonemic string may be used to generate plausible word hypotheses, while the language model is used to verify such hypotheses for compatibility and consistency. In general, one wants systems in which the role of knowledge sources is somewhat symmetric. They may be required to predict or verify depending on the context. The representations of knowledge required to perform these different roles will usually be different.

In CSR we have seen that at a given time one of several words might be possible given the acoustic evidence. This is what leads to the nondeterministic search, i.e., consideration and evaluation of an ordered list of alternate word sequences in the flow chart given in Fig. 10. This nondeterministic (and errorful) nature of decisions permeates all the levels of the speech decoding process, i.e., segmental, phonetic, phonemic, syllabic, word, phrase, and conceptual, and not just the word level. There is no such thing as error-free segmentation, error-free labels, and so on up the levels. This requires the representation of alternate sequences at all levels, not just the word level as in the case of CSR systems. Fig. 12 (from Reddy and Erman [122]) illustrates the consequences of this nondeterminism.

At the bottom of Fig. 12, we see the speech waveform for part of an utterance: '. . . all about . . . '. The "true" locations of phoneme and word boundaries are given below the waveform. In a recognition system, the choices of segment boundaries and labels to be associated with each of the segments are not as clear cut. (In fact, even getting trained phoneticians to agree on the "true" locations is often difficult.) A segmentation and labeling program might produce segment boundaries as indicated by the dotted lines connecting the waveform to the segment level. Given the segmental features, the phoneme represented by the first segment might be /aw/,

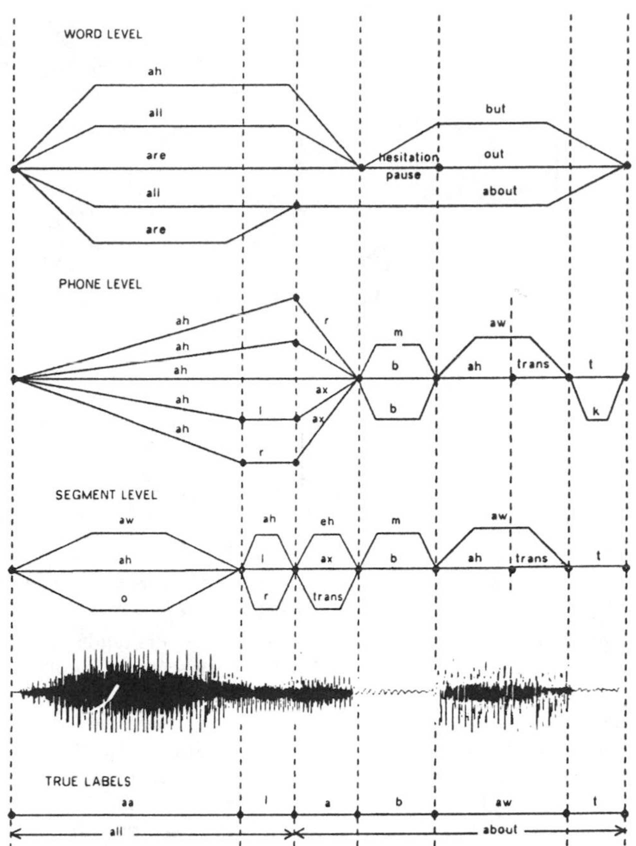

Fig. 12. Example of network representation of alternative choices at various levels. (From Reddy and Erman [122].)

/ah/, or /ow/. Similarly, several different labels can be given to each of the other segments. Given the necessary acoustic–phonetic rules, it is possible to combine, regroup, and delete segments, forming larger phoneme-size units, as shown in the figure. Note, for example, that /ah/ and /l/ are very similar, and it is not impossible that the minor parametric variability that caused the segment boundary at the lower level is just free variation. These phoneme hypotheses give rise to a multiplicity of word hypotheses such as 'ah but', 'all out', 'all about', 'all but', 'are about', and so on.

If, instead of selecting several alternate segmentations and following their consequences, we were to select a single segmentation and associate a single label with each segment, the resulting errors might make it impossible to verify and validate the correct word. Thus some form of network representation of alternate hypotheses at all levels is necessary in systems requiring high accuracy.

Even the lowest level decision about segmentation sometimes requires the active mediation of higher level knowledge such as the plausibility of a given word occurring in that position. Fig. 12 can be used to illustrate the point. The segment boundary at the word juncture of 'all' and 'about' is usually very difficult to find since the spectral characteristics of /l/ and the reduced vowel /ax/ tend to be very similar. In the event that a higher level process is fairly confident about this word sequence but there is no segment boundary, it could call upon the segmenter for a closer look, possibly using a different parametric representation. In general, SUS's require flexible means of cooperation and communication among different

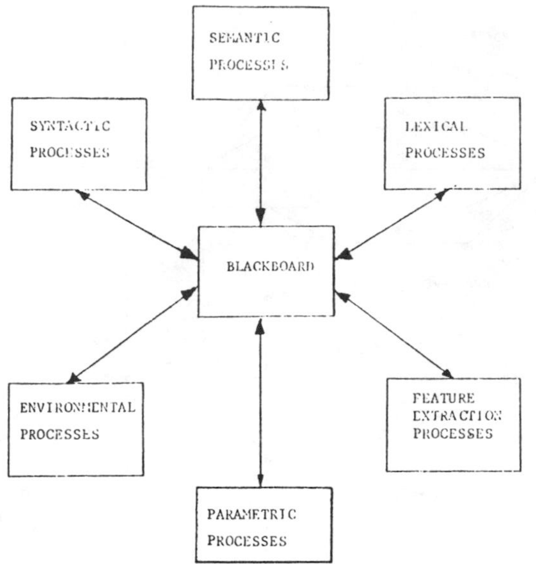

Fig. 13. Blackboard model used in Hearsay-II. (From Lesser *et al.* [86].)

knowledge sources (KS's). Since an SU system tends to have many more KS's than a CSR system, the system should be designed so that knowledge processes can easily be added and deleted.

Finally, the requirements of representation of *understanding, response generation, conversational context,* and *task* all add to the difficulty and overall complexity of an SUS.

Approaches to Speech Understanding: Given the difficulties that arise in SUS, it is clear that one needs significantly more sophisticated system design than those used in current CSR systems. At present, there is no clear agreement among researchers as to what an ideal system organization for an SUS might be.

In the VDMS system [127], the parser coordinates the operation of the system. In many respects the control flow resembles the one for CSR systems (Fig. 10) and is based on the best-first strategy. However, the simplistic notion of an ordered list of word sequences is replaced by a *parse net* mechanism which permits sharing of results and does not require strict left-to-right analysis of the utterance [115]. A language definition facility permits efficient internal representation of various KS's [128].

In the SPEECHLIS system [166], control strategies and system organization are derived through incremental simulation [168]. People located in different rooms simulate the various components and attempt to analyze an utterance by communicating via teletypewriter. Then one by one, people are replaced by computer algorithms having specified interface characteristics. A control strategy for SUS derived in this manner is described by Rovner *et al.* [131]. The final control structure is not available yet but is expected to be within the near future.

Perhaps the most ambitious of all the system organizations is the one used by the Hearsay-II system [86], [37]. Though it was designed with speech understanding systems in mind, it is viewed as one of the potential solutions to the problem of knowledge-based systems (KBS) architecture that is of general interest in artificial intelligence research. Other proposed solutions to the KBS architecture problem include Planner [62], production systems [106], and QA-4 [132].

Hearsay-II is based on a *blackboard* model (Fig. 13). The blackboard model conceives of each KS as an information gathering and dispensing process. When a KS generates a hypothesis about the utterance that might be useful for others, it broadcasts the hypothesis by writing it on the "blackboard"—a structurally uniform global data base. The hypothesis-and-test paradigm (see Section I-A) serves as the basic medium of communication among KS's. The way KS's communicate and cooperate with each other is to validate or reject each other's hypotheses. The KS's are treated uniformly by the system and are independent (i.e., anonymous to each other) and therefore relatively easy to modify and replace. The activation of a KS is data-driven, based on the occurrence of patterns on the blackboard which match the templates specified by the KS.

Most of the control difficulties associated with SUS appear to have a solution within the Hearsay framework. It is easy to delete, add, or replace KS's. The system can continue to function even in the absence of one or more of these KS's as long as there are some hypothesis generators and some verifiers in the aggregate. The blackboard consists of a uniform multilevel network (similar to the one in Fig. 12, but containing all the levels) and permits generation and linkage of alternate hypotheses at all the levels. A higher level KS can generate hypotheses at a lower level and vice versa. It is not necessary for the acoustic processing to be bottom-up and the language model to be top-down.

How does the recognition proceed in an asynchronously activated data-driven system such as Hearsay-II? Since there are not many systems of this type around, it is difficult for most people to visualize what happens. It is difficult to explain using flow charts which are primarily useful for explaining sequential flow of control. What we have here is an activity equivalent to a set of cooperating asynchronous parallel processors even when it runs on a uniprocessor. Generating and verifying hypotheses using several KS's is analogous to several persons attempting to solve a jigsaw puzzle with each person working on a different part of the puzzle but with each modifying his strategies based on the progress being made by the others.

What is important to realize is that within the Hearsay framework one can create the effects of a strictly bottom-up system, top-down system, or system which works one way at one time and the other way the next time, depending on cost and utility considerations. The ratings policy process, a global KS, combines and propagates ratings across levels facilitating focus of attention, goal-directed scheduling, and eventual recognition of the utterance. The focus-of-attention KS is used to determine an optimal set of alternative paths which should be explored further based on notions such as effort spent, desirability of further effort, important areas yet to be explored, and goal lists.

Knowledge Sources: Fig. 14 shows the design choices made by the three systems. Many of the low-level issues are common with CSR and do not require much discussion (see also Sections III, IV, and V). Here we will discuss the nature of the higher level knowledge sources used in each system.

The task for Hearsay-II is news retrieval, i.e., retrieval of daily wire-service news stories upon voice request by the user. The vocabulary size for the task is approximately 1200 words. The syntax for the task permits simple English-like sentences and uses the ACORN network representation developed by Hayes-Roth and Mostow [58]. The semantic and pragmatic model uses subselection mechanisms based on news items of

	Hearsay-II	Speechlis	VDMS
Microphone	Close speaking microphone	Close speaking microphone	Sony ECM-377 condenser microphone
Noise Level	Terminal room	Quiet office	Low (sound booth)
Parametric Rep.	LPC using Itakura metric	Formants and features	Formants and features
Segmentation	Parameter based	Feature based	Classification based
Labeling	Prototype matching	Heuristic	Heuristic
Word Hypothesis	Syllable based	Segment based	Syllable based
Word Verification	Markov Process	Analysis-by-Synthesis	Heuristic match with A-Matrix
Syntax	Restricted English	English-like	English-like
Semantics	Acorn net	Semantic net	Semantic net
Discourse Model	Topic based subselection	User model	Ellipsis and anaphora
Task	News retrieval	Travel Budget Manager	Submarine Data Base Management
Systems Control	Blackboard Model	Centralized Controller	Parser-Based

Fig. 14. Design choices of the three speech understanding systems. (Compiled from Lesser *et al.* [86], Woods [166], Ritea [127], and other related publications.)

1	2	3	4	5				6			
				Acoustic + Syntax				Acoustics + Syntax + Semantics			
Data set: Task/Speaker	Words in lexicon	No. of sentences	No. of words	%Sentences %Near miss	%Words	Average Time per sentence (sec)	Average Time per second of speech	%Sentences %Near miss	%Words	Average Time per sentence (sec)	Average Time per second of speech
1 Chess/Rn	31	14	82	43 100	87	11	6	100 100	100	9	5
2 Chess/Jb	31	19	86	74 95	93	12	9	100 100	100	8	6
3 Chess/Jb	31	21	105	15 50	69	15	8	48 90	88	13	7
4 Chess/(Tel) Bl	31	25	99	52 84	78	7	6	80 88	88	7	6
Totals		79	352	46 80	81	11	7	79 93	93	9	6

Fig. 15. Performance of Hearsay-I speech understanding system. (From Erman [35].) Column 1 gives data set number, task, and speaker identification. Column 2 gives number of words in task lexicon. Column 3 shows number of sentences in data set. Column 4 gives total number of word tokens in data set. Column 5 gives results for HS-I system recognition with Acoustics module and Syntax module both operating. First subcolumn indicates percent of sentences recognized completely correctly. "Near miss" (indicated below that number in first subcolumn) indicates percent of times that recognized utterance differed from actual utterance by at most one word of approximate similar phonetic structure. Second subcolumn gives percent of words recognized correctly. Mean computation times on PDP-10 computer (in seconds per sentence and in seconds per second of speech) are shown in subcolumns three and four. Column 6 shows results for recognition using all three sources of knowledge (for Chess task only): Acoustics, Syntax, and Semantics modules. Subcolumns are similar to those of Column 5.

the data, analysis of the conversation, and the presence of certain content words in the blackboard.

The task for SPEECHLIS is to act as an assistant to a travel budget manager. It permits interactive query and manipulation of a travel budget of a company. It is meant to help a manager keep track of the trips taken or proposed, and to produce summary information such as the total money spent or allocated. The vocabulary is about 1000 words. The syntax permits a wide variety of English sentences and is based on the augmented transition network (ATN) formalism developed by Woods [164]. The parser is driven by a modified ATN grammar [15], [16] which permits parsing to start anywhere, not necessarily left-to-right. The semantic component is based on a *semantic net* and uses *case frame tokens* to check for the consistency of completed syntactic constituents and the current semantic hypotheses [103]. Semantics is also used to focus attention and to produce a representation of the meaning of the utterance. A discourse model is used to predict what the user might say next.

The task for VDMS is to provide interactive query and retrieval of information from a "submarine data base." The vocabulary for the task is about 1000 words. The language definition facility [128] permits the speaker to communicate in relatively natural English. A semantic net representation along with strategies for net partitioning help to organize and condense the semantics of the task [60]. The pragmatic component [29] permits processing of simple forms of conversation-dependent ellipses and anaphora (see Section V-D).

Status: None of the three systems discussed here is working well enough to report performance statistics. Many component parts of these systems are working, but there are still weak links in the total systems that make such measurements meaningless. In the absence of these, it is useful to look at the performance of Hearsay-I to understand the potential role of semantics and other task-dependent knowledge in speech understanding systems. Fig. 15 shows performance results of Hearsay-I on the voice-chess task, both with and without the use of semantics. In a set of experiments using 79 utterances containing 352 words from three speakers (one speaker using telephone input), the sentence accuracies of the system increased from 46 to 79 percent by the use of task-dependent semantics. Response time also improved by about 10–20 percent (11–9 s). This speedup illustrates the fact that more complexity need not always mean slower systems. It is difficult to extrapolate how well other systems might perform from this lone example which used a powerful semantic module, i.e., a chess program, to predict legal moves. However, most researchers agree that without semantic and/or pragmatic knowledge, the systems will be unable to recognize or interpret some of the nongrammatical and non-well-formed sentences that usually occur in conversations.

Future Directions: It is too soon to draw any conclusions, but a few general observations can be made. The main scientific question to be answered in the next few years will be: is *understanding* a necessary prerequisite for *recognition* or can the simpler CSR systems do the job? If SU systems can achieve higher accuracies or recognize utterances faster on a given task than a CSR system, then the answer can be affirmative. It will always be the case for simple tasks that CSR systems, with their simpler program organization, are more likely to be adequate and cost-effective. What is not known are the tradeoffs that occur with large vocabulary English-like languages in complex task situations.

The second question is how to simplify the structure of the present SU systems while continuing to make effective use of all the available knowledge. Will SU systems price themselves out of the market by being more complex than most computer programs we write? The present systems are large, unwieldy, slow, and contain too many *ad hoc* decisions without the benefit of careful comparative evaluation of potential design choices. This is to be expected given their pioneering status. Once these systems are working, the most important task will be to study design alternatives that will significantly reduce the cost and/or increase the performance.

III. Signal Processing for Speech Recognition

One of the first decisions to be made in the design of a speech recognition system is how to digitize and represent speech in the computer. The tutorial-review paper, "Parametric Representations of Speech" by Schafer and Rabiner [137], provides a comprehensive and in-depth treatment of the digital techniques of speech analysis. Usually the first steps in the recognition process are the division of the connected speech into a sequence of utterances separated by pauses and the normalization of the signal to reduce variability due to noise and speaker. In this section, we shall review the signal processing techniques that have found to be useful in performing these tasks. The books by Fant [39] and Flanagan [44] are recommended for those interested in a thorough understanding of the theory and practice of speech analysis.

A. Parametric Analyses of Speech

Analysis of the speech signal was perhaps the single most popular subject of the papers on speech research in the 1950's and 1960's. The book by Flanagan [44] summarizes much of this work and provides an excellent description of the most commonly used speech analysis techniques, such as the short-time spectrum, formants, zero-crossings, and so on. In recent years, advances in computer architecture, graphics, and interactive use of systems have significantly altered the way speech research is conducted [105], and have tilted the balance in favor of digital rather than analog techniques. Here we will briefly mention some of the techniques that are commonly used in speech recognition research today.

The simplest digital representation of speech is pulse-code modulation (PCM). The changes in air pressure caused by the speech are sampled and digitized by a computer using an analog-to-digital converter. The speech is sampled from six to twenty thousand times a second in speech recognition research, depending on the frequency response desired. The speech is usually quantized at 9 to 16 bits per sample. Schafer and Rabiner [137] report that 11 bits is adequate for most purposes. The higher sample accuracy used in some systems [77], [175] provides for the wide dynamic range of signal levels observed across speakers. Conventional automatic gain control techniques produce signal distortions and are not preferred by researchers. It is easier to throw away the unneeded resolution later than to train speakers to speak at a uniform level of loudness.

Given a linear PCM representation of speech, one can derive other representations commonly used in speech recognition. Most of these representations are based on the assumption that parameters of speech remain unchanged over a short-time period. The commonly used *short-time spectrum* can be obtained using an analog filter bank or calculated from the PCM speech using digital filtering techniques or the fast Fourier transform (FFT).

The most widely used technique in speech recognition systems today is the LPC technique pioneered by Atal [1]–[5] and Itakura [68], [69], and extended by Markel [94] and Makhoul [91]. The tutorial-review papers by Makhoul [92], [93] discuss in detail the use of this technique in speech analysis and recognition. The theoretical foundations of LPC are based on the fact that the model of an acoustic tube whose input is impulses or low-level noise is mathematically tractable, i.e., the important parameters of the tube can be determined from its output, and that the model is good enough in estimating the response of the vocal tract. The basic ideal behind LPC is that, given the acoustic tube model of the vocal tract, the present can be estimated from the immediate past, i.e., a speech sample can be expressed as a linear function of the preceding P speech samples. The coefficients of the linear function are determined by least square error fitting of the short-time speech signal. Given the coefficients, one can derive other parametric representations of speech, such as spectrum, formants, and vocal tract shape. Besides linear predictive coding (LPC), other commonly used parametric representations in speech recognition are the smoothed short-time spectrum based on DFT processing [175] and measurements based on amplitude and zerocrossings [11]. Silverman and Dixon [175] state that they have found DFT based processing of speech to be more desirable in their system than LPC based methods.

B. End-Point Detection

Division of connected discourse into utterances, i.e., detection of the beginning and ending of individual phrases is usually called end-point detection. Accurate determination of the end points is not very difficult if the signal-to-noise ratio is high, say greater than 60 dB. But most practical speech recognition systems must work with much lower S/N ratios, sometimes as low as 15 to 20 dB. Under these conditions, weak fricatives and low-amplitude voiced sounds occurring at the end points of the utterance become difficult to detect, leading to unacceptable error rates in high-accuracy systems. It is possible to detect end points accurately even in the presence of noise by careful attention to the algorithms. Gold [51], Vicens [152], and Martin [96] report on specific algorithms used by their systems.

The only careful study of this problem so far appears in a paper by Rabiner and Sambur [118]. They use the overall energy measure to locate an approximate end-point interval (N_1, N_2) such that although part of the utterance may be outside the interval, the actual end points are not within this interval. Precise end points are obtained by extending this interval in both directions to include any low-amplitude unvoiced fricatives at the beginning and end using a strict threshold on a zero-crossing measure.

Martin [96] reports on the use of a pattern matching technique to distinguish speech sounds from breath noise, which has its own spectral characteristics. Vicens [152] detects and rejects high-energy impulse noises, such as opening of the lips (when using a close-speaking microphone) and teletypewriter noise, by their very short duration followed by a long pause.

C. Noise Normalization

The single most important factor that affects the reliability and repeatability of speech recognition systems at present is the lack of proper attention to the sources of noise, i.e., background noise, microphone (or telephone) frequency response, reverberation noise, and noise from quantization and aliasing. Systems tend to be reliable as long as these sources of noise are kept invariant, but show a significant drop in performance as soon as the situation is altered. There have been a few studies on recognition in noisy environments [96], [104], and on the use of telephone as input device [38], [70]. But there are many questions that still remain unanswered.

Many system designs respond to the problems of noise by refusing to deal with this source of variability and requiring a new training session each time the environment, the microphone, or the speaker is changed. This seems acceptable in the short run but systematic studies into noise normalization techniques and the factors affecting the potential tradeoffs will be needed eventually.

Background Noise: This type of noise is usually produced by air-conditioning systems, fans, fluorescent lamps, typewriters, computer systems, background conversation, footsteps, traffic, opening and closing doors, and so on. The designers of a speech recognition system usually have little control over these in real-life environments. This type of noise is additive in nature and usually steady state except for impulse noise sources like typewriters. Depending on the environment, the noise levels will vary from about 60 dB (A) to 90 dB (A). Many of the noise sources have energies concentrated over certain portions of the spectrum and are generally not representable by white-noise experiments.

The most commonly used technique to minimize the effects of background noise is to use a head-mounted close-speaking microphone. When a speaker is producing speech at normal conversational levels, the average speech level increases by about 3 dB each time the microphone-to-speaker distance is reduced by an inch (when the distances are small). In absolute terms, the speech level is usually around 90 to 100 dB when the speaker-to-microphone distance is less than 1 in. Some systems use the so-called noise-canceling close-speaking microphones which are somewhat adaptive to the noise levels in the environment [126]. It is important that a close-speaking microphone be head mounted; otherwise even slight movement of the speaker relative to the microphone will cause large fluctuations in the speech level. Close-speaking microphones may also exhibit somewhat poorer frequency response characteristics. Careful experimental studies are needed to determine the microphone-related factors that affect the performance of a speech recognition system. Another method often used to reduce background noise derived from air conditioning, 60-Hz electrical hum, etc., is to high-pass filter the signal. (Cut-off frequency $\approx$80 to 120 Hz.)

Two signal processing techniques are generally used to normalize the spectra so as to reduce the effects of noise and distortion: inverse filtering and spectrum weighting. Silverman and Dixon [175] use quadratic spectral normalization to compensate for amplitude variations. Itakura [70] uses a second-order inverse filter based on the long-time spectrum of the entire utterance. This is intended to normalize the gross spectral distribution of the utterance. One could also use an inverse filter based on the noise characteristics alone rather than the whole utterance. Spectrum weighting techniques attempt to ignore those parts of the spectrum where the S/N ratio is low. This can be achieved by subtraction of the log noise spectrum from the log speech spectrum. This is equivalent to $[S_t + N_t]/N$, where S_t and N_t are the short-time spectra of speech and noise at time T, and N is the long-time average spectrum of the noise [170]. Another technique is to extract features only from those frequency bands where the signal spectrum exceeds the noise spectrum by at least 6 dB or more. The larger the difference, the less the impact due to noise.

Telephone Noise: Use of the telephone as the input device for a speech recognition system introduces several problems: the restriction of the bandwidth to 300 to 3000 Hz, the uneven frequency response of the carbon microphone, burst noise, distortion, echo, crosstalk, frequency translation, envelope delay, clipping, and so on. It is not known at this time how each of these problems affects the accuracy and performance of a system. In the case of isolated word recognition systems, we know [70] that there is little effect in the case of relatively unambiguous vocabularies, but the accuracy drops significantly for ambiguous words, like in the alpha-digit list. Further studies are needed to suggest noise normalization techniques which will improve the accuracy for telephone input systems. Use of a different microphone headset connected to the telephone systems and preemphasis and/or postemphasis to normalize for the frequency response characteristics have been suggested [38]. Techniques suggested for background noise normalization would also be applicable here.

Reverberation Noise: In rooms which have hard reflecting surfaces, there is a significant reverberant field. Unlike background noise, which is additive, reverberation is a multiplicative noise and cannot easily be suppressed. If the reverberation measurement of an environment indicates a significant reverberation component, acoustic treatment of the room may be necessary. One can reduce the effects of reverberation by using a close-speaking microphone and locating the input station away from hard reflecting surfaces if possible.

Sampling Effects: Speech input is filtered by passing through a low-pass filter prior to the sampling process to eliminate undesired high frequencies (aliasing) of speech and high frequencies of noise. The characteristics of the filter, especially its rolloff near the cutoff frequency, are superimposed on the spectrum of the speech signal. It is not known whether this has any significant effect on the performance of the system.

Future Directions: We do not yet have a clear idea of which of the many possible techniques of noise normalization work well and which do not, and what the accuracy and performance tradeoffs are. We need many careful experimental studies. However, some basic issues are clear, although very few systems seem to have paid any attention to them. In high-noise environments, it will be difficult to detect, recognize, and distinguish between silence, weak fricatives (voiced and unvoiced), voice bars, voiced and unvoiced /h/, and nasals in some contexts. In systems using telephone input it will be difficult to detect and distinguish between most stops, fricatives, and nasals. Systems must provide for some form of noise adaptation at the symbol (usually phonemic) matching level if they are to be noise-insensitive.

IV. Task-Independent Knowledge

There are many aspects of processing that are common to both connected speech recognition (CSR) systems and speech understanding (SU) systems. The associated knowledge and techniques are: the speech sounds and symbols (phones and phonemes), features associated with speech sounds (acoustic–phonetics), rules governing the insertions and deletions of speech sounds (phonological rules), stress and intonation patterns of speech (prosodics), and matching of speech sounds with higher level linguistic units (syllables and words). The knowledge associated with these techniques is primarily dependent on the language and is usually independent of the task to be performed. In this section we will present the knowledge, techniques, and present state of accomplishment associated with these task-independent aspects of speech recognition, i.e., phonemic labeling, phonology, word hypothesis, and word verification.

In the following discussion, the use of the terms *phone*, *phoneme*, and *syllable* are somewhat different from the conventional usage of these terms in linguistic literature. In linguistics, the use of these terms is motivated by either perceptual or articulatory (production) considerations. Our use of the terms is acoustically motivated. Thus the minimally distinctive character of a phoneme is based on acoustic considerations, i.e., two phonemes are distinct if they are acoustically separable. We choose to use the same terms rather than invent some new ones because the intent is the same even through the criteria for distinguishabilty are different.

A. Phonemic Labeling

We have already seen, while discussing the difficulties of CSR systems (Section II-B), that some form of signal-to-symbol transformation is necessary and that attempting to match using reference patterns (as in the case of word recognition) can lead to unwieldy and unextensible CSR systems. The common technique adopted by CSR and SU systems is to attempt to transform the speech into a phonemic (or some such) string, which is then matched to the expected phones in the word. This transformation of the speech signal into a sequence of phonemic symbols usually involves feature detection, segmentation, and labeling. The tutorial-review paper by Broad and Shoup [21] presents some of the basic concepts associated with the phonemic labeling problem. The book by Fant [40] provides a comprehensive discussion of the features of speech sounds and their relationship to phonemic labels. Here we will outline the techniques useful in machine labeling of speech.

Feature detection usually represents the detection of silence, voicing, stress, and so on. The purpose of segmentation is to divide the continuous speech signal into discrete units based on some measure of acoustic similarity. Labeling schemes associate a phonemic symbol with each segmental unit. Before this symbol sequence can be used in matching, it is necessary to apply phonological rules (Section IV-B) to combine segments, change labels based on context, delete segments such as transitions, and so on.

Different systems do these operations in different orders. Some systems segment the data first, use the averaged segmental parameters to detect features such as voicing and stress, and then attempt labeling. Other systems classify and label speech every 10 ms and use the resulting labels in segmentation. The former tends to be less sensitive to noise and segment boundary effects. The commonly used paradigm is to detect features, then segment, and then label.

Not all connected speech recognition systems use segmentation and labeling prior to matching. The Dragon system [9] matches the phonemic representation of the word directly at the 10-ms level. Bakis [12] reports significantly improved performance on the continuous digit recognition experiment using the segmentation-free word template matching technique. However, such techniques are likely to run into serious difficulties with large vocabularies involving a wide variety of juncture phenomena.

1) Feature Extraction: There are a large number of potential features one can extract from speech [40]. Many of these tend to be unreliable, and it is difficult to devise detection algorithms for them. Hughes and Hemdal [65] and Itahashi *et al.* [67] have attempted detecting various distinctive features with a limited success. However, certain basic features are extracted by almost all the systems: silence, voicing, and stress. These are usually based on two measurements: energy and fundamental frequency (pitch period) of the speech signal. Schafer and Rabiner [137] present the basic concepts and techniques useful in extracting energy and pitch measurements. One common measure of energy is to sum the absolute values of the speech samples over a 5-ms region. The papers by Sondhi [147], Gold and Rabiner [52], and Gillmann [50], provide several alternate techniques for extracting pitch periods.

Silence detection is usually based on a threshold applied to the energy function. Weinstein *et al.* [159] use a threshold of about 3 dB over the background noise level. When the energy falls below this threshold it is classified as a silence. The silence segment is then extended on both sides as long as the energy in the adjacent frames stays below a slightly higher threshold.

Voicing decision is usually based on the results of pitch extraction. If the period shows wide variability, it is treated as unvoiced [52]. In addition, concentration of energy in the high-frequency regions (3700–5000 Hz) when compared with low-frequency regions (100–900 Hz) is also an indication of unvoicing [159].

Stress decisions are usually based both on energy and on the pitch period. Much of the recent work on stressed syllable detection is based on the work by Lea *et al.* [79], [81]. Lea gives an algorithm for detecting stressed syllables from the rise–fall patterns of the pitch period (F_0) contours and the local maxima of energy. Although F_0 contours fall gradually in each breath group, it is possible to detect those maxima related to stress and they usually show rises over the gradually falling contour.

In addition to such primary features, several systems [136], [127] use other measures such as normalized linear prediction error, frequency of 2-pole linear prediction model, first autocorrelation coefficient, and energy in the 5–10-kHz region. Each of these features measures some quality of the signal such as lack of high-frequency energy or presence of voicing.

2) Segmentation: It is often said that "the problem with segmentation is that you can't segment." That is to say, there is no simple machine algorithm which will give phonemic boundaries. However, if one is satisfied with acoustic boundaries, i.e., boundaries associated with significant changes in the acoustic characteristics of speech, then it is possible to devise automatic algorithms to segment speech. The papers by Fant and Lindblom [42], Reddy [119], Reddy and Vicens [125], Tappert *et al.* [148], Dixon and Silverman [30], [31], Baker [11], and Goldberg [53] illustrate several attempts to segment connected speech into phonemic units with the understanding that some phonemic boundaries may be missed and some acoustic boundaries may be inserted where there are no phonemic boundaries.

Why is segmentation difficult? Figs. 16 and 17 (from Goldberg [53]) give examples where a boundary may be missing or added based on acoustic evidence. Fig. 16 gives the oscillogram of part of the word sequence 'been measured.' Note that it is impossible to say where /n/ ends and /m/ begins (vide the time period 121 to 132 centiseconds). The labels indicated at the bottom of the figure indicate an arbitrary choice on the part of the human segmenter. Fig. 17 contains part of the waveform of the word 'samples' and the corresponding spectrogram. Note that there is a significant variation in the parameters in the last 4 centiseconds (from 75 to 79) of the vowel resulting from coarticulation. Any attempt to ignore this variation can lead to errors in other contexts. A segmentation program based on acoustic measurements would normally insert an extra segment even though there is not a corresponding phoneme.

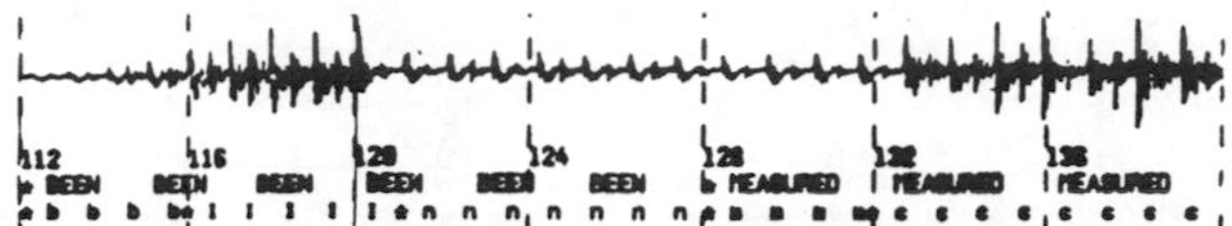

Fig. 16. Example of missing phoneme boundary, showing oscillogram (waveform) plot of part of the word sequence "been measured." Time scale is indicated on the first line below the plot in centisecond units. Second line shows a manually derived marker indicating which part of the waveform belongs to "been" and which part to "measured" (only parts of each word are visible in the plot). Third line shows manually derived markers indicating where various phonemes belonging to the words begin and end. The ending phoneme /n/ of the word "been" is assimilated with the beginning phoneme /m/ of the word "measured" as can be seen from the lack of any visible indication in the waveform. Boundary indicated at time 128 cs represents an arbitrary choice on the part of the human segmenter.

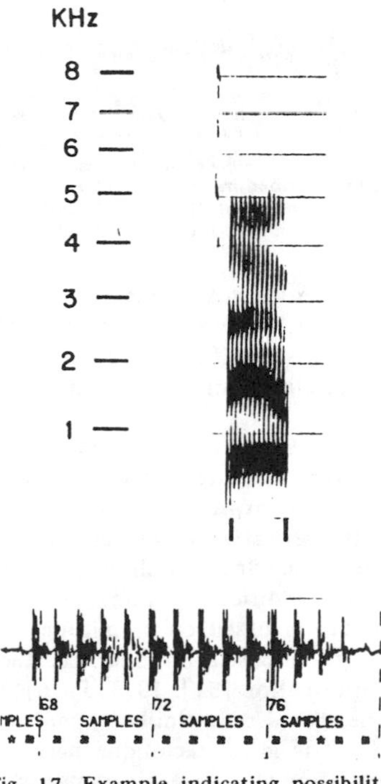

Fig. 17. Example indicating possibility of extra acoustic segments for a given phonetic segment. The waveform plot is similar to the one described in Fig. 16. The vowel /ae/ has significantly different parameters for the last 50 ms or so (from time unit 75 onwards) making it a candidate for an extra acoustic boundary.

There are many times when a boundary is expected but it is difficult to say exactly where it should be placed because of continuous variation. Fig. 18 illustrates an example of this. Looking at the waveform and the spectrogram for part of the word 'ratio,' it is difficult to say where /i/ ends and /o/ begins. Again the boundary indicated (* on line 3 between /i/ and /o/ at time 324) represents an arbitrary choice on the part of the human segmenter. If a machine segmentation program should place that boundary marker at a slightly different position (or time unit), it does not necessarily indicate an error of segmentation. In general, one will observe a few missing phonemic boundaries, some extra boundaries, and some cases in which the location of the boundary is shifted. These do not necessarily represent errors, but rather arise from the nature of the acoustic phenomena associated with phonemic symbols.

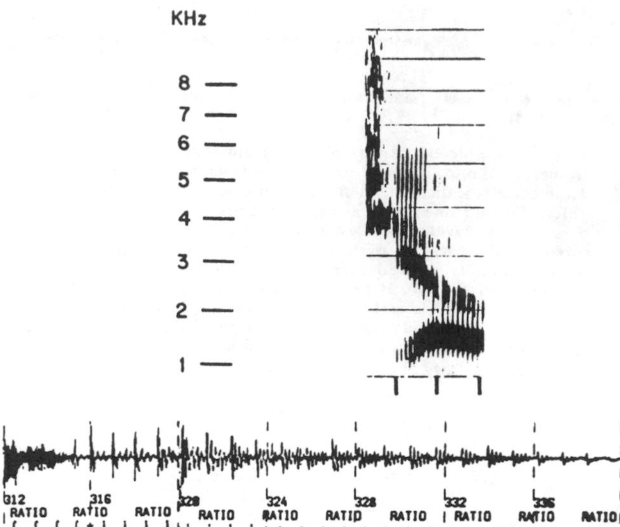

Fig. 18. Example of hard-to-place boundaries. The waveform plot is similar to the one described in Fig. 16. Note that it is difficult to say where /i/ ends and /o/ begins in the word "ratio"—boundary could be placed anywhere between time unit 324 and 330.

Another problem with segmentation is devising an appropriate acoustic similarity measure which indicates a boundary if and only if there is significant acoustic change. It is difficult to express in algorithm from intuitive notions of waveform similarity.

Segmentation techniques: Amplitude (or energy) is the single most important measure in segmentation [119]. It can be used to detect many of the boundaries. Sometimes it leads to extra segments in fricative sounds and missing segments in vowel/liquid sequences. Spectral characteristics of the sounds can be used to find additional boundaries that are missed by the gross segmentation based on amplitude. This additional segmentation may be based on heuristic techniques using speech specific information [31], [32], [136], [159], or algorithmic techniques based on a similarity metric on the parameter space [53]. The latter technique permits experimentation with and evaluation of different parametric representations of speech. The instantaneous frequency representation [11] yields the most accurate boundaries in nonsonorant speech (within 1 or 2 ms).

Fig. 19 shows typical segment boundaries placed by a machine segmenter [53]. The labels on the third and fourth rows under the waveforms in Fig. 19 show the human segmentation and labeling given for the utterance. The vertical lines indicate machine segmentation. Note that there are many more machine segments than there are phonemic boundaries. Examination of the waveform and spectrograms in the figure shows that many of the extra segments are in fact not errors in segmentation but a consequence of intraphone variability and transitions between phones.

Performance: There are many factors which must be considered in the evaluation of segmentation programs. Fig. 20 presents a list of some of the more important ones. Since reported performance evaluations of different programs may deal with only a few of these factors, direct comparisons are difficult to make.

Dixon and Silverman [31] report 6.9 percent missed segments with 10.5 percent extra segments over 6175 segments (8.5 min of speech). Recordings were made under sound booth conditions with high quality equipment. A single speaker was used and speaker specific training was employed. The segmenter also makes use of speech specific knowledge at the phonetic level. Dixon and Silverman report that recent work has further reduced these error rates to 5 percent missed and 6 percent extra.

Baker [11] reports 9.3 percent missed with 17.6 percent extra segments for 216 segments in 5 sentences spoken by 4 male and one female speaker. Recording conditions and equipment varied, and no speaker specific information at the phonetic level was used. The referent segmentation used in Baker's study included all segments indicated at the phonemic level. Hence, omissions of sounds by the speakers may have caused slightly higher missed segment rates than would be shown with a less conservative referent.

Goldberg [53] reports a 3.7 percent missed and 27.6 percent extra segments for 1085 segments in 40 sentences spoken under terminal room conditions (~65 dB (A)) using a close speaking microphone. Training was speaker specific and no speech specific knowledge was employed. The system was tested for several speakers with similar results. Goldberg introduces a model from signal detection theory to quantify the missed versus extra segment tradeoff. By adjusting a few thresholds, error rates (predicted by the model) of 11.7 percent missed and 11.7 percent extra can be achieved.

3) Labeling: Labeling is the process by which each segment is assigned a label. This can be done either heuristically [73], [120], [136], [159], based on speech specific information, or by using a nearest neighbor pattern classification technique [53], or both [31].

As in every other aspect of speech recognition, it is difficult to attempt comparative evaluation of different labeling schemes. There are three factors that affect accuracy and computation time of a labeling procedure: number of labels, number of alternate choices, and the correctness criteria. Weinstein *et al.* [159] report results of labeling accuracy for about 20 or the 35 APEL labels used in the Lincoln system. Dixon and Silverman [31] use 34 different phonemic class labels in their system. Goldberg [53] uses about 70 labels to account for various allophonic variations. The finer the desired phonemic transcription, the lower the accuracy.

The second factor that affects apparent accuracy of labeling is the *branching factor*, i.e., the number of alternate labels assigned to a segment, and is indicative of the degree of indecision of an algorithm. If you permit a large number of alternative choices, the correct label will appear sooner or later. Fig. 21 (from Goldberg [53]) illustrates the effects of the branching factor and the number of labels on accuracy. The figure shows that the labeling accuracy increases sharply when one considers several alternative choices. For example, the correct label appears as one of the choices 70–80 percent of the time if one considers 5 alternative choices (out of a possible 40) whereas it is the top choice only about 35 percent of the time.

The third and perhaps the most elusive factor is the label assigned to a segment by a human subject to be used for the evaluation of the machine labeler. Dixon *et al.* [174], [144] discuss the need for objective phonetic transcription and its importance in obtaining reliable performance statistics. Shockey and Reddy [142] show that subjective judgments of phoneticians seem to agree among themselves only about 51 percent of the time when labeling spontaneous connected speech in unfamiliar languages. Most of this variability is at-

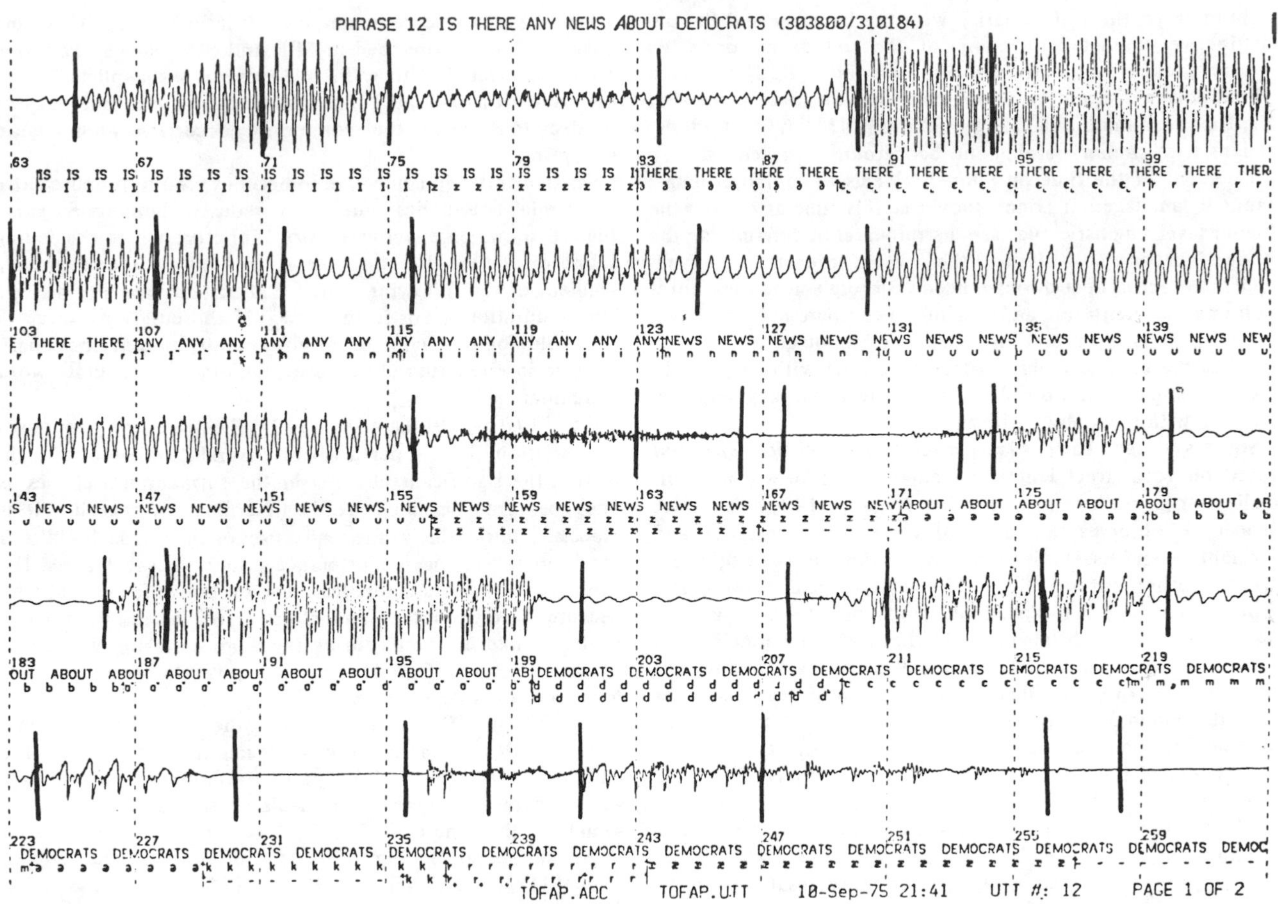

Fig. 19. Typical result of a machine segmentation "Is there any news about Democrats?" The waveform plot is similar to the one described in Fig. 16. Dark vertical lines indicate position of machine boundaries.

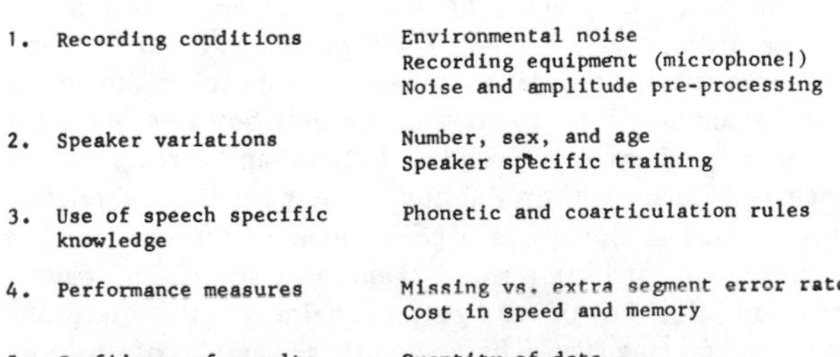

1. Recording conditions	Environmental noise Recording equipment (microphone!) Noise and amplitude pre-processing
2. Speaker variations	Number, sex, and age Speaker specific training
3. Use of speech specific knowledge	Phonetic and coarticulation rules
4. Performance measures	Missing vs. extra segment error rates Cost in speed and memory
5. Confidence of results	Quantity of data Nature and quality of "correct" segmentation (referent)

Fig. 20. Typical factors which may affect segmentation performance evaluations.

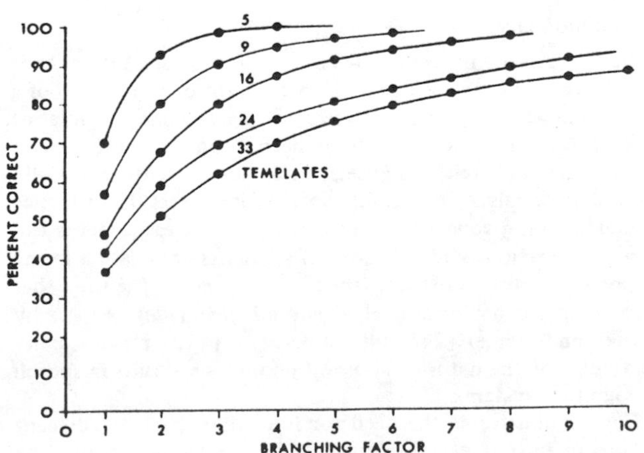

Fig. 21. Accuracy of labeling as a function of branching factor (number of choices per segment) and number of templates. The number below each curve indicates the number of template classes. The 5 classes consist of vowels, liquids, fricatives, nasals, and stops. Larger numbers of classes indicate finer subdivisions. The 33 classes are individual phonetic labels. (For further details, see Goldberg [53].)

tributable to the unfamiliarity with the language and the undistinctive character of many of the sounds in connected speech spoken by a native speaker. Carterette [22] says that phoneticians disagree on phonemic labels up to 20 percent of the time on a familiar language. Shoup [143] says that phoneticians with similar training and background disagree less than 10 percent of the time on phonetic labels while transcribing a familiar language. It is not known at this time how often the higher level linguistic cues are instrumental in determining the phone label and how often all the relevant information is available in the actual speech signal itself. Since we need some form of human segmentation and labeling to compare machine labeling with, it is clear that the accuracies reported are only as good as the manually derived labels we start with. Fig. 19 illustrates some of the problems with perceptual judgments associated with manually derived labels.

Some systems [159], [166] attempt *speaker normalization* based on vocal tract length estimates [155] or a vowel normalization procedure proposed by Gerstman [49]. The latter procedure observes the range of values for formant 1 and formant 2, and uses a linear scaling technique based on these values. Other systems [30], [53] achieve speaker normalization by using speaker-dependent prototype reference patterns associated with each label. Note that speaker normalization may be necessary and useful at many other levels besides the labeling level. Fig. 3 indicates many of the potential sources of improvement. In addition to vocal tract variations, one has to consider dialectal variations, vocabulary and grammatical preferences of the user, and a psychological model of the user predicting what action he might take next.

Performance: There are a few performance evaluations of labeling schemes given in the literature [31], [46], [53], [120], [159]. Of these, the performance results given by Dixon and Silverman [31] are the most comprehensive so far and are representative of the state of accomplishment to date in labeling connected speech. Dixon and Silverman report 61.7 percent accuracy at the phoneme level and 88.6 percent accuracy at the phoneme-class level.

B. Phonological Rules

In the preceding section, we saw how a speech utterance is segmented and each segment is labeled with one (or more) of a set of phonemic symbols. Here we will give some examples of knowledge and rules that have been found to be useful in combining and relabeling segmental units (with essentially phonemic labels). In natural continuous speech, the influence of surrounding vowels and consonants and stress patterns can lead to insertions and deletions of segments or variation in the expected acoustic characteristics of phonemes. The rules that govern this behavior are called *phonological rules.* Papers by Cohen and Mercer [24] and Oshika *et al.* [112] provide many examples of the nature and use of phonological rules in speech recognition systems.

Fig. 12 illustrates the need for rules that combine adjacent segments into larger sized units. In the word "about" the diphthong /aw/ is usually divided into two or more segments. Given the labels (or features) of individual segments, one can define diphthong detection rules which will combine the segments into larger units when an appropriate sequence of labels occurs. Often the onglide and offglide portion of a vowel are indicated as separate segments. In this case these segments are deleted using segment deletion rules. In Fig. 12, the initial part of /aa/ in "all" is an example of an onglide which has no phonemic significance of its own.

Fig. 22 gives some examples of insertion, deletion, and change rules that are used in CSR and SU systems. The comments associated with each rule explain the applicability of that rule. It is estimated that a few hundred such rules may be needed to explain the commonly occurring phonological variations.

Segment insertion rules are sometimes used to propose extra phonemic boundaries where no acoustic boundaries exist. Fig. 16 shows an example of word juncture where the ending sound of one word is the same as (or similar to) the beginning segment of the following word. This usually leads to a single longer duration acoustic segment. If the duration exceeds a threshold for that class of speech sounds, an extra boundary may be inserted (usually at the midpoint) to facilitate word matching.

Fig. 23 (from Oshika *et al.* [112]) illustrates the phonological variation that is pervasive in natural continuous speech. Notice the significant changes in the formant trajectories as one goes from isolated words to connected speech. It is especially noticeable in the realization of the words "you" and "the" in the connected utterance. In both these cases, the expected vowel characteristics have been significantly altered because of the context and stress. Any attempt to find a /u/-like sound in "you" during the word matching would lead to the rejection of that word as a possible choice for that portion of the utterance.

Fig. 23 also illustrates several other phonological phenomena. Note that a frication segment is inserted at the juncture of the words "did you" (pronounced as "did ja") where there was none in the isolated words. The fricative sounds at the juncture of "refresh screen" are merged into a single /sh/ sound, leading to the deletion of a segment. Oshika *et al.* [112] and Cohen and Mercer [24] provide a detailed discussion of the specification and use of phonological rules in speech recognition systems.

C. Prosodics

Prosodic features of speech, i.e., stress, intonation, rhythm, pauses, and tempo, augment the syntactic and semantic structure of language in helping to communicate the intended message. *Stress* patterns of speech help to distinguish between "light housekeeper" and "lighthouse keeper." *Intonation* helps to distinguish between "I will move, on Saturday" and "I will move on, Saturday." *Rhythm* in speech is illustrated by the example "John, who was the best boy in school, got the medal" where one usually observes an increase in the speech rate during the production of the parenthetical relative clause (almost as though each constituent of the sentence has to observe an equal-time rule). *Tempo* of speech and *pauses* provide additional distinctive patterns helpful in the interpretation of spoken language. These and other examples of prosodic knowledge, given in Lea *et al.* [81], illustrate the importance of prosodics in speech understanding research.

Stress and pause structure have been used to determine syntactic boundaries in utterances [81], [82], [111]. Although the boundaries cannot be placed exactly, they do indicate the general area within the utterance where a syntactic boundary may be expected. Rising and falling patterns of pitch contours have been used to determine whether an utterance is a question or an assertion. Research is presently under way [81] to determine other acoustic correlates of contrasting patterns of intonation, rhythm, and tempo in speech.

X → W/Y * Z means X can become W in the context of Y and Z

{ } means logical OR

( ) means enclosed segment is optional

;... indicates a comment

Insertion Rules

0 → (-) / n * s	; a silence segment may be inserted between /n/ and /s/
r → (s) (r) / t * i	; an /r/ occuring in the context of /t/ and /i/ may result in an optional fricative sound /s/
0 → (i) / t * u	; an /i/-like segment may appear in the context of /t/ and /u/

Deletion Rules

b → 0 / m *	; a /b/ might be missing when preceded by an /m/
{p, t, k} → 0 / * {p, t, k}	; an unvoiced stop may be missing in the context of another unvoiced stop

Substitution Rules

z → s / Unvoiced * Unvoiced	; a /z/ becomes devoiced in an unvoiced context
s → z / Voiced * Voiced	; an /s/ becomes voiced in a voiced context
{t, d} → Flap / Vowel_1 * Vowel_3	; an intervocalic /t/ or /d/ become flap-like

Fig. 22. Some typical phonological rules. (Compiled from Cohen and Mercer [24], Erman [35], and Hall [55].)

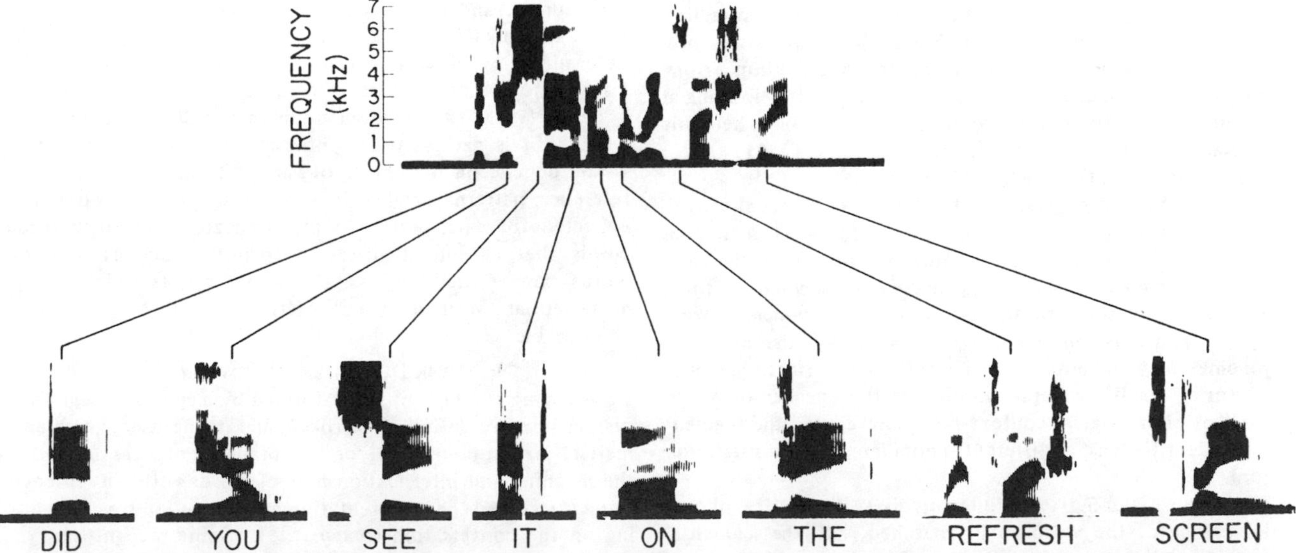

Fig. 23. Spectrograms of the words "did you see it on the refresh screen?" said in isolation, compared with spectrogram of the words in the continuous phrase. Note the significant differences in acoustic characteristics of the words "you" and "the" in the connected speech compared to the corresponding isolated words. (From Oshika *et al.* [112].)

Future Directions: It has been said that "prosodics play the role in spoken language that 'space' plays in written language." If this is so, we have been slow in making effective use of this source of knowledge. To be sure, amplitude (which is a measure of stress) has been used in segmentation and stress detection for a long time, but we are only just beginning to explore other uses of stress and intonation-related phenomena. Forgie [45] suggests that much of the nonlinguistic phenomena such as hesitation and stutter may be detectable from prosodic patterns of speech. This would make it easier to detect and ignore some of the speech-like noises and other nongrammaticality in spoken utterances. These considerations make prosodics an important area of study in speech recognition research.

D. Word Hypothesis

As the vocabularies get larger, it becomes expensive to match all the possible words that may appear in a given part of the utterance. In large vocabulary systems, the phonemic string is used to generate hypotheses for plausible words in a given location which are then verified by various higher level processes and/or more expensive low-level verifiers. There are two techniques presently being used in SU systems [100], [130], [146].

Rovner *et al.* [130] use partial sequences of phonemic descriptions and the expected phonemic patterns of the vocabulary to retrieve words from the lexicon that match the acoustic characteristics of the signal to some specified degree. The class of words scanned may be delimited by explicit enumeration, class membership, or phonemic length. Appropriate word boundary rules are used whenever an adjacent word is known.

Smith's word hypothesizer [146] detects syllables and uses them to retrieve and verify words that have matching syllable types. The syllable type is hypothesized using a Markov probability model to relate a sequence of phones to a sequence of states defining a syllable type. For each stressed syllable type, the program looks up all the words containing the same syllable type using an inverted lexicon, prunes away multisyllable words that do not match with adjacent syllable hypotheses, and rates and hypothesizes the remaining words. Smith reports that the program locates the correct word within the first two choices about 59 percent of the time given a 275-word vocabulary.

E. Word Verification

Matching and verification of hypothesized words, given the acoustic evidence from an unknown utterance, is basic to almost all speech recognition systems. In connected speech this usually implies matching the expected phonemic realizations of a given word with an unknown phonemic string possibly containing insertion, deletion, and substitution errors. Here we will illustrate the techniques employed by looking at the structure of three word verification techniques: heuristic matching [35], [55], stochastic matching [71], [150], [172], and analysis-by-synthesis [75], [12].

Heuristic Matching: Many of the connected speech recognition systems use this type of matching. Hall [55] of Lincoln Laboratories gives one of the clearest descriptions of the basic techniques involved. Matching process must account for three types of errors: some of the symbols in the phonemic string may be spurious (*insertion error*); some of the expected phonemes may be missing as a result of incorrect segmentation, or a result of being unsaid by the speaker (*deletion error*); or phonological context may have caused the segment to be identified as a different phoneme type (*substitution error*).

The basic matching techniques involves aligning the phonemic spelling of the word to be matched with the segmental (phone-like) labels while allowing for the possibility that some of the above types of error may have occurred. Alignment is usually based on the notion of "anchor points" in which stressed vowels and sibilants which are much less likely to be missed are aligned first, followed by the alignment of the remaining vowels and consonants. Once the alignment is completed, the degree of similarity between the word and the unknown phonemic string is defined as a weighted sum of the individual phoneme versus segment label similarity values. These similarity measures are usually available as a confusion matrix generated from a set of manually labeled training data.

Stochastic Matching: This type of matching is used in the IBM system [72], [150], [172] and in the Dragon system [7]. Given a finite-state representation of alternative pronunciations of a word with associated transition probabilities, a dynamic programming technique is used to perform matching left-to-right in a best-first manner. The best phonemic match and the corresponding likelihood are determined by matching all the possible phonemic variations of the word with the unknown segmental phoneme string. This technique, being more mathematically tractable, will probably become the standard technique in word matching. However, careful training procedures are needed to establish the transition probabilities in the graph representation of alternative pronunciations.

Analysis-by-Synthesis: Klatt [75] proposes the use of analysis-by-synthesis as the principal technique for word verification. He feels that phonological phenomena such as vowel reduction, flapping, palatalization, etc., are basically generative in nature and cannot be easily captured in terms of analytic rules. Klatt and Stevens' study of spectrogram reading [76] demonstrates the difficulty. In that study only 77 percent of the segments were correctly (or partially correctly) labeled during the analysis phase, while 97 percent of the words were correctly identified during verification.

Some form of analysis-by-synthesis procedure seems essential to transform an abstract representation of a word into an acoustic representation suitable for matching with the acoustic parametrization of the unknown utterance. Klatt gives the structure and description of an analysis-by-synthesis system which can be used as a word verification component. (see also Section IX of Jelinek [72].)

Future Directions: Whether matching must occur at the signal level, as in the case of analysis-by-synthesis, to achieve accurate recognition will depend on the success achieved by the heuristic and stochastic matching techniques. One would also have to investigate the store versus compute tradeoff in determining whether one can store a set of synthesized (or learned) reference patterns as in the case of word recognition systems (with the necessary juncture rules of course) or whether it is necessary to synthesize them each time. This would depend on the degree of variability and the number of reference patterns needed to cover the range of variability expected for each word. A mixed strategy in which those words that exhibit significant variability (such as function words) are verified by analysis-by-synthesis technique while all others are verified by one of the other techniques might be desirable.

V. Task-Dependent Knowledge

Specifying the task to be performed by a speech recognition system involves defining the *vocabulary* to be used, the grammatical structure of legal or acceptable sentences (*syntax*), the meaning and interrelationships of words within a sentence (*semantics*), and the representation and use of context depending on the conversation (*pragmatics*). Some recognition systems choose to ignore one or more of these KS's, partly because the notions of semantics and pragmatics are somewhat ill-defined and ill-understood at present, and partly because not all the KS's are necessary if the task is sufficiently restricted. The tutorial-review paper by Woods [167] presents a clear discussion of the role of syntax and semantics in speech. In this section, we will illustrate how these task-dependent KS's help to restrict and reduce the combinatorial explosion resulting from the error and uncertainty of the choices at the lower levels.

A major component of an SUS is to understand and respond to a message. There is a large body of literature on language understanding that is relevant. The books edited by Minsky [102], Simon [145], Rustin [133], Colby and Shank [138],

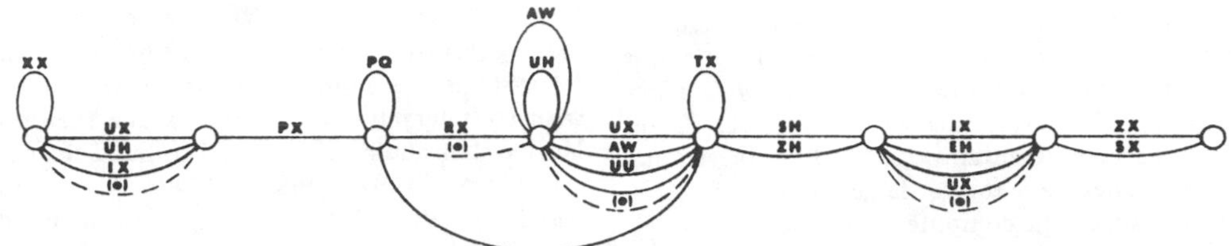

Fig. 24. Phonemic subgraph of the word "approaches" showing possible speaker variation. Branches corresponding to machine error phonemena and indications of second-order constraint have been omitted for clarity of representation. (From Paul *et al.* [114].)

Task	Size of Vocabulary	Language Entropy	Language EQV. Branching factor	Confusability Entropy	Confusability EQV. Branching factor
Digits	10	3.32	10	0.24	1.18
Alphabet	26	4.70	26	2.43	5.39
Alpha-digit	36	5.17	36	2.29	4.89
Chess	31	2.87	7.30	1.37	3.32
Lincoln	237	2.84	7.18		
Extended	411	3.36	12.61		
IBM	250	2.872	7.32		
Prog. language (no syntax)	37	5.21	37.00	1.92	3.78

Fig. 25. Confusability of some common vocabularies. (From Goodman [54].) The first two columns show the entropy per word (i.e., average number of bits it takes to represent a word in the language) and the equivalent branching factor. The last two columns show the confusability of the same vocabulary in terms of entropy (of a noisy channel) and branching factor. Note that the confusability of the digits vocabulary is low while the confusability of the alphabet ("aye," "bee," . . .) is much higher. Note that the average branching factors of the languages used by the systems shown in Figs. 9 and 11 are all less than 10 except for the extended Lincoln task.

Shank [139], and Bobrow and Collins [19] contain a number of the important papers in the natural language understanding area. In this section, we will restrict ourselves to those aspects of the task-dependent knowledge that are directly relevant to the problem of recognition of the utterance.

A. Vocabulary

The primary source of restriction in most speech recognition systems is the vocabulary. Performance of a system is not only affected by the size and dialectal variations of the vocabulary but also by the confusability among the words. The main design choice associated with this level is the representation of alternative pronunciations of the words. If the task permits, one might also wish to select words so as to minimize the confusability among them.

Representation of Phonemic Variation: Most of us know that words are pronounced differently in different contexts. The phrases "David and Robert" and "Fish'n chips" illustrate two different pronunciations of "and." The word "mostly" is sometimes pronounced without the /t/, as "mosly." What is not commonly realized is that much of this variability is rule governed and can be predicted by a set of phonological rules [24], [112]. Starting with a phonemic base form, one can create all possible alternative pronunciations. Early attempts represented each phonemic variation as a separate entry in the lexicon, but most present systems use a more compact network representation. Fig. 24 [114] illustrates the representation of many alternate pronunciations of "approaches" in the network form. Stress and syllable boundary information is also usually entered in the lexicon.

The lexical entries are sometimes preanalyzed to determine all the words that have the same syllable type and represented as an inverted dictionary where one can look up all the words that have the same syllable. This type of representation is useful in generating word hypotheses based on the phones and syllables observed in the symbolic representation of the unknown utterance.

Ambiguity: We saw in Section II how a system which gives 99 percent accuracy on a 200-word multisyllable vocabulary can drop to 89 percent accuracy on a 36-word alpha-digit list. This is because the letters of the alphabet (when pronounced as "aye," "bee," "cee," · · ·) are highly confusable. It is thus important to know not only the size of a vocabulary but also a measure of its confusability. Goodman [54] has studied the confusability of several vocabularies using both theoretical and experimental methods. Fig. 25 summarizes some of his results for several task domains. The first two columns show the entropy per word (i.e., average number of bits required to represent a word in the language) and equivalent branching factor. Thus for the digit sequence recognition task, where any of the 10 digits can follow at every choice point, the average branching factor is 10. However, the confusability of the digits vocabulary is not very high. Using the notion of entropy of a noisy channel, Goodman shows that, from a confusability point of view, the average branching factor for the digit task is only 1.18. For the spelling task (i.e., alphabet recognition task), the confusability is much higher, with a branching factor of 5.39.

Effect of Vocabulary Size on Accuracy: There have been no systematic studies in this area. The Lincoln system performance drops from 49 percent sentence accuracy to 28 percent when the vocabulary increases from 237 words to 411 words. (Note that the complexity of the language, as measured by the average branching factor, has also increased. Fig. 25 shows that the branching factor increased from 7.32 to 12.61—almost proportional to the increase in vocabulary in this case.) The Hearsay-I system shows a similar drop in performance in going from 30 to 194 words. What seems to be important is not so much the size but rather the confusability. In vocabularies that have not been carefully preselected, i.e., they might be assumed to have about the same percentage of words that are confusable, doubling the size of vocabulary seems to double the error rate. This linear increase is contrary to the earlier expectations that, as the vocabularies get larger, confusability among words (and hence the error rate) would only grow less than linearly. However, this linear increase should not be of concern if CSR systems can approach the accuracies being achieved by word recognition systems, i.e., greater than 99 percent accuracy at the word level.

Future Directions: Assuming that current trends in research and technology will continue, there is no reason, in principle at least, why we should not look toward *unlimited vocabulary recognition* systems. However, this will require significant advances in dictionary representation, word hypothesis, and word verification. There are several large phonemic dictionaries of English available in computer readable form [57]. Words that do not exist can be added using grapheme-to-phoneme translation techniques (see the paper by Jon Allen in this issue). Special techniques have to be devised to produce compact and easily retrievable representations of a dictionary containing on the order of a million entries.

Unstressed function words will always be a problem, whether we have a 1000-word system or an unlimited vocabulary system. To establish the feasibility of unlimited vocabulary recognition, we need to consider only the problems of locating and recognizing the rest of the words which can be expected to have at least one stressed syllable. Given the present and projected performances of word hypothesis procedures, fewer than one thousand of the million words are likely to be hypothesized around each stressed syllable. This candidate list can be further pruned to 10 or 20 words using stochastic word verification procedures discussed in Section IV. At this point the remaining words will have fine differences, such as between the words *sit* and *slit*. These will require analysis-by-synthesis, matching with prestored reference patterns for syllables, or some such technique. Any further ambiguities at this stage and prediction and detection of unstressed function words will require the active mediation of higher level processes, such as pragmatics.

B. Syntax

The grammatical structure of sentences can be viewed as principally a mechanism for reducing search by restricting the number of acceptable alternatives. Given a vocabulary of size N, if one permits any word to follow any other word such as "sleep roses dangerously young colorless," the number of possible sentences would be of the order N^L for utterances of less than L words in length. Syntactic structure imposes an ordering and mutually interdependent relationships among words such that only a subset of the N^L is in fact possible.

For example, the IBM New Raleigh task [10] containing 250 words permits only 1.4×10^7 sentences of the possible 250^8 ($\sim 10^{19}$), thereby reducing the search space by a factor of 10^{12}. A more meaningful measure for CSR systems is the average branching factor of the grammar, i.e., the average number of alternative word hypotheses possible at each point in the grammar. For the IBM New Raleigh task, this is about 8 out of the possible 250 words (with a maximum branching factor of about 24). Baker and Bahl [10] measure the complexity of a grammar in terms of the entropy of a word in the language. For the IBM task, the entropy was 2.87. (Note 2^{entropy} is also a measure of the average branching factor of the grammar.) One must also consider the confusability among the alternative words at each choice point. Fig. 25 (from [54]) shows the entropy and the average branching factor that can be expected as a result of the confusability of the vocabulary. Note that the average branching factors for several of the systems discussed in Section II are all less than 10.

Woods [165] proposes four categories to measure the constraint provided by a given grammar. The first two categories are finite-state grammars, the first one having a small branching factor (usually less than 30 at each choice point) and the second one having large branching factors (greater than 400 words at some choice points). Category III systems are artificial languages characterized by context-free grammars permitting recursion, and having large branching factors. Category IV systems are approximations to natural English grammars with considerably larger search space than even category III. Most systems built to data tend to be of the category I type.

Robinson [129] argues that the representation of grammar based on written language is likely to be of limited use. She proposes that the discovery of rules governing spoken language behavior and the development of performance grammars should be based on systematic study of conversational speech. She demonstrates some of the strategies and constraints operating in performance (and the rule-governed regularities they produce) by analysis of several task-oriented dialogs.

Representation: The most commonly used representation for grammars is some form of network representation. Woods [167] uses augmented transition network (ATN) grammars. An ATN consists of a finite-state transition diagram with embedded recursion added, and a set of registers which can hold arbitrary pieces of tree structure and can be modified depending on the actions (programs) associated with the arcs of the grammar. The ATN formalism is known to have the linguistic adequacy of a transformational grammar while providing more of the efficiency needed in parsing algorithms. The papers by Bates [15], [16], and Paxton [115] contain examples of the representation and use of transition network grammars.

Baker [7] and Jelinek, Bahl, and Mercer [71] view grammar as a probabilistic function of a Markov process and represents it as a finite-state network with transition probabilities including the self-transition probability (providing for recursion). Fig. 26 gives an illustration of Baker's representation of the chess grammar (transition probabilities not shown). This representation permits the Dragon system to determine the optimal match for the utterance using the dynamic programming algorithm.

C. Semantics

The term *semantics* means different things to different people. Here we use the term to denote the rules and relationships associated with the meaning of symbols. By this we mean the rules of language which tell us that the sequence of words "colorless yellow ideas" is not meaningful. It is not always possible to detect semantic inconsistency by looking at adjacent word pairs as in the previous example. The statements "Give me about a yard" and "Tell me about Tom" are acceptable, but "Give me about Tom" is not. Given a set of possibly disjoint words, semantic information must determine whether they are compatible and meaningful. The role of semantics in the recognition aspects of an SUS is analogous to that of syntax, i.e., it provides a mechanism for reducing search by restricting the number of acceptable alternatives. The papers by Woods [167], Nash-Webber [103], and Hendrix [60] illustrate the uses of semantic knowledge in speech understanding systems.

The principal technique used to represent this KS is a *semantic net*. Fig. 27 gives the structure of a semantic net fragment used by Hendrix [61]. A semantic net is used to represent objects, relationships among objects, events, rules, and situations. Such a net can be used to predict or verify possible word hypotheses in an unknown utterance. Given the concepts of *content* and *contains* and the meaning of the word "in," one may accept the statement "The bolts are in the box" and reject "The box is in the bolts" using such a semantic net.

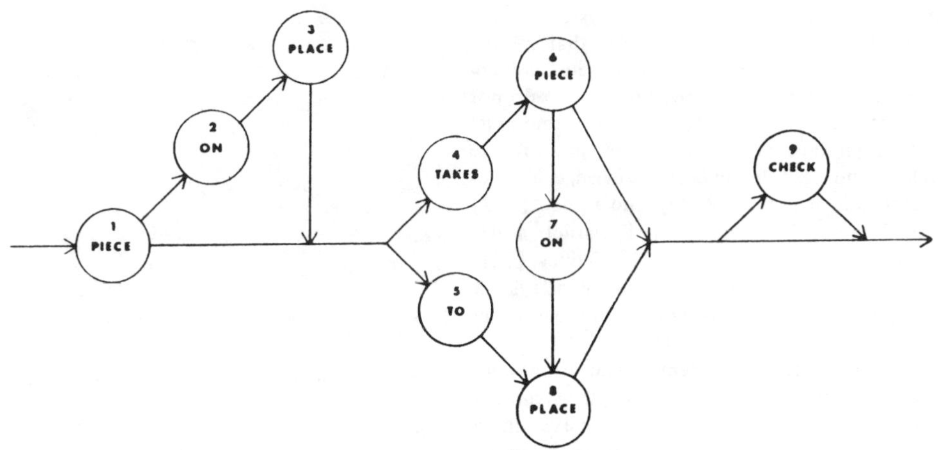

Fig. 26. Fragment of network grammar for Chess. (From Baker [7].)

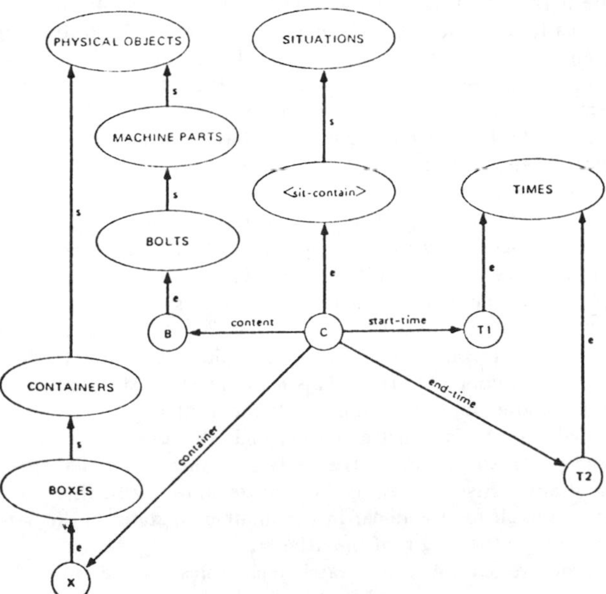

Fig. 27. Part of a typical semantic net. (From Hendrix [61].)

The chess task used by Hearsay-I [123] illustrates how knowledge about the partially recognized utterance can be used to constrain the hypotheses to a small set of words. For example, given that a word such as "captures" or "takes" appears in the partially recognized utterance, this information can be used to further restrict the search to the capture moves in a particular board position. This restricted set of moves is used to give high semantic preference to the key content words that may occur in the capture moves.

D. Pragmatics and Discourse Analysis

The term *pragmatics* usually leads to even more confusion and misunderstanding than *semantics*. Here we use it to mean conversation-dependent contextual information, i.e., task-related information accumulated so far through man–machine dialog. At a given point in the conversation, the user may use an elided (or non-well-formed) sentence or may use pronominal reference to a previous subject. For example, consider the sequence of questions, "How much does Tom weigh? How about John? What is his height?" It is obvious that in the second question one is asking for John's weight even though it does not appear explicitly. In the third question, does the term "his" refer to Tom or John? It is ambiguous, but the most plausible interpretation is that it refers to John, the subject of the immediately preceding utterance. Interpretation and validation of such questions based on pragmatics of the situation require the representation of dialog so that missing constituents can be inferred. Deutsch [29] uses a tree structure representation scheme for handling simple forms of ellipsis and anaphora.

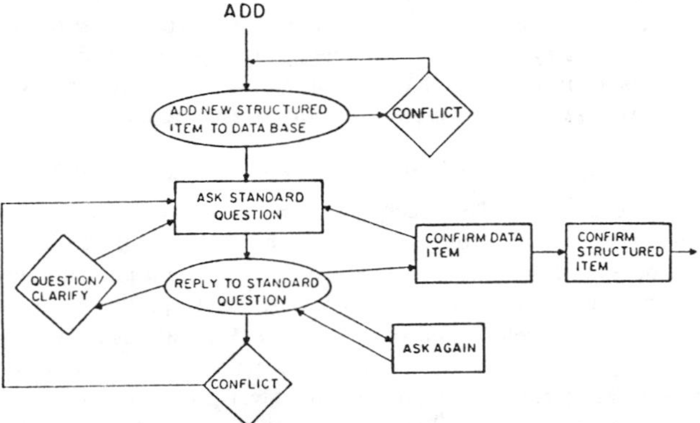

Fig. 28. User-oriented discourse model. (From Woods *et al.* [169].)

The other main role of pragmatics is to predict the user behavior (user model) based on the dialog. Fig. 28 is a transition network diagram indicating the common modes of interaction found in travel budget management dialog [167]. It illustrates various possible modes of interaction of the user such as: user adds a new item to the data base, system points out contradiction, user asks a question, system answers, user makes a change, and so on. If the pragmatic knowledge can accurately ascertain the state of the user, it can be used to achieve syntactic subselection, i.e., only a small set of all the possible grammatical constructs would be likely in that situation. We do not yet have any system which has made effective use of user models, but several are attempting to do so.

VI. System Organization

System organization is a catch-all term that describes the art of transforming ideas into working programs. Given that many of the problems of connected speech recognition and understanding are not well defined, the issue of system organization assumes added importance. We know that all the available sources of knowledge must communicate and cooperate in the presence of error and uncertainty. We do not know how to do it effectively or efficiently. The system must work smoothly with high-data-rate real-time input and provide facilities for speaker- and task-dependent knowledge acquisition. The tutorial-review paper by Reddy and Erman [122] and the papers by Newell [107], Baker [9], Barnett [14], Erman [35], Fennell [43], Jelinek *et al.* [71], Jelinek [72], and Lesser [85] provide more detailed discussions of system organization issues. In this section, we will briefly review the problems of system organization.

Many of the principal issues of system organization were raised and discussed in Section II while studying the structure of various types of speech recognition systems and examining what makes such systems difficult to realize. In particular, we have seen how various systems were organized to permit several diverse sources of knowledge to communicate and cooperate, how search strategies were devised to deal with error and ambiguity, and how knowledge is represented and used. In this section, we will discuss some of the related issues of system organization which were not covered earlier.

A. Control Strategies in the Presence of Ambiguity and Error

There are several sources of error and ambiguity in speech recognition. In spontaneous (nonmaximally differentiated) connected speech many expected features (and phones) may be missing. Variability due to noise and speaker leads to errors. Incomplete and/or inaccurate KS's at each level introduce more errors. In simple hierarchical systems, these errors propagate through various levels, compounding the error rate. Thus every system organization must cater to the inevitability of errors and handle them in a graceful manner.

Given the errorful nature of speech processing, one has to consider several alternative hypotheses (or interpretations) since the hypothesis with the highest rating may not be the correct one. In Fig. 12, we see how the problem of error is transformed into a problem of uncertainty by considering several plausible alternative hypotheses. At that point the problem becomes one of search through this multilevel network to discover the best path that is consistent with all the KS's. There are several search techniques developed in the field of artificial intelligence that become potentially useful. We will consider two of these techniques that have been used in speech recognition.

The commonly used strategy is *best-first search*. This technique is used in Hearsay-I, Lincoln, and in a modified form in the IBM system (see Section II-B and Section V of Jelinek [72]). This technique is best explained by an example [122]. In Fig. 29, we see a tree of possible alternatives that had arisen in the analysis of the utterance "Are your headaches severe?" We find that there are nine alternatives for the first word: "have," "are," "where," and six others. The ratings indicating the likelihood, which can be derived either mathematically [71] or heuristically [55], are given under each word. Given that the word "have" has the highest rating (470), we begin to explore that path. "Have" is followed by a single alternative "you." The combined rating for the sequence "have you" is given under "you." The rating of 455 makes the sequence "have you" better than the other alternative paths. Proceeding along this path, we have three alternative words that can follow "have you." The sequence "have you had" receives the

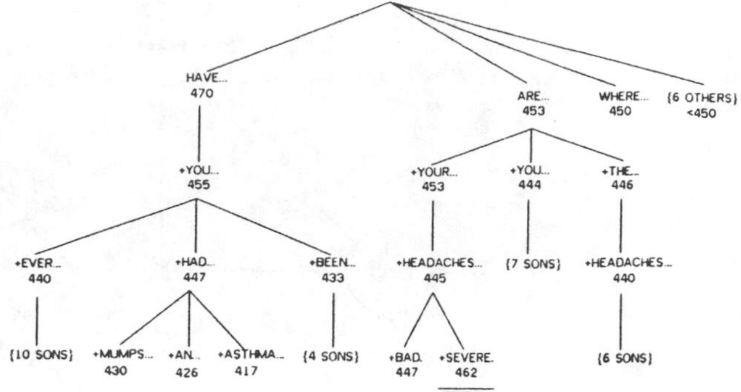

Fig. 29. Example of best-first search. (From Reddy and Erman [122].)

highest rating of 447 but is no longer the highest rated path. Search is suspended along this path and we begin exploring the alternatives that can follow "are." Of the three alternatives, the path "are your" has the highest rating of 453. Proceeding along this path, we get a rating of 445 for the sequence "are your headaches." Since this is lower than 447, we now suspend this search and resume search along the path "have you had." The highest rated sequence "have you had mumps" is lower than 445, so we resume the path of "are your headaches" again. Now we find that "are your headaches severe" has the highest rating of 462 and, being the end of a sentence, cannot proceed any further. We accept this as the most probable sentence and return it as the answer to the search.

Another technique that has been used in speech recognition is to *search all possible paths in parallel* but constrain the search only through those sequences which are valid paths in a specific network [7], [8]. This network is constructed to be an integrated representation of all the available KS's. Exponential growth is constrained through the use of a Markov assumption which limits the relevant context and collapses many alternative sequences to a single state. With this technique, search time is linear in the number of states in the network and in the length of the utterance.

There are several other search techniques, such as prosodically guided search [81], anchor points, focus of attention [86], a few alternative paths in parallel [90], and so on. The relative advantages and disadvantages of these techniques are not clearly understood.

B. Real-Time Input

Unlike most other forms of computer input, speech is critically *data directed*. That is, initiation and termination of the input depend on the incoming data rather than on program control. Thus a system must be prepared to continuously monitor the speech input device (analog-to-digital converter, filter bank, or what have you) to determine if the signal is speech or noise.

The *high data rates* associated with speech input (100 to 300 kbit/s) imply that a system cannot afford to have resident in primary memory more than a few seconds of speech data (usually no more than a single utterance). Thus the data must be immediately processed, placed in secondary storage, or played back. Keeping two high-data-rate devices serviced is not a major problem if the system is dedicated. However, if the system has a general-purpose operating system, special care must be taken to see that the device service overhead is low in order to avoid loss of data. This often becomes difficult to achieve with two active devices because of the costs associated with process synchronization, buffer service routines, and signal detection [35]. System primitives available within the system for performing these operations tend to be too slow and need to be reprogrammed.

C. Knowledge Acquisition

Every speech recognition system uses thresholds, templates, probabilities, and so on, based on measurements obtained on training data. In the case of word recognition systems, the problem is solved neatly since reference patterns capture noise, microphone, speaker, and phonological variability in a single step. In CSR systems, however, one has to deal with most of these sources of variability individually.

The first question that arises is what parameters will be seen when a sound is spoken. This depends not only on the parametric representation used but also on the speaker, the microphone used, and the noise in the environment. Systems using formant representation attempt to normalize speaker dependencies by estimating the shifts in formant trajectories, the length of the vocal tract of the speaker, etc. Systems that use prototype template matching require spectral templates (or some other parametric representation) for each sound to be recognized for each speaker. These in turn require a set of carefully manually segmented and labeled sentences for each speaker. Machine-aided segmentation and labeling has been attempted [6], but this requires a reasonable set of starting templates (the chicken and the egg problem).

The second question that arises is what phonemes are observed when a word (or a sequence of words) is spoken. Phonological rules predict some phenomena but they do not predict (at least not as yet) that a stop in some context can be three-quarters voiced and one-quarter unvoiced. Some systems attempt to accumulate such acoustic-phonetic phenomena from real data. Again, one needs manually labeled data or machine-labeled data for training of the system. Baker and Bahl [10] present the results of an interesting training method for automatically learning transition probabilities described in [71] and [72].

Many of the heuristic techniques used by various systems require substantial amounts of labeled data. This in turn necessitates the design of several interactive programs with graphical output for collection and validation of rules. Labeled data are also essential for systematic performance analysis of segmentation, labeling, syllable detection, word hypothesis, and word verification procedures.

VII. Conclusions

We have attempted to review the recent developments in speech recognition. The focus has been to review research progress, to indicate the areas of difficulty, why they are difficult, and how they are being solved. The paper is not intended as a survey of all known results in speech recognition and represents only one point of view of important issues, problems, and solutions.

The past few years have seen several conceptual and scientific advances in the field. We have already discussed many of these aspects earlier in the text. We will summarize them here.

1) For the first time we have available extensive analysis of connected speech. We know connected speech recognition is not impossible.
2) The role and use of knowledge are better understood. Almost all systems use knowledge to generate hypotheses and/or verify them.
3) Error and ambiguity can be handled within the framework of search.
4) Stochastic representations and dynamic programming provide a simple and effective solution to the matching problem.
5) Network representation of knowledge is a compact and computationally efficient way of generating and verifying hypotheses.
6) For the first time we have some techniques for the codification and use of phonological rules in speech recognition systems.
7) For the first time we have effective tools for the study of prosodics and the application of prosodic information to speech recognition.
8) There has been comparatively significant progress in the past five years in the areas of parameter extraction, formant tracking, feature detection, segmentation, and labeling.
9) Linear predictive coding and Itakura's distance metric represent effective digital techniques for analysis and matching at the signal level.

In spite of the significant progress, there are still several unsolved problem areas: signal processing associated with noise, telephone and speaker normalization, real-time live input providing graceful interaction with the user, careful and systematic performance analysis of the existing systems, and labeled data bases. In addition, continued progress is necessary in almost all the knowledge domains to establish optimal representation and use of different sources of knowledge.

We have indicated that it may be possible to build a $1000 isolated word recognition system, a $20 000 connected speech system, an unlimited vocabulary system, and so on. All of these seem feasible and can probably be realized within the next 10 years if the present momentum in speech recognition research can be continued. However, they may never be realized without significant and directed research effort. We are still far from being able to handle relatively unrestricted dialogs from a large population of speakers in uncontrolled environments. Many more years of intensive research seems necessary to achieve such a goal.

Acknowledgment

The author wishes to thank his colleagues L. Erman and A. Newell for their many valuable comments on various drafts of this paper, and also J. K. Baker, J. M. Baker, R. Dixon, J. Forgie, H. Goldberg, J. Shoup-Hummel, W. Lea, F. Jelinek, T. Martin, N. Neuburg, L. Rabiner, A. Rosenberg, H. Silverman, G. White, and J. Wolf for their comments on various parts of this paper.

References

[1] B. S. Atal and M. R. Schroeder, "Predictive coding of speech signals," in *Proc. 1967 Conf. Speech Communication and Processing*, pp. 360–361, Nov. 1967.

[2] ——, "Predictive coding of speech signals," in *Proc. Int. Congr. Acoustics*, C-5-4, Tokyo, Japan, Aug. 1968.

[3] ——, "Adaptive predicting coding of speech signals," *Bell Syst. Tech. J.*, vol. 49, no. 6, pp. 1973–1986, 1970.

[4] B. S. Atal and S. L. Hanauer, "Speech analysis and synthesis by linear prediction of the speech wave," *J. Acoust. Soc. Amer.*, vol. 50, no. 2, pp. 637–655, 1971.

[5] B. S. Atal, "Linear prediction of speech—Recent advances with applications to speech analysis," in [121, pp. 221–230].

[6] J. K. Baker, "Machine-aided labeling of connected speech," in *Working Papers in Speech Recognition II*, Tech. Rep., Comput. Sci. Dep., Carnegie-Mellon Univ., Pittsburgh, PA, 1973.
[7] —, "The DRAGON system–An overview," *IEEE Trans. Acoust., Speech, Signal Processing*, vol. ASSP-23, pp. 24–29, Feb. 1975.
[8] —, "Stochastic modeling as a means of automatic speech recognition," Ph.D. dissertation, Computer Sci. Dep., Carnegie-Mellon Univ., Pittsburgh, PA, 1975.
[9] —, "Stochastic modeling for automatic speech understanding," in [121, pp. 500–520].
[10] J. K. Baker and L. Bahl, "Some experiments in automatic recognition of continuous speech," in *Proc. 11th Annu. IEEE Computer Society Conf.*, pp. 326–329, 1975.
[11] J. M. Baker, "A new time-domain analysis of human speech and other complex waveforms," Ph.D. dissertations, Carnegie-Mellon Univ., Pittsburgh, PA, 1975.
[12] R. Bakis, "Continuous speech recognition via centisecond acoustic states," *J. Acoustic Society Amer.*, vol. 58 (to be presented at the 91st meeting of ASA).
[13] J. A. Barnett, "A vocal data management system," *IEEE Trans. Audio Electroacoust.*, vol. AU-21, pp. 185–188, June 1973.
[14] —, "Module linkage and communication in large systems," in [121, pp. 500–520].
[15] M. Bates, "The use of syntax in a speech understanding system," *IEEE Trans. Acoust., Speech, Signal Processing*, vol. ASSP-23, pp. 112–117, Feb. 1975.
[16] —, "Syntactic analysis in a speech understanding system," Ph.D. dissertation, Harvard Univ., Cambridge, MA, 1975. Also Rep. 3116, Bolt Beranek and Newman, Inc., Cambridge, MA, 1975.
[17] B. Beek, E. P. Neuburg, D. C. Hodge, R. S. Vonusa, and R. A. Curtis, "An assessment of the technology of automatic speech recognition for military application," NATO Rep. To be published by Rome Air Development Center, Rome, NY, 1976.
[18] D. G. Bobrow and D. H. Klatt, "A limited speech recognition system," in *Proc. AFIPS Fall Joint Computer Conf.*, vol. 33. Washington, DC: Thompson, 1968, pp. 305–318.
[19] D. G. Bobrow and A. Collins, *Representation and Understanding.* New York: Academic Press, 1975.
[20] R. Breaux and I. Goldstein, "Development of machine speech understanding for automated instructional systems," in *Proc. 8th NTECL/Industry Conf.*, Naval Training Equipment Center, Orlando, FL, Nov. 1975.
[21] D. J. Broad and J. E. Shoup, "Concepts for acoustic phonetic recognition," in [121, pp. 243–274].
[22] E. C. Carterette and M. H. Jones, *Informal Speech.* Berkeley, CA: Univ. of California Press, p. 16 ff, 1974.
[23] A. Chapanis, "Interactive human communication," *Sci. Amer.*, vol. 232, no. 3, pp. 36–42, 1975.
[24] P. S. Cohen and R. L. Mercer, "The phonological component of an automatic speech recognition system," in [121, pp. 275–320].
[25] E. E. David, Jr., and P. B. Denes, *Human Communication: A Unified View.* New York: McGraw-Hill, 1972.
[26] R. De Mori, S. Rivoira, and A. Serra, "A speech understanding system with learning capability," in *Proc. 4th Int. Joint Conf. Artificial Intelligence*, Tbilisi, USSR, 1975.
[27] M. Derkach, "Heuristic models for automatic recognition of spoken words," Quart. Progr. Status Rep., Speech Transmission Labs., KTH, Stockholm, Sweden, pp. 39–49, Jan–Mar. 1970.
[28] M. Derkach, R. Gumetsky, B. Gura, and L. Mishin, "Automatic recognition of simplified sentences constructed of the limited lexicon," in [41].
[29] B. G. Deutsch, "Discourse analysis and pragmatics," in [156, ch. VI].
[30] N. R. Dixon and H. F. Silverman, "A description of a parametrically controlled modular structure for speech processing," *IEEE Trans. Acoust., Speech, Signal Processing*, vol. ASSP-23, pp. 87–91, Feb. 1975.
[31] N. R. Dixon and H. F. Silverman, "A general language-operated decision implementation system (GLODIS): Its application to continuous speech segmentation," (to appear in *IEEE Trans. Acoust. Speech, Signal Processing*, vol. ASSP-24, 1976.
[32] —, "Some encouraging results for general purpose continuous speech recognition," in *Proc. 1975 Int. Conf. Cybernetics and Society*, San Francisco, CA, pp. 293–295, 1975.
[33] P. H. Dorn, "Whither data entry," *Datamation*, vol. 27, pp. 49–51, Mar. 1973.
[34] L. D. Erman, Ed., *Contributed Papers of IEEE Symp. Speech Recognition*, Carnegie-Mellon Univ., Pittsburgh, PA (IEEE Cat. 74CHO878-9 AE), 1974.
[35] —, "An environment and system for machine understanding of connected speech," Ph.D. dissertation, Comput. Sci. Dep., Stanford Univ., Tech. Rep., Comput. Sci. Dep., Carnegie-Mellon Univ., Pittsburgh, PA, 1974.
[36] —, "Overview of the Hearsay speech understanding research," *Comput. Sci. Res. Rev.*, Comput. Sci. Dep., Carnegie-Mellon Univ., Pittsburgh, PA, 1975.
[37] L. D. Erman and V. R. Lesser, "A multi-level organization for problem solving using many, diverse cooperating sources of knowledge," in *Proc. 4th Int. Joint Conf. Artificial Intelligence*, Tbilisi, USSR, 1975.
[38] L. D. Erman, and D. R. Reddy, "Implications of telephone input for automatic speech recognition," in *Proc. 7th Int. Congr. Acoustics*, vol. 3, Budapest, Hungary, 1971, pp. 85–88.
[39] C. G. M. Fant, "Automatic recognition and speech research," Quart. Progr. Status Rep., Speech Transmission Labs., KTH, Stockholm, Sweden, pp. 16–31, Jan–Mar. 1970.
[40] —, *Speech Sounds and Features.* Cambridge, MA: M.I.T. Press, 1973.
[41] —, Ed., *Proc. Speech Communications Seminar*, Stockholm, Sweden, 1974. To be published by Almquist and Wiksell Int. (Stockholm) and Wiley (New York), 1975.
[42] C. G. M. Fant and B. Lindblom, "Studies of minimal speech sound units," Quart. Progr. Status Rep., Speech Transmission Labs., KTH, Stockholm, Sweden, pp. 1–11, Apr.–June 1961.
[43] R. D. Fennell, "Multiprocess software architecture for AI problem solving," Ph.D. dissertation, Comput. Sci. Dep., Carnegie-Mellon Univ., Pittsburgh, PA, 1975.
[44] J. L. Flanagan, *Speech Analysis, Synthesis and Perception.* New York: Springer, 1972.
[45] J. W. Forgie, personal communication, 1975.
[46] J. W. Forgie and C. D. Forgie, "Results obtained from a vowel recognition computer program," *J. Acoust. Soc. Amer.*, vol. 31, pp. 1480–1489, 1959.
[47] J. W. Forgie *et al.*, "Speech understanding systems–semiannual Tech. Summary Rep.–May 1974," M.I.T. Lincoln Lab., Lexington, MA, 1974.
[48] J. W. Forgie, D. E. Hall, and R. W. Wiesen, "An overview of the Lincoln Laboratory speech recognition system," *J. Acoust. Soc. Amer.*, vol. 56, S27 (A), 1974.
[49] L. J. Gerstman, "Classification of self-normalized vowels, *IEEE Trans. Audio Electroacoust.*, vol. AU-16, pp. 78–80, Mar. 1968.
[50] R. A. Gillmann, "A fast frequency domain pitch algorithm," System Development Corp., Santa Monica, CA, unpublished rep., 1975.
[51] B. Gold, "Word recognition computer program," M.I.T. Lincoln Lab., Cambridge, MA, Tech. Rep. 456, 1966.
[52] B. Gold and L. Rabiner, "Parallel processing techniques for estimating pitch periods of speech in time domain," *J. Acoust. Soc. Amer.*, vol. 46, no. 2, pp. 422–449, 1969.
[53] H. G. Goldberg, "Segmentation and labeling of speech: A comparative performance evaluation," Ph.D. dissertation, Computer Science Department, Carnegie-Mellon University, Pittsburgh, PA, 1975.
[54] R. G. Goodman, "Language design for man-machine communication," Ph.D. dissertation (in preperation), Comput. Sci. Dep., Stanford Univ., Stanford, CA, 1976.
[55] D. E. Hall, "The linguistic module, Final report on speech understanding systems," M.I.T. Lincoln Lab., Lexington, MA, unpublished rep., 1974.
[56] D. E. Hall and J. W. Forgie, "Parsing and word matching in the Lincoln Laboratory speech recognition system," *J. Acoust. Soc. Amer.*, vol. 56, S27 (A), 1974.
[57] E. Hayden and J. Shoup, "SCRL computerized pronouncing dictionary," Speech Communication Res. Lab., Santa Barbara, CA, unpublished, 1975.
[58] F. Hayes-Roth and D. J. Mostow, "An automatically compilable recognition network for structured patterns," in *Proc. 4th Int. Joint Conf. Artificial Intelligence*, Tbilsi, USSR, 1975.
[59] F. Hayes-Roth and V. Lesser, "Focus of attention in a distributed logic speech understanding system," Comput. Sci. Dep., Carnegie-Mellon Univ., Pittsburgh, PA, Tech. Rep., 1976.
[60] G. G. Hendrix, "Expanding the utility of semantic networks through partitioning," in *Proc. 4th Int. Joint Conf. Artificial Intelligence,* Tbilisi, USSR, 1975.
[61] —, "Semantics," in [156, ch. V].
[62] C. Hewitt, "Description and theoretical analysis, (using schemata) of Planner: A language for proving theorems and manipulation models in a robot," M.I.T. Project MAC, Cambridge, MA, AI Memo. 251, 1972.
[63] D. R. Hill, "Man-machine interaction using speech," in *Advances in Computers*, F. L. Alt, M. Rubinoff, and M. C. Yovits, Eds., vol. II. New York: Academic Press, 1971, pp. 165–230.
[64] A. D. C. Holden, E. Strasbourger, and L. Price, "A computer programming system using continuous speech input," in [34].
[65] J. F. Hemdal and G. W. Hughes, "A feature based computer recognition program for the modeling of vowel perception," in [158, pp. 440–453].
[66] S. R. Hyde, "Automatic speech recognition: Literature, survey, and discussion," in [25].
[67] S. Itahashi, S. Makino, and K. Kido, "Discrete-word recognition utilizing a word dictionary and phonological rules," *IEEE Trans.*

Audio Electroacoust., vol. AU-21, pp. 239–249, June 1973.

[68] F. Itakura and S. Saito, "Analysis synthesis telephony based on the maximum likelihood method," in *Proc. 6th Int. Congr. Acoustics*, 1968, Paper C-5-5.

[69] ——, "A statistical method for estimation of speech spectral density and formant frequencies," *Electron. Commun. Japan*, vol. 53-A, no. 1, pp. 36–43, 1970.

[70] F. Itakura, "Minimum prediction residual principle applied to speech recognition," *IEEE Trans. Acoust., Speech, Signal Processing*,vol. ASSP-23, pp. 67–72, Feb. 1975.

[71] F. Jelinek, L. R. Bahl, and R. L. Mercer, "Design of a linguistic statistical decoder for the recognition of continuous speech," *IEEE Trans. Inform. Theory*, vol. IT-21, pp. 250–256, May 1975.

[72] F. Jelinek, "Continuous speech recognition by statistical methods," this issue, pp. 532–556.

[73] I. Kameny, "Comparison of the formant spaces of retroflexed and nonretroflexed vowels," *IEEE Trans. Acoust., Speech, Signal Processing*, vol. ASSP-23, pp. 38–49, Feb. 1975.

[74] D. H. Klatt, "On the design of a speech understanding system," in [41].

[75] ——, "Word verification in a speech understanding system," in [121, pp. 321–341].

[76] D. H. Klatt and K. N. Stevens, "On the automatic recognition of continuous speech: Implications from a spectrogram-reading experiment," *IEEE Trans. Audio Electroacoust.*, vol. AU-21, pp. 210–217, June 1973.

[77] J. S. Kriz, "A 16-bit A-D-A conversion system for high-fidelity audio research," *IEEE Trans. Acoust. Speech, Signal Processing*, vol. ASSP-23, pp. 146–149, 1975.

[78] W. A. Lea, "Establishing the value of voice communication with computers," *IEEE Trans. Audio Electroacoust.*, vol. AU-16, pp. 184–197, June 1968.

[79] ——, "Intonational cues to the constituent structure and phonemics of spoken English," Ph.D. dissertation, School of Elec. Eng., Purdue Univ., Lafayette, IN, 1972.

[80] ——, "Prosodic aids to speech recognition: IV–A general strategy for prosodically-guided speech understanding," Sperry Univac Rep. PX10791, 1974.

[81] W. A. Lea, M. F. Medress, and T. E. Skinner, "A prosodically guided speech understanding system," *IEEE Trans. Acoust. Speech, Signal Processing*, vol. ASSP-23, pp. 30–38, Feb. 1975.

[82] W. A. Lea and D. R. Kloker, "Prosodic aids to speech recognition: VI–Timing cues to linguistic structure and improved computer program," Univac Rep. Px11239, 1975.

[83] I. Lehiste, *Readings in Acoustic Phonetics.* Cambridge, MA: M.I.T. Press, 1967.

[84] ——, *Suprasegmentals.* Cambridge, MA: M.I.T. Press, 1970.

[85] V. R. Lesser, "Parallel processing in speech understanding: A survey of design problems," in [121, pp. 481–499].

[86] V. R. Lesser, R. D. Fennell, L. D. Erman, and D. R. Reddy, "Organization of the Hearsay-II speech understanding system," *IEEE Trans. Acoust. Speech, Signal Processing*, vol. ASSP-23, pp. 11–23, 1975.

[87] J. C. R. Licklinder, "Man computer symbiosis," in *Perspectives on the Computer Revolution*, Z. W. Pylyshyn, Ed. Englewood Cliffs, NJ: Prentice-Hall, 1970, pp. 306–318. (First published in *IRE Trans. Hum. Factors Electron.*, vol. HFE-1, 1960).

[88] N. Lindgren, "Machine recognition of human language," *IEEE Spectrum*, vol. 2, Mar., Apr., May, 1965.

[89] ——, "Speech–Man's natural communication," *IEEE Spectrum*, vol. 4, pp. 75–86, June 1967.

[90] B. Lowerre, "A comparative performance analysis of speech understanding systems," Ph.D. dissertation (in preparation), Comput. Sci. Dep., Carnegie-Mellon Univ., Pittsburgh, PA, 1976.

[91] J. Makhoul, "Spectral analysis of speech by linear prediction," *IEEE Trans. Audio Electroacoust.*, vol. AU-21, pp. 140–148, June 1973.

[92] ——, "Linear prediction: A tutorial review," *Proc. IEEE (Special Issue on Digital Signal Processing)*, vol. 63, pp. 561–580, Apr. 1975.

[93] ——, "Linear prediction in automatic speech recognition," in [121, pp. 183–220].

[94] J. D. Markel, "Digital inverse filtering–A new tool for formant trajectory estimation," *IEEE Trans. Audio Electroacoust.*, vol. AU-20, pp. 129–137, June 1972.

[95] T. B. Martin, "Acoustic recognition of a limited vocabulary in continuous speech," Ph.D. dissertation, Univ. of Pennsylvania, Philadelphia, 1970.

[96] ——, "Applications of limited vocabulary recognition systems," in [121, pp. 55–71].

[97] S. S. McCandless, "An algorithm for automatic formant extraction using linear prediction spectra," *IEEE Trans. Acoust., Speech, Signal Processing*, vol. ASSP-22, pp. 135–141, Apr. 1974.

[98] M. Medress, "Computer recognition of single-syllable English words," Ph.D. dissertation, M.I.T., Cambridge, MA, 1969.

[99] P. Mermelstein, "A phonetic-context controlled strategy for segmentation and phonetic labeling of speech," *IEEE Trans. Acoust., Speech, Signal Processing*, vol. ASSP-23, pp. 79–82, Feb. 1975.

[100] ——, "Automatic segmentation of speech into syllable units," *J. Acoust. Soc. Amer.*, vol. 58, pp. 880–883, 1975.

[101] G. A. Miller and S. Isard, "Some perceptual consequences of linguistic rules," *J. Verbal Learning Behavior*, vol. 2, pp. 217–228, 1963.

[102] M. L. Minsky, Ed., *Semantic Information Processing.* Cambridge, MA: M.I.T. Press, 1970.

[103] B. Nash-Webber, "Semantic support for a speech understanding system," *IEEE Trans. Acoust., Speech, Signal Processing*, vol. ASSP-23, pp. 124–128, Feb. 1975.

[104] R. B. Neely and D. R. Reddy, "Speech recognition in the presence of noise," in *Proc. 7th Int. Congr. Acoustics*, vol. 3, Budapest, 1971, pp. 177–180.

[105] E. P. Neuburg, "Philosophies of speech recognition," in [121, pp. 83–95].

[106] A. Newell, "Production systems: Models of control structures," in *Visual Information Processing*, W. C. Chase, Ed. New York: Academic Press, 1973, pp. 463–526.

[107] ——, "A tutorial on speech understanding systems," in [121, pp. 3–54].

[108] A. Newell, J. Barnett, J. Forgie, C. Green, D. Klatt, J. C. R. Licklinder, J. Munson, R. Reddy, and W. Woods, *Speech Understanding Systems: Final Report of a Study Group*, 1971. (Reprinted by North-Holland/American Elsevier, Amsterdam, Netherlands, 1973).

[109] A. Newell, F. S. Cooper, J. W. Forgie, C. C. Green, D. H. Klatt, M. F. Medress, E. P. Neuburg, M. H. O'Malley, D. R. Reddy, B. Ritea, J. E. Shoup, D. E. Walker, and W. A. Woods, "Considerations for a follow-on ARPA research program for speech understanding systems," available from Comput. Sci. Dep., Carnegie-Mellon Univ., Pittsburgh, PA, 1975.

[110] R. B. Ochsman and A. Chapanis, "The effects of 10 communication modes on the behavior of teams during co-operative problem-solving," *Int. J. Man-Machine Studies*, vol. 6, pp. 579–619, 1974.

[111] M. M. O'Malley, D. Kloker, and B. Dara-Abrams, "Recovering parentheses from spoken algebraic expressions," *IEEE Trans. Audio Electroacoust.*, vol. AU-21, pp. 217–220, June 1973.

[112] B. T. Oshika, V. W. Zue, R. V. Weeks, H. Nue, and J. Aurbach, "The role of phonological rules in speech understanding research," *IEEE Trans. Acoust., Speech, Signal Processing*, vol. ASSP-23, pp. 104–112, Feb. 1975.

[113] K. W. Otten, "Approaches to the machine recognition of conversational speech," in [63, pp. 127–163].

[114] J. E. Paul, A. S. Rabinowitz, J. P. Riganati, V. A. Vitols, and M. L. Griffith, "Automatic recognition of continuous speech: Further development of a hierarchical strategy," Rome Air Development Center, Rome, NY, RADC-TR-73-319, 1973.

[115] W. H. Paxton, "The parsing system," in [156, ch. III].

[116] J. R. Pierce, "Whither speech recognition?" *J. Acoust. Soc. Amer.*, vol. 46, pp. 1049–1051, 1969.

[117] L. C. Pols, "Real-time recognition of spoken words," *IEEE Trans. Comput.*, vol. C-20, pp. 972–978, Sept. 1971.

[118] L. R. Rabiner and M. R. Sambur, "An algorithm for determining the endpoints of isolated utterances," *Bell Syst. Tech. J.*, vol. 54, no. 2, pp. 297–315, 1975.

[119] D. R. Reddy, "Segmentation of speech sounds," *J. Acoust. Soc. Amer.*, vol. 40, pp. 307–312, 1966.

[120] ——, "Computer recognition of connected speech," *J. Acoust. Soc. Amer.*, vol. 42, pp. 329–347, 1967.

[121] ——, Ed., *Speech Recognition: Invited Papers of the IEEE Symp.* New York: Academic Press, 1975.

[122] D. R. Reddy and L. D. Erman, "Tutorial on system organization for speech understanding," in [121, pp. 457–479].

[123] D. R. Reddy, L. D. Erman, and R. B. Neely, "A model and a system for machine recognition of speech," *IEEE Trans. Audio Electroacoust.*, vol. AU-21, pp. 229–238, June 1973.

[124] D. R. Reddy and A. Newell, "Knowledge and its representation in a speech understanding system," in *Knowledge and Cognition*, L. W. Gregg, Ed. Washington, DC: L. Earlbaum Assoc., 1974, pp. 253–285.

[125] D. R. Reddy and P. J. Vicens, "A procedure for segmentation of connected speech," *J. Audio Eng. Soc.*, vol. 16, pp. 404–412, 1968.

[126] C. W. Reedyk, "Noise-cancelling electret microphone for lightweight head telephone sets," *J. Acoust. Soc. Amer.*, vol. 53, pp. 1609–1615, 1973.

[127] B. Ritea, "Automatic speech understanding systems," in *Proc. 11th Annu. IEEE Computer Society Conf.*, Washington, DC, Sept. 1975.

[128] J. J. Robinson, "The language definition," in [156, ch. IV].

[129] ——, "Performance grammars," in [121, pp. 401–427].

[130] P. J. Rovner, J. Makhoul, J. Wolf, and J. Colarusso, "Where the

words are: Lexical retrieval in a speech understanding system," in [34, pp. 160-164].

[131] P. J. Rovner, B. Nash-Webber, and W. Woods, "Control concepts in a speech understanding system," *IEEE Trans. Acoust., Speech, Signal, Processing*, vol. ASSP-23, pp. 136-140, Feb. 1975.

[132] J. F. Rulifson *et al.*, "QA4: A procedural calculus for intuitive reasoning," AI Center, Stanford Res. Inst., Menlo Park, CA, Tech. Note 73, 1973.

[133] R. Rustin, Ed., *Natural Language Processing.* New York: Algorithmics Press, 1973.

[134] T. Sakai and S. Nakagawa, "Continuous speech understanding system LITHAN," Dept. Inform. Sci., Kyoto Univ., Kyoto, Japan, Tech. Rep., 1975.

[135] M. R. Sambur and L. R. Rabiner, "A speaker-independent digit-recognition system," *Bell Syst. Tech. J.*, vol. 54, pp. 81-102, 1975.

[136] R. Schwartz and J. Makhoul, "Where the phonemes are: Dealing with Ambiguity in acoustic-phonetic recognition," *IEEE Trans. Acoust., Speech, Signal, Processing*, vol. ASSP-23, pp. 50-53, Feb. 1975.

[137] R. N. Schafer and L. R. Rabiner, "Parametric representations of speech," in [121, pp. 99-150].

[138] R. C. Shank and K. M. Colby, *Computer Models of Thought and Language.* San Francisco, CA: Freeman, 1973.

[139] R. C. Shank, Ed., *Conceptual Information Processing.* Amsterdam, Netherlands: North-Holland, 1975.

[140] D. E. Shanon, "Prediction and entropy of printed English," *Bell Syst. Tech. J.*, vol. 30, pp. 50-64, 1951.

[141] J. N. Shearme and P. F. Leach, "Some experiments with a simple word recognition system," *IEEE Trans. Audio Electroacoust.*, vol. AU-16, pp. 256-261, June 1968.

[142] L. Shockey and R. Reddy, "Quantitative analysis of speech perception," in [41].

[143] J. Shoup, personal communication, 1975.

[144] H. F. Silverman and N. R. Dixon, "An objective parallel evaluator of segmentation/classification performance for multiple systems," *IEEE Trans. Acoust., Speech, Signal, Processing*, vol. ASSP-23, pp. 92-99, Feb. 1975.

[145] H. A. Simon and L. Siklossy, Eds., *Representation and Meaning.* Englewood Cliffs, NJ: Prentice-Hall, 1972.

[146] A. R. Smith, "A word hypothesizer for the Hearsay II speech system," in *Proc. IEEE Int. Conf. Acoustics, Speech, and Signal Processing*, Philadelphia, PA, Apr. 1976.

[147] M. M. Sondhi, "New methods of pitch extraction," *IEEE Trans. Audio Electroacoust.*, vol. AU-16, pp. 262-266, 1968.

[148] C. C. Tappert, M. R. Dixon, A. S. Rabinowitz, and W. D. Chapman, "Automatic recognition of continuous speech utilizing dynamic segmentation, dual classification, sequential decoding and error recovery," Rome Air Development Center, Griffiss AFB, Rome, NY, Tech. Rep. TR-71-146, 1971.

[149] C. C. Tappert, N. R. Dixon, and A. S. Rabinowitz, "Application of sequential decoding for converting phonetic to graphic representation in automatic recognition of continuous speech (ARCS)," *IEEE Trans. Audio Electroacoust.*, vol. AU-21, pp. 225-228, June 1973.

[150] C. C. Tappert, "Experiments with a tree-search method for converting noisy phonetic representation into standard orthography," *IEEE Trans. Acoust., Speech, Signal, Processing*, vol. ASSP-23, pp. 129-135, Feb. 1975.

[151] V. M. Velichiko and N. G. Zagoruiko, "Automatic recognition of 200 words," *Int. J. Man-Machine Studies*, vol. 2, pp. 223-234, 1970.

[152] P. Vicens, "Aspects of speech recognition by computer," Ph.D. dissertation, Comput. Sci. Dep., Stanford Univ., Stanford, CA, 1969.

[153] G. Ya Vysotsky, B. N. Rudnyy, V. N. Trunin-Donskoy, and G. I. Tsemel, "Experiment in voice control of computers," *Izv. Akad. Nauk SSSR, Tekn. Kibern.*, no. 2, pp. 134-143, 1970.

[154] T. G. Von Keller, "On-line recognition system for spoken digits," *J. Acoust. Soc. Amer.*, vol. 49, pp. 1288-1296, 1971.

[155] H. Wakita, "An approach to vowel normalization," Speech Communication Res. Labs., Santa Barbara, CA, Tech. Rep., 1975.

[156] D. E. Walker, W. H. Paxton, J. J. Robinson, G. G. Hendrix, B. G. Deutsch, and A. E. Robinson, "Speech understanding research annual report," Artificial Intelligence Center, Stanford Res. Inst., Menlo Park, CA, Project 3804, 1975.

[157] D. E. Walker, "The SRI speech understanding system," *IEEE Trans. Acoust., Speech, Signal Processing*, vol. ASSP-23, pp. 397-416, Oct. 1975.

[158] Walthen-Dunn, Ed., *Models for the Perception of Speech and Visual Form.* Cambridge, MA: M.I.T. Press, 1967.

[159] C. J. Weinstein, S. S. McCandless, L. F. Mondshein, and V. W. Zue, "A system for acoustic-phonetic analysis of continuous speech," *IEEE Trans. Acoust., Speech, Signal Processing*, vol. ASSP-23, pp. 54-67, Feb. 1975.

[160] C. Wherry, "VRAS: Voice recognition and synthesis," Naval Air Development Center, 1975.

[161] G. M. White and R. B. Neely, "Speech recognition experiments with linear prediction, bandpass filtering, and dynamic programming," in *Proc. 2nd USA-Japan Computer Conf.*, Tokyo Japan, Aug. 1975. Also to appear in *IEEE Trans. Acoust., Speech, Signal Processing.*

[162] R. A. Wiesen and J. W. Forgie, "An evaluation of the Lincoln Laboratory speech recognition system," *J. Acoust. Soc. Amer.*, vol. 56, S27 (A), 1974.

[163] J. J. Wolf, "Speech recognition and understanding," in *Pattern Recognition*, K. S. Fu, Ed. New York: Springer, 1975.

[164] W. A. Woods, "Transition network grammars for natural language analysis," *Commun. Ass. Comput. Mach.*, vol. 13, no. 10, pp. 591-602, 1970.

[165] —, "Proposal for research on English language and speech understanding," Bolt Beranek and Newman, Inc., 1975.

[166] —, "Motivation and overview of SPEECHLIS: An experimental prototype for speech understanding research," *IEEE Trans. Acoust., Speech, Signal Processing*, vol. ASSP-23, pp. 2-10, 1975.

[167] —, "Syntax, semantics and speech," in [121, pp. 345-400].

[168] W. A. Woods and J. Makhoul, "Mechanical inference problems in continuous speech understanding," *Artificial Intelligence*, vol. 5, pp. 73-91, 1974.

[169] W. A. Woods, M. A. Bates, B. C. Bruce, J. J. Colarusso, C. C. Cook, L. Gould, J. I. Makhoul, B. L. Nash-Webber, R. M. Schwartz, and J. J. Wolf, "Speech understanding research at BBN, Final report on natural communication with computers," vol. I, Bolt Beranek and Newman, Inc., Rep. 2976, 1974.

[170] B. Yegnanarayana, "Effect of noise and distortion in speech on parametric extraction," in *Proc. IEEE Int. Conf. Acoustics, Speech, and Signal Processing*, Philadelphia, PA, Apr. 1976.

[171] N. G. Zagoruiko, "Automatic recognition of speech," Quart. Progr. Status Rep., Speech Transmission Labs., KTH, Stockholm, Sweden, pp. 39-49, Jan-Mar. 1970.

[172] L. R. Bahl and F. Jelinek, "Decoding for channels with insertions, deletions, and substitutions with applications to speech recognition," *IEEE Trans. Inform. Theory*, vol. IT-21, pp. 404-411, 1975.

[173] L. R. Bahl, J. K. Baker, P. S. Cohen, N. R. Dixon, F. Jelinek, R. L. Mercer, and H. F. Silverman, "Experiments in continuous speech recognition," to appear in *Proc. IEEE Int. Conf. Acoustics, Speech, and Signal Processing*, Philadelphia, PA, Apr. 1976.

[174] N. R. Dixon and C. C. Tappert, "Toward objective phonetic transcription—An on-line interactive technique for machine-processed speech data," *IEEE Trans. Man-Mach. Syst.*, vol. MMS-11, pp. 202-210, 1970.

[175] H. F. Silverman and N. R. Dixon, "A parametrically-controlled spectral analysis system for speech," *IEEE Trans. Acoust., Speech, Signal Processing*, vol. ASSP-22, pp. 362-381, 1974.

THE VALUE OF SPEECH RECOGNITION SYSTEMS

Wayne A. Lea
Speech Communications Research Laboratory

1-1. INTRODUCTION

Each reader of this book probably has some idea why it is valuable to have machines that can recognize spoken commands. Some of us could perhaps even offer explicit examples of how we would profitably use such systems if we could get access to them immediately. We all are aware of the growing importance of machines in business, school, government, and even in the home. One of our most frequent complaints about such machines is the difficulty of communicating with them in efficient and natural ways. Speech input seems to offer a truly natural mode for human-machine communication that, if attainable in a cost-effective way, would be unsurpassed in making computers and other mechanical devices truly cooperative servants of humankind, rather than increasing the demands on the human to adapt to the machine.

In this chapter, we shall first consider the many advantages of speech as an input modality for communication with machines (Sec. 1-2). Along with the advantages, we shall also consider the disadvantages, most of which can readily be alleviated, but which must not be neglected. We shall then compare speech with other input modalities, and discuss evidence that speech is the most effective single modality, and an integral part of the most effective multimodality communication links (Sec. 1-3).

Even if we acknowledge speech input to machines to be the best (or one of the best) machine-input modalities, we would find that knowledge to be of little use if speech recognition by machines were unattainable or if adequate systems were not practical. Consequently, we shall (in Sec. 1-4) define the dimensions of alternative system capabilities (isolated words versus connected speech, small versus large vocabulary of accepted words, number of speakers recognized, accuracy requirements, etc.) and consider how much recognition capability is needed to make a system useful for various applications. The ultimate practicality of speech recognition will depend upon the success of the various analysis techniques described throughout this book, and any others that are yet to be discovered, tested, and efficiently applied. While we can count on the scientists and engineers to come up with new ideas and algorithms for years to come, the ultimate utility of such advances will be determined by the commercial sources of devices, and the users in industry and government, who tailor those systems to real needs and test them in the crucible of field applications and repetitive conversations with machines. This book offers valuable tutorials about various important aspects of the inner workings of speech recognition systems (in Part II), and summaries of past, present, and future work in the field (in Chap. 4, and also in Parts III, IV, and V, respectively), but we need a solid foundation concerning why we want speech recognizers before we detail how they can be developed, tested, used, and improved.

1-2. ADVANTAGES AND DISADVANTAGES OF SPEECH INPUT TO MACHINES

Suppose you have a problem, and you intend to use your computer (or a command and control system, or the like) to help you solve it. Perhaps you are in industry, and would like to have the machine assist you in taking inventory of stock items whose stock numbers you could read and enter into the machine. Or perhaps while your hands and eyes are busy handling a large volume of items, you would like to dictate where objects go by commanding a computer that controls a conveyor system (such as some postal services have). Or perhaps you are involved with an airline reservation system and busy at other tasks. Or maybe you have a computer system that authorizes credit transactions, but you have a heavy turnover of employees who are unwilling to endure the tedium and pressure of receiving a large volume of telephone calls from merchants, all of whom have the same form of inquiry about the acceptability of a credit card and want the receiver of the call to check both the number and the amount to be charged to the account. Or maybe you're a manager who would like to communicate with that awesome machine down the hall without going through an expert programmer or some teletypewriting terminal--maybe you could go right through that telephone on your desk.

Alternatively, you might be an air traffic controller at a facility that uses a computer to assist in keeping information about the position, altitude, identity, fuel supply, and other critical conditions for a large number of aircraft in your vicinity. Or, you could be a forward observer in a military tactical situation where you would like to communicate with the gun control computer from your remote field site. Or you're in a crowded airplane cockpit with no room for another keyboard, display, or array of knobs, but you need another way of communicating to one more of the many aspects of the airborne system or a ground control facility. Or, perhaps you're "really far out", as an astronaut suited up for an extra-vehicular manuever in space.

You then are one of those to whom speech recognition advocates would try (or have tried) to sell their wares. Why? Does speech input offer special advantages in such cases as these? Indeed it does. We can see this more clearly by looking at the list of advantages of speech input given in Table 1-1. You will want to use speech wherever possible, because it is the human's most natural communication modality. It is thus a familiar, convenient, spontaneous part of the capabilities the human brings to the situation of interacting with machines. One distinct aspect of that spontaneity and naturalness will be a propensity to use that natural modality when communicating under stress conditions. Like a native English speaker in a foreign country, who will revert to his native language when in danger, when angry, or otherwise under stress, you will be more inclined under duress to speak (and speak correctly) in your native natural language than to type, punch buttons, or even speak an artificial code.

Untrained people speak but do not in all cases read, write, typewrite, or use buttons, knobs, or tactile devices with any efficiency. Speech thus requires no training, except for instructing you the user to confine your utterences to those which the machine can recognize or "understand". This latter aspect is one of the potential difficulties of using speech recognition facilities; namely, can you readily refrain from saying arbitrary sentences that the machine has not been programmed to understand, and rather constrain yourself to say only a restricted set of sentence structures and limited vocabulary (which may not necessarily be the most obvious way to say what was intended)? Once you speak, you are inclined to speak freely, forgetting any artificial constraints. "Habitability" (Watts, 1968; Klatt, 1977) is a common term for this desired ease of learning, and adhering to, constraints dictated by a restricted language. A habitable language is one for which you can be assured you won't keep getting system responses like "say again", "syntax error", "that doesn't compute", etc. The human's

Originally appeared in *Trends in Speech Recognition*, pp 3–18, Speech Science Publications (1986).

TABLE 1-1.

ADVANTAGES AND DISADVANTAGES OF SPEECH INPUT TO MACHINES

Advantage	Disadvantage
EFFECTIVE USE OF HUMAN COMMUNICATIVE ABILITIES	
• Human's Most Natural Modality Familiar, Convenient, Spontaneous,	but the user may say natural, yet unrecognizable utterances.
• Requires No Training of User,	except for how to constrain utterances to those recognizable by the machine.
• Human's Highest-Capacity Output Channel,	but slowed by pauses or unfamiliarity.
• Permits Multimodal Communication.	
• Simultaneous Communication with Humans and Machines,	but the user may forget which is being addressed.
COMPATIBILITY WITH UNUSUAL CIRCUMSTANCES	
• Possible in Darkness, Around Obstacles, and for the blind or handicapped.	
• Unaffected by weightlessness,	though this feature is rarely important.
• Only Slightly Affected by High Acceleration and Mechanical Constraints.	
• Permits Verifying Speaker's Identity,	but is sensitive to dialects and differences in pronunciation.
• Permits Monitoring Acoustical Environment,	but is susceptible to environmental noise and distortions.
• Requires no Panel Space, Displays, or Complex Apparatus,	but microphone must be worn or held.
MOBILITY AND FREEDOM FOR OTHER ACTIVITIES	
• Possible at a Distance and at Various Orientations,	but at a loss of privacy.
• Permits Simultaneous Use of Hands and Eyes for Other Tasks.	
• Permits Telephone to Serve as a Computer Terminal,	provided the potentially large speaker population, narrowband, noise, and distortions can be handled.

ability to adapt is, of course, quite impressive, and we might well expect that highly motivated users (e.g., trainees, subordinates under strict instructions, etc.) will accept and abide by even some of the most "unhabitable" forms of communication, but the more the machine adapts to the normal human speech mode (that is, the more versatile and structurally-unconstrained the interactive language), the more universally useful the speech input system will be. Such a trend will preserve the distinct "little or no training" feature of speech input to machines. In the meantime, as long as the machines are limited in what they can correctly understand, there will be *some* amount of user training required, but it is usually far less than that required for other computer input devices.

A word of caution is appropriate related to training users to speak to a machine. Several informal studies (e.g., Bobrow and Klatt, 1968) suggest that speakers are more consistent from time to time, and thus *less* prone to confuse the machine with unexpected differences in pronunciation, if they are instructed (or simply *allowed*) to speak "naturally", not to speak "carefully" or "clearly". The unusual articulations when users try to help the machine are so inconsistent from time to time that the conscientious user can do more harm than good if instructed to focus on the *manner* of speaking.

Since speech is the natural communication mode between humans, and can be heard both by humans and machines, speech could offer *simultaneous communication* with humans and machines. One distinct disadvantage that this might produce, however, is that the speaker might forget the machine's constraints on acceptable utterances as he or she turns from one utterance, directed at a human, to the next utterance, directed at the machine. Of course, the indiscriminate propagation of the speech signal in the vicinity of the speaker also jeopardizes the *privacy* of the human-to-computer communication link.

Another important advantage of speech is that it is the human's *highest-capacity* output communication channel. This has been quantitatively shown several times in the literature (Shannon and Weaver, 1949; Pierce and Korlin, 1957; Lea, 1968; Turn, 1974, p. 4). Spontaneous speech has a usual rate of around 2.0 to 3.6 words per second (Turn, 1974, p. 4). In contrast, only about 0.4 words per second are conveyed by handwriting or handprinting, while *skilled* typists can type about 1.6 to 2.5 words per second, and *unskilled* typists (that is, most computer users) can type only about 0.2 to 0.4 words per second. Newell et al. (1971) also reported that only about 1.2 to 1.5 words per second can be conveyed by using a touch-tone telephone. Chapanis, et al. (1977) found that even *experienced* typists only achieved about *18* words per minute in actual problem solving (thinking and typing), compared to about *176* words per minute in speech (thinking and speaking). Speech clearly offers the highest potential capacity for human-to-computer communication.

We must, however, qualify these statements about the high rate of information transfer with speech. If you only can speak in sequences of *isolated words*, where each word is clearly delimited by preceding and following pauses (silences), then some of the gain in rate of information transfer is lost. Martin (1976) reported that *average* speaking rates of about 0.5 to 1.1 isolated words per second (or, as he reported it, 30 to 70 words per minute) were achieved in factory environments by individuals using voice input systems, with peak rates (dictated by high workload) running close to 2.0 words per second. This overall performance is still somewhat better than the usual worker can accomplish by typewriting, keypunching, or button-pushing, but is less than the five-to-one (or larger) ratio obtained in comparing spontaneous connected speech with unskilled typewriting or handwriting, or the two-to-one ratio in comparing spontaneous speech with operating a touch-tone telephone.

Related to the issue of *rate* of information transfer between human and machine is the advantage of *multimodal communication*, which speech permits. Speech input may be combined with other input modalities, so that, for example, you can point to a specific position on a graphical input device and speak at the same time, etc. Multimodal communication of course increases the possible rates of information transfer, and it also permits choosing the best input method for each new problem, and provides redundancy and increased reliability (since, if one input channel fails, another back-up channel is available).

Although I don't believe the advantages of speech listed in the second part of Table 1-1 usually represent the major reasons why speech recognizers are bought and used, they are worthy of some consideration. Speech communication is possible in darkness, and around obstacles, because it propagates omni-directionally, without light. For aerospace applications, it may be of some interest that speech is unaffected by weightlessness, and less affected by high levels of acceleration and mechanical constraint than are other conventional mechanical modes of machine input, such as typewriting, button pushing, twisting knobs and thumb-wheels, or handwriting (Lea, 1970; Turn, 1974).

For example, Turn (1974, pp. 9-10) reported on two studies that showed that it took 4.0 g. acceleration to cause 10% reduction in recognition accuracy, while only 0.8 g. vibration caused 10% reduction in input accuracy when using push buttons, rotary dials, or thumb wheels. On the other hand, speech can be significantly distorted by unusual atmospheric composition and pressure, such as occur for deep sea divers and astronauts.

The same speech that may be used to instruct the machine might also be used to monitor the physical and psychological state of the speaker. This might be of some value in monitoring astronaut capabilities (Lea, 1968), detecting fatigue and emotion, and observing variabilities in the speaker's pronunciation, that need to be normalized for if successful recognition is to be maintained. More important for some applications is the ability to use spoken commands to verify a speaker's identity before permitting access to a secure area or a computer facility, or before disclosing credit information or other secrets. Other aspects of the acoustic environment can also be monitored by the speech input channel.

A primary difficulty with speech recognition is this ability of the input system to pick up other sounds in the environment that act as interfering noise, making accurate recognition more difficult. Speech recognizers that work very well in quiet laboratory environments may fail miserably in factories, computer rooms, or other field applications where acoustic noise is high. Part of the solution to such noise problems is to use close-talking (and noise-cancelling) microphones, that pick up the near-by speech better than the distant noises. Most commercial speech recognizers being used today are equipped with close-talking noise-cancelling microphones worn on light-weight headbands or mounted in telephone-like handsets. Another part of the solution to acoustic noise is to reduce the noise at its source, or to isolate the human from the noise by way of soundproofing and acoustic enclosures. This cannot always be done when the talker must be mobile or must simultaneously work with the very machines that are making the noise. Besides keeping the microphone away from the noise, the effects of noise can be reduced if the acoustic features used in the recognition decisions are less susceptible to distortions or confusions from noise. Rather than giving equal attention to all arbitrary aspects of acoustic patterns, we may endeavor to focus on robust features that are closely associated with linguistic (phonetic) contrasts but that are not markedly affected by noise. This is one primary reason for attempting to use formant frequencies, pitch, general spectral shapes and other phonetic features, in the more sophisticated speech recognizers that will be discussed throughout this book.

Another complication introduced by the acoustic environment is any bandwidth limitations and spectral distortions that may be intrinsic in the transducer and input communication system. Obviously, sibilants (e.g., s,z) and stop bursts, whose energy is distributed primarily at high frequencies, will be more difficult to reliably detect over telephones and narrowband radio channels. Recognizers must not rely upon such phonetic units if the expected input channel disallows their reliable detection.

One additional advantage of speech recognizers in certain specific applications (such as in crowded aircraft cockpits) is that there is no need for displays, buttons, or more panel space on the interactive consoles being used. The microphone that a pilot already wears or holds for other communications then serves adequately as a computer input device.

I believe that the advantages listed in the last part of Table 1-1 include the most important practical reasons for developing and using speech recognition facilities. Speech permits mobility and simultaneous performance of other tasks, which are unusual in computer input facilities. In using switches, typewriters, cathode ray tube displays, and even the more unusual graphical input devices ("RAND tablets") and "joy sticks", the user must either be in physical contact with the computer console or terminal or must be oriented in fixed directions to produce input commands and monitor computer outputs. With speech, you can walk around the room, read instruction manuals, and turn your back on the console, while still inputting to the computer. Your hands and eyes can be busy with other tasks, such as handling packages in an inventory or postal distribution situation, or measuring critical distances in a quality control or inspection task. You can perform other primary tasks like hands-on experiments or adjustment of equipment while speaking information into the computer. It is possible to be some distance from the microphone, or to hold it or have it mounted on a headband, and you may move your head, hands, and body without returning to a fixed position for computer input. If you like, you may sit at your desk and talk over the familiar telephone to the computer down the hall or across the country.

These are the most encouraging aspects of speech recognition technology, that have opened up new vistas for a variety of practical applications. We can talk all we want to about the academic virtues of speech or other modalities, but it truly strikes home, factory, and the pocketbook when work efficiency is increased, input errors are reduced, and good workers are freed from tedious unnatural tasks and constant movement of eyes and hands from work pieces to computer input devices. Martin and Welch (Chap. 2; cf. also Martin, 1976) and their colleagues and competitors (Herscher, 1977; Glenn, 1971) have found success in practical applications of speech recognizers for: control and inspection of television faceplates, inspecting pull-ring can lids, automobile assembly lines, inspecting incoming merchandise, automated handling of materials (packages, etc., as in distribution systems within post offices and nationwide chains of department stores), and "voice programming" by supervisory personnel who are unskilled in computer programming. Most satisfied customers who have bought and used speech recognizers have had overloaded workers whose hands and eyes were thereby freed to simultaneously handle other tasks.

1-3. EXPERIMENTAL EVALUATION OF VOICE INTERACTIONS

We have seen that speech has many advantages for human-to-computer communication, including being natural and fast, and also "liberating", so the user can move around and be involved in other tasks. What clinches the case in favor of speech recognition for me is the experimental evidence that voice communication is critical to the best single- and multi-modality communication links. In 1974, Ochsman and Chapanis (cf. also Chapanis , 1975) reported on experiments in which pairs of people communicated with each other via ten alternative communication channels that might be used in human-computer communications, and they determined which channels produced the most effective problem solving. Included in the study were five basic channels: voice (via microphones and speakers in adjoining rooms); typewriting (via slaved electric typewriters); handwriting (via a telautograph); closed circuit video ("TV without voice"), and visual contact (through a sound-insulated glass panel). The teams of two communicators were given problem-solving tasks like scheduling classes for a college student, finding faults in an automobile ignition system, and identifying small parts that match requested parts (such as light sockets). Each member of the team had part of the necessary information, and they needed to communicate to successfully complete the task. (Chapanis, 1975, reported similar studies with other problem solving tasks, including: equipment-assembly; retrieval of newspaper articles about a specific topic; and a map-searching problem in which the team tried to find the office of a physician closest to a hypothetical home address.)

There were several major conclusions from these experiments, all of which strongly support the value of voice interaction (and hence support speech recognition capabilities). Their most important conclusion was that "there is a sharp dichotomy between modes of communication involving voice and those modes of communication that do not" (Ochsman and Chapanis, 1974, pp. 617-618). Their data showed that "regardless of extra embellishments, communication via typewriter or handwriting cannot even approach speech in terms of speed or task efficiency" (p. 618).

More specifically, Ochsman and Chapanis found that the average time it took for the communicating team to solve a problem was about 12 minutes for communication involving voice and handwriting, and about 16 minutes for voice alone. Other voice-assisted combinations of voice and typewriting, voice and video, and a communication-rich mode involving all five basic channels had mean solution times within those 12 and 16 minute limits. On the other hand, the fastest hard-copy mode (handwriting and video, without voice) took about 23 minutes, or 46% more time than the slowest mode involving voice alone. They could very reasonably conclude that, "The single most important decision in the design of a telecommunications link should center around the inclusion of a voice channel." (p. 618).

The inclusion or exclusion of the voice channel not only accounted for 90% of the statistical variance between problem solving times for the various modes, but also accounted for 72% of the variance in channel-switching actions that reflected the user preferences for various modes. They measured how often the communicators used activation buttons, seeking to use a channel, and found there were about four times as many activations, or messages sent, per unit time with speech modes as with the non-speech modes (p. 599). Speech thus seems to be the most "interactive" mode, allowing the users to work faster, and yet initiate more messages or interactions within that shorter problem solving time.

Finally, they found that the amount of time spent in non-communicative activities (like reading information, searching through the information folio given to each communicator, handling parts, making notes, waiting, etc.) was much greater in the non-speech modes than in the oral modes (12.1 versus 5.3 minutes, respectively; p. 608). With speech, they could do these other activities simultaneously with communicating, rather than at separate times. This is experimental evidence for one of the most important advantages of speech mentioned in Sec. 1-2; namely, that, more than any other communication modality, speech permits you to communicate while your hands and eyes are busy at other tasks. Other evidence comes from "field experience"; most commercial speech recognizers have been purchased and effectively used in industry because the user's hands and eyes were busy at other tasks and faster non-interruptive communication was desired (and attained, with definite customer satisfaction).

Later experiments (Chapanis et al., 1977; Kelly and Chapanis, 1977; Michaelis, et al., 1977) showed it is possible to find a small "basic" vocabulary (of around 200-300 words) that allows effective performing of realistic tasks, provided the word list is carefully tailored to the application. Given no vocabulary limits, talkers used about 1200 different words. A few hundred carefully chosen words may thus be adequate in practical recognizers, but perhaps 1200 words are needed if the vocabulary is not tailored to the task and individual speakers.

1-4. THE POTENTIAL FOR RECOGNIZERS OF VARIOUS CAPABILITIES

Even though we know that speech input to computers is valuable to have, we must, for each specific application, face the question of whether we can ever achieve the design, construction, and practical use of adequate speech recognizers. Exactly what is "adequate" needs to be clarified, and related to the specific uses of various speech input capabilities. A fully versatile, rapidly-responding speech input system capable of correctly recognizing all of the arbitrary natural-language sentences spoken by any arbitrary talker, over any communication link, would probably make best use of the advantages of the speech modality. But such a system is not available, and won't be forthcoming in any foreseeable future, so that spoken communication between human and computer will involve a compromise between the human needs and desires and the computer's limited capabilities. A critical question for each potential application thus is, "How much recognition capability is really needed?"

Table 1-2 lists various dimensions of system capability that need to be considered in discussing system adequacy and specific task requirements. Many of the system design criteria associated with these dimensions will be discussed throughout this book, and need to be understood if we are to fully appreciate the value of speech recognizers and the difficulties involved in developing systems that are adequate for various applications.

The most basic dimension of relative capability of interest in speech recognizer design involves the form of speech to be processed. The easiest task is the recognition of isolated words taken from a small vocabulary of alternative words or short phrases. Larger vocabularies of up to several hundred isolated words or commands make the problem more difficult and only a few prototype systems with such capabilities have been developed. Recently, initial systems have been developed to slightly extend the isolated-word capability by using formatted sequences of isolated commands, with strict (syntactic and task-dictated) constraints on the acceptable sequences of isolated words or commands.

If the form of speech is continuous (uninterrupted), one of the next most simple recognition tasks is word spotting (equivalently, "keyword spotting"), which is the detection of each (or, at least, many) of the occurrences of selected "keywords" in the context of flowing speech. Keyword spotting is fairly simple in one sense, in that not all of the speech need be analyzed and classified into words or phrases; only the occasional occurrences of the keywords need to be detected. Usually the interesting ("information-carrying") keywords are prominently stressed and clearly articulated, and many of the problems with continuous speech (e.g., coarticulation, missing segments, etc.) are minimized in finding such words. Yet, in another sense, word spotting is difficult, because the context of the word is not known and cannot be used to reinforce or verify decisions. In addition, the primary purpose of keyword spotting is to survey large amounts of information taken from narrow-bandwidth, noisy radio links, and to select conversations about topics of special interest. Consequently, word spotting is difficult on some other dimensions listed in Table 1-2, since the speaker is unknown (and usually not

TABLE 1-2.

DIMENSIONS OF DIFFICULTY IN SPEECH RECOGNITION

INPUT CHARACTERISTICS	1. Form of Speech
	2. Speaker Population
	3. Transducer and Channel
LANGUAGE DESIGN	4. Vocabulary
	5. Syntactic Constraints
	6. Semantic Constraints
	7. Task Constraints
	8. Enhanceability
SYSTEM STRUCTURE	9. Control Strategy
	10. Knowledge Sources
	11. Scoring Procedures
PERFORMANCE CRITERIA	12. Recognition Accuracy
	13. Training the Machine
	14. Training the User; User Acceptance
	15. Speed
	16. Cost
	17. Time for delivery

cooperative), the channel distorts and adds noise, and the conversation is not limited by preselected vocabulary, syntax, or topic, and is naturally rather sloppily spoken (Beek, et al., 1977).

Another restricted recognizer of connected speech handles highly constrained (but continuously spoken) sequences of words, like strings of digits (telephone numbers, stock numbers, measurements, etc.) or carefully formatted sequences of words (air traffic control commands, fixed-length commands with each word selected from a predetermined small vocabulary, etc.). This demands more complete analysis of the utterance than word spotting, so that all words must be determined. However, for some applications, the vocabulary of possible words used at each point in an utterance can be preselected so that the words are largely unaffected by their context (so that coarticulation effects are minimal). Also, the structural variety is kept to a minimum by the strict format demanded for all acceptable sequences, and the words spoken in such strict formats are generally spoken with unusual care. (See **Chap. 18 and 19 of this book for example word-sequence recognizers.)**

Farther along on the spectrum of increasing recognition difficulties are two distinct system types: restricted sentence understanding and what I shall call autonomous continuous speech recognition. Restricted sentence understanding was introduced by the Speech Understanding Research (ARPA SUR) project sponsored by the USA Advanced Research Projects Agency, which will be described more fully in Part III of this book (cf. also Newell, et al., 1971). A sentence understanding system could potentially use all the forms of knowledge available to a native listener of a language, including: acoustic processing, phonetic segmentation and labelling (that is, finding and categorizing all the vowels and consonants in the continuous speech); coarticulation and sound structure ("phonological") rules of the language; expected patterns or sound structures of words (to be matched with the sound patterns in the speech being analyzed); prosodic information; syntactic constraints on allowable word and phrase sequences; semantic knowledge ("intended meanings"); and pragmatic constraints such as the expected flow of discourse, user preferences for certain ways of saying things, and the task-dictated constraints on what needs to be communicated to have the machine truly aid the human in performing the specific task. The basic dogma of speech understanding is that for a machine to "understand" speech requires more than mere recognition of the sound structure and wording of the sentence; higher level linguistic information (associated with syntax, intended meanings, and task contexts) is also needed, and the acoustic speech signal alone is not adequate for understanding enough so that the machine can give the correct ultimate response. This dogma is not endorsed by all workers in the field of speech recognition.

Recent work in speech understanding (and future work for years to come) is clearly restricted, in that systems are tailored to specific problems and specific subsets of acceptable natural-language sentences. For example, the HEARSAY I speech understanding system developed at Carnegie-Mellon University (CMU) was initially developed using the specific task of playing chess with the computer, with the human's moves spoken as highly formatted utterances like "Pawn to king four." (Reddy, et al., 1973). In understanding the spoken move, the computer used explicit knowledge about allowable chess moves, the current state of the chess board, acceptable ways to express the moves, etc.

Autonomous continuous speech recognition (or, as it is usually called, simply "continuous speech recognition") is well represented by an old notion of automatically transcribing speech into word sequences. "Autonomous" here refers to the idea that these recognizers are to operate independent of syntactic, semantic, or pragmatic knowledge (cf. Postal, 1968). By endeavoring to do an excellent job in recognizing the sound structure of continuous speech and thus to locate all the words, the developers of such systems hope to avoid the heavy dependence upon syntactic, semantic, and pragmatic constraints that "speech understanding systems" must rely upon. The system theoretically can then be used on several new tasks without major adjustments or reprogramming (provided the vocabulary is still maintained). Obviously, without the verification help of total linguistic and pragmatic information, such systems must have a very reliable word recognition capability, and must be able to handle the effects of almost any word on its neighboring words.

In the extreme, the autonomous continuous speech recognizer might be directed towards recognizing any arbitrary English (or other-language) sentence, and might be visualized as a voice dictation machine or "phonetic typewriter" that would turn any spoken utterance into the appropriate word sequence. For the foreseeable future, some practical constraints have to be placed on such a system, primarily through limiting the vocabulary. Also, many researchers believe that adequate success in autonomous recognition is difficult or impossible to achieve. Most known applications for speech recognizers permit (in fact, encourage) use of task restrictions and linguistic constraints. Ultimately, if the recognizer is to be more than a phonetic typewriter, and is to use incoming messages to alter its future responses in aiding the human, speech "understanding" does seem to be necessary and in line with the "bionic" model of duplicating the successful human listener.

We have defined the primary dimension for distinguishing speech recognizers, on the basis of the form of speech. It appears that each type of recognizer in that spectrum of recognition capabilities has its own potential value and specific applications. However, in the past, most commercial interest, and even much of the military field interest, in speech recognizers, has been dominated by the ready availability of isolated word recognizers. It seems to be a case of the available technology dictating to the application, rather than the application dictating what technology should be developed and used. Beek, et al. (1977, p. 315) noted that "There has never been a stated military requirement for CSR" (continuous speech recognition), but this may be due more to the military emphasis on using available technology than to the lack of real uses for such capabilities. A large number of military-sponsored projects in continuous speech recognition (cf. Beek, et al., 1977), of which the ARPA SUR project was the largest, suggest that significant military interest must exist in developing continuous speech recognizers. Recognition studies have been done for applications in aircraft cockpits, military tactical field-data entry, military training systems, voice input to cartographic processing systems, keyword spotting, and several other applications. A RAND report outlined a variety of military applications where various speech recognition capabilities may be useful (Turn, et al. 1974). Ultimately, the "burden of proof" is on the speech recognition advocate to show why speech recognition is useful in any specific application, and to determine what form of recognizer (handling isolated words, connected speech of specific formats, speech understanding, or whatever) is most appropriate to that application.

Another important dimension of difficulty is the speaker population that must be handled. While a system can be tailored specifically to a single talker, most applications demand some ability (immediately, or after some training or retraining) to handle more than one talker, perhaps as many as 10, or 100, or 1000 talkers, or (for surveillance of communication systems, or for nationwide credit card authorizations) an unlimited number of talkers. The talker may be (a) "cooperative" (that is, willing to help the machine by saying exactly what the machine wants, or saying it in such a clear way as to help the machine), (b) "not cooperative" (perhaps unaware of, or not committed to, the need to help, and yet not endeavoring to confuse the machine), or (c) "uncooperative" (that is, unwilling to help, and working to prevent the machine from correctly understanding). Machines are also sensitive to the sex of the talker, and his or her dialect, and these are also critical aspects of the difficulty introduced by the speaker population.

The transducer and communication channel used with a speech recognition system can also introduce several problems, including reduced bandwidth, low signal-to-noise ratio (that is, presence of considerable noise), and other distortions that are characteristic of microphones, telephones, and radio channels. Detection and classification of all the vowels and consonants can be handicapped by loss of high-and low-frequency energy, confusions introduced by noise, and spectral distortions that alter the apparent spectral content of the speech. It is easier to avoid all these problems by use of high quality broadband systems in quiet environments, but many systems (such as factory installations of word recognizers, word spotters, etc.) must deal with such complications. The ARPA SUR project made a tradeoff in complexities, by dealing with ambitious sentence understanding tasks but a fairly small number of speakers and quite high quality speech.

The vocabulary of recognizable words can vary in size from a few words like the ten digits, up to 100; 1000; 10,000; or some larger number of entries. The ARPA SUR project, for example, greatly extended the target vocabulary size, by seeking to handle 1000 words. In addition to the number of words in the vocabulary, the confusability of words in the vocabulary is also very important. It is more difficult to accurately recognize ten rhyming words that the ten digits zero (or "oh") to nine, and considerably easier to recognize ten other longer and more distinctive words, like the names of the ten largest cities in the USA, etc. In some applications, words can be carefully selected to be clearly distinct from all other words in the vocabulary (such as using the phonetically-rich word "negative" instead of the shorter less distinctive word "no").

Other language constraints may be used to restrict the difficulty of recognizing continuous speech. Syntactic constraints may range from simple constraints on what word can be next, based only on the identity of the previous word (so-called "Markov" models), to more complex constraints on phrase structure based on what are called context-free, context-sensitive, and "augmented transition network" (ATN) grammars which make more intricate use of the total structure of the sentence. Semantic constraints specify which word sequences are meaningful in the human-machine communications. Task constraints may exclude certain word sequences that cannot occur in the context of the previous human-computer discourse, the current state of the task environment (such as the current board positions in a chess game), and the expectations that certain speakers will use certain expressions. The more of these linguistic and situational constraints we use in a system, the more complex the system gets, but the better the chances of correct recognition can be (cf. Klatt, 1977).

Table 1-2 also includes the "enhanceability" of the language and system, meaning the ease with which new words or sentence structures could be incorporated into the system as time progresses and the changing usage demands some change in the vocabulary or other aspects of the language. We would hope that we need not start from scratch everytime the language or application is changed slightly. This aspect of recognizer design has been given little consideration in previous studies, but may be quite important to the long-term utility of a recognizer.

A speech recognizer may be structured in various ways, with various "knowledge sources", or components, communicating to each other in various ways, and an executive control strategy that schedules and gives attention to various components at successive times in the analysis. In essence, this involves an implementation of alternative "divide and conquer" strategies, such as the alternative control structures discussed by Goodman and Reddy in Chap. 10 of this book. Alternatively, the recognition system can be based on an integrated network representation such as used in HARPY (see Chap. 15) and the DRAGON and IBM systems (Jelinek, 1976), which use statistical knowledge and generalized mathematical models (what Newell, 1976, called "generalized input-output systems"), rather than separate linguistically-defined components.

In any system, the available acoustic data can sometimes be compatible with more than one interpretation (such as when a word sounds a lot like the word "speech" but it is also somewhat like the word "beach", or "peach", or "spits", etc.), and some procedure is needed for selecting the best first guess. Scoring procedures are then needed to define "nearest neighbors" or order of likelihood for alternative hypotheses. Such procedures also become particularly troublesome when several different types of information, or different knowledge sources, suggest different hypotheses, and the various "votes" for the competing alternatives need to be weighted so that a best choice can again be made. One of the more sophisticated scoring procedures was developed in the BBN HWIM system, to be described in Chapter 14.

Table 1-2 also lists six important PERFORMANCE CRITERIA that define system specifications that can dramatically affect the difficulty of attaining adequate recognizers. Recognition accuracy is the percentage of all utterances or units that are correctly identified, and the higher the demanded level of accuracy (such as 99%, rather that 95%, etc.) the more difficult the system development task will be. Most commercial isolated word recognizers achieve over 99% correct recognition when trained for the individual talker, but performance may drop significantly when speech of new talkers is processed, or the input channel picks up considerable noise or distortions. Occasionally a word will be rejected because it is not close enough to any one word to make a reliable decision. For word spotting systems, many more failures to locate keywords may be permitted, provided most of the important conversations are found from the correctly located words; however a false detection of a keyword when it wasn't really there is considered very undesirable in word spotting, since the intention is to weed out all conversations that aren't of interest. For continuous speech recognition or restricted speech understanding, one can speak of errors and accuracies at several levels, including identification of phonemes, words, sentence structures, and meanings. High accuracy requirements at each of these levels makes the recognition task very difficult. In judging the final performance for such complex systems and being guided toward future improvements, one needs to consider not only the overall final semantic accuracy or word sequence accuracy, but the accuracy of each of the components or knowledge sources, and the exact sources of error (or "weak spots") in system performance.

Another dimension of difficulty in the design of speech recognizers is the amount of training required by the machine. Can a new user come up to the machine and be accurately recognized without ever having trained the machine to his or her voice, or must the user initially say a small set of training words (one or more times) or say all the words in the vocabulary, or all the acceptable utterances, once, or more than once? For large vocabularies and a large range of alternative sentences or phrases that can be recognized, the need to say all alternative utterances becomes an unwieldy task. Recognizers that require little or no training are preferred, but are more difficult to develop.

Similarly, a system is to be preferred which requires little or no training of the user, so the user need not learn special ways of talking, unnatural constraints on acceptable sentence structures, highly limited vocabularies, or the need to speak formatted word sequences with pauses separating successive words. It is true that talking is pleasant and natural to the human, yet the user of a recognizer may be severely disturbed and possibly reduced in efficiency and reliability if he or she is radically restricted in "conversation" with the machine. To be forced to speak in only a highly restricted and "stilted" command language may be awkward and frustrating, and may thus reduce the acceptability of voice communication with computers. It would seem appropriate for advocates of speech recognition to determine what constraints on the vocabulary, syntax, semantics, and general "naturalness" and "expressive power" of an interactive language are most likely to be acceptable to the user of a recognition system. I know of only one study (Lea, 1968, 1969) of the operational acceptability to the user of practical constraints on vocabulary size, command or sentence structure, and verbal system response times, and that study has had virtually no effect on the design of useful speech recognizers. Behavioral studies of human operator performance could and should be performed to provide meaningful measures (such as error rates, times required to cooperatively solve problems, modality duty rates, etc.) of the effectiveness of restricted voice input systems. The final test of the value of the voice link between human and computer will be whether the users accept and use it with some low level of frustration and low error rate, and high efficiency.

Associated with efficiency is the speed of the machine; does it take minutes to get a computer response to a three-second command, or does it respond immediately (in real time)? While initial laboratory models can be permitted to take 10, or 100, or even 1000 times real time to process an utterance through all their algorithms and make a final decision, such delays are usually unacceptable in operational recognizers. Commercial word recognizers usually provide almost instantaneous responses, and this has been a part of their growing acceptability. Recently, researchers have become increasingly concerned with speeding up their computer software for recognition, not only to demonstrate the ultimate feasibility of useful real-time recognition, but also to reduce time required to do experiments and analyze enough data to develop reliable algorithms. Of course, such demands for high-speed analysis do increase the difficulty of designing adequate recognizers, but in another sense the resultant ability to process lots of data and carefully tune algorithms to near optimum conditions increases the chance of providing reliable and useful recognizers.

The cost of a system is an important design criterion. Past experience and standard commercial procedures suggest that commercial customers will not pay the development cost of initial prototype systems, so the developers of recognizers must handle initial developments under contracts or grants, or internal funds. After such development projects, product lines can be introduced at fixed prices. The initial cost of available commercial speech recognition devices range from tens of thousands of dollars for the reliable self-contained word recognizers down to a few hundred dollars for a hobbyist's speech hardware interface to be used with an available small computer. Recent hardware **advances suggest that most of the type of processing that has been done in** speech recognizers (such as spectral analysis, autocorrelation, and decision logic) will be possible to obtain on a single "chip" costing at most a few hundred dollars (White, 1977), so that initial costs of such recognizers will probably drop dramatically. In addition, recognizers of connected speech, such as the LOCUST version of HARPY (cf. Lowerre and Reddy, Chap. 15 of this book), will probably be available in the price range of the earlier word recognizers. Another aspect of cost is the cost per second of speech processed, which may or may not be expressed to include an amortizing of the initial purchase price of the recognizer. In any case, cost of a system will obviously be one of the important performance criteria.

Another criterion of some interest is the time for delivery. Commercial word recognizers are now "off the shelf" items, available for use within days, whereas the interested user will wait longer for more sophisticated recognizers. Within the next few years (after the writing of this chapter in 1978), commercial recognizers will probably be available that can handle vocabularies of 200 or more isolated words, or restricted (HARPY-like) forms of connected speech, with near-real-time performance. It appears there will be prototype word spotting systems within that same time period. However, interested users will probably have to wait some years before versatile recognizers are available that can handle substantial subsets of spoken natural-language sentences that are not severely restricted by a small speaker population, stilted syntax, pre-selected task domains, and considerable training of the machine and user. Some informed researchers are not optimistic about having versatile speech understanding systems ("that will accept and understand unrestricted discourse from all speakers") in our lifetime (Flanagan, 1976, p. 411).

1-5. SUMMARY

In summary, we have seen that while speech offers many advantages for communication with machines, there are a variety of ways in which we can put demands on the machine that increase the difficulty of achieving success. The very advantage of naturalness of speech can promote versatile unrestricted recognizers that are to handle unrestricted forms of speech, but some compromise is needed between the human's desires for fully natural expression and the machine's limited capability for dealing with arbitrary sentence structures, extensive vocabularies, and casually slurred articulations. The larger the speaker population, the more difficult the system design will be. Also, while we have seen that primary advantages of speech input include the mobility it permits and the freeing of hands and eyes for other tasks, the recognizer's task is compounded by pickup of environmental noise and distortions in telephone systems and other communication links. The recognizer's chance of success can be increased by alleviating noise and distortions, tuning to the specific speakers, and restricting the vocabulary, syntactic structures, possible semantic interpretations, and task-related alternatives about what can be said. The system can be structured to use various forms of knowledge to develop and score alternative hypotheses that the system control strategy can select among. The final performance evaluation or utility of a system then hinges on its accuracy, the training effort it requires, the user acceptability, the speed and cost, and its availability.

Certain applications clearly demand certain choices in system design. For example, word spotters must handle nearly unlimited speaker populations, noisy and distorted speech data, and unrestricted forms of conversational speech. However, for most applications, the design choices are less rigid, so that while it might be nice to allow any speaker to use a telephone, and say nearly any arbitrary utterance, with almost no machine errors and with immediate and inexpensive response, less versatility may be acceptable. One of the crucial questions for each developer (or purchaser) of speech recognizers will be, "How much speech recognition ability is really adequate for the intended application?" By carefully answering this question in each such circumstance, using the dimensions shown in Table 1-2, the speech recognition advocate can successfully develop and evaluate speech input facilities, and give further evidence about the actual value of speech recognition systems.

1-6. REFERENCES

BEEK, B., E.P. NEUBERG, and D.C. HODGE (1977) "An Assessment of the Technology of Automatic Speech Recognition for Military Applications", IEEE Trans. Acoustics, Speech, and Signal Processing, ASSP-25, No. 4, 310-322.

BOBROW, D.G. and D.H. KLATT (1968) "A Limited Speech Recognition System", BBN Report 1667, Final Report, Contract NAS 12-138, Bolt Beranek and Newman, Cambridge, MA.

CHAPANIS, A. (1975), "Interactive Human Communication", Scientific American, 232, No. 3, 36-42.

CHAPANIS, A., R.N. PARRISH, R.B. OCHSMAN, and G.D. WEEKS (1977), Studies in Interactive Communication: II. The Effects of Four Communication Modes on the Linguistic Performance of Teams during Cooperative Problem Solving, Human Factors, 19, No. 2, 101-126.

FLANAGAN, J.L. (1976), "Computers that Talk and Listen: Man-Machine Communication by Voice", Proc. IEEE, 64, No. 4, 405-415.

GLENN, J. (1971), Voice Initiated Cockpit Control and Integrating (VICCI) System Test for Environmental Factors, Scope Electronics, Inc., Reston, Va.

HERSCHER, M.B. (1977), "Real-Time Interactive Speech Technology at Threshold Technology, Inc.", presented at Workshop on Voice Technology for Interactive Real-Time Command and Control System Application, NASA Ames Res. Center, December 6-8, 1977.

KELLY, M.J. and A. CHAPANIS (1977), Limited Vocabulary Natural Language Dialogue, Intern. J. Man-Machine Studies, 9, 479-501.

KLATT, D.H. (1977), "Review of the ARPA Speech Understanding Project", J. Acoust. Soc. America, 62, No. 6, December, 1977, 1345-1366.

LEA, W.A. (1968), "Establishing the Value of Voice Communication with Computers", IEEE Trans. Audio & Electroacoustics, vol. AU-16, 184-197.

________(1969), The Impact of Speech Communication with Computers, Proc. Sixth Space Congress, Cocoa Beach, FL: Brevard Printers, pp. 15-19 to 15-31.

________(1970a), "Evaluating Speech Recognition Work", J. Acoustic. Soc. America, 47, No. 6, 1612-1614.

________(1970b), "Towards Versatile Speech Communication with Computers", Intern. J. Man-Machine Studies, 2, 107-155.

MARTIN, T.B. (1976), "Practical Applications of Voice Input to Machines", Proc. IEEE, 64, 487-500.

MICHAELIS, P.R., A. CHAPANIS, G.D. WEEKS, and M.J. KELLY (1977), Word Usage in Interactive Dialog with Restricted and Unrestricted Vocabularies, IEEE Trans. on Professional Communication, Vol. PC-20, No. 4, 214-221.

NEWELL, A., J. BARNETT, J. FORGIE, C. GREEN, D.H. KLATT, J.C.R. LICKLIDER, J. MUNSON, D.R. REDDY, and W.A. WOODS (1971), Speech Understanding Systems; Final Report of a Study Group, Carnegie-Mellon University, Pittsburgh, PA. (Reprinted by American Elsevier, Amsterdam, North-Holland, 1973).

OCHSMAN, R.B. and A. CHAPANIS (1974), "The Effects of 10 Communication Modes on the Behavior of Teams During Cooperative Problem Solving", Intern. J. Man-Machine Studies, 6, 579-619.

PIERCE, J.R. and J.E. KERLIN (1957), "Reading Rates and the Information Rate of a Human Channel, Bell System Techn. J., 36, 497-516.

POSTAL, P.M. (1968), Aspects of Phonological Theory. New York: Harper & Row.

REDDY, D.R., L.D. ERMAN, and R.B. NEELY (1973), "A Model and a System for Machine Recognition of Speech, IEEE Trans. Audio Electroacoustics, vol. AU-21, 229-238.

SHANNON, C.E. and W. WEAVER (1949), The Mathematical Theory of Communication, Urbana, IL: University of Illinois Press.

TURN, R. (1974), "The Use of Speech for Man-Computer Communication", RAND Report-1386-ARPA, RAND Corp., Santa Monica, CA.

________, A. HOFFMAN, and T. LIPPIATT (1974), "Military Applications of Speech Understanding Systems, Defense Advanced Research Projects Agency, Arlington, VA, Report 14-34, AD 787394, June 1974.

WATT, W.C. (1968), "Habitability", American Documentation, 19, 338-351.

WHITE, G.M. (1977), "Implications of Low-Cost Signal-Processing Devices for Speech Science", J. Acoust. Soc. America, 62, Suppl. No. 1, 536-537 (A).

Chapter 3

Speech Analysis

Introduction

The first question that arises during the design of a speech-recognition system is how to represent or encode the speech signal itself before its recognition is attempted. In principle, one could simply use a digitized waveform as input signal. However, at sampling rates of 10,000 samples per second or more, the amount of processing required would be prohibitive. The waveform also contains information that is considered redundant for speech recognition (for example, phase information) and can hurt recognition performance rather than help it. A number of encoding schemes have therefore been developed that attempt to provide a more compact representation of speech, while retaining and even enhancing the perceptually relevant cues in speech. These schemes have been studied extensively over the years, and their influence on recognition system performance has been evaluated experimentally. In the following analysis we present several key papers that introduce some of the most widely used forms of speech analysis.

Our first paper, *Digital Representations of Speech Signals* by Shafer and Rabiner is a good tutorial review of a variety of digital speech-processing techniques that have been employed in speech recognition. The paper first describes waveform-based analyses such as peak and energy measurements, zero crossings, and autocorrelations. These measurements are typically chosen because they are easy to compute and already represent important aspects of speech. Perceptually most relevant in speech is information contained in the power spectrum of the signal and particularly, the spectral envelope that highlights the "formants," i.e., the resonances of the vocal tract. Spectral-encoding strategies, therefore, seek to represent well or emphasize these resonances in the spectral domain. Important examples here are the use of filter banks [Flanagan 72], linear predictive coding [Markel 76], and cepstral analysis. More general introductory texts to digital signal processing include [Oppenheim 75] and [Rabiner 78].

The second paper, *Comparisons of Parametric Representations of Monosyllabic Word Recognition in Continously Spoken Sentences*, by Davis and Mermelstein, describes several common encoding techniques and evaluates the resulting coefficients in the light of speech-recognition performance. Beyond coding efficiency, it attempts to determine which of a number of analysis methods best enhances features that are relevant in improving speech-recognition-system performance. It finds variants of cepstral analysis among the most effective techniques given the particular recognition strategy (template matching) used.

Significant further compression of the signal can be achieved by *vector quantization* (VQ), as described in *Vector Quantization* by Gray. The basic idea behind vector quantization (VQ) is to replace an incoming vector of speech coefficients by one of a small number of representative protoypical vectors, called *codewords*. If a set of codewords (a "codebook") has been assembled that is reasonably close to most speech signals, an incoming speech vector can then be represented by the codebook index that identifies the closest matching codeword. VQ has been used with various speech-recognition approaches and has led to significant data reduction without noticable loss in recognition performance. Other detailed treatments on vector quantization can be found in [Makhoul 85] and [Linde 80]

More recently, speech processing techniques based on the human auditory system have been proposed [Lyon 84; Seneff 88; Cohen 89]. The motivation of auditory models is that humans recognize the speech signal only after it has been processed by the human auditory system. While other previously described representations can be resynthesized accurately, there is evidence that they do not represent the actual input to the human recognition process. In the final paper of this chapter, *A Joint Synchrony/Mean-Rate Model of Auditory Speech Processing* by Seneff, a speech-processing system based on properties of the human auditory system is described. After processing by a model of the nonlinear transduction stage in the cochlea, two output paths are produced. One path yields an energy measure based on neural discharge. The other produces a synchrony measure that captures the synchronous firing of auditory nerve in response to vowels. The first path has been successfully used for segmentation, and the latter applied to classification in MIT's SUMMIT Speech Recognition System [Zue 90].

References

[Cohen 89] Cohen, J.R. *Application of an Auditory Model to Speech Recognition.* The Journal of the Acoustical Society of America 85(6):2623-2629, June, 1989.

[Flanagan 72] Flanagan, J.L. *Speech Analysis; Synthesis and Perception.* Springer-Verlag, Berlin, 1972.

[Linde 80] Linde, Y., Buzo, A., Gray, R.M. *An Algorithm for Vector Quantizer Design.* IEEE Transactions on Communication COM-28 (1):84-95, January, 1980.

[Lyon 84] Lyon, R. *Computational Models of Neural Auditory Processing.* In IEEE International Conference on Acoustics, Speech, and Signal Processing, pp 36.1.1-4. May, 1984.

[Makhoul 85] Makhoul, J., Roucos, S., Gish, H. *Vector Quantization in Speech Coding.* Proceedings of the IEEE 73(11):1551-1588, November, 1985.

[Markel 76] Markel, J. D., Gray, A. H. *Linear Prediction of Speech.* Springer-Verlag, Berlin, 1976.

[Oppenheim 75] Oppenheim, A. V., Schafer, R. W. *Digital Signal Processing.* Prentice-Hall, Englewood Cliffs, N.J., 1975.

[Rabiner 78] Rabiner, L.R., Shafer, R.W. *Digital Processing of Speech Signals.* Prentice-Hall International, London, 1978.

[Seneff 88] Seneff, S. *A Joint Synchrony/Mean-Rate Model of Auditory Speech Processing.* Journal of Phonetics 16(1):55-76, January, 1988.

[Zue 90] Zue, V., Glass, M., Phillips, M., Seneff, S. *The Summit Speech Recognition System: Phonological Modelling and Lexical Access.* In IEEE International Conference on Acoustics, Speech, and Signal Processing. April, 1990.

Digital Representations of Speech Signals

RONALD W. SCHAFER, SENIOR MEMBER, IEEE, AND LAWRENCE R. RABINER, MEMBER, IEEE

Invited Paper

Abstract—**This paper presents several digital signal processing methods for representing speech. Included among the representations are simple waveform coding methods; time domain techniques; frequency domain representations; nonlinear or homomorphic methods; and finally linear predictive coding techniques. The advantages and disadvantages of each of these representations for various speech processing applications are discussed.**

I. Introduction

THE NOTION of a *representation* of a speech signal is central to almost every area of speech communication research. Often the form of representation of the speech signal is not singled out for special attention or concern but yet it is implicit in the formulation of a problem or in the design of a system. A good example of this situation is in telephony, where speech is, in fact, represented by fluctuations in electrical current for purposes of long distance transmission. In other situations, however, we must often pay strict attention to the choice and method of implementation of the representation of the speech signal. This is true, for example, in such diverse areas as speech transmission, computer storage of speech and computer voice response, speech synthesis, speech aids for the handicapped, speaker verification and identification, and speech recognition. In all of these areas, digital representations; i.e., representations as sequences of numbers, are becoming increasingly dominant. There are two basic reasons for this. First, through the use of small general purpose digital computers, speech researchers have been able to apply a wide variety of digital signal processing techniques to speech communication problems. These techniques cover a range of complexity and sophistication that is impossible to match with analog methods. Second, the recent and predicted future developments in integrated circuit technology make it possible to realize digital speech processing schemes economically as hardware devices having the same sophistication and flexibility as a computer program implementation.

The purpose of this paper is to survey the important and most useful methods for obtaining digital representations of speech signals. This is a formidable task since the number and variety of such methods is great. Thus we must begin by disclaiming any pretentions to completeness; we shall only try to point out the methods that in our view are the most useful in the technical and research areas of speech communication.

The organization of this paper is as follows. In Section II, we briefly review the speech production process and show how it can be modeled with a simple digital representation. We then discuss a class of waveform coding methods for representing speech in Section III. Included in this class are linear pulse-code modulation (PCM), delta modulation (DM), differential PCM, adaptive delta modulation, and finally adaptive differential PCM (DPCM). It is shown at the end of this section that if an adaptive predictor is incorporated in these models, the waveform coding technique becomes quite similar to the linear predictive coding method to be discussed in Section VII.

In Section IV, we discuss various time-domain representations of speech. Included in this section are the concepts of zero crossing analysis, autocorrelation functions, "peak-to-peak" type estimations, and the use of "energy" functions. In Section V, we discuss frequency domain representations of speech for which the concept of short-time spectrum analysis is dominant. Several examples of systems based on short-time spectrum analysis are given in this section.

In Section VI, we discuss the topic of homomorphic analysis of speech. In this section the concept of the cepstrum is introduced. Finally, in Section VII, we discuss the two basic methods of linear prediction analysis, explain their similarities and differences and discuss the basic concepts which are derivable from them including the spectrum, cepstrum, and autocorrelation function.

II. A Digital Model for Production of the Speech Signal [1]-[3]

A schematic diagram of the human vocal apparatus is shown in Fig. 1. The vocal tract is an acoustic tube that is terminated at one end by the vocal cords and at the other end by the lips. An ancillary tube, the nasal tract, can be connected or disconnected by the movement of the velum. The shape of the vocal tract is determined by the position of the lips, jaw, tongue, and velum.

Sound is generated in this system in three ways. Voiced sounds are produced by exciting the vocal tract with quasi-periodic pulses of air pressure caused by vibration of the vocal cords. Fricative sounds are produced by forming a constriction somewhere in the vocal tract, and forcing air through the constriction, thereby creating turbulence which produces a source of noise to excite the vocal tract. Plosive sounds are created by completely closing off the vocal tract, building up pressure, and then quickly releasing it. All these sources create a wide-band excitation of the vocal tract which in turn acts as a linear time-varying filter which imposes its transmission properties on the frequency spectra of the sources. The vocal tract can be characterized by its natural frequencies (or formants) which correspond to resonances in the sound transmission characteristics of the vocal tract.

A typical speech waveform is shown in Fig. 2, which illustrates some of the basic properties of the speech signal. We see, for example, that although the properties of the waveform change with time, it is reasonable to view the speech waveform as being composed of segments during which the signal properties remain

Manuscript received September 18, 1974; revised November 25, 1974.
R. W. Schafer was with the Bell Laboratories, Inc., Murray Hill, N.J. He is now with the Department of Electrical Engineering, Georgia Institute of Technology, Atlanta, Ga. 30332.
L. R. Rabiner is with the Bell Laboratories, Inc., Murray Hill, N.J. 07974.

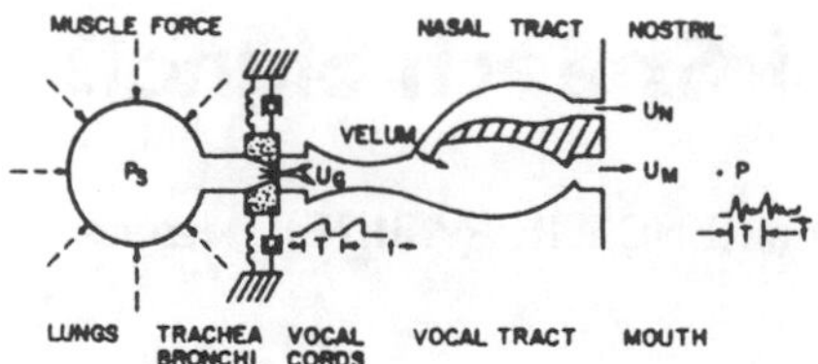

Fig. 1. Schematic diagram of mechanism of speech production. (After Flanagan *et al.* [2].)

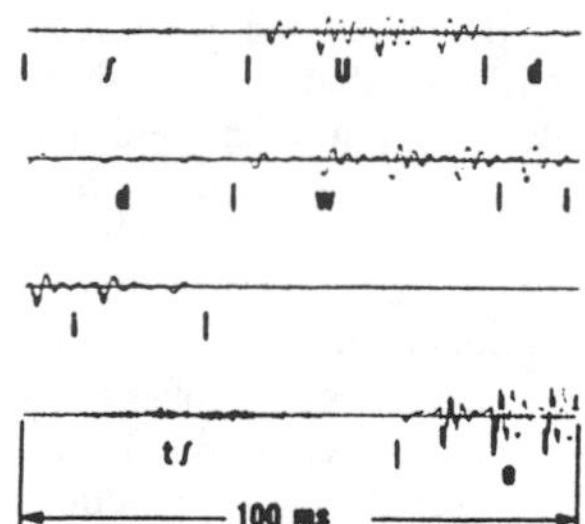

Fig. 2. An illustration of a speech waveform, corresponding to the utterance "*Should we chase*".

rather constant. Such segments are demarked in Fig. 2 below the waveform. These sample segments have the appearance either of a low-level random (unvoiced) signal (as in ʃ or tʃ in Fig. 2) or a high-level quasi-periodic (voiced signal) (as in *U* or *w* or *i*) with each period displaying the exponentially decaying response properties of an acoustic transmission system. We note that the dynamic range of the waveform is large; i.e., the peak amplitude of a voiced segment is much larger than the peak amplitude of an unvoiced segment.

Because the sound sources and vocal tract shape are relatively independent, a reasonable approximation is to model them separately, as shown in Fig. 3. In this digital model, samples of the speech waveform are assumed to be the output of a time-varying digital filter that approximates the transmission properties of the vocal tract and the spectral properties of the glottal pulse shape. Since, as is clear from Fig. 2, the vocal tract changes shape rather slowly in continuous speech (likewise its sound transmission properties) it is reasonable to assume that the digital filter in Fig. 3 has fixed characteristics over a time interval of on the order of 10 ms. Thus the digital filter may be characterized in each such interval by an impulse response or a set of coefficients for a digital filter. For voiced speech, the digital filter is excited by an impulse train generator that creates a quasi-periodic impulse train in which the spacing between impulses corresponds to the fundamental period of the glottal excitation.[1] For unvoiced speech, the filter is excited by a random number generator that produces flat spectrum noise. In both cases, an amplitude control regulates the intensity of the input to the digital filter.

This model is the basis of a wide variety of representations of speech signals. These are conveniently classified as either waveform representations or parametric representations depending upon whether the speech waveform is represented directly or whether the representation is in terms of time-varying parameters of the basic speech model. These representations range in complexity from simply samples of the speech wave-

[1] It is assumed that the effects of the glottal pulse shape are included in the digital filter.

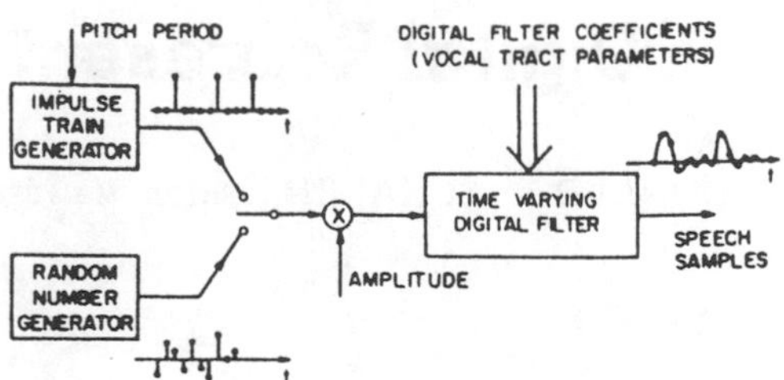

Fig. 3. Digital processing model for production of speech signals.

form taken periodically in time to estimates of the parameters of the model in Fig. 3. The choice of the digital representation is governed by three major considerations: processing complexity, information (bit) rate, and flexibility. By complexity, we mean the amount of processing required to obtain the chosen representation. In many cases processing complexity is a measure of cost of implementation of the system in hardware. A simple representation can generally be implemented more economically than a complex representation. Thus complexity is often the overriding consideration in some transmission applications where low terminal cost is crucial. Information or bit rate is a measure of the redundancy in the speech signal which has been removed by the processing. A low bit rate means that the digital representation of the speech signal can be transmitted over a low capacity channel, or stored efficiently in digital memory. Finally flexibility is a measure of how the speech can be manipulated or altered for applications other than transmission, e.g., voice response, speech recognition, or speaker verification. In general, greater complexity is the price paid to lower the bit rate and increase the flexibility. However, tradeoffs can generally be made among these three factors. In transmission and voice response applications the quality and intelligibility of the reconstituted speech are also prime considerations. Most of the techniques we will discuss are capable of producing good quality, highly intelligible speech, although some of the techniques are primarily analysis methods, and as such are limited to applications where the speech signal need not be reconstructed.

In the remainder of this paper, we will discuss a number of of digital representations that span the spectrum of possibilities in each of the above areas of concern. We shall begin with the simplest, least efficient and least flexible representation of speech and progress to more complex ones which have the greatest flexibility and lowest bit rate.

III. Digital Waveform Coding

Conceptually, the simplest digital representations of speech are concerned with direct representation of the speech waveform. Such schemes as PCM, DM, and DPCM are all based on Shannon's sampling theorem, which says that any bandlimited signal can be exactly reconstructed from samples taken periodically in time if the sampling rate is twice the highest frequency of the signal. We begin with a discussion of the simplest waveform coding technique; i.e., PCM.

A. PCM

In applying the sampling theorem to a digital representation of speech there are two main concerns. These are depicted in Fig. 4. If the signal bandwidth is W hertz, then the sampling period must be $T \leq 1/(2W)$. Since the samples $x(nT)$ of the signal generally take on a continuous range of values, they must be quantized for transmission or digital storage. If we repre-

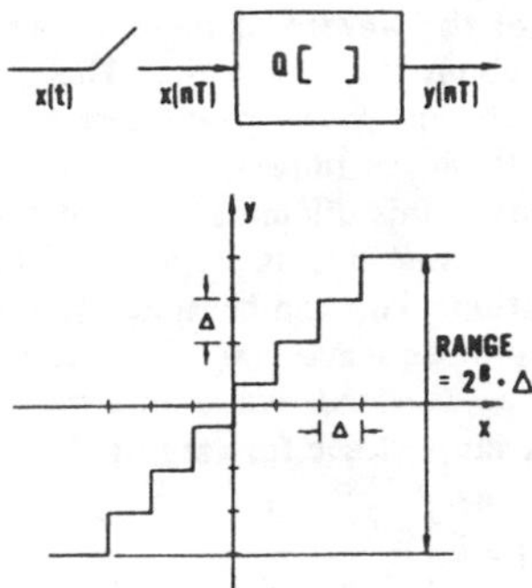

Fig. 4. Sampling and quantizing of an analog signal.

sent the samples as B-bit binary words, then the bit rate is $2BW$ bits/s. The value of W required for speech signals depends on the ultimate use of the samples. We know from measurements and theoretical studies that speech sounds such as fricatives have rather wide bandwidths (on the order of 10 kHz). On the other hand much of the information required for speech intelligibility is contained in the variation of the first three formant frequencies of voiced speech and these are typically below 3 kHz. Thus, a sampling rate between 6 kHz and 20 kHz is generally used. No matter what the sampling rate is, the speech signal must be suitably low-pass filtered prior to the sampling process to eliminate undesired high frequencies of the speech and high frequency noise.

The choice of the number of bits per sample B is also dependent upon the intended use of the samples. If our purpose is transmission or computer storage followed by conversion back to an analog signal, we are only concerned that the resulting analog signal be perceptually acceptable. Also, the sampling process just described is generally the first step in any digital speech analysis techniques. Since errors incurred in the sampling process will propagate to more refined digital representations, we are often justified in a very generous allotment of bits and sampling rate if the sampled speech wave is to undergo further processing. However it should be noted that the amount of processing required to implement most systems is proportional to sampling rate. Thus we should try to keep the sampling rate as low as possible, consistent with other objectives.

One objective measure of the fidelity of the PCM representation is the ratio of the signal power to the quantization noise power. If we define the quantization noise in Fig. 4 as the following:

$$e(nT) = x(nT) - Q[x(nT)] = x(nT) - y(nT)$$

then it can be shown [4], [7] that about 11 bits are required in order that the signal-to-noise ratio (SNR) be 60 dB. (This is often referred to as "toll quantity".) It is easily shown that the addition of one bit changes the SNR by 6 dB.

The preceding discussion can be summarized by stating that an adequate PCM representation for most purposes requires from 66 000 bits/s (11 bits × 6 kHz) to 220 000 bits/s (11 bits × 20 kHz). This is a very significant consideration in transmission or storage for processing on a computer.

Since we generally have little flexibility in lowering the sampling rate, as this is governed by other considerations, the main hope for lowering the overall bit rate is in reducing the number of bits/sample. The key to such reductions lies in considering one of the basic properties of the speech signal; namely, that speech has a wide dynamic range. We see from Fig. 4 that if B is fixed, then the step size Δ must be chosen so that $\Delta \cdot 2^B$ spans the maximum peak-to-peak range of the signal. Thus the quantizer step size is determined by the amplitude of the voiced segments of speech whereas a good representation of unvoiced segments requires a much smaller step size.

One solution to this problem is to use a nonlinear quantizer characteristic which distributes the quantization levels more densely for lower amplitudes than for high amplitudes. Based on empirical determinations of the amplitude distribution of speech signals, a logarithmic quantizer characteristic has been found to be nearly optimum [9]. Using a logarithmic quantizer, 7 bits/sample are sufficient to obtain toll quality. An alternative approach is the use of a time varying step size [5]-[7], i.e., an adaptive quantizer. When the signal level is low, a small step size is used; and when the signal amplitude is large, an appropriate large step size is used. The adjustment of the step size may be done by logical operations on the sequence of samples arising from adaptive quantization process [5]-[7].

B. Differential Quantization

Further reductions in bit rate for waveform quantization methods can be obtained by considering more of the detailed properties of the speech signal. Specifically, it is clear from Fig. 2 that there is a great deal of redundancy in the speech signal. Removal of some of this redundancy can yield a concomitant reduction in bit rate, at the expense of increased complexity in the signal processing algorithms. Fig. 5 depicts a general differential quantization scheme. The scheme is based on the fact that even for sampling at just the Nyquist rate ($T = 1/(2W)$), the correlation between successive samples is quite high and, as the sampling rate increases, the sample-to-sample correlation increases, approaching unity for very high sampling rates.

In the system of Fig. 5, let us assume that $\tilde{x}(n)$ is an estimate of the value of the speech sample $x(n) = x(nT)$. Then if the estimate is good, the variance of the difference $\delta(n) = x(n) - \tilde{x}(n)$ should be small, and thus the variance of the quantization error should be smaller than that incurred in quantizing the speech samples $x(n)$. The quantized difference signal $\hat{\delta}(n)$ when added to $\tilde{x}(n)$ produces a reconstructed signal $\hat{x}(n)$ which differs from $x(n)$ by only the quantization error of the difference signal; i.e.,

$$\begin{aligned} e(n) &= \delta(n) - \hat{\delta}(n) \\ &= [x(n) - \tilde{x}(n)] - [\hat{x}(n) - \tilde{x}(n)] \\ &= x(n) - \hat{x}(n). \end{aligned}$$

Due to the redundancy in the speech signal, it seems plausible that a given sample could be predicted as a linear combination of previous samples. In fact even the simplest linear combination may suffice; i.e., a constant times the previous sample. Therefore if the quantization error is small, $\hat{x}(n)$ will be a good approximation to $x(n)$ and

$$\tilde{x}(n) = a\hat{x}(n-1), \qquad a \approx 1 \tag{1}$$

will be a good estimate of $x(n)$. The z transform of (1) is

$$\tilde{X}(z) = az^{-1}\hat{X}(z).$$

Thus the predictor is characterized by the polynomial

$$P(z) = \frac{\tilde{X}(z)}{\hat{X}(z)} = az^{-1} \tag{2}$$

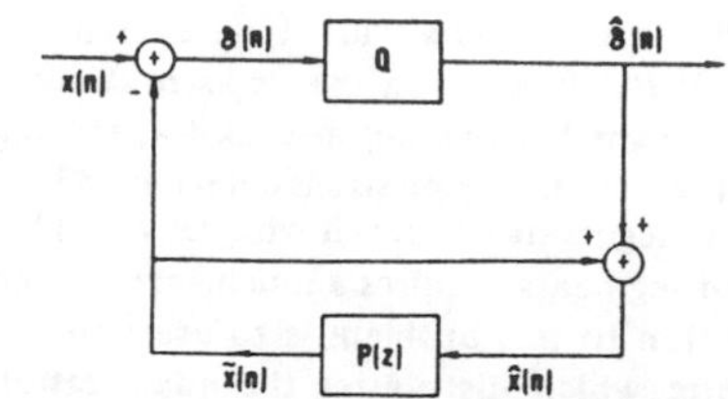

Fig. 5. General differential quantization scheme.

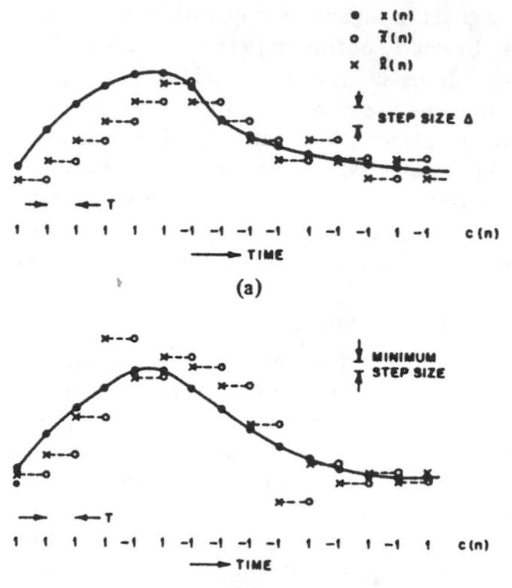

Fig. 6. Illustration of delta modulation. (a) Fixed step size. (b) Adaptive step size.

A more general predictor polynomial is of the form

$$P(z) = \sum_{k=1}^{p} a_k z^{-k}. \tag{3}$$

The basic principle of linear prediction is applied in more generality in Section VII.

In using differential quantization, we are free to choose the sampling rate, the quantizer and the predictor so as to reduce the bit rate. If the sampling rate is much higher than the Nyquist rate, the correlation between adjacent samples is very close to one and it is possible to use a 1-bit quantizer to obtain a good approximation to the input samples. This case, illustrated in Fig. 6(a), is called DM. In Fig. 6(a), we have illustrated how $x(n)$, $\tilde{x}(n)$, and $\hat{x}(n)$ vary with time. (We have shown the case where $a = 1$.) The quantized difference signal has the form

$$\hat{\delta}(n) = \Delta \cdot c(n)$$

where

$$c(n) = \begin{cases} +1, & \text{if } \delta(n) \geq 0 \\ -1, & \text{if } \delta(n) < 0 \end{cases}$$

and Δ is the fixed step size. Fig. 6(a) shows the two types of errors that are inherent in differential quantization schemes. On the left of the figure, the slope of the waveform is greater than the maximum rate of increase of the staircase approximation; i.e., for this choice of sampling period, Δ is too small to follow rapid changes in the waveform. This is called slope overload. On the right side of the figure, we see that in slowly varying parts of the waveform there is a tendency to oscillate up and down about the waveform. This is called granular distortion. In such regions we would like to have a smaller step size to reduce the magnitude of the quantization error.

One solution to this dilemma is to let the step size vary so that Δ becomes large during slope overload and small during granular distortion. This can be done by searching for patterns in the code word sequence $c(n)$. For example a run of +1's or −1's means slope overload, while an alternating pattern means granularity. A simple logic for varying the step size is [6]

$$\Delta(n) = \begin{cases} P\Delta(n-1), & \text{if } c(n) = c(n-1) \\ Q\Delta(n-1), & \text{if } c(n) \neq c(n-1). \end{cases}$$

The quantized difference signal is now

$$\hat{\delta}(n) = \Delta(n) \cdot c(n).$$

An optimum choice of the parameters is [6]

$$P = 1.5, \quad Q = 1/P.$$

This scheme is illustrated by Fig. 6(b). (Here, for simplicity we have assumed $P = 2$ and $a = 1$.) It can be seen that this adaptive delta modulator (ADM) is able to follow rapid increases in slope and also it is able to use a smaller step size in regions of granularity. In practice, limits are placed on the step size variation so that $\Delta_{min} \leq \Delta(n) \leq \Delta_{max}$. This prevents the step size both from becoming unreasonably large and from being driven to zero when the input to the differential quantizer is zero.

If we use a multibit quantizer in Fig. 5, then a lower sampling rate can be used. This case is DPCM. If the sampling rate is the Nyquist rate, then we can use two bits less in the quantizer than required for straight PCM for the same SNR [8]. Furthermore, we can adapt the quantizer step size to obtain further improvements. Schemes similar to the ADM system just described have been implemented for multi-bit quantizers. These are called adaptive DPCM (ADPCM) systems [5].

Such a representation has been used for storage of speech at 24 kbits/s for a computer voice response system [10], [11]. An interesting result of this work is the observation that the adaptive quantizing provides a simple means of finding the beginning and end of a speech utterance [10]. This is a problem that arises in many situations, including speech recognition, speaker verification and computer voice response.

IV. Time Domain Analysis Methods

The objective of digital waveform coding is to represent the speech waveform as accurately as possible so that an acoustic signal can be reconstructed from the digital representation. In many speech processing problems, however, we are not interested in reconstructing an acoustic signal but rather we are concerned with representing the speech signal in terms of a set of properties or parameters of the model discussed in Section II. Some rather simple, but useful, characterizations can be derived by simple measurements on the waveform itself; i.e., upon a PCM representation of the waveform.

The key to these, and, indeed, the key to all parametric representations, is the concept of short-time analysis. We note from Fig. 2 that if we select an arbitrary segment of the speech waveform of about 10- to 30-ms duration, then it is quite probable that the properties of the waveform remain roughly invariant over that interval. For example, we may select a voiced interval in which the speech signal is characterized by the fundamental period and the amplitude of each basic period. On the other hand, we may select an unvoiced segment where the signal is characterized by the lack of periodicity and the amplitude of the waveform. Since these properties vary from segment-to-segment, it is common to analyze speech on a time-varying basis by carrying out an analysis on short segments of speech selected at uniformly spaced time intervals.

A. Peak Measurements

It is only necessary to glance at Fig. 2 to see that during voiced intervals, the speech signal is characterized by a sequence of peaks that occur periodically at the fundamental frequency of the speech signal. In contrast, during unvoiced intervals the peaks are relatively smaller and do not occur in any discernible pattern. Thus the maximum peak amplitude during an analysis interval can serve as a simple indication of the amplitude of the signal and as an aid in distinguishing between voiced and unvoiced speech segments.

The time between corresponding peaks is, of course, equal to the fundamental period for voiced speech. This principle has been used in a number of schemes for determining the fundamental period or pitch period. A difficulty with this approach is that even over a short analysis interval, the speech signal is not exactly periodic. Since each period has a number of peaks, it is possible to make several different estimates of the period. A method for logically combining the results of several simple measurements of this kind to improve accuracy has been discussed by Gold and Rabiner [12], [13]. By careful choice of the basic measurements and careful design of the logic, the accuracy of the combined results is much greater than the accuracy of any of the individual estimates.

B. Energy Measurements

One of the simplest representations of a signal is its energy. In the case of a real discrete-time signal $x(n)$, the energy is defined in general as

$$E = \sum_{n=-\infty}^{\infty} x^2(n). \tag{4}$$

For nonstationary signals such as speech, it is often more appropriate to consider a time-varying energy calculation such as the following:

$$E(n) = \sum_{m=0}^{N-1} [w(m)x(n-m)]^2 \tag{5}$$

where $w(m)$ is a weighting sequence or window which selects a segment of $x(n)$, and N is the number of samples in the window. For the simple case of $w(m) = 1$, $E(n)$ is the sum of the squares of the N most recent values of $x(n)$. Fig. 7(a) shows how the energy measurement of (5) can be viewed in terms of filtering the sequence $x^2(n)$ by a finite impulse response (FIR) filter with impulse response $w^2(n)$.

It is to be expected that the function $E(n)$ would display the time varying amplitude properties of the speech signal. However, the definition of (5) requires careful interpretation. First there is the choice of window. The purpose of the window is to attach lower weight to speech samples which occurred further back in time, thus $w(m)$ generally tends to 0 monotonically as m gets larger. When one wants to apply equal weight to the entire interval, a rectangular window is used. The

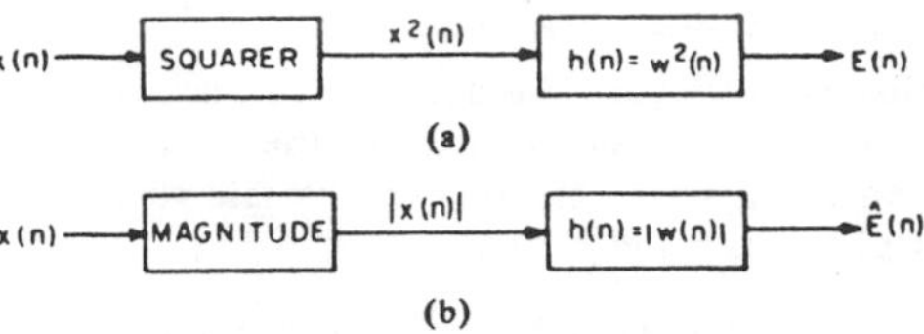

Fig. 7. (a) Implementation of short-time energy calculation using a finite impulse response digital filter. (b) An alternative definition of energy.

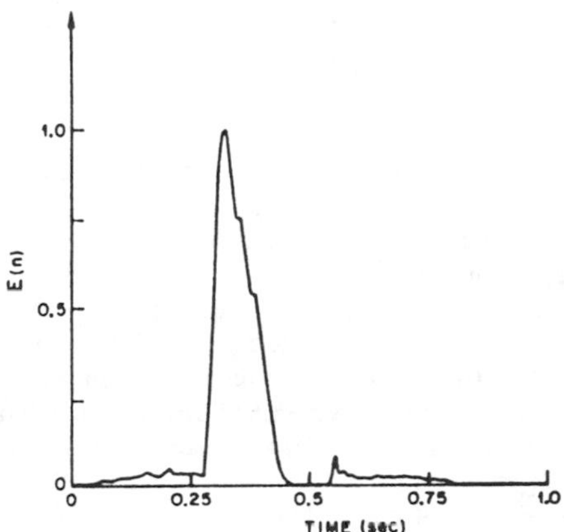

Fig. 8. Normalized energy for the word /six/.

second difficulty involves choice of measurement interval N. If N is too small, i.e., less than a pitch period, $E(n)$ of (6) will fluctuate very rapidly depending on exact details of the waveform. If N is too large, i.e., several pitch periods, $E(n)$ will have very little variation, and will not reflect the changing properties of the speech signal. A suitable practical choice of N is on the order of 100–200 for a 10-kHz sampling rate (i.e., 10–20 ms of speech).

The major significance of $E(n)$ is that it provides a good measure for separating voiced speech segments from unvoiced speech segments. $E(n)$ for unvoiced segments is much smaller than for voiced segments. Also the smaller the value of N, the less smearing there is in locating the exact instant at which unvoiced speech becomes voiced and vice versa. Furthermore, for very high quality speech, the energy can be used to separate unvoiced speech from silence.

One difficulty with energy measurements is that they are very sensitive to large signal levels (because they enter the computation as a square), thereby emphasizing large sample-to-sample variations in $E(n)$. One relatively simple way of alleviating this problem is to use as a measure of energy, the function

$$\hat{E}(n) = \sum_{m=0}^{N-1} |w(m)x(n-m)| \tag{6}$$

where the sum of absolute values is computed instead of the sum of squares. Fig. 7(b) shows an interpretation of (6) as a linear filtering operation on $|x(n)|$. Fig. 8 shows the energy function for the word six for a 10-ms rectangular window. It is easy to see the low energy fricative regions at the beginning and end of six, and the stop gap region during the /k/ for which the energy is almost zero. An example of the application of energy measurements is the speech recognition work of Reddy [14].

C. Zero Crossing Measurements

Another very simple time domain analysis method is based on zero crossing measurements. In the context of a digital implementation, a zero crossing can be said to occur between sampling instants n and $n - 1$ if

$$\text{sign}\,[x(n)] \neq \text{sign}\,[x(n-1)]\,. \tag{7}$$

This measurement is trivial to implement and is often used as a gross estimate of the frequency content of a speech signal. Its use is motivated by the observation that if the signal is a sinusoid of frequency f_0, then the average number of zero crossings is

$$n_z = 2f_0 \text{ crossings/s.} \tag{8}$$

However, the interpretation of zero crossing measurements for speech is much less precise, because of the broad frequency spectrum of most speech sounds. Nevertheless, very crude estimates of spectrum properties such as this may often suffice.

For example, it is well known that the energy of voiced speech tends to be concentrated below 3 kHz, whereas the energy of fricatives generally is concentrated above 3 kHz. Thus, zero crossing measurements (along with energy information) are often used in making a decision about whether a particular segment of speech is voiced or unvoiced. If the zero crossing rate is high, the implication is unvoiced; if the zero crossing rate is low, the segment is most likely to be voiced. Zero crossing measurements, coupled with a pitch detection scheme, provide a useful approach to estimation of excitation parameters [34]. Zero crossing measurements have also been useful as representations of speech signals for speech recognition [14].

In implementing zero crossing measurements digitally, there are a number of important considerations. Although the basic algorithm requires only a comparison of signs of two successive samples, special care must be taken in the sampling process. Noise, dc offset, and 60-Hz hum have disastrous effects on zero crossing measurements. Thus for zero crossing measurements a bandpass filter rather than a low-pass filter may be necessary prior to sampling to avoid the said difficulties. Also, the sampling period T determines the time resolution of the zero crossing measurements; thus fine resolution requires a high sampling rate. However, very crude quantization (1 bit in fact) is all that is necessary to preserve the zero crossing information.

D. Short-Time Autocorrelation Analysis

The autocorrelation function of a discrete-time signal $x(n)$ is defined as

$$\varphi(m) = \lim_{N \to \infty} \frac{1}{2N+1} \sum_{n=-N}^{N} x(n)\,x(n+m).$$

The autocorrelation function is useful for displaying structure in any waveform, speech being no exception. For example, if a signal is periodic with period P, i.e., $x(n+P) = x(n)$ for all n, then it is easily shown that

$$\varphi(m) = \varphi(m+P). \tag{9}$$

Thus periodicity in the autocorrelation function indicates periodicity in the signal. Also, an autocorrelation function that is sharply peaked around $m = 0$ and falls off rapidly to zero as m increases indicates a lack of predictable structure in the signal.

As we have observed, speech is not a stationary signal. However, the properties of the speech signal remain fixed over relatively long time intervals. As we have already seen, this leads to the notion of short-time analysis techniques that operate on short segments of the speech signal. For example consider a segment of N samples of the signal

$$x_l(n) = x(n+l), \qquad 0 \leqq n \leqq N-1 \tag{10}$$

where l denotes the beginning of the segment. Then the short-time autocorrelation function can be defined as

$$\varphi_l(m) = \frac{1}{N} \sum_{n=0}^{N'-1} x_l(n)x_l(n+m), \qquad 0 \leqq m \leqq M_0 - 1 \tag{11}$$

where M_0 denotes the maximum lag that is of interest. For example, if we wish to observe periodicity in a waveform, then we would require $M_0 > P$. The integer N' is for the moment unspecified.

We can interpret (11) as the autocorrelation of a segment of the speech signal of length N samples beginning at sample l. If $N' = N$, then data from outside the segment $l \leqslant n \leqslant N + l - 1$ is used in the computation. If $N' = N - m$, then only data from that interval is required. In this case, the segment is often weighted by a "window" function that smoothly tapers the ends of the segment to zero. In using the autocorrelation function to detect periodicity in speech, either choice is satisfactory; however, we shall see in Section VII that the distinction is important in analysis methods based on linear prediction. In either case, the direct computation of $\varphi_l(m)$ for $0 \leqq m \leqq M_0 - 1$ requires computational effort proportional to $M_0 \cdot N$. This can be a significant overhead factor.

Short-time analysis methods typically are applied to estimate parameters of the speech model discussed in Section II. The normal assumption is that although a sampling rate ranging from 6 kHz to 20 kHz may be necessary to preserve the essential features of the speech signal in a PCM representation, much lower sampling rates suffice for the slowly varying parameters of the model (50 to 100 Hz is typical). Suppose for example that the sampling rate of the speech signal is 10 kHz and the short-time autocorrelation is to be computed 100 times/s. The estimate of the autocorrelation is generally based upon from 20- to 40-ms segments of the speech signal. (For estimates of periodicity, the window must be long enough to encompass at least two periods of the speech signal.) Thus, for a 10-kHz sampling rate $200 \leqslant N \leqslant 400$, and the autocorrelation estimates must be computed by moving in increments of 100 samples.

In using the short-time autocorrelation function for pitch period estimation, it is desirable that the correlation function be sharply peaked so that a strong peak will stand out at multiples of P, the period. The correlation function of speech is not sharply peaked because there is a great deal of predictable structure in each period of the speech waveform. Sondhi [15] has given several methods of sharpening the peaks in the autocorrelation function. One of these called center clipping is illustrated in Fig. 9. The nonlinear operation of clipping out the middle of the speech waveform is very effective in reducing the sample to sample correlation of the signal. This is illustrated in Fig. 10 which shows a succession of short-time

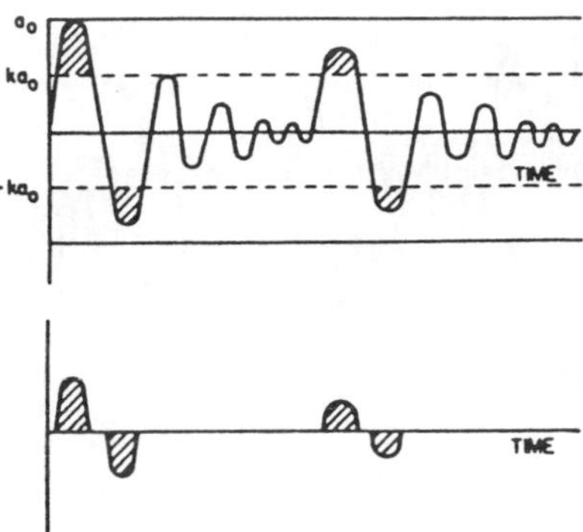

Fig. 9. Illustration of center clipping.

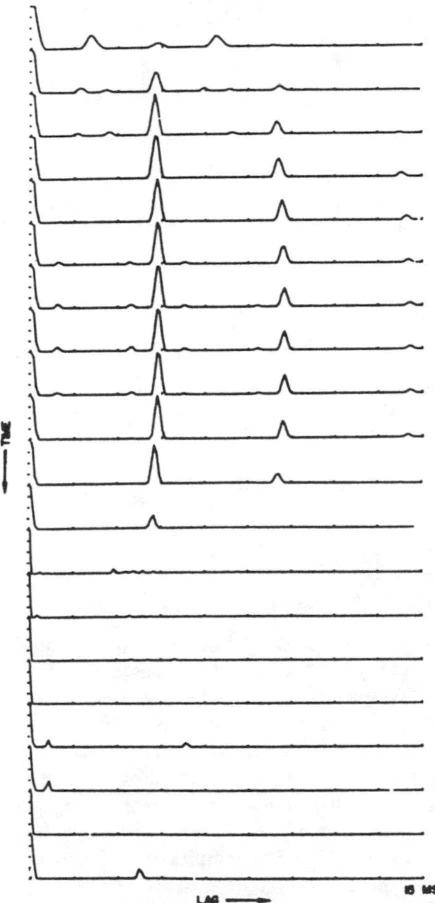

Fig. 10. Sequence of autocorrelation functions for center-clipped speech.

autocorrelation functions each estimated from 30-ms segments of center-clipped speech which are selected at intervals of 15 ms ($66\frac{2}{3}$-Hz sampling rate).

From a set of correlation functions of this type it is possible to estimate the pitch period simply by locating the strong peak that is in evidence during voiced intervals. Sondhi [15] gives a decision algorithm that formalizes this process. This scheme has been found to perform very well in situations where the speech is voiced but the wave shape is almost sinusoidal or when the fundamental frequency is missing [15].

V. Short-Time Spectrum Analysis

Short-time spectrum analysis has traditionally been one of the most important speech processing techniques. As we have previously stated, the fundamental assumption underlying any short-time analysis method is that over a long-time interval, speech is nonstationary but that over a sufficiently short-time interval it can be considered stationary. Thus, the Fourier transform of a short segment of speech should give a good spectral representation of the speech during that time interval. Measurement of the short-time spectrum is the basic operation in the channel vocoder [19], [26] the phase vocoder [18], spectrogram displays [21], [23], and some speech recognition systems [20]. Two methods are commonly used for implementing short-time Fourier analysis. The first uses a bank of bandpass filters. This method was originally used with analog filters and it can be implemented with even greater precision and flexibility with digital filters. The second method uses a fast Fourier transform (FFT) algorithm. This method is fundamentally digital and has no analog counterpart. When implemented on a computer, the FFT method is generally computationally superior to the bank-of-filters model.

A. Filter Banks for Short-Time Spectrum Analysis

Fig. 11 shows a simple way of implementing a short-time spectrum analyzer using a bank of bandpass filters. If the filter passbands are chosen to cover the speech band, then, roughly speaking, the outputs can be thought of as a Fourier representation of the input speech signal. If the filters are carefully designed, the sum of all the filter outputs will be a good approximation to the original speech signal [24]. This is the basis for communication systems such as the channel vocoder and the phase vocoder.

Based on some fundamental ideas of spectrum analysis, the discrete short-time spectrum of $x(n)$ is defined as

$$X_l(\omega) = \sum_{n=-\infty}^{l} x(n)\, h(l-n)\, e^{-j\omega n} \tag{12a}$$

$$= |X_l(\omega)|\, e^{j\theta_l(\omega)} \tag{12b}$$

$$= a_l(\omega) - jb_l(\omega). \tag{12c}$$

Equation (12) can be interpreted in a number of ways. As shown in Fig. 12, one interpretation is that $X_l(\omega)$ is the Fourier transform of a sequence $x(n)$ that is weighted by a "window" $h(l-n)$. Thus the short-time Fourier transform is a function of both frequency ω and the discrete time index l. A second interpretation follows if we assume that $h(n)$ is the impulse response of a low-pass digital filter. Assume that we wish to evaluate the short-time transform at frequency ω. Then $X_n(\omega)$ is seen to be the output of the low-pass filter with input $x(n)\, e^{-j\omega n}$. This is depicted in Fig. 13(a). To avoid complex arithmetic, the system of Fig. 13(a) is generally implemented as shown in Fig. 13(b) where the output parameters are $a_n(\omega)$ and $b_n(\omega)$, the real and imaginary parts of the spectrum. The bandwidth of the low-pass filter determines the frequency resolution. Typically, this bandwidth is on the order of 50 Hz. Thus the spectrum signals can be sampled at a much lower rate (~100 Hz) than the speech signal itself.

Using digital filters, it has been shown [24], [25] that the short-time Fourier transform can be a very good representation of the speech signal in the sense that the output obtained by summing appropriately modulated bandpass channels can be made indistinguishable from the input. This requires a bit

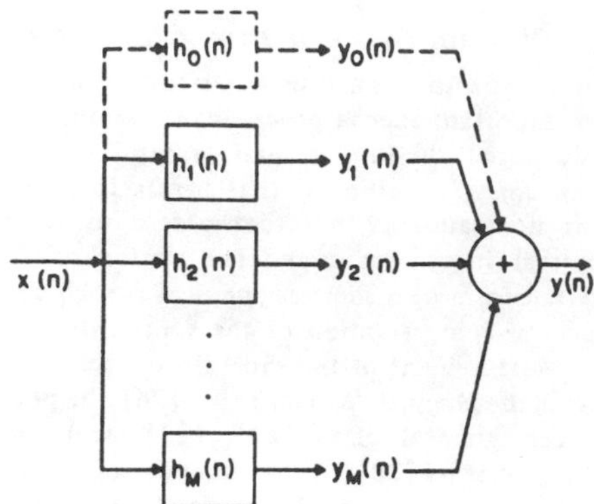

Fig. 11. A bank of bandpass filters.

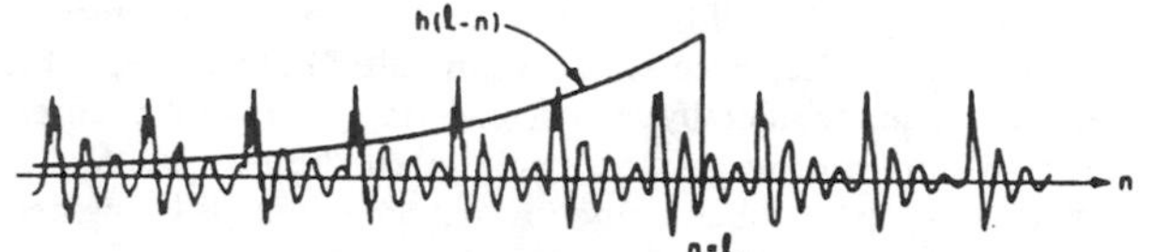

Fig. 12. Illustration of computation of the short-time Fourier transform.

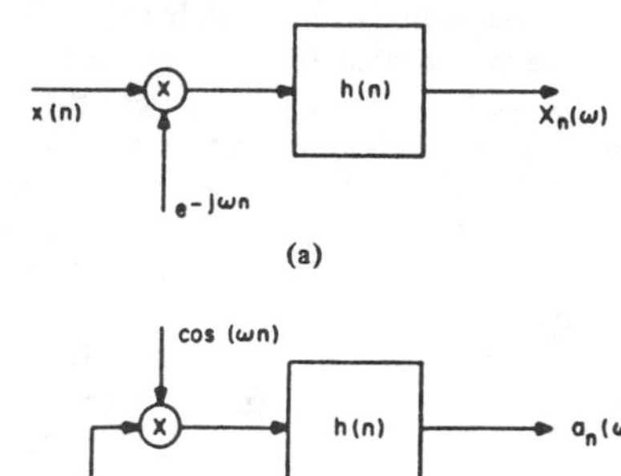

(a)

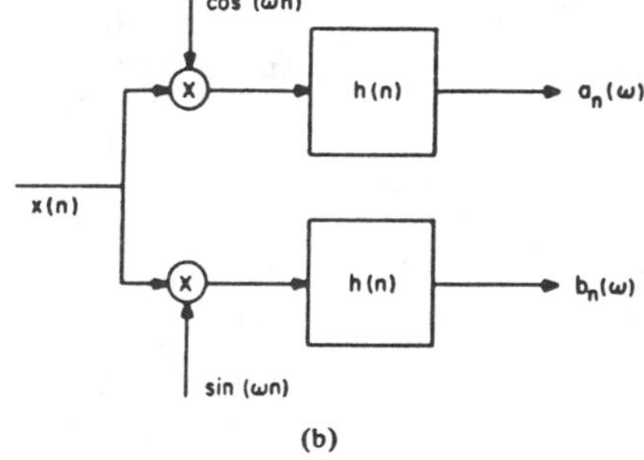

(b)

Fig. 13. Short-time Fourier analysis and synthesis for one channel centered at ω.

rate on the order of the bit rate required for comparable PCM representation. However, the resulting representation of the speech signal permits greater flexibility in the sense that the spectral parameters $a_n(\omega)$ and $b_n(\omega)$ provide information about the parameters of the speech model in a convenient and useful form. For example the time and frequency dimensions of a speech signal can be independently manipulated through simple manipulations of the spectral parameters [18].

B. Use of the FFT for Short-Time Spectrum Analysis

The FFT is a set of highly efficient algorithms for evaluating the discrete Fourier transform (DFT) expressions

$$F(k) = \sum_{n=0}^{M-1} f(n) \exp\left(-j\frac{2\pi}{M}kn\right), \quad k = 0, 1, \cdots, M-1 \quad (13)$$

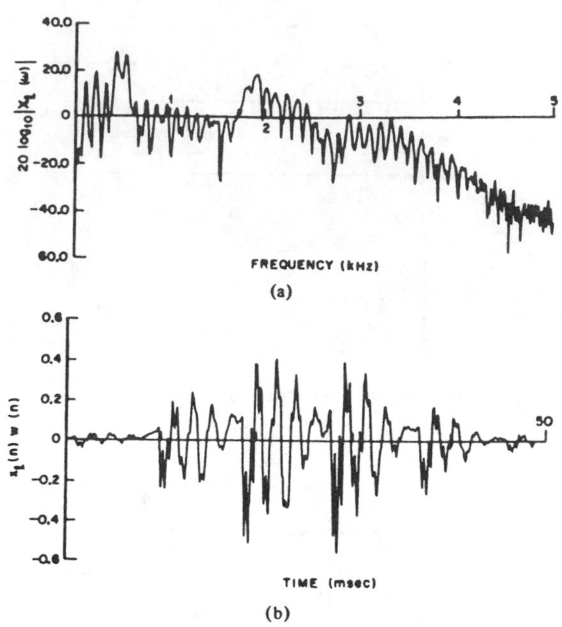

Fig. 14. (a) Log magnitude of the short-time transform. (b) Corresponding windowed speech segment. ($N = 500$.)

and

$$f(n) = \frac{1}{M}\sum_{k=0}^{M-1} F(k) \exp\left(j\frac{2\pi}{M}kn\right), \quad n = 0, 1, \cdots, M-1. \quad (14)$$

For using these expressions, it is convenient to define the short-time transform as

$$X_l(\omega) = \sum_{n=0}^{N-1} x_l(n)\, w(n)\, e^{-j\omega n} \quad (15a)$$

where

$$x_l(n) = x(n+l), \quad n = 0, 1, \cdots, N-1, \quad l = 0, L, 2L, \cdots. \quad (15b)$$

As in the case of the short-time autocorrelation function, we interpret (15a) as the Fourier transform of a segment of speech N samples long (weighted by a window $w(n)$), beginning at l. The frequency resolution of the spectrum measurement is inversely proportional to the window length N. This is illustrated in Fig. 14. Fig. 14(a) shows the short-time transform and Fig. 14(b) shows the corresponding windowed segment of speech data. A Hamming window [17] of length 50 ms was used. ($N = 500$ samples at a 10-kHz sampling rate.) Note that the individual harmonics of the pitch period are resolved in the short-time transform. Figs. 15(a) and (b) show the short-time transform and the windowed speech for $N = 50$ samples. (The speech segment is the first 50 samples of the segment shown in Fig. 14(b).) In this case the frequency resolution is much less than in Fig. 14. We note that the spectrum of Fig. 14 could be considered comparable to a conventional narrow-band spectrogram measurement while Fig. 15 is comparable to a conventional wide-band spectrogram analysis. In particular, Figs. 14 and 15 show typical spectral cross-sections at a particular time. In the first case, both the pitch information and vocal tract transfer function information is present while in the latter case only the general shape of the vocal tract transfer function is preserved.

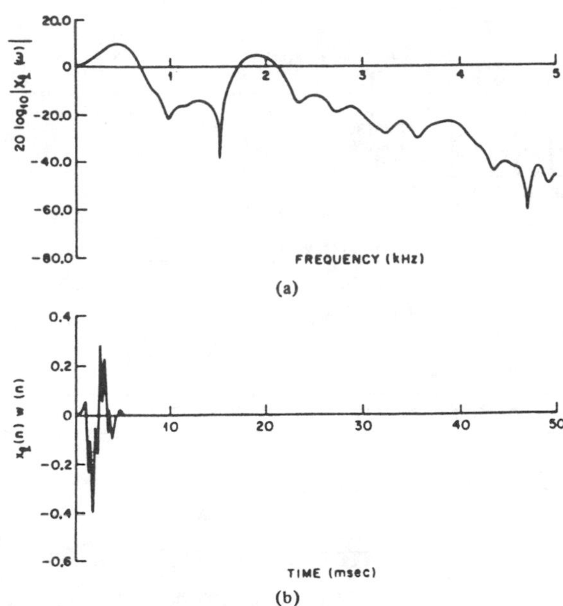

Fig. 15. (a) Log magnitude of the short-time transform. (b) Corresponding windowed speech segment. ($N = 50$.)

An FFT algorithm can be used to compute (15) at equally spaced frequencies $\omega_k = 2\pi k/M$, for $k = 0, 1, \cdots, M-1$. If $M \geq N$, then the sequence $x_l(n)w(n)$ must be augmented with $M - N$ zero valued samples to form a sequence of length M. In this case we can compute

$$X_l\left(\frac{2\pi}{M}k\right) = \sum_{n=0}^{N-1} x_l(n)\, w(n)\, e^{-j2\pi kn/M}, \qquad k = 0, 1, \cdots, M-1 \quad (16)$$

using an FFT algorithm.

On the other hand if $M < N$, we can take advantage of the periodicity of the complex exponential $\exp(-j2\pi kn/M)$ to express (15a) as

$$X_l\left(\frac{2\pi}{M}k\right) = \sum_{n=0}^{M-1} g(n)\, e^{-j2\pi kn/M}, \qquad k = 0, 1, \cdots, M-1 \quad (17a)$$

where

$$g(n) = \sum_{r=0}^{[N/M]} x_l(n+r)w(n+r) \quad (17b)$$

and $[N/M]$ means the largest integer in N/M. This latter feature of FFT spectrum analysis is useful whenever one wishes to only evaluate the transform at intervals of $\omega = 2\pi/M$ but at the same time wishes to obtain the better frequency resolution corresponding to a window of length N. Using the preceding approach, it is also possible to use the FFT to compute the outputs of a uniformly spaced bank of filters as required in a phase vocoder analyzer [24].

An important consequence of the definition of the short-time spectrum in (15) is that $|X_l(\omega)|^2/N$ is the Fourier trans-

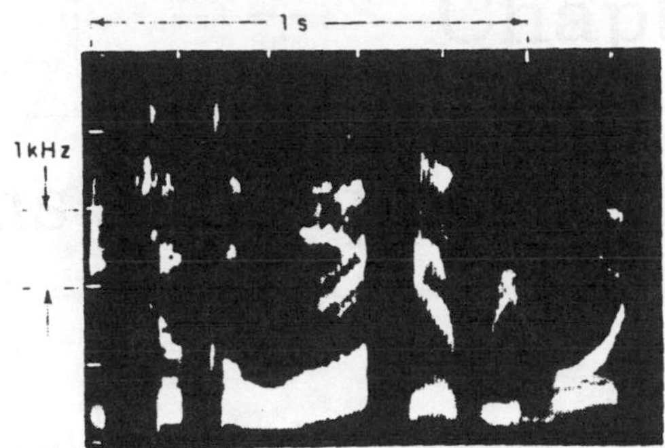

Fig. 16. An example of a spectrogram produced using digital spectrum analysis and computer graphics display. (After Oppenheim [23].)

form of the short-time autocorrelation function

$$R_l(m) = \frac{1}{N}\sum_{n=0}^{N-1-m} x_l(n)w(n)\, x_l(n+m)w(n+m). \quad (18)$$

That is,

$$R_l(m) = \frac{1}{2\pi}\int_{-\pi}^{\pi} \frac{|X_l(\omega)|^2}{N} e^{j\omega m}\, d\omega. \quad (19)$$

Furthermore, it can be shown that if $X_l(2\pi k/M)$ is computed with $M \geq 2N$, then $R_l(m)$ is the inverse of $|X_l(2\pi k/M)|^2/N$; i.e.,

$$R_l(m) = \frac{1}{M}\sum_{k=0}^{M-1} \frac{|X_l(2\pi k/M)|^2}{N} e^{\,j2\pi kn/M}, \qquad 0 \leq m \leq N-1. \quad (20)$$

If we suppose that $R_l(m)$ is required for $0 \leq m \leq M_0 - 1$, where M_0 is a large number, as in pitch detection, it may be most efficient to first compute the short-time transform using (16), and then compute the autocorrelation function using (20).

C. Short-Time Spectrum Representations of Speech

The short-time spectrum can serve directly as a representation of the speech signal as is the case in many vocoder systems [18], [19], [25], [26] and in some speech recognition systems [20]. In many cases, however, the short-time spectrum is computed as an intermediate step in the estimation of one or more of the time varying parameters of the speech model. In the narrow-band short-time spectrum as in Fig. 14(a), both pitch and vocal tract transfer function information are clearly in evidence, while the wide-band analysis, as in Fig. 15(a), does not preserve the pitch information. Thus there are a variety of methods for estimating fundamental frequency directly from the narrow-band short-time spectrum [22], [27]. Similarly there are a wide variety of methods of estimating parameters such as formant frequencies from the short-time spectrum [16], [26].

One of the most useful tools in speech science is the sound spectrograph. This device produces a plot of energy as a function of time and frequency; i.e., a display of the short-time spectrum. The basis analysis techniques of this section have been used to generate spectrographic displays that are similar to, but in many cases more elaborate and flexible than, con-

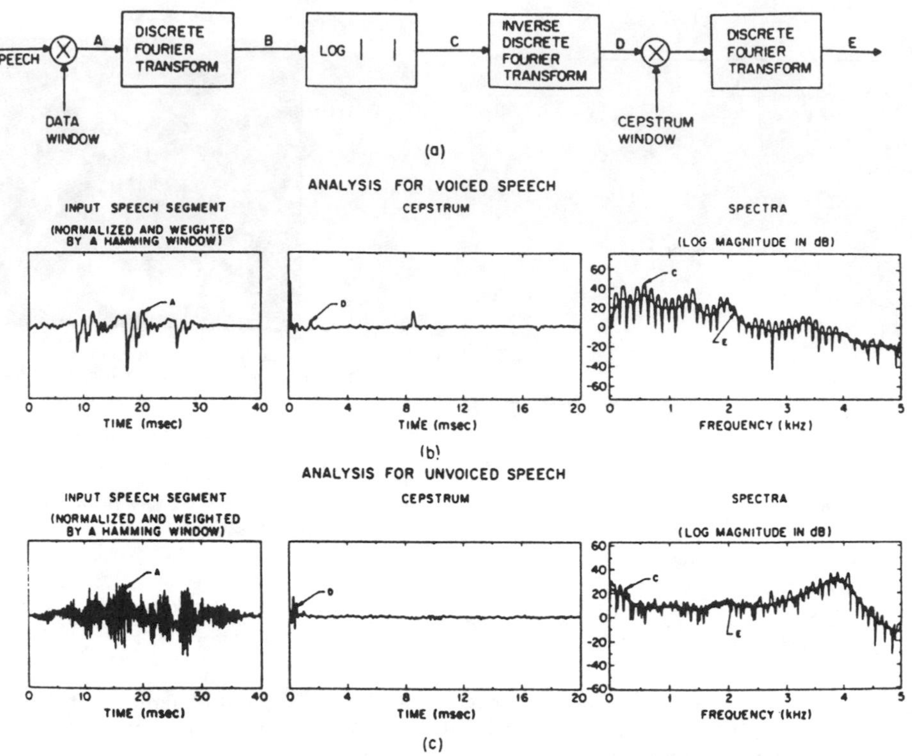

Fig. 17. Homomorphic processing of speech. (a) Basic operations. (b) Analysis for voiced speech. (c) Analysis for unvoiced speech.

ventional spectrograms [21], [23], [28]. As we have pointed out, there is great flexibility for computer spectral analysis in window length and shape or equivalently frequency resolution. Also, the spectrum can be shaped in a manner to enhance it for display, and it is possible to precisely correlate the speech waveform with the spectrographic display.

Such schemes have been implemented in a variety of ways but most of them use (15) to compute a set of short-time spectra at equally spaced time intervals. This set of spectra can be thought of as samples of the two dimensional function $X_l(\omega)$ which can be plotted as a frequency-time-intensity plot on an oscilloscope or television monitor. Using such techniques it has been possible to produce on-line spectrogram displays that are equal in quality to conventional spectrograms and far surpass them in flexibility and innovation. An example of one approach is shown in Fig. 16 [23].

VI. Homomorphic Speech Processing

Homomorphic filtering is a class of nonlinear signal processing techniques that is based on a generalization of the principle of superposition that defines linear systems. Such techniques have been applied in separating signals that have been combined by multiplication and convolution [31]. The application of these techniques to speech processing is again based on the assumption that although speech production is a time varying process, it can be viewed on a short-time basis as the convolution of an excitation function (either random noise or a quasiperiodic pulse train) with the vocal tract impulse response. Thus methods for separating the components of a convolution are of interest.

A. Fundamentals

A homomorphic system for speech analysis is shown in Fig. 17(a). We assume that the signal at A is the discrete convolution of the excitation and the vocal tract impulse response. Then the short-time Fourier transform (i.e., the spectrum of the windowed signal), computed using the FFT method of the previous section, is the product of the Fourier transforms of the excitation and the vocal tract impulse response. Taking the logarithm of the magnitude of the Fourier transform, we obtain at C the sum of the logarithms of the transforms of the excitation and vocal tract impulse response. Since the inverse discrete Fourier transform (IDFT) is a linear operation, the result at D (called the cepstrum of the input at A) is an additive combination of the cepstra of the excitation and vocal tract components. Thus, the effect of the operations, windowing, DFT, log magnitude, and IDFT is to approximately transform convolution into addition. The value of this transformation can be seen from Fig. 17(b), which depicts the results of such an analysis for voiced speech. The curve labeled A is the input speech segment that has been multiplied by a Hamming window. The rapidly varying curve labeled C is the log-magnitude of the short-time transform. It consists of a slowly varying component due to the vocal tract transmission, and a rapidly varying periodic component due to the periodic excitation. The slowly varying part of the log magnitude produces the low-time part of the cepstrum (D), and the rapidly varying periodic component of the log magnitude manifests itself in the strong peak at a time equal to the period of the input speech segment. If we assume that the vocal tract transfer function in the model of Fig. 3 is of the form of an all-pole model,

$$H(z) = \frac{A}{1 - \sum_{k=1}^{p} a_k z^{-k}} = A \prod_{k=1}^{p} \frac{1}{1 - z_k z^{-1}} \tag{21}$$

then the cepstrum of the vocal tract component of the convolution can be shown [30], [47] to be

$$\hat{h}(n) = \begin{cases} 0, & n < 0 \\ \log A, & n = 0 \\ \sum_{k=1}^{p} \frac{z_k^n}{n}, & n > 0. \end{cases} \tag{22}$$

If we assume that the excitation component is a periodic train of impulses, then it can be shown [30] that the cepstrum of the excitation component will also be a train of impulses with the same spacing as the input impulse train. This is clearly reflected in the cepstrum for voiced speech in Fig. 17(b). The important point is that the cepstrum consists of an additive combination in which (due to the $1/n$ falloff) the vocal tract and excitation components essentially do not overlap. The situation for unvoiced speech, shown in Fig. 17(c), is much the same with the exception that the random nature of the excitation component of the input speech segment (A) causes a rapidly varying random component in the log magnitude (C). Thus in the cepstrum (D), the low time components correspond as before to the slowly varying vocal tract transfer function; however, since the rapid variations of the log magnitude are not, in this case, periodic, there is no strong peak as for the voiced speech segment. Thus, the cepstrum serves as an excellent basis for estimating the fundamental period of voiced speech and for determining whether a particular speech segment is voiced or unvoiced [29].

The vocal tract transfer function, often called the spectrum envelope, can be obtained by removing the rapidly varying components of the log magnitude spectrum by linear filtering. One approach to this filtering operation involves computing the IDFT of the log magnitude spectrum (to give the cepstrum), multiplying the cepstrum by an appropriate window that only passes the short-time components, and then computing the DFT of the resulting windowed cepstrum. This method corresponds to the fast convolution method [45]-[49], in this case being applied to filter a function of frequency rather than a function of time. The results for voiced and unvoiced speech segments are labeled E in Figs. 17(b) and (c), respectively.

The smoothed spectrum obtained by the above method is in many respects comparable to a short-time spectrum obtained by direct analysis using a short data window. The major difference, however, is that the cepstrum method is based upon the initial computation of a narrow-band spectrum, which involves a wide time window, while the wide-band spectrum is computed using a very narrow-time window. The smoothing is done upon a narrow-band log-magnitude spectrum rather than upon the short-time Fourier transform itself, as is the case for wide-band analysis. Thus, for speech segments in which the basic parameters such as pitch period and formant frequencies are not changing, we should expect the cepstrum method to produce superior results to direct spectrum analysis. When the speech spectrum is changing rapidly, as in the case of a voiced/unvoiced boundary, the direct method may produce a better representation than the cepstrum method due to its shorter averaging time.

B. Estimation of Formant Frequencies and Pitch Period

The results depicted in Fig. 17 suggest algorithms for estimating basic speech parameters such as pitch period and formant frequencies. Specifically, voiced/unvoiced classification of the excitation is indicated by the presence or absence of a strong peak in the cepstrum [29]. The presence of a strong peak for voiced speech is dependent upon there being many harmonics present in the spectrum. In cases where this is not true, such as voiced stops, zero crossing measurements are helpful in distinguishing voiced from unvoiced speech [34]. If a strong peak is present, its location is a good indicator of the pitch period.

The smoothed spectrum retains peaks at the vocal tract resonances or formant frequencies. One approach to estimating the formants is to search the smooth spectra for peaks and then decide which peaks correspond to formants [34]. Another approach uses iterative methods to adjust the parameters of a model similar to (21) until a good match to the smooth spectrum is obtained [33].

An illustration of the use of homomorphic processing is given in Fig. 18. On the left are shown a sequence of cepstra computed at 20-ms intervals. The strong peak indicates that the speech is voiced during the entire interval. On the right are successive short-time spectra and homomorphically smoothed short-time spectra. The lines connecting the peaks of the smooth spectra show the formant frequencies automatically estimated from the spectrum peaks. The peak-picking approach is relatively simple except when two formants merge as in the third and fourth frames from the top and the last 4 frames from the bottom. In this case it is useful to evaluate the vocal tract transfer function on a contour which passes closer to the poles thereby sharpening the resonances [34].

Speech can be synthesized from formant and pitch data by using the estimated parameters to vary the parameters of the model of Fig. 3. With efficient coding of the parameters, speech is thus represented by about 1000 bits/s [2]. In addition to this high efficiency, the formant representation offers great flexibility in manipulating basic speech parameters. Also, since so much of the speech model is built into the representation, these parameters are very useful for other purposes such as speech recognition and speaker verification.

C. The Cepstrum as a Representation of Speech

The low-time samples of the cepstrum contain mostly information about the vocal tract transfer function $H(z)$ of (21). It can be shown [31], [47], that the following recurrence formula relates the vocal tract impulse response $h(n)$ to the cepstrum $\hat{h}(n)$ of (22):

$$h(n) = \begin{cases} \hat{h}(n)h(0) + \sum_{k=0}^{n-1} \left(\frac{k}{n}\right) \hat{h}(k)h(n-k), & 1 \leq n \\ e^{\hat{h}(0)}, & n = 0. \end{cases} \tag{23}$$

Also using (23) it is easily shown that the coefficients a_n in (21) are related to the cepstrum by

$$a_n = \hat{h}(n) - \sum_{k=0}^{n-1} \left(\frac{k}{n}\right) \hat{h}(k) a_{n-k}, \quad 1 \leq n \leq p. \tag{24}$$

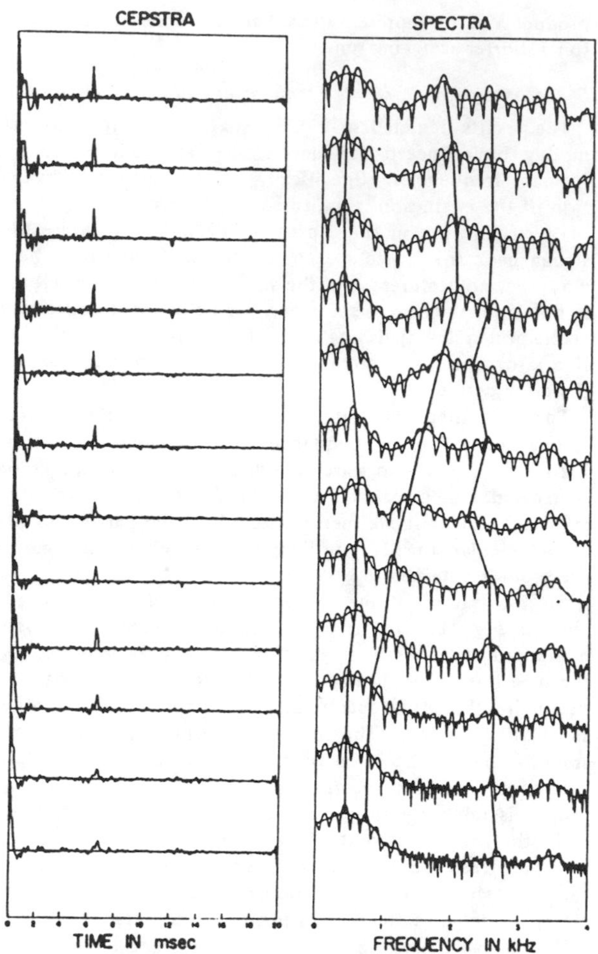

Fig. 18. Cepstra and spectra for a region of voiced speech.

Since the cepstrum contains all of the information of the short-time spectrum, it can be viewed as still another representation of the speech signal. This principle has been applied in a speech analysis synthesis scheme called the homomorphic vocoder [32]. In this system, the low-time cepstrum values and an estimate of pitch period serve as a representation of the speech signal from which an acoustic wave can be reconstructed.

VII. Linear Predictive Analysis

Among the most useful methods of speech analysis are those based upon the principle of linear prediction. These methods are important because of their accuracy and their speed of computation. In this section, we present a formulation of linear predictive analysis and discuss some of the issues which are involved in using it in practical speech applications.

The basic idea behind linear predictive coding (LPC) is that a sample of speech can be approximated as a linear combination of the past p speech samples. By minimizing the square difference between the actual speech samples and the linearly predicted ones, one can determine the predictor coefficients; i.e., the weighting coefficients of the linear combination. The basic philosophy of this scheme is reminiscent of and, in fact, related to the waveform quantization methods discussed in Section III [35]. There it was mentioned that a linear predictor can be applied in a differential quantization scheme to reduce the bit rate of the digital representation of the speech waveform. In this case, as in linear predictive analysis, the predictor coefficients must be adapted (i.e., updated regularly) to match the time-varying properties of the speech signal.

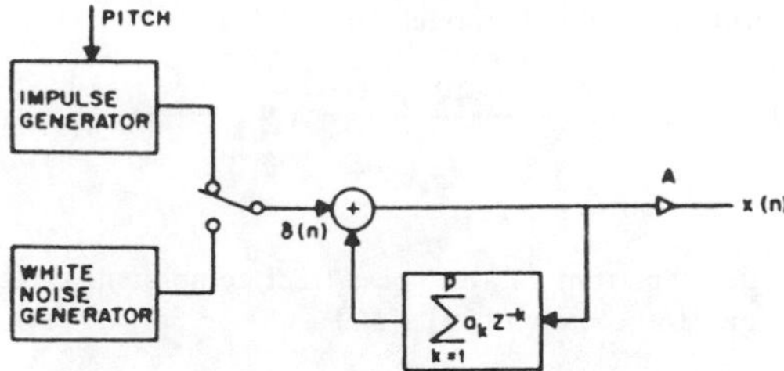

Fig. 19. Digital model for speech production.

A. Fundamental Principles

The use of linear predictive analysis is suggested by the digital model of Section II. Assume that samples of the speech signal are produced by the model of Fig. 3, where over a short time interval the linear system has the transfer function

$$H(z) = \frac{A}{1 - \sum_{k=1}^{p} a_k z^{-k}}. \tag{25}$$

For voiced speech, the system is excited by an impulse train and for unvoiced speech it is excited by random white noise as depicted in Fig. 19. Linear prediction analysis is based on the observation that for such a system the speech samples $x(n)$ are related to the excitation $\delta(n)$ by the following difference equation:

$$x(n) = \sum_{k=1}^{p} a_k x(n-k) + \delta(n). \tag{26}$$

Suppose that we process the speech signal with a linear predictor; i.e.,

$$\tilde{x}(n) = \sum_{k=1}^{p} \alpha_k x(n-k).$$

Then the predictor error is defined as

$$\epsilon(n) = x(n) - \tilde{x}(n) = x(n) - \sum_{k=1}^{p} \alpha_k x(n-k). \tag{27}$$

Note that in this case the prediction is based on the unquantized samples $x(n)$, whereas in Section III, the prediction was based on quantized samples $\hat{x}(n)$. It can be seen by comparing (26) and (27) that if $\alpha_k = a_k$, and if the speech signal really does obey the model of (26), then $\epsilon(n) = \delta(n)$. Therefore, between the excitation impulses of voiced speech, the prediction error should be very small if the predictor coefficients α_k are equal to the parameters a_k of the vocal tract transfer function. Thus the predictor polynomial

$$P(z) = 1 - \sum_{k=1}^{p} \alpha_k z^{-k}$$

is a good approximation to the denominator of the vocal tract transfer function.[2]

One approach for obtaining the predictor coefficients is based on minimizing the average squared prediction error over a short segment of the speech waveform. That is, we search for the values of α_k that minimize

$$E_l = \sum_{n=0}^{N-1} (x_l(n) - \tilde{x}_l(n))^2$$

$$= \sum_{n=0}^{N-1} \left(x_l(n) - \sum_{k=1}^{p} \alpha_k x_l(n-k) \right)^2 \qquad (28)$$

where $x_l(n)$ is a segment of speech that has been selected in the vicinity of sample l; i.e.,

$$x_l(n) = x(n+l).$$

There are two basic ways of choosing $x_l(n)$ each leading to procedures that are somewhat different in the details of their implementation and the results that are obtained. Leaving $x_l(n)$ unspecified for now, we can find the values of α_k that minimize E_l in (28) by setting $\partial E_l / \partial \alpha_i = 0$, $i = 1, 2, \cdots, p$, thus obtaining the equations

$$\sum_{n=0}^{N-1} x_l(n-i) x_l(n) = \sum_{k=1}^{p} \alpha_k \sum_{n=0}^{N-1} x_l(n-i) x_l(n-k),$$

$$1 \leqslant i \leqslant p. \qquad (29)$$

If we define

$$\varphi_l(i,k) = \sum_{n=0}^{N-1} x_l(n-i) x_l(n-k) \qquad (30)$$

then (29) can be written more compactly as

$$\sum_{k=1}^{p} \alpha_k \varphi_l(i,k) = \varphi_l(i,0), \qquad i = 1, 2, \cdots, p. \qquad (31)$$

This set of p equations in p unknowns can be solved for the unknown predictor coefficients that minimize the average squared prediction error for the segment $x_l(n)$. To do this, the quantities $\varphi_l(i,k)$ must be computed for $1 \leqslant i \leqslant p$ and $1 \leqslant k \leqslant p$. The details of this computation depend upon how $x_l(n)$ is defined.

By a simple substitution of variables, (30) can be written as

$$\varphi_l(i,k) = \sum_{n=-i}^{N-1-i} x_l(n) x_l(n+i-k)$$

$$= \sum_{n=-k}^{N-1-k} x_l(n) x_l(n+k-i). \qquad (32)$$

Clearly, $\varphi_l(i,k) = \varphi_l(k,i)$. We observe from (32) that values of $x_l(n)$ are required outside the interval $0 \leqslant n \leqslant N-1$. If we choose to supply the values outside this interval we note that we then require

$$x_l(n) = x(n+l), \qquad -p \leqslant n \leqslant N-2 \qquad (33)$$

to evaluate $\varphi_l(i,k)$. This method and its attendant details was proposed by Atal [36] and has come to be called the *covariance* method because of the similarity of the matrix $\varphi_l(i,k)$ to a covariance matric.

If we choose not to supply values of the signal outside the interval $0 \leqslant n \leqslant N-1$, then we must resort to using a finite duration window $w(n)$ to reduce the end effects thereby obtaining,

$$x_l(n) = \begin{cases} x(n+l)w(n), & 0 \leqslant n \leqslant N-1 \\ 0, & \text{otherwise.} \end{cases}$$

Using this definition of $x_l(n)$, (32) becomes

$$\varphi_l(i,k) = \sum_{n=0}^{N-1-(i-k)} x_l(n) x_l(n+i-k).$$

$$= \sum_{n=0}^{N-1-(k-i)} x_l(n) x_l(n+k-i)$$

$$\equiv r_l(i-k) = r_l(k-i). \qquad (34)$$

In this case (31) becomes

$$\sum_{k=1}^{p} \alpha_k r_l(|i-k|) = r_l(i), \qquad i = 1, 2, \cdots, p. \qquad (35)$$

From (34) and (18), it is clear that $r_l(n) = NR_l(n)$; i.e., $r_l(n)$ is equal (to within a constant multiplier) to the short-time autocorrelation function, which in turn is related to the short-time Fourier transform $X_l(\omega)$. Thus the method based on (35) is called the *autocorrelation method.* Methods of this type have been proposed by Itakura [38] (the maximum likelihood method) and Markel [41]-[43] (the inverse filter formulation).

The basic difference between the covariance method and the autocorrelation method is the necessity to use a window for the autocorrelation method. For the covariance method the section length is increased by augmenting p samples to enable the first p samples of the section ($x_l(n)$, $0 \leqslant n \leqslant p-1$) to be predicted from speech samples outside the section. Thus an equal number of samples go into the computation of $\varphi(i,j)$ for all indices i and j, and no window is required. For the autocorrelation method one is trying to predict the first p samples from speech samples outside the section. Since these samples are arbitrarily zero, a large error may result. To reduce the error a window is applied which smoothly tapers the signal to zero at the ends of the window.

At this point it is worth noting the mathematical and physical interpretations of using windows in the autocorrelation method. The process of multiplication of a signal by a window is equivalent to a circular convolution of the frequency response of the window with the speech spectrum. Thus a smearing occurs in the speech spectrum. The extent of this smearing depends on the section length N and the actual window used. However, it is clear that with the autocorrelation method, parameters such as formant bandwidths may not be accurately estimated. In many practical applications this is of little or no consequence; however, for vocoder applications it may be significant.

B. Details of Implementation

Both (31) and (35) are a set of p equations in p unknowns that can be expressed in matrix form as

$$\Phi \cdot a = \Psi. \qquad (36)$$

These equations may be solved for the predictor coefficients using any general procedure for solving linear equations. How-

[2] The effects of the glottal pulse shape are included in the predictor polynomial.

ever, if computational efficiency is important, as it usually is, some special properties of the matrix Φ can be exploited to reduce computation. In the case of (31) (the covariance method) Φ is symmetric and positive definite. Utilization of this fact leads to an efficient procedure for solving for the vector a of predictor coefficients that is based on matrix factorization. This method is called the square root method, or the Cholesky decomposition [37].

Similarly, for the autocorrelation method the matrix Φ is symmetric and positive definite and also has the property that the elements along any diagonal are equal. Such a matrix is called a Toeplitz matrix and in this case an even more efficient method for solving the equations can be found [43]. This method is called the Levinson method.

Since computational efficiency is an important consideration in any practical speech analysis scheme, it is worthwhile comparing these two methods of linear prediction in this sense. The square root method for solving the covariance method formulation requires on the order of p^3 operations (multiplications) whereas the Levinson method for solving the autocorrelation formulation requires on the order of p^2 operations. Thus the solution of the equation for the autocorrelation formulation is inherently faster computationally than for the covariance formulation. In particular, for $p = 14$, Makhoul and Wolf [39] note a ratio in computation time of 3.2 to 1 in favor of the autocorrelation method. However, this savings in computation is not significant when viewed in the total framework of the method for two reasons. First the time required to compute the matrix of correlations is significantly greater than the time to solve the matrix equation. For example, for $N = 150$, Makhoul and Wolf [39] note that it takes ten times longer to compute the matrix then to solve the matrix equations using the autocorrelation method. Thus the savings in computation of the Levinson method becomes much less significant. As a second consideration the value of N required for both methods is not the same. For the autocorrelation method (for 10-kHz sampling) a value of N in the range 150 to 300 is generally required. For the covariance method a much smaller value of N can be used if care is taken to begin the section after a pitch pulse. In fact, Atal reports using values of N on the order of 30 with good results [36]. Thus there are many factors which determine computational efficiency.

Another difference between the two methods concerns the roots of the predictor polynomial which are the poles of the digital filter that accounts for the vocal tract transmission properties. For stability of this system, the roots must be inside the unit circle of the z plane. This is not guaranteed by the covariance method [36]; however, given *sufficient computational accuracy* the autocorrelation method guarantees stability [39], [43].

Another consideration in using these two methods is the numerical stability of the matrix inversion. Wilkinson [44] has shown that the square-root method is very stable numerically; no such statement has been made for the Levinson method. Markel [43] has pointed out that when implemented with finite precision arithmetic, the Levinson method requires careful scaling, and it is beneficial if the speech spectrum has been equalized by a simple first-order network.

Until now we have dealt with considerations which can be easily quantified and for which definitive statements can be made. When one becomes seriously interested in using linear predictive methods, several other considerations are involved. These include the necessity for spectrum equalization prior to analysis; the effects of the analog prefilter prior to analog-to-digital (A/D) conversion; the effects of finite word length on the analysis; the desirability of various structures for implementing the system; and finally the ease of building the various alternatives in digital hardware. Markel [43] has provided some excellent insights into several of these issues but most of them are as yet unresolved.

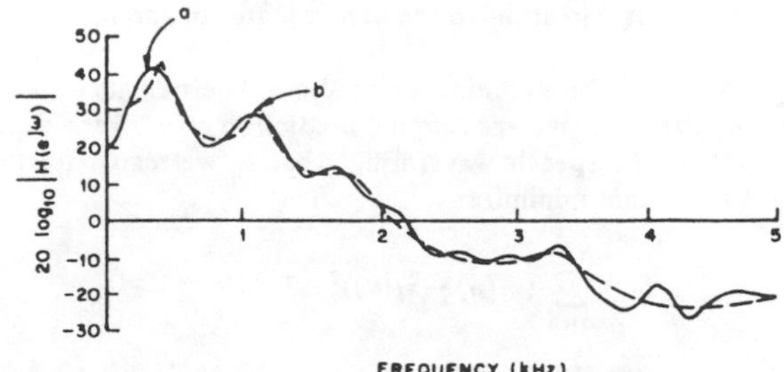

Fig. 20. Comparison of speech spectra. (a) Obtained by cepstrum smoothing. (b) Obtained by linear prediction.

C. Uses of Linear Prediction Analysis

Once the predictor coefficients have been obtained, they can be used in various ways to represent the properties of the speech signal.

1) Spectrum Estimation: If the predictor polynomial is assumed to represent the denominator of the vocal tract transfer function, we can obtain the frequency response of the vocal tract (for a particular segment of the speech signal) as

$$H(e^{j\omega T}) = \frac{A}{1 - \sum_{k=1}^{p} \alpha_k e^{-j\omega kT}}. \tag{37}$$

An example is shown in Fig. 20, where the spectrum obtained using (37) with the predictor coefficients estimated by the autocorrelation method is compared to that obtained by cepstrum smoothing for the same segment of speech. The formant frequencies are clearly in evidence in both plots, however, Fig. 20(b) has fewer extraneous peaks. This is because p was chosen so that at most 6 ($p = 12$) resonance peaks could occur. To determine the appropriate value of p for a given sampling rate, a good rule of thumb is to allow one pair of poles to account for radiation and glottal effects, and one pair of poles for each formant frequency expected in the frequency range $0 \leqslant \omega \leqslant \pi/T$. Thus, for a 10-kHz sampling rate we expect not more than 5 formant frequencies so $p = 12$ should give a good representation of the spectrum. For unvoiced speech it has been shown that a reasonably small prediction error can be obtained with a value of p on the order of 12 [36], [43].

Another point to notice is that the spectrum peaks in Fig. 20(a) are much broader than the peaks in Fig. 20(b). This is an inherent property of the homomorphic method since the Fig. 20(a) was obtained by smoothing the short-time log spectrum.

2) Formant Frequency Estimation: Smooth spectra such as Fig. 20(b) have been used in a peak picking algorithm to estimate formant frequencies in much the same manner as spectra such as Fig. 20(a) were used [41].

If p is chosen as discussed here, it can be assumed that the roots of the predictor polynomial will in general correspond to the formant frequencies. These roots can be obtained by factoring the predictor polynomial. An example is shown in Fig. 21. It is clear by comparing the plot of Fig. 21(b) to the spec-

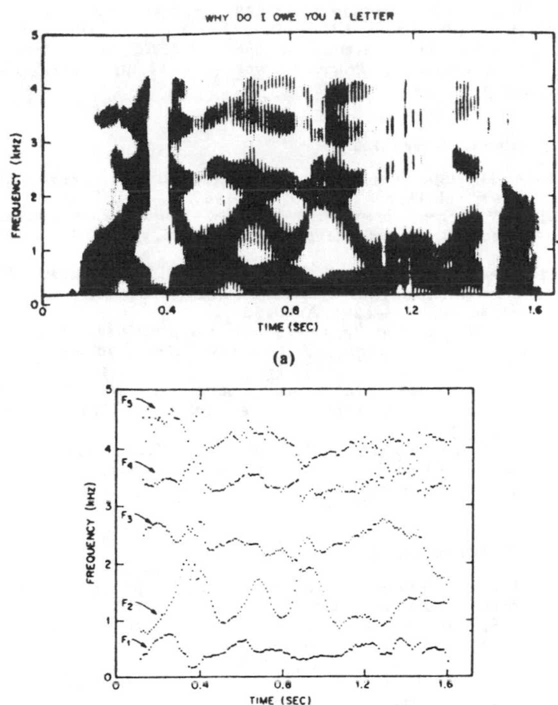

Fig. 21. (a) Spectrogram of predictor polynomial. (b) Roots of predictor polynomial (after Atal [36]).

trogram that the roots of the predictor polynomial are generally very good estimates of the formant frequencies. As with all formant analysis problems the difficulty in the problem lies in giving a particular formant label to a pole. Several reliable algorithms exist for doing this job [34], [41].

3) Pitch Detection: We recall that if we use the predictor coefficients as in our original formulation, then the prediction error

$$\epsilon(n) = x(n) - \sum_{k=1}^{p} \alpha_k x(n-k) \tag{38}$$

should appear very much like the excitation function $\delta(n)$ in Fig. 19. Thus it might be expected that the prediction error signal might be useful as a starting point for determining properties of the excitation; i.e., pitch period and voiced/unvoiced decision. Several procedures of this type have been suggested [40], [42].

4) Relation to the Cepstrum and Autocorrelation Function: In addition to the aforementioned, the basic linear prediction coefficients can be transformed directly into a number of other representations of the speech signal. For example by solving (24) for $\hat{h}(n)$, we obtain the recurrence formula

$$\hat{h}(n) = a_n + \sum_{k=0}^{n-1} \left(\frac{k}{n}\right) \hat{h}(k) a_{n-k} \tag{39}$$

relating the cepstrum of the vocal tract impulse response to the coefficients a_n in (25). Similarly it can be shown [35] that the autocorrelation function of the vocal tract impulse response defined as

$$r(m) = \sum_{n=0}^{\infty} h(n)h(n+m) \tag{40}$$

satisfies the recurrence formula

$$r(m) = \begin{cases} \sum_{k=1}^{p} a_k r(i-k), & m \geqq 1 \\ \sum_{k=1}^{p} a_k r(k) + 1, & m = 1. \end{cases} \tag{41}$$

5) Speech Synthesis: Finally, the predictor coefficients and excitation information can be used in the model of Fig. 19 to reconstruct a speech waveform [36]. In this case it is necessary to estimate the constant A in (25) as well as the parameters of the predictor polynomial. This can be done as part of the computation of the predictor coefficients [43] but in most cases A is simply chosen to match the energy of the synthetic speech to the energy of the original speech [36].

D. Discussion

The underlying structure of linear prediction analysis is that over short sections of speech one can accurately predict the current speech sample from the preceding p samples. Although a wide variety of different formulations of this method have arisen, the inherent similarities between methods are much larger than the supposed differences. To make all the decisions as to which particular method to use, what section duration etc., one must pay strict attention to the ultimate application of the method. Thus for most speech recognition applications, for example, the differences between formulations are *not* significant. For other more stringent applications, such as analysis/synthesis, the differences may indeed be quite significant and may mean the difference between an acceptable and a nonacceptable system.

VIII. Summary

In this paper, we have discussed a wide variety of digital representations of speech signals. These representations have varied in complexity, information rate, and flexibility from simple waveform coding schemes to analysis schemes such as homomorphic filtering and linear prediction analysis which are directed toward the estimation of the parameters of a detailed model of speech production. We have focused our attention almost exclusively on analysis techniques that are of wide applicability. The results of most of these techniques can be applied in a variety of speech processing applications including speech recognition, speech synthesis, and speaker verification.

References

General

[1] G. Fant, *Acoustic Theory of Speech Production*. The Hague, The Netherlands: Mouton, 1970.
[2] J. L. Flanagan, C. H. Coker, L. R. Rabiner, R. W. Schafer, and N. Umeda, "Synthetic voices for computers," *IEEE Spectrum*, vol. 7, pp. 22–45, Oct. 1970.
[3] J. L. Flanagan, *Speech Analysis, Synthesis and Perception*, 2nd ed. New York: Springer-Verlag, 1972.

Waveform Coding

[4] H. S. Black, *Modulation Theory*. Princeton, N.J.: Van Nostrand, 1953.

[5] P. Cummiskey, N. S. Jayant, and J. L. Flanagan, "Adaptive quantization in differential PCM coding of speech," *Bell Syst. Tech. J.*, pp. 1105-1118, Sept. 1973.
[6] N. S. Jayant, "Adaptive delta modulation with a one-bit memory," *Bell Syst. Tech. J.*, pp. 321-342, Mar. 1970.
[7] —, "Digital coding of speech waveforms," *Proc. IEEE.*, vol. 62, pp. 611-632, May 1974.
[8] R. A. McDonald, "Signal-to-noise and idle channel performance of DPCM systems—particular application to voice signals," *Bell Syst. Tech. J.*, pp. 1123-1151, 1966.
[9] J. Max, "Quantizing for minimum distortion," *IRE Trans. Inform. Theory*, vol. IT- pp. 7-12, Mar. 1960.
[10] L. H. Rosenthal, R. W. Schafer, and L. R. Rabiner "An algorithm for locating the beginning and end of an utterance using ADPCM coded speech," *Bell Syst. Tech. J.*, vol. 53, pp. 1127-1135, July-Aug. 1974.
[11] L. H. Rosenthal, L. R. Rabiner, R. W. Schafer, P. Cummiskey, and J. L. Flanagan, "A multiline computer voice response system utilizing ADPCM coded speech," *IEEE Trans. Acoust., Speech, and Sig. Processing*, vol. ASSP-22, pp. 339-352, Oct. 1974.

Time-Domain Methods

[12] B. Gold, "Note on buzz-hiss detection," *J. Acoust. Soc. Amer.*, vol. 36, pp. 1659-1661, 1964.
[13] B. Gold and L. R. Rabiner, "Parallel processing techniques for estimating pitch periods of speech in the time domain," *J. Acoust. Soc. Amer.*, vol. 46, no. 2, pp. 442-449, Aug. 1969.
[14] D. R. Reddy, "Computer recognition of connected speech," *J. Acoust. Soc. Amer.*, vol. 42, no. 2, pp. 329-347, Aug. 1967.
[15] M. M. Sondhi, "New methods of pitch detection," *IEEE Trans. Audio Electroacoust.*, vol. AU-16, pp. 262-266, June 1968.

Short-Time Spectrum Analysis

[16] C. G. Bell, H. Fujisaki, J. M. Heinz, K. N. Stevens, and A. S. House, "Reduction of speech spectra by analysis-by-synthesis techniques," *J. Acoust. Soc. Amer.*, vol. 33, pp. 1725-1736, Dec. 1961.
[17] R. B. Blackman and J. W. Tukey, *The Measurement of Power Spectra.* New York: Dover, 1959.
[18] J. L. Flanagan and R. M. Golden, "Phase vocoder," *Bell Syst. Tech. J.*, vol. 45, pp. 1493-1509, Nov. 1966.
[19] B. Gold and C. M. Rader, "Systems for compressing the bandwidth of speech," *IEEE Trans. Audio Electroacoust.*, vol. AU-15, pp. 131-135, Sept. 1967; and "The channel vocoder," *IEEE Trans. Audio Electroacoust.*, vol. AU-15, pp. 148-160, Dec. 1967.
[20] T. Martin, "Acoustic recognition of a limited vocabulary in continuous speech," Ph.D. dissertation, Univ. Pennsylvania, Philadelphia, 1970. (Available from Univ. Microfilms, Ann Arbor, Mich.)
[21] P. Mermelstein, "Computer generated spectrogram displays for on-line speech research," *IEEE Trans. Audio Electroacoust.*, vol. AU-19, pp. 44-47, Mar. 1971.
[22] A. M. Noll, "Pitch determination of human speech by the harmonic product spectrum, the harmonic sum spectrum, and a maximum likelihood estimate," in *Computer Processing in Communications Proceedings*, J. Fox, Ed. New York: Polytechnic Press, 1969.
[23] A. V. Oppenheim, "Speech spectrograms using the fast Fourier transform," *IEEE Spectrum*, vol. 7, pp. 57-62, Aug. 1970.
[24] R. W. Schafer and L. R. Rabiner, "Design of digital filter banks for speech analysis," *Bell Syst. Tech. J.*, vol. 50, no. 10, pp. 3097-3115, Dec. 1971.
[25] —, "Design and simulation of a speech analysis-synthesis system based on short-time Fourier analysis," *IEEE Trans. Audio Electroacoust.*, vol. AU-21, pp. 165-174, June 1973.
[26] M. R. Schroeder, "Vocoders: Analysis and synthesis of speech," *Proc. IEEE*, vol. 54, pp. 720-734, May 1966.
[27] M. R. Schroeder, "Period histogram and product spectrum: New methods for fundamental-frequency measurement," *J. Acoust. Soc. Amer.*, vol. 43, no. 4, pp. 829-834, Apr. 1968.
[28] H. R. Silverman and N. R. Dixon, "A parametrically controlled spectral analysis system for speech," *IEEE Trans. Acoustics, Speech, and Sig. Processing*, vol. ASSP-22, pp. 362-381, Oct. 1974.

Homomorphic Speech Analysis

[29] A. M. Noll, "Cepstrum pitch determination," *J. Acoust. Soc. Amer.*, vol. 41, pp. 293-309, Feb. 1967.
[30] A. V. Oppenheim and R. W. Schafer, "Homomorphic analysis of speech," *IEEE Trans. Audio Electroacoust.*, vol. AU-16, pp. 221-226, June 1968.
[31] A. V. Oppenheim, R. W. Schafer, and T. G. Stockham, Jr., "Nonlinear filtering of multiplied and convolved signals," *Proc. IEEE*, vol. 56, pp. 1264-1291, Aug. 1968.
[32] A. V. Oppenheim, "A speech analysis-synthesis system based on homomorphic filtering," *J. Acoust. Soc. Amer.*, vol. 45, pp. 458-465, Feb. 1969.
[33] J. Olive, "Automatic formant tracking in a Newton-Raphson technique," *J. Acoust. Soc. Amer.*, vol. 50, pt. 2, pp. 661-670, Aug. 1971.
[34] R. W. Schafer and L. R. Rabiner, "System for automatic formant analysis of voiced speech," *J. Acoust. Soc. Amer.*, vol. 47, no. 2, pp. 634-648, Feb. 1970.

Linear Prediction Analysis

[35] B. S. Atal and M. R. Schroeder, "Adaptive predictive coding of speech signals," *Bell Syst. Tech. J.*, vol. 49, 1970.
[36] B. S. Atal and S. L. Hanauer, "Speech analysis and synthesis by linear prediction of the speech wave," *J. Acoust. Soc. Amer.*, vol. 50, pt. 2, pp. 637-655, Aug. 1971.
[37] D. K. Faddeev and V. N. Faddeeva, *Computational Methods of Linear Algebra.* San Francisco, Calif.: Freeman, 1963.
[38] F. Itakura and S. Saito, "An analysis-synthesis telephony system based on maximum likelihood method," *Electronics Commun. Japan*, vol. 53A, pp. 36-43, 1970.
[39] J. I. Makhoul and J. J. Wolf, "Linear prediction and the spectral analysis of speech," Bolt, Beranek, and Newman Inc., Boston, Mass., BBN Rep. 2304, Aug. 31, 1972.
[40] J. N. Maksym, "Real-time pitch extraction by adaptive prediction of the speech waveform," *IEEE Trans. Audio Electroacoust.*, vol. AU-21, pp. 149-153, June 1973.
[41] J. D. Markel, "Digital inverse filtering—A new tool for formant trajectory estimation," *IEEE Trans. Audio Electroacoust.*, vol. AU-20, pp. 129-137, June 1972.
[42] J. D. Markel, "The sift algorithm for fundamental frequency estimation," *IEEE Trans. Audio Electroacoust.*, vol. AU-20, pp. 367-377, Dec. 1972.
[43] J. D. Markel, A. H. Gray, Jr., and H. Wakita, "Linear prediction of speech-theory and practice," Speech Communications Res. Lab., Santa Barbara, Calif., SCRL Monograph 10, Sept. 1973.
[44] J. H. Wilkinson, *Rounding Errors in Algebraic Processes.* Englewood Cliffs, N.J.: Prentice-Hall, 1963.

Digital Signal Processing

[45] B. Gold and C. M. Rader, *Digital Processing of Signals.* New York: McGraw-Hill, 1969.
[46] H. D. Helms, "Fast Fourier transform method of computing difference equations and simulating filters," *IEEE Trans. Audio Electroacoust.*, vol. AU-15, no. 2, pp. 85-90, June 1967.
[47] A. V. Oppenheim and R. W. Schafer, *Digital Signal Processing.* Englewood Cliffs, N.J.: Prentice-Hall, 1975.
[48] L. R. Rabiner and B. Gold, *Theory and Application of Digital Signal Processing.* Englewood Cliffs, N.J.: Prentice-Hall, 1975.
[49] T. G. Stockham, Jr., "High speed convolution and correlation," *AFIPS Proc.*, pp. 229-233, 1966.

Comparison of Parametric Representations for Monosyllabic Word Recognition in Continuously Spoken Sentences

STEVEN B. DAVIS, MEMBER, IEEE, AND PAUL MERMELSTEIN, SENIOR MEMBER, IEEE

Abstract—Several parametric representations of the acoustic signal were compared with regard to word recognition performance in a syllable-oriented continuous speech recognition system. The vocabulary included many phonetically similar monosyllabic words, therefore the emphasis was on the ability to retain phonetically significant acoustic information in the face of syntactic and duration variations. For each parameter set (based on a mel-frequency cepstrum, a linear frequency cepstrum, a linear prediction cepstrum, a linear prediction spectrum, or a set of reflection coefficients), word templates were generated using an efficient dynamic warping method, and test data were time registered with the templates. A set of ten mel-frequency cepstrum coefficients computed every 6.4 ms resulted in the best performance, namely 96.5 percent and 95.0 percent recognition with each of two speakers. The superior performance of the mel-frequency cepstrum coefficients may be attributed to the fact that they better represent the perceptually relevant aspects of the short-term speech spectrum.

I. Introduction

THE selection of the best parametric representation of acoustic data is an important task in the design of any speech recognition system. The usual objectives in selecting a representation are to compress the speech data by eliminating information not pertinent to the phonetic analysis of the data and to enhance those aspects of the signal that contribute significantly to the detection of phonetic differences. When a significant amount of reference information is stored, such as different speakers' productions of the vocabulary, compact storage of the information becomes an important practical consideration.

The choice of a basic phonetic segment bears closely on the representation problem because the decision to identify an unknown segment with a reference category is based on the parameters within the entire segment. The number of different reference segments is generally smaller than the number of possible unknown segments, and therefore the step of identifying an unknown with a reference entails a significant loss of information. One can minimize the loss of useful information by examining different parametric representations in the framework of the specific recognition system under consideration. However, since the choice of a segment is so basic to the decision as to what acoustic information is useful, the result of such a comparative examination of different representations is directly applicable only to the specific recognition system, and generalization to differently organized systems may not be warranted.

Manuscript received June 11, 1979; revised December 18, 1979 and March 10, 1980. This material is based upon work supported by the National Science Foundation under Grant BNS 7682023 to Haskins Laboratories.

S. B. Davis was with Haskins Laboratories, New Haven, CT 06510. He is now with Signal Technology, Inc., Santa Barbara, CA 93101.

P. Mermelstein was with Haskins Laboratories, New Haven, CT 06510. He is now with Bell-Northern Research and INRS-Telecommunications, University of Quebec, Nun's Island, Verdun, P.Q., Canada.

Fujimura [1] and Mermelstein [2] discussed in detail the rationale for use of syllable-sized segments in the recognition of continuous speech. The goal of the experiments reported here was to select an acoustic representation most appropriate for the recognition of such segments. The methods used to evaluate the representations were open testing, where the training data and test data were independently derived, and closed testing, where these data sets were identical. In each case, the same speaker produced both the reference and test data, which included the same words in a variety of different syntactic contexts. Although variation among speakers is an important problem in its own right, attention is focused here on speaker-dependent representations to restrict the different sources of variation in the acoustic data.

White and Neely [3] showed that the choice of parametric representations significantly affects the recognition results in an isolated word recognition system. Two of the best representations they explored were a 20 channel bandpass filtering approach using a Chebyshev norm on the logarithm of the filter energies as a similarity measure, and a linear prediction coding approach using a linear prediction residual [4] as a similarity measure. From the similarity of the corresponding results, they concluded that bandpass filtering and linear prediction were essentially equivalent when used with a dynamic programming time alignment method. However, that result may be due to the absence of phonetically similar words in the test vocabulary.

Because of the known variation of the ear's critical bandwidths with frequency [5], [6], filters spaced linearly at low frequencies and logarithmically at high frequencies have been used to capture the phonetically important characteristics of speech. Pols [7] showed that the first six eigenvectors of the covariance matrix for Dutch vowels of three speakers, expressed in terms of 17 such filter energies, accounted for 91.8 percent of the total variance. The direction cosines of his eigenvectors were very similar to a cosine series expansion on the filter energies. Additional eigenvectors showed an increasing number of oscillations of their direction cosines with respect to their original energies. This result suggested that a

0096-3518/80/0800-0357$00.75

compact representation would be provided by a set of mel-frequency cepstrum coefficients. These cepstrum coefficients are the result of a cosine transform of the real logarithm of the short-term energy spectrum expressed on a mel-frequency scale.[1]

A preliminary experiment [9] showed that the cepstrum coefficients were useful for representing consonantal information as well. Four speakers produced 12 phonetically similar words, namely *stick*, *sick*, *skit*, *spit*, *sit*, *slit*, *strip*, *scrip*, *skip*, *skid*, *spick*, and *slid*. A representation using only two cepstrum coefficients resulted in 96 percent correct recognition of this vocabulary. Given these encouraging results, it became important to verify the power of the mel-frequency cepstrum representation by comparing it to a number of other commonly used representations in a recognition framework where the other variables, including vocabulary, are kept constant.

This paper compares the performance of different acoustic representations in a continuous speech recognition system based on syllabic units. The next section describes the organization of the recognition system, the selection of the speech data, and the different parametric representations. The following section describes the method for generating the acoustic templates for each word by use of a dynamic-warping time-alignment procedure. Finally, the results obtained with the various representations are listed and discussed from the point of view of completeness in representing the necessary acoustic information.

II. Experimental Framework

A rather simple speech recognition framework served as the testbed to evaluate the various acoustic representations. Lexical information was utilized in the form of a list of possible words and their corresponding acoustic templates, and these words were assumed to occur with equal likelihood. No syntactic or semantic information was utilized. If such information had been present, it could have been used to restrict the number of admissible lexical hypotheses or assign unequal probabilities to them. Thus, in practice, instead of matching hypotheses to the entire vocabulary, the number of lexical hypotheses that one evaluates may be reduced to a much smaller number. This reduction would cause many of the hypotheses phonetically similar to the target word to be eliminated from consideration. Thus the high phonetic confusability of the test data may have resulted in a test environment that is more rigorous than would be encountered in practice.

A. Selection of Corpus

The performance of continuous speech recognition systems is determined by a number of distinct sources of acoustic variability, including speaker characteristics, speaking rate, syntax, communication environment, and recording and/or transmission conditions. The focus of the current experiments is acoustic recognition in the face of variability induced in words of the same speaker by variation of the surrounding words and by syntactic position. The use of a separate reference template for each different syntactic environment which a word might occupy would require exorbitant amounts of storage and training data. Thus an important practical requirement is to generate reference templates without regard to the syntactic position of the word. To avoid the problem of automatically segmenting complex consonantal clusters, the corpus was composed of monosyllabic target words that were semantically acceptable in a number of different positions in a given syntactic context. Since acoustic variation due to different speakers is a distinctly separate problem [10], it was considered advisable to restrict the scope of these initial experiments by using only speaker-dependent templates. That is, both reference and test data were produced by the same speaker.

The sentences were read clearly in a quiet environment and recorded using a high-quality microphone. These recording conditions were selected to establish the best performance level that one could expect the recognition system to attain. Environments with higher ambient noise, which may be encountered in a practical speech input situation, would undoubtedly detract from the clarity of the acoustic information and therefore result in lower performance.

The speech data comprised 52 different CVC words from two male speakers (*DZ* and *LL*), and a total of 169 tokens were collected from 57 distinct sentences (Appendix A). The sentences were read twice by each speaker in recording sessions separated in time by two months (denoted by *DZ*1, *DZ*2, *LL*1, and *LL*2). Thus the data consisted of a total of 676 syllables. To achieve the required variability, the selected words could be used as both nouns and verbs. For example, "*Keep* the *hope* at the *bar*" and "*Bar* the *keep* for the *yell*" are two sentences that allow syntactic variation but preserve the same overall intonation pattern. All the words examined carried some stress; the unstressed function words were not analyzed. The target words, all CVC's, included 12 distinct vowels, /i, I, e, ɛ, æ, ɔ, ʌ, U, u, ɝ, a, o/, some of which are normally diphthongized in English. Each vowel was represented in at least four different words, and these words manifested differences in both the prevocalic and postvocalic consonants. The consonants were comprised of simple consonants as well as affricates, but no consonantal clusters.

B. Segmentation

An automatic segmentation process [11] was initially considered as one way of delimiting syllable-sized units in continuously spoken text, but any such algorithm performs the segmentation task with a finite probability of error. In particular, weak unstressed function words sometimes appear appended to the adjacent words carrying stronger stress. Additionally, in this study, a boundary point located for an intervocalic consonant with high sonority may not consistently join that consonant to the word of interest. In order to avoid possible interaction between segmentation errors and poor parametric representations, manual segmentation and auditory evaluation was used to accurately delimit the signal

[1] Fant [8] compares Beranek's mel-frequency scale, Koenig's scale, and Fant's approximation to the mel-frequency scale. Since the differences between these scales are not significant here, the mel-frequency scale should be understood as a linear frequency spacing below 1000 Hz and a logarithmic spacing above 1000 Hz.

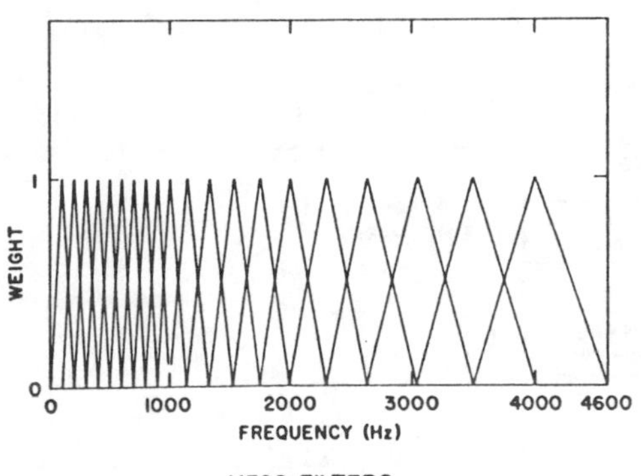

Fig. 1. Filters for generating mel-frequency cepstrum coefficients.

corresponding to the target words. The segmentation, as well as the subsequent analysis and recognition, was performed on a PDP-11/45 minicomputer with the Interactive Laboratory System [12].

In systems employing automatic segmentation, the actual recognition rates can be expected to be lower due to the generation of templates from imperfectly delimited words [13]. However, there is no reason to believe that segmentation errors would not detract equally from the recognition rates obtained for the various parametric representations.

C. Parametric Representations

The parametric representations evaluated in this study may be divided into two groups: those based on the Fourier spectrum and those based on the linear prediction spectrum. The first group comprises the mel-frequency cepstrum coefficients (MFCC) and the linear frequency cepstrum coefficients (LFCC). The second group includes the linear prediction coefficients (LPC), the reflection coefficients (RC), and the cepstrum coefficients derived from the linear prediction coefficients (LPCC). A Euclidean distance metric was used for all cepstrum parameters since cepstrum coefficients are derived from an orthogonal basis. This metric was also used for the RC, in view of the lack of an inherent associated distance metric. The LPC were evaluated using the minimum prediction residual distance metric [4].

Each acoustic signal was low-pass filtered at 5 kHz and sampled at 10 kHz. Fourier spectra or linear prediction spectra were computed for sequential frames 64 points (6.4 ms) or 128 points (12.8 ms) apart. In each case, a 256 point Hamming window was used to select the data points to be analyzed. (A window size of 128 points produced degraded results.)

For the MFCC computations, 20 triangular bandpass filters were simulated as shown in Fig. 1. The MFCC were computed as

$$\mathrm{MFCC}_i = \sum_{k=1}^{20} X_k \cos\left[i\left(k - \frac{1}{2}\right)\frac{\pi}{20}\right], \quad i = 1, 2, \cdots, M, \tag{1}$$

where M is the number of cepstrum coefficients, and X_k, $k = 1, 2, \cdots, 20$, represents the log-energy output of the kth filter.

The LFCC were computed from the log-magnitude discrete Fourier transform (DFT) directly as

$$\mathrm{LFCC}_i = \sum_{k=0}^{K-1} Y_k \cos\left(\frac{\pi i k}{K}\right), \quad i = 1, 2, \cdots, M, \tag{2}$$

where K is the number of DFT magnitude coefficients Y_k.

The LPC were obtained from a 10th order all-pole approximation to the spectrum of the windowed waveform. The autocorrelation method for evaluation of the linear prediction coefficients was used [14]. The RC were obtained by a transformation of the LPC which is equivalent to matching the inverse of the LPC spectrum with a transfer function spectrum that corresponds to an acoustic tube consisting of ten sections of variable cross-sectional area [15]. The reflection coefficients determine the fraction of energy in a traveling wave that is reflected at each section boundary.

The LPCC were obtained from the LPC directly as [14]

$$\mathrm{LPCC}_i = \mathrm{LPC}_i + \sum_{k=1}^{i-1} \frac{k-i}{i}\, \mathrm{LPCC}_{i-k}\mathrm{LPC}_k, \quad i = 1, 2, \cdots, 10. \tag{3}$$

The Itakura metric represents the distance between two spectral frames with optimal (reference) LPC and test $\widehat{\mathrm{LPC}}$ as

$$D\,[\mathrm{LPC}, \widehat{\mathrm{LPC}}] = \log \left| \frac{\mathrm{LPC}\, \hat{R}\, \mathrm{LPC}^T}{\widehat{\mathrm{LPC}}\, \hat{R}\, \widehat{\mathrm{LPC}}^T} \right| \tag{4}$$

where $\hat{R}$ is the autocorrelation matrix (obtained from the test sample) corresponding to $\widehat{\mathrm{LPC}}$. The metric measures the residual error when the test sample is filtered by the optimal LPC. Because of its asymmetry, the Itakura metric requires specific identification of the reference coefficients (LPC) and the test coefficients ($\widehat{\mathrm{LPC}}$). For computational efficiency, the denominator of (4) will be unity if $\hat{R}$ is expressed in unnormalized form. Then if $\hat{r}(n)$ denotes the unnormalized diagonal elements of $\hat{R}$, $r_{\mathrm{LP}}(n)$ denotes the unnormalized autocorrelation coefficients from the LPC polynomial, and the logarithm is eliminated, the distance may be expressed as [16]

$$D\,[\hat{r}, r_{\mathrm{LP}}] = \hat{r}(0)\, r_{\mathrm{LP}}(0) + 2 \sum_{i=1}^{10} \hat{r}(i)\, r_{\mathrm{LP}}(i). \tag{5}$$

III. Generation of Acoustic Templates

The use of templates to represent the acoustic information in reference tokens allows a significant computation reduction compared to use of the reference tokens themselves. The design of a template generation process is governed by the goal of finding the point in acoustic space that simultaneously minimizes the "distance" to all given reference items. Where the appropriate distance is a linear function of the acoustic variables, this goal can be realized by the use of classic pattern recognition techniques. However, phonetic features are not uniformly distributed across the acoustic data, and therefore perceptually motivated distance measures are nonlinear functions of those data. To avoid the computationally exorbitant procedure of simultaneously minimizing the set of nonlinear distances, templates are incrementally generated by introducing additional acoustic information from each reference token to the partial template formed from the previous used refer-

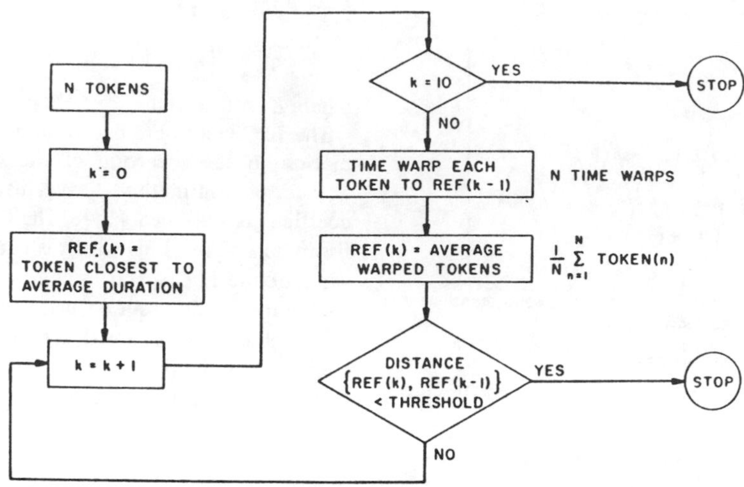

Fig. 2. Iterative algorithm for template generation.

ence tokens. Given a distance between two tokens, or between a token and a template, the new template can be located along the line whose extent measures that distance. Since only acoustically similar tokens are to be combined into individual templates, one may expect that this procedure will exploit whatever local linearization the space permits.

A. Template Generation Algorithms

In one algorithm [10], an initial template is chosen as the token whose duration is the closest to the average duration of all tokens representing the same word (Fig. 2). Then all remaining tokens are warped to the initial template. The warping is achieved by first using dynamic programming to provide a mapping (or time registration) between any token and the reference template. Following the notation in [17], let $T_i(m)$, $0 \leq m \leq M_i$, be a token contour for word replication i with duration M_i, $i = 1, 2, \cdots, I$, and let $R_1(m) = T_j(m)$ be the initial reference contour, where the duration of the jth token is closest to the average duration. For example, these contours may be vectors of cepstrum coefficients obtained at 10 ms intervals during the word. Then dynamic programming may be used to find mappings $m_i = w_i(n)$, $i = 1, 2, \cdots, I$, subject to boundary conditions at the endpoints, such that the total distance $D_T(i)$ between token i and the reference contour is minimal. A distance function D is defined for each pair of points (m, n). Then

$$D_T(i) = \min_{\{w_i(n)\}} \sum_{n=1}^{N} D[R_1(n), T_i(w_i(n))]. \tag{6}$$

With the aid of these mappings, a new reference contour may be defined as

$$R_2(n) = \frac{1}{I} \sum_{i=1}^{I} T[w_i(n)], \tag{7}$$

and the process is repeated until the distance between the current and previous templates is below some threshold. This procedure is not dependent on the order in which tokens are considered. However, it is computationally expensive to iterate to the final reference contour. Furthermore, there may be cases where there is no convergence [10].

A different algorithm can be used for phonetically similar words; this algorithm requires less computation effort and has no convergence problems. Furthermore, the algorithm allows a reference template to be easily updated with an accepted token during verification to allow for word variation over time. In this procedure [18], each successive token is warped with the current template to produce a new template for the next token (Fig. 3). For example,

$$R_1(n) = T_1(n),$$
$$R_2(n) = \tfrac{1}{2}[R_1(n) + T_2(w_2(n))],$$
$$R_3(n) = \tfrac{1}{3}[2R_2(n) + T_3(w_3(n))],$$
$$\vdots \qquad \vdots$$
$$R_I(n) = \frac{1}{I}[(I-1)R_{I-1}(n) + T_I(w_I(n))]. \tag{8}$$

Thus, the process ends with the Ith template.

While this algorithm has computational advantages over the first algorithm, the results become order dependent since the warping is sequential and nonlinear. If the tokens are used in a different order, a different template will result. For tokens obtained from the same speaker and spoken within the same context, order dependence is not a problem. However, for tokens obtained from different syntactic positions, order dependence is potentially a problem. Finally, if different speakers are involved, tokens will be less similar, and the order in which they are taken may greatly affect the final template. If clustering algorithms are used to generate multiple templates for each word [10], then each cluster may be viewed as a group in which order dependence may be a consideration.

B. Time Alignment

All but one of the parametric distance measures explored are derived from Euclidean functions of parameters pertaining to pairs of time frames. The appropriate time frames are chosen to best align the significant acoustic events in time. Because

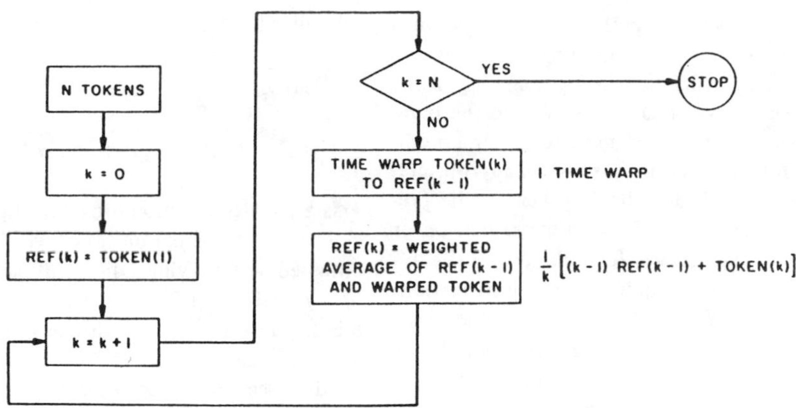

Fig. 3. Noniterative algorithm for template generation.

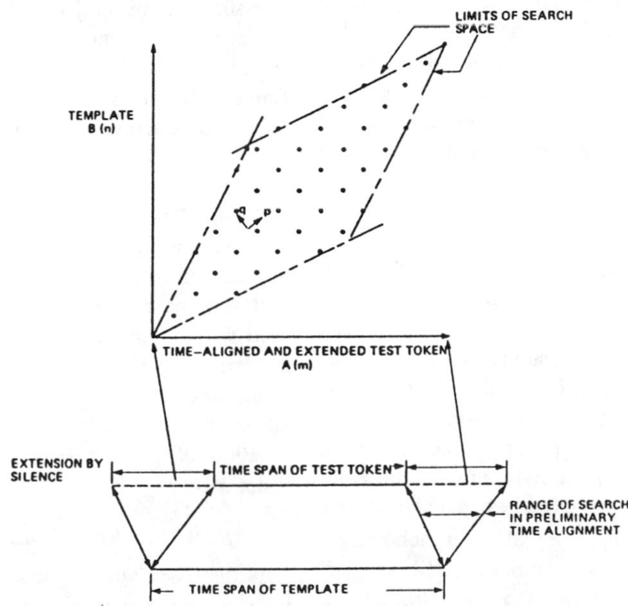

Fig. 4. Dynamic time alignment of speech samples.

the segments aligned are monosyllabic words, one can take advantage of a number of well-defined acoustic features to guide the alignment procedure. For example, the release of a prevocalic voiced stop or the onset of frication of a post-vocalic fricative manifest themselves by means of such acoustic features. The particular alignment procedure used meets these requirements without requiring explicit decisions concerning the nature of the acoustic events.

The alignment operation employed a modified form of the dynamic programming algorithm first applied to spoken words by Velichko and Zagoruyko [19] and subsequently modified by Bridle and Brown [20] and Itakura [4]. In view of the intent to use the same algorithm for template generation as for recognition of unknown tokens, a symmetric dynamic programming algorithm was utilized. Sakoe and Chiba [2] have recently shown that a symmetric dynamic programming algorithm yields better word recognition results than previously used asymmetric forms.

Execution of the algorithm proceeded in two stages (Fig. 4). First, the pair of tokens to be compared was time aligned by appending silence to the marked endpoints and linearly shifting the shorter of the pair, with respect to the longer, to achieve a preliminary distance minimum. Since monosyllabic words generally possess a prominent syllabic peak in energy, this operation ensured that the syllabic peaks were lined up before the nonlinear minimization process was started. Informal evaluation has shown that use of the preliminary alignment procedure yields better results than omitting the procedure or using a linear time warping procedure to equalize the time durations of the tokens. The two tokens, extended by silence where necessary, were then subjected to the dynamic programming search to find an improved distance minimum. The preliminary distance minimum, found as a result of the initial linear time alignment procedure, corresponded to the distance computed along the diagonal of the search space and represented in most cases a good starting point for the subsequent detailed search. Use of this preliminary time alignment and the additional invocation of a penalty function when the point selected along the dynamic programming path implied unequal time increments along the measured data, generally forced the optimum warping path to be near the diagonal, unless prominent acoustic information was present to indicate the contrary. For efficiency in programming, zeros (representing silence) were never really appended to the data, rather, the time shift was retained and used to trigger a modified Euclidean or Itakura distance measure when appropriate.

The use of silence to extend the syllable tokens in the preliminary time alignment, instead of linear time expansion or contraction as implied by asymmetric formulations of the dynamic programming algorithm, requires some justification. The comparison here is among syllable-sized units which generally possess an energy peak near the center regions and lesser energy near the ends. Based on a perceptual model, extension of the tokens by silence is clearly appropriate. Linear time scale changes would obscure equally the more significant duration information in the consonantal regions and less significant duration information in the vocalic regions. Discrimination between words like "pool" and "fool" depends critically on the duration of the prevocalic burst or fricative. The alignment ensures that the prominent vowel regions are lined up before time scale changes in the consonantal regions are examined.

C. Dynamic Warping Algorithm

The dynamic warping algorithm serves to estimate the similarity between an unknown token and a reference template. Additionally, it serves to align a reference token with a partial template to ensure that phonetically similar spectral frames are averaged in generating a composite template. Through the preliminary alignment procedure discussed above, the token or template, whichever is shortest, is extended by silence frames on both sides. The resulting multidimensional acoustic representations of the pair of patterns compared can be denoted by $A(m)$, $m = 1, 2, \cdots, M$ and $B(n)$, $n = 1, 2, \cdots, M$. For each pair of frames $\{A(m), B(n)\}$, a local distance function $D[A, B]$ can be defined for estimating the similarity at point $x'(m, n)$. A change of variables identifies $x'(m, n)$ as $x(p, q)$, where p and q are measured along and normal to the diagonal illustrated in Fig. 4. For each position along the diagonal $\{x(p, 0), 1 \leqslant p \leqslant M\}$, points along the normal $\{x(p, q), |q| \leqslant Q(p)\}$ are analyzed where the search space is limited by $|q| \leqslant Q(p)$. The $Q(p)$ define a region in the grid area delimited by lines with slopes $\frac{1}{2}$ and 2 passing through the corners $x(0, 0)$ and $x(M, 0)$.

In order for a grid point $x(p, q)$ to be an acceptable continuation of a path through some previous point $x(p - 1, q')$, it must satisfy two continuity conditions:

1) $|q - q'| \leqslant 1$—this condition restricts the path to follow nonnegative time steps along the time coordinates of the patterns; and

2) $|q - q''| \leqslant 1$, where $x(p - 2, q'')$ is the selected predecessor of the point $x(p - 1, q')$—this condition restricts any one time frame to participation in at most two local comparisons.

With the aid of these constraints, each point in the search is restricted to at most three possible predecessors. To establish the minimal distance subpath $D_T(p, q)$ leading back to the origin from the point $x(p, q)$, the cumulative distance leading to that point through each possible predecessor $x(p - 1, q')$ is minimized. Thus

$$D_T(p, q) = \min_{q'} \{D_T(p - 1, q') + D[A(p - q), B(p + q)]\, V(q - q')\}. \tag{9}$$

V is a penalty function introduced to keep the alignment path close to the diagonal unless a significant distance reduction is obtained by following a different path. By setting V to 1.5 for $|q - q'| = 1$ and 1.0 otherwise, unproductive searches far from the diagonal are avoided. Since all paths terminate at $x(M, 0)$, the total distance of the minimum distance path and therefore the distance between A and B is given by $D_T(M, 0)$.

The minimal distance subpath passes through the points $\{x(p, \hat{q}), 1 \leqslant p \leqslant M\}$. These points allow the identification of pairs of frames $A(p - \hat{q})$ and $B(p + \hat{q})$ that contributed to the minimal distance result. A new template $C(p)$, $p = 1, 2, \cdots, M$, can then be generated by appropriately averaging the frames $A(p - \hat{q})$ and $B(p + \hat{q})$, $p = 1, 2, \cdots, M$.

The one exception to template generation by weighted averaging occurs with the LPC. If two LPC vectors are averaged, stability of the resultant vector is not guaranteed. Therefore, LPC templates were generated in the space of LP-derived reflection coefficients. Since the reflection coefficients are bounded in magnitude by one, stability requirements are satisfied and the symmetric dynamic warping algorithm could be used without modification. Alternately, the templates could be derived in the space of LP-derived autocorrelation coefficients since stability is guaranteed from the result that a stable autocorrelation matrix is positive-definite and a linear combination of positive-definite matrices is positive-definite and hence stable.

D. Effects of Order In Generating a Template

As discussed above, the incremental addition of individual tokens to a previously formed template results in a final template whose values depend on the order of the tokens.

In a preliminary experiment utilizing the same database [18], ten sets of reference templates based on six MFCC were generated. Each set of templates used the reference tokens in random order. Independent test data were then matched with each set of templates on a per speaker basis. The average recognition scores and standard deviations were 94.76 ± 0.53 percent and 90.53 ± 0.48 percent for each speaker, respectively. Thus, random ordering of tokens for template generation did not change the results. At a 0.01 significance level, none of the rates for either speaker was significantly different from the respective mean. Thirty-two of the 52 different CVC word types were never misidentified. Errors were generally confined to the same test tokens of a word regardless of the template, and the most confusions were among test-reference pairs such as *wake-bait*, *book-hood*, and *burn-herd*.

The consistent rates among template sets indicated that the templates for any given word were relatively similar. To visualize such relationships, all of the pairwise distances for eight templates and four test tokens of *keep* were measured and fitted to an X–Y plane. The eight templates were arbitrarily chosen from among the 24 possible templates for four refer-

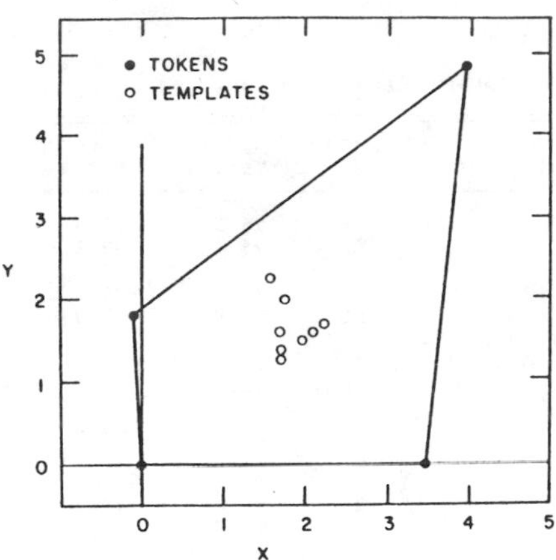

Fig. 5. X-Y coordinate plane for *keep*.

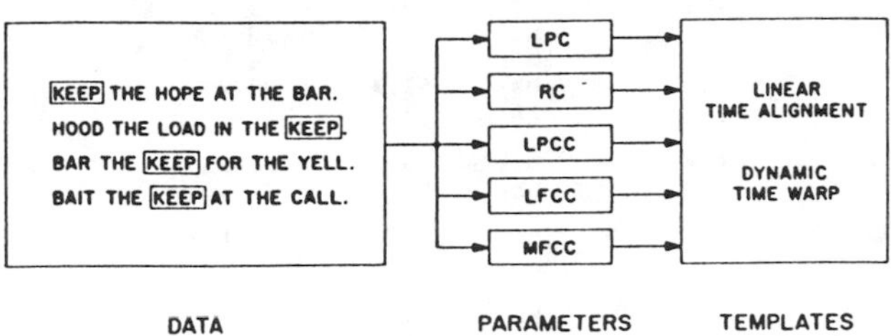

Fig. 6. Selection of monosyllabic words for template generation.

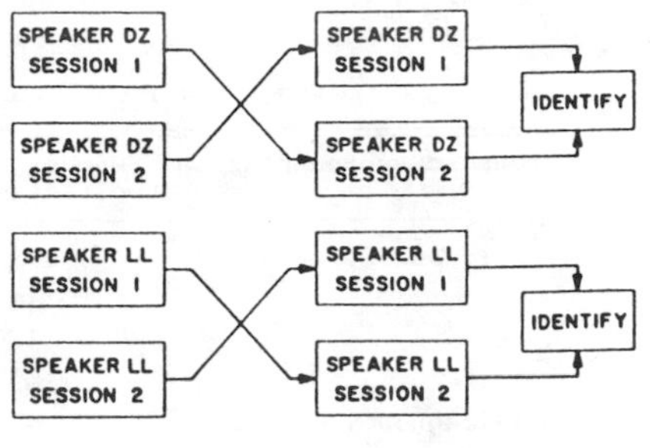

Fig. 7. Two-way speaker-dependent identification tests.

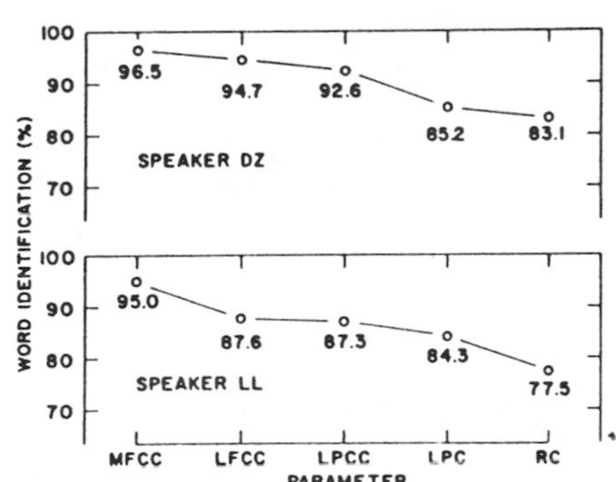

Fig. 8. Performance of parametric representations for recognition.

ence tokens from $DZ1$, and the four test tokens were obtained from $DZ2$. The fitting procedure was based on iterating (x, y) coordinates for each point (template or token) until the mean-square error in distances among the points was minimized. The coordinate plane is shown in Fig. 5. Regardless of ordering, the templates are close to each other and relatively far from the test tokens, thus illustrating the robustness of the technique for template generation.

IV. Recognition

For each parametric representation (MFCC, LFCC, LPCC, LPC, and RC), the following test procedure was used [22]. Each segmented token from sets $DZ1$, $DZ2$, $LL1$, and $LL2$ was analyzed and a matrix of coefficients (columns corresponding to coefficient number and rows corresponding to time frame) was stored (Fig. 6). Each set was used in turn as test and reference data. In the case of reference data, templates were formed on a per speaker-per session basis, using all tokens of each word (generally three to five in number) recorded in the session. Two types of testing were used: closed tests, where test and reference data were from the same session, e.g., reference $DZ1$ versus test $DZ1$, and open tests, where test and reference data were from different sessions, e.g., reference $DZ1$ versus test $DZ2$ (Fig. 7). For each test word, a warping was performed with each of the 52 reference templates, and the word was identified with the least distant template (maximum similarity). In a practical situation, alternative methods, such as vowel preselection and thresholding for early rejection, could be applied to reduce the computations and the number of comparisons. In this experiment, however, the emphasis was on methodology rather than efficiency.

The results are listed in Table I and displayed in Fig. 8 for open tests with 10 coefficients and 6.4 ms frames. Regardless of the frame separation, type of testing or speaker, these data indicate superior performance of the MFCC when compared with the other parametric representations. In fact, the performance of six MFCC was also better than any other ten coefficient set. In all cases, the 6.4 ms frame separation produced better performance. As previously stated, the window size was 25.6 ms, and using half the window size produced degraded results. Finally, speaker DZ, a male with exceptionally low fundamental frequency, was better recognized than speaker LL, a male with somewhat higher fundamental frequency. Speaker-dependent differences, however, require further systematic investigation.

Most confusions arose between pairs of words that were phonetically very similar. For example, of the eight misrecognitions using the MFCC parameters for speaker DZ, two were between *bar* and *mar*, two were between *pool* and *fool*, one each between *keep* and *heat*, *bait* and *wake*, *hook* and *rig*, and *hood* and *cause*. Note that by not using the average spectrum energy (the zeroth cepstrum coefficient) in these comparisons, the overall energy between time-aligned spectral frames has been equalized. Inclusion of the variation of overall energy with time might possibly assist discrimination between such highly confusable word pairs.

V. Conclusions

The similarity in rank order of the recognition rates by representation for each of the two speakers suggests that the performance differences among the various acoustic repre-

TABLE I
RECOGNITION RATES RESULTING FROM USE OF VARIOUS ACOUSTIC REPRESENTATIONS

Acoustic Representation	Number of Coefficients	Distance Metric	Frame Separation (ms)	Speaker	Open Test %	Closed Test %
mel-frequency cepstrum	10	Euclidean	6.4	DZ	96.5	99.4
				LL	95.0	99.1
			12.8	DZ	95.6	99.4
				LL	93.8	97.9
mel-frequency cepstrum	6	Euclidean	6.4	DZ	96.5	99.4
				LL	92.0	97.6
			12.8	DZ	95.0	98.8
				LL	90.2	97.6
linear-frequency cepstrum	10	Euclidean	6.4	DZ	94.7	99.1
				LL	87.6	98.2
			12.8	DZ	93.2	98.8
				LL	84.9	97.3
linear-prediction cepstrum	10	Euclidean	6.4	DZ	92.6	99.1
				LL	87.3	98.2
			12.8	DZ	91.7	98.2
				LL	86.4	96.7
linear-prediction spectrum	10	Itakura	6.4	DZ	85.2	97.9
				LL	84.3	95.2
reflection coefficients	10	Euclidean	6.4	DZ	83.1	97.1
				LL	77.5	97.0
			12.8	DZ	80.5	97.6
				LL	74.6	96.2

sentations are significant. These differences lead to the following specific conclusions.

1) Parameters derived from the short-term Fourier spectrum (MFCC and LFCC) of the acoustic signal preserve information that parameters from the LPC spectrum (LPCC, LPC, and RC) omit. Both spectral representations are considered adequate for vowels. However, it is the confusions between the consonants that are most frequent. The differences found may be due to the inaccurate representation of the consonantal spectra by the linear prediction technique.

2) The mel-frequency cepstra possess a significant advantage over the linear frequency cepstra. Specifically, MFCC allow better suppression of insignificant spectral variation in the higher frequency bands.

3) The cepstrum parameters (MFCC, LFCC, and LPCC), which correspond to various frequency smoothed representations of the log-magnitude spectrum, succeed better than the LPC and RC in capturing the significant acoustic information. A Euclidean distance metric defined on the cepstrum parameters apparently allows a better separation of phonetically distinct spectra. Since there is a unique transformation between a set of LPCC and the corresponding LPC and RC, these representations can be said to contain equivalent information. However, this transformation is nonlinear. Representing the acoustic information in the hyperspace of cepstrum parameters favors the use of a particularly simple distance metric.

4) Defining the metric on the basis of the Itakura distance is less effective than defining it on the basis of cepstrum distance. The point of optimality is the same, i.e., equality between cepstra implies zero difference in prediction residual energy. However, the Itakura distance is less successful in indicating the phonetic significance of the difference between a pair of spectra than the cepstrum distance.

5) The mel-frequency cepstrum coefficients form a particularly compact representation. Six coefficients succeed in capturing most of the relevant information. The importance of the higher cepstrum coefficients appears to depend on the speaker. Further data are required from additional speakers before firm conclusions can be reached on the optimal number of coefficients.

The results are limited by the restrictions on the speech data examined. In particular, consonant clusters, multisyllabic words, and unstressed monosyllabic words have not been studied. Expansion of the database along any one of these directions introduces additional representation problems. It is not obvious that the best representation for stressed words is also best for the much more elastic unstressed words. These questions are left for future studies.

It should be emphasized that the comparative ranking of the representations can be influenced by the choice of both the local and the integrated distance metrics. A Euclidean distance function is one of the simplest to implement. However, taking into account the probability distributions of the individual parameters should result in improved performance. Estimating these distributions requires considerable data. Yet, even if only a few parameters of these distributions are known, for example, the variance of the cepstrum coefficients, better local distance metrics could be designed. Despite the high recognition rates achieved so far, there is reason to believe that even better performance can be attained in the future.

The design of the mel-frequency cepstrum representation was motivated by perceptual factors. Evidently, an ability to capture the perceptually relevant information is an important advantage. The design of an improved distance metric may result from more accurate modeling of perceptual behavior. In particular, where a constant difference between spectra persists for a number of consecutive time frames, the contribution of that difference in the current distance computation is proportional to the duration of that difference. With the possible exception of very short durations, no perceptual justification exists for this property [5]. Nevertheless, the distance function must in some fashion combine different information from all the time frames constituting the signals compared. Further optimization of the integrated distance function represents an important challenge.

For each representation, a small but significant gain in recognition is achieved by decreasing the frame spacing from 12.8 ms to 6.4 ms. The average difference in the recognition rates is 1.7 percent. However, the computational complexity for any dynamic programming comparison varies as the square of the average number of frames constituting a word. Thus a significant computational penalty accompanies any increase in the frame rate. In contrast, the computations grow only linearly with the number of cepstrum coefficients. Since the recognition rates for six cepstrum coefficients and 6.4 ms frame spacing is quite comparable to the rate for ten coefficients and 12.8 ms frame spacing, increasing the number of coefficients and maintaining a somewhat coarser time resolution is computationally more advantageous than using fewer coefficients more frequently.

The principal conclusion of the study is that perceptually-based word templates are effective in capturing the acoustic information required to recognize these words in continuous speech. Due to the various limitations of this study, a conclusion that such high recognition rates are attainable with a complete automatic system operating in a practical environment is not warranted at this time. However, the results do encourage a continuing effort to optimize the performance of speech recognition systems by critical evaluation of each of the constituent components.

Appendix A

Sentences Used for Word Recognition

1. *Keep* the *hope* at the *bar.*
2. *Dig* this *rock* in the *heat.*
3. *Wake* the *herd* at the *head.*
4. *Check* the *lock* on the *seal.*
5. *Bang* this *bar* on the *head.*
6. *Call* a *mess* in the *case.*
7. *Cut* the *coat* for a *mop.*
8. *Foot* the *work* in the *mess.*
9. *Boot* the *back* of the *book.*
10. *Burn* your *check* in the *jar.*
11. *Mop* the *room* on the *watch.*
12. *Load* the *tar* for the *bait.*
13. *Tar* this *rig* in a *rush.*
14. *Fear* a *hood* on the *ship.*
15. *Rig* a *bait* for the *work.*
16. *Nail* that *book* to the *rock.*
17. *Yell* this *call* for the *wake.*
18. *Gang* the *bait* on the *coat.*
19. *Walk* the *watch* in the *hope.*
20. *Buff* one *book* for the *walk.*
21. *Hook* the *mop* on the *lock.*
22. *Pool* the *case* for the *man.*
23. *Hurl* his *bar* in the *muck.*
24. *Bomb* the *head* at the *wake.*
25. *Pose* this *seal* for the *gang.*
26. *Mar* the *watch* on the *hood.*
27. *Heat* the *foot* of the *fool.*
28. *Kill* the *herd* for the *load.*
29. *Case* your *ship* for the *cause.*
30. *Head* the *rush* for the *burn.*
31. *Back* the *pool* for the *check.*
32. *Watch* that *hook* with the *nail.*
33. *Rush* the *buff* at the *foot.*
34. *Hood* the *load* for the *keep.*
35. *Room* one *seal* in the *pool.*
36. *Herd* the *fool* with a *yell.*
37. *Rock* the *mop* with a *hurl.*
38. *Coat* the *cut* with the *tar.*
39. *Jar* the *bomb* with a *bang.*
40. *Seal* the *dig* in a *fear.*
41. *Ship* the *nail* in a *boot.*
42. *Bait* the *keep* with a *call.*
43. *Mess* his *work* in the *room.*
44. *Man* the *cut* at the *kill.*
45. *Cause* a *mar* on the *back.*
46. *Muck* the *gang* on the *walk.*
47. *Book* the *fool* on the *rig.*
48. *Fool* the *man* on the *rock.*
49. *Work* the *hurl* at the *dig.*
50. *Lock* your *man* in a *pose.*
51. *Hope* this *call* for the *heat.*
52. *Bar* the *keep* for the *yell.*
53. Put a *bang* in the *bomb.*
54. Set a *pose* in the *muck.*
55. *Pose* a *jar* on the *buff.*
56. *Kill* the *fear* in the *cause.*
57. *Mar* the *burn* on the *head.*

Acknowledgment

Drs. F. Cooper and P. Nye participated in numerous discussions of the experimental program, and their contribution is greatly appreciated.

References

[1] O. Fujimura, "The syllable as a unit of speech recognition," *IEEE Trans. Acoust., Speech, Signal Processing*, vol. ASSP-23, pp. 82-87, Feb. 1975.

[2] P. Mermelstein, "A phonetic-context controlled strategy for segmentation and phonetic labeling of speech," *IEEE Trans. Acoust., Speech, Signal Processing*, vol. ASSP-23, pp. 79-82, Feb. 1975.

[3] G. M. White and R. B. Neely, "Speech recognition experiments

with linear prediction, bandpass filtering, and dynamic programming," *IEEE Trans. Acoust., Speech, Signal Processing*, vol. ASSP-24, pp. 183–188, Apr. 1976.
[4] F. Itakura, "Minimum prediction residual principle applied to speech recognition," *IEEE Trans. Acoust., Speech, Signal Processing*, vol. ASSP-23, pp. 67–72, Feb. 1975.
[5] R. Feldtkeller and E. Zwicker, *Das Ohr als Nachrichtenempfanger*. S. Hirzel, Stuttgart, 1956.
[6] M. R. Schroeder, "Recognition of complex acoustic signals," *Life Sci. Res. Rep.*, T. H. Bullock, Ed., vol. 55, pp. 323–328, 1977.
[7] L. C. W. Pols, "Spectral analysis and identification of Dutch vowels in monosyllabic words," Doctoral dissertation, Free University, Amsterdam, The Netherlands, 1966.
[8] C. G. M. Fant, "Acoustic description and classification of phonetic units," *Ericsson Technics*, vol. 1, 1959; also G. Fant, *Speech Sounds and Features*. Cambridge, MA: MIT Press, 1973, pp. 32–83.
[9] P. Mermelstein, "Distance measures for speech recognition, psychological and instrumental," in *Pattern Recognition and Artificial Intelligence*, C. H. Chen, Ed. New York: Academic, 1976, pp. 374–388.
[10] L. R. Rabiner, "On creating reference templates for speaker-independent recognition of isolated words," *IEEE Trans. Acoust., Speech, Signal Processing*, vol. ASSP-26, pp. 34–42, Feb. 1978.
[11] P. Mermelstein, "Automatic segmentation of speech into syllabic units," *J. Acoust. Soc. Amer.*, vol. 58, pp. 880–883, Oct. 1975.
[12] L. L. Pfeifer, *Interactive Laboratory System Users Guide*, Signal Technology, Inc., Santa Barbara, CA, 1977.
[13] P. Mermelstein, "Recognition of monosyllabic words in continuous sentences using composite word templates," in *Conf. Rec., 1978 Int. Conf. Acoust., Speech, Signal Processing*, Tulsa, OK, 1978, pp. 708–711.
[14] J. D. Markel and A. H. Gray Jr., *Linear Prediction of Speech*. New York: Springer-Verlag, 1976.
[15] H. Wakita, "Direct estimation of the vocal tract shape by inverse filtering of acoustic speech waveforms," *IEEE Trans. Audio and Electroacoust.*, vol. AU-21, pp. 417–427, Dec. 1973.
[16] A. H. Gray, Jr. and J. D. Markel, "Distance measures for speech processing," *IEEE Trans. Acoust., Speech, Signal Processing*, vol. ASSP-24, pp. 380–391, Oct. 1976.
[17] L. R. Rabiner, A. E. Rosenberg, and S. E. Levinson, "Considerations in dynamic time warping algorithms for discrete word recognition," *IEEE Trans. Acoust., Speech, Signal Processing*, vol. ASSP-26, pp. 575–586, Dec. 1978.
[18] S. B. Davis, "Order dependence in templates for monosyllabic word identification," in *Conf. Rec., 1979 Int. Conf. Acoust., Speech, Signal Processing*, Washington, DC, 1979, pp. 570–573.
[19] V. M. Velichko and N. G. Zagoruyko, "Automatic recognition of 200 words," *Int. J. Man-Machine Studies*, vol. 2, pp. 223–234, 1970.
[20] J. S. Bridle and M. D. Brown, "An experimental automatic word recognition system," Joint Speech Research Unit, Ruislip, England, Tech. Rep. 1003, 1979.
[21] H. Sakoe and S. Chiba, "Dynamic programming algorithm optimization for spoken word recognition," *IEEE Trans. Acoust., Speech, Signal Processing*, vol. ASSP-26, pp. 43–49, Feb. 1978.
[22] S. B. Davis and P. Mermelstein, "Evaluation of acoustic parameters for monosyllabic word identification" (abstract), *J. Acoust. Soc. Amer.*, vol. 64, suppl. 1, p. S180, 1978.

Steven B. Davis (S'71–M'76) was born in Los Angeles, CA, in 1951. He received the B.S., M.S., and Ph.D. degrees in electrical engineering from the University of California, Santa Barbara, in 1972, 1973, and 1976, respectively.

In 1973 he held a summer fellowship at Woods Hole Oceanographic Institute, RI. In 1974 he joined the Speech Communications Research Laboratory, Inc. (SCRL), Santa Barbara, CA, where he worked on interactive systems for speech processing and acoustic analysis of pathological voices. In 1975 he was elected to *Who's Who Among Students in American Universities and Colleges.* From 1977 to 1978, he worked at Haskins Laboratories, New Haven, CT, where he was engaged in word recognition, articulatory synthesis, and applications of speech processing to linguistics and phonetics. In 1978 he rejoined SCRL, Los Angeles, CA, working on clinical techniques for detecting and evaluating pathological voices, and he began work at Signal Technology, Inc. (STI), Santa Barbara, in the area of telephone channel equalization for narrow-band speech processors. His current technical interests include speech recognition by computers and iterative software systems for digital signal processing.

Dr. Davis is a member of Eta Kappa Nu, Sigma Xi, the Acoustical Society of America, the IEEE Acoustics, Speech, and Signal Processing Society, and the IEEE Computer Society Technical Subcommittee on Speech Recognition and Understanding.

Paul Mermelstein (S'58–M'63–SM'77) was born in Czechoslovakia in 1939, and came to Canada in 1951. He received the B.Eng. degree in engineering physics from McGill University, Montreal, P.Q., Canada, in 1959 and went on to graduate work in electrical engineering at the Massachusetts Institute of Technology, Cambridge, MA, graduating with the D.Sc. degree in 1964.

From 1964 to 1973, he was a Technical Staff Member in the Speech and Communications Research Department, Bell Laboratories, Murray Hill, NJ. In 1973 he moved to Haskins Laboratories, New Haven, CT, pursuing research in speech recognition and speech perception. In 1977 he was appointed Manager of Speech Communications Systems Research for Bell-Northern Research, Nun's Island, Verdun P.Q., Canada. As part of a cooperative research program between BNR and INRS-Telecommunications, Université du Québec, he serves as Visiting Professor at INRS and Auxiliary Professor of Electrical Engineering at McGill University. His current technical interests include digital speech transmission, speech recognition and synthesis by computers, and human speech communication.

Dr. Mermelstein is a member of the Acoustical Society of America.

Vector Quantization

Robert M. Gray

A vector quantizer is a system for mapping a sequence of continuous or discrete vectors into a digital sequence suitable for communication over or storage in a digital channel. The goal of such a system is data compression: to reduce the bit rate so as to minimize communication channel capacity or digital storage memory requirements while maintaining the necessary fidelity of the data. The mapping for each vector may or may not have memory in the sense of depending on past actions of the coder, just as in well established scalar techniques such as PCM, which has no memory, and predictive quantization, which does. Even though information theory implies that one can always obtain better performance by coding vectors instead of scalars, scalar quantizers have remained by far the most common data compression system because of their simplicity and good performance when the communication rate is sufficiently large. In addition, relatively few design techniques have existed for vector quantizers.

During the past few years several design algorithms have been developed for a variety of vector quantizers and the performance of these codes has been studied for speech waveforms, speech linear predictive parameter vectors, images, and several simulated random processes. It is the purpose of this article to survey some of these design techniques and their applications.

DATA compression is the conversion of a stream of analog or very high rate discrete data into a stream of relatively low rate data for communication over a digital communication link or storage in a digital memory. As digital communication and secure communication have become increasingly important, the theory and practice of data compression have received increased attention. While it is true that in many systems bandwidth is relatively inexpensive, e.g., fiber optic and cable TV links, in most systems the growing amount of information that users wish to communicate or store necessitates some form of compression for efficient, secure, and reliable use of the communication or storage medium.

A prime example arises with image data, where simple schemes require bit rates too large for many communication links or storage devices. Another example where compression is required results from the fact that if speech is digitized using a simple PCM system consisting of a sampler followed by scalar quantization, the resulting signal will no longer have a small enough bandwidth to fit on ordinary telephone channels. That is, digitization (which may be desirable for security or reliability) causes bandwidth expansion. Hence data compression will be required if the original communication channel is to be used.

The two examples of image compression and speech compression or, as they are often called, image coding and speech coding, are probably the currently most important applications of data compression. They are also among the most interesting for study because experience has shown that both types of data exhibit sufficient structure to permit considerable compression with sufficiently sophisticated codes.

Such conversion of relatively high rate data to lower rate data virtually always entails a loss of fidelity or an increase in distortion. Hence a fundamental goal of data compression is to obtain the best possible fidelity for the given rate or, equivalently, to minimize the rate required for a given fidelity. If a system has a sufficiently high rate constraint, then good fidelity is relatively easy to achieve and techniques such as PCM, transform coding, predictive coding, and adaptive versions of these techniques have become quite popular because of their simplicity and good performance [1, 2, 3]. All of these techniques share a fundamental property: The actual quantization or coding or conversion of continuous quantities into discrete quantities is done on scalars, e.g., on individual real-valued samples of waveforms or pixels of images. PCM does this in a memoryless fashion; that is, each successive input is encoded using a rule that does not depend on any past inputs or outputs of the encoder. Transform coding does it by first taking block transforms of a vector and then scalar coding the coordinates of the transformed vector. Predictive coding does it by quantizing an error term formed as the difference between the new sample and a prediction of the new sample based on past coded outputs.

A fundamental result of Shannon's rate-distortion theory, the branch of information theory devoted to data compression, is that better performance can always be achieved by coding vectors instead of scalars, even if the data source is memoryless, e.g., consists of a sequence of independent random variables, or if the data compression system can have memory, i.e., the action of an encoder at each time is permitted to depend on past encoder inputs or outputs [4, 5, 6, 7, 8]. While some traditional compression schemes such as transform coding operate on vectors and achieve significant improvement over PCM, the quantization is still accomplished on scalars and hence these systems are, in a Shannon sense, inherently suboptimal: better performance is always achievable *in theory* by coding vectors instead of scalars, even if the scalars have been produced by preprocessing the original input data so as to make them uncorrelated or independent!

This theory had a limited impact on actual system design because 1) the Shannon theory does not provide constructive design techniques for vector coders, and 2) traditional scalar coders often yield satisfactory performance with enough adaptation and fine tuning. As a result, few design techniques for vector quantizers were considered in the literature prior to the late 1970's when it was found that a simple algorithm of Lloyd [9] for the iterative design of scalar quantization or PCM systems extended in a straightforward way to the design of memoryless vector quantizers, that is, of vector quantizers which encode successive input vectors in a manner not depending on previous encoder input vectors or their coded outputs. Variations of the basic algorithm have since proved useful for the design of vector quantizers with and without memory for a variety of data sources including speech waveforms, speech parameter vectors, images, and several random process models, the latter being useful for gauging the performance of the resulting codes with the optimal performance bounds of information theory.

This paper is intended as a survey of the basic design algorithm and many of its variations and applications. We begin with the simplest example of a memoryless vector quantizer, a vector generalization of PCM. For convenience we use the shorthand VQ for both vector quantization and vector quantizer. Necessary properties of optimal quantizers are described and an algorithm given which uses these properties to iteratively improve a code. For concreteness, we focus on two examples of distortion measures: the ubiquitous mean-squared error and the Itakura-Saito distortion. The first example, which is popular in waveform coding applications, provides a geometric flavor to the development; the second example, which is useful in voice coding applications, helps to demonstrate the generality and power of the technique.

Next, various techniques are described for designing the initial codes required by the algorithm. These techniques also indicate some useful structure that can be imposed on vector quantizers to make them more implementable. Several variations of the basic VQ are described which permit reduced complexity or memory or both at the expense of a hopefully tolerable loss of performance. These include tree-searched codes, product codes, and multistep codes.

We then turn from memoryless vector quantizers to those with memory: feedback vector quantizers such as vector predictive quantizers and finite-state vector quantizers. These codes are not yet well understood, but they possess a structure highly suited to VLSI implementation and initial studies suggest that they offer significant performance gains.

For comparison, we also briefly describe trellis encoding systems or "lookahead" or "delayed decision" or "multipath search" codes which use the same decoder as a feedback vector quantizer but which permit the encoder to base its decision on a longer input data sequence.

A final general code structure is described which uses vector quantization to adapt a waveform coder, which may be another VQ.

We next present a variety of simulation results describing the performance of various VQ systems on various data sources. Examples of all of the above VQ varieties are tested for waveform coding applications on two common data sources: a Gauss Markov source and real sampled speech. One bit per sample coders for these sources are compared on the basis of performance, memory requirements, and computational complexity. Both memoryless and simple feedback vector quantizers are studied for voice coding applications at a rate of 0.062 bits/sample and less and for image coding at a rate of 0.5 bit per sample. One example is given of a simple adaptive predictive vector quantizer for speech waveform coding.

By studying a variety of coding systems on common data sources, the results yield some general comparisons and trends among the various vector quantization techniques. The reader should, however, keep two caveats in mind when interpreting such quantitative results: First, the emphasis here is on low bit rate systems, e.g., speech coders using 1 bit per sample or less and image coders ½ bit per pixel. Comparisons favoring certain systems at such low rates may not be valid for the same systems at higher rates. Second, the numbers reported here are intended to provide comparisons for different systems used on common data sources; they can be compared with other numbers reported in the literature only with great care: the input data and the system design parameters such as sampling rate and pre- or post-filtering may be quite different.

Applications of vector quantization to real data sources such as sampled speech waveforms and images are still young and the algorithms do not yet incorporate the sophisticated "bells and whistles" of many well-established scalar quantization schemes. The preliminary experiments described here, using fairly simple vector quantizers with and without memory, demonstrate that the general approach holds considerable promise for some applications. For example, good quality vocoding systems using VQ and the Itakura-Saito distortion have been developed at 800 bits per second, a significant reduction in the bit rate previously required for comparable quality [10]. While the compression achieved so far in waveform coding and image coding applications using the squared-error distortion has not yet been as significant, we believe that it has yielded comparable or better performance at low rates than traditional scalar schemes of greater complexity. The quality of the ½ bit per pixel images shown here is promising given the simplicity of the coding scheme used.

We attempt to use the minimum of mathematics and a maximum of English in the presentation so as to focus on the intuitive ideas underlying the design and operation of vector quantizers. The detailed descriptions of the various algorithms can be found in the cited references. The reader is also referred to a recent tutorial by Gersho and Cuperman [11] which presents a brief overview of VQ applied to speech waveform coding.

MEMORYLESS VECTOR QUANTIZERS

In this section we introduce the basic definition of memoryless vector quantizers, their properties, and an algorithm for their design.

Quantization

Mathematically, a k-dimensional memoryless vector quantizer or, simply, a VQ (without modifying adjectives) consists of two mappings: an encoder γ which assigns to each input vector $\mathbf{x} = (x_0, x_1, \cdots, x_{k-1})$ a channel symbol $\gamma(\mathbf{x})$ in some channel symbol set $\mathbf{M}$, and a decoder β assigning to each channel symbol v in $\mathbf{M}$ a value in a reproduction alphabet $\hat{\mathbf{A}}$. The channel symbol set is often assumed to be a space of binary vectors for convenience, e.g., $\mathbf{M}$ may be the set of all 2^R binary R-dimensional vectors. The reproduction alphabet may or may not be the same as the input vector space; in particular, it may consist of real vectors of a different dimension.

If $\mathbf{M}$ has M elements, then the quantity $R = \log_2 M$ is called the *rate* of the quantizer in bits per vector and $r = R/k$ is the rate in bits per symbol or, when the input is a sampled waveform, bits per sample.

The application of a quantizer to data compression is depicted in the standard Fig. 1. The input data vectors might be consecutive samples of a waveform, consecutive parameter vectors in a voice coding system, or consecutive rasters or subrasters in an image coding system. For integer values of R it is useful to think of the channel symbols, the encoded input vectors, as binary R-dimensional vectors. As is commonly done in information and communication theory, we assume that the channel is noiseless, that is, that $U_n = \hat{U}_n$. While real channels are rarely noiseless, the joint source and channel coding theorem of information theory implies that a good data compression system designed for a noiseless channel can be combined with a good error correction coding system for a noisy channel in order to produce a complete system. In other words, the assumption of a noiseless channel is made simply to focus on the problem of data compression system design and not to reflect any practical model.

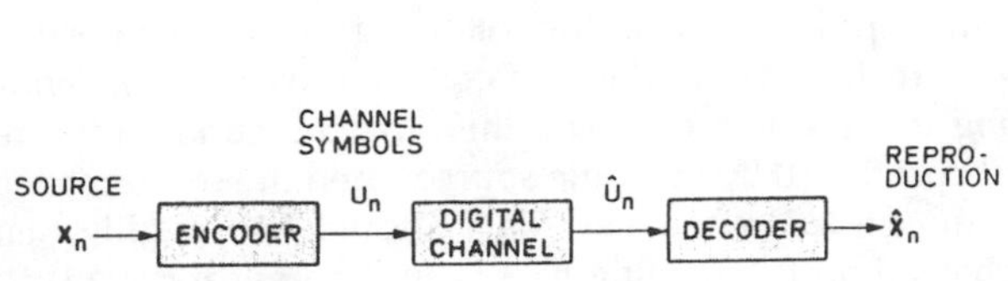

Figure 1. Data Compression System. The data or information source $\{X_n; n = 0, 1, \ldots\}$ is a sequence of random vectors. The encoder produces a sequence of channel symbols $\{U_n; n = 0, 1, 2, \ldots\}$. The sequence $\{\hat{U}_n; n = 0, 1, 2, \ldots\}$ is delivered to the receiver by the digital channel. The decoder then maps this sequence into the final reproduction sequence of vectors $\{\hat{X}_n; n = 0, 1, 2, \ldots\}$.

Observe that unlike scalar quantization, general VQ permits fractional rates in bits per sample. For example, scalar PCM must have a bit rate of at least 1 bit per sample while a k dimensional VQ can have a bit rate of only $1/k$ bits per sample by having only a single binary channel symbol for k-dimensional input vectors.

The goal of such a quantization system is to produce the "best" possible reproduction sequence for a given rate R. To quantify this idea, to define the performance of a quantizer, and to complete the definition of a quantizer, we require the idea of a distortion measure.

Distortion

A distortion measure d is an assignment of a cost $d(\mathbf{x}, \hat{\mathbf{x}})$ of reproducing any input vector $\mathbf{x}$ as a reproduction vector $\hat{\mathbf{x}}$. Given such a distortion measure, we can quantify the performance of a system by an average distortion $Ed(\mathbf{X}, \hat{\mathbf{X}})$ between the input and the final reproduction: A system will be good if it yields a small average distortion. In practice, the important average is the long term sample average or time average

$$\lim_{n\to\infty} \frac{1}{n} \sum_{i=0}^{n-1} d(\mathbf{X}_i, \hat{\mathbf{X}}_i) \tag{1}$$

provided, of course, that the limit makes sense. If the vector process is stationary and ergodic, then, with probability one, the limit exists and equals an expectation $E(d(\mathbf{X}, \hat{\mathbf{X}}))$. For the moment we will assume that such conditions are met and that such long term sample averages are given by expectations. Later remarks will focus on the general assumptions required and their implications for practice.

Ideally a distortion measure should be tractable to permit analysis, computable so that it can be evaluated in real time and used in minimum distortion systems, and subjectively meaningful so that large or small quantitative distortion measures correlate with bad and good subjective quality. Here we do not consider the difficult and controversial issues of selecting a distortion measure; we assume that one has been selected and consider means of designing systems which yield small average distortion. For simplicity and to ease exposition, we focus on two important specific examples:

(1) *The squared error distortion measure:* Here the input and reproduction spaces are k-dimensional Euclidean space

$$d(\mathbf{x}, \hat{\mathbf{x}}) = \|\mathbf{x} - \hat{\mathbf{x}}\|^2 = \sum_{i=0}^{k-1} (x_i - \hat{x}_i)^2,$$

the square of the Euclidean distance between the vectors. This is the simplest distortion measure and the most common for waveform coding. While not subjectively meaningful in many cases, generalizations permitting input-dependent weightings have proved useful and only slightly more complicated. For the squared-error distortion it is common practice to measure the performance of a system by the signal-to-noise ratio (or signal-to-quantization-noise ratio)

$$SNR = 10 \log_{10} \frac{E(\|X\|^2)}{E[d(X, \hat{X})]}.$$

This corresponds to normalizing the average distortion by the average energy and plotting it on a logarithmic scale: Large (small) SNR corresponds to small (large) average distortion.

(2) *The (modified) Itakura-Saito distortion:* This distortion measure is useful in voice coding applications where the receiver is sent a linear model of the underlying voice production process. The distortion measure is based on the "error matching measure" developed in the pioneering work of Itakura and Saito on the PARCOR or LPC approach to voice coding [12]. More generally, this distortion measure is a special case of a minimum relative entropy or discrimination measure; VQ using such distortion measures can be viewed as an application of the minimum relative entropy pattern classification technique introduced by Kullback [13] as an application of information theory to statistical pattern classification. (See also [14,15].)

We here introduce a minimum of notation to present a definition of the Itakura-Saito distortion measure. Details and generalizations may be found in [16,17,14,15]. Here the input vector can again be considered as a collection of consecutive waveform samples. Now, however, the output vectors have the form $\hat{\mathbf{x}} = (\alpha, a_1, a_2, \cdots, a_p)$, where α is a positive gain or residual energy term and where the a_i with $a_0 = 1$ are inverse filter coefficients in the sense that if

$$A(z) = \sum_{i=0}^{p} a_i z^{-i}$$

then the all-pole filter with z-transform $1/A(z)$ is a stable filter. Here the reproduction vectors may be thought of as all-pole models for synthesizing the reproduction at the receiver using a locally generated noise or periodic source, in other words, as the filter portion of a linear predictive coding (LPC) model in a vocoding (voice coding) system. The Itakura-Saito distortion between the input vector and the model can be defined in the time domain as

$$d(\mathbf{x}, \hat{\mathbf{x}}) = \frac{\mathbf{a}^t \mathbf{R}(\mathbf{x}) \mathbf{a}}{\alpha} - \ln \frac{\alpha_p(\mathbf{x})}{\alpha} - 1,$$

where $\mathbf{a}^t = (1, a_1, \cdots, a_p)$, $\mathbf{R}(\mathbf{x})$ is the $(p + 1) \times (p + 1)$ sample autocorrelation matrix of the input vector $\mathbf{x}$, and where $\alpha_p(\mathbf{x})$ is an input gain (residual energy) term defined as the minimum value of $\mathbf{b}^t \mathbf{R}(\mathbf{x}) \mathbf{b}$, where the minimum is taken over all vectors $\mathbf{b}$ with first component equal to 1. There are many equivalent forms of the distortion measure, some useful for theory and some for computation. Frequency domain forms show that minimizing the above distortion can be interpreted as trying to match the sample spectrum of the input vector to the power spectral density of the linear all-pole model formed by driving the filter with z-transform $1/A(z)$ by white noise with constant power spectral density $\sqrt{\alpha}$.

The above formula for the distortion is one of the simplest, yet it demonstrates that the distortion measure is indeed complicated—it is not a simple function of an error vector, it is not symmetric in its input and output arguments, and it is not a metric or distance. Because of the intimate connection of this distortion measure with LPC vocoding techniques, we will refer to VQ's designed using this distortion measure as LPC VQ's.

Average distortion

As the average distortion quantifies the performance of a system and since we will be trying to minimize this quantity using good codes, we pause to consider what the average means in theory and in practice.

As previously noted, in practice it is the long term sample average of (1) that we actually measure and which we would like to be small. If the process is stationary and ergodic, then this limiting time average is the same as the mathematical expectation. The mathematical expectation is useful for developing information theoretic performance bounds, but it is often impossible to calculate in practice because the required probability distributions are not known, e.g., there are no noncontroversial generally accepted accurate probability distributions for real speech and image data. Hence a pragmatic approach to system design is to take long sequences of training data, estimate the "true" but unknown expected distortion by the sample average, and attempt to design a code that minimizes the sample average distortion for the training sequence. If the input source is indeed stationary and ergodic, the resulting sample average should be nearly the expected value and the same code used on future data should yield approximately the same averages [18].

The above motivates a training sequence based design for stationary and ergodic data sources. In fact, even if the "true" probability distributions are known as in the case of a Gauss Markov source, the training sequence approach reduces to a standard Monte Carlo approach.

An immediate objection to the above approach, however, is whether or not it makes sense for real sources which may be neither stationary nor ergodic. The answer is an emphatic "yes" in the following sense: The desired property is that if we design a code based on a *sufficiently long* training sequence and then use the code on future data produced by the same source, then the performance of the code on the new data should be roughly that achieved on the training data. The theoretical issue is to provide conditions under which this statement can be made rigorous. For reasonable distortion measures, a sufficient condition for this to be true for memoryless VQ design is that the source be asymptotically mean stationary, it need not be either stationary nor ergodic [19,20,21,22,23]. Asymptotically mean stationary sources include all stationary sources, block (or cyclo) stationary sources, and asymptotically stationary sources. Processes such as speech which exhibit distinct short term and long term stationarity properties are well modeled by asymptotically mean stationary sources [21].

The key point here is that the general design approach using long training sequences does not require either ergodicity nor stationarity to have a solid mathematical foundation. In fact, the mathematics suggest the following pragmatic approach: Try to design a code which minimizes the sample average distortion for a very long training sequence. Then use the code on test sequences produced by the same source, but not in the training sequence. If the performance is reasonably close to the design values, then one can have a certain amount of confidence that the code will continue to yield roughly the same performance in the future. If the training and test performance are significantly different, then probably the training sequence is not sufficiently long. In other words, do not try to prove mathematically that a source is asymptotically mean stationary, instead try to design codes for it and then see if they work on new data.

Henceforth for brevity we will write expectations with the assumption that they are to be interpreted as shorthand for long term sample averages. (A sample average $L^{-1} \sum_{i=0}^{L-1} d(\mathbf{X}_i, \hat{\mathbf{X}}_i)$ is, in fact, an expectation with respect to the sample distribution which assigns a probability of $1/L$ to each vector in the training sequence.)

Properties of optimal quantizers

A VQ is optimal if it minimizes an average distortion $Ed\{\mathbf{X}, \beta[\gamma(\mathbf{X})]\}$. Two necessary conditions for a VQ to be optimal follow easily using the same logic as in Lloyd's [9] classical development for optimal PCM with a mean-squared error distortion measure. The following definition is useful for stating these properties: The collection of possible reproduction vectors $C = \{\text{all } \mathbf{y} : \mathbf{y} = \beta(v), \text{ some } v \text{ in } \mathbf{M}\}$ is called the *reproduction codebook* or, simply, *codebook* of the quantizer and its members called *codewords* (or templates). The encoder knows the structure of the decoder and hence all of the possible final output codewords.

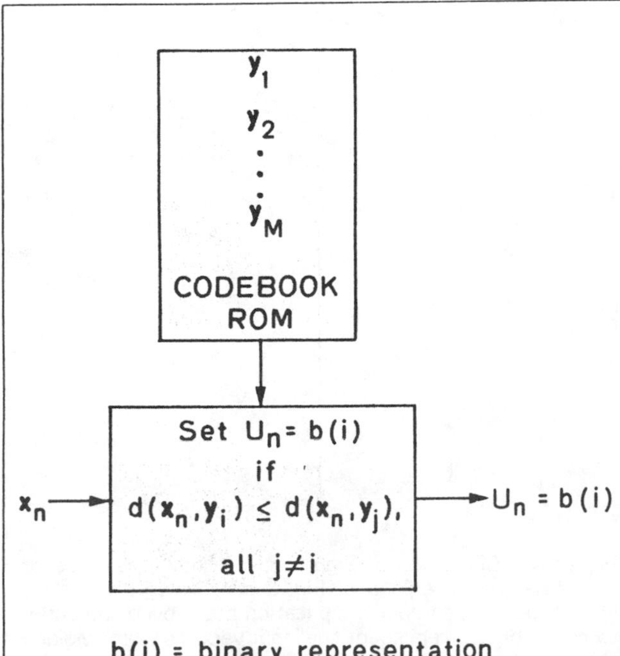

Figure 2. VQ Encoder. The distortion between the input vector and each stored codeword is computed. The encoded output is then the binary representation of the index of the minimum distortion codeword.

Property 1: Given the goal of minimizing the average distortion and given a specific decoder β, no memoryless quantizer encoder can do better than select the codeword v in $\mathbf{M}$ that will yield the minimum possible distortion at the output, that is, to select the channel symbol v yielding the minimum

$$d\{\mathbf{x}, \beta[\gamma(\mathbf{x})]\} = \min_{v \in \mathbf{M}} d[\mathbf{x}, \beta(v)] = \min_{y \in C} d(\mathbf{x}, y). \qquad (2)$$

That is, for a given decoder in a memoryless vector quantizer the best encoder is a minimum distortion or nearest neighbor mapping

$$\gamma(\mathbf{x}) = \min_{v \in \mathbf{M}}{}^{-1} d[\mathbf{x}, \beta(v)], \qquad (3)$$

where the inverse minimum notation means that we select the v giving the minimum of (2).

Gersho [24] calls a quantizer with a minimum distortion encoder a Voronoi quantizer since the Voronoi regions about a set of points in a space correspond to a partition of that space according to the nearest-neighbor rule. The word quantizer, however, is practically always associated with such a minimum distortion mapping. We observe that such a vector quantizer with such a minimum distortion encoder is exactly the Shannon model for a block source code subject to a fidelity criterion which is used in information theory to develop optimal performance bounds for data compression systems.

An encoder γ can be thought of as a partition of the input space into cells where all input vectors yielding a common reproduction are grouped together. Such a partition according to a minimum distortion rule is called a Voronoi or Dirichlet partition. A general minimum distance VQ encoder is depicted In Fig. 2.

A simple example of such a partition and hence of an encoder is depicted in Fig. 3 (a more interesting example follows shortly). Observe that this vector quantizer is just two uses of a scalar quantizer in disguise.

As the minimum distortion rule optimizes the encoder of a memoryless VQ for a decoder, we can also optimize the decoder for a given encoder.

Property 2: Given an encoder γ, then no decoder can do better than that which assigns to each channel symbol v the generalized centroid (or center of gravity or barycenter) of all source vectors encoded into v, that is,

$$\beta(v) = cent(v) = \min_{\hat{x} \in \hat{A}}{}^{-1} E(d(\mathbf{X}, \hat{\mathbf{x}}) \mid \gamma(\mathbf{X}) = v), \qquad (4)$$

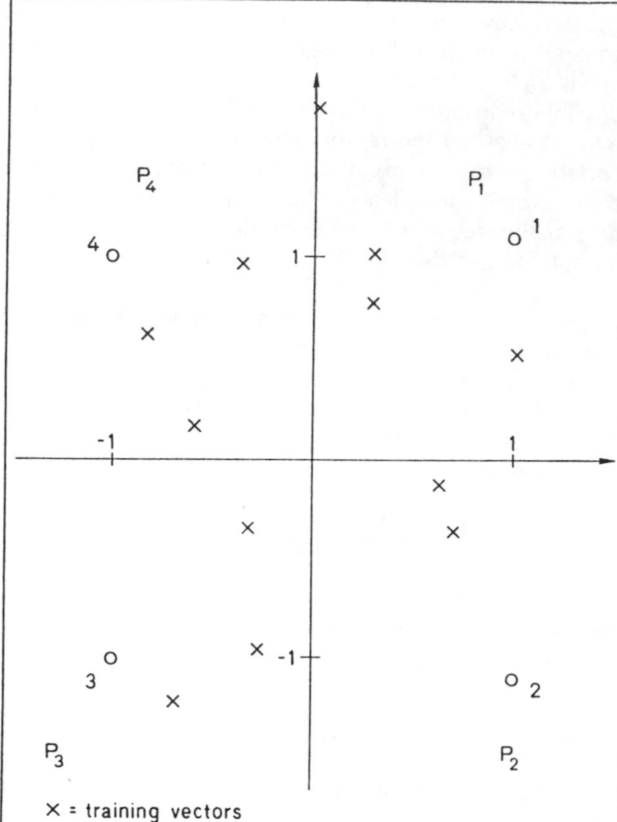

Figure 3. Two-Dimensional Minimum Distortion Partition. The four circles are the codewords of a two-dimensional codebook. The Voronoi regions are the quadrants containing the circles. The x's were produced by a training sequence of twelve two-dimensional Gaussian vectors. Each input vector is mapped into the nearest-neighbor codeword, that is, the circle in the same quadrant.

that is, $\beta(v)$ is the vector yielding the minimum conditional average distortion given that the input vector was mapped into v.

While minimizing such a conditional average may be quite difficult for an arbitrary random process and distortion measure, it is often easy to find for a sample distribution and a nice distortion measure. For example, the centroid in the case of a sample distribution and a squared-error distortion measure is simply the ordinary Euclidean centroid or the vector sum of all input vectors encoded into the given channel symbol, that is, given the sample distribution defined by a training sequence $\{\mathbf{x}_i;\ i = 0, 1, \ldots, L-1\}$, then

$$cent(v) = \frac{1}{i(v)} \sum_{\mathbf{x}_i : \gamma(\mathbf{x}_i) = v} x_i ,$$

where $i(v)$ is the number of indices i for which $\gamma(\mathbf{x}_i) = v$.

The Euclidean centroids of the example of Fig. 3 are depicted in Fig. 4. (The numerical values may be found in [25].) The new codewords better represent the training vectors mapping into the old codewords, but they yield a different minimum distortion partition of the input alphabet, as indicated by the broken line in Fig. 3. This is the key of the algorithm: iteratively optimize the codebook for the old encoder and then use a minimum distortion encoder for the new codebook.

The Itakura-Saito distortion example is somewhat more complicated, but still easily computable. As with the squared error distortion, one groups all input vectors yielding a common channel symbol. Instead of averaging the vectors, however, the sample autocorrelation matrices for all of the vectors are averaged. The centroid is then given by the standard LPC all-pole model for this average autocorrelation, that is, the centroid is found by a standard Levinson's recursion run on the average autocorrelation.

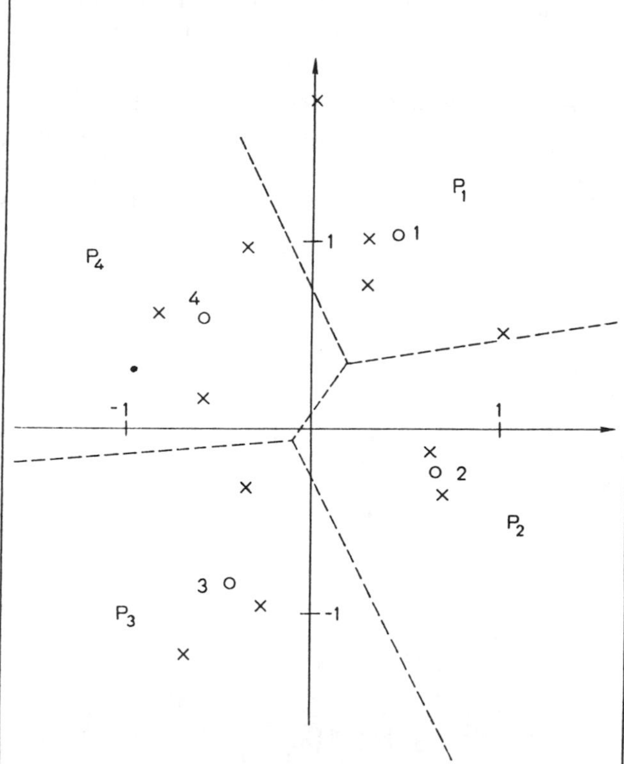

Figure 4. Centroids of Figure 3. The new centroids of the old Voronoi regions of Fig. 3 are drawn as circles. Note that the centroid computation has moved the codewords to better represent the input vectors which yielded those codewords, that is, if one used the same encoder (as in Fig. 3), but replaced the reproduction codewords produced at the decoder by these new centroids, the average distortion would decrease. The broken line delineates the new Voronoi regions for these codewords.

The generalized Lloyd algorithm

The fact that the encoder can be optimized for the decoder and vice versa formed the basis of Lloyd's original optimal PCM design algorithm for a scalar random variable with a known probability density function and a squared error distortion. The general VQ design algorithms considered here are based on the simple observation that Lloyd's basic development is valid for vectors, for sample distributions, and for a variety of distortion measures. The only requirement on the distortion measure is that one can compute the centroids. The basic algorithm is the following:

Step 0. Given: A training sequence and an initial decoder.

Step 1. Encode the training sequence into a sequence of channel symbols using the given decoder minimum distortion rule. If the average distortion is small enough, quit.

Step 2. Replace the old reproduction codeword of the decoder for each channel symbol v by the centroid of all training vectors which mapped into v in Step 1. Go to Step 1.

Means of generating initial decoders will be considered in the next section. Each step of the algorithm must either reduce average distortion or leave it unchanged. The algorithm is usually stopped when the relative distortion decrease falls below some small threshold. The algorithm was developed for vector quantizers, training sequences, and general distortion measures by Linde, Buzo, and Gray [25] and it is sometimes referred to as the LBG algorithm. Previously Lloyd's algorithm had been considered for vectors and difference distortion measures in cluster analysis and pattern recognition problems (e.g., MacQueen [26] and Diday and Simon [27]) and in two-dimensional quantization (e.g., Chen [28] and Adoul *et al.* [29]). Only recently, however, has it been extensively studied for vector quantization applications using several different distortion measures.

Before continuing, it should be emphasized that such iterative improvement algorithms need not in general yield truly optimum codes. It is known that subject to some mathematical conditions the algorithm will yield locally optimum quantizers, but in general there may be numerous such codes and many may yield poor performance. (See, e.g., [30].) It is often useful, therefore, to enhance the algorithm's potential by providing it with good initial codebooks and perhaps by trying it on several different initial codebooks.

INITIAL CODEBOOKS

The basic design algorithm of the previous section is an iterative improvement algorithm and requires an initial code to improve. Two basic approaches have been developed: One can start with some simple codebook of the correct size or one can start with a simple small codebook and recursively construct larger ones.

"Random" codes

Perhaps the simplest example of the first technique is that used in the k-means variation of the algorithm [26]: Use the first 2^R vectors in the training sequence as the initial codebook. An obvious modification more natural for highly correlated data is to select several widely spaced words from the training sequence. This approach is sometimes called random code generation, but we avoid this nomenclature because of its confusion with the random code techniques of information theory which are used to prove the performance bounds.

Product codes

Another example of the first approach is to use a scalar code such as a uniform quantizer k times in succession and then prune the resulting vector codebook down to the correct size. The mathematical model for such a code is a product code, which we pause to define for current and later use: Say we have a collection of codebooks C_i, $i = 0, 1, \ldots, m-1$, each consisting of M_i vectors of dimension k_i and having rate $R_i = \log_2 M_i$ bits per vector. Then the *product codebook* C is defined as the collection of all $M = \Pi_i M_i$ possible concatenations of m words drawn successively from the m codebooks C_i. The dimension of the product codebook is $k = \sum_{i=0}^{m-1} k_i$, the sum of the dimensions of the component codebooks. The product code is denoted mathematically as a Cartesian product:

$$C = \mathop{\times}_{i=0}^{m-1} C_i = \{\textit{all vectors of the form } (\hat{\mathbf{x}}_0, \hat{\mathbf{x}}_1, \cdots, \hat{\mathbf{x}}_{m-1});\ \hat{\mathbf{x}}_i \textit{ in } C_i;\ i = 0, 1, \ldots, m-1\}$$

Thus, for example, using a scalar quantizer with rate R/k k times in succession yields a product k-dimensional vector quantizer of rate R bits per vector. This product code can be used as an initial code for the design algorithm. The scalar quantizers may be identical uniform quantizers with a range selected to match the source, or they may be different, e.g., a positive codebook for a gain and uniform quantizers for $[-1, 1]$ for reflection coefficients in an LPC VQ system.

In waveform coding applications where the reproduction and input alphabets are the same—k-dimensional Euclidean space—an alternative product code provides a means of growing better initial guesses from smaller dimensional codes [31]. Begin with a scalar quantizer C_0 and use a two-dimensional product code $C_0 \times C_0$ as an initial guess for designing a two-dimensional VQ. On completion of the design we have a two-dimensional code, say C^2. Form an initial guess for a three dimensional code as all possible pairs from C^2 and scalars from C_0, that is, use the product code $C^2 \times C_0$ as an initial guess. Continuing in this way, given a good $k-1$ dimensional VQ described by a codebook C^{k-1}, an initial guess for a k-dimensional code design is the product code $C^{k-1} \times C_0$. One can also use such product code constructions with a different initial scalar code C_0, such as those produced by the scalar version of the next algorithm.

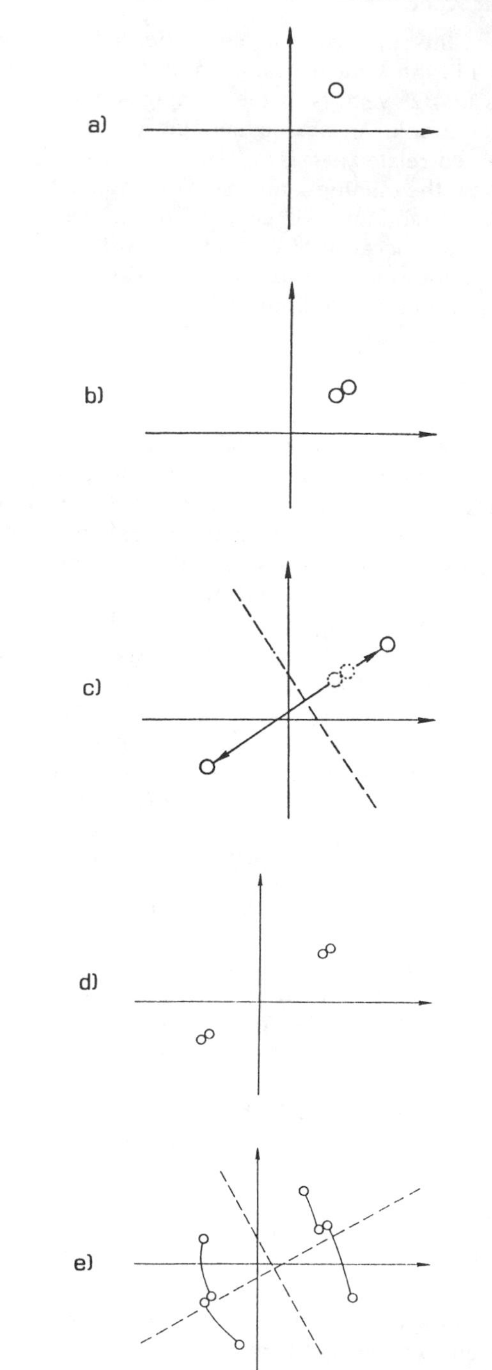

Figure 5. Splitting. A large code is defined in stages: at each stage each codeword of a small code is split into two new codewords, giving an initial codebook of twice the size. The algorithm is run to get a new better codebook. (a) Rate 0: The centroid of the entire training sequence. (b) Initial Rate 1: The one codeword is split to form an initial guess for a two word code. (c) Final Rate 1: The algorithm produces a good code with two words. The dotted line indicates the Voronoi regions. (d) Initial Rate 2: The two words are split to form an initial guess for a four word code. (e) Final Rate 2: The algorithm is run to produce a final four word code.

Splitting

Instead of constructing long codes from smaller dimensional codes, we can construct a sequence of bigger codes having a fixed dimension using a "splitting" technique [25, 16]. This method can be used for any fixed dimension, including scalar codes. Here one first finds the optimum 0 rate code — the centroid of the entire training sequence, as depicted in Fig. 5a for a two-dimensional input alphabet. This single codeword is then split to form two codewords (Fig. 5b). For example, the energy can be perturbed slightly to form a second distinct word or one might purposefully find a word distant from the first. It is convenient to have the original codeword a member of the new pair to ensure that the distortion will not increase. The algorithm is then run to get a good rate 1 bit per vector code as indicated in Fig. 5c. The design continues in this way in stages as shown: the final code of one stage is split to form an initial code for the next.

VARIATIONS OF MEMORYLESS VECTOR QUANTIZERS

In this section we consider some of the variations of memoryless vector quantization aimed at reducing the computation or memory requirements of a full search memoryless VQ.

Tree-searched VQ

Tree-searched vector quantizers were first proposed by Buzo *et al.* [16] and are a natural byproduct of the splitting algorithm for generating initial code guesses. We focus on the case of a binary tree for simplicity, but more general trees will provide better performance while retaining a significant reduction in complexity.

Say that we have a good rate 1 code as in Fig. 5c and we form a new rate two code by splitting the two codewords as in Fig. 5d. Instead of running a full search VQ design on the resulting 4-word codebook, however, we divide the training sequence into two pieces, collecting together all those vectors encoded into a common word in the 1 bit codebook, that is, all of the training sequence vectors in a common cell of the Voronoi partition. For each of these subsequences of training vectors, we then find a good 1-bit code using the algorithm. The final codebook (so far) consists of the four codewords in the two 1-bit codebooks designed for the two subsequences. A tree-searched encoder selects one of the words not by an ordinary full search of this codebook, but instead it uses the first one bit codebook designed on the whole sequence to select a second code and it then picks the best word in the second code. This encoder can then be used to further subdivide the training sequence and construct even better codebooks for the subsequences. The encoder operation can be depicted as a tree in Fig. 6.

The tree is designed one layer at a time; each new layer being designed so that the new codebook available from each node is good for the vectors encoded into the node. Observe that there are 2^R possible reproduction vectors as in the full search VQ, but now R binary searches are made instead of a single 2^R-ary search. In addition, the encoder

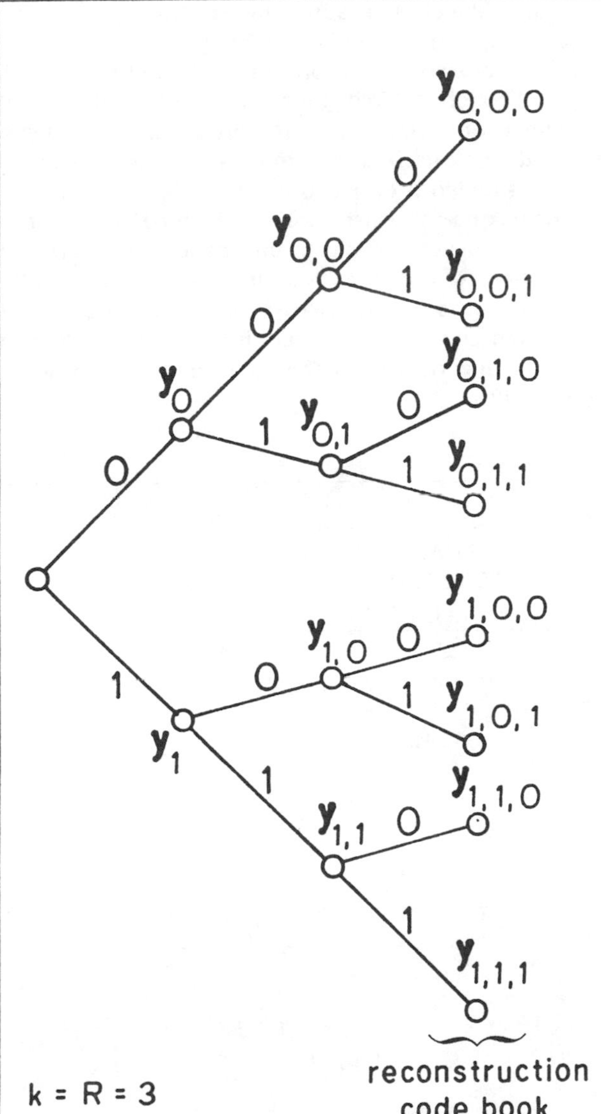

Figure 6. Tree-Searched VQ. A binary encoder tree is shown for a three-dimensional one bit per sample VQ. The encoder makes a succession of R minimum distortion choices from binary codebooks, where the available codebook at each level consists of labels of the nodes in the next level. The labels of the nodes of the final layer are the actual reproduction codewords. At each node the encoder chooses the minimum distortion available label and, if the new index is a 0 (1), sends a channel symbol of 0 (1) and advances up (down) to the next node. After R binary selections the complete channel codeword has been sent and the reproduction codeword specified to the decoder.

storage requirements have doubled. The encoder is no longer optimal for the decoder in the sense of Property 1 since it no longer can perform an exhaustive search of the codebook. The search, however, is much more efficient if done sequentially than is a full search. Thus one may trade performance for efficiency of implementation.

Nonbinary trees can also be used where at the ith layer codebooks of rate R_i are used and the overall rate is then $\Sigma_i R_i$. For example, a depth three tree for VQ of LPC parameter vectors using successive rates of 4, 4, and 2 bits per vector yields performance nearly as good as a full search VQ of the same total rate of 10 bits per vector, yet for the tree search one need only compute $2^4 + 2^4 + 2^2 = 36$ distortions instead of $2^{10} = 1028$ distortions [10].

Other techniques can be used to design tree-searched codes. For example, Adoul *et al.* [32] use a separating hyperplane approach. Another approach is to begin with a full search codebook and to design a tree-search into the codebook. One technique for accomplishing this is to first group the codewords into close disjoint pairs and then form the centroids of the pairs as the node label of the immediate ancestor of the pair. One then works backwards through the tree, always grouping close pairs. Ideally, one would like a general design technique for obtaining a tree search into an arbitrary VQ codebook with only a small loss of average distortion. Gersho and Cheng [33] have reported preliminary results for designing a variable-length tree search for an arbitrary codebook and have demonstrated its implementability for several small dimensional examples.

Multistep VQ

A multistep VQ is a tree-searched VQ where only a single small codebook is stored for each layer of the tree instead of a different codebook for each node of each layer. Such codes provide the computation reduction of tree-searched codes while reducing the storage requirements below that of even ordinary VQ's. The first example of such a code was the multistage codebook [34]. For simplicity we again confine interest to codes which make a sequence of binary decisions. The first layer binary code is designed as in the tree-searched case. This codebook is used to encode the training sequence and then a training sequence of error or residual vectors is formed. For waveform coding applications the error vectors are simply the difference of the input vectors and their codewords. For vocoding applications, the error vectors are residuals formed by passing the input waveform through the inverse filter $A(z)/\alpha$. The algorithm is then run to design a binary VQ for this vector training sequence of coding errors. The reconstruction for these two bits is then formed by combining the two codewords: For waveform coding this is accomplished by adding the first codeword to the error codeword. For voice coding this is accomplished by using the cascade of two all-pole filters for synthesis. This reproduction can then be used to form a "finer" error vector and a code designed for it. Thus an input vector is encoded in stages as with the tree-searched code, but now only R binary codebooks and hence $2R$ total codewords need to be stored. Observe that there are still 2^R possible final codewords, but we have not needed this much storage because the code can be constructed by adding different combinations of a smaller set of words. A multistage VQ is depicted in Fig. 7.

Product codes

Another useful structure for a memoryless VQ is a prod-

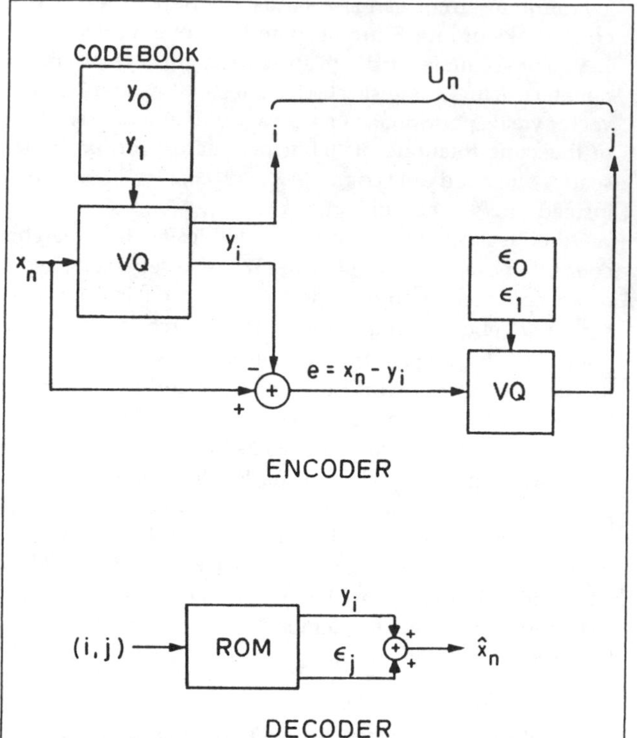

Figure 7. Multistage VQ with 2 Stages. The input vector is first encoded by one VQ and an error vector is formed. The second VQ then encodes the error vector. The two channel symbols from the two VQ's together form the complete channel symbol for the entire encoder. The decoder adds together the corresponding reproduction vectors.

uct code. In one extreme, multiple use of scalar quantizers is equivalent to product VQ's and are obviously simple to implement. More general product VQ's, however, may permit one to take advantage of the performance achievable by VQ's while still being able to achieve the higher rates required for good fidelity. In addition, such codes may yield a smaller computational complexity than an ordinary VQ of the same rate and performance (but different dimension). The basic technique is useful when there are differing aspects of the input vector that one might wish to code separately because of different effects, e.g., on dynamic range or finite word length implementation.

Gain/shape VQ

One example of a product code is a gain/shape VQ where separate, but interdependent, codes are used to code the "shape" and "gain" of the waveform, where the "shape" is defined as the original input vector normalized by removal of a "gain" term such as energy in a waveform coder or LPC residual energy in a vocoder. Gain/shape encoders were introduced by Buzo *et al.* [16] and were subsequently extended and optimized by Sabin and Gray [35, 36]. A gain/shape VQ for waveform coding with a squared-error distortion is illustrated in Fig. 8.

Figure 8 sketches the surprising fact that for the squared error case considered, the two-step selection of the product codeword is an optimal encoding for the given product codebook. We emphasize that here the encoder is optimal for the given product codebook or decoder, but the codebook itself is in general suboptimal because of the constrained product form. A similar property holds for the Itakura-Saito distortion gain/shape VQ. Thus in this case if one devotes R_s bits to the shape and R_g bits to the gain, where $R_s + R_g = R$, then one need only compute 2^{R_s} vector distortions and an easy scalar quantization. The full search encoder would require 2^R vector distortions, yet both encoders yield the same minimum distortion codeword!

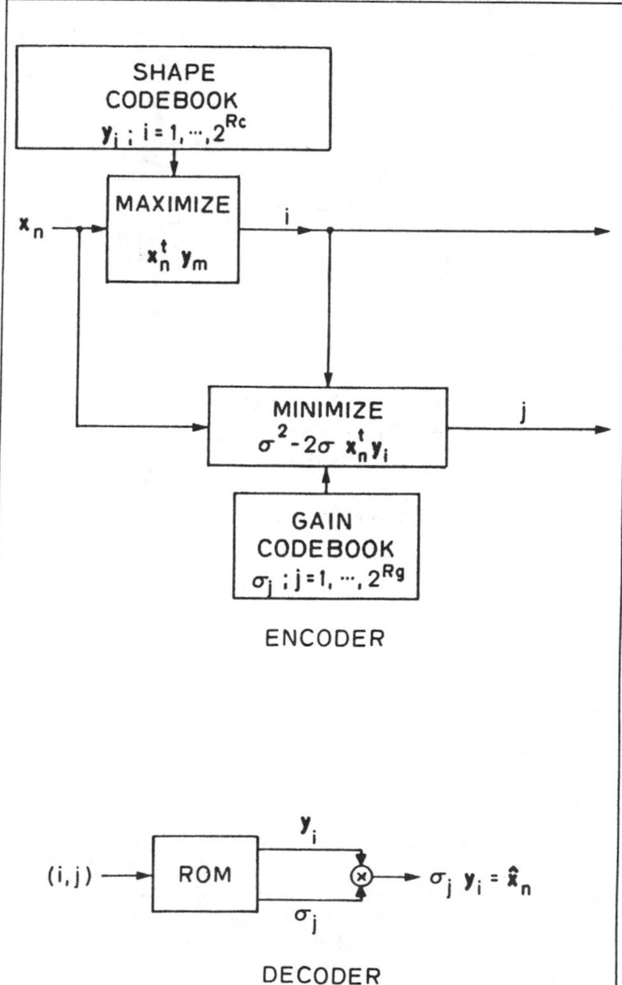

Figure 8. Gain/Shape VQ. First a unit energy shape vector is chosen to match the input vector by maximizing the inner product over the codewords. Given the resulting shape vector, a scalar gain codeword is selected so as to minimize the indicated quantity. The encoder yields the product codeword $\sigma_j y_i$ with the minimum possible squared error distortion from the input vector. Thus this multistep encoder is optimum for the product codebook.

Variations of the basic VQ algorithm can be used to iteratively improve a gain shape code by alternately optimizing the shape for the gain and vice versa. The resulting conditional centroids are easy to compute. The centroid updates can be made either simultaneously or alternately after each iteration [36].

One can experimentally determine the optimal bit allocation between the gain and the shape codebooks.

Separating mean VQ

Another example of a multistep product code is the separating mean VQ where a sample mean instead of an energy term is removed [37]. Define the sample mean $\langle \mathbf{x} \rangle$ of a k-dimensional vector by $k^{-1} \sum_{i=0}^{k-1} x_i$. In a separated mean VQ one first uses a scalar quantizer to code the sample mean of a vector, then the coded sample mean is subtracted from all of the components of the input vector to form a new vector with approximately zero sample mean. This new vector is then vector quantized. Such a system is depicted in Fig. 9. The basic motivation here is that in image coding the sample mean of pixel intensities in a small rectangular block represents a relatively slowly varying average background value of pixel intensity around which there are variations.

To design such a VQ, first use the algorithm to design a scalar quantizer for the sample mean sequence $\langle \mathbf{x}_j \rangle$, $j = 0,1,\ldots,L-1$. Let $q(\langle \mathbf{x} \rangle)$ denote the reproduction for $\langle \mathbf{x} \rangle$ using the quantizer. Then use the vector training sequence $\mathbf{x}_j - q(\langle \mathbf{x}_j \rangle)\mathbf{1}$, where $\mathbf{1} = (1,1,\ldots,1)$, to design a VQ for the difference. Like the gain/shape VQ, a product codebook and a multistep encoder are used, but unlike the gain/shape VQ it can be shown that the multistep encoder here does not select the best possible mean, shape pair, that is, the multistep encoder is not equivalent to a full search encoder.

Lattice VQ

A final VQ structure capable of efficient searches and memory usage is the lattice quantizer, a k-dimensional generalization of the scalar uniform quantizer. A lattice in k-dimensional space is a collection of all vectors of the form $\mathbf{y} = \sum_{i=0}^{n-1} a_i \mathbf{e}_i$, where $n \le k$, where $\mathbf{e}_0, \ldots, \mathbf{e}_{n-1}$ are a set of linearly independent vectors in $\mathbf{R}^k$, and where the a_i are arbitrary integers. A lattice quantizer is a quantizer whose codewords form a subset of a lattice. Lattice quantizers were introduced by Gersho [38] and the performance and efficient coding algorithms were developed for many particular lattices by Conway and Sloane [39, 40, 41] and Barnes and Sloane [42]. The disadvantage of lattice quantizers is that they cannot be improved by a variation of the Lloyd algorithm without losing their structure and good quantizers produced by the Lloyd algorithm cannot generally be well approximated by lattices. Lattice codes can work well on source distributions that are approximately uniform over a bounded region of space. In fact, lattices that are asymptotically optimal in the limit of large rate are known for this case in two and three dimensions and good lattices are known for dimensions up to 16.

Ideally, one would like to take a full search, unconstrained VQ and find some fast means of encoding having complexity more like the above techniques than that of the full search. For example, some form of multidimensional companding followed by a lattice quantizer as suggested by Gersho [24] would provide both good performance and efficient implementation. Unfortunately, however, no design methods accomplishing this goal have yet been found.

FEEDBACK VECTOR QUANTIZERS

Memory can be incorporated into a vector quantizer in a simple manner by using different codebooks for each input vector, where the codebooks are chosen based on past input vectors. The decoder must know which codebook is being used by the encoder in order to decode the channel symbols. This can be accomplished in two ways: 1) The encoder can use a codebook selection procedure that depends only on past encoder outputs and hence the codebook sequence can be tracked by the decoder. 2) The decoder is informed of the selected codebook via a special low-rate side channel. The first approach is called feedback vector quantization and is the

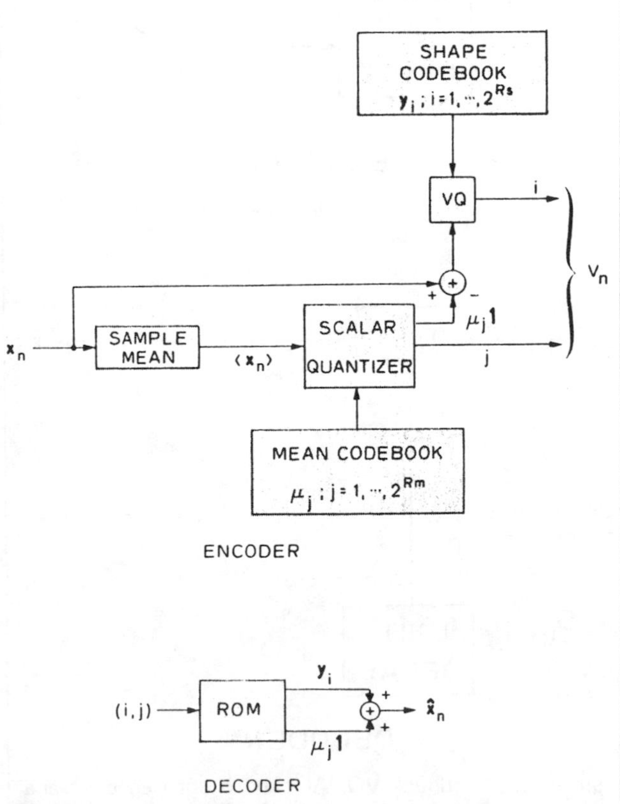

Figure 9. Separating Mean VQ. The sample mean of the input vector is computed, scalar quantized, and then subtracted from each component of the input vector. The resulting vector with approximately zero sample mean is then vector quantized. The decoder adds the coded sample mean to all components of the coded shape vector.

topic of this section. The name follows because the encoder output is "fed back" for use in selecting the new codebook. A feedback vector quantizer can be viewed as the vector extension of a scalar adaptive quantizer with backward estimation (AQB) [3]. The second approach is the vector extension of a scalar adaptive quantizer with forward estimation (AQF) and is called simply adaptive vector quantization. Adaptive VQ will be considered in a later section. Observe that systems can combine the two techniques and use both feedback and side information. We also point out that unlike most scalar AQB and AQF systems, the vector analogs considered here involve no explicit estimation of the underlying densities.

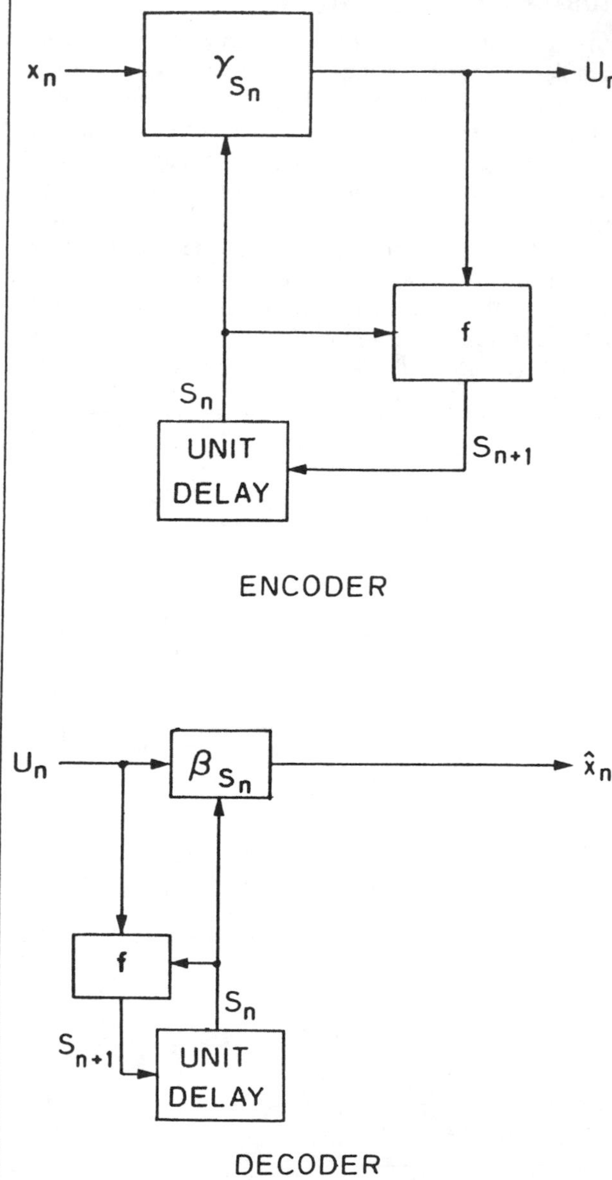

Figure 10. Feedback VQ. At time n both encoder and decoder are in a common state S_n. The encoder uses a state VQ γ_{S_n} to encode the input vector and then selects a new state for the next input vector. Knowing the VQ used and the resulting channel symbol, the decoder can produce the correct reproduction. Note that the state VQ's may be computed at each time from some rule or, if they are small in number, simply stored separately.

It should be emphasized that the results of information theory imply that VQ's with memory can do no better than memoryless VQ's in the sense of minimizing average distortion for a given rate constraint. In fact, the basic mathematical model for a data compression system in information theory is exactly a memoryless VQ and such codes can perform arbitrarily close to the optimal performance achievable using any data compression system. The exponential growth of computation and memory with rate, however, may result in nonimplementable VQ's. A VQ with memory may yield the desired distortion with practicable complexity.

A general feedback VQ can be described as follows [22]: Suppose now that we have a space **S** whose members we shall call states and that for each state s in **S** we have a separate quantizer: an encoder γ_s, decoder β_s, and codebook C_s. The channel codeword space **M** is assumed to be the same for all of the VQ's. Consider a data compression system consisting of a sequential machine such that if the machine is in state s, then it uses the quantizer with encoder γ_s and decoder β_s. It then selects its next state by a mapping called a next-state function or state-transition function f such that given a state s and a channel symbol v, then $f(v, s)$ is the new state of the machine. More precisely, given a sequence of input vectors $\{\mathbf{x}_n;\ n = 0, 1, 2, \ldots\}$ and an initial state s_0, then the subsequent state sequence s_n, channel symbol sequence v_n, and reproduction sequence $\hat{\mathbf{x}}_n$ are defined recursively for $n = 0, 1, 2, \ldots$ as

$$v_n = \gamma_{s_n}(\mathbf{x}_n), \qquad \hat{\mathbf{x}}_n = \beta_{s_n}(v_n), \qquad s_{n+1} = f(v_n, s_n). \quad (5)$$

Since the next state depends only on the current state and the channel codeword, the decoder can track the state if it knows the initial state and the channel sequence. A general feedback vector quantizer is depicted in Fig. 10. The freedom to use different quantizers based on the past without increasing the rate should permit the code to perform better than a memoryless quantizer of the same dimension and rate.

An important drawback of all feedback quantizers is that channel errors can accumulate and cause disastrous reconstruction errors. As with scalar feedback quantizer systems, this must be handled by periodic resetting or by error control or by a combination of the two.

If the state space is finite, then we shall call the resulting system a finite-state vector quantizer or FSVQ. For an FSVQ, all of the codebooks and the next-state transition table can all be stored in ROM, making the general FSVQ structure amenable to LSI or VLSI implementation [43].

Observe that a memoryless vector quantizer is simply a feedback vector quantizer or finite-state vector quantizer with only a single state. The general FSVQ is a special case of a tracking finite state source coding system [44] where the encoder is a minimum distortion mapping.

Three design algorithms for feedback vector quantizers using variations on the generalized Lloyd algorithm have been recently developed. The remainder of this section is devoted to brief descriptions of these techniques.

Vector predictive quantization

Cuperman and Gersho [45, 46] proposed a vector predictive coder or vector predictive quantizer (VPQ) which is a vector generalization of DPCM or predictive quantization. A VPQ is sketched in Fig. 11. For a fixed predictor, the VQ design algorithm is used to design a VQ for the prediction error sequence. Cuperman and Gersho considered several variations on the basic algorithm, some of which will be later mentioned.

Chang [47] developed an extension to Cuperman and Gersho's algorithm which begins with their system and then uses a stochastic gradient algorithm to iteratively improve the vector linear predictor coefficients, that is, to better match the predictor to the quantizer. The stochastic gradient algorithm is used only in the design of the system, not as an on line adaptation mechanism as in the adaptive gradient algorithms of, e.g., Gibson *et al.* [48] and Dunn [49]. A scalar version of this algorithm for improving the predictor for the quantizer was developed in unpublished work of Y. Linde.

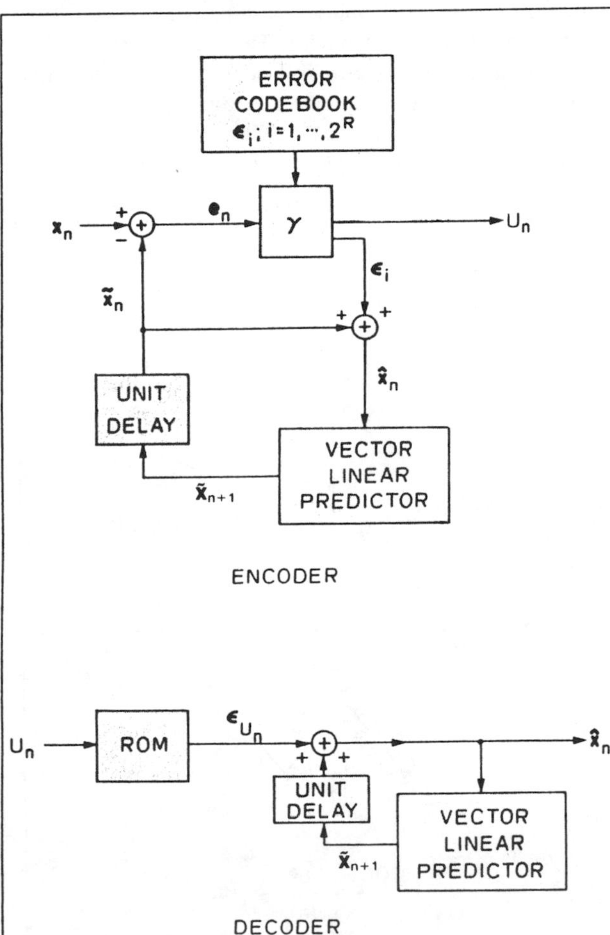

Figure 11. Vector Predictive Quantization. A linear vector predictor for the next input vector of a process given the previous input vector is applied to the previous reproduction of the input vector. The resulting prediction is subtracted from the current input vector to form an error vector which is vector quantized. The decoder uses a copy of the encoder and the received encoded error vectors to construct the reproduction.

Product/multistep FVQ

A second basic approach for designing feedback vector quantizers which is quite simple and works quite well is to use a product multistep VQ such as the gain/shape VQ or the separating mean VQ and use a simple feedback quantizer on the scalar portion and an ordinary memoryless VQ on the remaining vector. This approach was developed in [10] for gain/shape VQ of LPC parameters and in [37] for separating mean VQ of images. Both efforts used simple scalar predictive quantization for the feedback quantization of the scalar terms.

FSVQ

The first general design technique for finite-state vector quantizers was reported by Foster and Gray [50, 51]. There are two principal design components: 1. Design an initial set of state codebooks and a next-state function using an *ad hoc* algorithm. 2. Given the next-state function, use a variation of the basic algorithm to attempt to improve the state codebooks. The second component is accomplished by a slight extension of the basic algorithm that is similar to the extension of [52] for the design of trellis encoders: Encode the data using the FSVQ and then replace all of the reproduction vectors by the centroids of the training vectors which map into those vectors; now, however, the centroids are conditioned on both the channel symbol and the state. While such conditional averages are likely impossible to compute analytically, they are easily computed for a training sequence. For example, in the case of a squared error distance one simply forms the Euclidean centroid of all input vectors which correspond to the state s and channel symbol v in an encoding of the training sequence.

As with ordinary VQ, replacing the old decoder or codebook by centroids cannot yield a code with larger distortion. Unlike memoryless VQ, however, replacing the old encoder by a minimum distortion rule for the new decoder can in principal cause an increase in distortion and hence now the iteration is somewhat different: Replace the old encoder (which is a minimum distortion rule for the old decoder) by a minimum distortion rule for the new decoder. If the distortion goes down, then continue the iteration and find the new centroids. If the distortion goes up, then quit with the encoder being a quantizer for the previous codebook and the decoder being the centroids for the encoder. By construction this algorithm can only improve performance. It turns out, however, that in practice it is a good idea to not stop the algorithm if the distortion increases slightly, but to let it continue: it will almost always eventually drop back down in distortion and converge to something better.

The first design component is more complicated. We here describe one of the more promising approaches of [51] called the omniscient design approach. Say that we wish to design an FSVQ with K states and rate R bits per vector. For simplicity we label the states as 0 through K-1. First use the training sequence to design a memoryless VQ with K codewords, one for each state. We shall call these codewords state labels and this VQ the state quantizer. We call the output of the state VQ the "ideal next state" instead of a channel symbol. Next break up the training sequence into subsequences as follows: Encode the training sequence using the state VQ and for each state s collect all of training vectors which *follow* the occurrence of this state label. Thus for s the corresponding training subsequence consists of all input vectors that occur when the *current* ideal state is s. Use the basic algorithm to design a rate R codebook C_s for the corresponding training sequence for each s.

The resulting state VQ and the collection of codebooks for each state have been designed to yield good performance in the following communication system: The encoder is in an ideal state s chosen by using the state VQ on the last input vector. The encoder uses the corresponding VQ encoder γ_s described by the codebook C_s. The output of γ_s is the channel symbol. In order to decode the channel symbol, the decoder must also know the ideal state. Unfortunately, however, this ideal state cannot be determined from knowledge of the initial state and all of the received channel symbols. Thus the decoder must be omniscient in the sense of knowing this additional side information in order to be able to decode. In particular, this system is not an FSVQ by our definition. We can use the state quantizer and the various codebooks, however, to construct an FSVQ by approximating the omniscient system: Instead of forming the ideal next state by using the state VQ on the actual input vector (as we did in the design procedure), use the state VQ on the current reproduction vector in order to choose the next state. This will yield a state sequence depending only on encoder outputs and the original state and hence will be trackable by the decoder. This is analogous to the scalar practice of building a predictive coder and choosing the predictor as if it knew the past inputs, but in fact applying it to past reproductions.

Combining the previously described steps of (1) initial (state label) codebook design, (2) state codebooks and next-state function design, and (3) iterative improvement of code for given next-state function, provides a complete design algorithm.

In addition to the above design approach, techniques have been developed for iterating on (2) and (3) above in the sense of optimizing the next-state function for a given collection of codebooks. These algorithms, however, are more complicated and require ideas from the theory of adaptive stochastic automata. The reader is referred to [53] for a discussion of these improvement algorithms.

VECTOR TREE AND TRELLIS ENCODERS

As with scalar feedback quantizers, the actions of the decoder of a feedback VQ can be depicted as a directed graph or tree. A simple example is depicted in Fig. 12, where a merged tree or trellis can be drawn since the feedback VQ has only a finite number of states.

Instead of using the ordinary VQ encoder which is only permitted to look at the current input vector in order to decide on a channel symbol, one could use algorithms such as the Viterbi algorithm, M-algorithm or M,L-algorithm, Fano algorithm, or stack algorithm for a minimum cost search through a directed graph and search several levels ahead into the tree or trellis before choosing a channel symbol. This introduces an additional delay into the encoding of several vectors, but it ensures better long run average distortion behavior. This technique is called tree or trellis encoding and is also referred to as look-ahead coding, delayed decision coding, and multipath search coding. (See, e.g., [54, 52] for surveys.) We point out that a tree encoding system uses a tree to denote the

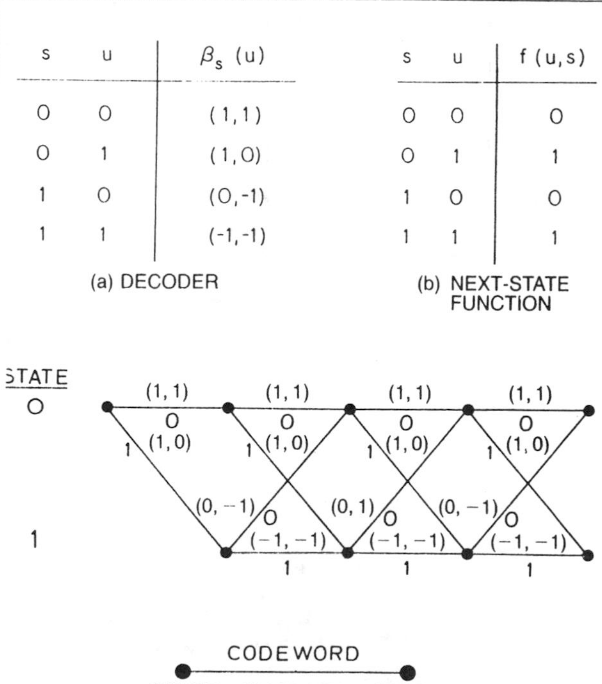

s	u	β_s (u)
0	0	(1,1)
0	1	(1,0)
1	0	(0,-1)
1	1	(-1,-1)

s	u	f (u,s)
0	0	0
0	1	1
1	0	0
1	1	1

Figure 12. Decoder trellis for a two state 1 bit per vector two dimensional waveform coder. The trellis depicts the possible state transitions for the given next-state function. The transitions are labeled by the corresponding decoder output (in parentheses) and channel symbol produced by the encoder.

operation on successive vectors by the decoder at successive times while a tree-searched VQ uses a tree to construct a fast search for a single vector at a single time.

A natural variation of the basic algorithm for designing FSVQ's can be used to design trellis encoding systems: Simply replace the FSVQ encoder which finds the minimum distortion reproduction for a single input vector by a Viterbi or other search algorithm which searches the decoder trellis to some fixed depth to find a good long term minimum distortion path. The centroid computation is accomplished exactly as with an FSVQ: each branch or transition label is replaced by the centroid of all training vectors causing that transition, that is, the centroid conditioned on the decoder state and channel symbol. Scalar and simple two dimensional vector trellis encoding systems were designed in [52] using this approach.

Trellis encoding systems are not really vector quantization systems as we have defined them since the encoder is permitted to search ahead to determine the effect on the decoder output of several input vectors while a vector quantizer is restricted to search only a single vector ahead. The two systems are intimately related, however, and a trellis encoder can always be used to improve the performance of a feedback vector quantizer. Very little work has yet been done on vector trellis encoding systems.

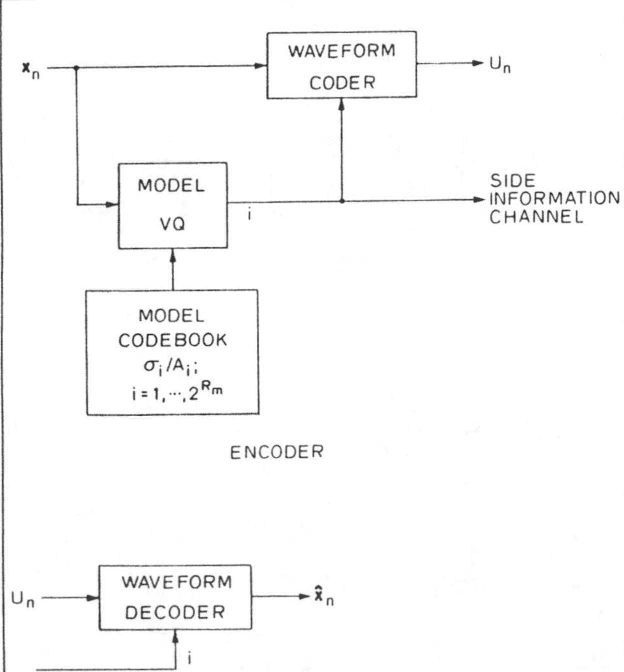

Figure 13. Adaptive VQ. The model VQ uses the Itakura-Saito distortion to select an LPC model to fit the input frame of many sample vectors. This selection in turn determines the waveform coder used to digitize the sample vectors. A side channel then informs the receiver which decoder to use on the channel symbols produced by the waveform coder.

ADAPTIVE VQ

As a final class of VQ we consider systems that use one VQ to adapt a waveform coder, which might be another VQ. The adaptation information is communicated to the receiver via a low rate side information channel.

The various forms of vector quantization using the Itakura-Saito family of distortion measures can be considered as model classifiers, that is, they fit an all-pole model to an observed sequence of sampled speech. When used alone in an LPC VQ system, the model is used to synthesize the speech at the receiver. Alternatively, one could use the model selected to choose a waveform coder designed to be good for sampled waveforms that produce that model. For example, analogous to the omniscient design of FSVQ one could design separate VQ's for the subsequences of the training sequence encoding into common models. Both the model index and the waveform coding index are then sent to the receiver. Thus LPC VQ can be used to adapt a waveform coder, possibly also a VQ or related system. This will yield a system typically of much higher rate, but potentially of much better quality since the codebooks can be matched to local behavior of the data. The general structure is shown in Fig. 13. The model VQ typically operates on a much larger vector of samples and at a much lower rate in bits per sample than does the waveform coder and hence the bits spent on specifying the model through the side channel are typically much fewer than those devoted to the waveform coder.

There are a variety of such possible systems since both the model quantizer and the waveform quantizer can take on many of the structures so far considered. In addition, as in speech recognition applications [55] the gain-independent variations of the Itakura-Saito distortion measure which either normalize or optimize gain may be better suited for the model quantization than the usual form. Few such systems have yet been studied in detail. We here briefly describe some systems of this type that have appeared in the literature to exemplify some typical combinations. All of them use some form of memoryless VQ for the model quantization, but a variety of waveform coders are used.

The first application of VQ to adaptive coding was by Adoul, Debray, and Dalle [32] who used an LPC VQ to choose a predictor for use in a scalar predictive waveform coder. Vector quantization was used only for the adaptation and not for the waveform coding. An adaptive VQ generalization of this system was later developed by Cuperman and Gersho [45, 46] who used an alternative classification technique to pick one of three vector predictors and then used those predictors in a predictive vector quantizer. The predictive vector quantizer design algorithm previously described was used, except now the training sequence was broken up into subsequences corresponding to the selected predictor and a quantizer was designed for each resulting error sequence. Chang [47] used a similar scheme with an ordinary LPC VQ as the classifier and with a stochastic gradient algorithm run on each of the vector predictive quantizers in order to im-

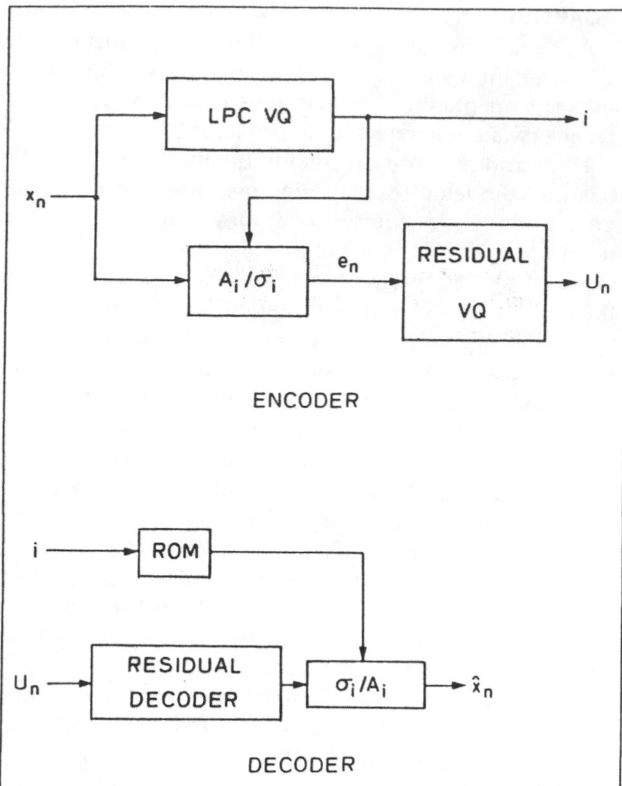

Figure 14. RELP VQ. An LPC VQ is used for model selection and a single VQ to waveform encode the residuals formed by passing the original waveform through the inverse filter $A/\sqrt{\alpha}$. The side information specifies to the decoder which of the model filters $\sqrt{\alpha}/A$ should be used for synthesis.

prove the prediction coefficients for the corresponding codebooks.

Rebolledo *et al.* [56] and Adoul and Mabilleau [57] developed vector residual excited linear predictive (RELP) systems. (See Fig. 14.) A similar system employing either a scalar or a simple vector trellis encoder for the waveform coder was developed by Stewart *et al.* [52]. Both of these systems used the basic algorithm to design both the model VQ and the waveform coders.

The RELP VQ systems yielded disappointingly poor performance at low bit rates. Significantly better performance was achieved by using the residual codebooks produced in the RELP design to construct codebooks for the original waveform, that is, instead of coding the model and the residual, code the model and use the selected model to construct a waveform coder for the original waveform as depicted in Fig. 15 [52]. For lack of a better name, this system might be called an inverted RELP because it uses residual codebooks to drive an inverse model filter in order to get a codebook for the original waveform.

Yet another use of LPC VQ to adapt a waveform coder was reported by Heron, Crochiere, and Cox [58] who used a subband/transform coder for the waveform coding and used the side information to adapt the bit allocation for the scalar parameter quantizers.

Many other variations on the general theme are possible and the structure is a promising one for processes such as speech that exhibit local stationarity, that is, slowly varying short term statistical behavior. The use of one VQ to partition a training sequence in order to design good codes for the resulting distinct subsequences is an intuitive approach to the computer-aided design of adaptive data compression systems.

EXAMPLES

We next consider the performance of various forms of vector quantizers on three popular guinea pigs: Gauss Markov sources, speech waveforms, and images. For the speech coding example we consider both waveform coders using the squared error distortion measure and vocoders using the Itakura-Saito distortion. The caveats of the introduction should be kept in mind when interpreting the results.

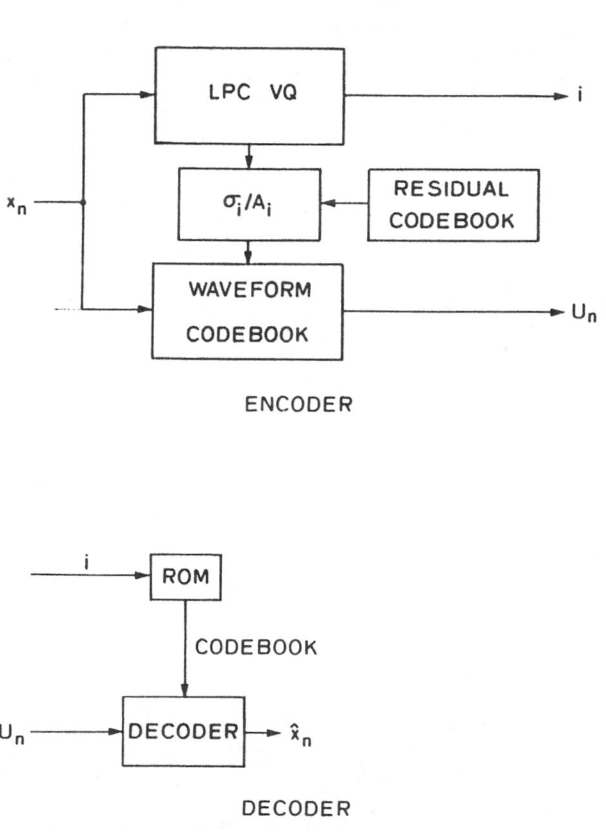

Figure 15. Inverted RELP. An LPC VQ is used to select a model filter σ/A. A waveform codebook is then formed by driving the model filter with all possible residual codewords from a RELP VQ design. Thus, unlike a RELP system, the original waveform (and not a residual) is matched by possible reproduction codewords.

The performance of the systems are given by SNR's for squared error and by an analogous quantity for the Itakura-Saito distortion: In both cases we measure normalized average distortion on a logarithmic scale, where the normalization is by the average distortion of the optimum zero rate code — the average distortion between the input sequence and the centroid of the entire input sequence. This quantity reduces to an SNR in the squared error case and provides a useful dimensionless normalized average distortion in general. We call this quantity the SNR in both cases. The SNR is given in tables instead of graphs in order to facilitate quantitative comparisons among the coding schemes.

TABLE I

MEMORYLESS VQ FOR A GAUSS MARKOV SOURCE.

	VQ			TSVQ			MVQ			G/SVQ		
k	SNR	n	M	SNR	n	M	SNR	n	M	SNR	n	M
1	4.4	2	2	4.4	2	2	4.4	2	2			
2	7.9	4	8	7.9	4	12	7.6	4	8	7.9	1	3
3	9.2	8	24	9.2	6	42	8.6	6	18	9.3	1	5
4	10.2	16	64	10.2	8	120	8.4	8	32	9.4	2	10
5	10.6	32	160	10.4	10	310	9.3	10	50	9.8	3	17
6	10.9	64	384	10.7	12	756	9.1	12	72	9.9	4	26
7	11.2	128	896	11.0	14	1778	9.4	14	98	10.2	4	31
8							9.9	16	128	10.6	5	43
9										10.9	6	57

Signal to Noise Ratios (SNR), number of multiplications per sample (n), and storage requirements of memoryless vector quantizers: full search memoryless VQ (VQ), binary tree-searched (TSVQ), binary multistage VQ (MVQ), and gain/shape VQ (G/SVQ). Rate = 1 bit/sample. k = vector dimension. Training Sequence = 60000 samples from a Gauss Markov Source with correlation coefficient 0.9.

TABLE II

FEEDBACK VQ OF A GAUSS MARKOV SOURCE.

	FSVQ1				FSVQ2				VPQ		
k	SNR	K	n	M	SNR	K	n	M	SNR	n	M
1	10.0	64	2	64	9.5	16	2	16	10.0	2	2
2	10.8	256	4	512	10.8	32	4	64	11.2	4	8
3	11.4	512	8	1536	11.1	64	8	192	11.6	8	24
4	12.1	512	16	2048	11.3	128	16	512	11.6	16	64

Signal to Noise Ratios (SNR), number of states (K), number of multiplications per sample (n), and storage (M) for feedback quantizers: FSVQ with number of states increased until negligible change (FSVQ1), FSVQ with fewer states (FSVQ2), VPQ. Rate = 1 bit/sample. k = vector dimension. Training Sequence = 60000 samples from a Gauss Markov Source with correlation coefficient 0.9.

Gauss Markov sources

We first consider the popular guinea pig of a Gauss Markov source. This source is useful as a mathematical model for some real data sources and its information theoretic optimal performance bounds as described by the distortion-rate function are known. For this example we consider only the squared error distortion. A Gauss Markov source or a first order Gauss autoregressive source $\{X_n\}$ is defined by the difference equation $X_{n+1} = aX_n + W_n$, where $\{W_n\}$ is a zero mean, unit variance, independent and identically distributed Gaussian source. We here consider the highly correlated case of $a = 0.9$ and vector quantizers of 1 bit/sample. The maximum achievable SNR as given by Shannon's distortion-rate function for this source and rate is 13.2 dB [7].

Various design algorithms were used to design vector quantizers for several dimensions for this source. Table I describes the results of designing several memoryless vector quantizers for a training sequence of 60,000 samples. Given are the design SNR (code performance on the training sequence), the number of multiplications per sample required by the encoder, and the number of real scalars that must be stored for the encoder codebook. The number of multiplications is used as a measure of encoder complexity because it is usually the dominant computation and because the number of additions required is usually comparable. It is given by n = (the number of codewords searched) × (dimension)/(dimension) = the number of codewords searched. The actual storage required depends on the number of bytes used to store each floating point number. Many (but not all) of the final codes were subsequently tested on different test sequences of 60,000 samples. In all cases the open test SNR's were within .25 dB of the design distortion. The systems considered are full search VQ's [25], binary tree-searched VQ's [59], binary multistage VQ's [47], and gain/shape VQ's [36]. The gain and codebook sizes for the gain/shape codes were experimentally optimized.

As expected, the full search VQ yields the best performance for each dimension, but the tree-searched VQ is not much worse and has a much lower complexity. The multistage VQ is noticeably inferior, losing more than 1 dB at the higher dimensions, but its memory requirements are small. The gain/shape VQ compares poorly on the basis of performance vs. rate for a fixed dimension, but it is the best code in the sense of providing the minimum distortion for a fixed complexity and rate.

For larger rates and lower distortion the relative merits may be quite different. For example, the multistage VQ is then capable of better performance relative to the ordinary VQ since the quantization errors in the various stages do not accumulate so rapidly. (See, e.g., [34].) Thus in this

TABLE III

MEMORYLESS VQ OF SAMPLED SPEECH.

	VQ				TSVQ			
k	SNRin	SNRout	n	M	SNRin	SNRout	n	M
1	2.0	2.1	2	2	2.0	2.1	2	2
2	5.2	5.3	4	8	5.1	5.1	4	12
3	6.1	6.0	8	24	5.5	5.5	6	42
4	7.1	7.0	16	64	6.4	6.4	8	120
5	7.9	7.6	32	160	7.1	6.9	10	310
6	8.5	8.1	64	384	7.9	7.5	12	756
7	9.1	8.4	128	896	8.3	7.8	14	1778
8	9.7	8.8	256	2048	8.9	8.0	16	4080

	MVQ				G/SVQ			
k	SNRin	SNRout	n	M	SNRin	SNRout	n	M
1	2.0	2.1	2	2				
2	4.3	4.4	4	8				
3	4.3	4.4	6	18	4.5	4.6	4	14
4	4.4	4.5	8	32	6.0	6.1	4	20
5	5.0	5.0	10	50	7.2	6.9	8	44
6	5.0	4.9	12	72	7.7	7.4	16	100
7	5.3	5.1	14	98	8.2	7.7	16	120
8	5.6	5.5	16	128	8.8	8.1	32	264
9					9.3	8.5	64	584
10					9.8	8.9	128	1288
11					10.4	9.3	256	2824

Signal to Noise Ratios inside training sequence (SNRin) of 640000 speech samples, Signal to Noise Ratios outside training sequence (SNRout) of 76800 speech samples, number of multiplications per sample (n), and storage requirements of memoryless vector quantizers: full search memoryless VQ (VQ), binary tree-searched (TSVQ), binary multistage VQ (MVQ), and gain/shape VQ (G/SVQ). Rate = 1 bit/sample. k = vector dimension.

case multistage VQ may be far better because if its much smaller computational requirements.

Table II presents results for three feedback VQ's for the same source. In addition to the parameters of Table I, the number of states for the FSVQ's are given. The first FSVQ and the VPQ were designed for the same training sequence of 60,000 samples. Because of the extensive computation required and the shortness of the training sequence for a feedback quantizer, only dimensions 1 through 4 were considered. The first FSVQ was designed using the omniscient design approach for 1 bit per sample, dimensions 1 through 4, and a variety of numbers of states. For the first example, the number of states was chosen by designing FSVQ's for more and more states until firther increases yielded negligible improvements [51]. It was found, however, that the performance outside of the training sequence for these codes was significantly inferior, by 1 to 2 dB for the larger dimensions. From the discussion of average distortion, this suggests that the training sequence was too short. Hence the second FSVQ design (FSVQ2) was run with a larger training sequence of 128,000 samples and fewer states. The test sequence for these codes always yielded performance within .3 dB of the design value. The VPQ test performance with within .1 dB of the design performance. The scalar predictive quantizer performance and the codebook for the prediction error quantizer are the same as the analytically optimized predictive quantization system of Arnstein [60] run on the same data.

Observe that the scalar FSVQ in the first experiment with 64 states yielded performance quite close to that of the scalar VPQ, which does not have a finite number of states. Intuitively the FSVQ is trying to approximate the infinite state machine by using a large number of states. The VPQ, however, is less complex and requires less memory and hence for this application is superior.

For comparison, the best 1 bit/sample scalar trellis encoding system for this source yields 11.25 dB for this source [52]. The trellis encoding system uses a block Viterbi algorithm with a search depth of 1000 samples for the encoder. It is perhaps surprising that in this example the VPQ and the FSVQ with the short delay of only 4 samples can outperform a Viterbi algorithm with a delay of 1000 samples. It points out, however, two advantages of feedback VQ over scalar trellis encoding systems: 1. The decoder is permitted to be a more general form of finite-state machine than the shift-register based nonlinear filter usually used in trellis encoding systems; and 2. the encoder performs a single full search of a small vector codebook instead of a Viterbi algorithm consisting of a tree search of a sequence of scalar codebooks. In other words, single short vector searches may yield better performance than a "look ahead" sequence of searches of scalar codebooks.

Speech waveform coding

The second set of results considers a training sequence of 640,000 samples of ordinary speech from four different male speakers sampled at 6.5 kHz. The reader is reminded that squared error is not generally a subjectively good distortion measure for speech. Better subjective quality may be obtained by using more complicated distortion measures such as the general quadratic distortion measures with input dependent weightings such as the arithmetic segmented distortions. The VQ design techniques extend to such distortion measures, but the centroid computations are more complicated. (See [30] for the theory and [45, 46] for the application of input-weighted quadratic distortion measures.)

Tables III and IV are the counterparts of Tables I and II for this source. Now, however, the SNR's of the codes on test sequences of samples outside of the training sequence (and by a different speaker) are presented for comparison. In addition, some larger dimensions are con-

TABLE IV
FEEDBACK VQ OF SAMPLED SPEECH.

	FSVQ					VPQ			
k	SNRin	SNRout	K	n	M	SNRin	SNRout	n	M
1	2.0	2.0	2	2	2	2.1	2.6	2	2
2	7.8	7.5	32	4	64	6.4	6.2	4	8
3	9.0	8.3	64	10	192	7.3	6.8	8	24
4	10.9	9.4	512	16	2048	8.0	7.6	16	64
5	12.2	10.8	512	32	2560				

Signal to Noise Ratios inside training sequence (SNRin) of 640000 speech samples, Signal to Noise Ratios outside training sequence (SNRout) of 76800 speech samples, number of states (K), number of multiplications per sample (n), and storage (M) for feedback quantizers: Rate = 1 bit/sample. k = vector dimension.

sidered because the longer training sequence made them more trustworthy. Again for comparison, the best known (nonadaptive) scalar trellis encoding system for this source yields a performance of 9 dB [52]. Here the trellis encoder uses the M-algorithm with a search depth of 31 samples. The general comparisons are similar to those of the previous source, but there are several differences. The tree-searched VQ is now more degraded in comparison to the full search VQ and the multistage VQ is even worse, about 3 dB below the full search at the largest dimension in comparison to about 1 dB for the Gauss Markov case. The complexity and storage requirements are the same except for the shape/gain VQ where different optimum selections of gain and shape codebook size yield different complexity and storage requirements. The VPQ of dimension 4 is inferior to the trellis encoder and the FSVQ of the same dimension. The four dimensional FSVQ, however, still outperforms the scalar trellis encoder.

Observe that an FSVQ of dimension 4 provides better performance inside and outside the training sequence than does a full search memoryless vector quantizer of dimension 8, achieving better performance with 16 4-dimensional distortion evaluations than with 512 8-dimensional distortion computations. The cost, of course, is a large increase in memory. This, however, is a basic point of FSVQ design—to use more memory but less computation.

TABLE V
LPC VQ AND FSVQ WITH AND WITHOUT NEXT STATE FUNCTION IMPROVEMENT.

		VQ		FSVQ1		FSVQ2		
R	r	SNRin	SNRout	SNRin	SNRout	SNRin	SNRout	K
1	.008	3.7	2.9					
2	.016	6.1	5.2	7.2	4.3	7.5	6.1	16
3	.023	7.3	6.2	8.4	5.9	9.0	7.5	16
4	.031	8.8	7.9	9.5	7.8	9.6	8.7	4
5	.039	9.7	8.8	10.6	8.9	10.7	9.3	4
6	.047	10.5	9.5					
7	.055	11.6	10.1					
8	.062	12.6	10.7					

Signal to Noise Ratios inside training sequence (SNRin) of 5000 vectors of 128 samples each, Signal to Noise Ratios outside training sequence (SNRout) of 600 vectors of 128 samples each: memoryless VQ, omniscient FSVQ design (FSVQ1), and for omnisicient FSVQ design with next-state function improvement (FSVQ2). K = number of states in FSVQ, R = rate in bits/vector, r = rate in bits/sample. Itakura-Saito distortion measure.

LPC VQ (vocoding)

Table V presents a comparison of VQ and FSVQ for vector quantization of speech using the Itakura-Saito distortion measure or, equivalently, vector quantization of LPC speech models [16, 14, 53]. The training sequence and test sequence are as above, but now the input dimension is 128 samples and the output vectors are 10th order all-pole models. The training sequence is now effectively shorter since it contains only 5000 input vectors of this dimension. As a result the test results are noticeably different than the design results. Because of the shortness of the training sequence, only FSVQ's of small dimension and few states were considered.

TABLE VI
ADAPTIVE VPQ.

	VPQ	
k	SNRin	SNRout
1	4.12	4.34
2	7.47	7.17
3	8.10	7.67
4	8.87	8.30

Signal to Noise Ratios inside training sequence (SNRin) of 5000 vectors, and Signal to Noise Ratios in test sequence (SNRout) of 600 vectors, rate = 1.023 bits/sample.

The table summarizes memoryless VQ and two FSVQ designs: the first FSVQ design used was a straightforward application of the design technique outlined previously and the second used the stochastic iteration next-state improvement algorithm of [53]. Observe that the next-state function improvement yields codes that perform better outside of the training sequence then do the ordinary FSVQ codes.

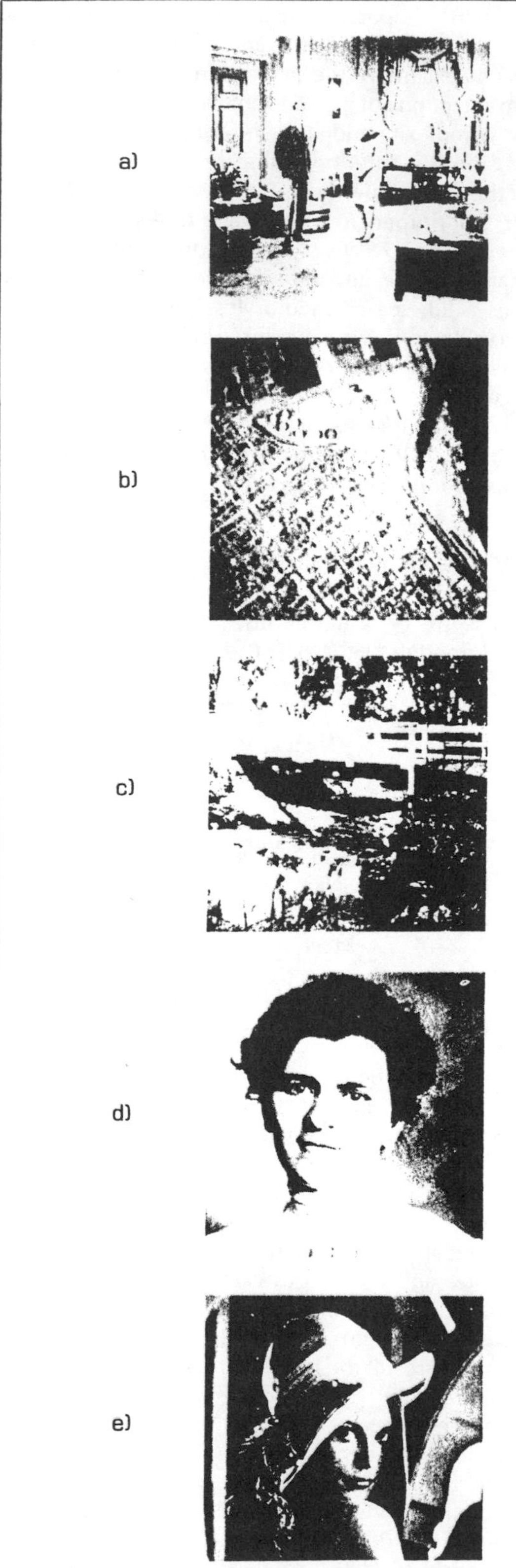

Figure 16. Image Training Sequence. The training sequence consisted of the sequence of 3 × 4 subblocks of the five 256 × 256 images shown.

Gain/shape VQ's for this application are developed in [16] and [36]. Tree-searched LPC VQ is considered for binary and nonbinary trees in combination with gain/shape codes in [16] and [10].

Adaptive coding

Table VI presents the results of a simple example of an adaptive VQ, here consisting of an LPC VQ with 8 codewords every 128 samples combined with VPQs of dimensions 1–4. Each of the 8 VPQs is designed for the subsequence of training vectors mapping into the corresponding LPC VQ model [47]. The rate of this system is $1 + 3/128 = 1.023$ bits/sample. The performance is significantly worse than the 10 dB achieved by a hybrid scalar trellis encoder of the same rate [52], but it improves on the nonadaptive VPQ by about ¾ dB. Adaptive vector quantizers are still quite new, however, and relatively little work on the wide variety of possible systems has yet been done.

Image coding

In 1980–1982 four separate groups developed successful applications of VQ techniques to image coding [61, 62, 63, 64, 65, 66, 67, 37]. The only real difference from waveform coding is that now the VQ operates on small rectangular blocks of from 9 to 16 pixels, that is, the vectors are really 2-dimensional subblocks of images, typically squares with 3 or 4 pixels on a side or 3 by 4 rectangles. We here consider both the basic technique and one variation. We consider only small codebooks of 6 bits per 4 × 3 block of 12 pixels for purposes of demonstration. Better quality pictures could be obtained at the same rate of ½ bit per pixel by using larger block sizes and hence larger rates of, say, 8 to 10 bits per block. Better quality could also likely be achieved with more complicated distortion measures than the simple squared error used.

Fig. 16 gives the training sequence of five images. Fig. 17a shows a small portion of the fifth image, an eye, magnified. Fig. 17b is a picture of the $2^6 = 64$ codewords. Fig. 17c shows the decoded eye. Fig. 18 shows the original, decoded image, and error image for the complete picture. The error image is useful for highlighting the problems encountered with the ordinary memoryless VQ. In particular, edges are poorly reproduced and the codeword edges make the picture appear "blocky." This problem was attacked by Ramamurthi and Gersho [62, 67] by constructing segmented (or union or composite) codes—separate codebooks for the edge information and the texture information where a simple classifier was used to distinguish the two in design. In [37] a feedback vector quantizer was developed by using a separating mean VQ with a predictive scalar quantizer to track the mean. Fig. 19 shows the original eye, ordinary VQ, and the feedback VQ. The improved ability to track edges is clearly discernible. Fig. 20 shows the full decoded image for feedback VQ together with the error pattern.

Although image coding using VQ is still in its infancy,

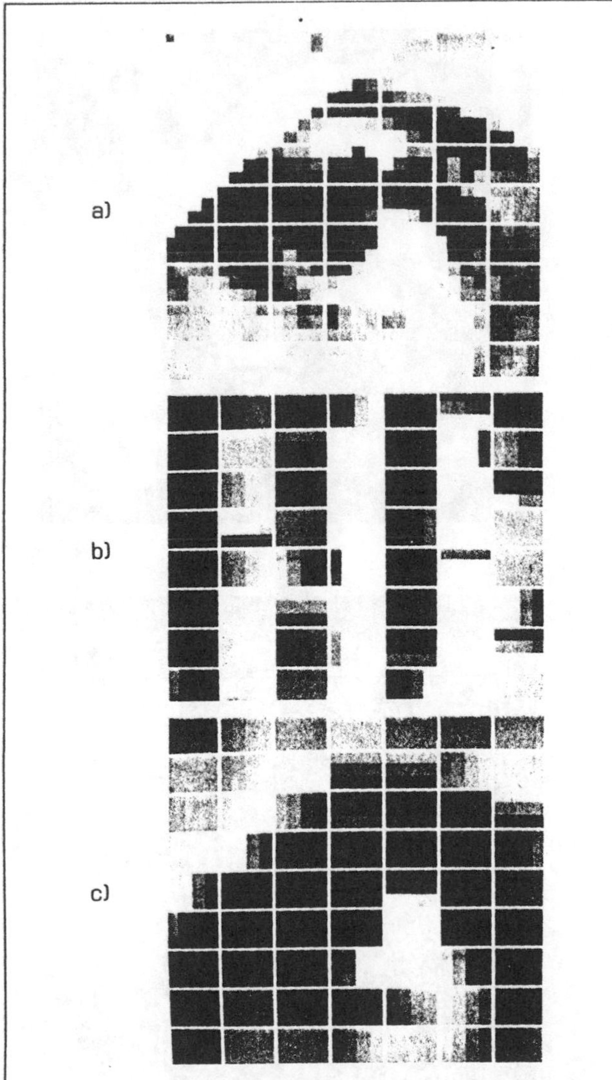

Figure 17. Basic Image VQ Example at ½ bit per pixel. (a) Original Eye Magnified (b) 6 bit codebook VQ codebook for 4 × 3 blocks (c) Decoded Image.

these preliminary experiments using only fairly simple memoryless and feedback VQ techniques with small codebooks demonstrate that the general approach holds considerable promise for such applications.

COMMENTS

We have described Lloyd's basic iterative algorithm and how it can be used to improve the performance of a variety of vector quantization systems, ranging from the fundamental memoryless full search VQ that serves as the basic model for data compression in information theory to a variety of feedback and adaptive systems that can be viewed as vector extensions of popular scalar compression systems. By a variety of examples of systems and code design simulations we have tried to illustrate some of the tradeoffs among performance, rate, complexity, and storage for these codes.

The basic structure of all of the VQ systems is well suited to VLSI implementation: a minimum distortion search algorithm on a chip communicating with off-board storage for codebooks and next-state transition functions. As new and better design algorithms are developed, the chips can be updated by simply reburning the codebook and transition ROM's.

The basic approach can also be incorporated into the design of some traditional scalar data compression schemes, an approach which Gersho calls "imbedded

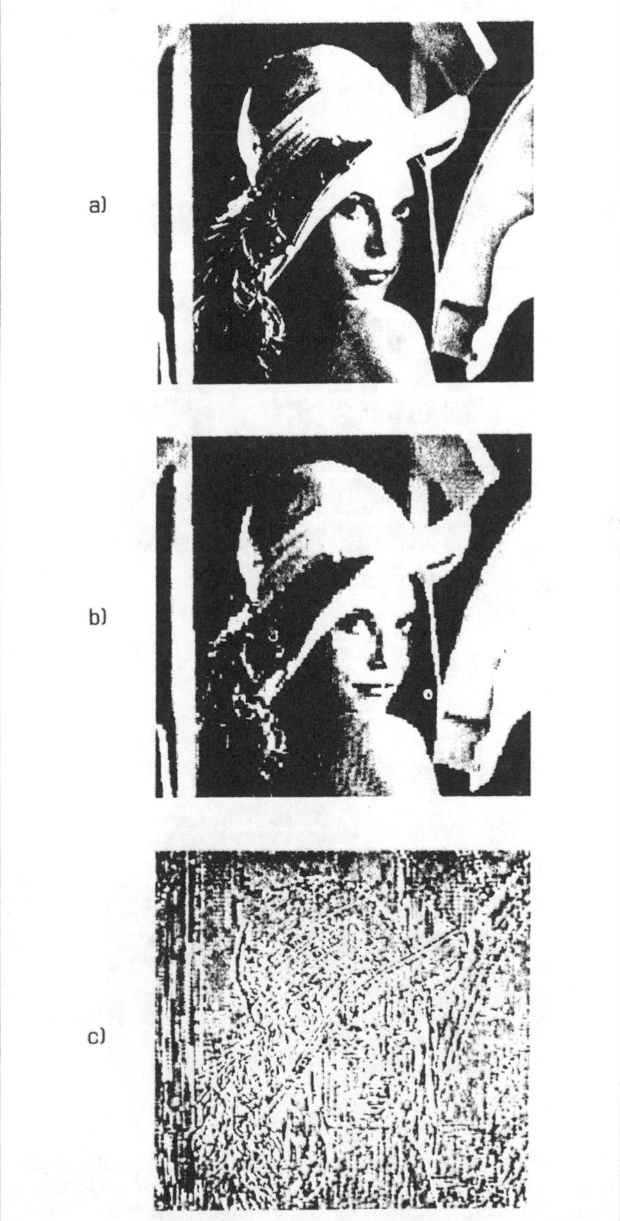

Figure 18. Full Image for Basic Example (a) Original (b) Decoded Image (c) Error Image.

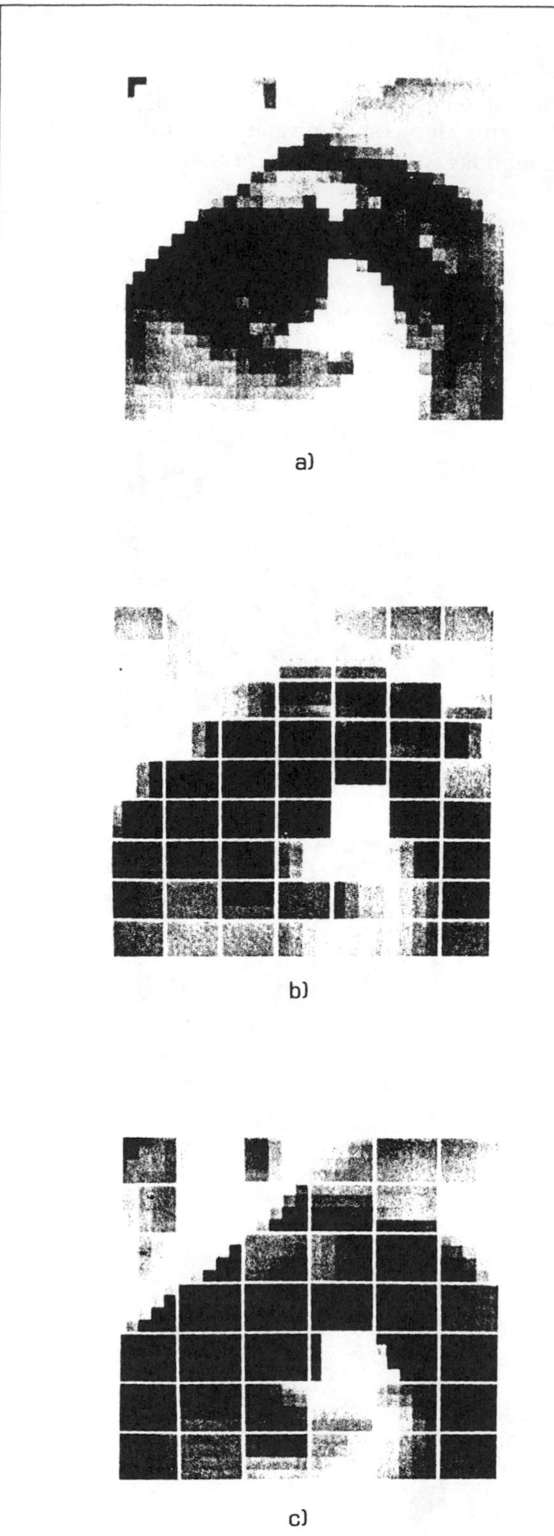

Figure 19. VQ vs. Separating Mean VQ at Rate ½ bit per pixel (a) Original Eye Magnified (b) VQ Decoded Image (c) Separating Mean VQ with DPCM Mean Coding Decoded Image.

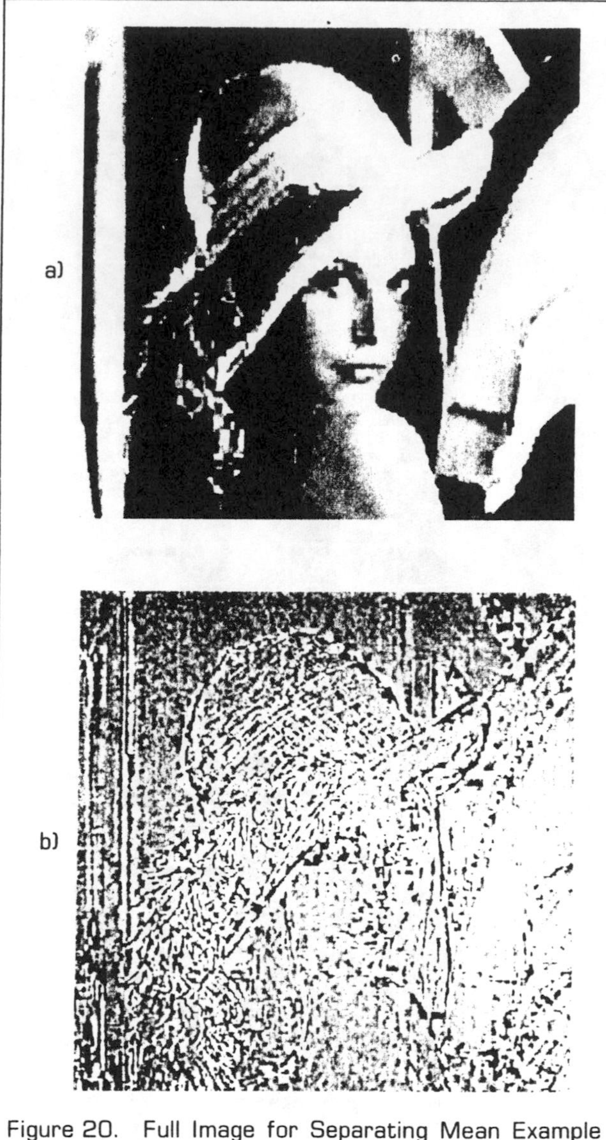

Figure 20. Full Image for Separating Mean Example (a) Decoded Image using Separating Mean VQ with DPCM Mean Coding (b) Error Image.

VQ" [11]. Such schemes typically enforce additional structure on the code such as preprocessing, transforming, splitting into subbands, and scalar quantization, however, and hence the algorithms may not have the freedom to do as well as the more unconstrained structures considered here. Even if the traditional schemes prove more useful because of existing DSP chips or intuitive variations well matched to particular data sources, the vector quantization systems can prove a useful benchmark for comparison.

Recently VQ has also been successfully used in isolated word recognition systems without dynamic time warping by using either separate codebooks for each utterance or by mapping trajectories through one or more codebooks [68, 69, 70, 71, 55, 72]. Vector quantization has also been used as a front end acoustic processor to isolated utterance and continuous speech recognition systems which then do approximately maximum likelihood linguistic decoding based on probabilities estimated using "hidden Markov" models for the VQ output data. [73, 74, 75].

Variations of the basic VQ design algorithm have been tried for several distortion measures, including the squared error, weighted squared error, the Itakura-Saito distortion, and an (arithmetic) segmented signal to noise ratio. (See, e.g., [30, 45, 46]). Other distortion measures are currently under study.

The algorithm has not yet been extended to some of the more complicated distortion measures implicit in noise masking techniques for enhancing the subjective performance of scalar quantization speech coding systems. Whether scalar systems designed by sophisticated techniques matched to subjective distortion measures will sound or look better than vector systems designed for mathematically tractable distortion measures remains to be seen. Whenever the subjective distortion measures can be quantified and a means found to compute centroids, however, the vector systems will yield better quantitative performance. Since the centroid computation is only done in design and not in implementation, it can be quite complicated and still yield useful results.

The generalized Lloyd algorithm is essentially a clustering algorithm and we have attempted to demonstrate its applicability to the design of a variety of data compression systems. Other clustering algorithms may yield better codes in some applications. For example, Freeman [76] proposed a design algorithm for scalar trellis encoding systems using the squared error distortion measure which replaced the Lloyd procedure by a conjugate gradient procedure for minimizing the average distortion for a long training sequence. He found that for a memoryless Gaussian source the resulting codes were superior to those obtained by the Lloyd procedure. It would be interesting to characterize the reasons for this superiority, e.g., the procedure may find a better local minimum or it may simply be numerically better suited for finding a continuous local minimum on a digital computer. It would also be interesting to consider variations of this approach for the design of some of the other systems considered here.

A survey article with many topics cannot provide complete descriptions or exhaustive studies of any of systems sketched. It is hoped, however, that these examples impart the flavor of vector quantizer design algorithms and that they may interest some readers to further delve into the recent and current work in the area.

ACKNOWLEDGMENT

The author gratefully acknowledges the many helpful comments from students and colleagues that aided the preparation of this paper.

Portions of the research described here were supported by the Army Research Office, the Air Force Office of Scientific Research, the National Science Foundation, the John Simon Guggenheim Memorial Foundation, and the Joint Services Electronics Program at Stanford University.

REFERENCES

[1] Davisson, L. D. and Gray, R. M., *Data Compression*, Dowden, Hutchinson, & Ross, Inc., Stroudsbug, PA (1976). Benchmark Papers in Electrical Engineering and Computer Science, Volume 14.

[2] Jayant, N. S., Editor, *Waveform coding quantization and Coding*, IEEE Press, NY (1976).

[3] Jayant, N. S. and Noll, P., *Digital Coding of Waveforms*, Prentice–Hall, Englewood Cliffs, NJ (1984).

[4] Shannon, C. E., "A mathematical theory of communication," *Bell Systems Technical Journal* 27 pp. 379–423, 623–656 (1948).

[5] Shannon, C. E., "Coding theorems for a discrete source with a fidelity criterion," *IRE National Convention Record, Part 4*, pp. 142–163 (1959).

[6] Gallager, R. G., *Information theory and reliable communication*, John Wiley & Sons, NY (1968).

[7] Berger, T., *Rate Distortion Theory*, Prentice-Hall Inc., Englewood Cliffs, NJ (1971).

[8] Viterbi, A. J. and Omura, J. K., *Principles of Digital Communication and Coding*, McGraw-Hill Book Company, New York (1979).

[9] Lloyd, S. P., *Least squares quantization in PCM*, Bell Laboratories Technical Note (1957). (Published in the March 1982 special issue on quantization).

[10] Wong, D., Juang, B.-H., and Gray, A. H., Jr., "An 800 bit/s vector quantization LPC vocoder," *IEEE Transactions on Acoustics Speech and Signal Processing* ASSP-30 pp. 770–779 (October 1982).

[11] Gersho, A. and Cuperman, V., "Vector Quantization: A pattern-matching technique for speech coding," *IEEE Communications Magazine*, (December 1983).

[12] Itakura, F. and Saito, S., "Analysis synthesis telephony based on the maximum liklihood method," *Proceedings of the 6th International Congress of Acoustics*, pp. C-17–C-20 (August 1968).

[13] Kullback, S., *Information Theory and Statistics*, Dover, New York (1969).

[14] Gray, R. M., Gray, A. H., Jr., Rebolledo, G., and Shore, J. E., "Rate distortion speech coding with a minimum discrimination information distortion measure," *IEEE Transactions on Information Theory* IT-27 (6) pp. 708–721 (Nov. 1981).

[15] Shore, J. E. and Gray, R. M., "Minimum-cross-entropy pattern classification and cluster analysis," *IEEE Transactions on Pattern Analysis and Machine Intelligence* PAMI-4 pp. 11–17 (Jan. 1982).

[16] Buzo, A., Gray, A. H., Jr., and Gray, R. M., and Markel, J. D., "Speech coding based upon vector quantization," *IEEE Transactions on Acoustics Speech and Signal Processing* ASSP-28 pp. 562–574. (October 1980).

[17] Gray, R. M., Buzo, A., Gray, A. H., Jr., and Matsuyama, Y., "Distortion measures for speech processing," *IEEE Transactions on Acoustics, Speech, and Signal Processing*, ASSP-28 pp. 367–376 (August 1980).

[18] Gray, R. M., Kieffer, J. C., and Linde, Y., "Locally opti-

mal block quantizer design," *Information and Control* 45 pp. 178–198 (May 1980).

[19] Gray, R. M. and Kieffer, J. C., "Asymptotically mean stationary measures," *Annals of Probability* 8 pp. 962–973 (Oct. 1980).

[20] Kieffer, J. C. and Rahe, M., "Markov channels are asymptotically mean stationary," *Siam Journal of Mathematical Analysis* 12 pp. 293–305 (1980).

[21] Fontana, R. J., Gray, R. M., and Kieffer, J. C., "Asymptotically mean stationary channels," *IEEE Transactions on Information Theory* IT-27 pp. 308–316 (May 1981).

[22] Kieffer, J. C., "Stochastic stability for feedback quantization schemes," *IEEE Transactions on Information Theory* IT-28 pp. 248–254 (March 1982).

[23] Sabin, M. J. and Gray, R. M., *Asymptotic properties of the generalized Lloyd algorithm,* Submitted for publication 1983.

[24] Gersho, A., "On the structure of vector quantizers," *IEEE Transactions on Information Theory* IT-28 pp. 157–166 (March 1982).

[25] Linde, Y., Buzo, A., and Gray, R. M., "An algorithm for vector quantizer design," *IEEE Transactions on Communications* COM-28 pp. 84–95 (January 1980).

[26] MacQueen, J., "Some methods for classification and analysis of multivariate observations," *Proc. of the Fifth Berkeley Symposium on Math. Stat. and Prob.* 1 pp. 281–296 (1967).

[27] Diday, E. and Simon, J. C., "Clustering analysis," in *Digital Pattern Recognition,* ed. K. S. Fu, Springer-Verlag, NY (1976).

[28] Chen, D. T. S., "On two or more dimensional optimum quantizers," *Proceedings, 1977 International Conference on Acoustics, Speech, and Signal Processing,* pp. 640–643 (1977).

[29] Adoul, J.-P., Morissette, S., and Rudko, M., "Bit-rate-halving algorithm for PCM-encoded speech using a new bidimensional data compression scheme," *Record of the 1979 IEEE International Conference on Acoustics Speech and Signal Processing,* pp. 432–435 (April 1979).

[30] Gray, R. M. and Karnin, E., "Multiple local optima in vector quantizers," *IEEE Transactions on Information Theory* IT-28 pp. 256–261 (March 1982).

[31] Abut, H., Gray, R. M., and Rebolledo, G., "Vector quantization of speech and speech-like waveforms," *IEEE Transactions on Acoustics Speech and Signal Processing* ASSP-30 pp. 423–435 (June 1982).

[32] Adoul, J.-P., Debray, J.-L., and Dalle, D., "Spectral distance measure applied to the optimum design of DPCM coders with L predictors," *Proceedings of the 1980 IEEE International Conference on Acoustics Speech and Signal Processing,* pp. 512–515 (April 1980).

[33] Gersho, A. and Cheng, D., "Fast nearest neighbor search for nonstructured Euclidean codes," *Abstracts of the 1983 IEEE International Symposium on Information Theory,* p. 88 (September 1983).

[34] Juang, B.-H. and Gray, A. H., Jr., "Multiple stage vector quantization for speech coding," *Proceedings of the IEEE International Conference on Acoustics Speech and Signal Processing* 1 pp. 597–600 (April 1982).

[35] Sabin, M. J. and Gray, R. M., "Product code vector quantizers for speech waveform coding," *Conference Record Globecom '82,* pp. 1087–1091 (December 1982).

[36] Sabin, M. J. and Gray, R. M., *Product code vector quantizers for waveform and voice coding, IEEE Trans. ASSP,* to appear, (April 1984).

[37] Baker, R. L. and Gray, R. M., "Differential vector quantization of achromatic imagery," *Proceedings of the International Picture Coding Symposium,* (March 1983).

[38] Gersho, A., "Asymptotically optimal block quantization," *IEEE Transactions on Information Theory* IT-25 pp. 373–380 (July 1979).

[39] Conway, J. H. and Sloane, N. J. A., "Voronoi regions of lattices, second moments of polytopes, and quantization," *IEEE Transactions on Information Theory* IT-28 pp. 211–226 (March 1982).

[40] Conway, J. H. and Sloane, N. J. A., "Fast quantizing and decoding algorithms for lattice quantizers and codes," *IEEE Transactions on Information Theory* IT-28 pp. 227–232 (March 1982).

[41] Conway, J. H. and Sloane, N. J. A., "On the Voronoi regions of certain lattices," *SIAM Journal of Alg. Disc. Math.,* (1983). in press

[42] Barnes, E. S. and Sloane, N. J. A., "The optimal lattice quantizer in three dimensions," *SIAM Journal of Alg. Disc. Math.* 4 pp. 30–41 (1983).

[43] Foster, J., Newkirk, J., and Gray, R. M., *VLSI implementation of a finite-state vector quantization waveform encoder,* submitted for publication 1983.

[44] Gaarder, N. T. and Slepian, D., "On optimal finite-state digital transmission systems," *IEEE Transactions on Information Theory* IT-28 pp. 167–186 (March 1982).

[45] Cuperman, V. and Gersho, A., "Adaptive differential vector coding of speech," *Conference Record, GlobeCom 82,* pp. 1092–1096 (December 1982).

[46] Cuperman, V. and Gersho, A., *Vector predictive coding of speech at 16 Kb/s,* Submitted for possible publication 1983.

[47] Chang, P. C., Ph.D. Research, Stanford University 1983.

[48] Gibson, J. D., Jones, S. K., and Melsa, J. L., "Sequentially adaptive prediction and coding of speech signals," *IEEE Transactions on Communications* COM-22 pp. 1789–1797 (November 1974).

[49] Dunn, J. G., "An experimental 9600-bit/s voice digitizer employing adaptive prediction," *IEEE Transactions on Communication Technology* COM-19 pp. 1021–1032 (December 1971).

[50] Foster, J. and Gray, R. M., "Finite-state vector quantization," *Abstracts of the 1982 International Sym-*

posium on Information Theory, (June 1982).

[51] Foster, J., Gray, R. M., and Ostendouf, M., *Finite-state vector quantization for waveform coding,* IEEE Trans. Info. Theory, to appear.

[52] Stewart, L. C., Gray, R. M., and Linde, Y., "The design of trellis waveform coders," *IEEE Transactions on Communications* COM-30 pp. 702–710 (April 1982).

[53] Ostendorf, M. and Gray, R. M., *An algorithm for the design of labeled-transition finite-state vector quantizers,* submitted for publication 1983.

[54] Fehn, H. G. and Noll, P., "Multipath search coding of stationary signals with applications to speech," *IEEE Transactions on Communications* COM-30 pp. 687–701 (April 1982).

[55] Shore, J. E. and Burton, D. K., "Discrete utterance speech recognition without time alignment," *IEEE Transactions on Information Theory* IT-29 pp. 473–491 (July 1983).

[56] Rebolledo, G., Gray, R. M., and Burg, J. P., "A multirate voice digitizer based upon vector quantization," *IEEE Transactions on Communications* COM-30 pp. 721–727 (April 1982).

[57] Adoul, J.-P. and Mabilleau, P., "4800 bps RELP vocoder using vector quantization for both filter and residual representation," *Proceedings of the IEEE International Conference on Acoustics Speech and Signal Processing* 1 p. 601 (April 1982).

[58] Heron, C. D., Crochiere, R. E., and Cox, R. V., "A 32-band subband/transform coder incorporating vector quantization for dynamic bit allocation," *Proceedings ICASSP,* pp. 1276–1279 (April 1983).

[59] Gray, R. M. and Linde, Y., "Vector quantizers and predictive quantizers for Gauss-Markov sources," *IEEE Transactions on Communications* COM-30 pp. 381–389 (Feb. 1982).

[60] Arnstein, D. S., "Quantization error in predictive coders," *IEEE Transactions on Communications* COM-23 pp. 423–429 (April 1975).

[61] Yamada, Y., Fujita, K., and Tazaki, S., "Vector quantization of video signals," *Proceedings of Annual Conference of IECE,* p. 1031 (1980).

[62] Gersho, A. and Ramamurthi, B., "Image coding using vector quantization," *Proceedings of the IEEE International Conference on Acoustics Speech and Signal Processing* 1 pp. 428–431 (April 1982).

[63] Baker, R. L. and Gray, R. M., "Image compression using non-adaptive spatial vector quantization," *Conference Record of the Sixteenth Asilomar Conference on Circuits Systems and Computers,* (October 1982).

[64] Murakami, T., Asai, K., and Yamazaki, E., "Vector quantizer of video signals," *Electronic Letters* 7 pp. 1005–1006 (Nov. 1982).

[65] Yamada, Y. and Tazaki, S., "Vector quantizer design for video signals," *IECE Transactions* J66-B pp. 965–972 (1983). (in Japanese)

[66] Yamada, Y. and Tazaki, S., "A method for constructing successive approximation vector quantizers for video signals," *Proceedings of the Annual Conference of the Institute of Television Engineers of Japan,* pp. 6–2 (1983).

[67] Ramamurthi, B. and Gersho, A., "Image coding using segmented codebooks," *Proceedings International Picture Coding Symposium,* (Mar. 1983).

[68] Hamabe, R., Yamada, Y., Murata, M., and Namekawa, T., "A speech recognition system using inverse filter matching technique," *Proceedings of the Ann. Conf. Inst. of Television Engineers,* (June 1981). (in Japanese)

[69] Shore, J. E. and Burton, D. K., "Discrete utterance speech recognition without time alignment," *Proceedings 1982 IEEE International Conference on Acoustics Speech and Signal Processing,* p. 907 (May 1982).

[70] Martinez, H. G., Riviera, C., and Buzo, A., "Discrete utterance recognition based upon source coding techniques," *Proceedings IEEE International Conference on Acoustics Speech and Signal Processing,* pp. 539–542 (May 1982).

[71] Rabiner, L., Levinson, S. E., and Sondhi, M. M., "On the application of vector quantization and hidden Markov models to speaker-independent isolated word recognition," *Bell System Technical Journal* 62 pp. 1075–1106 (April 1983).

[72] Shore, J. E., Burton, D., and Buck, J., "A generalization of isolated word recognition using vector quantization," *Proceedings 1983 International Conference on Acoustics Speech and Signal Processing,* pp. 1021–1024 (April 1983).

[73] Jelinek, F., Mercer, R. L., and Bahl, L. R., "Continuous speech recognition: statistical methods," in *Handbook of Statistics,* Vol. 2, P. R. Khrishaieh and L. N. Kanal, eds., North-Holland, pp. 549–573. (1982).

[74] Billi, R., "Vector quantization and Markov models applied to speech recognition," *Proc. ICASSP 82,* pp. 574–577, Paris (May 1982).

[75] Rabiner, L. R., Levinson, S. E., and Sondhi, M. M., "On the application of vector quantization and hidden Markov models to speaker-independent isolated word recognition," *BSTJ,* Vol. 62, pp. 1075–1105, (April 1983).

[76] Freeman, G. H., "The design of time-invariant trellis source codes," *Abstracts of the 1983 IEEE International Symposium on Information Theory,* pp. 42–43 (September 1983).

[77] Haoui, A. and Messerschmidt, D., "Predictive Vector Quantization," Proceedings of the IEEE International Conference on Acoustics, Speech, and Signal Processing (1984).

Robert M. Gray was born in San Diego, CA, on November 1, 1943. He received the B.S. and M.S. degrees from M.I.T. in 1966 and the Ph.D. degree from U.S.C. in 1969, all in Electrical Engineering. Since 1969 he has been with the Information Systems Laboratory and the Electrical Engineering Department of Stanford University, CA, where he is currently a Professor engaged in teaching and research in communication and information theory with an emphasis on data compression. He was Associate Editor (1977–1980) and Editor (1980–1983) of the *IEEE Transactions on Information Theory* and was a member of the IEEE Information Theory Group Board of Governors (1974–1980). He was corecipient with Lee D. Davisson of the 1976 IEEE Information Theory Group Paper Award. He has been a fellow of the Japan Society for the Promotion of Science (1981) and the John Simon Guggenheim Memorial Foundation (1981–1982). He is a fellow of the IEEE and a member of Sigma Xi, Eta Kappa Nu, SIAM, IMS, AAAS, and the Societé des Ingenieurs et Scientifiques de France. He holds an Advanced Class Amateur Radio License (KB6XQ).

Notes added in proof: A similar design technique for FSVQ was independently developed by Haoui and Messerschmidt [77]. It should be pointed out that the FSVQ design algorithm described here is incomplete in that it does not describe the methods used to avoid non-communicating collection of states and wasted states. These issues are discussed in [51].

A joint synchrony/mean-rate model of auditory speech processing

Stephanie Seneff

Research Laboratory of Electronics, Massachusetts Institute of Technology, Cambridge, MA 02139, U.S.A.

This paper describes a speech processing system that is based on properties of the human auditory system. A bank of critical-band filters defines the initial spectral analysis. Filter outputs are processed by a model of the nonlinear transduction stage in the cochlea, which accounts for such features as saturation, adaptation and forward masking. The parameters of the model were adjusted to match existing experimental results of the physiology of the auditory periphery. The output of this model is delivered to two parallel channels, each of which produces spectral representations appropriate for distinct subtasks of a speech recognition system. One path yields an overall energy measure for each channel that can be identified with the average rate of neural discharge. The outputs of this path appear to be useful for locating acoustic events and assigning segments to broad phonetic categories. In the other path, the extent of dominance of periodicities at each channel's center frequency is captured by a synchrony measure, which yields a spectral representation with enhanced spectral contrast, relative to the mean-rate spectrogram. The outputs of this stage show distinct formant peaks during sonorant regions, with smooth transitions over time, as well as preserving spectral prominences in the high-frequency region for fricatives and stops.

1. Introduction

The human auditory system, together with its central connections, is a speech recognizer with excellent performance. If a computational model could be designed that adequately reflects the transformations occurring in the auditory pathway, the resulting spectral representations should be superior to representations based on non-biological criteria commonly used in computer speech recognition algorithms. Due to a wealth of physiological data, particularly at the level of the auditory nerve, it is now possible to characterize many of the transformations that occur in the auditory periphery. Although many features of the auditory system have been characterized quite explicitly, it is still a difficult task to design a computer system that achieves a comparable level of performance, particularly when computational issues are taken into account.

Having chosen a design for the peripheral auditory model, the speech researcher is confronted with the task of modeling the processing which occurs in the more central regions of the auditory pathway. Beyond the periphery, the physiological properties of the system are not nearly so well-defined, and therefore the criteria for the design are open to considerably more speculation. Instead of trying to match the responses of a given system, one can only try to create a reasonable processing strategy that yields "promising" representations given a general knowledge about neural processing and about the important features to be preserved in speech signals.

The following section briefly reviews those properties of the auditory periphery which are relevant to the processing of speech. In Section 3 an auditory model for speech processing is described in detail and referred to the relevant physiological data discussed in Section 2. Section 4 compares the results produced by the model with physiological responses for a number of different experimental paradigms. The final section describes a model for synchrony detection and illustrates various outputs of the computer model for speech signals.

2. Brief review of relevant features of auditory system

Auditory physiologists have gathered considerable data describing the response of mammalian auditory-nerve fibers to spectrally simple (Kiang, Watanabe, Thomas & Clark, 1965; Johnson, 1974, 1980; Smith & Zwislocki, 1975) as well as more complex signals, such as synthetic speech (Young & Sachs, 1979; Sachs & Young, 1980). From these data it is clear that some form of frequency analysis is performed and that this operation is heavily influenced by such nonlinearities as response saturation and both long- and short-term adaptation.

The dynamics of the response to non-steady-state signals are important aspects to be captured by any model of auditory processing. The "instantaneous" discharge rate of auditory-nerve fibers is often significantly highest during the initial 15 ms of acoustic stimulation and decreases thereafter, until it reaches a steady-state level approximately 50 ms after signal onset. This decrease in response rate is referred to as "adaptation" (Smith & Zwislocki, 1975). Typically, there is a very rapid initial decay in rate immediately after onset, followed by a slower decay to a steady-state level[1]. The "rapid adaptation" is attributed in part (if not in full) to the refractory property of auditory-nerve fibers (Johnson & Swami, 1983). The slower, "short-term" adaptation is attributed to a depletion of neurotransmitter in the synaptic region between the inner hair cell and associated nerve fibers (Eggermont, 1973). Another important response property, possibly related to adaptation, is "forward masking". This occurs when the response to a particular sound is diminished as a consequence of a preceding, usually considerably more intense signal (Harris & Dallos, 1979).

In addition to the dynamics of the gross temporal *envelope* of the response discussed above, another important aspect of neural firing behavior involves the detailed time course of the probabilistic response to each cycle of the input signal. Auditory-nerve fibers tend to fire in a phase-locked fashion to low-frequency periodic stimuli. In other words, the intervals between nerve firings tend to be integral multiples of the stimulus period.

The detailed temporal patterns in the neural response are a potential source of more specific information about the frequencies present in the input signal. In response to

[1]The low- and (to a lesser extent) medium-spontaneous rate fibers do not exhibit the rapid adaptation typical of the more numerous high-spontaneous units (Rhode & Smith, 1986). However, the present model attempts to simulate only the more general characteristics of auditory-nerve fiber response and thus will ignore such differences among nerve fiber populations.

sinusoidal stimuli, the spectrum of the response pattern contains energy at the input frequency and its harmonics. The harmonics are introduced primarily as a consequence of half-wave rectification. Fibers responsive to the high-frequency components of a signal tend to synchronize only to the modulation envelope of the signal, which is correlated with the signal's fundamental frequency. Thus, there will typically be some degree of synchronization to the fundamental frequency in the response of high-frequency fibers despite the fact that they are incapable of phase-locking to the frequency components lying within their response areas. Such envelope synchrony may be useful for pitch processing (Delgutte, 1980; Delgutte & Kiang, 1984*a*).

2.1. *Responses to speech-like stimuli*

Only recently have researchers begun to examine the nerve fiber response characteristics to complex stimuli that more closely resemble natural speech. Noteworthy are the studies by Young & Sachs (1979) and Sachs & Young (1980) on the responses of cat auditory-nerve fibers to steady-state synthetic vowels, and the work by Delgutte (1980), Miller & Sachs (1983), Sinex & Geisler (1983) and Delgutte & Kiang (1984*a*, *b*, *c*), on the responses to other speech-like stimuli such as formant transitions, fricatives and stop-consonants. These researchers observed response patterns that were consistent, in many ways, with those obtained with less complex stimuli.

Young and Sachs were particularly interested in addressing the issue of whether discharge rate alone is sufficient for vowel identification, or whether some form of synchrony measure is required at a higher stage in the auditory system to determine the formant frequencies. They studied a large population of fibers, and computed the mean-rate response, as well as period histograms to synthetic vowel stimuli presented over a range of sound pressure levels. They found that the formant information was almost completely obliterated from the rate response of most fibers at the higher amplitudes, due to the saturation of their discharge rate[2].

Young and Sachs also tested the adequacy of a synchronized response measure for vowel representation. The measure, "average localized synchronized rate" (ALSR) was evaluated for the frequencies corresponding to harmonics of the fundamental. It is computed by averaging the spectral amplitude of the period histograms at a given frequency, nf_0, over a group of fibers whose characteristic frequencies (CFs) are close to that harmonic. This representation yields a more robust representation of the formants over a wide range of amplitudes. However, the ALSR measure is also sensitive to spurious peaks in the spectral representation which are the consequence of cochlear nonlinearities such as rectification. These nonlinearities introduce substantial energy at the second harmonic of a strong peak. Srulovicz & Goldstein (1983) have explored, within a theoretical framework, a similar model for a "central spectrum" using an approach which complements the experimental results of Young and Sachs.

3. Peripheral auditory model

The analysis system consists of a set of 40 independent channels which collectively cover the frequency range from 130 to 6400 Hz. The bandwidth of the channels is approximately

[2]However, the rate-place profiles for the low- and, to a lesser extent, the medium-spontaneous fibers were shown to contain some information relevant to the formant frequencies (see Geisler, 1988, and Sachs, Blackburn & Young, 1988, in this volume).

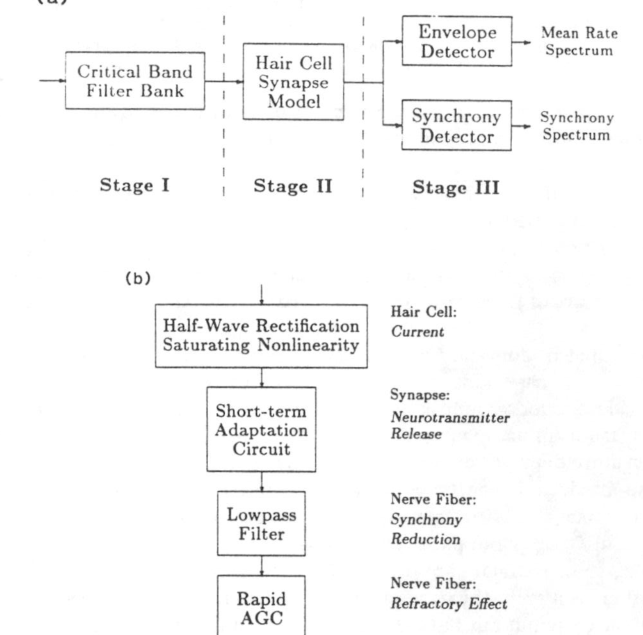

Figure 1. (a) The computer model. (b) The subcomponents of Stage II with suggested auditory system affiliations indicated at right.

0.5 Bark[3]. Although a larger number of channels would provide superior spatial resolution of the cochlear output, the amount of computation time required would be increased significantly. Thus, practical considerations of the model's design have kept the number of channels to the minimum required to provide the resolution required to produce a clear representation of the speech spectrum. In the future it may be possible to increase the number of channels and keep the computation time down by implementing the model in hardware.

The model is illustrated in Fig. 1(a). Each channel consists of a linear critical-band filter, followed by a nonlinear stage (Stage II), intended to capture the prominent features of the transformation from basilar membrane vibration to the probabilistic response properties of auditory-nerve fibers. The Stage II outputs include the detailed waveshape of the probabilistic response to individual cycles of the input stimulus. The nerve responses are never reduced to spike trains, as would be the case for single neurons. Rather, the outputs represent the probability of firing as a function of time for an ensemble of similar fibers acting as a group. The outputs are delivered to two parallel,

[3]A Bark corresponds to the width of one critical band, which is a unit of frequency resolution and energy integration derived from psychophysical experiments. A critical band is equal to approximately $f_c/6$ for frequencies greater than 1 kHz and becomes somewhat broader (on a logarithmic scale) in the low-frequency range. A concise definition is provided by Zwicker (1961).

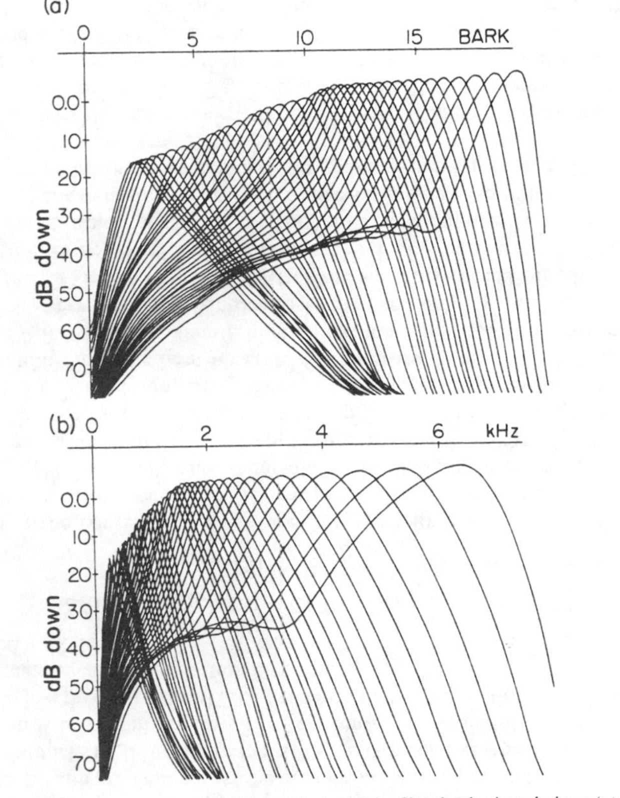

Figure 2. Frequency response characteristics of the filter bank plotted along (a) a Bark scale (Zwicker, 1961) and (b) a linear frequency scale.

non-interacting modules. One module determines the envelope amplitude, corresponding to the average discharge rate response. The other module measures the extent to which information near the center frequency (CF) of the linear filter dominates the output (i.e. determines the "synchronous response").

3.1. *Filter bank design*

The frequency response characteristics of the filters are shown in Fig. 2(a), plotted on a Bark-frequency scale (Zwicker, 1961), and in Fig. 2(b) on a linear scale. The analog speech signal is initially band-limited to 6.5 kHz and sampled at 16 kHz. In the interest of efficiency the filters were implemented as a cascade of complex high-frequency zero pairs (anti-resonances), with taps to individual tuned resonators after each zero pair. The high-frequency zeros serve to filter out energy above resonance, and help to produce a steep cutoff on the high-frequency side of the filter. The high-CF filters have broad low-frequency tails, such as are observed in neural data (Kiang *et al.*, 1965). The filters were designed by estimating the frequencies and bandwidths for the zeros, and then determining automatically the correct radius for the poles in the z-plane to match the critical-bandwidth criterion. The zeros could then be readjusted manually to improve the match to the desired filter shape. The details of this iterative interactive filter design process are discussed in Seneff (1984, 1985).

In traditional spectral analysis, speech is typically pre-emphasized prior to Fourier analysis. Some form of pre-emphasis can also be justified from an auditory standpoint. It has been determined experimentally that broad outer-ear resonances should result in a 10–20 dB boost in energy between about 1.5 and 5.0 kHz (Yost & Nielsen, 1977). The gains of the filters in the model are set so as to reflect these resonances, as shown in Fig. 2.

3.2. *Inner-hair-cell/synapse model*

Following the linear-filtering stage, each channel is processed independently through a nonlinear stage to model the transformation from basilar membrane vibration to auditory-nerve fiber responses. The model incorporates such nonlinearities as dynamic range compression and half-wave rectification, and also captures effects such as short-term adaptation, rapid adaptation, and forward masking. No attempt was made to model any long-term adaptation phenomena. The output of this stage represents a probability of firing.

The model consists of four subcomponents, as shown in Fig. 1(b): a half-wave rectifier, a short-term adaptation component, a lowpass filter, and a rapid Automatic Gain Control (AGC). Each component will be described in more detail in this section. The numerical values used for the parameters of the system are given in Section 4, since these were determined through comparisons with physiological data.

All of the components, except the lowpass filter, are nonlinear and therefore the final output is affected by the *ordering* of the components. A particular ordering can be justified in part by forming associations with elements of the auditory apparatus, as suggested to the right of each component in the figure. Such links can also aid in the design of each individual component.

The hair-cell current response, as measured for amphibians, shows a distinct directional sensitivity (Hudspeth & Corey, 1977). It is not clear if the electrical current is a direct link in the response mechanism; nonetheless, it is tempting to assume that half-wave rectification first occurs in the hair cell and, hence, this is the first component in the model. There seems to be no evidence for short-term adaptation in hair-cell current or voltage responses; therefore it is generally assumed that this effect is introduced in the synaptic region between the hair cell and the nerve fiber (Eggermont, 1973). The logical ordering is therefore to place this component second.

The AGC is assumed to be affiliated with the refractory phenomenon of nerve fibers; therefore, this component should be placed late in the series. Such an affiliation implies that the rapid-adaptation component of responses to onsets is due to the refractory phenomenon, a hypothesis proposed by Johnson & Swami (1983).

The lowpass filter is associated with the gradual loss of synchrony in nerve-fiber responses as stimulus frequency is increased. There are probably several loci where further synchrony loss is introduced; for example, ion diffusion can be viewed as a lowpass process. The filter must follow the half-wave rectifier, because it only makes sense after signal energy has been preserved through a d.c. component. If the filter precedes the adaptation circuit, the time constants of adaptation become significantly dependent on signal frequency. Therefore, it was decided to place the filter just before the AGC.

The model for the instantaneous half-wave rectifier is defined mathematically as follows:

$$\begin{aligned} y &= 1 + A \tan^{-1} Bx \quad x > 0 \\ &= e^{ABx} \qquad\qquad\quad x \leqslant 0 \end{aligned} \tag{1}$$

The parameter B can be viewed as an input gain, or, alternatively, as a mechanism for setting the operating range of the channel. This function is exponential for negative signals, linear but shifted (by a "spontaneous" rate of unity magnitude) for small positive signals, and compressive for larger signals, saturating at $1 + A\pi/2$. It is based on the measured hair-cell current responses as a function of a fixed displacement of the cilia as determined in the frog saculus by Hudspeth & Corey (1977).

The model for short-term adaptation is very similar to one proposed by Goldhor (1985). It consists of two separate mechanisms that influence the concentration of a substance, which could be thought of as a neurotransmitter or an ion. A model "membrane" allows flow of a supply from a source region at a rate that is proportional to the concentration gradient across the membrane, with a proportionality constant, μ_a. However, channels in this membrane are closed whenever the concentration in the supply region is too small (i.e. when the concentration gradient is *negative*). The substance is also lost through natural decay at a rate that is proportional to its concentration within the region, with a proportionality constant μ_b. Mathematically, the process can be expressed as follows:

$$\begin{aligned} dC(t)/dt &= \mu_a[S(t) - C(t)] - \mu_b C(t) \quad C(t) < S(t) \\ &= -\mu_b C(t) \qquad\qquad\qquad\quad C(t) \geqslant S(t) \end{aligned} \tag{2}$$

where $C(t)$ is the concentration of the substance within the region, and $S(t)$ is the concentration in the source region. The output of this system is the flow rate across the membrane, $\mu_a[S(t) - C(t)]$, which controls the probability of firing of the nerve fiber. A discrete realization is achieved by approximating d/dt by a first difference in time.

Goldhor showed that such a model, when applied using the *envelope* of the stimulus as the source concentration, $S(t)$, obeys certain linear response properties of short-term adaptation that have been observed for auditory data (Smith & Zwislocki, 1975) (see Section 4 for details). When a high-amplitude signal turns on abruptly, the flow rate is initially very high and then decreases exponentially, with a time constant, $\tau_1 = 1/(\mu_a + \mu_b)$, to a steady-state value. After the signal is turned off, the concentration gradient becomes negative, and the flow rate remains zero until $C(t)$ decays (exponentially with a time constant $\tau_2 = 1/\mu_b$) to the spontaneous concentration level. Thus, the time constant for recovery after offsets is longer than that for adaptation after onsets, a feature which also resembles the auditory-nerve response (Harris & Dallos, 1979).

Our system uses the same model, except that the detailed cycle-by-cycle behavior of the input signal is preserved in $S(t)$. In this case, the channel opens and closes for each period of the stimulus, and an adapted response is obtained only after the amount of substance gained while $S(t)$ is greater than $C(t)$, is exactly equal to the amount lost during the remaining portion of the cycle. One consequence is that the effective time constant for adaptation lies somewhere between the "open" time constant, τ_1, and the "closed" time constant, τ_2. The time constant for recovery, on the other hand, remains equal to τ_2.

The output of the adaptation stage is next processed through a lowpass filter that achieves two important effects: it reduces synchrony to high-frequency stimuli and it smooths the square-wave shape encountered in the half-wave response for saturating stimuli. The lowpass filter was realized as a cascade of n_{LP} leaky integrators, each with an identical time constant τ_{LP}. The two parameters, n_{LP} and τ_{LP}, were adjusted to match

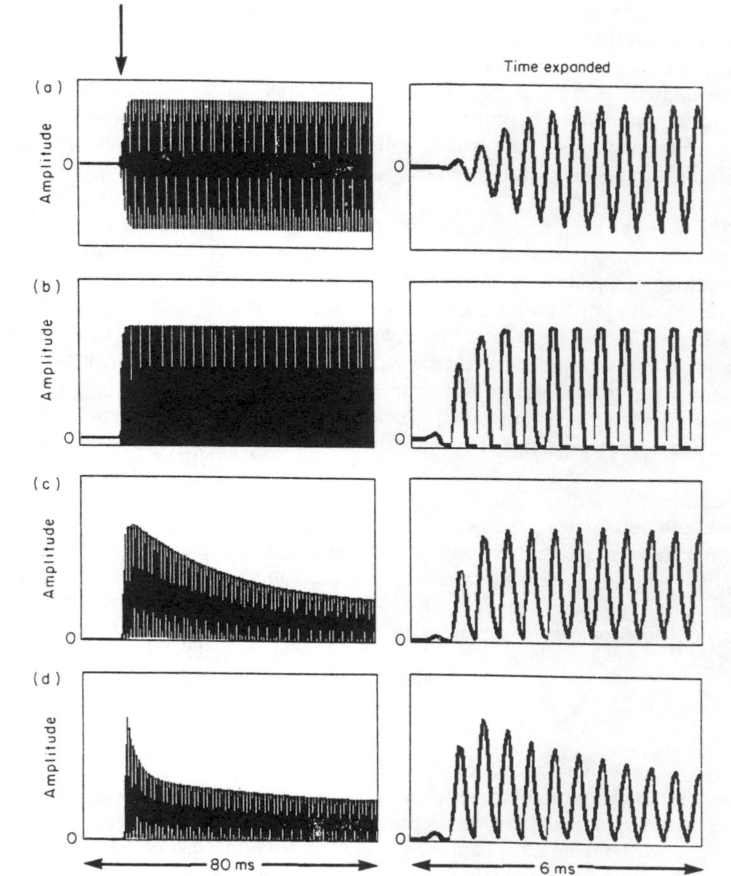

Figure 3. Responses at CF for the intermediate stages of the inner-hair-cell/synapse model in response to a 2-kHz signal presented at a high sound-pressure level: (a) after passing through a critical band filter, (b) after half-wave rectification, (c) after short-term adaptation and lowpass filtering, and (d) after the AGC. The arrow marks the center of the time-expanded region on the right.

available data on synchrony as a function of frequency (Johnson, 1974). The equation in the discrete domain for the resulting transfer function is:

$$H(z) = \left(\frac{1-\alpha}{1-\alpha z^{-1}}\right)^{n_{LP}}, \quad (3)$$

where α is the pole location on the real axis of the z-plane such that $\alpha^n = \exp(-1)$ at a sample count, n, corresponding to τ_{LP} ms.

The final component is the rapid AGC, which is defined as follows:

$$y[n] = \frac{x[n]}{1 + K_{AGC}\langle x[n]\rangle}, \quad (4)$$

where K_{AGC} is a constant and $\langle\,\rangle$ symbolizes "expected value of", obtained by processing $x[n]$ through the first-order lowpass filter, with time constant τ_{AGC}. This equation resembles in form the formula obtained theoretically by Johnson & Swami (1983) as a steady-state solution for a simple model of the refractory effect, where it is assumed that a response is locked out for a time interval Δ after a spike occurs:

$$y(t) = \frac{x(t)}{1 + \int_{t-\Delta}^{t} x(\alpha)d\alpha}. \quad (5)$$

Figure 3 shows the outputs of intermediate stages of the 2-kHz channel in response to a high-amplitude tone at CF. The envelope of the response over a long time interval is shown on the left, and the detailed wave shapes near tone onset are shown on the right. Figure 3(a) shows the response after only the linear filter of Stage I. Figure 3(b) shows the response after the instantaneous half-wave rectifier. The square-wave shapes introduced here are lost after the lowpass filter. The effects of the short-term adaptation component are apparent in the envelope response on the left in Fig. 3(c). The final AGC further alters the dynamics of the onset, to produce a trend quite typical of auditory-nerve fibers, as shown in Fig. 3(d).

4. Comparison of the model with physiological data

The system described above contains a number of parameters that can be adjusted according to a specific set of criteria based on relevant physiological data. The degree to which the model agrees with the relevant physiology provides a measure of the system's ability to adequately describe the essential properties underlying speech coding in the auditory periphery. The following physiological properties are considered to be significant with respect to speech representation in the auditory nerve:

(1) Temporal envelope of nerve-fiber discharge rate as a function of signal amplitude level, particularly during the initial 40 ms following stimulus onset (Delgutte, 1980).

(2) Forward masking effects as a function of masker sound-pressure level (Delgutte, 1980).

(3) Period histogram responses in steady-state conditions for single-formant stimuli, as a function of stimulus amplitude (Delgutte, 1980).

(4) Dynamic properties of discharge response to amplitude increments (Smith & Zwislocki, 1975).

(5) Synchrony falloff characteristics as a function of signal frequency (Johnson, 1974).

TABLE I. Fixed parameter values used for experiments

Half-wave			Adaptation		Lowpass		AGC	
A	B	G_{HW}	τ_1	τ_2	τ_{LP}	n_{LP}	τ_{AGC}	K_{AGC}
10	65	2.35	15 ms	120 ms	0.04 ms	4	3 ms	0.002

The parameters of the system were adjusted to match all of the above criteria as well as possible. Several iterations through the matching process were necessary to achieve convergence. Some surprising results emerged from the exercise. Most remarkable was that the τ_2 parameter of the Goldhor adaptation model had to be set to a much larger value than was anticipated in order to match the forward-masking data. Another discovery was that although the short-term adaptation component and the AGC component interact in a complex way, it is possible to set their parameters so that the equal-increment criterion imposed by the Smith and Zwislocki paradigm is reasonably well matched. Each of the above criteria is discussed in turn. For each example the relevant physiological data are compared with the response of the model.

In all instances the parameters of the model, as empirically determined, were set at fixed values, which are shown in Table I. Parameter B of the half-wave rectifier, an input gain term, is based on the assumption that the input speech signal has been normalized to a maximum amplitude of 1.0. The output of the half-wave rectifier was multiplied by a gain term, G_{HW}, which was adjusted to yield a final output that could be equated with firing rate. The lowpass filter has a very gradual falloff as a function of frequency. The response is down by 3 dB at 2 kHz, by 9 dB at 4 kHz and by 13 dB at 6 kHz.

4.1. *Tone onsets*

Delgutte (1980) plotted the envelope of the discharge pattern as a function of time in response to a sinusoidal signal presented over a large range of sound-pressure levels (Fig. 4). The experimental paradigm was simulated for the computer model and the resulting responses are shown in the right-hand column. Onset response characteristics are largely dominated in the model by the parameters of the rapid AGC component.

4.2. *Forward masking*

Delgutte's (1980) plot for a forward masking experiment are shown in Figure 5 (left), along with the results of the computer model (right). The plots are given as a function of adapter sound-pressure level, with the test-tone level held fixed. The main controlling factor of forward masking in the model is τ_2 of the short-term adaptation model.

4.3. *Formant period histograms*

Delgutte (1980) obtained plots of the period histograms of steady-state responses to a single-formant, vowel-like stimulus (i.e. a pulse train of frequency F_0 was passed through a resonator whose center frequency was set to F_1). Figure 6 compares the period histograms from a fiber (CF = formant frequency) with those produced by the model for signals presented over a wide range of sound-pressure levels. For both the physiological data and the model output, the bandwidth of the response appears to be broader

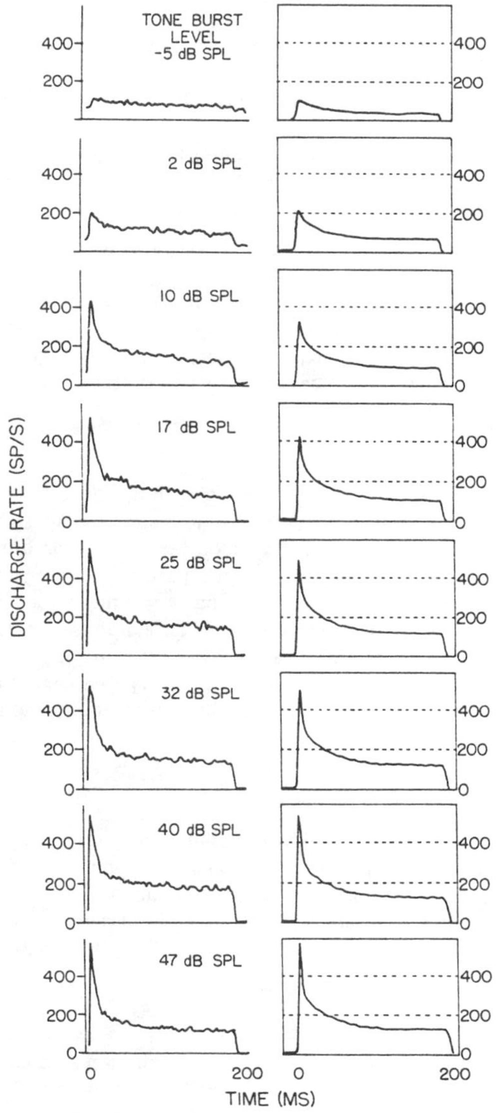

Figure 4. Response patterns of an auditory-nerve fiber to a tone burst as a function of signal amplitude (from Delgutte, 1980). The 180-ms burst has a rise/fall time of 2.5 ms, and a frequency of 770 Hz, approximately equal to the fiber CF. The post-stimulus-time (PST) histogram was computed with a bin width of 1.4 ms and then smoothed with a three-point smoother. Response patterns generated by the model for the same stimulus conditions. The response was smoothed with a 4.2-ms Hamming window.

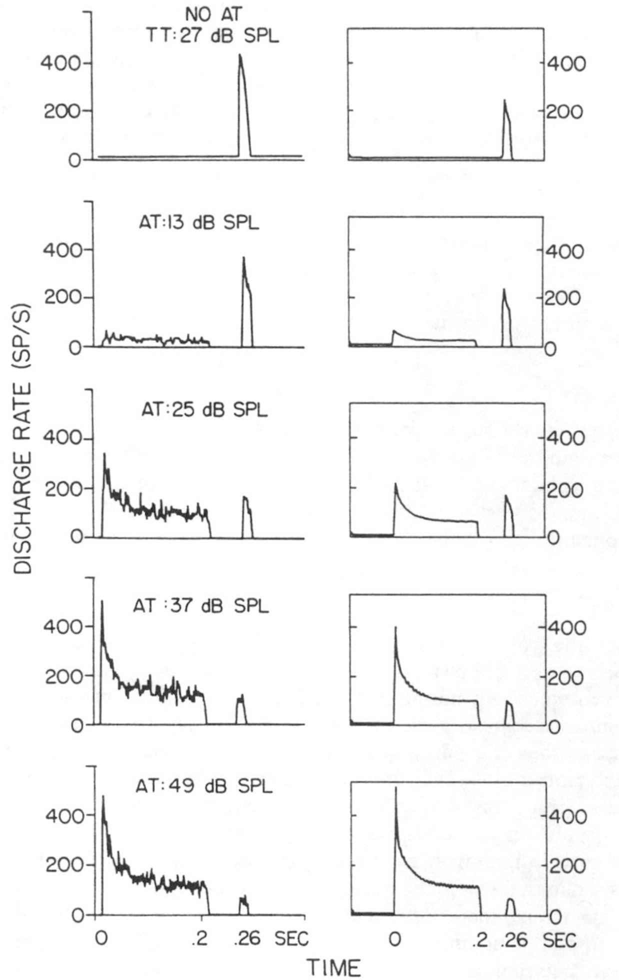

Figure 5. Left: response patterns of an auditory-nerve fiber to a 20-ms test tone preceded by a 200-ms adapting tone (from Delgutte, 1980). Both tones have a rise time of 2.5 ms and a frequency of 1220 Hz, approximately equal to the fiber CF. Histograms are computed with a 1-ms bin width, and were three-point smoothed. Right: response patterns for the computer model for the same stimulus conditions, using a 3-ms Hamming window for smoothing.

(i.e. the response decays more rapidly with each period) at intermediate amplitudes than at higher amplitudes, where saturation effects are dominating the response. Such domination at high signal amplitudes may well be related to the phenomenon of two-tone suppression (Sachs & Abbas, 1976; Javel, Geisler & Ravindran, 1978). The half-wave rectifier is the controlling factor in this steady-state phase-locked response characteristic, although the short-term adaptation component also plays a role.

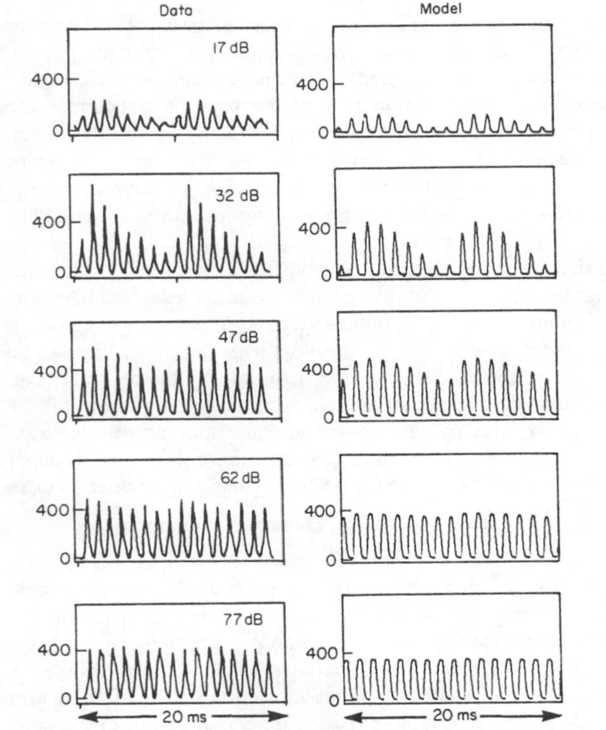

Figure 6. Left: response patterns of an auditory-nerve fiber to a single-formant synthetic stimulus as a function of signal amplitude. The stimulus has a formant frequency of 800 Hz, approximately equal to the fiber CF. Formant bandwidth is 70 Hz and the fundamental frequency is 100 Hz. The 10-ms period histogram, computed with a 50 μs bin width, is repeated twice in each case to show two pitch periods of the response. Right: response patterns generated by the model for the same stimulus conditions. The responses, in this case, are unsmoothed.

4.4. *Incremental responses*

Smith & Zwislocki (1975) measured the discharge rate of auditory-nerve fibers in response to abrupt increments of a sinusoid's amplitude. The amplitude, I, was incremented by an amount δI at a time $\tau = 150$ ms after initial onset. A post-stimulus-time histogram of the response was computed, and a difference between the response immediately preceding (R_τ^-) and following (R_τ^+) the amplitude increment was designated the "steady-state incremental response". This incremental response, defined as $IR = R_\tau^+ - R_\tau^-$, was then compared with an "onset incremental response", which is defined as the difference between the response to an onset signal at amplitude $I + \delta I$ and the response to a signal at amplitude I. Two important observations were: (1) the steady-state and onset IRs were approximately the same for signals of low-to-moderate sound-pressure level, and (2) the ratio of the response at signal onset, R_0, to the response during the steady-state portion, R_τ^-, was approximately equal to 2.5, regardless of the onset intensity level, I. This is the most difficult result to match with the model. The rapid AGC and the short-term adaptation tend to impose opposing constraints on the outputs. It is possible to obtain a fairly constant ratio of onset to steady-state response magnitude, but this ratio was consistently too large (3.0 instead of 2.5), as shown in Fig. 7(a). For the parameter settings shown in Table I, the 3-dB onset incremental response of the model was slightly larger than the 3-dB steady-state incremental response for low-amplitude signals. This response ratio became significantly smaller for more intense signals—a result which is in close agreement with the physiological data, as shown in Fig. 7(b).

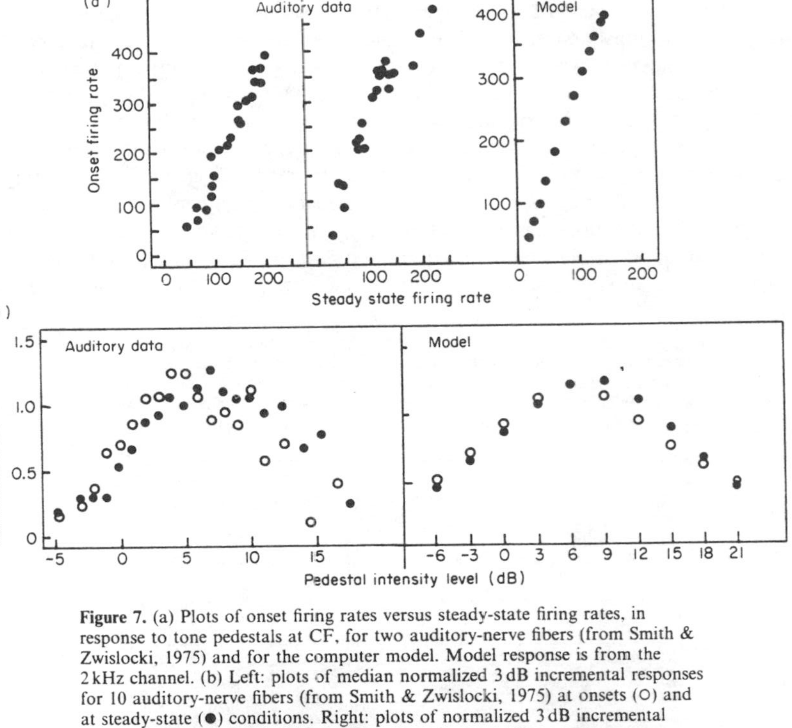

Figure 7. (a) Plots of onset firing rates versus steady-state firing rates, in response to tone pedestals at CF, for two auditory-nerve fibers (from Smith & Zwislocki, 1975) and for the computer model. Model response is from the 2 kHz channel. (b) Left: plots of median normalized 3 dB incremental responses for 10 auditory-nerve fibers (from Smith & Zwislocki, 1975) at onsets (○) and at steady-state (●) conditions. Right: plots of normalized 3 dB incremental responses for model at onsets (○) and at steady-state (●) conditions.

4.5. *Synchrony falloff*

Johnson (1974) provided a specific definition for a "synchronization index" applied to the period histograms of auditory-nerve fiber responses to sinusoidal signals. This index is the same as the normalized Fourier coefficient which is defined as:

$$S_f = \frac{A(F_0)}{A(0)}, \tag{6}$$

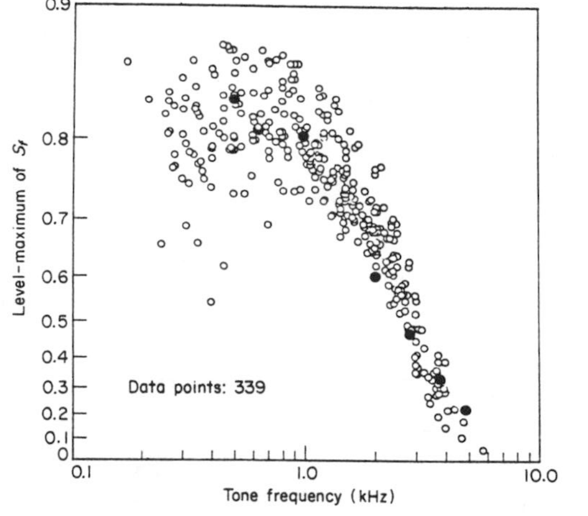

Figure 8. Scatter diagram of synchronization index (from Johnson, 1974) as a function of signal frequency (339 measurements from 233 units), compared with the model synchrony data (●).

where S_f is the synchronization index, $A(f)$ is the amplitude of the spectrum of the period histogram at frequency f, and F_0 is the signal frequency. Johnson measured S_f for a large number of fibers, using signals which did not always correspond to the fiber CF, and obtained the plot shown in Fig. 8. Points obtained by applying the same definition of synchrony to the model outputs are superimposed on Fig. 8 as closed circles. The primary component controlling the synchrony falloff in the model is the lowpass filter.

5. Output of the model for speech signals

Figure 9 shows an example of the Stage II outputs for a short segment of a male speaker's voiced speech, during the [e] of the word "make". Figure 9(a) is a wideband spectrogram of the signal, with a vertical bar indicating the point in time to which the channel outputs, shown in Fig. 9(b), refer. The 50-ms time-window includes approximately five pitch periods. The peaks are skewed slightly to the left for low frequencies, a feature that is present in the physiological data as well (Johnson, 1974). Figure 9(c) shows the output of the channel whose CF is nearest the vowel's second formant. A prominent component near the formant frequency is evident, in addition to the "envelope" periodicity at the fundamental frequency. Such formant periodicity is utilized by the synchrony algorithm in Stage III.

Figure 10 compares the outputs of Stages I and II outputs for the word "description" spoken by a female speaker. Each waveform is the output of one of the 40 channels, smoothed and downsampled to a 5-ms frame rate. The low-frequency channels are displayed at the bottom of the Figure. It is essential to represent Stage I outputs by a log-magnitude scale in place of a linear-magnitude representation; otherwise the formant peaks would overwhelm the remainder of the spectrum. A log-magnitude scale also corresponds to traditional analysis methods. Because of the saturating nonlinearity in the half-wave rectifier, as well as in the final AGC, a log representation is not appropriate

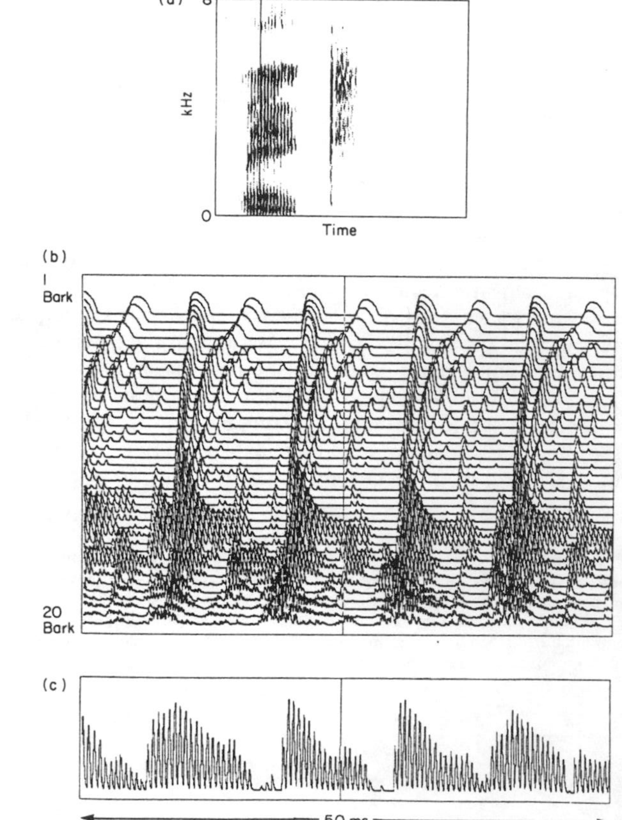

Figure 9. (a) Wideband spectrogram of the word "make", spoken by a male speaker. (b) Stage II outputs of 40 channels, with the *lowest* frequency channel at *top*, for five pitch periods during the vowel [e] at the time of the vertical bar in (a). (c) Output of a single channel near the frequency of the second formant at the same point in time as in (b).

for the outputs of Stage II. Magnitude at this level corresponds to "mean discharge rate", which is computed by dividing the number of spikes by the signal duration and scaling the result in units of seconds^{-1}. A phonetic transcription is provided below the channel outputs to facilitate segmentation.

Transitions from one phonetic segment to the next are more clearly delineated by onsets and offsets in the Stage II representation. All segment boundaries, except those associated with [rI], are well delineated in the Stage II representation. The closure intervals for both the [k] and [p] are flat valleys in the Stage II representation. There is clear evidence for forward masking here, particularly in the low-frequency region of the [pʃ] segment. The vowel [I] masks the low-frequency noise not only during the [p]-closure interval but also during the subsequent [ʃ]. Such masking phenomena should enhance

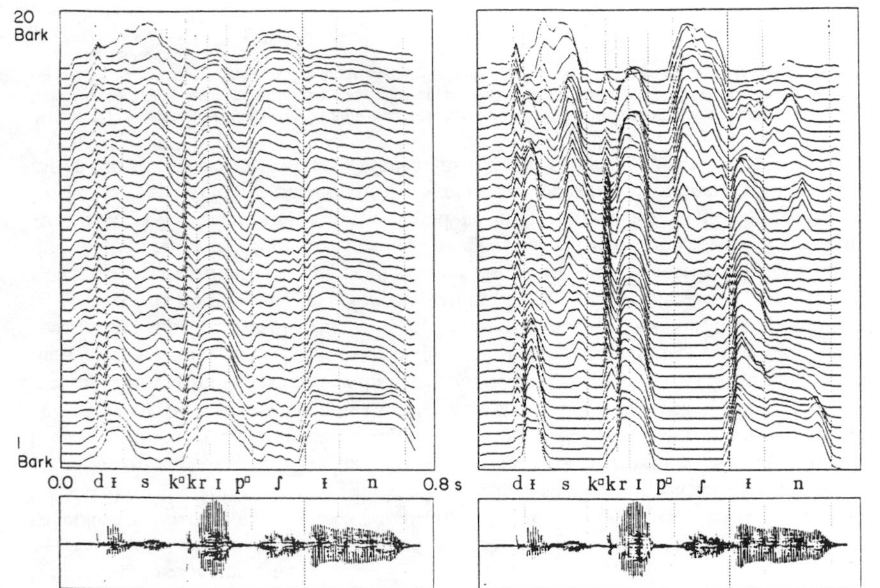

Figure 10. Left: log-magnitude response of Stage I outputs for the word "description" spoken by a female speaker, with the *lowest* frequency channel at the *bottom*. Right: magnitude response of Stage II outputs for the same word. The original waveform is shown below in each case. The dotted vertical lines denote the phonetic boundaries.

the contrast between vowels and fricatives. The boundary between the [ɪ] and the final [n] is very difficult to see in the Stage I representation. However, the Stage II nonlinearities serve to delineate this boundary. The stop-burst onsets for the [d] and the [k] are also much more sharply delineated after Stage II.

5.1. *The synchrony spectrogram*

The Stage II outputs, smoothed and downsampled, appear to be an excellent representation for locating transitions between phonemes, and thus could provide an adequate basis for phonetic segmentation. They may also be useful for broadly categorizing the resulting segments as *fricatives*, *closures*, *weak sonorants*, *vowels*, and so forth. However, these outputs, when displayed as a spectrogram, do not provide a precise estimate of the formant frequencies. This is to be expected because of the saturating nature and resulting limited dynamic range of auditory-nerve fibers. During the vocalic segments, many channels in the vicinity of the formant frequencies are responding at the saturation level and, as a consequence, the formant peaks become very broadly distributed.

The Stage II outputs do, however, contain significant information about the formant frequencies, which is discarded by the smoothing process. Such information is available as a dominant periodicity in the temporal response pattern. The ALSR calculation of Young & Sachs (1979) capitalized on such periodicity. We have chosen a somewhat different measure aimed at a similar goal. This "Generalized Synchrony Detector"

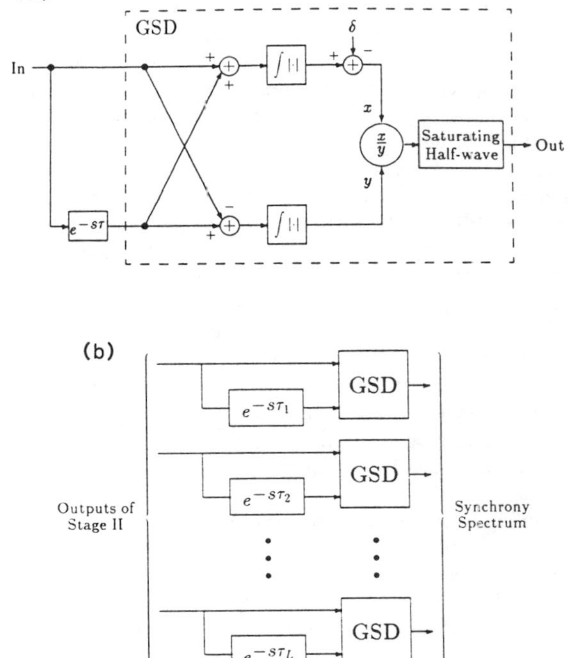

Figure 11. (a) Schematic diagram of the Generalized Synchrony Detector (GSD). (b) The synchrony branch of Stage III. Each channel output in Stage II is processed through a GSD tuned to the center frequency of the corresponding peripheral filter in Stage I. See text for details of GSD processing.

(GSD) was selected from a number of different possibilities because it offers certain advantages in representing the speech spectrum used to identify the phonetic content of the utterance. Our goal was to produce as clean a spectral representation as possible, one which would preserve prominent peaks at the formant resonances, while significantly reducing features of the spectrogram associated with the glottal excitation. We also sought to normalize for amplitude. Although pitch and loudness are certainly important perceptual attributes of the speech signal, we believe that a collection of distinct spectral representations, each of which is adapted to a specific assigned task, is to be preferred over a single complex representation which preserves all of the signal attributes.

The GSD is based on the ratio of the estimated magnitude of a sum waveform to the estimated magnitude of a difference waveform, as shown in Fig. 11(a). The inputs to the sum and difference computation are the GSD input signal and a delayed version of the input signal, with the delay period corresponding to the frequency to which the GSD is tuned. When the input to the GSD is perfectly periodic with the delay period, the magnitude of the difference waveform is zero. Hence, the ratio can become infinitely large during perfect synchrony. To constrain the response to be within reasonable limits, a final saturating nonlinearity is applied. In addition, a threshold is subtracted from the numerator in order to preclude a response from very weak signals. This threshold is set to a level slightly greater than the spontaneous discharge rate.

Figure 11(b) shows how the GSD is used to compute a synchrony spectrogram directly from the Stage II outputs. Each Stage II channel output is processed through a GSD tuned to the center frequency of the corresponding auditory filter in Stage I. Thus, if there is a prominent peak in the signal at a particular frequency, *f*, it will show up as a periodicity in the Stage II waveforms. Only the channel whose CF is closest to *f* will specifically detect the "correct" periodicity; its response will be correspondingly large. The output of adjacent channels will be significantly smaller because their tuned periodicity is inappropriate to that of the dominant signal.

This particular definition of synchrony was chosen for a number of reasons. First, because it measures a *periodicity* rather than a *frequency*, it avoids the problem of detecting synchrony to the second harmonic of a strong peak, such as was the case for the ALSR strategy[4]. Second, because the difference waveform in the denominator is balanced by a sum waveform in the numerator, this is effectively an *energy-normalized* scheme. Such normalization has the added advantage of significantly reducing temporal fluctuations in the response due to the envelope of the glottal excitation, which can be viewed as unwanted noise for this part of the recognition task. Finally, the algorithm is computationally simple, involving components that could reasonably be computed by neuron-like elements.

Harmonic structure due to the glottal excitation is usually completely obliterated in the synchrony spectrogram for male voices, but typically retained in the first-formant region for female voices. Harmonics between F_1 and F_2 are usually suppressed, because prominent energy at the first-formant frequency in the channel output destroys synchrony to the intermediate harmonics. Pitch striations over time are usually absent, due to the amplitude normalization process. Peaks at the formant frequencies are much narrower than in the envelope representation, thus making the synchrony spectrum more suitable for making fine distinctions.

The features of the synchrony branch of the system are illustrated in Fig. 12. A wideband spectrogram, an envelope spectrogram and a synchrony spectrogram are presented for the word "hesitate" spoken by a female speaker. The latter two are shown on a Bark-frequency scale (Zwicker, 1961). It is clear that the formant peaks are not well preserved in the envelope spectrogram, due mainly to the limited dynamic range of the nerve fibers. The formant resonances in the vowels are captured well by the synchrony measure. Furthermore, spectral peaks in regions of little energy, such as the initial [h] and the schwa, are enhanced relative to the wideband spectrogram. Perhaps surprisingly, the spectral prominences for obstruents in the high-frequency regions (i.e. in the [t] and the [z]) are accentuated by the synchrony algorithm, in spite of the fact that a good deal of synchrony to the stimulus frequency has been lost in Stage II. A possible explanation is that the synchrony measure incorporates energy at d.c., as well as energy at the CF. Any strong energy concentration in the signal at high frequencies is mostly converted to d.c. energy, which is passed by the synchrony measure. Prominent peaks in the input waveform well below the CF of high-frequency filters appropriately reduce the

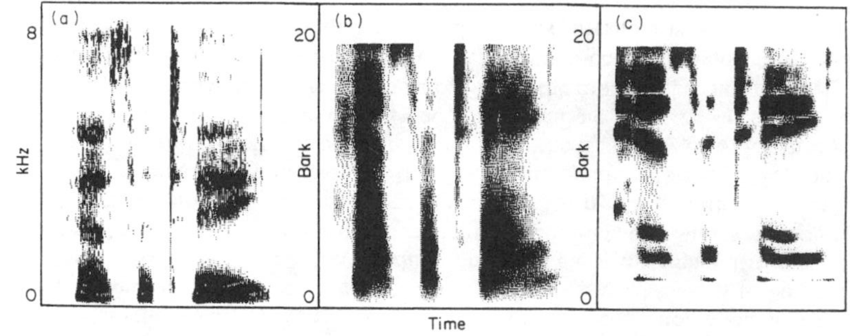

Figure 12. (a) Wideband spectrogram for the word "hesitate", spoken by a female speaker. (b) "Mean-rate" spectrogram for the same word, obtained by processing Stage II outputs through an envelope-detection scheme, corresponding to the top path of Stage III. (c) "Synchrony" spectrogram for the same word, obtained by processing Stage II outputs through a synchrony-detection scheme, corresponding to the bottom path of Stage III. The wideband spectrogram is shown on a linear-frequency scale, whereas the other two are displayed on a Bark scale.

synchronous response of such filters because the synchrony present in the signal is not of the appropriate frequency for these channels.

6. Summary and conclusions

This paper describes a relatively simple model for auditory processing of speech signals, which attains a reasonably good match to measured auditory responses for a number of different experimental paradigms. The model offers the hope of elucidating further the nature of the auditory response to speech. In addition, we anticipate that representations obtained from such a model will be well-suited to applications in computer speech recognition.

It is surprising that this model is capable of yielding such a close match to the Smith and Zwislocki data which show a constant ratio of onset to steady-state response and a close-to-equal incremental response characteristic for onset and steady-state conditions. Both the Goldhor adaptation model (when applied to a periodic signal rather than to the gross temporal envelope) and the AGC are nonlinear elements, yet a cascade of the two components results in an apparently linear overall response.

The model used for the AGC is a poor approximation of the refractory effect as it is currently understood. First, Equation (5) is only valid for steady-state conditions, and only exact for signals that are periodic with respect to Δ. Second, a leaky integrator yields an averaging window for $\langle x[n] \rangle$ that is exponential in shape, whereas a rectangular window is a much better approximation to the recovery function. Nonetheless, the value for K_{AGC} that was determined experimentally to best match auditory data is 0.002. This value corresponds to a 2-ms lockout period, which is of the correct order of magnitude. Perhaps a more realistic model for the refractory effect that would be appropriate during onsets, as well as steady states, would result in a better match to the dynamics of the onset envelope response.

It is not clear at what level of the auditory pathway a neural processing mechanism analogous to the Generalized Synchrony Detector should be sought. Nonetheless, such

[4]The GSD *does* detect synchrony at *half* the frequency of an input stimulus. This is a problem only for filters in the first formant region, since the high-frequency auditory filters typically have very steep slopes on the high-frequency side, such that input signals at twice the CF rarely trigger a response above the spontaneous rate.

a mechanism could be realized using simple units that are at least feasible neurologically. If the input to the GSD were a sequence of pulses instead of a waveform, then the difference waveform in the denominator would reduce to an XOR gate, with a suitably narrow time window over which the delayed input and the undelayed input "coincide". The division and half-wave rectification are functionally similar to an excitatory/inhibitory unit. This unit or "cell" would have a minimal response threshold, related to the silence threshold in Fig. 11(a), and a saturation level.

It is still premature to suggest that an auditory-based speech analysis system will pay off in speech recognition. There are emerging, however, strong indications that auditory-based representations are interesting and worthy of further study. We are now becoming more confident in the validity of the computer models, such that they may reveal interesting effects in auditory speech processing, which may lead the way to appropriate later-stage speech recognition strategies. We have described here a computer model that produces two distinct spectral-like representations for the speech signal, one based on the average discharge rate and the other based on the synchronous response. Several researchers in the speech group at M.I.T. are pursuing recognition strategies based on these representations. The mean-rate response outputs have been used successfully for locating acoustic boundaries and for making broad category decisions (Glass & Zue, 1986). Preliminary results using these outputs for syllable detection in continous speech are encouraging. The synchrony spectrogram has been applied to speaker-independent vowel recognition in continuous speech (Seneff, 1987). Preliminary results indicate superior performance with minimal computational load for the recognition stage.

The design of this system was influenced by interaction with several people. Among these are Bertrand Delgutte, Rich Goldhor, Don Johnson, Camp Searle, Ken Stevens, Tim Wilson and Victor Zue. Rob Kassel was very helpful in constructing some of the figures. The paper is much improved due to the careful reading of earlier versions by Katy Kline, Don Johnson, Ken Stevens, Steven Greenberg, Quentin Summerfield and an anonymous reviewer.

This research was supported by DARPA under Contract N00039-85-C-0254, monitored through Naval Electronic Systems Command.

References

Delgutte, B. (1980) Representation of speech-like sounds in the discharge patterns of auditory-nerve fibers, *Journal of the Acoustical Society of America*, **68**, 843–857.

Delgutte, B. & Kiang, N. Y. S. (1984*a*) Speech coding in the auditory nerve: I. Vowel-like sounds, *Journal of the Acoustical Society of America*, **75**, 866–878.

Delgutte, B. & Kiang, N. Y. S. (1984*b*) Speech coding in the auditory nerve: III. Voiceless fricative consonants, *Journal of the Acoustical Society of America*, **75**, 887–896.

Delgutte, B. & Kiang, N. Y. S. (1984*c*) Speech coding in the auditory nerve: IV. Sounds with consonant-like dynamic characteristics, *Journal of the Acoustical Society of America*, **75**, 897–907.

Eggermont, J. J. (1973) Analog modelling of cochlear adaptation, *Kybernetik*, **14**, 117–126.

Glass, J. R. & Zue, V. W. (1986) Signal representation for acoustic segmentation, *Proceedings of the First Australian Conference on Speech Science and Technology*, 124–129.

Geisler, C. D. (1988) Representation of speech sounds in the auditory nerve, *Journal of Phonetics*, **16**, 19–35.

Goldhor, R. S. (1985) *Representation of consonants in the peripheral auditory system: a modeling study of the correspondence between response properties and phonetic features*. Technical Report 505. Cambridge, MA: M.I.T.

Harris, D. M. & Dallos, P. (1979) Forward masking of auditory nerve fiber responses, *Journal of Neurophysiology*, **42**, 1083–1107.

Hudspeth, A. J. & Corey, D. P. (1977) Sensitivity, polarity and conductance change in the response of vertebrate hair cells to controlled mechanical stimuli, *Proceedings of the National Academy of Science, U.S.A.*, **74**, 2407–2411.

Javel, E., Geisler, C. D. & Ravindran, A. (1978) Two-tone suppression in the auditory nerve of the cat, *Journal of the Acoustical Society of America*, **63**, 1157–1163.

Johnson, D. H. (1974) The response of single auditory-nerve fibers in the cat to single tones: synchrony and average discharge rate. Ph.D. Thesis, Massachusetts Institute of Technology, Cambridge, MA.

Johnson, D. H. (1980) The relationship between spike rate and synchrony in responses of auditory-nerve fibers to single tones, *Journal of the Acoustical Society of America*, **68**, 1115–1122.

Johnson, D. H. & Swami, A. (1983) The transmission of signals by auditory-nerve fiber discharge patterns, *Journal of the Acoustical Society of America*, **74**, 493–501.

Kiang, N. Y. S., Watanabe, T., Thomas, E. C. & Clark, L. F. (1965) *Discharge patterns of single fibers in the cat's auditory nerve*, Cambridge, MA: M.I.T. Press.

Miller, M. I. & Sachs, M. B. (1983) Representation of stop consonants in the discharge patterns of auditory-nerve fibers, *Journal of the Acoustical Society of America*, **74**, 502–517.

Rhode, W. S. & Smith, P. H. (1985) Characteristics of tone-pip response patterns in relationship to spontaneous rate in cat auditory nerve fibers. *Hearing Research*, **18**, 159–168.

Sachs, M. B. & Abbas, P. J. (1976) Phenomenological model for two-tone suppression, *Journal of the Acoustical Society of America*, **60**, 1157–1163.

Sachs, M. B., Blackburn, C. C. & Young, E. D. (1988) Rate-place and temporal-place representations of vowels in the auditory nerve and anteroventral cochlear nucleus, *Journal of Phonetics*, **16**, 37–53.

Sachs, M. B. & Young, E. D. (1980) Effects of nonlinearities on speech encoding in the auditory nerve, *Journal of the Acoustical Society of America*, **68**, 858–875.

Seneff, S. (1984) Pitch and spectral estimation of speech based on an auditory synchrony model, *Proceedings of ICASSP-84*, San Diego, CA.

Seneff, S. (1985) *Pitch and spectral analysis of speech based on an auditory synchrony model*. RLE Technical Report 504. Cambridge, MA: M.I.T. Press.

Seneff, S. (1987) Vowel recognition based on line-formants derived from an auditory-based spectral representation, *Proceedings of the Eleventh International Congress of Phonetic Sciences*, Tallinn, Estonia, U.S.S.R.

Sinex, D. G. & Geisler, C. D. (1983) Responses of auditory-nerve fibers to consonant-vowel syllables, *Journal of the Acoustical Society of America*, **73**, 602–615.

Smith, R. & Zwislocki, J. J. (1975) Short-term adaptation and incremental responses of single auditory-nerve fibers, *Biological Cybernetics*, **17**, 169–182.

Srulovicz, P. & Goldstein, J. L. (1983) A central spectrum model: a synthesis of auditory-nerve timing and place cues in monaural communication of the frequency spectrum, *Journal of the Acoustical Society of America*, **73**, 1266–1276.

Yost, W. A. & Nielsen, D. W. (1977) *Fundamentals of hearing—an introduction*. New York: Holt, Rinehart and Winston.

Young, E. D. & Sachs, M. B. (1979) Representation of steady-state vowels in the temporal aspects of the discharge patterns of populations of auditory-nerve fibers, *Journal of the Acoustical Society of America*, **66**, 1381–1403.

Zwicker, E. (1961) Subdivision of the audible frequency range into critical bands (frequenzgruppen), *Journal of the Acoustical Society of America*, **33**, 248–249.

Chapter 4

Template-Based Approaches

Introduction

Template-based approaches to speech recognition have provided a family of techniques that have advanced the field considerably during the last two decades. The underlying idea is simple. A collection of prototypical speech patterns (the templates) are stored as reference patterns representing the dictionary of candidate words. Recognition is then carried out by matching an unknown spoken utterance with each of these reference templates and selecting the category of the best matching pattern. Usually templates for entire words are constructed. This has the advantage that errors due to segmentation or classification of smaller acoustically more variable units such as phonemes can be avoided. In turn, each word must have its own full reference template; template preparation and matching become prohibitively expensive or impractical as vocabulary size increases beyond a few hundred words. Nonetheless, many important lessons have been learned from template-based recognition that continue to be applied in most recognition systems today.

We begin this chapter with a tutorial overview of template-based recognition, *Isolated and Connected Word Recognition* by Rabiner and Levinson. This paper actually provides a general speech-recognition tutorial and overview; however, it is dominated by the templated-based approach. This paper provides a good description of template-based matching for both isolated words and connected speech recognition. In addition, it describes signal processing, syntax, semantics, and speech applications. These aspects are also applicable to other speech recognition paradigms.

The second paper, *Minimum Prediction Residual Principle Applied to Speech Recognition* by F. Itakura, is one of the classic papers in template-based recognition, as it demonstrated excellent performance for a small isolated word vocabulary and helped popularize the template-based approach. It introduced the use of linear predictive coefficients as a compact but effective encoding of the speech signal useful for speech recognition. For template matching, a minimum prediction residual is used as a distance measure between unknown test and the reference templates. Rather than matching test and reference frame by frame, it successfully applied dynamic programming as a technique to find an optimal time alignment between the unknown and reference patterns.

Human speech varies considerably in speaking rate, and a system based on template matching should dynamically stretch and compress the time axes between test and reference patterns. Optimal dynamic-programming strategies to achieve such time alignment were proposed and studied by Sakoe and Chiba in their pioneering work, *Dynamic Programming Algorithm Optimization for Spoken Word Recognition*, which represents an important description and summary of dynamic programming (DP)-based recognition techniques. DP-based strategies were explored in considerable detail in subsequent years under various names—dynamic programming, dynamic time warping, DTW, dynamic time alignment, and DP matching, to name a few.

While most of the earlier work was mostly aiming at speaker-dependent recognition, this restriction was soon to be removed. In 1979, Rabiner et al. introduced a speaker-independent template based isolated-word recognition system. Their paper, *Speaker-Independent Recognition of Isolated Words Using Clustering Techniques* used clustering techniques to automatically generate multiple templates for each word candidate to better represent speech patterns belonging to each word, despite considerable variability across speakers.

Many of the earlier systems were also only isolated-word recognition systems; that is, they could only recognize one word at a time. An endpoint-detection algorithm would typically identify the start and end time of the candidate word, and a user would have to pause between words to enter a string of words. Once again, this limitation was soon lifted. Several techniques were proposed that were able to search for an optimal *string* of words. While earlier work by Vintsyuk [Vintsyuk 71] had already proposed just such a technique, the first widely known connected-word recognition scheme was developed by Sakoe in *Two-Level DP-Matching—A Dynamic Programming Based Pattern Matching Algorithm for Connected Word Recognition*. This approach used a second-level dynamic-programming optimization step to find the best sequence of words given the optimal word time alignment for each possible word start and end time.

During the subsequent years several other connected-word recognition strategies emerged. One of these method is the level-building algorithm [Myers 81] that iteratively extends N-word hypotheses to N+1 words. This algorithm is described in the first paper in this section. Another algorithm, the one-stage strategy, was independently developed by Vintsyuk [Vintsyuk 71], by Bridle et al. [Bridle 82], and by Ney [Ney 84]. This one-stage strategy does not require several levels of optimization, and has a number of attractive properties. Its simplicity allows for efficient implementation, recognition of unknown length strings, and real-time performance (recognition results can be output before the speaker has finished the utterance) without loss in optimality. *The Use of a One-Stage Dynamic Programming Algorithm for Connected Word Recognition* by Ney reviews this elegant strategy.

References

[Bridle 82] Bridle, J.S., Brown, M.D., and Chamberlain, R.M. An Algorithm for Connected Word Recognition. In *ICASSP 82 Proceedings* Volume 2:899–902. IEEE ASSP, April, 1982.

[Myers 81] Myers, C.S., Rabiner, L.R. Connected Digit Recognition Using a Level Building DTW Algorithm. *IEEE Transactions on Acoustics, Speech, and Signal Processing* ASSP-29(3):351-363, June, 1981.

[Ney 84] Ney, H. The Use of a One-Stage Dynamic Programming Algorithm for Connected Word Recognition. *IEEE Transactions on Acoustics, Speech, Signal Processing* ASSP-32(2):263–271, April, 1984.

[Vintsyuk 71] Vintsyuk, T.K. Element-Wise Recognition of Continuous Speech Composed of Words from a Specified Dictionary. *Kibernetika* 7:133-143, March-April, 1971.

Isolated and Connected Word Recognition—Theory and Selected Applications

LAWRENCE R. RABINER, FELLOW, IEEE, AND STEPHEN E. LEVINSON, MEMBER, IEEE

(Invited Paper)

Abstract—**The art and science of speech recognition have been advanced to the state where it is now possible to communicate reliably with a computer by speaking to it in a disciplined manner using a vocabulary of moderate size. It is the purpose of this paper to outline two aspects of speech-recognition research. First, we discuss word recognition as a classical pattern-recognition problem and show how some fundamental concepts of signal processing, information theory, and computer science can be combined to give us the capability of robust recognition of isolated words and simple connected word sequences. We then describe methods whereby these principles, augmented by modern theories of formal language and semantic analysis, can be used to study some of the more general problems in speech recognition. It is anticipated that these methods will ultimately lead to accurate mechanical recognition of fluent speech under certain controlled conditions.**

I. INTRODUCTION

ALTHOUGH a great deal has been learned about the fundamental processes of speech production and speech perception, the goal of mechanical recognition of fluent speech remains elusive [1]-[5]. Speech recognition, however, has made major strides forward in the past decade, and it has advanced to the point where several commercial systems are currently available [6]-[11]. These commercial systems are predominantly isolated word, speaker-trained systems which achieve word accuracies greater than 95 percent in noisy environments. At least one system, however, is a speaker-independent, isolated word recognizer operating over dialed-up telephone lines [7], while another is a speaker trained system that can handle a connected string of words (typically digits) [8].

In the laboratory, equally impressive advances have been recorded for speech recognition. A wide range of systems based on isolated words (both speaker-trained, and speaker-independent) have been developed for use over dialed-up telephone lines [12]-[16]; and more recently speaker-independent, connected-word systems have been proposed for connected digit recognition [8], [17]-[19].

As the capabilities of the word recognizers have improved, the tasks to which they have been applied have become more sophisticated, and more difficult. Such tasks have included chess playing, data retrieval and management, airlines information and reservations, and automatic recognition of read text extracted from patents on lasers [20]-[23]. Much of this advanced research has been under the auspices of ARPA, and excellent summaries of this work are available in [4] and [24].

This paper is intended to be a tutorial in the concepts and theories underlying modern speech-recognition systems, both practical and experimental. Two aspects of the subject are given special attention. First, we treat speech recognition as a classical problem in pattern recognition and show how some fundamental ideas from signal processing, information theory, and computer science can be utilized to provide the capability of robust recognition of isolated words and simple connected-word sequences. We then describe methods whereby these principles, augmented by modern theories of formal language and semantic analysis, can be combined to study some of the more general problems of speech recognition. In particular, we show how these theories can be applied to improve the recognition accuracy of a nonideal acoustic pattern recognizer. It is anticipated that these investigations will ultimately afford accurate mechanical recognition of fluent speech provided that it is part of a "task-oriented" dialog, that is, it is restricted to pertain to a well-defined, carefully circumscribed topic.

The outline of this paper is as follows. We begin, in Section II, with an overview of the pattern-recognition aspects of speech recognition. In this section, we are concerned with methods for short-time spectral estimation and elaborate on the filter bank and linear prediction methods. We also discuss other aspects of the pattern-recognition paradigm including similarity measures, temporal alignment of speech patterns, and statistical decision strategies. We then describe, within this framework, the basic word-recognition system, giving some details of its implementation, operation, and performance.

Section III provides a discussion of the application of pattern-recognition techniques to the construction of speech-recognition systems designed to perform specific tasks. In these examples, the special requirements of each task influence the way the general theories are utilized and adapted.

A relatively straightforward application of the basic principles allows us to build a voice-operated telephone repertory dialer. This particular system exploits some rudimentary task constraints by partitioning the vocabulary into sets of which only one is appropriate to any of the specific types of commands to which the system can respond.

A more sophisticated kind of constraint is used to build a telephone directory listing retrieval system. Here the constraints implicit in a telephone directory are used to actually correct acoustic-recognition errors. In this context, we intro-

Manuscript received October 17, 1980; revised January 8, 1981.
The authors are with Bell Laboratories, Murray Hill, NJ 07974.

0090-6778/81/0500-0621$00.75

duce the notion of list searching on an incomplete or corrupted key. Later we will formalize and generalize this approach.

Finally we describe a system which recognizes strings of connected digits. This system is substantially different from the other two in that it recognizes strings of words uttered without pauses between them. This is made possible by an important generalization of the temporal-alignment procedure discussed earlier.

Each of these three systems represents an advance toward the ultimate goal of speech-recognition research, human/machine conversational-speech communciation. Over the years, this goal has proven to be a most elusive one. Part of the reason for the difficulty lies in the fact that extrapolation of the pattern-recognition paradigm does not provide a sufficiently general model of the speech-communication process. Thus in Section IV, we go on to consider some other disciplines which can be used to analyze some phenomena of speech not encompassed by the pattern-recognition model.

We begin with a brief description of the human speech-communication process including both the vocal and auditory apparatus and an abstract definition of communication. We then outline some parts of the theories of formal languages and semantic analysis which can be applied to speech recognition. In particular, we elaborate on a simple formalization of grammar which both dramatically increases the versatility and robustness of our speech-recognition machines and provides insights into the role of linguistic structure in speech recognition.

Next, we show how these theories can be implemented and how they increase the capabilities of our experimental speech-recognition systems. We first return to the notion of list searching. We formalize this procedure and present two algorithms. This discussion provides natural motivation for the notion of maximum-likelihood parsing leading to two different methods for continuous speech recognition. Finally, we develop some semantic theories which, when combined with the formal language theoretic results, permit us to simulate, in an elementary way, the entire speech-communication process.

We conclude with an evaluation of our current knowledge and experimental results, some directions for future research, and a few predictions of our ultimate accomplishments.

Although we have strived to describe the theory and framework of an arbitrary word recognizer in this paper, most of the examples and specific applications are derived from the research performed at Bell Laboratories. The advantage of this strategy is that the authors are familiar with this work and can accurately describe the theoretical principles, the results, and the conclusions drawn from this research. The disadvantage is that we are forced to omit describing, in detail, the work of our colleagues both in the commercial world and at universities and other research laboratories. We have, however, endeavored to reference outside work whenever possible, especially as it relates to the general principles we describe.

II. PATTERN-RECOGNITION MODEL FOR SPEECH RECOGNITION

Fig. 1 shows the canonic pattern-recognition model used in the majority of isolated word speech-recognition systems. There are three basic steps in the model:

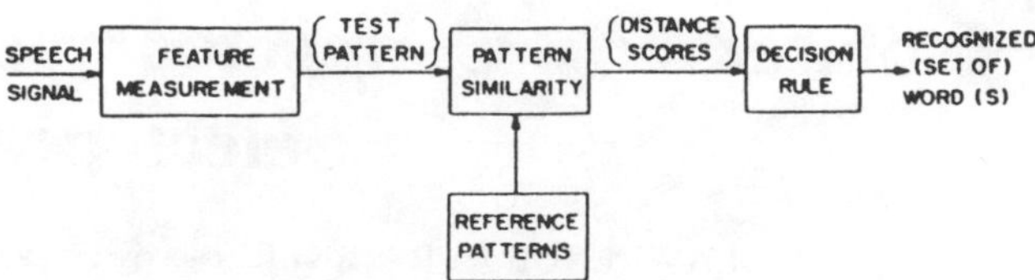

Fig. 1. Pattern-recognition model for speech recognition.

1) feature measurement;
2) pattern similarity determination;
3) decision rule.

The input to the model is the acoustic waveform of the spoken input[1] (typically a word, or a connected string of words). The output of the model is a "best" estimate of the word (or words) in the input. Often the output of the model is a set of estimates of the words in the input, ordered by similarity, allowing the final decision of what was actually spoken to be deferred to a higher level of processing in the recognition system.

Before going into detail about how the three steps in the model of Fig. 1 are actually performed, it is worthwhile to make two observations about the model. The first point concerns the model itself. Although modifications have been made to one or more steps, no viable alternative to the model of Fig. 1 has been proposed. The second point explains why this model has been used for so long and for so many applications. The answer is that the model

1) is invariant to different speech vocabularies, users, feature sets, pattern similarity algorithms, and decision rules;
2) is easy to implement;
3) works well in practice.

Either of these reasons alone provides justification for use of the model; however, the combination provides compelling reasons for its use. Therefore we will be using and referring to the pattern-recognition model of Fig. 1 throughout this paper.

A. Feature Measurement

For the purposes of this paper, feature measurement is basically a data-reduction technique whereby a large number of data points (in this case samples of the speech waveform recorded at an appropriate sampling rate) are transformed into a smaller set of features which are equivalent in the sense that they faithfully describe the salient properties of the acoustic waveform. For speech signals, data-reduction rates from 10 to 100 are generally practical.

For representing speech signals, a number of different feature sets have been proposed ranging from simple sets such as energy and zero crossing rates (usually in selected frequency bands), to complex, "complete" representations such as the short-time spectrum, linear-predictive coding (LPC), and the homomorphic model [2]. For recognition systems, the moti-

[1] An important, real-world, problem with the simple model of Fig. 1 is that the problem of speech (or endpoint) detection (i.e., finding the signal in the given acoustic background) is ignored. We shall return to this problem later in this section.

vation for choosing one feature set over another is often complex and highly dependent on constraints imposed on the system (e.g., cost, speed, response time, computational complexity, etc.). Three of the most important of these criteria are

1) computation time
2) storage
3) ease of implementation.

Of course the ultimate criterion is overall system performance (i.e., accuracy with which the recognition task is performed). However, this criterion is a complicated function of all system variables.

To illustrate the techniques used in measuring features for speech recognition, we now discuss two frequently used feature sets, namely, the filter bank model and the LPC model.

1) Filter Bank-Analysis of Speech: One of the most popular set of features used for speech recognition is the output of a bank of filters, as shown in Fig. 2 [25]-[28]. Throughout this paper, we will assume the speech signal $s(n)$ is in digital form, i.e., it has been digitized at a sampling rate of F_0 samples per second. We will also assume that all signal processing is performed digitally. In many practical cases, however, analog signal processing is used to obtain the feature sets. This is especially true for the model of Fig. 2, since inexpensive implementations of this particular structure are fairly straightforward [6], [7], [9]-[11].

In filter bank-analysis model, the speech signal is passed through a bank of Q bandpass filters covering the speech band from about 100 Hz to some upper cutoff frequency (typically between 3000 and 8000 Hz). The number of filters used, Q, varies from about 5 to as many as 32, and the filter spacing is generally linear until about 1000 Hz, and logarithmic beyond 1000 Hz.

The output of each bandpass filter is generally passed through a nonlinearity (e.g., a square-law detector or a full-wave rectifier) and low-pass filtered to give a signal which is proportional to the energy of the speech signal in the band. A logarithmic compressor is generally used to reduce the dynamic range of the intensity signal and the compressed output is resampled (decimated) at a low rate (generally twice the low-pass filter cutoff) for efficiency of storage. At a given time sample m, the parallel outputs $x_1(m)$, $x_2(m)$, $\cdots$, $x_Q(m)$ define a Qth order feature vector $X(m)$. The time course of X defines a pattern, i.e.

$$X(m) = \{x_1(m), x_2(m), \cdots, x_Q(m)\} \tag{1a}$$

$$P = \{X(1), X(2), \cdots, X(M)\}. \tag{1b}$$

The pattern so defined is used for training or testing the recognition system.

At the bottom of Fig. 2, we show schematically a typical bandpass and low-pass filter. The cutoff frequencies of the bandpass filter are denoted as f_{L1} and f_{H1}. Typically, the filter bandwidth

$$\Delta f = f_{H1} - f_{L1} \tag{2}$$

is about 100 Hz for the low-cutoff filters, and as large as 500-

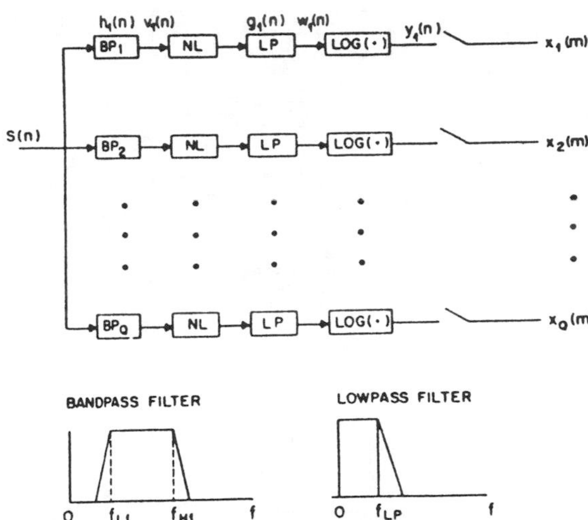

Fig. 2. Filter banks model for estimating recognition features from a bank of Q filters.

1000 Hz for the high-band filters. Implementations that have been used are as simple as two-pole Butterworth filters, and as complex as 511 point, linear phase, FIR digital filters [25]-[28].

The low-pass filter cutoff frequency f_{LP} is typically about 20-30 Hz, implying output feature sampling rates of from 40 to 60 Hz. For the value of $Q = 5$, with a 40 Hz sampling rate, it is seen that a total of about 200 features are required to represent 1 s of speech. For 8000 Hz sampled speech, this represents a 40:1 reduction in data rate.[2]

It should be clear that each branch of the filter bank model of Fig. 2 is measuring (approximately) the speech energy in the band covered by the bandpass filter of the branch. For many recognition systems, this feature set is supplemented by adding a zero-crossing counter at the output of the bandpass filter, as shown in Fig. 3. (The zero-crossing count is, to a first approximation, a measure of the formant frequency for wide bandwidth filters.) By incorporating zero crossings into the system, the number of features is doubled with little increase in computation or system complexity. To the extent that zero crossing and energy are independent parameters in each band, the information obtained about the speech is increased at little cost. However, as we will see later, there is increased cost in the decision making parts of the recognizer. Hence the doubling of the number of features is generally unadvisable unless the features are truly independent and information bearing.

2) LPC Feature Model For Recognition: Another commonly used feature set for recognition is the LPC based feature set for recognition is the LPC based feature set originally proposed by Itakura [12].

The basic idea behind linear predictive coding is that a given speech sample can be approximated as a linear combination of

[2] It should be noted that a significant amount of information is lost from the signal when it is represented by 200 features per second, i.e., one could not synthesize a high-quality replica of the original signal from these features.

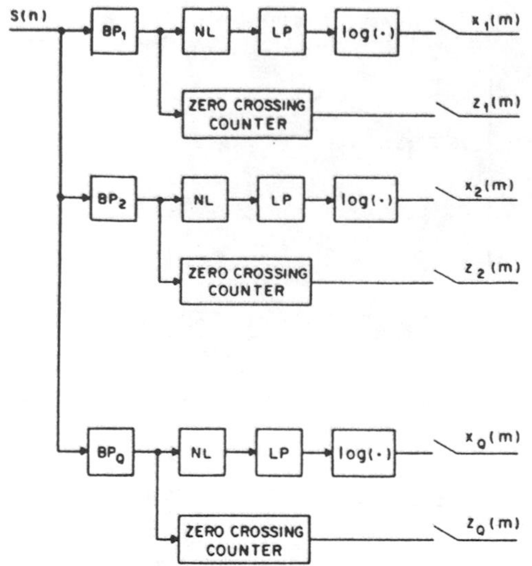

Fig. 3. The addition of zero-crossing measurements to the energy measurements of each band in the bank of filters model.

past speech samples. By minimizing the sum of the squared differences (over a finite interval) between the actual samples and the linearly predicted ones, a unique set of predictor coefficients can be determined. Linear-predictive coding can be readily shown to be closely related to the basic model of speech production in which the speech signal is modeled as the output of a linear, time-varying system excited by either quasi-periodic pulses (for voiced sounds) or random noise (for unvoiced sounds). The linear-predictive coding method provides a robust, reliable, and accurate method for estimating the parameters that characterize the linear, time-varying, system [2], [29], [30].

Fig. 4 shows a block diagram of the LPC-based feature analysis system. Unlike the bank of filters model, this system is a block processing model in which a frame of N samples of speech is processed, and a vector of features is measured. To obtain this vector, the speech signal is first preemphasized (to spectrally flatten the speech signal and to reduce computational instabilities associated with finite precision arithmetic [29]) using a fixed first-order digital system with transfer function

$$H(z) = 1 - az^{-1}, \qquad a = 0.95 \tag{3a}$$

giving the signal

$$\tilde{s}(n) = s(n) - as(n-1). \tag{3b}$$

The signal is next blocked into N sample sections (frames) for feature measurement. (Typical frame sizes are from 15 to 50 ms, i.e., $N = 150$ to 500 for a 10 kHz sampling rate.) Consecutive frames are spaced M samples apart. Clearly when $M < N$, there is overlap between adjacent frames. Such overlap inherently provides smoothing between vectors of feature coefficients. (Typical values of M are $M = N/3$, $M = N/2$, or $M = N$ for 3 to 1, 2 to 1, and no overlap, respectively.)

If we denote the lth frame of speech as $x_l(n)$, we have

$$x_l(n) = \tilde{s}(Ml + n), \qquad n = 0, 1, \cdots, N-1, \qquad l = 0, 1, \cdots, L-1 \tag{4}$$

where $l = 0$ is the first frame and $l = L - 1$ is the Lth frame of speech. In order to minimize the effects of trying to analyze a slice of the speech waveform, a smoothing window $w(n)$ is applied to the data to taper the speech samples to zero at the end of the frame, giving the windowed signal

$$\tilde{x}_l(n) = x_l(n) \cdot w(n). \tag{5a}$$

A typical smoothing window used in LPC analysis systems is the Hamming window defined as

$$w(n) = 0.54 - 0.46 \cos\left(\frac{2\pi n}{N-1}\right). \tag{5b}$$

The next step in the analysis is to perform an autocorrelation analysis of the windowed frame of data, giving

$$R_l(m) = \sum_{n=0}^{N-1-|m|} \tilde{x}_l(n)\tilde{x}_l(n+m), \qquad m = 0, 1, \cdots, p \tag{6}$$

where p is the order of the analysis system. (Typical values of p range from 8 to 12.) The feature set

$$X(l) = \{R_l(0), R_l(1), \cdots, R_l(p)\} \tag{7}$$

is often used as the analysis output of the LPC-based recognizer, since both reference and test patterns can be derived from the features of (7). However to perform both these tasks, a full LPC analysis is required in which a minimum mean squared error (in the time domain) all-pole fit to the spectrum of the frame of data is found by solving a set of linear simultaneous equations [29], [30]. The resulting all-pole model fit to the frame is of the form

$$A_l(z) = \frac{G}{1 + \sum_{m=1}^{p} a_l(m) z^{-m}} \tag{8a}$$

where G is a gain factor, and the set of coefficients $a_l(m)$, $m = 1, 2, \cdots, p$ define the all-pole model. If we define $a_l(0) = 1$, then we can define

$$A_l(z) = \frac{G}{\sum_{m=0}^{p} a_l(m) z^{-m}} \tag{8b}$$

and equivalently use the set $a_l(m)$ as the features for frame l.

To illustrate the LPC analysis method, Figs. 5 and 6 plots (for a 10 kHz sampling rate with $p = 14$) of

1) the windowed frame of data [part (a)];

2) the residual error (i.e., the signal which is not linearly predictable) by the model [part (b)];

3) the signal spectrum (as measured via an FFT) and the model spectrum [part (c)];

4) the spectrum of the error signal [part (d)] for the vowels /i/ (Fig. 5) and /a/ (Fig. 6). It can be seen from these figures

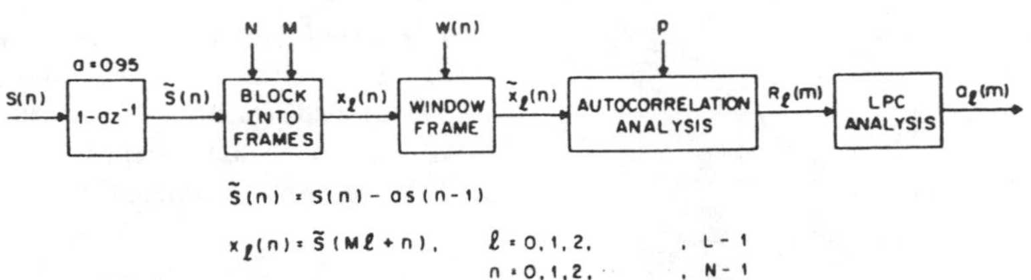

Fig. 4. Signal processing for extracting LPC features for recognition.

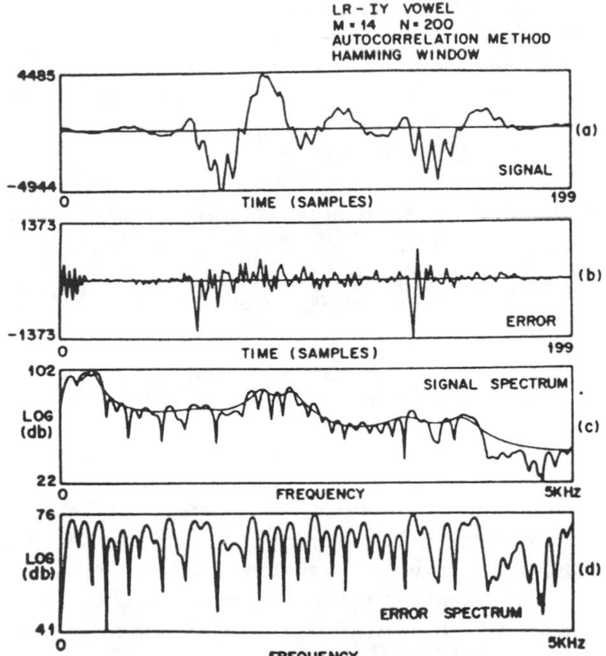

Fig. 5. Signals and spectra obtained from LPC model for vowel /i/.

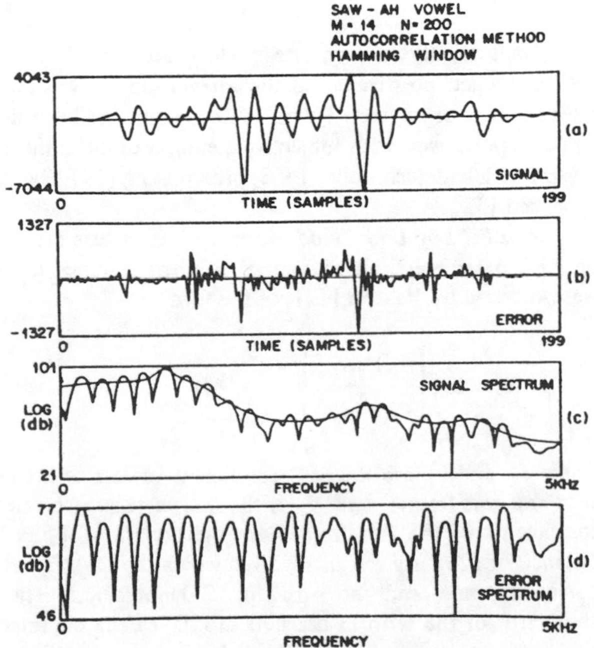

Fig. 6. Signals and spectra obtained from LPC model for vowel /a/.

that the LPC model provides a good fit to these simple vowel sounds.

B. Time Registration of Patterns

Once the patterns have been measured, the next step in the pattern-recognition model of Fig. 1 is to determine similarity between test and reference patterns. Because speaking rates vary greatly, pattern similarity involves both time alignment, and distance computation, and often these two are performed simultaneously.

Fig. 7 illustrates the function of time alignment between a test pattern $T(t)$ and a reference pattern $R(t)$ [12], [33], [35]. Our goal is to find an alignment function $w(t)$ which maps R onto the corresponding parts of T. The criterion for correspondence is that some measure of distance between the functions $D(T, R)$ be minimized by the mapping w. Thus, we seek $w(t)$ such that

$$D(T,R) = \min_{\{w(t)\}} \int_{t_0}^{t_1} d(t, w(t))G(t, w(t), \dot{w}(t))dt \tag{9a}$$

where $\{w(t)\}$ is the set of all monotonically increasing, continuous differentiable functions; $\dot{w}(t)$ is the derivative of $w(t)$; $d(t, w(t))$ is a metric $d(T(t), R(w(t)))$ which is the pointwise distance from R to T; and G is a weighting function.

Unfortunately, the variational problem of (9a) is not in general solvable so we discretize the problem by letting

$$T = \{T(1), T(2), \cdots T(NT)\} \tag{9b}$$

and

$$R = \{R(1), R(2), \cdots R(NR)\} \tag{9c}$$

after which a number of techniques including the classical dynamic programming method may be used. The "optimum" time-alignment path is a curve relating the m time axis of the reference pattern to the n time axis of the test pattern, of the form

$$m = w(n). \tag{10}$$

The constrained beginning and ending points of Fig. 7 can be formally expressed as constraints on $w(n)$ of the form

$$w(1) = 1 \tag{11a}$$

$$w(NT) = NR. \tag{11b}$$

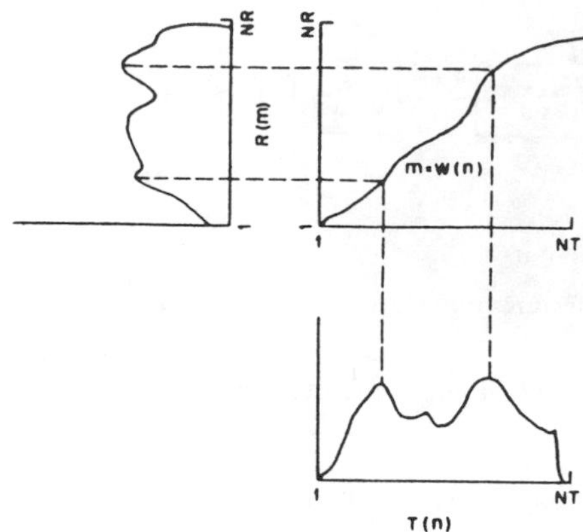

Fig. 7. Example of time registration of a test and a reference pattern.

Several techniques have been proposed for determining the alignment path w, including:

1) linear time alignment, i.e.

$$m = w(n) = (n-1)\frac{(NR-1)}{(NT-1)} + 1 \tag{12}$$

2) time event matching, i.e., times at which significant "events" occur in both reference and test patterns are found, and lined up in time

$$m_1 = w(n_1) \tag{13a}$$

$$m_2 = w(n_2) \tag{13b}$$

$$\vdots$$

$$m_Q = w(n_Q) \tag{13c}$$

and a functional fit to $w(n)$ is found based on these constraints. (Typically $w(n)$ is chosen to be a piecewise linear fit).

3) Correlation maximization, i.e., the warping function $w(n)$ is varied to maximize the correlation between reference and test patterns

$$R^* = \max_{w(n)} \sum_n (T(n)R(w(n))) \tag{14}$$

where the optimization is performed in a constrained manner.

4) Dynamic time warping, i.e., the warping curve is determined as the solution to the optimization problem

$$D^* = \min_{w(n)} \left[\sum_{n=1}^{NT} d(T(n), R(w(n))) \right] \tag{15}$$

where $d(T(n), R(w(n)))$ is the "distance" between frame n of the test pattern, and frame $w(n)$ of the reference pattern.

In the remainder of this section, we will develop the dynamic time-warping approach to registration of patterns since it has been shown to be extremely useful in a wide variety of speech-recognition systems [3], [8], [12], [15], [19], [23], [26], [31].

1) Frame-by-Frame Distance Measure: In order to implement the optimization of (15), the concept of distance between frames of features must be defined. Several possible distance measures can be used, depending on the form of the feature sets. For example, a simple Euclidean distance of the form

$$d(T,R) = \| T - R \| = \sum_{i=0}^{p} (T_i - R_i)^2 \tag{16}$$

where T_i and R_i are the ith components of the vectors T and R, respectively, is often used.

Other distance measures which have been used include:

a) Covariance Weighting: The distance is defined as

$$d(T,R) = (T-R)\tau^{-1}(T-R)^t \tag{17}$$

where τ^{-1} is the inverse of the covariance matrix of features, i.e.

$$\tau = \begin{bmatrix} \overline{R_0R_0} - \bar{R}_0{}^2 & \overline{R_0R_1} - \bar{R}_0\bar{R}_1 & \cdots & \overline{R_0R_p} - \bar{R}_0\bar{R}_p \\ \vdots & & & \\ \overline{R_pR_0} - \bar{R}_p\bar{R}_0 & & & \overline{R_pR_p} - \bar{R}_p{}^2 \end{bmatrix} \tag{18}$$

where the overbar corresponds to expected value. This type of weighting compensates for correlation between features, and tends to give equal weight to all features in the overall distance.

b) Spectral Distance: For this measure the log spectra of reference and test patterns are obtained, and the distance is given as

$$d(T,R) = \int_{\omega} [\log [T(e^{j\omega})] - \log [R(e^{j\omega})]]^q \, d\omega \tag{19}$$

where q is usually an even integer (to make the qth power of the difference positive), and the integration is over the frequency range of interest. This distance measure has been shown to correspond well with subjective measures of difference, and several efficient techniques for approximating (19) have been proposed [32].

c) LPC Log Likelihood Measure: For feature sets based on LPC parameters, an extremely efficient distance measure was proposed by Itakura [12], of the form

$$d(T,R) = \log \left[\frac{a_R V_T a_R{}^t}{a_T V_T a_T{}^t} \right] \tag{20}$$

where a_R and a_T are the LPC coefficient vectors of the reference and test frames, and V_T is the matrix of autocorrelation coefficients of the test frame. An interpretation of the LPC distance of (20) is given in Fig. 8 in which the subscript R denotes reference, and the subscript T denotes test. The denominator of the term in brackets in (20) can be obtained by passing the test signal $S_T(n)$ through the inverse LPC system

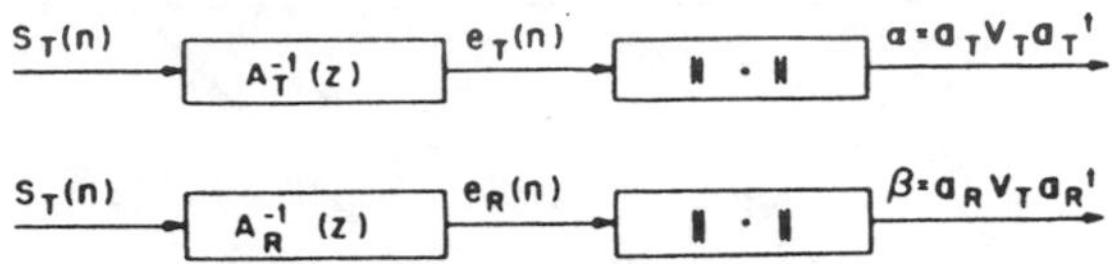

Fig. 8. Interpretation of LPC distance measure.

of the test, $A_T{}^{-1}(z)$ with response

$$A_T{}^{-1}(z) = \sum_{m=0}^{p} a_{mT} z^{-m} \tag{21}$$

giving the error signal

$$e_T(n) = \sum_{m=0}^{p} a_{mT} S_T(n-m) \tag{22}$$

and then by taking its energy giving

$$\alpha = \| e_T(n) \| = \sum_{n=0}^{N-1} [e_T(n)]^2. \tag{23}$$

Similarly, the numerator term can be obtained by passing the *same* test signal $S_T(n)$ through the inverse LPC system of the reference $A_R{}^{-1}(z)$ with response

$$A_R^{-1}(z) = \sum_{m=0}^{p} a_{mR} z^{-m} \tag{24}$$

giving the error signal

$$e_R(n) = \sum_{m=0}^{p} a_{mR} S_T(n-m) \tag{25}$$

with energy

$$\beta = \| e_R(n) \| = \sum_{n=0}^{N-1} [e_R(n)]^2. \tag{26}$$

Thus, from (20), (23), and (26) we get

$$d(T,R) = \log(\beta/\alpha) \tag{27}$$

showing that the distance between the two feature sets is related to the difference in LPC feature sets, which in turn is related to the differences in spectra between T and R frames. Markel and Gray [32] have quantified the interpretation of (20) as a spectral distance by showing it can be written as

$$d(T,R) = \log\left[\int_{-\pi}^{\pi} \left|\frac{A_R(e^{j\omega})}{A_T(e^{j\omega})}\right|^2 \frac{d\omega}{2\pi}\right] \tag{28}$$

i.e., an integrated square of the ratio of spectra between reference and test frames.

One of the most important aspects of any distance measure is the speed of computation, since distance calculations will be shown to be the most costly (time consuming) part of most recognition systems. As such any proposed distance measure which requires an inordinate amount of computation would not be a candidate for use in a practical system, no matter what its other advantages might be. On this basis, if we reexamine the four distance measures proposed in this section we get the following results:

1) Euclidean distance (16)–As proposed this distance measure requires $(p + 1)$ multiplications, $(p + 1)$ substractions, and $(p + 1)$ additions. By using a sum of magnitudes rather than squares, the multiplications can be eliminated in the computation.

2) Covariance weighting (17)–This distance measure requires about $(p + 1)^2$ multiplications and additions. For any reasonable size p, this computation is prohibitively large.

3) Spectral distance (19)–This distance requires the evaluation of an integral, or a discrete approximation to it. In either case the computation would be prohibitive; however Markel and Gray have proposed alternative measures which correlate well with (19), but with considerably reduced computation (e.g., the cosh measure) [32].

4) LPC distance (20)–As given in either (20), or as illustrated in Fig. 8, the computation of the LPC distance requires a large number of multiplications and additions. However Itakura [12] has shown that the distance d of (20) can be expressed (exactly) in the form

$$d(T,R) = \log\left[\sum_{m=0}^{p} \tilde{V}_T(m) R_R^a(m)\right] \tag{29}$$

where

$$V_T(m) = \frac{\tilde{V}_T(m)}{E_T} \tag{30}$$

where E_T is the normalized error of the LPC analysis of the test frame, and

$$R_R{}^a(m) = \sum_{k=0}^{p-m} a_R(k) a_R(k+m) \tag{31}$$

i.e., $R_R{}^a(m)$ is the autocorrelation of the finite vector

$$a_R = [1, a_R(1), a_R(2), \cdots, a_R(p)]. \tag{32}$$

Using (29), the computation of distance requires $(p + 1)$ multiplications and additions, and one log.

These results show that both the Euclidean and LPC distances are reasonable candidates for distance measures for recognition systems and both these measures have been widely used in practice.

2) Dynamic Time-Warping Framework: As described earlier, the dynamic-time warping (DTW) alignment problem (15) is to find the "optimal" warping path $w(n)$ which minimizes the accumulated distance D between test and reference patterns, subject to a set of path and endpoint constraints. A variety of formulations of the DTW problem, especially as applied to speech recognition, have been proposed by Sakoe and Chiba [33], and Myers *et al.* [34]. Rather than attempting to describe, or even summarize their work, we will just present a simple-minded approach that yields one DTW algorithm, [12], and then will briefly mention variants that have been proposed.

The basis behind most DTW algorithms is the realization that the solution to (15) is equivalent to finding the "best" path through a finite grid. As such, classical "path-finding" techniques could be used to solve the problem. In particular, it has been shown that a simple recursive technique could be used to find the best path in the grid. To see how this recursive solution is implemented, we must first define the minimum accumulated distance function $D_A(n, m)$ as the accumulated distance from the initial grid point $n = 1$, $m = 1$, to the grid point (n, m). If we assume that n represents the independent grid search variable, and that all valid paths through the grid correspond to monotonically increasing time indices, then we can write the recursion

$$D_A(n,m) = d(T_n, R_m) + \min_{q \leq m} [D_A(n-1, q)]. \tag{33}$$

As illustrated in Fig. 9, (33) says that the minimum accumulated distance to the grid point (n, m) consists of the local distance d between feature sets T_n and R_m, plus the minimum accumulated distance to the grid point $(n-1, q)$ where q is the set of m values such that a path exists between $(n-1, q)$ and (n, m). Fig. 9 shows an example in which there are only three valid paths to any grid point (n, m), i.e., from $(n-1, m)$, $(n-1, m-1)$, and $(n-1, m-2)$. It further shows a "nonlinear" constraint that if the best path to grid point $(n-1, m)$ came from grid point $(n-2, m)$, then no path can lead from $(n-1, m)$. Formally, we can express such local continuity constraints on the path (for the example of Fig. 9) as

$$w(n) - w(n-1) = 0, 1, 2 \quad \text{if } w(n-1) \neq w(n-2) \tag{34a}$$

$$= 1, 2 \quad \text{if } w(n-1) = w(n-2) \tag{34b}$$

giving the modified form of (33) as

$$D_A(n,m) = d(T_n, R_m) + \min [D_A(n-1, m) g(n-1, m), D_A(n-1, m-1), D_A(n-1, m-2)] \tag{35}$$

where .

$$g(n-1, m) = 1 \quad \text{if } w(n-1) \neq w(n-2) \tag{36a}$$

$$= \infty \quad \text{if } w(n-1) = w(n-2). \tag{36b}$$

The iteration of (35) is carried out over all valid m, for each value of n sequentially from $n = 1$ to $n = NT$, and the final desired solution is given as

$$D^* = D_A(NT, NR). \tag{37}$$

The optimum warping path $w(n)$ is determined by backtracking from the "end of the path" back to the beginning. For most word-recognition applications, the warping path need not be computed, only the accumulated distance D^* is required.

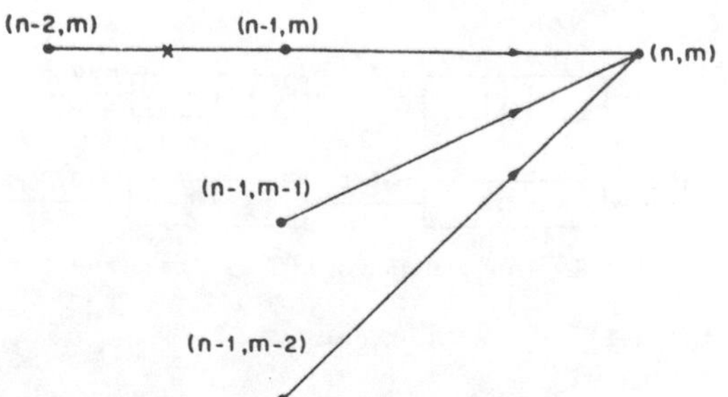

Fig. 9. One set of possible transitions to the grid point (n, m).

To illustrate a typical DTW warping region, Fig. 10 shows a grid size NT by NR. If the endpoint conditions of (11), and the local path constraints of (34) are used, the region in which the optimal warping path is required to lie is the shaded region in Fig. 10, i.e., a parallelogram bounded by lines of slope 2 and slope ½ from the grid extremal points (1, 1) and (NT, NR). The slope constraint of ½ is determined by the condition that the optimal path cannot be flat $(w(n) - w(n-1) = 0)$ for two consecutive frames, and the slope constraint of 2 is determined by the condition that no path to the grid point (n, m) can come from any grid point lower than $(n-1, m-2)$.

This simplified discussion has shown that in order to implement a DTW algorithm, several factors must be specified including:

1) endpoint constraints on the path;

2) local path continuity constraints, i.e., the possible types of motion (e.g., directions, slopes) of the path

3) global path constraints, i.e., the limitations on where the path can fall in the (n, m) plane

4) distance measure.

In addition, there are differences in implementation of a DTW algorithm depending on whether the reference or test pattern is along the independent-time axis. Both Sakoe and Chiba, and Myers *et al.* [33], [34] have studied the effects of varying the above factors on both speed and performance of the DTW algorithm in actual speech-recognition systems. They have found that only small differences are found in performance for a farily wide range in variation of DTW parameters.

One of the most interesting results that came out of the experiments by Myers *et al.* [34] in working with different variants of the DTW algorithm is illustrated in Fig. 11. This figure shows the size of the parallelogram in which the optimal path can lie for three different ratios of reference length NR to test length NT, namely, 1 to 2, 1 to 3/2, and 1 to 1. It can be seen that when $NT = (3/2)NR$, the size of the parallelogram shrinks considerably (i.e., the region of the optimal warping path is much more constrained), and when $NT = 2NR$, only a single warping path is valid, namely a linear expansion of the reference pattern by 2 to 1. As such all the advantages of DTW time alignment are wasted, the more incommensurate the lengths of the test and reference pattern. Myers *et al.*, realizing this result, proposed a scheme in which *both* reference and test patterns are *linearly* warped to a fixed standard length, prior to DTW alignment. This scheme is illustrated in Fig. 12. In this manner, the path region is maximized and the DTW algorithm

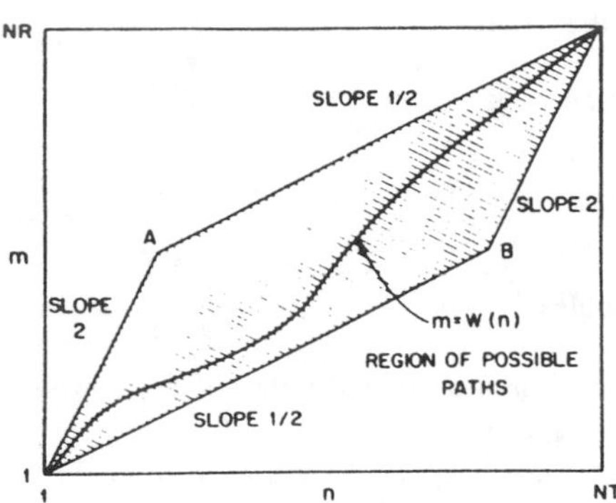

Fig. 10. Typical range for dynamic warping path with slope constraints of 2 to 1 and ½ to 1.

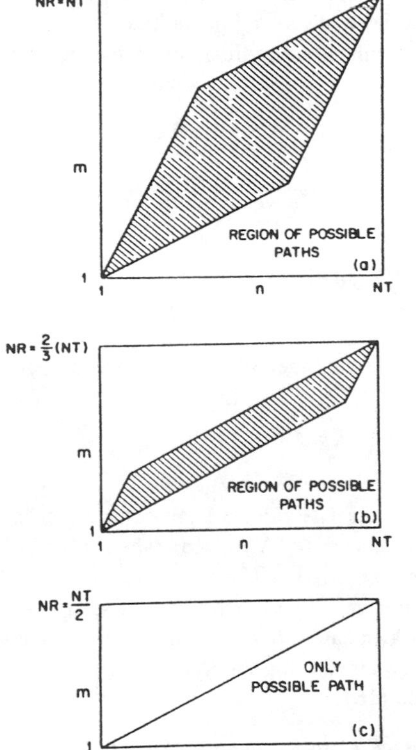

Fig. 11. The effects of relative duration of reference and test patterns on the range of the dynamic path.

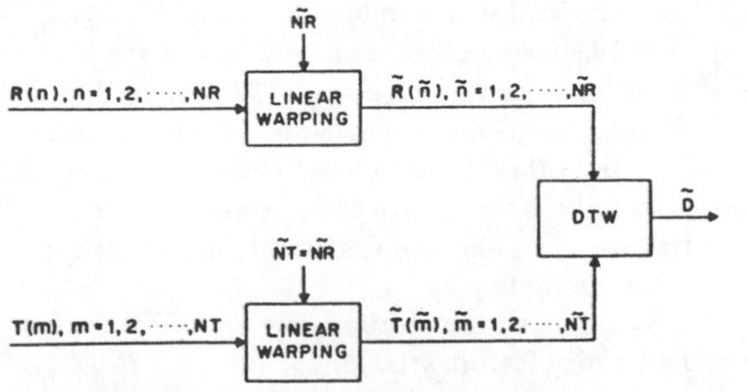

Fig. 12. A normalize-and-warp procedure for time alignment and distance computation.

has the best chance of matching the two patterns. Experimentation with this approach showed recognition performance comparable to or better than all other methods of dynamic time-warping alignment [34].

3) Endpoint Variants of DTW Algorithms: One of the major drawbacks in the simplified DTW algorithm presented in the preceding section is the assumption that the reference and test patterns must line up precisely at the initial and final frames. When reasonably accurate determination of the beginning and ending points of both patterns has been made, this constraint is acceptable and does not harm overall performance of the recognizer. However in cases where accurate endpoint detection cannot be made, the constrained endpoint DTW algorithm is inadequate. As such, several variations on the endpoint constraints have been proposed [35].

Fig. 13 illustrates three versions on the simple DTW algorithm discussed earlier. The first variant, called the constrained endpoints, 2 to 1 slope range (CE2-1) method is the one already discussed in which it is assumed that perfect alignment of endpoints of test and reference patterns exists. The second variant, called the unconstrained endpoints 2 to 1 slope range (UE2-1), retains all local path constraints, but relaxes the endpoint conditions to the set

$$1 \leq w(1) \leq 1 + \delta \tag{38a}$$

$$NR - \delta \leq w(NT) \leq NR \tag{38b}$$

where δ is an "offset" parameter of the DTW algorithm. Clearly, if $\delta = 0$, the UE2-1 DTW algorithm becomes identical to the CE2-1 method. Nonzero values of δ, however, increase the region of the (n, m) plane in which the path can lie, often significantly, as shown in Fig. 13(b).

The third variant of the DTW algorithm, called the unconstrained endpoints, local minimum (UELM) method, used the first relaxed endpoint constraint of (38a), but added tightened path constraints of the form

$$m^*(n-1) - \epsilon \leq m(n) \leq m^*(n-1) + \epsilon \tag{39}$$

where $m(n)$ is the range on m for searching for the optimum path for each value of n, $m^*(n-1)$ is the m index where $D_A(n-1, m)$ was minimum, i.e.

$$m^*(n-1) = \underset{m}{\text{argmin}} \, [D_A(n-1, m)] \tag{40}$$

and ϵ is a range width parameter. As shown in Fig. 13(c), the UELM algorithm tracks the *locally* optimum path in order to estimate the globally optimum path with reduced computation. Clearly the final endpoint constraint is eliminated since the path itself determines the final endpoint alignment. This variant of the DTW algorithm is useful in recognition applications where only one of the endpoints is even approximately known, e.g., word spotting, or connected word recognition.

4) Some General Comments on DTW Algorithms: It is generally agreed that the introduction of dynamic time warping as a method of registering two speech patterns is one of the major breakthroughs that have made speech recognition practical for a wide range of conditions. The importance of

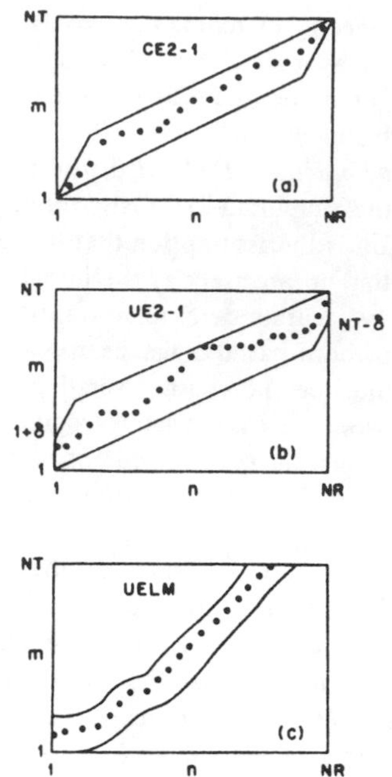

Fig. 13. Several variants on the simple DTW algorithm.

this class of methods has been manifest in a variety of areas including communications in which the classic algorithm of Viterbi for decoding convolutional codes has been shown to be a variant of a dynamic programming procedure [36], [37]. In the area of speech recognition, the importance of dynamic time warping was shown clearly by White and Neely [26] in experiments on isolated work recognition. These researchers showed that for polysyllabic words, distinct improvements in recognition performance were obtained over simple linear time alignment. We will see in later sections how dynamic time warping is a major component in systems for connected word recognition, as well as in syntactic processing for sentence recognition.

C. The Decision Rule for Recognition

The last major step in the pattern-recognition model of Fig. 1 is the decision rule which chooses which (reference) pattern (or patterns) most closely match the unknown test pattern. Although a variety of approaches are applicable here, only two decision rules have been used in most practical systems, namely, the nearest neighbor rule (NN rule) and the K-nearest neighbor rule (KNN rule).

The NN rule operates as follows. Assume we have V reference patterns, R^i, $i = 1, 2, \cdots V$, and for each pattern we obtain the average distance score D^i from the DTW algorithm. Then the NN rule is simply

$$i^* = \underset{i}{\operatorname{argmin}}\,[D^i] \tag{41}$$

i.e., choose the pattern, R^{i^*} with smallest average distance as the recognized pattern. In some applications, as we will see later, explicit choice of i^* is not required; instead an ordered (by distance) list of recognition candidates is used. In this case, the set of distances D^i is reordered to give a new set $D^{[i]}$ such that

$$D^{[1]} \leqslant D^{[2]} \leqslant \cdots \leqslant D^{[V]} \tag{42}$$

and the set of indices that gave the new ordering $[i]$ is retained, i.e.

$$[i] = \text{Table}\ (i) \tag{43}$$

where Table (i) is the original index of the ith element in the reordered distance array.

The KNN rule is applied when each reference entity (e.g., word) is represented by two or more reference patterns, e.g., as would be used to make the reference patterns independent of the talker. Thus if we assume there are P reference patterns for each of V reference words, and we denote the jth occurrence of the ith pattern as $R^{i,j}$, $1 \leqslant i \leqslant V$, $1 \leqslant j \leqslant P$, then if we denote the DTW distance for the jth occurrence of the ith pattern as $D^{i,j}$, and if we reorder the P distances of the ith word so that

$$D^{i,[1]} \leqslant D^{i,[2]} \leqslant \cdots \leqslant D^{i,[P]} \tag{44}$$

then for the KNN rule we compute the average distance(radius)

$$r^i = \frac{1}{K} \sum_{k=1}^{K} D^{i,[k]} \tag{45}$$

and we choose the index of the "recognized" pattern as

$$i^* = \underset{i}{\operatorname{argmin}}\ r^i \tag{46}$$

Similarly to the NN rule, we can compute an ordered list of averaged distances (r^i) for cases when a list of recognition candidates is required.

The importance of the KNN rule is seen when P is from 6 to 12, in which case it has been shown that a real statistical advantage is obtained using the KNN rule (with $K = 2$ or 3) over the NN rule [16].

D. The Overall Word-Recognition System

At this point, we are ready to look in more detail at the operation of a particular isolated word-recognition system. The system we will use is the one which we have studied at Bell Laboratories for a number of years [12], [13], [15], [16]. Fig. 14 shows a block diagram of the recognition system based on LPC features, and using a DTW algorithm with the log likelihood (LPC) distance measure. A careful examination of this, or any other, isolated word recognizer, shows that the system has three distinct modes of operation, namely:

1) training, i.e., the acquisition of feature sets for each word in the vocabulary.

2) clustering, i.e., the creation of word reference templates from the training feature sets.

3) testing, i.e., the recognition of an unknown pattern by comparison with each reference pattern.

It is worthwhile examining what goes on in each of these

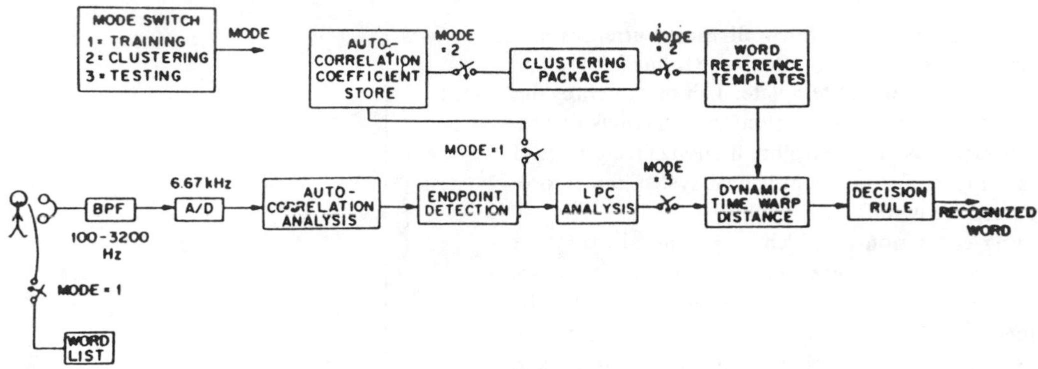

Fig. 14. Overall block diagram of LPC based isolated word-recognition system.

three modes more closely, as this will help explain how the recognizer actually works.

1) Training Mode: In the training mode, each speaker (for a speaker-trained system) or a set of speakers (for a speaker-independent system) recites each word of the desired vocabulary (one or more times) over some transmission system. For most of our own applications, the transducer used is the carbon button of standard telephone, and the transmission system is the standard telephone system for a dialed-up line (generally a local PBX). For commercial applications which do not require telephone transmission, generally a high-quality, close-talking, noise-canceling microphone is used to reduce the effects of the background environment (i.e., high-noise levels, extraneous conversation) on the speech quality.

The analog front end of the system of Fig. 14 consists of a standard bandpass filter from 100 to 3200 Hz (24 dB/octave attenuation skirts), followed by analog-to-digital (A/D) conversion at a 6.67 kHz rate (using a 15-bit convertor). From this point on, all processing is done digitally.

The next step in the processing is feature measurement in which a set of a autocorrelation coefficients are estimated every 15 ms (100 samples) using overlapping frames of 45 ms (300 samples) of speech which has been preemphasized and windowed.

At this point the process called endpoint detection must be carried out. Endpoint detection means literally finding the spoken word in the designated recording interval, i.e., separating the speech from the background sounds. This step is a crucial one in the recognizer for two reasions, namely:

1) Errors in endpoint location increase the probability of making recognition errors. Gross errors in endpoint location make reliable recognition impossible.

2) Proper lcoation of endpoints keeps the overall computation of the system to a minimum.

For reasonably quiescent recording conditions (i.e., a quiet room) endpoint location is a very simple procedure. However as the recording conditions degrade, the difficulty of endpoint location increases.

The technique used in the system of Fig. 14 is to use the contour (time pattern) of the zeroth autocorrelation coefficient (the signal energy) to locate endpoints by defining adaptive level and duration thresholds, and setting endpoints in terms of the energy contour exceeding the thresholds. Fig. 15 shows three examples of endpoints determined by the system for isolated spoken words. The endpoints of the word are denoted by the heavy vertical lines.

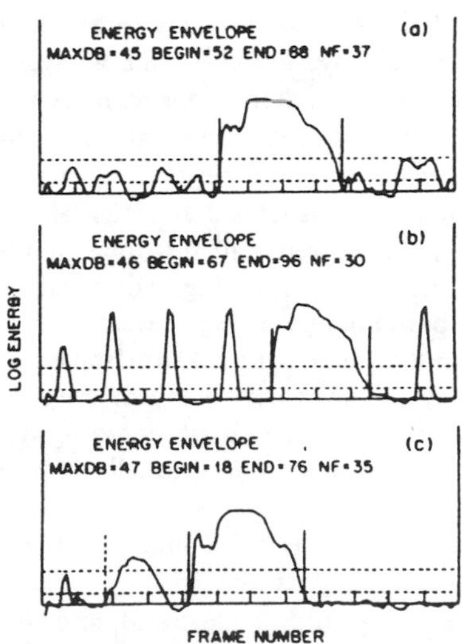

Fig. 15. Three cases of endpoint detection using energy contours.

In each of these examples the spoken word occurred in a background of conversation [Fig. 15(a)], line clicks [Fig. 15(b)], or extraneous lip noises [Fig. 15(c)] [38]. In all three cases, correct location of endpoints was made.

Following endpoint location the sets of autocorrelation coefficients within the spoken word are stored for use in the clustering mode. Thus, the training consists of iterative speaking and analysis of the vocabulary words, and storing the resulting feature sets in an appropriate place.

2) Clustering Mode: In the clustering mode, a conversion is made from isolated occurrences of feature sets for a word, to reference patterns to be used in the recognizer. There are three different methods which have been used to perform this conversion, namely:

1) direct conversion or casual training, in which a reference template is created for each occurrence of a feature set. Thus, if a speaker said each of vocabulary words two times during training, a total of $2V$ word templates are created. This method is used primarily in simple, speaker-trained systems where it is assumed that one or two spoken versions of each word are adequate for recognition.

2) Averaging conversion in which all the occurrences of a given word are averaged together (after some form of time alignment) to give a single reference template. This method provides a statistical gain over direct conversion since spurious recordings are downgraded by the averaging, if enough recordings of each word are made. For one commercial system ten recordings of each word are used for averaging [6].

3) Clustering conversion in which it is assumed that there are P occurrences of each vocabulary word, and they are grouped together to form Q clusters. Within each cluster the tokens (elements of the clustering analysis) have the property that they are "similar" (i.e., small distance to each other), and between clusters, the tokens have the property that they are dissimilar. For each such cluster, a single-word reference template is created using an averaging technique of the type discussed above. Clearly, the clustering analysis is most appropriate for obtaining speaker-independent templates; however it has been equally well applied to speaker-trained systems [39].

Fig. 16 illustrates the concepts of clustering for a set of 17 two-dimensional tokens (this is an articifial set). It can be seen that 15 of the 17 tokens fall into one of the three clusters labeled C1, C2, and C3 in Fig. 16. Each of these clusters would be represented by a single reference template. However it is also seen that two of the tokens (labeled A and B) are outliers, i.e., they are not close to any of the clusters. These outliers, if valid tokens (i.e., without recording artifacts) form single-element clusters are are individually represented as a template.

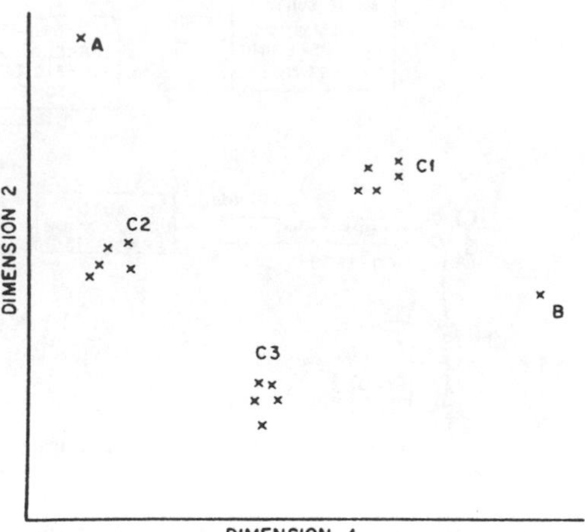

Fig. 16. Illustration of clustering of tokens in a two-dimensional space.

3) Testing Mode: The third mode of the recognition system proceeds initially as the training mode, i.e., a word is spoken, a set of features is measured, and the endpoint locations of the word are found. Following endpoint detection a full LPC analysis is performed on each frame of the word to give a test pattern $T(n), n = 1, 2, \cdots NT$ to be used in the DTW algorithm. This test pattern is optimally time aligned (using the normalize and warp procedure described above) with each of the V reference patterns, giving a distance score D_i, $i = 1, 2, \cdots, V$. The decision rule orders the distance scores and provides a best candidate or set of recognition candidates based on either the NN or KNN rules.

4) Illustration of the Recognizer Output: To set ideas firmly, Fig. 17 shows a plot of the minimum DTW accumulated distance function $D_A{}^*(n)$ versus n for each word in the vocabulary, where

$$D_A{}^*(n) = \min_m [D_A(n, m)]. \tag{47}$$

In this example, the spoken word was the letter /Q/ and the vocabulary consisted of the letters of the alphabet. A total of two templates were used for each vocabulary word. By looking at $D_A{}^*(NT)$ (i.e., at the right-hand edge of the plots), it can be seen that the two /Q/ templates achieved the smallest distance scores, and that the two /U/ templates achieved the next smallest scores. No other letter achieved an acceptably small distance to be considered. It can also be seen that from frame 10 to the end, the rate of accumulation of distance for /Q/ and /U/ were about the same, as might be expected phonetically.

Also shown in Fig. 17 are two recognition features that serve to reduce computation, and increase flexibility of the system. The first, called the rejection threshold, is a curve of accumulated distance which bounds the DTW search. Thus, if the minimum accumulated distance $D_A{}^*(n)$ at frame n exceeds the threshold $\hat{T}(n)$, then the DTW search is terminated and the reference template is given an infinite distance. As shown in Fig. 17, $\hat{T}(n)$ is generally of the form

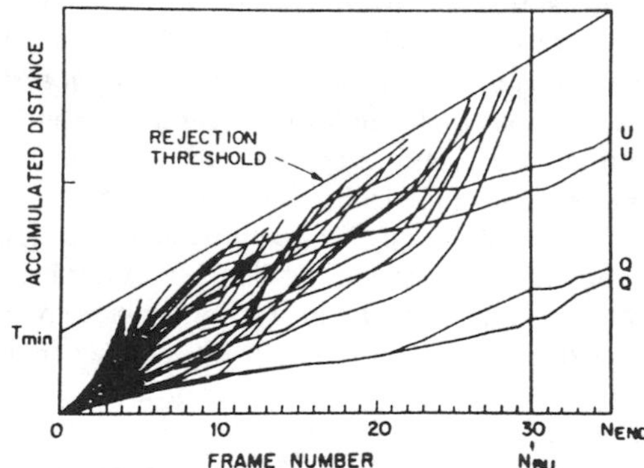

Fig. 17. Plots of accumulated distance versus frame number for a 26-word vocabulary and for the spoken test word /Q/.

$$\hat{T}(n) = (T_{\min} + (n-1)T_{\text{slope}}) \tag{48}$$

where $T_{\min}$ and T_{slope} are parameters of the distance function. (For our system $T_{\min} = 3.0$, $T_{\text{slope}} = 0.7$.)

The second extra recognition feature is the backup frame, labeled N_{BU} in Fig. 17. This is essentially an alternative word ending frame based on the assumption that a breath noise was made at the end of the word and included within the word interval. The backup frame is computed directly from the word energy contour [16], and is used as an early "stopping" frame in the DTW algorithm.

5) Some General Comments on the Word Recognizer: The system of Fig. 14 has several desirable features that have led to its use in a variety of applications, as will be discussed in Section III. These include the following.

1) It can be used as either a speaker-trained, or a speaker-independent system with no modifications.

2) It can be used with any word vocabulary.

3) It is modular in its three main steps, and alternative algorithms (i.e., new feature sets, DTW methods, etc.) can be readily used and tested.

4) It is an all-digital implementation.

The advantages have literally made the recognizer a single module in a number of larger task-oriented systems.

6) Results on Isolated Word Recognition Tests: The isolated word recognizer of Fig. 14 has been used in a wide variety of evaluation tests, and the results of these evaluations are given in Table I. This table gives overall recognition accuracy for different vocabularies and training modes. (The speaker mode column designates whether the system was used as a speaker-trained recognizer or a speaker-independent recognizer. It also designates the procedure used to obtain templates, where appropriate.) A quick glance at the table shows that recognition accuracy varies from 79 to 100 percent, and more importantly, it is seen that the accuracy is not a function of the vocabulary size, so much as it is a function of vocabulary complexity. Hence a small size vocabulary consisting of many similar sounding words (e.g., A, J, K, or B, D, E, G, P, T, V, Z, etc.) is considerably more complex than a vocabulary of 200 polysyllabic, distinctly different words (e.g., the Japanese cities list).

The results given in Table I are chronologically ordered. Hence, when the same vocabulary is tested with an improved system (e.g., 54-word vocabulary using clustered speaker-independent templates), the recognition accuracy will often show substantial improvement. A general result seen from the data in Table I is that high-recognition accuracy (>95 percent) can be obtained in a speaker-trained system by careful creation of word reference templates (even for highly complex vocabularies), and for a speaker independent system when noncomplex vocabularies are used.

More insight into the performance of the isolated word recognizer (operating in a speaker-independent mode) can be gained by examining the results presented in Fig. 18. This figure shows plots of recognition accuracy as a function of the number of templates per word used in the recognizer, the value of K for the KNN rule, the word candidate position, and the method used to obtain the word templates. Parts (a) and (b) of this figure are results for templates obtained from a sophisticated clustering procedure, and parts (c) and (d) are similar plots for templates obtained by random selection from the tokens used in the clustering. Parts (a) and (c) are results for the top recognition candidate, and parts (b) and (d) are results for the top five choices. If we first examine Fig. 18(a), we see the following.

1) For the clustered template set, recognition accuracy steadily increases as the number of templates per word increases from two to about eight, at which point no real increases in recognition accuracy are obtained.

2) For small numbers of templates per word, the KNN rule performs best with $K = 1$; for large numbers of templates per word, the KNN rule with $K = 2$ produces the highest accuracy.

For the vocabulary used in making these plots (i.e, the digits, the letters of the alphabet, and three command words), recognition accuracy goes from about 62 percent (one template per word), to about 79 percent (12 templates per word) for the top candidate.

TABLE I
RECOGNITION SCORES FOR SEVERAL ISOLATED WORD-RECOGNITION SYSTEMS

Reference	Vocabulary	Speaker Mode	Accuracy
Itakura [12]	200 Japanese cities	Trained - 1 Talker	97.3%
Itakura [12]	A-Z, 0-9	Trained - 1 Talker	88.6%
Rosenberg [13]	84 words, cities, numbers days, airports	Trained - 10 Talkers	91.6%
Rosenberg [45]	A-Z	Trained - 10 Talkers	79.5%
Rabiner [15]	54 Computer words	Independent - Pseudo-clustered, 8 Talkers	85.4%
Rabiner et. al. [16]	A-Z, 0-9, STOP ERROR, REPEAT	Independent - Clustered 28 Talkers	79%
Rabiner et. al. [16]	0-9	Independent - Clustered 110 Talkers	98.2%
Rabiner, Wilpon [40]	54 Computer words	Independent - Clustered 40 Talkers	96.5%
Rabiner, Wilpon [39]	A-Z, 0-9, STOP, ERROR, REPEAT	Trained-Clustered 3 Talkers	97%
Rabiner et. al. [41]	20 Names, 10 Digits, 7 Command Words	Trained - 6 Talkers	100%
Rabiner, Wilpon [42]	561 Words and Phrases	Trained - 2 Talkers	95%

Fig. 18(b) shows similar trends in accuracy scores for the top five recognition candidates with overall accuracy going from 88 to 98 percent as a function of the number of templates per word.

For the case of randomly chosen templates [Figs. 18(c) and (d)], it is seen that the same trends exist in the data. However, the absolute recognition scores are from 4 to 12 percent lower, conclusively demonstrating the performance improvements obtained from using clustered templates.

Based on the results given in Fig. 18, and those obtained in subsequent tests, the following general conclusions have been drawn.

1) Clustering methods are effective for finding structure in a group of tokens representing multiple occurrences of an isolated word, and can be used to provide a robust, accurate set of speaker-independent word-reference templates.

2) Performance obtained from clustered tokens is significantly better than performance obtained from randomly chosen tokens.

3) The KNN rule provides higher recognition accuracies for values of K of 2 and 3 than for $K = 1$ (NN rule) for a large number of templates per word.

4) Six to twelve templates per word are adequate for representing a large population of talkers (on the order of 100–1000).

These results have been used in the speaker-independent, isolated-word recognizer at Bell Laboratories, and the performance of the system has not changed in a three-year period,

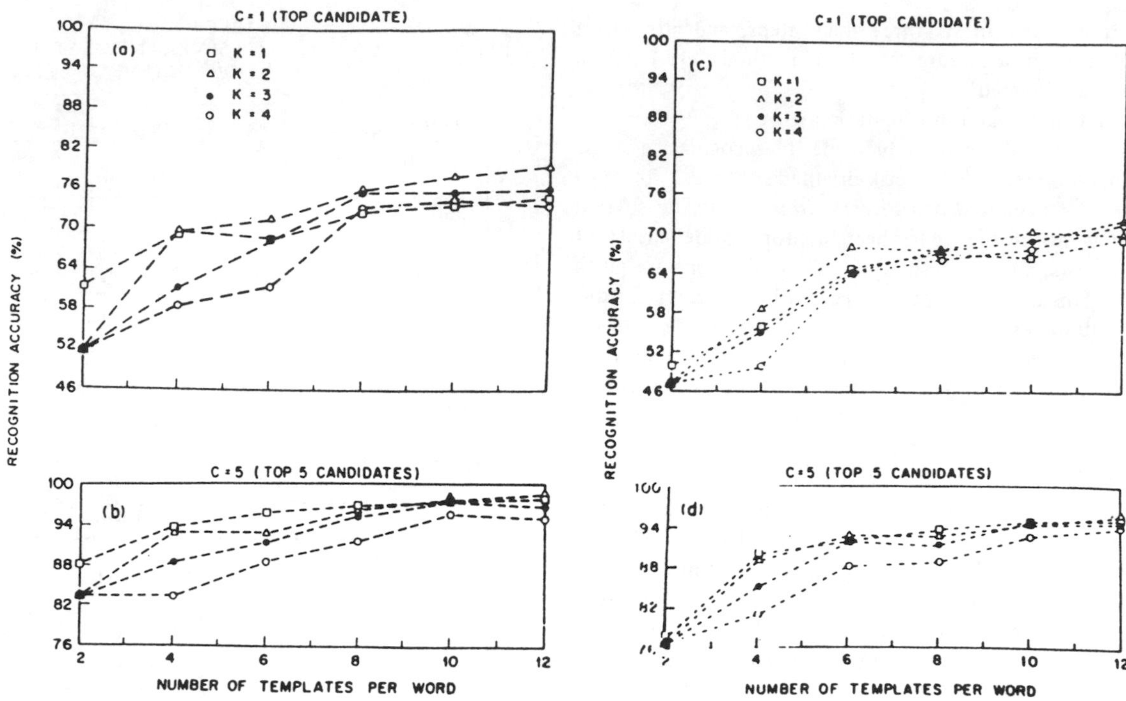

Fig. 18. Recognition accuracy for speaker-independent systems as a function of several recognition-system parameters.

even though the word templates were created at the beginning of the test period.

7) New Directions For Isolated Word-Recognition Systems: Although it might seem, from the discussion of the previous sections, that it has all been done, there remains several open issues in isolated word recognition that are the topics of active research. One such issue is the question of how to improve the performance of the system for complex vocabularies containing many similar sounding words. Although there is inherently no "perfect" solution to this problem, recent work by Rabiner and Wilpon [43] suggests that a two-pass approach to recognition can make improvements in the recognition accuracy. The way in which such a system would work is as follows. The vocabulary words are first grouped into "equivalence classes" based on phonetic and acoustic similarity. Using the equivalence class representation of the vocabulary, the first recognition pass would determine the equivalence class in which the unknown word occurred. The second pass of the recognizer would then use an optimally determined distance weighting curve to distinguish between "similar" words, i.e., words within the acoustic equivalence class. Preliminary results using such a system on the vocabulary of letters and digits indicates improvements in recognition accuracy of 3 to 8 percent.

Another place in which improvements can be made is in the endpoint location method. Errors in locating endpoints account for a large percentage of the errors made in most recognizers. Unfortunately, we have no panacea to this universal problem.

Finally, it is incumbent upon us to make some comments about practical (hardware) implementations of isolated word recognition systems. Commerically available systems cost from $100 to $80 000 per channel. The more sophisticated, higher performance systems (i.e., the type we have been discussing here) range from about $2000 to $80 000. With the advent of increased digital processing power of modern microprocessors, it is estimated that the costs of the high-performance systems will tumble to the $100 range in the foreseeable future (five-year time period). The system which we have discussed in this paper is currently being implemented in digital hardware [44] using an NMOS microprocessor (Intel 8086) in conjunction with a specially designed digital-speech processor based on the TRW 1010J high-speed multiplier-accumulator chip. A block diagram of the hardware configuration is given in Fig. 19. For a 40-word vocabulary (speaker-trained) a recognition time of about ¼ s is required. The parts cost of the system is about $1800 (including memory for 160 templates), and it is anticipated that such a system would cost about $300 wihin three years. Thus, it is felt that the high-performance word-recognition systems will become more ubiquitous in the foreseeable future as the cost falls sufficiently to justify its application.

8) Summary of Issues in Isolated Word Recognition: If we review the ideas we have been discussing in this section, we see that there are a number of factors that must be specified for the implementation of an isolated word recognition system. These factors include the following.

1) Speaker-trained or speaker-independent system. We have seen that this affects the training and the decision rule used.

2) Vocabulary complexity. This factor affects overall recognition accuracy.

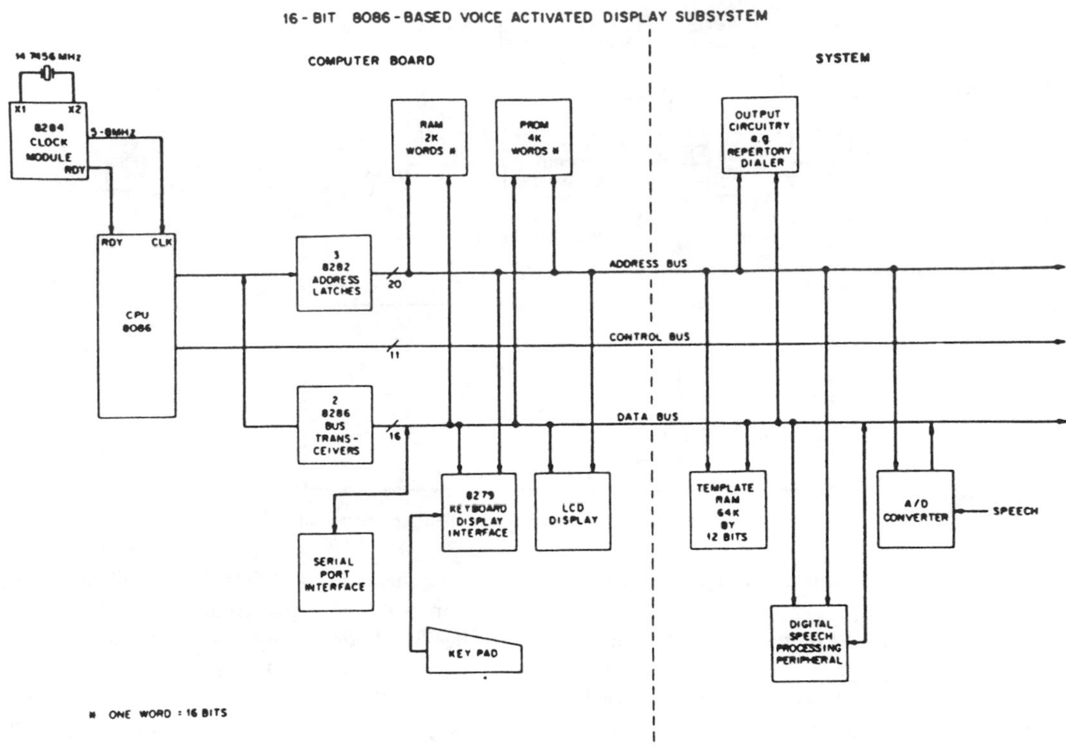

Fig. 19. Block diagram of a hardware structure for implementing the LPC-based isolated-word recognizer.

3) Transmission system (e.g., high-quality microphone, close talking, noise-cancelling microphone, telephone). This factor affects the endpoint location algorithm.

4) System complexity, e.g., the amount of computation for recognition. This factor affects the system response time.

Each of these factors must be taken into consideration for proper design of the isolated word recognition system.

III. TASK-ORIENTED APPLICATIONS OF ISOLATED WORD RECOGNITION

Although we have shown that isolated word-recognition systems will often perform adequately, the power of speech recognition lies in its ability to perform a given task reliably, i.e., when the isolated recognizer is only a single component in a larger, more general system. It will be shown in both this section, and in the following one, that the power of the isolated word recognizer is increased substantially when embedded in a higher level task. In this section, we will discuss three fairly simple task-oriented applications, namely:

1) a voice controlled repertory dialer system [41];
2) a directory listing retrieval system [45], [46];
3) a connected digit recognizer [8], [18], [19].

The task in each of these systems is specified by a simple set of rules which essentially limits the possible set of recognition outputs. Each of the sets of rules is specified as a table of possible recognition sequences at each point in the system. In Section IV, we will present a more theoretical approach to the idea of using task constraints to increase reliability and improve recognition performance.

A. Voice-Controlled Repertory Dialer System

A voice-controlled repertory dialer system is a speech recognizer which is capable of responding to single-word commands, and which can perform the following tasks:

1) build an inventory (a repertory) of spoken names for which the telephone number is determined (from voice input);

2) access any name from the repertory and have the associated telephone number dialed directly;

3) automatically dial any "all-digit" telephone number spoken into the system;

4) edit the repertory of spoken names to add names (and telephone numbers), delete names, and modify telephone numbers.

Thus, the voice controlled repertory dialer is essentially equivalent to a push-button repertory dialer with the button pushing being repalced by speech commands.

Fig. 20 shows a block diagram of the dialer system. The nominal vocabulary for using the system is the 17-word vocabulary consisting of

1) digits: 0–9

2) command words: Offhook, Hangup, Add, Delete, Modify, Error, Stop.

In addition the vocabulary for each user contains the set of names appearing in the repertory. This system could be classified a hybrid recognizer since the 17 command words could be recognized using speaker-independent templates, and the

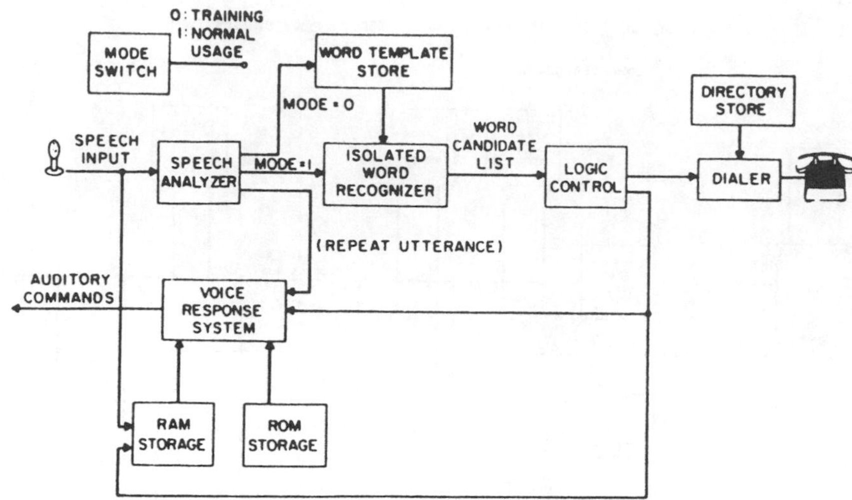

Fig. 20. Block diagram of the voice controlled repertory dialer system.

repertory names would be recognized using speaker-trained templates.

As seen in Fig. 20, the major components of the repertory dialer system are

1) real-time speech analyzer which measures LPC features (in real time) for the word recognizer;

2) an isolated word recognizer to determine the spoken word;

3) a voice-response system to guide the user as to when to speak, and to provide feedback as to the word (or words) recognized;

4) logic control to guide the operation of the system;

5) a dialer to outpulse the desired telephone number.

There are four major storage memories that are required in the system, namely:

1) a word template store to store the reference patterns;

2) a directory store to store telephone numbers associated with each directory name;

3) RAM voice response storage to store coded versions of the acoustic waveform of each name in the repertory;

4) ROM storage to store standard voice-response commands for prompting and feedback to the user.

The way in which the dialer operates is as follows. Initially the user must create his repertory. He does this by speaking the "Add" command, following a system prompt to speak (a double beep). The system asks the user to enter the new repertory name, and the acoustic waveform is stored (in coded format) in the RAM memory of the voice-response system. The system then obtains a recognition template for the name as well as the telephone number (spoken as a set of isolated digits), and stores this information in the template and directory stores, respectively. This process continues until all repertory names are entered. By using the "Delete" or "Modify" commands, names can be deleted from the repertory, or telephone numbers can be modified. These three editing commands (namely, Add, Delete, Modify) can be invoked at any time when the system is running.

Following training, the system can be used as a repertory dialer by speaking the command "Offhook" following a signal prompt. This command (acknowledged to the user by a single beep prompt) takes the telephone off the hook so a number can be dialed. Following the single beep the user can speak any previously recorded repertory name, or speak a sequence of isolated digits. The system verifies the recognition via the voice-response system and waits for an "Error" response. If none is recognized, the telephone number is dialed. If an error response is recognized, a request to repeat the spoken sequence is made, and the process continues.

There are several points worth noting about the voice dialer. The first is that all communication between the user and the system is by voice. No visual display of any type is needed to train or to use the system. The voice response commands (as stored in ROM memory) include the 13 phrases shown in Table II, and the 7 command words, and 10 digits of the vocabulary. RAM memory space has to be allocated for each of the names in the repertory—typically 10 to 20 names should be sufficient. If all voice response commands are coded to 24 kbits/s [47], [48], using a waveform coding technique like ADPCM, a total of about 720 000 bits (30 s × 24 000 bits/s) are required for ROM storage, and 360 000 bits (15 s × 24 000 bits/s) are required for RAM storage. With LPC coding, the storage requirements are reduced further by a factor of ten or more (although the coder/decoder costs increase substantially).

A second feature of the dialer is that the system responds only to isolated word inputs. Thus the user may hold a conversation while the dialer is operating, and the system will not be triggered unless an isolated version of one of the command words is recognized. In order for a word to be recognized, it must have a distance score within prescribed limits, and it must have a considerably smaller distance than the next likely recognition candidate. The likelihood of such events occurring during conversational speech is very small.

Another aspect of this system is that the vocabulary is partitioned for recognition into the following sets:

1) SET 1–7 command words
2) SET 2–L names, 10 digits, word STOP

TABLE II
PHRASES USED BY THE VOICE-RESPONSE SYSTEM OF THE REPERTORY DIALER

1. After each tone say the specified word.
2. Please repeat.
3. Please repeat the command.
4. Please repeat the number.
5. At the beep, speak the name to be added.
6. Please repeat the name to be added.
7. At the beep say the word (—).
8. Please enter phone number.
9. Please repeat the name to be deleted.
10. Please enter the name to be deleted.
11. Please enter new phone number.
12. Please verify.
13. Please repeat the name whose phone number is to be changed.
14. "Beep".

3) SET 3–10 digits
4) SET 4–STOP and ERROR.

Thus, in the worst case the recognizer must choose among $(L + 11)$ possible candidates. However, even for that case, more information is present in the task. If the recognizer finds a digit, the task knows that it must be part of a four-digit string. If no such string is found, the task can choose the best recognition candidate among the set of the names and the word STOP. Similarly, if a string of digits is spoken and the recognizer matches the first digit to a name, the task can correct the word to the most likely digit based on the recognition of subsequent digits.

To demonstrate the effectiveness of these simple task constraints on the recognition, the dialer system was tested on a vocabulary of 20 names (chosen from the Acoustics Research Department) and the 17 standard words. Six talkers (three male–three female) each spoke 170 full commands (a total of 770 words) over a two-week period. The commands were chosen to test the full range of the dialer system. The results of the test showed *no recognition errors for any talker.* This result conclusively demonstrates that a task-oriented recognizer can be implemented in a reliable manner if one can take advantage of some of the natural constraints of the task, the vocabulary, and the recognizer.

B. Directory Listing Retrieval System [45], [46]

Another interesting, task-oriented application of isolated word recognition is the problem of information retrieval from a directory. In particular we have studied the problem of retrieving a directory listing from a spoken spelled name. A

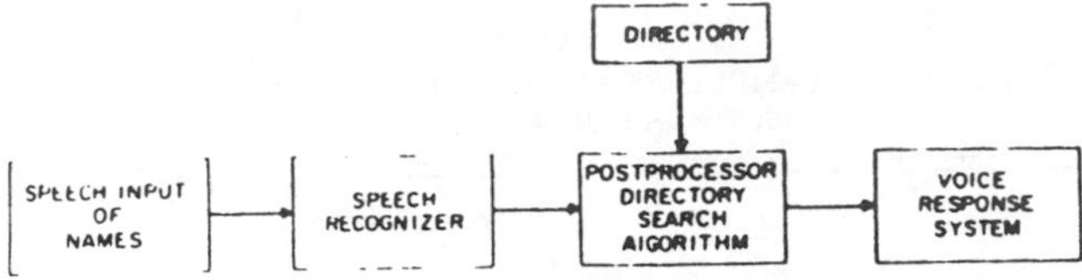

Fig. 21. Block diagram of directory listing retrieval system from speech input of names.

block diagram of a canonic directory listing retrieval system using speech input is shown in Fig. 21. The user provides to the system the required input information (in the form of spoken commands) which specifies an entry in the directory for which some information is desired. The directory search technique searches the directory to find the best match (in some sense) to the given input, and either provides directory information to the user (generally via a voice response system), or requests additional input information to help resolve ambiguity in the directory search.

In the system we have studied [45], [46], the input information is a sequence of isolated letters (for the last name) followed by the isolated command word /STOP/, followed by initials (whichever ones are known) and a final /STOP/ to denote the end of the string. Thus, a typical input would be of the form

L/E/E/STOP/K/STOP

for directory listing retrieval for the name Kim Lee. In speaking the above string of words, each word has to be spoken in isolation (i.e., a distinct pause or gap of at least 50 ms between words is required). In the system which was studied, only initials are used for the first and middle names, and any number of initials (from 0 to 2) can be used. Up to six letters of the last name are used since, for the directory that was investigated, almost no new information about the name is obtained for more than six letters of the last name.

The speech recognizer treats each separate input as an isolated word, and does speaker independent recognition using a 27-word vocabulary (A-Z, STOP) with 12 clustered templates per word. To illustrate a typical recognition output, Table III shows the sets of ordered (by distance) recognition candidates for the spoken string

R/A/B/I/N/E/STOP/L/R/STOP.

Only the smallest 10 distances are shown for each input in the string. A circle is drawn around the correct candidate for each string position. It can be seen that, for the example, two recognition errors were made, namely the letter /A/ in position 2 was recognized as the ninth candidate, and the letter /N/ in position 5 was recognized as the second candidate. As will be shown shortly, it is the job of the postprocessor directory search algorithm to use the distances generated by the recognizer to find the correct name in the directory.

Thus, the output of the speech recognizer is a matrix of (unordered) distance scores $\tilde{D}$, where the $\tilde{D}_{ij}$ entry is the recognition distance between distance between vocabulary

TABLE III
TYPICAL EXAMPLE OF THE CANDIDATES AND DISTANCE SCORES FOR A SPOKEN NAME

	Candidates/Distances									
WORD # 1	(R) .456	STOP .577	I .605	M .646	Y .723	L .750	F .782	N .820	S .834	X .840
WORD # 2	J .391	G .409	C .428	K .430	Z .465	T .490	U .539	D .541	(A) .573	P .605
WORD # 3	(B) .318	D .323	E .330	G .343	P .355	T .360	U .429	Z .458	C .557	A .614
WORD # 4	(I) .338	Y .376	R .600	ST .673	F .788	M .796	S .829	L .872	U .872	X .880
WORD # 5	M .468	(N) .478	X .563	F .577	STOP .579	S .613	L .655	U .783	U .786	K .799
WORD # 6	(E) .203	P .287	B .299	T .316	D .320	G .331	U .453	Z .468	A .549	C .555
WORD # 7	(STOP) .291	X .573	M .588	F .596	S .610	L .646	N .665	I .710	C .725	U .731
WORD # 8	(L) .288	Q .644	F .675	STOP .686	U .699	O .721	M .837	W .890	X .925	S .931
WORD # 9	(R) .268	I .531	Y .598	ST .604	M .612	L .677	F .713	S .769	O .778	N .791
WORD # 10	(STOP) .254	X .543	M .580	L .581	F .584	S .596	I .677	N .684	U .703	Q .751

RABINER LR

LOCATION IS: MH
ROOM NUMBER: 2D533

word i and the jth spoken word in the input string. If we assume there are P words in the vocabulary ($P = 27$) and an L word string was spoken, then $\tilde{D}$ is of the form

$$\tilde{D} = \begin{bmatrix} \tilde{D}_{1,1} & \tilde{D}_{1,2} & \cdots & \tilde{D}_{1,L} \\ \tilde{D}_{2,1} & \tilde{D}_{2,2} & & \cdot \\ \vdots & \vdots & & \cdot \\ \tilde{D}_{P,1} & \tilde{D}_{P,2} & \cdots & \tilde{D}_{P,L} \end{bmatrix} \tag{49}$$

The postprocessor search algorithm must find the string (or strings) in the directory which has minimum distance $D(S)$, where S is an L-component (letter) string defined as

$$S = (l_1, l_2, \cdots, l_L). \tag{50}$$

The distance of any string S can be computed from the matrix $\tilde{D}$ as

$$D(S) = D(l_1, l_2, \cdots, l_L) = \sum_{j=1}^{L} \tilde{D}_{l_j,j} \tag{51}$$

where we have used a natural correspondence between word numbers (l_j) and vocabulary words, i.e., letter A is word 1, letter B word 2, etc.

Based on (51), a string distance is defined for each string in the directory. The purpose of the search algorithm is to find the minimum-distance string with a small number of probes.

The key to the search algorithm that is used is the assumption that letter confusions in the word recognizer occur primarily with known classes of acoustically similar letters, i.e., B and V are confused, A and K and J, etc. Thus, even if a spoken letter is not recognized correctly (i.e., it does not have minimum distance) the acoustic class to which it belongs is recognized correctly most of the time. This characteristic of the recognizer is exploited by reogranizing the directory in terms of acoustically similar letter classes (rathern than alphabetically) and then by using a searching strategy that exploits this new classification scheme. Hence the manner in which the correct name is generally found is similar to the procedure used by a grade schooler in looking up in a dictionary the spelling of a word which he does not know how to spell. A first guess at the approximate name (spelling) is taken from the distance matrix and all names that are acoustically equivalent (in a specified sense) to this first guess are accessed, their string distances are calculated using (51) and a record is kept of the best name candidates. A second guess at the approximate name is taken from the distance matrix (in a fairly simple way) and again all acoustically similar names are accessed and their distances are calculated. When the best distance in a new acoustic name class becomes too large, the procedure terminates and the best name (or names) are output to the user. The details of the search procedure are given in [46] and [49] and will not be discussed here. Instead, we will highlight some of the performance characteristics of the overall directory listing retrieval system.

The performance of the word recognizer is best expressed as a curve showing the error rate $E(i)$ as a function of the rank i in the ordered distance vector, i.e., the percentage of letters which are not in the top i positions of the ordered distance vector. Fig. 22 shows such a curve for three cases, namely, the average for 20 talkers used to test the system, the curve for the best talker, and the curve for the worst talker. It can be seen that for the average talker, the correct letter is not found in the first position about 30 percent of the time, and, in fact, is not found in the top seven positions about 3 percent of the time. Thus the probability of recognizing a name based on the top recognition candidate for each letter position is rather low—on the order of 0.1, and thus the search algorithm essentially provides the leverage required to obtain high name accuracy in spite of low-word-recognition accuracy.

At the output of the directory search procedure, one of three conditions can occur, namely the following.

1) A single string has been found whose distance is sufficiently small to accept this string as the spoken name.

2) No string has been found whose distance is acceptably small. In the case, a request is made to the user to repeat the spoken input.

3) More than one string has been found whose string distances are sufficiently small, i.e., there is ambiguity as to what is the correct choice among several candidate strings. The way in which we handle such cases will be discussed below.

Based on the above possibilities, Table IV(a) shows the performance characteristicsof the overall directory testing retrieval system for the cases when 0, 1, or 2 (when possible) initials were specified for the Bell Laboratories directory of 18 000

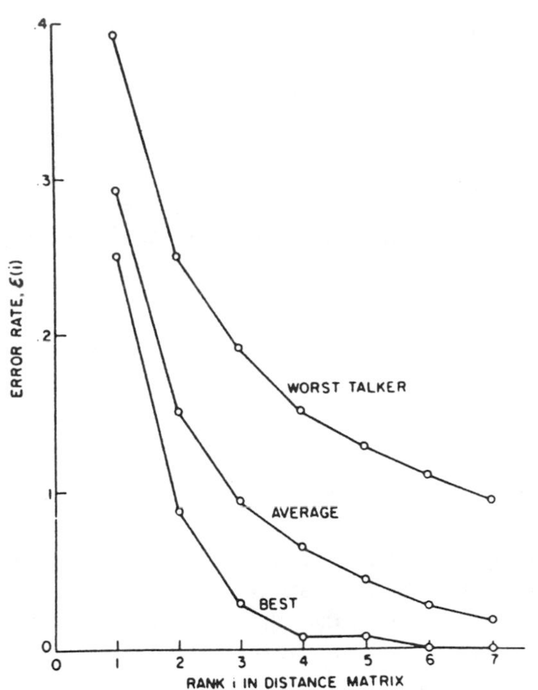

Fig. 22. Recognition error rate as a function of rank in the distance matrix for the worst, average, and best talkers.

TABLE IV
RESULTS ON THE DIRECTORY LISTING RETRIEVAL TASK. (a) ONE-PASS SEARCH. (b) TWO-PASS SEARCH.

NO INITIALS	CORRECT ANSWERS	ERRORS	UNRESOLVED
0	40.5	8.1	51.4
1	74.9	8.9	16.2
2	92.0	5.0	3.0

(a)

NO INITIALS	CORRECT	ERROR	UNRESOLVED
0	PASS 1: 34.9	1.5	---
	PASS 2: 92.4	2.6	5.0
1	PASS 1: 66.2	1.2	---
	PASS 2: 96.8	1.9	1.3
2	PASS 1: 87.8	0.8	---
	PASS 2: 98.3	1.1	0.6

(b)

names. It can be seen that for 0 initials, over half of the cases are unresolved, whereas for 2 initials specified, only 3 percent of the cases are unresolved. However, even for 2 initials, only 92 percent of the names are correctly determined, i.e., there is a 5 percent error rate. Such an error rate is too high for this system to be of any practical utility.

To improve the performance of the system, two modifications were made, as follows.

1) A distance threshold was defined such that two strings were defined as equivalent if the difference in their string distances was below this threshold.

2) When string ambiguity was found, a request for additional information (in this case the organization number at Bell Laboratories) was made and the recognizer was used a second time to recognize the new spoken input.

A flow diagram of this "two-pass" directory listing retrieval system is shown in Fig. 23. The acoustic recognizer and the directory search algorithm are seen to communicate via direct control paths, and from files in which all partial results are retained.

Table IV(b) illustrates the improvements in performance using the two-pass recognition-search strategy. For the case of 0 specified initials, the percentage of correct names jumps to 92.4 percent (after the second pass), whereas for two initials specified, a name accuracy of 98.3 percent with an error rate of 1.1 percent is attained. These improvements are truly significant, and again illustrate the leverage in improving recognition accuracy provided by a well-designed task.

C. Connected-Word Recognition Using Isolated Word-Reference Patterns

Interestingly, one of the most important applications of the techniques of isolated-word recognition has been the area of connected-word recognition. Before discussing this application, we must first define connected-word recognition, and distinguish it from continuous-speech recognition. In connected-word recognition, the spoken input is a sequence of words from a specified vocabulary, and the recognition is performed based on matching isolated word-reference templates. Typical examples include connected digit strings where the vocabulary is the set of 10 digits (0-9), or connected-letter recognition (e.g., for spelling names, words, etc.) where the vocabulary is the set of 26 letters (*A-Z*). Continuous-speech recognition, on the other hand, generally involves recognition from basic units of speech, e.g., phonemes, syllables, demisyllables, diphones, dyads, etc., and hence implies the need for some form of segmentation of the speech into the units, and labeling of the units. (There do exist speech recognizers (e.g., CMU's HARPY system) which combine aspects of both connected-word and continuous-speech recognition). It is generally acknowledged that continuous-speech recognition is a considerably more difficult problem than connected-word recognition. However, there are many applications where connected-word recognition serves a useful purpose.

A block diagram of a fairly general pattern-recognition structure for connected word recognition is given in Fig. 24. This block diagram is almost identical to the one for the isolated-word recognizer, with one major exception. This exception is the feedback loop shown at the output of the decision rule box which, at the end of each recognition (level), feeds back to the DTW algorithm a set of estimates of where in the test string the current local matches end. In this manner, the DTW algorithm can progressively build up a set of matches to the test string and, at the end of the search, determine an ordering of matches according to accumulated distance scores.

The remaining components of the connected-word recognizer, namely, the acoustic analyzer, the reference templates,

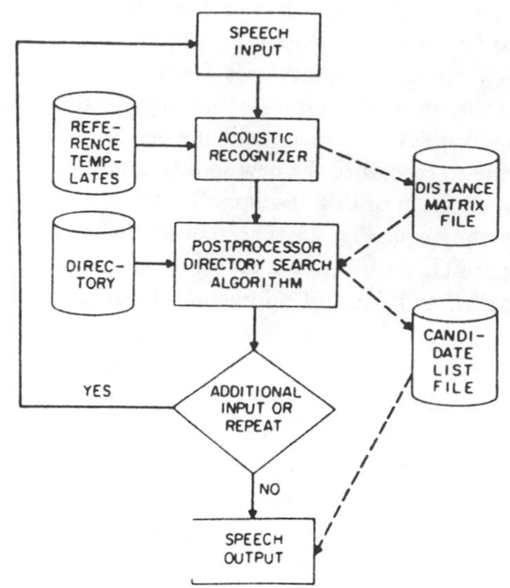

Fig. 23. Flow diagram of a two-pass directory listing retrieval system.

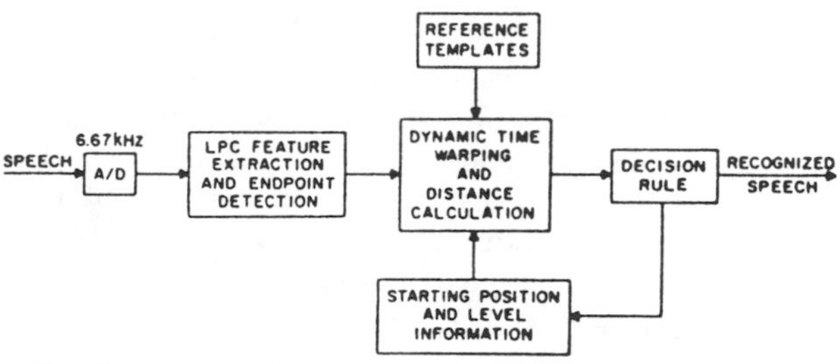

Fig. 24. Block diagram of a connected word-recognition system.

the DTW algorithm, and the decision rule are essentially the same as used for isolated-word recognition.[3] Thus, one key point about connected-word recognition is that the reference templates are isolated-word templates. The only other point of note is that the DTW algorithm cannot be a constrained end-point algorithm, since no word boundaries are known *a priori.* Hence, a DTW algorithm such as the UELM algorithm, must be used in this application.

To understand how the connected-word recognition is solved, we must first define some terms. We denote the unknown test string pattern as $T(m), m = 1, 2, \cdots, M$, where $T(m)$ represents a string (of unknown length) of words. The test string $T(m)$ is to be time registered with a sequence of L reference patterns $R_{q(1)}(n)$, $R_{q(2)}(n)$, $\cdots$, $R_{q(L)}(n)$, where each $R_{q(n)}$, $k = 1, 2, \cdots, L$ is one of a set of V reference patterns (the word vocabulary) R_v, $v = 1, 2, \cdots, V$. The length of the vth reference pattern is denoted as N_v. We define a "super" reference pattern [8], [50] $R_{q(1)q(2)}{}^s \cdots {}_{q(L)}$ as the concatenation of the L reference patterns $R_{q(1)}, R_{q(2)}, \cdots, R_{q(L)}$, i.e.

$$R^s = R_{q(1)} \oplus R_{q(2)} \oplus \cdots \oplus R_{q(L)} \tag{52}$$

[3] The decision rule, as in the isolated-word recognizer, chooses the word string with minimum distance. If one considers the class of all possible time warps for a string (or for a word), then alternative decision rules could be considered.

or

$$R^s(n) \begin{cases} = R_{q(1)}(n - \phi(0)) & 1 + \phi(0) \leq n \leq \phi(1) \\ = R_{q(2)}(n - \phi(1)) & 1 + \phi(1) \leq n \leq \phi(2) \\ \vdots & \\ = R_{q(L)}(n - \phi(L-1)) & 1 + \phi(L-1) \leq n \leq \phi(L) \end{cases} \tag{53}$$

where the length function $\phi(l)$ is defined [50] as

$$\phi(l) = \sum_{k=1}^{l} N_{q(k)} \tag{54a}$$

$$\phi(0) = 0. \tag{54b}$$

If we attempt a DTW match between $T(m)$ and $R^s(n)$, and we define the resulting distance at the end of the match as $D_{q(1)q(2)} \cdots {}_{q(L)}(M)$, then the "ideal" solution to the connected-word-recognition problem is the solution of the minimization

$$D^* = \min_L \left[\min_{q(1)q(2)\cdots q(L)} [D_{q(1)q(2)\cdots q(L)}(M)] \right] \tag{55}$$

i.e., the reference string, of length L words, which minimizes the accumulated distance is the best estimate of the test string.

It should be clear that, except for trivial cases, direct, exhaustive solution of (55) is impractical due to the excessive computation involved. For example for $L = 5$, $V = 10$ (i.e., a ten-word vocabulary with up to 5 words in a string), a total of

$$NS = 10^5 \text{ (five-word strings)} + 10^4 \text{ (four-word strings)} + \cdots + 10 \text{ (one-word strings)}$$

would have to be tested. As such there have been several approaches proposed for solving (55) in an efficient manner [8], [17], [18], [50], [51]. These approaches all attempt to reduce the computational loading by solving the minimization in a series of stages (levels) in which sufficient information is retained so that a series of string candidates is evaluated. Generally, the "best" string is retained as one of the candidates, and the vast majority of strings with poor distance scores are discarded.

It is impossible to discuss, in any detail, the different approaches to DTW algorithms for connected-word recognition. However, to illustrate the sophistication in these methods, we will discuss briefly the level building approach of Myers and Rabiner [50] as it serves to explain the general principles of operation of most of the methods.[4]

[4] The material in this section is taken directly from [19]. It has been shown that the level-building algorithm is related to the stack algorithm of Bahl and Jelinek [83].

1) The Level-Building Approach to Connected-Word Recognition: The manner in which the level-building algorithm is implemented for solving the minimization of (55) is illustrated in Figs. 25-26. Fig. 25 shows the simple case of obtaining the DTW distance between the test pattern $T(m)$, and a *given* super reference pattern $R^s = R_{q(1)} \oplus R_{q(2)} \oplus \cdots \oplus R_{q(L)}$, i.e., for fixed indices $q(1)q(2) \cdots q(L)$. A constrained endpoint DTW algorithm in which the slope of the warping function $w(m)$ is constrained to lie between ½ and 2 is used to find the best path within the parallelogram for matching T and R^s. This procedure could, in theory, be used to solve (55) by exhaustively testing every possible R^s and doing the minimization directly. However, as discussed previously, the amount of computation (V^L comparisons), even for modest values of L, is untractable.

In order to see how we can efficiently solve (55) we must examine, in more detail, the way in which the DTW algorithm is generally implemented for a fixed R^s and T. Fig. 26(a) shows a typical implementation of a constrained endpoint DTW algorithm. Generally, the computation to find the optimum warping path is performed in vertical stripes (i.e., m is indexed sequentially and a range on n is found in which the path is constrained to lie) as illustrated in this figure. An alternative way in which the computation could be performed is illustrated in Fig. 26(b). A set of horizontal lines has been drawn for different ending frames of the references within R^s. For this case the computation is done in vertical stripes again, however, the horizontal line formed by the end of each reference forms a constraint on the region in which the computing is done. As such, the computation is again done in vertical stripes until the partial region G_1 of the parallelogram is covered. In order to correctly pick up the computation for the second reference pattern (i.e., in region G_2) the accumulated distance scores for all paths that end at the first horizontal line (devoted by the heavy dots) must be retained, and used as initial conditions on distances. In this manner, the identical computation, as shown in Fig. 26(a) can be carried out by levels (i.e., words within the sequence of reference patterns) in a series of computations.

The significance of the above results is that the *level-building* approach to finding the best dynamic path (i.e., finding the best path for each reference pattern in the sequence) can be extended to the case of more than one reference pattern at each level, by computing all possible distances at the end of each level and retaining the best distance for each index m. Thus, if we define a range beginning variable $m_1(l)$ and a range ending variable $m_2(l)$, then in order to solve for the best match to the test pattern, for each value of m in the range $m_1(l) \leqslant m \leqslant m_2(l)$, at level l, we must keep track of three quantities, as follows.

1) Minimum accumulated distance, $\tilde{D}_l^B(m) = \min_{1 \leq v \leq V} [\tilde{D}_l^v(m)]$ where $\tilde{D}_l^v(m)$ is the accumulated distance for the vth reference pattern, at level l ending at frame m of the test pattern.

2) Best reference, $W_l(m) = \text{argmin}_{1 \leq v \leq V} [\tilde{D}_l^v(m)]$, i.e., the reference pattern leading to the minimum accumulated distance.

3) Backtracking pointer, $\tilde{F}_l^B(m) = \tilde{F}_l^{W_l(m)}(m)$, where $\tilde{F}_l^v(m)$ is the frame of the test pattern at level $l-1$ at which the best path to test frame m, at level l, for reference pattern R_v, ended, i.e., the best path to frame m of the test pattern, at the end of the lth level using reference R_v, began at frame $\tilde{F}_l^v(m) + 1$. This pointer basically keeps track of the ending frame of each path at the previous level. For level $l = 1$, it should be clear that $\tilde{F}_l^B(m) = 0$ for all m, since all paths started at frame 1 of the test pattern.

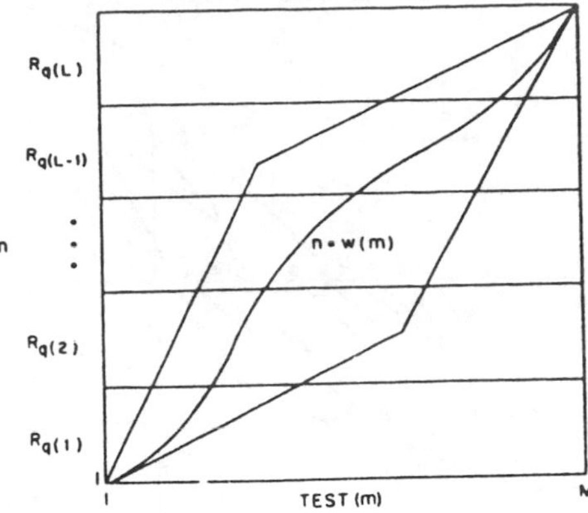

Fig. 25. Illustration of constrained endpoint DTW match of a sequence of reference patterns to a connected-word test string.

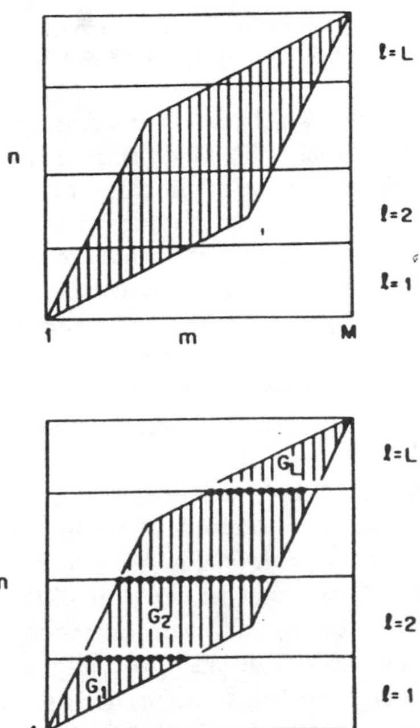

Fig. 26. Two possible implementations of constrained endpoint DTW algorithms.

Fig. 27 illustrates the operation of the level-building algorithm for a simple example where it is assumed that there are only two reference patterns, denoted as A and B, each of equal length. It is assumed that a string of length $L = 4$ is known to have been spoken. At the end of the first level, there are six possible ending values of m, and the reference pattern giving the smallest distance is denoted along the horizontal line at the end of the level. Similarly, at levels two and three best paths to each possible ending frame are noted by the refer-

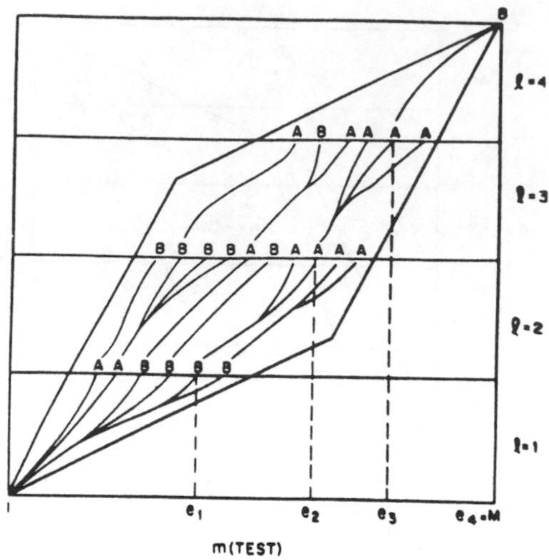

Fig. 27. Illustration of backtracking to recover the best sequence match in a four-level DTW match.

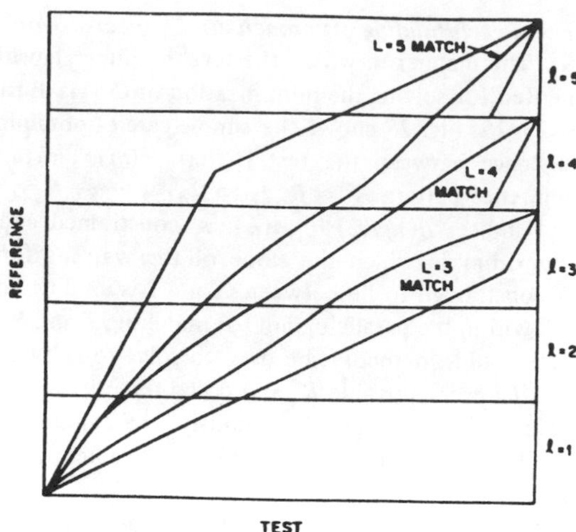

Fig. 28. Example of use of the level-building algorithm with several different length candidates.

ence, at that level, which gave minimum accumulated distance. Finally, at level four, only a single path is retained, as this is the optimum path which minimizes the distance of (55). To determine the best matching string, we must backtrack the path ending at $m = M$ to give the sequence BAAB as the best sequence of four reference patterns matching the test pattern. Also denoted in Fig. 27 are the test frame values e_l corresponding to the end of each reference in the best matching sequence. In principle, these values e_l could be used as best estimates of segmentation points between entries in the test pattern.

It should be noted that the level-building algorithm, as presented above, is capable of determining the best matching string to a test pattern of variable length. As such, the algorithm can generate several "best" matches, each of different lengths as shown in Fig. 28. The overall "best" match is defined as the match giving the smallest distance over all possible sequence lengths. The alternative length strings are useful for applications in which the length of the string is known *a priori*, e.g., telephone number dialing, credit-card codes, etc. In Fig. 28, we show best matches for strings of length $L = 3$, 4, and 5, for the given example.

A second point of note is that, by doubling the storage at each level, we can keep track of both a "best" path, and a second best path, to each frame m of the test pattern. In this manner, alternative estimates of reference strings can be estimated by using second best paths at any level in the warp. This important point is illustrated in Fig. 29, which shows a "best" path for an $L = 4$ length string, and a series of four alternative paths obtaining by substituting a second best distance alternative at each level in the warp. These paths are shown graphically in Fig. 29(a), and symbolically in Fig. 29(b). If we denote the best path by the sequence of arcs 1111, then the alternative paths 2111, 1211, 1121, and 1112. However, the arcs labeled 1's occurring before an arc labeled 2 in the alternative paths, need not be the same arcs labeled 1 for the best path, since we are now finding a best path to a different ending frame at each level. The set of distances associated with each of these suboptimum paths can be ordered to give an alternative list of strings as estimates for the spoken string.

Fig. 30 illustrates the application of the level-building algorithm to connected digit strings. In this plot, we show the log energy contour of the spoken string [part (a)] and a series of plots of the accumulated distance for each digit at each level. Fig. 30 is for the spoken string 51560. At the end of each level, the program prints out the best local estimate of the digit at each level (shown to the right of each level rectangle). The verticle dashed lines, at each level, denote the initial range of m for which the level allows paths to begin. The sloped dashed line at each level is a distance rejection threshold (similar to the one used for isolated words) to eliminate candidates which accumulate large distances. For this example, the best estimate, at each level, of the spoken digit is the actual spoken digit. At the end of the fourth level, the string 5157 matched to the end of the test string with an average distance score of 0.533. Three alternative strings, namely, 1157, 5957, and 5117, were also generated at this level by using the second-best distance candidates at each position in the string. At the fifth level, the string 51560 (the correct one) was obtained with an average distance score of 0.333. Alternate choices, at this level, included the strings 11560, 51570, 59560, 51160, and 51562 with average distance scores as shown on the figure.

The level-building DTW algorithm can be easily modified both to increase its efficiency and to increase its flexibility in handling various types of test input strings. To accomplish these tasks, a set of variables has been defined that can be independently controlled, and which influence the performance of the level-building algorithm. These variables include the following.

1) δ_{R_1} = region of uncertainty at the beginning of the reference pattern.

2) δ_{R_2} = region of uncertainty at the end of the reference pattern.

3) δ_{END} = region of uncertainty at the end of the test pattern.

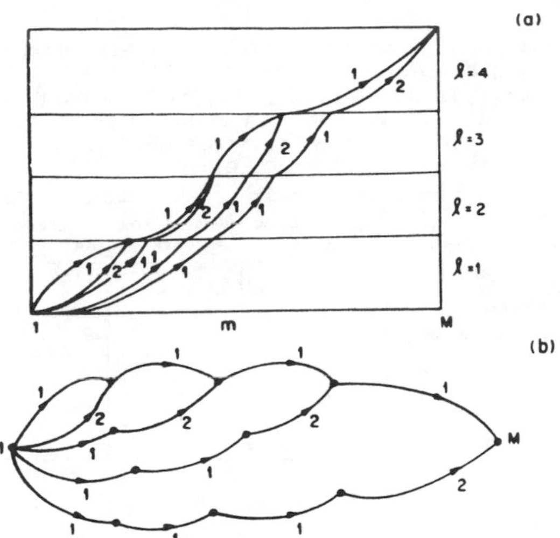

Fig. 29. Example illustrating how additional candidate strings are obtained in the level-building algorithm.

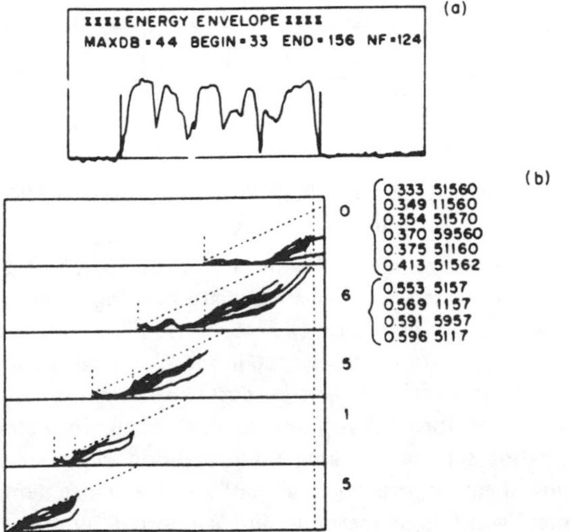

Fig. 30. Log energy contour and accumulated distance at each level of the level-building algorithm for the test string 51560.

4) M_T = distance multiplier to determine initial m-axis range, at each level, along the test pattern.

5) ϵ = range of DTW local warp along the reference pattern.

6) $T_{\min}, T_{\max}$ = threshold parameters on accumulated distance at each level.

7) KNN = K-nearest neighbor decision rule criterion.

The physical interpretations of some of these variables on the level-building paths are illustrated in Fig. 31. The variables δ_{R_1} and δ_{R_2} define regions, at the beginning and end of each reference pattern, in which the local path can begin or end, i.e., paths need not begin at frame 1 of each reference and end at the last frame, but instead the best beginning and ending frames, within the specified regions, are found and used for each path.

Similarly, the parameter δ_{END} defines a region at the end of the test pattern in which a total match can end, rather than strictly requiring each path to end at that frame $m = M$. This added flexibility allows for some margin of error in determining the ending frame of the test pattern.

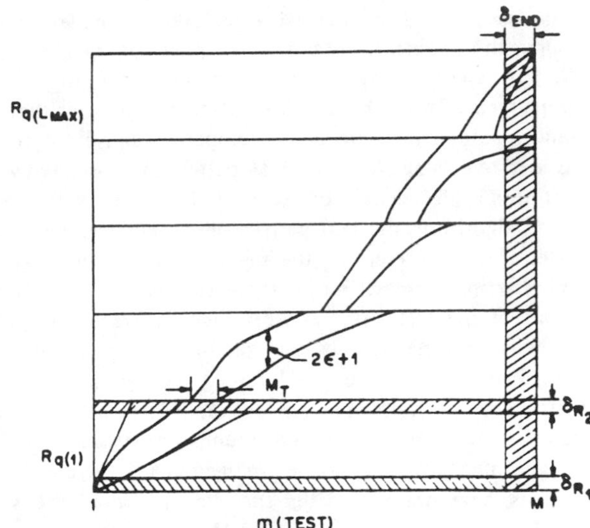

Fig. 31. Illustration of the level-building parameters $\delta_{R_1}, \delta_{R_2}, \delta_{end}, M_T$, and ϵ.

The parameters M_T and ϵ are range reduction parameters which reduce the size of the local regions G_l at level l, in which the dynamic path is constrained to lie. The parameter M_T is used to reduce the initial starting range (i.e., from $m_1(l)$ to $m_2(l)$) to the reduced range

$$S_l^{\,1} \leqslant m \leqslant S_l^{\,2} \tag{56}$$

where $S_l^{\,1}$ and $S_l^{\,2}$ are defined as

$$S_1^{\,1} = \text{largest } m \text{ such that } \tilde{D}_{l-1}{}^{B}(m)/m > M_T \cdot \phi_{l-1} \quad \text{for all } m < S_l^{\,1} \tag{57a}$$

$$S_l^{\,2} = \text{smallest } m \text{ such that } \tilde{D}_{l-1}{}^{B}(m)/m > M_T \cdot \phi_{l-1} \quad \text{for all } m > S_l^{\,2} \tag{57b}$$

where

$$\phi_{l-1} = \min_{1 \leqslant m \leqslant M} \left[\frac{\tilde{D}_{l-1}{}^{B}(m)}{m} \right] \tag{58}$$

is the minimum average distance at the end of level $l-1$. For practical values of M_T, the range of starting values of m can be reduced by about 50 percent.

Similarly, the parameter ϵ defines a range of width $2\epsilon + 1$ for searching in the n-direction, to find the best path for each reference at each level, as defined by Rabiner *et al.* in the UELM DTW algorithm [35]. At each frame m, along the test, the range along n is determined by examining a region within $\pm\epsilon$ frames (along n) of the minimum accumulated distance at frame $m-1$. This parameter is again primarily used to reduce the size of the search region.

The parameters $T_{\min}$ and $T_{\max}$ are used to terminate DTW searches on reference patterns which accumulate excessive incremental distance at any level l. Details of the incremental distance test are given in [16].

The last method for increasing flexibility of the level-building algorithm, namely, the use of the K-nearest neighbor rule (KNN) for speaker-independent recognition, is a difficult one to implement. This is because the KNN rule assumes that the distance scores which are being compared (and averaged) all are generated using the same test pattern. For isolated-word recognition, this assumption is valid; however, in the level-building algorithm, the best paths at level l and frame m, from two templates representing the same word, can begin at different starting frames. Hence, these two paths use different portions of the test string and cannot be averaged in a KNN rule. Thus, in general, it is not possible to compare distance scores directly with the KNN rule. However, a reasonable heuristic for the KNN rule can be applied, namely, that the distance scores from two reference templates (representing the same vocabulary word) may be averaged in a KNN rule if both templates have warping paths that "came from" the same word. To implement the revised KNN rule, for each token of the vth vocabulary word, we must keep track of the distance accumulated to frame m, and a pointer of the word (at the previous level) from which the best path began. For all frames where KNN (or more) tokens are defined to have come from the same word at the previous level, the KNN rule averages the KNN smallest distances, to give the word distance at frame m and level l.

2) Results on the Recognition of Connected-Digit Strings [19]: The level building DTW algorithm of the previous section was applied to the task of connected-digit recognition and the results of a series of performance evaluations are given in Table V. For these tests, a total of six talkers (three male, three female) each spoken 80 connected-digit strings. The strings varied in length from two to five digits, and were randomly chosen, but balanced to have an equal number of occurrences of each digit in each string length, on average. A total of 20 strings of each length were spoken. The strings were recorded over dialed-up telephone lines.

The recognizer was tested as both a speaker-trained system (one template per word) and a speaker-independent system (using the clustered, isolated-word templates described previously). Table V(a) shows the error rate scores for string errors (i.e., if any digit in the string was wrong, the whole string was in error), word errors, and string errors with "known length", i.e., only strings of the correct length were allowed. It is seen that string error rates of about 4.7 percent and word error rates of about 0.8 percent are attained for *both* speaker-trained and speaker-independent systems.

Table V(b) shows a breakdown of the string errors by talker (M for male, F for female). It is seen that the speaker-trained system performed better for males than for females, however, the speaker-independent system performed equally well for both males and females.

3) Summary: The area of connected-word recognition is one which is being investigated actively at a number of research laboratories. It is anticipated that as more experience and insight is gained into the strengths and weaknesses of the connected-word DTW algorithms, further applications of this promising technology will appear.

TABLE V
RESULTS ON CONNECTED-DIGIT RECOGNITION USING THE LEVEL-BUILDING ALGORITHM. (a) SIX TALKERS–THREE MALE, THREE FEMALE; 80 STRINGS PER TALKER; 20 EACH OF LENGTH 2, 3, 4, 5, DIGITS; BALANCED DIGITS WITHIN STRINGS. (b) NUMBER OF STRING ERRORS.

	STRING ERROR RATE	WORD ERROR RATE	STRING ERROR RATE-KNOWN LENGTH
SPEAKER TRAINED (Single Template Per Word)	4.8%	0.7%	3.8%
SPEAKER INDEPENDENT (12 Templates Per Word)	4.6%	0.9%	3.5%

(a)

TALKER	SPEAKER TRAINED	SPEAKER INDEPENDENT
LR (M)	3	1
JG (M)	3	7
SL (M)	2	3
KS (F)	6	3
CS (F)	3	5
SC (F)	6	3

(b)

IV. THE ROLE OF GRAMMAR AND SEMANTICS IN SPEECH RECOGNITION

In the foregoing discussion, automatic speech recognition has been treated as a classical pattern-recognition problem. The techniques presented all rest on the almost universally accepted fact that the intelligence in speech is largely encoded in the temporal variation of the short-time amplitude spectrum. It was, therefore, appropriate to have discussed methods for estimating spectra, tracking their variation in time and comparing them to prototypical patterns (reference templates). Armed with these methods and supported by the ever increasing computational power provided by a variety of electronic technologies, one can build robust speech-recognition devices which perform practical human/machine communication tasks on an economically competitive basis.

Not surprisingly, however, such machines are limited in their ability to effect versatile, fluent speech communication simply by extrapolation of the above discussed techniques. The reason is , of course, that speech is a complex code in which the intelligence of a message is represented both locally, by spectral features, and globally by a hierarchy of structural features. If we are to build devices which function with the richness and robustness of natural speech communication, the structural aspects must be considered. It is important to note, in passing, that this fact was appreciated by the earliest researchers of speech recognition (see, for example, Denes [52]). It is only now, however, that we have both the mathematics and the computers to model and study some of the global aspects of the speech code. Many of the modern speech-recognition systems rely heavily on the structural and linguistic aspects of speech [53]-[56], [28], [20], [21].

In this section, then, we shall investigate two levels of the hierarchy of structural information, grammar and semantics, and their application to mechanical speech recognition. For the purposes of our discussion, grammar is the surface structure of a message and includes, but is not limited to the phonetic structure of words and word order in sentences. Semantics is the deep structure of a message by which meaning is conveyed.

Let us begin by placing grammar and semantics in perspective with respect to the speech-communication process. Speech is a code used to convey information. Peirce [57] has distinguished among four aspects of natural language codes, symbolic, syntactic, semantic, and pragmatic. The symbols of a language are arbitrary and differ both from language to language and from the written to the spoken form of a given language. For written English, for example, the symbols are the 26 letters of the alphabet, a blank symbol or a space, and a few punctuation marks. For spoken English, the 40 or so basic sounds or phonemes are a reasonable choice. Although they are subject to substantial variation, they do correlate highly with measurable spectral parameters.

Syntax is the relationship of symbols to each other. Although we usually think of syntax as grammar, that is the way the words are concatenated to form sentences, syntax equally well describes the way spectral types form phonemes, phonemes form syllables, and syllables form words. The syntatic structure of a language is also arbitrary to the extent that any set of rules for forming sequences of symbols is legitimate so long as the sequences can actually be realized. In speech, for example, one would not expect to find sequences of phonemes which are anatomically impossible to articulate. Later we shall see that while syntatic rules are arbitrary, some sets are better than others in the sense that they provide for more robust communication.

Semantics is the relationship of symbols to reality. It is at this level of the communication hierarchy that the arbitrariness ends. Once certain symbols are chosen to represent specific aspects of the real world, certain constraints on the way symbols are arranged in sequences are automatically imposed if we are to have a faithful linguistic model of our universe.

The boundary between syntax and semantics is easily emphasized by an example. Consider the sentence: *The green colorless cloud pulled coldly on the fast shirt.* According to the rules of English grammar, the sentence is well formed. It is, however, clearly semantically anomalous and in ordinary conversation, would not be understood. The semantic constraints inherent in natural language, like those imposed by syntax, serve to make it more robust and must be exploited for the same purpose in constructing speech-recognition machines.

Pragmatics is the relationship between symbols and their users. Two different speakers, or the same speaker in two different contexts, will use the same symbol to mean entirely different things. This aspect of language is very difficult to formalize and will not be treated in this paper. The definition is given only for the sake of completeness.

Having defined the fundamental aspects of communication by natural language, we turn to the human speech-communication process to see how these fundamentals are manifest. We shall later use this understanding as a guide to the design of a speech-recognition machine.

Referring to Fig. 32, let us follow the processes which occur in the course of speech communication. A speaker wishing to convey a message must first formulate it in accordance with the semantic structure of the language. The conceptual representation must then be transformed into the corresponding linguistic encoding. Finally, neuromuscular activities must be coordinated so that the lungs, vocal cords, and articulatory organs of the vocal tract move in the proper sequence to produce the sound pressure wave which can be heard as speech.

The hearing process begins in the peripheral auditory system, where spectral analysis is performed by the exquisitely sensitive and selective filter bank called the cochlea. Spectral and temporal information is quantized, encoded, and transmitted via the auditory nerve to the auditory cortex of the brain where symbols are detected, the linguistic code is deciphered and the semantic content extracted whereupon the message is understood.

Even from this oversimplified account of the speech-communication process, several insights which have profound effect on our approach to human/machine speech communication may be derived. The first is the change in data rates which occurs at each stage in the process. The bit rates required after each transformation are shown in Fig. 32. These figures are derived from the "text to speech" synthesis system of Coker [58] and are, of course, only estimates. They serve, however, to empahsize the important fact that the speech signal is highly redundant. Clearly a mechanical speech recognizer should exploit this redundancy.

It is also apparent that speech communication involves cognitive processes which implies that the human capacity for speech communication is inextricably related to our intelligence. We should, therefore, not expect to achieve high-quality speech-recognition machines until we can simulate human intelligence.

One distinctive feature of intelligence is the transition from processing continua to manipulating discrete symbols. While the boundary is not always clearly demarked, its presence is unmistakable. In the speech-production process the change occurs somewhere between linguistic encoding and muscular actions. For the listener, the transition lies somewhere between the cochlear mechanics and linguistic decoding.

It is entirely appropriate that this paper reflect this characteristic transition. The first three sections have dealt with the signal processing and pattern-recognition aspects of speech recognition and were made precise in terms of classical applied mathematics. The formalisms used in the remainder of the presentation will be predominantly those of discrete, strictly nonnumerical computation. We shall encounter one striking exception which serves as a bridge between the two worlds and reminds us of their vague common boundary.

As for the speech-production mechanism, we can make rather faithful mathematical models of the process. In these representations there is a clear and intuitively appealing relationship between reality and abstraction. Coker *et al.* [59]

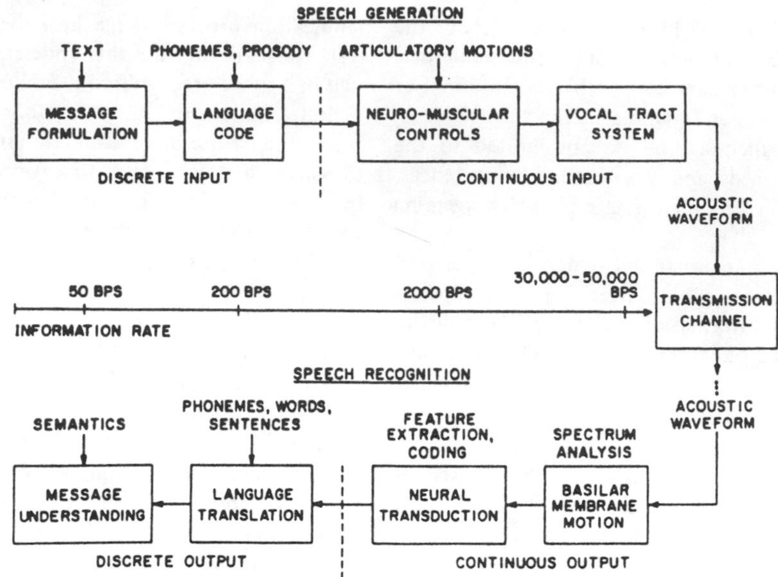

Fig. 32. Schematic representation of the human speech-communication process.

have built a speech-synthesis system in which messages in the form of ordinary text are linguistically encoded using a pronunciation dictionary and a table of prosodic rules for pitch, intensity and duration. The linguistic code is then transformed into a sequence of articulatory motions and the response of the vocal tract to an appropriate excitation fucntion is computed resulting in intelligible synthetic speech. Flanagan *et al.* [60] have investigated the dynamics of the vocal cords and have coupled it with an even more detailed vocal tract model in an effort to gain even more understanding of the physical mechanisms involved in speech production.

Unfortunately, the same kind of model of the mechanics of speech recognition is not available to us. We resort instead to a metaphorical model in which abstract formalisms are used instead of physical and physiological correlates. In fact, the formalisms which we use are the very simplest forms of a very rich mathematical discipline. Despite their obvious shortcomings, our models further our efforts to build speech-recognition machines in two ways. First, they exhibit some of the important phenomena observed in natural speech communications. In particular, they yield a explanation for and quantification of the simultaneous increases in versatility and robustness which are obtained by the addition of grammatical and semantic analyses. Second, they enable us to actually build more powerful speech-recognition devices. Thus we have pursued these models because of their analytical and experimental value.

A. Syntatic Analysis

We begin our discussion of higher level processing in speech recognition by considering systems of the form shown in Fig. 33. These systems operate as a two-level hierarchy in which the first level is an acoustic processor and the second, a language analyzer. Throughout this discussion, the acoustic processor will be assumed to be the isolated word recognizer described in Section II above. The language analyzer can be any of a number of devices, several of which will be described in this section.

1) Rudimentary Linguistic Analysis: Regardless of what the specifics of the language analyzer are, however, its conceptual description is the same. Suppose that the acoustic processor is capable of recognizing a vocabulary of a finite numer of words with a small but nonnegligible probability of error. Imagine that we wish to recognize messages composed of sequences of the vocabulary words (with clearly marked boundaries between words[5]) and that we have a list of all the messages of interest. When a message is processed acoustically, the transcirption may be corrupted (due to errors in either production or recognition). The language analyzer takes this possibly incorrect string of symbols and finds the message in the list which most closely matches, in a well-defined sense, the acoustic transcription. This message is then taken to be the actual utterance.

If the user of such a system is cooperative in the sense that he only utters sequences which are actually in the list, and if we have made the number of messages in the list smaller than the number of arbitrary sequences of vocabulary words, then we would expect the process to be able to correct errors in the acoustic transcription. At the same time, we may increase the versatility of the speech-recognition system by requiring that there be more messages than vocabulary words.

In order to implement the procedure exactly as described above, one need only define the best-match criterion used in searching the message list. Toward that end, we assume an n word vocabulary V_T where

$$V_T = \{v_j\}_{j=1}{}^n. \tag{59}$$

Since the acoustic processor recognizes a word by computing the distance from the unknown utterance to the prototype for

[5] Often the input is a sequence of isolated words with distinct pauses between words.

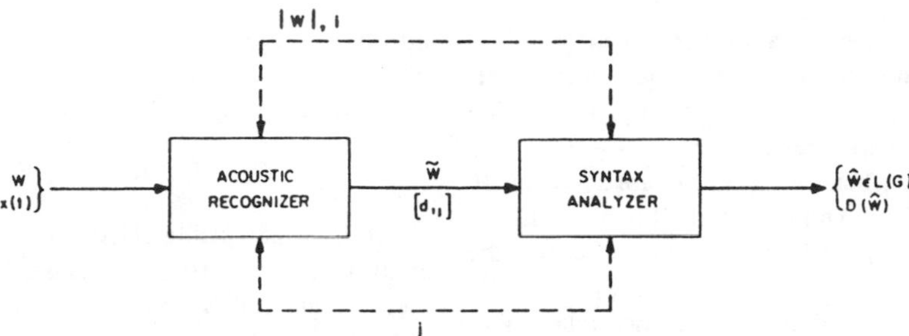

Fig. 33. Block diagram of two-level speech-recognition system.

each word in the vocabulary and then applying some decision rule, for an input string W consisting of the k words $v_{j_1} v_{j_2} \cdots v_{j_k}$, i.e.

$$W = v_{j_1} v_{j_2} \cdots v_{j_k} \tag{60}$$

the acoustic processor must compute all the distances for each of the k words. It is convenient to store these distances as a matrix,

$$D = [d_{ij}]\ 1 \leqslant i \leqslant k; \qquad 1 \leqslant j \leqslant n \tag{61}$$

in which d_{ij} is the distance from the ith word in the string v_{j_i} to the prototype for the jth vocabulary word v_j.

To describe the simplest form of the search procedure we denote the message list by L where

$$L = \{W_i\}_{i=1}^{N} \tag{62}$$

and each W_i is a string of the form of (60). If

$$W_i = v_{j_{i_1}} v_{j_{i_2}} \cdots v_{j_{i_k}} \tag{63}$$

then its distance $D(W_i)$ is given by

$$D(W_i) = \sum_{l=1}^{k} d_{l j_{i_l}} \tag{64}$$

which we can compute for $1 \leqslant i \leqslant N$. Then ordering the list of distances so that

$$D(W_{m_1}) \leqslant D(W_{m_2}) \leqslant \cdots \leqslant D(W_{m_N}) \tag{65}$$

the input W is recognized as W_{m_1}. The obvious drawback to this method is that the amount of computation grows linearly with N. For many otherwise practical tasks, this is prohibitive.

The computational burden could be greatly reduced if we could enumerate strings of symbols in order of their distances. When a string X is found such that $X \in L$, then the search terminates and $W = X$. An efficient procedure for so enumerating the strings has been devised by Aho *et al.* [61].

The algorithm of Aho *et al.* for enumerating the Cartesian product of ordered sets is as follows. Sort the matrix D on its second subscript so that for each i, $1 \leqslant i \leqslant k$ we have

$$d_{ij_1} \leqslant d_{ij_2} \leqslant \cdots \leqslant d_{ij_n}. \tag{66}$$

Note that in this process we have ordered the vocabulary symbols with $v_{j_{i_1}}$ having the highest likelihood. Clearly then the string of minimum distance $\hat{W}_1$ is just $v_{1j_1} v_{2j_1} \cdots v_{kj_1}$ and its distance D_1 is given by

$$D_1 = \sum_{i=1}^{k} d_{i1}. \tag{67}$$

The key observation is that if $\hat{W}_k$ is the kth most likely string, having distance D_k, then the $k+1$st most likely string, $\hat{W}_{k+1}$, differs from one of $\hat{W}_1, \hat{W}_2 \cdots \hat{W}_k$ in only one position and in that one position the second subscript advances by exactly 1. So, for example,

$$W_2 = v_{1j_1} v_{2j_2} \cdots v_{l-1,j_1} \cdots v_{lj_2} v_{l+1,j_1} \cdots v_{kj_1} \tag{68}$$

for some l such that $1 \leqslant l \leqslant k$. The corresponding distance D_2 is just

$$D_2 = \left[\sum_{\substack{i=1 \\ i \neq l}}^{k} d_{i1}\right] + d_{l2}. \tag{69}$$

Comparing (69) to (67) we see that the right-hand sides differ by only one term, the lth, and in that term the second subscript differs only by one.

The above discussion suggests the following simple algorithm. Given D_m for some m, compute all string distances which differ from D_m in only one term and, in that one term term, have a second subscript which is larger by one. Store these distances in a sorted list or priority queue. Delete D_m from the queue. The smallest entry remaining on the list is D_{m+1} and the corresponding string is easily found if the subscripts are maintained on a parallel queue.

The priority queue can be implemented in the form of a binary tree as described by Knuth [62]. Using this data structure, only $M \log_2 M$ operations are required to find the M smallest string distances. The tree need have at most M nodes so that the storage is not excessive. Of course, we have no assurance that one of $\hat{W}_1, \hat{W}_2, \cdots, \hat{W}_M$ is actually in L unless $M = n^k$. So if we restrict M to some tractably small size, we must be prepared for search failures. There are, of course, other methods for searching L. One is based on organizing L as a tree and applying sequential decoding techniques [85].

Aldefeld *et al.* [49] have derived a method which combines the certainty of the exhaustive search technique with the efficiency of the Cartesian product algorithm. The underlying idea is to impose an equivalence relation, $\equiv$, on V_T. One way to do this is to let $v_i \equiv v_j$ whenever v_i and v_j are acoustically similar. The algorithm will still work however if membership in equivalence classes is assigned arbitrarily. Let us denote the number of classes by N_V.

Once defined, we can extend the equivalence relation to strings of vocabulary words by letting

$$v_1 v_2 \cdots v_k \equiv v_1' v_2' \cdots v_k' \quad \text{iff } v_j \equiv v_j' \text{ for } 1 \leqslant j \leqslant k. \tag{70}$$

Based on the classification of letters and strings we may define string-class distances. Let $h(v_1 v_2 \cdots v_k)$ be the set of all strings equivalent to $v_1 v_2 \cdots v_k$. Then the distance of $h(v_1 v_2 \cdots v_k)$, $D(h(v_1 v_2 \cdots v_k))$, is defined by

$$D(h(v_1 v_2 \cdots v_k)) = \min \{D(v_1' v_2' \cdots v_k') \mid v_1' v_2' \cdots v_k' \equiv v_1 v_2 \cdots v_k\} \tag{71}$$

meaning that the string-class distance is the least distance of any of its members. Equation (71) can be easily evaluated according to

$$D(h(v_1 v_2 \cdots v_k)) = \sum_{i=1}^{k} \min \{d_{ij_i} \mid v_{j_i} \equiv v_i\}. \tag{72}$$

The new search algorithm is now easily described. Given a D matrix, the string class distances are computed in increasing order by the Cartesian product algorithm. Each class is searched by the exhaustive search technique for the string within L which has the minimum distance. When the next class distance exceeds the distance of the best string found thus far, the algorithm terminates and the current best string is the string of minimum distance. Maximum efficiency of the algorithm is achieved by selecting a value of N_V so that a balance is maintained between the number of string classes and the number of strings in each class.

The list searching method of language analysis has been implemented and has proven to be very effective for the problem of retrieving telephone directory information by spoken spelled queries.[6] In the first of several experiments, Rosenberg and Schmidt [45] used a vocabulary consisting of just the 26 letters of the alphabet and a message list in the form of the 18 000 entry Bell Laboratories telephone directory. Using a heuristic search procedure they obtained 92 percent correct directory information with an acoustic process of 79 percent accuracy on individual letters using templates obtained from each individual talker.

Subsequently, the equivalence class algorithm was implemented and tested on the same problem by Aldefeld *et al.* [49]. A block diagram of the system has already been given in Fig. 21. For convenience the vocabulary was partitioned into two classes C_1 and C_2 where

$$C_1 = \{B, C, D, E, G, O, P, Q, T, U, VW, Z\} \tag{73a}$$

$$C_2 = \{A, F, H, I, J, K, L, M, N, R, S, X, Y, \text{blank}\} \tag{73b}$$

resulting in 256 string classes, for strings of eight words, with an average of 70 strings per class. The telephone directory was then reorganized, storing equivalence classes sequentially on a disk file.

Again using an acoustic processor with an error rate of 20 percent on letters, a 1.4 percent error rate on directory retrievals was measured. On the average, only 1.2 percent of the directory was searched for a query. As discussed previously, these results show that some very simple linguistic processing can greatly enhance our speech-recognition capabilities.

B. Applying Formal Language Theory to Linguistic Processing

The list search technique described above has an obvious limitation. It will not work if there is no explicit list of messages. Unfortunately, this is exactly the case in Natural Language communication. There is no explicit list of all the possible sentences of English, for example, which might occur. What people seem to have, however, is a set of rules which enables them to generte whatever part of the list is needed in a given conversation. In this section, we shall see how the essence of this process is captured by elementary formal language theory and how this theory can be advantageously applied to speech recognition.

1) Definitions and Nomenclature: We shall use the symbol $L(G)$ to denote a language generated by a grammar G. The grammar is a function of four arguments: $G = G(V_N, V_T, S, P)$. As in the case of lists of messages discussed in the previous section, V_T is a finite set of symbols out of which sentences are composed. V_N is another finite set of symbols disjoint with V_T and whose members never appear in sentences. $S \in V_N$ is a distinguished symbol called the start symbol. The heart of the grammar is a finite set of transformations called production rules and represented by P. The transformations map strings of symbols from V_N and V_T into other such strings. This is written as

$$\alpha \to \beta; \alpha, \beta \epsilon \{V_N \cup V_T\}^* \tag{74}$$

where the asterisk means the set of all strings of elements of the designated set.

A string of symbols $W = w_1 w_2 \cdots w_k$ where $w_i \in V_T$ for $1 \leqslant i \leqslant k$ is said to be a sentence in the language, written $W \in L(G)$, if and only if there exists a sequence of production rules wich map S into W. That is

$$S => \alpha_1; \alpha_1 => \alpha_2; \cdots; \alpha_r => W \tag{75}$$

which we signify by $S \overset{*}{=}> W$.

Different forms of production rules lead to languages of different complexity. Chomsky [63] has formulated a taxonomy of languages, often referred to as the Chomsky hierarchy, based on the form of the production rules required for genera-

[6] The reader may want to refer to Section III-B for a general discussion of the directory listing retrieval system.

tion. From this seminal work has developed a very beautiful and important branch of mathematics called formal language theory which is essential to the study of both natural languages and artificial ones such as programming languages. In this section, we shall look briefly at one tiny aspect of formal language theory which has a bearing on speech recognition. Readers interested in further study of formal language theory should consult Hopcroft and Ullman [64].

If we restrict the form of production rules to

$$A \to aB \tag{76a}$$

or

$$C \to b \tag{76b}$$

where $A, B, C \in V_N$; $a, b \in V_T$, we get the set of Chomsky type 3, or regular, grammars. Linguists are fond of reminding us that this simplest of formal grammars does not have the richness of structure to generate a natural language. It does, however, allow us to generate nontrivial subsets of natural language appropriate to a specific topic.

Regular languages have the additional advantage of a graphic representation of the type shown in Fig. 34. This particular graph is called a state transition diagram and can be used in both a generative and analytical mode. Each transition from one state to another corresponds to a production rule in the grammar G.

The state diagram can be used to generate sentences in the language by beginning in state 1 and making transitions from state to state until a final state, denoted by an asterisk, is reached. As each transition is made, the vocabulary word associated with it is appended to the string formulated thus far. It is not customary to use the state diagram in this generative sense but rather to use P as the generator of the language.

The traditional use for the state transition diagram is to parse a sentence W, that is to determine if $W \in L(G)$, and if so what sequence of production rules form the derivation $S \overset{*}{=} > W$. In terms of the state diagram, parsing is searching the graph for a path, beginning at state 1 and terminating at some final state, the labels on whose transitions, read in sequence, are the string under analysis. If no such path exists, then the string, W does not parse and we write $W \notin L(G)$. As we shall see presently, there are efficient ways of performing the search. Later on we shall discuss the significance of the path or state sequence corresponding to a given sentence.

For the moment, let us revisit Fig. 33 in the context of the present discussion. The acoustic processor operates exactly as before producing the distance matrix D. The language analyzer, in this case, finds the sentence $\hat{W} \in L(G)$ whose total distance

$$D(\hat{W}) = \sum_{i=1}^{k} d_{ij_i} \tag{77}$$

is minimized. Then $\hat{W} = v_{j_1} v_{j_2} \cdots v_{j_k}$ and the procedure for finding it and its derivation is called a maximum-likelihood parsing technique. This technique, too, can be described in terms of the graph searching explanation of parsing given above. One simply assigns the appropriate entry of D to each state transition and then searches for the shortest path, i.e., the one of minimal total distance, from state 1 to a final state having exactly one transition for each row of D.

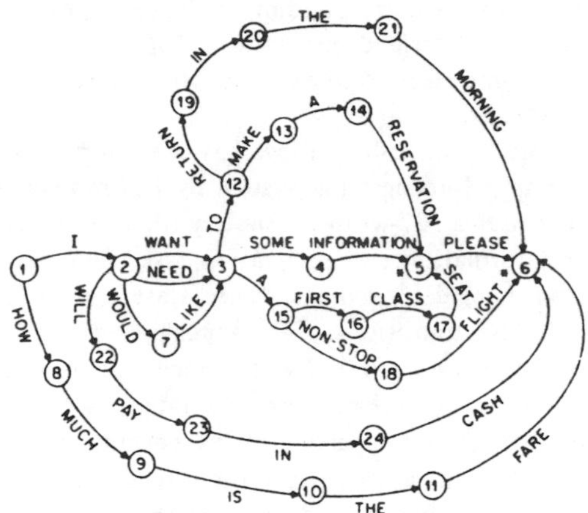

Fig. 34. Example of a state diagram representation of a regular language.

This search can be performed efficiently by a dynamic programming technique due to Dijkstra [65]. Let $Q = \{q_1, q_2, \cdots, q_N\}$ be the set of states in the state transition diagram. We then use two matrices $[\Phi_{iq}]$ and $[\Psi_{iq}]$ with $0 \leqslant i \leqslant k$, where there are k rows in D, and $1 \leqslant q \leqslant N$.

Initially we set

$$\Phi_{iq} = \begin{cases} 0 & \text{for } q = 1; i = 0 \\ \infty & \text{otherwise} \end{cases} \tag{78a}$$

and

$$\Psi_{iq} = 0 \qquad \forall i, q. \tag{78b}$$

The entries of $[\Phi_{iq}]$ and $[\Psi_{iq}]$ are computed recursively according to

$$\Phi_{iq} = \min_{\Delta} \{\Phi_{i-1,s} + d_{ij}\} \tag{79}$$

where Δ is the set of all transitions from state s to state q labeled by v_j. Then

$$\Psi_{iq} = \Psi_{i-1,s^*} v_{j^*} \tag{80}$$

where s^* and j^* minimize the right-hand side of (79).

If we define z to be the final state for which Φ_{kz} is minimum, then

$$\hat{W} = \Psi_{kz} \tag{81a}$$

and

$$D(\hat{W}) = \Phi_{kz}. \tag{81b}$$

The state sequence corresponding to $\hat{W}$, say $\bar{q}$, can be found using a method described by Levinson [66]. The significance of $\bar{q}$ will become clear from our discussion of semantic information processing.

The algorithm described above has been implemented and tested in a speech-recognition system by Levinson *et al.* [22]. The system uses a 127-word vocabulary designed for an airline timetable information and reservation task. Syntatic analysis is based on a regular grammar whose state diagram has 144 states and 450 transitions. The language generated by the grammar contains over 6×10^9 sentences. Using an acoustic processor having an 11.7 percent error rate on words, an overall word error rate after parsing of 0.4 percent was obtained. This corresponds to a sentence error rate of 3.9 percent for sentences with an average length of seven words. This result should be compared with a sentence error rate, without the parsing stage, of 58 percent!

By means of a computer simulation, Levinson [66] has investigated the error correcting properties of maximum-likelihood parsing algorithms. The result of a simulation based on the airline task language is shown in Fig. 35. Shown is a plot of word error probability as a function of the simulation control parameter σ. This parameter controls the variance of the probability density function for the distance from a test utterance to a prototype for that word. As σ increases, therefore, the vocabulary words are made to appear less distinct acoustically.

The upper curve shows that as σ increases, the error rate for acoustic recognition grows rapidly until it reaches its asymptotic value of $(1 - (1/127))$ or 0.992, the rate which would be obtained by random selection. The lower curve shows the error rates obtained when acoustic recognition is supplemented by maximum-likelihood parsing. The degradation in recognition accuracy is greatly retarded, especially in the region of realistic acoustic error rates from 5-10 percent.

Similar simulations on several different languages, including some more complex than the simple type 3 variety, have been performed by Levinson *et al.* [67]. The same qualitative behavior as is shown in Fig. 35 was always observed. There were, however, differences in asymptotic error rates and slopes of the curves. These differences are a function of some intrinsic properties of the languages under consideration.

In order to gain a more quantitative understanding of the differences between languages and how these differences affect the error correcting capability of maximum-likelihood parsing, we shall resort to the statistical properties of formal languages. In an early paper, Shannon [68] observed that readers of English could accurately guess at letters missing from text and he related this predictability property of language to a precise statistical measure of information, entropy. Shannon devised a number of methods for estimating the entropy of natural language. Following Shannon [84], Sondhi and Levinson [69] have shown how the entropy $H(L(G))$ of the regular language $L(G)$ may be exactly determined from its state-transition diagram.

The key quantity characterizing the state diagram is its connectivity matrix, defined by

$$c_{ij} = \text{number of transitions from } q_i \text{ to } q_j \qquad (82)$$

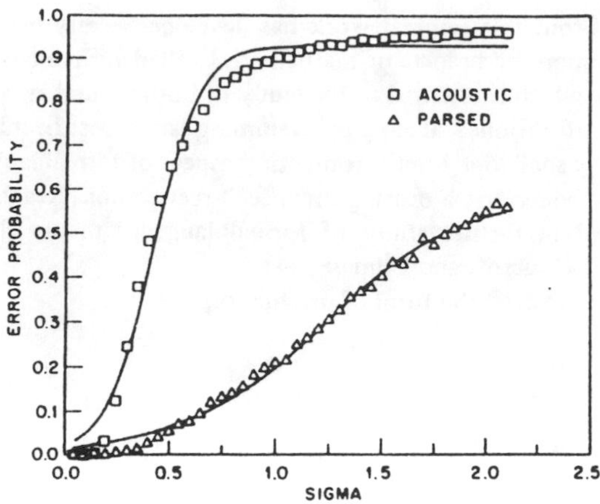

Fig. 35. Stimulation results showing the effects of maximum-likelihood parsing.

and $1 \leq i, j \leq N$. We can use the connectivity matrix to compute the number of sentences, N_k, of length k in $L(G)$ from

$$N_k = \vec{e}_1 C^k \vec{f}^T \qquad (83)$$

where $\vec{e}_1$ is the first N component unit vector and $\vec{f}$ is an N vector of 1's and 0's whose ith component is 1 iff q_i is a final state. The superscript T signifies matrix transposition. Then, since

$$\sum_{k=0}^{\infty} C^k = (I - C)^{-1} \qquad (84)$$

where I is the $N \times N$ identity matrix, the total number of sentences in the language $|L(G)|$ is just

$$|L(G)| = \vec{e}_1 (I - C)^{-1} \vec{f}^T \qquad (85)$$

and the average sentence length $|\bar{W}|$ is given by

$$|\bar{W}| = \frac{\sum_k kN_k}{|L(G)|}. \qquad (86)$$

If we now assume that $|L(G)| < \infty$ and the sentences are equiprobable, then we can compute the N_k, $|L(G)|$ and $|\bar{W}|$ from (83)-(85) which in turn allows us to compute the entropy $H_{eq}(L(G))$ from

$$H_{eq}(L(G)) = \frac{\log_2 |L(G)|}{|\bar{W}|}. \qquad (87)$$

If the assumption of equiprobably sentences is not realistic, we can also compute the maximum entropy obtained under any probability distribution of sentences. In this case, we can show that [64]

$$H_{max}(L(G)) = -\log_2 (x_0) \qquad (88)$$

where x_0 is chosen so that

$$1 - \sum_k N_k x_0{}^k = 0. \qquad (89)$$

The acoustic word recognizer can be regarded as a noisy channel and, as such, can be characterized by its equivocation $H(x \mid y)$, which is a measure of the uncertainty in the spoken word x given the recognized word y. We can extend the notion of equivocation to sentences by defining the uncertainty in the spoken sentence given the acoustically recognized one according to

$$H(W \mid \tilde{W}) = \mid \bar{W} \mid H(x \mid y). \tag{90}$$

where

$$H(x \mid y) = \sum_{x \in V_T} \sum_{y \in V_T} p(x \mid y) p(x) \log_2 \left[\frac{p(x \mid y) p(x)}{p(y)} \right]. \tag{91}$$

The probabilities of confusion $p(x \mid y)$ can be experimentally measured; the prior probabilities of words $p(x)$ can be computed by the method given in [69]. Then the probability of occurrence of the word y at the output of the recognizer $p(y)$ can be calculated from

$$p(y) = \sum_{x \in V_T} p(x \mid y) p(x). \tag{92}$$

Finally, from an inequality due to Fano [70], it follows immediately that

$$H(W \mid \tilde{W}) \eta \leqslant \frac{H(P_e)}{\mid \bar{W} \mid} + P_e H_{eq}(L(G)) \tag{93}$$

where P_e is the probability of sentence error; $H(P_e)$ is defined as

$$H(P_e) = P_e \log_2 P_e + (1 - P_e) \log_2 (1 - P_e) \tag{94}$$

and the efficiency of the language η is given by

$$\eta = \frac{H_{eq}(L(G))}{\log_2 (\mid V_T \mid)}. \tag{95}$$

Since the entropy of the language is less than or equal to the logarithm of the vocabulary size, $\eta \leqslant 1$.

Equation (93) is not guaranteed to give a good estimate of P_e. However, for the speech-recognition system based on the flight information and reservation task language, the computation gives $p_e \geqslant 0.038$. The observed probability of error on 351 sentences was 0.039! The significance of (93) is that it enables us to estimate error probability in terms of measurable and computable properties of the task language and the acoustic recognizer. Since one has great flexibility in designing task languages for speech recognition, the grammars can be matched to word recognizers to yield robust communication.

C. Recognition of Connected and Continuous Speech

The discussion thus far has been predicated on the existence of a method of segmenting a sentence into its component words. In the experiments just described, the issue of segmentation was completely circumvented by requiring speakers to speak sentences with brief pauses between words. Sentences uttered in this manner can be segmented reliably on the basis of the temporal variation of energy in the speech waveform. Obviously, energy minima of sufficient duration signal word boundaries. With the location of the words so marked in the input utterance, isolated word recognizers of the type discussed in the first part of this paper serve well in the role of the acoustic processor shown in Fig. 33.

In continuous speech, however, no such pauses between words exist and segmentation becomes an error-prone process. In this section, we describe two basic methods for recognizing continuous speech in the presence of unreliable segmentation. The first is a syntax-directed method which matches isolated word templates to a continuous-speech stream. In this case, one copes with the segmentation problem by generating many hypothetical segmentations and choosing the best. The second method places the burden of correcting segmentation errors on the language analyzer by endowing it with the ability to insert missing segments and delete extra ones. A noteworthy aspect of this approach is that it has been implemented both for word-sized segments and more fundamental linguistic units, phonemes. The later method was used in a recognition system for fluent Japanese speech.

1) Syntax Directed Approach to Connected-Word Recognition: The origins of our syntax-directed architecture are found in some early attempts to improve the efficiency of the system for recognition of sentences composed of isolated words. Recall that in this system, the acoustic processor computes an entire D matrix. Since not all vocabulary words can occur in all word positions in the sentence, many of the entries of D are unused. The goal of these experiments then was to eliminate these unnecessary and costly distance computations. A solution to this problem was offered by Levinson and Rosenberg [71] in which a communication path was provided between the acoustic processor and the language analyzer (the dashed lines in Fig. 33). In this system, the language analyzer provides the acoustic processor with a list of those words which can occur in a given word position in the sentence being processed and the acoustic processor computes only those entries in the distance matrix. Besides providing a substantial reduction in computation, this "hypothesize and test" structure immediately suggests a method for connected-word recognition. We refer to this type of speech recognition as connected-word recognition because it is based on isolated-word templates and requires reasonable care of articulation although no pauses between words are required.

The system which was implemented by Levinson and Rosenberg [51] is shown in Fig. 36. The main components of the system are a parser similar to that described above, and an isolated-word recognizer which uses the UELM method of dynamic time registration discussed in Section II-B3).

Referring to the diagram of Fig. 36, the interaction between the parser and the time alignment subroutine is as follows. Based on its present state, the parser specifies that a vocabulary word, say v, should occur approximately at time t_b. The UELM algorithm matches the input speech beginning at t_b to a reference template for the word v. The distance of the match D_v is returned along with the computed endpoint t_e. This endpoint will then serve as a nominal beginning point for the next word in the candidate sentence.

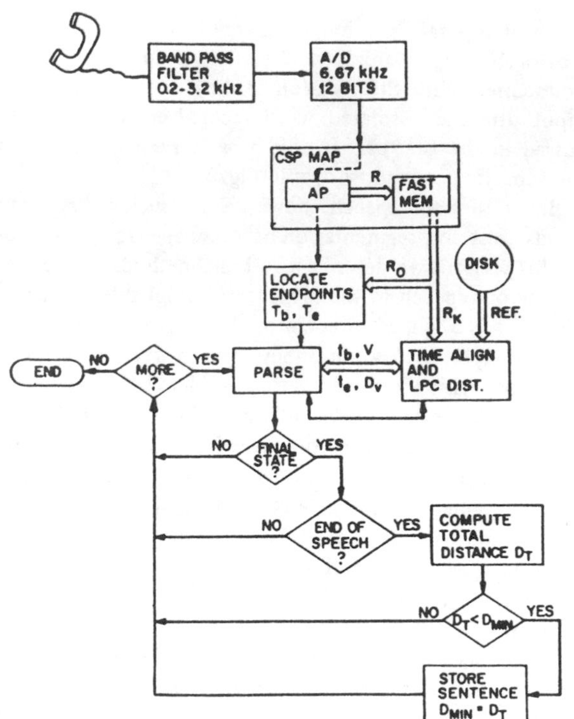

Fig. 36. Block diagram of the syntax-directed speech-recognition system.

The dynamic programming recursion by which the parser is implemented is identical to that of (78)–(80), except that a third matrix $[\Theta_{iq}]$ is added to keep track of the implicit segmentation performed by the UELM procedure. Initially, we set

$$\Theta_{iq} = \begin{cases} 1 & \text{for } i = 0, q = 1 \\ \infty & \text{otherwise} \end{cases} \tag{96}$$

where the initial values simply indicate that the parser must be in its initial state at the onset time of the speech input. Then we add the following to the basic recursion:

$$\Theta_{iq} = \Theta_{i-1,s^*} + \tau_{j^*} \tag{97}$$

where τ_{j^*} is the duration, in frames, of the segment of the input sentence to which the template for word v_{j^*} was aligned. Thus, when the parser continues a sentence from state q, it will begin the time alignment at frame $\Theta_{i+1,q}$.

After the evaluation of each word hypothesis, the parser checks to see if a final state has been reached. If the present state is not a final state, processing continues. Otherwise, a further check is performed to determine whether or not the last word terminated close to the endpoint of the input speech. If not, processing continues. Otherwise, a candidate sentence has been completed. If the newly generated sentence has a smaller metric than any previously produced, it is saved. Otherwise, it is discarded and processing continued.

The three step recursion of (79), (80), and (97) is performed by applying every transition in the state diagram once for each of $i = 0, 1, 2 \cdots$ thus building many candidate sentences in a strictly left to right fashion. Parsing continues until, for some i, every transition has been used without adding any word to any candidate sentence. Due to the rather liberal compression and expansion allowed by the time-alignment procedure, candidate sentences of a wide range of lengths are often generated. Usually, candidate sentences containing many more or may fewer words than were present in the input are poor ones. The final recognition of the input is the surviving candidate sentence when the termination criteria have all been satisfied.

The system has been tested on a set of 100 sentences ranging in length from 4 to 11 words and spoken by two male speakers. The median word-recognition rate was 90 percent and the sentence accuracy recorded was 75 percent. These results, which are significantly poorer than those obtained in the case of sentences with pauses between words, reflect the increased difficulty of the connected-speech task.

The principal shortcoming of the system can be seen from Fig. 37 in which are plotted the empirically determined probability density functions of the metrics for correct words (HITS), $p_H(d)$, and incorrect ones (ERRORS), $p_E(d)$. The equal error threshold occurs at $d = 0.528$ and the corresponding error probability is 0.275. Thus it may be seen that while the probability is high that a word having a small distance is correct, there is a substantial likelihood that a correct word will have a large distance. Since the parser maintains only the best path to each state, one such large distance can cause the parser to abandon an otherwise correct path. Since the segmentation will then not match that of the true sentence, the correct path will not usually be recovered. The obvious solution is to retain more than one candidate sentence for each state.

2) Explicit Segmentation and Labeling for Continuous-Speech Recognition: The principal advantage of the syntax-directed approach to connected-word recognition is that by using word size templates we implicitly have good representations of coarticulation effects within word boundaries. Unfortunately, the coarticulation effects across word boundaries in fluent speech are not well accounted for by reference patterns derived from isolated words. One approach to this problem is to use an explicit segmentation and labeling scheme in conjunction with a parser which can correct the segmentation errors which will certainly occur.

To illustrate the power of such a parser, consider the following example derived from the toy language shown in Fig. 34. Suppose that the sentence "I NEED A FIRST CLASS SEAT" was incorrectly segmented with the article "A" being deleted. But suppose that all other words were recognized correctly with low distances. A parser which assumes correct segmentation would interpret the input as either "I NEED A NONSTOP FLIGHT" or some other five word sentence depending on the values in the distance matrix. In any event, it cannot get the correct sentence because it has six segments (words) and the parser cannot alter the number of segments. The parser we shall describe in this section has the desirable property of being able to insert and delete segments, and, by that means, will derive the correct sentence from the erroneously segmented transcription of our example.

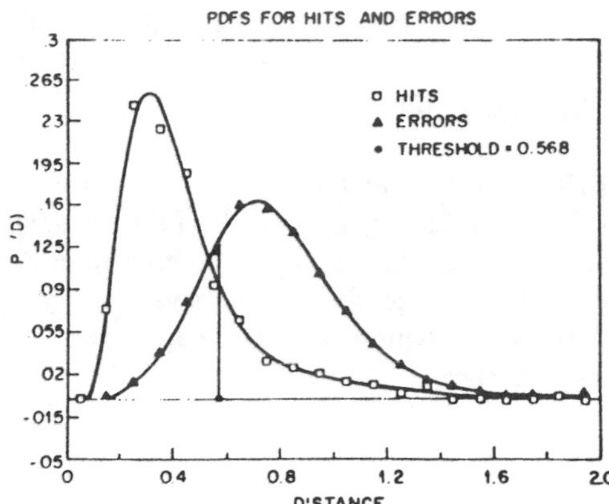

Fig. 37. Probability density functions for correct and incorrect words in connected-speech recognition.

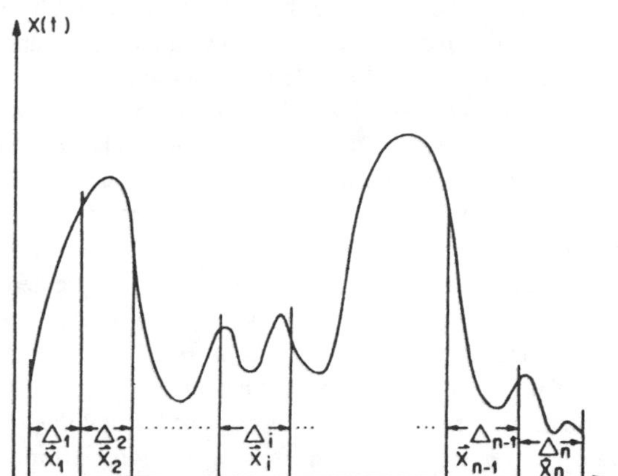

Fig. 38. Example illustrating segmentation of an acoustic waveform.

The ability of a parser to function in the presence of segmentation errors is especially important for large vocabulary continuous-speech recognition tasks because, as the vocabulary grows, it becomes unfeasible to have reference templates for each word. Rather, one would like to use a smaller set of "universal" templates in terms of which one can construct the entire lexicon of a chosen natural language. One such set is the set of phonemes which are the "atomic sounds" of spoken language. It is here that algorithmic parsers, such as those we are discussing, shine, because their operation is independent of the grammar and/or symbols used. In this section, we shall describe just such a parser for fluent Japanese based on a 27-phoneme representation of that language.

The parser which we describe below requires the acoustic processor to segment and label the speech waveform as shown in Fig. 38. The acoustic processor must place segment boundaries in the speech stream so that the segments, $\Delta_1, \Delta_2, \cdots, \Delta_k$, correspond to the vocabulary symbols which the recognizer and parser know. These segments, which are not necessarily of equal length, are then analyzed and feature vectors $\vec{x}, \vec{x}_2, \cdots, \vec{x}_k$ are extracted. The feature vectors are then used to compute the entries of the D matrix in which there will be one row for each segment of the waveform. The difference between this distance matrix and the one used earlier is that previously each row of D corresponded to a real-word position in the sentence; whereas, in this case, the segments are not certain to correspond one-for-one to symbols. Some segments may be superfluous while others may actually contain several symbols. In this segmentation and labeling paradigm, the parser must be able to correct such segmentation errors.

The parser, which is described in detail by Levinson [72] requires two dynamic programming algorithms, one nested inside the other. The outer and main one is similar to a procedure due to Wagner [73] which was used to correct spelling errors in text. The second and inner procedure uses the algorithm of Dijkstra cited earlier.

The outer dynamic program uses two rectangular matrices $[\Phi_{iq}]$ and $[\Psi_{iq}]$ where $1 \leqslant i \leqslant k$, $1 \leqslant q \leqslant N$ and k is the number of rows of D. These two matrices are initialized exactly as in (78a) and (78b). The basic recursion is then given by

$$\Phi_{iq} = \min_{1 \leqslant s \leqslant N} \{\Phi_{i-1,s} + E_{sqi}\} \tag{98a}$$

and

$$\Psi_{iq} = \Psi_{1-1,s_0} \cdot \beta^* \tag{98b}$$

where E_{sqi} is the length, in terms of D, of the shortest path from state s to state q based on the ith segment, β^* is the corresponding sentence fragment, and $s_0{}^*$ is the state for which (98a) is minimized.

Equations (98a) and (98b) have a very simple interpretation. They say that the best path from state 1 to state q based on the ith segment of the input is just the best path from state 1 to state s concatenated to the best path from state s to state q. It is important to note that there are no restrictions on the number of symbols in β; therefore the ith segment may account for zero symbols, in which case the segment is deleted; one symbol meaning that the segment is correct; or many symbols in which case all symbols except one are inserted.

To actually calculate E_{qsi} and β, we use Dijkstra's algorithm; there is, however, an added complication. If the length of β is greater than one then one symbol comes from the ith segment and all others are inserted. Since we do not know which symbol is the real one, all possibilities must be tried. For this reason, the algorithm requires three dimensional arrays $[\phi_{rlp}]$ and $[\psi_{rlp}]$. Initially

$$\phi_{rlp} = \begin{cases} 0 & \text{for } l = 0, p = s \text{ and } \forall r \\ \infty & \text{otherwise} \end{cases} \tag{99a}$$

and

$$\psi_{rlp} = 0 \qquad \forall r, l, p. \tag{99b}$$

Then the basic recursion proceeds according to

$$\phi_{rmy} = \min_{\Delta} \{\phi_{r,m-1,t} + h_{ij_m}\} \tag{100}$$

where Δ is the set of all transitions from state t to state y with a label of v_j and

$$h_{ij_m} = \begin{cases} d_{ij_m} & \text{for } m = r \\ \xi(d_{ij_m}) & \text{for } m \neq r. \end{cases} \tag{101}$$

That is, when $m = r$ we are taking the symbol from the ith segment and thus using its distance from the D matrix. In all other cases, we are inserting a symbol and its score is some function of that entry $\xi(d_{ij_m})$. The other part of the recursion is given by

$$\psi_{rmy} = \psi_{r,m-1,t^*} \cdot v_j^* \tag{102}$$

where t^* and v_j^* minimizes (100). Then

$$E_{sqi} = \min_l \left\{ \min_{1<r<l} \{\phi_{rlq}\} \right\} \tag{103}$$

and

$$\beta = \psi_{r^* l^* q} \tag{104}$$

where r^* and l^* minimize (103).

Finally, substituting E_{sqi} from (102) into (98a) and β from (104) into (98b) we get

$$D(\hat{W}) = \min_z \{\Phi_{kz}\} \tag{105}$$

where the minimization is over all final states z. In some cases it is desirable to bias $\hat{D}(W)$ in favor of longer sentences by normalizing by the length of Ψ_{kz}. The optimal sentence $\hat{W}$ is determined from

$$\hat{W} = \Psi_{kz^*}$$

where z^* minimizes (105).

The speech-recognition task on which the parser was tested is described in detail by Shikano and Kohda [53] and Nakatsu and Kohda [54]. We give only a brief description here. The task of the system is railroad seat reservations. An input consists of a sequence of up to eight phrases spoken in fluent Japanese and separated by pauses of approximately 0.5 s duration. Each phrase except one specifies one item of information necessary to obtain a reservation. The other phrase is the verb of the sentence comprising all of the phrases. The phrases need not occur in any order, except that the verb, if present, must be last; nor must all phrases be present. The sentences are composed from a 112-word vocabulary while the words are represented in terms of just 27 phonemes.

The acoustic processor segments each phrase first into syllables and then phonemes. The distance matrix is derived from this second segmentation and passed to the parser. The parser analyzes each phrase in terms of each of eight grammars. The best phrases from each grammar are selected and their scores entered in another distance matrix D defined by

$$d_{ij} = D(\hat{W}_j \mid G_i) 1 \leqslant i \leqslant 8, 1 \leqslant j \leqslant N_w \tag{107}$$

where $\hat{D}(W_j \mid G_i)$ denotes the minimum distance for the jth phrase in the sentence when parsed into the ith grammar. The number of phrases in the sentence is represented by N_w.

Since at most one phrase can be generated by any grammar and the verb, if present must be last, we minimize the total phrase distance

$$T = \sum_{i=1}^{N_w} d_{i_j j} \tag{108}$$

subject to the constraints that $i_k \neq i_l$ for $k \neq l$ and $i_j = 3$ only for $j = N_w$. The latter constraint is because G_3 is the grammar for verb phrases. The minimization is accomplished by means of the Cartesian product algorithm described earlier and from it, the maximum-likelihood sentence is derived.

The system was tested on 20 sentences comprising 124 phrases spoken by each of four male subjects. The accuracy of the acoustic recognition which formed the input to the parser was as follows. Phonemes were correctly classified 64 percent of the time. Of the errors, 23 percent were due to simple substitutions. The remaining 16 percent involved segmentation faults. Under these conditions, an overall correct phrase-recognition rate of 68 percent was achieved. In absolute terms, this constitutes an unacceptably high error rate, but in comparison with the error rate which is observed, using the acoustic processor alone it becomes a striking demonstration of the power of linguistic analysis in speech recognition.

D. Modeling the Speech-Communication Process

Although the ultimate purpose of speech-recognition research is to enable natural spoken language human/machine communication, the systems described thus far simply transcribe speech. In this section we describe a complete system for human/machine speech communication. The system utilizes acoustic, syntactic, and semantic processing to effect a true dialog. The user of the system must speak in sentences with pauses between words and the machine responds in a similar fashion. The system is highly robust and operates on line in a few times real time on a laboratory minicomputer. Details of the system as implemented for the airline timetable task, are given by Levinson and Shipley [74]. The following overview, however, will be useful for these discussions.

A block diagram of the system is shown in Fig. 39. From the figure we see that speech in the form of a sentence W is input to the word recognizer which operates in conjunction with the parser in the syntax directed mode discussed earlier. The output of the parser is the maximum-likelihood sentence $\hat{W}$ and its derivation or state sequence $\bar{q}$. The semantic processor takes $\bar{q}$ and $\hat{W}$ and interprets them in the context of the conversation stored in the u-model (universe) to generate "actions" which involve searching the Official Airline Guide data base, altering the context of the conversation, and formulating an appropriate response.

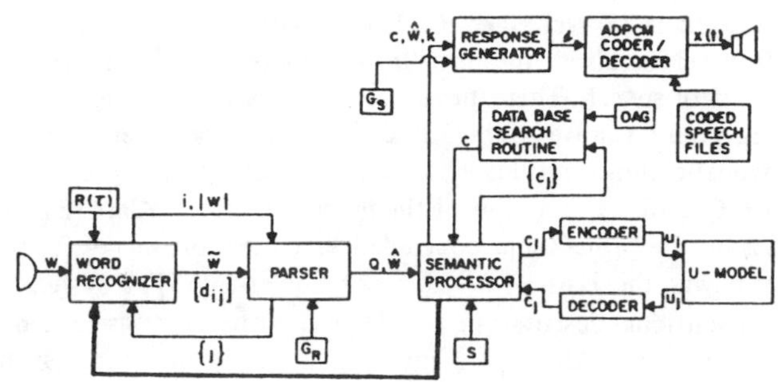

Fig. 39. Block diagram of the conversational-mode speech-recognition system.

The data base search routine can take a set of items $\{c_j\}$ and either match it to a complete flight description C or determine in what way the set is insufficient. A complete flight description can be used to answer a question and/or update the u-model.

The response generator takes the current flight description C, the input sequence $\hat{W}$, and a semantic code K, and generates a reply to $\hat{W}$ using the grammar G_s. The reply is first represented by a string of symbols each of which is a code for one word of a sentence S. A subroutine controls an ADPCM coder/decoder, uses S to access a file of precoded isolated words, and concatenates them into a spoken rendition of the reply.

1) Semantic Processing: The semantic analysis which is performed by the system is based on the following abstraction of the communication process. For A to communicate with B, both must have a model or internal representation of the subject. A takes the state of his model and encodes it in a message which he transmits to B. B decodes the message in terms of his subject model and alters its state accordingly. Communication takes place to the extent that B's model is isomorphic to the state A's would be in had he received the same message.

This abstraction poses two requirements. First we must have some way of defining states of a "world-model" and second, there must be a mechanism for changing states. In our system, the states are implicitly defined by the semantic structure of the task language. The language has 19 semantic categories such as *information, reservation, flight choice, seat selection,* etc. These define 15 parameters of the task model such as *destination, day of the week, departure time,* etc. The particular values which are assigned to the parameters determine the state of the model, for example, *destination* = BOSTON, *day of the week* = TUESDAY, *departure time* = MORNING. The state of the U-model is changed by instructions called "actions" which mediate between the input, the data base, and the task model.

Semantic processing, then, occurs in two stages. First, there is a decoding stage in which it is determined from the input which "actions" are to be executed. Then the "actions" must actually be performed. Semantic decoding is simply a mapping

$$S: \{Q \times V_T\} \rightarrow A \tag{109}$$

where Q is the set of states of the diagram of G and A is the set of "actions" which we shall define precisely below. Thus, if $\hat{W} = \hat{w}_1 \hat{w}_2 \cdots \hat{w}_k$ is a sentence which has been recognized by the acoustic processor and parser and $\bar{q} = q_0 q_1 \cdots q_k$ is its state sequency then

$$S(q_i, \hat{w}_i) = \alpha_i \in A \text{ for } 1 \leqslant i \leqslant k. \tag{110}$$

The "actions" α_i are nothing more than instructions for the classical finite state machine. Thus an action is just the four-tuple

$$\alpha_i = \alpha_i(X, U_p, K, U_N) \tag{111}$$

which is understood to mean, if the task model is presently in state U_p and the input contains the set of words $X \in V_T^*$, then change the state of the task model to U_N and issue output code K which will be used by the response generator to construct the reply $R(\hat{W})$.

The semantic processor has five mechanisms for changing states in the U-model: default values, data base lookup, direct translation from the input, derivation from the present state, and computation based on information and procedures not reflected in the current state of the U-model.

There are 126 entries in the semantic decoding table S, and 37 instructions in the "action" set A. These are stored in a static portion of memory while the U-model and the subroutines, which are special purpose procedures for changing its state, are stored in dynamic memories.

The following sample dialog gives an idea of the level of sophistication of the conversations in which the system can participate.

Machine: This is the Bell Laboratories flight information system. May I help you?
User: I want one first class seat on flight number three one to Denver on Sunday.
M: I am sorry, the flight is not available on Sunday.
U: I would like to leave on Saturday.
M: Flight number three one leaves New York at nine forty five A.M.; arrives in Denver at one ten P.M.
U: What is the flight time?
M: The flight time is five hours and twenty five minutes.
U: How many stops are there on the flight?
M: This flight makes one stop.
U: I want a nonstop flight.
M: I am sorry there are no nine A.M. nonstop flights.
U: I want to go at four P.M.
M: Flight number one six leaves New York at four fifty P.M.; arrives in Denver at seven P.M.
U: What stops are there on the flight?
M: This flight makes no stops.
U: Is a meal served on the flight?
M: Dinner is served.
U: How much is the fare?
M: The round-trip first-class fare is three hundred sixty dollars.
U: What plane is on the flight?
M: The aircraft is a Douglas DC ten.

U: I prefer the Boeing seven four seven.
M: The aircraft is a Douglas DC ten.
U: Please repeat the departure time.
M: The departure time is four fifty P.M.
U: I will take flight number six five.
M: I am sorry there is no flight six five to Denver.
U: Please repeat the flight number.
M: The flight number is one six.
U: I want flight one six.
M: Your reservation on flight number one six to Denver on Saturday is confirmed. Thank you.

The dialog is stilted but communication is effected. The important result derived from this experimental system is that by combining several simple systems, a synergistic effect is achieved in which the combination can perform tasks of a sophistication greater than would be expected on the basis of the complexity of the components.

The system is also highly robust. It was evaluated on a corpus of 351 sentences spoken by five male and two female speakers. After syntactic processing, 21 sentences contained word-recognition errors. However after semantic analysis 15 of these were correctly understood despite the errors and correct responses were made. In the remaining six cases, a semantic anomaly was detected causing the machine to pose a question to the user who could then correct the problem. Thus we achieved a recognition accuracy of more than 98 percent and when recognition errors occurred, communication did not break down. Thus, we see that in making even this crude model of speech communication, a surprising level of robustness is obtained. This indicates that to make progress in speech recognition one needs not only to improve the individual components, but also to treat the problem in total and design better control structures to coordinate the components.

V. CONCLUSION

In the previous section of the paper, we have discussed the application of higher level processing to the problem of speech recognition. We discussed grammatical analysis from the standpoint first of list searching and then parsing within a formal language theoretical framework. This formulation lead to an analytical understanding of how syntactic information makes speech communication more robust. We have described four experimental systems which utilize syntactic information to improve speech-recognition accuracy. We then discussed semantic processing and showed how it could be used to build a conversational-mode speech-recognition system. A summary of these five systems and some of their pertinent specifications is shown in Table VI. The main conclusion that can be drawn from this table is that as better high-level processing is included, thereby simulating cognitive and intelligence related processes, more sophisticated and robust human/machine communication is obtained.

At the end of such a presentation, it is appropriate to address the question of directions for further research. This is a highly speculative venture and workers in the field have had little success in predicting what would be an instructive next step. In 1973, Newell *et al.* [75] argued cogently that the next frontier involved the intelligence related and structural aspects of speech. Their thesis was that only higher level processing could resolve ambiguities in the necessarily error-ridden acoustic transcription. Thus was born the ARPA project. In 1976, after termination of the herculean effort, Klatt [24] assessed the project and concluded that the most successful system was the HARPY machine of Lowerre [55], a system of conventional design using the classical syntax analysis described in this paper. Although many insights were gained through the HEARSAY [20] and HWIM [21] systems, they did not meet the original design specification. In a recent survey of speech-recognition research, Lea and Shoup [76] concluded that the new frontier is acoustic and prosodic analysis. So we have made a complete cycle.

We suspect that what is truly needed is a better understanding of all levels of the speech communication process from acoustics and phonetics to pragmatics. We suggest that some potentially fruitful investigations into certain aspects of the speech communication process have been conspicuously absent from the research forum. These are the study of adaptive schemes, the relation of speech recognition to speech synthesis and the incorporation of models of hearing and perception in acoustic analysis.

In humans, speech is an acquired ability not present at birth. Perhaps it is too difficult a process to emulate by a deterministic program but rather must be learned by adapting to an environment. The detailed Markov model and careful statistical analysis which is unique to the speech-recognition system of Jelinek [56] and Bahl *et al.* [77] is probably well suited to be part of an adaptive or self-organizing strategy.

Presently there are several systems which synthesize speech from text [59], [78], [79]. The state of the art in synthesis is advanced in comparison to that of recognition. Flanagan [80] has suggested that the discrepancy in performance indicates that there is a great deal of information about speech embedded in these synthesis systems that is presently not, but should be, used in recongition.

Finally, from models of the peripheral auditory system of Allen [81] and Hall [82] it is becoming clear that the ear performs a kind of spectral analysis which cannot be approximated by conventional methods. Perhaps these models can provide the extreme selectivity and nonlinear effects which are needed to improve acoustic analysis.

As for the ultimate limits of our ability to provide spoken natural language human/machine communication, we tend to be conservative in our estimates. We believe that disciplined discourse in artificial languages about carefully circumscribed topics with computers will be possible and economically viable in the not-too-distant future. At the present moment, the worthy goal of unconstrained speech communication seems quite beyond our reach.

ACKNOWLEDGMENT

The authors would like to acknowledge the contributions of several of their colleagues to the work described in this paper. Dr. James L. Flanagan has been the leader of the effort to bring speech-recognition research to prominence at Bell Laboratories,

TABLE VI
SUMMARY OF PERFORMANCE OF SEVERAL SPEECH-RECOGNITION SYSTEMS

Task	Input Speech	Vocabulary	Type of Processing	Accuracy	Remarks
Airline Timetable Information and Reservations	Sentences With Pauses Between Words	127 Words	Isolated Word Recognition With Maximum Likelihood Parsing	> 96% on Sentences	Reference [66] Speaker Trained
Telephone Directory Assistance	Spelled Names With Pauses Between Letters	26 Letters	Maximum Likelihood List Searching Isolated Word Recognition	> 98% Correct Information Retrieval	Uses 18,000 Name BTL Directory Speaker Independent References [46,49]
Airline Timetable Information and Reservations	Carefully Articulated Sentences, No Pauses Between Words	127 Words	Syntax-Directed Dynamic Programming Time Registration	75% Sentences 90% Words	Speaker Trained Reference [71]
Train Seat Reservations	Fluent Japanese Phrases	112 Words 27 Phonemes	Segmentation and Labelling Maximum Likelihood Parsing Corrects Segmentation Errors	68% Phrases	Speaker Independent References [72,53,54]
Airline Timetable Information and Reservations	Sentences With Pauses Between Words	127 Words	Isolated Word Recognition Maximum Likelihood Parsing Semantic Analysis	> 98% Sentences and Error Detection	Speaker Trained Reference [74] Conducts Spoken Dialog Official Airline Guide Data Base

and he has provided guidance, insight, and numerous valuable suggestions and advice. Dr. Aaron Rosenberg has been involved with almost every aspect of the recognition problem and has made substantial research contributions. Dr. Fumitada Itakura was responsible for the earliest recognition systems upon which this paper is based. Cory Myers has been primarily responsible for much of our understanding of dynamic time-warping algorithms and their application to isolated and connected word recognition. We also thank Cory for his diligent reading and comments on the paper. Finally, we acknowledge the contributions of Jay Wilpon in the implementation of many of the systems described in this paper.

REFERENCES

[1] J. L. Flanagan, *Speech Analysis, Synthesis, and Recognition*, 2nd ed. New York: Springer-Verlag, 1972.
[2] L. R. Rabiner and R. W. Schafer, *Digital Processing of Speech Signals*. Englewood Cliffs, NJ: Prentice-Hall, 1978.
[3] N. R. Dixon and T. B. Martin, Eds., *Automatic Speech and Speaker Recognition*. New York: IEEE Press, 1979.
[4] W. Lea, Ed., *Trends in Speech Recognition*. Englewood Cliffs, NJ: Prentice-Hall, 1980.
[5] D. R. Reddy, Ed., *Speech Recognition*. New York: Academic, 1974.
[6] T. B. Martin, "Practical applications of voice input to machines," *Proc. IEEE*, vol. 64, pp. 487–501, Apr. 1976.
[7] S. Moshier, "Talker independent speech recognition in commercial environments," in *Speech Commun. Papers, 97th ASA Meeting*, June 1979, pp. 551–553.
[8] H. Sakoe, "Two-level DP-matching—A dynamic programming based pattern matching algorithm for connected word recognition," *IEEE Trans. Acoust., Speech, Signal Processing*, vol. ASSP-27, pp. 588–595, Dec. 1979.
[9] Interstate Electronics Corp., Voice Data Entry System, unpublished tech. descriptions.
[10] Centigram Corp., Mike, unpublished tech. descriptions.
[11] Heuristics Corp., Speechlab, unpublished tech. description.
[12] F. Itakura, "Minimum prediction residual principle applied to speech recognition," *IEEE Trans. Acoust., Speech, Signal. Processing*, vol. ASSP-23, pp. 67–72, Feb. 1975.
[13] A. E. Rosenberg and F. Itakura, "Evaluation of an automatic word recognition system over dialed-up telephone lines," *J. Acoust. Soc. Amer.*, suppl. 1, vol. 60, p. S12, 1976.
[14] M. R. Sambur and L. R. Rabiner, "A speaker-independent digit-recognition system," *Bell Syst. Tech. J.*, vol. 54, pp. 81–102, Jan. 1975.
[15] L. R. Rabiner, "On creating reference templates for speaker independent recognition of isolated words, *IEEE Trans. Acoust., Speech, Signal Processing*, vol. ASSP-26, pp. 34–42, Feb. 1978.
[16] L. R. Rabiner, S. E. Levinson, A. E. Rosenberg, and J. G. Wilpon, "Speaker-independent recognition of isolated words using clustering techniques," *IEEE Trans. Acoust., Speech, Signal Processing*, vol. ASSP-27, pp. 336–349, Aug. 1979.
[17] J. S. Bridle and M. D. Brown, "Connected word recognition using whole word templates," in *Proc. Inst. Acoust.*, Autumn 1979.
[18] L. R. Rabiner and C. E. Schmidt, "Application of dynamic time warping to connected digit recognition," *IEEE Trans. Acoust., Speech, Signal Processing*, vol. ASSP-28, pp. 337–388, Aug. 1980.
[19] C. S. Myers and L. R. Rabiner, "Connected digit recognition using a level building DTW algorithm," *IEEE Trans. Acoust., Speech, Signal Processing*, vol. ASSP-29, June 1981.
[20] V. R. Lesser, R. D. Fennell, L. D. Erman, and D. R. Reddy, "Organization of the hearsay II speech understanding system," *IEEE Trans. Acoust., Speech, Signal Processing*, vol. ASSP-23, pp. 11–24, Feb. 1975.
[21] J. J. Wolf and W. A. Woods, "The HWIM speech understanding system," in *Conf. Rec. 1977 IEEE Int. Conf. Acoust., Speech, Signal Processing*, May 1977, pp. 784–787.
[22] S. E. Levinson, A. E. Rosenberg, and J. L. Flanagan, "Evaluation of a word recognition system using syntax analysis," *Bell Syst. Tech. J.*, vol. 57, pp. 1619–1626, May–June 1978.
[23] F. Jelinek, L. R. Bahl, and R. L. Mercer, "Design of a linguistic decoder for the recognition of continuous speech," *IEEE Trans. Inform. Theory*, vol. IT-21, pp. 250–256, May 1975.
[24] D. H. Klatt, "Review of the ARPA speech understanding project," *J. Acoust. Soc. Amer.*, vol. 62, pp. 1345–1366, Dec. 1977.
[25] J. S. Bridle and M. D. Brown, "An experimental automatic word-recognition system: Interim report," JSRU Res. Rep. 1003, Dec. 1974.
[26] G. M. White and R. B. Neely, "Speech recognition experiments

with linear prediction, bandpass filtering, and dynamic programming," *IEEE Trans. Acoust., Speech, Signal Processing*, vol. ASSP-24, pp. 183–188, Apr. 1976.

[27] H. F. Silverman and N. R. Dixon, "A comparison of several speech-spectra classification methods," *IEEE Trans. Acoust., Speech, Signal Processing*, vol. ASSP-24, pp. 289–295, Aug. 1976.

[28] D. R. Reddy, L. D. Erman, and R. B. Neely, "A model and a system for machine recognition of speech," *IEEE Trans. Audio Electroacoust.*, vol. AU-21, pp. 229–238, June 1973.

[29] J. D. Markel and A. H. Gray Jr., *Linear Prediction of Speech*. New York: Springer-Verlag, 1976.

[30] J. Makhoul, "Linear prediction: A tutorial review," *Proc. IEEE*, vol. 63, pp. 561–580, Apr. 1975.

[31] G. M. White, "Dynamic programming, the Viterbi algorithm, and low cost speech recognition," in *Proc. 1978 IEEE Int. Conf. Acoust., Speech, Signal Processing*, pp. 413–417, Apr. 1978.

[32] A. H. Gray, Jr. and J. D. Markel, "Distance measures for speech processing," *IEEE Trans. Acoust., Speech, Signal Processing*, vol. ASSP-24, pp. 380–391, Oct. 1976.

[33] H. Sakoe and S. Chiba, "Dynamic programming algorithm optimization for spoken word recognition," *IEEE Trans. Acoust., Speech, Signal Processing*, vol. ASSP-26, pp. 43–49, Feb. 1978.

[34] C. S. Myers, L. R. Rabiner, and A. E. Rosenberg, "Performance tradeoffs in dynamic time warping algorithms for isolated word recognition," *IEEE Trans. Acoust., Speech, Signal Processing*, vol. ASSP-28, pp. 622–635, Dec. 1980.

[35] L. R. Rabiner, A. E. Rosenberg, and S. E. Levinson, "Considerations in dynamic time warping for discrete word recognition," *IEEE Trans. Acoust., Speech, Signal Processing*, vol. ASSP-26, pp. 575–582, Dec. 1978.

[36] A. J. Viterbi, "Error bounds for convolutional codes and an asymptotically optimum decoding algorithm," *IEEE Trans. Inform. Theory*, vol. IT-13, pp. 260–269, Apr. 1967.

[37] G. D. Forney, Jr., "The Viterbi algorithm," *Proc. IEEE*, vol. 61, pp. 268–278, Mar. 1973.

[38] L. F. Lamel, "Methods of endpoint detection for isolated word recognition," M.S. thesis, Massachusetts Inst. Technol., Feb. 1980.

[39] L. R. Rabiner and J. G. Wilpon, "Application of clustering techniques to speaker-trained isolated word recognition," *Bell Syst. Tech. J.*, vol. 58, pp. 2217–2233, Dec. 1979.

[40] ——, "Speaker independent isolated word recognition for a moderate size (54 word) vocabulary," *IEEE Trans. Acoust., Speech, Signal Processing*, vol. ASSP-27, pp. 583–587, Dec. 1979.

[41] L. R. Rabiner, J. G. Wilpon, and A. E. Rosenberg, "A voice-controlled repertory-dialer system," *Bell Syst. Tech. J.*, vol. 59, pp. 1153–1163, Sept. 1980.

[42] L. R. Rabiner and J. G. Wilpon, "Application of isolated word recognition to large vocabularies," unpublished.

[43] ——, "A two pass system for isolated word recognition," *Bell Syst. Tech. J.*, vol. 60, pp. 739–766, May–June 1981.

[44] J. G. Ackenhusen and L. R. Rabiner, "Microprocessor implementation of an LPC-based isolated word recognizer," *BTL Microprocessor Symp.*, Sept. 1980.

[45] A. E. Rosenberg and C. E. Schmidt, "Automatic recognition of spoken spelled names for obtaining directory listings," *Bell Syst. Tech. J.*, vol. 58, pp. 1797–1823, Oct. 1979.

[46] B. Aldefeld, L. R. Rabiner, A. E. Rosenberg, and J. G. Wilpon, "Automated directory listing retrieval system based on isolated word recognition," *Proc. IEEE*, vol. 68, pp. 1364–1379, Nov. 1980.

[47] P. Cummiskey, N. S. Jayant, and J. L. Flanagan, "Adaptive quantization in differential PCM coding of speech," *Bell Syst. Tech. J.*, vol. 52, pp. 1105–1118, Sept. 1973.

[48] L. R. Rabiner and R. W. Schafer, "Digital techniques for computer voice response: Implementations and applications," *Proc. IEEE*, vol. 64, pp. 416–433, Apr. 1976.

[49] B. Aldefeld, S. E. Levinson, and T. G. Szymanski, "A minimum distance search technique and its application to automatic directory assistance," *Bell Syst. Tech. J.*, vol. 59, pp. 1343–1356, Oct. 1980.

[50] C. S. Myers and L. R. Rabiner, "A dynamic time warping algorithm for connected word recognition," *IEEE Trans. Acoust., Speech, Signal Processing*, vol. ASSP-29, Apr. 1981.

[51] S. E. Levinson and A. E. Rosenberg, "A new system for continuous speech recognition—Preliminary results," in *Proc. ICASSP-79*, pp. 239–243, Apr. 1979.

[52] P. B. Denes, "The design and operation of a mechanical speech recognizer at University College, London," *J. Brit. IRE*, vol. 19, pp. 219–229, Apr. 1959.

[53] K. Shikano and M. Kohda, "A linguistic processor in a conventional speech recognition system," *Rev. ECL*, vol. 26, pp. 1486–1504, 1978.

[54] R. Nakatsu and M. Kohda, "An acoustic processor in a conversational speech recognition system," *Rev. ECL*, vol. 26, pp. 1505–1520, 1978.

[55] B. T. Lowerre, "The HARPY speech recognition system," Ph.D. dissertation, Carnegie Mellon Univ., Pittsburgh, PA, 1976.

[56] F. Jelinek, "Continuous speech recognition by statistical methods," *Proc. IEEE*, vol. 64, pp. 532–556, Apr. 1976.

[57] C. S. Peirce, *Collected Papers of Charles Sanders Peirce*, C. Hartstone and P. Weirs, Eds. Cambridge, MA: Harvard Univ. Press, 1935.

[58] C. H. Coker, "A model of articulatory dynamics and control," *Proc. IEEE*, vol. 64, pp. 452–460, Apr. 1976.

[59] C. H. Coker, N. Umeda, and C. P. Browman, "Automatic synthesis from ordinary english text," *IEEE Trans. Audio Electroacoust.*, vol. AU-21, pp. 293–298, Feb. 1973.

[60] J. L. Flanagan, K. Ishizaka, and K. Shipley, "Synthetic speech from a dynamic model of the vocal cords and vocal tract," *Bell Syst. Tech. J.*, vol. 54, pp. 485–506, Mar. 1975.

[61] A. V. Aho, T. G. Szymanski, and M. Yannakakis, "Enumerating the Cartesian product of ordered sets," in *Proc. 14th Annu. Conf. Information Sciences and Systems*, Princeton, NJ, Mar. 1980.

[62] D. E. Knuth, *The Art of Computer Programming, Vol. 3: Sorting and Searching*. Reading, MA: Addison-Wesley, 1973, pp. 422 ff.

[63] N. Chomsky, "On certain formal properties of grammars," *Inform. Contr.*, vol. 2, pp. 137–167, 1959.

[64] J. E. Hopcroft and J. D. Ullman, *Formal Languages and Their Relation to Automata*. Reading, MA: Addison-Wesley, 1969.

[65] E. W. Dijkstra, "A note on two problems in connection with graphs," *Num. Math.*, vol. 1, pp. 269–271, 1959.

[66] S. E. Levinson, "The effects of syntactic analysis on word recognition accuracy," *Bell Syst. Tech. J.*, vol. 57, pp. 1627–1644, May–June 1977.

[67] S. E. Levinson, R. J. Lipton, and L. Snyder, "Some results on maximum *a posterori* probability parsing," in *Proc. 1976 Conf. Inform. Sciences and Systems*, Baltimore, MD, Apr. 1976.

[68] C. E. Shannon, "Prediction and entropy of printed english," *Bell Syst. Tech. J.*, vol. 1, pp. 50–64, Jan. 1951.

[69] M. M. Sondhi and S. E. Levinson, "Computing relative redundancy to measure grammatical constraint in speech recognition tasks," in *Proc. Int. Conf. Acoust., Speech, Signal Processing*, Tulsa, OK, Apr. 1978, pp. 409–412.

[70] R. M. Fano, *Transmission of Information, A Statistical Theory of Communications*. New York, NY: M.I.T. Press and Wiley, 1961, pp. 186 ff.

[71] S. E. Levinson and A. E. Rosenberg, "Some experiments with a syntax directed speech recognition system," in *Proc. Int. Conf. Acoust., Speech, Signal Processing*, Tulsa, OK, Apr. 1978, pp. 700–703.

[72] S. E. Levinson, "An algorithm for maximum likelihood parsing of speech in the presence of segmentation errors and an experimental performance evaluation," *IEEE Trans. Acoust., Speech, Signal Processing*, to be published.

[73] R. A. Wagner, "Order-*n* correction for regular languages," *Commun. Ass. Comput. Mach.*, vol. 17, pp. 265–269, May 1974.

[74] S. E. Levinson and K. L. Shipley, "A conversational mode airline information and reservation system using speech input and output," *Bell Syst. Tech. J.*, vol. 59, pp. 119–137, Jan. 1980.

[75] A. Newell, J. Barnett, J. W. Forgie, C. C. Green, D. H. Klatt, J. C. R. Licklider, J. Munson, D. R. Reddy, and W. A. Woods, *Speech Understanding Systems: Final Report of a Study Group*. Amsterdam, The Netherlands: North Holland/American Elsevier, 1973.

[76] W. A. Lea and J. E. Shoup, "Gaps in the technology of speech understanding," in *Proc. Int. Conf. Acoust., Speech, Signal Processing*, Tulsa, OK, Apr. 1978, pp. 405–408.

[77] L. R. Bahl, R. Bakis, P. S. Cohen, A. G. Cole, F. Jelinek, B. L. Lewis, and R. L. Mercer, "Further results on the recognition of a

continuously read natural corpus," in *Proc. Int. Conf. Acoust., Speech, Signal Processing*, Denver, CO, Apr. 1980, pp. 872–875.

[78] O. Fujimura, M. J. Macchi, and J. B. Lovins, "Demisyllables and affixes for speech synthesis," in *Proc. 9th Int. Congress Acoust.*, vol. 1 (Madrid, Spain), July 1977, p. 513.

[79] J. Allen, "Synthesis of speech from unrestricted text," *Proc. IEEE*, vol. 64, pp. 433–442, Apr. 1976.

[80] J. L. Flanagan, "Computers that talk and listen: Man–machine communication by voice," *Proc. IEEE*, vol. 64, pp. 405–415, Apr. 1976.

[81] J. B. Allen, "Cochlear micromechanics—A mechanism for transforming mechanical to neural tuning within the cochlea," *J. Acoust. Soc. Amer.*, vol. 62, pp. 930–939, 1977.

[82] J. L. Hall, "Two tone suppression in a non-linear model of the basilar membrane," *J. Acoust. Soc. Amer.*, vol. 61, pp. 802–810, 1977.

[83] L. R. Bahl and F. Jelinek, "Decoding for channels with insertions, deletions and substitutions with applications to speech recognition," *IEEE Trans. Inform. Theory*, vol. IT-21, pp. 404–411, 1975.

[84] C. E. Shannon, "A mathematical theory of communication," *Bell Syst. Tech. J.*, vol. 27, pp. 379–423, 1948.

[85] F. Jelinek, "Fast sequential decoding algorithm using a stack," *IBM J. Res. Development*, vol. 13, pp. 675–678, 1969.

Lawrence R. Rabiner (S'62–M'67–SM'75–F'75) was born in Brooklyn, NY, on September 28, 1943. He received the S.B. and S.M. degrees simultaneously in June 1964, and the Ph.D. degree in electrical engineering in June 1967, all from the Massachusetts Institute of Technology, Cambridge, MA.

From 1962 through 1964, he participated in the cooperative plan in electrical engineering at Bell Laboratories, Whippany, NJ, and Murray Hill, NJ. He worked on digital circuitry, military communications problems, and problems in binaural hearing. Presently, he is engaged in research on speech communications and digital signal-processing techniques at Bell Laboratories, Murray Hill. He is coauthor of the books *Theory and Application of Digital Signal Processing* (Prentice-Hall, 1975) and *Digital Processing of Speech Signals* (Prentice-Hall, 1978).

Dr. Rabiner is a member of Eta Kappa Nu, Sigma Xi, Tau Beta Pi, and a Fellow of the Acoustical Society of America. He is a former President of the IEEE S-ASSP Ad Com, and is currently a member of the S-ASSP Technical Committee on Digital Signal Processing, former member of the S-ASSP Technical Committee on Speech Communication, former Associate Editor of the S-ASSP TRANSACTIONS, member of the PROCEEDINGS OF THE IEEE Editorial Board, and a former member of the Technical Committee on Speech Communication of the Acoustical Society.

Stephen E. Levinson (S'72–M'74) was born in New York, NY, on September 27, 1944. He received the B.A. degree in engineering sciences from Harvard University, Cambridge, MA, in 1966, and the M.S. and Ph.D. degrees in electrical engineering from the University of Rhode Island, Kingston, RI, in 1972 and 1974, respectively.

From 1966–1969, he was a Design Engineer at Electric Boat Division of General Dynamics in Groton, CT. From 1974–1976, he held a J. Willard Gibbs Instructorship in Computer Science at Yale University. In 1976, he joined the technical staff at Bell Laboratories, Murray Hill, NJ, where he is pursuing research in the areas of speech recognition and cybernetics.

Dr. Levinson is a member of the Association for Computing Machinery and the Acoustical Society of America, and is Chairman of the IEEE Computer Society Technical Committee on Speech Recognition and Understanding.

Minimum Prediction Residual Principle Applied to Speech Recognition

FUMITADA ITAKURA, MEMBER, IEEE

Abstract—A computer system is described in which isolated words, spoken by a designated talker, are recognized through calculation of a minimum prediction residual. A reference pattern for each word to be recognized is stored as a time pattern of linear prediction coefficients (LPC). The total log prediction residual of an input signal is minimized by optimally registering the reference LPC onto the input autocorrelation coefficients using the dynamic programming algorithm (DP). The input signal is recognized as the reference word which produces the minimum prediction residual. A sequential decision procedure is used to reduce the amount of computation in DP. A frequency normalization with respect to the long-time spectral distribution is used to reduce effects of variations in the frequency response of telephone connections.

The system has been implemented on a DDP-516 computer for the 200-word recognition experiment. The recognition rate for a designated male talker is 97.3 percent for telephone input, and the recognition time is about 22 times real time.

I. INTRODUCTION

RECENTLY time-domain speech analysis based on linear predictability of signal waveform has been successfully adopted for efficient coding of a redundant speech signal [1], [2]. Motivated by these successes, several efforts have been made toward application of the linear predictor coefficients (LPC) for speech recognition [3], [4]. But the immediate use of LPC as feature parameters was not so successful as might be expected [5]. The lack of success may be partly due to the fact that the feature space spanned by LPC is too complicated to introduce a simple and effective measure of distance between elements in the space.

Manuscript received March 29, 1974; revised October 2, 1974. This paper was presented at the IEEE Symposium on Speech Recognition, Carnegie-Mellon University, Pittsburgh, Pa., April 15–19, 1974.

The author is with the Acoustics Research Department, Bell Laboratories, Murray Hill, N. J. 07974 and the Electrical Communications Laboratories, Nippon Telephone and Telegraph Public Corporation, Musashino, Tokyo, Japan.

It may be natural to raise the question: what kind of distance measure should be used in the framework of the linear prediction technique? In order to discuss this question, let us consider a more simplified problem; given a short segment of signal, what is the optimal distance measure to test a hypothesis that the segment can be regarded as one generated by a model having specified LPC? The answer to this question might be extended to test a more complicated hypothesis; namely, that some input utterance can be regarded as a word having a specified pattern of LPC.

In this paper, an approach to this problem will be described from a statistical point of view, and it will be shown that the log likelihood ratio, which is the best criterion to test the hypothesis, is reduced to the logarithm of the ratio of prediction residuals, and can be used as a powerful distance measure. This result is applied to automatic recognition of isolated words, wherein a sequential likelihood ratio test is adopted to reduce the amount of computation.

II. DISTANCE MEASURE FOR AN ALL-POLE MODEL

An all-pole model of speech signal is as follows. The discrete-time signal $x(n)$ ($t = nT$, when T is the interval between samples) in a stationary segment of signal satisfies the system of difference equations

$$x(n) + a(1)x(n-1) + \cdots + a(p)x(n-p) = e(n) \tag{1}$$

where $\{a(i)\}$ are constants and $\{e(n)\}$ is a white noise or a quasi-periodic signal, with mean-squared value s. Because p is usually much less than the period of $\{e(n)\}$, $\{e(n)\}$ can be regarded as an uncorrelated signal as far as correlations between $q(<p)$ adjacent samples are concerned. In this paper, $\{-a(i)\}$ or simply $\{a(i)\}$ is called the LPC, and the mean-squared value s of $\{e(n)\}$, or power, is called the prediction residual.

The problem in this section is to derive a measure of distance, or dissimilarity, between a segment of signal $\mathbf{X} = (x(1),\cdots,x(N))$ and the model defined by (1). Here, for mathematical tractability, we assume that $\{e(n)\}$ is a Gaussian white noise. Then a set of parameters $\mathbf{P} = (s,a(1),\cdots,a(p))$ specifies the conditional joint probability density $p(\mathbf{X}/\mathbf{P})$, and if $N \gg p$, the logarithm of $p(\mathbf{X}/\mathbf{P})$ is approximately given by [6], [7]

$$L(\mathbf{X}/\mathbf{P}) = -(N/2)[\log 2\pi s + (1/s)\mathbf{a}\mathbf{V}\mathbf{a}'] \tag{2}$$

where $\mathbf{a}$ is a row vector $(1,a(1),\cdots,a(p))$, and

$$\mathbf{V} = [v(|i-j|)], \qquad (i,j = 0,1,\cdots p)$$

is a correlation matrix whose elements are defined by

$$v(i) = (1/N)\sum_{n=1}^{N-i} x(n)x(n+i). \tag{3}$$

Supposing that we have no knowledge about the absolute value of s and s is a free parameter (Case I), it is replaced by its estimate which maximizes $L(\mathbf{X}/\mathbf{P})$

$$\partial L(\mathbf{X}/\mathbf{P})/\partial s = 0, \qquad s = \mathbf{a}\mathbf{V}\mathbf{a}' \tag{4}$$

thus, from (2), we obtain

$$L'(\mathbf{X}/\mathbf{a}) = \max_{s} L(\mathbf{X}/\mathbf{P})$$

$$= -(N/2)\log \mathbf{a}\mathbf{V}\mathbf{a}' + C. \tag{5}$$

The vector $\hat{\mathbf{a}}$ which maximizes $L'(\mathbf{X}/\mathbf{a})$ is determined as a solution of the following system of equations:

$$\sum_{j=0}^{p} v(i-j)\hat{a}(j) = 0, \qquad (i = 1,\cdots,p) \tag{6}$$

and the maximum value is as follows:

$$L''(X) = \max_{\mathbf{a}} L'(\mathbf{X}/\mathbf{a})$$

$$= -(N/2)\log \hat{\mathbf{a}}\mathbf{V}\hat{\mathbf{a}}' + C. \tag{7}$$

$L''(\mathbf{X})$ is the maximum value of the likelihood function when both s and $\mathbf{a}$ are assumed to be free parameters (Case II). From (5) and (7), the likelihood ratio for the Case I and II of free parameters is proportional to

$$d(\mathbf{X}/\mathbf{a}) = \log(\mathbf{a}\mathbf{V}\mathbf{a}'/\hat{\mathbf{a}}\mathbf{V}\hat{\mathbf{a}}'). \tag{8}$$

The quadratic forms $\mathbf{a}\mathbf{V}\mathbf{a}'$ and $\hat{\mathbf{a}}\mathbf{V}\hat{\mathbf{a}}'$ in (8) are prediction residuals, when the input signal $\mathbf{X}$ is operated by the model LPC $\mathbf{a}$ and the estimated LPC $\hat{\mathbf{a}}$, respectively.

If the model defined by $\mathbf{a}$ is close to the actual process which generates $\mathbf{X}$, then the $\hat{\mathbf{a}}$, which is the maximum likelihood estimate of $\mathbf{a}$, are close to the $\mathbf{a}$ and $d(\mathbf{X}/\mathbf{a})$ is close to zero; if not, $d(\mathbf{X}/\mathbf{a})$ is significantly large. More precisely, $d(\mathbf{X}/\mathbf{a})N$ will be asymptotically a χ^2 variate with p degrees of freedom, if $\mathbf{X}$ is a realization of a model having $\mathbf{a}$ as the parameter (null hypothesis) [12]. If the $d(\mathbf{X}/\mathbf{a})N$ is larger than the $\chi^2_{1-\alpha}(p)$, then the null hypothesis should be rejected at a given probability α of false rejection. In this sense, $d(\mathbf{X}/\mathbf{a})$ can be regarded as a distance measure between $\mathbf{X}$ and the hypothesized model (1) specified by LPC $\mathbf{a}$.

For small deviation of $\hat{\mathbf{a}}$ from $\mathbf{a}$, the distance of (8) can be approximated by

$$d'(\mathbf{X},\mathbf{a}) = [(\mathbf{a}-\hat{\mathbf{a}})\mathbf{V}(\mathbf{a}-\hat{\mathbf{a}})']/[\hat{\mathbf{a}}\mathbf{V}\hat{\mathbf{a}}']. \tag{8'}$$

This measure is apparently different from those which might be intuitively suggested in the space of $\{a(i)\}$ such as

$$d = (\mathbf{a}-\hat{\mathbf{a}})\mathbf{W}(\mathbf{a}-\hat{\mathbf{a}})'. \tag{9}$$

The main difference is in that, the weighting of the quadratic form in (9) is a constant matrix $\mathbf{W}$, while that of (8') depends on the autocorrelation $\mathbf{V}$ of $\mathbf{X}$. This dependence of the weighting matrix on $\mathbf{V}$, or equivalently on $\hat{\mathbf{a}}$, is a natural consequence from the fact that the covariance characteristics of estimation error of $\mathbf{a}$ depends on the location of $\hat{\mathbf{a}}$ in the space of LPC. It is well known that the estimated covariance matrix of $(\mathbf{a}-\hat{\mathbf{a}})$ is proportional to the inverse of $\mathbf{V}/[\hat{\mathbf{a}}\mathbf{V}\hat{\mathbf{a}}']$ [12]. In the distance measure of (8'), the weighting for the difference $(\mathbf{a}-\hat{\mathbf{a}})$ is automatically adjusted in accordance with the probable error of the estimated parameter $\hat{\mathbf{a}}$.

Equation (8) can be rewritten in the form

$$d(\mathbf{X}/\mathbf{a}) = c + \log[(\mathbf{b}\mathbf{r})/(\hat{\mathbf{a}}\mathbf{r})] \tag{10}$$

where $(\mathbf{xy})$ means the inner product of two vectors. $\mathbf{r} = (v(i)/v(0))$, $(i = 0,\cdots,p)$, $c = \log(\mathbf{aa})$, and $\mathbf{b}$ is a vector $(1,b(1),\cdots,b(p))$ whose elements are defined by

$$b(i) = 2\sum_{j=0}^{p-i} a(j)a(j+i)/(\mathbf{aa}). \tag{11}$$

The $\{b(i)/2\}$'s are the autocorrelation coefficients associated with the inverse filter of the all-pole model. The c is the log power of its impulse response. These modified parameters $\mathbf{b}$ and c are more convenient to compute $d(\mathbf{X}/\mathbf{a})$ than the $\mathbf{a}$ themselves.

III. ISOLATED WORD RECOGNITION

Each isolated word to be recognized can be expressed as a time pattern of LPC, which is called the reference pattern. The process in recognition is to find a reference pattern which produces the minimum distance to an input utterance.

Reference Pattern: The reference pattern $\mathbf{R}(k)$ for each word is stored as a matrix of the form

$$\mathbf{R}(k) = [c(m;k),\mathbf{b}(m;k)]$$
$$(m = 1,\cdots,M(k), k = 1,\cdots,K) \tag{12}$$

where $c(m;k)$ and $\mathbf{b}(m;k)$ are the modified parameters of LPC at the mth segment of the kth reference pattern, $M(k)$ is the number of segments in the reference pattern $\mathbf{R}(k)$, and K is the number of words to be recognized. Elements of the matrix $\mathbf{R}(k)$ are computed from a training utterance using (3), (6), and (11).

Recognition: An input utterrance is expressed as a time pattern of autocorrelation coefficients at the first p delays

$$\mathbf{r}(n), \qquad n = 1,\cdots,N \tag{13}$$

where N is the number of segments in the input utterance. The distance between the nth segment of the input and the mth segment of a reference pattern $\mathbf{R}(k)$ is

$$d(n,m;k) = c(m;k)$$
$$+ \log[(\mathbf{b}(m;k)\mathbf{r}(n))/(\hat{\mathbf{a}}(n)\mathbf{r}(n))]. \tag{14}$$

The value of $(\hat{\mathbf{a}}(n)\mathbf{r}(n))$ is obtained in the process of solving the linear equation (6).

If we assume statistical independence of $d(n,m;k)$ for $n = 1,\cdots,N$, it is reasonable to sum up $d(n,m;k)$ over the entire input utterance to give the total distance between the input and the reference pattern. Of course, m must be determined as a function of n

$$m = w(n). \tag{15}$$

This function $w(n)$, which maps the input time axis onto the reference time axis, is called the time-warping function. This function should satisfy some boundary conditions as well as some continuity conditions. For brevity in the following discussion, it is assumed that $w(n)$ is subject to the following conditions.

Boundary Conditions:

$$w(1) = 1, \qquad w(N) = M(k). \tag{16}$$

Continuity Conditions:

$$\begin{aligned} w(n+1) - w(n) &= 0, 1, 2 \qquad (w(n) \neq w(n-1)) \\ &= 1, 2 \qquad (w(n) = w(n-1)). \end{aligned} \tag{17}$$

Fig. 1 shows the domain of possible (n,m) coordinates and an example of $w(n)$. The continuity conditions imply

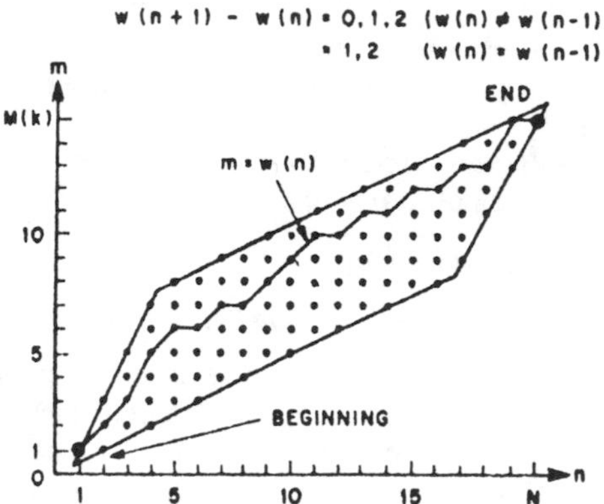

Fig. 1. An example of time-warping function. The parallelogram shows the possible domain of (n,m) coordinates.

that the ratio of instantaneous speed of the input utterance to that of the reference is bounded between 1/2 and 2 at every point. Let us denote the minimum value of the sum of $d(n,m;k)$ for all possible choices of the time-warping function by

$$D(k) = \min_{\{w(n)\}} \sum_{n=1}^{N} d(n,w(n);k). \tag{18}$$

$D(k)$ is a distance between the input utterance and a hypothesized word k. A decision can be made on the basis of the minimum distance among $D(k), k = 1,2,\cdots,K$.

IV. DYNAMIC PROGRAMMING AND SEQUENTIAL DECISION

The distance $D(k)$ in (18) can be efficiently computed using the algorithm of dynamic programming (DP) [8]-[10]. Let us introduce the partial distance measure, in which the boundary conditions are $w(1) = 1$ and $w(n) = m$, and the continuity conditions are the same as the above, denoted by

$$D(n,m;k) = \min_{\{w(j)\}} \sum_{j=1}^{n} d(j,w(j);k). \tag{19}$$

Then there follows the recurrence relation;

$$\begin{aligned} D(n+1,m;k) = d(n+1,m;k) + \min\ (&D(n,m;k) \\ &\cdot g(n,m), \\ &D(n,m-1;k), D(n,m-2;k)) \end{aligned} \tag{20}$$

where

$$\begin{aligned} g(n,m) &= 1(w(n) \neq w(n-1)), \\ &= \infty\,(w(n) = (n-1)). \end{aligned} \tag{21}$$

In the recurrence relation (20), it is assumed that $d(n,m;k)$ outside the allowable domain in the (n,m) coordinates, shown in Fig. 1, is infinitely large. $D(k)$ is found at the last stage in this recurrence formula, that is, $D(k) = D(N,M(k);k)$.

As shown in the recurrence relation, at every lattice point, $d(n,m;k)$ must be calculated; therefore the amount of computation to obtain $D(k)$ is approximately proportional to the number of lattice points, which is nearly

$$L = (2N - M(k) + 1)(2M(k) - N + 1)/3. \tag{22}$$

For example, if $N = 40$, $M(k) = 40$, $K = 200$, the total number of lattice points to be examined in recognizing one word is nearly 112 000, and the processing time is 49 s, if one lattice point is processed in 420 μs, as is the case described later.

One method to reduce the computation time might be the procedure of sequential decisions. Now, let us define $D(n;k)$ by

$$D(n;k) = \min_{m} D(n,m;k). \tag{23}$$

$D(n;k)$ is the minimum distance between the first n segments of the input and a reference pattern $\mathbf{R}(k)$. If a reference pattern $\mathbf{R}(k^*)$ coincides with the input, it is expected that $D(n;k^*)$ takes lower values for all stages n. Therefore, if $D(n;k)$ is sufficiently large compared with probable excursion of $D(n;k^*)$, the reference pattern can be immediately rejected at an early stage without examining further segments. If not, the next stage is examined.

The threshold for rejection should be as low as possible under the constraint that the probability of false rejection is sufficiently small. Although it is desirable to get a threshold $T(n)$ which meets this requirement theoretically, it is difficult to find it in practice.[1] But, if we notice that the final decision is made on the basis of the relative values of $D(k)$, $T(n)$ might be determined depending on the actual realization of $D(n;k)$. The method used in the experiment is as follows.

[1] If the reference pattern $R(k^*)$ is the true one and the assumptions of the model and the statistical independence of $d(n,m;k^*)$ for $n = 1,2,\cdots,N$ hold, the optimal $T(n)$ is given by $x_{1-\alpha}{}^2(pn)$, where α is the probability of false rejection.

The rejection threshold is assumed to be of the form

$$T(n) = S(n) + M \quad (24)$$

where M is a constant decision margin and $S(n)$ is the variable part of $T(n)$ and is updated at every stage in the DP. Initially $S(n)$ is so selected that it is not less than $D(n;k^*)$ for all cases when k^* coincides with the input word. Beginning with $n = 1$, $D(n;k)$ is sequentially computed. If $D(n;k)$ is less than $T(n)$ at the stage n, $S(n)$ is replaced by $D(n;k)$ to give a new threshold which will be used to compute $D(n;k + 1)$. If a reference which is similar to the input is found, the threshold $T(n)$ is set to a lower value. Thereafter only references similar to the input are examined in detail and other references will be rejected at earlier stages. In the final decision only reference patterns which arrived at the last stage N are candidates for the recognized word. If no reference arrives at the last stage, the input is rejected as an inadequate input.

V. EXPERIMENTAL PROCEDURE AND RESULTS

The recognition scheme described earlier has been implemented on a DDP-516 computer for a 200-word recognition experiment. The flow chart of the system is shown in Fig. 2. The 200 words are Japanese geographical names and were pronounced by a male speaker. The mean duration of the reference utterances is 600 ms, and the mean number of syllables is 3.5.

Speech Input: The experimental arrangement for the isolated word recognition is shown in Fig. 3. Each utterance is inputted to the computer using a conventional telephone set dialed through the Bell Laboratories PBX. The telephone set is placed beside the computer console and the noise level around it is about 68 dB(A). After passing through a lowpass filter whose 6 dB cutoff frequency is 3.0 kHz, the speech is sampled at 6.667 kHz and temporarily stored in disc memory. Each utterance is made within a fixed time interval of 1.2 s after listening to the start signal or manually pressing an initiating switch.

Autocorrelation Analysis: Hamming window of 200 samples (30 ms) is applied to the digitized signal. The window is advanced in steps of 100 samples (15 ms) to get the next segment. The instantaneous power within each window is computed, and if it exceeds the noise level, the first eight coefficients are computed. The speech signal duration is detected automatically by examining the power envelope from the forward and backward and neglecting low-level noise.

Normalization of Long-Time Spectrum: The gross spectral distribution of the input signal may be greatly affected by physical factors, such as transducer and line response, as well as by human factors, such as stress and physical condition. These factors may have serious effects on the stability of the system using LPC. Therefore, we have applied a normalization technique of input spectral distribution in the following way. The first two autocorrelation coefficients are averaged over the utterance interval after weighting by the instantaneous power level. For every utterance, a second-order inverse filter is designed by solving a two-variable linear equation. This filter is used to normalize the gross spectral distribution of the utterance. This is done by convolving the original autocorrelation coefficients and the autocorrelation coefficients of the impulse response of the second order inverse filter. The first six normalized autocorrelation coefficients are used to make both the reference patterns to recognize unknown inputs.

Making a Reference Pattern: The reference pattern for each word is generated by the method described in Section III. In this experiment p is 6, $\overline{M(k)}$, the average number of reference segments is about 40 (600 ms), and K, the number of words, is 200. The memory capacity for storing all the reference patterns is $(p + 1)\overline{M(k)}K = 56\,000$ words, and each computer word consists of 16 bits.

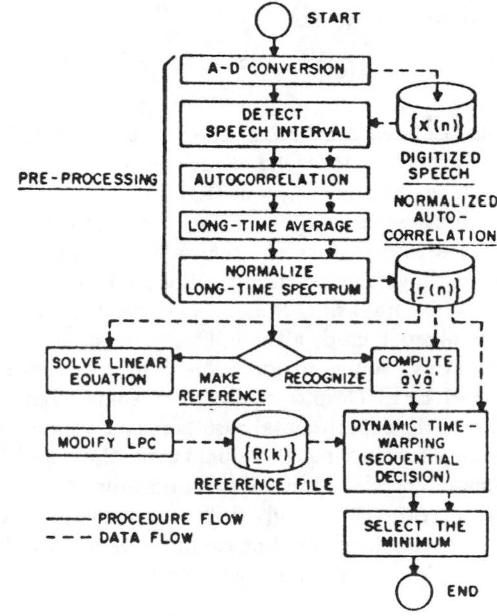

Fig. 2. Flow chart of isolated word recognition.

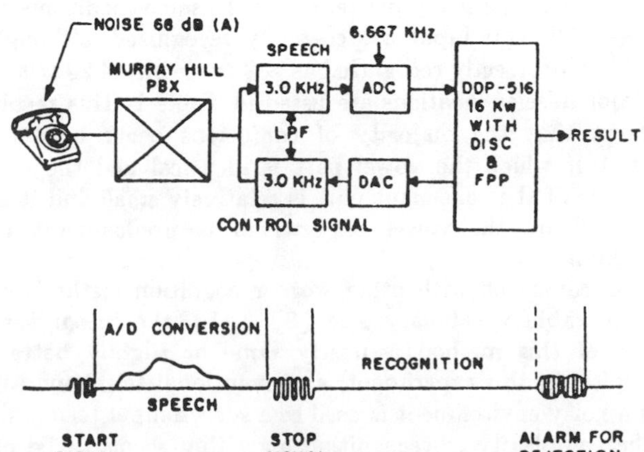

Fig. 3. Experimental arrangement of on-line isolated word recognition.

Recognition and Result: The recognition procedure has been described in Sections III and IV. The major processing in this phase is to compute the distance $d(n,m;k)$ defined by (14), and it is programmed using assembly language. The base of the logarithm is set to 2, and $\log x(1/2 \leq x < 1)$ is approximated by $2(x - 1)$. The computation time for the basic recurrence formula (20) at every lattice point is 420 μs including the computation of $d(n,m;k)$. The threshold margin is chosen as $M = 4$ on the basis of preliminary experiments. The average number of lattice points actually examined is 69 per reference pattern; that is, only 12 percent of L expressed by (22) in which the sequential decision scheme is not used. The total recognition time including the autocorrelation analysis and other preprocessing is about 12 s for one utterance, which is 22 times real time. The recognition rate is 97.3 percent and the rejection rate is 1.65 percent, when the designated talker inputs 2000 test utterances over an time span of three weeks.

VI. DISCUSSION

The main objective of this study is not to develop a particular isolated word recognition system, but is focused to assess experimentally the effectiveness of the proposed distance measure and the sequential decision scheme based on the distance. For this reason, the word recognition system is a straightforward realization of the proposed method without any ad hoc modification. Some parameters, such as intensity, voicing and pitch patterns, are intentionally not used, although they must be crucial in discriminating some words which have very similar patterns of LPC. Despite existence of some room for improvement, the experimental results may give a promising impression, considering the quality of the input signal and vocabulary size. But it must be admitted that the recognition rate is strongly influenced by a particular choice of vocabulary set. For example, if the vocabulary set is the English alphabet and digit

$$\{A,B,\cdots,Y,Z,1,2,\cdots,9,0\},$$

the recognition rate was 88.6 percent for 720 test utterances by the same speaker under the same conditions as in V. All digit input are correctly recognized, although "H" is incorrectly recognized as "8" twice out of 20 trials. Major misclassifications are listed in Table I. This result shows that the majority of confusions occur between pairs in which the vowel part is identical and the difference of the consonant part is relatively small and it is masked by the vowel part which is predominant in duration.

As compared with other word recognition methods of comparable vocabulary size [8], [11], the recognition rate of this method is nearly same or slightly better, despite, in this experiment, a conventional telephone set in a noisy environment is used as a speech input terminal. The complexity of recognition algorithm seems to be of the same order, judging from the processing time per word using computers of similar speed.

VII. CONCLUSION

A new measure of distance for an all-pole model of speech has been derived on the basis of the likelihood ratio criteria and is applied to automatic recognition of isolated words. An algorithm to find to the best match between the input pattern and a reference pattern is derived, in which the dynamic programming technique is used in conjunction with a sequential decision scheme. The system is implemented on a DDP-516 computer to recognize 200 isolated words. The validity of the scheme has been confirmed experimentally. Further work is in progress to test the system for a greater number of talkers and for telephone connections switched over greater distances.

TABLE I
MAJOR MISRECOGNITIONS IN ALPHABET-DIGIT RECOGNITION

INPUT	RECOGNIZED	NO. of ERRORS
V	B or D	15
B	D	10
P	T or D	9
E	T	9
N	M	5
I	Y	5
	SUB TOTAL	53
	OTHER ERRORS	29
	TOTAL ERRORS / TOTAL TRIALS	82 / 720
	ERROR RATE	=11.4%

ACKNOWLEDGMENT

The author wishes to thank J. L. Flanagan for his guidance and stimulating discussions, and to acknowledge the help received from C. H. Coker and A. E. Rosenberg during implementation of the system.

REFERENCES

[1] F. Itakura and S. Saito, "Analysis synthesis telephony based on the maximum likelihood method," in *Proc. Int. Congr. Acoust.*, Tokyo, Japan, Rep. C-5-6, 1968.
[2] B. S. Atal and S. L. Hanauer, "Speech analysis and synthesis by linear prediction of speech waveform," *J. Acoust. Soc. Amer.*, vol. 50, pp. 637–655, 1971.
[3] M. Kohda, S. Hashimoto, and S. Saito, "Spoken digit mechanical recognition," *Trans. Inst. Electron. Commun. Eng. (Japan)*, vol. 55-D, no. 3, 1972
[4] Y. Nakano, A. Ichikawa, and K. Nakata, "Evaluation of various parameters in spoken digits recognition," presented at the IEEE Conf. Speech Communication and Processing, Cambridge, Mass., Apr. 1972, Paper C4.
[5] H. Fujisaki and Y. Sato, "Evaluation and comparison of features in speech recognition," Faculty Eng., Univ. of Tokyo, Tokyo, Japan, Annu. Rep. Eng. Res. Inst., 1973, vol. 32, pp. 213–218.
[6] F. Itakura and S. Saito, "A statistical method for estimation of speech spectral density and formant frequencies," *Trans. Inst. Electron. Commun. Eng. (Japan)*, vol. 53-A, pp. 36–43, 1970.
[7] S. Saito, T. Fukumura, and F. Itakura, "Statistically optimum discrimination of speech spectra," *J. Acoust. Soc. Japan*, vol. 23, no. 5, 1967.
[8] V. M. Velichiko and N. G. Zagoruiko, "Automatic recognition of 200-words," *Int. J. Man-Machine Studies*, vol. 2, pp. 223–234, 1970.
[9] H. Sakoe and S. Chiba, "A dynamic programming approach to continuous speech recognition," in *Proc. Int. Congr. Acoust.*, Budapest, Hungary, Rep. 20-C-13, 1971.
[10] ——, "Comparative study of DP-pattern matching techniques for speech recognition," Speech Res. Group, Acoust. Soc. Japan, Rep. S73-22, 1973.
[11] D. R. Reddy, "Segment synchronization problem in speech recognition," *J. Acoust. Soc. Amer.*, vol. 46, no. 1, p. 89, 1969.
[12] H. B. Mann and A. Wald, "On the statistical treatment of linear difference equations," *Econometrica*, vol. 11, pp. 173–217, 1943.

Dynamic Programming Algorithm Optimization for Spoken Word Recognition

HIROAKI SAKOE AND SEIBI CHIBA

Abstract—This paper reports on an optimum dynamic programming (DP) based time-normalization algorithm for spoken word recognition. First, a general principle of time-normalization is given using time-warping function. Then, two time-normalized distance definitions, called symmetric and asymmetric forms, are derived from the principle. These two forms are compared with each other through theoretical discussions and experimental studies. The symmetric form algorithm superiority is established. A new technique, called slope constraint, is successfully introduced, in which the warping function slope is restricted so as to improve discrimination between words in different categories. The effective slope constraint characteristic is qualitatively analyzed, and the optimum slope constraint condition is determined through experiments. The optimized algorithm is then extensively subjected to experimental comparison with various DP-algorithms, previously applied to spoken word recognition by different research groups. The experiment shows that the present algorithm gives no more than about two-thirds errors, even compared to the best conventional algorithm.

I. Introduction

It is well known that speaking rate variation causes nonlinear fluctuation in a speech pattern time axis. Elimination of this fluctuation, or time-normalization, has been one of the central problems in spoken word recognition research. At an early stage, some linear normalization techniques were examined, in which timing differences between speech patterns were eliminated by linear transformation of the time axis. Reports on these efforts indicated that any linear transformation is inherently insufficient for dealing with highly complicated fluctuation nonlinearity as well as that time-normalization significantly improves recognition accuracy.

DP-matching, discussed in this paper, is a pattern matching algorithm with a nonlinear time-normalization effect. In this algorithm, the time-axis fluctuation is approximately modeled with a nonlinear warping function of some carefully specified properties. Timing differences between two speech patterns are eliminated by warping the time axis of one so that the maximum coincidence is attained with the other. Then, the time-normalized distance is calculated as the minimized residual distance between them. This minimization process is very efficiently carried out by use of the dynamic programming (DP) technique. The basic idea of DP-matching has been reported in several publications [1]-[3], where it has been shown by preliminary experiment on Japanese digit words that a recognition accuracy as high as 99.8 percent has been achieved, indicating the DP-matching effectiveness.

This paper reports an optimum algorithm for DP-matching through theoretical discussions and experimental studies. Investigations were made, based on the assumption that speech patterns are time-sampled with a common and uniform sampling period, as in most general cases. One of the problems discussed in this paper involves the relative superiority of either a symmetric form of DP-matching or an asymmetric one. In the asymmetric form, time-normalization is achieved by transforming the time axis of a speech pattern onto that of the other. In the symmetric form, on the other hand, both time axes are transformed onto a temporarily defined common axis. Theoretical and experimental comparisons show that the symmetric form gives better recognition than the asymmetric one. Another problem discussed concerns slope constraint technique. Since too much of the warping function flexibility sometimes results in poor discrimination between words in different categories, a constraint is newly introduced on the warping function slope. Detailed slope constraint condition is optimized through experimental studies. As a further investigation, the optimized algorithm is experimentally compared with several varieties of the DP-algorithm, which have been applied to spoken word recognition by some research groups [3]-[6]. The optimized algorithm superiority is established, indicating the validity of this investigation.

Manuscript received February 17, 1977; revised September 7, 1977.

The authors are with Central Research Laboratories, Nippon Electric Company, Limited, Kawasaki, Japan.

II. DP-Matching Principle

A. General Time-Normalized Distance Definition

Speech can be expressed by appropriate feature extraction as a sequence of feature vectors.

$$A = a_1, a_2, \text{------}, a_i, \text{------}, a_I$$

$$B = b_1, b_2, \text{------}, b_j, \text{------}, b_J. \quad (1)$$

Consider the problem of eliminating timing differences between these two speech patterns. In order to clarify the nature of time-axis fluctuation or timing differences, let us consider an i - j plane, shown in Fig. 1, where patterns A and B are developed along the i-axis and j-axis, respectively. Where these speech patterns are of the same category, the timing differences between them can be depicted by a sequence of points $c = (i, j)$:

$$F = c(1), c(2), \text{------}, c(k), \text{------}, c(K), \quad (2)$$

where

$$c(k) = (i(k), j(k)).$$

This sequence can be considered to represent a function which approximately realizes a mapping from the time axis of pattern A onto that of pattern B. Hereafter, it is called a warping function. When there is no timing difference between these

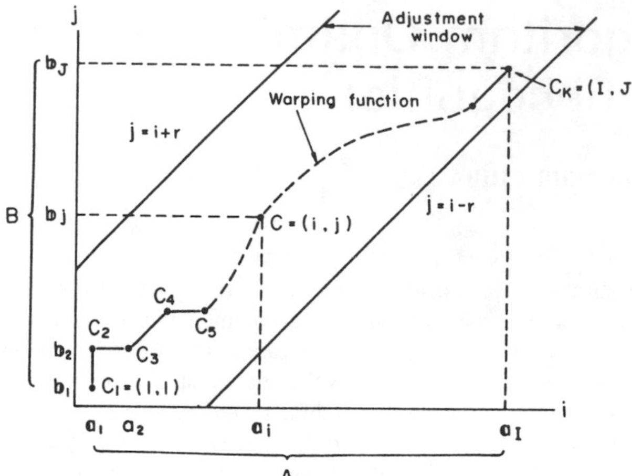

Fig. 1. Warping function and adjustment window definition.

patterns, the warping function coincides with the diagonal line $j = i$. It deviates further from the diagonal line as the timing difference grows.

As a measure of the difference between two feature vectors a_i and b_j, a distance

$$d(c) = d(i,j) = \| a_i - b_j \| \tag{3}$$

is employed between them. Then, the weighted summation of distances on warping function F becomes

$$E(F) = \sum_{k=1}^{K} d(c(k)) \cdot w(k) \tag{4}$$

(where $w(k)$ is a nonnegative weighting coefficient, which is intentionally introduced to allow the $E(F)$ measure flexible characteristic) and is a reasonable measure for the goodness of warping function F. It attains its minimum value when warping function F is determined so as to optimally adjust the timing difference. This minimum residual distance value can be considered to be a distance between patterns A and B, remaining still after eliminating the timing differences between them, and is naturally expected to be stable against time-axis fluctuation. Based on these considerations, the time-normalized distance between two speech patterns A and B is defined as follows:

$$D(A,B) = \operatorname*{Min}_{F} \left[\frac{\sum_{k=1}^{K} d(c(k)) \cdot w(k)}{\sum_{k=1}^{K} w(k)} \right] \tag{5}$$

where denominator $\Sigma\, w(k)$ is employed to compensate for the effect of K (number of points on the warping function F).

Equation (5) is no more than a fundamental definition of time-normalized distance. Effective characteristics of this measure greatly depend on the warping function specification and the weighting coefficient definition. Desirable characteristics of the time-normalized distance measure will vary, according to speech pattern properties (especially time axis expression of speech pattern) to be dealt with. Therefore, the present problem is restricted to the most general case where the following two conditions hold:

Condition 1: Speech patterns are time-sampled with a common and constant sampling period.

Condition 2: We have no *a priori* knowledge about which parts of speech pattern contain linguistically important information.

In this case, it is reasonable to consider each part of a speech pattern to contain an equal amount of linguistic information.

B. Restrictions on Warping Function

Warping function F, defined by (2), is a model of time-axis fluctuation in a speech pattern. Accordingly, it should approximate the properties of actual time-axis fluctuation. In other words, function F, when viewed as a mapping from the time axis of pattern A onto that of pattern B, must preserve linguistically essential structures in pattern A time axis and vice versa. Essential speech pattern time-axis structures are continuity, monotonicity (or restriction of relative timing in a speech), limitation on the acoustic parameter transition speed in a speech, and so on. These conditions can be realized as the following restrictions on warping function F (or points $c(k) = (i(k), j(k))$.

1) Monotonic conditions:

$$i(k-1) \leqq i(k) \text{ and } j(k-1) \leqq j(k).$$

2) Continuity conditions:

$$i(k) - i(k-1) \leqq 1 \text{ and } j(k) - j(k-1) \leqq 1.$$

As a result of these two restrictions, the following relation holds between two consecutive points.

$$c(k-1) = \begin{cases} (i(k),\ j(k)-1), \\ (i(k)-1,\ j(k)-1), \\ \text{or } (i(k)-1,\ j(k)). \end{cases} \tag{6}$$

3) Boundary conditions:

$$i(1) = 1,\ j(1) = 1, \text{ and}$$

$$i(K) = I,\ j(K) = J. \tag{7}$$

4) Adjustment window condition (see Fig. 1):

$$| i(k) - j(k) | \leqq r \tag{8}$$

where r is an appropriate positive integer called window length. This condition corresponds to the fact that time-axis fluctuation in usual cases never causes a too excessive timing difference.

5) Slope constraint condition:

Neither too steep nor too gentle a gradient should be allowed for warping function F because such deviations may cause undesirable time-axis warping. Too steep a gradient, for example, causes an unrealistic correspondence between a very short pattern A segment and a relatively long pattern B segment. Then, such a case occurs where a short segment in consonant or phoneme transition part happens to be in good coincidence with an entire steady vowel part. Therefore, a restriction called a slope constraint condition, was set upon the warping function F, so that its first derivative is of discrete form. The slope constraint condition is realized as a restriction on the possible relation among (or the possible configuration of) several consecutive points on the warping function, as is shown in Fig. 2(a) and (b). To put it concretely, if point $c(k)$ moves forward in the direction of i (or j)-axis consecutive m times, then point

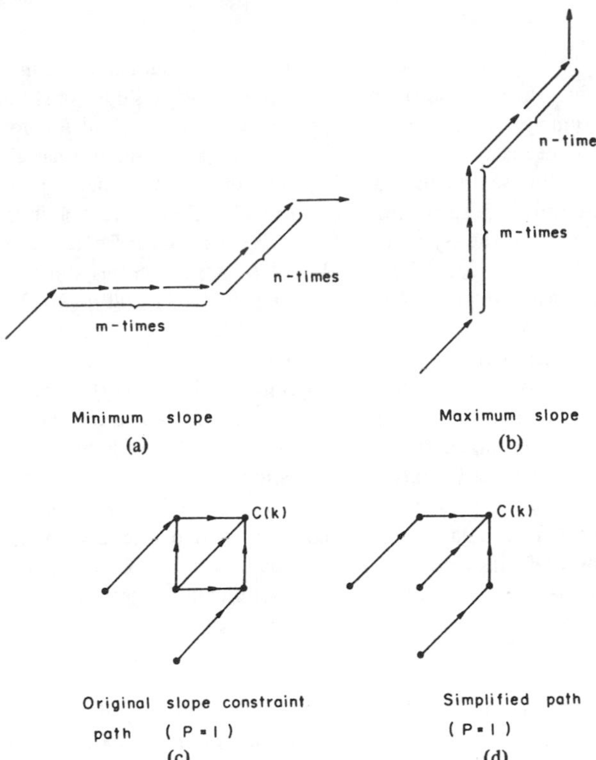

Fig. 2. Slope constraint on warping function.

$c(k)$ is not allowed to step further in the same direction before stepping at least n times in the diagonal direction. The effective intensity of the slope constraint can be evaluated by the following measure

$$P = n/m. \tag{9}$$

The larger the P measure, the more rigidly the warping function slope is restricted. When $p = 0$, there are no restrictions on the warping function slope. When $p = \infty$ (that is $m = 0$), the warping function is restricted to diagonal line $j = i$. Nothing more occurs than a conventional pattern matching no time-normalization. Generally speaking, if the slope constraint is too severe, then time-normalization would not work effectively. If the slope constraint is too lax, then discrimination between speech patterns in different categories is degraded. Thus, setting neither a too large nor a too small value for p is desirable. Section IV reports the results of an investigation on an optimum compromise on p value through several experiments.

In Fig. 2(c) and (d), two examples of permissible point $c(k)$ paths under slope constraint condition $p = 1$ are shown. The Fig. 2(c) type is directly derived from the above definition, while Fig. 2(d) is an approximated type, and there is another constraint. That is, the second derivative of warping function F is restricted, so that the point $c(k)$ path does not orthogonally change its direction. This new constraint reduces the number of paths to be searched. Therefore, the simple Fig. 2(d) type is adopted afterward, except for the $p = 0$ case.

C. Discussions on Weighting Coefficient

Since the criterion function in (5) is a rational expression, its maximization is an unwieldv problem. If the denominator in (5)

$$N = \sum_{k=1}^{K} w(k) \tag{10}$$

(called normalization coefficient) is independent of warping function F, it can be put out of the bracket, while simplifying the equation as follows:

$$D(A,B) = \frac{1}{N} \min_{F} \left[\sum_{k=1}^{K} d(c(k)) \cdot w(k) \right]. \tag{11}$$

This simplified problem can be effectively solved by use of the dynamic programming technique. There are two typical weighting coefficient definitions which enable this simplification. They are as follows.

1) Symmetric form:

$$w(k) = (i(k) - i(k-1)) + (j(k) - j(k-1)), \tag{12}$$

then

$$N = I + J, \tag{13}$$

where I and J are lengths of speech patterns A and B, respectively [see (1)].

2) Asymmetric form:

$$w(k) = (i(k) - i(k-1)), \tag{14}$$

then

$$N = I. \tag{15}$$

(Or equivalently, $w(k) = (j(k) - j(k-1))$, then $N = J$.)

The basic concepts of the symmetric and asymmetric forms were originally defined by Sakoe and Chiba [3]. The problem of their relative superiority has been left unsolved.

If it is assumed that time axes i and j are both continuous, then, in the symmetric form, the summation in (5) means an integration along the temporarily defined axis $l = i + j$. In the asymmetric form, on the other hand, the summation means an integration along time axis i. As a result of this difference, time-normalized distance is symmetric, or $D(A,B) = D(B,A)$, in the symmetric form, though not in the asymmetric form. Another more important result, caused by the difference in the integration axis, is that, as is shown in Fig. 3, weighting coefficient $w(k)$ reduces to zero in the asymmetric form, when the point in warping function steps in the direction of j-axis, or $c(k) = c(k-1) + (0, 1)$. This means that some feature vectors b_j are possibly excluded from the integration in the asymmetric form. On the contrary, in the case of symmetric form, minimum $w(k)$ value is equal to 1, and no exclusion occurs. Since discussions here are based on the assumption that each part in a speech pattern should be treated equally, an exclusion of any feature vectors from integration should be avoided as long as possible. It can be expected, therefore, that the symmetric form will give better recognition accuracy than the asymmetric form. However, it should be noted that the slope constraint reduces the situation where the point in warping function steps in the j-axis direction. The difference in performance between the symmetric one and asymmetric one will gradually vanish as the slope constraint is intensified.

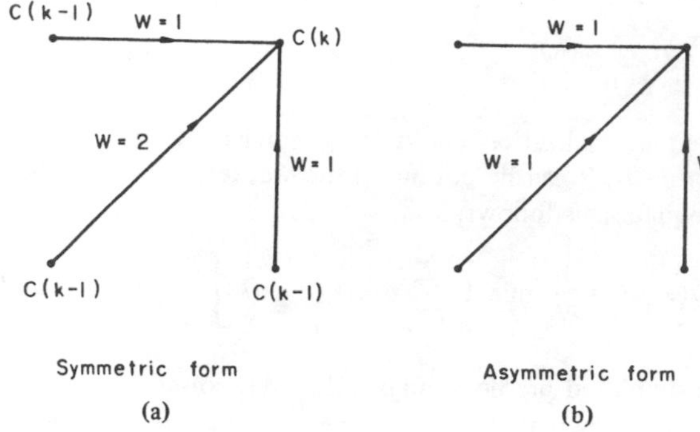

Fig. 3. Weighting coefficient $W(k)$ for both symmetric and asymmetric forms.

III. Practical DP-Matching Algorithm

A. DP-Equation

A simplified definition of time-normalized distance $D(A, B)$ given by (11) is one of the typical problems to which the well-known DP-principle [7] can be applied. The basic algorithm for calculating (11) is written as follows.

Initial condition:

$$g_1(c(1)) = d(c(1)) \cdot w(1). \tag{16}$$

DP-equation:

$$g_K(c(k)) = \min_{c(k-1)} [g_{k-1}(c(k-1)) + d(c(k)) \cdot w(k)]. \tag{17}$$

Time-normalized distance:

$$D(A, B) = \frac{1}{N} g_K(c(K)). \tag{18}$$

It is implicitly assumed here that $c(0) = (0, 0)$. Accordingly, $w(1) = 2$ in the symmetric form, and $w(1) = 1$ in the asymmetric form. By realizing the restriction on the warping function described in Section II-B and substituting (12) or (14) for weighting coefficient $w(k)$ in (17), several practical algorithms can be derived. As one of the simplest examples, the algorithm for symmetric form, in which no slope constraint is employed (that is $P = 0$), is shown here.

Initial condition:

$$g(1, 1) = 2d(1, 1). \tag{19}$$

DP-equation:

$$g(i, j) = \min \begin{bmatrix} g(i, j-1) + d(i, j) \\ g(i-1, j-1) + 2d(i, j) \\ g(i-1, j) + d(i, j) \end{bmatrix}. \tag{20}$$

Restricting condition (adjustment window):

$$j - r \leqq i \leqq j + r. \tag{21}$$

Time-normalized distance:

$$D(A, B) = \frac{1}{N} g(I, J), \quad \text{where } N = I + J. \tag{22}$$

Calculation details are briefly depicted in Section III-B.

The algorithm, especially the DP-equation, should be modified when the asymmetric form is adopted or some slope constraint is employed. In Table I, algorithms are summarized for both symmetric and asymmetric forms, with various slope constraint conditions. In this table, DP-equations for asymmetric forms are shown in some improved form. The first expression in the bracket of the asymmetric form DP-equation for $P = 1$ (that is, $g(i-1, j-2) + (d(i, j-1) + d(i, j))/2$) corresponds to the case where $c(k-1) = (i(k), j(k)-1)$ and $c(k-2) = (i(k-1)-1, j(k-1)-1)$. Accordingly, if the definition in (14) is strictly obeyed, $w(k)$ is equal to zero while $w(k-1)$ is equal to 1, thus completely omitting the $d(c(k))$ from the summation. In order to avoid this situation to a certain extent, the weighting coefficient $w(k-1) = 1$ is divided between two weighting coefficients $w(k-1)$ and $w(k)$. Thus, $(d(i, j-1) + d(i, j))/2$ is substituted for $d(i, j-1) + 0 \cdot d(i, j)$ in this expression. Similar modifications are applied to other asymmetric form DP-equations. In fact, it has been established, by a preliminary experiment, that this modification significantly improves the asymmetric form performance.

B. Calculation Details

DP-equation or $g(i, j)$ must be recurrently calculated in ascending order with respect to coordinates i and j, starting from initial condition at $(1, 1)$ up to (I, J). The domain in which the DP-equation must be calculated is specified by

$$1 \leqq i \leqq I, \quad 1 \leqq j \leqq J,$$

and

$$j - r \leqq i \leqq j + r \text{ (adjustment window).}$$

A practical procedure for calculating the time-normalized distance is shown in Fig. 4 as a flowchart.

IV. Experiments and Results

A. Experiment Outline

In order to quantitatively evaluate various types of DP-matching, several recognition experiments were conducted. The speech analyzer used through these experiments was a 10-channel bandpass filter bank which covered up to a 5.9-kHz frequency range. The output of each channel was time-sampled every 18 ms and was digitized in order that it could be fed into the digital computer (NEAC-3100). Automatic gain control effect was realized by dividing each filter output level by their sum total, at every sampling period. The so-called time-frequency amplitude pattern thus obtained was stored on a digital magnetic tape file. Recognition experiments were conducted for the speech pattern read out of this file. The recognition scheme used was the forced decision pattern matching method, where the input pattern (unknown) was decided to be of the same category as the reference pattern to which the maximum coincidence (that is the minimum time-normalized distance) was achieved. Distance $d(i, j)$ was measured by the Chebyshev norm, which was employed in the previous work [2]. Reference patterns were adapted to each speaker. That is, one repetition of the complete vocabulary, pronounced by each speaker, was used as the reference patterns for each speaker.

TABLE I
SYMMETRIC AND ASYMMETRIC DP-ALGORITHMS WITH SLOPE CONSTRAINT CONDITION $P = 0, \frac{1}{2}, 1$, AND 2

P	Schematic explanation	Symmetric / Asymmetric		DP-equation g(i, j) =
0		Symmetric	min	g(i,j-1)+d(i,j) g(i-1,j-1)+2d(i,j) g(i-1,j)+d(i,j)
		Asymmetric	min	g(i,j-1) g(i-1,j-1)+d(i,j) g(i-1,j)+d(i,j)
1/2		Symmetric	min	g(i-1,j-3)+2d(i,j-2)+d(i,j-1)+d(i,j) g(i-1,j-2)+2d(i,j-1)+d(i,j) g(i-1,j-1)+2d(i,j) g(i-2,j-1)+2d(i-1,j)+d(i,j) g(i-3,j-1)+2d(i-2,j)+d(i-1,j)+d(i,j)
		Asymmetric	min	g(i-1,j-3)+(d(i,j-2)+d(i,j-1)+d(i,j))/3 g(i-1,j-2)+(d(i,j-1)+d(i,j))/2 g(i-1,j-1)+d(i,j) g(i-2,j-1)+d(i-1,j)+d(i,j) g(i-3,j-1)+d(i-2,j)+d(i-1,j)+d(i,j)
1		Symmetric	min	g(i-1,j-2)+2d(i,j-1)+d(i,j) g(i-1,j-1)+2d(i,j) g(i-2,j-1)+2d(i-1,j)+d(i,j)
		Asymmetric	min	g(i-1,j-2)+(d(i,j-1)+d(i,j))/2 g(i-1,j-1)+d(i,j) g(i-2,j-1)+d(i-1,j)+d(i,j)
2		Symmetric	min	g(i-2,j-3)+2d(i-1,j-2)+2d(i,j-1)+d(i,j) g(i-1,j-1)+2d(i,j) g(i-3,j-2)+2d(i-2,j-1)+2d(i-1,j)+d(i,j)
		Asymmetric	min	g(i-2,j-3)+2(d(i-1,j-2)+d(i,j-1)+d(i,j))/3 g(i-1,j-1)+d(i,j) g(i-3,j-2)+d(i-2,j-1)+d(i-1,j)+d(i,j)

Experiments were conducted in three parts. The first part was carried out with the objectives of comparing the performances of symmetric form DP-matching and asymmetric form DP-matching, and optimizing the slope constraint condition. In the second part, further optimization of the slope constraint condition was investigated. In the final part of the experiments, the algorithm thus optimized was compared with several DP-algorithms proposed by different research groups.

B. Experiment (I)

The objective of this experiment was to compare symmetric form DP-matching and asymmetric form DP-matching performances, and to determine the best compromise for the slope constraint intensity (parameter P). Speech data used in this experiment were Japanese digit words (see Table II) isolatedly spoken by 10 male speakers. Six repetitions of the 10 digit words were made by each speaker. Then, for each speaker, each of the six repetitions was used as a reference pattern set. For each reference pattern set, the remaining five repetitions were supplied to recognition. Therefore, 10 (persons) $\times$ 6 (reference pattern sets) $\times$ 50 (input patterns) = 3000 (recognition tests) were conducted. The DP-matching subjected to this experiment covered both symmetric and asymmetric forms, with slope constraint condition of $P = 0, \frac{1}{2}, 1$, and 2. In each case, window length r was set equal to 6, which covered the utmost ± 108 ms timing difference. A linear time-normalization method was also tested where the time axis of the input pattern was adjusted to that of the reference pattern with linear transformation.

Results are shown in Fig. 5 as two error rate curves. In this

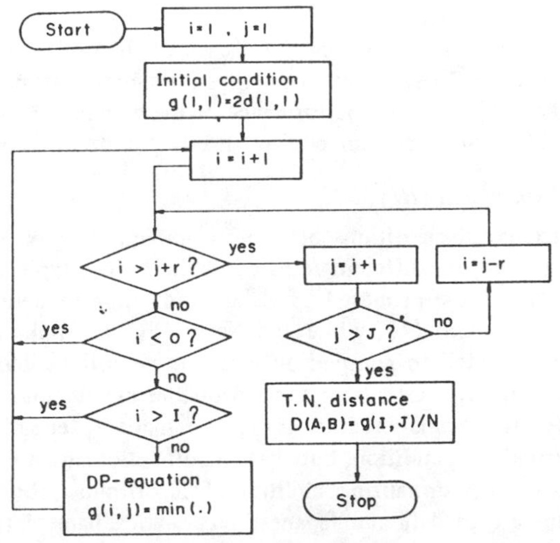

Fig. 4. DP-matching flowchart.

figure, it can be seen that the performance of the asymmetric form DP-matching is evidently inferior to that of the symmetric one, and that the difference in performance between them tends to vanish gradually as the slope constraint is intensified. It can also be seen that symmetric form DP-matching performance is utterly unaffected by a slope constraint of up to $P = 1$. On the other hand, the asymmetric form DP-matching performance is very effectively improved by slope constraint. The optimum condition is $P = 1$. When the slope constraint is intensified beyond $P = 1$, the performance of the asym-

TABLE II
TEN JAPANESE DIGITS AND THEIR PHONEMIC TRANSCRIPTIONS

0	1	2	3	4	5	6	7	8	9
rei	itʃi	ni	san	jon	go	roku	nana	hatʃi	kju

metric form, as well as that of the symmetric one tends to be degraded. Since extremely intensified slope constraint does not give any time-normalization, it is naturally understood that further growth in slope constraint will result in some worse performance than that of linear time-normalization method (0.8 percent error).

C. Experiment (II)

In order to further examine the effect of the slope constraint on the symmetric form DP-matching performance, another experiment was carried out for a 50-Japanese geographical name vocabulary. This vocabulary includes such confusing pairs of words as "Chiba"-"Shiga", "Okayama"-"Wakayama", "Fukushima"-"Tokushima", and "Hyogo"-"Kyoto". Each of two male speakers and two female speakers uttered six repetitions of the complete vocabulary. The first repetitions of each speaker were used as the reference patterns. The remaining five repetitions of each speaker were used as unknown input patterns, thus providing 4 (persons) X 50 (vocabulary size) X 5 (repetitions) = 1000 (recognition tests). The window length r here was set equal to 8, which covered utmost ±144 ms timing difference.

Results are shown in Fig. 6 for each of the slope constraint conditions. These results show that the slope constraint has a marked effect on the performance of the symmetric form DP matching, too. Optimum performance is also attained at $P = 1$.

D. Experiment (III)

Various DP-algorithms have been applied to spoken word recognition, by different research groups. Four typical ones, including those proposed by Sakoe and Chiba [3], Velichko and Zagoruyko [4], White and Neely [5], and Itakura [6], were subjected to comparison with the algorithms described in this paper. Details of each algorithm are summarized in Table III. Some modifications were made to equalize the experimental condition, but these modifications are not harmful to time-normalizing abilities of algorithms. Both the Japanese digit data and Japanese geographical name data were again used as test data. Results are shown in Table IV. From these results, it can be observed that the symmetric form DP-matching with slope constraint $P = 1$, described in this paper, is the best of various DP-algorithms applied to spoken word recognition.

V. DISCUSSIONS

From the results shown in Fig. 5, it can be observed that the symmetric form DP-matching performance is significantly superior to that of the asymmetric one. It can also be seen that the difference in performance between them tends to decrease as the slope constraint grows. These observations completely agree with the theoretical discussions presented in Section II, indicating the validity of this investigation.

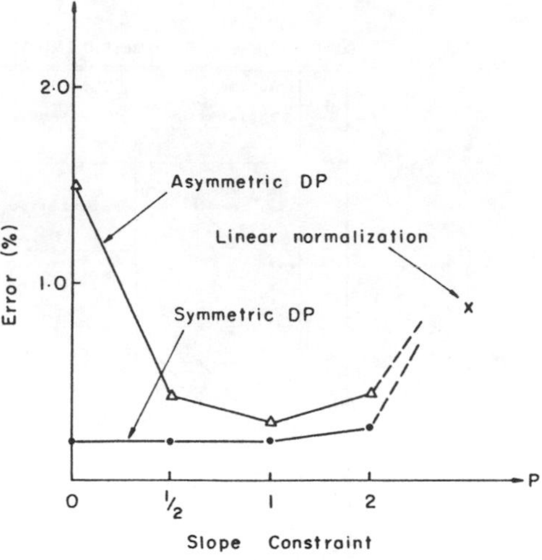

Fig. 5. Experiment (I) results (for Japanese digit words).

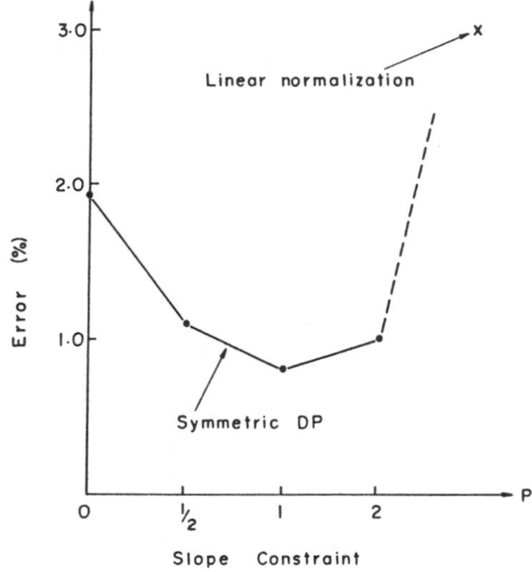

Fig. 6. Experiment (II) results (for 50 Japanese geographical names).

From Figs. 5 and 6, it can be determined that the slope constraint condition with $P = 1$ is the optimum point for both symmetric and asymmetric forms. Moreover, as can be seen from Table I, the DP-equation for $P = 1$ is of the most simple form, next to that for $P = 0$. Thus, the slope constraint condition with $P = 1$ is favorable for computational economy, as well as for best performance. The slope constraint hardly affects the performance of the symmetric form DP-matching in case of Japanese digit vocabulary. This is perhaps due to the fact that, in case of Japanese digit words, the vocabulary size is so small and the separation between the words in the vocabulary is inherently so good that an optimally high recognition accuracy was achieved even without slope constraint. Nevertheless, the usefulness of the slope constraint for the symmetric form was established by the experiment on the Japanese geographical name data. Summing up these discussions, the symmetric form with slope constraint condition $P = 1$ is the optimum condition, when the speech patterns are time-sampled with a common and uniform sampling period.

TABLE III

FOUR VARITIES OF DP-ALGORITHMS SUBJECTED TO COMPARISON IN EXPERIMENT (III)

Algorithm	Initial Condition $g(1, 1) =$	Normalization Coefficient N	DP-equation $g(i, j) =$
Sakoe and Chiba [3]	$d(1, 1)$	I	$\min \begin{bmatrix} g(i-1, j) + d(i, j) \\ g(i-1, j-1) + d(i, j) \\ g(i-1, j-2) + d(i, j) \end{bmatrix}$
Velichko and Zagoruyko [4]	$a(1, 1)$	$\max\ [I, J]$	$\max \begin{bmatrix} g(i, j-1) \\ g(i-1, j-1) + a(i, j) \\ g(i-1, j) \end{bmatrix}$ where $a(i, j) = 1-d(i, j)$
White and Neely [5]	$d(1, 1)$	$(I + J)$	$\min \begin{bmatrix} g(i-1, j) + d(i, j) \\ g(i-1, j-1) + d(i, j) \\ g(i, j-1) + d(i, j) \end{bmatrix}$
Itakura [6]	$d(1, 1)$	I	$\min \begin{bmatrix} g(i-1, j) + \alpha \cdot d(i, j) \\ g(i-1, j-1) + d(i, j) \\ g(i-1, j-2) + d(i, j) \end{bmatrix}$ where $\alpha = \infty \quad (i(k-1) = i(k-2))$, $\alpha = 1 \quad (i(k-1) \neq i(k-2))$

The optimized algorithm was experimentally compared with several DP-algorithms, including those reported by other research groups. Results show that the present algorithm gives considerably better performance, for both Japanese digit data and Japanese geographical name data. This superiority can be attributed to careful investigations made to realize a pattern matching algorithm with rational characteristics of comparing each part of speech pattern evenly as far as possible.

As for the computational time, NEAC-3100 computer (index modified addition/substruction execution time is 8 μs) required about 3 s for each digit word recognition and about 30 s for geographical name recognition. These computational times scarcely depended upon the employed DP-equation. Recent high-speed digital integrated circuit devices and pipeline processor techniques made it feasible to realize the real time DP-matching operation. Actually, a DP-matching processor has been constructed which recognizes 60 geographical names in 300 ms after the utterance [8].

TABLE IV

EXPERIMENT (III) RESULTS

Algorithm \ Test data	Error rate (%): Japanese digit words	Error rate (%): 50 Japanese Geographical names
Sakoe and Chiba Symmetric P = 1 (in this paper)	0.2	0.8
Sakoe and Chiba Asymmetric P = 1 (in this paper)	0.3	1.3
Sakoe and Chiba [3]	0.3	1.5
Velichko and Zagoruyko [4]	2.0	2.7
White and Neely [5]	0.33	1.3
Itakura [6]	0.4	1.3
Linear method	0.87	5.9

VI. CONCLUSIONS

The optimum DP-algorithm, applied to speech recognition, was investigated. Two forms of pattern matching method, symmetric and asymmetric forms, were proposed along with a new technique called slope constraint. These varieties were then compared through theoretical and experimental investigations. Conclusions are as follows.

1) The symmetric form gives better recognition accuracy than the asymmetric form.

2) Slope constraint is actually effective. Optimum performance is attained when the slope constraint condition is $P = 1$.

The validity of these results was ensured by a good agreement between theoretical discussions and experimental results.

The optimized algorithm was then experimentally compared with several other DP-algorithms applied to spoken word recognition by different research groups, and the superiority of the algorithm described in this paper was established.

ACKNOWLEDGMENT

The authors wish to thank Y. Kato for his encouragement throughout this research.

REFERENCES

[1] H. Sakoe and S. Chiba, "A similarity evaluation of speech patterns by dynamic programming" (in Japanese), presented at the Dig. 1970 Nat. Meeting, Inst. Electron. Comm. Eng. Japan, p. 136, July 1970.

[2] —, "A dynamic programming approach to continuous speech recognition," in *1971 Proc. 7th ICA*, *Paper 20 C13*, Aug. 1971.

[3] —, "Comparative study of DP-pattern matching techniques for speech recognition" (in Japanese), in *1973 Tech. Group Meeting Speech, Acoust. Soc. Japan, Preprints (S73-22)*, Dec. 1973.

[4] V. M. Velichko and N. G. Zagoruyko, "Automatic recognition of 200 words," *Int. J. Man-Machine Stud.*, vol. 2, p. 223, June 1970.

[5] G. White and R. Neely, "Speech recognition experiments with linear prediction, bandpass filtering, and dynamic programming," *IEEE Trans. Acoust., Speech, Signal Processing*, vol. ASSP-24, pp. 183-188, Apr. 1976.

[6] F. Itakura, "Minimum prediction residual principle applied to speech recognition," *IEEE Trans. Acoust., Speech, Signal Processing*, vol. ASSP-23, pp. 67-72, Feb. 1975.

[7] R. Bellman and S. Dreyfus, *Applied Dynamic Programming*. New Jersey: Princeton Univ. Press, 1962.

[8] S. Tsuruta, H. Sakoe, and S. Chiba, "Real-time speech recognition system by minicomputer with DP processor" (in Japanese), in *1974 Tech. Group Meeting Speech, Acoust. Soc. Japan, Preprints (S74-30)*, Dec. 1974.

Speaker-Independent Recognition of Isolated Words Using Clustering Techniques

LAWRENCE R. RABINER, FELLOW, IEEE, STEPHEN E. LEVINSON, MEMBER, IEEE, AARON E. ROSENBERG, MEMBER, IEEE, AND JAY G. WILPON

Abstract—A speaker-independent isolated word recognition system is described which is based on the use of multiple templates for each word in the vocabulary. The word templates are obtained from a statistical clustering analysis of a large database consisting of 100 replications of each word (i.e., once by each of 100 talkers). The recognition system, which accepts telephone quality speech input, is based on an LPC analysis of the unknown word, dynamic time warping of each reference template to the unknown word (using the Itakura LPC distance measure), and the application of a K-nearest neighbor (KNN) decision rule. Results for several test sets of data are presented. They show error rates that are comparable to, or better than, those obtained with speaker-trained isolated word recognition systems.

I. Introduction

Although there are a large number of factors which influence the implementation of a discrete word recognizer, perhaps two of the most important ones are vocabulary size and degree of speaker dependence. These factors are illustrated in Fig. 1 which also shows the areas in which the most current word recognition research is being performed. For speaker-dependent systems, vocabulary sizes of from 40 to 1000 words have been investigated [1]-[4], with vocabulary sizes of from 100 to 200 words being most typical of modern systems. For speaker-independent systems, vocabulary sizes of from 2 to 50 words have been used with varying degrees of success [5]-[10]. Error rates associated with such systems range from 20 percent (for the larger vocabulary sizes or the more difficult vocabularies) to less than 1 percent (for the easier or smaller vocabularies).

Although most word recognition systems are either speaker-dependent or speaker-independent the dichotomy between these two categories is more one of implementation than of structure. For statistical pattern recognition systems, a speaker-dependent word recognizer can be used as a speaker-independent word recognizer (and vice versa) by interchanging the set of reference templates. Recently, several attempts have been made at "bridging the gap" between completely speaker-dependent and completely speaker-independent word recognizers by using multiple templates per word instead of the usual single template per word [8]-[10]. In addition, increasingly sophisticated pattern recognition or clustering algorithms have been used to aid in the optimal selection of the word templates [11]. As such, these word recognizers fall midway between the classic speaker-independent and speaker-dependent recognizers, as illustrated in Fig. 1.

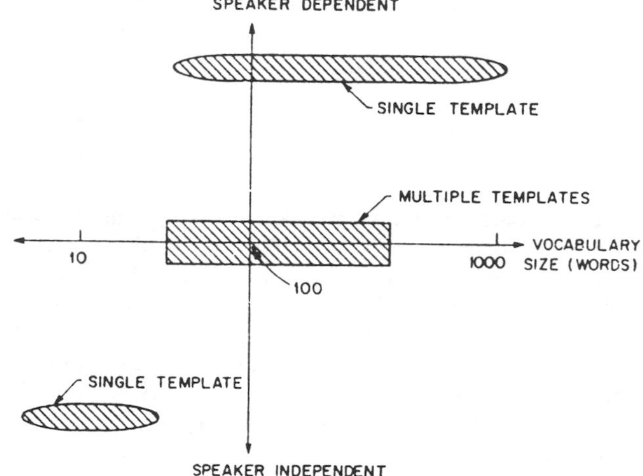

Fig. 1. Illustration of the range of recent isolated word recognition systems as a function of vocabulary size and degree of speaker dependence.

The purpose of this paper is to describe some recent results on speaker-independent recognition of isolated words based on word templates obtained from a statistical clustering analysis. In building the recognition system, many aspects were considered, such as time alignment procedures, endpoint robustness by means of a backup frame, rejection thresholding, and statistical decision rules. The theory of these procedures is described in Section II. The cluster analysis which is central to these investigations is described briefly in Section III. Extensive test results are provided in Section IV. In particular, we have evaluated each of the aspects discussed in Section II independently to observe its contribution to the overall system performance. Finally, we summarize in Section V by presenting an error analysis, a comparison of our results with those of other researchers and directions for further studies.

II. Word Recognition System

Fig. 2 shows a block diagram of the word recognition system. The speech signal was recorded using a standard telephone line, bandpass filtered from 100 to 3200 Hz, and sampled at a 6.67 kHz rate. The first step in the digital processing of Fig. 2 is endpoint detection to determine points in time at which the unknown word begins and ends. The major causes of errors

Manuscript received September 8, 1978; revised January 15, 1979.
The authors are with the Acoustics Research Department, Bell Laboratories, Murray Hill, NJ 07974.

0096-3518/79/0800-0336$00.75 © 1979 IEEE

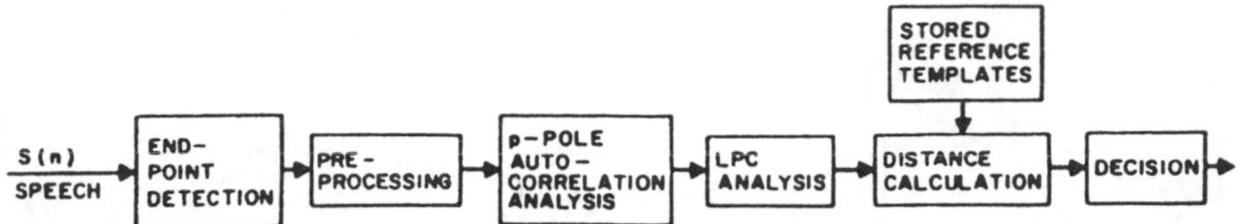

Fig. 2. Block diagram of the word recognition system.

in endpoint detection are clicks on the lines and heavy breathing at the ends of words. Special care was taken to minimize the possibility of endpoint errors. In particular, a backup ending point was calculated to account for mouth clicks, breath noise, etc. at the end of the utterance. The calculation for the backup point was as follows. We denote the detected frames of the word as having indices $i = 1, 2, \cdots, N_{END}$. For each frame we denote the zeroth autocorrelation coefficient as $R_i(0)$. We then define the function $g(i)$ as

$$g(i) = \sum_{j=1}^{i} \frac{R_j(0)}{R_{\max}} \tag{1}$$

where

$$R_{\max} = \max_i \, [R_i(0)]. \tag{2}$$

The backup frame N_{BU} is calculated as the largest index i satisfying the constraint

$$g(i) < g(N_{END}) - S \tag{3}$$

where S is an empirically determined threshold. (It was set to 0.001 in our simulations.) The backup frame is used as an alternative endpoint for the distance calculations to be described later.

Following endpoint detection, the speech is preemphasized using a simple first-order digital filter with z transform

$$H(z) = 1 - az^{-1} \tag{4}$$

where a value of $a = 0.95$ was used in our simulations. Extensive experimental evidence has shown that preemphasis serves to reduce the variance of the distance calculations used in the recognition system when LPC parameters are used as the feature set, and the autocorrelation method of analysis is used [12].

The next step in the recognition system is to perform a p-pole autocorrelation analysis of the word. A value of $p = 8$ was used for the telephone quality speech. The autocorrelation coefficients were calculated from overlapping frames of length $N = 300$ samples (45 ms) using a Hamming window on the data. A total of 67 frames/s (i.e., every 15 ms) were calculated. Each frame of autocorrelation coefficients was then converted to linear prediction coefficients (LPC), using the autocorrelation method, for subsequent processing and/or storage as reference patterns.

A. Dynamic Time Warping

The recognition phase is essentially a matching process in which an unknown sample pattern of autocorrelation coefficients is compared with an ensemble of stored reference patterns (templates). The reference patterns may be from a designated speaker (for speaker-dependent systems) or a "universal" set (for speaker-independent systems). In the comparison, a frame-by-frame scan of the sample pattern is carried out against each reference pattern. A distance score (or measure of dissimilarity) is calculated and accumulated using a dynamic programming technique [1], [13]-[15] as the scan proceeds. A simple decision rule which is often used designates the vocabulary item corresponding to the reference pattern with the lowest accumulated distance as the recognized word. A somewhat more powerful decision rule is discussed later in this section.

The use of a dynamic programming algorithm provides an efficient procedure for obtaining a nonlinear time alignment between each reference pattern and the unknown sample. By means of a simple recursion formula, a sequence of frames through each reference pattern is generated, associated with a minimum accumulation of distance from beginning to end. The use of a nonlinear time alignment has been shown to be a significant factor in the performance of the recognizer, especially for polysyllabic words [1].

B. Variants of the Time-Warping Algorithm

Recently, several variants on the basic dynamic time-warping algorithm have been proposed [14]-[15]. These modified dynamic time-warping algorithms account for misregistrations between the unknown sample and the reference patterns due to errors in the word endpoints. In addition, Sakoe and Chiba [14] have proposed a modified version of the algorithm which is symmetrical in the time alignment procedure, i.e., neither the unknown sample nor the reference guides the frame-by-frame matching process, but instead a parametric index (which is a function of both time scales) is used.

The three versions of the dynamic time warping algorithm proposed by Rabiner *et al.* [15] have been studied in the context of the recognition system of Fig. 2. These three algorithms and their properties are as follows.

1) CE2-1–Constrained Endpoints, 2-to-1 Range of Slopes: This algorithm is the one proposed by Itakura [1] in which the starting and ending points are assumed to be in perfect registration, and the dynamic path is assumed to be in a fixed parallelogram whose slopes are 2 and $\frac{1}{2}$ at the edges.

2) UE2-1–Unconstrained Endpoints, 2-to-1 Range of Durations: For this version, the boundary conditions are relaxed and it is assumed that a region of width of δ frames exists in which the initial and final frames could be mapped. (A value of δ of 5 frames (75 ms) was used in our implementation.) The dynamic path was again assumed to lie within a fixed parallelogram whose slopes are 2 and $\frac{1}{2}$ at the edges.

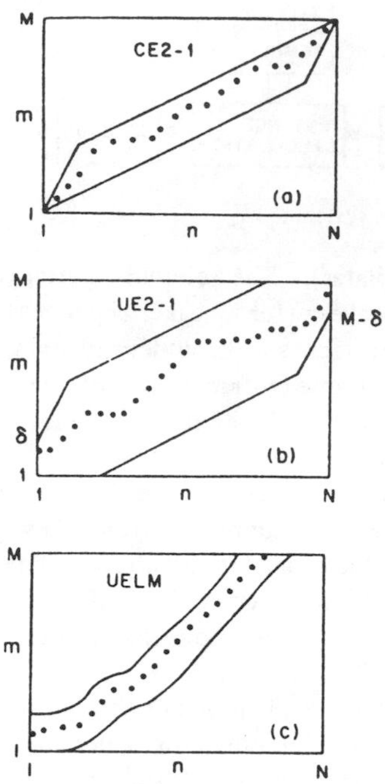

Fig. 3. Typical warping paths for the three dynamic time-warping techniques used in the recognition system.

3) UELM–Unconstrained Endpoints, Local Minimum: For this version, both the endpoint constraints are relaxed, and the allowable region of dynamic paths is constrained to follow the locally optimum path to within a range of $\pm\epsilon$ frames. A value of ϵ of 4 frames (60 ms) was used in our implementation.

Fig. 3 provides a summary of the three dynamic warping algorithms described above. Typical warping functions and the boundaries of the allowable regions of dynamic paths are shown in this figure.

C. Rejection Threshold

To speed up the distance calculation by eliminating unlikely reference patterns, an accumulated distance rejection threshold was used. If we denote the minimum accumulated distance at frame j as D_j, and the rejection threshold is denoted as T_j, then if

$$D_j > T_j \tag{5}$$

where

$$T_j = [T_{\min} + (j - 1)T_{\text{slope}}] \cdot N \tag{6}$$

($T_{\min} = 0.3$, $T_{\text{slope}} = 0.7$ (typically), and N is the number of frames of the test sample), the scan is aborted at frame j and the vocabulary item corresponding to the reference pattern is rejected as a candidate for recognition. Generally, the minimum threshold $T_{\min}$ and the slope T_{slope}, are chosen to ensure that a sufficient number of candidates are not rejected. We discuss the effect of raising and lowering the rejection thresholds later in this paper.

Fig. 4 shows a plot of typical accumulated distances versus frame number for a recognition test. The rejection threshold is shown as the straight line at which the scans terminate. It is not unusual for the vast majority of incorrect words to be eliminated by the rejection threshold. Also shown in this figure is the back-up frame N_{BU}. For scans which fall below the rejection threshold until the backup frame, the total average distance for the entire scan is the quantity D, defined as

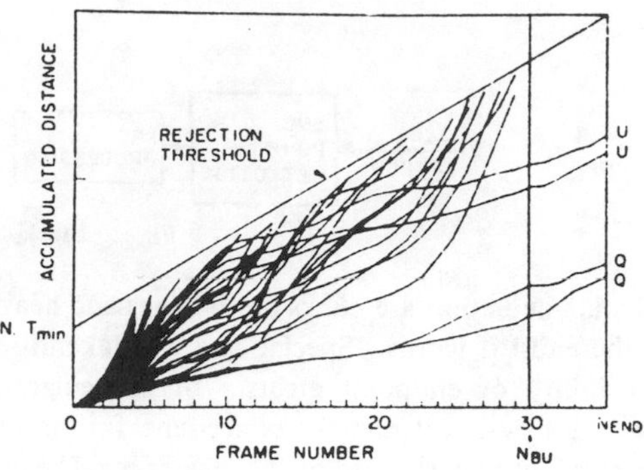

Fig. 4. Accumulated distance versus frame number for the test word Q.

$$D = \min\left[\frac{D_{BU}}{N_{BU}}, \frac{D_{END}}{N_{END}}\right] \tag{7}$$

where N_{BU} is the frame number of the backup frame, N_{END} is the frame number of the ending frame, D_{BU} is the accumulated distance to the backup frame, and D_{END} is the accumulated distance to the ending frame (which may not be the last frame in the unknown word due to the boundary conditions of the warping algorithm). Thus, the backup frame serves as an alternate estimate of the endpoint of the unknown word, and if the accumulated distance rises rapidly after the backup frame, it is assumed that it is due to endpoint errors, and (7) uses the smaller accumulated average distance for the word.

D. Decision Rule for Recognition

For recognition systems in which a single (or perhaps 2) reference template(s) per word are used, the decision rule which is generally used is the nearest neighbor rule for which the vocabulary item whose average accumulated distance D is minimum is chosen. Thus, if we denote the candidate words by the index j, $j = 1, 2, \cdots, J$, then the nearest neighbor (NN) rule is

$$\text{Choose } i = i^* \ni D[x, x^{(i^*)}] \leq D[x, x^{(j)}] \qquad 1 \leq j \leq J \tag{8}$$

where $D[x, x^{(j)}]$ is the average distance between the unknown x and the reference template $x^{(j)}$.

For recognition systems in which multiple reference templates are used for each word, the decision rule can be made more sophisticated. For example, the K-nearest neighbor (KNN) rule can be used in which the vocabulary item whose average distance of the K-nearest neighbors to the unknown sample is minimum is chosen as the recognized word. If we denote the kth nearest neighbor of the jth word to the unknown sample x as $D[x, x_{[k]}^{(j)}]$, then for the KNN rule we compute the quantity r_j defined as

$$r_j = \frac{1}{K}\sum_{k=1}^{K} D[x, x_{[k]}^{(j)}] \tag{9}$$

and we recognize the unknown word as word j^* such that

$$r_{j^*} \leq r_j, \quad j = 1, 2, \cdots, J. \tag{10}$$

It is shown in the Appendix that the quantity r_j of (9) is monotonically related to an estimate of the local probability density function of the jth word. We shall see later that this estimator is well suited to our data.

It should be noted that for $K = 1$, the K-nearest neighbor decision rule becomes the nearest neighbor rule. In this paper we discuss results of recognition tests with values of K from 1 to 4 and for reference data with up to 12 templates per vocabulary word.

E. Other Considerations in the Recognition System

In general, the result of a recognition trial is a single vocabulary item. However, for some applications it is useful to give a *set* of candidate items rather than a single word [3]-[4]. Usually, the list of choices is ordered by the distance scores. Such a result is useful when the recognition output is itself subject to further processing. An example of such a system is the spoken spelled name recognizer for directory assistance proposed by Rosenberg and Schmidt [4]. In this system up to five word candidates were retained for each letter in the spelled name, and a directory search was used to resolve the correct candidate for each letter. For this system a median acoustic error rate of 20 percent led to a median string (name obtained from the directory search) error rate of 4 percent.

Another general comment about the recognition system of Fig. 2 is that the *only* feature that determines whether the recognition system is speaker-trained or speaker-independent is the reference template store. Thus, this recognition system is versatile enough to be used in a wide variety of applications.

III. Generation of Multiple Templates by Clustering

In order to implement a speaker-independent word recognizer, the variations among speakers in pronouncing the same word must be accounted for. One way of accomplishing this task is to select a gross set of features which are characteristic of the phonetic content of the word (e.g., nasality, fricative sound, vowel type, etc.) and rely on meausrements which are capable of predicting the presence or absence of such features [1]. Another possibility is to use an arbitrary set of features (e.g., formant frequencies, cepstral coefficients, LPC coefficients) and to form statistics on the variability of the features both in time and across talkers [16]. Each of the above solutions attempts to find a single charactprization of each vocabulary word which is either independent of speakers, or can account for speaker variability in statistical terms.

Another possible solution, and the one which we have used, is to rely on statistical pattern clustering methods to obtain not just one, but a multiplicity of patterns which characterize the variability of the features (for a single word) across different talkers [11]. The basic assumption is that repetitions of a word by different speakers can be clustered into groups such that differences in the features within the group are small, but differences between groups within a word are relatively large. As such, each group or cluster can be represented by a single template, and the word can be represented by whatever number of templates are required to "span the space" of talkers. The local density of training words is a measure of the probability density function for the given word. (See the Appendix for further clarification of this point.) Thus, clusters with the largest number of tokens are those closest to a maximum of the probability density function for the word.

There are a number of important issues which are involved in implementing a set of clustering algorithms for isolated word data [11]. Although clustering techniques have become highly developed [17]-[19], it is still more of an art than a science to arbitrarily cluster data without making assumptions as to the form of its probability density function. Clustering is particularly a problem when the data are characterized by a set of distances (between pairs of words) rather than a set of features in a multidimensional space. In the latter case we can only indirectly estimate the probability density function of the data. Thus, one of the issues in clustering is to decide which types of algorithms are applicable to the given set of data.

Another important issue is the question of how to characterize the data within a cluster. One simple and effective way is to choose an element of the cluster which best (in some sense) characterizes the cluster. Another possibility is to combine the tokens within the cluster using some averaging technique. Intuitively, it is appealing to use a real token as the reference template (rather than some artificially created average). It is not clear how averaging affects the characteristic properties of the templates. However, for clusters with a small number of tokens, averaging may have some advantages.

Other important issues in clustering include deciding how many clusters to use in representing the data, setting thresholds for providing natural separations between clusters, modifying feature-dependent algorithms to use distance data, and the question of whether using distance data from other words will enhance the process of clustering a given word.

To handle a large speech data base of isolated words, a sophisticated clustering system was implemented [11]. In Section III-A we list the procedures used to cluster the data base. Then we discuss the actual data base used and present some statistics on the clustering output.

A. Clustering Algorithms

A series of four procedures was used to cluster the isolated word data. These were

1) the chainmap [18],
2) the shared nearest neighbor procedure [18],
3) the k-means iteration [20], and
4) Isodata [21].

Each of these procedures was used interactively on a matrix of distances between pairs of repetitions of a given word to produce a stable set of clusters for which σ the ratio of average intercluster distance to average intracluster distance, was maximized [11]. The total number of clusters per word is a variable which is determined interactively by examining the outputs of each of the above procedures and deciding whether to increase or decrease the total number of clusters in order to increase σ.

TABLE I
WORDS IN THE VOCABULARY

1. A	21. U
2. B	22. V
3. C	23. W
4. D	24. X
5. E	25. Y
6. F	26. Z
7. G	27. STOP
8. H	28. ERROR
9. I	29. REPEAT
10. J	30. ZERO
11. K	31. ONE
12. L	32. TWO
13. M	33. THREE
14. N	34. FOUR
15. O	35. FIVE
16. P	36. SIX
17. Q	37. SEVEN
18. R	38. EIGHT
19. S	39. NINE
20. T	

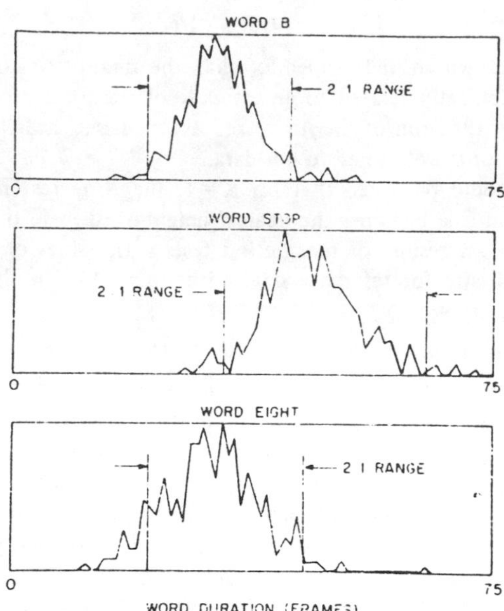

Fig. 5. Histogram plots of the durations of the words B, STOP, and EIGHT.

B. Speech Database

To test the recognition and clustering algorithm, the 39 word vocabulary of Table I was used. Included in the vocabulary were the letters of the alphabet, the digits, and the control words STOP, ERROR and REPEAT. This vocabulary is one which is suitable for a wide range of applications [4].

A group of 100 speakers (50 male, 50 female) recorded the complete vocabulary a total of four times each on different days. Recordings were made in a soundproof booth over a standard telephone line and recorded on analog tape. Each of the 15 600 words was manually edited to eliminate artifacts at the beginning and end of the utterances, and the autocorrelation frames for each word were stored in a file.

The first replication of each talker was used for training the system. Thus, for each vocabulary word, a total of 100 repetitions were used for clustering. If we denote the ith word for the jth speaker as $x^{(ij)}$, and the distance (dynamic time-warped) between the ith word for the lth speaker, and the ith word for the jth speaker as

$$d_{lj}^{(i)} = \frac{d[x^{(il)}, x^{(ij)}] + d[x^{(ij)}, x^{(il)}]}{2}, \tag{11}$$

then the input data to the clustering package for the ith word was the set of paired distances $d_{lj}^{(i)}$, $1 \leqslant l \leqslant 100$, $1 \leqslant j \leqslant 100$. The averaging of distances in (11) is done because, in general, the distance between tokens is not symmetric. Because of the imposed symmetry of (11), we get

$$d_{lj}^{(i)} = d_{jl}^{(i)} \tag{12}$$

and thus only the lower triangular matrix $d_{lj}^{(i)}$, $1 \leqslant l \leqslant 100$, $1 \leqslant j \leqslant l$ is required.

Since the quantity $d[x^{(i)}, x^{(j)}]$ is determined by dynamically time-warping token $x^{(j)}$ to token $x^{(i)}$, it is possible that the distance is not defined for some pairs of tokens due to the slope constraints in some of the time-warping algorithms [1], [11]. Thus, prior to the distance calculation [(11)], a histogram of the durations of each of the 100 repetitions of each word was made, and a sliding window was used to find the range of the word durations such that the maximum number of repetitions satisfied the constraints and could be used in the clustering. Those repetitions falling outside the window were eliminated from the clustering.

Fig. 5 shows the plots of the histograms of word durations (for all four replications) for three of the words in the vocabulary (B, STOP, EIGHT). Included in the plots is the 2-to-1 range in which the maximum number of repetitions of the word occurred. (For the UELM time-warping algorithm, no slope constraint existed, and thus all 100 repetitions of each word were clustered.) For the entire 39 word vocabulary, the number of repetitions that were excluded (in the first replication) because of the slope constraint varied from 1 (for the word B) to 12 (for the word EIGHT), and the total number of words excluded was 152 out of 3900 words. A total of 4 talkers of the 100 spoke, 82 of the 152 excluded words; thus these talkers were effectively excluded from the training set about half the time.

C. Results of the Clustering of Word Data

The clustering algorithms of Section III-A were used interactively on the speech database to give an ordered set of clusters for each word in the vocabulary. The paired distance data were obtained from each of the three dynamic time-warping algorithms discussed in Section II-B. Table II presents a summary of the main statistics associated with each of the sets of clusters. In this table are shown, for each time-warping

TABLE II
STATISTICS OF THE WORD CLUSTERS FOR THE THREE DYNAMIC TIME WARPING ALGORITHMS

	CE2-1			UE2-1			UELM		
	AVG	MIN	MAX	AVG	MIN	MAX	AVG	MIN	MAX
Number of Clusters Per Word	13	8	19	13	9	18	14	9	19
Number of Outliers Per Word	8	3	16	13	5	19	9	4	16
Quality Ratio (σ)	2.95	2.41	3.88	3.38	2.67	4.68	3.20	2.54	4.17
Size of Largest Cluster	24	12	36	20	12	34	21	10	36

algorithm, the average and the minimum and maximum values of:

1) the number of clusters per word, where a cluster is a set with 2 or more tokens of the (approximately) 100 tokens being clustered;

2) the number of outliers per word, where an outlier is a token that falls outside all the word clusters for that word;

3) the σ or quality ratio for the word; and

4) the size (numbers of tokens) of the largest cluster.

From Table II we see that the number of clusters per word ranged from 6 to 19 and the average was about 13 for all 3 algorithms. The average number of outliers, however, for the UE2-1 case was 50 percent larger than for the other 2 cases. At the same time, however, the σ or quality ratio of the UE2-1 clusters was significantly larger than for the other 2 cases. This result is subject to some interpretation. The σ measure has the property that as the number of clusters increase, the σ ratio can become unbounded (i.e., as the number of clusters becomes equal to the number of data points, the average intracluster distance becomes 0 and σ becomes infinite). Thus, increases in σ are meaningful if the number of data points falling within the nonoutlier clusters stays the same, or increases.

It is of interest to examine the distribution of tokens among the clusters. An important question is whether the tokens are distributed uniformly among the clusters, or do a relatively small number of clusters account for most of the tokens. To answer this question, the function $g_n(l)$, which represents the accumulated number of tokens in the l largest clusters for the nth word, was computed. The range on l was 1 to 10 (representing the 10 largest clusters for each word), and the range of n was 1 to 39. From $g_n(l)$, the average across n was computed for each value of l and is plotted in Fig. 6 for each of the three time-warping algorithms. Also included in the plots are individual curves for the word with the fewest number of tokens in the 10 largest clusters, and the word with the largest number of tokens in the 10 largest clusters. These curves serve to approximately delineate the range of $g_n(l)$ for each warping algorithm. The plots show a highly nonuniform distribution of tokens within the clusters. They also show that, on average, about 80 percent of the tokens are included in the 10 largest clusters.

For each of the five largest clusters for each word, histograms were made of the estimated probability density functions of the distance of the tokens within the cluster and of the durations of the words. No unusual distributions of the duration

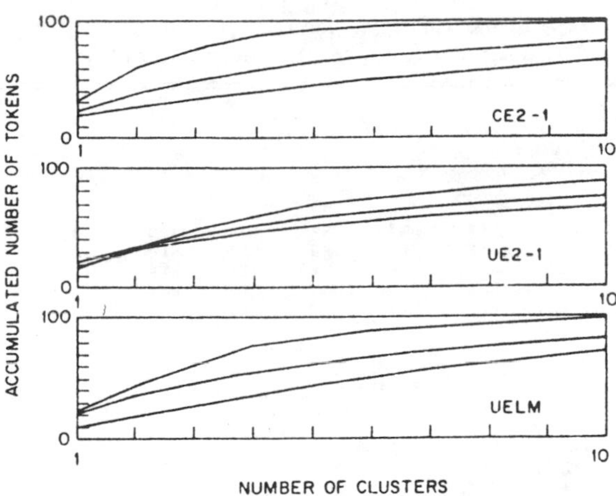

Fig. 6. The average, minimum, and maximum number of data points included within the first l clusters (as a function of l) for the CE2-1 algorithm, the UE2-1 algorithm, and the UELM algorithm.

of tokens within the cluster were found for any of the clusters. The only correlation between clusters and physical quantities that was observed was the tendency of the largest clusters to consist almost entirely of tokens by either male speakers or female speakers, but not both together. The histograms of distances were essentially Gaussian with mean distances of about 0.2 to 0.4.

IV. RECOGNITION RESULTS

To test the clustering analysis, several recognition tests were performed. In this section we describe the different data test sets which were generated, and then describe the individual experiments which were done.

A. *Recognition Test Sets*

Four distinct test sets of data were generated to test both the recognition system of Section II, and the clustering analysis of Section III. We denote the individual test sets as TS1 to TS4. The test material was as follows.

TS1–Each of 10 talkers (5 male, 5 female) spoke the 39 word vocabulary once over a dialed-up telephone line. The 10 talkers were all subjects who were *not* part of the original 100 talker database used for the clustering analysis. A new dialed connection was used for each talker. On-line editing (manual) of the endpoints was done on this data set to correct gross errors made in recording, e.g., erroneous clicks, pops, etc. which were not part of the recording process. A total of 390 words were in TS1.

TS2–Each of 8 new talkers (4 male, 4 female) spoke the 39 word vocabulary once over dialed-up telephone lines. Again the 8 talkers were not in the original training set. A high speed array processor (CSP MAP-200) performed the autocorrelation analysis of the input speech in real time and thus no manual editing of the endpoints was performed. A total of 312 words were in TS2.

TS3–This test set consisted of a random selection of talkers and words from the 100 talker database. The random selection was made from the three replications of the original recordings which were not used in the training set. For each of the 39 words, a random selection of 10 of the 300 tokens

TABLE III
RECOGNITION ACCURACIES (%) FOR CLUSTERS FROM THE CE2-1 ALGORITHM AND FOR THE RANDOMLY CHOSEN CLUSTERS

	$K = 1$		$K = 2$		$K = 3$		$K = 4$	
l	CE2-1	Random	CE2-1	Random	CE2-1	Random	CE2-1	Random
$C = 1$ (Top Candidate)								
2	61.2	49.9	51.6	47.1				
4	69.2	55.8	69.4	58.6	60.9	55.0	58.3	49.6
6	68.4	64.8	71.2	68.1	68.1	64.0	61.2	64.3
8	72.3	67.4	75.6	67.6	75.1	67.9	73.0	66.3
10	73.3	66.6	77.6	70.4	75.3	69.1	74.0	67.9
12	74.6	69.7	79.2	69.9	75.8	72.0	73.3	71.5
$C = 2$ (2 Top Candidates)								
2	75.3	59.1	66.3	55.0				
4	82.5	70.7	82.0	70.7	74.5	67.4	69.4	63.3
6	84.1	80.7	83.3	80.7	80.7	79.7	74.0	74.0
8	85.4	81.2	87.9	81.2	85.9	79.4	83.3	75.8
10	87.4	80.7	87.9	83.3	86.6	83.0	86.1	81.5
12	87.4	82.5	89.0	82.3	87.4	84.1	85.9	83.8
$C = 5$ (5 Top Candidates)								
2	88.2	77.4	83.3	76.9				
4	93.6	89.5	92.8	88.7	88.4	84.8	83.3	80.7
6	95.6	91.5	92.6	92.3	91.3	91.5	88.4	87.7
8	96.7	93.3	96.1	92.3	95.1	91.0	91.5	88.4
10	97.4	94.6	97.7	94.1	97.4	94.6	95.6	92.3
12	97.9	94.4	98.5	95.4	96.7	94.6	94.9	93.8

(100 talkers times 3 replications) was made. A total of 390 words were in TS3.

TS4—This test set consisted of all the tokens from the training set which were out of range for the constrained dynamic warping algorithms, i.e., tokens which were unusually long, or short as compared to the average duration for the word. This set represents an extremely difficult test set because of the extremes of the duration of the words. The number of words in the test set was 162, and the words were nonuniformly distributed across the vocabulary, as mentioned earlier.

B. Recognition Experiments and Results

1) Recognition as a Function of the Number of Templates per Word: The purpose of the first recognition experiment was to measure recognition accuracy as a function of the number of templates per word in the training set. For this purpose the reference templates were chosen from the CE2-1 clustering results. The test set was TS1. For all the recognition experiments to be described in this paper, results were obtained for values of K (in the K-nearest neighbor rule) from $K = 1$ to $K = 4$. The results of this first test are given in Table III (the columns labeled random will be described later) and Fig. 7. The results are given as the mean accuracy (averaged over talkers) for each nearest neighbor rule (K) as a function of the number of templates per word (l), and the number of ordered candidates that were considered (C). The word templates were chosen in descending order based on the size of the cluster, i.e., the $l = 1$ template was the cluster center of the largest cluster, the $l = 2$ template was the cluster center of the next largest cluster, etc. For $C = 1$, only the top candidate was considered. The results for this case are shown in Fig. 7(a). It is seen that the recognition accuracy is about 61

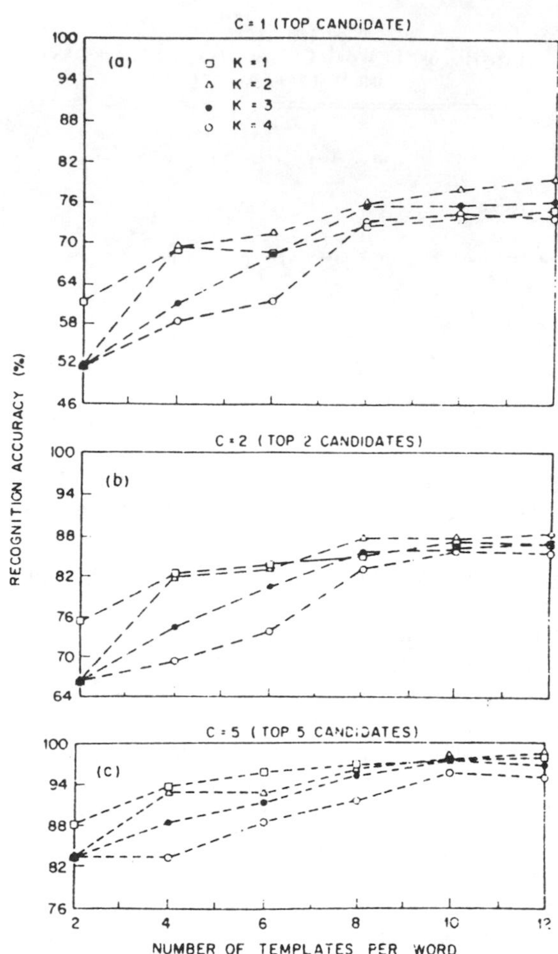

Fig. 7. Recognition accuracy (percent) as a function of the number of templates per word for the CE2-1 clusters with $K = 1, 2, 3, 4$, and $C = 1, 2$, and 5.

percent for $K = 1$ and $l = 2$, and about 51 percent for $K = 2$ and $l = 2$. As l increases, the $K = 2$ and $K = 3$ nearest neighbor rules yield higher recognition accuracies than the $K = 1$ or $K = 4$ rules. For $l = 12$ templates per word (the most used in our tests), the final recognition accuracy (for $C = 1$) was 79 percent for the $K = 2$ rule, and from 3 to 5 percent lower for the other rules.

Similar behavior of the curves of recognition accuracy versus l (for different K values) is seen for the $C = 2$ top candidates [Fig. 7(b)], and for the $C = 5$ top candidates [Fig. 7(c)]. For the best two candidates, the recognition accuracy goes from about 75 percent (for the $K = 1$ rule) to 89 percent (for the $K = 2$ rule) as the number of templates per word goes from 2 to 12. For the top five candidates, the highest accuracy goes from 88 to 98.5 percent for a similar range of l.

The overall shape of the curve of recognition accuracy versus l (for all the values of K and C) shows a sharp rise near $l = 2$ and a gradual steadying off near $l = 10$ to 12. Thus, increases in the number of templates per word beyond 12 would produce marginal (if any) increases in recognition accuracy.

2) Comparisons of the Three Dynamic Warping Algorithms: A series of tests was performed to compare the recognition rates using the CE2-1, UE2-1 and UELM dynamic warping

TABLE IV
RECOGNITION ACCURACIES (%) FOR THE FOUR TEST SETS

	C = 1				C = 2				C = 5			
Clusters	K = 1	K = 2	K = 3	K = 4	K = 1	K = 2	K = 3	K = 4	K = 1	K = 2	K = 3	K = 4
CE2-1	75	79	76	73	87	89	87	86	98	99	97	95
UE2-1	69	74	74	74	84	84	86	85	97	96	96	96
UELM	68	73	73	72	84	87	87	85	95	96	96	95

(a)

	C = 1				C = 2				C = 5			
Clusters	K = 1	K = 2	K = 3	K = 4	K = 1	K = 2	K = 3	K = 4	K = 1	K = 2	K = 3	K = 4
CE2-1	74	76	72	71	86	88	89	88	96	98	97	97
UE2-1	72	73	74	71*	85	86	85	83	96	95	96	95
UELM	65	68	68	66	82	82	80	80	92	92	92	91

(b)

	C = 1				C = 2				C = 5			
Clusters	K = 1	K = 2	K = 3	K = 4	K = 1	K = 2	K = 3	K = 4	K = 1	K = 2	K = 3	K = 4
CE2-1	79	82	82	82	90	91	91	91	99	98	99	99
UE2-1	75	80	80	81	90	92	91	91	98	99	99	98
UELM	71	76	75	76	86	87	90	89	95	97	97	97

(c)

	C = 1				C = 2				C = 5			
Clusters	K = 1	K = 2	K = 3	K = 4	K = 1	K = 2	K = 3	K = 4	K = 1	K = 2	K = 3	K = 4
CE2-1	60	65	69	62	75	81	80	80	90	93	91	91
UE2-1	59	67	70	70	78	82	83	80	91	92	94	93
UELM	62	70	72	70	81	82	83	80	91	95	97	97

(d)

algorithms. All four test sets (TS1-TS4) were used in these tests. A total of $l = 12$ templates per word were used in each test. Table IV shows the average recognition accuracy for each set of data for each dynamic warping algorithm, as a function of K (nearest neighbor rule) and C (number of candidates).

Table IV(a) shows that the CE2-1 algorithm consistently performed as well or better than the other two warping algorithms for the data of TS1. For $K = 1$ and 2, the CE2-1 algorithm gave recognition accuracies from 1 to 6 percent higher than the next best warping method. For $K = 3$, the differences in error rate were small, but remained consistent. For $K = 4$, the differences between all three methods were small.

Tables IV(b) and IV(c) shows that for the data of TS2 and TS3, the CE2-1 again performed consistently as well as or better than the other two algorithms. Higher recognition accuracies of from 1 to 5 percent were obtained for different values of K and C.

The data of Table IV(d), however, show that for the data of TS4 (the out-of-range candidates) the recognition accuracy of all three dynamic warping methods fell considerably for $C = 1$ and $C = 2$. The data show that the UELM performed consistently the best and achieved recognition accuracies of 97 percent for $K = 3$ and $K = 4$ for $C = 5$ top candidates, whereas the CE2-1 and UE2-1 algorithms had from 3 to 6 percent lower accuracies for these cases. For $C = 1$ and $C = 2$, the peak recognition accuracies of 72 percent and 83 percent were considerably lower than for the earlier test sets of data.

3) Effects of Changes of the Rejection Threshold on Recognition Accuracy: All the preceding recognition tests were run using a fixed linear rejection threshold on the dynamic warping accumulated distance. The threshold was of the form

$$R(n) = R_{min}(N) + (R_{max} - R_{min}) \frac{(n - 1)}{(N - 1)} (N) \qquad n = 1, 2, \cdots, N \quad (13)$$

where R_{min} was chosen to be 0.3 and R_{max} was chosen to be 1.0, and N was the number of frames of the test (unknown) utterance. The quantities R_{min} and R_{max} can be shown to be related to the anticipated range of LPC distances for a given frame based on the distribution of LPC distances [1], [22]. One short experiment was run to show the effects of adjusting R_{min} and R_{max} on the recognition accuracy. For this experiment, the test set was TS1 and the templates from the CE2-1 training set were used. Again a total of 12 templates per word were used. The results are given in Table V. This experiment showed that when R_{min} and R_{max} were raised by 50 percent (allowing more templates to go to termination in the dynamic warping), *no change* occurred in the recognition accuracy. However, when R_{min} and R_{max} were lowered by 50 percent (rejecting a greater percentage of templates), an increase in error rate of from 2 to 8 percent occurred for different values of K and C. These tests conclusively showed the validity of the chosen values of R_{min} and R_{max} for this system.

4) Effect of the Backup Frame: One brief experiment was run again using the test data of TS1, and the reference data of the CE2-1 templates (12 per word) in which the backup frame was eliminated (i.e., the backup frame was chosen as the last frame in the utterance). The results of this experiment are also given in Table V. It can be seen that without the backup frame, a small but consistent increase in error rate occurs for different values of K and C. Increases of up to 3 percent ($K = 2$, $C = 1$) of the error rate can be seen in the table. These results, however, should not be considered con-

TABLE V
RECOGNITION ACCURACY AS A FUNCTION OF REJECTION THRESHOLD AND BACKUP FRAME

			C = 1				C = 2				C = 5			
R_{min}	R_{max}	BU	K = 1	K = 2	K = 3	K = 4	K = 1	K = 2	K = 3	K = 4	K = 1	K = 2	K = 3	K = 4
0.3	1.0	Yes	75	79	76	73	87	89	87	86	98	99	97	95
0.15	0.6	Yes	71	74	72	71	82	83	82	81	90	91	90	90
0.5	1.5	Yes	75	79	76	73	87	90	87	86	98	99	97	95
0.3	1.0	No	75	76	75	74	87	89	88	86	98	97	97	95

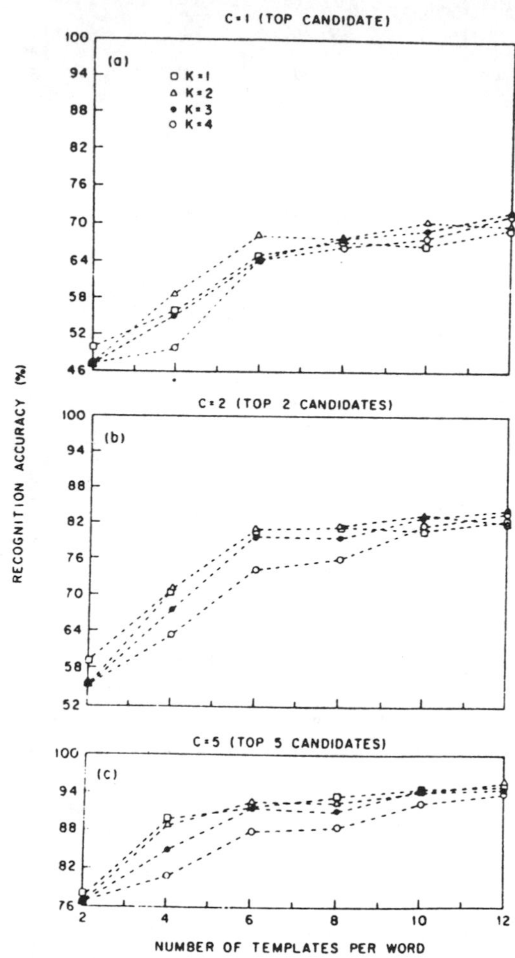

Fig. 8. Recognition accuracy (percent) as a function of the number of templates per word for random templates with $K = 1, 2, 3, 4$, and $C = 1, 2$, and 5.

clusive since the endpoints of the words of TS1 were manually corrected to eliminate clicks, pops, etc. A more definitive test needs to be done to check the utility of the backup frame.

5) Results Obtained Using Random Templates: To verify that the clustering analysis was providing any benefit, a set of templates was selected by choosing at random l out of the 100 templates for each word. Using the data of TS1, the recognition accuracy was measured as a function of l and C for $K = 1$ to 4 using the random templates. The results are given in Table III (columns labeled random) and Fig. 8. It can be seen (by comparing the random and the clustered results of Table III) that decreases in recognition accuracy of from 1 to 16 percent are the result of using randomly selected templates. For $K = 2, l = 12$ the differences in recognition accuracy are

9.3 percent for $C = 1$ (top candidate)
6.7 percent for $C = 2$ (top 2 candidates)
3.1 percent for $C = 5$ (top 5 candidates).

Although as l and C get large and the differences in accuracy decrease, there are substantial differences in recognition accuracy for all values of K, l, and C. Thus, this analysis shows the effectiveness of the clustering algorithms.

Similar comparisons were made for the data of TS2 and TS3 for a value of $l = 12$ templates per word. The results are entirely consistent with those of TS1; namely, significantly increased error rates for the randomly chosen templates.

6) Digit Recognition Results: Since the digits (zero to nine) were a subset of the 39 word vocabulary, it was a simple matter to perform an experiment to see how well digits spoken in isolation could be recognized using the clustered digit data. Thus, a test set was created with 2100 digits from 110 talkers, 100 of which were in the training set (using replications 3 and 4 of their data, which, of course, were *not* used in the training), and 10 who were not in the training set. The reference templates were obtained from the CE2-1 clusters for the digits. A total of 12 clusters per digit were used. The overall accuracies for the top candidate ($C = 1$) was 97.5 percent ($K = 1$), 98.2 percent ($K = 2$), 98.1 percent ($K = 3$), and 97.9 percent ($K = 4$). For the top 2 candidates ($C = 2$), the accuracies were within 0.1 percent of 99.6 percent for all 4 values of K. For the 10 talkers not in the original training set, the accuracy was 97 percent for $C = 1$, $K = 1$, 100 percent for $C = 1$, $K = 2$, and $K = 3$, and 98 percent for $C = 1$, $K = 4$.

7) Ratio Test Threshold: Based on the interpretation of the K-nearest neighbor distance $d_i(x)$ as being an estimate of the probability density function of the ith word at the point x (where x represents an unknown sample), the ordered distance data provide an interesting and useful way of setting a threshold to give a possible "no decision" as the outcome of each recognition trial. The assumption is made that if the average distances to two classes are essentially the same, the distributions have significant overlap in the region of x, and it is impossible to perform reliable recognition. The rule we have studied is a simple one. If we denote the ordered K-nearest neighbor distances as $d_{i_1}(x), d_{i_2}(x), \cdots, d_{i_q}(x)$ with

$$d_{i_1}(x) \leqslant d_{i_2}(x) \leqslant \cdots \leqslant d_{i_q}(x), \tag{14}$$

then a rejection occurs if

$$D_R = \frac{d_{i_1}(x)}{d_{i_2}(x)} \leqslant \frac{1}{T} \tag{15}$$

and a classification of the unknown as word i_1 occurs if the inequality of (15) is reversed.

To illustrate this rule, Fig. 9, shows a series of plots of recognition accuracy, rejection rate, and error rate as a function of the parameter $1/T$ for values of $1/T$ from 1.0 to 2.0. The plot of Fig. 9(a) is for the digit experiment with $K = 2$ ($C = 1$, of course). It can be seen that the error rate for the digits can be kept below 0.5 percent with a 3.9 percent rejection rate for a value of $1/T = 1.1$.

Fig. 9(b) shows results for $K = 2$ for the data of TS1 using 12 templates per word obtained from the CE2-1 algorithm. Fig. 9(c) shows results for TS2 and Fig. 9(d) shows results for TS3 with the same set of templates as for the data of Fig. 9(b). It can readily be seen that the error rate decreases substantially as $1/T$ goes from 1.0 to 1.1, and gradually beyond $1/T = 1.1$. For words in which D_R of (15) was in the range 1.0 to 1.1 [for the full vocabulary tests of Fig. 9(b) to 9(d)] about half the time the recognition result was in error. Since about 25 percent of the words fell into this range, the decrease of about 12.5 percent in error rate (for $1/T = 1.1$) generally brought the error rate down to around 6-8 percent, with a reject rate of about 25 percent. Further increases in $1/T$ brought about significantly larger increases in rejection rate with only small decreases in error rate.

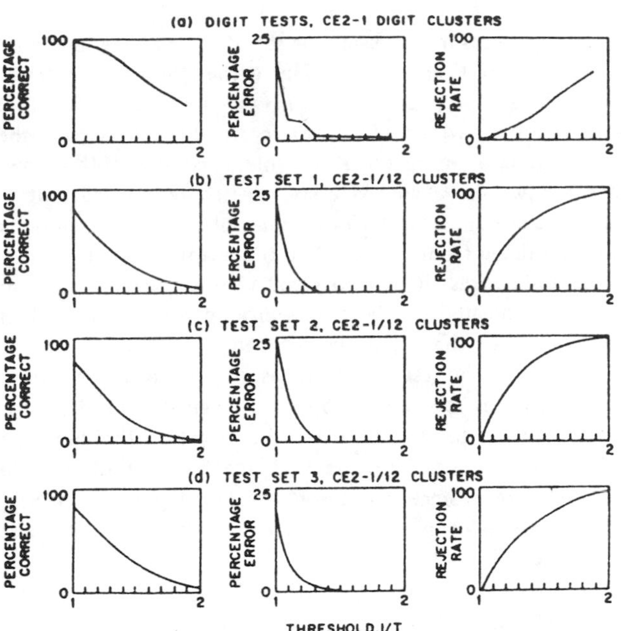

Fig. 9. Curves of recognition rate ($P(C)$) and error rate ($P(E)$) as a function of the rejection threshold T for: a) digit tests, b) test set 1, c) test set 2, and d) test set 3.

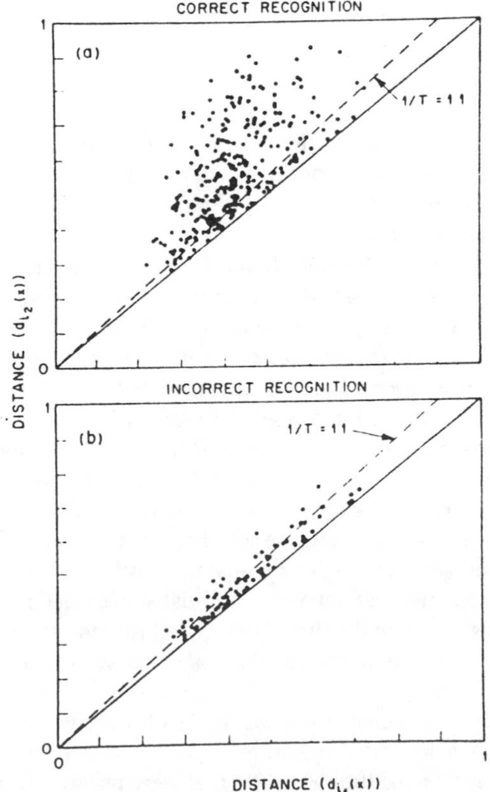

Fig. 10. Plots of the distance of the second candidate versus the distance of the first candidate for: a) words recognized correctly, and b) words incorrectly recognized.

To illustrate that a threshold of the type given in (15) (i.e., a ratio test) is more suitable than an absolute distance threshold, Fig. 10 shows plots of the quantity $d_{i_1}(x)$ versus $d_{i_2}(x)$

for all the words in TS1 using the set of 12 templates per word from the CE2-1 algorithm. The dashed line in the figure shows the set of points where $d_{i_2}(x) = 1.1\, d_{i_1}(x)$. Fig. 10(a) shows data for words which were correctly recognized as the first candidate (using the $K = 2$ rule), and Fig. 10(b) shows data for words which were incorrectly recognized. It is readily seen that in both cases, values of $d_{i_1}(x)$, the minimum distance, range from about 0.2 to 0.8. However, for the misrecognized words the quantity $d_{i_2}(x)$ was generally close to $d_{i_1}(x)$ as indicated by the points around the diagonal. It is this observation that led to the decision rule of (15).

We reiterate the result that, in cases in which absolute word identification is required (as opposed to giving an ordered list of candidates), the use of a decision rejection threshold can substantially reduce error rate at the expense of a finite rejection rate. Since rejections are data-dependent [(15)], cases in which an inherently high *a posteriori* error rate exist are rejected.

V. Discussion

In this paper we had several goals. These were:

1) to investigate a supervised algorithm for clustering words using only accumulated LPC distances between words,

2) to study the effects of variations on the dynamic time-warping algorithm on both clustering and the resulting recognition accuracy.

3) to study a novel decision rule which was linked to a multiple template (cluster) representation of the vocabulary words, and

4) to compare recognition accuracies obtained from multiple templates for each word and used in a speaker-independent manner to those obtained in systems which were trained to the individual speaker.

The discussion in Sections II and III, and the data of Section IV have provided partial answers to many of our original questions. The key results have been the following.

1) The pattern recognition clustering algorithms have provided an effective method of finding structure in the speech data. Evaluations of the resulting clusters in terms of both a quality measure of clustering and in terms of recognition accuracies have shown the data to fall naturally into a small number of clusters each of which could be adequately represented by a single point, the so-called cluster center. Recognition accuracies on test sets containing both new talkers and talkers from the test set were essentially identical across all conditions. This result shows that the clustered data provide, to a first approximation, a universal data set for the given vocabulary words.

2) The constrained endpoint (CE2-1) warping algorithm provided the highest recognition accuracies for almost all the data sets and recognition variables that were tested. For words which were anomolously long, or short, the UELM warping algorithm provided the best results.

3) The $K = 2$ and $K = 3$ nearest neighbor decision rules provided a significant improvement in recognition accuracy over the $K = 1$ (minimum distance) and $K = 4$ rules. This result was anticipated based on the interpretation of the KNN rule distance as an estimate of the local probability density function of the ith word. For a finite set of clusters which are used to "span the entire space" of the ith word, large values of K would be anticipated to give poor results due to sparse sampling of the space.

4) To obtain the best results in the recognition tests, conservative thresholds are required for the rejection threshold to guarantee that at least two or three valid candidates from each cluster set are used to give the KNN estimate of distance. The use of a backup frame to provide protection against spurious, nonspeech sounds at the end of a word provided a small but consistent increase in recognition accuracy.

5) The error rate of the system could be reduced at the expense of a finite rejection rate for applications in which a specified error rate had to be maintained. A simple, effective measurement was discussed which automatically identified those trials with which a high probability of error was associated.

6) High accuracies were obtained (98.2 percent) for speaker-independent digit recognition.

7) Experiments with randomly selected templates clearly showed the superiority of the clustering methods in giving an efficient representation of the structure for each word class.

In the remainder of this section we analyze the types of recognition errors that were made, compare the recognition accuracies that we obtained to those of other investigators, and discuss relevant issues that remain to be investigated.

A. Analysis of Recognition Errors

To analyze the performance of the overall recognition systems, the results of test sets 1, 2, and 3 were merged (using reference data obtained from the CE2-1 warping algorithm with 12 clusters per word), and a confusion matrix of errors was obtained for the $C = 1$ (first candidate) condition using $K = 2$ (nearest neighbor rule). A series of subsets of the resulting confusion matrix are given in Table VI. It is readily seen that the vast majority of confusions occur within classes of high acoustical and phonetic similarity. We have identified six such classes, namely:

1) the set of i sounds–b, c, d, e, g, p, t, v, z, 3,
2) the set of eI sounds–a, j, k, 8, h,
3) the set of e sounds–l, m, n,
4) the set of final fricatives with e or I–f, s, x, 6,
5) the set of aI sounds–i, y, 5,
6) the set of u sounds–q, u, 2.

A total of about 75 percent of the errors occurred *within* each of the six classes, with the majority occurring within Class 1. An error rate of less than 2.5 percent is obtained for the remaining eleven words of the vocabulary. Based on both previous experience and similar experiments with this vocabulary [4], it is felt that the overall error rate of this recognition system is fundamentally controlled by the acoustic similarities between words within each class (especially for band-limited) telephone speech), and not by the clustering results or any particular aspect of the recognition system.

B. Comparisons With Other Recognition Results

The full 39 word vocabulary has been used in two previous research projects by Itakura [1] and Rosenberg and Schmidt

TABLE VI
CONFUSIONS AMONG SUBCLASSES OF THE 39 WORD VOCABULARY

Recognized Word

	B	C	D	E	G	P	T	V	Z	3	Other
B	8		2	2		4	1	8	3		
C		23	1				1		2		1
D	3		7	3		4	4	6	1		
E	6		1	18				3			
G			2		19		3		2		2
P	2	1	2			14	7	1	1		
T	2	1	3	1	2	2	13	2	2		
V	1		3	1				16	5	1	1
Z		3					1	3	20		1
3		1	1			1		1		22	2

	A	J	K	H	8	Other
A	17	2	5		1	3
J		22	5			1
K	2	7	19			
H				25	3	3
8				1	24	

	L	M	N	Other
L	27			1
M	2	20	4	2
N		5	19	4

	F	S	X	6
F	24	2	1	1
S	2	25	1	
X		1	27	
6				28

	I	Y	5	Other
I	19	5	2	2
Y		27		1
5	2		24	2

	Q	U	2	Other
Q	22	3	3	
U	1	27		
2	4	1	21	2

[4]. Itakura tested the vocabulary on a single speaker for which the system was trained. Itakura reported a recognition accuracy of 88.6 percent on the top candidate. This score was about 9 percent higher than those obtained here. However, there were several speakers (of the 28 tested here) who had the same or higher recognition accuracy than Itakura; thus, it is difficult to assess our results based on Itakura's score.

Rosenberg and Schmidt trained their system to each of 10 talkers who recited 364 letters which spelled a group of 50 names with initials [4]. For this group of talkers, average recognition accuracies of

1) 79 percent for $C = 1$ (top candidate),
2) 88.5 percent for $C = 2$ (2 top candidates, and
3) 96 percent for $C = 5$ (5 top candidates),

were obtained.

The average recognition accuracies obtained across 28 talkers (merged test sets), none of whom individually trained the system, were

1) 79 percent for $C = 1$,
2) 89.3 percent for $C = 2$, and
3) 98.5 percent for $C = 5$.

Thus, our average recognition accuracies for speaker-independent recognition were comparable or somewhat higher than those of a speaker trained system. Since Rosenberg and Schmidt used only the letters, these comparisons are not strictly valid. However, they do serve to illustrate that carefully chosen word templates can yield essentially equivalent recognition scores for speaker-trained and speaker-independent systems.

For the digit vocabulary, we compare our results to those of Sambur and Rabiner [23] for speaker-independent recognition of isolated digits, Martin [5] for speaker-dependent recognition of isolated digits, and Rosenberg and Itakura [2] for speaker-dependent recognition of isolated digits. The results obtained by these investigators were

1) 95.6 percent accuracy by Sambur and Rabiner,
2) 99.5 percent accuracy by Martin, and
3) 96 percent accuracy by Rosenberg and Itakura.

Clearly the digit recognition accuracies obtained from multiple templates are essentially comparable to or better than those obtained in earlier investigations.

C. Issues for Further Investigation

Although we have attempted to explore a number of issues related to both clustering of word data for creating templates and recognition, there remain a number of interesting questions which require subsequent investigation. These include the following.

1) The applicability of the clustering approach to speaker-dependent recognition systems.

2) The effects of a totally unsupervised clustering of data on the quality of the clusters, and the resulting recognition accuracy.

3) The applicability of the ordered list of word candidates from the speaker-independent recognizer to a spelled spoken-speech system as described by Rosenberg and Schmidt [4].

4) The effects of averaging tokens within a cluster to give a cluster template, rather than choosing a cluster center based on minimax distance.

We hope to investigate these issues more fully in subsequent research.

VI. SUMMARY

In this paper we have discussed the suitability of using sophisticated pattern recognition techniques to provide multiple speaker-independent word templates for an isolated word recognition system. We have shown that such methods do indeed provide templates which give recognition accuracies that are comparable to equivalent recognition systems that are trained to an individual talker.

APPENDIX
THE GENERALIZED K-NEAREST NEIGHBOR DECISION RULE

Consider the set of points $\{X_1, X_2, \cdots, X_n\}$ and the point Z shown in Fig. 11. The set $\{X_i\}_{i=1}^n$ is a set of n observations drawn from a random process characterized by the probability density function $f(Z)$. The point Z is an arbitrary point in the observation space. As shown in Fig. 11, X_2 is the nearest neighbor to Z; X_1 is its second nearest neighbor; X_3 is its third, and so on. In general, we shall designate the Kth nearest neighbor to Z by $Z_{[K]}$ and we have

$$\|Z - Z_{[1]}\| \leqslant \|Z - Z_{[2]}\| \leqslant \cdots \leqslant \|Z - Z_{[K]}\| \leqslant \cdots \leqslant \|Z - Z_{[n]}\|. \quad (A1)$$

We define r_K as the average distance from Z to its K-nearest neighbors; thus

$$r_K = \frac{1}{K} \sum_{j=1}^{K} \|Z - Z_{[j]}\|. \quad (A2)$$

Following Fraser [24], we define the tolerance region T as the hypersphere of radius r_K centered at Z. We denote its volume as $\Phi(Z)$. For convenience we shall designate the complement of T in the observation space as T^*. Finally, let m be the number of observations in T. Clearly, $1 \leqslant m < K$.

Let $\hat{f}(Z)$ be an estimate of $f(Z)$ where

$$\hat{f}(Z) = \frac{K}{n} \cdot \frac{1}{\Phi(Z)}. \quad (A3)$$

It can be shown that $\hat{f}(Z)$ is a consistent estimator of $f(Z)$, i.e.,

$$\lim_{n \to \infty} \|\hat{f}(Z) - f(Z)\| = 0. \quad (A4)$$

The proof of (A4) is identical to that given by Loftsgaarden and Queensberry [25] with r_K substituted for $\|Z - Z_{[K]}\|$, the distance from Z to its Kth nearest neighbor. We shall not reproduce the proof here.

Nonparametric density estimators similar to that of (A3) have been studied by Loftsgaarden and Queensberry [25], Cover and Hart [26], and Patrick and Fischer [27]. These estimators lead to the nearest neighbor, majority vote, and generalized nearest neighbor decision rules, respectively. However, these estimators have different properties from that of (A3). To see what the differences are we define the coverage C_T of a tolerance region to be the probability that an observation drawn from $f(Z)$ will fall in the region; thus

$$C_T = P_r\{X \epsilon T\} = \int_T f(\xi)\, d\xi. \quad (A5)$$

Since T is defined in terms of the observations which are random variables, C_T is a random variable with $0 \leqslant C_T \leqslant 1$ and having density function, say, $g(C_T)$.

In the case when C_T is independent of $f(Z)$, that is, if the coverage of the tolerance region is independent of the underlying statistics of the observations, T is said to be distribution-free. The estimates described in the references [25]-[27] cited above are all based upon distribution-free tolerance regions.

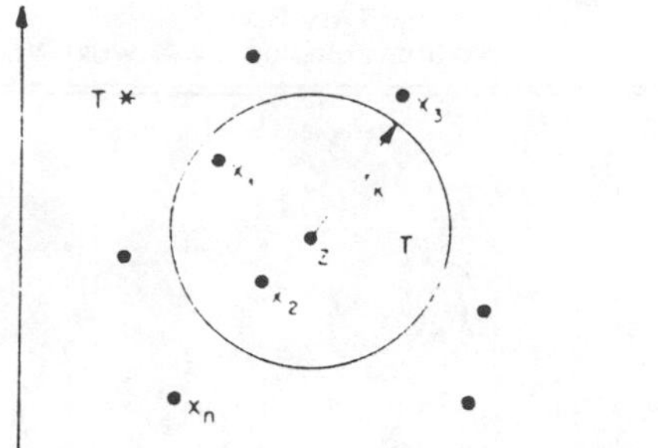

Fig. 11. Points in the observation space.

Using an argument similar to that given by Wilks [28], we see that the tolerance regions as defined above are not distribution-free. We first note that the probability that exactly m observations lie in T, and $n - m$ lie in T^* is given by the binomial distribution

$$P_r[|\{X_i \epsilon T\}| = m] = \frac{n!}{n!(n-m)!} C_T^m (1 - C_T)^{n-m} \quad (A6)$$

from which it follows that $g(C_T)$ has the beta distribution $\beta(m, n-m)$, independent of $f(Z)$.

However, the value of m varies between 1 and $K - 1$ depending on Z, even for a fixed set of observations, so that the density function for the coverage of T is the finite mixture

$$g(C_T) = \sum_{m=1}^{K-1} W_m \beta(m, n-m) \quad (A7)$$

in which the weights W_m depend on $f(Z)$. Thus, the tolerance regions as defined here are "nearly" distribution-free in the sense that their coverages are restricted to a parametric family of distributions. We shall see the significance of this later.

To describe the decision rule imagine that the n observations are taken from M classes, $\omega_1, \omega_2, \cdots \omega_M$, and ω_i has n_i observations and class-conditional density function $f(Z|\omega_i)$. The Bayes decision rule says assign the unknown observation Z to the class for which the conditional density function at Z is the largest, or

$$Z \epsilon \omega_i \text{ iff } f(Z|\omega_i) \geqslant f(Z|\omega_l) \quad 1 \leqslant l \leqslant M. \quad (A8)$$

Now consider the decision rule

$$Z \epsilon \omega_i \text{ iff } \frac{1}{K_i} \sum_{j=1}^{K_i} \|Z - Z_{[j]}^{(i)}\| \leqslant \frac{1}{K_l} \sum_{j=1}^{K_l} \|Z - Z_{[j]}^{(l)}\| \; \forall l \quad (A9)$$

where $Z_{[j]}^{(i)}$ is the jth nearest observation to Z in ω_i and $K_l \leqslant \sqrt{n}$. The decision rule of (A8) is simply: assign an unknown observation to the class for which the average distance to its K_i-nearest neighbors is minimum.

By definition of r_K, (A9) becomes

$$Z \epsilon \omega_i \text{ iff } r_{K_i} \leqslant r_{K_l} \quad 1 \leqslant l \leqslant M, \quad (A10)$$

and since $\Phi(Z)$ varies inversely with r_K according to

$$\Phi(Z) = \frac{N\Gamma\left(\frac{N}{2}\right)}{2r_K^N \pi^{(N/2)}} \tag{A11}$$

where N is the dimensionality of the observation space and $\Gamma(\cdot)$ is the gamma function. We have

$$Z\epsilon\omega_i \text{ iff } \frac{K_i}{N_i\Phi_i(Z)} \geqslant \frac{K_l}{N_l\Phi_l(Z)} \quad \forall l \tag{A12}$$

where the subscripts are class indices. Finally, from (A8) we have

$$Z\epsilon\omega_i \text{ iff } \hat{f}(Z|\omega_i) \leqslant \hat{f}(Z|\omega_l) \qquad 1 \leqslant l \leqslant M \tag{A13}$$

which is exactly Bayes' rule, (A8).

Patrick [29] has observed that while distribution-free tolerance regions provide satisfactory density estimates, better estimates may be obtained if the tolerance regions are constructed in a way that takes into account the special properties of the data.

The peculiarities of the data with which we are most concerned are the small sample size and occasional artifacts introduced by the time alignment procedure. The effect of the small sample size is to make the variance of the estimator of (A3) large which, in turn, introduces classification errors. Averaging the distance to the K-nearest neighbors reduces the variance by a factor of $1/K$. The nonlinear time registration procedure sometimes forces the distance from a sample to an incorrect template to be uncharacteristically small. Clearly, the averaging operation will mitigate the adverse effects of pathologically small distances.

We have compared the decision rule of (A9) to the nearest neighbor rule of Loftsgaarden and Queensberry [26] and that of Patrick and Fischer [27] in which a sample is classified according to the distances of its kth nearest neighbor in each class. On test set TS1, our rule showed improvements of 6.6 and 8.5 percent over the Patrick and Fischer scheme for $K = 2$ and $K = 3$, respectively, and 4.6 and 1.2 percent improvements over the nearest neighbor rule for $K = 2$ and $K = 3$, respectively.

Acknowledgment

The authors wish to acknowledge the programming support and assistance of C. Schmidt for data input and analysis for the clustering phase of the system.

References

[1] F. Itakura, "Minimum prediction residual applied to speech recognition," *IEEE Trans. Acoust., Speech, Signal Processing*, vol. ASSP-23, pp. 67-72, Feb. 1975.

[2] A. E. Rosenberg and F. Itakura, "Evaluation of an automatic word recognition system over dialed-up telephone lines," *J. Acoust. Soc. Amer.*, vol. 60, suppl. 1, p. S12 (abstr.), Nov. 1976.

[3] S. E. Levinson, A. E. Rosenberg, and J. L. Flanagan, "Evaluation of a word recognition system using syntax analysis," *Bell Syst. Tech. J.*, vol. 57, pp. 1619-1626, May-June 1978.

[4] A. E. Rosenberg and C. E. Schmidt, "Recognition of spoken spelled names applied to directory assistance," *J. Acoust. Soc. Amer.*, vol. 62, suppl. 1, p. 563 (abstr.), Dec. 1977.

[5] T. B. Martin, "Practical applications of voice input to machines," *Proc. IEEE*, vol. 64, pp. 487-501, Apr. 1976.

[6] J. N. Shearme and P. F. Leach, "Some experiments with a simple word recognition system," *IEEE Trans Audio Electroacoust.*, vol. AU-16, pp. 256-261, June 1968.

[7] B. Gold, "Word recognition computer program," Res. Lab Electron., Massachusetts Inst. Tech., Cambridge, Tech. Rep. 452, June 1966.

[8] P. B. Scott, "VICI-A speaker independent word recognition system," in *Conf. Rec. 1976 IEEE Int. Conf. Acoust., Speech, Signal Processing*, Philadelphia, PA, Apr. 1976, pp. 210-213.

[9] L. R. Rabiner, "On creating reference templates for speaker-independent recognition of isolated words," *IEEE Trans. Acoust., Speech, Signal Processing*, vol. ASSP-26, pp. 34-42, Feb. 1978.

[10] V. N. Gupta, J. K. Bryan, and J. N. Gowdy, "A speaker-independent speech recognition system based on linear prediction," *IEEE Trans. Acoust., Speech, Signal Processing*, vol. ASSP-26, pp. 27-33, Feb. 1978.

[11] S. E. Levinson, L. R. Rabiner, A. E. Rosenberg, and J. G. Wilpon, "Application of clustering techniques to speaker-independent word recognition," to be published.

[12] L. R. Rabiner, B. S. Atal, and M. R. Sambur, "LPC prediction error-Analysis of its variation with the position of the analysis frame," *IEEE Trans. Acoust., Speech, Signal Processing*, vol. ASSP-25, pp. 434-442, Oct. 1977.

[13] H. Sakoe and S. Chiba, "A dynamic programming approach to continuous speech recognition," in *Proc. Int. Congress on Acoustics*, Budapest, Hungary, Paper 20 C-13, 1971.

[14] H. Sakoe and S. Chiba, "Dynamic programming algorithm optimization for spoken word recognition," *IEEE Trans. Acoust., Speech, Signal Processing*, vol. ASSP-26, pp. 43-49, Feb. 1978.

[15] L. R. Rabiner, A. E. Rosenberg, and S. E. Levinson, "Considerations in dynamic time-warping algorithms for discrete word recognition," *IEEE Trans. Acoust., Speech, Signal Processing*, vol. ASSP-26, Oct. 1978.

[16] M. R. Sambur and L. R. Rabiner, "A statistical decision approach to the recognition of connected digits," *IEEE Trans. Acoust., Speech, Signal Processing*, vol. ASSP-24, pp. 550-558, Dec. 1976.

[17] J. T. Tou and R. C. Gonzalez, *Pattern Recognition Principles*. Reading, MA: Addison-Wesley, 1974.

[18] E. A. Patrick, *Fundamentals of Pattern Recognition*. Englewood Cliffs, NJ: Prentice-Hall, 1972.

[19] R. O. Duda and P. E. Hart, *Pattern Classification and Scene Analysis*. New York: Wiley, 1973.

[20] J. Mac Queen, "Some methods for classification and analysis of multivariate data," in *Proc. 5th Berkeley Symp. Probability and Statistics*, Berkeley, CA, 1967.

[21] G. H. Ball and D. J. Hall, "Isodata-An iterative method of multivariate analysis and pattern classification," in *Proc. IFIPS Congress*, 1965.

[22] J. M. Tribolet and L. R. Rabiner, "Statistical properties of the log likelihood ratio for LPC coefficients," to appear in *IEEE Trans. Acoust., Speech, Signal Processing*, 1979.

[23] M. R. Sambur and L. R. Rabiner, "A speaker-independent digit-recognition system," *Bell Syst. Tech. J.*, vol. 54, pp. 81-102, Jan. 1975.

[24] D. A. S. Fraser, *Nonparametric Methods in Statistics*. New York. Wiley, 1957.

[25] D. O. Loftsgaarden and C. P. Queensberry, "A nonparametric estimate of a multivariate density function," *Ann. Math. Statist.*, vol. 36, 1965.

[26] T. M. Cover and P. E. Hart, "Nearest neighbor pattern classification," *IEEE Trans. Inform. Theory*, vol. IT-13, p. 21-27, Jan. 1967.

[27] E. A. Patrick and F. P. Fischer, "A generalized K-nearest neighbor rule," *Inform. Contr.*, vol. 16, 1970.

[28] S. S. Wilks, "Determination of sample sizes for setting tolerance limits," *Ann. Math. Statist.*

[29] E. A. Patrick, *Fundamentals of Pattern Recognition*. Englewood Cliffs, NJ: Prentice-Hall, 1973, 12, 1941.

Two-Level DP-Matching—A Dynamic Programming-Based Pattern Matching Algorithm for Connected Word Recognition

HIROAKI SAKOE

Abstract–This paper reports a pattern matching approach to connected word recognition. First, a general principle of connected word recognition is given based on pattern matching between unknown continuous speech and artificially synthesized connected reference patterns. Time-normalization capability is allowed by use of dynamic programming-based time-warping technique (DP-matching). Then, it is shown that the matching process is efficiently carried out by breaking it down into two steps. The derived algorithm is extensively subjected to recognition experiments.

It is shown in a talker-adapted recognition experiment that digit data (one to four digits) connectedly spoken by five persons are recognized with as high as 99.6 percent accuracy. Computation time and memory requirement are both proved to be within reasonable limits.

I. Introduction

Connected word recognition is one of the most interesting problems at the present stage of speech recognition research since isolated word recognition techniques have been improved up to a practically high level [4], [8]. There are two reasons why this problem is so focused. First of all, connected speech input improves data input rate, as well as recognition system operational facility. Numeric data input, involving pronouncing numbers on a digit-by-digit basis, would be unacceptably slow and irritating work. Apart from these practical aspects, connected word recognition research should be emphasized from more long-term viewpoints, as well. This research will result in some key techniques for natural continuous speech recognition.

The target of this investigation is a talker-dependent high-accuracy recognition system, which deals with word-connected speech involving a limited vocabulary. The basic recognition strategy employed is the so-called pattern matching method. Though it is simple in principle, it is a very effective and efficient recognition method, as long as it is performed on a word unit basis.

Recent dynamic programming-based time-normalization technique (DP-matching [1]-[4]) has greatly improved its practical effectiveness. The pattern matching method also possesses many convenient features. It can be applied to different situations without any recognition algorithm modification. Vocabulary change or system adaptation to individual speakers is easily performed by updating the reference pattern. Furthermore the pattern matching method works fairly well for any foreign language. In this paper pattern matching is carried out between speech patterns with quasi-continuous time axes. Here, the term "quasi-continuous" means that time sampling is made with a relatively short (10 ms or so) constant period. It is well known that the resulting speech pattern is then very redundant. From the computational economy standpoint, quasi-continuous sampling will be insufficient. Some phonemic level segmention is naturally expected to reduce the redundancy. In spite of these well-known factors, preliminary segmentation is utterly discarded in this investigation. It is considered that computational efficiency improvement is a secondary problem, coming after the establishment of a more reliable recognition principle.

Two-level DP-matching discussed in this paper is a connected word recognition method based on pattern matching. It employs no preliminary segmentation in principle. Pattern matching is made on a whole connected word basis, that is, between unknown continuous and artificially synthesized connected reference patterns. The time-normalizing feature is given through the use of dynamic programming. It is shown that the matching process is efficiently carried out by breaking it down into two steps, word level matching and phrase level matching. Two execution algorithms are derived which are suitably applicable to the computer simulation experiment and the real-time recognition system, respectively. High-level recognition performance was established through several connected word recognition experiments. Computation time and memory requirements are both estimated to be within reasonable limits.

II. Connected Word Recognition Principle

A. Preliminary Discussions

As the result of the discussions in Section I, it has been decided that recognition should be made based on pattern matching with word unit reference patterns. In such a simplified case, the principal problems are considered to be segmentation, time-normalization, and coarticulation problems.

Segmentation is now a word level problem. In other words, this segmentation means separating a continuous speech into word units. This word level segmentation seems much easier than the phoneme or syllable level segmentation. Actually, Sambur and Rabiner [9] have reported a segmentation rule applied to English digit words. Their rule, however, was

Manuscript received August 11, 1978; revised April 10, 1979 and July 23, 1979.

The author is with Central Research Laboratories, Nippon Electric Company, Kawasaki, Japan.

0096-3518/79/1200-0588$00.75 © 1979 IEEE

specially designed for a specific vocabulary. It seems difficult to generalize their rule to a point where it would be applicable to an arbitrarily selected word set recognition. As vocabulary size grows, the rule will become more complicated. As long as the segmentation is imperfect, highly complicated recognition rules will be required to compensate for the imperfection. These considerations suggest the desirability of not making any segmentation prior to recognition, as was proposed by Sakoe and Chiba [2], [3]. In other words, the word boundary decision should be made in parallel with the word category decision.

Time-normalization is one of the central problems, even in isolated word recognition research. There should be much more time-normalization effort made in connected word recognition because time-axis fluctuation is much more violent in the continuous speech context than in the isolated speech context. Fortunately, dynamic programming-based pattern-matching technique, or DP-matching, has almost completely solved the problem [1]-[4]. In the early stage of DP-matching evolution a trial application is made to the connected word recognition problem [2], [3]. It has been reported that DP-matching is one of the most promising approaches to connected word recognition.

In the present study, no active effort is made to normalize or avoid the coarticulation effect. Instead, it is expected that in the case of word-unit-based recognition, the coarticulation effect is less severe than in the case of phoneme-unit-based recognition. Besides, multiple reference pattern use will solve the problem to a certain practical extent.

B. Time-Normalization Based on Dynamic Programming

In the proposed connected word recognition algorithm dynamic programming, or DP-matching, plays an essential role. A summarized description is given here on the DP-matching algorithm. Let

$$A = \mathbb{a}_1, \mathbb{a}_2, \cdots, \mathbb{a}_i, \cdots, \mathbb{a}_I$$

$$B = \mathbb{b}_1, \mathbb{b}_2, \cdots, \mathbb{b}_j, \cdots, \mathbb{b}_J \tag{1}$$

be two speech patterns. Each of them is represented as a sequence of feature vectors with quasi-continuous time axis i or j. The time-normalized distance measure between these two speech patterns is defined as

$$D(A,B) = \min_{j=j(i)} \left[\sum_{i=1}^{I} d(i,j) \right] \tag{2}$$

where $d(i,j)$, vector distance, is the distance between vectors $\mathbb{a}_i$ and $\mathbb{b}_j$. Warping function $j(i)$ is subjected to monotonic condition, continuous condition, etc., so that it can well approximate the actual time-axis fluctuation property. (See Sakoe and Chiba [4].) The minimization problem (2) is very efficiently solved by the use of dynamic programming.

The above definition is essentially the same as the asymmetric form distance given by Sakoe and Chiba [4]. It has been reported that the symmetric form distance shows significantly better performance than the asymmetric one. The reason why the asymmetric form distance is employed, in spite of its relative inferiority, will be made clear through the discussion in Section II-D.

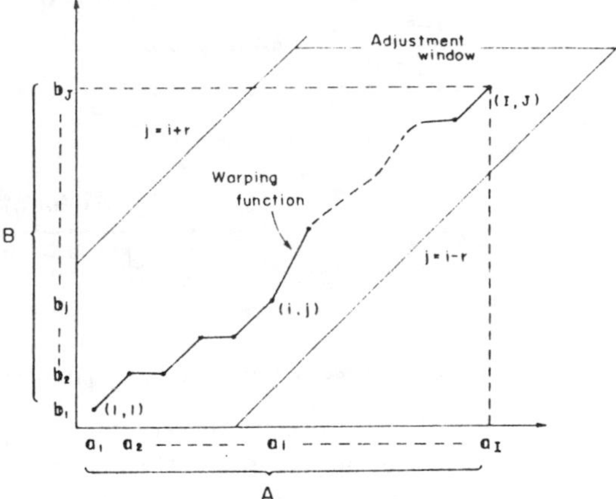

Fig. 1. DP-matching principle.

In order to give a basis for computational efficiency estimation in the following discussions, the computation time consumed in a DP-matching process is analyzed here. The DP-matching algorithm is intuitively well explained by the i-j plane shown in the Fig. 1. The asymmetric form DP-equation [4]

$$g(i,j) = \min \begin{bmatrix} g(i-1, j-2) + (d(i, j-1) + d(i,j))/2 \\ g(i-1, j-1) + d(i,j) \\ g(i-2, j-1) + d(i-1, j) + d(i,j) \end{bmatrix} \tag{3}$$

is recurrently calculated in the adjustment window $|i - j| \leqq r$ starting from point $(1, 1)$ up to (I, J). Therefore, computation time consumed by one DP-matching process is nearly proportional to $(2r + 1) \times J$. This product is used as the basis for algorithm efficiency evaluation.

C. Connected Word Recognition Principle

Let $1, 2, \cdots, n, \cdots, N$ represent an N word vocabulary. The reference pattern of word n is represented as

$$B^n = \mathbb{b}^n_1, \mathbb{b}^n_2, \cdots, \mathbb{b}^n_j, \cdots, \mathbb{b}^n_{J^n}. \tag{4}$$

Let

$$C = \mathbb{c}_1, \mathbb{c}_2, \cdots, \mathbb{c}_i, \cdots, \mathbb{c}_I \tag{5}$$

be an unknown input speech pattern. This input speech may be a single word speech or a multiple word speech. Hereafter, it is called connected speech or a phrase. The basic concept of the proposed recognition principle is shown in Fig. 2. An operator "⊕" is employed (meaning concatenating two speech patterns) as, for example,

$$B^m \oplus B^n = \mathbb{b}^m_1, \mathbb{b}^m_2, \cdots, \mathbb{b}^m_{J^m}, \mathbb{b}^n_1, \mathbb{b}^n_2, \cdots, \mathbb{b}^n_{J^n}. \tag{6}$$

An approximated phrase reference pattern $\overline{B}$ of words $n(1)$, $n(2), \cdots, n(k)$ is synthesized by concatenating their reference patterns as

$$\overline{B} = B^{n(1)} \oplus B^{n(2)} \oplus \cdots \oplus B^{n(k)}.$$

Pattern matching is made between unknown input pattern C and above synthesized reference pattern $\overline{B}$, providing a

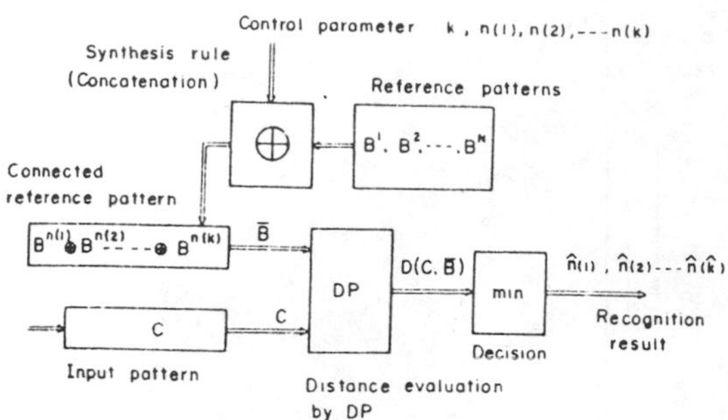

Fig. 2. Proposed connected word recognition principle.

distance $D(C, \overline{B})$. These processes are repeated, changing the number of words k and indexes $n(1), n(2), \cdots, n(k)$. When the above process is carried out until all repeated permutations of the indexes are exhausted, optimum parameters $k = \hat{k}$ and $n(x) = \hat{n}(x)$, $x = 1, 2, \cdots \hat{k}$ are determined, which give minimum distance $D(C, \overline{B})$. Then, decision is made that input pattern C comprises $\hat{k}$ words $\hat{n}(1), \hat{n}(2, \cdots, \hat{n}(\hat{k})$. Mathematically, this principle is formulated in the following minimization problem format.

$$T = \min_{k, n(x)} [D(C, B^{n(1)} \oplus B^{n(2)} \oplus \cdots \oplus B^{n(x)} \oplus \cdots \oplus B^{n(k)})]. \tag{8}$$

This recognition scheme needs no preliminary segmentation because pattern matching is made on a whole phrase basis. Thus, erroneous recognition possibility caused by inaccurate segmentation is completely excluded. Accordingly, a significantly higher performance is expected compared with traditional preliminary segmentation making approaches.

The minimization problem (8), however, is not an easy problem to be solved by the so-called direct search, or exhaustive comparison, method. It consumes a prohibitively enormous amount of computation because all possible concatenations of the reference patterns must be tested.

Sakoe and Chiba [2], [3] reported an approximate solution method for this problem. Their method is called the previous method in the following part of this paper. It worked fairly well for two-digit connected speech. Nevertheless, when word connection was further increased, recognition accuracy became rapidly degraded. It should be noted, however, that they made use of an interesting property of dynamic programming which gives solutions for a set of different boundary conditions in parallel.

On the premise that the syllable level (VCV-unit) segmentation is made on a preliminary stage, Nakatsu and Kohda [5] gave a solution method for problem (8). It is a complete and efficient method, as long as it is applied after accurate segmentation is made. On the other hand, the present investigation is on a quasi-continuous time axis basis, as declared in Section I of this paper. The following sections report an efficient segmentation-free recognition algorithm based on the efforts reported by Sakoe and Chiba and by Nakatsu and Kohda.

D. Minimization Process Decomposition

In this section the minimization problem (8) is broken down into two steps: one for word unit level, and one for the whole

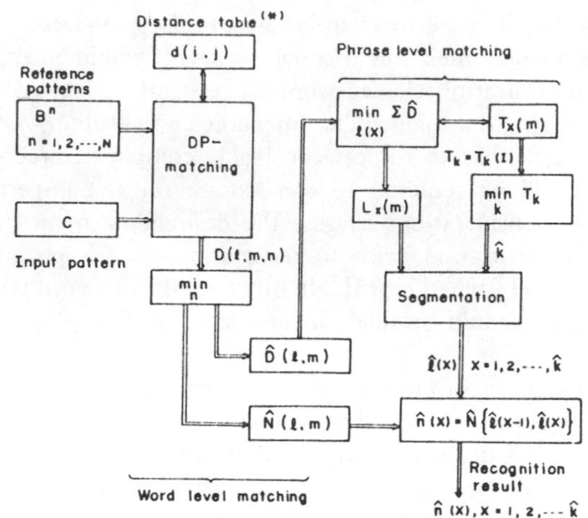

Fig. 3. Schematic diagram of two-level DP-matching. (*) Vector distance table is used only in Algorithm (I).

connected speech level (or phrase level). A partial pattern $C(l, m)$ for input pattern C is defined as follows:

$$C(l, m) = \mathfrak{c}_{l+1}, \mathfrak{c}_{l+2}, \cdots, \mathfrak{c}_m. \tag{9}$$

$(k - 1)$ word boundary timings $l(1), l(2), \cdots, l(k - 1)$ are assumed on the input pattern C time axis while breaking down input pattern C into k partial patterns

$$C = C(l(0), l(1)) \oplus C(l(1), l(2)) \oplus \cdots \oplus C(l(k - 1), l(k)) \tag{10}$$

where $l(0) = 0$ and $l(k) = I$. Asymmetric form distance (2) holds the following property in relation to the speech pattern breakdown:

$$D(C, B^m \oplus B^n) = \min_l [D(C(0, l), B^m) + D(C(l, I), B^n)]. \tag{11}$$

By putting (10) into (8), and repeatedly applying the relation in (11), we obtain

$$T = \min_{k, l(x)} \left[\sum_{x=1}^{k} \min_{n(x)} [D(l(x - 1), l(x), n(x))] \right] \tag{12}$$

where notation $D(l, m, n)$ is an abbreviation of $D(C(l, m), B^n)$, that is, a distance between partial pattern $C(l, m)$ and reference pattern B^n. Note that relation (11) does not hold for the symmetric form distance defined in [4]. Accordingly, (12) will not result. This is the reason why the asymmetric form distance definition (2) is adopted, in spite of its performance inferiority to the symmetric form distance definition.

There are two minimization problems involved in (12). They are efficiently solved by the following two step algorithm. Fig. 3 explains the algorithm.

1) Word Level Matching Process: Calculate and memorize. *Partial distance:*

$$\hat{D}(l, m) = \min_n [D(l, m, n)]. \tag{13}$$

Partial decision:

$$\hat{N}(l, m) = \underset{n}{\operatorname{argmin}}\, [D(l, m, n)] \tag{14}$$

for every combination of l and m, where $0 \leqq l < m \leqq I$. (Operator "$\underset{n}{\text{argmin}}$" means to find optimum parameter n.)

2) Phrase Level Matching Process: Solve the minimization problems

$$T_k = \min_{l(x)} \left[\sum_{x=1}^{k} \hat{D}(l(x-1), l(x)) \right] \tag{15}$$

and then,

$$T = \min_{k}\, [T_k] \tag{16}$$

yielding optimum parameters $k = \hat{k}$ and $l(x) = \hat{l}(x)$, where $x = 1, 2, \cdots, \hat{k}$.

Thus, the minimization problem (8) is broken down into two steps. Resulting optimum parameters $\hat{k}$ and $\hat{l}(x)$, with the above memorized partial decisions $\hat{N}(l, m)$, give the following recognition result.

3) Decision Making Process:

$$\hat{n}(x) = \hat{N}(\hat{l}(x-1), \hat{l}(x)), \tag{17}$$

where

$$x = 1, 2, \cdots, \hat{k}.$$

Algorithm details are given in the following section, where it is shown that both of the above two steps are very efficiently carried out by use of the dynamic programming algorithm. This is the reason why the proposed algorithm is called two-level DP-matching.

III. Practical Two-Level DP-Matching Algorithm

A. Basic Operations

In the word level matching process, (13) and (14) are calculated. The process is divided into two operations: DP-matching computation between partial pattern $C(l, m)$ and reference pattern B^n, and simple comparison of resulting distances $D(l, m, n)$, $n = 1, 2, \cdots, N$. A large amount of the computations is occupied by the DP-matching operation. Distances $D(l, m, n)$ must be calculated for every possible combination of l, m, and n. Fortunately, dynamic programming inherently has a convenient property which simultaneously furnishes solutions for different boundary conditions. This is well explained by the following concrete algorithm description and the i-j plane in Fig. 4. DP-matching for partial patterns, $C(l, m)$ beginning at $i = l + 1$, is executed by a DP-equation (3) calculation with the initial condition $g(l+1, 1) = d(l+1, 1)$ within the adjustment window $l + j - r \leqq i \leqq l + j + r$ up to $j = J^n$. When the above process is completed, we obtain $(2r + 1)$ distances $D(l, m, n) = g(m, J^n)$ simultaneously within the adjustment window at $j = J^n$

$$l + J^n - r \leqq m \leqq l + J^n + r. \tag{18}$$

Originally, adjustment window length was set so that it can cover the actual timing difference between reference pattern and input pattern. There is no need to take into account those

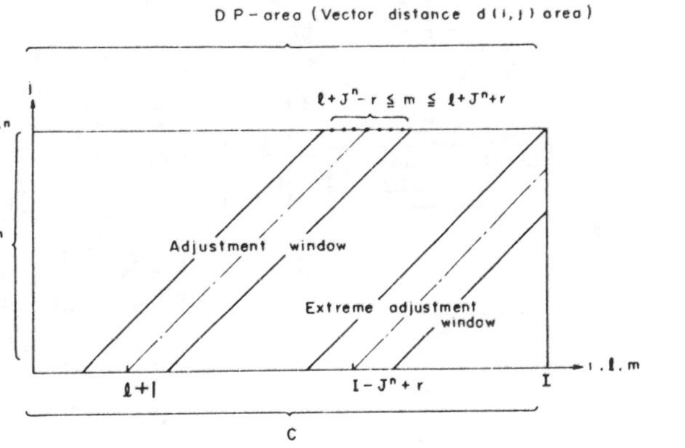

Fig. 4. Word level matching in Algorithm (I). Vector distances are calculated in $1 \leqq i \leqq I$ and $1 \leqq j \leqq J^n$. DP-matching is repeated scanning $0 \leqq l \leqq I - J^n + r$.

partial patterns whose ending points m are separated from the adjustment window (18). Thus, it has been shown that one DP-matching operation gives all necessary distances $D(l, m, n)$ for a current (l, n) value. The above DP-matching property cuts down computation time considerably. The variable l domain is, as is seen from Fig. 4,

$$0 \leqq l \leqq I - J^n + r. \tag{19}$$

Of course, $1 \leqq n \leqq N$.

In the phrase level matching process, minimization problem (15) is solved, again using the dynamic programming algorithm

Initial condition: $T_0(0) = 0$

$$\text{DP-equation: } T_x(m) = \min_{l}\, [\hat{D}(l, m) + T_{x-1}(l)], \tag{20}$$

where $m = 1, 2, \cdots, I$, and $x = 1, 2, \cdots, \bar{k}$. ($\bar{k}$ is a prespecified maximum word number.) Along with the above DP-equation calculation, optimum parameter

$$L_x(m) = \underset{l}{\operatorname{argmin}}\, [\hat{D}(l, m) + T_{x-1}(l)] \tag{21}$$

is determined and memorized to form an $L_x(m)$ table.

After completion of the above process, T_k is given by $T_k = T_k(I)$, where $k = 1, 2, \cdots, \bar{k}$. Optimum word number $\hat{k}$ becomes definite, as

$$\hat{k} = \underset{k}{\operatorname{argmin}}\, [T_k]. \tag{22}$$

(Operator "$\underset{k}{\text{argmin}}$" means to find optimum parameter k.)

Then, optimum word boundaries $\hat{l}(x)$ are decided by refering to the $L_x(m)$ table as

$$\hat{l}(\hat{k}) = I$$

$$\hat{l}(x) = L_{x+1}[\hat{l}(x+1)], x = \hat{k} - 1, \hat{k} - 2, \cdots, 1. \tag{23}$$

Decision is made based on the above resulting optimum word boundaries $\hat{l}(1), \hat{l}(2), \cdots, \hat{l}(k)$, as is shown by (17).

The above described basic operations are executable in different computational ways. Two typical versions of practical algorithms are described in the following. One is a computer simulation suitable algorithm. Instead of occupying relatively

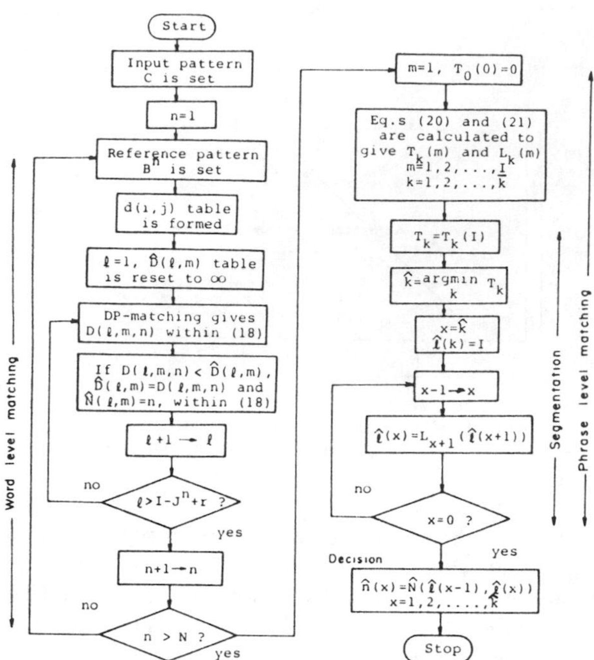

Note - Operator "argmin" means to find optimum parameter k.

Fig. 5. Algorithm (I) flowchart.

large working memories, it performs a two-level DP-matching process with minimum computation effort. The other algorithm is devised for a real-time recognition system. Although this method is rather complicated, much of its operations can be performed in parallel with speech pattern input. Besides, the working memory requirement is quite reasonable.

B. Algorithm (I)

In general, much of the computation for two-level DP-matching is consumed in the word level process, in particular in the DP-equation (3) calculation. In more detail, the calculation of vector distance $d(i, j) = \|c_i - b_j\|$ in the DP-equation (3) takes up a considerable part of the computations because both vectors c_i and b_j are usually more than ten-dimensional. Therefore, duplicate calculations of the same distances $d(i, j)$ should be avoided for any combination of i and j. In the case of nonreal-time recognition, where the recognition process starts after an input speech pattern C has been completely fed into the system, all necessary vector distances $d(i, j)$ can be calculated to form a distance table. The table is two dimensionally organized so that it covers the $I \times J^n$ square shown in Fig. 4. Algorithm details are shown in the Fig. 5 flowchart. The schematic diagram is roughly the same as that of Fig. 3. For the DP-equation (3) calculation, vector distances $d(i, j)$ are provided from this distance table. Therefore, duplicate vector distance calculation does not occur, in spite of the wide intersection of directly consecutive DP-matching adjustment windows $l+j-r \leq i \leq l+j+r$ and $l+j-r+1 \leq i \leq l+j+r+1$. DP-matching with a reference pattern is repeatedly preformed with its adjustment window incrementally shifted, along with partial pattern beginning timing l. As DP-matching has completely scanned the Fig. 4 distance table, or more definitely, when partial pattern beginning point l is incrementally changed to exhaust the region (19), the table is refreshed for the next reference pattern.

TABLE I
TYPICAL DIMENSIONS IN FIVE DIGIT NUMERICAL RECOGNITION CASE*

Parameter (unit)	Exhaustive Comparison	Two Level DP
Input pattern length I (frame)	100	100
Reference pattern length J (frame)	100 (5-digit connected)	20 (per digit average)
J_{max} (frame)	-	25
J_{min} (frame)	-	15
Vocabulary size N (word)	10	10
Number of words connected K (word)	5	5
Window length (frame)	40 (=0.4xJ)	8 (=0.4xJ)

* Speech pattern sampling period is assumed to be 18 ms.

In this algorithm version phrase level matching begins after the word level matching process is accomplished. Therefore, complete sets of partial distances $\hat{D}(l, m)$ and partial decisions $\hat{N}(l, m)$ must be memorized so that they can be accessed during the phrase level matching and decision making processes. Address l, or partial pattern beginning timing, takes values within (19). Address m, or partial pattern ending timing, depending on l value, takes value within (18) for each reference pattern B^n. Therefore, address m must cover their union

$$l + J_{\min} - r \leq m \leq l + J_{\max} + r \tag{24}$$

where $J_{\min} = \min_n [J^n]$ and $J_{\max} = \max_n [J^n]$. Referring to Table I, a numerical example of an actual case, it can be seen that the memory requirement for these two-dimensionally organized tables is of some considerable size (2900 words for each table, which may further grow in proportion to input pattern length I). In addition, a distance table and input pattern buffer occupy a sizable memory area. However, these memory requirements are not so unreasonable when the algorithm is coded on a general purpose computer. Therefore, it can be said that this algorithm is especially suitable to computer-simulated experiment application.

With relation to the phrase level matching process, there is little to supplement. When (20) and (21) are calculated, parameter l should be in

$$m - J_{\max} - r \leq l \leq m - J_{\min} + r, \tag{25}$$

which comes from the condition in (24). Obviously, those partial distances $\hat{D}(l, m)$, for which $l < 0$, should be counted out. Or, more precisely, parameter l should be within $\max [0, m - J_{\max} - r] \leq l \leq m - J_{\min} + r$.

C. Algorithm (II)

It is obvious that a DP-matching process can be executed in a time-reversed fashion. The initial condition is given at (m, J^n). Time-reversed DP-equation (which is obtained from (3) by substituting $i+1, i+2, j+1$ and $j+2$ for $i-1, i-2, j-1$ and $j-2$, respectively) is recurrently computed in descending order with relation to i and j. Then, distance $D(l, m, n) =$

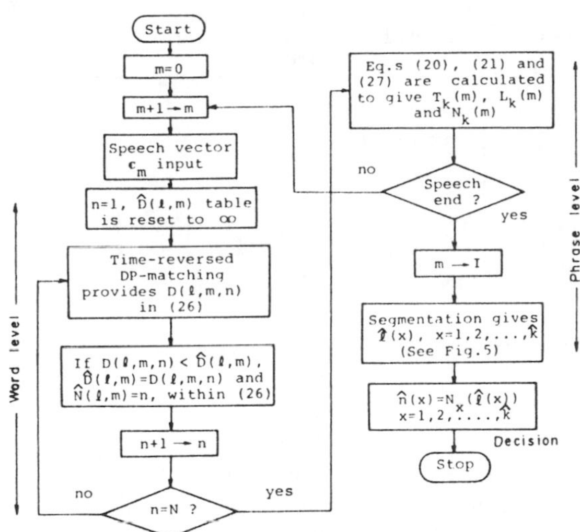

Fig. 6. Algorithm (II) flowchart.

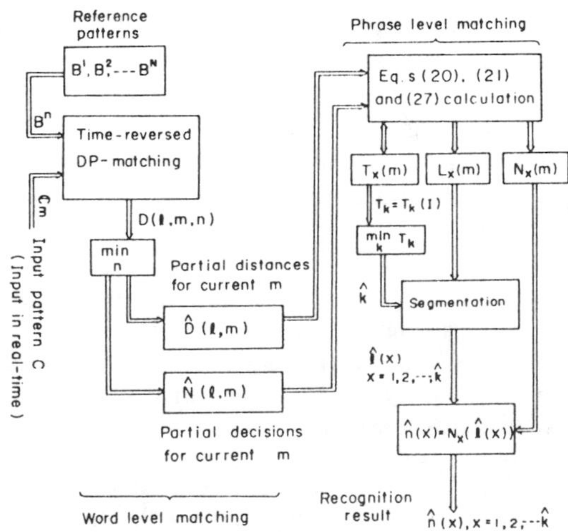

Fig. 7. Schematic diagram of Algorithm (II).

$g(l+1, 1)$ is yielded for each l within

$$m - J^n - r \leqq l \leqq m - J^n + r. \tag{26}$$

When the above DP-matching processes have been repeatedly performed for all reference patterns B^n, partial distances $\hat{D}(l, m)$ and partial decisions $\hat{N}(l, m)$ are completely furnished within (25) for a current m value. In phrase level matching, $T_x(m)$ in (20) can be computed as soon as all partial distances $\hat{D}(l, m)$, for which l values are within (25), are prepared.

These considerations lead to a real-time processing algorithm, shown in the Fig. 6 flowchart and Fig. 7 schematic diagram. Word level and phrase level matching operations proceed in parallel, synchronized with input pattern vector c_m feed-in-timing. Partial decisions $\hat{N}(l, m)$, also, are subjected to processing along with (20) calculation, as follows:

$$N_x(m) = \hat{N}(\hat{l}, m) \tag{27}$$

where $\hat{l}(=L_x(m))$ is the optimum l value which attains (20) minimization.

Buffer memories for $\hat{D}(l, m)$ and $\hat{N}(l, m)$, for which address l is within (25), can be refreshed every time new input vector C_m is fed in. Therefore, each of them now is of one-dimensiοal organization, and occupies only $(J_{\max} - J_{\min} + 2r + 1)$ words [this comes from (25)]. Besides, there is no need for buffering whole input pattern C nor whole vector distances $d(i, j)$.

In this algorithm a word level matching process, which intrinsically consumes many computations, is embedded into the input utterance duration. Therefore, a relatively large amount of computation requirement, caused by duplicate calculation of vector distance $d(i, j)$, does not matter so much in practice. This real-time processing feature, as well as the smallest memory requirement, implies that this algorithm is the most promising one for real-time system implementation.

D. Efficiency Evaluation

Here, the proposed algorithm efficiency is quantitatively analyzed in comparison with the case where the minimization problem in (8) is solved by Fig. 2's exhaustive comparison method. The numerical example in Table I is used as a typical case. In the exhaustive comparison method, $N^k = 10^5$ connected reference patterns are synthesized to be subjected to the DP-matching operation. It is assumed that the number of words k in the input pattern is known to be 5. The adjustment window length r is set so that it covers a ±40 percent timing difference, or $r = 0.4J$. Therefore, as was described in Section II-B, approximately 8.1×10^3 times DP-equation computations are consumed for each synthesized reference pattern. Thus, total DP-equation computation is estimated to amount to 8.1×10^8. In the proposed method, about $I \times N$ times DP-matching process must be repeated. Reference patterns are now of word units ($J = 20$). Therefore, it is estimated that total DP-equation iterations are about 3.4×10^5 times. Thus, it is known that the efficiency of the proposed method is more than 10^3 times as high as that of the exhaustive comparison method.

The above evaluation is made using the comparison scale of DP-equation iteration times. It is obvious that Algorithm (I) is much faster than the above estimation because duplicate vector distance calculation is omitted. In the Algorithm (II) case, the above estimation holds as long as the computation amount is concerned. However, it should be noted that, in Algorithm (II), much of its computations can be performed in parallel with real-time speech pattern input.

There are many varieties of practical algorithms differing from the ones described above. However, it seems that those which employ less working memories take more computations. The two above algorithms appear to be the most suitable ones for the computer simulation system and for a real-time system, respectively.

E. Word Number Specification Technique

It is feared, in connected word recognition, that word number decision errors might eventually occur. Here, "word number decision errors" means such case where two-word connected speech is recognized as three words, for example. Differing from substitution error, this is a problem peculiar to connected word recognition. Where input format (word connection number) is prespecified, there is a way to eliminate or diminish this type of error. Let word connection number k be specified as $k \in K$, where K is a set of integers. Parameter k in (22) is subjected to condition $k \in K$. When the word connection number is uniquely specified, as $K = \{3\}$ for example, word number decision error can be completely excluded. If $K = \{1, 3, 5\}$ or $K = \{2, 4, 6\}$ for example, then much of the word number decision errors will be prevented. At least, insertion or deletion of one word will be eliminated.

IV. Experiments and Results

A. Experiment Outline

In order to quantitatively evaluate the two-level DP-matching algorithm, several recognition experiments were conducted. The experimental system used was quite the same as that used in the previous report [4] (NEAC-3100 computer and vocoder type spectrum analyzer), except that a 16-channel spectrum analyzer was used instead of a 10-channel one. Experiments were conducted in four parts. In the first three parts, Japanese digit words (See Sakoe and Chiba [4]) were used as the test vocabulary. Digit words, though being few in number, are one of the most difficult word sets to recognize, when connectedly spoken. Each of them is relatively short in duration. Accordingly, they suffer heavy distortions from coarticulation. In the final part of the experiments, a 50 geographical name vocabulary was tested.

The recognition algorithm used in these experiments was Algorithm (I). It occupied about 20 kW memories, including those for the working area, and not including those for reference pattern storage. The word level process was coded by assembler language, and the phrase level and decision making processes were coded by Fortran language. Adjustment window length r was set equal to 8 (which covered the utmost ±144 ms timing difference) by some preliminary experiments. Reference patterns were adapted for each speaker. More precisely, one (in the case of geographical name recognition) or two (in the case of digit recognition) complete repetitions of isolated utterances made by each speaker were used as reference patterns.

B. Experiment (I)

The objective of this experiment was to compare the proposed method with the previous method [2], [3]. The speech data used were three-digit continuous numerals spoken by one male speaker. 200 utterances, which include a total of 600 digits, were subjected to a recognition test. When the previous method was used, ten of them were misrecognized, or digit error rate was $10/600 = 1.7$ percent. The proposed method, on the other hand, made no error. This comparison established the present algorithm superiority.

According to visual inspection, it was observed that the word boundary decision was made quite reasonably in most cases. Relatively large errors were observed when the same vowels appeared on both sides of a word boundary (for example, 2 - 1, /*ni - it ʃ i*/). It could be understood that accurate segmentation is very difficult in such cases. In spite of these segmentation errors, no erroneous recognition occurred. This is probably because the high time-normalization capability of the present algorithm makes it possible to recognize the abnormal partial pattern with incorrect endpoints.

TABLE II
EXPERIMENT (II) RESULT (FOR ONE TO FOUR DIGIT NUMERALS SPOKEN BY FIVE PERSONS)

Number of Digits Connected		1	2	3	4	Personal Accuracy (%)
Speaker	A(*) — Error Count	0	0	0	0	100
	B(*)	0	0	1	0	99.8
	C	0	0	0	1	99.8
	D	0	2	0	2	99.2
	E	0	0	0	5	99.0
Averaged Accuracy (%)		100	99.6	99.9	99.2	99.6

* : Well-experienced speaker

C. Experiment (II)

The objectives of this experiment were to investigate the algorithm performance in more general cases. Speech data, including up to four-digit numerals, were gathered from five male speakers. Each speaker made 50 utterances for each of one- (isolated) to four-digit connection. Recordings were made by reading a randomly ordered numeral list in a well noise-controlled room. 200 utterances, which include 500 digits, were recorded for each speaker. Thus, a total of 1000 utterances, or 2500 digits uttered by five speakers were subjected to a recognition test.

Experimental results are shown in Table II for each speaker. It is observed that connectedly-spoken numerals are recognized with as high as 99.6 percent accuracy. With relation to speaker individuality, it should be noted that no speaker made more than one percent error.

D. Experiment (III)

In this experiment the effectiveness of the word number specification technique was investigated [7]. When two persons tested a total of 800 numerical data (one- to four-digit) without word number specification, 16 recognition errors occurred, including 13 word number decision errors and three substitution errors. Then, the word number specification was employed, where specification was given by $K = \{1, 3, 5\}$ when isolated or three-digit numerals were tested, or by $K = \{2, 4\}$ otherwise. In this case, all the word number decision errors were eliminated without increasing any substitution error. Thus, it has been shown that the word number specification is a practical way of improving recognition system reliability.

D. Experiment (IV)

In the final part of the experiments nonnumerical word recognition was investigated. A 50 geographic name vocabulary appearing in [4] was used. One speaker made 200 utterances in the three-word connected manner. All of them were correctly recognized. It should be noted that such confusing word pairs as "Wakayama"-"Okayama," "Tokushima"-"Fukushima," and "Hyogo"-"Kyoto" were correctly recognized in the connected speech context.

V. Discussions

Experiment (I) results show that the present connected word recognition algorithm gives much better performance than the previous algorithm [2], [3]. The algorithm performance was extensively tested through Experiments (II), (III), and (IV). High recognition performance of the present algorithm has been established. High recognition accuracy of the algorithm should be attributed in part to the fact that preliminary segmentation is excluded from the recognition process. Word boundaries are determined in principle so that the optimum matching is attained between input pattern and connected reference patterns. This unique property, along with the high time-normalization capability, made it possible to recognize an arbitrarily selected word set with a practically high accuracy.

With relation to the computational aspect, the proposed algorithm may not be very concise or easy. In the experiments, NEAC-3100 computer (index modified addition time is 8 μs) took about ten seconds per digit. Thus, in spite of computational technique improvement throughout Section II and III, a considerable amount of computation time is still necessitated. Fortunately, recent high-speed integrated circuit devices and a pipeline processing technique have made it feasible to realize real-time recognition. Actually, a real-time recognition system has been constructed for practical use. It has been proved that it recognizes a 120 word vocabulary connected speech in real-time, based on Algorithm (II). The details of this real-time system have been reported by Tsuruta *et al.* [6].

Present investigations have been made with the target of a speaker-adaptive-type recognition system. However, the proposed algorithm is quite general, and it seems effective enough to be applied to speaker-independent (or training-free) recognition as a basic strategy. Two-level DP-matching will be able to solve a certain part of the problems which will appear along the time axis.

VI. Conclusions

A connected word recognition principle, which needs no preliminary segmentation, has been described. The principle realizes an optimum recognition in the sense that recognition is performed by attaining the best match between input pattern and artificially synthesized connected reference patterns. Two execution algorithms were derived, suitably applicable to the computer simulation system and the real-time recognition system, respectively. In these algorithms dynamic programming was effectively employed in two steps: first, to normalize intraword time-axis fluctuation, and then to make interword boundary decision. High-level recognition performance was proved by recognition experiments. Noticeable features of the algorithm are as follows:

1) The intrinsically unreliable preliminary segmentation process is completely discarded. Word boundary decision is accomplished simultaneously with word category decision.

2) Time-normalization capability is inherenthy high by use of dynamic programming-based time warping (DP-matching).

3) The algorithm is fast enough to realize a real-time system when recent high-speed digital hardware techniques are employed.

4) The algorithm is quite general in the sense that it is independent of vocabulary, language, and word connection number. High-level recognition performance comes from the above features 1) and 2).

Acknowledgment

The author wishes to thank Y. Kato and S. Chiba for their guidance and encouragement throughout this research. He also thanks S. Tsuruta for his help in conducting a certain part of the experiments. Finally, this paper has been improved by the insightful comments of anonymous referees.

References

[1] H. Sakoe and S. Chiba, "A similarity evaluation of speech patterns by dynamic programming" (in Japanese), *Dig. 1970 Nat. Meeting of Inst. Electron. Commun. Eng. Japan*, Aug. 1970.

[2] ——, "A dynamic programming approach to continuous speech recognition," presented at 7th ICA, Aug. 1971, Paper 20 C 13.

[3] ——, "Recognition of continuously spoken words based on time-normalization by dynamic programming," *J. Acoust. Soc. Japan*, vol. 77, Sept. 1971.

[4] ——, "Dynamic programming algorithm optimization for spoken word recognition," *IEEE Trans. Acoust., Speech, Signal Processing*, vol. ASSP-26, Feb. 1978.

[5] R. Nakatsu and M. Kohda, "Computer recognition of spoken connected words based on VCV syllable unit" (in Japanese), Rep. 1974 Autumn Meeting of Acoust. Soc. Japan, Oct. 1974.

[6] S. Tsuruta, H. Sakoe, and S. Chiba, "DP-100 connected speech recognition system," presented at INTELCOM 1979, Feb. 1979.

[7] H. Sakoe, "A connected word recognition algorithm with reduced word number decision error," Rep. 1978 Spring Meeting of Acoust. Soc. Japan, May 1978.

[8] S. Chiba, M. Watri, and T. Watanabe, "A speaker-independent word recognition system," presented at 4th Int. Joint Conf. on Pattern Recognition, Nov. 1978.

[9] M. R. Sambur and L. R. Rabiner, "A statistical decision approach to the recognition of connected digits," *IEEE Trans. Acoust., Speech, Signal Processing*, vol. ASSP-24, Dec. 1976.

The Use of a One-Stage Dynamic Programming Algorithm for Connected Word Recognition

HERMANN NEY

Abstract—This paper is of tutorial nature and describes a one-stage dynamic programming algorithm for the problem of connected word recognition. The algorithm to be developed is essentially identical to one presented by Vintsyuk [1] and later by Bridle and Brown [2]; but the notation and the presentation have been clarified. The derivation used for optimally time synchronizing a test pattern, consisting of a sequence of connected words, is straightforward and simple in comparison with other approaches decomposing the pattern matching problem into several levels. The approach presented relies basically on parameterizing the time warping path by a single index and on exploiting certain path constraints both in the word interior and at the word boundaries. The resulting algorithm turns out to be significantly more efficient than those proposed by Sakoe [3] as well as Myers and Rabiner [4], while providing the same accuracy in estimating the best possible matching string. Its most important feature is that the computational expenditure per word is independent of the number of words in the input string. Thus, it is well suited for recognizing comparatively long word sequences and for real-time operation. Furthermore, there is no need to specify the maximum number of words in the input string. The practical implementation of the algorithm is discussed; it requires no heuristic rules and no overhead. The algorithm can be modified to deal with syntactic constraints in terms of a finite state syntax.

I. Introduction

ONE of the most promising approaches to connected word recognition is the technique of dynamic programming [5]. For isolated word recognition, several authors have shown that the problem of nonlinearly time aligning speech patterns with no fixed time scale can be efficiently solved by dynamic programming [6]-[8]. Vintsyuk [1], Bridle and Brown [2], and Sakoe [3] have formulated the connected word recognition problem as an optimization problem similar to the isolated word recognition problem. One of the attractive features of this formulation is the small amount of *a priori* information and training that is required: only the reference patterns for each individual word need to be known. Another advantage is that the three operations of word boundary detection, nonlinear time alignment, and recognition are performed simultaneously; thus, recognition errors due to errors in word boundary detection or to time alignment errors are not possible. The algorithm is forced to match the complete words, and as a result of this, the word boundaries are determined automatically. In comparison, methods based on prespecified segmentation rules [9] or on statistical estimation for segmentation [10] require either detailed knowledge of the vocabulary dependent segmentation rules or an extensive training of the segmentation algorithm. There have been other systems like DRAGON [11] and HARPY [12], which model the recognition problem as an optimization problem as well, but which are based on subword units for the recognition as opposed to whole word templates. Meanwhile, a number of systems for connected word recognition have been developed which are based on the algorithm described in this paper [13]-[16].

Although Vintsyuk had formulated his algorithm already in 1971, his algorithm was not commonly known. Thus, later, Sakoe independently derived a two-level algorithm to solve the optimization problem. On the first level, all reference patterns are systematically matched against all possible subsections of the pattern. This matching operation is the same as for the nonlinear time alignment in isolated word recognition. On the second level, using the distance scores generated, the optimal estimate of the unknown sequence of words is obtained by minimizing the total distance of all possible word sequences. In a recent paper, Myers and Rabiner derived another solution to the optimization problem of connected word recognition [4]. They made use of the property that the matching of all possible word sequences can be performed by successive concatenation of reference patterns. Thus they obtained what they called a level building algorithm.

This paper is essentially tutorial. Its purpose is to present a clear description of the connected word recognition problem and its solution by a one-stage dynamic programming algorithm, to discuss the advantages of the one-stage algorithm and to compare it with other algorithms. The one-stage algorithm is basically identical to the algorithms given by both Vintsyuk [1] and by Bridle and Brown [2]. However, a straightforward formulation and derivation of the algorithm is given. The derivation is based on parameterizing the time warping path by a single index and treating the optimization criterion directly as a function of this time warping path. This approach is much simpler than the approaches used by both Sakoe [3] and by Myers and Rabiner [4], and it results in a computationally more efficient algorithm. The constraints imposed on the path are described in terms of two types of transition rules: transition rules for the word interior and for the word boundaries. Carrying out the optimization using these path constraints and dynamic programming leads to a one-stage algorithm, for which there are no multiple optimization levels as in the other approaches. Unlike the level building of Myers and Rabiner, the one-stage algorithm needs no prespecified maximum number of words in the input string. What is most important, the

Manuscript received February 15, 1982; revised February 7, 1983, July 29, 1983, and October 14, 1983.

The author is with Philips GmbH Forschungslaboratorium Hamburg, D-2000 Hamburg 54, Germany.

0096-3518/84/0400-0263$01.00 © 1984 IEEE

one-stage algorithm requires no more computational expenditure than the corresponding case of isolated word recognition with no adjustment window. The implementational aspects of the one-stage algorithm are described, and its computational and storage requirements are compared with the two-level algorithm of Sakoe and the level building algorithm of Myers and Rabiner. Finally, the algorithm is modified to deal with a finite state syntax.

II. Formulation of the Pattern Matching Problem

In the following, we will present a simple approach to the pattern matching problem for connected word recognition, the reason being that the simplification due to parameterizing the time warping path by a single index is most significant and provides some insights that immediately reveal how to arrive at a practical implementation of the algorithm.

Assume an unknown input or test pattern consisting of $i = 1, \cdots, N$ time frames, where a time frame is represented by a vector of features. The input pattern is known to be composed of individual words, which are chosen from a prespecified vocabulary. The words of the vocabulary correspond to a set of K reference patterns or templates obtained from single word utterances spoken in isolation. The word templates are distinguished by the index $k = 1, \cdots, K$. The time frames of the template k are denoted as $j = 1, \cdots, J(k)$, where $J(k)$ is the length of the template k.

The ultimate goal of connected word recognition is to determine that sequence $q(1), \cdots q(R)$ of templates that best matches the input pattern, where the criterion of match needs further specification. The concatenation of the templates $q(1), \cdots, q(R)$ is referred to as "super" reference pattern. Since this unknown "super" reference pattern may be handled like a single utterance pattern, the matching procedure is the same as in the case of isolated word recognition. Based on this consideration, it is obvious what specification and constraints to apply to the time warping procedure. Instead of decomposing the matching procedure into a single template matching level and a word string constructing level, as it was done in the other approaches mentioned [3], [4], we want to treat the matching procedure as a one-stage procedure [1], [2].

The basic idea is illustrated in Fig. 1. The time frames i of the test pattern and the time frames j of each template k define a set of grid points (i, j, k). Each grid point (i, j, k) is associated with a local distance measure $d(i, j, k)$ defining a measure of dissimilarity between the corresponding acoustic events. The connected word recognition problem can be regarded as one of finding the path through the set of grid points (i, j, k) which provides the best match between the test pattern and the unknown sequence of templates. The path is often referred to as time warping path. The three parameters i, j, k are of different characters: the time parameters i and j tend to change more or less uniformly in ascending order, whereas the template number k is constant for comparatively long subsections of the path and can change only after the path has passed a template boundary with $j = J(k)$. However, for deriving the algorithm, it is crucial to treat the three parameters as mathematically equivalent. Formally, the path W is given as a sequence of grid points

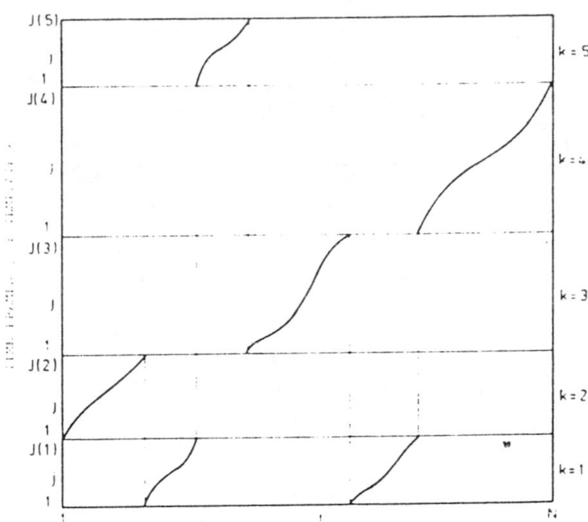

Fig. 1. The connected word recognition problem. The optimal path provides the unknown sequence of words as well as the nonlinear time alignment between the corresponding sequence of templates and the input pattern.

$$W = (w(1), w(2), \cdots, w(l), \cdots, w(L)) \tag{1}$$

where $w(l) = (i(l), j(l), k(l))$ and l is the path parameter for indexing the ordered set of path elements. The criterion for the matching procedure is the global distance, i.e., the sum over the local distances along a given path. The problem of connected word recognition can now be stated as the minimization problem

$$\min_W \sum_l d(w(l)) \tag{2}$$

i.e., minimize the global distance with respect to all allowed paths. From the best path, the associated sequence of templates can be uniquely recovered as is clear from Fig. 1.

In addition to minimizing the global distance, the time warping path is required to obey certain continuity constraints implied by the physical nature of the patterns to be matched. These constraints apply to consecutive points of the path. The constraints result from the requirement of the preservation of time order along the time axes and from the requirement of time continuity implying that no time frame, i.e., acoustic event, be omitted in the sequence $i(1), \cdots, i(l), \cdots, i(L)$. The continuity constraints determine the possible preceding points for a given path point (i, j, k) and are therefore also referred to as transition rules. A possible disadvantage of the global distance definition as given in (2) is that the global distance depends on the path length, and thus shorter paths are favored. This problem will be studied later in connection with the details of the dynamic programming algorithm.

Due to the concatenation of single word templates to a "super" reference pattern, it is convenient to distinguish between two types of transition rules: transition rules in the template interior called within-template transition rules and

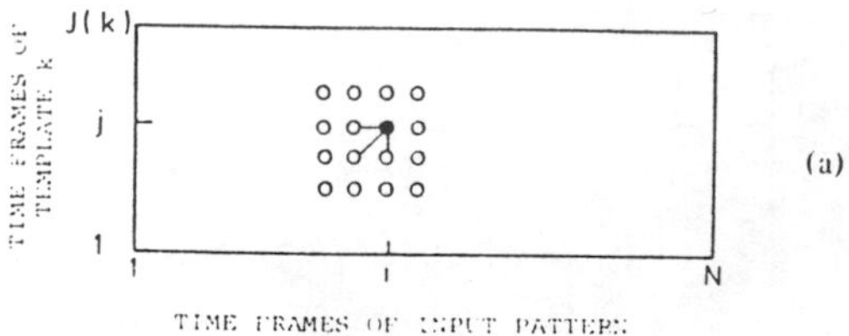

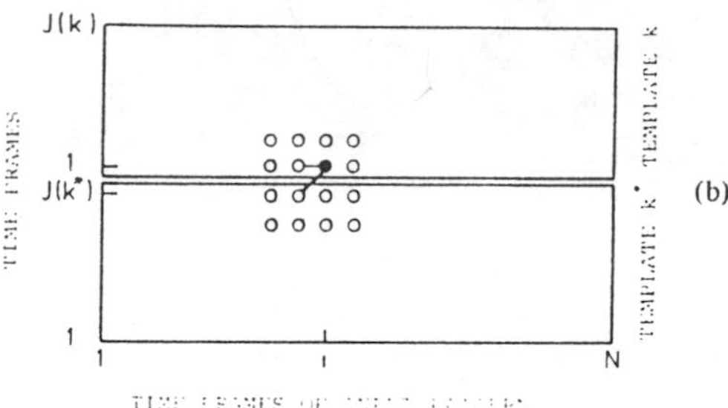

Fig. 2. (a) Within-template transition rules. (b) Illustration of between-template transition rules.

transition rules at the template boundaries called between-template transition rules. These two types of transition rules are illustrated in Fig. 2. For within-template transitions the following relation holds between two consecutive points:

$$\text{if } w(l) = (i, j, k), j > 1, \text{ then}$$

$$w(l-1) \in \{(i-1, j, k), (i-1, j-1, k), (i, j-1, k)\} \qquad (3a)$$

i.e., the point (i, j, k) can be reached only from one of the points $(i-1, j, k)$, $(i-1, j-1, k)$, $(i, j-1, k)$ as shown in Fig. 2(a). For transition at template boundaries where $j = 1$, the between-template transition rules are shown in Fig. 2(b):

$$\text{if } w(l) = (i, 1, k), \text{ then}$$

$$w(l-1) \in \{(i-1, 1, k);$$

$$(i-1, J(k^*), k^*): k^* = 1, \cdots, K\}. \qquad (3b)$$

Since the point $(i, 1, k)$ corresponds to the beginning frame of the template k, it is necessary that it can be reached from the ending frame of any template k^* including k itself. The between-template transition rules depend heavily on how the single words can be combined and must therefore be changed in the case of syntactic constraints as will be shown later. The coarticulation problem at the word boundaries is tackled by matching the interior parts of the words such that the word boundaries are correctly treated automatically. Finally, there are endpoint constraints requiring that the time warping path begins at a beginning frame of any template and ends at the ending frame of any template.

III. Derivation of the Algorithm Using Dynamic Programming

In this section, an algorithm for solving the minimization problem (2) and thus finding the best path W is derived by use of dynamic programming. The concept of dynamic programming is especially useful in solving combinatorial optimization problems of the type of (2) which can be broken down into a sequence of optimization steps and in which there are only a small number of possible choices or decisions to be taken at each optimization step [17]. The philosophy of dynamic programming is based primarily on the "principle of optimality" which is due to R. Bellman [5]. Its application to the minimization problem (2) says: If the best path goes through a grid point (i, j, k), then the best path includes, as a portion of it, the best partial path to the grid point (i, j, k).

In order to utilize this "principle of optimality," we define a minimum accumulated distance $D(i, j, k)$ along any path to the grid point (i, j, k). Since the accumulated distance $D(i, j, k)$ is a sum of local distances, it can be decomposed in the same way as the path into the accumulated distance along the best path to its predecessors and the local distance associated with the grid point (i, j, k) itself. To obtain the best path, we have to select the predecessor with the minimum total distance. Thus for the template interior, i.e., $j > 1$, we obtain the following using the within-template transition rules (3a):

$$D(i, j, k) = d(i, j, k) + \min\{D(i-1, j, k),$$

$$D(i-1, j-1, k), D(i, j-1, k)\}. \qquad (4a)$$

At the template boundaries with $j = 1$, the between-template transition rules (3b) yield

$$D(i, 1, k) = d(i, 1, k) + \min\{D(i-1, 1, k);$$

$$D(i-1, J(k^*), k^*): k^* = 1, \cdots, K\}. \qquad (4b)$$

For grid points at the beginning frame of the test pattern, the transition rules must be modified, since there is no preceding frame on the time axis of the test pattern. A grid point $(1, j, k)$ can be reached only from a grid point $(1, j-1, k)$.

Equations (4a) and (4b) are the typical recurrence relations of dynamic programming. By using these recurrence relations, the accumulated distances $D(i, j, k)$ can be recursively evaluated point by point. Evidently, the recursive evaluation is made possible by the transition rules which imply an ordered arrangement of grid points.

By way of summary, a complete algorithm for connected word recognition is given as follows.

Step 1) Initialize $D(1, j, k) = \sum_{n=1}^{j} d(1, n, k)$.

Step 2)
- a) For $i = 2, \cdots, N$, do steps 2b-2e.
- b) For $k = 1, \cdots, K$, do steps 2c-2e.
- c) $D(i, 1, k) = d(i, 1, k) + \min\{D(i-1, 1, k); D(i-1, J(k^*), k^*): k^* = 1, \cdots, K\}$.
- d) For $j = 2, \cdots, J(k)$, do step 2e.
- e) $D(i, j, k) = d(i, j, k) + \min\{D(i-1, j, k), D(i-1, j-1, k), D(i, j-1, k)\}$.

Step 3) Trace back the best path from the grid point at a template ending frame with minimum total distance using the array $D(i, j, k)$ of accumulated distances.

Step 3 of this algorithm recovers the unknown sequence of words in the input pattern by tracing back the decisions taken by the "minimum" operator at each grid point. For this backtracking procedure, the entire array of accumulated distances $D(i, j, k)$ must have been stored during the recursion. Although this storage requirement of the algorithm is not necessarily intractable even on today's microprocessors, it will be shown in the following section that the storage requirement can be significantly reduced by special techniques.

A drawback of the algorithm formulated so far results from the dependence of the global criterion (2) on the path length. An easy consideration shows that for path segments with a slope greater than 1, the number of local distances per input frame increases, whereas it remains constant for path segments with a slope smaller than 1. Ideally, the global criterion should be independent of the slope of the path in order to allow all types of time axis distortion. At the same time, however, the optimal path is likely to deviate only rarely from the diagonal direction, i.e., to have a slope 1, since speaking rate variations tend to be small. There is no general solution known to this problem. Sakoe and Chiba [8] describe two within-word transition rules for which the path slopes are always $\frac{1}{2}$, 1, or 2, and the path length is equal to the number of test frames processed. The Itakura constraints [7] lead to the same path length normalization, i.e., no time distortion penalties for slopes between $\frac{1}{2}$ and 2. Locally variable penalties for time distortion can be introduced as illustrated in Fig. 3. Depending on the three directions horizontal, diagonal and vertical, the local distance is multiplied by the weights $(1 + a)$, 1, and b prior to evaluating the dynamic programming recursion:

$$\begin{aligned} D(i,j,k) = \min \{&(1+a) \cdot d(i,j,k) + D(i-1,j,k), \\ &d(i,j,k) + D(i-1,j-1,k), \\ &b \cdot d(i,j-1,k) + D(i,j-1,k)\}. \end{aligned}$$

The reformulation of the global criterion (2) is omitted since it is trivial.

Fig. 3 indicates also what is the number of local distances per input frame for slopes 2, 1, and $\frac{1}{2}$. Typical values of the weights a and b are in the order of 1, e.g., $a = 1$ and $b = \frac{1}{2}$.

IV. Practical Implementation of the Algorithm

The final aim of the algorithm is to determine the unknown sequence of words. In order to accomplish this, it is sufficient to know at which time frame i of the test pattern the best path has started for a given ending point of a given template k.

The details of the best path within the templates are of no primary importance to the recognition problem. Another important aspect for reducing the storage requirement is evident from the structure of loops in the algorithm presented in the previous section. To perform the dynamic programming recursions for a time frame i, only a small portion from the complete array $D(i, j, k)$ of accumulated distances is needed, namely the elements corresponding to the preceding time frame i: $\{D(i-1, j, k): k = 1, \cdots, K; j = 1, \cdots, J(k)\}$. The grid points associated with these elements form a vertical cut through the time plane of Fig. 1. This column of storage will be simply referred to as column array of accumulated distances and denoted as $D(j, k)$. Thus, using only one column of storage from the array $D(i, j, k)$, the dynamic programming recursions (3a) and (3b) can be carried out by proceeding along

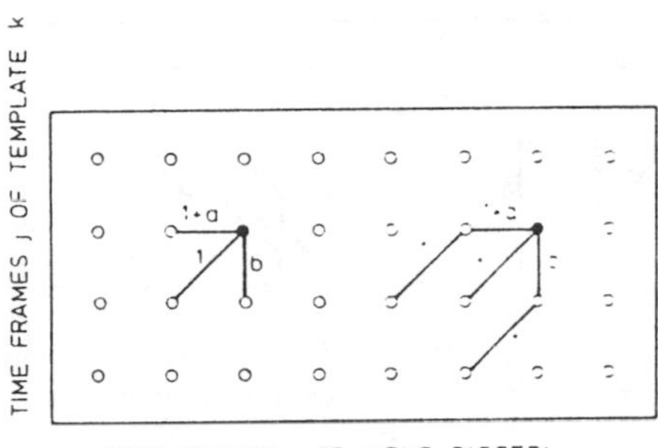

Fig. 3. Time distortion penalties as provided by slope dependent weights $1 + a$, 1, b: The number of local distances per input frame is thus $1 + (a/2)$ for $\frac{1}{2}$, 1 for slope 1 and $1 + b$ for slope 2.

the time axis of the test pattern and updating the storage column point by point.

This technique for storage reduction is analogous to the case of isolated word recognition, where all that is wanted is the minimum total distance as a matching score between the test pattern and the template. The essential difference, however, is that some form of backtracking must be added to enable the algorithm to recover the unknown sequence of words. Bridle *et al.* [13] refer to the following technique for backtracking as Vintsyuk's algorithm [1]. A similar backtracking procedure was proposed by Myers and Rabiner [4]. The backtracking information must be recorded during the evaluation of the dynamic programming recursion. For the path leading to the grid point (i, j, k), there is a unique starting point at the line $j = 1$ in the same template k. Hence, for each grid point, a backpointer $B(i, j, k)$ can be defined as that value of the ending frame of the preceding word from which the path to the grid point (i, j, k) has come. Fig. 4 illustrates the basic concept of the backpointers for the three preceding grid points of the grid point (i, j, k). Originally, the array of backpointers depends on the index triple (i, j, k) in the same way as the array $D(i, j, k)$ of accumulated distances.

Since, as stated above, we are only interested in the backpointers of the grid points $(i, J(k), k)$ at the template boundaries, we can reduce the array of backpointers $B(i, j, k)$ to a column array of backpointers $B(j, k)$ (in Fig. 1) as in the case of the array $D(i, j, k)$, and update it point by point according to where the best path has come from. A "from template" array $T(i)$ must be used to record the index k_0 of the template with minimum accumulated distance at its ending frame $J(k_0)$ for each frame i of the test pattern. Formally, this is expressed as

$$\begin{aligned} T(i) = k_0 &= \operatorname{argmin} \{D(i, J(k), k) \\ &\mathrel{\hat{=}} D(J(k), k): k = 1, \cdots, K\}, \end{aligned}$$

where the operator "argmin $\{f(x): x = x_0, \cdots, x_n\}$" means to find the optimum argument x which minimizes $f(x)$. Additionally, a "from frame" array $F(i)$ must be introduced in order to retain the backpointer $B(J(k_0), k_0) \mathrel{\hat{=}} B(i, J(k_0), k_0)$ to the ending frame of the preceding word after the test pattern i has been processed. Thus the "from frame" array $F(i)$ keeps track of the frame along the test pattern time axis from which the best path to the grid point $(i, J(k_0), k_0)$ has come. In other words, the "from frame" array keeps track of

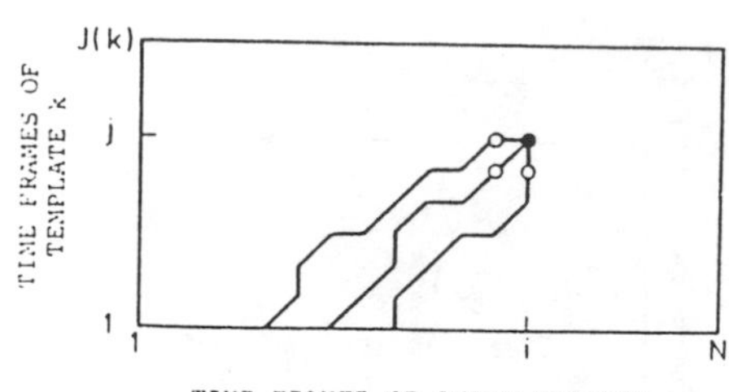

Fig. 4. Backpointers from the three preceding grid points (i, j, k) to their corresponding starting frames.

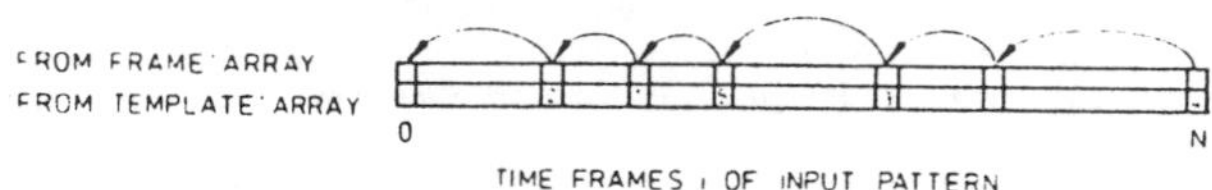

Fig. 5. The backtracking procedure.

potential word boundaries, and the "from template" array keeps track of the respective decision about the recognized word.

The concept of the "from template" and of the "from frame" arrays is closely related to the between-template transition rules, which are the characteristic of this approach presented as opposed to the other approaches. It is crucial to realize that for each time frame i, only the best template, i.e., the template with minimum accumulated distance at its ending frame, and the corresponding word boundary must be kept track of in order to be able to determine the optimal global path.

Fig. 5 shows an example of the backtracking procedure for recovering the unknown sequence of words for the example in Fig. 1. For the last time frame of the test pattern, the "from template" array records the template with minimum total distance at its ending frame. The "from frame" array points to the ending frame of the preceding word on the test pattern time axis. For this ending point, the "from template" array again contains the index of the best preceding word and the corresponding "from frame" array points again back to the ending frame of the preceding word. Obviously, the "from frame" array contains indices into itself and the "from template" array. This backtracking is continued until the zeroth frame of the test pattern has been reached. Thus for the optimal word boundaries we obtain the sequence (in reverse order)

$$N, F(N), F(F(N)), \cdots,$$

and for the optimal word sequence, we obtain the sequence (in reverse order)

$$T(N), T(F(N)), T(F(F(N))), \cdots.$$

In summary, the array $D(i, j, k)$ of accumulated distances along with the associated array $B(i, j, k)$ of backpointers has been substituted by four smaller arrays. These arrays are as follows.

The column array of accumulated distances

$$D(j, k): \hat{=} D(i, j, k),$$

the column array of backpointers

$$B(j, k): \hat{=} B(i, j, k),$$

the "from template" array

$$T(i): = \operatorname{argmin} \{D(i, J(k), k): k = 1, \cdots, K\},$$

the "from frame" array

$$F(i): = B(J(T(i)), T(i)) \hat{=} B(i, J(T(i)), T(i)).$$

The savings achieved by using these arrays instead of the original array $D(i, j, k)$ are considerable: instead of $N \cdot \bar{J} \cdot K$, where $\bar{J}$ denotes the average length of a template, only $2 \cdot (\bar{J} \cdot K + N)$ storage locations are required.

Fig. 6 shows a schematic diagram of the complete algorithm using the arrays introduced above and provides a short verbal description of the one-stage dynamic programming algorithm for connected word recognition.

In order to allow for the possibility of pauses between the words in the word string, it is useful to include an additional silence template in the set of templates. This technique can also be used for refining the detection of the beginning and ending points of the complete word string as it was proposed by Bridle *et al.* [13].

These authors also suggested an extension of the algorithm to deal with nonvocabulary words. They introduced a so-called pseudotemplate consisting of only one frame to which a fixed "distance" is assigned independent of with which input frame it is matched. Thus, the algorithm is able to reject a portion of the input utterance if the similarity is not sufficient.

The connected word recognition algorithm described so far starts the traceback from the end of the word string. However, it is possible to recognize the initial portion of the word string before its end has been spoken, which is very desirable for a real time operation of the recognition system. This is clear from the observation that if there is a section shared by all candidate paths, that section is necessarily part of the globally optimal path [13], [14]. Thus, by tracing back all candidate paths for a given input frame and determining the point where they all meet, the initial portion of the word string can be recognized. This recognition is irrevocable in the sense that no subsequent input can change the decision about the recognized words. In order to carry out this premature traceback, it is in fact sufficient that decisions about the recognized words as such, and not about the path details, are the same for all candidate paths.

V. Syntactic Constraints

In this section, the algorithm is modified in order to include a syntactic analysis for a finite state syntax. For connected word recognition, it is suitable to incorporate the syntactic analysis into the recognition process itself. It is worth noting that any lexicon of legal word strings can be described in terms of a finite state syntax. Clearly, syntactic constraints must affect the between-word transition rules. Each word as it starts can be reached only from words that may legally precede it according to the syntactic constraints. Thus, we define for each word k a "from predecessor" set $P(k)$ as the set of all vocabulary words which can precede the word k. Fig. 7(a) illustrates the method. For convenience, START and STOP are added as pseudowords to the vocabulary $\{A, B, C\}$. The arcs of the finite state network are associated with the words of the vocabulary. The finite state network shown in Fig. 7(a) is

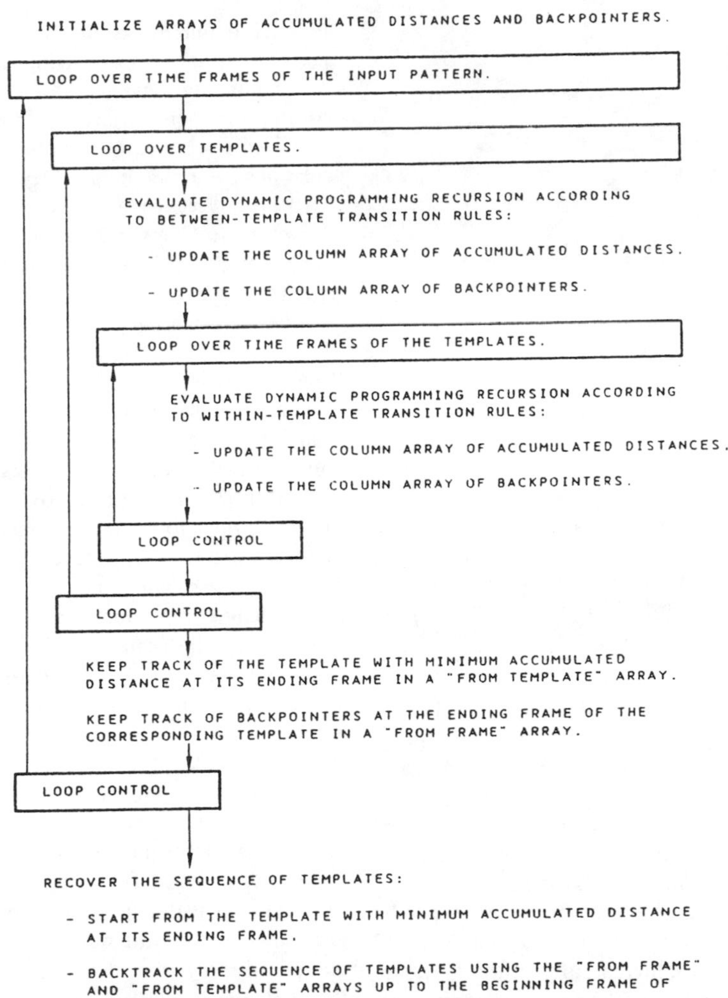
INITIALIZE ARRAYS OF ACCUMULATED DISTANCES AND BACKPOINTERS.
LOOP OVER TIME FRAMES OF THE INPUT PATTERN.
LOOP OVER TEMPLATES.
EVALUATE DYNAMIC PROGRAMMING RECURSION ACCORDING TO BETWEEN-TEMPLATE TRANSITION RULES:
- UPDATE THE COLUMN ARRAY OF ACCUMULATED DISTANCES.
- UPDATE THE COLUMN ARRAY OF BACKPOINTERS.
LOOP OVER TIME FRAMES OF THE TEMPLATES.
EVALUATE DYNAMIC PROGRAMMING RECURSION ACCORDING TO WITHIN-TEMPLATE TRANSITION RULES:
- UPDATE THE COLUMN ARRAY OF ACCUMULATED DISTANCES.
- UPDATE THE COLUMN ARRAY OF BACKPOINTERS.
LOOP CONTROL
LOOP CONTROL
KEEP TRACK OF THE TEMPLATE WITH MINIMUM ACCUMULATED DISTANCE AT ITS ENDING FRAME IN A "FROM TEMPLATE" ARRAY.
KEEP TRACK OF BACKPOINTERS AT THE ENDING FRAME OF THE CORRESPONDING TEMPLATE IN A "FROM FRAME" ARRAY.
LOOP CONTROL
RECOVER THE SEQUENCE OF TEMPLATES:
- START FROM THE TEMPLATE WITH MINIMUM ACCUMULATED DISTANCE AT ITS ENDING FRAME.
- BACKTRACK THE SEQUENCE OF TEMPLATES USING THE "FROM FRAME" AND "FROM TEMPLATE" ARRAYS UP TO THE BEGINNING FRAME OF THE INPUT PATTERN.

Fig. 6. Schematic diagram of the one-stage dynamic programming algorithm.

uniquely specified in terms of the "from predecessor" sets:

$$P(A) = \{\text{START}\},$$
$$P(B) = \{A, B\},$$
$$P(C) = \{\text{START}, A, B\},$$
$$P(\text{STOP}) = \{C\}.$$

In general, however, the "from predecessor" sets may depend on the position or context of the word in the finite state network. An example is shown in Fig. 7(b) where the word B requires two different "from predecessor" sets depending on its position. To deal with this problem of position dependence, we use the following method: we make several copies of each word, such that the finite state network is uniquely described by the "from predecessor" sets. For the example in Fig. 7(b), we have to make two copies B_1 and B_2 of the word B as shown in Fig. 7(c). Thus, we obtain the four-word vocabulary $\{A, B_1, B_2, C\}$ and the "from predecessor" sets:

$$P(A) = P(B_1) = \{\text{START}\},$$
$$P(B_2) = P(C) = \{A, B_2\},$$
$$P(\text{STOP}) = \{B_1, C\}.$$

This method of making copies can also be used for prescribing the number of words in the word strings as illustrated in Fig. 7(d). The legal word strings described by the network of Fig. 7(d) consist of three words from the vocabulary $\{A, B\}$.

The recognition algorithm can treat the copies of a word as if they were different words. Given the "from predecessor" sets, the syntactic constraints are then captured by the following modification of the recurrence relation for the between-word transitions:

$$D(i, 1, k) = d(i, 1, k) + \min \{D(i-1, 1, k);$$
$$D(i-1, J(k^*), k^*): k^* \in P(k)\}$$

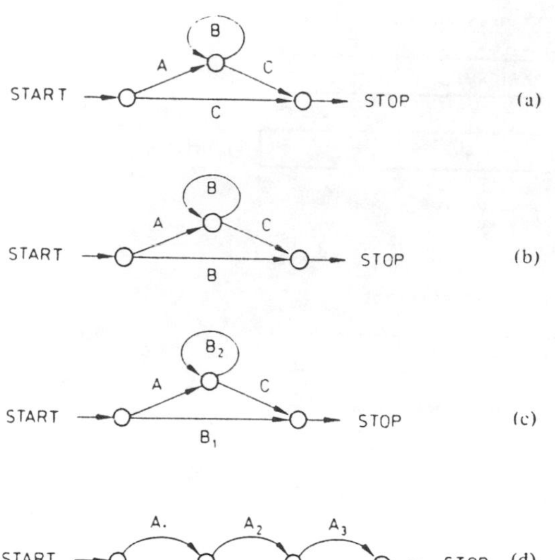

Fig. 7. Four examples (a), (b), (c), (d) of finite state networks as syntactic constraints for building up word strings from the vocabulary words A, B, C.

where the index k now indexes the word copies instead of the word classes. The recurrence relation for the within-word transitions is not changed. Note that the finite state networks need not be loop free, which was already indicated by Fig. 7.

Since now the optimal preceding word depends on the word under consideration, it is necessary to have a "from template" array $T(i)$ and a "from frame" array $F(i)$ for each word copy. For the several copies of a word, the local distances need to be calculated only once for one copy and can then be "copied" for the other copies. As a result, there is no significant increase in computational expenditure due to the syntactic constraints. The major part of the computation time is consumed in the most inner loop by the calculation of the local distance $d(i, j, k)$, which is a distance measure between feature vectors of dimension ten and more. Hence, the additional costs for the computation and updating of the backpointers, which is carried out in parallel with the computation of the accumulated distances, are negligible in comparison with the local distance calculations. There is, however, an increase in storage costs since each word copy must have its individual arrays for the accumulated distances and the backpointers.

VI. Comparison With Other Approaches

It is instructive to compare the different approaches to connected word recognition with respect to computational and storage requirements. Myers and Rabiner [4] present such a comparison between the two-level algorithm of Sakoe [3], their original level building algorithm and a reduced level building algorithm, which results from the level building algorithm by restricting the search region for the best path. In the following, we will extend their comparison to include the one-stage dynamic programming algorithm. Since, as we have seen, syntactic constraints do not significantly affect the computational requirements of the one-stage algorithm, the comparison is made for word strings with no syntactic constraints.

The computational and storage requirements of the four algorithms are summarized in Table I. The computational requirements are measured as the number of local distance calculations, which is the product of basic time warps multiplied by the (average) size of a time warp, i.e., the area covered by it. According to Myers and Rabiner [4], the storage requirements include only the storage locations for those arrays that are specific to the different algorithms. Thus the storage locations for the reference patterns as well as the arrays of accumulated distances and backpointers are not considered in general. However, as will be seen later, there will be an exception for the one-stage algorithm.

In the two-level algorithm of Sakoe, a time warp is carried out for each of the N time frames of the input pattern and for each of the K templates with average length $\overline{J}$. Each time warp covers a stripe around the diagonal line of bandwidth $(2R + 1)$: the warp size is then $\overline{J} \cdot (2R + 1)$. As a result, the number of local distance calculations is $N \cdot K \cdot \overline{J} \cdot (2R + 1)$. To start up the matching procedure on the second level, the socalled phrase level, the accumulated distance and the index of the best template must be stored for each of the $(2R + 1)$ pairs of beginning and ending points and for each time frame of the input pattern. Thus, the number of storage locations is $2 \cdot N \cdot (2R + 1)$.

In the level building algorithm of Myers and Rabiner, $M \cdot K$ time warps are performed, where M is a prespecified number for the maximum number of words, i.e., levels, in the input string. Each time warp covers an area of $\overline{J} \cdot N/3$ grid points. The factor $\frac{1}{3}$ is due to the Itakura constraints imposed on the local slope of the time warping path. These constraints result in a global restriction of the search area for the path. Hence, the total number of distance calculations is $M \cdot K \cdot \overline{J} \cdot N/3$. At each of the M levels and for each of the N time frames of the input pattern, the accumulated distance, the best template and the starting position on the input pattern time axis must be kept track of. This requires $3 \cdot N \cdot M$ storage locations. The level building algorithm turns out to be equivalent to the one-stage algorithm with a prescribed maximum number of words in the string: the levels correspond to the copies made of each template as described in the preceding section. For the reduced level algorithm, the size of a time warp is $\overline{J} \cdot (2R + 1)$, where R is a range parameter and defines a reduced search region for the path. It is worthwhile noting, however, that the reduced level algorithm is not guaranteed to find the globally optimal sequence of words.

The one-stage algorithm performs one time warp for each template. Strictly speaking, the term time warp is not appropriate for this algorithm, since actually only one global time warp is performed. However, the area covered by this global time warp as shown in Fig. 1 can be thought of as decomposed into smaller time warps for each template, as far as local distance computations are concerned. Each of these smaller time warps is of size $\overline{J} \cdot N$. Hence, the total number of local distance computations is $K \cdot \overline{J} \cdot N$. Since the one-stage algorithm must

TABLE I
COMPUTATIONAL COMPARISONS OF DYNAMIC PROGRAMMING ALGORITHMS FOR CONNECTED WORD RECOGNITION AND TYPICAL COMPUTATIONAL REQUIREMENTS FOR VOICE DIALING (i.e., 12 DIGITS IN A STRING)

	Two-Level Algorithm	Level Building Algorithm	Reduced Level Building Algorithm	One-Stage Algorithm
Number of basic time warps	$K \cdot N$	$K \cdot M$	$K \cdot M$	K
Size of time warps	$\bar{J} \cdot (2R + 1)$	$\bar{J} \cdot N/3$	$\bar{J} \cdot (2R + 1)$	$\bar{J} \cdot N$
Total computation	$K \cdot N \cdot \bar{J} \cdot (2R + 1)$	$K \cdot M \cdot \bar{J} \cdot N/3$	$K \cdot M \cdot \bar{J} \cdot (2R + 1)$	$K \cdot \bar{J} \cdot N$
Storage	$2 \cdot N \cdot (2R + 1)$	$3 \cdot N \cdot M$	$3 \cdot N \cdot M$	$2 \cdot (N + K \cdot \bar{J})$
Number of basic time warps	3600	120	120	10
Size of time warps	875	4200	875	12600
Total computation	3150000	504000	105000	126000
Storage	18000	12960	12960	1420

where $\bar{J} = 35$ = average length of a template
$K = 10$ = number of templates
$M = 12$ = maximum number of words in the input string, e.g., for voice dialing (5 + 7) digits
$N = 360$ = length of the input string
$R = 12$ = range parameter for time warping

keep track of the accumulated distances and backpointers for all vocabulary words at a time, it is appropriate to include the accumulated distances and the backpointers in the storage costs. Thus, the storage locations required are $2 \cdot (\bar{J} \cdot K + N)$ as shown in Section IV. The above considerations show the one-stage algorithm to be the only algorithm that calculates each local distance exactly once. Furthermore, the amount of computation and storage required for the one-stage algorithm is independent of the maximum allowed number of words in the input string as opposed to the level building algorithm and its reduced version.

Computational reductions by pruning techniques are also applicable to the one-stage algorithm [12]-[14]. They are based on the observation that candidate paths with accumulated distances significantly larger than the minimum accumulated distance for the input frame under consideration are very unlikely to result in the optimal path. Candidate paths with accumulated distances exceeding a threshold set relative to the best path candidate for the input frame considered can be removed from the subsequent operations.

Hence, the pruning operation requires the following additional computational steps to be performed for each grid point in connection with the evaluation of the dynamic programming recursion: one comparison for determining the minimum of the accumulated distances and three comparisons concerning the accumulated distances of the predecessor grid points for deciding whether to prune the grid point under consideration or not. As a result, the pruning overhead involves four comparisons per grid point, which definitely require less than a few percent of the overall computation time per grid point without pruning. For the pruned grid point or the corresponding path candidate, no local distance is calculated. The pruning technique results in an adjustment window of varying size [13]: when there is a very well defined minimum for the accumulated distances, only a few path candidates are retained; on the other hand, when there is no clear minimum at all, all or nearly all path candidates are expanded. A conservative estimate of the reduction factor achieved by pruning is three or more; apart from a few extra storage locations, there is no increase in storage requirements.

Table I gives also a numerical comparison of the computational and storage requirements of the four algorithms for some typical parameter values:

$$M = 12, \quad K = 10, \quad N = 360, \quad \bar{J} = 35, \quad R = 12.$$

Such parameter values are appropriate for the application of voice dialing, where there are, e.g., twelve digits in the input string: five digits for the area code and seven digits for the telephone number. For such long digit strings, it may be useful to include the endpoint detection in the recognition algorithm as described in Section V. Apart from the parameters M and N, the values are the same as chosen by Myers and Rabiner [4]. Table I shows for this example that the one-stage algorithm requires only $\frac{1}{25}$ of the computational amount of the two-level algorithm of Sakoe and only $\frac{1}{4}$ of the computational amount of the level building algorithm of Myers and Rabiner. As for the storage requirements, the one-stage algorithm offers a reduction factor of 9 or more as compared to the three other algorithms. Only the reduced level building algorithm does with a computational amount comparable with the one-stage algorithm, however, without ensuring the global optimality of the solution. Moreover, by using pruning the computational expenditure of the one-stage algorithm could be reduced further.

VII. Summary

In this paper, a tutorial presentation of a one-stage dynamic programming algorithm for connected word recognition and its relation to other dynamic programming algorithms has been given. The one-stage algorithm is basically the same as the algorithms given by Vintsyuk [1] and developed by Bridle and Brown [2]. The derivation of the one-stage algorithm is based on parameterizing the time warping path by one single index and results in a one-stage dynamic programming algorithm. The dynamic programming strategy performs three functions simultaneously: the time alignment, the word boundary detection and the classification itself. Thus, the problem of concatenating reference patterns of a connected word string is solved in a highly efficient manner. The main features of the one-stage algorithm include the following.

1) For input strings with no syntactic constraints, the algorithm is independent of a prespecified maximum number of words in the input string.

2) The computational effort is proportional to the number of time frames in the reference patterns and in the input string; each local distance between a reference frame and an input frame is calculated exactly once. In particular, the computational effort per input frame turns out to be exactly the same as in the case that the input string consists of isolated words and an isolated word recognition with no adjustment window is performed for each word.

3) The algorithm lends itself to a straightforward and simple implementation.

4) Syntactic constraints, formulated in terms of finite state syntaxes, can be dealt with by simple modifications of the algorithm and increase the computational expenditure only negligibly.

Acknowledgment

The author thanks the reviewers for helpful and constructive comments.

References

[1] T. K. Vintsyuk, "Element-wise recognition of continuous speech composed of words from a specified dictionary," *Kibernetika*, vol. 7, pp. 133–143, Mar.–Apr. 1971.

[2] J. S. Bridle and M. D. Brown, "Connected word recognition using whole word templates," in *Proc. Inst. Acoust. Autumn Conf.*, Nov. 1979, pp. 25–28.

[3] H. Sakoe, "Two-level DP-matching–A dynamic programming-based pattern matching algorithm for connected word recognition," *IEEE Trans. Acoust., Speech, Signal Processing*, vol. ASSP-27, pp. 588–595, Dec. 1979.

[4] C. S. Myers and L. R. Rabiner, "A level building dynamic time warping algorithm for connected word recognition," *IEEE Trans. Acoust., Speech, Signal Processing*, vol. ASSP-29, pp. 284–297, Apr. 1981.

[5] R. Bellman, *Dynamic Programming*. Princeton, NJ: Princeton Univ. Press, 1957.

[6] T. K. Vintsyuk, "Speech discrimination by dynamic programming," *Kibernetika*, vol. 4, pp. 81–88, Jan.–Feb. 1968.

[7] F. Itakura, "Minimum prediction residual principle applied to speech recognition," *IEEE Trans. Acoust., Speech, Signal Processing*, vol. ASSP-23, pp. 67–72, Feb. 1975.

[8] H. Sakoe and S. Chiba, "Dynamic programming algorithm optimization for spoken word recognition," *IEEE Trans. Acoust., Speech, Signal Processing*, vol. ASSP-26, pp. 43–49, Feb. 1978.

[9] M. R. Sambur and L. R. Rabiner, "A statistical decision approach to the recognition of connected digits," *IEEE Trans. Acoust., Speech, Signal Processing*, vol. ASSP-24, pp. 550–558, Dec. 1976.

[10] R. Zelinski and F. Class, "A segmentation procedure for connected word recognition based on estimation principles," in *Proc. 1981 IEEE Int. Conf. Acoust., Speech, Signal Processing*, Atlanta, GA, pp. 960–963, Mar.–Apr. 1981.

[11] J. K. Baker, "The DRAGON system–An overview," *IEEE Trans. Acoust., Speech, Signal Processing*, vol. ASSP-23, pp. 24–29, Feb. 1975.

[12] B. T. Lowerre, "The HARPY speech recognition system," Ph.D. dissertation, Carnegie Mellon Univ., Dep. Comp. Sci., Pittsburgh, PA, Apr. 1976.

[13] J. S. Bridle, M. D. Brown, and R. M. Chamberlain, "An algorithm for connected word recognition," in *Proc. 1982 IEEE Conf. Acoust., Speech, Signal Processing*, Paris, France, May 1982, pp. 899–902.

[14] P. F. Brown, J. C. Spohrer, P. H. Hochschild, and J. K. Baker, "Partial traceback and dynamic programming," in *Proc. 1982 IEEE Conf. Acoust., Speech, Signal Processing*, Paris, France, May 1982, pp. 1629–1632.

[15] J. Peckham, J. Green, J. Canning, and P. Stephens, "Logos–A real-time hardware continuous speech recognition system," in *Proc. 1982 IEEE Conf. Acoust., Speech, Signal Processing*, Paris, France, May 1982, pp. 863–866.

[16] H. Ney, "Connected utterance recognition using dynamic programming," in *Proc. 3rd Cong. FASE, DAGA*, Goettingen, Germany, Sept. 1982, pp. 915–918.

[17] —, "Dynamic programming as a technique for pattern recognition," in *Proc. 6th Int. Conf. Pattern Recogn.*, Munich, Germany, Oct. 1982, pp. 1119–1125.

Hermann Ney was born in Saarlouis, Germany, in 1952. He received the Diplom degree in physics from Goettingen University, Goettingen, Germany, in 1977 and the Dr.-Ing. degree in electrical engineering from Braunschweig Technical University, Braunschweig, Germany, in 1982.

Since 1977, he has been with Philips Research Laboratories, Hamburg, where he has worked on speaker verification via telephone lines, digital signal processing, word recognition, and speech recognition. His work has concentrated on the application of dynamic programming to the problem of decision making in context, such as nonlinear time alignment, nonlinear smoothing, and pitch contour determination. He is particularly interested in the application of mathematical techniques in signal processing research and in pattern recognition research. He is currently responsible for research on continuous speech recognition.

Chapter 5

Knowledge-Based Approaches

Introduction

While template-based approaches have been very effective in the design of a variety of speech recognition systems, they provided little insight about human speech processing, thereby making error analysis and knowledge-based system enhancement difficult. On the other hand, a large body of linguistic and phonetic literature [Lehiste 67; Flanagan 72] provided insights and understanding to human-speech processing. The desire to incorporate this knowledge of human-speech perception has stimulated attempts in most laboratories around the world.

In its pure form, knowledge-engineering design involves the direct and explicit incorporation of experts' speech knowledge into a recognition system. This knowledge is usually derived from careful study of spectrograms and is incorporated using rules or procedures. Pure knowledge engineering was also motivated by the interest and research in expert systems. However, this approach has only had limited success, largely due to the difficulty in quantifying expert knowledge. Another difficult problem is the integration of many levels of human knowledge—phonetics, phonotactics, lexical access, syntax, semantics, and pragmatics, for example. Implementing these individually and cascading them was soon found to be inadequate. Alternatively, combining independent and asynchronous knowledge sources optimally remains an unsolved problem.

In more indirect forms, knowledge has also been used to guide the design of the models and algorithms of other techniques, such as template matching and stochastic modeling. This form of knowledge application makes an important distinction between knowledge and algorithms—"Algorithms enable us to solve problems. Knowledge enables the algorithms to work better" [V.Zue]. This form of knowledge-based system enhancement has contributed considerably to the design of all successful strategies reported in this book. It plays an important role in the selection of a suitable input representation, the definition of units of speech, or the design of the recognition algorithm itself.

Based on considerable study of the acoustic-phonetic properties of speech and the observation that a spectrogram does indeed contain all the information needed for recognition (spectrogram reading), *The Use of Speech Knowledge in Automatic Speech Recognition*, by Zue, advocated increased use of speech knowledge in speech-recognition algorithms. Zue demonstrates that speech parameters contain much irrelevant information and high variability, and proposes a number of ways to identify relevant information, and reduce variability. Specific suggestions include the use of perceptually based models (see Paper 3.4) and measurements, robust features (see Paper 5.2, below) and perceptual distances [Klatt 82]. Furthermore, Zue advocates the utilization of known constraints, such as phonotactic constraints [Huttenlocher 84] and prosodic constraints (see Paper 8.5).

The second paper, *Feature-Based Speaker Independent Recognition of English Letters*, by Cole et al. describes a system that was carefully designed around a specific acoustically difficult task, the recognition of English letters. Within this task domain, the authors systematically studied numerous spectrograms of human speech in search of robust, salient, acoustic-phonetic features, independent of speaker. Once such features were determined, procedures were developed that would attempt to identify these features automatically in the signal. Statistical pattern-recognition techniques were used to combine the feature measurements into an overall output decision. For the recognition of isolated short utterances (letters), this knowlege-engineering approach, tailored to the task, lead to excellent performance.

While knowledge engineering appears to be manageable for small vocabularies and isolated words, it becomes a formidable task when confronted with the enormous number of acoustic-phonetic, lexical, syntactic, semantic, and prosodic facts and the subtle interactions between them. The task must be broken up into modules; some form of learning should take place. An example of a complex knowledge-based system is described in the paper *Recognition of Speaker-Dependent Continuous Speech with KEAL* by Mercier, et al. KEAL is a knowledge-based system that combines speaker-independent segmentation and speaker-dependent phonetic discrmination to create a phonetic lattice. Then, a word lattice is generated using dynamic programming, which is parsed by a context-free grammar parser. The idea of lattice parsing [Adams 86; Zue 90] facilitates modularity, but faces the dilemma between growing enormous lattices and losing correct words from the lattice as the size of the vocabulary increases.

An early attempt at designing and integrating multiple knowedge sources into an overall continuous-speech-recognition system was given by the *Hearsay II Speech Understanding System*, described by Erman and Lesser. Developed under a DARPA-sponsored, five-year research effort, it demonstrated a full system design in which multiple, parallel, knowledge sources interact by way of a blackboard. Each knowledge source receives input and is triggered by information on the blackboard. Each knowledge source, in turn, writes the results of its processing back to the blackboard. One of the promising notions developed by this system was the idea of multiple, parallel, knowledge sources that interact with each other ("opportunistic scheduling") given activity from the input or other knowledge sources. While producing good performance results, HEARSAY II was later outperformed by a simpler search-based recognition system, HARPY (see Chapter 9). Nonetheless, it introduced novel concepts that have inspired the design of many other Artificial Intelligence systems beyond speech systems.

Another Artificial Intelligence approach was taken in *Learning and Plan Refinement in a Knowledge-Based System for Automatic Speech Recognition* by De Mori, Lam, and Gilloux. The task here was speaker-independent, connected letter recognition. The design of the system was carried out in a semiautomatic fashion as planning activity, where plan refinement is triggered by inadequate performance. The system consists of a society of experts, whose activities ("spontaneous" or "on request") are organized into plans to achieve a goal. It incorporates plan refinement and inductive learning to improve system performance. This approach obtained good overall system performance and greater flexibility and extensibility.

References

[Adams 86] Adams, D. A., Bisiani, R. The Carnegie Mellon University Distributed Speech Recognition System. In *Speech Technology*, pp 14–23. March/April, 1986.

[Flanagan 72] Flanagan, J.L. *Speech Analysis; Synthesis and Perception*. Springer-Verlag, Berlin, 1972.

[Hatazaki 89] Hatazaki, K., Komori, Y., Kawabata, T., Shikano, K. Phoneme Segmentation Using Spectrogram Reading Knowledge. In *IEEE International Conference on Acoustics, Speech, and Signal Processing*, pp 393–396. April, 1989.

[Haton 84] Haton, J.-P. Knowledge-based and Expert Systems in Automatic Speech Recognition. In DeMori, R. (editor), *New Systems and Architectures for Automatic Speech Recognition and Synthesis*. Dordrecht, Reidel, Netherlands, 1984.

[Huttenlocher 84] Huttenlocher, D.P., Zue, V.W. A Model of Lexical Access Based on Partial Phonetic Information. In *IEEE International Conference on Acoustics, Speech, and Signal Processing*, pp 26.4.1–4. May, 1984.

[Klatt 82] Klatt, D.H. Prediction of Perceived Phonetic Distance from Critical-Band Spectra. In *IEEE International Conference on Acoustics, Speech, and Signal Processing*, pp 1278–1281. May, 1982.

[Lehiste 67] Lehiste, I. *Readings in Acoustic Phonetics.* MIT Press, Cambridge, Massachusetts, 1967.

[Wolf 80] Wolf, J.J., Woods, W.A. The HWIM Speech Understanding Systems. *Trends in Speech Recognition.* Speech Science Publications, Apple Valley, Minn., 1980.

[Zue 90] Zue, V., Glass, M., Phillips, M., Seneff, S. The Summit Speech Recognition System: Phonological Modelling and Lexical Access. In *IEEE International Conference on Acoustics, Speech, and Signal Processing*. April, 1990.

The Use of Speech Knowledge in Automatic Speech Recognition

VICTOR W. ZUE, MEMBER, IEEE

Invited Paper

In automatic speech recognition, the acoustic signal is the only tangible connection between the talker and the machine. While the signal conveys linguistic information, this information is often encoded in such a complex manner that the signal exhibits a great deal of variability. In addition, variations in environment and speaker can introduce further distortions that are linguistically irrelevant. This paper has three aims: 1) to discuss the nature of variabilities, 2) to describe the kinds of speech knowledge that may help us understand variabilities; and 3) to advocate and suggest specific procedures for the increased utilization of speech knowledge in automatic speech recognition.

I. Introduction

Automatic speech recognition by machine is a topic that has lured and fascinated engineers and speech scientists alike for over forty years. For many, the ability to converse freely with a machine represents the ultimate challenge to our understanding of the production and perception processes involved in human speech communication. In addition to being a provocative topic, automatic speech recognition is fast becoming a necessity. With the recent surge in the use of computers for information processing and the corresponding increases in the workload of human users, there is a growing need to incorporate voice as an added mode of human/machine communication.

The last decade has witnessed significant advances in speech recognition technology, to the extent that speech recognition devices with limited capabilities are now available commercially. These devices are usually able to deal only with a small number of acoustically distinct words spoken by a known talker,[1] and their performance varies widely as a function of the particular device, vocabulary, talker, and operating environment [1], [2]. These systems utilize little or no speech-specific knowledge, but rely instead primarily on general-purpose pattern-recognition algorithms. While such techniques are adequate for a small class of well-constrained speech recognition problems, their extendability to multiple speakers, large vocabularies, and/or continuous speech is highly questionable. In fact, even for the applications that these devices are designed to serve, their performance typically falls far short of human performance.

It is interesting to contrast today's prevailing pattern-matching approaches with some of the earlier efforts that focused on the explicit use of speech knowledge [3], [4]. Systems developed during the much publicized ARPA speech understanding project in the early 1970s provide some good examples. In these systems, the acoustic signal was first *segmented* and *labeled* into phoneme-like units,[2] and the resulting string was used for lexical and syntactic analysis. Words in the lexicon were represented in terms of phonemic spellings, and the grammar was usually described by conventional linguistic means. The abandonment of these phonetically based approaches in favor of general pattern-matching techniques has been partially motivated by our inability to reliably extract phonetic information from the speech signal. This failure in phonetic recognition is a direct reflection of the painfully slow advances made in acoustic phonetics and phonology, as well as our ignorance of a signal representation that would be appropriate for speech recognition. In contrast, general pattern-recognition techniques offer well-defined algorithms that can be easily described and implemented. Their performance is sufficiently enticing that more and more people find such techniques an attractive alternative. Despite their near-term success, however, many researchers have come to the conclusion that these solutions may not "scale up" to substantially more complex tasks.

This paper advocates the increased utilization of speech knowledge in speech recognition algorithms. We know that the acoustic signal conveys not only *linguistic* information but also *extralinguistic* information about such matters as

Manuscript received January 19, 1985; revised July 1, 1985. This research was supported by DARPA under Contract N00039-85-C-0254, monitored through Naval Electronic Systems Command.

The author is with the Department of Electrical Engineering and Computer Science and the Research Laboratory of Electronics, Massachusetts Institute of Technology, Cambridge, MA 02139, USA.

[1]A notable exception to this statement is the large vocabulary, isolated word recognition system developed by Fred Jelinek and his colleagues at IBM. See the article by Jelinek (this issue) for a description of the IBM accomplishments.

[2]A phoneme is the smallest sound unit in a language. Words that differ in their phonemic form will result in different linguistic meanings. For example, the words "bit" and "pit" both have three phonemes, but they differ in the first phoneme.

0018-9219/85/1100-1602$01.00 ©1985 IEEE

the identity of the speaker, his or her physiological and psychological states, and the acoustic environment. Successful speech recognition is possible only if we can determine ways to extract the linguistic information while discarding other information that is irrelevant.

The organization of the paper is as follows: After discussing the nature of the encoding of phonetic information in the speech signal, I point out some of the causes of acoustic-phonetic variability in the speech signal. The intent is not to be exhaustive but to illustrate the complex and diverse nature of the problem. Next, strategies for dealing with these variabilities in automatic speech recognition are described, with particular emphasis placed on the use of segmental phonetic information, distributional constraints, and signal representation based on auditory modeling. I also present a recognition model that incorporates these knowledge sources. This paper ends with a discussion of how speech knowledge may be represented and utilized in order to improve recognition performance. It is my hope that the last part of this paper will both dispel some of the myths associated with terminology and help bridge the polarizing positions often found in the literature. It is not my intent to make this article a review of the research. Accordingly, the references cited are more for illustration than for completeness. The reader seeking an overview of the field is referred to some excellent review articles in the literature [3]–[7]. The IEEE TRANSACTIONS ON ACOUSTICS, SPEECH, AND SIGNAL PROCESSING; the *Journal of the Acoustical Society of America*; and the proceedings of the annual IEEE International Conference on Acoustics, Speech, and Signal Processing are also valuable sources of further information.

II. WHY IS PHONETIC RECOGNITION DIFFICULT?

A. *The Complex Encoding of Phonetic Information*

Studies of the way language is organized provide strong evidence that underlying the production and perception of speech is a sequence of discrete segments that are concatenated in time. These segments, called phonemes, are assumed to have unique articulatory and acoustic correlates. While an essentially infinite number of articulatory gestures can be produced by the human vocal apparatus, the inventory of these basic sound units is remarkably limited. However, speech is generated through the closely coordinated and continuous movements of a set of articulators with different degrees of sluggishness. As a result, the acoustic properties of a given phoneme can change as a function of the immediate phonetic environment. This contextual influence, known as coarticulation, is responsible for the overlap of phonetic information in the acoustic signal from segment to segment, and for the smearing of segmental boundaries.

An illustration of how phonetic information manifests itself in the acoustic signal is provided in Fig. 1. This spectrogram shows a male speaker's recording of the sentence "Two plus seven is less than ten," with the

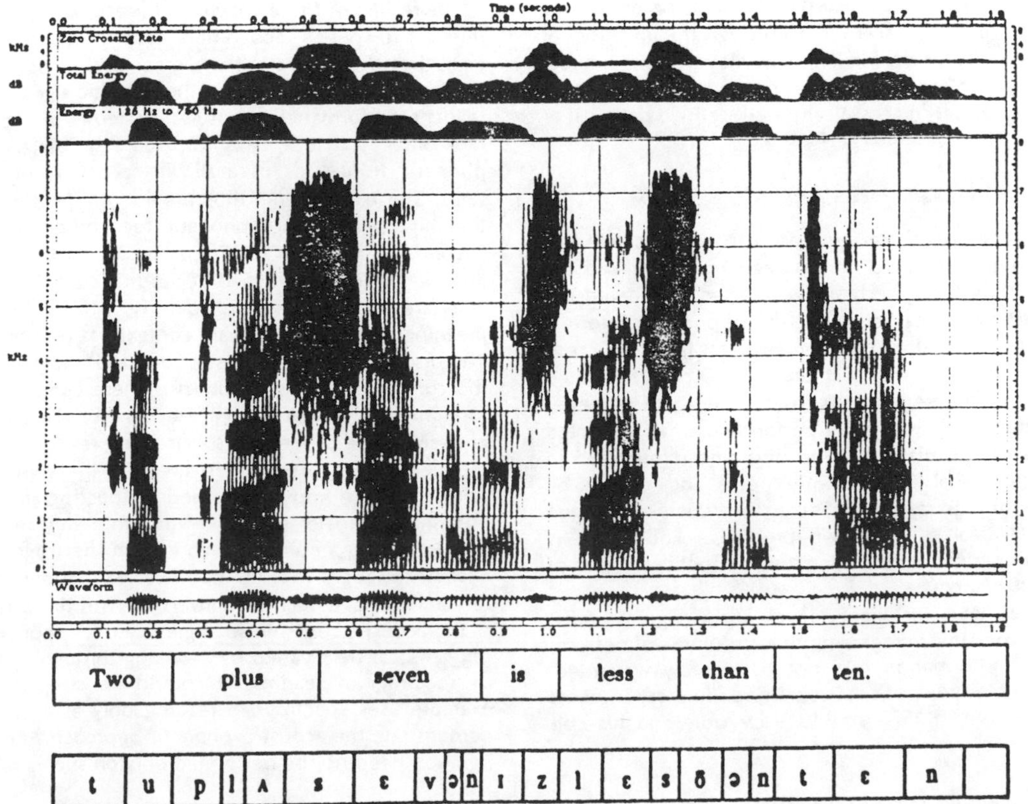

Fig. 1. A Speech Spectrogram. Digital spectrogram of the sentence "Two plus seven is less than ten," spoken by a male talker. The spectrogram illustrates some of the allophonic variations often found in continuous speech.

time-aligned orthographic and phonetic transcription immediately underneath. The sentence contains a number of interesting examples of the influence of local context on the acoustic properties of underlying phonemes. The first and last words of the sentence both start with the phoneme /t/. While these two segments exhibit some similar acoustic properties, such as the closure preceding the sudden high-frequency burst release and the delay in voicing onset, close examination of the spectrogram also reveals some major differences. The burst frequency is lower for the first /t/ than for the second, a direct consequence of anticipatory coarticulation caused by the rounded vowel /u/ in the first word. By the same token, the acoustic similarities among the three tokens of the vowel /ɛ/—in the words "seven," "less," and "ten"—are overshadowed by the apparent differences. The second /ɛ/ is influenced by the adjacent /l/, such that the second formant[3] shows articulatory undershoot, whereas the third /ɛ/ is heavily nasalized, as evidenced by the smearing of the first formant. There are several far more subtle contextual influences in this spectrogram. For example, the spectra of the strident fricatives in the words "is" and "less" both tilt upward near the end of the segment, but for different reasons. In the first case, the tilt is due to the following lateral consonant and is often accompanied by a brief period of epenthetic silence, followed by a vertical striation signifying the lateral release. In the second case, the upward tilt is due to the following dental fricative, which is more anterior in its place of articulation than the /s/.

Fig. 1 serves to illustrate the contextual influences on phonetic segments. In many cases, the contextual modifications are so severe that similarities in the same underlying segments are hard to discern. Even though the inventory of basic sound units for a given language may be quite limited, automatic speech recognition does not reduce to the recognition of a small set of acoustically well-defined patterns, or templates.

B. *Spectrogram-Reading Experiments*

In automatic speech recognition, the acoustic signal is the only tangible connection between the talker and the machine. While the speech signal is often considered the primary information carrier, extraction of phonetic information from the signal alone has met with very limited success. Until the mid-1970s, the best phonetic recognizer could recognize phonetic segments with an accuracy of no better than 60 percent [3]. Such poor performance has prompted researchers to speculate that the phonetic information in the acoustic signal is inherently noisy and cannot be extracted with high reliability. Some researchers even argue that a great deal of top-down predictive knowledge is necessary in order to determine the phonetic content of unknown utterances.

While the need for higher level knowledge is indisputable, the pessimism regarding the usefulness of bottom-up phonetic information may not be entirely warranted. The results of a series of spectrogram-reading experiments conducted between 1978 and 1979 by Cole and his colleagues suggest that the acoustic signal contains far richer phonetic information than previously believed [8]–[10]. In these experiments, a trained spectrogram reader was asked to examine spectrograms of unknown utterances recorded by unknown speakers and to provide a phonetic transcription based on such a visual representation. The spectrogram reader was presented with isolated words (e.g., "elephant") and regular English sentences (e.g., "The soldiers knew the battle was won."), as well as syntactically and semantically anomalous sentences (e.g., "Wake jungle gasoline sudden bright.").

The performance of the spectrogram reader was measured against the transcriptions provided by three phoneticians who listened to the utterances. The reader was able to locate almost all of the segments found by the phoneticians (97 percent for continuous speech, and 100 percent for isolated words). The segment labels produced by the reader agreed with those produced by the phoneticians between 81 and 93 percent of the time, depending on the test material and the criteria for evaluation. Closer examination of the results reveals a number of insights into the methods used. Over 85 percent of the segments have only one or two labels associated with them,[4] suggesting that the reader was able to find reliable acoustic cues most of the time. There was a tendency for consonants to be identified more accurately than vowels. Finally, higher level knowledge about the syntactic and semantic structure of English was rarely used while interpreting spectrograms. Performance was, in fact, slightly *better* on sequences of unrelated words and nonsense words than on normal English sentences.

The results of these spectrogram-reading experiments are relevant to speech recognition research in several respects. First, they demonstrate that a great deal of phonetic information can be derived from the acoustic signal alone. The reader's performance, measured in terms of accuracy and rank-order statistics, was considerably better than the phonetic front-ends of available speech recognition systems. The experiments thus provide an "existence proof" that high-performance phonetic recognition is attainable. Second, spectrogram reading is based on the recognition and integration of a myriad of acoustic cues. Some of these cues are relatively easy to identify, while others are not meaningful until the relevant context has been established. The discovery of the acoustic cues and, more importantly, the control strategies for utilizing these cues, are the keys to high-performance phonetic recognition. Finally, protocol analysis of the process of spectrogram reading reveals that the decoding process often involves the use of explicit rules. Thus the knowledge used in spectrogram reading is potentially transferable to others, both humans and machines. In fact, a number of courses in spectrogram reading have been taught over the past five years, and many speech researchers have become conversant with this procedure.

The acoustic cues and strategies used for phonetic decoding can best be gleaned by "walking through" an example of spectrogram reading. It should be stressed that our example uses spectrogram reading only as a *paradigm* to demonstrate the acoustic–phonetic approach. Phonetic recognition need not be performed only on such a representa-

[3] The term *formants* refers to the resonant frequencies of the vocal tract. On a wide-band spectrogram, formants appear as horizontal, ribbon-like dark bands that vary with time.

[4] The average number of labels per segment is 1.5.

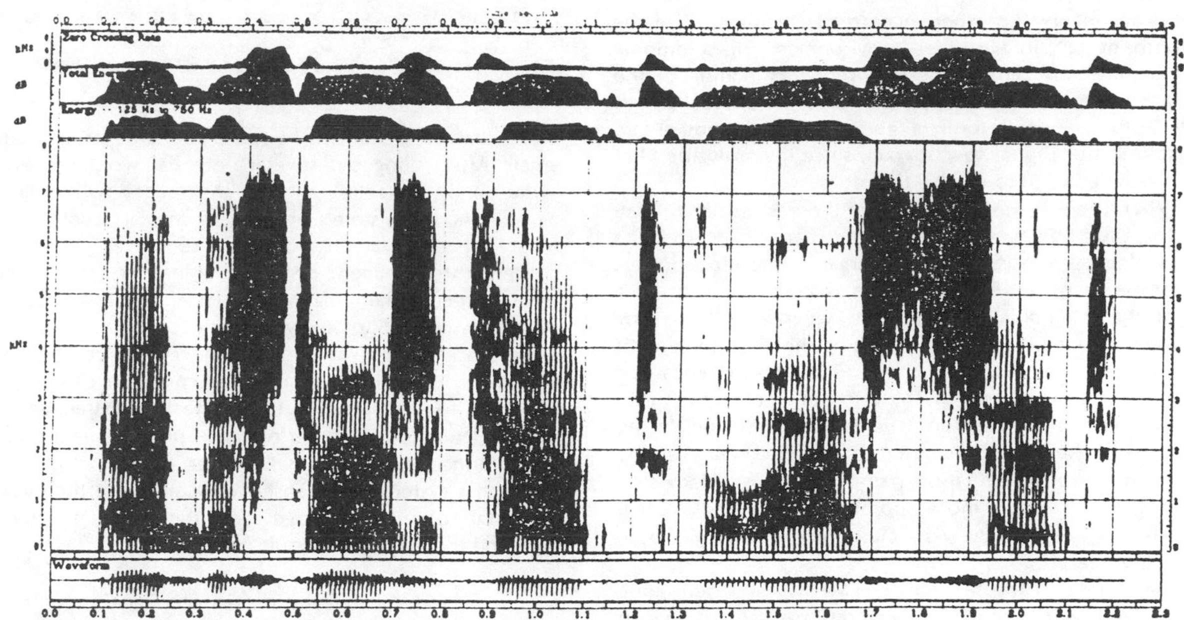

Fig. 2. A Speech Spectrogram. Digital spectrogram of an unknown utterance. The waveform and several parameters are also displayed to complement the information available on a spectrographic display.

tion of the speech signal; in fact, as we shall see, some acoustic information is poorly represented in a spectrogram.

Fig. 2 shows the spectrogram of an unknown utterance recorded by a male speaker. There is a well-enunciated glottal stop at the beginning of the sentence ($t = 0.1$ s), suggesting that the first word begins with a vowel, with no preceding consonant. The glottal stop appears as an irregularity in the fundamental frequency, which is visible in both the time waveform and the spectrogram. (Another cue for the absence of a preceding consonant is the absence of noticeable rising F1 transition, typical from a consonant to a vowel. Since F1 and F2 are both high in the middle of the vowel (around 800 and 1900 Hz, respectively), the most likely choice for the vowels is /æ/. (/ɛ/ might be a second choice, but the long duration of the vowel makes it a *distant* second choice.)

Following the vowel is a region of low acoustic output except in the low-frequency portion. Since the energy drops abruptly from the preceding vowel, the phoneme is probably a voiced stop. The identity of the stop can be determined by a process of elimination. If the stop were a labial stop (/b/), one would expect all formants to fall sharply at the end of the vowel. If it were a velar stop (/g/), one would expect F2 and F3 to move toward each other. Since there is little motion in F2 or F3 at the end of the vowel, the most likely candidate is a /d/. It might be supposed that the burst of energy following the stop gap ($t = 0.31$ s) is the burst of the /d/. However, it is instead associated with the voiced fricative /ð/, which is often realized in a stop-like manner when preceded by a consonant. The stop is therefore unreleased. A true /d/ burst would be stronger in amplitude and lower in frequency than the frication noise generated for /ð/. (See, for example, the stop burst at $t = 0.5$ s.)

Following the phoneme /ð/ is a short, moderately front vowel, possibly an unstressed /ɪ/. After the short vowel is a strong fricative (a definite /s/) followed by a short gap and a burst of energy ($t = 0.5$ s) that exhibits frequency characteristics typical of a dental stop (/d,t/). Since there is little aspiration following the burst, a /d/ or an unaspirated /t/ are the likely choices. The stop could therefore be either a /d/ with a boundary preceding it (since /sd/ is not an allowable English cluster), or a /t/ in a cluster with the /s/ (since /t/ is not aspirated in such a case). The vocalic portion following the stop release shows significant movement in F2 and F3. Since F3 is quite low, especially for the second half of the vocalic segment, a postvocalic /r/ is proposed. The vowel counterpart of /r/ is ruled out because F2 is much too low. After taking into account the formant transitions resulting form the preceding alveolar stop and the following /r/, we propose a low back vowel such as /ɔ/ or /o/.

After the /r/ is another strong alveolar fricative that must be either /s/ or /z/. Since it is short and there are some clear voicing striations (especially at the onset and below 4 kHz), the phoneme is probably a /z/. This conjecture is further corroborated by the strength of the low-frequency energy parameter. Following the /z/ is a very short vowel that is easily overlooked. This vowel, based on duration and formant frequencies, can only be a front-reduced /ɪ/. The release following the stop gap is aspirated, suggesting the presence of a voiceless stop. The second and third formant transitions during the aspiration and during the preceding schwa clearly indicate a velar stop, i.e., a /k/.

The vowel following the /k/ is rather long with a very high F1. The high F1 suggests /a/ or /æ/. The latter is ruled out because F2 is too low (compare with the first vowel). Notice that there is also considerable motion in F2, suggesting the possibility of a diphthong. However, F1 seems to be quite steady, although somewhat diffuse and weak in energy. An experienced reader will recognize the diphthong |a^{w}| in a nasalized environment. The additional nasal pole and zero in the low-frequency portion of the vowel spectra cause the appearance of an unusually high F1. Both the nasal formant and the vowel formant are visible in this digital spectrogram, since the analyzing filter is narrow enough to resolve them.

When there is a nasalized vowel there is usually a nasal. In this case, however, the nasal is very hard to find. In fact a phonological rule involving homorganic nasal-stop clusters must be invoked. The rule states that the duration of a homorganic nasal is greatly reduced when it is followed by a *voiceless* stop [11]. Since F2 is rising slightly at the end of the vowel, /nt/ is a likely choice. The stop gap ends in a strong burst with spectral characteristics indicating an alveolar place of articulation. It is tempting to associate the burst with the /t/ in the /nt/ cluster. However, the stop gap is quite long in duration, particularly unusual for a stop in a cluster. Thus a more appropriate hypothesis is that another /t/ follows the /nt/ cluster and the first /t/ is, in fact, unreleased.

The release of the second /t/ ($t = 1.21$ s) is quite long and is followed by yet another consonant that is low in amplitude. Phonotactic considerations rule out the possibility of this /t/ forming a cluster with another consonant. Thus the aspiration of the /t/ probably includes a devoiced schwa, a common acoustic realization of an unstressed "to" in continuous speech. The weak consonant following the aspirated /t/ is voiced, as evidenced by the periodicities in the waveform. The only candidates are the two voiced fricatives /v, ð/ or the voiced stop /b/. (/d/ and /g/ are not probable in light of the relatively weak release.) Given our previous discussion on the realization of /ð/ following another consonant, /ð/ appears to be the most logical choice. The consonant is followed by a schwa, which is followed by an intervocalic sonorant. The slow formant transitions suggest that the sonorant is either a /w/ or an /l/. /l/ is the more likely candidate because of the distinct separation of F1 and F2 and the rather marked discontinuity leading into the following vowel.

This vowel is relatively long and fairly steady-state, with a reasonably high F1 and mid-range F2. The only vowel to fit this category is /æ/. Note that the second formant for this /æ/ is somewhat lower than that of the first /æ/ we encountered. This is due to the coarticulatory effect of the /l/, which tends to lower the second formant of front and central vowels. After the /æ/ is another /s/, extremely long in duration with a fading of energy midway through. The length alone suggests that there must be more than one segment. In fact, this pattern is characteristic of the /sts/ cluster, with the /t/ closure never completely formed.

The final vowel is clearly nasalized, and, as in the previous nasalized vowel, no distinct nasal murmur is observable. The spectral characteristics of the release enable us to propose another /nt/ cluster. The first formant for the vowel is very difficult to locate, a problem often encountered with nasalized vowels. In such situations one learns to rely mainly on F2. The only vowels in English that can have such a second formant value are /ɛ/ and /æ/. Since the vowel is not very long, especially for the last segment of an utterance, /ɛ/ is probably a better choice than /æ/.

The string of phonemes that we have proposed thus far is shown in Fig. 3. Even with an open lexicon, the number of

ʔ æ̇ d ð ɪ s t ɔ r z ɪ k ɑ• n t t ə̣ ð ə l æ s t s ɛ n t
  ɛ   z d o   æ

Fig. 3. Proposed Phoneme String for the Utterance Shown in Fig. 2.

words that can be formed from this phoneme string is quite small. After ruling out several potential word strings on syntactic or semantic grounds, the reader will probably accept "Add the store's account to the last cent" as the most likely candidate for a complete sentence.

We see that phonetic decoding, at least as demonstrated from a spectrogram reading exercise, requires that one selectively attend to many acoustic cues, interpret their significance in light of other evidence, and combine the inferences to reach a decision. If a computer can be programmed to simulate this task of feature extraction and logical deduction, high-performance phonetic recognizers are, in principle, achievable. However, the task of developing such a system is immensely difficult, given the incomplete state of our knowledge about the important acoustic cues and the ways they should be combined.

C. *Sources of Variability in the Speech Signal*

Phonetic recognition by computers has met with limited success because of variability in the acoustic realization of utterances, which can come from diverse sources [12]. First, *acoustic variabilities* can result from changes in the environment as well as in the position and characteristics of the transducer. Second, *within-speaker variabilities* can result from changes in the speaker's physiological or psychological state, speaking rate, or voice quality. Third, differences in sociolinguistic background, dialect, and vocal tract size and shape can contribute to *across-speaker variabilities*.

Some of these variabilities may have little effect on phonetic distinctiveness, whereas others will have dire consequences. For example, Carlson, Granstrom, and Klatt found that changes in spectral tilt and formant bandwidth do not contribute significantly to changes in phonetic perception of a synthetic vowel /æ/ [13]. In contrast, dialectal differences and changes in speaking rate are known to affect both the phonetic form [14] and the application of many low-level phonological processes [15]. The development of truly speaker-independent speech recognition systems will require a complete understanding of the sources of variability in the speech signal. On the one hand, we must strive for better models for signal representation that are insensitive to irrelevant acoustic changes yet able to retain or enhance the acoustic cues important for phonetic distinctions. On the other hand, the contextual influences of phonetic units, either within or across word boundaries, must also be quantified.

The results of the spectrogram-reading experiments point out the importance of knowledge about the acoustic cues for phonetic segments, particularly the contextual influences. The identity of underlying phonetic segments is determined by a complex problem-solving paradigm in which cues are observed and hypotheses are verified utilizing contextual constraints. Traditionally, allophonic variations such as those found in Figs. 1 and 2 have often been viewed as one of the major sources of difficulty for speech recognition, since they represent undesirable distortions, or noise, imposed on the canonic characteristics of the phonemes. However, spectrogram-reading experiments indicate that knowledge about allophonic variations is in fact helpful for phonetic decoding. There is also increasing evidence that such variations may be sources of information for both human and machine recognition [16],[17]. For example, Church was able to parse detailed phonetic strings into syllables and other suprasegmental constituents by exploiting knowledge about allophonic variations [18]. The resulting representation was demonstrated to be extremely effective for reducing the number of candidate words during lexical access.

III. Dealing with Variabilities

Successful phonetic recognition crucially depends on our ability to deal with variabilities. Not only must we extract and utilize information from phonetic variabilities during recognition, we must also learn to disregard or deemphasize acoustic variabilities that are irrelevant. In this section, I will address two areas of research that are potentially useful for dealing with variabilities. Specifically, I will discuss how a representation of the speech signal based on known properties of the human auditory system may help to reduce irrelevant acoustic variabilities and enhance phonetic contrasts. I will also discuss some research results suggesting that knowledge about constraints on the sound patterns of a given language can be exploited during phonetic recognition. Finally, I will present a recognition model that takes these results into consideration.

A. *Signal Representation Based on Auditory Modeling*

Current speech recognition systems perform significantly worse than humans on the same task, even under ideal circumstances [1],[19]. When the operating conditions deteriorate, the difference between human and machine performance becomes even more dramatic. There is clearly much to be learned from studying the process by which human listeners decode the speech signal. While little is known about the decoding process beyond the eighth cranial nerve, recent advances in auditory physiology and psychophysics have begun to shed some light on the nature of representations of the speech signal in the human peripheral auditory system.

For the most part, current speech recognition strategies are based on a spectral representation of the speech signal that borrows heavily from models of speech production. Such models are very useful for characterizing the signal and for helping to identify the basic acoustic attributes that are important for phonetic identity [20]–[22]. Such models are also clearly appropriate in analysis/synthesis systems, where the goal is to produce as accurate a reconstruction as possible of the measured signal. Often, the form of spectral representation that is used for synthesis is assumed also to be appropriate for recognition. Yet the two tasks are really quite different, and there is no reason to believe that what works for synthesis is suitable for recognition. The human brain obviously recognizes the signal only after it has been processed through the human auditory system. It is quite clear from studies of the peripheral auditory system that what is available at the level of the eighth cranial nerve is not a close copy of the log magnitude spectrum. Yet a standard approach to evaluate the effectiveness of a particular method of generating a spectral representation, even one intended to be used for recognition purposes, is to apply some error metric to measure the deviation of the representation from the log spectrum.

In recent years, the auditory system has begun to play a larger role in motivating the design of some speech recognition front-end systems. It was long ago recognized that the ear performs a kind of frequency analysis on the incoming signal; we can even characterize with some confidence the shapes of the auditory filters. The concept of the "critical band" emerged originally from psychophysical data [23], but neurophysiologists have since confirmed its general validity from studies of nerve fiber responses to tones and tone complexes [24]. The ear performs a frequency analysis with better frequency resolution at the low-frequency end of the scale than at the high-frequency end. This design makes sense in terms of speech because sonorants, which are predominantly low-frequency sounds, benefit from a long integration window and good frequency resolution, whereas good temporal resolution is needed to detect and characterize the predominantly high-frequency sounds like stop bursts. Searle *et al.* [25], among others, have made use of this critical-band concept in the design of a constant-Q filter bank, which was utilized in a stop-consonant identification task.

Although a bank of filters appropriately designed is a good first step in an attempt to emulate the auditory system, to obtain a representation that is at all similar to what the brain processes we must go much further with the model. The nonlinearities that take place in the transformation from basilar membrane vibration to nerve fiber spike sequences grossly distort the spectral shape. Some pioneering work by Sachs and Young [26] on the responses of a large population of nerve fibers in the cat's ear to synthetic speech-like stimuli indicates that a representation based on average firing rate would be decidedly inadequate for characterizing the formant structure. They demonstrate that it is possible to obtain a much more adequate spectral representation, and one that shows stability over changes in signal level, by examining the *temporal patterns* in the spike sequences. Nerve fibers respond to stimuli in a phase-locked or synchronous fashion; that is, the intervals between firings tend to cluster near multiples of the stimulus period [27]. Sachs and Young advocate that by making use of this synchronous response it is possible to recover much more of the relevant spectral information in the signal than by simply counting the number of spikes.

As a result of these pioneering findings, many researchers have begun to propose speech signal representations that take into account these known properties of the auditory system [28]–[33]. One such representation, proposed by Seneff [33], processes the output of the peripheral auditory system through a so-called Generalized Synchrony Detector, designed to capture the essence of synchronous firing in the auditory nerve in response to vowel-like stimuli. The resulting spectral representation often shows enhanced peaks at the formant frequencies. An example of the outputs of Seneff's system is shown for the word "joke," spoken by a male speaker, in Fig. 4. Part (a) of this figure shows the conventional wide-band spectrogram. The spectrogram in part (b) was obtained by processing the output of a model of the auditory periphery through the synchrony detection algorithm. The frequency scales for the two spec-

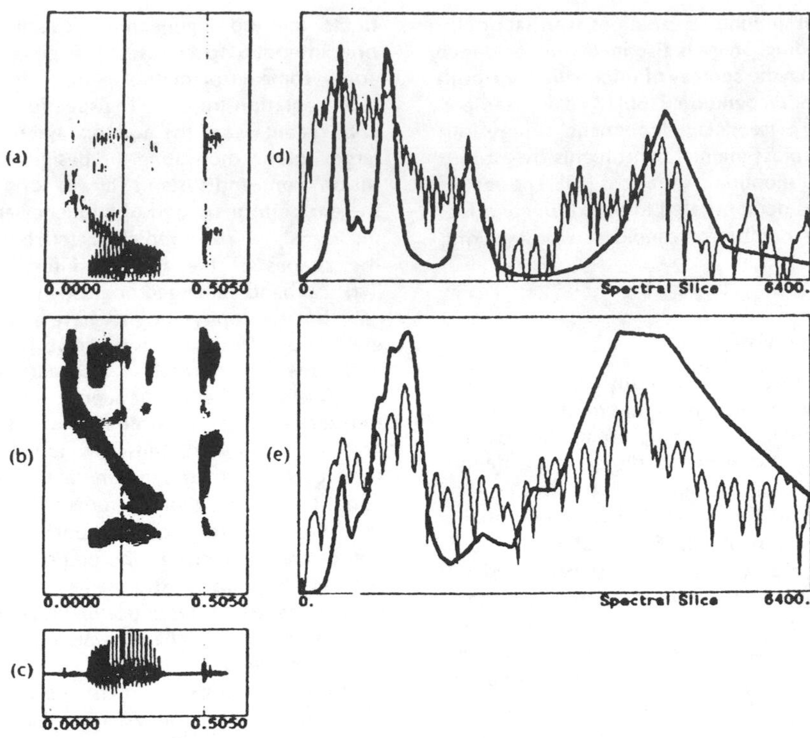

Fig. 4. Spectral Representation Based on Auditory Modeling. A comparison of the spectrograms and spectra of conventional wide-band analysis and output of the synchrony analysis proposed by Seneff.

trograms are linear and critical-band-like, respectively. Comparing the two spectrograms, we see that the formant peaks as well as the major concentration of spectral energy for consonants are enhanced by the synchrony processing. Furthermore, detailed temporal variations during voiced portions are reduced considerably in part (b), making such a representation potentially better suited for further signal processing such as formant tracking. Parts (d) and (e) of Fig. 4 compare the short-time spectrum of the two representations during the vowel portion of the word (as marked by the first cursor) and during consonantal release (as marked by the second cursor). For ease of visual comparison, the spectra from synchrony processing are converted back to a linear scale, thus making the higher formants appear wider. In both cases, we see that the representation based on auditory modeling retains and enhances cues in the signal that are known to be important for phonetic distinction. Preliminary results indicate that spectral representations such as this one generally have the property of not deteriorating drastically with the addition of background noise. Proper utilization of knowledge in auditory modeling may indeed result in speech recognition front-ends that are more robust.

B. *Utilization of Constraints*

Turning now to allophonic variations in the speech signal, one can choose to deal with this problem by increasing the inventory of recognition units, so that each of these units corresponds to one of the allophones. However, even with a substantially improved knowledge base, such an approach may still have serious drawbacks. It is often difficult to make fine phonetic distinctions (for example, distinguishing between "sue" and "shoe") reliably across a wide range of speakers. Furthermore, the application of context-dependent rules often requires the specification of the correct context, a process that is prone to error. (For example, the identification of a retroflexed /t/ in the word "tree" depends upon correctly identifying the retroflex consonant /r/.) Problems such as these suggest that a detailed phonetic transcription of an unknown utterance may not by itself be a desirable aim for the early application of phonetic knowledge.

1) Segmental Constraints: Detailed segmental representation of the speech signal constitutes but one of the sources of encoded phonetic information. The sound patterns of a given language are limited not only by the inventory of basic sound units, but also by the allowable combinations of these sound units. For example, we know that there are fewer than fifty consonant clusters that can start a word in American English, and that syllable-final nasal-stop combinations (such as "camp," "hand," and "thank") must agree in their places of articulation. Knowledge about such constraints is presumably very useful in speech communication, since it provides native speakers with the ability to fill in phonetic details that are otherwise unavailable or distorted.

These so-called *phonotactic* constraints have been studied by linguists and phonologists for many decades. However, the magnitude of their constraining power has only recently been demonstrated through a set of studies [34]–[37], utilizing a large dictionary containing many thousands of words. The words are given different phonological representations, and distributional constraints of the lexicon are then investigated. In one such study, all 20 000 words in the Merriam Pocket Dictionary (MPD) were mapped into six categories that roughly correspond to the manners of articulation.[5] One can define an *equivalence class* as the collection of words having the same representation. Thus for example, the words "speed," "steep," and "scout" all belong to the same equivalence class:

[STRONG-FRICATIVE][STOP][VOWEL][STOP]

It was found that even at this broad phonetic level, the sizes of the equivalence classes were quite small. Table 1 summarizes the results of this experiment.

Table 1 Representing Words by Broad Phonetic Categories

	MPD (Equally Weighted)	MPD (Frequency Weighted)
Expected class size	22	34
Median class size	4	25
Maximum class size	223	223
% of unique classes	32	6

We see that the maximum class size corresponds to about 1 percent of the size of the lexicon, and that almost one-third of the words are uniquely represented at this broad phonetic level. The expected value of the class size, even after normalization in terms of frequency of usage, is still a fraction of a percent of the entire lexicon. It should be noted that results such as these are not restricted to the English language. Studies of Swedish, German, Italian, and French [38] reveal constraints of about the same magnitude.

These findings about phonological constraints have serious implications for speech recognition. They suggest that in itself a complete and detailed phonetic analysis of the speech signal not only is undesirable from an error propagation standpoint, but may indeed be unnecessary. Broad phonetic analysis by its nature focuses on acoustic cues that are more invariant against contextual influences. That such a representation is also able to capture important phonological constraints imposed by the language suggests that large-scale lexical candidate reduction may be possible. Once the list of potential word candidates has been reduced to a small set, differential diagnosis techniques can be employed to focus on the specific acoustic cues that can distinguish among the remaining words. Furthermore, knowing the exact phonetic context will permit us to use detailed phonetic knowledge with greater confidence. If "tree" is a candidate word, then the verification process can use the predictive knowledge of the retroflexed context, as specified by the following /r/. The recognition algorithm will then be able to focus its attention on the detection of the retroflexed /t/, as opposed to a generic /t/.

As another example, suppose the word spoken is "speed," and the broad phonetic analysis returns the pattern:

[STRONG-FRICATIVE][STOP][HIGH-FRONT-VOWEL][STOP]

[5]Manners of articulation define classes of speech sounds that are produced with similar, general articulatory maneuvers. For example, /m, n, ŋ/ belong to the manner class NASALS, whereas /p, t, k, b, d, g/ belong to the class STOPS.

Based on this analysis, lexical access may well return the following set of words from the MPD:

skate
skid
skip
skit
spade
speak
speed
spit
stake
state
steak
steed
steep
stick

For this example, it is clear that further identification of the first phoneme would be unnecessary, since all word candidates have the same initial phoneme. Instead attention should be focused on the following stop. This can only be an unaspirated voiceless stop, for the context clearly precludes a voiced stop from consideration. As a result, one need utilize only those cues that help distinguish /p/ from /t/ from /k/ in the syllable initial /s/-cluster environment.

2) Differential Encoding of Phonetic Information: The encoding of the phonetic information is not uniform throughout the signal. It has long been suggested that stressed syllables represent *islands of reliability* where the acoustic cues for phonetic segments are particularly robust. Evidence for this observation comes from diverse sources. For example, phoneme monitoring experiments for human speech perception show that speech errors in stressed syllables are detected faster than those in unstressed syllables [39], suggesting that phonemes around stressed syllables are easier to recognize. Analysis of spectrogram reading results also indicates that accuracy is higher for sounds around stressed syllables. In addition, automatic speech recognition front-ends typically recognize phonemes around stressed syllables more accurately, again suggesting that the acoustic cues in these regions are more reliable. These observations have prompted some researchers to propose recognition strategies that focus attention on speech sounds in stressed syllables.

To illustrate the point of differential encoding of phonetic information, Fig. 5 shows the distribution of the voice-onset time (VOT) for stop consonants preceding stressed and unstressed vowels. While VOT has long been recognized as a reliable measure of the voicing contrast between voiced and voiceless stops in English, almost all of the analysis results were obtained for prestressed stops. We can see from Fig. 5 that the VOTs for voiced and voiceless stops occupy essentially disjoint regions when the stops precede stressed vowels, whereas when they precede unstressed vowels, the VOTs overlap significantly. Thus VOT may be a robust acoustic measure for stops in the prestressed position, but its utility is greatly curtailed in the unstressed position.

In addition to providing information on the reliability of acoustic cues, lexical stress information is useful for speech recognition because it provides yet another source of constraint. Recent studies show that knowledge of the stress

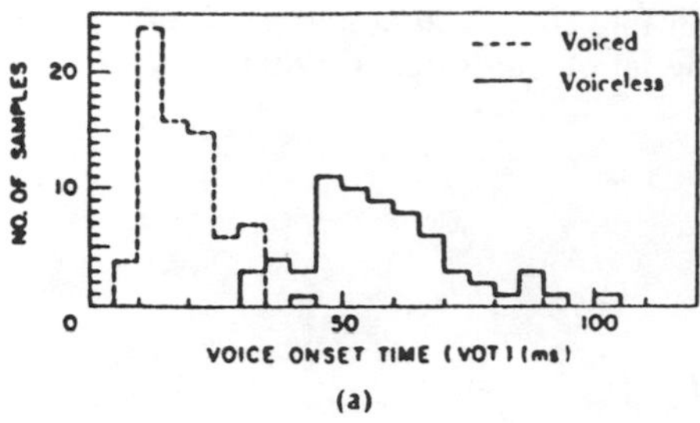

(a)

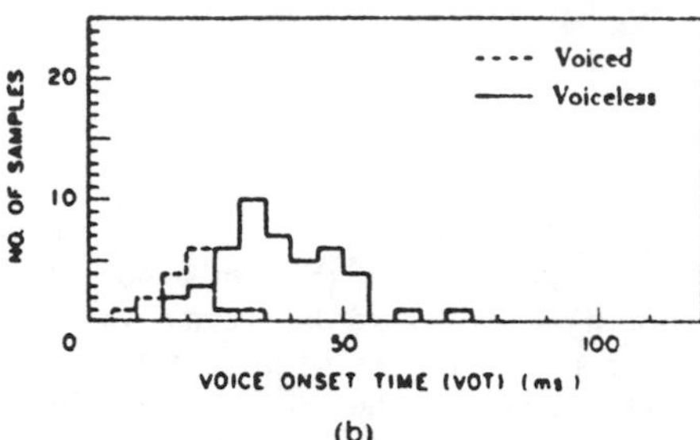

(b)

Fig. 5. A VOT Histogram. Histograms comparing the distribution of VOT for voiceless and voiced stops preceding (a) stressed vowels, and (b) unstressed vowels. The data are collected from one hundred sentences, spoken by five talkers

pattern of a word can significantly reduce the number of word candidates [40]. In one such study, the approximately 16 000 polysyllabic words in the MPD were represented by the stress pattern alone. Thus for example, the word "classify" was represented by the pattern:

[S][R][U]

where S, U, and R, denote stressed, unstressed, and reduced syllables, respectively. The expected value for the size of the equivalence class was found to be approximately 3000. In other words, one can expect to reduce the word candidates by a factor of almost five using stress information alone. When this information is coupled with the broad phonetic representation described earlier, a further reduction of the size of the equivalence classes is obtained [37]. This result is shown in the first column of Table 2, where the words have been weighted by the frequency of usage.

Table 2 Representing Words by Broad Phonetic Categories and Lexical Stress Information

	Entire Word	Stressed Syllable Only	Unstressed Syllable Only
Expected class size	26	40	2013
Median class size	8	22	1725
Maximum class size	223	261	3703

Another study attempted to identify the amount of phonetic richness of unstressed and stressed syllables. The results clearly indicate that the phonemes in unstressed syllables provide little lexical constraint compared to those in stressed syllables. For the experiment, a comparison was made between two conditions: in one, entire stressed syllables were replaced by "placeholders" and phonemes in unstressed syllables were mapped into broad categories; in the other, stressed and unstressed syllable modes were reversed. Thus the word "piston" in one case is represented by the pattern:

[STOP][VOWEL][STRONG-FRICATIVE][*]

where * is the unstressed syllable marker, whereas in the other case it is represented by:

[*][STOP][VOWEL][NASAL]

where * is the stressed syllable marker. The results of these experiments are summarized in the second and third columns of Table 2. Comparing the first two columns of Table 2, we see that the expected value, the median, and the maximum of the class size all increase by a relatively small amount when segmental information around stressed syllables is used for lexical access, suggesting that the stressed syllable provides almost as much constraint as the entire word. When segmental information around unstressed syllables is used for lexical access, as shown in the third column of Table 2, all the corresponding measures increase drastically. From these results one may conclude that phonemes in stressed syllables provide significantly more constraining power than those in unstressed syllables. This conclusion, together with the observation that acoustic information may not be robust around unstressed syllables, suggests that the emphasis in phonetic recognition should be placed on stressed syllables. Not only are the phonemes around unstressed syllables highly variable in their acoustic properties, they do not provide a great deal of constraint even if correctly recognized.

C. A Model for Automatic Speech Recognition by Machine

A possible recognition model that incorporates some of the previously discussed ways of dealing with variabilities is shown in Fig. 6. The input speech signal is first transformed

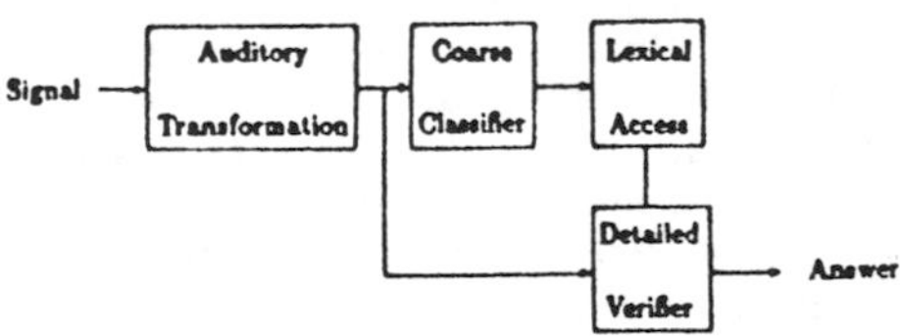

Fig. 6. A Speech Recognition Model. A proposed speech recognition model that attempts to incorporate features for dealing with variabilities.

into a representation that takes into account known properties of the human auditory system such as critical-band frequency analysis, dynamic range compression, temporal and frequency masking, adaptation and onset enhancement, and synchrony processing. From various stages of this transformation, acoustic parameters are extracted and used to classify the utterance into broad phonetic categories. The coarse classification also includes prosodic analysis that identifies regions where the speech signal is likely to be more robust. The outcomes of these analyses are used for lexical access. The constraints imposed by the language on possible sound patterns should significantly reduce the number of word candidates. Once the phonetic context has been specified following lexical access, differential diagnosis techniques are used, in conjunction with detailed acoustic cues from the signal, to select the correct answer from the small set of candidate words.

Note that the proposed recognition model is essentially a hypothesis-test, or analysis-by-synthesis, model. It has been proposed in the past for speech analysis [41] as well as for speech perception [42]. The success of such a model relies heavily on the assumption that the number and the dimensionality of the hypotheses remain small. In our case, this is achieved through large-scale hypothesis pruning utilizing a proper set of constraints. Once the number of hypotheses becomes manageable, attention can be directed toward detailed acoustic cues that will enable us to make fine phonetic distinctions. The model is also computationally efficient since detailed acoustic cues are not computed until it is necessary. During verification, the acoustic cues can be determined in a prioritized manner as well. However, the computational savings should be considered a side benefit; the primary appeal of the model stems from its ability to deal with variability. The coarse analysis is desirable because the resulting representation is relatively invariant across contexts and yet implicitly captures lexical and phonotactic constraints. Since detailed phonetic recognition is often error-prone, deferring this process will minimize error propagation.

To successfully implement such a model, mechanisms must be provided to insure that correct word candidates are not accidentally pruned, since this would result in unrecoverable error. Errors of this sort occur for two reasons: either the coarse classifier makes a mistake, or the lexicon does not anticipate a particular phonetic realization for the word by the speaker. This problem can be alleviated by permitting the lexical access procedure to accept reasonable insertions, deletions, and substitutions. If the errors are indeed reasonable, one would expect the correct word candidates to have better scores than the incorrect ones. Fig. 7 shows the result of such a "soft failure" lexical access scheme for the continuous-digit recognition tasks [43]. In

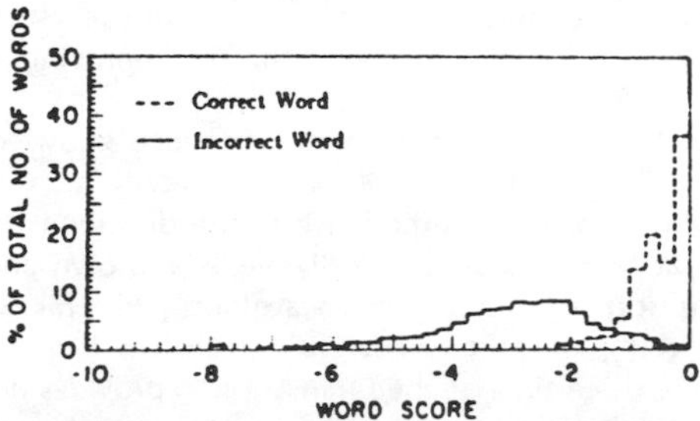

Fig. 7. Histograms of Word Scores for Correct and Incorrect Words. Histograms of word scores for correct (shown in solid lines) and incorrect (shown in dashed lines) word candidates in a continuous digit recognition system by Chen [43]. The scores are obtained from unknown talkers based on training data from a different set of talkers. Scores are expressed in terms of log probabilities.

this implementation, lexical access is accomplished by finding the best alignment between the output of the classifier and the words in the lexicon, where the path constraints and scoring metrics are derived from performance statistics of the coarse classifier. Thus each word is given a score that indicates the relative goodness of the match. We see that the scores associated with the correct word candidates are consistently lower than those for incorrect words. If the words are rank ordered in terms of their scores, the stack can then be pruned by a predetermined threshold.

While the discussion leading to this model has focused on isolated words, the model can, in principle, deal with continuous speech as well. Instead of working with a set of word candidates, the verifier would deal with a *lattice* of word candidates. Provisions would then be made to determine and compare the relative goodness of words and word strings, subject to phonological, syntactic, and semantic constraints. Recent lexical studies using larger linguistic units such as syllables and metrical feet [44] show that these units exhibit constraints of similar magnitude. Using these large units may prove to be a more elegant way of accommodating continuous speech.

IV. Speech Knowledge Utilization

Proper utilization of speech knowledge is important to successful speech recognition. In this section, I will attempt to describe several issues relevant to knowledge utilization. The intent is to suggest ways to benefit from the speech knowledge that we as a research community have acquired over the years. While there is still a vast amount of this knowledge to be uncovered, we must be mindful of procedures that will enable us to apply such knowledge as it becomes available.

A. *Template Matching versus Feature Extraction: An Unnecessary Dichotomy*

One of the most popular approaches to speech recognition over the past ten years has been template matching. In this approach, words are typically represented in the form of spectral sequences as a function of time. Recognition is achieved by using a pre-defined similarity measure to compare the unknown token against stored templates. In many cases, time-alignment algorithms are used to account for some variability in speech rate. While template-matching systems can achieve high performance with a small set of acoustically distinct words, some researchers question the ability of such systems to ultimately make fine phonetic distinctions among a wide range of talkers [19]. As an alternative, they propose a feature-based approach to speech recognition, in which one must first identify a set of acoustic "features" that capture the phonetically relevant information in the speech signal. With this knowledge, algorithms can be developed to extract the features from the speech signal. A classifier is then used to combine the features and arrive at a recognition decision. It is argued that a feature-based system is better able to perform fine phonetic distinctions than a template-matching scheme, and is thus inherently superior.

Drawing a sharp division between these two approaches is somewhat artificial and perhaps unnecessary. Template matching is a technique often used in pattern recognition, whereby an unknown is compared with prototypes in order to determine which one it most closely resembles. By this definition, feature-based speech recognition systems that use multivariate Gaussian models for classification also perform template matching. In this case, the statistical classifier merely uses a feature vector as the pattern. Similarly, if one regards spectrum amplitude and LPC coefficients as features, then spectrum-based techniques are feature-based as well. What is most important is whether and to what extent speech-specific knowledge is being utilized for recognition. Template matching and feature-based systems really represent different points along a continuum.

One of the most serious problems with a template-matching approach is the difficulty of defining distance measures that are sensitive enough for fine phonetic distinctions but insensitive to irrelevant spectral changes. One manifestation of this problem is the excessive weight given to perceptually unimportant frame-to-frame variations in the spectrum of a long steady-state vowel. In this regard, speech perception experiments utilizing synthetic stimuli can often help. If certain aspects of the signal are known to be perceptually salient, one could concentrate on preserving those aspects of the signal. Following a set of studies where synthetic stimuli were manipulated to uncover phonetically relevant cues, Klatt has proposed a number of distance metrics that are intended to be sensitive to phonetic differences and insensitive to irrelevant acoustic differences [45]. Such a distance metric might improve the performance of template-matching systems, since it includes speech knowledge in the measurement of spectral distances.

B. The Use of Speech Knowledge to Improve Existing Algorithms

As we stated at the onset, this paper advocates the increased utilization of speech-specific knowledge in speech recognition. We see that the speech signal is a special kind of signal. It is produced with constraints imposed by the language, and by the human production and perception mechanisms. Future successes in speech recognition, in our opinion, will rely heavily on our ability to properly incorporate such knowledge into recognition systems.

There are at least two levels at which speech knowledge can be introduced. First, the acoustic attributes that are useful in signifying phonetic contrasts must be uncovered, and reliable algorithms to automatically extract these attributes must be determined. These are problems in the areas of *signal processing* and *feature extraction*. Although we have made significant headway in this direction, we have by no means reached a point of identifying a complete set of acoustic attributes or prescribing a method for their extraction. For example, there does not yet exist a formant tracker that can determine formant frequencies reliably, especially in regions where the direction and the extent of formant transitions provide important information about the place of articulation for consonants. These formant transitions may be readily apparent on a spectrogram. The human visual system, however, is a very sophisticated device, capable of integrating subtle patterns, in a way not yet understood, to arrive at the relevant information [46].

A second area for the application of speech knowledge is in determining *how* the acoustic attributes should be combined in order to make phonetic distinctions. These are the problems of *knowledge representation* and *control strategy*. In this area, we are probably many years away from reaching a full understanding. As an example, consider the problem of *cue integration*. It has long been known that a given phonetic contrast is often signified by many acoustic cues. In American English, the voicing characteristics of a stop consonant can be signified by such cues as a) the duration of the voice-onset time (VOT), b) the prevoicing during closure, c) the extent of the first formant transition, d) the amplitude of the burst release, e) the fundamental frequency contour, and f) the duration of the preceding vowel [47]. Some of the cues may be redundant, and others may be absent in certain environments. For example, if the stop is not released (as the /t/ in "basketball"), then those cues related to the release will not be present, thus rendering a decision strategy based on VOT or burst spectrum useless. How these cues should be integrated to form a unified phonetic perception is a problem that many have tackled with little success. As a result, some researchers have found comfort in using statistical algorithms to combine the various acoustic attributes for recognition.

One of the most successful attempts in this direction is the FEATURE system developed by Cole and his colleagues [19]. FEATURE is designed to recognize isolated letters of the alphabet, a very difficult task due to the similarity of the lexical items. Cole *et al.*'s approach in the development of the feature-based system involves the following three steps: 1) the acoustic features are determined through studies of various visual displays of a large body of data, 2) algorithms for feature extraction are then created, and 3) classification is done by taking into account inter- and intra-feature variabilities, using statistical techniques. Cole *et al.* claim that the system design was inspired by experimental results in acoustic phonetics, speech perception, and spectrogram reading that indicate the presence of multiple acoustic cues as well as the trading relations among the various cues. However, the system falls short of specifying a procedure for combining these features for phonetic recognition; instead it directly classifies the lexical items in terms of traditional, statistical techniques for pattern classification. Nevertheless, this system offers the best results anywhere for the task of alphabet recognition. A conclusion that may be drawn is that even with little knowledge about how the acoustic cues should be combined, a set of speech-specific acoustic cues can be of great value in improving system performance.

To further illustrate the power of speech knowledge to improve the performance of existing algorithms, we draw from our own recent experience in the development of a system at MIT that automatically aligns a known phonetic transcription with the speech waveform [48]. This work is an integral part of an effort to establish a large speech database, since time-aligned transcription provides pointers to specific phonetic events in the waveform. Perhaps just as important, the development of such a system provides a testing ground for phonetic recognition algorithms, since the task is one of locating phonetic events when the local context is known. The system is structured to have three modules. First, a set of k-means classifiers is used to delineate the speech signal into regions that correspond to broad phonetic class. These regions provide islands of reliability for future processing. Next, a path-finding algorithm is used to align the transcription with the broad class segments. Following the initial alignment, further segmentation is performed on more subtle and context-dependent transitions. An evaluation of the system's performance on more than 4 min of continuous speech revealed that over

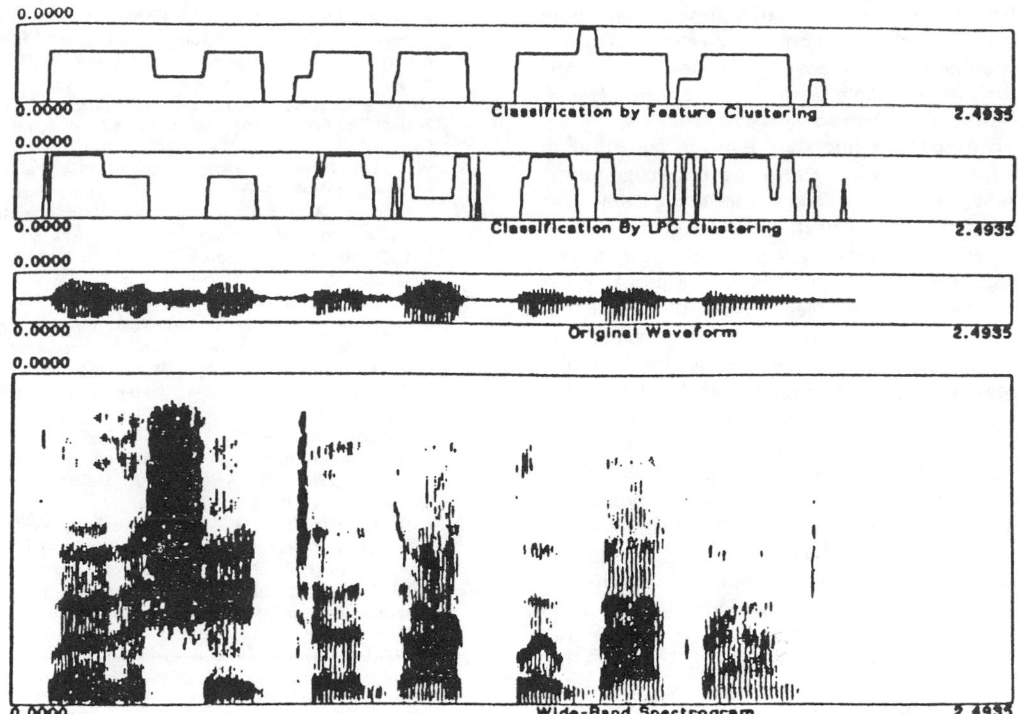

Fig. 8. Automatic Alignment System by Leung [48]. A comparison of k-means clustering results using LPC parameters and Itakura distance metric versus results using sets of acoustic attributes specially selected to enhance phonetic contrast. The sentence is "Glue the sheet to the dark blue background," spoken by a male talker.

95 percent of the phonetic segments were successfully aligned, thus significantly reducing the need for a human expert.

Throughout the development of the system, it was found that existing algorithms can be made more powerful by the judicious application of speech knowledge. By structuring the initial classifiers in a binary decision tree, for example, specific acoustic attributes can be selected to ehance a particular phonetic contrast. Fig. 8 shows a typical comparison of this procedure with an LPC-based classifier using the Itakura distance metric [49]. In this figure, the outputs of the four-way classifier have been converted to a level-coded waveform for ease of visual comparison. As illustrated in this example, we consistently found that the feature-based classifier outperforms the LPC-based classifier in that the resulting classes are both stable and phonetically meaningful, suggesting that proper selection of acoustic measurements for classification has its payoffs.

The path-finding algorithm used in this system is not unlike the popular dynamic programming algorithms [50], [51]. In this case, however, the alignment is performed at the segmental level, so that phonetic rules can be used to severely constrain the search space. As illustrated in Fig. 9, the path alternatives, shown as open circles, are so limited that finding the correct alignment is often trivial.

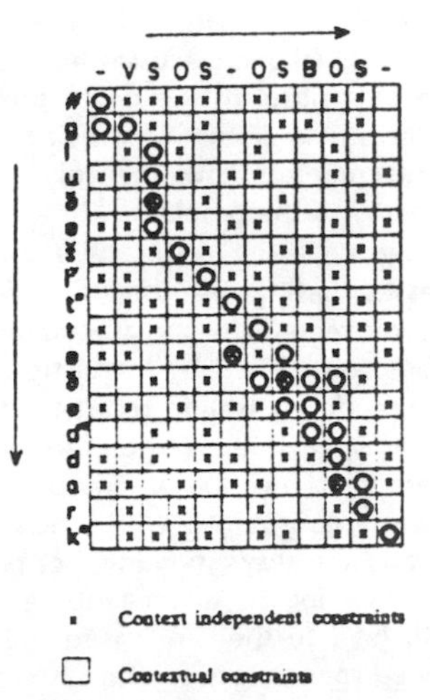

Fig. 9. Automatic Alignment System by Leung [48]. An example of path finding in which phonetic rules are used to limit the possible paths. The open circles represent cells to which the alignment path can traverse

C. *The Importance of Ignorance Modeling*

While we are making steady progress toward a better understanding of the complex relationship between the speech signal and its underlying linguistic forms, there is no denying that our knowledge is still very limited. We must concede that decades may pass before we are in command of this knowledge. Aside from diligently chipping away at the problem, is there anything that can and should be done in the near term?

It is our belief that speech knowledge can potentially improve recognition algorithms. The improvement may come in the form of better signal representation, more reliable methods to extract phonetically relevant acoustic measures, and perceptually based measures of phonetic similarity. *Algorithms* enable us to solve problems, *knowledge* enables the algorithms to work better.

Perhaps an even more important issue in our effort to incorporate speech knowledge into speech recognition is *admitting what we do not know and doing something about it.* Makhoul and Schwartz [52] have argued that powerful speech-recognition systems in the last decade have attained surprisingly high performance primarily because they have effective mechanisms to model our ignorance. In their view, systems that utilize dynamic time warping have an ignorance model for dealing with the effect of speaking rate on the speech signal. Similarly, the use of the probabilistic hidden Markov modeling for speech recognition [53], [54] is another successful attempt at modeling our ignorance. In the IBM system, speech sounds are represented by a structure whose parameters are probability density functions. The estimation of the parameters requires a substantial amount of training data but needs little human interaction. In all these cases, simple but self-optimizing mathematical procedures can outperform human intuition, simply because human intuition is still not well developed. While we should continue to strive for the acquisition of speech knowledge and mechanisms to incorporate it into recognition systems, we should also be mindful of the fact that sophisiticated ignorance models can make optimal use of whatever knowledge we do have.

V. Concluding Remarks

This paper describes the nature of some of the information in the speech signal and discusses how speech-specific knowledge can be helpful in the development of speech recognition systems. The discussion is by no means exhaustive. The lack of complete coverage only helps to underscore the immensity of the problem.

The speech signal is the result of a complex set of encoding processes starting with the linguistic concept and ending with the movements of the articulators. The encoding processes are constrained by linguistic rules, many of them language-specific, as well as by articulatory dynamics. In our view, the speech-recognition problem is one in which we attempt to decode utterances by using our knowledge of these constraints. While the exact nature of the constraints and the ways they interact remain mysterious, we must strive for an understanding of these constraints that will lead to their increased utilization in the future in advanced speech recognition systems.

Acknowledgment

The author would like to thank J. Allen, R. Cole, D. Klatt, S. Seneff, and K. Stevens for reading and offering valuable comments on earlier versions of this paper, and K. Kline for editorial assistance.

References

[1] G. D. Doddington and T. B. Schalk, "Speech recognition: Turning theory to practice," *IEEE Spectrum*, vol. 18, no. 9, pp. 26–32, Sept. 1981.

[2] National Research Council's Committee on Computerized Speech Recognition Technologies, *Automatic Speech Recognition in Severe Environments.* Washington, DC: Nat. Acad Press, 1984.

[3] D. H. Klatt, "Review of the ARPA Speech Understanding Project," *J. Acoust. Soc. Amer.*, vol. 62, no. 6, pp. 1345–1366, Dec. 1977.

[4] W. A. Lea, *Trends in Speech Recognition.* Englewood Cliffs NJ: Prentice-Hall, 1980.

[5] S. R. Hyde, "Automatic speech recognition: Literature, survey and discussion," in *Human Communication: A Unified View* E. E. David and P. B. Denes, Eds. New York: McGraw-Hill, 1972, pp. 399–438.

[6] J. J. Wolf, "Speech recognition and understanding," in *Pattern Recognition*, K. S. Fu, Ed. New York: Springer, 1975.

[7] D. R. Reddy, "Speech recognition by machine: A review *Proc. IEEE*, vol. 64, no. 4, pp. 501–531, Apr. 1976.

[8] V. W. Zue and R. A. Cole, "Experiments on spectrogram reading," in *Proc. ICASSP-79*, pp. 116–119, 1979.

[9] R. A. Cole, A. I. Rudnicky, V. W. Zue, and D. R. Reddy "Speech as patterns on paper," in *Perception and Production of Fluent Speech*, R. A. Cole, Ed. Hillsdale, NJ: Lawrence Erlbaum Assoc., 1980, pp. 3–50.

[10] R. A. Cole and V. W. Zue, "Speech as eyes see it," in *Attention and Performance VIII*, R. S. Nickerson, Ed. Hillsdale, NJ: Lawrence Erlbaum Assoc., 1980, pp. 475–494.

[11] V. W. Zue and M. Laferriere, "Acoustic study of medial /t, d/ in American English," *J. Acoust Soc. Amer.*, vol. 66, no. 4, pp. 1039–1050, Oct. 1979.

[12] D. H. Klatt, "The problem of variability in speech recognition and in models of speech perception," in *Variability and Invariance in Speech Processes*, J. S. Perkell and D. H. Klatt, Eds. Hillsdale, NJ: Lawrence Erlbaum Assoc., 1985.

[13] R. Carlson, B. Granstrom, and D. Klatt "Vowel perception The relative perceptual salience of selected acoustic manipulations," *Speech Transmission Lab. Quart. Progress Rep.*, STL-QPSR 3-4, pp. 73–83, 1979.

[14] W. Labov, "Sources of inherent variation in the speech process," in *Variability and Invariance in Speech Processes*, J. S. Perkell and D. H. Klatt, Eds. Hillsdale, NJ: Lawrence Erlbaum Assoc., 1985.

[15] K. C. Moore and V. W. Zue, "The effect of speech rate on the application of low-level phonological rules," *J. Acoust. Soc Amer.*, vol. 77, suppl. 1, p. S53, 1985.

[16] L. Nakatani and K. Dukes, "Locus of segmental cues for word juncture," *J. Acoust Soc. Amer.*, vol. 62, no. 3, pp. 714–719 Sept. 1977.

[17] K. W. Church, "Phrase-structure parsing: A method for taking advantage of allophonic constraints," Ph.D. dissertation, Mass Inst. Technol., Cambridge, MA, 1983.

[18] D. Kahn, "Syllable-based generalization of English phonology," Ph.D. dissertation, Mass. Inst. Technol., Cambridge, MA, 1968.

[19] R. A. Cole, R. M. Stern, and M. J. Lasry, "Performing fine phonetic distinctions: Templates versus features," in *Variability and Invariance in Speech Processes*, J. S. Perkell and D H Klatt, Eds. Hillsdale, NJ: Lawrence Erlbaum Assoc., 1985.

[20] G. Fant, *Acoustic Theory of Speech Production.* The Hague The Netherlands: Mouton & Co. N.V., 1970.

[21] J. L. Flanagan, *Speech Analysis Synthesis and Perception* Berlin, Germany: Springer-Verlag, 1972.

[22] L. R. Rabiner and R. W. Schafer, *Digital Processing of Speech Signals.* Englewood Cliffs, NJ: Prentice-Hall, 1978.

[23] H. Fletcher, "Auditory patterns," *Rev. Mod. Phys.*, vol. 12, pp. 47–65, 1940.

[24] N. Y-S. Kiang, T. Watanabe, E. C. Thomas, and L. F. Clark *Discharge Patterns of Single Fibers in the Cat's Auditory Nerve*, Research Monograph No. 35. Cambridge, MA: MIT Press, 1965.

[25] C. L. Searle, J. J. Zachary, and S. G. Rayment, "Stop consonant discrimination based on human audition," *J. Acoust. Soc Amer.*, vol. 65, no. 3, pp. 799–809, Mar. 1979.

[26] M. B. Sachs and E. D. Young, "Effects of nonlinearities on speech encoding in the auditory nerve," *J. Acoust. Soc Amer* vol. 68, no. 3, pp. 858–875, Sept. 1980.

[27] D. H. Johnson, "The response of single auditory-nerve fibers

in the cat to single tones: Synchrony and average discharge rate," Ph.D dissertation, Mass. Inst. Technol., Cambridge, MA, 1974.

[28] R. Lyon, "A computational model of filtering, detection, and compression in the cochlea," in *Proc. ICASSP-79*, pp. 1282–1285, 1982.

[29] D. H. Klatt, "Speech processing strategies based on auditory models," in *The Representation of Speech in the Peripheral Auditory System*, R. Carlson and B. Granstrom, Eds. New York: Elsevier/North-Holland, 1982, pp. 181–196.

[30] P. Srulovicz and J. L. Goldstein, "A central spectrum model: A synthesis of auditory-nerve timing and place cues in monaural communication of frequency spectrum," *J. Acoust. Soc. Amer.*, vol. 73, no. 4, pp. 1266–1276, Apr. 1983.

[31] B. Delgutte, "Speech coding in the auditory nerve: II. Processing schemes for vowel-like sounds," *J. Acoust. Soc. Amer.*, vol. 75, no. 3, pp. 879–886, Mar. 1984.

[32] R. Goldhor, "Representation of consonants in the peripheral auditory system: A modeling study of the correspondence between response properties and phonetic features," Ph.D. dissertation, Mass. Inst. Technol., Cambridge, MA, 1985.

[33] S. Seneff, "Pitch and spectral analysis of speech based on an auditory synchrony model," Ph.D. dissertation, Mass. Inst. Technol., Cambridge, MA, 1985.

[34] T. H. Crystal, M. K. Hoffmann, and A. S. House, "Statistics of phonetic category representation of speech for application to word recognition," Communication Research Division Working Paper No. 528, Institute for Defense Analysis, Princeton, NJ, 1977.

[35] D. W. Shipman and V. W. Zue, "Properties of large lexicons: Implications for advanced isolated word recognition systems," in *Proc. ICASSP-82*, pp. 546–549, 1982.

[36] D. P. Huttenlocher and V. W. Zue, "A model of lexical access based on partial phonetic information," in *Proc. ICASSP-84*, pp. 26.4.1–4, 1984.

[37] D. P. Huttenlocher, "Acoustic-phonetic and lexical constraints in word recognition: Lexical access using partial phonetic information," S.M. thesis, Mass. Inst. Technol., Cambridge, MA, 1984.

[38] R. Carlson, K. Elenius, B. Granstrom, and S. Hunnicutt, "Phonetic and orthographic properties of the basic vocabulary of five European languages," *Speech Transmission Lab. Quart. Progress Rep.*, STL-QPSR 1-2, 1985.

[39] A. Cutler and D. J. Foss, "On the role of sentence stress in sentence processing," *Language and Speech*, vol. 20, pp. 1–10, 1977.

[40] A. M. Aull, "Lexical stress and its application in large vocabulary speech recognition," S.M. thesis, Mass. Inst. Technol., Cambridge, MA, 1984.

[41] C.G. Bell, H. Fujisaki, J.M. Heinz, and K.N. Stevens, "Reduction of speech spectra by analysis-by-synthesis techniques," *J. Acoust. Soc. Amer.*, vol. 33, pp. 1725–1736, 1961.

[42] K. N. Stevens and A. S. House, "Speech perception," in *Foundations of Modern Auditory Theory*, J. Tobias and E. Schuber, Eds. New York: Academic Press, 1970.

[43] F. R. Chen, "Acoustic-phonetic constraints in continuous speech recognition: A case study using the digit vocabulary," Ph.D. dissertation, Mass. Inst. Technol., Cambridge, MA, 1985.

[44] D. P. Huttenlocher and M. Withgott, personal communication.

[45] D. H. Klatt, "Prediction of perceived phonetic distance from critical-band spectra: A first step," in *Proc. ICASSP-82*, IEEE Catalog No. 82-CH1746-7, pp. 1278–1281, 1982.

[46] D. Marr, *Vision*. San Francisco, CA: W. H. Freeman & Co., 1982.

[47] D. H. Klatt, "Voice onset time, frication and aspiration in word-initial consonant clusters," *J. Speech Hearing Res.*, vol. 18, pp. 686–706, 1975.

[48] H. C. Leung, "A procedure for automatic alignment of phonetic transcriptions with continuous speech," S.M. thesis, Mass. Inst. Technol., Cambridge, MA, 1985.

[49] F. Itakura, "Minimum prediction residual principle applied to speech recognition," *IEEE Trans. Acoust., Speech, Signal Process.*, vol. ASSP-23, no. 1, pp. 67–72, Feb. 1975.

[50] H. Sakoe and S. Chiba, "A dynamic programming approach to continuous speech recognition," in *Proc. Int. Congr. Acoustics* (Budapest, Hungary), paper 20C-13.

[51] L. R. Rabiner and C. S. Myers, "Connected digit recognition using a level-building DTW algorithm," *IEEE Trans. Acoust., Speech, Signal Process.*, vol. ASSP-29, no. 3, June 1981.

[52] J. Makhoul and R. Schwartz, "Ignorance modeling," in *Variability and Invariance in Speech Processes*, J. S. Perkell and D. H. Klatt, Eds. Hillsdale, NJ: Lawrence Erlbaum Assoc., 1985.

[53] F. Jelinek, "Continuous speech recognition by statistical methods," *Proc. IEEE*, vol. 64, pp. 532–556, 1976.

[54] L. R. Bahl, A. G. Cole, F. Jelinek, R. L. Mercer, A. Nadas, D. Nahamoo, and M. A. Picheny, "Recognition of isolated word sentences from a 5000-word vocabulary office correspondence task," in *Proc. ICASSP-83*, pp. 1065–1067, 1983.

Performing Fine Phonetic Distinctions: Templates versus Features

Ronald A. Cole, Richard M. Stern and Moshé J. Lasry
Department of Computer Science
Carnegie-Mellon University
Pittsburgh, Pennsylvania

INTRODUCTION

Despite intensive research in computer speech recognition during the past 10 years, there is still a very large gap between human and machine recognition of speech. Human speech perception is robust and flexible: A person can recognize a novel sentence produced by an unfamiliar talker in a background of other conversations. By comparison, computer speech-recognition systems typically require training to each new speaker and perform well only when word choice is limited to a small number of acoustically distinct items.

Considering the amount of effort that has been devoted to speech recognition research, the "front-end" performance of speech-recognition systems is surprisingly poor. Systems developed during the ARPA speech-understanding project achieved first choice segmental recognition accuracies of 50% to 60% (Klatt, 1977). This is not accurate enough to recognize words unless vocabulary choice is highly constrained, and the items at each choice point are acoustically distinct.[1]

The problem is that computer systems are unable to perform fine phonetic distinctions: Today's systems are unable to discriminate among acoustically similar segments with sufficient accuracy to recognize the words of a language. Failure to correctly identify a single segment can and often will result in word recognition errors (e.g., "big" could be perceived as "pig," "beg," or "bid"). Thus, fine phonetic distinctions must be continuously and accurately performed in order to recognize speech. Until phonetic information can be extracted from speech at levels approaching human performance, it will not be possible to construct truly extensible speech understanding systems.

[1] The best front-end performance was provided by HWIM (Hear What I Mean), a feature-based recognition system developed at Bolt, Baranek, and Newman (Woods, Bates, Brown, Bruce, Cook, Klovstad, Makhoul, Nash-Webber, Schwartz, Wolf, & Zue, 1976.)

TEMPLATE MATCHING

Almost all current systems use some form of time-normalized template matching to extract the linguistic information from the stimulus. By template matching, we refer to the time-frame-by-time-frame spectral comparison of an input utterance to a set of reference templates. In this section, we argue that template matching systems are unable to perform fine phonetic distinctions because spectral templates do not capture the acoustic-phonetic events that are necessary to identify most phonetic segments.

In 1975, Itakura published his classic article on isolated word recognition using the dynamic programming (DP) time normalization algorithm (Itakura, 1975; Sakoe & Chiba, 1971, 1978). In essence, the DP algorithm finds the best frame-by-frame spectral match between a test and reference pattern by stretching or folding the temporal axis of either the test or the reference in a nonlinear fashion. For a single speaker, Itakura obtained 97.3% accuracy on a 200-word vocabulary of Japanese geographical names using telephone speech (3 kHz), 8 LPC coefficients, a 30 msec sampling window and a 15 msec sampling rate. These results demonstrated that, even with substantial data reduction, DP template matching can produce high-recognition scores for some vocabularies.[1]

Itakura's research, and many subsequent studies, have shown that DP template matching systems will produce high recognition accuracies in a speaker-dependent mode as long as the vocabulary items are acoustically distinct. The critical importance of the acoustic similarity of the vocabulary items was noted by Itakura: "...the recognition rate is strongly influenced by a particular choice of vocabulary set. For example, if the vocabulary set is the English alphabet and digits, the recognition rate was 88.6% for 720 utterances by the same speaker under the same conditions..." But even this result is misleading, since almost all of the errors obtained in the alphadigit task occurred among a few confusable items. For example, the digits (which are acoustically distinct) were never confused, while the letters M - N, I - Y, and B, D, E, P, T, and V were recognized about 60% of the time.

Following Itakura's study, a number of experiments investigated the performance of template matching algorithms with confusable vocabularies.

[1] Template matching systems work well with small vocabularies of unambiguous words. In general, these systems work best in a speaker-dependent mode, but good speaker-independent results can be achieved for small vocabularies by using several templates for each word. The particular set of templates is determined by applying clustering algorithms to a data base provided by many speakers (Rabiner and Wilpon, 1979).

Originally appeared in J. S. Perkell and D. M. Klatt (eds) *Variability and Invariance in Speech Processes*, Lawrence Erlbaum Assocs., Hillsdale, N.J., 1986.

Most experiments used the *alphadigit* vocabulary, the English letters (A) through (Z) and the digits (0) (pronounced "zero") through (9). As Lamel and Zue (1982) point out, the alphadigit vocabulary is one of the most difficult in isolated word recognition (it is also one of the most important for many applications, such as directory assistance). All but three of the items are monosyllabic, so that number of syllables cannot be used to discriminate among the items. Most important, the letters and digits form highly confusable subsets. Rabiner, Levinson, Rosenberg and Wilpon (1979) identify the following six subsets: (a) (B C D E G P T V Z 3), (b) (A J K 8 H), (c) (L M N), (d) (F S X 6), (e) (I Y 5), (f) (Q U 2). Almost all errors occur within these sets; confusions rarely occur across sets.

Table 15.1 summarizes experiments which use template matching with confusable vocabularies. Almost all of these studies include several experimental conditions where effects of different representations and algorithmic variations are explored. Rather than detail each of these conditions, we report the range of results over all conditions.

The results shown in Table 15.1 are consistent across experiments. Recognition accuracy for the alphadigit vocabulary is typically between 60–80% for telephone bandwidth speech and 80-90% for speech sampled at higher rates.[3]

The ability of template matching systems to perform fine phonetic distinctions is illustrated best by recognition rates obtained for the "E set": (B, C, D, E, G, P, T, V, Z, 3). Recognition of these letters is about 60% (Rabiner, Levinson, Rosenberg, & Wilpon, 1979; Waibel & Yegnanarayana, 1981). But even this error rate is an overestimate of the ability of template matching to perform fine phonetic distinctions, since many letter pairs in the E set are not acoustically confusable. For example, B versus C, D versus C, B versus Z, and E versus C, should not be considered fine phonetic distinctions. Examination of the E-set confusions reported by Rabiner et al., (1979) and Waibel and Yegnanarayana (1981) reveals that the letters B, D, E, are recognized at less than 50% accuracy.

One of the main reasons that template-matching systems perform poorly with confusable vocabularies is that all parts of an utterance are given equal weight during recognition. Clearly, in order to discriminate among B and D, we would like to give more weight to information at the beginning of the utterance. Template matching systems give equal weight to each time frame. Thus, when trying to discriminate B from D, irrelevant variation in the vowel part of the utterance can outweigh the more important information

[3] The only disparate data point is the 98% accuracy reported by White and Neely (1976). This result represents performance for a single speaker (GW) who is a sophisticated user of speech-recognition machines. As Dixon and Silverman (1981) note, the significant variables in template-matching studies are the vocabulary items and the speakers; all other variables produce small variations in performance. The 98% reported by White and Neely can be attributed to the particular speaker used in that experiment.

TABLE 15.1

Template Matching Studies With Confusable Vocabularies

Experiment	*Data*	*Speakers*	*Representation*	*Upper Freq.(kHz)*	*Recognition Rate(%)*
Itakura (1975)	Alphadigit	1	LPC - 8	3.0	87
White & Neely (1976)	Alphadigit	1	LPC - 14 and Filter Bank	5.0	91-98
Rabiner et al.[a] (1979)	Alphadigit	100	LPC - 8	3.2	59-82
Rabiner & Wilpon[a] (1979)	Alphadigit	100	LPC - 8	3.2	65-86
Das (1980)	Alphadigit	8	5 Freq. coeff.	4.5	81-90
Dixon & Silverman (1981)	Alphadigit	22	12 filter bands	5.0	80-82
	Confusable words[b]	22			70-76
Rabiner & Wilpon[a] (1981)	Alphadigit	100	LPC - 8	3.2	84-88
Bradshaw, Cole & Li (1982)	Alphadigit	8	16 mel scale coefficients	4.6	84-93
Lamel & Zue (1982)	Alphadigit	10	27 log scale coefficients	4.8	84-89
E-set results					
Rabiner, et al.	E set[c]				57
Waibel & Yegnanarayana (1981)	E set	8	16 mel scale coefficients	4.6	58-60
Bradshaw, et al.	E set				63-84

[a] Speaker-independent, averaging 12 templates per word determined by clustering algorithms.

[b] B, V, thee, in'valid, inva'lid, dressed, add rest, addressed, saline, sailing.

[c] E set = B, C, D, E, G, P, T, V, Z, 3.

at the beginning of the utterance. Dynamic programming approaches to speech-recognition fail to focus attention on the most informative parts of an utterance.

A possible solution to this problem is to automatically focus on the informative parts of an utterance. Rabiner and Wilpon (1981) developed a two-pass recognition approach for classifying digits and letters. During the first pass, the utterance was classified as belonging to one of the confusable sets. During the second pass, a locally weighted distance was used to provide optimal separation among the words in each class. Recognition improvements of from 3% to 7% were obtained. Bradshaw, Cole, and Li (1982) used a similar procedure to evaluate performance on letters in the "E set." They obtained an improvement in recognition accuracy from 63% to 84%.

Research in acoustic phonetics and speech perception suggests why template matching systems are unable to perform fine phonetic distinctions. These experiments show that there are many different cues to each phonetic distinction, and listeners make use of all available cues (Cole & Scott, 1974b). For example, Lisker (1978) has provided a catalogue of 16 different cues to the voicing of stops in intervocalic position. Moreover, the various cues to a particular phonetic distinction are distributed across both frequency and time. Thus, it is necessary to identify and integrate diverse sources of information to arrive at a phonetic percept.

To summarize, in order to perform fine phonetic distinctions, it is necessary to extract a number of acoustic features from the speech signal—features such as formant frequencies and formant trajectories—and integrate these features to define a phonetic category. Since these features occur at different times in the signal and covary among each other, the information needed to perform fine distinctions cannot be captured by comparing individual spectral slices. We therefore conclude that speech-recognition systems which use template matching technology will not be able to achieve human levels of performance.

FEATURE-BASED RECOGNITION

Feature-based recognition is an alternative to frame-by-frame spectral matching. The idea behind feature-based recognition is to identify and automatically extract those acoustic features from the speech signal that are needed to identify phonetic events.

Figure 15.1 illustrates the advantage of using carefully chosen features and multivariate classification for determining speaker-independent categories for vowels. The figure includes four schematic spectrograms of the vowels "eh" and "ih" that show substantially different formant frequencies for the male and female tokens of each vowel. However, the *relationships* among the formant frequencies define a speaker-independent pattern for each vowel; "eh' consists of equally spaced formants, while "ih" has about twice the frequency

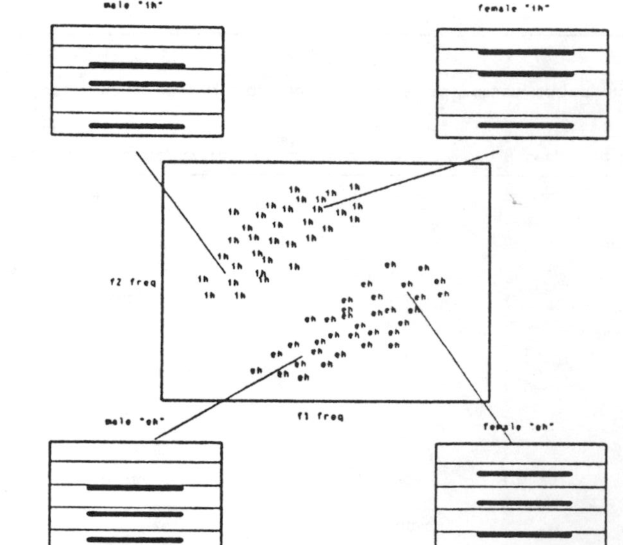

FIG. 15.1. Schematic spectrograms, and comparisons of the first two formant frequencies, of two vowels from male and female speakers.

separation between the first and second formants as between the second and third. The central panel in the figure is a two-dimensional projection of the first two formants. The vowels group into two separate regions that are speaker-independent descriptions of the vowels "eh" and 'ih'.

The feature-based system described below was motivated by spectrogram reading experiments performed with our colleague Victor Zue (Cole, Rudnicky, Zue & Reddy, 1980; Cole & Zue, 1980). These studies showed that it is possible to identify acoustic features on speech spectrograms which form speaker-independent patterns for phonetic segments. Our studies with Victor Zue suggested the following strategy for developing a feature-based speech-recognition system:

- Study various types of visual displays of speech to determine the features that are needed to discriminate among phonetic segments. There will be several different features needed for each fine phonetic distinction, and these features are likely to be distributed across both frequency and time.
- Create algorithms to extract the features from speech.
- Determine the best way to use the featural information to specify speaker-independent patterns for phonetic events. The classifier must be able to take into account the manner in which features

covary, so that it will be possible to capture trading relations among features.

FEATURE: A feature-based speech recognition system

Research leading to the development of FEATURE began in 1980, when the first author intensively studied speech spectrograms of letters and digits. The goal was to acquire knowledge about the speaker-independent characteristics of English letters and digits. The data base consisted of 2,880 broadband speech spectrograms. The spectrograms displayed 10 tokens of each of the letters A through Z and the digits 0 through 9 produced by four male and four female speakers.

After two weeks of study, the reader was able to identify letters and digits on spectrograms with about 2% error. When a new speaker was encountered, the same pattern emerged. During the first "run" through a set of letters and digits (one spectrogram of each letter and digit) the reader produced one to three errors, and these occurred on confusable items such as P–T, B–D, R–4, I–5. After studying the spectrograms of the confusable items, the reader was able to discover reliable features for each new speaker. We were thus able to show that it is possible to learn to read spectrograms of letters and digits after a short period of intensive study, and to specify the features that distinguish confusable items.

On the basis of knowledge gained during this experiment, we developed a feature-based, speaker-independent isolated letter recognition system. FEATURE consists of the following modules:

- A program that detects the onset of speech and creates a file containing the digitized waveform.
- Signal processing routines that transform speech into a set of representations from which features can be extracted.
- A set of feature-extraction routines that measure formant frequencies, formant slopes, and other features.
- Statistical classification routines that use the feature values to classify letters at each of a series of decision points until a single letter is identified.
- A program that uses feedback to modify the expected feature values at each decision point.

Representation. The signal processing routines produce a set of data structures that are used by the feature extraction algorithms. These vectors and arrays vary as a function of time and include information about (a) the spectrum; (b) pitch; (c) zero crossings; (d) total energy; (e) energy in a low frequency band; (f) energy in a mid-frequency band; and (g) energy in a high-frequency band.

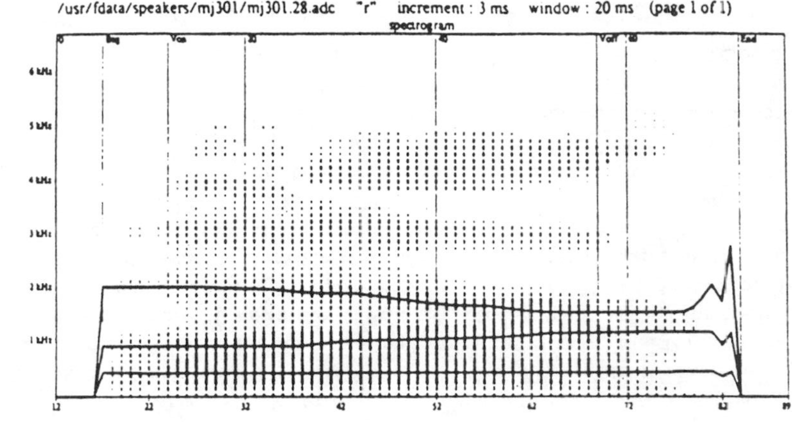

FIG. 15.2. Spectrogram of the letter "R" using digital spectral representation. The lines are drawn automatically using the formant extraction algorithms.

The spectral representation consists of 54 coefficients compressed from a sequence of 256-point DFTs. The 54 coefficients are computed every 3 msec over 20 msec of speech. The coefficients span the range from 63 to 6,093 Hz. The bandwidth of each coefficient is 250 Hz, and coefficients overlap by 125 Hz. Most of the feature detection algorithms (such as the formant frequency estimators) use this array. Figure 15.2 shows a typical spectrogram of the letter (R) generated from this array. The formant tracks are drawn automatically by our formant estimation algorithms.

Segmentation. Four points are located in each utterance: the beginning of the utterance, the vowel onset, the vowel offset and the endpoint of the utterance. These four points are used as temporal anchors for the feature extraction algorithms.

Feature Extraction. Features were discovered through examination of visual displays of the representations produced by the signal processing routines. The most useful display was the computer-generated spectrogram using the coefficient values in the spectral array. In general, the features used to make fine phonetic distinctions correspond to the acoustic cues reported in the acoustic-phonetic literature. These include:

- The frequencies of the first three formants in the vowel portion of the sound (used to discriminate among different vowels).
- The trajectories of the first three formants in the vowel portion of the sound (e.g., E set versus U set; I versus Y versus R; M versus N).

- The maximum and minimum frequencies of the first three formants between vowel onset and vowel offset (I Y R versus A, L, O),
- The duration of aperiodic energy before vowel onset (voiced versus voiceless stops, CV versus V and VC syllables).
- The duration of aperiodic energy after vowel offset (VC versus V and CV syllables).
- The attack characteristics of the sound (T versus Z; P versus Z; P versus V)
- The ratio of high frequency energy to low frequency energy before vowel onset (B, P, V versus D, T, Z) or after vowel offset (F versus S).

In all, about 50 different features were used to discriminate among the letters of the English alphabet.

Decision Strategy. The hierarchical decision tree shown in Figure 15.3 was used to classify letters. By using a decision-tree structure we were able to reduce the problem of choosing one of 26 letters on the basis of observed values of up to 50 features to a series of decisions between smaller numbers of candidate sets, using a relatively small number of features at a time. For example, at the fourth level, letters are classified into groups of vowels on the basis of formant frequencies. At the later levels, where fine phonetic distinctions are performed, just those measures that are needed to discriminate the confusable letters are used. This approach significantly reduces the dimensionality of the decision space within which the classifications are performed.

The combinations of features actually used at each node of the decision tree were selected automatically. Specifically, a principal components analysis was first performed to reduce the dimensionality of the decision space, and to avoid linearly dependent combinations of the original 50 features. At each node of the decision tree a discriminant analysis was performed to determine sets of linear combinations of features that maximized the ratio of class-to-class covariance to the average covariance within a given decision class. *A posteriori* probabilities of the letters given the observed combinations of feature values were evaluated at each node of the decision tree, using the methods described below. At each subsequent node of a given branch of the decision tree, new linear combinations of feature values were selected that were approximately uncorrelated with the combinations of features that were used to evaluate probabilities at previous nodes along the branch. Because these sets of features were assumed to be uncorrelated, the overall *a posteriori* probabilities of each letter were obtained by multiplying the probabilities calculated at the nodes of the decision tree along the branch ending with that letter. The letter with greatest *a posteriori* probability was the one recognized by the classifier.

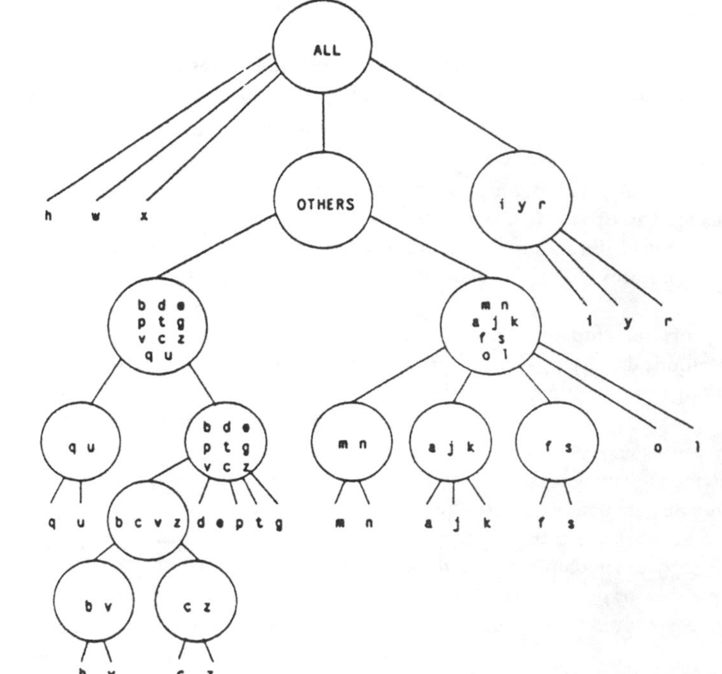

FIG. 15.3. Decision tree used in classifying the letters of the alphabet.

Dynamic Speaker Adaptation. Even when features are designed to be speaker-independent, it is often the case that individual speakers will produce unusual values for some features for some letters. The tuning program produces a running estimate of the expected feature values for individual speakers using maximum *a posteriori* probability (MAP) estimation techniques. After each utterance, the program optimally combines the feature values obtained from the observations thus far with *a priori* statistics obtained from the training data. The amount by which new observations shift the running estimates depends on the sample-to-sample variability of the observed data compared to the speaker-to-speaker variability of the expected feature values. The program also exploits correlations from feature to feature for a given letter and from letter to letter. This component of the system is discussed in further detail in the section "Tuning to Individual Speakers" below.

Performance. The data base used to develop feature extraction algorithms consisted of four tokens of each letter produced by 23 male and 20 female speakers. Data were then collected for a new set of 19 speakers (10 male and 9 female) who also recorded four tokens of each letter.

In evaluating the classifier, the new speakers were divided into subgroups of 10 speakers and 9 speakers. The classifier was trained on the original 43 speakers plus one of the two subgroups then tested on the other subgroup. FEATURE classified the letters of the alphabet with an average error rate of 11.2% across the two groups. The error rate on the E set was 16.7%. This compares favorably to speaker-dependent error rates of 60% obtained with template matching algorithms on the E set.

An important property of feature-based systems is that errors can be analyzed to determine what feature extraction algorithms need to be improved in order to eliminate confusions. For example, the most common substitution that we observed in the E set was P classified as B. Examination of the feature values for these letters revealed that, in each case, the error occurred because of a short Voice Onset Time (more characteristic of B than P). Further analysis revealed that Voice Onset Time was too short because of an error in the automatic location of the vowel onset. If we can eliminate this problem, we will decrease the current error rate by 1%. This seems like a small improvement, but many such improvements will result in a system that can perform fine phonetic distinctions as well as human listeners.

VARIABILITY AND FEATURES

The success of FEATURE depends critically on knowledge of variability in speech. Estimates of the variance and covariance of feature values within letters, across letters, within speakers, and across speakers forms the basis for both the classification of letters and dynamic adaptation to new speakers. Since the theme of this volume is the nature of variability in speech, this section presents a review of the of the sources of variability in speech that are used in classification and dynamic adaptation in FEATURE.

Bayesian Classification

FEATURE classifies letters using Bayesian classification methods. In this section, we briefly review the principles of Bayesian classification, concentrating on the ways in which the optimal classification procedures make use of variance and covariance in classifying data.

Decisions in Bayesian classification are made on the basis of which class of utterance is the most probable, given the specific values of the features that are extracted by the system. We adopt the notation C_i to indicate the ith decision class, the vector $\mathbf{x}$ to indicate the set of observed feature values, and $P(C_i|\mathbf{x})$ to represent the *a posteriori* conditional probability of the decision class C_i being correct given the observed features $\mathbf{x}$. The Bayesian classifier, then, chooses the class C_i for which $P(C_i|\mathbf{x})$ is maximum. This probability is calculated by applying Bayes rule

$$P(C_i|\mathbf{x}) = p(\mathbf{x}|C_i)P(C_i)/p(\mathbf{x}) \tag{1}$$

In most applications it is sufficient to compare the numerators of the above expression for the various decision classes since the denominator is the same in each case.

In order to implement Bayesian classification, it is necessary to estimate or compute $P(C_i)$, the *a priori* probabilities of the various letters, and $p(\mathbf{x}|C_i)$, the probability distribution of each feature vector given that a particular letter has been presented to the classifier. In our current implementation of FEATURE, we assume that letters are equiprobable, and that the statistics of the feature values can be reasonably approximated as jointly gaussian random variables. The gaussian assumption is almost certainly inadequate when large numbers of features are considered at once, but it was adopted as a first working hypothesis because it is the only probability density function that can be easily applied to a large number of statistically correlated features.

Equation (1) can be evaluated directly for the various C_i since explicit analytic expressions for $p(\mathbf{x}|C_i)$ are specified by the multivariate gaussian assumption. Since the general results are available in any standard text on pattern classification (e.g. Duda and Hart, 1973), we will only illustrate through the use of several simple examples how optimal Bayesian classification, and FEATURE in particular, makes use of various types of variance and invariance in recognizing speech.

VARIANCE OF INDIVIDUAL FEATURES

Let us first consider the simplest possible recognition task in which we are recognizing samples from an alphabet of only two letters on the basis of the observed values x of a single feature. Intuitively we would expect that the decision rule for classification should depend on the means and variances of x given that utterances from either decision class 1 or decision class 2 are presented to the system, as well as the *a priori* probability of either class being presented.

If the feature value x has the same variance for the two decision classes, the gaussian assumption leads to the decision rule

Choose class 1 if $x < \gamma$ (2a)

Choose class 2 if $x > \gamma$ (2b)

where $\gamma = (m_1 + m_2)/2 + \sigma \ln [P(C_1)/P(C_2)]$

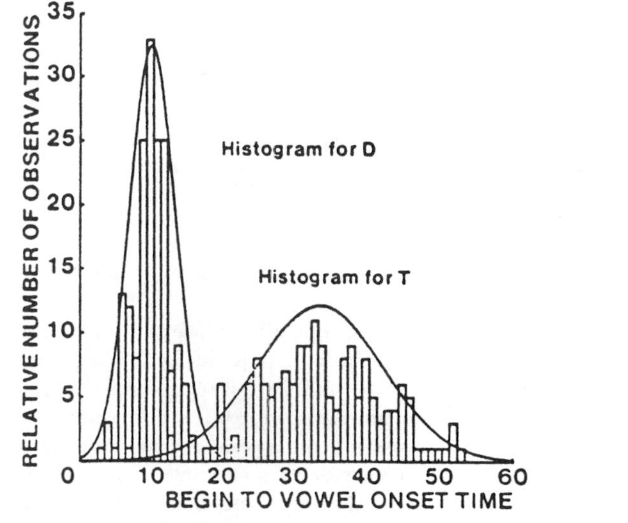

FIG. 15.4. Histograms and Gaussian probability densities for the time between the beginning of an utterance and vowel onset (in arbitrary units) for the letters D and T.

The symbols m_1 and m_2 represent the means of the feature values x given class 1 or class 2 respectively, and σ is the standard deviation of x for the two decision classes. In effect this decision rule partitions the possible values of x into two regions separated by the criterion γ. If C_1 and C_2 are equiprobable, the criterion γ is halfway between m_1 and m_2, so an unknown utterance is assigned to the class with the "closest" mean value along the x continuum. If $P(C_1)$ and $P(C_2)$ are not equal, the criterion γ shifts so as to assign ambiguous samples (i.e. values of x that are close to the midpoint between m_1 and m_2) to the class of letters with greater *a priori* probability. The amount of criterion shift is controlled by the standard deviation of the feature values σ. Specifically, larger values of σ imply that the particular feature value x is more intrinsically variable. In such a case the criterion is shifted so that the final decision is more heavily influenced by the *a priori* probabilities of the decision classes, and decisions are less dependent on the specific values of ambiguous observations.

In general, the variance of the feature values will depend on which class of letters is presented. For example, Figure 15.4 shows histograms of values of a feature measuring the time from the beginning of an utterance to the onset of voicing for the letters D and T, with gaussian probability densities superimposed over the histograms. The histograms represent data from 42 speakers, and the validity of the gaussian assumption can be evaluated by comparing the shapes of the histograms to the smooth curves. As can be

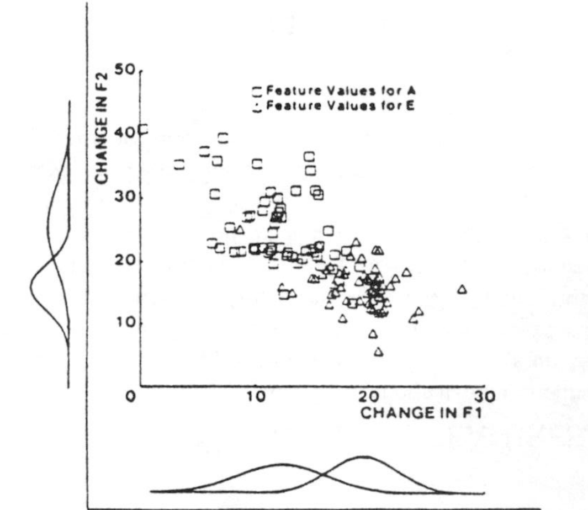

FIG. 15.5. Two-dimensional scatter plot of two frequency-based features for the letters A and E.

seen from the figure, the standard deviation of this feature is about 2.7 times as large when the letter T is presented to the recognizer than when D is presented. The decision boundaries specified by the Bayesian classifier under the assumption that the letters are equiprobable are at the points of intersection of the probability densities. If the variance of a feature differs from class to class, the decision boundary shifts away from the mean value of the class with the greater variance. In a two-class problem, this has the effect of causing observations that fall about halfway between the two mean feature values to be assigned to the decision class producing greater variance in the features, which is what would be desired intuitively.

Covariance of Sets of Features

In order to achieve the best recognition performance possible it is necessary to consider not only the individual means and variances of each of these features but also the covariance of the features as well. The reason for this is shown in Figure 15.5, which displays a two-dimensional histogram of values of features measuring the first and second formant frequencies at the time of vowel onset for the letters A and E. The bell-shaped curves along the coordinate axes of the figure are proportional to the probability density functions characterizing the two features for each of the letters, if we accept the gaussian assumption as valid. The fact that these probability densities overlap quite a bit indicates that recognition performance based on the observed values of either of these features independently would be relatively poor. On the other hand, the observed feature values separate into two well-defined clouds if we consider the histograms as points in a two-dimensional space. This separability indicates that a classifier can be constructed that will achieve good recognition performance for these two letters if it incorporates knowledge of the expected correlation of the two features for each letter, as well as statistics describing the behavior of each of the features considered separately.

If all the letters are equiprobable, the assumption of multivariate gaussian probabilities for the features in the Bayesian classifier leads to a classification rule that essentially minimizes the "distance" in the vector space of the observed feature values from the centroid of the cloud of histogram points observed for the ith letter to be recognized. This measure of distance accommodates differences in variance among the features, as well as correlations of the two features. For example, if the cloud of feature values is ellipsoidal in shape, an observation that falls along the major axis of the ellipse would be closer to the center of the cloud in the sense of the distance measure used by the classifier than a second observation that is equally distant in the usual Euclidean sense, but located along the minor axis. In the two-feature case shown in Figure 15.5, this decision rule partitions the two-dimensional space of possible observations into regions corresponding to each possible decision.

As an example of the improvement in performance that can be obtained by making use of correlation of the feature values, we compared the classification error rate for the letters of the E set with and without considering these correlations. Training on three groups of 28 speakers and testing on 14 other speakers, we observed an error rate of 12.5% for the E-set letters when the features were considered independently, compared to 10.1% errors when the classifier was able to exploit correlations among the features.[4] We expect that the improvement in performance obtained by considering featural correlation will be even greater in discriminating vowel sounds.

Tuning to Individual Speakers

A third way in which variability is important in FEATURE is in dynamic adaptation or "tuning" to the acoustical characteristics of individual speakers. Even though the features used in the system were designed to be speaker independent, the variation of individual feature values for a given letter is frequently smaller within a given speaker than from speaker to speaker. For example, across all speakers the average second formant frequency before the onset of the nasal murmur may be 1200 Hz in M and 1800 Hz in N, but a particular speaker may produce average values of 1800 Hz for M 2400 Hz for N. In such cases, the performance of the recognition system can be greatly improved by adapting the statistical parameters of the feature values to the individual speakers.

In our research in dynamic adaptation, we have primarily been concerned with enabling the system to update its estimates of the mean values of the features for a given letter when spoken by a particular individual. FEATURE begins by recognizing utterances according to mean feature values estimated by averaging training data from a representative set of speakers. The system then adapts to the characteristics of an individual speaker after it is informed by user feedback which letter had actually been spoken.

The goal of the dynamic adaptation component of FEATURE is to combine in some optimal fashion the *a priori* information representing the average behavior of all speakers with the *a posteriori* information gained when the system receives samples of speech from the individual presently using the system. We have used another Bayesian technique, maximum *a posteriori* probability (MAP) estimation, to accomplish this task. (Classical MAP estimation has been applied to many types of statistical problems, including estimation of vocal tract length [Kirlin, 1978]). In our dynamic adaptation of the system's representation of the feature mean values to individual speakers, we choose the mean vector M to maximize the *a posteriori* probability

$$p(M|\mathrm{x}) = \frac{p(\mathrm{x}|M)}{p(\mathrm{x})} \qquad (3)$$

where $p(\mathrm{x}|M)$ is the conditional probability density for the observed feature values given a particular mean vector for a specific letter, and $p(\mathrm{x})$ and $p(M)$ are the *a priori* probability densities for the mean vectors and the observations, respectively. While this expression is obviously very similar to Equation (1), we note that x now represents the complete set of observed feature values for all utterances presented to the recognition system, rather than just the observations used for a single classification.

The MAP estimate obtained when the mean values of the features as well as the data are assumed to be gaussian is indeed a linear combination of the average across all speakers of the mean values of the features in the training data, and the sample mean of the feature values observed up to the present utterance. The relative weighting of this *a priori* and *a posteriori* information is determined by the ratio of within-speaker variability to across-speaker variability of the observed values of a given feature, and a small value of this ratio indicates that the performance of a given feature is more likely to be improved by dynamic adaptation to individual speakers. Our

[4] The classification procedure used in this evaluation and the evaluation cited in the next section was similar to the procedure described above except that classification decisions are made at each node on the basis of observed values of hand-selected features. In addition, "hard decisions" were made in that only the decision class with the greatest *a posteriori* probability at any given node was considered at subsequent decision nodes.

analysis of these variances indicates that formant estimates and other spectral features derive the most benefit from tuning to individual speakers. The values of features that record temporal events (such as the interval between the beginning of an utterance and vowel onset) tend to be more speaker independent.

An important innovation of FEATURE is that we characterize the mean feature values as random variables that may be correlated from class to class. This approach enables the system to use samples of the letter ⟨M⟩, for example, to update estimates of the expected feature values for the letter ⟨N⟩ as well as ⟨M⟩. As a result, the system adapts more rapidly to individual speakers than it would if all the mean values of the features were assumed to be statistically independent, but at the cost of greater computational complexity and storage requirements.

We have compared the performance of an earlier implementation of FEATURE with and without the use of tuning to individual speakers (Stern & Lasry, 1983). After four presentations of the entire alphabet (with feedback to the system indicating which letter had been presented) the system's error rate using multivariate Bayesian classification alone dropped from 12.5% to 6.1%. Similarly, the error rate for confusing the letters B, D, P, and T dropped from 8.1% to 1.7%, and the error rate for confusing the letters M and N dropped from 8.4% to 4.2%.

CONCLUSION

We have demonstrated that a recognition system based on perceptually-derived features of speech can significantly outperform systems based on more traditional spectral matching approaches, such as dynamic programming, when the recognition task requires that fine phonetic distinctions be performed. Our feature-based system can recognize the letters of the English alphabet with a speaker-independent error rate of about 11%. These error rates decrease considerably when the system is permitted to adapt to the acoustical characteristics of individual speakers. The system achieves an error rate of 16.7% on the confusable E set. In contrast, most template-based systems recognize the English alphabet with an error rate of 15% to 30%, and they classify the E-set letters with error rates of 20% to 40%.

We find it interesting that FEATURE emulates some of the important characteristics of human speech perception. Decisions about phonetic events are based on many different features distributed across both frequency and time. For example, a decision about the letter V is based on onset information, the fricative spectrum, changes in formant frequencies after vowel onset, and several other features. The manner in which these features covary is taken into account when using multivariate statistics.

ACKNOWLEDGMENTS

This research was sponsored in part by the National Science Foundation, Grant MCS-7825824 and in part by the Defense Advanced Research Projects Agency (DOD), ARPA Order No. 3597, monitored by the Air Force Avionics Laboratory Under Contract F33615-78-C-1551.

The views and conclusions contained in this document are those of the authors and should not be interpreted as representing the official policies, either expressed or implied, of the Defense Advanced Research Projects Agency or the US Government.

Many additional researchers in the Carnegie-Mellon University speech group contributed significantly to the software implementations of the FEATURE system, including Michael Phillips, Scott Brill, Andrew Pilant, Philippe Specker, and Robert Brennan. The classifier using automatic feature selection was created and implemented by Alan Rogers.

Victor W. Zue: Comment

In order to comment on the system described in Chapter 15, it is necessary to first understand the state of the art. Today's isolated word recognition (IWR) systems share several features. These systems generally require clear pauses, typically 200 ms, between words and usually operate in a speaker-dependent mode. That is, systems must be trained for a particular speaker's voice. Treating each word as a unit, recognition is performed by matching the parameters of the input signal to the stored templates for the vocabulary items. The stored template that best matches with the input is selected to be the intended word. The scoring algorithm uses time-alignment procedures (the most successful being dynamic programming) designed to account for the inherent variability of the speech signal. These IWR systems usually operate on a small vocabulary of 10 to 200 items.

Despite intensive effort in speech recognition over the past years, there is still a very large gap between human and machine performance. Human speech recognition is robust and flexible: A person can recognize a novel sentence produced by unfamiliar talkers in hostile acoustic environments. In contrast, computer speech-recognition systems typically require training for each speaker, and the performance is very poor for acoustically confusable words. For example, as mentioned by Cole, et al., template-matching systems typically recognize only 60% of the confusable E-set of the letters of the alphabet.

Cole and his colleagues argue that in order to perform fine phonetic distinctions, one must identify and extract acoustic features from the speech signal that are needed to specify phonetic events. Their system, called FEATURE, is designed to recognize the letters of the English alphabets. It is motivated by experimental results in acoustic phonetics, speech perception, and spectrogram reading, indicating the presence of multiple acoustic cues and the trading relations among the various cues. Their approach in the development of the feature-based system involves the following three steps: (1) the acoustic features are determined through studies of various visual displays of a large body of data; (2) algorithms for feature extraction are then created; and (3) classification is done by taking into account interfeature and intrafeature variabilities, using statistical techniques. I think the FEATURE system is one of the most exciting milestones of speech recognition in recent years. Measured in terms of performance, the FEATURE system offers the best recognition results anywhere for the task of alphabet recognition. It constitutes an existence-proof that a feature-based system can outperform the so-called template-matching systems. By incorporating dynamic adaptation through feedback, the system gradually adjusts its performance to a given speaker. This second characteristic of the system is both attractive and essential. Having said this, I now offer some critical comments.

First, Cole contrasts his feature-based approach with the template-matching approach in which the spectrum is used directly for recognition. Strictly speaking, however, this use of the term "feature based" to distinguish such approaches from spectral ones is inappropriate. In the pattern classification literature, template matching refers to techniques for answering questions of the form "Does the input contain an instance of some previously-specified object?" by comparing the unknown with a prototype. Using this definition, feature-based speech-recognition systems which use multivariate gaussian models for classification also perform template matching. Similarly, spectrum amplitudes may be regarded as features so that spectrum-based techniques are "feature-based" as well. What is more important is whether and how much speech-specific knowledge is being utilized for recognition. In the development of the FEATURE system, Cole utilized an enormous amount of speech knowledge by literally examining thousands of spectrograms to discover the acoustic cues. It represents one of the most massive efforts to derive acoustic cues for phonetic contrasts.

One of the most serious problems with a template-matching approach is that it is difficult to define distance measures which are sensitive enough for fine phonetic distinctions but insensitive to irrelevant spectral changes. One manifestation of this problem is that perceptually-unimportant frame-to-frame variations in the spectrum of a long steady-state vowel are given excessive weight. Klatt (Chapter 14) has proposed a number of distance metrics which are intended to be sensitive to phonetic differences and insensitive to irrelevant acoustic differences. Such a distance metric may improve the performance of template-matching systems, since it includes speech knowledge in the measurement of spectral distances.

Second, in a feature-based approach, there are several levels where acoustic-phonetic knowledge can be introduced. On one hand, one must uncover acoustic attributes that are useful in signifying phonetic contrasts. On the other hand, one must also determine how these attributes should be combined to make the phonetic distinction. The FEATURE system selects a set of acoustic attributes that are well motivated. However, the system falls short of specifying the procedure for how these features should be combined for phonetic recognition, and instead classifies the lexical items directly in terms of traditional, statistical techniques for pattern classification. A conclusion that one may draw is that, even with no knowledge about how the acoustic cues should be combined, a set of speech-specific acoustic cues can go a long way in improving system performance.

Third, the FEATURE system is developed for a specific task. Whether the system can be extended to other tasks is not entirely clear. In the system, the four temporal anchors clearly play an important role in the extraction of acoustic attributes. It is doubtful that such anchors can reliably be obtained for a different lexicon. The lexical items of the FEATURE system are relatively simple; i.e., they represent a very small subset of the possible CV and VC combinations used in American English. As consonant clusters and more vowels are introduced, it remains to be seen whether the basic approach is still viable. One task that comes to mind, in order to answer the question of extendibility, is the recognition of a variety of CVs. It would also be of interest to see how system performance degrades when noise, either stationary or transient, is added to the speech signal.

Finally, we come to the question of variability and invariance, which is the theme of this volume. Variabilities in the speech signal can be due to speaker-specific factors, ranging from physiological to sociolinguistic ones. They can also appear as a consequence of contextual influence. The system developed by Cole and his colleagues shows that a judicious selection of well-motivated acoustic attributes will enable variabilities to be captured in the variance and covariance of the feature values. On the other hand, the dependence of system performance on speakers is somewhat alarming. The error rate for the best and worst speaker differ by an order of magnitude. By the authors' own admissions, the performance of their system is still a long way from human performance on the same task.

My comments should not be interpreted as being overly critical of Cole's work. I really intend to point out the magnitude of the problem facing speech-recognition researchers. Cole and his colleagues have made significant contributions to this field. However, there is much much more to be done. Success is more likely to be measured in decades, rather than years.

John Makhoul and Richard Schwartz: Ignorance Modeling

It has become quite clear that our knowledge, either of speech perception or in extracting features that are useful in automatic speech recognition, is very limited. Furthermore, part of that knowledge may, in fact, be erroneous or it may be used erroneously in speech-recognition systems.

Our conclusion from these observations is that, in incorporating our knowledge in a speech-recognition system, we should not neglect to *model our ignorance*. In fact, we believe that, in the last decade or so, high-performance speech-recognition systems have achieved their performance exactly because they had better ignorance models than other systems. We shall demonstrate what we mean by modeling ignorance using some examples.

In template-matching approaches to word recognition, one often computes the similarity of two spectra by using a simple Euclidean type of distance measure. Such distance measures are really ignorance models of perceptual distance between two spectra. Euclidean distances have certain desirable mathematical properties that are found to be useful in recognition, but certainly are not optimal.

In matching the templates of two words, we know that speech changes dynamically in time but don't know exactly how. We use dynamic time warping (Sakoe & Chiba, 1978) as our ignorance model for how speech varies in time. The model basically accepts that we don't know how to warp one word template to compare it to another, so we will try all possibilities (within limits) and pick the warp that gives the minimum distance between templates. This is a mathematical solution with certain desirable properties which result in improved recognition performance, but certainly not optimal performance.

Our final example of an ignorance model, and certainly one of the most powerful, is the probabilistic hidden-Markov model developed at the Institute for Defense Analyses (Baum, 1972) and used most successfully at IBM (Bahl, Jelinek, & Mercer, 1983). At IBM, a phoneme is represented by a hidden-Markov model with a structure that incorporates only a very small amount of speech knowledge. The model parameters are probability density functions that are estimated from training data. One of the major features of the estimation procedure is that while it requires a large amount of training data, computing resources, and storage, it requires relatively little human interaction. The IBM experience has been that, often, a simple but self-optimizing procedure outperforms human intuitions about speech as they are incorporated into automatic recognition systems.

Future speech research should be directed at producing knowledge and intuition that could be incorporated in the design of recognition systems, especially in minimizing the amount of training necessary for optimal performance, and eventually leading to virtually speaker-independent systems. Simultaneously, the search should continue for more sophisticated ignorance models that can make optimal use of what little knowledge we do have.

John Holmes: Comment

Victor Zue has already said much of what I was going to say. The main aspect I am unhappy about in Cole's paper is the presentation of template matching and the use of features as a dichotomy. Even assuming one regards the use of templates in the traditional way involving fairly crude pattern matching, there is no reason why there should not be a lot more speech-specific knowledge put into the patterns that are compared.

If the processes I suggested after Klatt's paper (Chapter 14) were adopted, highlighting in the measurement space such aspects as formant transitions and stop bursts, the template-matching approach would become much more like a feature-based system. I personally believe that the right sort of dynamic-programming algorithm, using a more speech-related measurement space, might have more explanatory power than the type of tree-structured process that Cole and his colleagues have described.

Recognition of speaker-dependent continuous speech with KEAL

G. Mercier
D. Bigorgne
L. Miclet
L. Le Guennec
M. Querre

Indexing terms: Speech recognition, Acoustics, Training

Abstract: A description of the speaker-dependent continuous speech recognition system KEAL is given. An unknown utterance is recognised by means of the following procedures: acoustic analysis, phonetic segmentation and identification, word and sentence analysis. The combination of feature-based, speaker-independent coarse phonetic segmentation with speaker-dependent statistical classification techniques is one of the main design features of the acoustic-phonetic decoder. The lexical access component is essentially based on a statistical dynamic programming technique which aims at matching a phonemic lexical entry containing various phonological forms, against a phonetic lattice. Sentence recognition is achieved by use of a context-free grammar and a parsing algorithm derived from Earley's parser. A speaker adaptation module allows some of the system parameters to be adjusted by matching known utterances with their acoustical representation. The task to be performed, described by its vocabulary and its grammar, is given as a parameter of the system. Continuously spoken sentences extracted from a 'pseudo-Logo' language are analysed and results are presented.

1 Introduction

KEAL is a continuous and understanding speech recognition system which aims at recognising continuously spoken utterances involved in oral man-machine communication. This paper related results reached by this recognition part of KEAL [16].

Roughly speaking, KEAL is a hierarchical bottom-up speech recognition system [7], which tries to combine statistical, structural and knowledge-based recognition techniques. For instance, its acoustic-phonetic decoder is based on speaker-independent deductive rules able to segment input speech signals into phones and to recognise the main coarse phonetic features characterising these segments. In parallel, speaker-dependent linear discriminant functions allow these first phonetic hypotheses to be refined. The lexical decoder of KEAL is essentially based on a statistical dynamic programming method which aims at matching a phonemic lexical entry containing various phonetic knowledge against a phonetic lattice [19]. Sentence recognition is achieved by use of a context-free grammar (CFG) sentence recogniser [14].

Different experimental tasks are currently under investigation. In this paper, we describe recognition experiments of spoken sentences extracted from the 'pseudo-Logo' task domain. 'Logo' is a well-known natural programming language used to teach computer science to children.

Paper 6465I, first received 18th January 1988 and in revised form 22nd September 1988

The authors are with the Centre National d'Études des Télécommunications, Route de Trégastel, BP 40, 22301 Lannion Cedex, France

2 Main components of KEAL

2.1 Global architecture of KEAL

Fig. 1 shows the mutual disposition of the modules of KEAL. This current version consists of four modules, mostly bottom-up from the acoustic decoder to the syntactic analyser, accompanied by a learning component; this last module works either for extracting the phonetic individualities of a speaker, or for adapting the system (tuned on one given speaker or some 'average speaker') to another one; the latter procedure uses the lexical decoder as a matcher between a known utterance and its recognition before tuning. We shall now describe briefly each of these modules.

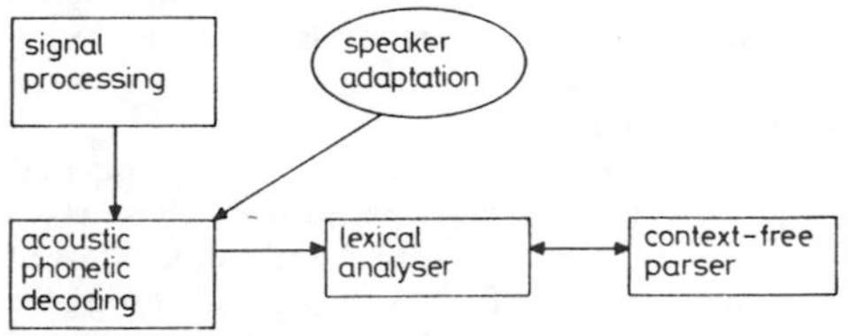

Fig. 1 *Architecture of KEAL*

2.2 Speech processing and acoustic parameters extraction

Acoustic analysis is carried out by an n-channel, mel-scaled vocoder (usual values for the system parameter n are 14, 16 or 29); the acoustic spectrum is computed every 13.3 ms or 10 ms. The energy within each frequency band is measured by a signal processing routine computing a 256-point discrete Fourier transform (DFT) and using a 20 ms window.

The value $n = 14$ corresponds to our basic channel vocoder; the frequency bandwidth of each channel is logarithmically distributed from 250 Hz to 4300 Hz and the frequency bandwidth covered by the first 12 channels corresponds to the telephone bandwidth. The experiments described in the following Sections were driven using this channel vocoder.

The system can be activated by also using a mel-scaled 29-channel vocoder which covers a larger frequency band: 100–6240 Hz. Until now, this latter vocoder was only used for designing new rules aimed at recognising the place of articulation of stop consonants and was not used for the experiments described here. The 16-channel vocoder is another mel-scaled vocoder covering the frequency band 220–5320 Hz; it was not used for the current tests.

The basic analysis frame rate used for our experiments was 13.3 ms. While offering a slightly better temporal signal description, the 10 ms option was not used for the tests because some time duration parameters were not adjusted to this frame rate analysis.

Additional parameters such as voiced–unvoiced decisions, pitch, signal amplitude, and spectral centres of gravity are also measured and used by the phonetic recogniser.

2.3 Phonetic recognition

This module is decomposed into a sequence of step activations: sentence onset detection, centisecond labelling, segmentation into pseudosyllables and phones, primary phonetic feature recognition and phone recognition. A speaker-independent set of rules and speaker-dependent linear decision functions are used for this acoustic-phonetic decoding.

The phonetic module output is a sequence of segments (called a phonetic spectrum or lattice). Among the segment attributes, a probability weighting factor and a list of phonemes, ordered with decreasing likelihood, are given.

These different steps are now described in more detail.

2.3.1 Sentence onset detection: This detection is based on several criteria, refining progressively the precise detection of the speech limits.

First the mean energy of the speech signal is computed and the frame with the maximum energy located and then the amplitudes of its formants are measured. These values are used to normalise thresholds, making it possible to decide whether the beginning and ending frames are possible speech frames. This decision is made by means of rules for comparing the energy levels of each frame to the normalised thresholds.

A second set of rules is applied after the centisecond frame labelling function has been performed. These rules are based on the detection of the first and the last vowel of the speech signal. All the frames at the beginning and at the end of the utterance which are too far from these vowels are considered as noise and are excluded.

2.3.2 Vocalic/nonvocalic centisecond frame labelling: Based on a set of rules and of acoustic cues derived from the basic parameters, each speech frame is labelled as 'consonant', 'vowel' or 'silence'. The assignment of this label starts with the computation of the energies and centres of gravity of the energy distribution in the low, middle, high and total frequencies. Then, for each frame, rules for comparing these parameters either to normalised thresholds, either between them or to the parameters computed on the neighbouring frames are applied.

The closure parts of stops are mostly detected by simple energy criteria. The following rule allows most of fricatives |s| and |ʃ| and sometimes |z| and |ʒ| to be detected:

IF the spectral centre of gravity is greater than some normalised threshold, THEN the frame is labelled 'consonant'.

The following rule tries to detect some unvoiced consonants like |f| and |ʃ| or liquids not detected by simpler rules:

IF the three following conditions are verified, THEN the frame is labelled 'consonant':

(*a*) maxbf < formax
(*b*) $E[250–450] < E[450–650]$
(*c*) $E[450–650] < E[650–850]$

where 'maxbf' represents the amplitude of the low frequency energy maximum, 'formax' represents the amplitude of the highest energy maximum over the speech signal augmented by 30 dB, and $E[a–b]$ is the energy between the frequencies a and b.

Special rules are designed for the detection of vowels such as |i|, |y| and |u| characterised by a lower energy in comparison to the other vowels. Conversely, consonants such as |v|, |ʒ|, nasals or liquids which are sometimes characterised by high energies are also detected by complex rules. About thirty rules are necessary to get this vocalic/nonvocalic decision.

2.3.3 Open/closed and front/back detection: Rules for this feature detection were designed and optimised by Bonneau and Rossi [2] using an expert system and were then implemented in KEAL. Three cues, based on a comparison of energies computed in selected frequency bands, are used, one for measuring the degree of openness and the two others the degree of acuteness. The frequency bands involved in the measurement of the degree of openness are included in the low frequencies (less than 1050 Hz), whereas the degree of acuteness tends to be linked to higher frequencies (from 850 Hz to 3500 Hz). These frequency ranges are tuned according to the mean pitch value. The cues are computed on three selected frames after the vocalic nuclei have been located and a probability of acuteness and openness is assigned to these frames by means of rules, taking into account the values of the cues.

2.3.4 Voiced/unvoiced detection: Voiced consonant frames are separated from unvoiced consonant frames by taking into account the following parameters: the F_0 measurement, the energies in the band 250–650 Hz, and the ratio between low- and high-frequency energies.

2.3.5 Fricative detection: This detection is based on the following parameters: the zero-crossing counts of the signal derivative, the high- to low-frequency energy ratio and the spectral centre of gravity. Other cues, measuring the degree of flatness of a spectrum, are also computed. By means of these latter cues, fricatives such as |v| can be detected.

2.3.6 Nasal consonant detection: The value of the spectral centre of gravity is compared to some thresholds and the comparison of the maxima and minima of energies in the low- and high-frequencies provides the main cues for assigning the label 'potentially nasal' to each frame.

2.3.7 Fine phonetic frame labelling: In parallel with the preceding speaker-independent rules which allow a feature label to be assigned to centisecond frames, speaker-dependent linear decision functions are used to assign a 'phone' label to each frame. This is done after the 'vocalic/nonvocalic' decision has been taken. These linear decision functions are defined as follows: each centisecond sample is represented by a vector $X(t)$, the first co-ordinates of which correspond to the differences of energies between consecutive vocoder channels; the following co-ordinates correspond to the energy of the spectrum, the centre of gravity of the total energy distribution, the energies defined inside four frequency subbands and the centre of gravity of the energy distribution in these subbands, respectively; for the consonant frames, two parameters, measuring the local temporal variations of the total energy and of the centre of gravity between the current frame and the preceeding one, are added.

Within each category (vocalic, nonvocalic), it is possible to distinguish between a number m of different phones. Each phone usually has a compact representation in the space in which the centisecond vector sample points $X(t) = \{x_1(t), x_2(t), \ldots, x_i(t), \ldots, x_n(t)\}$ are represented.

The labelling algorithm makes use of a separation of this space by hyperplanes, which are determined by 'fitting' to the clusters as in Chaplin and Levadi [4]. The best fit is determined by a least-square procedure during a training stage [10].

To label a sample $X(t)$, m functions $F_i\{X(t)\}$ depending on the distance of the vector $X(t)$ to each hyperplane are computed. The $mF_i(t)$ values are compared and the sample $X(t)$ is assigned the three phone labels corresponding to the three greatest values of $F_i(t)$, ranked in decreasing order.

2.3.8 Segmentation into pseudosyllables: The basic principle behind this segmentation is the search for the syllable vowel nucleus. This is done in three steps:

(*a*) First, the energy curve measuring the weighted energy in the frequency band 250–4300 Hz is split into consecutive segments each containing an energy maximum. Consecutive short segments for which there is not a significant maximum energy in the low frequency range (250–850 Hz) are concatenated. Conversely, long segments, for which there exists a significant maximum in the low frequency range or enough vocalic frames, are split into two segments.

(*b*) These segments, or pseudosyllables, are then investigated to see whether or not they contain a vocalic nucleus. The following acoustic features are computed:

(i) The low-frequency energies measured at four instants of time, corresponding respectively to the peaks of the preceding and current segments and to the minima of energy before and after the current peak of energy.

(ii) The amplitudes of the first formant computed at the same instant of time.

(iii) The number of 'vowel' frames in the segment.

(iv) A measure of dissimilarity between the current potential vocalic nucleus and the preceding one.

(v) A feature indicating the presence of a significant proportion of 'voiced' frames surrounded by 'unvoiced' frames.

If a pseudosyllable does not contain a vocalic nucleus, or if it is too short or too similar to the neighbouring vocalic nuclei, it is merged with the preceding or the following segment.

(*c*) At the end of this process, the boundaries of the pseudosyllables are determined. This is done by taking the stationary portion between two vocalic nuclei which contains the least energy and designating its first frame as the boundary.

2.3.9 Segmentation into phones: An obvious property of the speech signal is that it is composed of a sequence of stationary or transient events that can be displayed, for instance, by the magnitude of the derivative with respect to time $P(t)$ of the spectral envelope. Consecutive low values of $P(t)$ delimit a stationary portion in the signal, which may contain the main features for certain phonemes, whereas high values of this curve indicate a transient event between phones which may include essential features of one or both of these phones.

In KEAL, vowels are first located within the zone around the energy maximum of each syllable. In addition this zone must contain a sufficient proportion of 'vowel' frames. Sequences of stationary and transient events are then located between each vocalic nucleus. These segments form the new framework within which the main phonetic features will be identified.

2.3.10 Recognition of Vocalic segments: Two alternative vowel recognition procedures are available:

(*a*) A rule feature-based vowel recognition which aims at being speaker independent. According to the procedure described above, the features 'front', 'back', 'open', 'closed' are detected on three frames: the centre of the vowel and the middle of the first and second half of the vowel. A plausibility is assigned to each feature and to each of these frames. Oral-nasal distinction rules are also under development. They are based on a search for flat spectra in the frames belonging to the second part of the vowel. These frames are also characterised by an energy which is lower than the energy of the frames belonging to the first part.

(*b*) The second vowel recognition procedure is very simple; it comprises the computation of m mean values $G(i)$ of the sequence of centisecond samples representing the vowel segment, with

$$G(i) = \frac{1}{l} \sum_{t=t_1}^{t=t_l} F_i(t)$$

where l is the number of centisecond samples in the segment and $F_i(t)$ is the function defined in Section 2.3.7. The phonetic labels that correspond to the highest values of the function $G(i)$ represent the phonetic hypotheses. These values are then combined with the plausibilities obtained by the feature decision rules to eliminate or to make new hypotheses as follows. If the plausibility $P(b)$ of the 'back' feature is greater than 0.7, then each value $G(i)$ corresponding to a front candidate $|i|$ is decreased by the value $G(i)*f$ where $f = P(b)*a$ and a is a factor lying between 0 and 0.25. Similar procedures are applied when the plausibilities of the features 'front', 'open' or 'closed' are greater than 0.7. This recognition strategy is effectively used in the configuration we evaluate here. The oral nasal distinction was not taken into account.

2.3.11 Consonant recognition: Here again two parallel procedures are performed:

(*a*) The feature-based procedure takes into account the centisecond frame feature labelling and new features such as stops or liquids or places of articulation are hypothesised:

(i) For each stationary segment placed between two vocalic nuclei, the proportion of 'voiced' and 'unvoiced' frames is measured and the degree of voiceness or voicelessness is given by this measure. For stops, a second cue, voice onset time (VOT), is measured within the transient segment after the closure. In KEAL, this VOT is a function of the number of voiced or unvoiced frames at the beginning of the burst.

(ii) The feature 'fricative' is assigned if the segment is composed of sufficient frames with the centisecond frame label 'fricative'. Before this assignment, the frame 'fricative' label is refined by comparing the spectrum of each possible fricative frame to the spectrum of the frames corresponding to the energy maxima of the preceding and following vowels.

(iii) A stationary segment will be labelled 'nasal' if it is composed of sufficient 'potentially-nasal spectral frames' and if some contextual and temporal criteria (comparison of each frame spectrum to the neighbouring vocalic spectra) are fulfilled for each frame.

(iv) A liquid |l| or |r| will be detected after a plosive sound if there is at least one maximum in the energy curve together with sufficient energy at low frequencies.

(v) Three main cues are currently considered for recognising the places of articulation of plosives: change in the first spectral centre of gravity, the frequency region in which the spectral energy maximum of the burst is located and change in the amplitude of the signal during the burst. This recognition has to be improved by taking into account the vocalic context.

(*b*) As for vowels, the linear discriminant approach comprises the computation of m mean values $G(i)$ of the sequence of centisecond samples representing the consonant segment, with

$$G(i) = \frac{1}{l} \sum_{t=t_1}^{t=t_l} F_i(t)$$

Before computing the $F_i(t)$ functions, the vector sample points $X(t)$ are modified; global temporal parameters computed along the segment are added to the preceding co-ordinates defined in Section 2.3.7. These co-ordinates represent, for instance, the highest jump of the energy or of the spectral centre of gravity within the segment.

For each segment, the highest values of $G(i)$, correspond to the best phonetic hypotheses. These values and hypotheses are combined with the feature rule-based hypotheses and plausibilities to produce new hypotheses which are stored in the phonetic lattice.

2.3.12 Building the phonetic lattice: The output of the acoustic phonetic decoder is given in the form of segments, each with the following information: reliability value, beginning and ending time of the segment, candidate phones ranked by likelihood score, number of the syllable to which the segment belongs. The average temporal position of each phonetic candidate within its segment is another feature of the phonetic lattice.

Each segment is also weighted by a value measuring the evidence that there is a phone in the position where the segment is detected. This weight depends upon three main factors: energy of the segment, duration and feature labelling evidence. This last factor is measured during the feature-based labelling procedure. For instance, a liquid between two vowels can be very short; however, if the feature labelling procedure has detected the feature 'liquid' with a high plausibility, the weight of this segment will be high (that is 1.00).

These parameters, recorded in the phonetic lattice, are used by the lexical and syntactic analysers to score the lexical and syntactic hypotheses.

2.4 Training and speaker-adaptation

The coefficients of the linear discriminant functions used to separate the phone classes are determined by means of two consecutive procedures:

(*a*) The phonetic segment references necessary for building the training phonetic set are automatically extracted by using an alignment program based on a dynamic programming algorithm described in the following Section. This program maps the acoustic phonetic lattice given by KEAL onto an ideal phonemic transcription of the syllables, words or sentences which form the reference data set. The temporal position of each ideal phoneme is found in the phonetic lattice and it is consequently possible to extract automatically its acoustic representation. In the case of mapping errors, the limits of the segments have eventually to be adjusted (or deleted) by hand to provide the correct acoustic samples.

(*b*) A stochastic approximation program which minimises a least-square criterion on this set of acoustic phone references, supplies the phonetic analyser with the optimal coefficients W of the linear discriminant functions. In fact, two optimal sets W are computed (one for vowels and another one for consonants).

2.5 Lexical analysis

Lexical decoding is a dynamic programming process matching each phonemic symbol spectrum of each lexical entry to a portion of a phonetic lattice produced by the phonetic decoder.

2.5.1 The lexicon: Each lexical entry contains the following information: orthographic form, phonemic symbol spectrum and syntactic category. Only the phonemic symbol spectrum is used by the lexical decoder. Here, spectrum is a sequence of segments:

$$(v_0, \ldots, v_j, \ldots, v_m)$$

with

$$v_j = (z_j, (q_j^1, \ldots, q_j^l, \ldots, q_j^s))$$

The sequence q_j^1 to q_j^s represents different allophonic forms of a phoneme. These characterise contextual and individual pronunciations of this phoneme within a given word; for instance, the digit '0', the standard phonemic form of which is |z e r o|, is represented in the lexicon by the following sequence: |z(e ɛ) r o|; the phonemic form |ɛ| corresponds to an opening of |e| in the context |r|.

Voicing, devoicing, opening and nasalisation are the main phonetic modifications introduced in the lexicon.

Some phonetic segments v_j can be optional. This possibility is represented by the parameter z_j which has the value 0 if the current phoneme can be deleted and 1 in the other cases. This is an interesting way of representing phonological phenomena such as possible phoneme deletions or possible liaisons (insertion of extra phonemes between two consecutive words).

2.5.2 The algorithm: This lexical decoder runs from left to right, performing all the computations needed by a phonetic segment before processing the next one. Moreover, it can be driven by the upper levels, working in this case on a fraction of the lexicon and on a specified sequence of phonetic segments.

The search space is a finite pattern of squares (i, j). The x-axis is the phonetic symbol lattice produced by the phonetic decoder. This phonetic lattice is a sequence of n segments (index i):

$$(u_0, \ldots, u_i, \ldots, u_n)$$

with

$$u_i = (p_i, (q_i^{\alpha_1}, \ldots, q_i^{\alpha_l}, \ldots, q_i^{\alpha_s}))$$

where

p_i weights the evidence that there is a segment u_i to be detected

α_l is a phonetic symbol

$q_i^{\alpha_l}$ weights the independent evidence of the labelling of u_i by α_l

For each word v, the y-axis is composed of the phonemic symbol spectrum representing the various pronunciations of this lexical entry (index j). A local dissimilarity measure $p(i, j)$ is used and a cumulative penalty $P(i, j)$ at point (i, j) is to be minimised to get the optimal match.

$$P(i, j) = P(i', j') + p(i, j)$$

where $p(i, j)$ depends upon the kind of transition from (i', j') to (i, j). $p(i, j)$ is defined by

$$p(i, j) = \min\,(p_{su}, p_{in}, p_{de}, p_{sp}, p_{me})$$

The transition leading to (i, j) may come from

(*a*) $(i-1, j-1)$, the diagonal, normal path, called the substitution (*su*) path.

(*b*) $(i, j-1)$, the vertical, non-diagonal path, called the deletion path (*de*) when the jth phoneme is missing or the merging path (*me*) when two phonemes are merged in one segment in the lattice and are both detected in this segment.

(*c*) $(i-1, j)$, the horizontal, non-diagonal path, called the insertion path (in) when an extra segment is inserted in the lattice after the $(i-1)$th segment; this path is identified as a spreading path (*sp*) when the jth phoneme of the lexical entry is detected in the segments $i-1$ and i.

These five local penalties are defined by the following equations:

$$p_{su} = (1 - x_i^j)y_i + pm(1 - y_i)z_j$$

$$p_{in} = pin\ y_i$$

$$p_{sp} = \min_{d \in \Delta}(1 - x_d^j) + \begin{cases} pm(1 - \sum_\Delta y_d)z_j & \text{if } \sum_\Delta y_d < 1 \\ psp(\sum_\Delta y_d - 1) & \text{otherwise} \end{cases}$$

$$p_{de} = pde \cdot z_j$$

$$p_{me} = (1 - x_i^j)y_i f + pme(1 - y_i f)z$$

where f is a penalty sigmoid function taking its value in the interval [0, 1]; the value taken by f is lower when the temporal distance between the two phones which are merged in the same segment is higher.

y_i is the weight of the ith segment of the phonetic lattice

z_j is the weight of the jth segment of the lexical entry taking for the moment the value 0 or 1 if the segment is optional or not

Δ is the set of the consecutive spread phones d

pin, *psp*, *pde* are penalty factors for insertion, spreading and deletion paths; *pm* is a penalty factor when the weight of the segment is less than 1; all these factors are statistically optimised [8]

$$x_i^j = \max_{\alpha_1, \ldots, \alpha_l, \ldots, \alpha_s} sim(j, l) \cdot q_i^{\alpha_l}$$

$sim(j, l)$ is a statistically established similarity between each phonetic symbol l of the set used by the phonetic decoder and each phonetic symbol j of the set used in the description of the lexicon. (These two sets are not necessarily identical; this allows for the use of archiphonemes in some places and fine allophones in others; it also allows for a first pass of lexical decoding based on broad-class mapping in the case of large vocabularies.)

The optimal global path can sometimes be missed because the spreading penalty p_{sp} is not additive: a minimum over consecutive spreadings is computed. In fact, it seems that the probability of missing the optimal solution is very low.

With the use of a low-score threshold, the output of the lexical decoder is a lexical lattice. The lattice elements are: identification of lexicon entries, total penalty, length-normalised score and mapping path of the word on phonetic segments. This dynamic programming decoder can be optionally completed by a word verification module using a set of phonological and prosodic rules which can modify the score of the detections and even reject some of them [19].

For the purpose of parameter optimisation, and also for comparing different versions, a method for evaluating the efficiency of the lexical decoder was designed. It is based on the assumption that a restriction of the output of the lexical decoder to those detections that begin and end in some predefined place is a statistically valid representation of the behaviour of a decoder. If we know that a given word has been uttered between, say, t_1 and t_2, we examine the detections beginning in $[t_{1-o}, t_{1+g}]$ and ending in $[t_{2-g}, t_{2+o}]$ where o and g are the allowed overlaps and gaps between successive detections ($o = g = 2$ phonetic segments). These detections can be ordered by decreasing score, after these scores have been modified to account for gaps and overlaps relative to the correct boundaries of the uttered word. One of these detections is the first to have an entry in the lexicon which is a variant of the uttered word: it is the 'target'. The lower the rank of the target, the better the lexical decoder has performed. A global test has been conducted on 26 sentences and 6 speakers (438 uttered words) with hand-verified automatic mappings on speech data, with a 250 entry lexicon, representing 122 different words. It appears that the last version of our lexical decoder, without any verification, ranks the targets at 2.34 on average. An earlier version ranks the targets, without any verification, at 3.56, and with elaborate verifications at 2.75. For this reason, we used only the optimised version in the following experiments.

2.6 Sentence recognition

The sentence recogniser used in KEAL has been implemented by Quinton [14] and uses the context-free grammar formalism. This module reconstructs the uttered sentence as a complete string of words, starting from the lexical lattice obtained at the previous step. It is required that this string be generated by the context-free grammar of the running application, which is a data of KEAL. The general strategy of the parsing is based on a lattice parser similar to that of Earley [6], which was designed to perform several analyses in parallel; the string to be analysed is read from left to right, and the syntactic information corresponding to the part of the string which has been read is summarised by 'configurations' stored in a stack. The term 'configuration' refers to a set of syntactic structures, whose roots are the beginnings of a right part of a rule, and whose leaves are a substring of the sentence to be analysed.

Sentence: oriente la tortue au cap optique

Basic phonetic transcription: o r i j ã t l a t o r t u o k a p o p t i k

PHONETIC LATTICE

Number of segment	:	0	1	2	3	4	5	6	7	8	9
Weight of segment	:	1.00	1.00	1.00	1.00	1.00	1.00	1.00	1.00	1.00	1.00
Number of syllable	:	0	1	1	2	2	3	3	4	4	4
Beginning of segment	:	14	22	25	31	32	42	51	61	62	67
End of segment	:	20	24	30	31	41	50	55	62	66	73
Phone candidates	!	oi	w	(i)	(y)	oi	b	(a1)	(t)	oi	s
	!	an	(r)	u	uu	o	d	oe	p	(o)	(r)
	!	(o)		ei		r1	g	ai	k	r1	f
	!	r1		eu		a	y	eu		o1	ch
	!	on		r1		o1	m			a	j
	V	o1		ou		(an)	z			oe	w
Number of segment	:	10	11	12	13	14	15	16	17	18	19
Weight of segment	:	1.00	0.50	1.00	0.73	1.00	1.00	1.00	1.00	0.25	1.00
Number of syllable	:	5	5	5	6	6	7	7	8	8	8
Beginning of segment	:	78	79	82	89	89	102	105	116	118	118
End of segment	:	78	81	88	89	96	105	109	117	118	121
Phone candidates	!	(t)	ch	(u)	(uu)	ou	(k)	(a)	(p)	m	(o)
	!	p	s	i	l	(o)	p	a1	b	w	ou
	!	k	f	ei		o1	t	ai	k	g	o1
	V		j			i	g	un	g	r	eu
Number of segment	:	20	21	22	23	24					
Weight of segment	:	1.00	0.25	1.00	1.00	0.50					
Number of syllable	:	9	9	9	9	9					
Beginning of segment	:	127	135	138	147	157					
End of segment	:	134	137	143	159	160					
Phone candidates	!	k	s	(i)	(k)	y					
	!	(t)	f	u		j					
	!	(p)	j	ei		ch					
	V		ch	ou							

SENTENCE DETECTIONS

—Detection number 1, score = 899, cumulated penalty = 2531
'oriente la_tortue_au cap optique'

Detected word	Identified phones	Location	Word penalty
oriente	o.r.i.y._d.	[0 5]	817
la_tortue_au	_a.t.o.r.t.u._au.	[6 14]	1291
cap	k.a.p.	[15 17]	0
optique	w.o._t._i.k._	[18 23]	210

—Detection numero 2, score = 849, cumulated penalty = 3784
'oriente la_tortue_au un moins six'

Detected word	Identified phones	Location	Word penalty
oriente	o.r.i.y._d.	[0 5]	817
la_tortue_au	_a.t.o.r.t.u._au.	[6 14]	1291
un	h.un.	[15 16]	219
moins	m.oi.	[17 19]	445
six	s.i.	[20 22]	125

Fig. 2 *Phonetic lattice and identified sentences for the French utterance 'Oriente la tortue au cap optique'*
The position of each word of the identified sentence within the phonetic lattice is also given by the interval $[i\ j]$ where i is the beginning segment and j the last segment of the mapping path. 'Right' detected phonemes are encircled

In order to reduce the number of configurations to be analysed, the parsing process is represented as a search problem in a state-space graph. This runs from left to right in a beam-search fashion. The cumulated penalty of a syntactic hypothesis is obtained by summing the penalties of the words composing this hypothesis; in the case of an overlap or gap between consecutive words, insertion or overlapping penalties are added, following the formula given for computing the penalty of a word. Pruning is done with the values of the best length-normalised scores of aggregated phrases. The beam-search strategy has been chosen as the best of several possibilities (best-first with backtracking, sequential decoding). The output of the syntactic decoder is a set of parsed sentences ordered by their score (cf. Fig. 2). This score is computed from the total penalty *py* using the following formula:

$$\text{Score} = \left(1 - \frac{py}{nb}\right) \cdot 1000$$

where nb is the number of segments of the phonetic lattice.

We may first consider that a sentence is said to be recognised only when the totality of its ordered words is the best solution retained by this algorithm. This is a severe measure of the final performance of a speech recognition system. Another, complementary figure of merit can be used at this level: the percentage of words that, after syntactic decoding, have been correctly found at their correct location in the corpus of utterances. These two basic assessment methods will be used to evaluate the overall performances of KEAL (cf. the last Section).

Fig. 2 shows the phonetic lattice and the first two recognised sentences, with their score and their tree structure, for the command: 'oriente la tortue au cap optique' (orient the tortoise in the direction of the lightpen).

3 Task description

Each word of the vocabulary is described by means of a sequence of basic units. At the lexical level, the basic units of the KEAL system are the phonemes. Each word usually has a standard phonemic form and possibly one, two or more phonemic variants. Some sequences of phonemes, such as the diphone | w a |, being difficult to separate into two different sounds, are considered as basic units. In this case, this particular diphone is named | oi | as in the word | s ois an t | ('soixante' or '60').

The lexicon is composed of 123 basic words, from which each sentence can be generated by means of a context-free grammar. This dictionnary is speaker independent.

At the phonetic level, the set of phonemes is divided into two main classes: vowels and consonants (some phonemes, such as | r |, can belong to both classes).

Within each class, some allophonic units are introduced so as to have homogeneous classes of phonemes; for instance, the phonemes | r |, | l |, | a | and | o | have two allophones. Each stop consonant is itself divided into two segments corresponding to the occlusion part and to the burst part, respectively. These phonetic segments correspond to the following set: | p |, | p1 |; | t |, | t1 |; | k |, | k1 |; | b |, | b1 |; | d |, | d1 |; | g |, | g1 |.

The context-free grammar of the pseudo-Logo sentences comprises 72 nonterminal or syntactic categories, 105 terminal or lexical categories and 100 rules. The perplexity figure of the corpus is 21. This perplexity, as defined by Sondhi and Levinson [17], represents the average number of lexical hypotheses, at each instant of analysis, after the syntactic constraints have been applied.

4 Experiments

4.1 Speech data

Speech collected from nine speakers (4 female and 5 male speakers) is recorded and digitised at a sampling rate of 12.8 kHz and the FFT implemented every 13.3 ms. The log-energy in each of 14 critical bands is computed. This speech data is divided into two sets:

(*a*) a training set comprising 73 short task-independent sentences uttered once by each speaker.

(*b*) a test set comprising 39 pseudo-Logo sentences per speaker.

4.2 Speaker training phase

For each speaker, a reference set of phones is automatically extracted from the training set by means of the automatic alignment program, which maps each phonetic lattice given by the phonetic analyser on to the ideal phonetic transcription of each training sentence.

This phonetic reference set is then checked or improved manually, in case mapping errors have occurred. From this set, two new sets of coefficients (corresponding to vowels and consonants, respectively), representing the optimal hyperplanes separating the phones in each of these two classes, are computed. Accordingly, for each speaker, at the end of the training time, the system is provided with these two sets of speaker-dependent coefficients which are used to refine the first phonetic recognition given by the rule-based part of the acoustic-phonetic decoding module.

5 Results

5.1 Evaluation of the segmentation

A first evaluation of the phonetic segmentation of the 39 sentences of the 'pseudo-Logo' test set is given in Table 1. Each of these sentences was spoken once by seven speakers. These results are obtained automatically by means of the alignment program, which maps the ideal phonetic string of each sentence onto the phonetic lattice given by KEAL as can be seen from Fig. 3. The ideal phonetic string is the same for each speaker. As indicated in Fig. 4, the alignment program automatically computes the confusion matrices for vowels and consonants. The last two columns of these matrices correspond to the number of phonemes inserted (including spread phones) and omitted (including merged phones). The average percentages of omissions and insertions are given in Table 1. Some comments on these results are necessary:

(*a*) Insertion errors are overestimated because the weight which is assigned to each segment is taken into account by the lexical analyser in computing the score of a particular detection. For instance, in Fig. 2 the segments numbered 11, 13, 18, 21 and 24 have the weights 0.50, 0.73, 0.25, 0.25, and 0.50, respectively, which leads to the real insertion of 2.23 segments; however, the evaluation program has considered each of these segments as a full segment leading to 5 insertions.

Table 1: Results of segmentation for 7 speakers and 39 Logo sentences uttered by each speaker

Actual number of segments to be found	5601
Average length of sentences (in segments)	20
Omission percentage (including merging)	3.5
Insertion percentage (including spreading)	10.5

(*b*) In Fig. 4, it can be noticed that the most frequent insertions correspond to the fricatives | s | and | ch |, which are often spread (c.f., for instance, Fig. 3 where a spreading of the phone | ch | is shown). In fact, these spread segments are penalised much less than normal insertions by the lexical analyser. This spreading can be viewed as a loop on the 'phone' state when each word in the lexicon is represented by a 'phonetic' network. The same comment can be made on merged phones, where two consecutive phones are found in the same segment; these errors are also less important than normal omissions; they are the less important because the relative temporal position of both merged phonemes inside the corresponding segment can be taken into account by the lexical

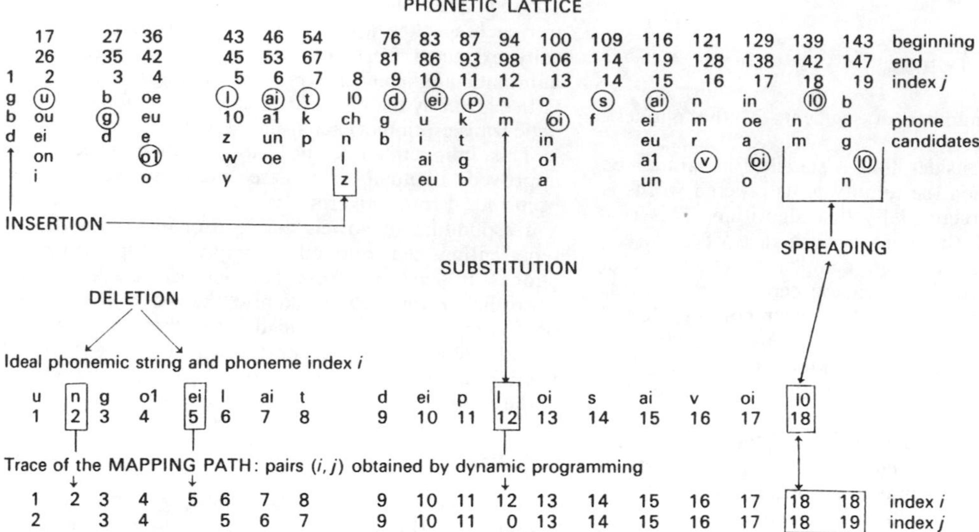

Output of the alignment program recorded in the phonetic data base

Extracted phones	Centisecond samples beginning	end	Preceding phone	Following phone
u	17 ⟷	26		n
g	27 ⟷	35	n	o
o1	36 ⟷	42	g	ei
l	43 ⟷	45	ei	ai
ai	46 ⟷	53	l	t
t	54 ⟷	67	ai	d
d	76 ⟷	81	t	ei
ei	83 ⟷	86	d	p
p	87 ⟷	93	ei	l
oi	100 ⟷	106	l	s
s	109 ⟷	114	oi	ai
ai	116 ⟷	119	s	v
v	121 ⟷	128	ai	oi
oi	129 ⟷	138	v	l
l0	139 ⟷	142	oi	

Fig. 3 *Example of the mapping results given by the alignment program and used for automatic labelling, extraction of phones (phonetic data base) and evaluation of the phonetic decoder*

The sentence is 'une goelette deploie ses voiles' ('a schooner's sails are spreading'). An alignment of the phone i from the ideal phonemic transcription with the segment j of the phonetic lattice allows the phonetic label i to be given to the acoustic spectra belonging to the segment j

Right identified phones are encircled

decoder. This temporal position is an attribute of the phonetic lattice.

(*c*) The omission error is twice as great for consonants as for vowels and more than 50% of the omissions in the case of consonants are due to the phoneme |l|, which is often present in grammatical words such as 'le', 'la', 'l'', and sequences of short coarticulated strings such as 'de la'.

5.2 Evaluation of the phonetic decoder

For each speaker a confusion matrix is automatically extracted. This confusion matrix is obtained by considering the phoneme present in the first line of the phonetic lattice to be the recognised phoneme when there is a mapping between a phoneme of the ideal phonetic string and its corresponding column in the phonetic lattice. When there is a spreading of a phoneme in two or more segments, it is considered to have been recognised when it is on the top of one of these columns. When there is a merging of two phonemes, not more than one can be recognised at the top of the column, that is, in first position. When a phoneme is characterised by allophones (for instance |r|, which has three allophones in the phonetic lattice, |r|, |r0|, |r1|) then if one of these allophones is at the top of the corresponding column of the phonetic lattice, it is considered to have been recognised in position 1. In the same manner, when the phoneme or one of its allophones is present in the second line of the right column of the phonetic lattice, it is considered to have been recognised in the second position, and in the same manner for the third and following best choices.

These results are summarised in Table 2. The first column indicates the rate of recognition, including errors due to omission. The second column gives the rate of identification, that is the omitted phonemes are excluded from the total number of phonemes for computing the percentage of identification. These percentages are probably slightly underestimated because the alignment

Table 2: Average of the phonetic decoding results for 7 speakers (4 females and 3 males) and 39 pseudo-Logo utterances

Rank	Cumulative percentage of phones in rank	
	Recognised (including omission errors)	Identified (excluding omitted phones)
1	52%	54%
2	69%	71%
3	77%	80%
4	81%	84%
5	84%	87%
Total number of phones	5601	5392

Identified phones

	i	ei	ai	a	o	ou	u	e	oe	in	an	on	un	o1	a1	r1	oi	au	eu	an	oa	ay	a2	i1	ins	omi
i	36	1			1		4					1				1				2					1	1
ei		19																	1						2	0
ai			7							2															0	2
a				14						4							4		3						2	0
o			2		16	4											1		5						0	2
ou						3																			2	0
u							18																		0	0
e	1																								0	0
oe									2					1											1	0
in										1															0	0
an																									0	0
on	1						2					3				1				1					1	1
un				5					1				4							1					0	0
o1						2			7	5				20	1		2		1						0	0
a1			6						2	3			2		33				4						0	0
r1		3					2									3			1						0	0
oi				1					2								2								1	0
au																									0	0
eu							1			1						1			31						2	0
an				1	1							8	2			1	2			3					0	0
oa																									0	0
ay																									0	0
a2																									0	0
i1																									0	0
	i	ei	ai	a	o	ou	u	e	oe	in	an	on	un	o1	a1	r1	oi	au	eu	an	oa	ay	a2	i1		

	p	t	k	b	d	g	f	s	ch	v	z	j	l	r	m	n	gn	y	w	uu	p1	t1	k1	b1	d1	g1	r0	10	v0	ins	omi
p	23	11	2	6																										3	0
t	3	44	1	2	2	1		2			1																			4	2
k	7	15	6	1	1	1																								0	0
b				2												1														6	0
d		1		6	19	1		1	1		1					4		1												5	8
g				3	1	2			1																					1	0
f							2	1	3																					0	0
s								26	10			1																		13	1
ch								3	8																					12	0
v				1								1	1		2	1														1	0
z					2			2		2	11	2	1			1		3												0	0
j								2				4																		2	0
l				3	1	3			3	5		1	15			5		1		4										7	11
r		1		1	1			12	4		1		2	12	2	2			2											0	1
m								1							9	5				1										3	0
n																12														6	0
gn																														0	0
y								1				1						3												1	1
w					3										1															2	3
uu										1		1								3										1	0
p1																														0	0
t1																														0	0
k1																														0	0
b1																														0	0
d1																														0	0
g1																														0	0
r0							1		3				1					1									1			0	0
10										2						1														3	0
v0																														0	0
	p	t	k	b	d	g	f	s	ch	v	z	j	l	r	m	n	gn	y	w	uu	p1	t1	k1	b1	d1	g1	r0	10	v0		

Fig. 4 *Confusion matrices for one speaker*

The last two columns correspond to the number of inserted (or spread) and omitted phones

program makes some errors of mapping and an improvement of about 3% of recognition which are mainly due to improvements in the alignment programs has been noted. However this program has the main advantage to be automatic and reproducible and avoids human interference in the assessment process.

The individual phonetic identification percentage is shown in Fig. 5. A variation of about 10% can be observed among the speakers.

5.3 Evaluation of the lexical and syntactic decoders

The percentage of correct sentence recognition obtained by using the context-free parser of KEAL on the test set is 81.5% (264 sentences out of 324). At word level the recognition percentage is 91% (1172 out of 1287). This latter percentage is obtained by computing the percent-

Table 3: Speaker-dependent correct word and sentence recognition percentages for 9 speakers

	Female speakers			Male speakers					
	AB	MG	DD	JN	CG	JM	RV	GU	JS
Word recognition	89	91	94	94	94	86	83	93	98
Sentence recognition	80	87	93	80	80	77	67	88	88

age of words identified correctly in the first sentence hypothesis given by KEAL. Detailed results obtained with the sentence recogniser are shown in Table 3.

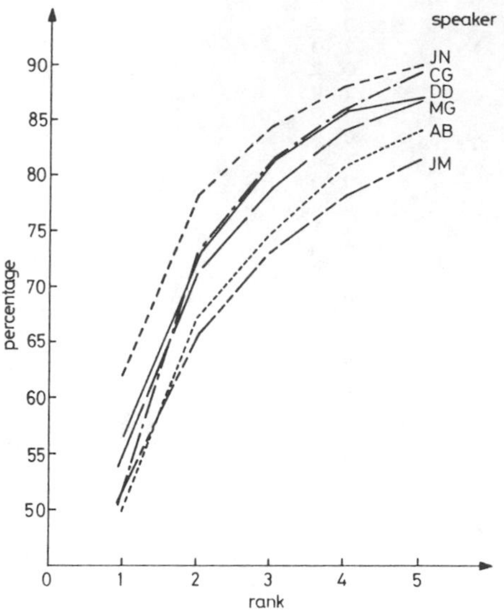

Fig. 5 *Phonetic identification percentage for six different speakers*

6 Conclusions

The results show that a reasonable continuous speech recognition performance can be obtained, even with a partially rule-based, bottom-up approach. Of course, there are several possible ways to improve these results.

The phonetic lattice can be refined by adding new contextual rules and by improving the set of basic allophones. In particular, recognition of the place of articulation of the stops has to be improved. A comparison of the linear decision functions with the 'K-nearest neighbour' technique and the optimisation of the coordinate space representation is currently being undertaken [12].

We also hope to improve the level of word recognition by introducing statistical contextual error models and by including a lexical verification module taking into account fine acoustic phonetic rules which can be applied to sequences of known coarticulated phones. It is hoped that the use of prosodic parameters will improve the levels of word and sentence recognition [18].

The recognition part of KEAL is to be modified to become the recognition component of a natural language dialogue system able to provide voice access to data bases. For this purpose a new linguistic parser, ALOEMDA, has been designed. This new parser is an extension of an algorithm described by Winograd [20] to the ATN (Augmented Transition Networks) grammar formalism and lexical lattice input. ALOEMDA [5] is an active chart parser in which semantic or conceptual restrictions are processed simultaneously with syntactic conditions. The semantic representation is very similar to that developed by Poessio and Rullent [13] and by Brietzmann and Ehrlich [3] and is based on the case frame notion of a head concept, modified by related concepts, thus playing some role. The head recognition allows predictions to be made as to the remaining part of the utterance as well as confirming previous partial results.

This linguistic module is driven by a dialogue management module [1], from which it receives a set of predictions. The output to the dialogue module is the semantic representation of the best solution. By means of these two new modules, the system is expected to handle larger vocabularies (about 500 words).

7 References

1 BIGORGNE, D., COZANNET, A., GUYOMARD, M., MERCIER, G., MICLET, L., QUERRE, M., and SIROUX, J.: 'A versatile speaker-dependent continuous speech understanding system'. ICASSP 88, **1**, New York, 1988, pp. 303–306

2 BONNEAU, A., and ROSSI, M.: 'Recognition of French vowels by expert system SERAC'. Proceedings of 11th Int. Congress of Phonetic sciences, **5**, Tallin, USSR, 1987, pp. 282–285

3 BRIETZMANN, A., and EHRLICH, U.: 'The role of semantic processing in an automatic speech understanding system'. Proceedings of COLING-86, Bonn, 1986, pp. 596–598

4 CHAPLIN, W.G., and LEVADI, V.S.: 'A generalization of the linear threshold decision algorithm to multiple classes' *in* TOU, J.T. (Ed.): 'Computer and information and Sciences. Vol. II' (Academic Press, 1967), pp. 337–355

5 COZANNET, A.: 'ALOEMDA, analyseur linguistique pour l'oral et l'écrit'. Proceedings of 6th RFIA Conference, Antibes, France, November 1987, pp. 381–390

6 EARLEY, J.: 'An efficient context-free parsing algorithm', *Comm. ACM*, 1970, **13**, (2), pp. 94–102

7 LEA, W.A.: 'Trends in automatic speech recognition' (Prentice-Hall, New York, 1980)

8 MATHAN, L.: 'Optimisation du decodeur lexical KAPHRADE de KEAL'. Rapport de stage, CNET, 1988, pp. 1–69

9 MERCIER, G., and GERARD, M.: 'L'apprentissage des paramètres de reconnaissance phonétique dans un système de reconnaissance de la parole continue'. Proc. du congrès de reconnaissance des formes et d'intelligence artificielle, Nancy, Septembre 1981, pp. 641–652

10 MERCIER, G.: 'Acoustic-phonetic decoding and adaptation in continuous speech recognition' *in* HATON, J.P. (Ed.): Proceedings of NATO Advanced Study Institute on Automatic speech analysis and recognition, (D. Reidel, Bonas, 1981), pp. 69–99

11 MERCIER, G., LE GUENNEC, L., and LAFACE, P.: 'Recognition of Italian numbers and connected digits'. Report of P1015 ESPRIT project, 1987

12 MICLET, L., and MERCIER, G.: 'Evaluation of the acoustic decoder of the "KEAL" speech recognition system'. Proceedings of 9th International Conference on Pattern Recognition, Rome, Italy, 1988

13 POESSIO, M., and RULLENT, C.: 'Modified case frame parsing for speech understanding systems'. Proceedings of IJCAI 87, Milan, 1987, pp. 622–625

14 QUINTON, P.: 'Contribution à la reconnaissance de la parole: utilisation des méthodes heuristiques pour la reconnaissance des phrases'. Thèse d'état, Rennes, 1980

15 SAKOE, H., and CHIBA, S.: 'Dynamic programming algorithm optimization for spoken word recognition', *IEEE Trans.*, 1978, **26**, pp. 43–49

16 SIROUX, J., and GILLET, D.: 'A system for man-machine communication using speech', *Speech Commun.*, 1985, **4**, (4), pp. 289–315

17 SONDHI, M.M., and LEVINSON, S.E.: 'Computing relative redundancy to measure grammatical constraints in speech recognition tasks'. Proceedings of IEEE ICASSP, Tulsa, USA, 1978, pp. 409–412

18 VAISSIERE, J.: 'The use of prosodic parameters in automatic speech recognition'. Invited Lecture presented at meeting of Nato Advanced Study Institute on Recent advances on speech understanding and dialogue systems, Bad Windscheim, FRG, 5th–18th July, 1987 (Ed. H. NIEMANN *et al.*) (Springer-Verlag, Berlin Heidelberg, 1988), pp. 71–99

19 VIVES, R.: 'Vérification des hypothèses proposées par un analyseur lexical d'un système de reconnaissance automatique de la parole'. Proceedings of 4th FASE Symposum, Venise, 1985, pp. 277–280

20 WINOGRAD, T.: 'Language as a cognitive process. Part 1: Syntax' (Addison Wesley, 1983)

16.

THE HEARSAY-II SPEECH UNDERSTANDING SYSTEM: A TUTORIAL[1]

Lee D. Erman
Carnegie-Mellon University

Victor R. Lesser
The University of Massachusetts

16-1. INTRODUCTION

In 1971-72, the Hearsay-I speech understanding system was developed at Carnegie-Mellon University -- the first of a series of such systems. Hearsay-I [Reddy Erman & Neely 73, Reddy Erman Fennell & Neely 73] was a successful attempt to solve the problem of machine understanding of speech in specialized task domains. In this early system, the size of the vocabulary (fewer than 100 words) and complexity of the grammar were very limited. Experiences with Hearsay-I led to the more generalized Hearsay-II architecture [Lesser Fennell Erman & Reddy 75, Erman & Lesser 75, Lesser & Erman 77] in order to handle more difficult problems (e.g., larger vocabularies and less-constrained grammars).

The active development of Hearsay-II extended over three years. During this period, a number of different knowledge-source configurations were constructed within the Hearsay-II framework. The most important of these are called configurations C0 (January, 1975), C1 (January, 1976), and C2 (September, 1976). This last configuration was very successful: it came close to the original ARPA performance goals set out in 1971 to be met by the end of 1976 [Newell et al, 73]. Its performance in September, 1976, was 90% correct semantic interpretation of sentences over a 1011-word vocabulary and constrained syntax [CMU 77].

This presentation is divided into three major sections. First, the Hearsay-II system architecture is presented (Sec. 16-2). The next section (Sec. 16-3) discusses in detail the C2 configuration -- the particular types of knowledge that are contained in this configuration, and how this knowledge interacts in order to recognize spoken utterances. Section 16-4 contains a detailed example of C2 recognizing an utterance.

16-2. THE HEARSAY-II ARCHITECTURE

The Hearsay-II architecture is based on the view that the inherently errorful nature of processing connected speech can be handled only through the effective and efficient cooperation of multiple, diverse sources of knowledge. Additionally, the experimental approach needed for system development requires the ability to add and replace sources of knowledge and to explore different control strategies. Thus, such changes must be relatively easy to accomplish; there must also be ways to evaluate the performance of the system in general and the roles of the various sources of knowledge and control strategies in particular. This ability to experiment conveniently with the system is especially crucial because the amount of knowledge is large and many people are needed to introduce and validate it.

A major focus of the design of the Hearsay-II system was the development of a framework for experimenting with the representation of and cooperation among these diverse sources of knowledge. Based on our experiences with Hearsay-I, we expected to need types of knowledge and interaction patterns whose details could not be anticipated at the outset of the project. Therefore, instead of designing a specific speech understanding system, we considered Hearsay-II as a model for a class of systems and a framework within which specific configurations of that general model could be constructed and studied. One can think of Hearsay-II as a high-level system for programming speech understanding systems of a certain type -- i.e., those that conform to the Hearsay-II model.

In the Hearsay-II architecture, each of the diverse types of knowledge needed to solve the speech problem is encapsulated in a _knowledge source_ (KS). For speech understanding, typical KSs incorporate information about syntax, semantics, acoustic-phonetics, prosodics, syllabification, coarticulation, etc. The C2 configuration has about ten KS modules. KSs are kept separate, anonymous, and as independent as possible, in order to make the creation, modification, and testing of KS modules as easy as possible.

As one knowledge source makes errors and creates ambiguities, other KSs must be brought to bear to correct and clarify those actions. This KS cooperation should occur as soon as possible after the introduction of an error or ambiguity in order to limit its ramifications. The mechanism used for providing this high degree of cooperation is the _hypothesize-and-test_ paradigm. In this paradigm, solution-finding is viewed as an iterative process. Two kinds of KS actions occur: 1) the creation of an _hypothesis_, an "educated guess" about some aspect of the problem (e.g., that a particular word was spoken during a specified portion of the utterance), and 2) tests of the plausibility of some hypothesis or sets of hypotheses. For both of these steps, the KS uses _a priori_ knowledge about the problem, as well as the previously generated hypotheses. This "iterative guess-building" terminates when some subset of the hypotheses generated describes the spoken utterance "well-enough" to satisfy some halting criteria.

16-2.1 The Blackboard

The requirement that knowledge sources be independent implies that the functioning (and very existence) of each must not be necessary or crucial to the others. On the other hand, the KSs are required to cooperate in the iterative guess-building, using and correcting one another's guesses; this implies that there must be interaction among the KSs. These two opposing requirements have led to a design in which each KS interfaces to the others externally in a uniform way that is identical across KSs and in which no knowledge source knows which or how many other KSs exist. The interface is implemented as a dynamic global data structure, called the _blackboard_.

The blackboard is partitioned into distinct information levels (e.g., "phrase", "word", "syllable", and "phone"); each level holds a different representation of the problem space. The current state of problem solution is represented in terms of _hypotheses_ on the blackboard. An hypothesis is an interpretation of a portion of the spoken utterance at a particular level (e.g., an hypothesis might be that the word 'today' occurred from millisecond 100 to millisecond 600 in the utterance). All hypotheses, no matter what their level, have a uniform attribute-value structure. For example, each

1 This work was supported at Carnegie-Mellon University by the Defense Advanced Research Projects Agency (F44620-73-C-0074) and is monitored by the Air Force Office of Scientific Research.

hypothesis has attributes containing its level, begin- and end-time within the utterance (which can include notions of fuzziness), and plausibility ratings. The level and time attributes place a two-dimensional structure on hypotheses which partitions the blackboard and can be used for addressing hypotheses. Note that two or more hypotheses at the same level with significantly overlapping times are competitors; i.e., they represent competing interpretations of a portion of the utterance.

Hypotheses at different levels are connected through an and/or directed graph structure. Through these connections, hypotheses at each level can be described approximately as abstractions of hypotheses at the next lower level. A partial solution (i.e., a group of hypotheses) at one level can be used to constrain the search at an adjacent level. For example, consider a KS which can predict and rate words based on acoustic information and another KS which knows about the grammar of the language. The first KS can generate a set of candidate word-hypotheses. The second KS can use these hypotheses to generate phrase hypotheses which can be used, in turn, to predict words likely to precede or follow. These predictions can now constrain the search for the first KS.

16-2.2 Knowledge-Source Activation

Each knowledge source is activated in a data-directed manner, based on the occurrence on the blackboard of patterns of hypotheses specific to its interests. For example, a KS which knows how to make hypotheses about words given hypotheses about syllables is activated whenever any KS creates new syllable hypotheses. Once activated, a KS may examine the blackboard, typically in the vicinity of the hypotheses that activated it. Based on its knowledge, the KS may then modify those hypotheses or other hypotheses, or create new hypotheses. Such actions establish new patterns on the blackboard; these patterns may cause other KSs to be activated. This mechanism for KS activation implements a data-directed form of the hypothesize-and-test paradigm.

Each KS has two major components: a precondition and an action. The purpose of the precondition is to find a subset of hypotheses that is appropriate for action by the KS and to invoke the KS on that subset; the subset is called the stimulus frame of the KS instantiation. For example, the precondition of the KS that generates word hypotheses based on syllables looks for new syllable hypotheses. To keep from having to fire continuously to search the blackboard, each precondition declares the primitive kinds of blackboard changes in which it is interested. Each precondition is triggered only when such primitive changes occur (and is then given pointers to all of them). Whenever a precondition is executed, it checks all blackboard events in which it is interested that have occurred since the last time it was executed. For example, a "new hypothesis" to an executing precondition is any hypothesis which was created since the last time the precondition was executed.

The action part of a KS is a program for applying the knowledge to the stimulus frame and making appropriate changes to the blackboard. A stylized description of the likely action that the KS instantiation will perform (if and when it is allowed to execute) is called the response frame. For example, a response frame for the syllable-based word hypothesizer indicates that the action will be to generate hypotheses at the word level and in a time area that includes at least that of the stimulus frame. The stimulus and response frames, which are generated by the precondition component of the KS, provide information for comparing the desirability of execution of a KS instantiation to that of other KS instantiations; this information is used for the scheduling of KS instantiations.

16-2.3 Scheduling of Knowledge-Sources

At any point, there are, in general, a number of pending tasks to execute -- both invoked knowledge sources and triggered preconditions. (In practice, the number of pending tasks often exceeds 200.) If very, very large amounts of processing power (and memory) were available, one could consider actually activating all KSs in all their possible contexts. This would expand the blackboard with many (competing) hypotheses. Assuming this would eventually terminate (i.e., at some point no new contexts are created), a decision process could then try to pick from all the competing hypotheses that subset which best describes the data -- this would be the system's "solution" to the problem. Because of this combinatoric explosion of possibilities (caused mostly by the problems of variability and incompleteness in the signal and errorfulness of the KSs), this complete expansion is not feasible. Therefore, the control strategy can pick only a small subset of the applicable KS activations; this can be thought of as exploring a limited portion of the (potential) fully-expanded blackboard.

This selection process is implemented by a scheduler which calculates a priority for each waiting task and selects for execution the task with the highest priority. The priority calculation attempts, based on the specific stimulus and response frames of the actions, to estimate the usefulness of the action in fulfilling the overall system goal of recognizing the utterance. A more detailed explanation of the scheduler is contained in the next section and in [Hayes-Roth & Lesser 77].

16-2.4 The Hearsay-II Implementation

Based on the architecture just described, a high-level programming system was constructed to provide an environment for programming knowledge sources, configuring groups of them into systems, and executing them. Because KS interactions occur via the blackboard (triggering on patterns, accessing hypotheses, and making modifications) and the blackboard has a uniform structure, KS interactions are also uniform. Thus, one set of facilities can serve all KSs. Facilities are provided for

- o defining the levels on the blackboard,
- o configuring groups of KSs into runnable systems,
- o accessing and modifying hypotheses on the blackboard,
- o activating and scheduling KSs.

These facilities, along with other utilities for debugging and user (researcher) interaction, are called the Hearsay-II 'kernel'. The kernel is the high-level environment for creating and testing KSs and configurations of them [Erman & Lesser 78].

Hearsay-II is implemented in the SAIL programming system [Reiser 76], an Algol-60 dialect which has a sophisticated compile-time macro facility as well as a large number of data structures (including lists and sets) and control modes which are implemented fairly efficiently. The Hearsay-II kernel provides a high-level environment for KSs at compile-time by extending SAIL's data types and syntax through declarations of procedure calls, global variables, and complex macros. This extended SAIL provides an explicit structure for the specification of a KS and its interaction with other KSs (through the blackboard). The high-level environment also provides mechanisms that enable KSs to specify to the kernel (usually in non-procedural ways) a variety of information which the kernel uses when configuring a system, scheduling KS activity, and controlling user interaction.

The knowledge in a KS is represented using SAIL data structures and code, in whatever form the KS developer finds appropriate. The kernel environment provides the facilities for structuring the interface between this knowledge and other KSs, via the blackboard. For example, the syntax KS contains a grammar for the specialized task language that is to be recognized; this grammar is in a compact, network form. The KS also contains procedures for searching this network, for example, to parse a sequence of words. The kernel provides facilities (1) for triggering this KS whenever new word hypotheses appear on the blackboard, (2) for the KS to read those word hypotheses (in order to find the sequence of words to be parsed), and (3) for the KS to create new hypotheses on the blackboard, indicating the structure of the parse.

16-3. THE KNOWLEDGE-SOURCES OF SEPTEMBER, 1976

In this section, a description of the September, 1976, version of the Hearsay-II system -- configuration C2 -- is given in terms of the functions and interactions of its knowledge sources. Included is an example run of the system.

The task for the system is to answer questions about and retrieve documents from a collection of computer science abstracts (in the area of artificial intelligence). Example sentences are

"Which abstracts refer to theory of computation?"
"List those articles."
"What has McCarthy written since nineteen seventy-four?"

The vocabulary contains 1011 words (in which each extended form of a root, e.g., the plural of a noun, is counted separately, if it appears). The grammar which defines the legal sentences is context free and includes recursion. The style of the grammar is such that there are many more non-terminals than in conventional syntactic grammars; the information contained in the greater number of nodes provides semantic and pragmatic constraint within the grammatical structure. For example, in place of 'Noun' in a conventional grammar, this grammar includes such non-terminals as 'Topic', 'Author', 'Year', 'Publisher', etc.

The grammar allows each word to be followed, on the average, by seventeen other words of the vocabulary.[2] The standard deviation of this measure is very high (about 51), since some words can be followed by many others (up to 300 in several cases). For the sentences used for performance testing, the average length is seven words and the average number of words that can follow any initial portion of the sentence is thirty-four.

Figure 16-1 gives a schematic of configuration C2 as it was operational in September, 1976. The levels are indicated by solid horizontal lines and are labeled at the left. KSs are indicated by vertical arcs with the circled end indicating the level where its stimulus frame is and the pointed end indicating the level of its response frame. The name of a KS is connected to its arc by a dashed horizontal line.

16-3.1 Signal Acquisition, Parameter Extraction, Segmentation, Labeling (SEG)

An input utterance is spoken into a medium-quality Electro-Voice RE-51 close-speaking headset microphone in a fairly noisy environment (>65 db). The audio signal is low-passed filtered and 9-bit sampled at 10 KHz. All subsequent processing, as well as controlling the A/D converter, is digital and is done on a time-shared PDP-10 computer. Four parameters (called "ZAPDASH") are derived by simple algorithms operating directly on the sampled signal [Goldberg Reddy & Gill 77]. These parameters are extracted in real-time and are used initially to detect the beginning and end of the utterance.

The ZAPDASH parameters are next used by the SEG knowledge-source as the basis for an acoustic segmentation and classification of the utterance. This

2 Actually, a family of grammars was generated, varying in the number of words (terminals) and in the number and complexity of sentences allowed. The grammar described here and used in most of the testing is called "X05".

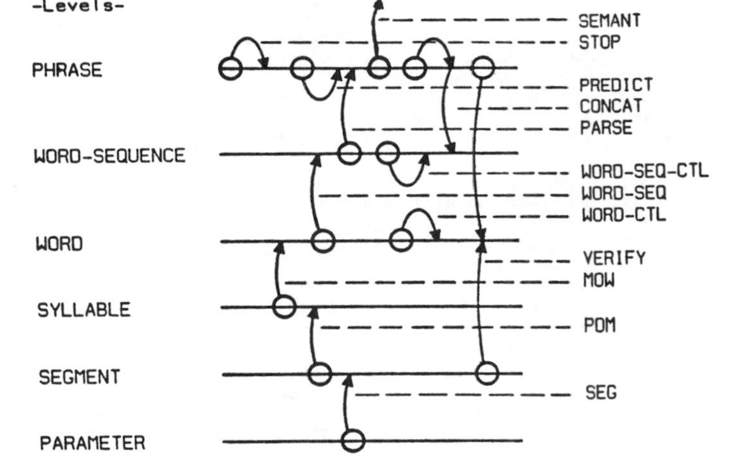

Figure 16-1. The levels and knowledge sources of configuration C2.

segmentation is accomplished by an iterative refinement technique: First, silence is separated from non-silence; then, the non-silence is broken down into the sonorant and non-sonorant regions, etc. Eventually, five classes of segments are produced: silence, sonorant peak, sonorant non-peak, fricative, and flap. Associated with each classified segment is its duration, absolute amplitude, and amplitude relative to its neighboring segments (i.e., local peak, local value, or plateau). The segments are contiguous and non-overlapping, with one class designation for each.

Finally, the SEG KS does a finer labeling of each segment. The labels are allophonic-like; there are currently 98 of them. Each of the 98 labels is defined by a vector of auto-correlation coefficients [Itakura 75]. These templates are generated from speaker-dependent training data that have been hand-labeled. The result of the labeling process, which matches the central portion of each segment against each of the templates using the Itakura metric, is a vector of 98 numbers; the i'th number is an estimate of the (negative log) probability that the segment represents an occurrence of the i'th allophone in the label set.

16-3.2 Word Spotting (POM, MOW, WORD-CTL)

The initial generation of words, bottom-up, is accomplished by a three-step process.

First, using the labeled segments as input, the POM knowledge source [Smith 76] generates hypotheses for likely syllable classes. This is done by first identifying syllable nuclei and then "parsing" outward from each nucleus. The syllable-class parsing is driven by a probabilistic "grammar" of "syllable-class -> segment" productions; the rules and their probabilities are learned by an off-line program which is trained on hand-labeled utterances. (The current training, which is speaker-dependent, uses 60 utterances containing about 360 word tokens.) For each nucleus position, several competing syllable-class hypotheses are generated -- typically three to eight.

The syllable classes are used to hypothesize words. Each of the 1011 words in the vocabulary is specified by a pronunciation description. For word hypothesization purposes, an inverted form of the dictionary is kept, in which there is associated with each syllable-class all the words which have some pronunciation containing that syllable-class. The MOW KS [Smith 76] looks up each hypothesized syllable class and generates word candidates from among those words containing that syllable-class. For each word that is multi-syllabic, all of the syllables in one of the pronunciations must match above a threshold. Typically, about 50 words of the 1011-word vocabulary are generated at each syllable nucleus position.[3]

Finally, the generated word candidates are rated and their begin- and end-times adjusted by the WIZARD procedure [McKeown 77]. For each word in the vocabulary, WIZARD has a network which describes the possible pronunciations. This rating is calculated by finding the path through the network which best matches the labeled segments, using the distances associated with each label for each segment; the rating is then based on the difference between this best path and the segment labels.[4]

The result of the processing to this point is a set of words. Each word includes a begin-time, an end-time, and a confidence rating. MOW selects a subset of these words, based on their times and ratings, to be hypothesized; it is these selected word hypotheses that form the base for the "top-end" processing. Typically, these hypotheses include about 75% of the words actually spoken (i.e., "correct" word hypotheses). Each correct hypothesis has a rating which ranks it on the average about three, as compared to the five to twenty-five or so incorrect hypotheses which compete with it (i.e., which significantly overlap it in time). The non-selected words are retained internally by MOW for possible later hypothesization.

The amount of hypothesization that MOW does is controlled by the WORD-CTL ('Word Control') KS. WORD-CTL creates "goal" hypotheses at the word level; these are interpreted by MOW as indicating how many word hypotheses to attempt to create in each time area. One can think of MOW as a generator of word hypotheses (from the candidates it creates internally) and WORD-CTL as embodying the policy of how many to hypothesize. This clear separation of policy from mechanism has facilitated experimentation with various control schemes. For example, a trivial change to WORD-CTL, such that goal hypotheses are generated only at the start of the utterance ("left-hand end"), results in MOW creating word hypotheses only at the start, thus forcing all top-end processing to be left-to-right.

WORD-CTL fires at the start of processing of an utterance in order to create goal hypotheses. Subsequently, it may re-trigger if the over-all search process stagnates; this condition is recognized as there being no waiting KS instantiations above a certain priority (as described in Sec. 16-3.3.8) or as the global measures of current state of the problem solution not having increased in the last several KS executions.

16-3.3 Top-End Processing

16-3.3.1 Word-Island Generation (WORD-SEQ, WORD-SEQ-CTL) - The WORD-SEQ knowledge source [Lesser Hayes-Roth Birnbaum & Cronk 77] has the job of generating, from the word hypotheses generated bottom-up, a small set (about three to ten) of word sequence hypotheses. Each of these sequences, or *islands*, can be used as the basis for expansion into larger islands, hopefully culminating in an hypothesis that spans the entire utterance. Multi-word islands are used rather than single-word islands because of the relatively poor reliability of ratings of single words as well as the limited syntactic constraint supplied by single words.

WORD-SEQ uses two kinds of knowledge to generate multi-word islands:

- A table derived from the grammar indicates for every ordered pair of words in the vocabulary (1011 x 1011) whether that pair can occur in that order in some sentence of the defined language. This binary table (which contains about 1.7% "1"'s) thus defines "language-adjacency".
- Acoustic-phonetic knowledge, embodied in the JUNCT ('juncture') procedure, is applied to pairs of word hypotheses and is used to decide if that pair might be considered to be time-adjacent in the utterance. JUNCT uses the dictionary pronunciations and examines the segments at their juncture (gap or overlap) in making its decision.

WORD-SEQ takes the highest-rated single words and generates multi-word sequences by expanding them with other hypothesized words that are both time- and language-adjacent. This expansion is controlled by heuristics based on the number and ratings of competing word hypotheses. The best of these words sequences (which occasionally includes single words) are hypothesized.

The WORD-SEQ-CTL ('Word-Sequence-Control') KS controls the amount of hypothesization that WORD-SEQ does by creating "goal" hypotheses which are interpreted by WORD-SEQ as indicating how many hypotheses to create. This provides the same kind of separation of policy and mechanism achieved in the MOW/WORD-CTL pair of KSs. WORD-SEQ-CTL fires at the start of processing of an utterance in order to create the goal hypotheses. Subsequently, WORD-SEQ-CTL triggers if stagnation is recognized; it then modifies the word-sequence goal hypotheses, thus stimulating WORD-SEQ to generate new word-sequence islands from which the search may be be more fruitful. WORD-SEQ will generate the additional hypotheses by decomposing word-sequence islands already on the blackboard or by re-generating islands which were initially discarded because their ratings were too low.

16-3.3.2 Word-Sequence Parsing (PARSE) - Because the syntactic constraint used in the generation of the word sequences is only pair-wise, a sequence longer than two words might not be syntactically acceptable. The PARSE knowledge source of the SASS module [Hayes-Roth Erman Fox & Mostow 77, Hayes-Roth Mostow & Fox 78] can parse a word sequence of arbitrary length, using the full constraints given by the language. This parsing does not require that the word sequence form a complete non-terminal in the grammar nor that the sequence be sentence-initial or sentence-final -- the words need only occur contiguously somewhere in some sentence of the language. If a sequence hypothesis does not parse, the hypothesis is marked as "rejected". Otherwise, a *phrase hypothesis* is created. Associated with the phrase hypothesis is the word sequence of which it is composed, as well as information about the way (or ways) the words parsed.

16-3.3.3 Word Predictions from Phrases (PREDICT) - The PREDICT knowledge source of the SASS module can, for any phrase hypothesis, generate predictions of all words which can immediately precede and all which can immediately follow that phrase in the language. In doing the computation to generate these predictions, this KS uses the parsing information attached to the phrase hypothesis by the parsing component.

16-3.3.4 Word Verification (VERIFY) - An attempt is made to verify the existence of or reject each such predicted word, in the context of its

3 Since the September, 1976, version, the POM and MOW KSs have been replaced by Noah [Smith 77, Smith & Sambur 78 (section 7-3.2.2.3)]. This KS outperforms POM-MOW on the 1011-word vocabulary (in both speed and accuracy) and is able to handle much larger vocabularies -- it has a performance degradation which is only logarithmic in vocabulary size in the range of 500 to 19,000 words.

4 WIZARD is, in effect, a miniature version of the HARPY speech recognition system [Lowerre 76, Lowerre & Reddy 78], except that it has one network for each word, rather than one network with all words and all sentences.

predicting phrase. This verification is handled by the VERIFY knowledge source. If verified, a confidence rating for the word must also be generated. First, if the word has been hypothesized previously and passes the test for time-adjacency (by the JUNCT procedure), it is marked as verified and the word hypothesis is associated with the prediction. (Note that a single word hypothesis may thus become associated with several different phrases.) Second, a search is made of the internal store created by MOW to see if the candidate can be matched by a previously-generated candidate which had not been hypothesized. Again, JUNCT makes a judgment about time-adjacency. Finally, WIZARD compares its word-pronunciation network to the segments in an attempt to verify the prediction.

For each of these different kinds of verification, the approximate begin-time (end-time) of the word being predicted to the right (left) of the phrase is taken to be the end-time (begin-time) of the phrase. The end-time (begin-time) of the predicted word is not known and, in fact, one requirement of the verification step is to generate an approximate end-time (begin-time) for the verified word. In general, several different "versions" of the word may be generated which differ primarily in their end-times; since no context to the right (left) of the predicted word is given, several different estimates of the end (beginning) of the word may be plausible based solely on the segmental information.

16-3.3.5 Word-Phrase Concatenation (CONCAT) - For each verified word and its predicting phrase, a new and longer phrase may be generated. This process, accomplished by the CONCAT knowledge source of SASS, which is similar to the PARSE knowledge source, involves parsing the words of the original phrase augmented by the newly verified word. The extended phrase is then hypothesized and includes a rating based on the ratings of the words that compose it.

If a verified word is already associated with some other phrase hypothesis, CONCAT tries to parse that phrase with the predicting phrase. If successful, a new, larger phrase hypothesis is created which represents the merging of the two phrases.

16-3.3.6 Complete Sentences and Halting Criteria (STOP) - Two unique "word" hypotheses are generated before the first and after the last segment of the utterance to denote begin and end of utterance, respectively. These same "words" are included in the syntactic specification of the language and appear as the first and last terminals of every complete sentence. Thus, any verified phrase that includes these as its extreme constituents is a complete sentence and spans the entire utterance. Such a sentence becomes a candidate for selection as the system's recognition result.

In general, the control and rating strategies do not guarantee that the first such complete spanning hypothesis found will have the highest rating of all possible spanning sentence hypotheses that might be found if the search were allowed to continue, so the system does not just stop with the first one generated. However, the characteristics of such an hypothesis are used by the STOP knowledge source to prune from further consideration other partial hypotheses which, because of their low ratings, are unlikely to be extendible into spanning hypotheses with ratings higher than the best already-discovered spanning sentence. This heuristic pruning procedure is based on the form of the ratings function (i.e., how the rating of the phrase is derived from its constituent words). The pruning procedure considers each partial phrase and uses the ratings of other word hypotheses in the time areas not covered by the phrase to determine if the phrase might be extendible to a phrase rated higher than the spanning hypothesis; if not, the partial phrase is pruned. This pruning process and the rating and halting policies are discussed in [Mostow 77].

The recognition processing finally halts in one of two ways: First, there may be no more partial hypotheses left to consider for predicting and extending. Because of the combinatorics of the grammar and the likelihood of finding some prediction that is rated at least above the absolute rejection threshold, this form of termination happens when the pruning procedure has been effective and has eliminated all competitors. Second, the expenditure of a predefined amount of computing resources (time or space) also halts the recognition process; the actual thresholds used are set according to the past performance of the system on similar sentences (i.e., of the given length and over the same vocabulary and grammar).

Once the recognition process is halted, a selection of one or more phrase hypotheses is made to represent the result. If at least one spanning sentence hypothesis was found, the highest-rated such hypothesis is chosen; otherwise, a selection of several of the highest-rated of the partial phrase hypotheses is made, biasing the selection to the longest ones which tend to overlap (in time) the least.

16-3.3.7 Hypothesis Ratings (RPOL) - The RPOL KS runs in high priority immediately after any KS action that creates a new hypothesis or that modifies an existing hypothesis. RPOL uses rating information on the hypothesis, as well as rating information on hypotheses to which the stimulus hypothesis is connected, to calculate the over-all rating of the stimulus hypothesis.

16-3.3.8 Attention Focussing - The top-end processing operations include (a) word-island generation, (b) word sequence parsing, (c) word prediction from phrases, (d) word verification, and (e) word-phrase concatenation. Of these, (c), (d), and (e) are the most frequently performed. Typically, there are a number of these actions waiting to be performed at various places in the utterance. The selection at each point in the processing of which of these actions to perform is a problem of combinatoric control, since the execution of each action usually generates other actions to be done.

To handle this problem, the Hearsay-II system has a statistically-based scheduler [Hayes-Roth & Lesser 77] which calculates a priority for each action and selects, at each time, the waiting action with the highest priority. The priority calculation attempts to estimate the usefulness of the action in fulfilling the over-all system goal of recognizing the utterance. The calculation is based on the stimulus and response frames specified when the action is triggered. For example, the word verifier is triggered whenever words are predicted from a phrase hypothesis; the information passed to the scheduler in order to help calculate the priority of this instantiation of the verifier includes such things as the time and rating of the predicting phrase (in the stimulus frame) and the number of words predicted (as given in the response frame). In addition to the action-specific information, the scheduler keeps track of the overall state of the system in terms of the kinds and quality of hypotheses in each time area.

16-3.4 Interpretation and Response (SEMANT, DISCO)

The SEMANT knowledge-source [Fox & Mostow 77] accepts the word sequence(s) result of the recognition process and generates an interpretation in an unambiguous format for interaction with the data base that the speaker is querying. The interpretation is constructed by actions associated with "semantically interesting" non-terminals (which have been pre-specified for the grammar) in the parse tree(s) of the recognized sequence(s). If recognition results in two or more partial sequences, SEMANT constructs a consistent interpretation based on all of the partial sentences, taking into account for each partial sentence its rating, temporal position, and semantic consistency, as compared to the other partial sentences.

The DISCO ('discourse') knowledge-source [Hayes-Roth Gill & Mostow 77] accepts the formatted interpretation of SEMANT and produces a response to the speaker. This response is often the display of a selected portion of the queried data base. In order to retain a coherent interpretation across sentences, DISCO has a finite-state model of the discourse which is updated with each interaction.

16-4. AN EXAMPLE OF RECOGNITION

Following is a description of the recognition of the utterance "ARE ANY BY FEIGENBAUM AND FELDMAN?" by configuration C2 of Hearsay-II.[5] Each major step of the processing is shown; a step usually corresponds to the action of a knowledge source. Execution of the preconditions is not shown explicitly, nor is indication given of knowledge-source instantiations which are never scheduled. Also, executions of RPOL are not shown.

The name of the KS activated at each step follows the step number. If the KS name is followed by an asterisk, this indicates that the hypotheses in the stimulus frame of this KS instantiation are all correct. Single numbers in parentheses after hypotheses are their ratings (on a scale of 0-100). All times given are in centi-second units; thus the duration of the whole utterance, which was 2.25 seconds, is 225. When begin- and end-times of hypotheses are given, they appear as two numbers separated by a colon (e.g., 52:82). Hypotheses which are correct are marked with an asterisk.

The waveform of the spoken utterance is shown in Fig. 16-2.a. The "correct" word boundaries (determined by human inspection) is shown in Fig. 16-2.b for reference. The remaining sections of Fig. 16-2 contain all the hypotheses created by the KSs on the blackboard (except that the goal hypotheses created by WORD-CTL and WORD-SEQ-CTL are not shown). Each hypothesis is indicated by a box; the hypotheses are grouped by level -- segment, syllable, word, word-sequence, and phrase. Within each hypothesis box, the number preceding the colon indicates the step number in which the hypothesis was created. The symbol following the colon names the hypothesis. At the word level and above, a "*" following the symbol indicates that the hypothesis is correct. The trailing number within the hypothesis box is the rating, on a scale of 0 (lowest) to 100.

None of the links between hypotheses are shown in Fig. 16-2. In general, each hypothesis is connected via multiple binary links to hypotheses above and below it. For example, a word hypothesis has downward links connecting it to each of the syllables which compose it and upward links connecting it to each phrase and/or word-sequence in which it takes part.

1. KS: WORD-CTL
   Stimulus: Start of processing.
   Action: Create goal hypotheses at the word level. These will control the amount of hypothesization that MOW will do.

2. KS: WORD-SEQ-CTL
   Stimulus: Start of processing.
   Action: Create goal hypotheses at the word-sequence level. These will control the amount of hypothesization that WORD-SEQ will do.

3. KS: SEG
   Stimulus: Creation of ZAPDASH parameters for the utterance.
   Action: Create segment hypotheses with vector of estimated allophone

5 For reasons of clarity, the description differs from the actual run in a few details.

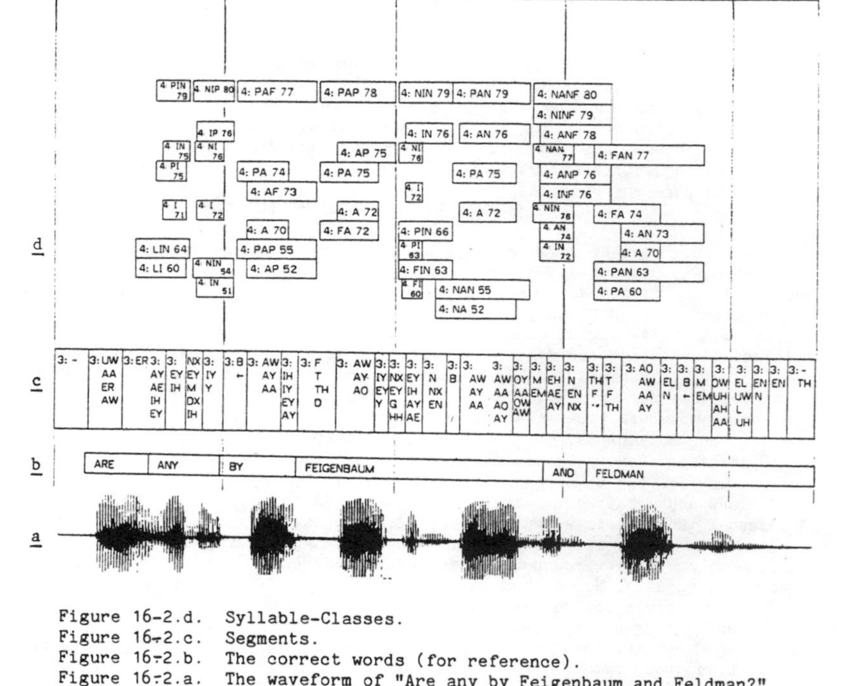

Figure 16-2.d. Syllable-Classes.
Figure 16-2.c. Segments.
Figure 16-2.b. The correct words (for reference).
Figure 16-2.a. The waveform of "Are any by Feigenbaum and Feldman?".

Fig. 16-2. The example utterance.

probabilities. (The several highest-rated labels of each segment are shown in Fig. 16-2.c.)

4. KS: POM
   Stimulus: New segment hypotheses.
   Action: Create syllable-class hypotheses.

Figure 16-2.d shows the syllable-class hypotheses created. Each class name is made up of single-letter codes representing classes of phones, as follows:

Code	Phone-class	Phones in class
A	A-like	AE,AA,AH,AO,AX
I	I-like	IY,IH,EY,EH,IX,AY
U	U-like	OW,UH,U,UW,ER,AW,OY,EL,EM,EN
L	liquid	Y,W,R,L
N	nasal	M,N,NX
P	stop	P,T,K,B,D,G,DX
F	fricative	HH,F,TH,S,SH,V,DH,Z,ZH,CH,JH,WH

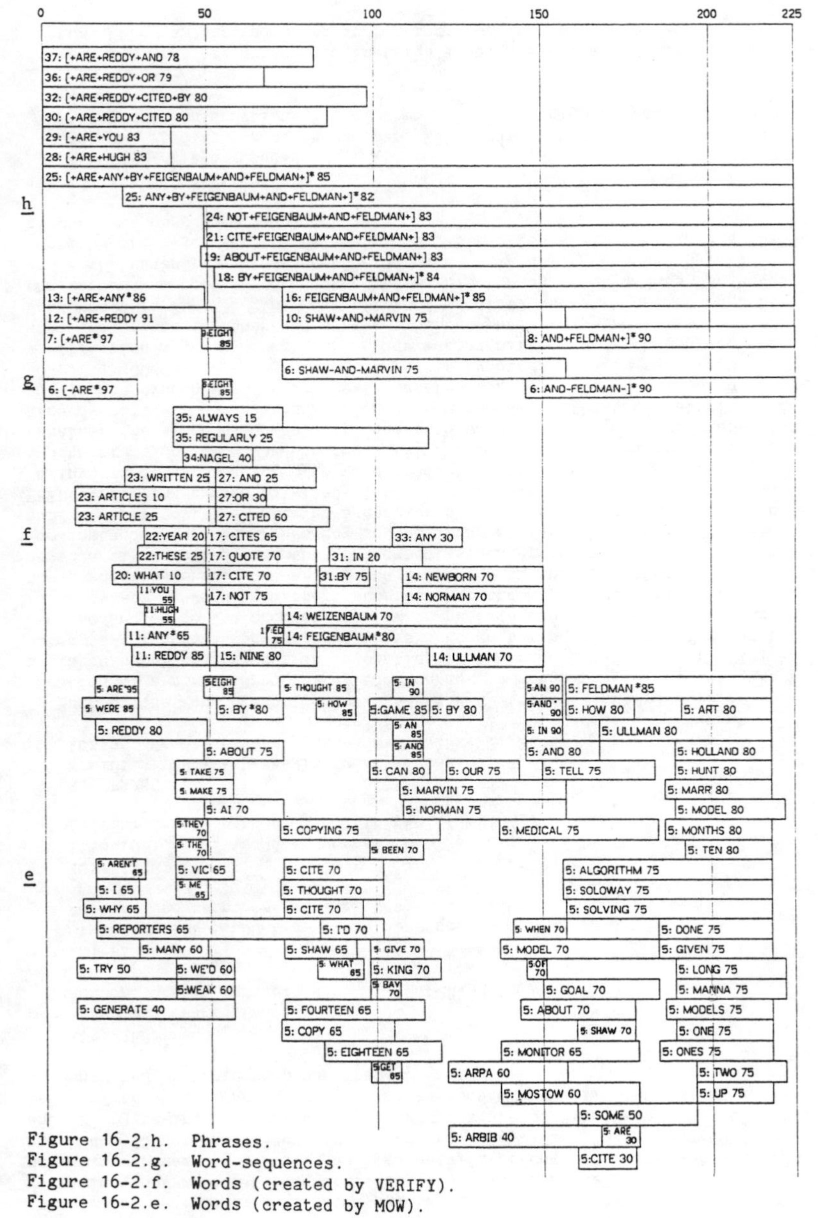

Figure 16-2.h. Phrases.
Figure 16-2.g. Word-sequences.
Figure 16-2.f. Words (created by VERIFY).
Figure 16-2.e. Words (created by MOW).

Fig. 16-2 (continued).

5. KS: MOW
   Stimulus: New syllable hypotheses.[6]
   Action: Create word hypotheses.

Steps 1, 3, 4, and 5 comprise the low level, bottom-up processing; this results in a selection of word hypotheses (created in step 5). Figure 16-2.e depicts these word hypotheses.

Four words (ARE, BY, AND, and FELDMAN) of the six in the utterance were correctly hypothesized; 86 incorrect hypotheses were generated. The 90 words that were hypothesized represents approximately 1.5% of the 1011-word vocabulary for each one of the 6 words in the utterance.

6. KS: WORD-SEQ
   Stimulus: New words created bottom-up.
   Action: Create 4 word-sequence hypotheses: AND-FELDMAN-]*(90,145:225), [-ARE*(97,0:28), SHAW-AND-MARVIN(75,72:157), EIGHT(85,48:57).

Step 6 results in the generation of 4 multi-word sequences. (See Fig. 16-2.g.) These will be used as initial, alternative anchor points for additional searching. Note that two of these islands are correct, each representing an alternative search path that potentially can lead to a correct interpretation of the utterance.

In earlier versions of KS configuration of the system (e.g., C1), low-level processing was not done in the serial, lock-step manner as in steps 3, 4, and 5 (i.e., level-to-level, where each level is completely processed before processing on the next higher level is begun). Rather, processing was done in an asynchronous, data-directed manner (i.e., as interesting hypotheses were generated at one level, they were immediately propagated to and processed by KSs operating at higher levels). It was found that the asynchronous processing at these lower levels (e.g., segment, syllable, and word) was inappropriate because there was not enough accuracy in credibility ratings of hypotheses to form hypothesis islands that could direct the search reliably. It is only with the word-sequence hypotheses produced in step 6 that the reliability of the hypothesis ratings is high enough that selective search can be employed. This conclusion is substantiated by experiments with several island-driving strategies [Lesser Hayes-Roth Birnbaum & Cronk 77].

High level processing on the multi-word sequences is accomplished by the following KSs: PARSE, PREDICT, VERIFY, CONCAT, STOP, and WORD-SEQ-CTL. Since an execution of the VERIFY KS will often immediately follow the execution of the PREDICT KS (each on the same hypothesis), we have combined the descriptions of these two KS executions into one step for ease of understanding.

Steps 7 through 10 involve the PARSE KS. The PARSE KS verifies whether a multi-word sequence (created in step 6) is a legal language fragment of the grammar. If the sequence is grammatical, a phrase hypothesis is constructed from it; otherwise, the sequence is marked rejected. In this example, all four multi-word sequences were verified to be valid language fragments. However, if a multi-word sequence had been rejected, the WORD-SEQ KS might be reinvoked to generate additional multi-word sequences in the time area of the rejected sequence. WORD-SEQ would generate the additional hypotheses by decomposing word-sequence islands already on the blackboard or by re-generating islands which were initially discarded because their ratings were too low. Additional word-sequence hypotheses might also be generated in response to the modification of "goal" hypotheses at the word-sequence level by the WORD-SEQ-CTL.

6 MOW will also be re-invoked upon a modification to the word goal hypotheses by WORD-CTL.

The scheduling strategy is so parameterized that processing at the phrase level is delayed until an adequate number of highly-rated phrase hypothesis islands are generated. This strategy is not built directly into the scheduler, but rather is accomplished (1) by appropriately setting external scheduling parameters (i.e., the high setting of the priorities of WORD-SEQ and PARSE KS actions in contrast to those of PREDICT, VERIFY, and CONCAT),[7] and (2) by taking into account the current state of hypotheses on the phrase level of the blackboard in evaluating the usefulness of potential KS actions as described by their response frames.

7. KS: PARSE*
   Stimulus: [-ARE* (word sequence)
   Action: Create phrase: [+ARE* (97,0:28)

8. KS: PARSE*
   Stimulus: AND-FELDMAN-]* (word sequence)
   Action: Create phrase: AND+FELDMAN+]* (90,145:225)

9. KS: PARSE
   Stimulus: EIGHT (word sequence)
   Action: Create phrase: EIGHT (85,48:57)

10. KS: PARSE
    Stimulus: SHAW-AND-MARVIN (word sequence)
    Action: Create phrase: SHAW+AND+MARVIN (75,72:157)

Each of the four executions of the PARSE KS (steps 7-10) results in the creation of a phrase hypothesis; each phrase is shown in Fig. 16-2.h. Each of these hypotheses causes an invocation of the PREDICT KS. The PREDICT KS attempts to extend a phrase hypothesis through the predictions of words that can, according to the grammar, follow or precede the hypothesis. Its action is to attach a "word-predictor" attribute to the hypothesis which specifies the predicted words. Not all of these PREDICT KS instantiations are necessarily executed (and thus indicated as a step in the execution history). For instance, further processing on the phrases [+ARE and AND+FELDMAN+] is sufficiently positive that the scheduler never executes the instantiation of PREDICT for the phrase SHAW+AND+MARVIN (created in step 10). In turn, VERIFY is invoked by the placing of a word-predictor attribute on a phrase hypothesis. For each word on the attribute list that VERIFY verifies (against the segmental data), it creates a word hypothesis (if one does not already exist) and the word is placed on a "word-verification" attribute of the phrase hypothesis. (Such newly-created word hypotheses are shown in Fig. 16-2.f.) CONCAT is then invoked on phrase hypotheses which have word-verification attributes attached. For each verified word, the phrase and new word are parsed together and a new, extended phrase hypothesis is created (and shown in Fig. 16-2.h). If all word predictions to the right or left of the phrase had been rejected, the phrase hypothesis is marked as "rejected", as is the underlying word-sequence hypothesis if all the phrase hypotheses it supports are rejected. (Note that this last action will re-trigger WORD-SEQ to generate more word sequences.)

11. KS: PREDICT & VERIFY*
    Stimulus: [+ARE* (phrase)
    Action: Predict (from the grammar) 292 words to right. Reject (using the acoustic information) 277 of them. The four highest-rated of the fifteen verified words are REDDY(85,26:52), ANY*(65,24:49), HUGH (55,30:39), and YOU(55,28:39).

12. KS: CONCAT
    Stimulus: [+ARE* (phrase), REDDY (word)
    Action: Create phrase: [+ARE+REDDY (91,0:52)

13. KS: CONCAT*
    Stimulus: [+ARE* (phrase), ANY* (word)
    Action: Create phrase: [+ARE+ANY* (86,0:49)

In steps 11 through 13, the highly-rated phrase [+ARE is extended and results in the generation of the additional phrases [+ARE+REDDY and [+ARE+ANY. These phrases, however, are not immediately extended because the predicted words REDDY and ANY are not rated sufficiently high. Instead, the scheduler, pursuing a strategy more conservative than strict best-first, investigates phrases that look almost as good as the best one. This scheduling strategy results in the execution of the PREDICT and VERIFY KSs on two of the other initial phrase islands: AND+FELDMAN+] and EIGHT.

14. KS: PREDICT & VERIFY*
    Stimulus: AND+FELDMAN+]* (phrase)
    Action: Predict 100 words to left. Reject 76 of them. The best of the verified 24 (in descending rating order) are FEIGENBAUM*(80,72:150), WEIZENBAUM(70,72:150), ULLMAN(70,116:150), NORMAN(70,108:150), and NEWBORN(70,108:150)

15. KS: PREDICT & VERIFY
    Stimulus: EIGHT (phrase)
    Action: Predict the word NINE to right and verify it (80,52:82). Predict SEVEN to left, reject prediction.

The attempted extension of the phrase EIGHT at step 15 is not successful -- none of the grammatically predicted words is acoustically verified, even using a lenient threshold. Thus, this phrase is marked rejected and is dropped from further consideration.

16. KS: CONCAT*
    Stimulus: FEIGENBAUM* (word), AND+FELDMAN+]* (phrase)
    Action: Create phrase: FEIGENBAUM+AND+FELDMAN+]* (85,72:225)

Beginning with step 16, the highly-rated left word extension FEIGENBAUM to the phrase AND+FELDMAN+] looks sufficiently promising that processing now continues in a more depth-first manner along the path FEIGENBAUM+AND+FELDMAN+] through step 25.[8] Processing on the path [+ARE+REDDY does not resume until step 26.

17. KS: PREDICT & VERIFY*
    Stimulus: FEIGENBAUM+AND+FELDMAN+]* (phrase)
    Action: Predict eight words to left. Reject one (DISCUSS). Find two already on blackboard: BY*(80,52:72) and ABOUT(75,48:72). Verify five others: NOT(75,49:82), ED(75,67:72), CITE(70,49:82), QUOTE(70,49:82), CITES(65:49:82).

---

7 These settings are determined empirically by observing a number of training runs. They are not adjusted during test runs of the system.

8 The rating on an hypothesis is only one parameter used by the scheduler to assign priorities to waiting KS instantiations. In particular, the length of an hypothesis is also important. Thus, FEIGENBAUM with a rating of 80 looks better than REDDY with a rating of 85 because it is much longer.

In steps 18 through 24, alternative word extensions of FEIGENBAUM+AND+FELDMAN+] are explored. As a result of this exploration, the phrase BY+FEIGENBAUM+AND+FELDMAN+] is considered the most credible.

18. KS: CONCAT
Stimulus: BY* (word), FEIGENBAUM+AND+FELDMAN+]* (phrase)
Action: Create phrase: BY+FEIGENBAUM+AND+FELDMAN+]* (84,52:225)

19. KS: CONCAT
Stimulus: ABOUT (word), FEIGENBAUM+AND+FELDMAN+]* (phrase)
Action: Create phrase: ABOUT+FEIGENBAUM+AND+FELDMAN+] (83,48:225)

20. KS: PREDICT & VERIFY
Stimulus: ABOUT+FEIGENBAUM+AND+FELDMAN+] (phrase)
Action: Predict one word to left: WHAT. Verify it (10,20:49).

21. KS: CONCAT
Stimulus: CITE (word), FEIGENBAUM+AND+FELDMAN+] (phrase)
Action: Create phrase: CITE+FEIGENBAUM+AND+FELDMAN+] (83,49:225)

22. KS: PREDICT & VERIFY
Stimulus: CITE+FEIGENBAUM+AND+FELDMAN+] (phrase)
Action: Predict four words to left. Reject two of them: BOOKS, PAPERS. Verify THESE(25,28:49), YEAR(20,30:49).

23. KS: PREDICT & VERIFY*
Stimulus: BY+FEIGENBAUM+AND+FELDMAN+]* (phrase)
Action: Predict ten words to left. Reject five: ABSTRACTS, ARE, BOOKS, PAPERS, REFERENCED. Find two already on blackboard: ANY*(65,24:49), THESE(25,28:49). Verify three more: ARTICLE(25,9:52), WRITTEN (25,24:52), ARTICLES(10,9:52).

24. KS: CONCAT
Stimulus: NOT (word), FEIGENBAUM+AND+FELDMAN+]*
Action: Create phrase: NOT+FEIGENBAUM+AND+FELDMAN+] (83,49:225)

25. KS: CONCAT*
Stimulus: ANY* (word), BY+FEIGENBAUM+AND+FELDMAN+]* (phrase)
Action: Create phrase: ANY+BY+FEIGENBAUM+AND+FELDMAN+]* (82,24:225) [+ARE+ANY+BY+FEIGENBAUM+AND+FELDMAN+]* (85,0:225) is also created, from [+ARE+ANY and BY+FEIGENBAUM+AND+FELDMAN+].

In step 25, the word ANY is concatenated onto the phrase BY+FEIGENBAUM+AND+FELDMAN+]. However, instead of only creating this new combined phrase, the CONCAT KS also notices that the word ANY is the last word of the phrase [+AND+ANY; this leads the CONCAT KS to merge the two adjacent phrases [+ARE+ANY and BY+FEIGENBAUM+AND+FELDMAN+] into a single enlarged phrase, after first ascertaining that the resulting phrase is grammatically allowed. This merging bypasses the several single-word PREDICT, VERIFY, and CONCAT actions that would be necessary to generate the enlarged hypothesis from either of the two original hypotheses in an incremental fashion. Thus, the recognition process is sped up, not only because the several single-word actions are eliminated, but also because KS actions on competing non-correct hypotheses are avoided since these actions do not appear to the scheduler as attractive as actions on the new, enlarged hypothesis. Such mergings occur in approximately half of the runs on the 1011-word grammar with the small branching factor ("X05"); in grammars with higher branching factors, the merging of phrase hypotheses occurs with even higher frequency.

It has been our experience that, just as a multi-word island is more credible than the individual words that compose it, so a merged phrase hypothesis is more credible than its two constituent phrases. For example, about 80% of the mergings in X05 runs produce correct hypotheses. In more complex grammars, this statistic drops to about 35%, but there are correspondingly more phrase mergings that occur.

The newly-created merged phrase also happens to be a complete sentence; i.e., it has begin- and end-of-utterance markers at as its extreme constituents. Thus, it is a candidate for the interpretation of the utterance.

26. KS: STOP
Stimulus: [+ARE+ANY+BY+FEIGENBAUM+AND+FELDMAN+]* (complete phrase)
Action: Deactivation of several score hypotheses.

STOP responds to the creation of a complete phrase. STOP tests each phrase hypothesis on the blackboard to see whether there is any possibility of extending it to produce a complete phrase that is rated higher than the one just created. It performs this heuristic test by trying to combine the phrase, just based on simple time adjacency constraints, in the best possible way with words already hypothesized. Each phrase that cannot be extended by this process into a word sequence that spans the entire utterance and is better than the newly created complete phrase is discarded. Subsequently, the RPOL KS (whose executions are not shown here) will discard hypotheses as they are created if they also cannot pass the same test.

Of the hypotheses not discarded, extensions to the phrase [+ARE now appear as the most likely candidates to produce new and better complete phrases. This search for better complete phrases results, in steps 27 through 36, in the examination of numerous alternative extensions, each of which is promising.

27. KS: PREDICT & VERIFY
Stimulus: [+ARE+REDDY
Action: Predict three words to right. Verify CITED(60,52:86), OR (30,52:67), AND(25,52:82).

28. KS: CONCAT
Stimulus: [+ARE (phrase), HUGH (word)
Action: Create phrase: [+ARE+HUGH (83,0:39)

29. KS: CONCAT
Stimulus: [+ARE (phrase), YOU (word)
Action: Create phrase: [+ARE+YOU (83,0:39)

30. KS: CONCAT
Stimulus: [+ARE+REDDY (phrase), CITED (word)
Action: Create phrase: [+ARE+REDDY+CITED (80,0:86)

31. KS: PREDICT & VERIFY
Stimulus: [+ARE+REDDY+CITED (phrase)
Action: Predict two words to right. Verify BY(75,83:98), IN(20,86:114).

32. KS: CONCAT
Stimulus: [+ARE+REDDY+CITED (phrase), BY (word)
Action: Create phrase: [+ARE+REDDY+CITED+BY (80,0:98)

33. KS: PREDICT & VERIFY
Stimulus: [+ARE+REDDY+CITED+BY (phrase)
Action: Predict one word to right. Verify ANY(30,105:126).

34. KS: PREDICT & VERIFY
Stimulus: [+ARE+HUGH (phrase)
Action: Predict one word to right. Verify NAGEL(40,42:63).

35. KS: PREDICT & VERIFY
Stimulus: [+ARE+YOU (phrase)
Action: Predict three words to right. Reject USUALLY. Verify REGULARLY (25,39:116), ALWAYS(15,39:72).

36. KS: CONCAT
Stimulus: [+ARE+REDDY (phrase), OR (word)
Action: Create phrase: [+ARE+REDDY+OR (79,0:67)

37. KS: CONCAT
Stimulus: [+ARE+REDDY (phrase), AND (word)
Action: Create phrase: [+ARE+REDDY+AND (78,0:82)

38. KS: STOP
Stimulus: Stagnation
Action: Stop search and accept [+ARE+ANY+BY+FEIGENBAUM+AND+FELDMAN+]*.

KS STOP is again executed; this execution is caused by the lack of any KS instantiations that are rated sufficiently high. STOP here makes a decision to terminate the search process and accept the phrase [+ARE+ANY+BY+FEIGENBAUM+AND+FELDMAN+] as the correct interpretation.

39. KS: SEMANT*
Stimulus: Recognized utterance: [+ARE+ANY+BY+FEIGENBAUM+AND+FELDMAN+]
Action: SEMANT parses the utterance, using the same grammar, but with semantic routines on some of the non-terminal nodes. The execution of these routines incrementally produces the following structure:

```
F:[ U:( [ ARE ANY BY FEIGENBAUM AND FELDMAN ] )
    N:( $PRUNE!LIST
        S:($PRUNE!LIST!AUTHOR K:(A:(( FEIGENBAUM * FELDMAN)))) )
  ]
```

"F" denotes the total message. "U" contains the utterance itself. "N" indicates the main type of the utterance (e.g., REQUEST, HELP, etc.), "S" the sub-type. "K" denotes the different attributes associated with the utterance (e.g., "A" is the author and "T" is the topic). This structure is passed on to the discourse component, which queries the data base and responds to the speaker.

16-5. CONCLUSIONS

The Hearsay-II system has been successful. It came very close to meeting the ARPA performance goals: In September, 1976, the C2 configuration achieved correct semantic interpretation of 90% of a test set of utterances (with 73% of the utterances being recognized word-for-word correctly). This performance was with the highly constrained "X05" grammar over the 1011-word vocabulary. The test set contained twenty-two utterances, averaging seven words each. These utterances were totally new to the system and were run "blind". The processing time averaged 85 mipss (million instructions per second of speech) on a PDP-10 computer. (Subsequently, some trivial implementation modifications reduced the processing costs to about 60 mipss.)

In addition to its successful performance, the structure of the system is interesting. An attempt was made from the start to develop a clean model for the kinds of complex interactions that would be required of the various sources of knowledge. Although the system was modified substantially as experience was gained, it retained its fidelity to that model, indicating its validity. A detailed discussion of the evolution of the architecture with respect to the model can be found in [Lesser & Erman 77]. Several other problem areas have been attacked with organizations strongly influenced by the Hearsay-II structure: image understanding [Prager et al 77], reading comprehension [Rumumelhart 76], protein-crystallographic analysis [Engelmore & Nii 77], signal understanding [Nii & Feigenbaum 78], and complex learning [Soloway 77].

16-6. ACKNOWLEDGMENTS

Raj Reddy has provided much of the vision and energy for this work, most of the central ideas in the Hearsay model, and much technical expertise in many of the knowledge sources in the Hearsay-II system. Richard Fennell and Rick Hayes-Roth have been particularly instrumental in formulating and testing the Hearsay-II architecture. All members of the CMU "speech group" have contributed to this work; their substantial efforts are gratefully acknowledged. Lucy Erman and Mark Fox have made helpful suggestions for this paper.

16-7. REFERENCES

Abbreviations: ASSP -- Acoustics, Speech, and Signal Processing
CMU -- Computer Science Dept., Carnegie-Mellon Univ., Pittsburgh, Pa.
IJCAI -- International Joint Conference on Artificial Intelligence

CMU Computer Science Speech Group (1977). Summary of the CMU Five-year ARPA effort in speech understanding research. Technical Report, CMU.

Engelmore,R.S. & H.P.Nii (1977). A knowledge-based system for the interpretation of protein x-ray crystallographic data. Technical Report Stan-CS-77-589, Stanford Univ., Stanford, CA.

Erman,L.D. & V.R.Lesser (1975). A multi-level organization for problem solving using many diverse cooperating sources of knowledge. Proc. 4IJCAI, Tbilisi, USSR, 483-490.

Erman,L.D. & V.R.Lesser (1978). System engineering techniques for artificial intelligence systems. In A.Hanson and E.Riseman (Eds.), Computer Vision Systems, Academic Press, 1978.

Fox,M.S. & D.J.Mostow (1977). Maximal consistent interpretations of errorful data in hierarchically modelled domains. Proc. 5IJCAI, Cambridge, Mass., 165-171.

Goldberg,H., R.Reddy, & G.Gill (1977). The ZAPDASH parameters, feature extraction, segmentation, and labeling for speech understanding systems. In [CMU 77], 10-11.

Itakura,F. (1975). Minimum prediction residual principle applied to speech recognition. IEEE Trans. ASSP, 23, 67-72.

Hayes-Roth,F., L.D.Erman, M.Fox, & D.J.Mostow (1977). Syntactic processing in Hearsay-II. In [CMU 77], 16-18.

Hayes-Roth,F., G.Gill, and D.J.Mostow (1977). Discourse analysis and task performance in the Hearsay-II speech understanding system. In [CMU 77], 24-28.

Hayes-Roth,F. & V.R.Lesser (1977). Focus of attention in the Hearsay-II system. Proc. 5IJCAI, Cambridge, Mass., 27-35.

Hayes-Roth,F., D.J.Mostow, & M.Fox (1978, in press). Understanding speech in the Hearsay-II system. In Natural Language Communication with Computers. L.Bloc (Ed.) Springer-Verlag, Berlin.

Lesser,V.R., R.D.Fennell, L.D.Erman, & D.R.Reddy (1975). Organization of the Hearsay-II speech understanding system. IEEE Trans. ASSP, 23, 11-23.

Lesser,V.R. & L.D.Erman (1977). A retrospective view of the Hearsay-II architecture. Proc. 5IJCAI, Cambridge, Mass., 790-800.

Lesser,V.R., F.Hayes-Roth, M.Birnbaum, & R.Cronk (1977). Selection of word islands in the Hearsay-II speech understanding system. Proc. IEEE Inter. Conf. ASSP, Hartford, Conn., 791-794.

Lowerre,B.T. (1976). The Harpy speech recognition system. Technical Report, CMU (Ph.D. Dissertation).

Lowerre,B.T. & R.Reddy (1978). The Harpy speech understanding system. In Trends in Speech Recognition, W.A.Lea (Ed.), Prentice-Hall (this book), Chap. 15.

McKeown,D.M. (1977). Word verification in the Hearsay-II speech understanding system. Proc. 1977 IEEE Inter. Conf. ASSP., Hartford, Conn., 795-798.

Mostow,D.J. (1977). A halting condition and related pruning heuristic for combinatorial search. In [CMU 77], 158-166.

Newell,A., J.Barnett, J.Forgie, C.Green, D.Klatt, J.C.R.Licklider, J.Munson, R.Reddy, & W.Woods (1973). Speech Understanding Systems: Final Report of a Study Group. North-Holland. (Originally appeared in 1971.)

Nii,H.P. & E.A.Feigenbaum (1978). Rule-based understanding of signals. In D.A.Waterman & F.Hayes-Roth (Eds.) Pattern-Directed Inference Systems, Academic Press.

Prager,J., P.Nagin, R.Kohler, A.Hanson, & E.Riseman (1977). Segmentation processes in the VISIONS system. Proc. 5IJCAI, Cambridge, Mass., 642-643.

Reddy,D.R., L.D.Erman, & R.B.Neely (1973). A model and a system for machine recognition of speech. IEEE Trans. Audio and Electroacoustics, AU-21, 229-238.

Reddy,D.R., L.D.Erman, R.D.Fennell, & R.B.Neely (1973). The Hearsay speech understanding system: An example of the recognition process. Proc. 3IJCAI, Stanford, Cal., 185-193.

Reiser,J.F. (1976). SAIL. Stanford Artificial Intelligence Lab., Memo AIM-289.

Rumelhart, D. E. (1976). Toward an interactive model of reading. Technical Report 56, Center for Human Information Processing, Univ. of Cal. at San Diego.

Smith,A.R. (1976). Word hypothesization in the Hearsay-II speech system. Proc. IEEE Int. Conf. ASSP, Philadelphia, Pa., 549-552.

Smith,A.R. (1977). Word hypothesization for large-vocabulary speech understanding systems. Technical Report, CMU (Ph.D. Dissertation).

Smith,A.R. & M.R.Sambur (1978). Hypothesizing and verifying words for speech recognition. In Trends in Speech Recognition, W.A.Lea (Ed.), Prentice-Hall (this book), Chap. 7.

Soloway,E.M. & E.M.Riseman (1977). Levels of pattern description in learning. Proc. 5IJCAI, Cambridge, Mass., 801-811.

Learning and Plan Refinement in a Knowledge-Based System for Automatic Speech Recognition

RENATO DE MORI, LILY LAM, AND MICHEL GILLOUX

***Abstract*—This paper shows how a semiautomatic design of a speech recognition system can be done as a planning activity. Recognition performances are used for deciding plan refinement. Inductive learning is performed for setting action preconditions. Experimental results in the recognition of connected letters spoken by 100 speakers are presented.**

***Index Terms*—Automatic speech recognition, connected speech recognition, inductive learning, letter recognition, network of actions, planning, stochastic rules.**

I. Introduction

IMPORTANT achievements have been recently obtained in Automatic Speech Recognition (ASR) using global pattern matching or stochastic decoding.

Global pattern matching methods compare data with prototypes and have a computational complexity that is proportional to the number of prototypes. This number grows with the number of speakers to be recognized and with the vocabulary size. Prototype clustering has been shown to be useful for reducing the number of prototypes to be used for multispeaker recognition [1]. Nevertheless, concatenating word or syllable prototypes for multispeaker recognition of connected speech involving large vocabularies does not allow us to take into account coarticulation effects across the segments that are concatenated. This consideration partially explains why such an approach did not produce good recognition results [2]. Another successful approach is based on vector-quantization for producing symbols to be used by a stochastic model of the language [3]. Systems that have been developed so far based on this principle perform well on isolated words and constrained protocols and are speaker-dependent. Furthermore, they do not perform equally well with different speakers.

The introduction of procedures in order to achieve multispeaker recognition of isolated or connected words in limited vocabularies has also been attempted using procedural networks [4], [5]. Procedures are associated with transitions between states of the network. In the systems proposed so far, a procedure computes a similarity between a segment of the input signal and vector prototypes. More knowledge can be used in these procedures in order to achieve better performance in complex tasks such as the multispeaker recognition of connectedly spoken letters. Knowledge about speech recognition can be distributed into procedures conceived as *perceptual plans*. These plans must be capable of implementing various recognition strategies involving focus of attention. Recognition strategies may use invariant properties, when they are known to be reliable enough, speaker normalization techniques, when they are appropriate, or statistical methods.

Knowledge about *speaking modes* or speaking styles should also be taken into account. Some sounds, for example, are characterized for some speakers (and for a number of speech synthesizers) by formant transitions. Our recent experience on the analysis and recognition of plosive sounds has shown that formants offer good discriminant cues in some cases but not always. We argue, based on this experience, that a truly speaker-independent system must have knowledge about different speaking modes. In a speaking mode, for example, formant transitions, represented by transitions of spectral lines, have a high discrimination power for a class of sounds. In another speaking mode, broad-band energy concentrations may have a better discriminating power for the same class of sounds. Different speakers may use different speaking modes and styles because of their anatomy, education, and mood.

With a knowledge-based approach, the speech signal is *described* in terms of sequences of sets of *acoustic properties*. Descriptions can be insufficient for decoding the speech waveform but cannot be wrong because they represent events of the signal and not interpretations of it.

Conceiving plans capable of extracting property descriptions of the speech waveform is the topic addressed in this paper. Plans must be capable of extracting different sets of properties in short-time intervals for the same class of sounds in order to be able to characterize different speaking modes. Plan operators should be executed when some *preconditions* are met. Preconditions are expressions of *acoustic properties* detected in the signal. Characterization of speaking modes is implicit in precondition expressions.

Phonetic knowledge can be used in many ways. It can suggest algorithms to be incorporated into sensory pro-

Manuscript received January 3, 1986; revised May 26, 1986. Recommended for acceptance by T. Pavlidis. This work was supported by the Natural Sciences and Engineering Research Council of Canada under Grant A2439. This paper is dedicated to the memory of Professor King-Sun Fu.

R. De Mori is with the School of Computer Science, McGill University, Montreal, P. Q. H3A 2K6, Canada.

L. Lam is with the Department of Computer Science, Concordia University, Montreal, P.Q. H3G 1M8, Canada.

M. Gilloux is with the Centre National d'Etudes de Telecommunications, B. P. 40, Lannion 22301, France.

IEEE Log Number 8612808.

cedures and the contextual constraints that have to be satisfied when the procedures are invoked. Phonetic knowledge can also help in setting initial conditions for learning algorithms requiring a preliminary alignment of the data to be learned. For example, Markov Models can be used for representing positions of spectral lines along the frequency axis in stationary acoustic segments [6]. Formant target values and their expected variations can be used as initial mean values and standard deviations associated with some states of the Markov Model.

Some descriptions can appear sufficient after a number of experiments involving a set of speakers or a set of speaking modes. These descriptions can become insufficient when new speaking modes are observed. In such a case, conditions for generating descriptions can be made more specific through a revised learning phase. Should this operation appear not feasible, new acoustic properties have to be extracted and discriminant descriptions become preconditions for *refinement*.

In a recent paper [7], a paradigm based on an *Expert System Society* (ESS) for ASR has been proposed. The task of each Expert of the Society is obtained by decomposing the signal interpretation task into components such that each component uses homogeneous knowledge. Examples of Expert's knowledge are signal processing, acoustic phonetics, lexicon, and phonology. The possibility that each Expert executes several activities in parallel has also been investigated. Each Expert may have a set of "spontaneous activities" and a set of activities executed "on request." Both types of activities have the purpose of achieving some *goal* such as the extraction and description of an acoustic property or the generation of phoneme hypotheses. The organization of such activities into plans together with *plan refinement* is the major contribution of this paper.

In order to prove the validity of this conception method, a particularly difficult subset of the spoken alphabet, namely the E1 set, has been chosen. Experiments in the recognition of connectedly spoken letters from 100 speakers will be reported.

Section II of this paper introduces Networks of Actions. Section III introduces plane refinement. Section IV gives details of the actions used for the recognition of the letters belonging to the E1 set spoken connectedly. Section V is about inductive learning and truth maintenance. Section VI presents experimental results with a nonstochastic model. Section VII proposes a stochastic model of rule application for solving ambiguities. Sections III and V describe how Artificial Intelligence (AI) techniques have been used for designing the ASR system as a planning system. The reader who is just interested in the structure and the performance of the recognition system may skip these sections.

II. On the Use of Networks of Actions as Recognition Paradigm

A. The Elaboration-Decision Paradigm

This section discusses how the objective of producing accurate descriptions of essential properties of speech segments can be achieved through a Network of Action Hierarchies [8]. Actions to be performed for recognition are selected using the *elaboration-decision* paradigm [9]. Elaboration may involve the execution of sensory procedures or of inferences that will provide information about the signal to be interpreted.

Actions can consist of the generation of phonemic hypotheses based on decision table or of the execution of other elaboration-decision cycles.

Decisions are controlled by rules obtained during a planning phase with *inductive learning*.

The execution of an action of the hierarchy may be conditioned by the verification of some events called **precondition** and may consist in the application of a terminal decision-making *operator* or in the activation of a more detailed sequence of actions belonging to a lower level of the hierarchy. In such a case, the node of the hierarchy that will be expanded into a more detailed plan is considered to represent an **abstract action.**

The hierarchy of actions is executed according to the following algorithm:

```
action hierarchy execution algorithm
  begin
    next-action := spontaneous activities;
    elaboration-decision (next-action)
  end
procedure elaboration-decision (next-action)
  begin
    elaboration-phase (next-action)
    decision-phase (rule set (next-action), result)
    if (result = execution (new action)) then elabo-
      ration-decision (new-action)
    else the most detailed descriptions or hypotheses
      are generated
  end
```

During the *elaboration phase*, a sequence of operators corresponding to the action chosen in the previous decision cycle is applied in a specific context. The execution of such a subplan (action) may result in the generation of structured descriptions of acoustic properties called *objects* or in the updating of existing objects.

Objects are part of a network of data descriptions called the Data Description Network (DDN).

The just described paradigm has been applied to a limited but very difficult problem, i.e., the multispeaker recognition of connectedly spoken letters and digits belonging to the E1 set. The E1 set is defined as follows:

$$\text{E1} = \{B, C, D, E, G, K, P, T, V, 3\} \tag{1}$$

The choice of this protocol has many motivations. First, it is a very difficult one because all the letters in E1 end with the same vowel and the acoustic properties of the letters have to be detected in a short time interval at the onset of the vowel. Other authors (see for example [15]) report on the difficulties of this recognition task.

The letter Z is not included in the E1 set because its correct pronounciation does not end with |i:|. Rather the

TABLE I
ALPHABET FOR PRIMARY ACOUSTIC CUES (PAC)

Symbol	Attributes	Description
LPK	tb,te,m1,zx,rmin	long peak of total energy (TE)
SPK	"	short peak of TE
MPK	"	peak of TE of medium duration
LOWP	"	low energy peak of TE
LNS	tb,te,zx,rmin	long nonsonorant tract
MNS	"	medium duration nonsonorant tract
LVI	tb,te,m1,zx,rmin	long vocalic tract adjacent to a LNS or a MNS in a TE peak
MVI	tb,te,m1,zx,rmin	medium vocalic tract adjacent to a LNS or a MNS in a TE peak
LDD	emin,tb,te,zx	long deep dip of total energy
SDD	"	short deep dip of total energy
LMD	"	long dip of total energy with medium depth
SMD	"	short dip of total energy with medium depth
LHD	"	long non-deep dip of total energy
SHD	"	short non-deep dip of total energy

Attribute description

Attribute	Description
tb	time of beginning
te	time of end
m1	maximum signal energy in the peak
emin	minimum total energy in a dip
zx	maximum zero-crossing density of the signal
rmin	minimum value of the ratio between high and low frequency energies

letter *K* has been included because the diphthong | æi | can be confused with | i: |.

The E1 set is a good example for studying different speaking modes. Speakers of different mother tongues pronounce some letters of the E1 set differently. Some, for example, tend to pronounce plosive sounds with aspiration and some others not. Studying connected letters in a multispeaker environment is useful for performing a voice-activated access to a file system and, in general, for introducing spelling facilities into an ASR system. In order to take into account different speaking modes, phoneme symbols are generated with indexes. An index specifies the *mode* in which a phoneme has been perceived by the system. For example | b_3 | may indicate the phoneme | b | hypothesized with scarce buzz-bar evidence. A spontaneous activity describes suprasegmental speech properties called Primary Acoustic Cues (PAC) using an alphabet and algorithms introduced in [7]. Description phrases are the contexts in which preconditions of first actions of the hierarchies are evaluated. Further execution of actions selected by the decision phases produce objects thus enriching the already existing contexts.

Table I shows the alphabet for PAC's. Table II shows the most frequent preconditions based on PAC's as an example of a Rule-set. This Rule-set is used in the decision phase after the execution of the spontaneous activity. If phrases of PAC symbols correspond to more than one element of the vocabulary to be recognized, then there is an active confusion set and further actions have to be executed. Rules in Table II are applied according to the order indicated in the table. The first rule that can be applied determines the next action. Some rules have been compacted and new symbols have been introduced in order to keep Table II small. The experimental condition with which these rules were inferred are described in Section VI.

TABLE II
EXAMPLE OF DESCRIPTION PHRASES FOR THE E1 SET

No.	Precondition					Confusion set
1	(MNS+LNS)	SI	MD	LPK		3
2	DD	SI1	(MNS+SNS)	SI	MD LPK	3
3	DD	SI	(MNS+SNS)	SI1	MD LPK	3
4	DD	LOWP	(SMD+ϵ)	LPK		v
5	SHD	MPK	LPK			v
6	DD	MPK	MD	LPK		p
7	LDD	SPK	LHD	LPK		k
8	DD	(MNS+ϵ)	SSI	(SMD+ϵ)	LPK	k
9	SMD	(LVI+LPK)				b, g, v
10	MNS	MVI	LPK			g, t, z
11	MNS	LVI				g, v, z, c
12	LNS					3, c, t
13	(SDD+SMD)	SNS				d, k, t, v
14	SDD	MNS				d, g, k, t, v, 3
15	SDD	LNS				c, g, t, z
16	LDD	SNS				d, e, g, k, t, v, 3
		. . .				
41	SDD	LPK				b, d, v
		. . .				
45	LDD	LPK+LVI				b, d, e, k, p, v, 3
		. . .				
74	LDD	MNS	MVI			g, k, t
		.				
76	LDD	MNS				c, d, g, k, t, v, 3

ABBREVIATIONS

SI1 = MVI+SSI
SI = MVI+SSI+ϵ
MD = SMD+SHD+LMD+LHD
DD = LDD+SDD
ϵ = the empty symbol

Fig. 1 shows the general scheme of an action hierarchy and the planning system that generates its compiled version. Each expansion of an action represents a plan refinement. Each refinement is a subplan consisting of a sequence of operators. A detailed example will be described in Section IV.

B. Possible ASR Architectures

This subsection contains a brief discussion on how the Network of Action paradigm can be used in conjunction with some of the ASR architectures which are popular today. A scheme for a possible architecture is shown in Fig. 2(a). The purpose of the scheme is that of combining classical vector-quantization methods and knowledge-based methods for obtaining descriptions of acoustic properties to be used by a recognition program.

Classical vector-quantization could be performed by a unit indicated in Fig. 2(a) as "distance-based centisecond labeling." Another unit called "knowledge-based centisecond labeling" attempts to label each speech spectrum using knowledge of spectral morphologies. A third unit called "Asynchronous Description of Speech Segments" (ADSS) is the one that will be described and used for the experiments reported in this paper. Knowledge-based descriptions of speech segments can be used concurrently with frame-based vector quantizers as input to a stochastic decoder. The symbols produced can be unambiguous descriptions of acoustic properties or weighted phoneme or phonetic hypotheses.

Another possible architecture incorporating networks of plans can be based on a cascade of Augmented Transition

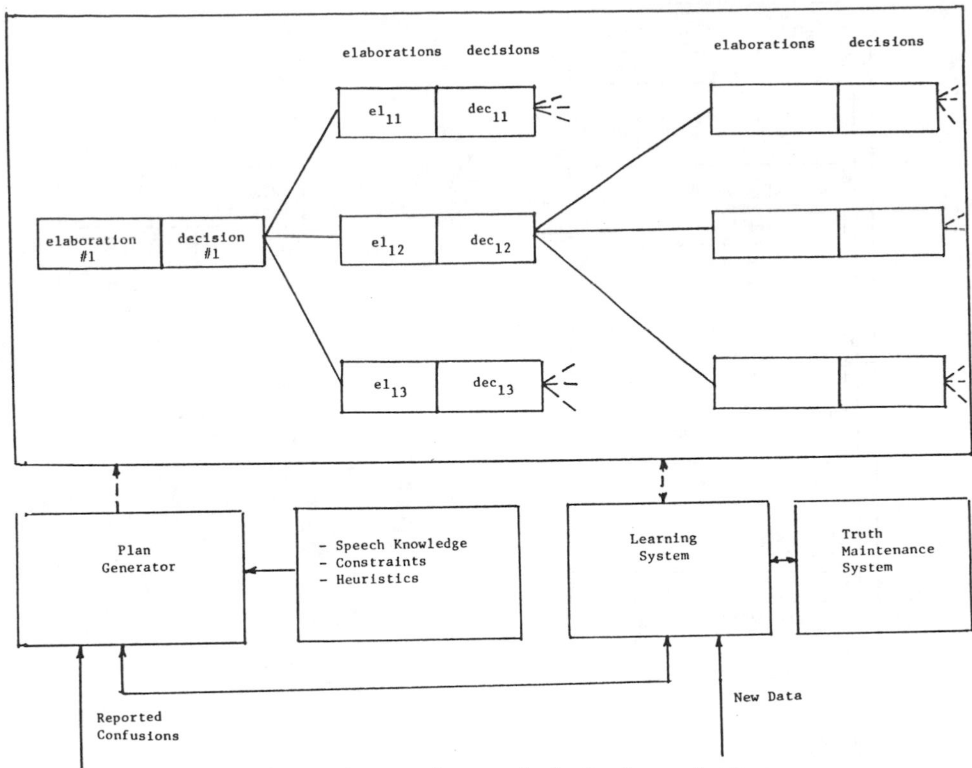

Fig. 1. Scheme for generating network of actions in compiled form.

Networks (ATN) or just Transition Networks (TN) according to the scheme shown in Fig. 2(b). Here a linguistic unit W_k such as, for example, a word is represented by a TN.

A transition of TN may imply a PUSH to a subnetwork. At the lowest level of the cascade of networks there is a procedural network S_{ki} whose procedures associated to transitions can be networks of actions NA_{kij}. An implementation of this architectural model is actually in development and will be described in a future paper.

Lexical ATN's, procedural networks, and signal processing programs invoked by procedural networks can be implemented in different specialized processors as suggested in [7].

III. Development of Perceptual Plans

This section describes methodologies and tools that have been developed in order to build in a semiautomatic manner the Network.

The design of a Network for ASR is a planing activity where refinements are decided based on recognition confusions that are considered unacceptable. Refinement is seen as the expansion of an action into a more detailed plan. In such a case the action that is expanded will be seen as an abstract one.

Interesting planning systems are proposed in recent literature. A report by Stefik [10] critically compares existing systems and discusses the differences between HEARSAY II [11], one of the most popular knowledge-based speech understanding systems developed so far, and hierarchical systems as the one proposed in this paper.

A paper by Wilkins [13] discusses the major problems in automatic planning and points out the advantages of an evolutionary approach to planning especially in large real-world problems. Such an evolutionary approach allows interaction with users throughout the planning and plan execution processes. Our approach belongs to this category as, indeed, it has to deal with a real-world problem. Reasoning about actions, a core problem in planning, is rather peculiar in our case. In fact, actions produce *descriptions of speech signals* that are expected to *discriminate* among segments corresponding to different sounds. The discrimination power of a description cannot be predicted; it has to be evaluated by experiments.

The evolution of a plan goes through the following cycle:

plan evolution cycle
begin
  definition of spontaneous activities for extracting descriptions for precondition #1
  repeat
    perform experiments;
    learning and generalization;
    elimination of actions producing descriptions ruled out by generalization;
    refinement for discriminating cases that remain confused after learning;
  until discrimination is satisfactory for a large population of speakers.
end

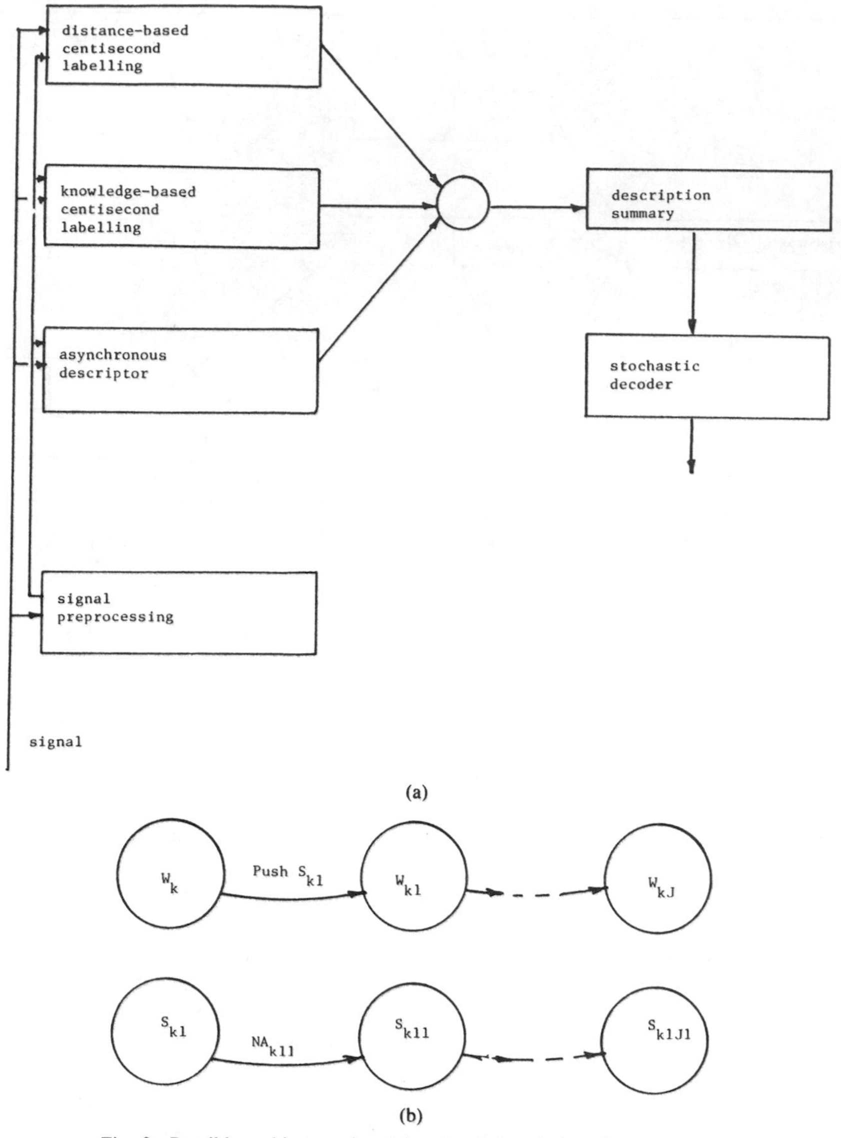

Fig. 2. Possible architecture involving signal description plans. (a) Data-driven Architecture. (b) Model-driven Architecture.

The new actions are actually decided and implemented by a human expert who uses the planning and the learning programs. He bases his decision on his knowledge, the type of patterns that require better discriminant descriptions and the statistics of the ambiguous descriptions of these patterns as obtained by the available system.

A Plan Generation Expert System (PGES), written in OPS5 [12] contributes to producing the Network of Actions. It uses speech knowledge for suggesting acoustic properties that can solve a problem in a given context (for example {b, d} distinction in the absence of burst evidence). PGES uses also Speech Knowledge and proposes signal processing algorithms (operators) for extracting suggested acoustic properties. Constraints are associated by PGES to operators. A final phase of *constraint satisfaction* is performed by PGES which produces a plan as an acceptable sequence of operators useful for refining a plan which produced descriptions with unsatisfactory discrimination power.

With such an approach, different researchers from different laboratories can provide suggestions for acoustic properties and operators together with constraints and, perhaps, performances. PGES can generate consistent plans from knowledge contributed by different sources and eventually rank plan candidates according to performance and computational complexities. Computationally complex plans should not be introduced unless experimental evidence requires their use.

Table II is made of rules that can be interpreted as having the form:

$$\text{antecedent} \rightarrow \text{consequent} \tag{2}$$

where "antecedent" is a sequence of PAC's and "consequent" can be, at the beginning, either an action for generating a single hypothesis or the indication of a confusion set requiring further plan refinement.

An example of rule in Table II is:

$$(\text{MNS})\,(\text{MVI})\,(\text{SHD})\,(\text{LPK}) \rightarrow \text{generate ``3''}.$$

This rule means that if a tract of medium duration having the characteristic of frication noise (MNS) is followed by a sonorant tract of medium duration (MVI) which is followed by a "short high dip" followed by a vocalic peak of the signal energy (LPK), then the label is "3". For example, an object that is part of DDN and matches the precondition of the previous rule could be:

$$((\text{MNS}\ (t_{b1}, t_{e1}, \cdots)$$
$$\text{MVI}\ (t_{b2}, t_{e2}, \cdots)$$
$$\text{SHD}\ (t_{b3}, t_{e3}, \cdots)$$
$$\text{LPK}\ (t_{b4}, t_{e4}, \cdots)).$$

Each PAC descriptor is followed by a list of attributes, starting with the beginning time t_{bj} and the end time t_{ej}. PAC descriptions do not overlap.

The "antecedents" of Table II are matched against the DDN. As a perfect match is found, the hypothesis "3" is generated and no further action is taken.

As rules in Table II do not have a rich enough discrimination power because they are only based on PAC's, plan refinement is used for producing new actions capable of extracting other properties with better discrimination power when required. New actions can also be provided for splitting segments containing more than one letter.

After the first set of experiments, confusions for each rule are detected and represented by *confusion sets*. Confusion statistics are also collected. A "*reasoning about actions*" *phase* takes place at this point trying to find out for each confusion set, a set and an application sequence of *physical operators* that can be applied, when preconditions represented by the antecedent expression are verified, in order to resolve the confusion described by the confusion sets.

An example of a confusion set is the following:

(LDD) (LPK) → (plosives, vowels or sonorant sounds after a pause) (3)

An example of *metaknowledge* used for proposing actions is the following:

(LDD) (LPK) *and* (confusion set [e, b]) → operators for buzz-bar detection (4)

Each physical operator can be applied under some *constraints*. An example of constraint is the following:

burst-analysis **and** burst-detection → must precede (burst-detection, burst-analysis) (5)

In practice, PGES architecture exploits some important features of rule-based programming. An opportunistic planning strategy is implemented by using *goals* and *contexts* (see [12] for more details). Goals force the reasoning to achieve different sequences of tasks, while contexts impose the system to use only those rules that are consistent with a set of acoustic properties which were found insufficient for an efficient discrimination among the hypotheses of a confusion set.

```
Task 1: input confusion set
Task 2: selection of useful acoustic properties

        (p BURST-REQ
            (GOAL ↑VALUE TASK2)
            (PROP ↑NAME BURST ↑STATUS UNDET)
            (LETTER ↑VALUE <<K B T D P>>)
            (LETTER ↑VALUE <<E V>>)

        →

            (MODIFY PROP ↑STATUS YES))

Task 3: input contexts

Task 4: selection of useful algorithms

        (P BURST-ALG-REQ
            (GOAL ↑VALUE TASK4)
            (CONTEXT ↑VALUE <<LDD-LPK SDD-LPK LDD-LVI ...>>)
            (PROP ↑NAME BURST ↑STATUS YES)

        →

            (make ENVELOPE-ALG ↑STATUS REQUEST ↑RESULT UNDET)

            (make BROAD-BAND-2-4K-ALG ↑STATUS REQUEST ↑RESULT UNDET))

Task 5: Review of plan inconsistencies and final phase of plan generation
```

Fig. 3. Chain of task in the planning system.

A chain of tasks together with an example of an OPS5 rule for the most relevant tasks is shown in Fig. 3. OPS5 is based on frame representations where ↑x indicates a slot whose name is x and what follows is the slot value. If the value of the goal of PGES is TASK2, then the rule for requesting a burst analysis is considered. If the rule has not been applied before, then the status of the property BURST is undetermined (UNDET). If there is at least one letter in the confusion set belonging to the set {K, B, T, D, P} and at least one letter belonging to the set {E, V} then burst detection can be a useful discriminant property and the status of the property BURST becomes YES. The context for the algorithms which execute BURST detection is a PAC description that is introduced by TASK 3.

Task 4 produces the request of execution of algorithms and considers them executed once the contexts they are supposed to produce has been provided to the system. For example, when the request of execution of the burst algorithm is presented to the user of PGES, the operator BURST-ALG is inserted into the plan and PGES will ask the user to provide the results of BURST-ALG that will constitute the context for further task execution. These results will fill the slot ↑RESULT of the frame BURST-ALG. A complete definition of OPS5 with all the details of the language can be found in [12]. There are actually about 60 rules in this system.

IV. Some Details of the Recognition Process

The speech signal is first analyzed on the basis of loudness, zero-crossing rates and broad-band energies as described in [7]. The result of this analysis is a string of

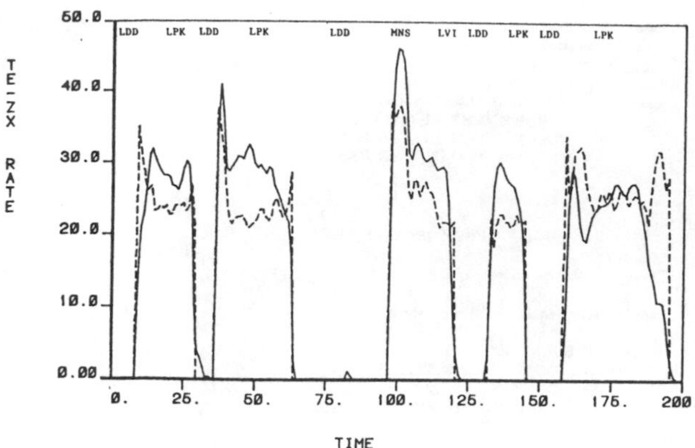

Fig. 4. Example of primary acoustic cues. Time is in centiseconds. Total Energy (TE) is in dB. Zero crossing rate (ZX) is represented by the number of crossings of a band across the zero value divided by four in a 10 ms interval.

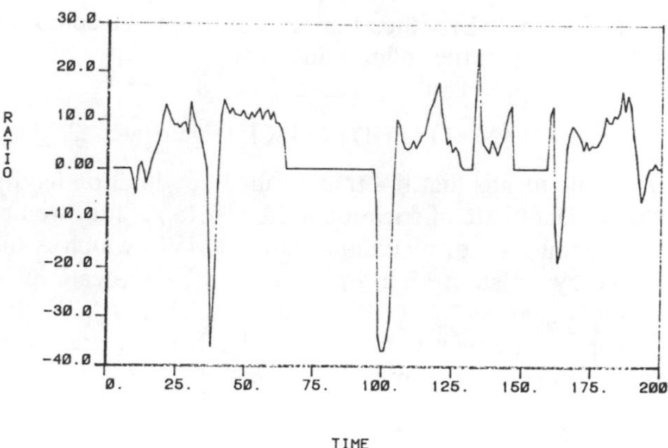

Fig. 5. Low to high frequency energy ratio.

symbols and attributes. Symbols belong to an alphabet of Primary Acoustic Cues (PAC) whose definition is recalled in Table I.

The use of coarse acoustic properties (PAC) for segmenting continuous speech into acoustic segments has been described in a previous paper [7]. The segmentation algorithm based on an attributed grammar has been simplified, in such a way that a preliminary segmentation is performed first based only on signal energy deep dips and frication intervals. Each *acoustic segment* obtained in this way may contain one or more syllables but it never contains less than one vowel. Each acoustic segment could be further described following the scheme shown in Fig. 1.

Fig. 4 shows the loudness curve (thick line) and the zero crossing rate of the first derivative of the signal (dashed line) for the sequence of elements of the E1 set EDTBP. The speaker is an anglophone female student. This example will be the running example of this Section. Fig. 5 shows the ratio between low (0.2–0.6 kHz) and high (5–7 kHz) frequency energy for this particular utterance. Deep dips in the ratio are burst indicators for D, T, and P. This parameter is used for describing frication noise (LNS, MNS) together with peaks of the zero crossing rate.

The three curves in Figs. 4 and 5 are processed by a linguistic descriptor that produces the following PAC description:

LDD	LPK		(12, 30)
LDD	LPK		(40, 65)
LDD	MNS	LVI	(104, 122)
LDD	LPK		(132, 146)
LDD	LPK		(165, 196)

Time references are in centiseconds and are reported only for the vocalic tracts.

An action hierarchy is then applied for interpreting the consonantal segment of every syllable.

Fig. 6 shows the more abstract part of the action hierarchy. PAC extraction and segmentation is a preliminary spontaneous activity that is followed by a decision phase where a rule-set is applied. Rules are made of preconditions and actions. Preconditions are sequences of PAC's. Actions describe what acoustic properties are worth to be extracted given the suprasegmental morphology described by the PAC expression.

For the sake of simplicity only the action corresponding to rule (1.45.1) is shown in Fig. 6. The precondition for this rule is (LDD) (LPK + LVI). The symbol + represents here logical disjunction. This PAC morphology may correspond to a vowel after a pause, to the consonants | v | or | g | or to plosive consonants for which burst is not evident in the loudness curve. This precondition represents a speaking mode that is rather frequent for | b | and is one of the most difficult to analyze. The action to be executed in this case is the analysis of the (deep dip) | (peak) transition. Useful operators are those that detect voicing, the existence of burst and some temporal relations among the onset of the energies in various bands because delays in these onset times are cues for the presence of plosive sounds.

The approach is that of extracting a *redundant set* of cues so that the final decision about the acoustic properties that describes them is reliable.

According to Fig. 6, the activity "dip peak analysis" is refined by a more detailed subplan which is produced by the planning system introduced in the previous section. As broad-band energies have to be analyzed at the end of the buzz-bar and when the signal envelope starts rising, the chaining order shown in Fig. 6 is obtained.

If there is enough evidence for burst and if there is still a need of discriminating among classes, then a rule of rule-set (1.45) will invoke the execution of a burst analysis action.

OP11 in Fig. 6 produces an envelope description by analyzing the signal amplitude before and after preemphasis. Envelope samples are obtained every millisecond (ms) by taking the absolute value of the difference between the absolute maximum and the absolute minimum

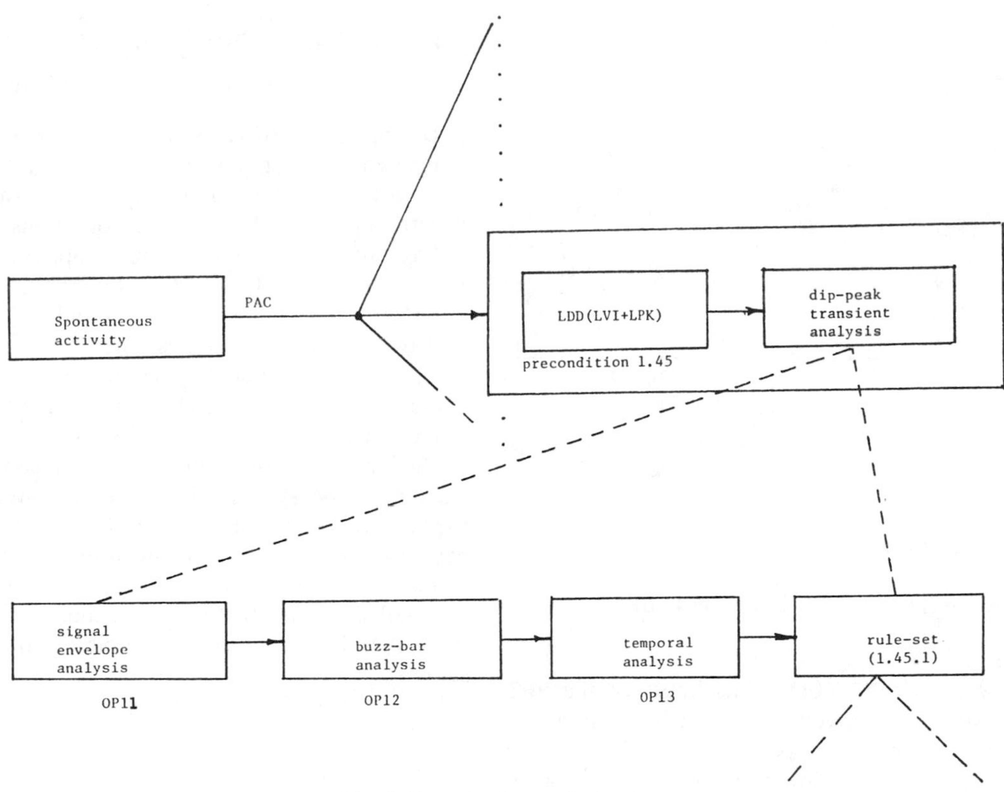

Fig. 6. Example of network of actions.

of the signal in a 3 ms interval. The envelope description is based on the following alphabets:

A111 = {SHORT—STEP(ST1),
LONG—STEP(ST2),
NO—STEP(ST0)}

A112 = {HIGH LOW FREQUENCY ENERGY(BZ1),
ABSENCE OF BUZZ INDICATOR IN THE ENVELOPE (BZ0)}

A113 = {POSSIBLE BURST (PB1),
ABSENCE OF BURST EVIDENCE (PBO}

A114 = {STRONG BURST EVIDENCE (BU1),
NO STRONG BURST EVIDENCE (BU0)}. (5)

The description produced by Op11 as well as those produced by OP12 and OP13 are attached to the DDN describing the segment under analysis.

Fig. 7 shows the envelope curve in the energy dip preceding the onset of |b|. The time reference 0 in Fig. 7 corresponds to frame 27 in Fig. 3. the unit of time axis is number of samples divided by 10. There are 20 000 samples per second. Because of the shape of the envelope, the 10 ms segment between 500 and 700 is described as (ST0, BZ1, PB1, BU0). The peak in the signal envelope is described by PB1 (possible burst). As there is no evidence of burst in the waveform in the peak envelope (long zero-crossing intervals) BU0 expresses no burst evidence. The bar in the envelope before the peak is described by BZ1. As there is no step in the envelope before the peak, a descriptor STO is produced. Descriptors are represented in Fig. 7.

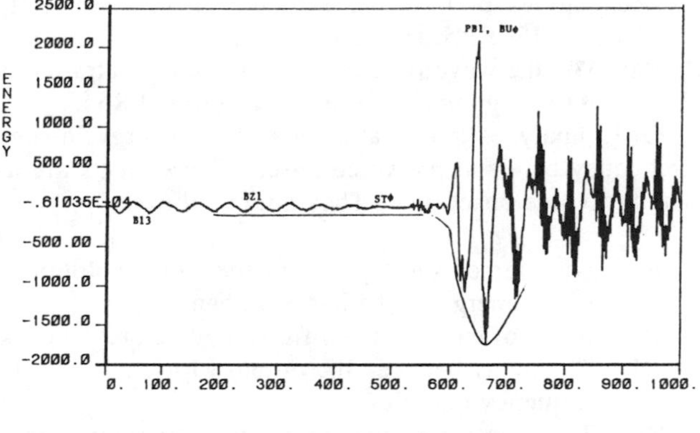

Fig. 7. Details of an envelope curve. Time unit is 0.5 ms. Signal amplitude unit is 2.5 mV.

OP12 describes the buzz-bar by analyzing the shape of the time waveform and of the spectra before the voice onset. The alphabets of the descriptions it produces are:

$$BZA1 = \{BI1, BI2, BI3, BI4, BI5\} \quad (6)$$

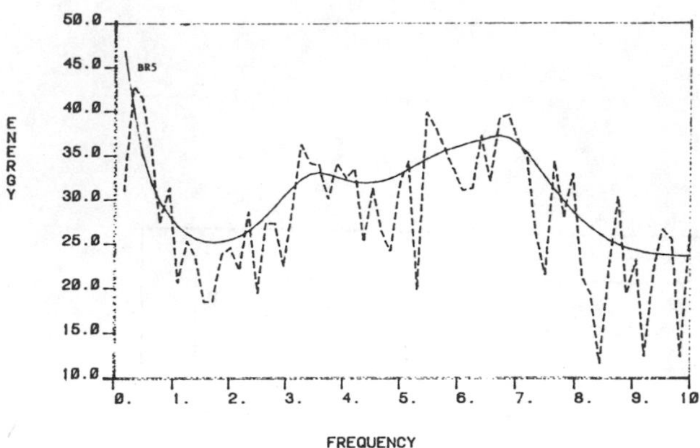

Fig. 8. Buzz spectrum, LPC (continuous line), FFT (dotted line). Frequency unit is 1 kHz. Energy is in dB.

for the time waveform and

$$BZA2 = \{BR1, BR2, BR3, BR4, BR5\} \quad (7)$$

for the spectra.

Fig. 8 shows the LPC (continuous line) and the FFT (dashed line) spectra computed before the TE peak onset. The consistent low frequency peak in the FFT spectrum is the cue for buzz-bar. The low frequency oscillations in Fig. 7 are other buzz cues.

BI1 and BR1 mean no buzz and the other symbols describe degrees of buzz-bar evidence: (BI2, BR2: little evidence; BI5, BR5: strong evidence).

Based on the waveform of Fig. 7 and the spectra shown in Fig. 8 the segment is described as (BI3, BR5).

Op13 analyzes temporal events of the energy in some frequency bands at the voice onset. These events are related to voice onset time. They are as follows.

- NP Number of short peaks in the time evolution of the energy in the 2–4 kHz band.
- RE A bar of energy at low frequency before the peak.
- DL The delay between the onset of low and high frequency energies.
- ZQ The duration of the largest zero-crossing interval of the signal at the onset.
- DR Minimum value in a dip of ratio between low and high frequency energies. (8)

The first two cues in (8) represent morphologies described by the alphabets: {NP0, · · ·, NP5}, {RE0, RE1}. Intervals of parameters in (8) are coded with symbols {DL1, · · ·, DL5}. {ZQ1, · · ·, ZQ5}, {DR1, · · ·, DR5}. From a dip-peak transition, a vector of values of (NP, RE, DL, ZQ, DR) is extracted and represented by a conjunction of symbols according to the intervals the parameters fall into. Intervals are determined after clustering vectors corresponding to the same letter and intersecting clusters of different letters.

The description obtained by OP11, OP12, and OP13 for the |b| in the interval (0.27–0.35 s) is the following:

Descr. 1.45: {PB1 ST0 BZ1 BU0 RE0 NP1 DR4 DL2 ZQ4 BI3 BR5}

During the *decision phase* competing preconditions are compared with data descriptions. A simple *fuzzy algebra* is used for ordering competing action candidates if data descriptions partially match preconditions. In such a case voting criteria combine different supports from different sources into a Similarity Measurement (SM) ($0 \geq SM \geq 1$). More details on SM can be found in [7].

If two or more candidates emerge with high and close similarity values, then they define an *active confusion set*. If the ASR is already considering an active confusion set in the same time interval, then the intersection of the two confusion sets becomes the new active confusion set considered by the system. The highest scored precondition expression is used for deciding the new action that is expected to produce a better discrimination between all the elements of the new active confusion set. The cycle is repeated until satisfactory discrimination is obtained or the system has exhausted its possibility of executing new actions.

For our example the following similarity measures were found:

Letter	SM	Rule component
d	1.000	(2)
b	1.000	(3)
p	0.888	(7)
p	0.824	(8)
p	0.812	(1)
p	0.771	(14)
k	0.757	(12)
e	0.729	(6)
b	0.669	(4)
3	0.656	(10)
d	0.556	(13)

In our example the active confusion set contains two letters [b, d] and the refinement is based on a more detailed analysis of the burst and transition of spectral lines. The refinement action is decided by another packet or rules whose preconditions are conjunctions of symbols belonging to the following alphabets: {A112, A113, A114, NP}. In our example, the refinement action is chosen by the precondition:

Pr 1.45: {PB1 BZ1 BU0 NP1}

The execution of a refinement action is followed by the computation of other similarity values. This cycle is repeated until the active confusion set contains a single hypothesis. If all the possible refinements have been performed and the active confusion set still contains more than one hypothesis then the stochastic component described in Section VII is applied. The refinement action contains the calculation of burst spectra and the description of spectral profiles as well as other properties like, center of gravity, frequency above which there is 70 per-

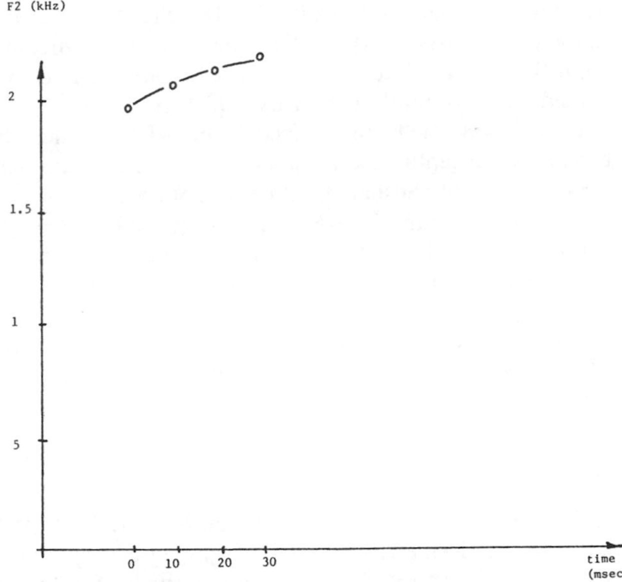

Fig. 9. Example of a formant property.

cent of the spectral energy and other parameters whose details are omitted for the sake of brevity.

In the particular example under analysis, the system has tracked the time evolution of the major energy concentration in the frequency band of the second formant obtaining the curve of Fig. 9. Based on a rule on the curve slope it has decided that the letter was | b |.

V. Learning of Preconditions

Preconditions for operator application for expanding an abstract action with a more detailed plan are logical expressions of predicates. Predicates are defined over relations between acoustic properties. The preconditions of rule-sets can be collected from experiments, but, in order to speed up the learning procedure, they have to be generalized.

The approach to learning taken in this paper is *incremental*. Although statistics of cue expressions for acoustic properties are taken into account, learning is conceived in such a way that if there are enough instances of property expressions for a given speaker, a generalization of these instances is performed even if its *a priori* probability is low compared to descriptions produced by other speakers.

Acoustic cues of a speech segment are represented by *predicates*. Instances of a class are described by conjunctions of predicates.

Conjunctions of predicates describing the same class are *generalized* into new expressions and their statistics are collected.

As long as generalizations do not introduce confusions they are accepted (believed). When new instances from new speakers show that some generalizations introduce unacceptable confusions, these generalizatons are not accepted any more (disbelieved). For this purpose, each generalization has a list of support based on positive and negative examples. As far as the number of negative examples is small (e.g., less than ten cases) the generalization can be accepted if the number of positive examples supporting it is remarkably higher than the number of negative ones. When the number of negative examples of a generalization becomes substantial (e.g., greater or equal to ten), the generalization is disbelieved. During recognition, only the most general rules describing disjoint sets for each class are kept in a rule-set.

Incremental learning has to produce a set of rules that is the most consistent with the examples in certain time.

In order to allow dynamic preservation of consistency among the set of rules, an algorithm is proposed which uses the *Truth Maintenance System* (TMS) formalism and which is reminiscent of previous work by Whitehill [16].

A generalization algorithm derives from two conjunctions C1 and C2 a conjunction of predicates C3 that is more general than both C1 and C2, i.e., C3 $\Rightarrow$ C1 and C3 $\Rightarrow$ C2, where $\Rightarrow$ means in this case "more general than."

The generalized rules themselves are the nodes of a TMS.

An example of a rule is a conjunction of predicates, like:

$$X3 \quad Y4 \quad W1 \quad Z5 : Bn_i \tag{9}$$

The left-hand side (LHS) of the expression is an instance of the class B and it has been observed n_i times for class B.

Each predicate represents the presence of an acoustic cue and belongs to a description alphabet. Thus:

$$X3 \in \Sigma X, \; Y4 \in \Sigma Y, \text{ etc.}$$

Before proceeding to generalization, expectations about each class are established based on acoustic-phonetic knowledge. These expectations are expressed, for each class as *subsets* of the alphabets ΣX, ΣY, $\cdots$.

For example the expectation EB for class B is expressed as follows:

$$EB = \{EBX, EBY, EBW, EBZ\} \tag{10}$$

where $EBX \subseteq \Sigma X$, $EBY \subseteq \Sigma Y$, etc.

Expectations of different classes may overlap but the selector of acceptable expressions in the learning system will always have expressions for different classes that do not overlap.

Let us assume we have the following observations for class B:

$$IB1 = X3 \quad Y4 \quad W1 \quad Z5 : Bn_i$$
$$IB2 = X2 \quad Y4 \quad W3 \quad Z5 : Bn_j \tag{11}$$

and that the expectation EB is:

$$EBX = \Sigma X$$
$$EBY = (Y2, Y3, Y4)$$
$$EBW = (W1 \quad W2 \quad W3)$$
$$EBZ = \Sigma Z \tag{12}$$

This means that the expectations for class B concerning the properties described by the alphabet ΣX can be any symbol of the alphabet ΣX = (X1, X2, · · ·), the properties described by the alphabet ΣY = (Y1, Y2, · · ·) are expected to belong to the subset (Y2, Y3, Y4) and so on according to the (12).

Two levels of generalizations will be generated by the system:

$$\text{level 1: } GB1 = (X2 + X3)\,Y4(W1 + W3)\,Z5 : B(n_i + n_j)$$

$$\text{level 2: } GB2 = Y4(W1 + W2 + W3)\,Z5 : B(n_i + n_j) \tag{13}$$

The two generalizations are related as follows:

$$GB2 \Rightarrow GB1$$

In GB2 the "dropping condition" has been applied to the predicates of ΣX. The choice of GB1 or GB2 will be made by the selector depending on the expressions considered for other classes.

For those descriptions that do not match expectations only level-1 generalization is performed because it is expected that anomalies are the major causes of confusions.

Let us assume, as an example, that

$$\Sigma X = A111$$
$$\Sigma Y = A112$$
$$\Sigma W = BZA1$$
$$\Sigma Z = BZA2$$

as defined by (5), (6), (7), and that Xi = STi, Yi = BZi, Wi = BIi, Zi = BRi.

Let us also assume that the class B is the phoneme |b| and that the following expectations hold:

$$EBX = \Sigma X = A111$$
$$EBY = Y1 = BZ1$$
$$EBW = (W3, W4, W5) = (BI3, BI4, BI5)$$
$$EBZ = (Z3, Z4, Z5) = (BR3, BR4, BR5)$$

Let us assume that the following observations have been made:

IB1 = ST0 BZ1 BI3 BR5 (5 times)

IB2 = ST1 BZ1 BI5 BR3 (7 times)

The following generalizations are possible:

level-1: GB1 = (ST0 + ST1) BZ1(BI3 + BI5)(BR3 + BR5):B(12 times)

level-2: GB2 = (BI3 + BI4 + BI5)(BR3 + BR4 + BR5):B(12 times)

The level-2 generalizations implies that the "step" cue is not relevant for |b| and that there must be buzz indicators from BI3 and BR3 up. Level-2 generalization can be accepted and kept until counter-examples are found.

Descriptions with unexpected levels of buzz must be considered exceptions and should not be generalized with the descriptions consistent with expectations.

Some overlapping between level-1 generalizations for two classes is tolerated. It may lead to the evidence that plan refinement is needed for the descriptions common to two or more classes.

Possible generalizations are maintained by the TMS whose basic elements are nodes containing relations of the type:

CONJ : CONC

Each node represents a rule of left-hand-side (LHS) CONJ and right-hand-side (RHS) CONC, having a support list SL whose IN and OUT part are, respectively, the list of nodes with RHS CONC and LHS less general than CONJ and the list of nodes with RHS different from CONC and LHS less general than CONC. With each node are kept the numbers of consistent examples (PE for positive evidence) and unconsistent examples (NE for negative evidence).

Lastly, each node has a STATUS property which is IN when the corresponding rule is believed to be true and OUT otherwise. A node is IN, i.e., its STATUS is IN if and only if all the nodes in the IN part and all the nodes in the OUT part of its SL are respectively IN and OUT and the numbers of examples in PE and NE satisfy a given predicate P.

P is true if $NE < 10$ and $PE \geq 2NE$. When NE becomes greater or equal to 10, it is assumed that there is enough negative evidence for a generalization that it cannot be believed, so the status of the corresponding node is OUT. Nodes that are OUT because their $NE \geq 10$ will never become IN so they can be ignored and deleted. This keeps small both the time and space complexity of the learning system because generalizations on supports having $NE \geq 10$ are not even attempted.

When a new example is learned, node statistics are updated or a new node is created if necessary and this node is generalized with the existing ones to generate new nodes that are themselves generalized with other ones. Then the PE and NE of the concerned nodes are updated and STATUS properties are modified when necessary and propagated through the nodes in order to maintain consistency. The stability of this process is guaranteed together by the definitions of SL and the predicate P. An outline of the algorithm is described in Table III in a Pascal-like form.

For each class, a characteristic rule is derived from the network of nodes whose LHS is the disjunction of LHSs of all IN nodes with the class appearing at RHS. The selector attempts to eliminate redundancies so that the most general non overlapping expressions for each class are used for recognition.

TABLE III
LEARNING ALGORITHM IN PASCAL-LIKE FORM

```
procedure LearnExample (EXAMPLE)
  NEWNODE :- NIL
  For every node N in ListOfNodes do
    if RHS(N) - Concept(EXAMP       th
        if MoreGeneralThan(LHS(N),Conjunction(EXAMPLE)
        then Push(EXAMPLE,PE(N)) ;
        if Equivalent(LHS(N),Conjunction(EXAMPLE))
        then NEWNODE :- N
     end
     else
       if MoreGeneralThan(LHS(N),Conjunction(EXAMPLE))
       Then Push(EXAMPLE,NE(N)) ;
  unless NN # NIL do
    begin
      NN :- MakeNode(Conjunction(EXAMPLE),Concept(EXAMPLE))
      AddNode(NN)
    end
  if P(PE(NN),NE(NN)) and EveryIn(In(SL(NN))) and EveryOut(Out(SL(NN)))
  then TruthMaintain(NN,in) else TruthMaintain(NN,out)
endproc

procedure AddNode (NODE)
  for every node N in ListOfNodes do
    unless N - NODE do
      if RHS(N) - RHS(NODE)
      then
        case
          MoreGeneralThan(LHS(N),LHS(NODE))
            Push(NODE,In(SL(N)))
          MoreGeneralThan(LHS(NODE),LHS(N))
            begin
              Push(N,In(SL(NODE)))
              PE(NODE) :- Union(PE(NODE),PE(N))
            end
        else
          begin
            NC :- Generalize(LHS(NODE),LHS(N)),RHS(NODE)))
            AddNode(MakeNode(NC,RHS(NODE)))
          end
      else
        case
          MoreGeneralThan(LHS(N),LHS(NODE))
            Push(NODE,Out(SL(N)))
          MoreGeneralThan(LHS(NODE),LHS(N))
            begin
              Push(N,Out(SL(NODE)))
              NE(NODE) :- Union(NE(NODE),PE(N))
            end
  endproc
```

VI. EXPERIMENTAL RESULTS BASED ON NONSTOCHASTIC KNOWLEDGE APPLIED ON THE TRANSIENTS

The proposed approach has been tested in a multi-speaker environment. An initial learning phase was performed on a corpus of 1000 connected pronounciations of symbols of the E1 set in strings EGP3V and KCBTD of five symbols each. The strings were pronounced by five male speakers, and five female speakers. Each speaker pronounced them ten times.

Knowledge acquisition consisted in plan refinement as well as in precondition learning. PAC expressions shown in Table II have been learned based on these data.

After the first 10 speakers were analyzed and knowledge was determined and updated, an overall error rate of 3 percent was achieved in the learning set consisting of 1000 samples.

The rules of the planning system do not necessarily produce a single hypothesis. Failure to generate the expected hypothesis is considered an *error*, while the generation of the expected hypothesis together with other candidates is considered an *ambiguity*.

In the learning set, 9 percent of the cases resulted in ambiguities. The average number of ambiguous hypotheses generated in this 9 percent was 2.2.

The experiments continued by presenting to the system data collected from successive sets always containing new speakers. Each set was made of 10 speakers randomly chosen among a large student population with predominance of Francophones and Anglophones. Each speaker in each set was asked to pronounce two sequences of elements of the E1 set. Sequences were 5 letters long and each sequence was generated at random by a computer program with the only constraint that |e| could appear only at the beginning of the sequence. This fact as well as the number of letters of each sequence were not known to the recognition program. Most of the newly generated sequences were different.

Performances were computed *before* refinement so that the system knowledge was used for recognizing phrases of speakers that were not previously analyzed by the system. Nevertheless, after the analysis of each set of speakers, plan, and precondition refinements were performed.

The evolutions of the error rate and of the number of cases correctly classified without ambiguities are shown in Fig. 10(a) and (b). An *error* is considered here and in the following a misclassification of an *individual letter*. For each speaker set, the average values as well as the values corresponding to the speakers with the best and worst performances are reported. Fig. 10(c) shows the percentage of candidates that were correctly classified with a single hypothesis generation or in a set of two hypotheses. The effects of learning are evident especially after the first sets of speakers for which the random generation of samples created coarticulation instances or new situations that were not previously known to the system. Typical examples involved |v|, |3|, and |c| at the beginning of the sequence.

After the first 5 sets for which results were reported in Fig. 10 were analyzed, all the utterances corresponding to these 5 sets (500 utterances, 50 speakers) and the 10 sets used for initial learning (1000 utterances, 10 speakers) were processed again for recognition and statistics of rule application were collected in order to prepare a stochastic model that will be described in the next section.

VII. STOCHASTIC MODEL BASED ON RULES

Inductive learning of rules is supposed to characterize different speaking modes through chains of property descriptions for short time intervals whose duration typically varies between 10 and 50 ms. Some properties may have a large scope both backward and forward.

Variations of parameter values and minor distortions of the inferred rules can be characterized by stochastic networks. Fig. 11 shows, as an example, the network for |d|. Each rule whose precondition is made of PAC's corresponds to a transition from the initial state.

A priori probabilities of rule application have been in-

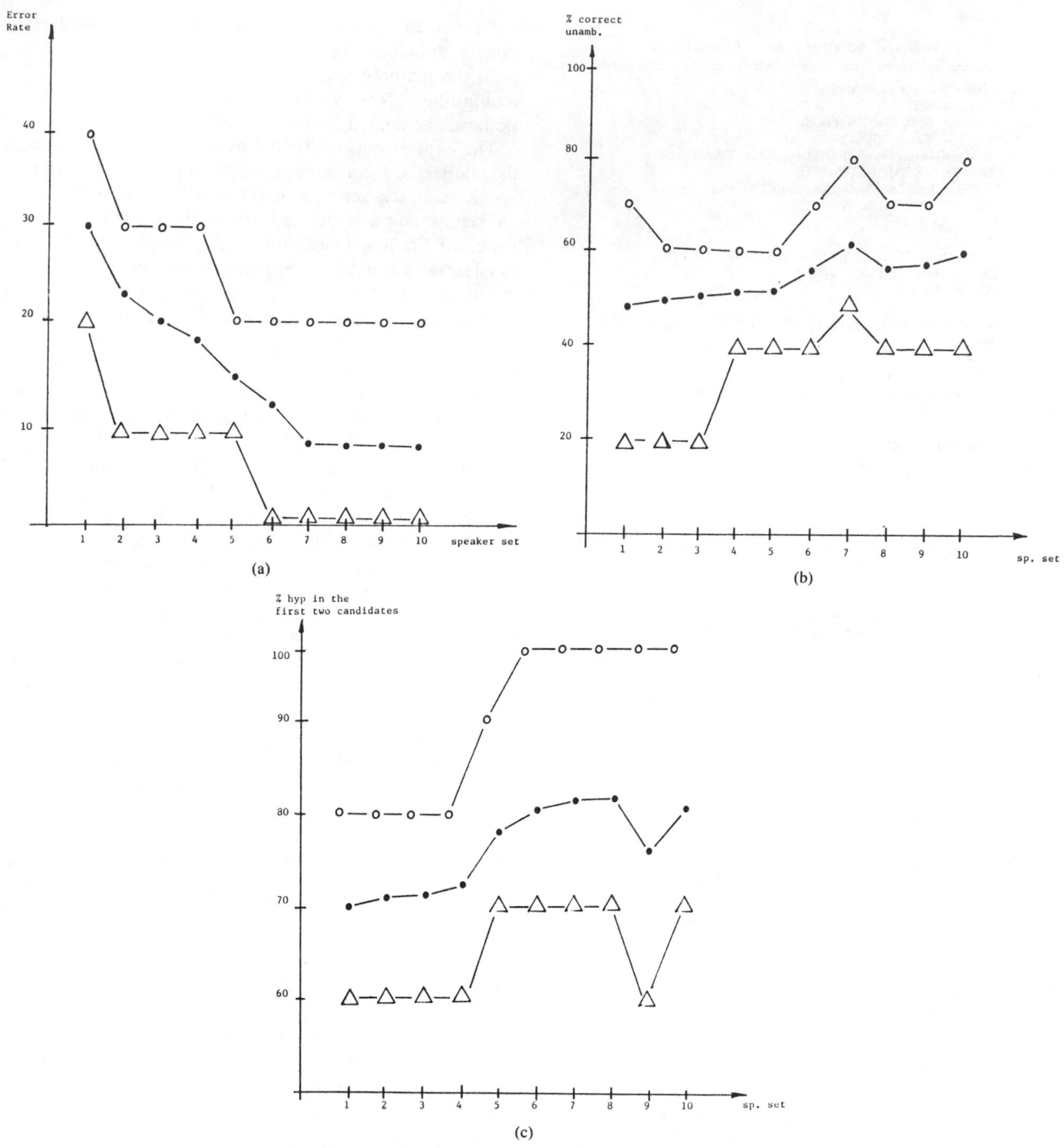

Fig. 10. System performances before knowledge refinement as function of successive refinements performed after the successive analysis of test sets pronounced by ten new speakers at each learning steps. Average values are represented by thick points. Maximum values are represented by circles and minimum values are represented by triangles. (a) Percent of cases correctly classified without ambiguities. (b) Percent of errors. (c) Percent of cases where the right hypothesis was generated unambiguously or in a set of two.

ferred using 1500 data as described in Section VI. Some of the inferred probabilities are reported in Fig. 11. Notice that PAC preconditions are mutually exclusive.

Fig. 11 shows the networks derived after rule 45 is applied according to the preconditions shown in Table IV. *A priori* probabilities are shown for each precondition.

Each morphology class described by qualitative symbols is associated with a different transition in the net-

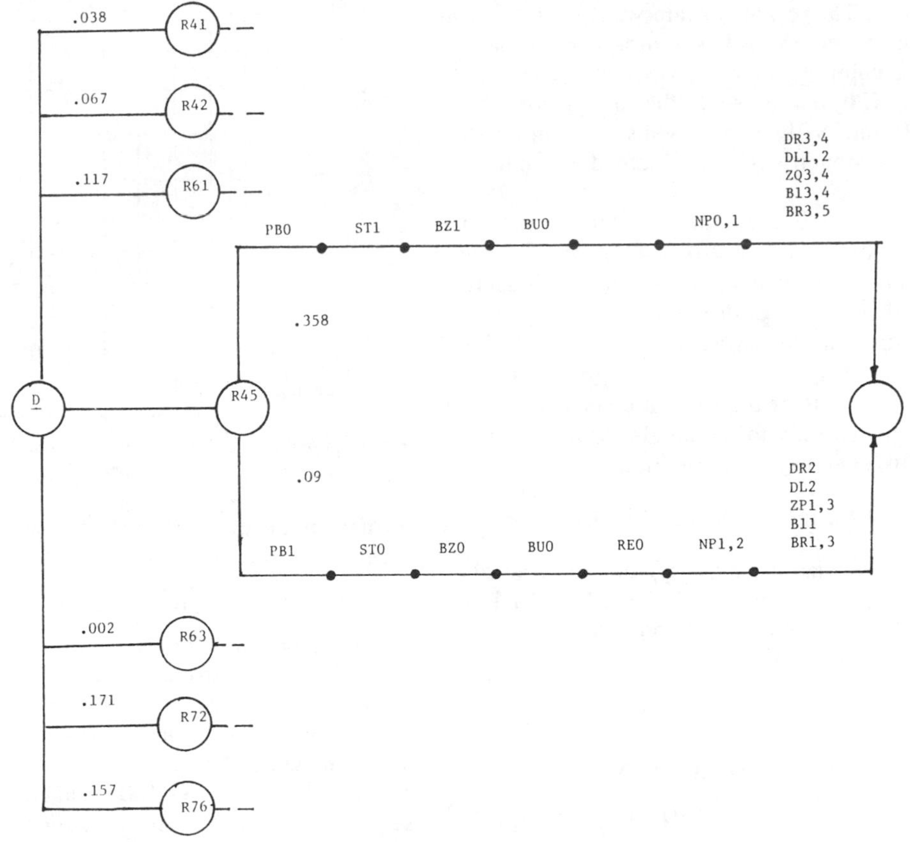

Fig. 11. Example of a stochastic network derived from a set of rules.

TABLE IV
RULES (45.1)

rule number	precondition		letter
1	BZ0 ST0 RE0 NP0 NP1	DR3 DR4 DL1 DL2 ZQ2 ZQ4 BI1 BI2 BR2 BR2	p
2	PB0 ST1 BZ1 BU0 NP0 NP1	DR3 DR4 DL1 DL2 ZQ3 ZQ4 BI3 BI4 BR3 BR5	d
3	BI0 STBI1 BZ1 BU0 NP0 NP1	DR3 DR4 DL1 DL2 ZQ3 ZQ4 BI3 BI4 BR3 BR5	b
4	PB0 ST1 BZ0 BU0 BU1 RE0 RE1 NP0 NP1	DR4 DR4 DL1 DL2 ZQ4 ZQ5 BI1 BI4 BR3 BR3	p
5	PB0 ST0 BU0 RE0 NP0 NP1	DR3 DR4 DL1 DL2 ZQ3 ZQ5 BI1 BI1 BR2 BR4	b
6	PB0 ST0 BU0 BZ0 NP0 NP1	DR3 DR4 DL1 DL2 ZQ2 ZQ4 BI1 BI2 BR2 BR3	e
7	PB1 ST0 BU1 BZ0 RE0 NP0 NP1	DR2 DR4 DL1 DL2 ZQ2 ZQ5 BI2 BI2 BR4 BR4	p
8	PB1 ST0 BZ0 BU0 RE0 NP1	DR2 DR3 DL2 DL2 ZQ5 ZQ5 BI4 BI4 BR4 BR5	p
9	PB0 ST0 BZ1 BU RE0 NP0	DR4 DR4 DL1 DL1 ZQ1 ZQ1 BI1 BI1 BR2 BR2	e
10	PB0 ST0 BZ1 BU0 RE0 NP1	DR2 DR2 DL4 DL4 ZQ4 ZQ4 BI2 BI2 BR3 BR3	3
11	PB0 ST1 BZ1 BU0 RE0 NP0	DR3 DR4 DL4 DL4 ZQ1 ZQ3 BI4 BI4 BR3 BR3	v
12	PB1 ST0 BZ0 BU0 RE0 NP1	DR2 DR3 DL2 DL2 ZQ1 ZQ3 BI1 BI1 BR1 BR2	k
13	PB1 ST0 BZ0 BU0 RE0 NP1 NP2	DR2 DR2 DL2 DL2 ZQ1 ZQ3 BI1 BI1 BR1 BR3	d
14	PB1 ST0 BZ1 BU0 RE0 NP1	DR3 DR3 DL1 DL1 ZQ4 ZQ4 BI1 BI1 BR2 BR2	p
15	PB0 ST0 BU0 RE0 NP0 NP1	DR3 DR4 DL1 DL2 ZQ2 ZQ4 BI1 BI1 BR2 BR2	v
16	PB0 ST0 RZ1 RE0 NP0	DR4 DR4 DL1 DL1 ZQ1 ZQ1 BI1 BI1 BR2 BR2	e

work. All the parameters are grouped and associated with a single transition. The parameter intervals are also shown in Fig. 11. For example, DR3, 4 represents the interval obtained by the union of intervals DR3 and DR4 for the parameter DR. NP0, 1 represents the disjunction of the properties NP0 and NP1, x represents a "don't care" condition on the property RE as obtained by inductive learning.

Having captured a model of the *structure* of speaking modes, it is possible now to perform a *stochastic generalization* by using the knowledge obtained with inductive learning for setting *initial conditions*.

Initial conditions can be set as follows. If a transition is associated with a single symbol, then a probability distribution on the symbols of the same alphabet is set with a high value assigned only to the single symbol. For example, ST1 will generate the distribution

$$\{(ST0, .01); (ST1, .98); (ST2, .01)\}$$

If a transition is associated with n symbols of a vocabulary of N symbols, then a probability equal to 0.01 is assigned to the $(N - n)$ symbols not appearing in the transition and a probability of $(1 - 0.01(N - n))/n$ is associated with the others.

For example, NP0, 1 will generate the distribution:

$$\{(NP0, .48)\ (NP1, .48); (NP2, .01); (NP3, .01); (NP4, .01); (NP5, .01)\}$$

If a transition is associated to a "don't care" symbol x, then all the symbols of the alphabet will appear with equal probability.

For example, x on RE will generate the distribution

$$\{(RE0, .5); (RE1, .5)\}$$

Parameter intervals can be seen as 3σ values of Gaussian distributions with mean just in the middle of the interval.

Forward-backward algorithms can be applied for refining the statistics of these stochastic automata.

Stochastic generalizations were performed only for those subnetworks for which there were enough data available. In the other cases, *a priori* probabilities of rule application were used for disambiguating multiple generation of letter hypotheses.

An additional feature described in [14] was used for recognizing the dipthong |æi| of |k|.

The confusions reported in Fig. 12 refer to a test set containing 500 data from 50 new speakers.

Errors are now due to two cases, namely fault in generating the right hypothesis or fault of selecting the right hypothesis when disambiguation is performed using stochastic networks.

A total of 23 errors due to segmentation were found on individual letters and 58 confusion errors were reported in a corpus of 500 letters pronounced by 50 speakers. Confusions are summarized in Fig. 12, making the overall performance of the system in a multispeaker evironment equal to 84 percent.

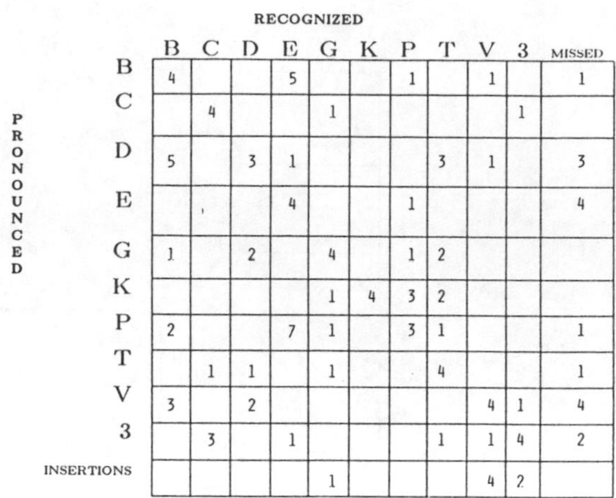

RECOGNIZED

PRONOUNCED	B	C	D	E	G	K	P	T	V	3	MISSED
B	4			5			1		1		1
C		4			1					1	
D	5		3	1				3	1		3
E				4			1				4
G	1		2		4		1	2			
K					1	4	3	2			
P	2			7	1		3	1			1
T		1	1		1			4			1
V	3		2						4	1	4
3		3		1				1	1	4	2
INSERTIONS					1				4	2	

Fig. 12. Confusions on a test set containing 500 data from 50 different speakers.

VIII. Conclusions

A paradigm for the recognition of connectedly spoken letters has been introduced and tested. Ten speakers, each pronouncing twenty sequences of five letters each, have been used for an initial setting of the knowledge base. Then knowledge refinement has been performed on data collected from another 100 speakers, each pronouncing 2 sequences of 5 letters each. Sequences were generated at random and were different for every speaker. Statistics of rule application were collected on the data of the first 50 speakers and used for disambiguating competing hypotheses for the other 50 speakers. An overall recognition rate of 84 percent for individual letters for the last 50 speakers was obtained.

The idea of using a number of phonetically significant properties in a recognition system based on the planning paradigm appears very promising. The analysis of the behavior of each plan and of the errors generated by their application suggests the actions that have to be taken in order to improve recognition accuracy.

Rule 45 is the most frequently used and the one responsible for most of the errors. In particular, the 14 confusions of |b|, |d|, |p|, and |3| with |e| are due to the fact that the system has not been able to correctly detect and process the transient at the vowel onset. Transients in such a case are difficult to analyze and the system tends to see the cues of |e| rather than those of the consonant that is supposed to preceed it.

Planning and inductive learning are still interactive and involve human activities, but they are aimed towards characterization of speaking modes and speech styles. Different speaking modes and styles can be well characterized using descriptions of acoustic properties that represent different phonetic events.

Finer variations of characterstic descriptions of acoustic properties can be represented and learned using stochastic methods. Letters exhibit little redundance because they are very short sounds. This justifies the introduction of a relatively large number of acoustic properties for characterizing a short time segment. *Redundancy* helps in reducing ambiguities.

Using different descriptions for the same letter allows one to recognize pronounciations of rare speaking modes provided that descriptions do not interfere with similar descriptions of other letters in other speaking modes.

Critical problems, as one can see from Fig. 12, are the distinction |d| versus |b| due to the fact that when the burst cues for |d| are not very evident, the system tends to apply the rule that a weak burst is more likely for |b| than for |d|. Other errors are due to misrecognition of voicing (confusion |d|, |t|) and to the incorrect classification of frication noise (confusion |3|, |c|). A few errors may be due to a wrong pronounciation of the speakers. In fact, perceptual tests were not performed in order to assess if the speakers really pronounced what they saw on the screen.

The use of suprasegmental features described by PAC's is very effective for locating signal segments where properties have to be extracted even if a few problems remain to be fixed. In addition to the reference made in [15] to the difficulties encountered in the automatic recognition of elements of the E-set spoken in isolation, it is worth mentioning a report by Cole, Stern, and Larsy [17]. In this report, the Authors propose a new method based on the classification of feature parameters for recognizing letters of the E-set spoken in isolation. They mention they achieved a recognition rate of 10.1 percent on a population of 42 speakers. The authors made a literature review on the recognition of alphadigit data and on the performance of the system, proposed before which did not perform as well as their system on the E-set.

The results reported in this paper are not as good as the ones described in [17], but they refer to a more difficult test that is the recognition of *connected* letters, pronounced by many speakers. The approach proposed in this paper is probably not the ultimate solution to the problem of recognizing connected letters spoken by many speakers, but clearly shows some achievements which make it worth pursuing the effort of refining knowledge in a flexible programming environment like the one just proposed.

The research will continue with the analysis of letters and digits including dipthongs and also towards the characterization of rare speaking modes of speakers with different mother tongue.

References

[1] S. E. Levinson, L. R. Rabiner, A. E. Rosenberg, and J. G. Wilpon, "Interactive clustering techniques for selecting speaker independent reference templates for isolated word recognition," *IEEE Trans. Acoust. Speech, Signal Processing*, vol. ASSP-27, pp. 134–141, Apr. 1979.

[2] A. E. Rosenberg, L. R. Rabiner, J. G. Wilpon, and D. Kahn, "Demisyllable-based isolate word recognition system," *IEEE Trans. Acoust., Speech, Signal Processing*, vol. ASSP-31, pp. 713–726, June 1983.

[3] L. R. Bahl, F. Jelinek, R. L. Mercer, "A maximum likelihood approach to continuous speech recognition," *IEEE Trans. Pattern Anal. Machine Intell.*, vol. PAMI-5, pp. 177–190, Mar. 1983.

[4] G. Kopec and M. Bush, "Network-based isolated digit recognition using vector quantization," *IEEE Trans. Acoust., Speech, Signal Processing*, vol. ASSP-33, p. 850, Aug. 1985.

[5] M. Bush and G. Kopec, "Network-based connected digit recognition using vector quantization," in *Proc. IEEE Int. Conf. Acoust., Speech, Signal Processing*, Tampa, FL, 1985, pp. 1197–1200.

[6] E. Merlo, R. De Mori, M. Palakal, and G. Mercier, "A continuous parameter and frequency domain based Markov model," in *Proc. Int. Conf. Acoust., Speech, Signal Processing*, Tokyo, Japan, Apr. 1986, pp. 1597–1600.

[7] R. De Mori, P. Laface, and Y. Mong, "Parallel algorithms for syllable recognition in continuous speech," *IEEE Trans. Pattern Anal. Machine Intell.*, vol. PAMI-6, pp. 56–69, Jan. 1985.

[8] E. D. Sacerdoti, "The nonlinear nature of plans," in *Proc. Int. Joint Conf. Artificial Intell.*, Tbilisi, Georgia, USSR, Sept. 1975, pp. 115–135.

[9] J. E. Laird, "Universal subgoaling," Dep. Comput. Sci., Carnegie-Mellon Univ., Pittsburgh, PA, Rep. CMU-CS-84-129, May 1984.

[10] M. J. Stefik, "Planning with constraints," Stanford Heuristic Programming Project, Memo HPP-80-2; Dep. Comput. Sci. Rep. STAN-CS-80-784, Jan. 1980.

[11] L. D. Erman, F. Hayes-Roth, V. R. Lesser, and D. R. Reddy, "The HEARSAY-II speech understanding system, integrating knowledge to resolve uncertainty," *ACM Comput. Surveys*, vol. 12, pp. 213–253, 1980.

[12] L. Brownston, R. Farrel, E. Kant, and N. Martin, *Programming Expert Systems in OPS5.* Reading, MA: Addison-Wesley, 1985.

[13] D. E. Wilkins, "Domain-independent planning: Representation and plan generation," *Artificial Intell.*, vol. 22, no. 3, pp. 269–302, Apr. 1984.

[14] R. De Mori and M. Palakal, "On the use of a taxonomy of time-frequency morphologies for automatic speech recognition," in *Proc. Int. Joint Conf. Artificial Intell.* (IJCAI-85), Los Angeles, CA, pp. 876–879.

[15] N. Nocerino, F. Soong, L. Rabiner, and D. Klatt, "Comparative study of several distortion measures for speech recognition," in *Proc. IEEE Int. Conf. Acoust., Speech, Signal Processing*, Tampa, FL, Mar. 1985, pp. 25–28.

[16] S. B. Whitehill, "Self correcting generalization," in *Proc. AAAI-80*, 1980, pp. 240–242.

[17] R. A. Cole, R. M. Stern, and M. J. Larsy, "Performing fine phonetic distinctions: Templates vs. features," Dep. Elec. Eng., Carnegie-Mellon Univ., Pittsburgh, PA, Internal Rep., 1984.

Renato De Mori received the Doctorate degree in electronic engineering from Politecnico di Torino, Torino, Italy, in 1967.

He was an Assistant and an Associate Professor at Politecnico di Torino from 1969 to 1976. In 1976 he became Professor and Chairman of the Institute for Computer Science, University of Torino. He was confirmed as Full Professor in Italy in 1979. In 1982 he joined Concordia University, Montreal, P.Q., Canada as a Professor in the Department of Computer Science, and was appointed

Chairman in 1984. As of January 1986, he is a Professor and the Director of the School of Computer Science at McGill University, Montreal, P.Q., Canada.

Dr. De Mori acted as a member of the Program Committees and as Chairman of Sessions at the World IFIP, Pattern Recognition, and Artificial Intelligence Conferences. He is Associate Editor of the journels *Computer Speech and Language* (New York: Academic), *Signal Processing, Speech Communication,* and *Pattern Recognition Letters* (Amsterdam, The Netherlands: North-Holland). He is author of 3 books and over 100 papers, mostly published in international journals and in the proceedings of international conferences devoted to computer systems, pattern recognition, and artificial intelligence. He is Vice-President of the Canadian Society for Computational Studies of Intelligence, Chairman of the Computing and Information System Committee of the Natural Science and Engineering Council of Canada, Chairman of the Technical Committee on Automatic Speech Recognition of the International Association for Pattern Recognition, General Chairman of the Canadian Conference on Artificial Intelligence, Montreal, 1986, and Program Co-Chairman of COMPRINT-85, Montreal, 1985, an IEEE Computer Society-ACM sponsored conference on computer aided technologies. He is a member of IEEE Computer Society, Association for Computing Machinery, AAAI, EURASIP, was on the Board of Directors of the Centre de Recherche en Informatique de Montréal (CRIM), is member of the Canadian CAD/CAM Council, and is in the Scientific Council of the Centre National d'Etudes de Télécommunications (CNET), Lannion-A, France.

Lily Lam was born in Hong Kong in 1949. She received the B.Sc. degree with first class honours from the University of Hong Kong in 1971, and the Master's degree in computer science from McGill University, Montreal, P.Q., Canada, in 1978.

She has been with the Department of Computer Science of Concordia University, Montreal, P.Q., Canada, as an analyst since 1978 where she has participated in various projects in research and development. Her interests include speech processing and recognition, VLSI design, and programming methodology.

Michel Gilloux was born in Nice, France, in 1958. He graduated from Ecole Polytechnique, Paris, in 1980 and Ecole Nationale Supérieure des Télécommunications, Paris, in 1982.

He is currently an Engineer at Centre National d'Etudes des Télécommunications, Lannion, France. His main research interest is in knowledge representation and natural language processing.

Chapter 6

Stochastic Approaches

Introduction

Stochastic modeling entails the use of probabilistic models to deal with uncertain or incomplete information. In speech recognition, uncertainty and incompleteness arise from many sources; for example, confusable sounds, speaker variabilities, contextual effects, and homophones words. Thus, stochastic models are a particularly suitable approach to speech recognition.

The most popular stochastic approach today is *hidden Markov modeling*. A hidden Markov model (HMM) is characterized by a finite-state Markov model and a set of output distributions. The transition parameters in the Markov chain models temporal variabilities, while the parameters in the output distributions model spectral variabilities. These two types of variabilities are the essence of speech recognition.

Hidden Markov models owe their success to the existence of several elegent and efficient algorithms. For training, the forward-backward algorithm estimates the transition and output parameters automatically and efficiently. This algorithm has a firm mathematical foundation, as it is an instance of the E-M (estimate-maximize) algorithm [Baum 72]. Yet, it is an extremely efficient algorithm, with complexity linear in the length of the input speech. The efficiency of the forward-backward algorithm enables HMM-based systems to learn their parameters from large bodies of data. Its drawback is the inaccurate Markov assumption; namely, that acoustic realizations and durations depend only on the current state and are conditionally independent of the past. In spite of this, the solid mathematical foundation and efficient learning algorithm for HMMs have led to a mature technology, upon which many successful systems have been built (see Chapter 9).

Compared to template-based approaches, hidden Markov modeling is more general and has a firmer mathematical foundation. A template-based model is simply a continuous density HMM (see below) with identity covariance matrices and a slope-constrained topology. Although templates can be trained on fewer instances, they lack the probabilistic formulation of full HMMs and, typically, underperform HMMs.

Compared to knowledge-based approaches, HMMs enable easy integration of knowledge sources into a compiled architecture. A negative side effect of this is that HMMs do not provide much insight on the recognition process. As a result, it is often difficult to analyze the errors of an HMM system in an attempt to improve its performance. Nevertheless, prudent incorporation of knowledge has significantly improved HMM-based systems.

Three fundamental HMM papers are included in this chapter. The first paper, *A Tutorial on Hidden Markov Models and Selected Applications in Speech Recognition* by Lawrence Rabiner, is an excellent introduction to HMMs. This paper gives the HMM algorithms, as well as their derivation and the underlying theory. It also provides several applications developed at AT&T Bell Laboratories. This paper provides a very readable introduction to the topic. A more detailed coverage of HMMs is given in [Huang 90].

The second paper, *Stochastic Modeling for Automatic Speech Understanding* by James Baker, is a classic paper that introduced the use of hidden

Markov models for speech recognition. This paper contains a succinct introduction to the problem, followed by discussions of basic HMM algorithms. It also enumerates a number of other interesting applications of HMMs, such as word spotting, segmentation, transcription, pitch tracking, and part-of-speech assignment.

The paper *A Maximum Likelihood Approach to Continuous Speech Recognition* by Bahl, Jelinek, and Mercer, is the most frequently cited paper on hidden Markov modeling. In addition to theory and HMM algorithms, the authors also discuss several very important new ideas. One of these is stack decoding, an A*-based search algorithm [Nilsson 80]. Another is deleted estimation [Jelinek 80], which increases the robustness of estimates from insufficient data, a problem that plagues HMMs. The paper also presented a number of ideas and experiments that demonstrate the power of HMMs.

All previous papers were based on discrete HMMs, which first reduces real-valued speech vectors into (usually about 200) discrete symbols. This quantization process undoubtedly sacrifices some accuracy. In view of this, continuous density HMMs [Poritz 86; Paul 86; Rabiner 88] are proposed to model the output distribution as a mixture Gaussian density. Perhaps the best example of a well-designed continuous-density system is Rabiner, Wilpon, and Soong's *High Performance Connected Digit Recognition Using Hidden Markov Models*. Their results showed much better performance than discrete HMMs[1]. This paper represents a milestone on speaker-independent connected-digit recognition.

Another paper on continuous-density HMMs was written by Bahl, Brown, de Souza, and Mercer. This paper, *Speech Recognition with Continuous-Parameter Hidden Markov Models*, however, has a different emphasis. The authors argued that while continuous-density HMMs are not subject to quantization errors, they must make assumptions (e.g. mixture Gaussian) about the data, which are invariably false due to finite training data. In view of this problem, they propose an alternate training algorithm, maximum mutual information estimation (MMIE). MMIE maximizes the information between the word sequence and the speech. Given an acoustic sequence Y, and the corresponding word sequence W, MMIE not only tries to increase $Pr(Y \mid W)$ (as does MLE), but also tries to decrease $Pr(Y \mid W')$ for incorrect words W'. Training against negative exemplars increases the importance of a correct recognition. Discriminative HMMs have gained considerable attention in the recent years. Other interesting approaches to discriminative HMMs include [Bahl 87; Doddington 89].

A final paper related to continuous-density HMMs is *Semi-Continuous Hidden Markov Models for Speech Recognition* by Huang and Jack. Semi-continuous HMMs (SCHMM) were proposed as a combination of continuous and discrete HMMs. SCHMMs can be viewed as discrete HMMs whose quantized codewords are Gaussian distributions that are trained jointly with transition and output parameters of the HMMs. This enables training of a large number of mixtures per state, since the mixtures are shared by all the states. SCHMMs are also more trainable than continuous HMMs because the total number of Gaussians is typically smaller. Huang and Jack showed that SCHMMs can outperform both discrete and continuous HMMs, while requiring only slightly more computation than discrete HMMs. Similar results were obtained by Bellagarda [Bellegarda 89].

One important research area for large-vocabulary recognition is subword modeling, or selecting a good set of HMMs that model units smaller than a word. Although phonetic models appear to be the most natural, because phones are highly affected by context, phone models have distributions that are too broad for optimal discrimination. One solution is the use of context-dependent HMMs, as described in *Context-Dependent Phonetic Hidden Markov Models for Continuous Speech Recognition* by Lee[2]. This paper describes several types of context-dependent phonetic models, including word-dependent phone models [Chow 86, Lee 88], triphone models [Schwartz 85], and generalized triphone models [Lee 89]. Detailed results show substantial improvements through contextual modeling. Also described are deleted interpolation of contextual models, and an information-theoretic subword-model-clustering procedure. Context-dependent

1. It should be noted that for some tasks, discrete HMMs still seem to perform as well as, if not better than, continuous HMMs. Which works better largely depends on the task and the data.

2. Context-dependent models were first introduced by BBN, and are described briefly in Chapter 9.

phonetic modeling is a good example of utilization of speech knowledge (see Paper 5.1, phonotactics).

A shortcoming of standard HMMs is that each observation is assumed to depend only on the HMM state, and conditionally independent of the past. With each observation limited to about 20 milliseconds, this severely limits the scope of HMMs. One attempt to ameliorate this problem is the use of differential coefficients (see Papers 6.4 and 6.7 by Rabiner and by Lee). However, these simple slope measures cannot fully decorrelate the long-term correlations inherent in speech. In view of this, a technique was proposed by Roucos and Dunham, *A Stochastic Segment Model for Phoneme-Based Continuous Speech Recognition*, is described in the final paper of this chapter. Stochastic segment models (SSM) are stochastic templates that model the distribution of entire segments. In theory, it can use arbitrary methods for time alignment and can use full-covariance matrices to model entire segments. In practice, linear resampling was used for alignment, and some independence was assumed. This paper pinpointed a serious shortcoming in HMMs, and proposed an interesting solution that led to some performance improvements. As more training data and faster computers become available, SSMs may serve as a basis for better stochastic models in the future.

References

[Bahl 87] Bahl, L.R., Brown, P.F., de Souza, P.V., Mercer, R.L., *Estimating Hidden Markov Model Parameters so as to Maximize Speech Recognition Accuracy.* Technical Report RC 13121 (#58589), IBM Thomas J. Watson Research Center, September, 1987.

[Baum 72] Baum, L. E. An Inequality and Associated Maximization Technique in Statistical Estimation of Probabilistic Functions of Markov Processes. In *Inequalities* 3:1-8, 1972.

[Bellegarda 89] Bellegarda, J.R., Nahamoo, D. Tied Mixture Continuous Parameter Models for Large Vocabulary Isolated Speech Recognition. In *IEEE International Conference on Acoustics, Speech, and Signal Processing,* pp 13–16. May, 1989.

[Chow 86] Chow, Y. L., Schwartz, R., Roucos, S., Kimball, O., Price, P., Kubala, F., Dunham, M., Krasner, M., Makhoul, J. The Role of Word-Dependent Coarticulatory Effects in a Phoneme-Based Speech Recognition System. In *IEEE International Conference on Acoustics, Speech, and Signal Processing.* April, 1986.

[Doddington 89] Doddington, G.R. Phonetically Sensitive Discriminants for Improved Speech Recognition. In *IEEE International Conference on Acoustics, Speech, and Signal Processing.* May, 1989.

[Huang 90] Huang, X.D., Ariki, Y., Jack, M.A. *Hidden Markov Models for Speech Recognition.* Edinburgh University Press, Edinburgh, 1990.

[Jelinek 80] Jelinek, F., Mercer, R.L. Interpolated Estimation of Markov Source Parameters from Sparse Data. In E.S. Gelsema and L.N. Kanal (eds.), *Pattern Recognition in Practice*, pages 381–397. North-Holland Publishing Company, Amsterdam, 1980.

[Lee 88] Lee, K.F., Hon, H.W. Large-Vocabulary Speaker-Independent Continuous Speech Recognition. In *IEEE International Conference on Acoustics, Speech, and Signal Processing.* April, 1988.

[Lee 89] Lee, K.F. *Automatic Speech Recognition: The Development of the SPHINX System.* Kluwer Academic Publishers, Boston, 1989.

[Nilsson 80] Nilsson, N.J. *Principles of Artificial Intelligence.* Morgan Kaufmann Publishers, San Mateo, Calif. 1980.

[Paul 86] Paul, D. B., Lippmann, R. P., Chen, Y., Weinstein, C. Robust HMM-Based Techniques for Recognition of Speech Produced under Stress and in Noise. In *Speech Tech.* April, 1986.

[Poritz 86] Poritz, A.,B., Richter, A.G. On Hidden Markov Models in Isolated Word Recognition. In *IEEE International Conference on Acoustics, Speech, and Signal Processing.* April, 1986.

[Rabiner 88] Rabiner, L.R., Wilpon, J.G., Soong, F.K. High Performance Connected Digit Recognition Using Hidden Markov Models. In *IEEE International Conference on Acoustics, Speech, and Signal Processing.* April, 1988.

[Schwartz 85] Schwartz, R., Chow, Y., Kimball, O., Roucos, S., Krasner, M., Makhoul, J. Context-Dependent Modeling for Acoustic-Phonetic Recognition of Continuous Speech. In *IEEE International Conference on Acoustics, Speech, and Signal Processing.* April, 1985.

A Tutorial on Hidden Markov Models and Selected Applications in Speech Recognition

LAWRENCE R. RABINER, FELLOW, IEEE

Although initially introduced and studied in the late 1960s and early 1970s, statistical methods of Markov source or hidden Markov modeling have become increasingly popular in the last several years. There are two strong reasons why this has occurred. First the models are very rich in mathematical structure and hence can form the theoretical basis for use in a wide range of applications. Second the models, when applied properly, work very well in practice for several important applications. In this paper we attempt to carefully and methodically review the theoretical aspects of this type of statistical modeling and show how they have been applied to selected problems in machine recognition of speech.

I. Introduction

Real-world processes generally produce observable outputs which can be characterized as signals. The signals can be discrete in nature (e.g., characters from a finite alphabet, quantized vectors from a codebook, etc.), or continuous in nature (e.g., speech samples, temperature measurements, music, etc.). The signal source can be stationary (i.e., its statistical properties do not vary with time), or nonstationary (i.e., the signal properties vary over time). The signals can be pure (i.e., coming strictly from a single source), or can be corrupted from other signal sources (e.g., noise) or by transmission distortions, reverberation, etc.

A problem of fundamental interest is characterizing such real-world signals in terms of signal models. There are several reasons why one is interested in applying signal models. First of all, a signal model can provide the basis for a theoretical description of a signal processing system which can be used to process the signal so as to provide a desired output. For example if we are interested in enhancing a speech signal corrupted by noise and transmission distortion, we can use the signal model to design a system which will optimally remove the noise and undo the transmission distortion. A second reason why signal models are important is that they are potentially capable of letting us learn a great deal about the signal source (i.e., the real-world process which produced the signal) without having to have the source available. This property is especially important when the cost of getting signals from the actual source is high. In this case, with a good signal model, we can simulate the source and learn as much as possible via simulations. Finally, the most important reason why signal models are important is that they often work extremely well in practice, and enable us to realize important practical systems—e.g., prediction systems, recognition systems, identification systems, etc., in a very efficient manner.

These are several possible choices for what type of signal model is used for characterizing the properties of a given signal. Broadly one can dichotomize the types of signal models into the class of deterministic models, and the class of statistical models. Deterministic models generally exploit some known specific properties of the signal, e.g., that the signal is a sine wave, or a sum of exponentials, etc. In these cases, specification of the signal model is generally straightforward; all that is required is to determine (estimate) values of the parameters of the signal model (e.g., amplitude, frequency, phase of a sine wave, amplitudes and rates of exponentials, etc.). The second broad class of signal models is the set of statistical models in which one tries to characterize only the statistical properties of the signal. Examples of such statistical models include Gaussian processes, Poisson processes, Markov processes, and hidden Markov processes, among others. The underlying assumption of the statistical model is that the signal can be well characterized as a parametric random process, and that the parameters of the stochastic process can be determined (estimated) in a precise, well-defined manner.

For the applications of interest, namely speech processing, both deterministic and stochastic signal models have had good success. In this paper we will concern ourselves strictly with one type of stochastic signal model, namely the hidden Markov model (HMM). (These models are referred to as Markov sources or probabilistic functions of Markov chains in the communications literature.) We will first review the theory of Markov chains and then extend the ideas to the class of hidden Markov models using several simple examples. We will then focus our attention on the three fundamental problems[1] for HMM design, namely: the

Manuscript received January 15, 1988; revised October 4, 1988.
The author is with AT&T Bell Laboratories, Murray Hill, NJ 07974-2070, USA.
IEEE Log Number 8825949.

[1]The idea of characterizing the theoretical aspects of hidden Markov modeling in terms of solving three fundamental problems is due to Jack Ferguson of IDA (Institute for Defense Analysis) who introduced it in lectures and writing.

0018-9219/89/0200-0257$01.00 © 1989 IEEE

evaluation of the probability (or likelihood) of a sequence of observations given a specific HMM; the determination of a best sequence of model states; and the adjustment of model parameters so as to best account for the observed signal. We will show that once these three fundamental problems are solved, we can apply HMMs to selected problems in speech recognition.

Neither the theory of hidden Markov models nor its applications to speech recognition is new. The basic theory was published in a series of classic papers by Baum and his colleagues [1]-[5] in the late 1960s and early 1970s and was implemented for speech processing applications by Baker [6] at CMU, and by Jelinek and his colleagues at IBM [7]-[13] in the 1970s. However, widespread understanding and application of the theory of HMMs to speech processing has occurred only within the past several years. There are several reasons why this has been the case. First, the basic theory of hidden Markov models was published in mathematical journals which were not generally read by engineers working on problems in speech processing. The second reason was that the original applications of the theory to speech processing did not provide sufficient tutorial material for most readers to understand the theory and to be able to apply it to their own research. As a result, several tutorial papers were written which provided a sufficient level of detail for a number of research labs to begin work using HMMs in individual speech processing applications [14]-[19]. This tutorial is intended to provide an overview of the basic theory of HMMs (as originated by Baum and his colleagues), provide practical details on methods of implementation of the theory, and describe a couple of selected applications of the theory to distinct problems in speech recognition. The paper combines results from a number of original sources and hopefully provides a single source for acquiring the background required to pursue further this fascinating area of research.

The organization of this paper is as follows. In Section II we review the theory of discrete Markov chains and show how the concept of hidden states, where the observation is a probabilistic function of the state, can be used effectively. We illustrate the theory with two simple examples, namely coin-tossing, and the classic balls-in-urns system. In Section III we discuss the three fundamental problems of HMMs, and give several practical techniques for solving these problems. In Section IV we discuss the various types of HMMs that have been studied including ergodic as well as left-right models. In this section we also discuss the various model features including the form of the observation density function, the state duration density, and the optimization criterion for choosing optimal HMM parameter values. In Section V we discuss the issues that arise in implementing HMMs including the topics of scaling, initial parameter estimates, model size, model form, missing data, and multiple observation sequences. In Section VI we describe an isolated word speech recognizer, implemented with HMM ideas, and show how it performs as compared to alternative implementations. In Section VII we extend the ideas presented in Section VI to the problem of recognizing a string of spoken words based on concatenating individual HMMs of each word in the vocabulary. In Section VIII we briefly outline how the ideas of HMM have been applied to a large vocabulary speech recognizer, and in Section IX we summarize the ideas discussed throughout the paper.

II. Discrete Markov Processes[2]

Consider a system which may be described at any time as being in one of a set of N distinct states, $S_1, S_2, \cdots, S_N$, as illustrated in Fig. 1 (where $N = 5$ for simplicity). At regularly spaced discrete times, the system undergoes a change of state (possibly back to the same state) according to a set of probabilities associated with the state. We denote the time instants associated with state changes as $t = 1, 2, \cdots$, and we denote the actual state at time t as q_t. A full probabilistic description of the above system would, in general, require specification of the current state (at time t), as well as all the predecessor states. For the special case of a discrete, first order, Markov chain, this probabilistic description is truncated to just the current and the predecessor state, i.e.,

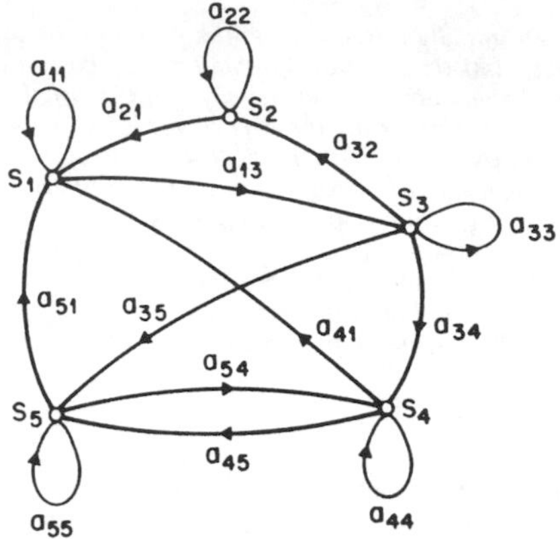

Fig. 1. A Markov chain with 5 states (labeled S_1 to S_5) with selected state transitions.

$$P[q_t = S_j | q_{t-1} = S_i, q_{t-2} = S_k, \cdots] = P[q_t = S_j | q_{t-1} = S_i]. \tag{1}$$

Furthermore we only consider those processes in which the right-hand side of (1) is independent of time, thereby leading to the set of state transition probabilities a_{ij} of the form

$$a_{ij} = P[q_t = S_j | q_{t-1} = S_i], \quad 1 \le i, j \le N \tag{2}$$

with the state transition coefficients having the properties

$$a_{ij} \ge 0 \tag{3a}$$

$$\sum_{j=1}^{N} a_{ij} = 1 \tag{3b}$$

since they obey standard stochastic constraints.

The above stochastic process could be called an observable Markov model since the output of the process is the set of states at each instant of time, where each state corresponds to a physical (observable) event. To set ideas, consider a simple 3-state Markov model of the weather. We assume that once a day (e.g., at noon), the weather is

[2] A good overview of discrete Markov processes is in [20, ch. 5].

observed as being one of the following:

State 1: rain or (snow)
State 2: cloudy
State 3: sunny.

We postulate that the weather on day t is characterized by a single one of the three states above, and that the matrix A of state transition probabilities is

$$A = \{a_{ij}\} = \begin{bmatrix} 0.4 & 0.3 & 0.3 \\ 0.2 & 0.6 & 0.2 \\ 0.1 & 0.1 & 0.8 \end{bmatrix}.$$

Given that the weather on day 1 ($t = 1$) is sunny (state 3), we can ask the question: What is the probability (according to the model) that the weather for the next 7 days will be "sun-sun-rain-rain-sun-cloudy-sun $\cdots$"? Stated more formally, we define the observation sequence O as $O = \{S_3, S_3, S_3, S_1, S_1, S_3, S_2, S_3\}$ corresponding to $t = 1, 2, \cdots, 8$, and we wish to determine the probability of O, given the model. This probability can be expressed (and evaluated) as

$$\begin{aligned} P(O|\text{Model}) &= P[S_3, S_3, S_3, S_1, S_1, S_3, S_2, S_3|\text{Model}] \\ &= P[S_3] \cdot P[S_3|S_3] \cdot P[S_3|S_3] \cdot P[S_1|S_3] \\ &\quad \cdot P[S_1|S_1] \cdot P[S_3|S_1] \cdot P[S_2|S_3] \cdot P[S_3|S_2] \\ &= \pi_3 \cdot a_{33} \cdot a_{33} \cdot a_{31} \cdot a_{11} \cdot a_{13} \cdot a_{32} \cdot a_{23} \\ &= 1 \cdot (0.8)(0.8)(0.1)(0.4)(0.3)(0.1)(0.2) \\ &= 1.536 \times 10^{-4} \end{aligned}$$

where we use the notation

$$\pi_i = P[q_1 = S_i], \quad 1 \le i \le N \tag{4}$$

to denote the initial state probabilities.

Another interesting question we can ask (and answer using the model) is: Given that the model is in a known state, what is the probability it stays in that state for exactly d days? This probability can be evaluated as the probability of the observation sequence

$$O = \{\underset{1}{S_i}, \underset{2}{S_i}, \underset{3}{S_i}, \cdots, \underset{d}{S_i}, \underset{d+1}{S_j} \neq S_i\},$$

given the model, which is

$$P(O|\text{Model}, q_1 = S_i) = (a_{ii})^{d-1}(1 - a_{ii}) = p_i(d). \tag{5}$$

The quantity $p_i(d)$ is the (discrete) probability density function of duration d in state i. This exponential duration density is characteristic of the state duration in a Markov chain. Based on $p_i(d)$, we can readily calculate the expected number of observations (duration) in a state, conditioned on starting in that state as

$$\bar{d}_i = \sum_{d=1}^{\infty} d p_i(d) \tag{6a}$$

$$= \sum_{d=1}^{\infty} d(a_{ii})^{d-1}(1 - a_{ii}) = \frac{1}{1 - a_{ii}}. \tag{6b}$$

Thus the expected number of consecutive days of sunny weather, according to the model, is $1/(0.2) = 5$; for cloudy it is 2.5; for rain it is 1.67.

A. Extension to Hidden Markov Models

So far we have considered Markov models in which each state corresponded to an observable (physical) event. This model is too restrictive to be applicable to many problems of interest. In this section we extend the concept of Markov models to include the case where the observation is a probabilistic function of the state—i.e., the resulting model (which is called a hidden Markov model) is a doubly embedded stochastic process with an underlying stochastic process that is *not* observable (it is hidden), but can only be observed through another set of stochastic processes that produce the sequence of observations. To fix ideas, consider the following model of some simple coin tossing experiments.

Coin Toss Models: Assume the following scenario. You are in a room with a barrier (e.g., a curtain) through which you cannot see what is happening. On the other side of the barrier is another person who is performing a coin (or multiple coin) tossing experiment. The other person will not tell you anything about what he is doing exactly; he will only tell you the result of each coin flip. Thus a sequence of *hidden* coin tossing experiments is performed, with the observation sequence consisting of a series of heads and tails; e.g., a typical observation sequence would be

$$\begin{aligned} O &= O_1 \, O_2 \, O_3 \cdots O_T \\ &= \mathcal{H} \, \mathcal{H} \, \mathcal{T} \, \mathcal{T} \, \mathcal{T} \, \mathcal{H} \, \mathcal{T} \, \mathcal{T} \, \mathcal{H} \cdots \mathcal{H} \end{aligned}$$

where $\mathcal{H}$ stands for heads and $\mathcal{T}$ stands for tails.

Given the above scenario, the problem of interest is how do we build an HMM to explain (model) the observed sequence of heads and tails. The first problem one faces is deciding what the states in the model correspond to, and then deciding how many states should be in the model. One possible choice would be to assume that only a single biased coin was being tossed. In this case we could model the situation with a 2-state model where each state corresponds to a side of the coin (i.e., heads or tails). This model is depicted in Fig. 2(a).[3] In this case the Markov model is observable, and the only issue for complete specification of the model would be to decide on the best value for the bias (i.e., the probability of, say, heads). Interestingly, an equivalent HMM to that of Fig. 2(a) would be a degenerate 1-state model, where the state corresponds to the single biased coin, and the unknown parameter is the bias of the coin.

A second form of HMM for explaining the observed sequence of coin toss outcome is given in Fig. 2(b). In this case there are 2 states in the model and each state corresponds to a different, biased, coin being tossed. Each state is characterized by a probability distribution of heads and tails, and transitions between states are characterized by a state transition matrix. The physical mechanism which accounts for how state transitions are selected could itself be a set of independent coin tosses, or some other probabilistic event.

A third form of HMM for explaining the observed sequence of coin toss outcomes is given in Fig. 2(c). This model corresponds to using 3 biased coins, and choosing from among the three, based on some probabilistic event.

[3]The model of Fig. 2(a) is a memoryless process and thus is a degenerate case of a Markov model.

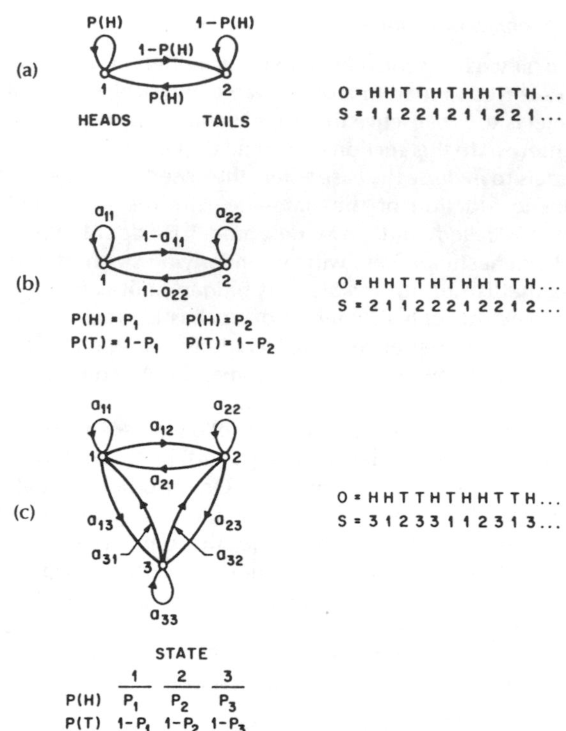

Fig. 2. Three possible Markov models which can account for the results of hidden coin tossing experiments. (a) 1-coin model. (b) 2-coins model. (c) 3-coins model.

Given the choice among the three models shown in Fig. 2 for explaining the observed sequence of heads and tails, a natural question would be which model best matches the actual observations. It should be clear that the simple 1-coin model of Fig. 2(a) has only 1 unknown parameter; the 2-coin model of Fig. 2(b) has 4 unknown parameters; and the 3-coin model of Fig. 2(c) has 9 unknown parameters. Thus, with the greater degrees of freedom, the larger HMMs would seem to inherently be more capable of modeling a series of coin tossing experiments than would equivalently smaller models. Although this is theoretically true, we will see later in this paper that practical considerations impose some strong limitations on the size of models that we can consider. Furthermore, it might just be the case that only a single coin is being tossed. Then using the 3-coin model of Fig. 2(c) would be inappropriate, since the actual physical event would not correspond to the model being used—i.e., we would be using an underspecified system.

The Urn and Ball Model[4]: To extend the ideas of the HMM to a somewhat more complicated situation, consider the urn and ball system of Fig. 3. We assume that there are N (large) glass urns in a room. Within each urn there are a large number of colored balls. We assume there are M distinct colors of the balls. The physical process for obtaining observations is as follows. A genie is in the room, and according to some random process, he (or she) chooses an initial urn. From this urn, a ball is chosen at random, and its color is recorded as the observation. The ball is then replaced in the urn from which it was selected. A new urn is then selected

[4]The urn and ball model was introduced by Jack Ferguson, and his colleagues, in lectures on HMM theory.

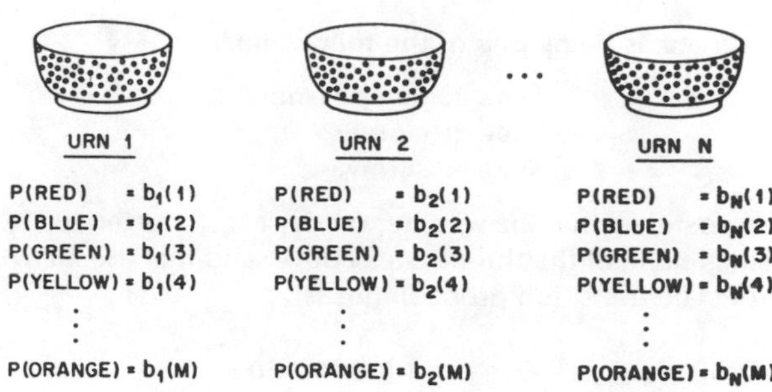

Fig. 3. An N-state urn and ball model which illustrates the general case of a discrete symbol HMM.

according to the random selection process associated with the current urn, and the ball selection process is repeated. This entire process generates a finite observation sequence of colors, which we would like to model as the observable output of an HMM.

It should be obvious that the simplest HMM that corresponds to the urn and ball process is one in which each state corresponds to a specific urn, and for which a (ball) color probability is defined for each state. The choice of urns is dictated by the state transition matrix of the HMM.

B. Elements of an HMM

The above examples give us a pretty good idea of what an HMM is and how it can be applied to some simple scenarios. We now formally define the elements of an HMM, and explain how the model generates observation sequences.

An HMM is characterized by the following:

1) N, the number of states in the model. Although the states are hidden, for many practical applications there is often some physical significance attached to the states or to sets of states of the model. Hence, in the coin tossing experiments, each state corresponded to a distinct biased coin. In the urn and ball model, the states corresponded to the urns. Generally the states are interconnected in such a way that any state can be reached from any other state (e.g., an ergodic model); however, we will see later in this paper that other possible interconnections of states are often of interest. We denote the individual states as $S = \{S_1, S_2, \cdots, S_N\}$, and the state at time t as q_t.

2) M, the number of distinct observation symbols per state, i.e., the discrete alphabet size. The observation symbols correspond to the physical output of the system being modeled. For the coin toss experiments the observation symbols were simply heads or tails; for the ball and urn model they were the colors of the balls selected from the urns. We denote the individual symbols as $V = \{v_1, v_2, \cdots, v_M\}$.

3) The state transition probability distribution $A = \{a_{ij}\}$ where

$$a_{ij} = P[q_{t+1} = S_j | q_t = S_i], \quad 1 \le i, j \le N. \tag{7}$$

For the special case where any state can reach any other state in a single step, we have $a_{ij} > 0$ for all i, j. For other types of HMMs, we would have $a_{ij} = 0$ for one or more (i, j) pairs.

4) The observation symbol probability distribution in state j, $B = \{b_j(k)\}$, where

$$b_j(k) = P[v_k \text{ at } t | q_t = S_j], \quad 1 \le j \le N \qquad 1 \le k \le M. \tag{8}$$

5) The initial state distribution $\pi = \{\pi_i\}$ where

$$\pi_i = P[q_1 = S_i], \quad 1 \le i \le N. \tag{9}$$

Given appropriate values of N, M, A, B, and π, the HMM can be used as a generator to give an observation sequence

$$O = O_1 O_2 \cdots O_T \tag{10}$$

(where each observation O_t is one of the symbols from V, and T is the number of observations in the sequence) as follows:

1) Choose an initial state $q_1 = S_i$ according to the initial state distribution π.
2) Set $t = 1$.
3) Choose $O_t = v_k$ according to the symbol probability distribution in state S_i, i.e., $b_i(k)$.
4) Transit to a new state $q_{t+1} = S_j$ according to the state transition probability distribution for state S_i, i.e., a_{ij}.
5) Set $t = t + 1$; return to step 3)if $t < T$; otherwise terminate the procedure.

The above procedure can be used as both a generator of observations, and as a model for how a given observation sequence was generated by an appropriate HMM.

It can be seen from the above discussion that a complete specification of an HMM requires specification of two model parameters (N and M), specification of observation symbols, and the specification of the three probability measures A, B, and π. For convenience, we use the compact notation

$$\lambda = (A, B, \pi) \tag{11}$$

to indicate the complete parameter set of the model.

C. The Three Basic Problems for HMMs[5]

Given the form of HMM of the previous section, there are three basic problems of interest that must be solved for the model to be useful in real-world applications. These problems are the following:

Problem 1: Given the observation sequence $O = O_1 O_2 \cdots O_T$, and a model $\lambda = (A, B, \pi)$, how do we efficiently compute $P(O|\lambda)$, the probability of the observation sequence, given the model?

Problem 2: Given the observation sequence $O = O_1 O_2 \cdots O_T$, and the model λ, how do we choose a corresponding state sequence $Q = q_1 q_2 \cdots q_T$ which is optimal in some meaningful sense (i.e., best "explains" the observations)?

Problem 3: How do we adjust the model parameters $\lambda = (A, B, \pi)$ to maximize $P(O|\lambda)$?

Problem 1 is the evaluation problem, namely given a model and a sequence of observations, how do we compute the probability that the observed sequence was produced by the model. We can also view the problem as one of scoring how well a given model matches a given observation sequence. The latter viewpoint is extremely useful. For example, if we consider the case in which we are trying to choose among several competing models, the solution to Problem 1 allows us to choose the model which best matches the observations.

Problem 2 is the one in which we attempt to uncover the hidden part of the model, i.e., to find the "correct" state sequence. It should be clear that for all but the case of degenerate models, there is no "correct" state sequence to be found. Hence for practical situations, we usually use an optimality criterion to solve this problem as best as possible. Unfortunately, as we will see, there are several reasonable optimality criteria that can be imposed, and hence the choice of criterion is a strong function of the intended use for the uncovered state sequence. Typical uses might be to learn about the structure of the model, to find optimal state sequences for continuous speech recognition, or to get average statistics of individual states, etc.

Problem 3 is the one in which we attempt to optimize the model parameters so as to best describe how a given observation sequence comes about. The observation sequence used to adjust the model parameters is called a training sequence since it is used to "train" the HMM. The training problem is the crucial one for most applications of HMMs, since it allows us to optimally adapt model parameters to observed training data—i.e., to create best models for real phenomena.

To fix ideas, consider the following simple isolated word speech recognizer. For each word of a W word vocabulary, we want to design a separate N-state HMM. We represent the speech signal of a given word as a time sequence of coded spectral vectors. We assume that the coding is done using a spectral codebook with M unique spectral vectors; hence each observation is the index of the spectral vector closest (in some spectral sense) to the original speech signal. Thus, for each vocabulary word, we have a training sequence consisting of a number of repetitions of sequences of codebook indices of the word (by one or more talkers). The first task is to build individual word models. This task is done by using the solution to Problem 3 to optimally estimate model parameters for each word model. To develop an understanding of the physical meaning of the model states, we use the solution to Problem 2 to segment each of the word training sequences into states, and then study the properties of the spectral vectors that lead to the observations occurring in each state. The goal here would be to make refinements on the model (e.g., more states, different codebook size, etc.) so as to improve its capability of modeling the spoken word sequences. Finally, once the set of W HMMs has been designed and optimized and thoroughly studied, recognition of an unknown word is performed using the solution to Problem 1 to score each word model based upon the given test observation sequence, and select the word whose model score is highest (i.e., the highest likelihood).

In the next section we present formal mathematical solutions to each of the three fundamental problems for HMMs.

[5]The material in this section and in Section III is based on the ideas presented by Jack Ferguson of IDA in lectures at Bell Laboratories.

We shall see that the three problems are linked together tightly under our probabilistic framework.

III. Solutions to the Three Basic Problems of HMMs

A. Solution to Problem 1

We wish to calculate the probability of the observation sequence, $O = O_1 O_2 \cdots O_T$, given the model λ, i.e., $P(O|\lambda)$. The most straightforward way of doing this is through enumerating every possible state sequence of length T (the number of observations). Consider one such fixed state sequence

$$Q = q_1 q_2 \cdots q_T \tag{12}$$

where q_1 is the initial state. The probability of the observation sequence O for the state sequence of (12) is

$$P(O|Q, \lambda) = \prod_{t=1}^{T} P(O_t|q_t, \lambda) \tag{13a}$$

where we have assumed statistical independence of observations. Thus we get

$$P(O|Q, \lambda) = b_{q_1}(O_1) \cdot b_{q_2}(O_2) \cdots b_{q_T}(O_T). \tag{13b}$$

The probability of such a state sequence Q can be written as

$$P(Q|\lambda) = \pi_{q_1} a_{q_1 q_2} a_{q_2 q_3} \cdots a_{q_{T-1} q_T}. \tag{14}$$

The joint probability of O and Q, i.e., the probability that O and Q occur simultaneously, is simply the product of the above two terms, i.e.,

$$P(O, Q|\lambda) = P(O|Q, \lambda)\, P(Q, \lambda). \tag{15}$$

The probability of O (given the model) is obtained by summing this joint probability over all possible state sequences q giving

$$P(O|\lambda) = \sum_{\text{all } Q} P(O|Q, \lambda)\, P(Q|\lambda) \tag{16}$$

$$= \sum_{q_1, q_2, \cdots, q_T} \pi_{q_1} b_{q_1}(O_1)\, a_{q_1 q_2} b_{q_2}(O_2) \cdots a_{q_{T-1} q_T} b_{q_T}(Q_T). \tag{17}$$

The interpretation of the computation in the above equation is the following. Initially (at time $t = 1$) we are in state q_1 with probability π_{q_1}, and generate the symbol O_1 (in this state) with probability $b_{q_1}(O_1)$. The clock changes from time t to $t + 1$ ($t = 2$) and we make a transition to state q_2 from state q_1 with probability $a_{q_1 q_2}$, and generate symbol O_2 with probability $b_{q_2}(O_2)$. This process continues in this manner until we make the list transition (at time T) from state q_{T-1} to state q_T with probability $a_{q_{T-1} q_T}$ and generate symbol O_T with probability $b_{q_T}(O_T)$.

A little thought should convince the reader that the calculation of $P(O|\lambda)$, according to its direct definition (17) involves on the order of $2T \cdot N^T$ calculations, since at every $t = 1, 2, \cdots, T$, there are N possible states which can be reached (i.e., there are N^T possible state sequences), and for each such state sequence about $2T$ calculations are required for each term in the sum of (17). (To be precise, we need $(2T - 1)N^T$ multiplications, and $N^T - 1$ additions.) This calculation is computationally unfeasible, even for small values of N and T; e.g., for $N = 5$ (states), $T = 100$ (observations), there are on the order of $2 \cdot 100 \cdot 5^{100} \approx 10^{72}$ computations! Clearly a more efficient procedure is required to solve Problem 1. Fortunately such a procedure exists and is called the forward-backward procedure.

The Forward-Backward Procedure [2], [3][6]: Consider the forward variable $\alpha_t(i)$ defined as

$$\alpha_t(i) = P(O_1 O_2 \cdots O_t, q_t = S_i|\lambda) \tag{18}$$

i.e., the probability of the partial observation sequence, $O_1 O_2 \cdots O_t$, (until time t) *and* state S_i at time t, given the model λ. We can solve for $\alpha_t(i)$ inductively, as follows:

1) Initialization:

$$\alpha_1(i) = \pi_i b_i(O_1), \quad 1 \le i \le N. \tag{19}$$

2) Induction:

$$\alpha_{t+1}(j) = \left[\sum_{i=1}^{N} \alpha_t(i) a_{ij}\right] b_j(O_{t+1}), \quad 1 \le t \le T-1, \quad 1 \le j \le N. \tag{20}$$

3) Termination:

$$P(O|\lambda) = \sum_{i=1}^{N} \alpha_T(i). \tag{21}$$

Step 1) initializes the forward probabilities as the joint probability of state S_i and initial observation O_1. The induction step, which is the heart of the forward calculation, is illustrated in Fig. 4(a). This figure shows how state S_j can be

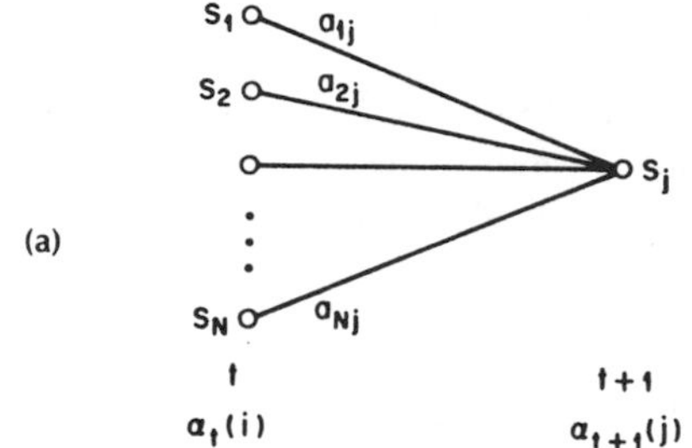

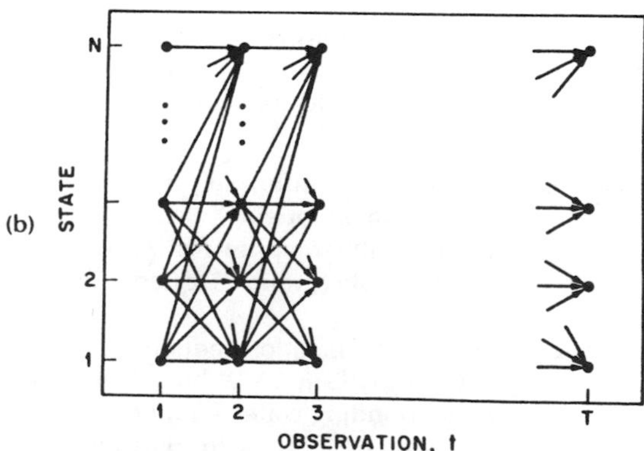

Fig. 4. (a) Illustration of the sequence of operations required for the computation of the forward variable $\alpha_{t+1}(j)$. (b) Implementation of the computation of $\alpha_t(i)$ in terms of a lattice of observations t, and states i.

[6] Strictly speaking, we only need the forward part of the forward-backward procedure to solve Problem 1. We will introduce the backward part of the procedure in this section since it will be used to help solve Problem 3.

reached at time $t+1$ from the N possible states, S_i, $1 \le i \le N$, at time t. Since $\alpha_t(i)$ is the probability of the joint event that $O_1 O_2 \cdots O_t$ are observed, and the state at time t is S_i, the product $\alpha_t(i)a_{ij}$ is then the probability of the joint event that $O_1 O_2 \cdots O_t$ are observed, and state S_j is reached at time $t+1$ via state S_i at time t. Summing this product over all the N possible states S_i, $1 \le i \le N$ at time t results in the probability of S_j at time $t+1$ with all the accompanying previous partial observations. Once this is done and S_j is known, it is easy to see that $\alpha_{t+1}(j)$ is obtained by accounting for observation O_{t+1} in state j, i.e., by multiplying the summed quantity by the probability $b_j(O_{t+1})$. The computation of (20) is performed for all states j, $1 \le j \le N$, for a given t; the computation is then iterated for $t = 1, 2, \cdots, T-1$. Finally, step 3) gives the desired calculation of $P(O|\lambda)$ as the sum of the terminal forward variables $\alpha_T(i)$. This is the case since, by definition,

$$\alpha_T(i) = P(O_1 O_2 \cdots O_T, q_T = S_i|\lambda) \tag{22}$$

and hence $P(O|\lambda)$ is just the sum of the $\alpha_T(i)$'s.

If we examine the computation involved in the calculation of $\alpha_t(j)$, $1 \le t \le T$, $1 \le j \le N$, we see that it requires on the order of N^2T calculations, rather than $2TN^T$ as required by the direct calculation. (Again, to be precise, we need $N(N+1)(T-1) + N$ multiplications and $N(N-1)(T-1)$ additions.) For $N = 5$, $T = 100$, we need about 3000 computations for the forward method, versus 10^{72} computations for the direct calculation, a savings of about 69 orders of magnitude.

The forward probability calculation is, in effect, based upon the lattice (or trellis) structure shown in Fig. 4(b). The key is that since there are only N states (nodes at each time slot in the lattice), all the possible state sequences will remerge into these N nodes, no matter how long the observation sequence. At time $t = 1$ (the first time slot in the lattice), we need to calculate values of $\alpha_1(i)$, $1 \le i \le N$. At times $t = 2, 3, \cdots, T$, we only need to calculate values of $\alpha_t(j)$, $1 \le j \le N$, where each calculation involves only N previous values of $\alpha_{t-1}(i)$ because each of the N grid points is reached from the same N grid points at the previous time slot.

In a similar manner,[7] we can consider a backward variable $\beta_t(i)$ defined as

$$\beta_t(i) = P(O_{t+1} O_{t+2} \cdots O_T | q_t = S_i, \lambda) \tag{23}$$

i.e., the probability of the partial observation sequence from $t+1$ to the end, given state S_i at time t and the model λ. Again we can solve for $\beta_t(i)$ inductively, as follows:

1) Initialization:

$$\beta_T(i) = 1, \qquad 1 \le i \le N. \tag{24}$$

2) Induction:

$$\beta_t(i) = \sum_{j=1}^{N} a_{ij} b_j(O_{t+1}) \beta_{t+1}(j),$$
$$t = T-1, T-2, \cdots, 1, \; 1 \le i \le N. \tag{25}$$

The initialization step 1) *arbitrarily* defines $\beta_T(i)$ to be 1 for all i. Step 2), which is illustrated in Fig. 5, shows that in order to have been in state S_i at time t, and to account for the

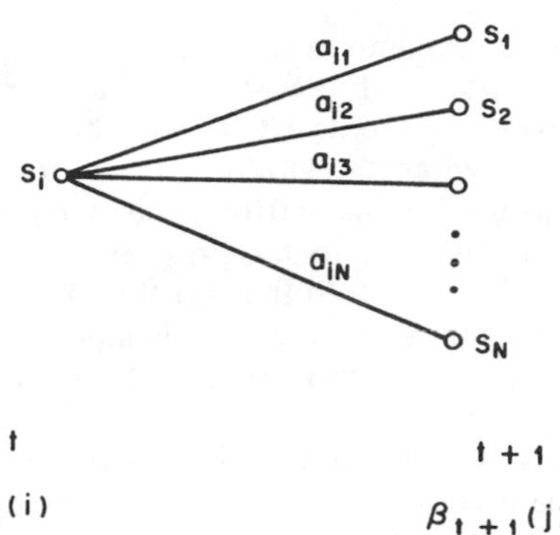

Fig. 5. Illustration of the sequence of operations required for the computation of the backward variable $\beta_t(i)$.

observation sequence from time $t+1$ on, you have to consider all possible states S_j at time $t+1$, accounting for the transition from S_i to S_j (the a_{ij} term), as well as the observation O_{t+1} in state j (the $b_j(O_{t+1})$ term), and then account for the remaining partial observation sequence from state j (the $\beta_{t+1}(j)$ term). We will see later how the backward, as well as the forward calculations are used extensively to help solve fundamental Problems 2 and 3 of HMMs.

Again, the computation of $\beta_t(i)$, $1 \le t \le T$, $1 \le i \le N$, requires on the order of N^2T calculations, and can be computed in a lattice structure similar to that of Fig. 4(b).

B. Solution to Problem 2

Unlike Problem 1 for which an exact solution can be given, there are several possible ways of solving Problem 2, namely finding the "optimal" state sequence associated with the given observation sequence. The difficulty lies with the definition of the optimal state sequence; i.e., there are several possible optimality criteria. For example, one possible optimality criterion is to choose the states q_t which are *individually* most likely. This optimality criterion maximizes the expected number of correct individual states. To implement this solution to Problem 2, we define the variable

$$\gamma_t(i) = P(q_t = S_i | O, \lambda) \tag{26}$$

i.e., the probability of being in state S_i at time t, given the observation sequence O, and the model λ. Equation (26) can be expressed simply in terms of the forward-backward variables, i.e.,

$$\gamma_t(i) = \frac{\alpha_t(i)\,\beta_t(i)}{P(O|\lambda)} = \frac{\alpha_t(i)\,\beta_t(i)}{\sum_{i=1}^{N} \alpha_t(i)\,\beta_t(i)} \tag{27}$$

since $\alpha_t(i)$ accounts for the partial observation sequence $O_1 O_2 \cdots O_t$ and state S_i at t, while $\beta_t(i)$ accounts for the remainder of the observation sequence $O_{t+1} O_{t+2} \cdots O_T$, given state S_i at t. The normalization factor $P(O|\lambda) = \Sigma_{i=1}^{N} \alpha_t(i), \beta_t(i)$ makes $\gamma_t(i)$ a probability measure so that

$$\sum_{i=1}^{N} \gamma_t(i) = 1. \tag{28}$$

Using $\gamma_t(i)$, we can solve for the individually most likely state q_t at time t, as

$$q_t = \operatorname*{argmax}_{1 \le i \le N} [\gamma_t(i)], \qquad 1 \le t \le T. \tag{29}$$

[7]Again we remind the reader that the backward procedure will be used in the solution to Problem 3, and is not required for the solution of Problem 1.

Although (29) maximizes the expected number of correct states (by choosing the most likely state for each t), there could be some problems with the resulting state sequence. For example, when the HMM has state transitions which have zero probabilty ($a_{ij} = 0$ for some i and j), the "optimal" state sequence may, in fact, not even be a valid state sequence. This is due to the fact that the solution of (29) simply determines the most likely state at every instant, without regard to the probability of occurrence of *sequences* of states.

One possible solution to the above problem is to modify the optimality criterion. For example, one could solve for the state sequence that maximizes the expected number of correct pairs of states (q_t, q_{t+1}), or triples of states (q_t, q_{t+1}, q_{t+2}), etc. Although these criteria might be reasonable for some applications, the most widely used criterion is to find the *single* best state sequence (path), i.e., to maximize $P(Q|O, \lambda)$ which is equivalent to maximizing $P(Q, O|\lambda)$. A formal technique for finding this single best state sequence exists, based on dynamic programming methods, and is called the Viterbi algorithm.

Viterbi Algorithm [21], [22]: To find the single best state sequence, $Q = \{q_1 q_2 \cdots q_T\}$, for the given observation sequence $O = \{O_1 O_2 \cdots O_T\}$, we need to define the quantity

$$\delta_t(i) = \max_{q_1, q_2, \cdots, q_{t-1}} P[q_1 q_2 \cdots q_t = i, O_1 O_2 \cdots O_t|\lambda] \tag{30}$$

i.e., $\delta_t(i)$ is the best score (highest probability) along a single path, at time t, which accounts for the first t observations and ends in state S_i. By induction we have

$$\delta_{t+1}(j) = [\max_i \delta_t(i) a_{ij}] \cdot b_j(O_{t+1}). \tag{31}$$

To actually retrieve the state sequence, we need to keep track of the argument which maximized (31), for each t and j. We do this via the array $\psi_t(j)$. The complete procedure for finding the best state sequence can now be stated as follows:

1) Initialization:

$$\delta_1(i) = \pi_i b_i(O_1), \quad 1 \le i \le N \tag{32a}$$

$$\psi_1(i) = 0. \tag{32b}$$

2) Recursion:

$$\delta_t(j) = \max_{1 \le i \le N} [\delta_{t-1}(i) a_{ij}] b_j(O_t), \quad 2 \le t \le T, \quad 1 \le j \le N \tag{33a}$$

$$\psi_t(j) = \operatorname*{argmax}_{1 \le i \le N} [\delta_{t-1}(i) a_{ij}], \quad 2 \le t \le T, \quad 1 \le j \le N. \tag{33b}$$

3) Termination: (34a)

$$P^* = \max_{1 \le i \le N} [\delta_T(i)]$$

$$q_T^* = \operatorname*{argmax}_{1 \le i \le N} [\delta_T(i)]. \tag{34b}$$

4) Path (state sequence) backtracking:

$$q_t^* = \psi_{t+1}(q_{t+1}^*), \quad t = T-1, T-2, \cdots, 1. \tag{35}$$

It should be noted that the Viterbi algorithm is similar (except for the backtracking step) in implementation to the forward calculation of (19)–(21). The major difference is the maximization in (33a) over previous states which is used in place of the summing procedure in (20). It also should be clear that a lattice (or trellis) structure efficiently implements the computation of the Viterbi procedure.

C. Solution to Problem 3 [1]–[5]

The third, and by far the most difficult, problem of HMMs is to determine a method to adjust the model parameters (A, B, π) to maximize the probability of the observation sequence given the model. There is no known way to analytically solve for the model which maximizes the probability of the observation sequence. In fact, given any finite observation sequence as training data, there is no optimal way of estimating the model parameters. We can, however, choose $\lambda = (A, B, \pi)$ such that $P(O|\lambda)$ is locally maximized using an iterative procedure such as the Baum–Welch method (or equivalently the EM (expectation-modification) method [23]), or using gradient techniques [14]. In this section we discuss one iterative procedure, based primarily on the classic work of Baum and his colleagues, for choosing model parameters.

In order to describe the procedure for reestimation (iterative update and improvement) of HMM parameters, we first define $\xi_t(i, j)$, the probability of being in state S_i at time t, and state S_j at time $t+1$, given the model and the observation sequence, i.e.

$$\xi_t(i, j) = P(q_t = S_i, q_{t+1} = S_j|O, \lambda). \tag{36}$$

The sequence of events leading to the conditions required by (36) is illustrated in Fig. 6. It should be clear, from the

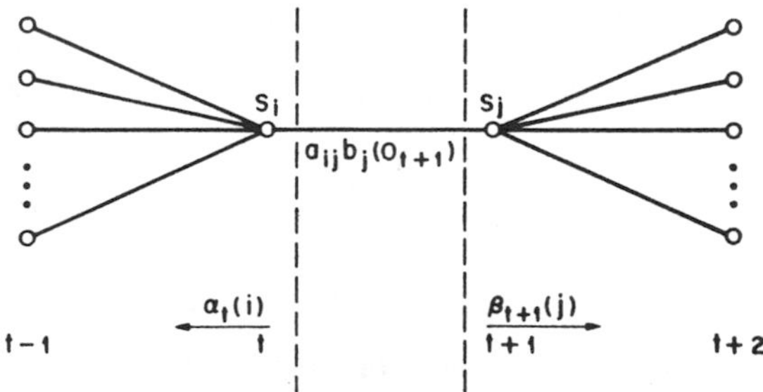

Fig. 6. Illustration of the sequence of operations required for the computation of the joint event that the system is in state S_i at time t and state S_j at time $t+1$.

definitions of the forward and backward variables, that we can write $\xi_t(i, j)$ in the form

$$\xi_t(i, j) = \frac{\alpha_t(i)\, a_{ij} b_j(O_{t+1})\, \beta_{t+1}(j)}{P(O|\lambda)} = \frac{\alpha_t(i)\, a_{ij} b_j(O_{t+1})\, \beta_{t+1}(j)}{\sum_{i=1}^{N} \sum_{j=1}^{N} \alpha_t(i)\, a_{ij} b_j(O_{t+1})\, \beta_{t+1}(j)} \tag{37}$$

where the numerator term is just $P(q_t = S_i, q_{t+1} = S_j, O|\lambda)$ and the division by $P(O|\lambda)$ gives the desired probability measure.

We have previously defined $\gamma_t(i)$ as the probability of being in state S_i at time t, given the observation sequence and the model; hence we can relate $\gamma_t(i)$ to $\xi_t(i, j)$ by summing over j, giving

$$\gamma_t(i) = \sum_{j=1}^{N} \xi_t(i, j). \tag{38}$$

If we sum $\gamma_t(i)$ over the time index t, we get a quantity which can be interpreted as the expected (over time) number of times that state S_i is visited, or equivalently, the expected number of transitions made from state S_i (if we exclude the time slot $t = T$ from the summation). Similarly, summation of $\xi_t(i, j)$ over t (from $t = 1$ to $t = T - 1$) can be interpreted as the expected number of transitions from state S_i to state S_j. That is

$$\sum_{t=1}^{T-1} \gamma_t(i) = \text{expected number of transitions from } S_i \tag{39a}$$

$$\sum_{t=1}^{T-1} \xi_t(i, j) = \text{expected number of transitions from } S_i \text{ to } S_j. \tag{39b}$$

Using the above formulas (and the concept of counting event occurrences) we can give a method for reestimation of the parameters of an HMM. A set of reasonable reestimation formulas for π, A, and B are

$$\bar{\pi}_i = \text{expected frequency (number of times) in state } S_i \text{ at time } (t = 1) = \gamma_1(i) \tag{40a}$$

$$\bar{a}_{ij} = \frac{\text{expected number of transitions from state } S_i \text{ to state } S_j}{\text{expected number of transitions from state } S_i} = \frac{\sum_{t=1}^{T-1} \xi_t(i, j)}{\sum_{t=1}^{T-1} \gamma_t(i)} \tag{40b}$$

$$\bar{b}_j(k) = \frac{\text{expected number of times in state } j \text{ and observing symbol } v_k}{\text{expected number of times in state } j} = \frac{\sum_{\substack{t=1 \\ \text{s.t. } O_t = v_k}}^{T} \gamma_t(j)}{\sum_{t=1}^{T} \gamma_t(j)}. \tag{40c}$$

If we define the current model as $\lambda = (A, B, \pi)$, and use that to compute the right-hand sides of (40a)–(40c), and we define the reestimated model as $\bar{\lambda} = \bar{A}, \bar{B}, \bar{\pi})$, as determined from the left-hand sides of (40a)–(40c), then it has been proven by Baum and his colleagues [6], [3] that either 1) the initial model λ defines a critical point of the likelihood function, in which case $\bar{\lambda} = \lambda$; or 2) model $\bar{\lambda}$ is more likely than model λ in the sense that $P(O|\bar{\lambda}) > P(O|\lambda)$, i.e., we have found a new model $\bar{\lambda}$ from which the observation sequence is more likely to have been produced.

Based on the above procedure, if we iteratively use $\bar{\lambda}$ in place of λ and repeat the reestimation calculation, we then can improve the probability of O being observed from the model until some limiting point is reached. The final result of this reestimation procedure is called a maximum likelihood estimate of the HMM. It should be pointed out that the forward-backward algorithm leads to local maxima only, and that in most problems of interest, the optimization surface is very complex and has many local maxima.

The reestimation formulas of (40a)–(40c) can be derived directly by maximizing (using standard constrained optimization techniques) Baum's auxiliary function

$$Q(\lambda, \bar{\lambda}) = \sum_{Q} P(Q|O, \lambda) \log [P(O, Q|\bar{\lambda})] \tag{41}$$

over $\bar{\lambda}$. It has been proven by Baum and his colleagues [6], [3] that maximization of $Q(\lambda, \bar{\lambda})$ leads to increased likelihood, i.e.

$$\max_{\bar{\lambda}} [Q(\lambda, \bar{\lambda})] \Rightarrow P(O|\bar{\lambda}) \geq P(O|\lambda). \tag{42}$$

Eventually the likelihood function converges to a critical point.

Notes on the Reestimation Procedure: The reestimation formulas can readily be interpreted as an implementation of the EM algorithm of statistics [23] in which the E (expectation) step is the calculation of the auxiliary function $Q(\lambda, \bar{\lambda})$, and the M (modification) step is the maximization over $\bar{\lambda}$. Thus the Baum–Welch reestimation equations are essentially identical to the EM steps for this particular problem.

An important aspect of the reestimation procedure is that the stochastic constraints of the HMM parameters, namely

$$\sum_{i=1}^{N} \bar{\pi}_i = 1 \tag{43a}$$

$$\sum_{j=1}^{N} \bar{a}_{ij} = 1, \quad 1 \leq i \leq N \tag{43b}$$

$$\sum_{k=1}^{M} \bar{b}_j(k) = 1, \quad 1 \leq j \leq N \tag{43c}$$

are automatically satisfied at each iteration. By looking at the parameter estimation problem as a constrained optimization of $P(O|\lambda)$ (subject to the constraints of (43)), the techniques of Lagrange multipliers can be used to find the values of π_i, a_{ij}, and $b_j(k)$ which maximize P (we use the notation $P = P(O|\lambda)$ as short-hand in this section). Based on setting up a standard Lagrange optimization using Lagrange multipliers, it can readily be shown that P is maximized when the following conditions are met:

$$\pi_i = \frac{\pi_i \dfrac{\partial P}{\partial \pi_i}}{\sum_{k=1}^{N} \pi_k \dfrac{\partial P}{\partial \pi_k}} \tag{44a}$$

$$a_{ij} = \frac{a_{ij} \dfrac{\partial P}{\partial a_{ij}}}{\sum_{k=1}^{N} a_{ik} \dfrac{\partial P}{\partial a_{ik}}} \tag{44b}$$

$$b_j(k) = \frac{b_j(k) \dfrac{\partial P}{\partial b_j(k)}}{\sum_{\ell=1}^{M} b_j(\ell) \dfrac{\partial P}{\partial b_j(\ell)}}. \tag{44c}$$

By appropriate manipulation of (44), the right-hand sides of each equation can be readily converted to be *identical* to the right-hand sides of each part of (40a)–(40c), thereby showing that the reestimation formulas are indeed exactly correct at critical points of P. In fact the form of (44) is essentially that of a reestimation formula in which the left-hand side is the reestimate and the right-hand side is computed using the current values of the variables.

Finally, we note that since the entire problem can be set up as an optimization problem, standard gradient techniques can be used to solve for "optimal" values of the model parameters [14]. Such procedures have been tried and have been shown to yield solutions comparable to those of the standard reestimation procedures.

IV. Types of HMMs

Until now, we have only considered the special case of ergodic or fully connected HMMs in which every state of the model could be reached (in a single step) from every other state of the model. (Strictly speaking, an ergodic model has the property that every state can be reached from every other state in a finite number of steps.) As shown in Fig. 7(a), for an $N = 4$ state model, this type of model has the property that every a_{ij} coefficient is positive. Hence for the example of Fig. 7a we have

$$A = \begin{bmatrix} a_{11} & a_{12} & a_{13} & a_{14} \\ a_{21} & a_{22} & a_{23} & a_{24} \\ a_{31} & a_{32} & a_{33} & a_{34} \\ a_{41} & a_{42} & a_{43} & a_{44} \end{bmatrix}.$$

For some applications, in particular those to be discussed later in this paper, other types of HMMs have been found to account for observed properties of the signal being modeled better than the standard ergodic model. One such model is shown in Fig. 7(b). This model is called a left-right model or a Bakis model [11], [10] because the underlying state sequence associated with the model has the property that as time increases the state index increases (or stays the same), i.e., the states proceed from left to right. Clearly the left-right type of HMM has the desirable property that it can readily model signals whose properties change over time—e.g., speech. The fundamental property of all left-right

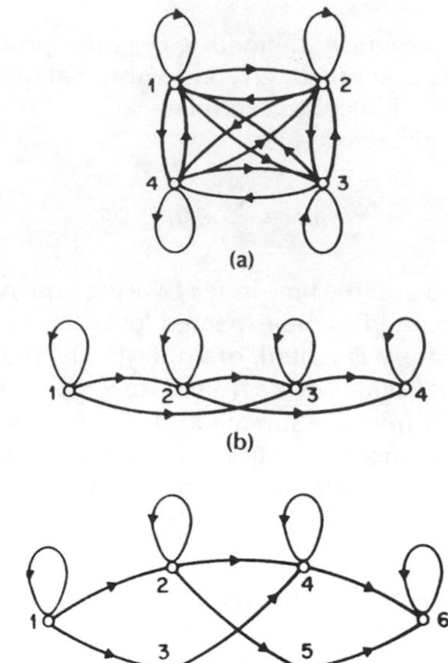

Fig. 7. Illustration of 3 distinct types of HMMs. (a) A 4-state ergodic model. (b) A 4-state left-right model. (c) A 6-state parallel path left-right model.

HMMs is that the state transition coefficients have the property

$$a_{ij} = 0, \quad j < i \tag{45}$$

i.e., no transitions are allowed to states whose indices are lower than the current state. Furthermore, the initial state probabilities have the property

$$\pi_i = \begin{cases} 0, & i \neq 1 \\ 1, & i = 1 \end{cases} \tag{46}$$

since the state sequence must begin in state 1 (and end in state N). Often, with left-right models, additional constraints are placed on the state transition coefficients to make sure that large changes in state indices do not occur; hence a constraint of the form

$$a_{ij} = 0, \quad j > i + \Delta \tag{47}$$

is often used. In particular, for the example of Fig. 7(b), the value of Δ is 2, i.e., no jumps of more than 2 states are allowed. The form of the state transition matrix for the example of Fig. 7(b) is thus

$$A = \begin{bmatrix} a_{11} & a_{12} & a_{13} & 0 \\ 0 & a_{22} & a_{23} & a_{24} \\ 0 & 0 & a_{33} & a_{34} \\ 0 & 0 & 0 & a_{44} \end{bmatrix}.$$

It should be clear that, for the last state in a left-right model, that the state transition coefficients are specified as

$$a_{NN} = 1 \tag{48a}$$

$$a_{Ni} = 0, \quad i < N. \tag{48b}$$

Although we have dichotomized HMMs into ergodic and left-right models, there are many possible variations and combinations possible. By way of example, Fig. 7(c) shows a cross-coupled connection of two parallel left-right HMMs. Strictly speaking, this model is a left-right model (it obeys all the a_{ij} constraints); however, it can be seen that it has certain flexibility not present in a strict left-right model (i.e., one without parallel paths).

It should be clear that the imposition of the constraints of the left-right model, or those of the constrained jump model, essentially have no effect on the reestimation procedure. This is the case because any HMM parameter set to zero initially, will remain at zero throughout the reestimation procedure (see (44)).

A. Continuous Observation Densities in HMMs [24]-[26]

All of our discussion, to this point, has considered only the case when the observations were characterized as discrete symbols chosen from a finite alphabet, and therefore we could use a discrete probability density within each state of this model. The problem with this approach, at least for some applications, is that the observations are continuous signals (or vectors). Although it is possible to quantize such continuous signals via codebooks, etc., there might be serious degradation associated with such quantization. Hence it would be advantageous to be able to use HMMs with continuous observation densities.

In order to use a continuous observation density, some restrictions have to be placed on the form of the model probability density function (pdf) to insure that the parameters of the pdf can be reestimated in a consistent way. The most general representation of the pdf, for which a reestimation procedure has been formulated [24]-[26], is a finite mixture of the form

$$b_j(\mathbf{O}) = \sum_{m=1}^{M} c_{jm} \mathfrak{N}[\mathbf{O}, \boldsymbol{\mu}_{jm}, \mathbf{U}_{jm}], \quad 1 \le j \le N \tag{49}$$

where $\mathbf{O}$ is the vector being modeled, c_{jm} is the mixture coefficient for the mth mixture in state j and $\mathfrak{N}$ is any log-concave or elliptically symmetric density [24] (e.g., Gaussian), with mean vector $\boldsymbol{\mu}_{jm}$ and covariance matrix $\mathbf{U}_{jm}$ for the mth mixture component in state j. Usually a Gaussian density is used for $\mathfrak{N}$. The mixture gains c_{jm} satisfy the stochastic constraint

$$\sum_{m=1}^{M} c_{jm} = 1, \quad 1 \le j \le N \tag{50a}$$

$$c_{jm} \ge 0, \quad 1 \le j \le N, 1 \le m \le M \tag{50b}$$

so that the pdf is properly normalized, i.e.,

$$\int_{-\infty}^{\infty} b_j(x)\, dx = 1, \quad 1 \le j \le N. \tag{51}$$

The pdf of (49) can be used to approximate, arbitrarily closely, any finite, continuous density function. Hence it can be applied to a wide range of problems.

It can be shown [24]-[26] that the reestimation formulas for the coefficients of the mixture density, i.e., c_{jm}, $\boldsymbol{\mu}_{jk}$, and $\mathbf{U}_{jk}$, are of the form

$$\bar{c}_{jk} = \frac{\sum_{t=1}^{T} \gamma_t(j, k)}{\sum_{t=1}^{T} \sum_{k=1}^{M} \gamma_t(j, k)} \tag{52}$$

$$\bar{\boldsymbol{\mu}}_{jk} = \frac{\sum_{t=1}^{T} \gamma_t(j, k) \cdot \mathbf{O}_t}{\sum_{t=1}^{T} \gamma_t(j, k)} \tag{53}$$

$$\bar{\mathbf{U}}_{jk} = \frac{\sum_{t=1}^{T} \gamma_t(j, k) \cdot (\mathbf{O}_t - \boldsymbol{\mu}_{jk})(\mathbf{O}_t - \boldsymbol{\mu}_{jk})'}{\sum_{t=1}^{T} \gamma_t(j, k)} \tag{54}$$

where prime denotes vector transpose and where $\gamma_t(j, k)$ is the probability of being in state j at time t with the kth mixture component accounting for $\mathbf{O}_t$, i.e.,

$$\gamma_t(j, k) = \left[\frac{\alpha_t(j)\, \beta_t(j)}{\sum_{j=1}^{N} \alpha_t(j)\, \beta_t(j)}\right] \left[\frac{c_{jk} \mathfrak{N}(\mathbf{O}_t, \boldsymbol{\mu}_{jk}, \mathbf{U}_{jk})}{\sum_{m=1}^{M} c_{jm} \mathfrak{N}(\mathbf{O}_t, \boldsymbol{\mu}_{jm}, \mathbf{U}_{jm})}\right].$$

(The term $\gamma_t(j, k)$ generalizes to $\gamma_t(j)$ of (26) in the case of a simple mixture, or a discrete density.) The reestimation formula for a_{ij} is identical to the one used for discrete observation densities (i.e., (40b)). The interpretation of (52)-(54) is fairly straightforward. The reestimation formula for c_{jk} is the ratio between the expected number of times the system is in state j using the kth mixture component, and the expected number of times the system is in state j. Similarly, the reestimation formula for the mean vector $\boldsymbol{\mu}_{jk}$ weights each numerator term of (52) by the observation, thereby giving the expected value of the portion of the observation vector accounted for by the kth mixture component. A similar interpretation can be given for the reestimation term for the covariance matrix $\mathbf{U}_{jk}$.

B. Autoregressive HMMS [27], [28]

Although the general formulation of continuous density HMMs is applicable to a wide range of problems, there is one other very interesting class of HMMs that is particularly applicable to speech processing. This is the class of autoregressive HMMs [27], [28]. For this class, the observation vectors are drawn from an autoregression process.

To be more specific, consider the observation vector $\mathbf{O}$ with components $(x_0, x_1, x_2, \cdots, x_{K-1})$. Since the basis probability density function for the observation vector is Gaussian autoregressive (or order p), then the components of $\mathbf{O}$ are related by

$$\mathbf{O}_k = -\sum_{i=1}^{p} a_i \mathbf{O}_{k-i} + e_k \tag{55}$$

where e_k, $k = 0, 1, 2, \cdots, K-1$ are Gaussian, independent, identically distributed random variables with zero mean and variance σ^2, and a_i, $i = 1, 2, \cdots, p$, are the autoregression or predictor coefficients. It can be shown that for large K, the density function for $\mathbf{O}$ is approximately

$$f(\mathbf{O}) = (2\pi\sigma^2)^{-K/2} \exp\left\{-\frac{1}{2\sigma^2}\, \delta(\mathbf{O}, \mathbf{a})\right\} \tag{56}$$

where

$$\delta(\mathbf{O}, \mathbf{a}) = r_a(0)\, r(0) + 2 \sum_{i=1}^{p} r_a(i)\, r(i) \tag{57a}$$

$$\mathbf{a}' = [1, a_1, a_2, \cdots, a_p] \tag{57b}$$

$$r_a(i) = \sum_{n=0}^{p-i} a_n a_{n+i} \qquad (a_0 = 1),\ 1 \le i \le p \tag{57c}$$

$$r(i) = \sum_{n=0}^{K-i-1} x_n x_{n+i} \qquad 0 \le i \le p. \tag{57d}$$

In the above equations it can be recognized that $r(i)$ is the autocorrelation of the observation samples, and $r_a(i)$ is the autocorrelation of the autoregressive coefficients.

The total (frame) prediction residual α can be written as

$$\alpha = E\left[\sum_{i=1}^{K} (e_i)^2\right] = K\sigma^2 \tag{58}$$

where σ^2 is the variance per sample of the error signal. Consider the normalized observation vector

$$\hat{\mathbf{O}} = \frac{\mathbf{O}}{\sqrt{\alpha}} = \frac{\mathbf{O}}{\sqrt{K\sigma^2}} \tag{59}$$

where each sample x_i is divided by $\sqrt{K\sigma^2}$, i.e., each sample is normalized by the sample variance. Then $f(\hat{\mathbf{O}})$ can be written as

$$f(\hat{\mathbf{O}}) = \left(\frac{2\pi}{K}\right)^{-K/2} \exp\left(-\frac{K}{2}\,\delta(\hat{\mathbf{O}}, \mathbf{a})\right). \tag{60}$$

In practice, the factor K (in front of the exponential of (60)) is replaced by an *effective* frame length $\hat{K}$ which represents the effective length of each data vector. Thus if consecutive data vectors are overlapped by 3 to 1, then we would use $\hat{K} = K/3$ in (60), so that the contribution of each sample of signal to the overall density is counted exactly once.

The way in which we use Gaussian autoregressive density in HMMs is straightforward. We assume a mixture density of the form

$$b_j(\mathbf{O}) = \sum_{m=1}^{M} c_{jm} b_{jm}(\mathbf{O}) \tag{61}$$

where each $b_{jm}(\mathbf{O})$ is the density defined by (60) with autoregression vector $\mathbf{a}_{jm}$ (or equivalently by autocorrelation vector $\mathbf{r}_{a_{jm}}$), i.e.,

$$b_{jm}(\mathbf{O}) = \left(\frac{2\pi}{K}\right)^{-K/2} \exp\left\{-\frac{K}{2}\,\delta(\mathbf{O}, \mathbf{a}_{jm})\right\}. \tag{62}$$

A reestimation formula for the sequence autocorrelation, $r(i)$ of (57d), for the jth state, kth mixture, component has been derived, and is of the form

$$\bar{\mathbf{r}}_{jk} = \frac{\sum_{t=1}^{T} \gamma_t(j, k) \cdot \mathbf{r}_t}{\sum_{t=1}^{T} \gamma_t(j, k)} \tag{63a}$$

where $\gamma_t(j, k)$ is defined as the probability of being in state j at time t and using mixture component k, i.e.,

$$\gamma_t(j, k) = \left[\frac{\alpha_t(j)\,\beta_t(j)}{\sum_{j=1}^{N} \alpha_t(j)\,\beta_t(j)}\right]\left[\frac{c_{jk} b_{jk}(\mathbf{O}_t)}{\sum_{k=1}^{M} c_{jk} b_{jk}(\mathbf{O}_t)}\right]. \tag{63b}$$

It can be seen that $\bar{\mathbf{r}}_{jk}$ is a weighted sum (by probability of occurrence) of the normalized autocorrelations of the frames in the observation sequence. From $\bar{\mathbf{r}}_{jk}$, one can solve a set of normal equations to obtain the corresponding autoregressive coefficient vector $\bar{\mathbf{a}}_{jk}$, for the kth mixture of state j. The new autocorrection vectors of the autoregression coefficients can then be calculated using (57c), thereby closing the reestimation loop.

C. Variants on HMM Structures—Null Transitions and Tied States

Throughout this paper we have considered HMMs in which the observations were associated with states of the model. It is also possible to consider models in which the observations are associated with the arcs of the model. This type of HMM has been used extensively in the IBM continuous speech recognizer [13]. It has been found useful, for this type of model, to allow transitions which produce no output—i.e., jumps from one state to another which produce no observation [13]. Such transitions are called null transitions and are designated by a dashed line with the symbol ϕ used to denote the null output.

Fig. 8 illustrates 3 examples (from speech processing tasks) where null arcs have been successfully utilized. The example of part (a) corresponds to an HMM (a left–right model) with a large number of states in which it is possible to omit transitions between any pair of states. Hence it is possible to generate observation sequences with as few as 1 observation and still account for a path which begins in state 1 and ends in state N.

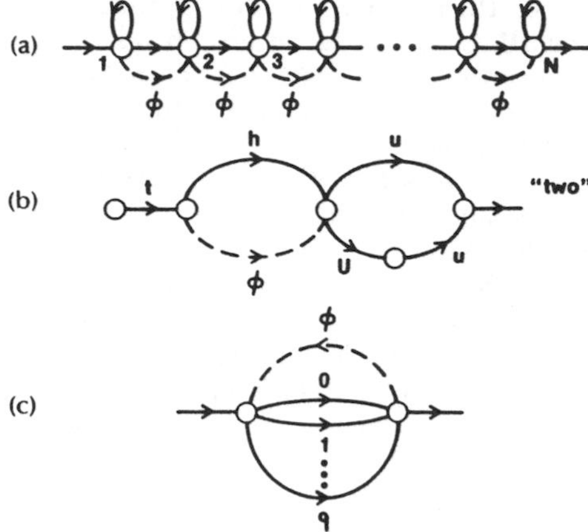

Fig. 8. Examples of networks incorporating null transitions. (a) Left–right model. (b) Finite state network. (c) Grammar network.

The example of Fig. 8(b) is a finite state network (FSN) representation of a word in terms of linguistic unit models (i.e., the sound on each arc is itself an HMM). For this model the null transition gives a compact and efficient way of describing alternate word pronunciations (i.e., symbol delections).

Finally the FSN of Fig. 8(c) shows how the ability to insert a null transition into a grammar network allows a relatively simple network to generate arbitrarily long word (digit) sequences. In the example shown in Fig. 8(c), the null transition allows the network to generate arbitrary sequences of digits of arbitrary length by returning to the initial state after each individual digit is produced.

Another interesting variation in the HMM structure is the concept of parameter tieing [13]. Basically the idea is to set up an equivalence relation between HMM parameters in different states. In this manner the number of independent parameters in the model is reduced and the parameter estimation becomes somewhat simpler. Parameter tieing is used in cases where the observation density (for example) is known to be the same in 2 or more states. Such cases occur often in characterizing speech sounds. The technique is especially appropriate in the case where there is insufficient training data to estimate, reliably, a large number of model parameters. For such cases it is appropriate to tie model parameters so as to reduce the number of parameters (i.e., size of the model) thereby making the parameter estimation problem somewhat simpler. We will discuss this method later in this paper.

D. Inclusion of Explicit State Duration Density in HMMs[8] *[29], [30]*

Perhaps the major weakness of conventional HMMs is the modeling of state duration. Earlier we showed (5) that the inherent duration probability density $p_i(d)$ associated with state S_i, with self transition coefficient a_{ii}, was of the form

$$\begin{aligned} p_i(d) &= (a_{ii})^{d-1}(1 - a_{ii}) \\ &= \text{probability of } d \text{ consecutive observations in state } S_i. \end{aligned} \tag{64}$$

For most physical signals, this exponential state duration density is inappropriate. Instead we would prefer to explicitly model duration density in some analytic form. Fig. 9

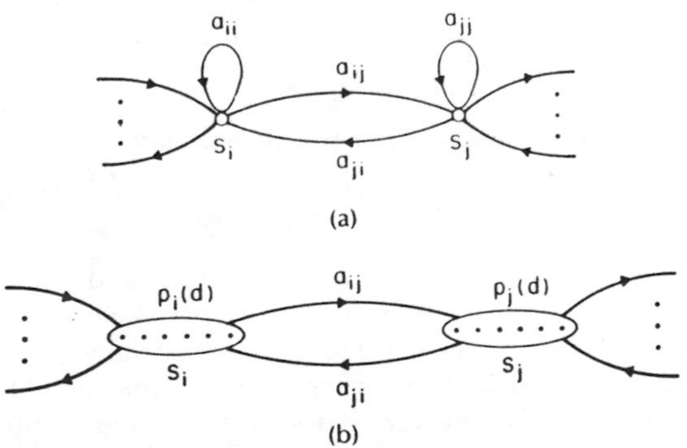

Fig. 9. Illustration of general interstate connections of (a) a normal HMM with exponential state duration density, and (b) a variable duration HMM with specified state densities and no self transitions from a state back to itself.

illustrates, for a pair of model states S_i and S_j, the differences between HMMs without and with explicit duration density. In part (a) the states have exponential duration densities based on self-transition coefficients a_{ii} and a_{jj}, respectively. In part (b), the self-transition coefficients are set to zero, and an explicit duration density is specified.[9] For this case, a transition is made only after the appropriate number of observations have occurred in the state (as specified by the duration density).

Based on the simple model of Fig. 9(b), the sequence of events of the variable duration HMM is as follows:

1) An initial state, $q_1 = S_i$, is chosen according to the initial state distribution π_i.
2) A duration d_1 is chosen according to the state duration density $p_{q_1}(d_1)$. (For expedience and ease of implementation the duration density $p_q(d)$ is truncated at a maximum duration value D.)
3) Observations $O_1 O_2 \cdots O_{d_1}$ are chosen according to the joint observation density, $b_{q_1}(O_1 O_2 \cdots O_{d_1})$. Generally we assume independent of observations so that $b_{q_1}(O_1 O_2 \cdots O_{d_1}) = \Pi_{t=1}^{d_1} b_{q_1}(O_t)$.
4) The next state, $q_2 = S_j$, is chosen according to the state transition probabilities, $a_{q_1q_2}$, with the constraint that $a_{q_1q_2} = 0$, i.e., no transition back to the same state can occur. (Clearly this is a requirement since we assume that, in state q_1, exactly d_1 observations occur.)

A little thought should convince the reader that the variable duration HMM can be made equivalent to the standard HMM by setting $p_i(d)$ to be the exponential density of (64).

Using the above formulation, several changes must be made to the formulas of Section III to allow calculation of $P(O|\lambda)$ and for reestimation of all model parameters. In particular we assume that the first state begins at $t = 1$ and the last state ends at $t = T$, i.e., entire duration intervals are included with the observation sequence. We then define the forward variable $\alpha_t(i)$ as

$$\alpha_t(i) = P(O_1 O_2 \cdots O_t, S_i \text{ ends at } t|\lambda). \tag{65}$$

We assume that a total of r states have been visited during the first t observations and we denote the states as $q_1, q_2, \cdots, q_r$ with durations associated with each state of $d_1, d_2, \cdots, d_r$. Thus the constraints of (65) are

$$q_r = S_i \tag{66a}$$

$$\sum_{s=1}^{r} d_s = t. \tag{66b}$$

Equation (65) can then be written as

$$\begin{aligned} \alpha_t(i) = \sum_q \sum_d \pi_{q_1} \cdot p_{q_1}(d_1) \cdot P(O_1 O_2 \cdots O_{d_1}|q_1) \\ \cdot a_{q_1q_2} p_{q_2}(d_2)\, P(O_{d_1+1} \cdots O_{d_1+d_2}|q_2) \cdots \\ \cdot a_{q_{r-1}q_r} p_{q_r}(d_r)\, P(O_{d_1+d_2+\cdots+d_{r-1}+1} \cdots O_t|q_r) \end{aligned} \tag{67}$$

where the sum is over all states q and all possible state durations d. By induction we can write $\alpha_t(j)$ as

$$\alpha_t(j) = \sum_{i=1}^{N} \sum_{d=1}^{D} \alpha_{t-d}(i)\, a_{ij} p_j(d) \prod_{s=t-d+1}^{t} b_j(\mathbf{O}_s) \tag{68}$$

where D is the maximum duration within any state. To initialize the computation of $\alpha_t(j)$ we use

$$\alpha_1(i) = \pi_i p_i(1) \cdot b_i(\mathbf{O}_1) \tag{69a}$$

$$\alpha_2(i) = \pi_i p_i(2) \prod_{s=1}^{2} b_i(\mathbf{O}_s) + \sum_{\substack{j=1 \\ j \neq i}}^{N} \alpha_1(j)\, a_{ji} p_i(1)\, b_i(\mathbf{O}_2) \tag{69b}$$

[8] In cases where a Bakis type model is used, i.e., left-right models where the number of states is proportional to the average duration, explicit inclusion of state duration density is neither necessary nor is it useful.

[9] Again the ideas behind using explicit state duration densities are due to Jack Ferguson of IDA. Most of the material in this section is based on Ferguson's original work.

$$\alpha_3(i) = \pi_i p_i(3) \prod_{s=1}^{3} b_i(\mathbf{O}_s) + \sum_{d=1}^{2} \sum_{\substack{j=1 \\ j \neq i}}^{N} \alpha_{3-d}(j)\, a_{ji} p_i(d) \cdot \prod_{s=4-d}^{3} b_i(\mathbf{O}_s) \tag{69c}$$

etc., until $\alpha_D(i)$ is computed; then (68) can be used for all $t > D$. It should be clear that the desired probability of O given the model λ can be written in terms of the α's as

$$P(O|\lambda) = \sum_{i=1}^{N} \alpha_T(i) \tag{70}$$

as was previously used for ordinary HMMs.

In order to give reestimation formulas for all the variables of the variable duration HMM, we must define three more forward-backward variables, namely

$$\alpha_t^*(i) = P(O_1\, O_2 \cdots O_t,\, S_i \text{ begins at } t+1|\lambda) \tag{71}$$

$$\beta_t(i) = P(O_{t+1} \cdots O_T|S_i \text{ ends at } t,\, \lambda) \tag{72}$$

$$\beta_t^*(i) = P(O_{t+1} \cdots O_T|S_i \text{ begins at } t+1,\, \lambda). \tag{73}$$

The relationships between α, α^*, β, and β^* are as follows:

$$\alpha_t^*(j) = \sum_{i=1}^{N} \alpha_t(i) a_{ij} \tag{74}$$

$$\alpha_t(i) = \sum_{d=1}^{D} \alpha_{t-d}^*(i)\, p_i(d) \prod_{s=t-d+1}^{t} b_i(\mathbf{O}_s) \tag{75}$$

$$\beta_t(i) = \sum_{j=1}^{N} a_{ij}\beta_t^*(j) \tag{76}$$

$$\beta_t^*(i) = \sum_{d=1}^{D} \beta_{t+d}(i)\, p_i(d) \prod_{s=t+1}^{t+d} b_i(\mathbf{O}_s). \tag{77}$$

Based on the above relationships and definitions, the reestimation formulas for the variable duration HMM are

$$\overline{\pi}_i = \frac{\pi_i \beta_0^*(i)}{P(O|\lambda)} \tag{78}$$

$$\overline{a}_{ij} = \frac{\sum_{t=1}^{T} \alpha_t(i)\, a_{ij}\beta_t^*(j)}{\sum_{j=1}^{N}\sum_{t=1}^{T} \alpha_t(i)\, a_{ij}\beta_t^*(j)} \tag{79}$$

$$\overline{b}_i(k) = \frac{\sum_{\substack{t=1 \\ \text{s.t. } O_t = k}}^{T} \left[\sum_{\tau<t} \alpha_\tau^*(i) \cdot \beta_\tau^*(i) - \sum_{\tau<t} \alpha_\tau(i)\, \beta_\tau(i) \right]}{\sum_{k=1}^{M} \sum_{\substack{t=1 \\ \text{s.t. } O_t = v_k}}^{T} \left[\sum_{\tau<t} \alpha_\tau^*(i) \cdot \beta_\tau^*(i) - \sum_{\tau<t} \alpha_\tau(i)\, \beta_\tau(i) \right]} \tag{80}$$

$$\overline{p}_i(d) = \frac{\sum_{t=1}^{T} \alpha_t^*(i)\, p_i(d)\, \beta_{t+d}(i) \prod_{s=t+1}^{t+d} b_i(\mathbf{O}_s)}{\sum_{d=1}^{D}\sum_{t=1}^{T} \alpha_t^*(i)\, p_i(d)\, \beta_{t+d}(i) \prod_{s=t+1}^{t+d} b_i(\mathbf{O}_s)}. \tag{81}$$

The interpretation of the reestimation formulas is the following. The formula for $\overline{\pi}_i$ is the probability that state i was the first state, given O. The formula for $\overline{a}_{ij}$ *is almost the same as for the usual HMM except it uses the condition that the alpha terms in which a state ends at t,* join with the beta terms in which a new state begins at $t + 1$. The formula for $\overline{b}_i(k)$ (assuming a discrete density) is the expected number of times that observation $O_t = v_k$ occurred in state i, normalized by the expected number of times that any observation occurred in state i. Finally, the reestimation formula for $\overline{p}_i(d)$ is the ratio of the expected number of times state i occurred with duration d, to the expected number of times state i occurred with any duration.

The importance of incorporating state duration densities is reflected in the observation that, for some problems, the quality of the modeling is significantly improved when explicit state duration densities are used. However, there are drawbacks to the use of the variable duration model discussed in this section. One is the greatly increased computational load associated with using variable durations. It can be seen from the definition and initialization conditions on the forward variable $\alpha_t(i)$, from (68)–(69), that about D times the storage and $D^2/2$ times the computation is required. For D on the order of 25 (as is reasonable for many speech processing problems), computation is increased by a factor of 300. Another problem with the variable duration models is the large number of parameters (D), associated with each state, that must be estimated, in addition to the usual HMM parameters. Furthermore, for a fixed number of observations T, in the training set, there are, on average, fewer state transitions and much less data to estimate $p_i(d)$ than would be used in a standard HMM. Thus the reestimation problem is more difficult for variable duration HMMs than for the standard HMM.

One proposal to alleviate some of these problems is to use a parametric state duration density instead of the non-parametric $p_i(d)$ used above [29], [30]. In particular, proposals include the Gaussian family with

$$p_i(d) = \mathfrak{N}(d, \mu_i, \sigma_i^2) \tag{82}$$

with parameters μ_i and σ_i^2, or the Gamma family with

$$p_i(d) = \frac{\eta_i^{\nu_i} d^{\nu_i - 1} e^{-\eta_i d}}{\Gamma(\nu_i)} \tag{83}$$

with parameters ν_i and η_i and with mean $\nu_i\eta_i^{-1}$ and variance $\nu_i\eta_i^{-2}$. Reestimation formulas for η_i and ν_i have been derived and used with good results [19]. Another possibility, which has been used with good success, is to assume a uniform duration distribution (over an appropriate range of durations) and use a path-constrained Viterbi decoding procedure [31].

E. Optimization Criterion—ML, MMI, and MDI [32], [33]

The basic philosophy of HMMs is that a signal (or observation sequence) can be well modeled if the parameters of an HMM are carefully and correctly chosen. The problem with this philosophy is that it is sometimes inaccurate—either because the signal does not obey the constraints of the HMM, or because it is too difficult to get reliable estimates of all HMM parameters. To alleviate this type of problem, there has been proposed at least two alternatives to the standard maximum likelihood (ML) optimization procedure for estimating HMM parameters.

The first alternative [32] is based on the idea that several HMMs are to be designed and we wish to design them all at the same time in such a way so as to maximize the discrimination power of each model (i.e., each model's ability to distinguish between observation sequences generated by the correct model and those generated by alternative models). We denote the different HMMs as λ_ν, $\nu = 1, 2, \cdots, V$. The standard ML design criterion is to use a separate training sequence of observations O^ν to derive model parameters for each model λ_ν. Thus the standard ML optimization yields

$$P_\nu^* = \max_{\lambda_\nu} P(O^\nu|\lambda_\nu). \tag{84}$$

The proposed alternative design criterion [31] is the maximum mutual information (MMI) criterion in which the average mutual information I between the observation sequence O^ν and the *complete* set of models $\lambda = (\lambda_1, \lambda_2, \cdots, \lambda_V)$ is maximized. One possible way of implementing this[10] is

$$I_\nu^* = \max_{\lambda} \left[\log P(O^\nu|\lambda_\nu) - \log \sum_{w=1}^{V} P(O^\nu|\lambda_w)\right] \tag{85}$$

i.e., choose λ so as to separate the correct model λ_ν from all other models on the training sequence O^ν. By summing (85) over all training sequences, one would hope to attain the most separated set of models possible. Thus a possible implementation would be

$$I^* = \max_{\lambda} \left\{\sum_{\nu=1}^{V} \left[\log P(O^\nu|\lambda_\nu) - \log \sum_{w=1}^{V} P(O^\nu|\lambda_w)\right]\right\}. \tag{86}$$

There are various theoretical reasons why analytical (or reestimation type) solutions to (86) cannot be realized. Thus the only known way of actually solving (86) is via general optimization procedures like the steepest descent methods [32].

The second alternative philosophy is to assume that the signal to be modeled was not necessarily generated by a Markov source, but does obey certain constraints (e.g., positive definite correlation function) [33]. The goal of the design procedure is therefore to choose HMM parameters which minimize the discrimination information (DI) or the cross entropy between the set of valid (i.e., which satisfy the measurements) signal probability densities (call this set Q), and the set of HMM probability densities (call this set P_λ), where the DI between Q and P_λ can generally be written in the form

$$D(Q\|P_\lambda) = \int q(y) \ln (q(y)/p(y))\, dy \tag{87}$$

where q and p are the probability density functions corresponding to Q and P_λ. Techniques for minimizing (87) (thereby giving an MDI solution) for the optimum values of $\lambda = (A, B, \pi)$ are highly nontrivial; however, they use a generalized Baum algorithm as the core of each iteration, and thus are efficiently tailored to hidden Markov modeling [33].

It has been shown that the ML, MMI, and MDI approaches can *all* be uniformly formulated as MDI approaches.[11] The three approaches differ in either the probability density attributed to the source being modeled, or in the model effectively being used. None of the approaches, however, assumes that the source has the probability distribution of the model.

[10] In (85) and (86) we assume that all words are equiprobable, i.e., $p(w) = 1/V$.

[11] Y. Ephraim and L. Rabiner, "On the Relations Between Modeling Approaches for Speech Recognition," to appear in IEEE Transactions on Information Theory.

F. Comparison of HMMs [34]

An interesting question associated with HMMs is the following: Given two HMMs, λ_1 and λ_2, what is a reasonable measure of the similarity of the two models? A key point here is the similarity criterion. By way of example, consider the case of two models

$$\lambda_1 = (A_1, B_1, \pi_1) \quad \lambda_2 = (A_2, B_2, \pi_2)$$

with

$$A_1 = \begin{bmatrix} p & 1-p \\ 1-p & p \end{bmatrix} \quad B_1 = \begin{bmatrix} q & 1-q \\ 1-q & q \end{bmatrix}$$

$$\pi_1 = [1/2 \;\; 1/2]$$

and

$$A_2 = \begin{bmatrix} r & 1-r \\ 1-r & r \end{bmatrix} \quad B_2 = \begin{bmatrix} s & 1-s \\ 1-s & s \end{bmatrix} \quad \pi_2 = [1/2 \;\; 1/2].$$

For λ_1 to be equivalent to λ_2, in the sense of having the same statistical properties for the observation symbols, i.e., $E[O_t = v_k|\lambda_1] = E[O_t = v_k|\lambda_2]$, for all v_k, we require

$$pq + (1-p)(1-q) = rs + (1-r)(1-s)$$

or, by solving for s, we get

$$s = \frac{p + q - 2pq}{1 - 2r}.$$

By choosing (arbitrarily) $p = 0.6$, $q = 0.7$, $r = 0.2$, we get $s = 13/30 \approx 0.433$. Thus, even when the two models, λ_1 and λ_2, look ostensibly very different (i.e., A_1 is very different from A_2 and B_1 is very different from B_2), statistical equivalence of the models can occur.

We can generalize the concept of model distance (dissimilarity) by defining a distance measure $D(\lambda_1, \lambda_2)$, between two Markov models, λ_1 and λ_2, as

$$D(\lambda_1, \lambda_2) = \frac{1}{T} [\log P(O^{(2)}|\lambda_1) - \log P(O^{(2)}|\lambda_2)] \tag{88}$$

where $O^{(2)} = O_1 O_2 O_3 \cdots O_T$ is a sequence of observations *generated* by model λ_2 [34]. Basically (88) is a measure of how well model λ_1 matches observations generated by model λ_2, relative to how well model λ_2 matches observations generated by itself. Several interpretations of (88) exist in terms of cross entropy, or divergence, or discrimination information [34].

One of the problems with the distance measure of (88) is that it is nonsymmetric. Hence a natural expression of this measure is the symmetrized version, namely

$$D_s(\lambda_1, \lambda_2) = \frac{D(\lambda_1, \lambda_2) + D(\lambda_2, \lambda_1)}{2}. \tag{89}$$

V. Implementation Issues for HMMs

The discussion in the previous two sections has primarily dealt with the theory of HMMs and several variations on the form of the model. In this section we deal with several practical implementation issues including scaling, multiple observation sequences, initial parameter estimates, missing data, and choice of model size and type. For some of these implementation issues we can prescribe exact analytical solutions; for other issues we can only provide some seat-of-the-pants experience gained from working with HMMs over the last several years.

A. Scaling [14]

In order to understand why scaling is required for implementing the reestimation procedure of HMMs, consider the definition of $\alpha_t(i)$ of (18). It can be seen that $\alpha_t(i)$ consists of the sum of a large number of terms, each of the form

$$\left(\prod_{s=1}^{t-1} a_{q_s q_{s+1}} \prod_{s=1}^{t} b_{q_s}(\mathbf{O}_s)\right)$$

with $q_t = S_i$. Since each a and b term is less than 1 (generally significantly less than 1), it can be seen that as t starts to get big (e.g., 10 or more), each term of $\alpha_t(i)$ starts to head exponentially to zero. For sufficiently large t (e.g., 100 or more) the dynamic range of the $\alpha_t(i)$ computation will exceed the precision range of essentially any machine (even in double precision). Hence the only reasonable way of performing the computation is by incorporating a scaling procedure.

The basic scaling procedure which is used is to multiply $\alpha_t(i)$ by a scaling coefficient that is independent of i (i.e., it depends only on t), with the goal of keeping the scaled $\alpha_t(i)$ within the dynamic range of the computer for $1 \le t \le T$. A similar scaling is done to the $\beta_t(i)$ coefficients (since these also tend to zero exponentially fast) and then, at the end of the computation, the scaling coefficients are canceled out exactly.

To understand this scaling procedure better, consider the reestimation formula for the state transition coefficients a_{ij}. If we write the reestimation formula (41) directly in terms of the forward and backward variables we get

$$\overline{a_{ij}} = \frac{\sum_{t=1}^{T-1} \alpha_t(i)\, a_{ij} b_j(O_{t+1})\, \beta_{t+1}(j)}{\sum_{t=1}^{T} \sum_{j=1}^{N} \alpha_t(i)\, a_{ij} b_j(O_{t+1})\, \beta_{t+1}(j)}. \tag{90}$$

Consider the computation of $\alpha_t(i)$. For each t, we first compute $\alpha_t(i)$ according to the induction formula (20), and then we multiply it by a scaling coefficient c_t, where

$$c_t = \frac{1}{\sum_{i=1}^{N} \alpha_t(i)}. \tag{91}$$

Thus, for a fixed t, we first compute

$$\alpha_t(i) = \sum_{j=1}^{N} \hat{\alpha}_{t-1}(j)\, a_{ij} b_j(O_t). \tag{92a}$$

Then the scaled coefficient set $\hat{\alpha}_t(i)$ is computed as

$$\hat{\alpha}_t(i) = \frac{\sum_{j=1}^{N} \hat{\alpha}_{t-1}(j)\, a_{ij} b_j(O_t)}{\sum_{i=1}^{N} \sum_{j=1}^{N} \hat{\alpha}_{t-1}(j)\, a_{ij} b_j(O_t)}. \tag{92b}$$

By induction we can write $\hat{\alpha}_{t-1}(j)$ as

$$\hat{\alpha}_{t-1}(j) = \left(\prod_{\tau=1}^{t-1} c_\tau\right) \alpha_{t-1}(j). \tag{93a}$$

Thus we can write $\hat{\alpha}_t(i)$ as

$$\hat{\alpha}_t(i) = \frac{\sum_{j=1}^{N} \alpha_{t-1}(j) \left(\prod_{\tau=1}^{t-1} c_\tau\right) a_{ij} b_j(O_t)}{\sum_{i=1}^{N} \sum_{j=1}^{N} \alpha_{t-1}(j) \left(\prod_{\tau=1}^{t-1} c_\tau\right) a_{ij} b_j(O_t)} = \frac{\alpha_t(i)}{\sum_{i=1}^{N} \alpha_t(i)} \tag{93b}$$

i.e., each $\alpha_t(i)$ is effectively scaled by the sum over all states of $\alpha_t(i)$.

Next we compute the $\beta_t(i)$ terms from the backward recursion. The only difference here is that we use the *same* scale factors for each time t for the betas as was used for the alphas. Hence the scaled β's are of the form

$$\hat{\beta}_t(i) = c_t \beta_t(i). \tag{94}$$

Since each scale factor effectively restores the magnitude of the α terms to 1, and since the magnitudes of the α and β terms are comparable, using the same scaling factors on the β's as was used on the α's is an effective way of keeping the computation within reasonable bounds. Furthermore, in terms of the scaled variables we see that the reestimation equation (90) becomes

$$\overline{a_{ij}} = \frac{\sum_{t=1}^{T-1} \hat{\alpha}_t(i)\, a_{ij} b_j(O_{t+1})\, \hat{\beta}_{t+1}(j)}{\sum_{t=1}^{T-1} \sum_{j=1}^{N} \hat{\alpha}_t(i)\, a_{ij} b_j(O_{t+1})\, \hat{\beta}_{t+1}(j)} \tag{95}$$

but each $\hat{\alpha}_t(i)$ can be written as

$$\hat{\alpha}_t(i) = \left[\prod_{s=1}^{t} c_s\right] \alpha_t(i) = C_t \alpha_t(i) \tag{96}$$

and each $\hat{\beta}_{t+1}(j)$ can be written as

$$\hat{\beta}_{t+1}(j) = \left[\prod_{s=t+1}^{T} c_s\right] \beta_{t+1}(j) = D_{t+1} \beta_{t+1}(j). \tag{97}$$

Thus (95) can be written as

$$\overline{a_{ij}} = \frac{\sum_{t=1}^{T-1} C_t \alpha_t(i)\, a_{ij} b_j(O_{t+1})\, D_{t+1} \beta_{t+1}(j)}{\sum_{t=1}^{T-1} \sum_{j=1}^{N} C_t \alpha_t(i)\, a_{ij} b_j(O_{t+1})\, D_{t+1} \beta_{t+1}(j)}. \tag{98}$$

Finally the term $C_t D_{t+1}$ can be seen to be of the form

$$C_t D_{t+1} = \prod_{s=1}^{t} c_s \prod_{s=t+1}^{T} c_s = \prod_{s=1}^{T} c_s = C_T \tag{99}$$

independent of t. Hence the terms $C_t D_{t+1}$ cancel out of both the numerator and denominator of (98) and the exact reestimation equation is therefore realized.

It should be obvious that the above scaling procedure applies equally well to reestimation of the π or B coefficients. It should also be obvious that the scaling procedure of (92) need not be applied at every time instant t, but can be performed whenever desired, or necessary (e.g., to prevent underflow). If scaling is not performed at some instant t, the scaling coefficients c_t are set to 1 at that time and all the conditions discussed above are then met.

The only real change to the HMM procedure because of scaling is the procedure for computing $P(O|\lambda)$. We cannot merely sum up the $\hat{\alpha}_T(i)$ terms since these are scaled already.

However, we can use the property that

$$\prod_{t=1}^{T} c_t \sum_{i=1}^{N} \alpha_T(i) = C_T \sum_{i=1}^{N} \alpha_T(i) = 1. \tag{100}$$

Thus we have

$$\prod_{t=1}^{T} c_t \cdot P(O|\lambda) = 1 \tag{101}$$

or

$$P(O|\lambda) = \frac{1}{\prod_{t=1}^{T} c_t} \tag{102}$$

or

$$\log [P(O|\lambda)] = -\sum_{t=1}^{T} \log c_t. \tag{103}$$

Thus the log of P can be computed, but not P since it would be out of the dynamic range of the machine anyway.

Finally we note that when using the Viterbi algorithm to give the maximum likelihood state sequence, no scaling is required if we use logarithms in the following way. (Refer back to (32)–(34).) We define

$$\phi_t(i) = \max_{q_1, q_2, \cdots, q_t} \{\log P[q_1\, q_2 \cdots q_t,\, O_1\, O_2 \cdots O_t|\lambda]\} \tag{104}$$

and initially set

$$\phi_1(i) = \log (\pi_i) + \log [b_i(O_1)] \tag{105a}$$

with the recursion step

$$\phi_t(j) = \max_{1 \le i \le N} [\phi_{t-1}(i) + \log a_{ij}] + \log [b_j(O_t)] \tag{105b}$$

and termination step

$$\log P^* = \max_{1 \le i \le N} [\phi_T(i)]. \tag{105c}$$

Again we arrive at $\log P^*$ rather than P^*, but with significantly less computation and with no numerical problems. (The reader should note that the terms $\log a_{ij}$ of (105b) can be precomputed and therefore do not cost anything in the computation. Furthermore, the terms $\log [b_j(O_t)]$ can be precomputed when a finite observation symbol analysis (e.g., a codebook of observation sequences) is used.

B. Multiple Observation Sequences [14]

In Section IV we discussed a form of HMM called the left-right or Bakis model in which the state proceeds from state 1 at $t = 1$ to state N at $t = T$ in a sequential manner (recall the model of Fig. 7(b)). We have already discussed how a left-right model imposes constraints on the state transition matrix, and the initial state probabilities (45)–(48). However, the major problem with left-right models is that one cannot use a single observation sequence to train the model (i.e., for reestimation of model parameters). This is because the transient nature of the states within the model only allow a small number of observations for any state (until a transition is made to a successor state). Hence, in order to have sufficient data to make reliable estimates of all model parameters, one has to use multiple observation sequences.

The modification of the reestimation procedure is straightforward and goes as follows. We denote the set of K observation sequences as

$$O = [O^{(1)}, O^{(2)}, \cdots, O^{(K)}] \tag{106}$$

where $O^{(k)} = [O_1^{(k)}\, O_2^{(k)} \cdots O_{T_k}^{(k)}]$ is the kth observation sequence. We assume each observation sequence is independent of every other observation sequence, and our goal is to adjust the parameters of the model λ to maximize

$$P(O|\lambda) = \prod_{k=1}^{K} P(O^{(k)}|\lambda) \tag{107}$$

$$= \prod_{k=1}^{K} P_k. \tag{108}$$

Since the reestimation formulas are based on frequencies of occurrence of various events, the reestimation formulas for multiple observation sequences are modified by adding together the individual frequencies of occurrence for each sequence. Thus the modified reestimation formulas for $\overline{a}_{ij}$ and $\overline{b}_j(\ell)$ are

$$\overline{a}_{ij} = \frac{\sum_{k=1}^{K} \frac{1}{P_k} \sum_{t=1}^{T_k-1} \alpha_t^k(i)\, a_{ij} b_j(O_{t+1}^{(k)})\, \beta_{t+1}^k(j)}{\sum_{k=1}^{K} \frac{1}{P_k} \sum_{t=1}^{T_k-1} \alpha_t^k(i)\, \beta_t^k(i)} \tag{109}$$

and

$$\overline{b}_j(\ell) = \frac{\sum_{k=1}^{K} \frac{1}{P_k} \sum_{\substack{t=1 \\ \text{s.t. } O_t = v_\ell}}^{T_k-1} \alpha_t^k(i)\, \beta_t^k(i)}{\sum_{k=1}^{K} \frac{1}{P_k} \sum_{t=1}^{T_k-1} \alpha_t^k(i)\, \beta_t^k(i)} \tag{110}$$

and π_i is not reestimated since $\pi_1 = 1$, $\pi_i = 0$, $i \neq 1$.

The proper scaling of (109)–(110) is now straightforward since each observation sequence has its own scaling factor. The key idea is to remove the scaling factor from each term before summing. This can be accomplished by writing the reestimation equations in terms of the scaled variables, i.e.,

$$\overline{a}_{ij} = \frac{\sum_{k=1}^{K} \frac{1}{P_k} \sum_{t=1}^{T_k-1} \hat{\alpha}_t^k(i)\, a_{ij} b_j(O_{t+1}^{(k)})\, \hat{\beta}_{t+1}^k(j)}{\sum_{k=1}^{K} \frac{1}{P_k} \sum_{t=1}^{T_k-1} \hat{\alpha}_t^k(i)\, \hat{\beta}_t^k(i)}. \tag{111}$$

In this manner, for each sequence $O^{(k)}$, the same scale factors will appear in each term of the sum over t as appears in the P_k term, and hence will cancel exactly. Thus using the scaled values of the alphas and betas results in an unscaled $\overline{a}_{ij}$. A similar result is obtained for the $\overline{b}_j(\ell)$ term.

C. Initial Estimates of HMM Parameters

In theory, the reestimation equations should give values of the HMM parameters which correspond to a local maximum of the likelihood function. A key question is therefore how do we choose initial estimates of the HMM parameters so that the local maximum is the global maximum of the likelihood function.

Basically there is no simple or straightforward answer to the above question. Instead, experience has shown that either random (subject to the stochastic and the nonzero value constraints) or uniform initial estimates of the π and

A parameters is adequate for giving useful reestimates of these parameters in almost all cases. However, for the B parameters, experience has shown that good initial estimates are helpful in the discrete symbol case, and are essential (when dealing with multiple mixtures) in the continuous distribution case [35]. Such initial estimates can be obtained in a number of ways, including manual segmentation of the observation sequence(s) into states with averaging of observations within states, maximum likelihood segmentation of observations with averaging, and segmental k-means segmentation with clustering, etc. We discuss such segmentation techniques later in this paper.

D. Effects of Insufficient Training Data [36]

Another problem associated with training HMM parameters via reestimation methods is that the observation sequence used for training is, of necessity, finite. Thus there is often an insufficient number of occurrences of different model events (e.g., symbol occurrences within states) to give good estimates of the model parameters. One solution to this problem is to increase the size of the training observation set. Often this is impractical. A second possible solution is to reduce the size of the model (e.g., number of states, number of symbols per state, etc). Although this is always possible, often there are physical reasons why a given model is used and therefore the model size cannot be changed. A third possible solution is to interpolate one set of parameter estimates with another set of parameter estimates from a model for which an adequate amount of training data exists [36]. The idea is to simultaneously design both the desired model as well as a smaller model for which the amount of training data is adequate to give good parameter estimates, and then to interpolate the parameter estimates from the two models. The way in which the smaller model is chosen is by tieing one or more sets of parameters of the initial model to create the smaller model. Thus if we have estimates for the parameters for the model $\lambda = (A, B, \pi)$, as well as for the reduced size model $\lambda' = (A', B', \pi')$, then the interpolated model, $\bar{\lambda} = (\bar{A}, \bar{B}, \bar{\pi})$, is obtained as

$$\bar{\lambda} = \epsilon\lambda + (1 - \epsilon)\lambda' \tag{112}$$

where ϵ represents the weighting of the parameters of the full model, and $(1 - \epsilon)$ represents the weighting of the parameters of the reduced model. A key issue is the determination of the optimal value of ϵ, which is clearly a function of the amount of training data. (As the amount of training data gets large, we expect ϵ to tend to 1.0; similarly for small amounts of training data we expect ϵ to tend to 0.0.) The solution to the determination of an optimal value for ϵ was provided by Jelinek and Mercer [36] who showed how the optimal value for ϵ could be estimated using the forward-backward algorithm by interpreting (112) as an expanded HMM of the type shown in Fig. 10. For this expanded model the parameter ϵ is the probability of a state transition from the (neutral) state $\tilde{s}$ to the model λ; similarly $(1 - \epsilon)$ is the probability of a state transition from $\tilde{s}$ to the model λ'. Between each of the models, λ and λ', and $\tilde{s}$, there is a null transition. Using the model of Fig. 9, the value of ϵ can be estimated from the training data in the standard manner. A key point is to segment the training data T into two disjoint sets, i.e., $T = T_1 \cup T_2$. Training set T_1 is first used to train models λ and λ' (i.e., to give estimates of (A, B, π) and (A', B', π')). Training set T_2 is then used to give an estimate of ϵ, assuming the models λ and λ' are fixed. A modified version of this training procedure, called the method of deleted interpolation [36], iterates the above procedure through multiple partitions of the training set. For example one might consider a partition of the training set such that T_1 is 90 percent of T and T_2 is the remaining 10 percent of T. There are a large number of ways in which such a partitioning can be accomplished but one particularly simple one is to cycle T_2 through the data, i.e., the first partition uses the last 10 percent of the data as T_2, the second partition uses the next-to-last 10 percent of the data as T_2, etc.

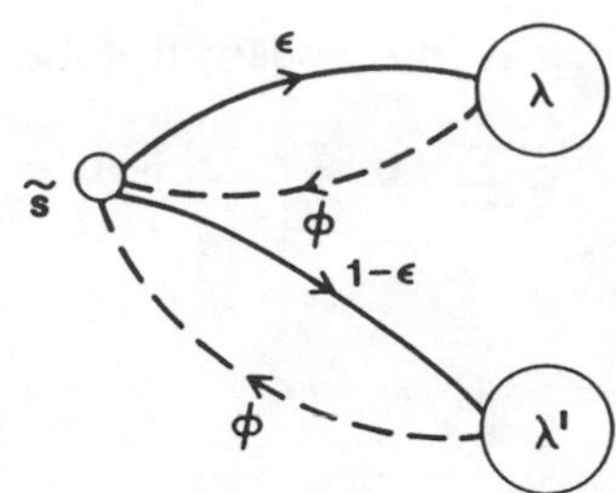

Fig. 10. Example of how the process of deleted interpolation can be represented using a state diagram.

The technique of deleted interpolation has been successfully applied to a number of problems in speech recognition including the estimation of trigram word probabilities for language models [13], and the estimation of HMM output probabilities for trigram phone models [37], [38].

Another way of handling the effects of insufficient training data is to add extra constraints to the model parameters to insure that no model parameter estimate falls below a specified level. Thus, for example, we might specify the constraint, for a discrete symbol model, that

$$b_j(k) \geq \delta \tag{113a}$$

or, for a continuous distribution model, that

$$U_{jk}(r, r) \geq \delta. \tag{113b}$$

The constraints can be applied as a postprocessor to the reestimation equations such that if a constraint is violated, the relevant parameter is manually corrected, and all remaining parameters are rescaled so that the densities obey the required stochastic constraints. Such post-processor techniques have been applied to several problems in speech processing with good success [39]. It can be seen from (112) that this procedure is essentially equivalent to a simple form of deleted interpolation in which the model λ' is a uniform distribution model, and the interpolation value ϵ is chosen as the fixed constant $(1 - \delta)$.

E. Choice of Model

The remaining issue in implementing HMMs is the choice of type of model (ergodic or left-right or some other form), choice of model size (number of states), and choice of observation symbols (discrete or continuous, single or multi-mixture, choice of observation parameters). Unfortunately, there is no simple, theoretically correct, way of making such choices. These choices must be made depending on the signal being modeled. With these comments we end our discussion of the theoretical aspects of hidden Markov models, and proceed to a discussion of how such models have been applied to selected problems in speech recognition.

VI. Implementation of Speech Recognizers Using HMMs

The purpose of this, and the following sections, is to illustrate how the ideas of HMMs, as discussed in the first 5 sections of this paper, have been applied to selected problems in speech recognition. As such, we will not strive to be as thorough or as complete in our descriptions as to what was done as we were in describing the theory of HMMs. The interested reader should read the material in [6], [10], [12], [13], [39]–[46] for more complete descriptions of individual systems. Our main goal here is to show how specific aspects of HMM theory get applied, not to make the reader an expert in speech recognition technology.

A. Overall Recognition System

Fig. 11 shows a block diagram of a pattern recognition approach to continuous speech recognition system. The key signal processing steps include the following:

1) Feature Analysis: A spectral and/or temporal analysis of the speech signal is performed to give observation vectors which can be used to train the HMMs which characterize various speech sounds. A detailed discussion of one type of feature analysis is given later in this section.

2) Unit Matching System: First a choice of speech recognition unit must be made. Possibilities include linguistically based sub-word units such as phones (or phone-like units), diphones, demisyllables, and syllables [38], as well as derivative units such as fenemes, fenones, and acoustic units [13]. Other possibilities include whole word units, and even units which correspond to a group of 2 or more words (e.g., and an, in the, of a, etc). Generally, the less complex the unit (e.g., phones), the fewer of them there are in the language, and the more complicated (variable) their structure in continuous speech. For large vocabulary speech recognition (involving 1000 or more words), the use of sub-word speech units is almost mandatory as it would be quite difficult to record an adequate training set for designing HMMs for units of the size of words or larger. However, for specialized applications (e.g., small vocabulary, constrained task), it is both reasonable and practical to consider the word as a basic speech unit. We will consider such systems exclusively in this and the following section. Independent of the unit chosen for recognition, an inventory of such units must be obtained via training. Typically each such unit is characterized by some type of HMM whose parameters are estimated from a training set of speech data. The unit matching system provides the likelihoods of a match of all sequences of speech recognition units to the unknown input speech. Techniques for providing such match scores, and in particular determining the best match score (subject to lexical and syntactic constraints of the system) include the stack decoding procedure [7], various forms of frame synchronous path decoding [37], and a lexical access scoring procedure [46].

3) Lexical Decoding: This process places constraints on the unit matching system so that the paths investigated are those corresponding to sequences of speech units which are in a word dictionary (a lexicon). This procedure implies that the speech recognition word vocabulary must be specified in terms of the basic units chosen for recognition. Such a specification can be deterministic (e.g., one or more finite state networks for each word in the vocabulary) or statistical (e.g., probabilities attached to the arcs in the finite state representation of words). In the case where the chosen units are words (or word combinations), the lexical decoding step is essentially eliminated and the structure of the recognizer is greatly simplified.

4) Syntactic Analysis: This process, much like lexical decoding, places further constraints on the unit matching system so that the paths investigated are those corresponding to speech units which comprise words (lexical decoding) and for which the words are in a proper sequence as specified by a word grammar. Such a word grammar can again be represented by a deterministic finite state network (in which all word combinations which are accepted by the grammar are enumerated), or by a statistical grammar (e.g., a trigram word model in which probabilities of sequences of 3 words in a specified order are given). For some command and control tasks, only a single word from a finite set of equiprobable is required to be recognized and therefore the grammar is either trivial or unnecessary. Such tasks are often referred to as isolated word speech recognition tasks. For other applications (e.g., digit sequences) very simple grammars are often adequate (e.g., any digit can be spoken and followed by any other digit). Finally there are tasks for which the grammar is a dominant factor and, although it adds a great deal of constraint to the recognition process, it greatly improves recognition performance by the resulting restrictions on the sequence of speech units which are valid recognition candidates.

5) Semantic Analysis: This process, again like the steps of syntactic analysis and lexical decoding, adds further constraints to the set of recognition search paths. One way in which semantic constraints are utilized is via a dynamic model of the state of the recognizer. Depending on the recognizer state certain syntactically correct input strings are eliminated from consideration. This again serves to make the recognition task easier and leads to higher performance of the system.

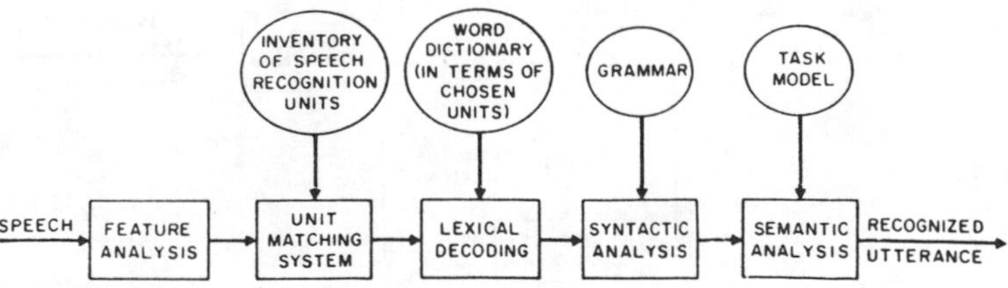

Fig. 11. Block diagram of a continuous speech recognizer.

There is one additional factor that has a significant effort on the implementation of a speech recognizer and that is the problem of separating background silence from the input speech. There are at least three reasonable ways of accomplishing this task:

1) Explicitly detecting the presence of speech via techniques which discriminate background from speech on the basis of signal energy and signal durations. Such methods have been used for template-based approaches because of their inherent simplicity and their success in low to moderate noise backgrounds [48].
2) Build a model of the background silence, e.g., a statistical model, and represent the incoming signal as an arbitrary sequence of speech and background, i.e.,

$$\text{signal} = (\text{silence}) - \text{speech} - (\text{silence})$$

where the silence part of the signal is optional in that it may not be present before or after the speech [49].
3) Extend the speech unit models so that background silence is included (optionally) within the first and/or last state of the model, and therefore silence inherently gets included within all speech unit models.

All three of these techniques have been utilized in speech recognition systems.

Instead of discussing the general continuous speech recognition system further, we now present specialized applications to illustrate how HMM technology can be utilized. First we present a system where the basic speech unit is the word, where the task is to recognize a single spoken word, and where there is no task syntax or semantics to constrain the choice of words. This task is generally referred to as isolated word recognition. Next we discuss a slightly more complicated task in which the basic speech unit is still the word, but where the task is to recognize a continuous utterance consisting of words from the vocabularly. Included in such a task is the problem of recognizing a spoken string of digits. We again consider the case where there is no task syntax or semantics to constrain the choice of words, i.e., any digit can follow any other digit. Recognition tasks of this type have been referred to as connected word recognizers because the continuous speech is recognized as a concatenated sequence of word models. This is technically a misnomer because it is truly a continuous speech recognition problem. However, the terminology has become established and we continue its use.

B. Isolated Word Recognition

As our first example, consider using HMMs to build an isolated word recognizer. Assume we have a vocabulary of V words to be recognized and that each word is to be modeled by a distinct HMM.[12] Further assume that for each word in the vocabulary we have a training set of K occurrences of each spoken word (spoken by 1 or more talkers) where each occurrence of the word constitutes an observation sequence, where the observations are some appropriate representation of the (spectral and/or temporal) characteristics of the word. (We will return to the question of what specific representation is used later in this section.) In order to do isolated word speech recognition, we must perform the following:

1) For each word v in the vocabulary, we must build an HMM λ^v, i.e., we must estimate the model parameters (A, B, π) that optimize the likelihood of the training set observation vectors for the vth word.
2) For each unknown word which is to be recognized, the processing of Fig. 12 must be carried out, namely measurement of the observation sequence $O = \{O_1 O_2 \cdots O_T\}$, via a feature analysis of the speech corresponding to the word; followed by calculation of model likelihoods for all possible models, $P(O|\lambda^v)$, $1 \le v \le V$; followed by selection of the word whose model likelihood is highest, i.e.,

$$v^* = \underset{1 \le v \le V}{\operatorname{argmax}} [P(O|\lambda^v)]. \tag{114}$$

The probability computation step is generally performed using the Viterbi algorithm (i.e., the maximum likelihood path is used) and requires on the order of $V \cdot N^2 \cdot T$ computations. For modest vocabulary sizes, e.g., $V = 100$ words, with an $N = 5$ state model, and $T = 40$ observations for the

[12]An excellent description of an isolated word, large vocabulary, speech recognizer based on sub-word units is given in the description of the IBM TANGORA system [50]. Another good reference which compares the effects of continuous and discrete densities using a 60 000 word vocabulary is [46].

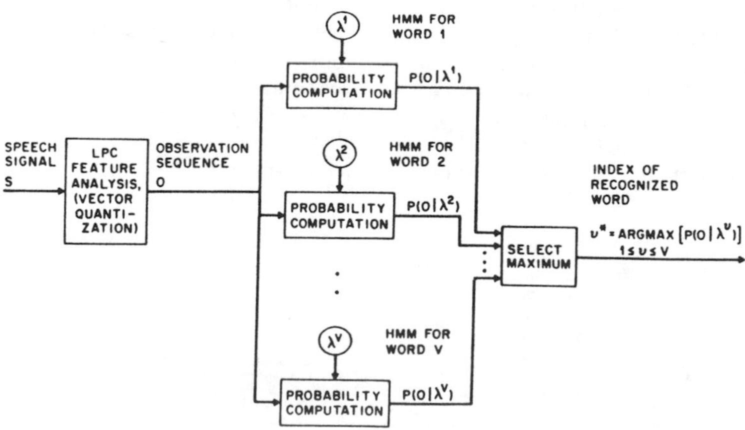

Fig. 12. Block diagram of an isolated word HMM recognizer.

unknown word, a total of 10^5 computations is required for recognition (where each computation is a multiply, and add, and a calculation of observation density, $b(O)$). Clearly this amount of computation is modest as compared to the capabilities of most modern signal processor chips.

C. LPC Feature Analysis [51]–[54]

One way to obtain observation vectors O from speech samples s is to perform a front end spectral analysis. (We assume that we are processing only the speech samples corresponding to the spoken word—i.e., all background before and after the spoken word has been eliminated by an appropriate word detection algorithm.) The type of spectral analysis that is often used (and the one we will describe here) is called linear predictive coding (LPC), and a block diagram of the steps that are carried out is given in Fig. 13. The overall system is a block processing model in which a frame of N_A samples is processed and a vector of features O_ℓ is computed. The steps in the processing are as follows:

1) Preemphasis: The digitized (at a 6.67 kHz rate for the examples to be discussed here) speech signal is processed by a first-order digital network in order to spectrally flatten the signal.

2) Blocking into Frames: Sections of N_A consecutive speech samples (we use $N_A = 300$ corresponding to 45 ms of signal) are used as a single frame. Consecutive frames are spaced M_A samples apart (we use $M_A = 100$ corresponding to 15-ms frame spacing, or 30-ms frame overlap).

3) Frame Windowing: Each frame is multiplied by an N_A-sample window (we use a Hamming window) $w(n)$ so as to minimize the adverse effects of chopping an N_A-sample section out of the running speech signal.

4) Autocorrelation Analysis: Each windowed set of speech samples is autocorrelated to give a set of $(p + 1)$ coefficients, where p is the order of the desired LPC analysis (we use $p = 8$).

5) LPC/Cepstral Analysis: For each frame, a vector of LPC coefficients is computed from the autocorrelation vector using a Levinson or a Durbin recursion method. An LPC derived cepstral vector is then computed up to the Qth component, where $Q > p$ and $Q = 12$ in the results to be described later in this section.

6) Cepstral Weighting: The Q-coefficient cepstral vector $c_\ell(m)$ at time frame ℓ is weighted by a window $W_c(m)$ of the form [55], [56]

$$W_c(m) = 1 + \frac{Q}{2}\sin\left(\frac{\pi m}{Q}\right), \quad 1 \le m \le Q \tag{115}$$

to give

$$\hat{c}_\ell(m) = c_\ell(m) \cdot W_c(m). \tag{116}$$

7) Delta Cepstrum: The time derivative of the sequence of weighted cepstral vectors is approximated by a first-order orthogonal polynomial over a finite length window of $(2K + 1)$ frames, centered around the current vector [57], [58]. ($K = 2$ in the results to be presented; hence a 5 frame window is used for the computation of the derivative.) The cepstral derivative (i.e., the delta cepstrum vector) is computed as

$$\Delta\hat{c}_\ell(m) = \left[\sum_{k=-K}^{K} k\hat{c}_{\ell-k}(m)\right] \cdot G, \quad 1 \le m \le Q \tag{117}$$

where G is a gain term chosen to make the variances of $\hat{c}_\ell(m)$ and $\Delta\hat{c}_\ell(m)$ equal. (A value of G of 0.375 was used.)

The observation vector $\mathbf{O}_\ell$ used for recognition and training is the concatenation of the weighted cepstral vector, and the corresponding weighted delta cepstrum vector, i.e.,

$$\mathbf{O}_\ell = \{\hat{c}_\ell(m), \Delta\hat{c}_\ell(m)\} \tag{118}$$

and consists of 24 coefficients per vector.

D. Vector Quantization [18], [39]

For the case in which we wish to use an HMM with a discrete observation symbol density, rather than the continuous vectors above, a vector quantizer (VQ) is required to map each continuous observation vector into a discrete codebook index. Once the codebook of vectors has been obtained, the mapping between continuous vectors and

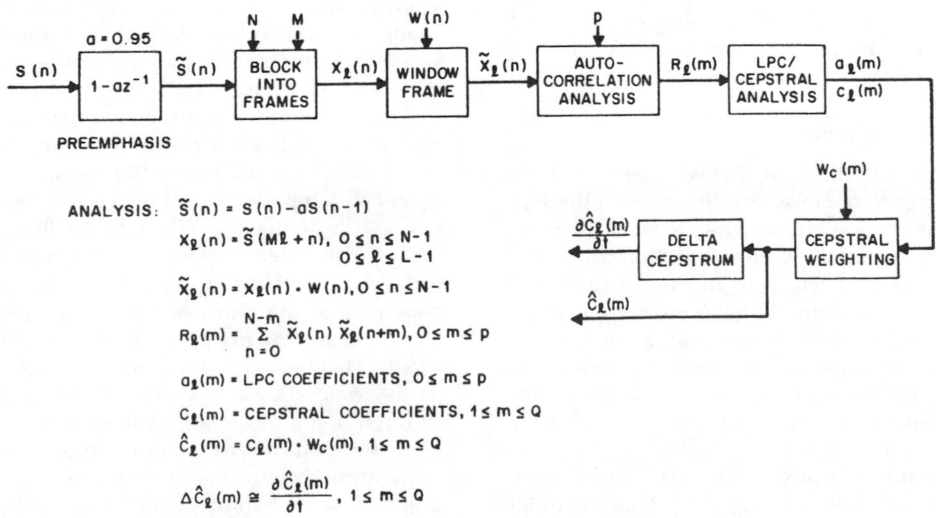

Fig. 13. Block diagram of the computations required in the front end feature analysis of the HMM recognizer.

codebook indices becomes a simple nearest neighbor computation, i.e., the continuous vector is assigned the index of the nearest (in a spectral distance sense) codebook vector. Thus the major issue in VQ is the design of an appropriate codebook for quantization.

Fortunately a great deal of work has gone into devising an excellent iterative procedure for designing codebooks based on having a representative training sequence of vectors [18]. The procedure basically partitions the training vectors into M disjoint sets (where M is the size of the codebook), represents each such set by a single vector (v_m, $1 \le m \le M$), which is generally the centroid of the vectors in the training set assigned to the mth region, and then iteratively optimizes the partition and the codebook (i.e., the centroids of each partition). Associated with VQ is a distortion penalty since we are representing an entire region of the vector space by a single vector. Clearly it is advantageous to keep the distortion penalty as small as possible. However, this implies a large size codebook, and that leads to problems in implementing HMMs with a large number of parameters. Fig. 14 illustrates the tradeoff of quantization

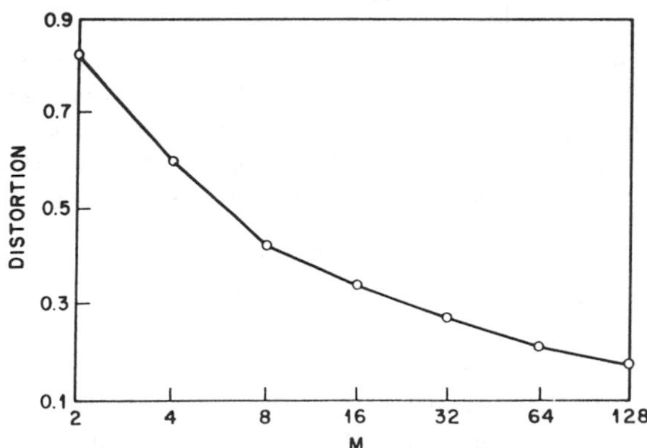

Fig. 14. Curve showing tradeoff of VQ average distortion as a function of the size of the VQ, M (shown of a log scale).

distortion versus M (on a log scale). Although the distortion steadily decreases as M increases, it can be seen from Fig. 14 that only small decreases in distortion accrue beyond a value of $M = 32$. Hence HMMs with codebook sizes of from $M = 32$ to 256 vectors have been used in speech recognition experiments using HMMs.

E. Choice of Model Parameters

We now come back to the issue that we have raised several times in this paper, namely how do we select the type of model, and how do we choose the parameters of the selected model. For isolated word recognition with a distinct HMM designed for each word in the vocabulary, it should be clear that a left-right model is more appropriate than an ergodic model, since we can then associate time with model states in a fairly straightforward manner. Furthermore we can envision the physical meaning of the model states as distinct sounds (e.g., phonemes, syllables) of the word being modeled.

The issue of the number of states to use in each word model leads to two schools of thought. One idea is to let the number of states correspond roughly to the number of sounds (phonemes) within the word—hence models with from 2 to 10 states would be appropriate. The other idea is to let the number of states correspond roughly to the average number of observations in a spoken version of the word, the so-called Bakis model [11]. In this manner each state corresponds to an observation interval—i.e., about 15 ms for the analysis we use. In the results to be described later in this section, we use the former approach. Furthermore we restrict each word model to have the same number of states; this implies that the models will work best when they represent words with the same number of sounds.

To illustrate the effect of varying the number of states in a word model, Fig. 15 shows a plot of average word error

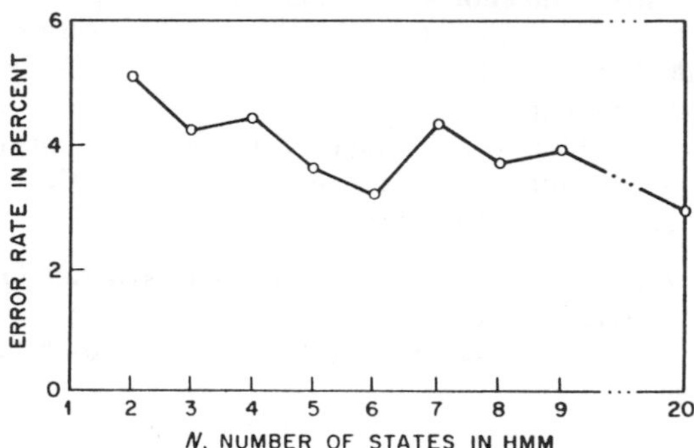

Fig. 15. Average word error rate (for a digits vocabulary) versus the number of states N in the HMM.

rate versus N, for the case of recognition of isolated digits (i.e., a 10-word vocabulary). It can be seen that the error is somewhat insensitive to N, achieving a local minimum at $N = 6$; however, differences in error rate for values of N close to 6 are small.

The next issue is the choice of observation vector and the way it is represented. As discussed in Sections VI-C and VI-D, we have considered LPC derived weighted cepstral coefficients and weighted cepstral derivatives or (for autoregressive HMMs) the autocorrelation of the LPC coefficients as the observation vectors for continuous models; for discrete symbol models we use a codebook to generate the discrete symbols. For the continuous models we use as many as $M = 9$ mixtures per state; for the discrete symbol models we use codebooks with as many as $M = 256$ codewords. Also, for the continuous models, we have found that it is preferable to use diagonal covariance matrices with several mixtures, rather than fewer mixtures with full covariance matrices. The reason for this is simple, namely the difficulty in performing reliable reestimation of the off-diagonal components of the covariance matrix from the necessarily limited training data. To illustrate the need for using mixture densities for modeling LPC observation vectors (i.e., eighth-order cepstral vectors with log energy appended as the ninth vector component), Fig. 16 shows a comparison of marginal distributions $b_j(O)|_{O=\cdots O_n\cdots}$ against a histogram of the actual observations within a state (as determined by a maximum likelihood segmentation of all the training observations into states). The observation vectors are ninth order, and the model density uses $M = 5$ mixtures. The covariance matrices are constrained to be diagonal for each individual mixture. The results of Fig. 16 are for the first model state of the word "zero." The need for values of $M > 1$ is clearly seen in the histogram of the

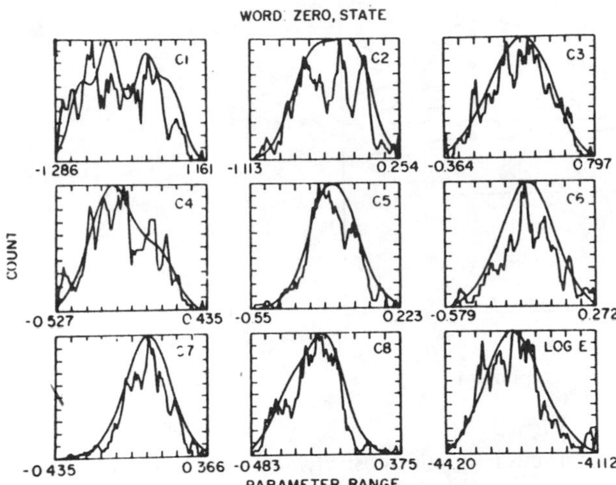

Fig. 16. Comparison of estimated density (jagged contour) and model density (smooth contour) for each of the nine components of the observation vector (eight cepstral components, one log energy component) for state 1 of the digit zero.

first parameter (the first cepstral component) which is inherently multimodal; similarly the second, fourth, and eight cepstral parameters show the need for more than a single Gaussian component to provide good fits to the empirical data. Many of the other parameters appear to be well fitted by a single Gaussian; in some cases, however, even $M = 5$ mixtures do not provide a sufficiently good fit.

Another experimentally verified fact about the HMM is that it is important to limit some of the parameter estimates in order to prevent them from becoming too small. For example, for the discrete symbol models, the constraint that $b_j(k)$ be greater than or equal to some minimum value ϵ is necessary to insure that even when the kth symbol never occurred in some state j in the training observation set, there is always a finite probability of its occurrence when scoring an unknown observation set. To illustrate this point, Fig. 17

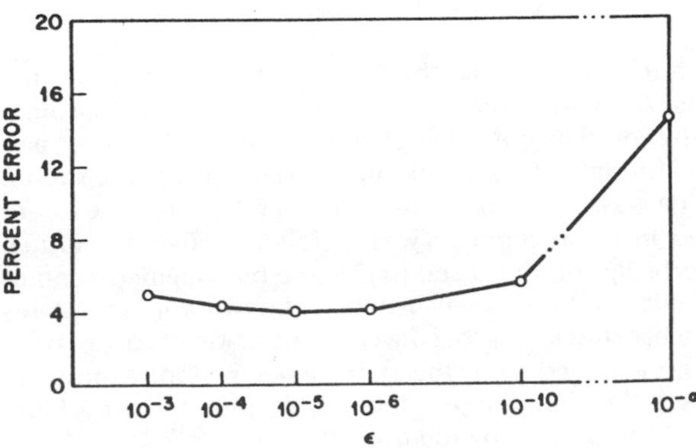

Fig. 17. Average word error rate as a function of the minimum discrete density value ϵ.

shows a curve of average word error rate versus the parameter ϵ (on a log scale) for a standard word recognition experiment. It can be seen that over a very broad range ($10^{-10} \leq \epsilon \leq 10^{-3}$) the average error rate remains at about a constant value; however, when ϵ is set to 0 (i.e., $10^{-\infty}$), then the error rate increases sharply. Similarly, for continuous densities it is important to constrain the mixture gains c_{jm} as well as the diagonal covariance coefficients $U_{jm}(r, r)$ to be greater than or equal to some minimum values (we use 10^{-4} in all cases).

F. Segmental k-Means Segmentation into States [42]

We stated earlier that good initial estimates of the parameters of the $b_j(O_t)$ densities were essential for rapid and proper convergence of the reestimation formulas. Hence a procedure for providing good initial estimates of these parameters was devised and is shown in Fig. 18. The training

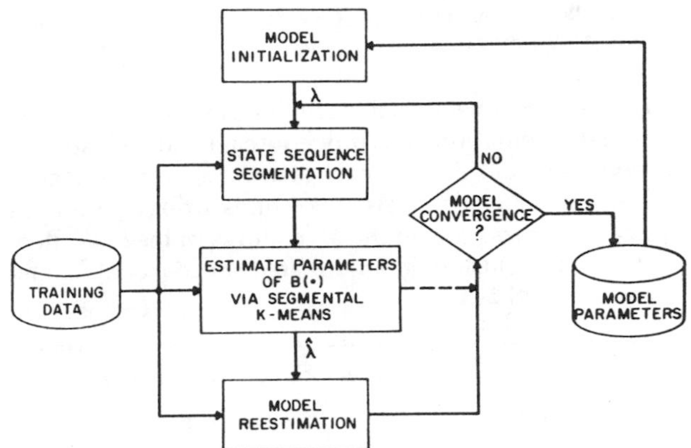

Fig. 18. The segmental k-means training procedure used to estimate parameter values for the optimal continuous mixture density fit to a finite number of observation sequences.

procedure is a variant on the well-known K-means iterative procedure for clustering data.

We assume we have a training set of observations (the same as is required for parameter reestimation), and an initial estimate of all model parameters. However, unlike the one required for reestimation, the initial model estimate can be chosen randomly, or on the basis of any available model which is appropriate to the data.

Following model initialization, the set of training observation sequences is segmented into states, based on the current model λ.[13] This segmentation is achieved by finding the optimum state sequence, via the Viterbi algorithm, and then backtracking along the optimal path. This procedure is illustrated in Fig. 19 which shows a log-energy plot, an accumulated log-likelihood plot, and a state segmentation for one occurrence of the word "six." It can be seen in Fig. 19 that the states correspond roughly to the sounds in the spoken word "six."

The result of segmenting each of the training sequences is, for each of the N states, a maximum likelihood estimate of the set of the observations that occur within each state S_j according to the current model. In the case where we are using discrete symbol densities, each of the observation vectors within a state is coded using the M-codeword codebook, and the updated estimate of the $b_j(k)$ parameters is

$$\hat{b}_j(k) = \text{number of vectors with codebook index } k \text{ in state } j \text{ divided by the number of vectors in state } j.$$

[13] The current or initial model could be one created from another set of talkers, or it could be one created from a uniform segmentation of each word into states.

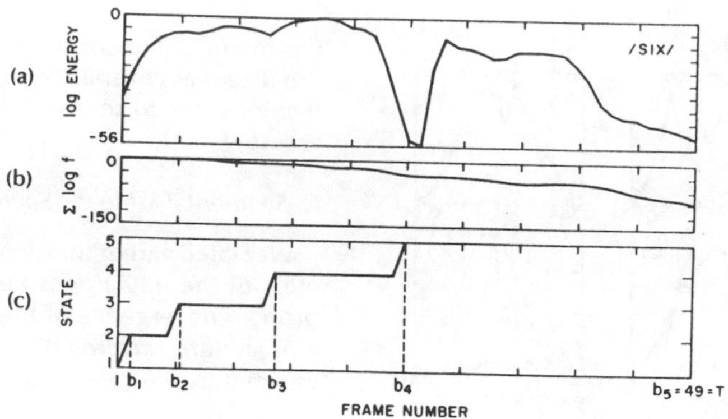

Fig. 19. Plots of: (a) log energy; (b) accumulated log likelihood; and (c) state assignment for one occurrence of the word "six."

In the case where we are using continuous observation densities, a segmental K-means procedure is used to cluster the observation vectors within each state S_j into a set of M clusters (using a Euclidean distortion measure), where each cluster represents one of the M mixtures of the $b_j(O_t)$ density. From the clustering, an updated set of model parameters is derived as follows:

$\hat{c}_{jm}$ = number of vectors classified in cluster m of state j divided by the number of vectors in state j

$\hat{\mu}_{jm}$ = sample mean of the vectors classified in cluster m of state j

$\hat{U}_{jm}$ = sample covariance matrix of the vectors classified in cluster m of state j.

Based on this state segmentation, updated estimates of the a_{ij} coefficients can be obtained by counting the number of transitions from state i to j and dividing it by the number of transitions from state i to any state (including itself).

An updated model $\hat{\lambda}$ is obtained from the new model parameters and the formal reestimation procedure is used to reestimate all model parameters. The resulting model is then compared to the previous model (by computing a distance score that reflects the statistical similarity of the HMMs). If the model distance score exceeds a threshold, then the old model λ is replaced by the new (reestimated) model $\bar{\lambda}$, and the overall training loop is repeated. If the model distance score falls below the threshold, then model convergence is assumed and the final model parameters are saved.

G. Incorporation of State Duration into the HMM

In Section IV-C we discussed the theoretically correct method of incorporating state duration information into the mechanics of the HMM. We also showed that the cost of including duration density was rather high; namely a D^2-fold increase in computation and a D-fold increase in storage. Using a value of $D = 25$ (as is required for word recognition), the cost of the increased computation tended to make the techniques not worth using. Thus the following alternative procedure was formulated for incorporating state duration information into the HMM.

For this alternative procedure, the state duration probability $p_j(d)$ was measured directly from the segmented training sequences used in the segmental K-means procedure of the previous section. Hence the estimates of $p_j(d)$ are strictly heuristic ones. A typical set of histograms of $p_j(d)$ for a 5-state model of the word "six" is shown in Fig. 20. (In this figure the histograms are plotted versus normalized duration (d/T), rather than absolute duration d.) It can be

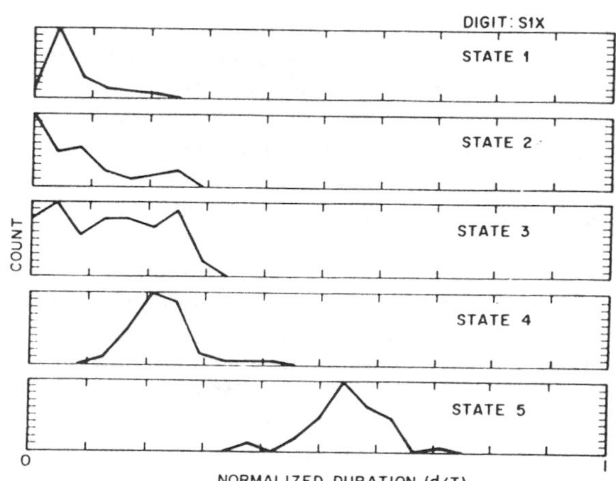

Fig. 20. Histograms of the normalized duration density for the five states of the digit "six."

seen from Fig. 20 that the first two states account for the initial /s/ in "six"; the third state accounts for the transition to the vowel /i/; the fourth state accounts for the vowel; and the fifth state accounts for the stop and the final /s/ sound.

The way in which the heuristic duration densities were used in the recognizer was as follows. First the normal Viterbi algorithm is used to give the best segmentation of the observation sequence of the unknown word into states via a backtracking procedure. The duration of each state is then measured from the state segmentation. A postprocessor then increments the log-likelihood score of the Viterbi algorithm, by the quantity

$$\log \hat{P}(q, O|\lambda) = \log P(q, O|\lambda) + \alpha_d \sum_{j=1}^{N} \log [p_j(d_j)] \quad (119)$$

where α_d is a scaling multiplier on the state duration scores, and d_j is the duration of state j along the optimal path as determined by the Viterbi algorithm. The incremental cost of the postprocessor for duration is essentially negligible, and experience has shown that recognition performance is essentially as good as that obtained using the theoretically correct duration model.

H. HMM Performance on Isolated Word Recognition

We conclude this section on isolated word recognition using HMMs by giving a set of performance results (in terms of average word error rate) on the task of recognizing isolated digits in a speaker independent manner. For this task, a training set consisting of 100 occurrences of each digit by 100 talkers (i.e., a single occurrence of each digit per talker) was used. Half the talkers were male; half female. For testing the algorithm, we used the initial training set, as well as three other independent test sets with the following characteristics:

TS2: the same 100 talkers as were used in the training; 100 occurrences of each digit

TS3: a new set of 100 talkers (50 male, 50 female); 100 occurrences of each digit

TS4: another new set of 100 talkers (50 male, 50 female); 100 occurrences of each digit

The results of the recognition tests are given in Table 1. The recognizers are the following:

LPC/DTW: Conventional template-based recognizer using dynamic time warping (DTW) alignment

LPC/DTW/VQ: Conventional recognizer with vector quantization of the feature vectors ($M = 64$)

HMM/VQ: HMM recognizer with $M = 64$ codebook

HMM/CD: HMM recognizer using continuous density model with $M = 5$ mixtures per state

HMM/AR: HMM recognizer using autoregressive observation density

Table 1 Average Digit Error Rates for Several Recognizers and Evaluation Sets

Recognizer Type	Evaluation Set: Original Training	TS2	TS3	TS4
LPC/DTW	0.1	0.2	2.0	1.1
LPC/DTW/VQ	—	3.5	—	—
HMM/VQ	—	3.7	—	—
HMM/CD	0	0.2	1.3	1.8
HMM/AR	0.3	1.8	3.4	4.1

It can be seen that, when using a VQ, the performance of the isolated word recognizer degrades in both the conventional and HMM modes. It can also be seen that the performances of the conventional template-based recognizer, and the HMM recognizer with a continuous density model are comparable. Finally Table 1 shows that the autoregressive density HMM gives poorer performance than the standard mixture density model.

VII. Connected Word Recognition Using HMMs [59]–[63]

A somewhat more complicated problem of speech recognition, to which HMMs have been successfully applied, is the problem of connected word recognition. The basic premise of connected word recognition is that the recognition is based on individual word models (as opposed to models of speech units smaller than words). The recognition problem (once the appropriate word models have been derived) is to find the optimum sequence (concatenation) of word models that best matches (in a maximum likelihood sense) an unknown connected word string. In this section we discuss one method (called the level building approach) for solving for such optimum sequences of word models. An alternative method for obtaining the optimum sequence of words is a frame (time) synchronous Viterbi search [31]. There are several practical advantages of the frame synchronous search (e.g., ease of real-time hardware implementation, ease of path pruning, etc.) but these do not affect the optimality of the two methods. For convenience, we restrict our discussion to the recognition of strings of connected digits.

A. Connected Digit Recognition from Word HMMs Using Level Building

A block diagram of the overall level building connected digit recognizer is given in Fig. 21. There are essentially three steps in the recognition process:

1) Spectral Analysis: The speech signal $s(n)$ is converted to either a set of LPC vectors or a set of cepstral and delta

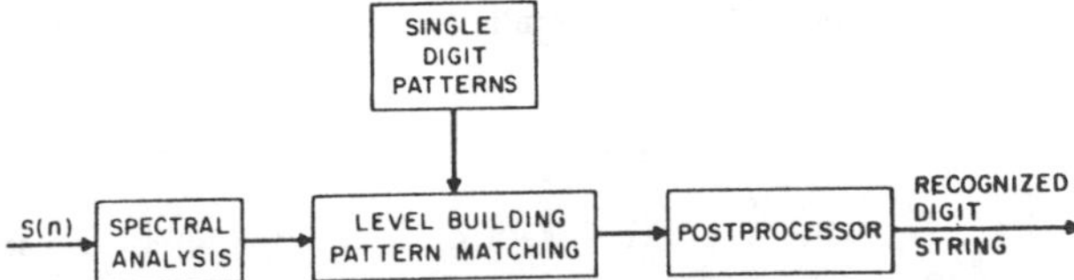

Fig. 21. Block diagram of level building, connected digit recognizer.

cepstral vectors. This defines the observation sequence $\boldsymbol{O}$ of the unknown connected digit string.

2) Level Building[14] Pattern Matching: The sequence of spectral vectors (the observations) of the unknown connected digit string is matched against the single word HMMs using a Viterbi scoring algorithm. The output of this process is a set of candidate digit strings, generally of different lengths (i.e., different number of digits per string), ordered by log probability scores.

3) Postprocessor: The candidate digit strings are subjected to further validity tests (e.g., duration), to eliminate unreasonable (unlikely) candidates. The postprocessor chooses the most likely digit string from the remaining (valid) candidate strings.

Individual digits are each characterized by an HMM of the type shown in Fig. 22. (Transitions between words are handled by a switch mode from the last state of one word model, to the first state of another word model, in the level building implementation.) The parameters of the HMMs used for characterizing digits are the following:

1) $N = 5$ or 8 states for digit models trained from observations of a single talker, and $N = 8$ or 10 states, for

[14] A level is a word position in a string. Hence a 5 digit string would have at least 5 level outputs, one for each digit in the string.

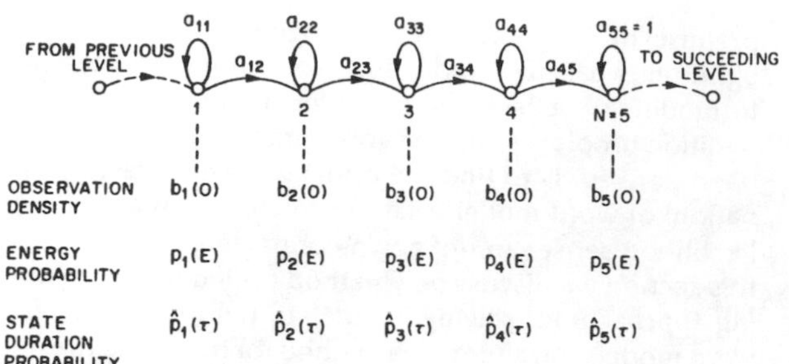

Fig. 22. HMM characterization of individual digits for connected digit recognition.

digit models trained from observations of more than a single talker.

2) Continuous observation mixture densities with $M = 3$ or 5 mixtures per state for single talker models and $M = 9$ mixtures per state for multiple talker models.
3) Energy probability $p_j(\epsilon)$ where ϵ_t is the dynamically normalized log energy of the frame of speech used to give observation vector O_t, and $p_j(\cdot)$ is a discrete density of log energy values in state j. The density is derived empirically from the training data.
4) State duration density $p_j(d)$, $1 \le d \le D = 25$.

In addition to the observation density, log energy probability, and state duration density, each word HMM λ^v is also characterized by an overall word duration density $p_v(D)$ of the form

$$p_v(D) = \mathfrak{N}(\overline{D}_v, \sigma_v^2) \tag{120}$$

where $\overline{D}_v$ is the average duration for word v, σ_v^2 is the variance in duration for word v, and $\mathfrak{N}$ is the normal density.

B. Level Building on HMMs

The way in which level building is used on HMMs is illustrated in Fig. 23. If we denote the set of V word HMMs as λ^v, $1 \le v \le V$, then to find the optimum sequence of HMMs that match O (i.e., maximize the likelihood), a sequence of Viterbi matches is performed. For each HMM λ^v, and at each level ℓ, we do a Viterbi match against O, starting at frame (observation interval) 1 on level 1, and retain for each possible frame t the following:

1) $P_\ell^v(t)$, $1 \le t \le T$, the accumulated log probability to frame t, at level ℓ, for reference model λ^v, along the best path.
2) $F_\ell^v(t)$, $1 \le t \le T$, a backpointer indicating where the path started at the beginning of the level.

To compute $P_\ell^v(t)$, we need a local measure for the probability that observation O_t, with log energy ϵ_t, occurred in state j of model λ^v. We use, as the observation density, the function

$$\hat{b}_j^v(O_t) = b_j^v(O_t) \cdot [p_j^v(\epsilon_t)]^{\gamma_\epsilon} \cdot K_1 \tag{121}$$

where γ_ϵ (set to 0.375) is a log energy scaling coefficient and K_1 is a normalization constant. The state transition coefficients enter the calculation of $P_\ell^v(t)$ via the dynamic programming optimization in determining the Viterbi path.

At the end of each level ℓ (where the level corresponds to word position within the string), a maximization over v is performed to get the best model at each frame t as follows:

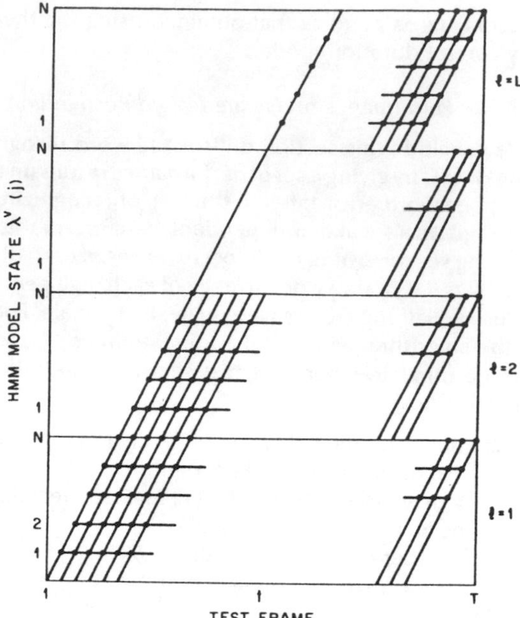

Fig. 23. Illustration of how HMMs are applied in the level building algorithm.

$$P_\ell^B(t) = \max_{1 \le v \le V} P_\ell^v(t), \qquad 1 \le t \le T \tag{122a}$$

$$W_\ell^B(t) = \operatorname*{argmax}_{1 \le v \le V} P_\ell^v(t), \qquad 1 \le t \le T \tag{122b}$$

$$F_\ell^B(t) = F_\ell^{W_\ell^B(t)}(t), \qquad 1 \le t \le T \tag{122c}$$

where $W_\ell^B(t)$ records the number of the word model which gave the best score at frame t, level ℓ, and $F_\ell^B(t)$ records the backpointer of the best word model.

Each new level begins with the initial best probability at the preceding frame on the preceding level and increments the Viterbi score by matching the word models beginning at the new initial frame. This process is repeated through a number of levels equivalent to the maximum expected number of digits in any string (e.g., typically 7).

At the end of each level, a best string of size ℓ words ($1 \le \ell \le L$) with probability $P_\ell^B(T)$ is obtained by backtracking using the backpointer array $F_\ell^B(t)$ to give the words in the string. The overall best string is the maximum of $P_\ell^B(T)$ over all possible levels ℓ.

C. Training the Word Models [59], [61]

The key to success in connected word recognition is to derive word models from representative connected word strings. We have found that although the formal reestimation procedures developed in this paper work well, they are costly in terms of computation, and equivalently good parameter estimates can be obtained using a segmental K-means procedure of the type discussed in Section VI. The only difference in the procedure, from the one discussed earlier, is that the training connected word strings are first segmented into individual digits, via a Viterbi alignment procedure, then each set of digits is segmented into states, and the vectors within each state are clustered into the best

M cluster solution. The segmental K-means reestimation of the HMM parameters is about an order of magnitude faster than the Baum-Welch reestimation procedure, and all our experimentation indicates that the resulting parameter estimates are essentially identical in that the resulting HMMs have essentially the same likelihood values. As such, the segmental K-means procedure was used to give all the results presented later in this section.

D. Duration Modeling for Connected Digits

There are two forms of durational information used in scoring connected digit sequences, namely word duration and state duration. The way in which word duration information is incorporated into the model scoring is as follows. At the end of each level, for each frame t, the accumulated probability $P_\ell^B(t)$ is modified by determining the word duration $\tau_v(t)$ as

$$\tau_v(t) = t - F_\ell^B(t) + 1 \tag{123}$$

and then multiplying the accumulated probability by the word duration probability, i.e.,

$$\hat{P}_\ell^v(t) = P_\ell^v(t) \cdot [\mathfrak{N}(\tau_v(t), \overline{D}_v, \sigma_v^2)]^{\gamma_{WD}} \cdot K_2 \tag{124}$$

where γ_{WD} (set to 3.0) is a weighting factor on word durations, and K_2 is a normalization constant.

State duration probabilities are incorporated in a postprocessor. The level building recognizer provides multiple candidates at each level (by tracking multiple best scores at each frame of each level). Hence overall probability scores are obtained for R^L strings of length L digits, where R is the number of candidates per level (typically $R = 2$). Each of the R^L strings is backtracked to give both individual words and individual states within the words. For an L-word string, if we denote the duration of state j at level ℓ as $\Delta_\ell(j)$, then, for each possible string, the postprocessor multiplies the overall accumulated probability $P_L^B(T)$ by the state duration probabilities, giving

$$\hat{P}_L^B(T) = P_L^B(T) \cdot \prod_{\ell=1}^{L} \prod_{j=1}^{N} [p_j^{w(\ell)}(\Delta_\ell(j))]^{\gamma_{SD}} \cdot K_3 \tag{125}$$

where γ_{SD} (set to 0.75) is a weighting factor on state durations, $w(\ell)$ is the word at level ℓ, and K_3 is a normalization constant. The computation of (125) is performed on all R^L strings, and a reordered list of best strings is obtained. The incremental cost of the postprocessor computation is negligible compared to the computation to give $P_L^B(T)$, and its performance has been shown to be comparable to the performance of the internal duration models.

E. Performance of the Connected Digit HMM Recognizer

The HMM-based connected digit recognizer has been trained and tested in 3 modes:

1) Speaker trained using 50 talkers (25 male, 25 female) each of whom provided a training set of about 500 connected digit strings and an independent testing set of 500 digit strings.
2) Multispeaker in which the training sets from the 50 talkers above were merged into a single large training set, and the testing sets were similarly merged. In this case a set of 6 HMMs per digit was used, where each HMM was derived from a subset of the training utterances.
3) Speaker independent based on the TI training and testing databases. Both the training and testing sets had about 113 talkers (different ones were used in each set) and the talkers were divided into 22 dialectal groups. In this case a set of 4 HMMs per digit was used.

In each of the above databases there were variable length digit strings with from 1 to 7 digits per string.

The performance of the HMM connected digit recognizer, in these modes, is given in Table 2, where the entries in the table are average string error rates for cases in which the string length was unknown apriori (UL), and for cases in which the string length was known apriori (KL). Results are given both for the training set (from which the word models were derived), and for the independent test set.

Table 2 Performance of the HMM Connected Digit Recognizer in Three Modes

Mode	Training Set		Testing Set	
	UL	KL	UL	KL
Speaker trained (50 talkers)	0.39	0.16	0.78	0.35
Multispeaker (50 talkers)	1.74	0.98	2.85	1.65
Speaker independent (112/113 talkers)	1.24	0.36	2.94	1.75

VIII. HMMs for Large Vocabulary Speech Recognition [6]–[13], [31], [37], [38], [51], [64]–[66]

Although HMMs have been successfully applied to problems in isolated and connected word recognition, the anticipated payoff of the theory, to problems in speech recognition, is in its application to large vocabulary speech recognition in which the recognition of speech is performed from basic speech units smaller than words. The research in this area far outweights the research in any other area of speech processing and is far too extensive to discuss here. Instead, in this section we briefly outline the ideas of how HMMs have been applied to this problem.

In the most advanced systems (e.g., comparable to those under investigation at IBM, BBN, CMU and other places), the theory of HMMs has been applied to the representation of phoneme-like sub-words as HMMs; representation of words as HMMs; and representation of syntax as an HMM. To solve the speech recognition problem, a triply embedded network of HMMs must be used. This leads to an expanded network with an astronomical number of equivalent states; hence an alternative to the complete, exhaustive search procedure is required. Among the alternatives are the stack algorithm [7] and various forms of Viterbi beam searches [31]. These procedures have been shown to be capable of handling such large networks (e.g., 5000 words with an average word branching factor of 100) in an efficient and reliable manner. Details of these approaches are beyond the scope of this paper.

In another attempt to apply HMMs to continuous speech recognition, an ergodic HMM was used in which each state represented an acoustic-phonetic unit [47]. Hence about 40–50 states are required to represent all sounds of English. The model incorporated the variable duration feature in each state to account for the fact that vowel-like sounds have vastly different durational characteristics than consonant-like sounds. In this approach, lexical access was used in conjunction with a standard pronouncing dictionary to determine the best matching word sequence from the output of the sub-word HMM. Again the details of this recognition system are beyond the scope of this paper. The purpose of this brief discussion is to point out the vast potential of HMMs for characterizing the basic processes of speech production; hence their applicability to problems in large vocabulary speech recognition.

A. Limitations of HMMs

Although use of HMM technology has contributed greatly to recent advances in speech recognition, there are some inherent limitations of this type of statistical model for speech. A major limitation is the assumption that successive observations (frames of speech) are independent, and therefore the probability of a sequence of observations $P(O, O_2 \cdots O_T)$ can be written as a product of probabilities of individual observations, i.e.,

$$P(O, O_2 \cdots O_T) = \prod_{i=1}^{T} P(O_i).$$

Another limitation is the assumption that the distributions of individual observation parameters can be well represented as a mixture of Gaussian or autoregressive densities. Finally the Markov assumption itself, i.e., that the probability of being in a given state at time t only depends on the state at time $t - 1$, is clearly inappropriate for speech sounds where dependencies often extend through several states. However, in spite of these limitations this type of statistical model has worked extremely well for certain types of speech recognition problems.

IX. Summary

In this paper we have attempted to present the theory of hidden Markov models from the simplest concepts (discrete Markov chains) to the most sophisticated models (variable duration, continuous density models). It has been our purpose to focus on physical explanations of the basic mathematics; hence we have avoided long, drawn out proofs and/or derivations of the key results, and concentrated primarily on trying to interpret the meaning of the math, and how it could be implemented in practice in real world systems. We have also attempted to illustrate some applications of the theory of HMMs to simple problems in speech recognition, and pointed out how the techniques could be (and have been) applied to more advanced speech recognition problems.

Acknowledgment

The author gratefully acknowledges the major contributions of several colleagues to the theory of HMMs in general, and to the presentation of this paper, in particular. A great debt is owed to Dr. J. Ferguson, Dr. A. Poritz, Dr. L. Liporace, Dr. A. Richter, and to Dr. F. Jelinek and the various members of the IBM group for introducing the speech world to the ideas behind HMMs. In addition Dr. S. Levinson, Dr. M. Sondhi, Dr. F. Juang, Dr. A. Dembo, and Dr. Y. Ephraim have contributed significantly to both the theory of HMMs as well as the author's perspective and knowledge as to how the theory is best applied to problems of speech recognition.

References

[1] L. E. Baum and T. Petrie, "Statistical inference for probabilistic functions of finite state Markov chains," *Ann. Math. Stat.*, vol. 37, pp. 1554–1563, 1966.
[2] L. E. Baum and J. A. Egon, "An inequality with applications to statistical estimation for probabilistic functions of a Markov process and to a model for ecology," *Bull. Amer. Meteorol. Soc.*, vol. 73, pp. 360–363, 1967.
[3] L. E. Baum and G. R. Sell, "Growth functions for transformations on manifolds," *Pac. J. Math.*, vol. 27, no. 2, pp. 211–227, 1968.
[4] L. E. Baum, T. Petrie, G. Soules, and N. Weiss, "A maximization technique occurring in the statistical analysis of probabilistic functions of Markov chains," *Ann. Math. Stat.*, vol. 41, no. 1, pp. 164–171, 1970.
[5] L. E. Baum, "An inequality and associated maximization technique in statistical estimation for probabilistic functions of Markov processes," *Inequalities*, vol. 3, pp. 1–8, 1972.
[6] J. K. Baker, "The dragon system—An overview," *IEEE Trans. Acoust. Speech Signal Processing*, vol. ASSP-23, no. 1, pp. 24–29, Feb. 1975.
[7] F. Jelinek, "A fast sequential decoding algorithm using a stack," *IBM J. Res. Develop.*, vol. 13, pp. 675–685, 1969.
[8] L. R. Bahl and F. Jelinek, "Decoding for channels with insertions, deletions, and substitutions with applications to speech recognition," *IEEE Trans. Informat. Theory*, vol. IT-21, pp. 404–411, 1975.
[9] F. Jelinek, L. R. Bahl, and R. L. Mercer, "Design of a linguistic statistical decoder for the recognition of continuous speech," *IEEE Trans. Informat. Theory*, vol. IT-21, pp. 250–256, 1975.
[10] F. Jelinek, "Continuous speech recognition by statistical methods," *Proc. IEEE*, vol. 64, pp. 532–536, Apr. 1976.
[11] R. Bakis, "Continuous speech word recognition via centisecond acoustic states," in *Proc. ASA Meeting* (Washington, DC), Apr. 1976.
[12] F. Jelinek, L. R. Bahl, and R. L. Mercer, "Continuous speech recognition: Statistical methods," in *Handbook of Statistics, II*, P. R. Krishnaiad, Ed. Amsterdam, The Netherlands: North-Holland, 1982.
[13] L. R. Bahl, F. Jelinek, and R. L. Mercer, "A maximum likelihood approach to continuous speech recognition," *IEEE Trans. Pattern Anal. Machine Intell.*, vol. PAMI-5, pp. 179–190, 1983.
[14] S. E. Levinson, L. R. Rabiner, and M. M. Sondhi, "An introduction to the application of the theory of probabilistic functions of a Markov process to automatic speech recognition," *Bell Syst. Tech. J.*, vol. 62, no. 4, pp. 1035–1074, Apr. 1983.
[15] B. H. Juang, "On the hidden Markov model and dynamic time warping for speech recognition—A unified view," *AT&T Tech. J.*, vol. 63, no. 7, pp. 1213–1243, Sept. 1984.
[16] L. R. Rabiner and B. H. Juang, "An introduction to hidden Markov models," *IEEE ASSP Mag.*, vol. 3, no. 1, pp. 4–16, 1986.
[17] J. S. Bridle, "Stochastic models and template matching: Some important relationships between two apparently different techniques for automatic speech recognition," in *Proc. Inst. of Acoustics*, Autum Conf., pp. 1–8, Nov. 1984.
[18] J. Makhoul, S. Roucos, and H. Gish, "Vector quantization in speech coding," *Proc. IEEE*, vol. 73, no. 11, pp. 1551–1588, Nov. 1985.
[19] S. E. Levinson, "Structural methods in automatic speech recognition," *Proc. IEEE*, vol. 73, no. 11, pp. 1625–1650, Nov. 1985.
[20] A. W. Drake, "Discrete—state Markov processes," Chapter 5 in *Fundamentals of Applied Probability Theory*. New York, NY: McGraw-Hill, 1967.
[21] A. J. Viterbi, "Error bounds for convolutional codes and an asymptotically optimal decoding algorithm," *IEEE Trans. Informat. Theory*, vol. IT-13, pp. 260–269, Apr. 1967.
[22] G. D. Forney, "The Viterbi algorithm," *Proc. IEEE*, vol. 61, pp. 268–278, Mar. 1973.
[23] A. P. Dempster, N. M. Laird, and D. B. Rubin, "Maximum like-

lihood from incomplete data via the EM algorithm," *J. Roy. Stat. Soc.*, vol. 39, no. 1, pp. 1–38, 1977.

[24] L. A. Liporace, "Maximum likelihood estimation for multivariate observations of Markov sources," *IEEE Trans. Informat. Theory*, vol. IT-28, no. 5, pp. 729–734, 1982.

[25] B. H. Juang, "Maximum likelihood estimation for mixture multivariate stochastic observations of Markov chains," *AT&T Tech. J.*, vol. 64, no. 6, pp. 1235–1249, July–Aug. 1985.

[26] B. H. Juang, S. E. Levinson, and M. M. Sondhi, "Maximum likelihood estimation for multivariate mixture observations of Markov chains," *IEEE Trans. Informat. Theory*, vol. IT-32, no. 2, pp. 307–309, Mar. 1986.

[27] A. B. Poritz, "Linear predictive hidden Markov models and the speech signal," in *Proc. ICASSP '82* (Paris, France), pp. 1291–1294, May 1982.

[28] B. H. Juang and L. R. Rabiner, "Mixture autoregressive hidden Markov models for speech signals," *IEEE Trans. Acoust. Speech Signal Processing*, vol. ASSP-33, no. 6, pp. 1404–1413, Dec. 1985.

[29] M. J. Russell and R. K. Moore, "Explicit modeling of state occupancy in hidden Markov models for automatic speech recognition," in *Proc. ICASSP '85* (Tampa, FL), pp. 5–8, Mar. 1985.

[30] S. E. Levinson, "Continuously variable duration hidden Markov models for automatic speech recognition," *Computer, Speech and Language*, vol. 1, no. 1, pp. 29–45, Mar. 1986.

[31] B. Lowerre and R. Reddy, "The HARPY speech understanding system," in *Trends in Speech Recognition*, W. Lea, Editor. Englewood Cliffs, NJ: Prentice-Hall, 1980, pp. 340–346.

[32] L. R. Bahl, P. F. Brown, P. V. de Souza, and R. L. Mercer, "Maximum mutual information estimation of hidden Markov model parameters for speech recognition," in *Proc. ICASSP '86* (Tokyo, Japan), pp. 49–52, Apr. 1986.

[33] Y. Ephraim, A. Dembo, and L. R. Rabiner, "A minimum discrimination information approach for hidden Markov modeling," in *Proc. ICASSP '87* (Dallas, TX), Apr. 1987.

[34] B. H. Juang and L. R. Rabiner, "A probabilistic distance measure for hidden Markov models," *AT&T Tech. J.*, vol. 64, no. 2, pp. 391–408, Feb. 1985.

[35] L. R. Rabiner, B. H. Juang, S. E. Levinson, and M. M. Sondhi, "Some properties of continuous hidden Markov model representations," *AT&T Tech. J.*, vol. 64, no. 6, pp. 1251–1270, July–Aug. 1985.

[36] F. Jelinek and R. L. Mercer, "Interpolated estimation of Markov source parameters from sparse data," in *Pattern Recognition in Practice*, E. S. Gelesma and L. N. Kanal, Eds. Amsterdam, The Netherlands: North-Holland, 1980, pp. 381–397.

[37] R. Schwartz *et al.*, "Context-dependent modeling for acoustic-phonetic recognition of continuous speech," in *Conf. Proc. IEEE Int. Conf. on Acoustics, Speech, and Signal Processing*, pp. 1205–1208, Apr. 1985.

[38] K. F. Lee and H. W. Hon, "Large-vocabulary speaker-independent continuous speech recognition," in *Conf. Proc. IEEE Int. Conf. on Acoustics, Speech, and Signal Processing*, pp. 123–126, Apr. 1988.

[39] L. R. Rabiner, S. E. Levinson, and M. M. Sondhi, "On the application of vector quantization and hidden Markov models to speaker-independent isolated word recognition," *Bell Syst. Tech. J.*, vol. 62, no. 4, pp. 1075–1105, Apr. 1983.

[40] ——, "On the use of hidden Markov models for speaker-independent recognition of isolated words from a medium-size vocabulary," *AT&T Tech. J.*, vol. 63, no. 4, pp. 627–642, Apr. 1984.

[41] R. Billi, "Vector quantization and Markov source models applied to speech recognition," in *Proc. ICASSP '82* (Paris, France), pp. 574–577, May 1982.

[42] L. R. Rabiner, B. H. Juang, S. E. Levinson, and M. M. Sondhi, "Recognition of isolated digits using hidden Markov models with continuous mixture densities," *AT&T Tech. J.*, vol. 64, no. 6, pp. 1211–1222, July–Aug. 1986.

[43] A. B. Poritz and A. G. Richter, "Isolated word recognition," in *Proc. ICASSP '86* (Tokyo, Japan), pp. 705–708, Apr. 1986.

[44] R. P. Lippmann, E. A. Martin, and D. B. Paul, "Multistyle training for robust isolated word speech recognition," in *Proc. ICASSP '87* (Dallas, TX), pp. 705–708, Apr. 1987.

[45] D. B. Paul, "A speaker stress resistant HMM isolated word recognizer," in *Proc. ICASSP '87* (Dallas, TX), pp. 713–716, Apr. 1987.

[46] V. N. Gupta, M. Lennig and P. Mermelstein, "Integration of acoustic information in a large vocabulary word recognizer," in *Conf. Proc. IEEE Int. Conf. on Acoustics, Speech, and Signal Processing*, pp. 697–700, Apr. 1987.

[47] S. E. Levinson, "Continuous speech recognition by means of acoustic-phonetic classification obtained from a hidden Markov model," in *Proc. ICASSP '87* (Dallas TX), Apr. 1987.

[48] J. G. Wilpon, L. R. Rabiner, and T. Martin, "An improved word detection algorithm for telephone quality speech incorporating both syntactic and semantic constraints," *AT&T Bell Labs Tech. J.*, vol. 63, no. 3, pp. 479–498, Mar. 1984.

[49] J. G. Wilpon and L. R. Rabiner, "Application of hidden Markov models to automatic speech endpoint detection," *Computer Speech and Language*, vol. 2, no. 3/4, pp. 321–341, Sept./Dec. 1987.

[50] A. Averbuch *et al.*, "Experiments with the TANGORA 20,000 word speech recognizer," in *Conf. Proc. IEEE Int. Conf. on Acoustics, Speech, and Signal Processing*, pp. 701–704, Apr. 1987.

[51] B. S. Atal and S. L. Hanauer, "Speech analysis and synthesis by linear prediction of the speech wave," *J. Acoust. Soc. Am.*, vol. 50, pp. 637–655, 1971.

[52] F. I. Itakura and S. Saito, "Analysis-synthesis telephony based upon the maximum likelihood method," in *Proc. 6th Int. Congress on Acoustics* (Tokyo, Japan), pp. C17–20, 1968.

[53] J. Makhoul, "Linear prediction: A tutorial review," *Proc. IEEE*, vol. 63, pp. 561–580, 1975.

[54] J. D. Markel and A. H. Gray, Jr., *Linear Prediction of Speech*. New York, NY: Springer-Verlag, 1976.

[55] Y. Tokhura, "A weighted cepstral distance measure for speech recognition," *IEEE Trans. Acoust. Speech Signal Processing*, vol. ASSP-35, no. 10, pp. 1414–1422, Oct. 1987.

[56] B. H. Juang, L. R. Rabiner, and J. G. Wilpon, "On the use of bandpass liftering in speech recognition," *IEEE Trans. Acoust. Speech Signal Processing*, vol. ASSP-35, no. 7, pp. 947–954, July 1987.

[57] S. Furui, "Speaker independent isolated word recognition based on dynamics emphasized cepstrum," *Trans. IECE of Japan*, vol. 69, no. 12, pp. 1310–1317, Dec. 1986.

[58] F. K. Soong and A. E. Rosenberg, "On the use of instantaneous and transitional spectral information in speaker recognition," in *Proc. ICASSP '86* (Tokyo, Japan), pp. 877–880, Apr. 1986.

[59] L. R. Rabiner, J. G. Wilpon, and B. H. Juang, "A segmental *k*-means training procedure for connected word recognition," *AT&T Tech. J.*, vol. 65, no. 3, pp. 21–31, May–June 1986.

[60] L. R. Rabiner and S. E. Levinson, "A speaker-independent, syntax-directed, connected word recognition system based on hidden Markov models and level building," *IEEE Trans. Acoust. Speech Signal Processing*, vol. ASSP-33, no. 3, pp. 561–573, June 1985.

[61] L. R. Rabiner, J. G. Wilpon, and B. H. Juang, "A model-based connected digit recognition system using either hidden Markov models or templates," *Computer, Speech, and Language*, vol. 1, no. 2, pp. 167–197, Dec. 1986.

[62] H. Bourlard, Y. Kamp, H. Ney, and C. J. Wellekens, "Speaker-dependent connected speech recognition via dynamic programming and statistical methods," in *Speech and Speaker Recognition*, M. R. Schroeder, Ed. Basel, Switzerland: Karger, 1985, pp. 115–148.

[63] C. J. Wellekens, "Global connected digit recognition using Baum-Welch algorithm," in *Proc. ICASSP '86* (Tokyo, Japan), pp. 1081–1084, Apr. 1986.

[64] A. M. Derouault, "Context dependent phonetic Markov models for large vocabulary speech recognition," in *Proc. ICASSP '87* (Dallas, TX), Paper 10.1.1, pp. 360–363, Apr. 1987.

[65] B. Merialdo, "Speech recognition with very large size dictionary," in *Proc. ICASSP '87* (Dallas, TX), Paper 10.2.2, pp. 364–367, Apr. 1987.

[66] Y. L. Chow *et al.*, "BYBLOS: The BBN continuous speech recognition system," in *Proc. ICASSP '87* (Dallas, TX), Paper 3.7.1, pp. 89–92, Apr. 1987.

Lawrence R. Rabiner (Fellow, IEEE) was born in Brooklyn, NY, on September 28, 1943. He received the S.B. and S.M. degrees, both in 1964, and the Ph.D. degree in electrical engineering, in 1967, all from the Massachusetts Institute of Technology, Cambridge, MA.

From 1962 through 1964 he participated in the cooperative plan in electrical engineering at Bell Laboratories, Whippany, and Murray Hill, NJ. He worked on digital circuitry, military communications problems, and problems in binaural hearing. Presently he is engaged in research on speech recognition and digital signal processing techniques at Bell Laboratories, Murray Hill. He is coauthor of the books *Theory and Application of Digital Signal Processing* (Prentice-Hall, 1975), *Digital Processing of Speech Signals* (Prentice-Hall, 1978), and *Multirate Digital Signal Processing* (Prentice-Hall, 1983).

Dr. Rabiner is a member of Eta Kappa Nu, Sigma Xi, Tau Beta Pi, The National Academy of Engineering, and a Fellow of the Acoustical Society of America.

STOCHASTIC MODELING FOR AUTOMATIC SPEECH UNDERSTANDING

James K. Baker
IBM T.J. Watson Research Center
Yorktown Heights, New York 10598

There are many situations in automatic speech recognition/understanding in which decisions have to be made based on incomplete or uncertain information. Stochastic modeling is a flexible general method for handling such situations. Stochastic modeling consists of employing a specific probabilistic model for the uncertainty or incompleteness of the information. The uncertainty in automatic speech recognition arises for many reasons. The acoustic signal is ambiguous because the acoustic cues for the individual speech sounds become reduced or are deleted in normal continuous speech. Automatic segmentation and labeling procedures make insertion, deletion and substitution errors in addition to the fundamental ambiguity of the signal. Other sources of knowledge, such as syntax and semantics, seldom limit the possible word candidates to a single word, so although their information may be precise, it is incomplete in terms of making a decision on a unique word for a given place in the utterance.

An abstract model for these situations of uncertainty is that there are two sequences of random variables: Y(1), Y(2), Y(3),..., Y(T) and X(1), X(2), X(3),...,X(T). The X's represent some sequence which we wish to know, but which we are not able to observe directly (for example, the words in an utterance). The Y's represent some sequence which are related to the X's and which we can observe or which we have already deduced by other means (for example, the sequence of acoustic parameter values). Stochastic modeling consists of formulating a probabilistic model for generating sequences of X's and for producing a sequence of Y's based on the sequence of X's. These models can then be used to make inferences in a speech recognition system. When a sequence of Y's is observed, techniques are used for finding the sequence of X's which best fits the observed sequence of Y's -- that is, the sequence of X's which, according to the model, is the sequence which is the most likely to produce the observed sequence of Y's.

In this paper a specific class of stochastic models is discussed -- models based on the theory of a probabilistic function of a Markov process. First the properties of the general model are discussed and then some examples are considered of situations in automatic speech analysis in which such models can be applied.

Let Y(1), Y(2), Y(3),..., Y(T) be a sequence of random variables representing the external (acoustic) observations. Let X(1), X(2), X(3),..., X(T) be a sequence of random variables representing the internal states of a stochastic process such that the probability distributions of the Y's depend on the values of the X's, but the X's are not directly observed. As a convenient abbreviation we use a bracket and colon notation to represent sequences. Thus, Y[1:T] represents Y(1), Y(2), Y(3),..., Y(T) and X[1:T] represents X(1), X(2), X(3),..., X(T). Let y[1:T] be the observed sequence of values for the random variables Y[1:T].

We wish to make inferences about the sequence X[1:T] in light of the knowledge of y[1:T]. For example, we would like to know the conditional probability PROB(X(t)=j | Y[1:T]=y[1;T]) for each t and j (the conditional probability of a specific internal state at a specific time, given the entire sequence of external observations). Assuming we have a model for speech production, we can evaluate the _a priori_ probability PROB(X[1:T]). Assuming a model for the generation of acoustic events associated with a specific sequence of internal states, we can evaluate the conditional probability PROB(Y[1:t] =y[1:T] | X[1:T]=x[1:T]) (That is, the model yields conditional probabilities of external observations, given the sequence of internal states). Thus we know the conditional probabilities in the generative or synthetic form.

We can compute the desired conditional probabilities using Bayes' formula

$$(1)\ \mathrm{PROB}(X(t)=j \mid Y[1{:}T]=y[1{:}T]) = \mathrm{PROB}(X(t)=j,\ Y[1{:}T]=y[1{:}T]/\mathrm{PROB}(Y[1{:}T]=y[1{:}T])$$

if we can evaluate the factors on the right hand side. The numerator is given by

(2) $\mathrm{PROB}(X(t)=j,\ Y[1{:}T]=y[1{:}T])$

$$=\Sigma_{x[1:T],x(t)=j}\ \mathrm{PROB}(X[1{:}T]=x[1{:}T]Y[1{:}T]=y[1{:}T])$$

$$=\Sigma_{x[1:T],x(t)=j}\ \mathrm{PROB}(Y[1{:}T]=y[1{:}T] \mid X[1{:}T]=x[1{:}T])\mathrm{PROB}(X[1{:}T]=x[1{:}T])$$

where the sum is taken over all possible sequences x[1:T] subject to the restriction x(t)=j. (The joint probability of an internal sequence and an external sequence is the product of the a priori probability of the internal sequence and conditional probability of the external sequence given by the model. The probability for the event X(t)=j is obtained by summing over all internal sequences which meet that restriction.) We can evaluate the a priori probability that Y[1:T] would be y[1:T] as

(3) $\mathrm{PROB}(Y[1{:}T]=y[1{:}T])$

$$=\Sigma_{x[1:T]}\ \mathrm{PROB}(Y[1{:}T]=y[1{:}T] \mid X[1{:}T]=x[1{:}T])\mathrm{PROB}(X[1{:}T]=x[1{:}T])$$

where the sum is taken over all possible sequences x[1:T]. (The total probability of an external sequence is the sum of its joint probability with all possible internal sequences.)

Therefore

(4) $\mathrm{PROB}(X(t)=j \mid Y[1{:}T]=y[1{:}T])$

$$=\mathrm{PROB}(X(t)=j,\ Y[1{:}T]=y[1{:}T])/\mathrm{PROB}(Y[1{:}T]=y[1{:}T])$$

$$=\frac{\Sigma_{x[1:T],x(t)=j}\ \mathrm{PROB}(Y[1{:}T]=y[1{:}T] \mid X[1{:}T]=x[1{:}T])\mathrm{PROB}(X[1{:}T]=x[1{:}T])}{\Sigma_{x[1:T]}\ \mathrm{PROB}(Y[1{:}T]=y[1{:}T] \mid X[1{:}T]=x[1{:}T])\mathrm{PROB}(X[1{:}T]=x[1{:}T])}$$

where the sum in the denominator is taken over all sequences x[1:T] and the sum in the numerator is taken over all such sequences subject to the restriction x(t)=j. (This is the probability of the internal event X(t)=j conditional on the observed external sequence, as desired.)

The derivation of equation (4) is just a standard application of Bayes' theorem. It represents a formal inversion of the conditional probabilities from the generative form to the analytic form. (Note: The word "analytic" is used here in a special sense. "Analytic" means "taking apart" as opposed to "synthetic," "generative," or "putting together." In terms of speech, the generative form predicts the observations (Y's) in terms of the internal sequence (X's). The analytic form computes the a posteriori probability of the X's conditional on the observed Y's.) The speech-recognition knowledge sources provide the conditional probabilities in a generative form. They must be converted into an analytic form to make inferences about a particular utterance from the observed acoustics. However, the formal inversion formula given in equation (4) is not computationally practical since in general the set of all possible sequences x[1:T] is prohibitively large. It is necessary to apply the restrictions of a more specific model to obtain a computationally efficient formula.

The model used in this paper is that the sequences represent a probabilistic function of a Markov process. Specifically, it is assumed that the conditional probability that X(t)=j given X(t-1) is independent of t and of the values of X[1:t-2] and that the conditional probability that Y(t)=k given X(t) and X(t-1) is independent of t and of the values of any of the other X's and Y's. Let $B=\{b_{i,j,k}\}$ and $A=\{a_{i,j}\}$ be arrays such that

$$(5)\ PROB(Y(t)=y(t) \mid X[1{:}t]=x[1{:}t],\ Y[1{:}t-1]=y[1{:}t-1])$$
$$=PROB(Y(t)=y(t) \mid X(t-1)=x(t-1), X(t)=x(t))$$
$$=b_{x(t-1),x(t),y(t)}$$

and

$$(6)\ PROB(X(t)=x(t) \mid X[1{:}t-1]=x[1{:}t-1])$$
$$=PROB(X(t)=x(t) \mid X(t-1)=x(t-1))$$
$$=a_{x(t-1),x(t)}$$

This restriction to a Markov model is the fundamental assumption which allows the computations to be practical. In the Markov model the conditional probabilities depend only on X(t) and X(t-1) and not on the entire sequence X[1:T] as in equations (1) to (4). This specialization makes it possible to evaluate the desired conditional probabilities by an indirect but computationally efficient procedure.

The Markov assumption might be parapharased by saying that the conditional probabilities are independent of context, but such a simple statement would be misleading. Since the state speace of the Markov process for our speech recognition application has not yet been formulated, the assumption of the Markov properties should be regarded as a prescription to be followed in the formulation of the state space. Specifically, two situations which differ in "relevant" context must be assigned two separate states in the state space of the random variables X[1:T]. Then all "relevant" context is included in the state space description, and the conditional probabilities are indeed independent of further context. The fundamental assumption that we are making is that it is possible to meet this prescription and still have a state space of manageable size.

Under the assumptions of equations (5) and (6) we have

$$(7)\ PROB(X[1{:}s]=x[1{:}s])=PROB(X(1)=x(1))(\Pi_{t=2,s}\ a_{x(t-1),x(t)})$$

(The a priori probability of a given internal state sequence is the product of the transition probabilities for all the transitions in the sequence.) To simplify, add a special extra state to the Markov process; let x(0) be this special state and define $a_{x(0),j}$ =PROB(X(1)=j). Similar conventions are assumed throughout this paper, unless specifically mentioned otherwise. Then

$$(8)\ PROB(X[1{:}s]=x[1{:}s])=\Pi_{t=1,s}\ a_{x(t-1),x(t)}$$

also

$$(9)\ PROB(Y[1{:}s]=y[1{:}s] \mid X[1{:}s]=x[1{:}s])=\Pi_{t=1,s}\ b_{x(t-1),x(t),y(t)}$$

(the model-defined probability of an external sequence, conditional on the internal sequence) where $b_{x(0),j,k}$ is defined appropriately. Combining (8) and (9) yields

$$(10)\ PROB(X[1{:}s]=x[1{:}s],\ Y[1{:}s]=y[1{:}s])=\Pi_{t=1,s}\ a_{x(t-1),x(t)}\ b_{x(t-1),x(t),y(t)}$$

(the joint probability of an internal sequence and an external sequence as given by the Markov model).

To make possible the efficient computation of the sums in equations (3) and (4), we introduce the probabilities of partial sequences of states and observations (Baum). Using (2) with t=T=s and using (10), we can set

(11) $\alpha(s,x(s))=\text{PROB}(X(s)=x(s),\ Y[1:s]=y[1:s])$

$$=\Sigma_{x[1:s-1]}\Pi_{t=1,s}a_{x(t-1),x(t)}b_{x(t-1),x(t),y(t)}$$

where the sum is over all possible sequences x[1:s-1]. (This is the joint probability of the partial external sequence, up to time s, and the event that the process is in state x(s) at time s.) Let

(12) $\beta(s,x(s))=\text{PROB}(X(s)=x(s)\ Y[s+1:T]=y[s+1:T])$

$$=\Sigma_{x[s+1:T]}\Pi_{t=s+1,T}a_{x(t-1),x(t)}b_{x(t-1),x(t),y(t)}$$

where the sum is over all possible sequences x[s+1:T]. (This is the joint probability of the partial external sequence from time s+1 to the end, and the event that processis in state x(s) at time s.) The benefit of introducing the functions α and β is that the values of $\alpha(s,j)$ for a given s can be computed from the values of $\alpha(s-1,j)$. Similarly, β for a given s can be computed from the values of β for s+1.

In fact

(13) $\alpha(s,j)=\Sigma_i\alpha(s-1,i)a_{i,j}b_{i,j,y(s)}$

(because every sequence x[1:s] must have x(s-1)=i for some i) and

(14) $\beta(s,j)=\Sigma_i\beta(s+1,i)a_{j,i}b_{j,i,y(s+1)}$

But $\alpha(T,j)=\text{PROB}(X(T)=j,Y[1:T]=y[1:T])$ hence

(15) $\text{PROB}(Y[1:T]=y[1:T])=\Sigma_j\alpha(T,j)$

We can compute the conditional probability distribution for X(t)

(16) $\text{PROB}(X(t)=j\mid Y[1:T]=y[1:T])$

$$=\text{PROB}(X(t)=j,\ Y[1:T])/\text{PROB}(Y[1:T]=y[1:T])$$

$$=\alpha(t,j)\beta(t,j)/\Sigma_i\alpha(T,i)$$

In speech recognition problems, we usually want to know the particular sequence x[1:T] which maximizes the joint probability PROB(X[1:T]=x[1:T],Y[1:T]=y[1:T]). Again, the problem can be solved by induction from partial sequences (Bellman). Let

(17) $\gamma(t,j)=\text{Max}_{x[1:t-1]}\text{PROB}(X[1:t-1]=x[1:t-1],\ X(t)=j,\ Y[1:t]=y[1:t])$

Then γ may be computed by

(18) $\gamma(t,j)=\text{Max}_i\gamma(t-1,i)a_{i,j}b_{i,j,y(t)}$

Notice that equation (18) is just like equation (13) except that Max has been substituted for Σ. It is convenient to save "back-pointers" while computing γ. Therefore, let $I(t,j)$ be any value of i for which the maximum is achieved in equation (18). Then a sequence x[1:T] for which PROB(X[1:T]=x[1:T],Y[1:T]=y[1:T]) is maximized is obtained by

(19) $x(T)=j$, where j is any index such that $\gamma(T,j)=\mathrm{Max}_i\,\gamma(T,i)$

and

(20) $x(t)=I(t+1,x(t+1)),\ t=T-1,T-2,\ldots,2,1$

So far the analysis has assumed that the matrices A and B are fixed and known. However, if A and B are not known but must be estimated, than the α and β computed above may be used to obtain a Bayesian <u>a posteriori</u> re-estimation of A and B. The matrix A is re-estimated by

$$(21)\ \hat{a}_{i,j} = \frac{\Sigma_{t=1,T-1}\ \mathrm{PROB}(X(t)=i,X(t+1)=j \mid Y[1:T]=y[1:T],\{a_{i,j}\},\{b_{i,j,k}\})}{\Sigma_{t=1,T-1}\mathrm{PROB}(X(t)=i \mid Y[1:T]=y[1:T],\{a_{i,j}\},\{b_{i,j,k}\})}$$

$$= \frac{\Sigma_{t=1,T-1}\alpha(t,i)a_{i,j}b_{i,j,y(t+1)}\beta(t+1,j)}{\Sigma_{t=1,T-1}\alpha(t,i)\beta(t,i)}$$

The matrix B is re-estimated by

$$(22)\ \hat{b}_{i,j,k} = \frac{\Sigma_{t=1,T-1,y(t+1)=k}\ \mathrm{PROB}(X(t)=i,X(t+1)=j \mid Y[1:T]=y[1:T],\{a_{i,j}\},\{b_{i,j,k}\})}{\Sigma_{t=1,T-1}\mathrm{PROB}(X(t)=i,\ X(t+1)=j \mid Y[1:T]=y[1:T],\{a_{i,j}\},\{b_{i,j,k}\})}$$

$$= \frac{\Sigma_{t=1,T-1,y(t+1)=k}\alpha(t,i)a_{i,j}b_{i,j,k}\beta(t+1,j)}{\Sigma_{t=1,T-1}\alpha(t,i)a_{i,j}b_{i,j,y(t+1)}\beta(t+1,j)}$$

In fact it can be shown (Baum) that

$$(23)\ \mathrm{PROB}(Y[1:T]=y[1:T] \mid \{\hat{a}_{i,j}\},\{\hat{b}_{i,j,k}\}) \geq \mathrm{PROB}(Y[1:T]=y[1:T] \mid \{a_{i,j}\},\{b_{i,j,k}\})$$

Hence the re-estimation given by equations (21) and (22) may be used iteratively in an attempt to obtain $\{a_{i,j}\}$ and $\{b_{i,j,k}\}$ which maximize PROB(Y[1:T]=y[1:T] | $\{a_{i,j}\},\{b_{i,j,k}\}$). Thus we can obtain an approximation to maximum likelihood estimates for $\{a_{i,j}\}$ and $\{b_{i,j,k}\}$.

In re-estimating the matrices A and B, the special structure of the speech recognition problem can be used to good advantage. Although it is convenient to use a single integrated model for the actual analysis and recognition of utterances, the re-estimation of the structural matrices can be performed separately for each of the levels in the hierarchy. Also note that any entry in A or B which is zero remains zero in the re-estimations of equations (21) and (22). Therefore we are able to maintain and utilize the sparseness of these matrices in the re-estimation process.

The general model of a probabilistic function of a Markov process can be applied to some degree to almost any situation in which there is an observed sequence (Y's) which depends probabilistically on an unobserved sequence (X's). Let's consider several examples of such situations in automatic speech analysis.

ISOLATED WORD RECOGNITION (ITAKURA, WHITE)

One method of isolated word recognition involves matching the sequence of acoustic parameters in the word to be recognized against a set of prototypes, where each prototype is the sequence of acoustic parameters for an instance of a word in the lexicon. Assuming that we have a method for measuring the match between the acoustic parameter values for an elementary segment in the prototype and an elementary segment in the word to be recognized, we still must take account of the fact that protions of the word to be recognized may be spoken faster or more slowly than the corresponding protions of the prototype. In matching a given word and a given prototype, we have a hidden stochastic process in which the observed sequence (Y's) consists of the sequence of acoustic parameters for the word to be recognized, and the internal sequence represents the information as to how the times in the word to be recognized correspond to the times in the prototype.

Specifically, we let Y(t) be the acoustic parameter values observed for the elementary segment at time t in the word to be recognized, and we let X(t)=s if the elementary segment at time t in the word to be recognized corresponds to the elementary segment at time s in the prototype. The possibility of a portion of the word being faster or slower than the prototype is represented by conditional probabilities such as those given in equation (24)

$$(24)\begin{cases} \text{PROB}(X(t)=s \mid X(t-1)=s)=a \\ \text{PROB}(X(t)=s \mid X(t-1=s-1)=1-a-b \\ \text{PROB}(X(t)=s \mid X(t-1)=s-2)=b \end{cases}$$

where a and b are parameters which can be estimated by experiment. Thus the matrix $A=\{a_{i,j}\}$ of equation (6) is determined by equation (24). Note that $a_{i,j}=0$ unless j is equal to i or i+1 or i+2. The conditional probability in equation (5) is estimated by the procedure which matches an elementary segment of the word with an elementary segment of the prototype. Thus, we have modeled the situation as a probabilistic function of a Markov process and can find the best internal sequence by using equations (18) and (20). The problem can also be viewed as one of finding the best path through the following network.

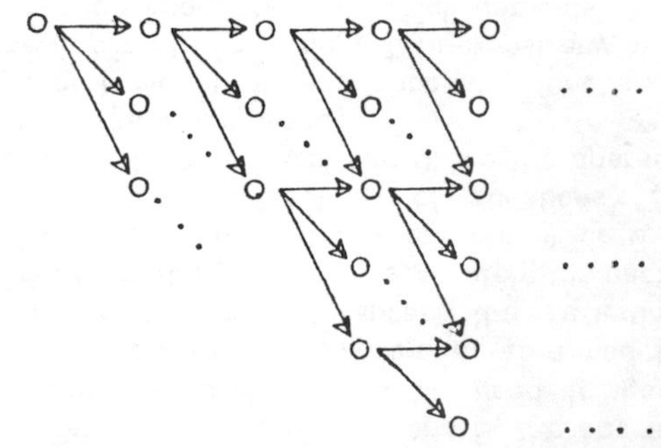

Figure 1. Dynamic Time Warping Network

The node in row s and column t of this network corresponds to the event X(t)=s. The state space network is a simple linear network, as shown in Figure 2.

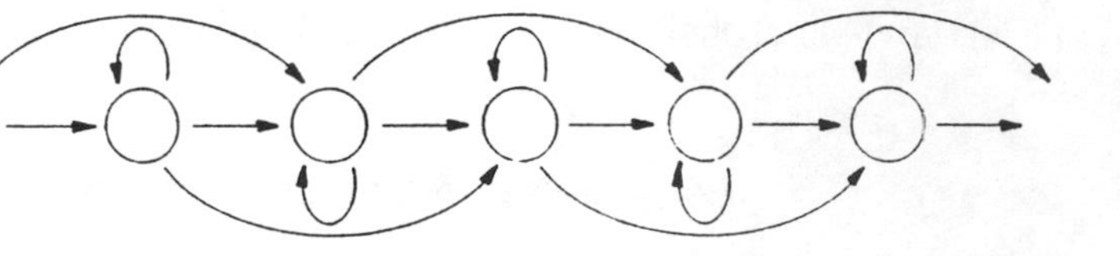

Figure 2. Isolated Word Recognition

A model similar to this one has been used successfully for automatic recognition of isolated words (Itakura).

WORD SPOTTING (BAKIS, BRIDLE)

Suppose we wish to find all instances of a particular word in a long recording of continuous speech. If we have a prototype for the word then we can formulate a model which is similar to the one we used for isolated word recognition, except there is an extra state in the network to represent all acoustic segments which occur between instances of the word, and the network loops back to allow repeated instances of the word. The schematic network is shown in Figure 3.

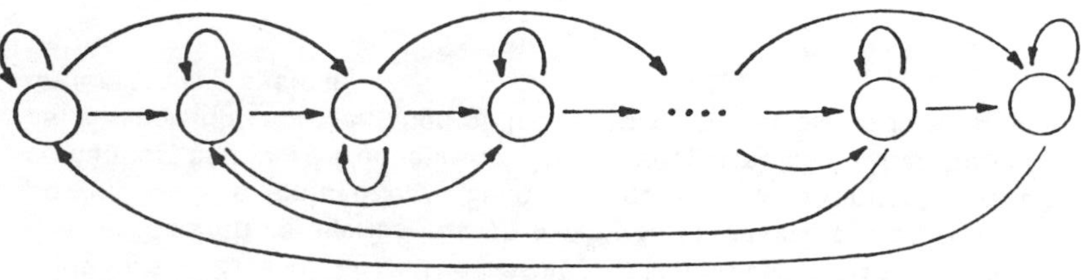

Figure 3. Word Spotting

If either in the isolated word recognition or in the word spotting we desire to construct prototypes not just from a single instance of a lexical item but rather from a collection of instances, then we must find which elementary segments in each instance corresponds with each elementary segment in the combined prototype. This correspondence can be found by equations (13) and (14) and we can automatically train for a generalization of the parameters a and b in equation (24) by the re-estimation procedure of equations (22) and (23). A word spotting procedure based on a model similar to the one described here, with a training procedure, has proven to be very successful (Bakis).

MACHINE AIDED SEGMENTATION (BAKER)

Automatic segmentation of continuous speech into acoustic segments corresponding to a broad phonetic transcription is a component of many speech recognition systems, but it is difficult to achieve high accuracy. A much simpler segmentation problem results if we assume that we have available a phonetic transcription of the utterance and merely want to know the times at which the given phones occur. Abstractly, this problem is just like that of comparing an isolated word to a prototype. The Markov model is again a simple linear network. In this case, however, the match and dynamic time warping is performed on an entire sentence. The prototype is constructed by concatenating prototypes for each of the phones in the given transcription.

MACHINE-AIDED PHONETIC TRANSCRIPTION (BAHL)

Suppose we are given an orthographic transcription of a sentence and wish to estimate the phonetic transcription. Given any sequence of words and a list of phonological rules, there exist automatic procedures (Cohen and Mercer) for applying the phonological rules to baseforms obtained from a phonemic dictionary to yield a network representation of all possible surface forms, that is, all possible prounounciations of the sentence. A simple example of such a network is shown in Figure 4.

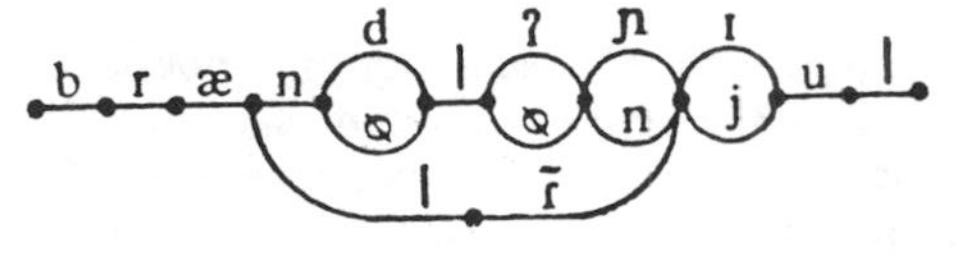

Figure 4. Phonetic Transcription

Each arc in this network corresponds to a particular phone. For each arc in the network we substitute a small network which represents a prototype for the phone corresponding to the arc. We can now use equations (18) and (20) to find the best path through this expanded network. The transition probabilities in this model are determined from the probabilities associated with the frequency of application of each of the phonological rules (conditional on the context of the rule being satisfied). These statistics can be estimated by an automatic procedure similar to the one represented by equations (22) and (23). Such a machine-aided phonetic transcriber has recently been successfully trained (Bahl).

PITCH TRACKING

Let the state space for the Markov process be a set of quantized values for the pitch frequency, plus a special state representing unvoiced speech. The transition probabilities are estimated from the frequencies of occurence of corresponding pitch changes in a set of training utterances. The random variable Y(t) is a vector of elementary pitch estimates. The conditional probability distribution for a typical component of Y(t) would have most of the probability clustered around the true pitch frequency, but also might have modes at half the true frequency or twice the true frequency, and so forth. The Bayesian estimate of X(t) given by equation (16) is then the best estimate of the pitch frequency at time t taking into account the whole sequence of elementary estimates Y[1:T] and the known (statistical) constraints on the rate of change of X. Thus the stochastic model allows us to combine estimates from an arbitrary number of elementary estimators and to use past, present and future pitch estimates to compute X(t).

FORMANT TRACKING

The state space for formant tracking is a vector of quantized frequencies, one element for each formant. The random variable Y(t) would be a list of frequencies that are candidates for formant frequencies (for example, they could be the peaks in a smoothed spectrum). In addition to the Markov process with time index t, there is a little Markov process whose index is the formant number. The little Markov process is run repeatedly, once for each time t. This little Markov process determines which formant corresponds to which candidate frequency and which formants correspond to no candidate frequencies at all. The state space variable for the little Markov process is a vector (C,M) where C is the number of candidate frequencies that are less than or equal to the current formant frequency, and M is a boolean variable indicating whether the current formant corresponds to any of the candidate frequencies. The transition network restricts C to be non-decreasing and the transition probabilities reflect the probabilities of missing peaks, two formants with a single peak, and so forth. The transition probabilities can be estimated by training on speech samples for which the formants have been tracked by hand.

DETERMINING SYNTACTIC-SEMANTIC CATEGORIES (RICH)

The grammatical categories of the words in a sentence are constrained by the syntax and can be used for prediction in a probabilistic sense. For example, a noun is frequently preceded by an adjective, but is less frequently followed by an adjective. Using a probabilistic function of a Markov process, we can generalize this notion, associating the words with arbitrary categories whether grammatically determined or otherwise. The random variable Y(t) in this model is the word which occurs at position t in a long sequence of words. The random variable X(t) is the category at position t. The words do not need to be assigned to disjoint categories. Category membership is represented by the conditional probability distributions PROB(Y(t)=w | X(t)=c), which includes word frequency information. It is possible to re-estimate the parameters of the Markov process by equations (22) and (23). The result would correspond to associating the words with categories in such a way as to maximize the predictive power of the categories. Such categories could reflect syntax, semantics, and word frequencies. These categories could then be used as a simplified representation of the syntax and semantics in a speech understanding system.

LINGUSTIC SEQUENTIAL DECODING

(Tappert et al., Paul et al., Jelinek et al.)

Speech recognition may be viewed as a sequential decoding problem. That is, we may view the sequence of labels produced by an automatic segmentation and labeling program as the true sequence of phones transmitted over a noisy channel. Sequential decoding algorithms developed for decoding convolution codes have been adapted to speech recognition/understanding problems. If we represent the true sequence of phones as a Markov process, then the output of the noisy channel is a probablistic function of a Markov process. Equations (18) and (20) correspond to an algorithm known in communications theory as the Viterbi algorithm (Viterbi). There are other algorithms for sequential decoding, which are also based on maximizing the a posteriori probability according to such a stochastic model, and several of them have been successfully applied to speech recognition (Tappert et al., Jelinek et al.).

INTEGRATED SPEECH RECOGNITION NETWORK (Baker)

The DRAGON speech recognition system extends the Markov model to include not only the linguistic decoder but also the lexical, phonological, and acoustic-phonetic knowledge. In addition semantics, both intra-sentence and inter-sentence, could be introduced. By formulating the entire speech recognition system in terms of a single abstract model, a great conceptual simplicity is achieved. Each knowledge source is represented as a probabilistic function of a Markov process, in a manner similar to that used in the examples above. The individual processes are organized into a hierarchy and the integrated system is also a probabilistic function of a Markov process. This integrated system could be treated by any of the sequential decoding techniques used in the linguistic sequential decoders, but in the DRAGON system an optimal search strategy has been adopted which performs the recognition by applying equations (18) and (20).

These equations correspond to searching all possible paths through the network to find the optimum path. In the application to an integrated speech recognition system, this search represents a search of all possible sentences of the language (constrained only by the length of the observed sequence of acoustic parameters), of all possible pronunciations of each sentence, and of all possible time warpings to match each such pronunciation to the observed acoustic sequence. It might seem that such an exhaustive search is impossible, but the essential feature of the Markov model is that it permits such a search to be performed with the number of computations being a linear function of the length of the utterance, as shown in equations (18) and (20).

The number of computations in each application of equation (18) is related to the number of pairs i,j for which $a_{i,j}$ is non-zero. If the integrated speech recognition network is too large and too complex, then optimal search would be impractical even though the time of computation is linear in the length of the utterance. To demonstrate that it is possible to satisfy the prescription to include all "relevant" context in the representation of the Markov state space and still obtain a network of manageable size, the DRAGON system has been implemented for several speech recognition tasks. Each task is based on a specialized language for a specific interactive computer task. The most complex task implemented so far is an interactive formant tracking task. The language has an infinite number of possible sentences, with about 16^n sentences of length n words. The lexicon and grammar are designed to fit the task: no restriction was placed on either the lexicon or the grammar to prevent acoustical confusions (for example, "Hamming" and "Hanning" are both used as possible window types and are syntactically equivalent).

The current implementation of the DRAGON system has been tested on a total of 61 sentences from three speech understanding tasks. An earlier test on 17 sentences including a fourth task gave comparable results. Detailed statistics of the performance on the 61 sentences are given in Tables 1-3. Since the number of words in the sentence output by the system is not necessarily the same as the number of words in the actual input sentence, there is no unique way to calculate the percentage of words correctly recognized. The statistic (words corrct)/(words in) ranges from 85.2% to 94.6%; the statistic (words correct)/(words out) ranges from 89% to 93.9%. The statistic (utterances correct)/(number of utterances) is 68.1%, 80.9% and 44.4%, respectively for the three tasks.

These statistics demonstrate that the concepts of stochastic modeling of knowledge sources and optimal search are viable. Note that this level of performance is achieved by a simplified system with no semantic knowledge, no explicit phonological rules, only one pronunciation modeled for each word, and a very simple set of acoustic parameters. Each of these limitations is a feature merely of the current implementation, in each case a more sophisticated model can easily be substituted. An experiment is being done to compare the performance of the HEARSAY system and the DRAGON system on the same set of sentences (Lowerre).

TASK: VOICE CHESS

PHRASE#	#IN	#OUT	#CORRECT	#SEMCOR	LENGTH	MAIN	ACO
1	5	5	5	5	2450	21.2	16.2
2	6	6	6	6	2740	21.8	16.0
3	5	5	5	5	2590	21.1	15.5
4	9	9	8	8	3990	21.9	16.6
5	3	3	3	3	2130	22.1	15.8
6	11	11	11	11	5800	21.0	15.6
7	5	5	5	5	2430	21.4	16.0
8	5	6	5	5	2300	22.9	15.6
9	6	6	4	4	2970	22.1	15.5
10	4	4	4	4	2120	22.0	15.8
11	3	3	3	3	1800	22.2	16.1
12	7	7	6	6	3410	22.6	15.9
13	5	5	5	5	2370	21.7	16.1
14	8	8	8	8	3920	21.2	15.6
15	6	6	6	6	3260	21.2	15.3
16	6	6	6	6	3160	20.6	15.3
17	7	7	6	6	3800	22.1	15.3
18	6	6	5	5	2870	21.1	15.3
19	6	6	6	6	2930	22.0	15.3
20	5	5	5	5	2210	21.6	15.3
21	6	6	5	5	3050	21.0	16.1
22	6	6	6	6	2630	20.0	16.0

(WORDS CORRECT)/(WORDS IN) = .946
(WORDS CORRECT)/(WORDS OUT) = .939
(WORDS SEMANTICALLY CORRECT)/(WORDS OUT) = .939

#IN = NUMBER OF WORDS IN ACTUAL (INPUT) PHRASE
#OUT = NUMBER OF WORDS IN OUTPUT PHRASE
#CORRECT = NUMBER WORDS CORRECTLY RECOGNIZED
#SEMCOR = NUMBER WORDS SEMANTICALLY CORRECT (ERROR IRRELEVANT TO TASK)
LENGTH = DURATION OF PHRASE IN MILLISECONDS
MAIN = (COMPUTATION TIME OF MAIN RECOGNITION ROUTINE)/LENGTH
ACO = (COMPUTATION TIME OF ACOUSTICS MODULE)/LENGTH
APPROXIMATE AMOUNT OF CORE NEEDED = 60K

Table 1

In evaluating the computation time and storage requirements, note that these figures are given only as a rough guide to what is possible. No attempt has been made to optimize the programs in terms of either computation time or storage requirements. The indicated computation time is the amount of central processor time used in running time used in running the program on a PDP-10 computer. The most important fact about the computation time is that for a given task the computation time is essentially proportional to the length of the utterance.

TASK: MEDICAL QUESTIONNAIRE

PHRASE*	*IN	*OUT	*CORRECT	*SEMCOR	LENGTH	MAIN	ACO
1	3	3	3	3	1340	37.2	20.8
2	3	3	3	3	1240	38.4	19.6
3	4	3	1	1	1740	37.2	21.0
4	4	4	4	4	1720	38.1	19.6
5	4	3	0	0	1740	37.1	21.1
6	4	4	4	4	2120	36.4	19.6
7	4	4	4	4	1580	38.3	19.6
8	4	4	4	4	2120	37.8	19.6
9	4	4	4	4	2370	38.0	19.7
10	4	4	4	4	1880	36.0	19.6
11	4	4	4	4	2050	36.7	19.7
12	5	5	5	5	2600	35.9	19.6
13	5	5	5	5	1990	38.2	19.6
14	6	6	6	6	2400	36.0	19.7
15	6	7	3	6	2510	36.0	20.8
16	6	6	6	6	2640	35.7	19.7
17	4	4	4	4	2730	35.1	19.6
18	5	5	5	5	2170	37.5	19.7
19	5	5	4	4	1820	37.4	19.6
20	4	4	4	4	2090	37.0	19.7
21	4	4	4	4	2180	37.9	19.7

(WORDS CORRECT)/(WORDS IN) = .880
(WORDS CORRECT)/(WORDS OUT) = .890
(WORDS SEMANTICALLY CORRECT)/(WORDS OUT) = .923

*IN = NUMBER OF WORDS IN ACTUAL (INPUT) PHRASE
*OUT = NUMBER OF WORDS IN OUTPUT PHRASE
*CORRECT = NUMBEER WORDS CORRECTLY RECOGNIZED
*SEMCOR = NUMBER WORDS SEMANTICALLY CORRECT
(ERROR IRRELEVANT TO TASK)
LENGTH = DURATION OF PHRASE IN MILLISECONDS
MAIN = (COMPUTATION TIME OF MAIN RECOGNITION ROUTINE)/LENGTH
ACO = (COMPUTATION TIME OF ACOUSTICS MODULE)/LENGTH
APPROXIMATE AMOUNT OF CORE NEEDED = 80K

Table 2

A point of major significance is that the computation time does not depend on how well the recognition proceeds. On the Voice Chess task the HEARSAY system takes, on the average, about 10 to 12 times real time for the complete recognition process, which is nearly 4 times as fast as the DRAGON system. However, the HEARSAY system uses a best-first search technique, so its computation time can vary greatly depending on how many errors are made in intermediate recognition decisions. With most search techniques, decisions in the recognition process control the direction of search and errors in early decisions can greatly increase the computation time. In fact, programs based on such techniques sometimes have to be terminated because they exhaust the available time or storage before they complete the analysis of an utterance. The DRAGON system uses a complete optimal search which takes the same length of time no matter how much noise there is in the data or how many errors there are in the recognition process.

TASK: INTERACTIVE FORMANT TRACKING

PHRASE*	*IN	*OUT	*CORRECT	*SEMCOR	LENGTH	MAIN	ACO
1	6	6	6	6	2170	126.9	18.7
2	9	8	8	8	4270	119.4	18.7
3	8	8	8	8	3730	119.4	18.3
4	9	8	7	7	3690	118.5	18.6
5	7	7	5	5	3490	123.7	18.6
6	9	9	9	9	5670	115.9	18.5
7	10	10	10	10	4510	121.2	18.4
8	7	7	7	7	3200	124.5	18.3
9	11	11	10	11	5120	118.1	17.6
10	7	6	6	6	3300	120.0	17.5
11	4	4	4	4	3070	119.6	18.5
12	10	9	8	8	4480	118.0	18.7
13	4	4	4	4	2760	124.0	18.8
14	4	3	0	0	2300	131.2	18.5
15	10	9	8	9	4260	126.3	19.2
16	11	11	7	8	5160	119.7	18.7
17	10	10	8	9	4060	121.9	17.9
18	6	6	6	6	3110	123.4	17.9

(WORDS CORRECT)/(WORDS IN) = .852
(WORDS CORRECT)/(WORDS OUT) = .890
(WORDS SEMANTICALLY CORRECT)/(WORDS OUT) = .919

*IN = NUMBER OF WORDS IN ACTUAL (INPUT) PHRASE
*OUT = NUMBER OF WORDS IN OUTPUT PHRASE
*CORRECT = NUMBER WORDS CORRECTLY RECOGNIZED
*SEMCOR = NUMBER WORDS SEMANTICALLY CORRECT
(ERROR IRRELEVANT TO TASK)
LENGTH = DURATION OF PHRASE IN MILLISECONDS
MAIN = (COMPUTATION TIME OF MAIN RECOGNITION ROUTINE)/LENGTH
ACO = (COMPUTATION TIME OF ACOUSTICS MODULE)/LENGTH
APPROXIMATE AMOUNT OF CORE NEEDED = 120K

Table 3

The amount of computation time required does depend on the size and complexity of the task. As a rough measure of complexity, the vocabulary sizes for the Voice Chess, Medical Questionaire, and Formant Tracking tasks are, respectively, 24 words, 76 words, and 195 words. In terms of the number of possible sentences, the Formant Tracking task is by far the most complex. It has a recursive grammar and the language has approximately 16" sentences of length n. Notice that, although the computation time is greater for the more complex task, the level of performance remains high.

CONCLUSIONS

This collection of examples demonstrates that stochastic modeling is a versatile and valuable procedure for automatic speech analysis. Many situations in speech analysis can be represented as a hidden stochastic process. Stochastic modeling allows us to make inferences about the internal or hidden process from its influence on an external process which we observe. The possible applications of these techniques are as many as we have the ingenuity to model. Their success in any application is dependent on our care in constructing the model.

REFERENCES

Bahl, Lalit R., personal communication.

Baker, James K., "Machine-Aided Labeling of Connected Speech," in "Working Papers in Speech Recognition -- II," Computer Science Department, Carnegie-Mellon University, 1972.

Baker, James K., "The DRAGON System -- an Overview," Proc. IEEE Symposium on Speech Recognition, Pittsburgh, Pa., 1974, pp. 22-26.

Bakis, Raimo, personal communication.

Baum, Leonard E., "An Inequality and Associated Maximization Technique in Statistical Estimation for Probabilistic Functions of a Markov Process," Inequalities, Vol. III, 1972, pp. 1-8.

Bellman, Richard E., Dynamic Programming, Princeton University Press, 1957.

Bridle, John, personal communication.

Cohen, P. S. and R. L. Mercer, "The Phonological Component of an Automatic Speech-Recognition System," Proc. IEEE Symposium on Speech Recognition, Pittsburgh, Pa., 1974, pp. 177-187.

Itakura, F., "Minimum Prediction Residual Principle Applied to Speech Recognition," Proc. IEEE Symposium on Speech Recognition, Pittsburgh, Pa., 1974, pp. 101-105.

Jelinek, Fredrick, Lalit Bahl, and Robert L. Mercer, "Design of a Linguistic Statistical Decoder for the Recognition of Continuous Speech," Proc. IEEE Symposium on Speech Recognition, Pittsburgh, Pa., pp. 255-260.

Lowerre, Bruce T., "Comparison of Two Speech Understanding Systems," JASA, Vol. 56, Supplement, Fall 1974, p. 527.

Paul, J. E., A. S. Rabinowitz, J. P. Raganati, V. A. Vitols, and M. L. Griffith, "Automatic Recognition of Continuous Speech: Further Development of a Hierarchial Strategy," RADC-TR-73-319, 1973.

Rich, Elaine, personal communication.

Tappert, C. C., N. R. Dixon, A. S. Rabinowitz, and W. D. Chapman, "Automatic Recognition of Continuous Speech Utilizing Dynamic Segmentation, Dual Classification, Sequential Decoding, and Error Recovery," IBM, RADC-TR-71-146, 1971.

Viterbi, A. J., "Error Bounds for Convolutional Codes and an Asymtotically Optimum Decoding Algorithm," IEEE Transactions on Information Theory, Vol. IT-13, April, 1967.

White, George, personal communication.

A Maximum Likelihood Approach to Continuous Speech Recognition

LALIT R. BAHL, MEMBER, IEEE, FREDERICK JELINEK, FELLOW, IEEE, AND ROBERT L. MERCER

Abstract—Speech recognition is formulated as a problem of maximum likelihood decoding. This formulation requires statistical models of the speech production process. In this paper, we describe a number of statistical models for use in speech recognition. We give special attention to determining the parameters for such models from sparse data. We also describe two decoding methods, one appropriate for constrained artificial languages and one appropriate for more realistic decoding tasks. To illustrate the usefulness of the methods described, we review a number of decoding results that have been obtained with them.

Index Terms—Markov models, maximum likelihood, parameter estimation, speech recognition, statistical models.

I. INTRODUCTION

THE AIM of research in automatic speech recognition is the development of a device that transcribes natural speech automatically. Three areas of speech recognition research can be distinguished: 1) *isolated word recognition* where words are separated by distinct pauses; 2) *continuous speech recognition* where sentences are produced continuously in a natural manner; and 3) *speech understanding* where the aim is not transcription but understanding in the sense that the system (e.g., a robot or a database query system) responds correctly to a spoken instruction or request. Commercially available products exist for isolated word recognition with vocabularies of up to several hundred words.

Although this article is confined to *continuous speech recognition* (CSR), the statistical methods described are applicable to the other two areas of research as well. Acoustics, phonetics, and signal processing are discussed here only as required to provide background for the exposition of statistical methods used in the research carried out at IBM.

Products which recognize continuously spoken small vocabularies are already on the market but the goal of unrestricted continuous speech recognition is far from being realized. All current research is carried out relative to task domains which greatly restrict the sentences that can be uttered. These task domains are of two kinds: those where the allowed sentences are prescribed *a priori* by a grammar designed by the experimenter (referred to as *artificial* tasks), and those related to a limited area of natural discourse which the experimenter tries to model from observed data (referred to as *natural* tasks). Examples of natural tasks are the text of business letters, patent applications, book reviews, etc.

Manuscript received February 23, 1981; revised September 28, 1982.
The authors are with the IBM T. J. Watson Research Center, Yorktown Heights, NY 10598.

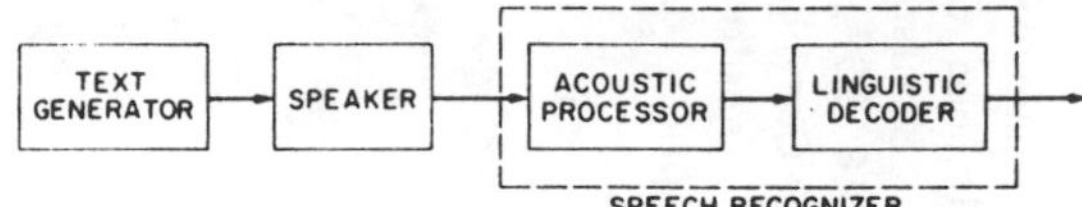

Fig. 1. A continuous speech recognition system.

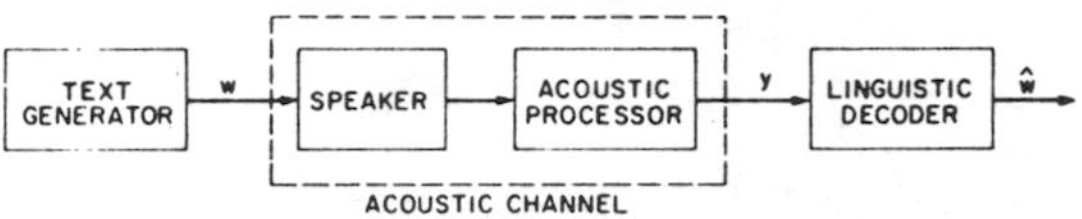

Fig. 2. The communication theory view of speech recognition.

In addition to the constraint imposed by the task domain, the experimental environment is often restricted in several other ways. For example, at IBM speech is recorded with a headset microphone; the system is tuned to a single talker; the talker is prompted by a script, false starts are eliminated, etc.; recognition often requires many seconds of CPU time for each second of speech.

The basic CSR system consists of an *acoustic processor* (AP) followed by a *linguistic decoder* (LD) as shown in Fig. 1. Traditionally, the acoustic processor is designed to act as a phonetician, transcribing the speech waveform into a string of phonetic symbols, while the linguistic decoder translates the possibly garbled phonetic string into a string of words. In more recent work [1]-[6], the acoustic processor does not produce a phonetic transcription, but rather produces a string of labels each of which characterizes the speech waveform locally over a short time interval (see Section II).

In Fig. 2, speech recognition is formulated as a problem in *communication theory*. The speaker and acoustic processor are combined into an *acoustic channel*, the speaker transforming the text into a speech waveform and the acoustic processor acting as a data transducer and compressor. The channel provides the linguistic decoder with a noisy string from which it must recover the message—in this case the original text. One is free to modify the channel by adjusting the acoustic processor but unlike in communications, one cannot choose the code because it is fixed by the language being spoken. It is possible to allow feedback from the decoder to the acoustic processor but the mathematical consequences of such a step are not well understood. By not including feedback we facilitate a consistent and streamlined formulation of the linguistic decoding problem.

The rest of this article is divided as follows. Section II gives a brief summary of acoustic processing techniques. Section

III formulates the problem of linguistic decoding and shows the necessity of statistical modeling of the text and of the acoustic channel. Section IV introduces Markov models of speech processes. Section V describes an elegant linguistic decoder based on dynamic programming that is practical under certain conditions. Section VI deals with the practical aspects of the sentence hypothesis search conducted by the linguistic decoder. Sections VII and VIII introduce algorithms for extracting model parameter values automatically from data. Section IX discusses methods of assessing the performance of CSR systems, and the relative difficulty of recognition tasks. Finally, in Section X we illustrate the capabilities of current recognition systems by describing the results of certain recognition experiments.

II. Acoustic Processors

An acoustic processor (AP) acts as a data compressor of the speech waveform. The output of the AP should 1) preserve the information important to recognition and 2) be amenable to statistical characterization. If the AP output can be easily interpreted by people, it is possible to judge the extent to which the AP fulfills requirement 1).

Typically, an AP is a signal processor, which transforms the speech waveform into a string of parameter vectors, followed by a pattern classifier, which transforms the string of parameter vectors into a string of labels from a finite alphabet. If the pattern classifier is absent, then the AP produces an unlabeled string of parameter vectors. In a *segmenting* AP, the speech waveform is segmented into distinct phonetic events (usually phones[1]) and each of these varying length portions is then labeled.

A *time-synchronous* AP produces parameter vectors computed from successive fixed-length intervals of the speech waveform. The distance from the parameter vector to each of a finite set of standard parameter vectors, or prototypes, is computed. The label for the parameter vector is the name of the prototype to which it is closest.

In early acoustic processors, prototypes were obtained from speech data labeled by an expert phonetician. In more recent acoustic processors, prototypes are obtained automatically from unlabeled speech data [3], [4].

A typical example of a time-synchronous AP is the IBM centisecond acoustic processor (CSAP). The acoustic parameters used by CSAP are the energies in each of 80 frequency bands in steps of 100 Hz covering the range from 0-8000 Hz. They are computed once every centisecond using a 2 cs window. The pattern classifier has 45 prototypes corresponding roughly to the phones of English. Each prototype for a given speaker is obtained from several samples of his speech which has been carefully labeled by a phonetician.

III. Linguistic Decoder

The AP produces an output string $\boldsymbol{y}$. From this string $\boldsymbol{y}$, the linguistic decoder (LD) makes an estimate $\hat{\boldsymbol{w}}$ of the word string $\boldsymbol{w}$ produced by the text generator (see Fig. 1). To minimize the probability of error, $\hat{\boldsymbol{w}}$ must be chosen so that

$$P(\hat{\boldsymbol{w}}|\boldsymbol{y}) = \max_{\boldsymbol{w}} P(\boldsymbol{w}|\boldsymbol{y}). \tag{3.1}$$

By Bayes' rule

$$P(\boldsymbol{w}|\boldsymbol{y}) = \frac{P(\boldsymbol{w})\,P(\boldsymbol{y}|\boldsymbol{w})}{P(\boldsymbol{y})}. \tag{3.2}$$

Since $P(\boldsymbol{y})$ does not depend on $\boldsymbol{w}$, maximizing $P(\boldsymbol{w}|\boldsymbol{y})$ is equivalent to maximizing the likelihood $P(\boldsymbol{w}, \boldsymbol{y}) = P(\boldsymbol{w})\ P(\boldsymbol{y}|\boldsymbol{w})$. Here $P(\boldsymbol{w})$ is the *a priori* probability that the word sequence $\boldsymbol{w}$ will be produced by the text generator, and $P(\boldsymbol{y}|\boldsymbol{w})$ is the probability with which the acoustic channel (see Fig. 1) transforms the word string $\boldsymbol{w}$ into the AP output string $\boldsymbol{y}$.

To estimate $P(\boldsymbol{w})$, the LD requires a probabilistic model of the text generator, which we refer to as the *language model.* For most artificial tasks, the language modeling problem is quite simple. Often the language is specified by a small finite-state or context-free grammar to which probabilities can be easily attached. For example, the *Raleigh* language (see Section IV) is specified by Fig. 7 where all words possible at any point are considered equally likely.

For natural tasks the estimation of $P(\boldsymbol{w})$ is much more difficult. Linguistics has not progressed to the point that it can provide a grammar for a sizable subset of natural English, which is useful for speech recognition. In addition, the interest in linguistics has been in specifying the sentences of a language, but not their probabilities. Our approach has been to model the text generator as a Markov source, the parameters of which are estimated from a large sample of text.

To estimate $P(\boldsymbol{y}|\boldsymbol{w})$, the other component of the likelihood, the LD requires a probabilistic model of the acoustic channel, which must account for the speaker's phonological and acoustic-phonetic variations and for the performance of the acoustic processor. Once models are available for computing $P(\boldsymbol{w})$ and $P(\boldsymbol{y}|\boldsymbol{w})$, it is in principle possible for the LD to compute the likelihood of each sentence in the language and determine the most likely $\hat{\boldsymbol{w}}$ directly. However, even a small artificial language such as the Raleigh language has several million possible sentences. It is therefore necessary in practice to carry out a suboptimal search. A dynamic programming search algorithm, the applicability of which is limited to tasks of moderate complexity, is described in Section V. A more general tree search decoding algorithm is described in Section VI.

IV. Markov Source Modeling of Speech Processes

Notation and Terminology

By a Markov source, we mean a collection of states connected to one another by transitions which produce symbols from a finite alphabet. Each transition t from a state s has associated with it a probability $q_s(t)$ which is the probability that t will be chosen next when s is reached. From the states of a Markov source we choose one state as the initial state and one state as the final state. The Markov source then assigns probabilities to all strings of transitions from the initial state to the final state. Fig. 3 shows an example of a Markov source.

[1] For an introductory discussion of phonetics, see Lyons [7, pp. 99–132].

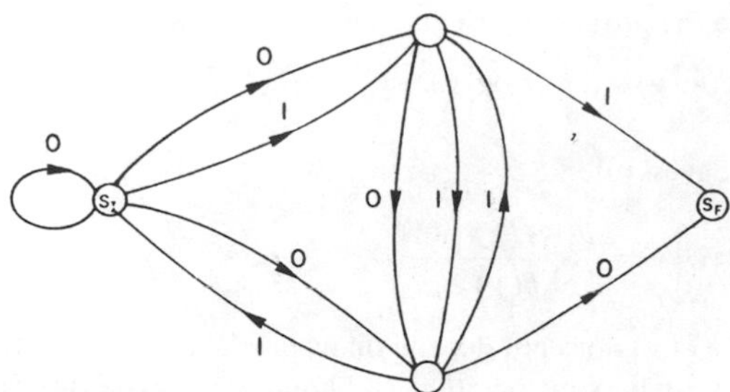

Fig. 3. A Markov source.

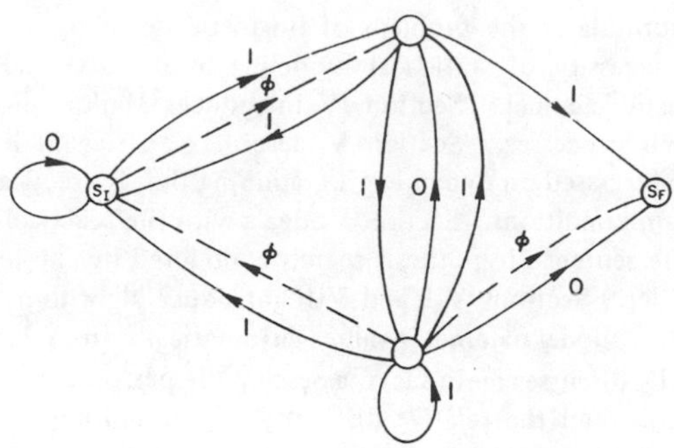

Fig. 4. A Markov source with null transitions.

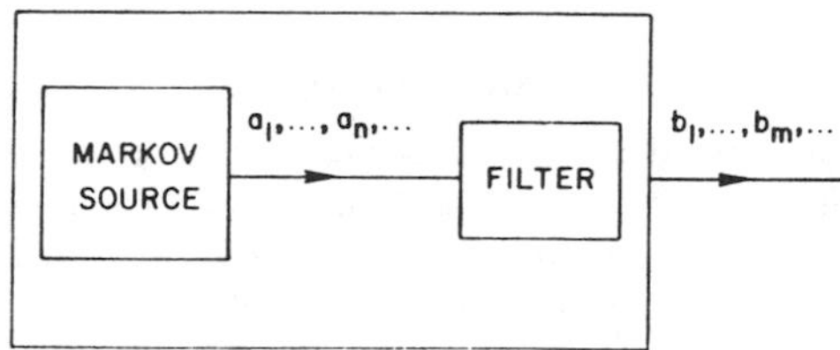

Fig. 5. A filtered Markov source.

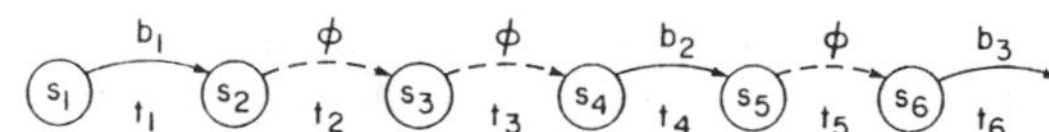

Fig. 6. A sequence of transitions to illustrate spanning. b_1 spans t_1; b_2 spans t_2, t_3, t_4; and b_3 spans t_5, t_6.

We define a Markov source more formally as follows. Let $\mathcal{S}$ be a finite set of states, $\mathcal{T}$ a finite set of transitions, and $\mathcal{A}$ a finite alphabet. Two elements of $\mathcal{S}$, s_I and s_F are distinguished as initial and final states, respectively. The structure of a Markov source is a 1-1 mapping M: $\mathcal{T} \to \mathcal{S} \times \mathcal{A} \times \mathcal{S}$. If $M(t) = (l, a, r)$ then we refer to l as the predecessor state of t, a as the output symbol associated with t, and r as the successor state of t; we write $l = L(t)$, $a = A(t)$, and $r = R(t)$.

The parameters of a Markov source are probabilities $q_s(t)$, $s \in \mathcal{S} - \{s_F\}$, $t \in \mathcal{T}$, such that

$$q_s(t) = 0 \quad \text{if } s \neq L(t)$$

and

$$\sum_t q_s(t) = 1, \quad s \in \mathcal{S} - \{s_F\}. \tag{4.1}$$

In general, the transition probabilities associated with one state are different from those associated with another. However, this need not always be the case. We say that state s_1 is tied to state s_2 if there exists a 1-1 correspondence $T_{s_1 s_2}$: $\mathcal{T} \to \mathcal{T}$ such that $q_{s_1}(t) = q_{s_2}(T_{s_1 s_2}(t))$ for all transitions t. It is easily verified that the relationship of being tied is an equivalence relation and hence induces a partition of $\mathcal{S}$ into sets of states which are mutually tied.

A string of n transitions [2] $\boldsymbol{t}_1^n$ for which $L(t_1) = s_I$ is called a path; if $R(t_n) = s_F$, then we refer to it as a complete path. The probability of a path $\boldsymbol{t}_1^n$ is given by

$$P(\boldsymbol{t}_1^n) = q_{s_I}(t_1) \prod_{i=2}^{n} q_{R(t_{i-1})}(t_i). \tag{4.2}$$

Associated with path $\boldsymbol{t}_1^n$ is an output symbol string $\boldsymbol{a}_1^n = A(\boldsymbol{t}_1^n)$. A particular output string $\boldsymbol{a}_1^n$, may in general arise from more than one path. Thus, the probability $P(\boldsymbol{a}_1^n)$ is given by

$$P(\boldsymbol{a}_1^n) = \sum_{\boldsymbol{t}_1^n} P(\boldsymbol{t}_1^n)\, \delta(A(\boldsymbol{t}_1^n), \boldsymbol{a}_1^n) \tag{4.3}$$

where

$$\delta(a, b) = \begin{cases} 1 & \text{if } a = b \\ 0 & \text{otherwise.} \end{cases} \tag{4.4}$$

A Markov source for which each output string $\boldsymbol{a}_1^n$ determines a unique path is called a *unifilar* Markov source.

[2] $\boldsymbol{t}_1^n$ is a short-hand notation for the concatenation of the symbols $t_1, t_2, \cdots, t_n$. Strings are indicated in boldface throughout.

In practice it is useful to allow transitions which produce no output. These null transitions are represented diagrammatically by interrupted lines (see Fig. 4). Rather than deal with null transitions directly, we have found it convenient to associate with them the distinguished latter ϕ. We then add to the Markov source a filter (see Fig. 5) which removes ϕ, transforming the output sequence $\boldsymbol{a}_1^n$ into an observed sequence $\boldsymbol{b}_1^m$, where $b_i \in \mathcal{B} = \mathcal{A} - \{\phi\}$. Although more general sources can be handled, we shall restrict our attention to sources which do not have closed circuits of null transitions.

If $\boldsymbol{t}_1^n$ is a path which produces the observed output sequence $\boldsymbol{b}_1^m$, then we say that b_i spans t_j if t_j is the transition which produced b_i or if t_j is a null transition immediately preceding a transition spanned by b_i. For example, in Fig. 6, b_1 spans t_1; b_2 spans t_2, t_3, and t_4; and b_3 spans t_5 and t_6.

A major advantage of using Markov source models for the text generator and acoustic channel is that once the structure is specified, the parameters can be estimated automatically from data (see Sections VII and VIII). Furthermore, computationally efficient algorithms exist for computing $P(\boldsymbol{w})$ and $P(\boldsymbol{y}|\boldsymbol{w})$ with such models (see Sections V and VI). Markov source models also allow easy estimation of the relative difficulty of recognition tasks (see Section IX).

The Language Model

Since the language model has to assign probabilities to strings of words, it is natural for its output alphabet to be the vocabulary of the language. However, the output alphabet can include shorter units such as word stems, prefixes, suffixes,

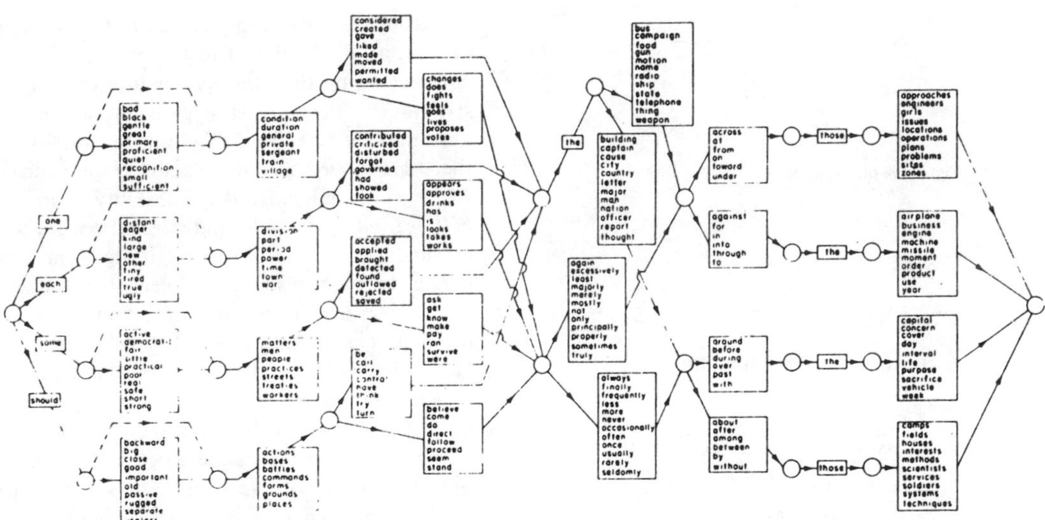

Fig. 7. Grammar of the Raleigh language.

etc., from which word sequences can be derived. Fig. 7 is the model of the artificial Raleigh language which has been used in some of our experiments. The output alphabet is the 250-word vocabulary of the language. For diagrammatic convenience, sets of transitions between pairs of states have been replaced by single transitions with an associated list of possible output words.

For natural languages, the structure of the model is not given *a priori*. However,

$$P(\mathbf{w}_1^n) = P(w_1)\,P(w_2|w_1)\,P(w_3|\mathbf{w}_1^2)\cdots P(w_n|\mathbf{w}_1^{n-1})$$

$$= \prod_{k=1}^{n} P(w_k|\mathbf{w}_1^{k-1}) \tag{4.5}$$

and so it is natural to consider structures for which a word string $\mathbf{w}_1^{k-1}$ uniquely determines the state of the model. A particularly simple model is the N-gram model where the state at time $k - 1$ corresponds to the $N - 1$ most recent words $w_{k-N+1}, \cdots, w_{k-1}$. This is equivalent to using the approximation

$$P(\mathbf{w}_1^n) \cong \prod_{k=1}^{n} P(w_k|\mathbf{w}_{k-N+1}^{k-1}).$$

N-gram models are computationally practical only for small values of N. In order to reflect longer term memory, the state can be made dependent on a syntactic analysis of the entire past word string $\mathbf{w}_1^{k-1}$, as might be obtained from an appropriate grammar of the language.

The Acoustic Channel Model

The AP is deterministic and hence the same waveform will always give rise to the same AP output string. However, for a given word sequence, the speaker can produce a great variety of waveforms resulting in a corresponding variation in the AP output string. Some of the variation arises because there are many different ways to pronounce the same word (this is called phonological variation). Other factors include rate of articulation, talker's position relative to the microphone, ambient noise, etc.

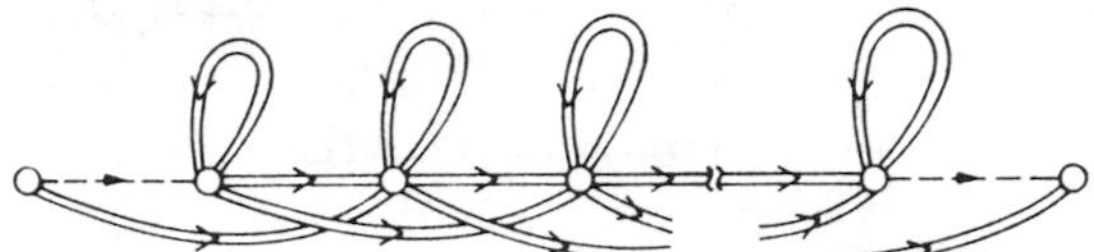

Fig. 8. A word-based Markov subsource.

We will only consider the problem of modeling the acoustic channel for single words. Models for word strings can be constructed by concatenation of these simpler, single word models. Fig. 8 is an example of the structure of a Markov source for a single word. The double arcs represent sets of transitions, one for each symbol in the output alphabet. The straight-line path represents pronunciations of average length, while the transitions above and below can lengthen and shorten the pronunciation, respectively. Since the pronunciation of a word depends on the environment in which it occurs, it may be necessary in practice to make the parameters of the model depend on the phonetic environment provided by the preceding and following words.

Since the same sounds can occur in many different words, portions of one model will be similar to portions of many other models. The number of parameters required to specify all the word models can be reduced by modeling sounds or phones rather than words directly. This leads to a two-level model in which word strings are transformed into phone strings which are then transformed into AP output strings. Using this approach, the acoustic channel model is built up from two components: a set of *phonetic subsources*, one for each word; and a set of *acoustic subsources*, one for each phone.

Let $\mathcal{P}$ be the alphabet of phones under consideration. A phonetic subsource for a word is a Markov source with output alphabet $\mathcal{P}$ which specifies the pronunciations possible for the word and assigns a probability to each of them. Fig. 9 shows the structure of a phonetic Markov subsource for the word

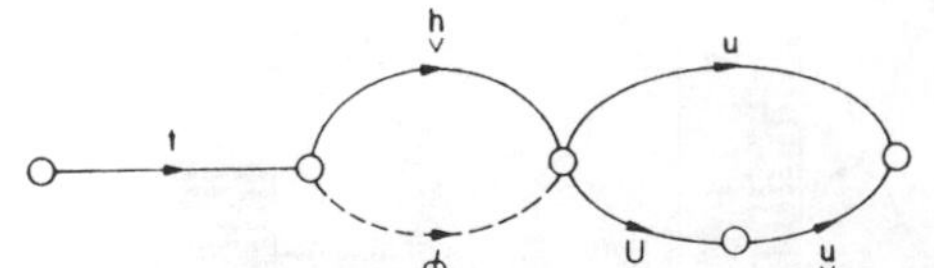

Fig. 9. A phonetic Markov subsource.

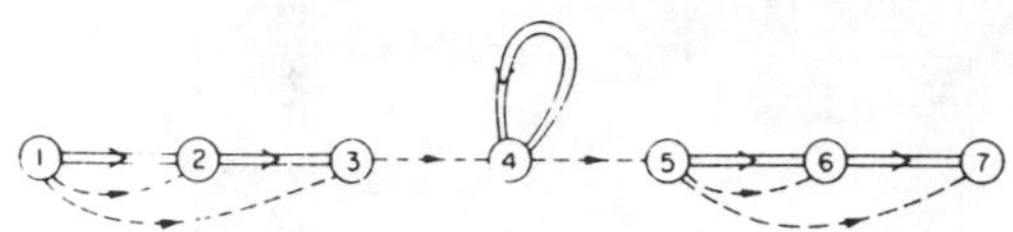

Fig. 10. An acoustic Markov subsource.

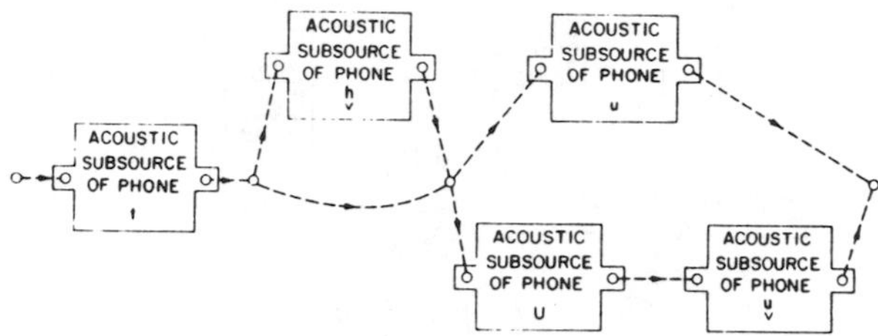

Fig. 11. A phone-based Markov source based on the phonetic subsource of Fig. 9.

two. The structures of these subsources may be derived by the application of phonological rules to dictionary pronunciations for the words [8].

An acoustic subsource for a phone is a Markov source with output alphabet $\mathcal{Y}$ which specifies the possible AP output strings for that phone and assigns a probability to each of them. Fig. 10 shows the structure of an acoustic Markov subsource used with the IBM Centisecond Acoustic Processor.

By replacing each of the transitions in the phonetic subsource by the acoustic subsource for the corresponding phone, we obtain a Markov source model for the acoustic channel. This embedding process is illustrated in Fig. 11.

Whereas the structure of the phonetic subsources can be derived in a principled way from phonological rules, the structures of the word model in Fig. 8 and the phone model in Fig. 9 are fairly arbitrary. Many possible structures seem reasonable; the ones shown here are very simple ones which have been used successfully in recognition experiments.

V. Viterbi Linguistic Decoding

In the preceding section we have shown that acoustic subsources can be embedded in phonetic subsources to produce a model for the acoustic channel. In a similar fashion we can embed acoustic channel word models in the Markov source specifying the language model by replacing each transition by the model of the corresponding word. The resulting Markov source is a model for the entire stochastic process to the left of the linguistic decoder in Fig. 1. Each complete path $\boldsymbol{t}_1^n$ through the model determines a unique word sequence $\boldsymbol{w}_1^k = W(\boldsymbol{t}_1^n)$ and a unique AP output string $\boldsymbol{y}_1^m = Y(\boldsymbol{t}_1^n)$ and has the associated probability $P(\boldsymbol{t}_1^n)$. Using well known minimum-cost path-finding algorithms, it is possible to determine for a given AP string $\boldsymbol{y}_1^m$, the complete path $\boldsymbol{t}_1^n$ which maximizes the probability $P(\boldsymbol{t}_1^n)$ subject to the constraint $Y(t_1^n) = \boldsymbol{y}_1^m$. A decoder based on this strategy would then produce as its output $W(\boldsymbol{t}_1^n)$. This decoding strategy is not optimal since it may not maximize the likelihood $P(\boldsymbol{w}, \boldsymbol{y})$. In fact, for a given pair $\boldsymbol{w}, \boldsymbol{y}$ there are many complete paths $\boldsymbol{t}$ for which $W(\boldsymbol{t}) = \boldsymbol{w}$ and $Y(\boldsymbol{t}) = \boldsymbol{y}$. To minimize the probability of error, one must sum $P(\boldsymbol{t})$ over all these paths and select the $\boldsymbol{w}$ for which the sum is maximum. Nevertheless, good recognition results have been obtained using this suboptimal decoding strategy [1], [2], [9].

A simple method for finding the most likely path is a dynamic programming scheme [10] called the Viterbi Algorithm [11]. Let $\tau_k(s)$ be the most probable path to state s which produces output $\boldsymbol{y}_1^k$. Let $V_k(s) = P(\tau_k(s))$ denote the probability of the path $\tau_k(s)$. We wish to determine $\tau_m(s_F)$.[3] Because of the Markov nature of the process, $\tau_k(s)$ can be shown to be an extension of $\tau_{k-1}(s')$ for some s'. Therefore, $\tau_k(s)$ and $V_k(s)$ can be computed recursively from $\tau_{k-1}(s)$ and $V_{k-1}(s)$ starting with the boundary conditions $V_0(s_I) = 1$ and $\tau_0(s_I)$ being the null string. Let $C(s, a) = \{t \mid R(t) = s, A(t) = a\}$. Then

$$V_k(s) = \max \{\max_{t \in C(s, y_k)} V_{k-1}(L(t))\, q_{L(t)}(t), \quad \max_{t \in C(s,\phi)} V_k(L(t))\, q_{L(t)}(t)\}. \tag{5.1}$$

If the maximizing transition t is in $C(s, y_k)$ then $\tau_k(s) = \tau_{k-1}(L(t)) \cdot t$; otherwise t must be in $C(s, \phi)$ and $\tau_k(s) = \tau_k(L(t)) \cdot t$, where $\cdot$ denotes concatenation. Note that in (5.1) $V_k(s)$ depends on $V_k(L(t))$ for $t \in C(s, \phi)$. $V_k(L(t))$ must therefore be computed before $V_k(s)$. Because closed circuits of null loops are not allowed,[3] it is possible to order the states $s_1, s_2, s_3, \cdots$, such that $t \in C(s_k, \phi)$ and $L(t) = s_j$ only if $j < k$. If we then compute $V_k(s_1)$, $V_k(s_2)$, etc., in sequence, the necessary values will always be available when required.

Many shortcuts to reduce the amount of computation and storage are possible and we will briefly mention some of the more useful ones. If logarithms of probabilities are used, no multiplications are necessary and the entire search can be carried out with additions and comparisons only. Computation and storage needs can be reduced by saving for each k, only those states having relatively large values of $V_k(s)$. This can be achieved by first computing $V_k(\max) = \max_s V_k(s)$ and then eliminating all states s having $V_k(s) < \Delta V_k(\max)$ where Δ is an appropriately chosen threshold. This makes the search suboptimal, but in practice there is little or no degradation in performance if the threshold Δ is chosen with care.

This type of search can be used quite successfully on artificial tasks such as the Raleigh language task, where the number of states is of the order of 10^5.

In addition to its application to suboptimal decoding, the Viterbi algorithm can be used to align an AP output string $\boldsymbol{y}$ with a known word string $\boldsymbol{w}$, by determining the most likely path $\boldsymbol{t}$ which produces $\boldsymbol{y}$ when $\boldsymbol{w}$ is uttered. The path $\boldsymbol{t}$ specifies a sequence of phones which the algorithm puts into correspondence with the symbols forming the sequence $\boldsymbol{y}$. Inspec-

[3]See Section IV, Notation and Terminology.

tion of this alignment allows the experimenter to judge the adequacy of his models and provides an intuitive check on the performance of the AP.

VI. Stack Linguistic Decoding

In the previous section we presented a decoding procedure which finds the most likely complete path $\boldsymbol{t}$ for a given AP output string $\boldsymbol{y}$. This decoding method is computationally feasible only if the state space is fairly small, as is the case in most artificial tasks. However, in the Laser task (described in Section X), the number of states is of the order of 10^{11} which makes the Viterbi search unattractive. Furthermore, the procedure is suboptimal because the word string corresponding to the most likely path $\boldsymbol{t}$ may not be the most likely word string. In this section we present a graph-search decoding method which attempts to find the most likely word string. This method can be used with large state spaces.

Search methods which attempt to find optimal paths through graphs have been used extensively in information theory [12] and in artificial intelligence [13]. Since we are interested in finding the most likely word string, the appropriate graph to search is the word graph generated by the language model. When a complete search of the language model graph is computationally impractical, some heuristic must be used for reducing the computation. Here we describe one specific heuristic method that has been used successfully. To reduce the amount of computation, a left-to-right search starting at the initial state and exploring successively longer paths can be carried out. To carry out this kind of search we need to define a likelihood function which allows us to compare incomplete paths of varying length. An obvious choice may seem to be the probability of uttering the (incomplete) sequence $\boldsymbol{w}$ and producing some initial subsequence of the observed string $\boldsymbol{y}$, i.e.,

$$\sum_{i=0}^{n} P(\boldsymbol{w}, \boldsymbol{y}_1^i) = P(\boldsymbol{w}) \sum_{i=0}^{n} P(\boldsymbol{y}_1^i | \boldsymbol{w}). \tag{6.1}$$

The first term on the right-hand side is the *a priori* probability of the word sequence $\boldsymbol{w}$. The second term, referred to as the acoustic match, is the sum over i of the probability that $\boldsymbol{w}$ produces an initial substring $\boldsymbol{y}_1^i$ of the AP output string $\boldsymbol{y}$. Unfortunately, the value of (6.1) will decrease with lengthening word sequences $\boldsymbol{w}$, making it unsuitable for comparing incomplete paths of different lengths. Some form of normalization to account for different path lengths is needed. As in the Fano metric used for sequential decoding [12], it is advantageous to have a likelihood function which increases slowly along the most likely path, and decreases along other paths. This can be accomplished by a likelihood function of the form

$$\Lambda(\boldsymbol{w}) = \sum_{i=0}^{n} P(\boldsymbol{w}, \boldsymbol{y}_1^i)\, \alpha^{n-i} \sum_{w'} P(\boldsymbol{w}', \boldsymbol{y}_{i+1}^n | \boldsymbol{w}, \boldsymbol{y}_1^i). \tag{6.2}$$

If we consider $P(\boldsymbol{w}, \boldsymbol{y}_1^i)$ to be the cost associated with accounting for the initial part of the AP string $\boldsymbol{y}_1^i$ by the word string $\boldsymbol{w}$, then $\Sigma_{\boldsymbol{w}'} P(\boldsymbol{w}', \boldsymbol{y}_{i+1}^n | \boldsymbol{w}, \boldsymbol{y}_1^i)$ represents the expected cost of accounting for the remainder of the AP string $\boldsymbol{y}_{i+1}^n$ with some continuation $\boldsymbol{w}'$ of $\boldsymbol{w}$. The normalizing factor α can be varied to control the average rate of growth of $\Lambda(\boldsymbol{w})$ along the most likely path. In practice, α can be chosen by trial and error.

An accurate estimate of $\Sigma_{\boldsymbol{w}'} P(\boldsymbol{w}', \boldsymbol{y}_{i+1}^n | \boldsymbol{w}, \boldsymbol{y}_1^i)$ is, of course, impossible in practice, but we can approximate it by ignoring the dependence on $\boldsymbol{w}$. An estimate of $E(\boldsymbol{y}_{i+1}^n | \boldsymbol{y}_1^i)$, the average value of $P(\boldsymbol{w}', \boldsymbol{y}_{i+1}^n | \boldsymbol{y}_1^i)$, can be obtained from training data. In practice, a Markov-type approximation of the form

$$E(\boldsymbol{y}_{i+1}^n | \boldsymbol{y}_1^i) = \prod_{j=i+1}^{n} E(y_j | \boldsymbol{y}_{j-k}^{j-1}) \tag{6.3}$$

can be used. Using $k = 1$ is usually adequate.

The likelihood used for incomplete paths during the search is then given by

$$\Lambda(\boldsymbol{w}) = P(\boldsymbol{w}) \sum_{i=0}^{n} P(\boldsymbol{y}_1^i | \boldsymbol{w})\, \alpha^{n-i} E(\boldsymbol{y}_{i+1}^n | \boldsymbol{y}_1^i). \tag{6.4}$$

For complete paths, the likelihood is

$$\Lambda(\boldsymbol{w}) = P(\boldsymbol{w})\, P(\boldsymbol{y}_1^n | \boldsymbol{w}), \tag{6.5}$$

i.e., the probability that $\boldsymbol{w}$ was uttered and produced the complete output string $\boldsymbol{y}_1^n$.

The likelihood of a successor path $\boldsymbol{w}_1^k = \boldsymbol{w}_1^{k-1} w_k$ can be computed incrementally from the likelihood of its immediate predecessor $\boldsymbol{w}_1^{k-1}$. The *a priori* probability $P(\boldsymbol{w}_1^k)$ is easily obtained from the language model using the recursion

$$P(\boldsymbol{w}_1^k) = P(\boldsymbol{w}_1^{k-1})\, P(w_k | \boldsymbol{w}_1^{k-1}). \tag{6.6}$$

The acoustic match values $P(\boldsymbol{y}_1^i | \boldsymbol{w}_1^k)$ can be computed incrementally if the values $P(\boldsymbol{y}_1^i | \boldsymbol{w}_1^{k-1})$ have been saved [14].

A search based on this likelihood function is easily implemented by having a stack in which entries of the form ($\boldsymbol{w}$, $\Lambda(\boldsymbol{w})$) are stored. The stack, ordered by decreasing values of $\Lambda(\boldsymbol{w})$, initially contains a single entry corresponding to the initial state of the language model. The term stack as used here refers to an ordered list in which entries can be inserted at any position. At each iteration of the search, the top stack entry is examined. If it is an incomplete path, the extensions of this path are evaluated and inserted in the stack. If the top path is a complete path, the search terminates with the path at the top of the stack being the decoded path.

Since the search is not exhaustive, it is possible that the decoded sentence is not the most likely one. A poorly articulated word resulting in a poor acoustic match, or the occurrence of a word with low *a priori* probability can cause the local likelihood of the most likely path to fall, which may then result in the path being prematurely abandoned. In particular, short function words like *the*, *a*, and *of*, are often poorly articulated, causing the likelihood to fall. At each iteration, all paths having likelihood within a threshold Δ of the maximum likelihood path in the stack are extended. The probability of prematurely abandoning the most likely path depends strongly on the choice of Δ which controls the width of the search. Smaller values of Δ will decrease the amount of search at the expense of having a higher probability of not finding the most likely path. In practice, Δ can be adjusted by trial and error to give a satisfactory balance between recognition accuracy and computation time. More complicated likelihood functions and extension strategies have also been used but they are beyond the scope of this paper.

VII. Automatic Estimation of Markov Source Parameters from Data

Let $P_i(t, \boldsymbol{b}_1^m)$ be the joint probability that $\boldsymbol{b}_1^m$ is observed at the output of a filtered Markov source and that the ith output b_i spans t.[3]

The *count*

$$c(t, \boldsymbol{b}_1^m) \triangleq \sum_{i=1}^{m} P_i(t, \boldsymbol{b}_1^m)/P(\boldsymbol{b}_1^m) \tag{7.1}$$

is the Bayes *a posteriori* estimate of the number of times that the transition t is used when the string $\boldsymbol{b}_1^m$ is produced. If the counts are normalized so that the total count for transitions from a given state is 1, then it is reasonable to expect that the resulting relative frequency

$$f_s(t, \boldsymbol{b}_1^m) \triangleq \frac{c(t, \boldsymbol{b}_1^m)\,\delta(s, L(t))}{\sum_{t'} c(t', \boldsymbol{b}_1^m)\,\delta(s, L(t'))} \tag{7.2}$$

will approach the transition probability $q_s(t)$ as m increases.

This suggests the following iterative procedure for obtaining estimates of $q_s(t)$.

1) Make initial guesses $q_s^o(t)$.
2) Set $j = 0$.
3) Compute $P_i(t, \boldsymbol{b}_1^m)$ for all i and t based on $q_s^j(t)$.
4) Compute $f_s(t, \boldsymbol{b}_1^m)$ and obtain new estimates $q_s^{j+1}(t) = f_s(t, \boldsymbol{b}_1^m)$.
5) Set $j = j + 1$.
6) Repeat from 3.

To apply this procedure, we need a simple method for computing $P_i(t, \boldsymbol{b}_1^m)$. Now $P_i(t, \boldsymbol{b}_1^m)$ is just the probability that a string of transitions ending in $L(t)$ will produce the observed sequence $\boldsymbol{b}_1^{i-1}$, times the probability that t will be taken once $L(t)$ is reached, times the probability that a string of transitions starting with $R(t)$ will produce the remainder of the observed sequence. If $A(t) = \phi$, then the remainder of the observed sequence is $\boldsymbol{b}_i^m$, if $A(t) \neq \phi$ then, of course, $A(t) = b_i$ and the remainder of the observed sequence is $\boldsymbol{b}_{i+1}^m$. Thus if $\alpha_i(s)$ denotes the probability of producing the observed sequence $\boldsymbol{b}_1^i$ by a sequence of transitions ending in the state s, and $\beta_i(s)$ denotes the probability of producing the observed sequence $\boldsymbol{b}_i^m$ by a string of transitions starting from the state s, then

$$P_i(t, \boldsymbol{b}_1^m) = \begin{cases} \alpha_{i-1}(L(t))\, q_{L(t)}(t)\, \beta_i(R(t)) & \text{if } A(t) = \phi \\ \alpha_{i-1}(L(t))\, q_{L(t)}(t)\, \beta_{i+1}(R(t)) & \text{if } A(t) = b_i. \end{cases} \tag{7.3}$$

The probabilities $\alpha_i(s)$ satisfy the equation [15]

$$\alpha_o(s) = \delta(s, s_I) + \sum_t \alpha_o(L(t))\, \gamma(t, s, \phi) \tag{7.4a}$$

$$\alpha_i(s) = \sum_t \alpha_{i-1}(L(t))\, \gamma(t, s, b_i) + \sum_t \alpha_i(L(t))\, \gamma(t, s, \phi) \quad i \geqslant 1 \tag{7.4b}$$

where

$$\gamma(t, s, a) = q_{L(t)}(t)\, \delta(R(t), s)\, \delta(A(t), a). \tag{7.5}$$

As with the Viterbi algorithm described in Section V, the absence of null circuits guarantees that the states can be ordered so that $\alpha_i(s_j)$ may be determined from $\alpha_{i-1}(s)$, $s \in \mathcal{S}$, and $\alpha_i(s_k)$, $k < j$.

The probabilities $\beta_i(s)$ satisfy the equations

$$\beta_m(s_F) = 1 \tag{7.6a}$$

$$\beta_i(s) = \sum_t \beta_i(R(t))\, \xi(t, s, \phi) + \sum_t \beta_{i+1}(R(t))\, \xi(t, s, b_i) \quad i \leqslant m, s \neq s_F \tag{7.6b}$$

where $\beta_{m+1}(s) = 0$ and

$$\xi(t, s, a) = q_{L(t)}(t)\, \delta(L(t), s)\, \delta(A(t), a). \tag{7.7}$$

Step 3) of the iterative procedure above then consists of computing α_i in a forward pass over the data, β_i in a backward pass over the data, and finally $P_i(t, \boldsymbol{b}_1^m)$ from (7.3). We refer to the iterative procedure together with the method described for computing $P_i(t, \boldsymbol{b}_1^m)$ as the Forward-Backward Algorithm.

The probability, $P(\boldsymbol{b}_1^m)$, of the observed sequence $\boldsymbol{b}_1^m$ is a function of the probabilities $q_s(t)$. To display this dependence explicitly, we write $P(\boldsymbol{b}_1^m, q_s(t))$. Baum [16] has proven that $P(\boldsymbol{b}_1^m, q_s^{j+1}(t)) \geqslant P(\boldsymbol{b}_1^m, q_s^j(t))$ with equality only if $q_s^j(t)$ is a stationary point (extremum or inflexion point) of $P(\boldsymbol{b}_1^m, \cdot)$. This result also holds if the transition distributions of some of the states are known and hence held fixed or if some of the states are tied[4] to one another thereby reducing the number of independent transition distributions.

When applied to a Markov source language model based on N-grams as described in Section IV the Forward-Backward Algorithm reduces simply to counting the number of times $K(w|\boldsymbol{w}_1^{N-1})$, that w follows the sequence $\boldsymbol{w}_1^{N-1}$, and setting

$$q_{\boldsymbol{w}_1^{N-1}}(w) = \frac{K(w|\boldsymbol{w}_1^{N-1})}{\sum_w K(w|\boldsymbol{w}_1^{N-1})}. \tag{7.8}$$

This is equivalent to maximum likelihood estimation of the transition probabilities.

When applied to a Markov source model for the acoustic channel, the Forward-Backward Algorithm is more interesting. Let us first consider the word-based channel model indicated in Fig. 8. A known text $\boldsymbol{w}_1^n$ is read by the speaker and processed by the acoustic processor to produce an output string $\boldsymbol{y}_1^m$. The Markov source corresponding to the text is constructed from the subsources for the words with the assumption that states of the source which arise from the same subsource state are tied. The Forward-Backward Algorithm then is used to estimate the transition probabilities of the subsources from the output string $\boldsymbol{y}_1^m$. To obtain reliable estimates of the subsource transition probabilities, it is necessary that each word in the vocabulary occur sufficiently often in

[4] For definition of tying, see Section IV, Notation and Terminology. For details of the Forward-Backward Algorithm extended to machines with tied states, see [15].

the text w_1^n. For large vocabularies this may require an exorbitant amount of reading.

The use of the phone-based model shown in Fig. 10 can overcome this problem. The Markov source for the text is constructed from phonetic and acoustic subsources as described in Section IV. States in the source arising from the same acoustic subsource state are assumed to be tied. In addition, states from different phonetic subsources are assumed to be tied if transitions leaving the states result from the same phonological rules. With these assumptions the training text can be considerably shorter since it need only include sufficiently many instances of each phone and each phonetic rule.

VIII. Parameter Estimation from Insufficient Data

It is often the case in practice that the data available are insufficient for a reliable determination of all of the parameters of a Markov model. For example, the trigram model for the *Laser Patent Text* corpus [18] used at IBM Research is based on 1.5 million words. Trigrams which do not occur among these 1.5 million words are assigned zero probability by maximum likelihood estimation, a degenerate case of the Forward-Backward Algorithm. Even though each of these trigrams is very improbable, there are so many of them that they constitute 23 percent of the trigrams present in new samples of text. In other words, after looking at 1.5 million trigrams the probability that the next one seen will never have been seen before is roughly 0.23. The Forward-Backward Algorithm provides an adequate probabilistic characterization of the training data but the characterization may be poor for new data. A method for handling this problem, presented in detail in [15], is discussed in this section.

Consider a Markov source model the parameters of which are to be estimated from data b_1^m. We assume that b_1^m is insufficient for the reliable estimation of all of the parameters.

Let $\hat{q}_s(t)$ be forward-backward estimates of the transition probabilities based on b_1^m and let $*\hat{q}_s(t)$ be the corresponding estimates obtained when certain of the states are assumed to be tied. Where the estimates $\hat{q}_s(t)$ are unreliable, we would like to fall back to the more reliably estimated $*\hat{q}_s(t)$, but where $\hat{q}_s(t)$ is reliable we would like to use it directly.

A convenient way to achieve this is to choose as final estimates of $q_s(t)$ a linear combination of $\hat{q}_s(t)$ and $*\hat{q}_s(t)$. Thus we let $\tilde{q}_s(t)$ be given by

$$\tilde{q}_s(t) = \lambda_s \hat{q}_s(t) + (1 - \lambda_s) *\hat{q}_s(t) \tag{8.1}$$

with λ_s chosen close to 1 when $\hat{q}_s(t)$ is reliable and close to 0 when it is not.

Fig. 12(a) shows the part of the transition structure of the Markov source related to the state s. Equation (8.1) can be interpreted in terms of the *associated* Markov source shown in Fig. 12(b), in which each state is replaced by three states. In Fig. 12(b), $\hat{s}$ corresponds directly to s in Fig. 12(a). The null transitions from $\hat{s}$ to s and s^* have transition probabilities equal to λ_s and $1 - \lambda_s$, respectively. The transitions out of s have probabilities $q_s(t) = \hat{q}_s(t)$ while those out of s^* have probabilities $*q_s(t) = *q_s(t)$. The structure of the associated Markov source is completely determined by the structure of the original Markov source and by the tyings assumed for obtaining more reliable parameter estimates.

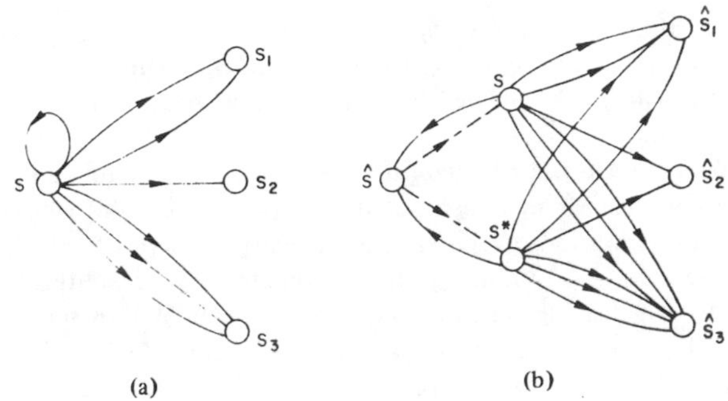

Fig. 12. (a) Part of transition structure of a Markov source. (b) The corresponding part of an associated interpolated Markov source.

The interpretation of (8.1) as an associated Markov source immediately suggests that the parameters λ_s be determined by the Forward-Backward (FB) Algorithm. However, since the λ parameters were introduced to predict as yet unseen data, rather than to account for the training data b_1^m, the FB Algorithm must be modified. We wish to extract the λ values from data that was not used to determine the distributions $q_s(t)$ and $*q_s(t)$ [see (8.1)]. Since presumably we have only b_1^m at our disposal, we will proceed by the *deleted interpolation* method. We shall divide b_1^m into n blocks and for $i = 1, \cdots, n$ estimate λ from the ith block while using $q_s(t)$ and $*q_s(t)$ estimates derived from the remaining blocks.

Since the λ_s values should depend on the reliability of the estimate $q_s(t)$, it is natural to associate them with the estimated relative frequency of occurrence of the state s. We thus decide on k relative frequency ranges and aim to determine corresponding values $\lambda(1), \cdots, \lambda(k)$. Then $\lambda_s = \lambda(i)$ if the relative frequency of s was estimated to fall within the ith range.

We partition the state space $\mathcal{S}$ into subsets of tied states $\mathcal{S}_1^*, \mathcal{S}_2^*, \cdots, \mathcal{S}_r^*$ and determine the transition correspondence functions $T_{s,s'}$ for all pairs of tied states s, s'. We recall from Section IV that then $*q_s(t) = *q_{s'}(T_{s,s'}(t))$ for all pairs $s, s' \in \mathcal{S}_i$, $i = 1, \cdots, r$. If $L(t) \in \mathcal{S}_i$, then $\mathcal{T}(t) = \{t' | t' = T_{L(t),s'}(t), s' \in \mathcal{S}_i^*\}$ is the set of transitions that are tied to t. Since $T_{L(t),L(t)}(t) = t$, then $t \in \mathcal{T}(t)$.

We divide the data b_1^m into n blocks of length $l (m = nl)$. We run the FB Algorithm in the ordinary way, but on the last iteration we establish separate counters

$$c_j(t, b_1^m) \triangleq \sum_{i=1}^{(j-1)l} P_i(t, b_1^m) + \sum_{i=jl+1}^{m} P_i(t, b_1^m)$$

$$j = 1, 2, \cdots, n \tag{8.2}$$

for each *deleted* block of data. The above values will give rise to detailed distributions

$$q_s(t, j) = \frac{c_j(t, b_1^m)\, \delta(s, L(t))}{\sum_{t'} c_j(t', b_1^m)\, \delta(s, L(t'))} \tag{8.3}$$

and to tied distributions

$$*q_s(t) = \frac{\delta(s, L(t)) \sum_{t' \in \mathcal{T}(t)} c_j(t', b_1^m)}{\sum_{t'} \delta(s, L(t')) \sum_{t'' \in \mathcal{T}(t')} c_j(t'', b_1^m)}. \tag{8.4}$$

Note that $q_s(t, j)$ and $*q_s(t, j)$ *do not* depend directly on the output data belonging to the jth block. Thus the data in the jth block can be considered *new* in relation to these probabilities.

We now run the FB Algorithm on data b_1^m to determine the λ values based on n associated Markov sources which have fixed distributions over transitions leaving the states s and s^*. These λ values are obtained from estimates of probabilities of transitions leaving the states $\hat{s}$ of the associated Markov source [see Fig. 12(b)]. Only k counter pairs pertaining to the values $\lambda(i)$ and $1 - \lambda(i)$ being estimated are established. When running on the data of the jth block, the jth associated Markov source is used based on the probabilities $q_s(t, j)$ and $*q_s(t, j)$. The values λ_s used in the jth block are chosen by computing the frequency estimates

$$q(s, j) = \frac{\sum_t c_j(t, b_1^m)\, \delta(s, L(t))}{\sum_{t'} c_j(t', b_1^m)} \tag{8.5}$$

and setting $\lambda_s = \lambda(i)$ if $q(s, j)$ belonged to the ith frequency range. Also, the λ_s counts estimated from the jth block are then added to the contents of the ith counter pair.

After λ values have been computed, new test data is predicted using an associated Markov source based on probabilities

$$q_s(t) = \frac{\delta(s, L(t)) \sum_{j=1}^{n} c_j(t, b_1^m)}{\sum_{t'} \delta(s, L(t')) \sum_{j=1}^{n} c_j(t', b_1^m)} \tag{8.6}$$

$$*q_s(t) = \frac{\delta(s, L(t)) \sum_{t' \in \mathcal{T}(t)} \sum_{j=1}^{n} c_j(t', b_1^m)}{\sum_{t'} \delta(s, L(t')) \sum_{t'' \in \mathcal{T}(t')} \sum_{j=1}^{n} c_j(t'', b_1^m)} \tag{8.7}$$

and λ_s values chosen from the derived set $\lambda(1), \cdots, \lambda(k)$, depending on the range within which the estimate

$$q(s) = \frac{\sum_t \delta(s, L(t)) \sum_{j=1}^{n} c_j(t, b_1^m)}{\sum_{t'} \sum_{j=1}^{n} c_j(t', b_1^m)} \tag{8.8}$$

falls. It might appear that the convergence of the estimation of the interpolation weights $\lambda(i)$ needs proving since it involves the use of different fixed distributions $q(s, j)$ over different blocks $j = 1, \cdots, n$. However, some thought will reveal that the problem can be reformulated in terms of a single move complex Markov source, some of whose parameters are tied and others fixed. This source is identical to the trellis that is needed to carry out the λ estimation. The process consists of carrying out the Forward-Backward Algorithms for estimating the parameters of the complex Markov source, and thus converges by the Baum theorem [16].

This approach to modeling data generation is called *deleted interpolation*. Several variations are possible some of which are described in [15]. In particular, it is possible to have v different tying partitions of the state space corresponding to transition distributions ${}^{(i)}q_s(t), i = 1, \cdots, v$, and to obtain the final estimates by the formula

$$\tilde{q}_s(t) = \sum_{i=1}^{v} \lambda_i(s)\, {}^{(i)}q_s(t) \tag{8.9}$$

with $\lambda_i(s)$ values determined by the Forward-Backward Algorithm.

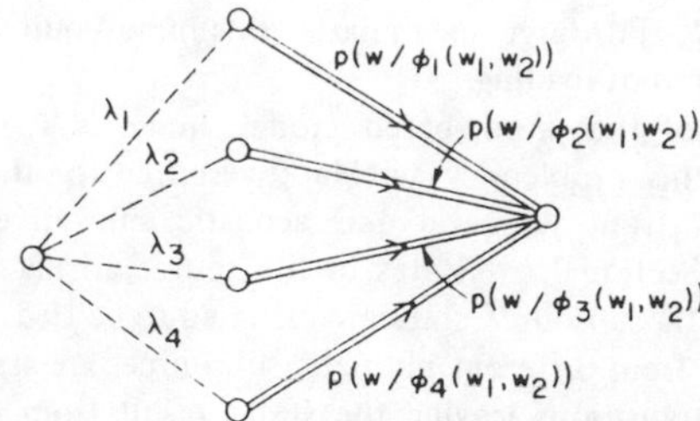

Fig. 13. A section of the interpolated trigram language model corresponding to the state determined by the word pair w_1, w_2.

We illustrate this deleted interpolation algorithm with an application to the trigram language model for the laser patent text corpus used at IBM.

Let $\pi(w)$ be the syntactic part of speech (e.g., noun, verb, etc.) assigned to the word w. Let $\phi_i, i = 1, \cdots, 4$ be functions classifying the language model states $w_1 w_2$ as follows:

$$\begin{aligned} \phi_1(w_1 w_2) &= \{(w_1 w_2)\} \\ \phi_2(w_1 w_2) &= \{(w w_2) \mid \pi(w) = \pi(w_1)\} \\ \phi_3(w_1 w_2) &= \{(w w') \mid \pi(w) = \pi(w_1),\ \pi(w') = \pi(w_2)\} \\ \phi_4(w_1 w_2) &= \{\text{all pairs of words}\}. \end{aligned} \tag{8.10}$$

Let $K(\phi_i(w_1 w_2))$ be the number of times that members of the set $\phi_i(w_1 w_2)$ occur in the training text. Finally, partition the state space into sets

$$\begin{aligned} \phi_5(w_1 w_2) = \{ww' \mid K(\phi_j(ww')) &= K(\phi_j(w_1 w_2)) = 1 \\ j &= 1, 2, \cdots, i - 1, \\ K(\phi_i(ww')) &= K(\phi_i(w_1 w_2)) > 1\} \end{aligned} \tag{8.11}$$

which will be used to tie the associated states $w_1 w_2$ according to the frequency of word pair occurrence. Note that if $K(\phi_1(w_1 w_2)) \geqslant 2$, then $\phi_5(w_1 w_2)$ is simply the set of all word pairs that occurred in the corpus exactly as many times as $w_1 w_2$ did. A different λ distribution will correspond to each different set (8.11). The language model transition probabilities are given by the formula

$$\hat{P}(w_3 \mid w_1 w_2) = \sum_{i=1}^{4} \lambda_i(\phi_5(w_1 w_2))\, P_i(w_3 \mid \phi_i(w_1 w_2)). \tag{8.12}$$

Fig. 13 illustrates this graphically. We use deleted interpolation also in estimating the probabilities associated with the acoustic channel model.

IX. A Measure of Difficulty for Finite State Recognition Tasks

Research in continuous speech recognition has led to the development of a number of artificial tasks. In order to compare the performance of different systems on sentences from different tasks, it is necessary to have a measure of the intrinsic difficulty of a task. Although vocabulary size is almost always mentioned in the description of an artificial task, by itself it is practically useless as a measure of difficulty. In this section we describe *perplexity*, a measure of difficulty based on well established information theoretic principles. The experimental results described in the next section show a clear correlation between increasing perplexity and increasing error rate.

Perplexity is defined in terms of the information theoretic concept of entropy. The tasks used in speech recognition can be adequately modeled as *unifilar*[3] Markov sources. Let $P(w|s)$ be the probability that word w will be produced next when the current state is s. The entropy, $H_s(w)$ associated with state s is

$$H_s(w) = -\sum_w P(w|s)\log_2 P(w|s). \tag{9.1}$$

The entropy $H(w)$ of the task is simply the average value of $H_s(w)$. Thus if $\pi(s)$ is the probability of being in state s during the production of a sentence, then

$$H(w) = \sum_s \pi(s)\, H_s(w). \tag{9.2}$$

The perplexity $S(w)$ of the task is given in terms of its entropy $H(w)$ by

$$S(w) = 2^{H(w)}. \tag{9.3}$$

Often, artificially constrained tasks specify the sentences possible without attaching probabilities to them. Although the task perplexity depends on the probabilities assigned to the sentences, Shannon [17] has shown that the maximum entropy achievable for a task with N possible sentences of average length l is $1/l \log_2 N$. Hence the maximum perplexity is $N^{1/l}$. If all the sentences for the task could be arranged as a regular tree, the number of branches emanating from a node would be $N^{1/l}$. So, for artificially constrained tasks, perplexity can be thought of as the average number of alternative words at each point. For the Raleigh task of Fig. 7, the number of alternative words ranges from 1 to 24, and the perplexity is 7.27.

For natural language tasks, some sentences are much more probable than others and so the maximum perplexity is not useful as a measure of difficulty. However, the perplexity, which can be computed from the probabilities of the sentences, remains a useful measure. Information theory shows that for a language with entropy H, we can ignore all but the most probable 2^{lH} strings of length l and still achieve any prescribed error rate.

The definition of perplexity makes no use of the phonetic character of the words in the vocabulary of the language. Two tasks may have the same perplexity but one may have words that are substantially longer than the other, thereby making recognition easier. This problem can be overcome by considering the sentences of the task to be strings of phonemes rather than strings of words. We can then compute the phoneme level perplexity of the two tasks and normalize them to words of equal length. In this way the perplexity of the task with the greater average word length will be lowered relative to that of the other task.

Some pairs of phonemes are more confusable than others. It is possible therefore to have two tasks with the same phoneme level perplexity, one of which is much easier to recognize than the other, simply because its words are acoustically farther apart. We can take this into account by considering the joint probability distribution $P(\mathbf{w}, \mathbf{y})$ of word sequences $\mathbf{w}$ and acoustic sequences $\mathbf{y}$ and determining from it the conditional entropy $H(\mathbf{w}|\mathbf{y})$. $\mathbf{y}$ could be the output string from a particular acoustic processor or simply the time waveform itself. Unfortunately, this is far too difficult to compute in practice.

Perplexity reflects the difficulty of recognition when a complete search can be performed. The effect on the error rate of performing an incomplete search may be more severe for one language than for another, even though they have the same perplexity. However, as the results in the next section show, there is a clear correlation between perplexity and error rate.

X. Experimental Results

The results given in this section, obtained before 1980, are described in detail in [3], [5], [6], [18], [19].

Table I shows the effect of training set size of recognition error rate. 200 sentences from the Raleigh Language (100 training and 100 test) were recognized using a segmenting acoustic processor and a stack algorithm decoder. We initially estimated the acoustic channel model parameters by examining samples of acoustic processor output. These parameter values were then refined by applying the Forward-Backward Algorithm to training sets of increasing size. While for small training set sizes performance on training sentences should be substantially better than on test sentences, for sufficiently large training set sizes performance on training and text sentences should be about equal. By this criterion a training set size of 600 sentences is adequate for determining the parameters of this acoustic channel model. Notice that even a training set size as small as 200 sentences leads to a substantial reduction in error rate as compared to decoding with the initially estimated channel model parameters.

The power of automatic training is evident from Table I in the dramatic decrease in error rate resulting from training even with a small amount of data. The results in Table II further demonstrate the power of automatic training. Here, three versions of the acoustic channel model are used, each weaker than the previous one. The "complete acoustic channel model" result corresponds to the last line of Table I. The acoustic channel model in this case is built up from phonetic subsources and acoustic subsources as described in Section IV. The phonetic subsources produce many different strings for each word reflecting phonological modifications due to rate of articulation, dialect, etc. The "single pronunciation" result is obtained with an acoustic channel model in which the phonetic subsources allow only a single pronunciation for each word. Finally, the "spelling-based pronunciation" result is obtained with an

TABLE I
EFFECT OF TRAINING SET SIZE ON ERROR RATE

Training Set Size	% of Sentences Decoded Incorrectly	
	Test	Training
0	80%	–
200	23%	12%
400	20%	13%
600	15%	16%
800	18%	16%
1070	17%	14%

TABLE II
EFFECT OF WEAK ACOUSTICS CHANNEL MODELS

Model Type	% of Sentences Decoded Incorrectly
Complete Acoustic Channel Model	17%
Single Pronounciation	25%
Spelling-Based Pronounciation	57%

TABLE III
DECODING RESULTS FOR SEVERAL DIFFERENT ACOUSTIC PROCESSORS WITH THE RALEIGH LANGUAGE

Acoustic Processor	Error Rate	
	Sentence	Word
MAP	27%	3.6%
CSAP	2%	0.2%
TRIVIAL	2%	0.2%

TABLE IV
RECOGNITION RESULTS FOR SEVERAL TASKS OF VARYING PERPLEXITY

	Vocabulary		Word Error Rate	
Task	Size	Perplexity	Segmenting AP	Time-Synchronous AP
CMU-AIX05	1011	4.53	0.8%	0.1%
Raleigh	250	7.27	3.1%	0.6%
Laser	1000	24.13	33.1%	8.9%

acoustic channel model in which the single pronunciation allowed by the phonetic subsources is based directly on the letter-by-letter spelling of the word. This leads to absurd pronunciation models for some of the words. For example, *through* is modeled as if the final *g* and *h* were pronounced. The trained parameters for the acoustic channel with spelling-based pronunciations show that letters are often deleted by the acoustic processor reflecting the large number of silent letters in English spelling. Although the results obtained in this way are much worse than those obtained with the other two channel models, they are still considerably better than the results obtained with the complete channel model using parameters estimated by people.

Table III shows results on the Raleigh Language for several different acoustic processors. In each case the same set of 100 sentences was decoded using the stack decoding algorithm. MAP is a segmenting acoustic processor, while CSAP and TRIVIAL are nonsegmenting acoustic processors. Prototypes for CSAP were selected by hand from an examination of speech data. Those for TRIVIAL were obtained automatically from a Viterbi alignment of about one hour of speech data.

Table IV summarizes the performance of the stack decoding algorithm with a segmenting and a time-synchronous acoustic processor on three tasks of varying perplexity. The Raleigh task has been described earlier in the paper. The Laser task is a natural language task used at IBM. It consists of sentences from the text of patents in laser technology. To limit the vocabulary, only sentences made entirely from the 1000 most frequent words in the complete laser corpus are considered. The CMU-AIX05 task [20] is the task used by Carnegie-Mellon University in their Speech Understanding System to meet the ARPA specifications [21]. All these results were obtained with sentences spoken by a single talker in a sound-treated room. Approximately 1000 sentences were used for estimating the parameters of the acoustic channel model in each of the experiments. There is a clear correlation between perplexity and error rate. The CMU-AIX05 task has the largest vocabulary but the smallest perplexity. Note that for each of the tasks, the performance of the time-synchronous acoustic processor is considerably better than that of the segmenting acoustic processor.

ACKNOWLEDGMENT

We would like to acknowledge the contributions of the following present and past members of the Continuous Speech Recognition Group at the IBM Thomas J. Watson Research

Center: J. K. Baker, J. M. Baker, R. Bakis, P. Cohen, A. Cole, R. Dixon, B. Lewis, E. Muckstein, and H. Silverman.

References

[1] R. Bakis, "Continuous speech recognition via centisecond acoustic states," presented at the 91st Meeting Acoust. Soc. Amer., Washington, DC, Apr. 1976; also IBM Res. Rep. RC-5971, IBM Res. Center, Yorktown Heights, NY, Apr. 1976.

[2] B. T. Lowerre, "The Harpy speech recognition system," Ph.D. dissertation, Dep. Comput. Sci., Carnegie-Mellon Univ., Pittsburgh, PA, 1976.

[3] L. R. Bahl, R. Bakis, P. S. Cohen, A. G. Cole, F. Jelinek, B. L. Lewis, and R. L. Mercer, "Recognition results with several acoustic processors," in *Proc. IEEE Int. Conf. Acoust., Speech, Signal Processing*, Washington, DC, Apr. 1979, pp. 249-251.

[4] J. M. Baker, "Performance statistics of the hear acoustic processor," in *Proc. IEEE Int. Conf. Acoust., Speech, Signal Processing*, Washington, DC, Apr. 1979, pp. 262-265.

[5] L. R. Bahl, J. K. Baker, P. S. Cohen, N. R. Dixon, F. Jelinek, R. L. Mercer, and H. F. Silverman, "Preliminary results on the performance of a system for the automatic recognition of continuous speech," in *Proc. IEEE Int. Conf. Acoust., Speech, Signal Processing*, Philadelphia, PA, Apr. 1976, pp. 425-429.

[6] L. R. Bahl, J. K. Baker, P. S. Cohen, A. G. Cole, F. Jelinek, B. L. Lewis, and R. L. Mercer, "Automatic recognition of continuously spoken sentences from a finite state grammar," in *Proc. IEEE Int. Conf. Acoust., Speech, Signal Processing*, Tulsa, OK, Apr. 1978, pp. 418-421.

[7] J. Lyons, *Introduction to Theoretical Linguistics*. Cambridge, England: Cambridge Univ. Press, 1969.

[8] P. S. Cohen and R. L. Mercer, "The phonological component of an automatic speech-recognition system," in *Speech Recognition*, D. R. Reddy, Ed. New York: Academic, 1975, pp. 275-320.

[9] J. K. Baker, "The DRAGON system–An overview," *IEEE Trans. Acoust., Speech, Signal Processing*, vol. ASSP-23, pp. 24-29, Feb. 1975.

[10] R. E. Bellman, *Dynamic Programming*. Princeton, NJ: Princeton Univ. Press, 1957.

[11] G. D. Forney, Jr., "The Viterbi algorithm," *Proc. IEEE*, vol. 61, pp. 268-278, Mar. 1973.

[12] F. Jelinek, "A fast sequential decoding algorithm using a stack," *IBM J. Res. Develop.*, vol. 13, pp. 675-685, Nov. 1969.

[13] N. J. Nilsson, *Problem-Solving Methods in Artificial Intelligence*. New York: McGraw-Hill, 1971.

[14] L. R. Bahl and F. Jelinek, "Decoding for channels with insertions, deletions, and substitutions with applications to speech recognition," *IEEE Trans. Inform. Theory*, vol. IT-21, pp. 404-411, July 1975.

[15] F. Jelinek and R. L. Mercer, "Interpolated estimation of Markov source parameters from sparse data," in *Proc. Workshop Pattern Recognition in Practice*, May 21-23, 1980. Amsterdam, The Netherlands: North-Holland.

[16] L. E. Baum, "An inequality and associated maximization technique in statistical estimation of probabilistic functions of Markov processes," *Inequalities*, vol. 3, pp. 1-8, 1972.

[17] C. E. Shannon, "Prediction and entropy of printed English," *Bell Syst. Tech. J.*, vol. 30, pp. 50-64, 1951.

[18] L. R. Bahl, J. K. Baker, P. S. Cohen, F. Jelinek, B. L. Lewis, and R. L. Mercer, "Recognition of a continuously read natural corpus," in *Proc. IEEE Int. Conf. Acoust., Speech, Signal Processing*, Tulsa, OK, Apr. 1978, pp. 422-424.

[19] L. R. Bahl, R. Bakis, P. S. Cohen, A. G. Cole, F. Jelinek, B. L. Lewis, and R. L. Mercer, "Further results on the recognition of a continuously read natural corpus," in *Proc. IEEE Int. Conf. Acoust., Speech, Signal Processing*, Denver, CO, Apr. 1980, pp. 872-875.

[20] D. R. Reddy *et al.*, "Speech understanding systems final report," Dep. Comput. Sci., Carnegie-Mellon Univ., 1977.

[21] A. Newell, J. Barnett, J. W. Forgie, C. Green, D. Klatt, J. C. R. Licklider, J. Munson, D. R. Reddy, and W. A. Woods, *Speech Understanding Systems: Final Report of a Study Group*. Amsterdam, The Netherlands: North-Holland, 1973.

Lalit R. Bahl (S'66-M'68) received the B.Tech. (Hons.) degree from the Indian Institute of Technology, Kharagpur, India, in 1964 and the M.S. and Ph.D. degrees in electrical engineering from the University of Illinois, Urbana, in 1966 and 1968, respectively.

Since 1968 he has been at the IBM Thomas J. Watson Research Center in Yorktown Heights, NY. Since 1979 he has been Manager of the Natural Language Speech Recognition Group. During 1969-1974 he was also Adjunct Associate Professor in the Department of Electrical Engineering and Computer Science, Columbia University, New York, NY. His research interests include speech recognition, information theory, coding theory, and communication theory.

Frederick Jelinek (S'55-M'62-SM'69-F'74) was born in Prague, Czechoslovakia, on November 18, 1932. He received the S.B., S.M., and Ph.D. degrees in electrical engineering from the Massachusetts Institute of Technology, Cambridge, in 1956, 1958, and 1962, respectively.

Since June 1972 he has been with the Computer Sciences Department, IBM Thomas J. Watson Research Center, Yorktown Heights, NY, where he manages research on automatic recognition (transcription) of speech. He has been an Instructor at M.I.T. (1959-1962), a Visiting Lecturer at Harvard University (1962), a Professor of Electrical Engineering at Cornell University (1962-1974), a Visiting Scientist at M.I.T. Lincoln Laboratory (1964-1965), and a Visiting Scientist at IBM Thomas J. Watson Research Center (1968-1969). His principal interests are in speech recognition and information theory. His is the author of *Probabilistic Information Theory* (New York: McGraw-Hill, 1968).

Dr. Jelinek was the President of the IEEE Group on Information Theory in 1977 and was the recipient of the 1969-1970 Information Theory Group Prize Paper Award.

Robert L. Mercer was born in San Jose, CA, on July 11, 1946. He received the B.S. degree in physics and mathematics from the University of New Mexico, Albuquerque, in 1968 and the M.S. and Ph.D. degrees in computer science from the University of Illinois, Urbana, in 1970 and 1972, respectively.

Since 1972 he has been a Research Staff member, Computer Sciences Department, and is currently Manager of Real-Time Speech Recognition at the IBM Thomas J. Watson Research Center, Yorktown Heights, NY.

Dr. Mercer is a member of Sigma Xi, Phi Beta Kappa, and Phi Kappa Phi.

High Performance Connected Digit Recognition Using Hidden Markov Models

LAWRENCE R. RABINER, FELLOW, IEEE, JAY G. WILPON, SENIOR MEMBER, IEEE, AND FRANK K. SOONG, MEMBER, IEEE

***Abstract*—Algorithms for connected word recognition based on whole word reference patterns have become increasingly sophisticated and have been shown capable of achieving high recognition performance for small or syntax-constrained, moderate size vocabularies in a speaker trained mode. In particular, it has been demonstrated that for a vocabulary of digits, in a speaker trained mode, very high string accuracy is achievable using either hidden Markov models (HMM) or templates as the digit reference patterns. In this paper we use an enhanced analysis feature set consisting of both instantaneous and transitional spectral information and test the HMM-based connected digit recognizer in speaker trained, multispeaker, and speaker independent modes. For the evaluation, we used both a 50 talker connected digit database recorded over local, dialed-up telephone lines, and the Texas Instruments, 225 adult talker, connected digits database which has been widely distributed through the National Bureau of Standards. Using these databases, the performance that was achieved was 0.35, 1.65, and 1.75 percent string error rates for known length strings, for speaker trained, multispeaker, and speaker independent modes, respectively, and 0.78, 2.85, and 2.94 percent string error rate for unknown length strings of up to 7 digits in length for the 3 modes. Several experiments were carried out to determine the best set of conditions (e.g., training, recognition parameters, etc.) for recognition of digits. The results, and the interpretation, of these experiments will be described in this paper.**

I. Introduction

THE problem of recognizing strings of connected digits is crucial to a number of applications such as voice dialing of telephone numbers, automatic data entry, credit card entry, PIN (personal identification number) entry, entry of access codes for transactions, etc. In the last several years, several highly successful algorithms for recognizing spoken connected word strings from word prototypes have evolved [1]–[5]. These algorithms, all based on statistical pattern recognition methods, have achieved great success when applied to the problem of connected digit recognition [5]–[7]. The reasons for this success are twofold: namely, the fact that the recognition algorithms are optimal in the sense that they find the string of digit reference patterns that best (in some objective sense) matches the spoken digit string, and the development of highly successful training procedures which derive the digit reference patterns from a training set of fluent, connected, digit strings [5]–[9].

Manuscript received February 9, 1988; revised November 5, 1988.
The authors are with AT&T Bell Laboratories, Murray Hill, NJ 07974.
IEEE Log Number 8928735.

Earlier investigations showed that when a reasonable size training set was available for deriving the digit reference patterns, a fairly good recognizer could be implemented using either hidden Markov model (HMM) or template characterizations of the digits, with the HMM-based system achieving somewhat higher performance than the template based approach [7]. For such systems, the highest performance scores were achieved in a speaker trained mode (typical string accuracies of from 98 to 99 percent); however, performance was found to degrade seriously in either a multispeaker or a speaker independent mode. Bush and Kopec found that by incorporating acoustic–phonetic knowledge into the recognizer, improved performance on speaker independent, connected digit recognition resulted [5]. Their results, which used some manual segmentation in order to bootstrap the training, showed speaker independent, connected digit string accuracies of from 96 to 97 percent.

In an effort to improve performance of the fully automatic connected digit recognition algorithms, a major change was made in the front end spectral analysis. The analysis feature vector used for recognition, nominally an extended cepstral vector derived from LPC analysis, was augmented by the so-called delta cepstrum information [10], [11]. (The delta cepstrum vector is the least squares fit of the time derivative of each of the cepstral parameters, defined over a finite time window.) The resulting augmented analysis vector characterizes both the *short-time spectrum* (via the cepstrum) and the *short-time spectral derivative* (via the delta cepstrum). The motivation behind this change was the observation that, by including information about the time derivative of the cepstral vector, a more complete 2-dimensional (time and frequency) spectral representation of the time-varying speech signal is obtained, and the performance of a vector quantization (VQ) based talker verification system improved dramatically (error rate decreased by a factor of 2) [11].

The new analysis feature set was tested in the HMM-based connected digit recognizer in speaker trained, multispeaker, and speaker independent modes, and was found to effectively reduce the string error rates by factors of 2 or more, often with considerably less computation than used previously [7]. In particular, digit string error rates of 0.78, 2.85, and 2.94 percent were obtained for *unknown length* (UL) strings of from 1 to 7 digits for speaker trained, multispeaker, and speaker independent tests, respectively. Comparable rates for *known length* (KL) strings were 0.35, 1.65, and 1.75 percent, respectively.

The organization of this paper is as follows. In Section II we review the fundamentals of the HMM connected digit recognizer. In this section we define precisely the way in which the new analysis feature vector is computed. In Section III we describe the experimental evaluation of the improved system in each of the three modes in which it was tested, namely, speaker trained, multispeaker, and speaker independent. Finally, in Section !V, we summarize the results and point out the relevance to general problems in speech recognition.

II. Review of HMM Connected Digit Recognizer

A fairly comprehensive description of the complete connected digit recognizer is given in [7]. Thus, in this section, we will give only an overview of the recognition system, and then will focus on the improved front end spectral analysis.

A block diagram of the overall level building, connected-digit recognizer is shown in Fig. 1. There are essentially three steps in the recognition algorithm, as follows.

1) Spectral analysis—The speech signal, $s(n)$, is converted to a set of LPC derived cepstral (weighted) and delta-cepstral (weighted) vectors.

2) Level building pattern matching—The sequence of spectral vectors of the unknown speech signal is matched against a set of stored single-digit patterns (hidden Markov models) using the level building algorithm with Viterbi matching within levels. The output of this process is a set of candidate digit strings, generally of different lengths (i.e., different number of digits per string).

3) Postprocessor—The output candidate strings from level building are subjected to further validity tests, e.g., state duration, to eliminate unreasonable candidates. The postprocessor chooses the most likely digit string from the remaining (valid) candidate strings.

In the remainder of this section we expand further on the LPC spectral analysis (since this is fundamentally different from the one used in previous studies), and on the form of the HMM's. All other signal processing in the recognizer is essentially identical to that described in [7].

A. LPC Spectral Analysis

The LPC front end processing for recognition is shown in Fig. 2. The overall system is a block processing model in which a frame of N samples is processed and a vector of features is computed. (Strictly speaking, as we will see below, this is not correct since the system uses a 5 frame window to compute the delta cepstrum vector.) The steps in the processing are as follows.

1) Preemphasis—The digitized (at a 6.67 kHz rate) speech signal is processed by a first-order digital network in order to spectrally flatten the signal.

2) Blocking into frames—Sections of N consecutive speech samples (we use $N = 300$ corresponding to 45 ms

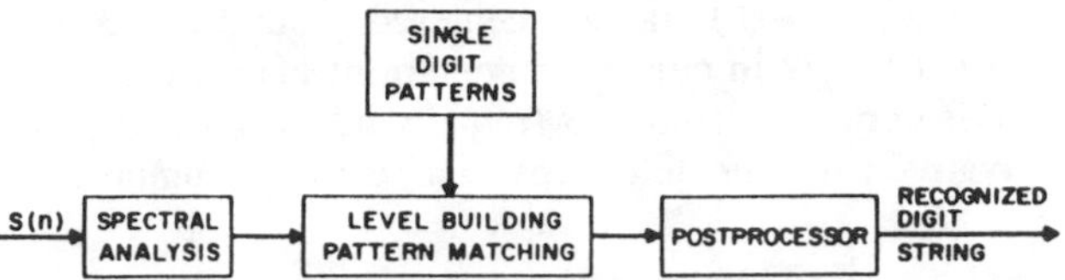

Fig. 1. Block diagram of connected digit recognizer.

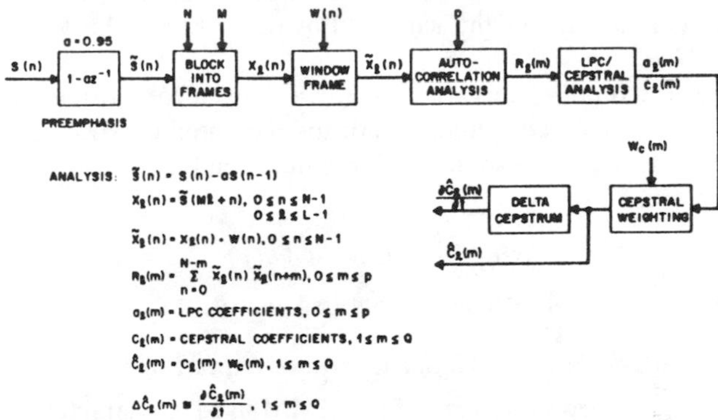

Fig. 2. Block diagram of improved front end LPC analysis incorporating instantaneous and transitional cepstral information.

of signal) are used as a single frame. Consecutive frames are spaced M samples apart (we use $M = 100$ corresponding to 15 ms frame spacing, or 30 ms frame overlap).

3) Frame windowing—Each frame is multiplied by an N-sample window (we use a Hamming window) so as to minimize the adverse effects of chopping an N-sample section out of the speech signal.

4) Autocorrelation analysis—Each windowed set of speech samples is autocorrelated to give a set of $(p + 1)$ coefficients, where p is the order of the desired LPC analysis (we use $p = 8$).

5) LPC/cepstral analysis—For each frame, vectors of LPC coefficients are computed from the autocorrelation vector using a Levinson or a Durbin recursion method. The LPC derived cepstral vector is then computed up to the Qth component, where $Q > p$, and $Q = 12$ in our implementation.

6) Cepstral weighting—The Q-coefficient cepstral vector, $c_l(m)$, at time frame l, is weighted by the window, $W_c(m)$, of the form [12], [13]

$$W_c(m) = \left[1 + \frac{Q}{2}\sin\left(\frac{\pi m}{Q}\right)\right], \qquad 1 \le m \le Q \quad (1)$$

to give

$$\hat{c}_l(m) = c_l(m) \cdot W_c(m). \quad (2)$$

(In theory, the use of cepstral weighting is irrelevant for diagonal covariance HMM's. However, since we used the weighted cepstal coefficients in the design of a codebook for choosing mixture parameters, based on a Euclidean distance, the weighting is relatively important.)

7) Delta cepstrum—The time derivative of the sequence of weighted cepstral vectors is approximated by a first-order orthogonal polynomial over a finite length win-

dow of $(2K + 1)$ frames, centered around the current vector. ($K = 2$ in our implementation; hence, the derivative is computed from a 5 frame window.) The cepstral derivative (i.e., the delta cepstrum vector) is computed as

$$\Delta \hat{c}_l(m) = \left[\sum_{k=-K}^{K} k\hat{c}_{l-k}(m) \right] \cdot G, \qquad 1 \le m \le Q \quad (3)$$

where G is a gain term so that the variances of $\hat{c}_l(m)$ and $\Delta \hat{c}_l(m)$ are about the same. (For our system, the value of G was 0.375.)

The overall observation vector, $\boldsymbol{O}_l$, used for scoring the HMM's is the concatenation of the weighted cepstral vector, and the corresponding weighted delta cepstrum vector, i.e.,

$$\boldsymbol{O}_l = \left\{ \hat{c}_l(m), \Delta \hat{c}_l(m) \right\}, \quad (4)$$

and consists of 24 coefficients per vector.

B. Hidden Markov Model Characterization of Words

Fig. 3 shows the form of the HMM used to characterize individual digits [14]–[16]. (Transitions between words are handled by a switch mode from the last state of one word model, to the first state of another word model, in the level building implementation.) The models are first-order left-to-right Markov models with N states.[1] (We have used values of N from 5 to 10.)[2] Each state, j, is characterized by the following.

1) A state transition vector, $\boldsymbol{a}_j$, with components a_{ji} = probability of making a transition to state i (at the next transition instant), given that the system is currently in state j. For the ergodic models of Fig. 3, a_{ji} satisfies the constraints

$$a_{ji} = 0, \qquad i < j, \qquad \text{and for } i > j + 1 \quad (5)$$

since we allow transitions from state j only to itself or to state $j + 1$.

2) A state observation density, $b_j(\boldsymbol{O})$, of the form

$$b_j(\boldsymbol{O}) = \sum_{m=1}^{M} c_{mj} N[\boldsymbol{O}, \mu_{mj}, U_{mj}] \quad (6)$$

i.e., a continuous mixture density where $\boldsymbol{O}$ is the observation vector (e.g., cepstral coefficient vector resulting from the LPC analysis), c_{mj} is the mixture weight for the mth component in state j, N represents a multivariate normal density, μ_{mj} is the mean vector for mixture m in state j, and U_{mj} is the covariance matrix for mixture m in state j. Typically, we use anywhere from $M = 1$ to $M = 9$ mixture components. In practice, we have observed that components of $\boldsymbol{O}$ are essentially uncorrelated. Hence, we

[1]We use the notation N to represent the number of states in an HMM, and use M to represent the number of mixtures per state. Previously we used N and M as the number of samples per frame in the LPC analysis and the shift per frame. This should cause no confusion as we will not refer to the LPC-analysis parameters again in the math.

[2]The choice of values of number of states, N, and number of mixtures open state, M, for the word vocabulary is somewhat of an art, and is highly dependent on both the vocabulary words and the amount of training data. No simple rules for such choices are known.

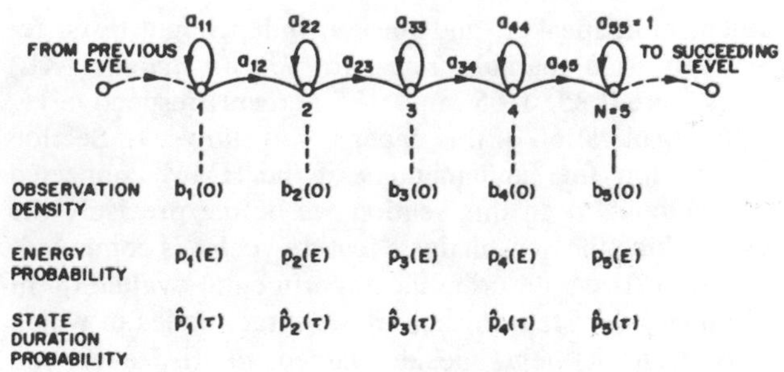

Fig. 3. Form of word HMM used to characterize individual digits.

assume that all components of $\boldsymbol{O}$ are statistically uncorrelated. Thus, U_{mj} becomes a diagonal covariance matrix, and (6) can be expressed simply as

$$b_j(\boldsymbol{O}) = \sum_{m=1}^{M} c_{mj} \frac{\prod_{d=1}^{D} \exp\left[-\left(O(d) - \mu_{mjd}\right)^2 / 2\sigma_{mjd}^2 \right]}{(2\pi)^{D/2} \left(\prod_{d=1}^{D} \sigma_{mjd}^2 \right)^{1/2}} \quad (7)$$

where $\boldsymbol{O}^{(d)}$ is the dth component of the observation vector, D is the number of components in $\boldsymbol{O}$, μ_{mjd} is the dth component of μ_{mj}, and σ_{mjd}^2 is the dth covariance of U_{mj}.

3) Energy probability, $p_j(\epsilon)$, where ϵ is the dynamically normalized frame energy, and p_j is a nonparametric discrete density of energy values in state j obtained empirically from training data. The energy values are computed on a log scale (i.e., in decibels), and the energy probabilities are quantized into 25 3-dB regions from 0 dB (absolute peak over a syllable length window) down to −75 dB and suitably normalized (based on a training set) so that

$$\sum_{i=1}^{25} p_j(\epsilon_i) = 1. \quad (8)$$

The choice of a 75 dB range on energy values reflects the range of variability of talkers, channels, and speech levels within a given channel.

4) State duration probability, $\hat{p}_j(\tau)$, where τ is the number of frames spent in state j, and $\hat{p}_j$ is an empirically measured, discrete density of duration values in state j. State durations are inherently quantized and are limited to values of 25 (frames) or less. Again, the state duration probabilities are normalized so that

$$\sum_{\tau_i=1}^{25} \hat{p}_j(\tau_i) = 1. \quad (9)$$

In addition to the observation density, energy probability, and state-duration probability, each HMM (for each word, v) is also characterized by an overall word-duration density, $p_v(D)$, of the form

$$p_v(D) = N[\overline{D}_v, \sigma_v^2] \quad (10)$$

where $\overline{D}_v$ is the average duration for word v, σ_v^2 is the variance in duration for word v, and N is the normal density.

Based on the above, the process of building an HMM, of the type shown in Fig. 3, to characterize a word, requires estimation of

1) $2N - 2$ values of a_{ij}, the state transition coefficients;
2) NM values of c_{mj}, the mixture gains;
3) NMD values of μ_{mjd}, the mean values of the observations;
4) NMD values of $[U_{mj}]_d$, the diagonal covariances of the observations;
5) $25N$ values of $p_j(\epsilon)$, the energy probability;
6) $25N$ values of $\hat{p}_j(\tau)$, the state-duration density; and
7) the value of $\overline{D}_v$ and of σ_v^2, the average and variance of overall word duration.

All these parameters are estimated (or measured) from a training set as discussed in the next section.

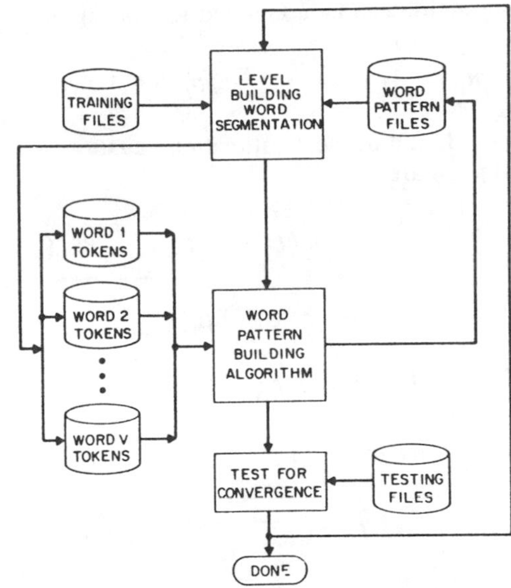

Fig. 4. Block diagram of the segmental k-means training procedure.

C. Training the Hidden Markov Models

In the case of building digit models from connected-digit training strings, the first step in building digit models is to segment optimally the digit strings into individual digits. For this task, a segmental k-means training procedure has been shown to be an effective way of converging at the optimum string segmentation [6]. A block diagram of the segmentation procedure is given in Fig. 4.

We assume that an initial set of word-pattern files is available. These initial files can equally well be a set of templates or HMM's. The templates or models can be a speaker independent set, a speaker trained set, or a designated training speaker set.

Give the initial word-pattern files and the training files (which consist of digit strings of various lengths), a level-building word-segmentation algorithm (of the type discussed in Section II-C) is used to optimally segment the training strings into individual word tokens which are stored in word-token files. A word-pattern-building algorithm (i.e., a model-estimation procedure for HMM's) is used to give an updated set of word patterns. The above procedure is iterated until the difference between the word patterns in consecutive iterations is sufficiently small [6].

1) Building HMM's for Each Word: Given a training set of W tokens of a word, the training problem for the HMM-based recognizer is to get optimal estimates of the complete set of HMM parameters for one or more models. The case of multiple models is essentially identical to that of single models. The only difference is that the training set is first clustered (using standard clustering procedures) and then a model is built for each cluster. Hence, we will concentrate here on parameter estimation for a single HMM from a finite training set of word tokens.

We have considered, and used, two methods for obtaining estimates of the HMM parameters, namely, the Baum–Welch reestimation procedure, and a segmental k-means loop based on segmentation of the words into individual states.

The Baum–Welch reestimation procedure is the standard method for estimation of the HMM parameters [14], [15]. Consider a single observation sequence, O, corresponding to a single word token. Let $O = O_1O_2 \cdots O_T$. We define the forward calculation, $\alpha_t(i)$, as

$$\alpha_t(i) = \text{Prob}\,(O_1O_2 \cdots O_t \quad \text{and state } i \text{ at } t \mid \lambda) \tag{11}$$

i.e., the probability of being in state i, at time t given the model λ. We compute $\alpha_t(i)$ recursively, i.e.,

$$\alpha_t(i) = \left[\sum_{j=1}^{N} \alpha_{t-1}(j)a_{ji}\right]\left(b_i(O_t) \cdot p_i(\epsilon_t)^{\gamma_\epsilon}\right) \tag{12}$$

where $p_i(\epsilon_t)^{\gamma_\epsilon}$ is a weighted probability that energy ϵ_t occurs in state i. Similarly, we define the backward function $\beta_t(j)$ as

$$\beta_t(j) = \text{Prob}\,(O_{t+1}O_{t+2} \cdots O_t \mid \text{state } j \text{ at } t \text{ and } \lambda). \tag{13}$$

We compute $\beta_t(j)$ recursively as

$$\beta_t(j) = \left[\sum_{i=1}^{N} \alpha_{ji}\left[b_i(O_{t+1})\, p_i(\epsilon_{t+1})^{\gamma_\epsilon}\right] \beta_{t+1}(i)\right]. \tag{14}$$

To complete the reestimation picture, we need a third function, $\rho_t(j, m)$, defined as

$$\rho_t(j, m) = \text{Prob}\,(O_1O_2 \cdots O_t, \text{ state } j, \text{ mixture } m \text{ at } t \mid \lambda). \tag{15}$$

The ρ function can be computed recursively as

$$\rho_t(j, m) = \sum_{i=1}^{N} \alpha_{t-1}(i)\, a_{ij} \left[c_{mj} b_j^{(m)}(O_t)\, p_j(\epsilon_t)^{\gamma_\epsilon}\right]. \quad (16)$$

Using α, β, and ρ, the reestimation equations for a, c, μ, U, and $p(\epsilon)$ are

$$\bar{a}_{ij} = \frac{\sum_{t=1}^{T-1} \alpha_t(i)\, a_{ij} b_j(O_{t+1})\, p_j(\epsilon_{t+1})^{\gamma_\epsilon}\, \beta_{t+1}(j)}{\sum_{t=1}^{T} \alpha_t(i)\, \beta_t(i)}, \quad 1 \le i, j \le N; \quad (17)$$

$$\bar{c}_{mj} = \frac{\sum_{t=1}^{T} \rho_t(j, m)\, \beta_t(j)}{\sum_{t=1}^{T} \alpha_t(j)\, \beta_t(j)}, \quad 1 \le m \le M, \quad 1 \le j \le N; \quad (18)$$

$$\bar{\mu}_{mjd} = \frac{\sum_{t=1}^{T} \rho_t(j, m)\, \beta_t(j) O_t^{(d)}}{\sum_{t=1}^{T} \rho_t(j, m)\, \beta_t(j)}, \quad 1 \le m \le M, \quad 1 \le j \le N, \quad 1 \le d \le D; \quad (19)$$

$$\bar{U}_{mjrs} = \frac{\sum_{t=1}^{T} \rho_t(j, m)\, \beta_t(j)(O_t^{(r)} - \mu_{mjr})(O_t^{(s)} - \mu_{mjs})}{\sum_{t=1}^{T} \rho_t(j, m)\, \beta_t(j)}, \quad 1 \le m \le M, \quad 1 \le j \le N, \quad 1 \le r, s \le D; \quad (20)$$

$$\bar{p}_j(\epsilon(k)) = \frac{\sum_{t\,\mathrm{s.t.}\,\epsilon_t = \epsilon(k)} \alpha_t(j)\, \beta_t(j)}{\sum_{t=1}^{T} \alpha_t(j)\, \beta_t(j)}. \quad (21)$$

Equations (11)-(21) are readily extended to the case of multiple training sequences [14].

The basic problem with the reestimation equations is the amount of computation associated with implementing equations (11)-(21) with large scale problems, e.g., 2500 training tokens and eight-state five-mixture models. To alleviate this difficulty, a segmental k-means algorithm was used to provide estimates of c, μ, U, and $p(\epsilon)$. This method segments each training token into states by determining the optimal (Viterbi) alignment of the current model with each training token. All frames for a given word, in a given state, are used as input to a clustering algorithm (i.e., a vector quantizer design procedure) which determines the best M cluster solution (codebook). The reestimate of the c's is just the number of vectors in a given cluster, divided by the total number of vectors in the state. The μ and U for each cluster are determined from the vectors within each cluster. The transition coefficients are reestimated based on the average duration in a state, and the energy probability histogram is measured from the vectors occurring in the state. Similarly, the state duration probability is measured from the training-set segmentation into states, and the overall word duration and variance is measured directly from the initial k-means segmentation into words.

The segmental k-means reestimation of the HMM parameters is faster than the Baum–Welch reestimation procedure, and all our experimentation indicates that the resulting parameter estimates are essentially identical in that the resulting HMM's had essentially the same likelihood values. As such, we have extensively used the segmental k-means procedure, and all results to be presented here are based on this algorithm.

D. Level Building on HMM's

The way in which level building is used on HMM's is illustrated in Fig. 5. If we denote the set of V word HMM as λ_v, $1 \le v \le V$, then to find the optimum sequence of HMM's that match O (i.e., that maximize the likelihood), a sequence of Viterbi matches is performed. For each HMM, λ_v, we do a Viterbi match against O, starting at frame 1, level 1, and retain for each possible frame, i, the following:

1) $P_l^v(i)$, the accumulated probability to frame i, at level l, for reference model λ_v, along the best path; and
2) $F_l^v(i)$, a backpointer indicating where the path started at the beginning of the level.

To compute $P_l^v(i)$, we need a local measure for the probability that observation O_i occurred in state j of model λ_v. The one we use is of the form

$$p_j^v(O) = b_j^v(O_i) \cdot \left[p_j^v(\epsilon_i)\right]^{\gamma_\epsilon} \cdot K_1 \quad (22)$$

where γ_ϵ is an energy-scaling coefficient, and K_1 is a normalization constant (which depends on γ_ϵ) such that (22) is a true probability. The value used for γ_ϵ in our experiments was 0.375. The state transition coefficients enter the calculation of $P_l^v(i)$ via the dynamic programming optimization in determining the Viterbi path.

At the end of each level, l, a maximization over v is performed to get the best model, at each frame, i, as follows:

$$P_l^B(i) = \max_{1 \le v \le V} P_l^v(i) \quad (23a)$$

$$W_l^B(i) = \operatorname*{argmax}_{1 \le v \le V} P_l^v(i) \quad (23b)$$

$$F_l^B(i) = F^{W_l^B(i)}(i). \quad (23c)$$

A best string of size l words ($1 \le l \le L$) with probability $P_l^B(I)$ is obtained by backtracking using the backpointer array $F_l^B(i)$ to give the words in the string. The overall best string is the maximum of $P_l^B(i)$ over all possible levels, l.

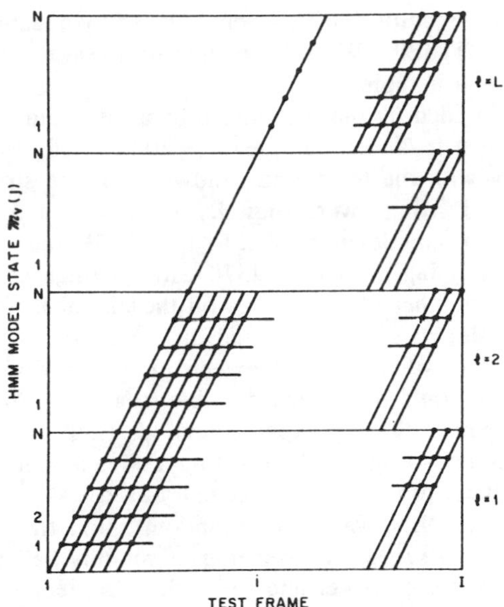

Fig. 5. Illustration of how level building is used with hidden Markov models.

E. *Use of Duration (State, Word) in HMM Scoring*

In the process of determining the best set of models that match a given input string, for each frame, i, of the test sequence, we use a local measure of the probability that the observation, O_i, occurred in state j of model v. If we denote this probability as p_i, then we have

$$p_i = b_j^v(O_i) \cdot \left[p_j^v(\epsilon_i)\right]^{\gamma_\epsilon} \cdot K_1 \tag{24}$$

as the local probability measure. For convenience, a "local distance" can be obtained by taking the negative log of p_i, giving

$$\begin{aligned} d_i &= -\log(p_i) \\ &= -\log\left(b_j^v(O_i)\right) - \gamma_\epsilon \log\left(p_j^v(\epsilon_i)\right) - \log K_1. \end{aligned} \tag{25}$$

The major problem associated with scoring HMM models using (24) or (25) is that there is no durational information incorporated, either explicitly or implicitly, into the local distance measure. The implicit state duration density is exponential because of the Markov property of the model, i.e., the probability of duration τ in state j is proportional to $(a_{jj})^\tau$. Clearly, such a duration density is incorrect in almost all cases. There are several ways in which other duration densities could be incorporated into the HMM scoring including the "Ferguson" internal model in which an explicit duration density is used (this work by Ferguson is unpublished), the Levinson model in which a parametric form of duration density is used [17], and a postprocessor model in which duration is accounted for in a postprocessor [16]. (In this case, the exponential duration density is still explicitly present in the model.) Since both the Ferguson and Levinson models significantly increase the computation associated with scoring, we have opted for the simpler postprocessor duration model.

The way in which word and state durations are incorporated into the model scoring is as follows. At the end of each level, for each frame, the accumulated probability, $P_l^B(i)$, is modified by determining the word duration, $\tau_w(i)$, as

$$\tau_w(i) = i - F_l^B(i) + 1 \tag{26}$$

and then multiplying the accumulated probability by the word duration probability, i.e.,

$$\hat{P}_l^B(i) = P_l^B(i) \cdot \left[N(\tau_w(i), \overline{D}, \sigma^2)\right]^{\gamma_{wD}} \cdot K_2 \tag{27}$$

where N is a normal density with mean $\overline{D}$ and variance σ^2, and where γ_{wD} is a weighting factor on word durations, and K_2 is a normalization constant which depends on γ_{wD} and which makes (27) a true probability. The value used for γ_{wD} in our experiments was 3.

State duration probabilities are incorporated in a postprocessor. The level-building recognizer provides multiple candidates at each level. Hence, overall probability scores are provided for R^L strings of length L, where R is the number of candidates per level (typically $R = 2$). Each of the R^L strings is backtracked to give individual words and individual states within the words. For an L-word string, if we denote the duration of state j at level l as $\Delta_l(j)$, then, for each possible string, the postprocessor multiplies the overall accumulated probability, $\hat{P}_L^B(I)$, by the state-duration probabilities, giving

$$\hat{P}_L^B(I) = P_L^B(I) \cdot \prod_{l=1}^{L} \prod_{j=1}^{N} \left[\hat{p}_j^{v(l)}(\Delta_l(j))\right]^{\gamma_{SD}} \cdot K_3 \tag{28}$$

where γ_{SD} is a weighting factor on state durations, and K_3 is a normalization constant which depends on γ_{SD}. The value used for γ_{SD} in our experiments was 0.75. The computation of (28) is performed for all $(R)^L$ strings, and a reordered list of best strings is obtained. The incremental cost of the postprocessor computation is negligible compared to the computation to give $\hat{P}_L^B(I)$, and its performance has been shown to be comparable to the performance of the internal duration models [16].

F. *Comments*

It is worth noting that a frame synchronous implementation (rather than the level synchronous used here), suitable for real-time processing, has been developed and shown to yield results identical to those of the current system [18]. Also, a real-time implementation of the system has been built using a processor board, called the ASPEN (AT&T Systolic Processor Ensemble) board, with 8 DSP-32 chips (AT&T), an AT&T PC 6300+ personal computer, and a special purpose LPC spectral analysis board (again based on a DSP-32 chip) [19].

III. Experimental Evaluation and Results

To evaluate the performance of the connected-digit recognizer, in speaker trained, multispeaker, and speaker independent modes, two databases were used.

The first database consisted of 50 talkers (25 male, 25 female) drawn from the local, nontechnical, population (i.e., all talkers were native New Jersey residents). Each talker recorded 1200 connected-digit strings in about five sessions, during a 1-week period, over local dialed-up telephone lines. A new line was used for each recording session. The digits vocabulary consisted of the 10 digits (zero to nine); the word "oh" was excluded. Each talker recorded an equal number of strings with from 1 to 7 digits. Within each string, the digits were selected at random; however, during the test there was a constraint that there be an equal number of occurrences of each digit. All recordings were made in a reasonably quiet environment; however, because of line variations and talker loudness variations, some recordings had very bad signal-to-noise ratios (i.e., on the order of 10–20 dB). A check was made on each recorded string to guarantee that the correct string was spoken. Subsequent checking of a part of the database showed that the checking process was itself error prone and in fact at least 155 of the recorded strings which passed the first check had some type of recording problem. Because of the inexperience of the 50 talkers, a rather large number of the spoken strings were unusable (generally because of gross speaking errors in which only partial or incomplete strings were spoken), and about 21 percent of the 60 000 recorded strings (i.e., 12 600 strings) were eliminated. The talker with the most difficulty had about 50 percent of his strings (604 of 1200) eliminated; the talker with the least difficulty had only 47 of 1200 strings eliminated. Overall there remained 47 336 strings in the database. We denote the 50-talker database as DB50 in tables and in the text. This database was used in the speaker trained, and multispeaker evaluations.

The second database, which was used to evaluate the connected digit recognizer in a speaker independent mode, was the TI connected digits database [20], as distributed by the National Bureau of Standards. This database contained connected digit strings from 225 adult talkers[1] (equally distributed among male and female talkers), and was conveniently divided into training and testing sets, for consistency of comparison of results among the different researchers using this database. This database was dialectically balanced with an equal mix of talkers from 22 dialectical regions. At least 10 talkers (5 male, 5 female) from each dialectical region were included in the database. The vocabulary consisted of 11 words, namely, the 10 digits and "oh." Each talker spoke 77 sequences of these digits, consisting of 2 tokens of each of the 11 digits in isolation, and 11 sequences of each of 2, 3, 4, 5, and 7 digits (i.e., no 6-digit sequences were spoken). Digits were selected at random without replacement with one exception, namely, the digits zero and "oh" never occurred in the same string. The digit strings were recorded in an acoustically treated sound room using a high quality microphone (Electro Voice RE-16 Dynamic Cardiod). All recorded strings were verified by a team of listeners at TI [20]. We refer to this database as DBTI in figures and in tables.

[1]Included in the TI database were connected digit strings from children. These strings were not used in our evaluations.

As provided by the National Bureau of Standards, the digitized strings were sampled at a 20 kHz rate. For consistency with the telephone bandwidth of the strings of DB50, all strings were digitally filtered to a 3.2 kHz bandwidth, and downsampled to a 6.67 kHz rate. A total of 8568 training strings and 8578 testing strings were used (a small number of the strings on the digital tapes were unreadable). It should be noted that many of the strings had distinct silence gaps between groups of digits. Although it would have been possible to account for these silence gaps either by explicit methods (i.e., reendpoint the recorded strings) or by creating a silence model, neither of these procedures was actually used.

Database DB50 was split (at random) into a training set and a testing set, each consisting of roughly half the utterances for each talker and for each string length in the database. The training and testing sets for DBTI were specified by TI as an integral part of the database. The training sets were used to derive additional word HMM's; the independent test sets were used to measure system performance. The segmental k-means training procedure was always bootstrapped from word models derived from the isolated digits within the database [6].

A. Speaker Trained Mode Results

For the speaker trained case, two sizes of HMM's were studied, namely, 1 with 5 states and 3 mixtures per state (the same size model as was used in [7]), and 1 with 8 states and 5 mixtures per state. (The choice of these operating points is somewhat arbitrary and was based on previous experience with representing digits by HMM's.) The results of the recognition runs for the speaker trained case are given in Table I. Table I(a) gives string error rates (in percent) for unknown length (UL) and known length (KL) strings, for both the training set and the independent testing set, for the two HMM's that were studied. (All results for speaker trained runs were obtained using DB50.) Table I(b) gives a breakdown of the string error rates for unknown length strings as a function of the number of digits in the string.

The results given in Table I show the following.

1) Recognition performance is uniformly better for the larger model (8 states) than for the smaller model (5 states).

2) String error rates on the testing set are about twice as large as on the training set, although the absolute differences in error rates are still small.

3) String error rates for KL strings are about half those of UL strings for both the training and testing sets.

4) UL string error rates increase uniformly with the number of digits in the string, up to about 4 digits per string; for longer strings the error rates are much larger (around 1.4 percent), and are relatively insensitive to the number of digits in the string. (The reason for such behavior is unclear; the only explanation is that the average

TABLE I

(a) String Error Rates (Percent), for Speaker Trained Mode, for Unknown Length (UL), and Known Length (KL) Strings on DB50, for Two Sizes of HMM. (b) String Error Rates (Percent), for Speaker Trained Mode, for Unknown Length Strings, as a Function of the Number of Digits in the String, on DB50, for Two Sizes of HMM

HMM	Training Set		Testing Set	
	UL	KL	UL	KL
8 states, 5 mixtures/state	0.39	0.16	0.78	0.35
5 states, 3 mixtures/state	0.62	0.29	1.02	0.47

(a)

HMM	Number of Digits in String						
	1	2	3	4	5	6	7
8 states, 5 mixtures/state	0.11	0.28	0.50	0.59	1.51	1.43	1.21
5 states, 3 mixtures/state	0.38	0.40	0.94	0.89	1.78	1.52	1.36

(b)

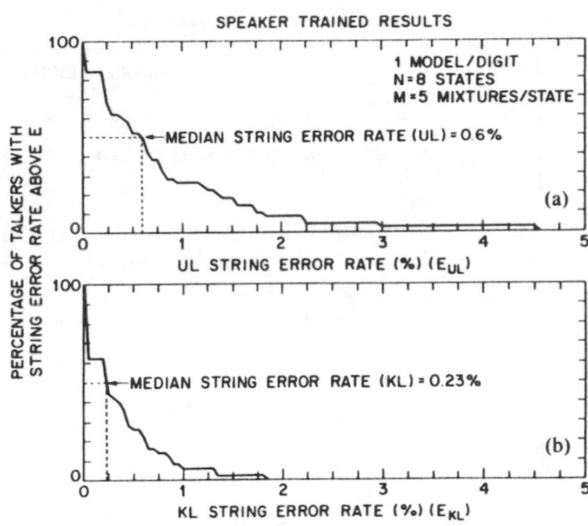

Fig. 6. Cumulative plots of percentage of talkers with testing set string error rates above a threshold for the speaker trained case; (a) for UL strings; (b) for KL strings.

rate of articulation for strings of length 4–7 digits, for this database, is approximately constant [7].)

The results given in Table I are based on the 23 750 strings spoken by the 50 talkers in the experiment. One interesting statistic is the individual speaker performance. This performance is illustrated in Fig. 6 which shows a cumulative plot of the percentage of talkers with testing string error rates above some threshold, E, for both UL [part (a)] and KL [part (b)] strings. It can be seen that for UL strings, the median string error rate is 0.6 percent (slightly lower than the average string error rate of 0.78 percent) and the talker with the highest error rate had 4.6 percent string errors. Similarly, for KL strings, the median string error rate is 0.23 percent (again slightly smaller than the average rate of 0.35 percent) and the talker with the highest error rate had 1.8 percent string errors.

B. Multispeaker Mode Results

For the multispeaker mode, using the training set of DB50, recognition systems were studied with from 1 to 6 models for each digit. The way in which multiple models were created was as follows. First, all the training strings were used to create a set of digit HMM's. (Two things should be noted here; first, only one-fourth of the set of training strings were used, i.e., about 6000 strings, because of computational constraints in the clustering algorithms; second, based on experience and intuition, we only considered models with $N = 10$ states, $M = 9$ mixtures per state.) Using a single model per digit set (designed using standard methods), the 6000 training strings were optimally segmented into individual digits, and these digit tokens were clustered into from 1 to 6 clusters for each of the 10 digits. An individual HMM was designed for each of the clusterings, thereby leading to sets of HMM's with from 1 to 6 models per digit.

The results of the recognition tests in the multispeaker mode are given in Table II which shows string error rate breakdowns for training and testing sets, and as a function of the number of digits per string for cases with from 1 to 6 models per digit. The results in Table II show the following.

TABLE II

(a) String Error Rates (Percent), for Multispeaker Mode, for Unknown Length (UL), and Known Length (KL) Strings on DB50, as a Function of the Number of Models per Digit, for an HMM with 10 States, 9 Mixtures/State. (b) String Error Rates (Percents), for Multispeaker Mode, for Unknown Length Strings, as a Function of the Number of Digits in the String and the Number of Models per Digit, on DB50, for an HMM with 10 States, 9 Mixtures/State

Number of Models Per Digit	Training Set		Testing Set	
	UL	KL	UL	KL
1	4.89	2.30	5.61	2.53
2	3.43	1.81	4.14	2.17
3	2.84	1.45	3.59	1.86
4	2.54	1.42	3.23	1.77
5	1.98	1.12	3.12	1.79
6	1.74	0.98	2.85	1.65

(a)

Number of Models Per Digit	Number of Digits in String						
	1	2	3	4	5	6	7
1	0.30	2.65	4.15	6.58	8.60	8.59	9.37
2	0.19	1.99	3.06	4.52	6.30	6.61	7.07
3	0.22	1.57	2.62	3.84	5.31	5.83	6.42
4	0.22	1.59	2.15	3.40	5.13	5.40	5.27
5	0.14	1.59	2.27	3.51	4.52	5.15	5.18
6	0.22	1.57	1.97	3.10	4.59	4.34	4.68

(b)

1) String error rates are significantly reduced by using more than 1 model per digit. For the training set, string error rates are reduced by a factor of about 2.5 as the number of models per digit is increased from 1 model/digit to 6 models/digit; for the testing set the comparable reduction in error rate is about 1.7 to 1.

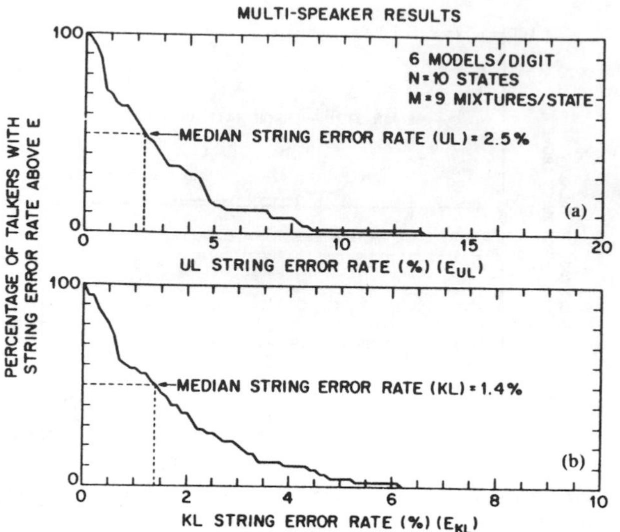

Fig. 7. Cumulative plots of percentage of talkers with testing set string error rates above a threshold for the multispeaker case; (a) for UL strings; (b) for KL strings.

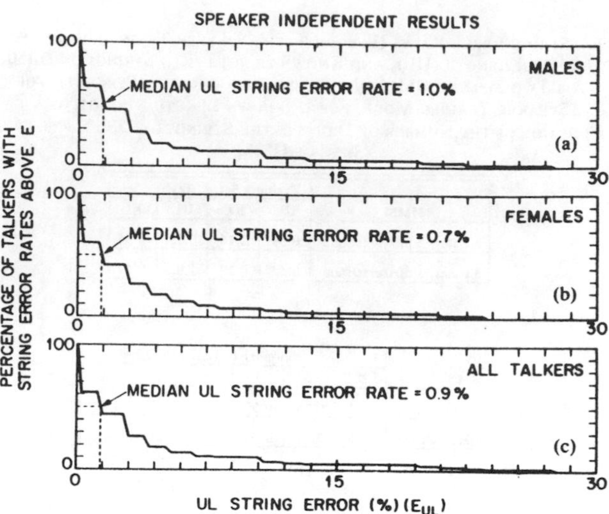

Fig. 8. Cumulative plots of percentage of talkers with testing set UL string error rates above a threshold for the speaker independent case; (a) for male talkers; (b) for female talkers; (c) for the combined talker set.

2) String error rates for training and testing sets are considerably closer than they were for the speaker trained case of Table I.

3) For the case of 6 models per digit, the resulting string error rates on the independent test set were 2.85 percent for unknown length strings and 1.65 percent for known length strings.

4) The error rates for isolated digits are very low (0.22 percent for 6 models per digit); the string error rates rise uniformly for 2-5 digit strings, then flatten off at a rate of about 4.5 percent.

Fig. 7 shows a cumulative plot, for the testing set, of the percentage of talkers with string error rate above a rate, E, for UL [part (a)], and KL [part (b)] strings, respectively. The median error rates of 2.5 percent (UL strings) and 1.4 percent (KL strings) are slightly lower than the average string error rates of 2.85 and 1.65 percent. The talker with the highest string error rate had 13 percent string errors (UL) and 6 percent string errors (KL). (Note that the scales in parts (a) and (b) of Fig. 8 are different.)

C. Speaker Independent Mode Results

For the speaker independent tests of the recognizer, database DBTI was used. The specified training set was used to create from 1 to 6 models per digit, in a manner similar to the one used in the multispeaker case. All 8565 training strings were used to create each set of models. The complete set of 8578 testing strings was used to evaluate the recognizer performance on the testing set. (The reader is reminded that, for this database, the vocabulary included the digits "oh" and zero, as well as one to nine.)

The results of the speaker independent recognition tests are given in Table III. The form of the table is the same as was used for Table II in the previous section. The results show the following.

TABLE III

(a) String Error Rates (Percent), for Speaker Independent Mode, for Unknown Length (UL), and Known Length (KL) Strings, on DBTI, as a Function of the Number of Models per Digit, for an HMM with 10 States, 9 Mixtures/State. (b) String Error Rates (Percent), for Speaker Independent Mode, for Unknown Length Strings, as a Function of the Number of Digits in the String, and the Number of Models per Digit, on DBTI, for an HMM with 10 States, 9 Mixtures/State

Number of Models Per Digit	Training Set		Testing Set	
	UL	KL	UL	KL
1	2.84	1.19	4.35	2.15
2	1.90	0.71	3.64	1.88
3	1.52	0.53	3.10	1.67
4	1.24	0.36	2.94	1.75
5	1.13	0.34	3.01	1.89
6	1.05	0.35	3.01	1.90

(a)

Number of Models Per Digit	Number of Digits in String					
	1	2	3	4	5	7
1	0.69	2.20	5.13	5.90	7.13	8.73
2	0.61	1.96	3.99	5.33	6.64	6.37
3	0.49	1.79	3.42	4.43	5.74	5.39
4	0.69	1.79	3.10	3.77	5.08	5.47
5	0.61	1.79	3.59	4.18	5.16	5.14
6	0.73	1.55	3.42	4.02	5.41	5.22

(b)

1) For the training set there is a reduction in string error rate of about 3 to 1 as the number of models per digit increases from 1 to 6; for the independent testing set the reduction in string error rate is only a factor of 1.5 for UL strings and 1.2 for KL strings.

2) A very large difference in performance exists between the training and testing sets, both for UL and KL strings. For example, for 6 models per digit, the string

error rate for UL strings is a factor of 3 smaller; for KL strings the error rates differ by a factor of 5.5.

3) The string error rates on the testing set level off at about 3–4 models per digit; for 4 models per digit the UL string error rate is 2.94 percent, the KL string error rate is 1.75 percent.

4) The isolated digit error rate for 6 models per digit is 0.73 percent; string error rates for UL strings increase uniformly from 2 to 5 digits per string. For 7 digit strings, the string error rate is essentially equal to that of 5 digit strings since no possibility of digit insertions existed, i.e., the maximum string length allowed was 7 digits.

Fig. 8 shows cumulative plots, for the testing set based on UL strings, of the percentage of talkers with string error rate above a threshold, E_{UL}, for the male talkers [part (a)], the female talkers [part (b)], and the combined talker set [part (c)]. Table IV gives a breakdown according to the number of string errors (out of the 77 spoken strings per talker), for males and females. The median UL string error rates are 1 percent for males, 0.7 percent for females, and 0.9 percent for the combined population. The UL string error rates are lower, by a factor of about 3, than the average error rates reported in Table III using 3 models per digit, showing that a large percentage of the string errors were generated by a small fraction of the talkers. This result was noted by Bush and Kopec [5].

TABLE IV
DISTRIBUTION OF STRING ERRORS FOR UL STRINGS IN THE TESTING SET BASED ON USING THREE MODELS PER DIGIT

	Number of String Errors												
Gender	0	1	2	3	4	5	6	7	8	9	10	>10	Total
Men	20	10	10	5	2	1	0	0	3	0	1	3(15,18,22)	55
Women	23	10	9	7	3	2	1	0	1	1	0	2(16,18)	57

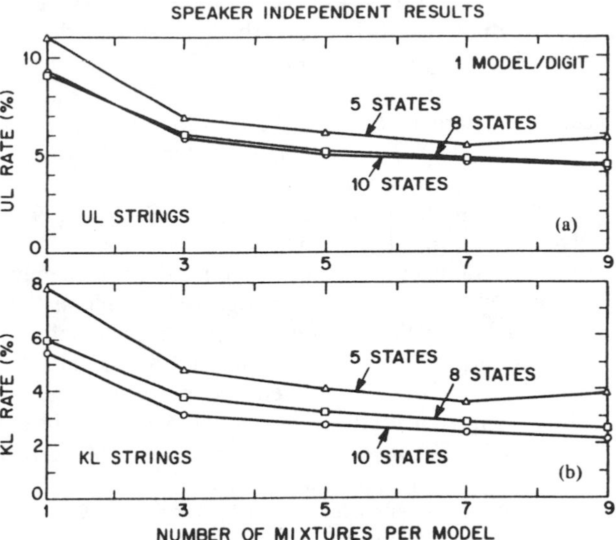

Fig. 9. Plots of testing set string error rates as a function of the number of mixtures per model for the speaker independent case; (a) UL strings, (b) KL strings.

D. Effects of Number of States, Number of Mixtures Per State

To demonstrate the effects of using fewer than 9 mixtures per state, or fewer than 10 states in each word HMM, an experiment was run using the DBTI database, in which a set of HMM's were designed with $N = 5$, 8, and 10 states, and with $M = 1$, 3, 5, 7, and 9 mixtures per state. In each case, for reasons related to computation, only a single HMM was designed for each digit; hence, the string error rates will be no better than the results in the first row of Table III(a). The results of this experiment, in the form of string error rates for UL strings [part (a)] and KL strings [part (b)], as a function of M, for different values of N, are given in Fig. 9. It can be seen that as M goes from 1 to 3, a significant reduction in string error rate occurs. Further increases in M result in small reductions in string error rate. Eventually, for large enough M, a statistical fluctuation in string error rate results. The effects of N are also clear. As N goes from 5 to 8, a significant reduction in string error rate results; however, as N goes from 8 to 10, there is no real performance difference for UL strings, but for KL strings there is a significant performance improvement.

E. Effects of Using Delta Cepstrum or Cepstrum Alone

Two brief experiments were carried out, using database DBTI, in which the feature set for recognition (the observation vectors) was changed from the combination of weighted cepstrum and weighted delta cepstrum to just the weighted delta cepstrum alone, or just weighted bandpass cepstrum alone (as was used in [7]). For these tests, a one-model-per-digit system was used with 10 states and 9 mixtures per state for each model. The results for these tests showed the following.

1) The error rates on the testing set, using just the weighted delta cepstrum coefficients, were 10.2 percent for UL strings, and 4.3 percent for KL strings, as contrasted to 4.35 percent for UL strings, and 2.15 percent for KL strings using the combined cepstrum.

2) The error rates on the testing set, using just the weighted cepstrum coefficients, were 12.7 percent for UL strings and 6.4 percent for KL strings.

These results show that the information in the "instantaneous" and "transitional" feature is somewhat complementary and that the combination of the feature sets gave much better performance than either of the individual feature sets. Whether or not further gains could be achieved using higher order transitional features is an open question of interest.

One last experiment was tried, based on work by Furui [10], in which the observation vector was created by adding the weighted delta cepstrum to the weighted cepstrum to create a feature set with only 12 components. The results using this additive set of features were the following (again with 1 model per digit, 10 states, and 9 mixtures per state).

1) The error rates on the testing set were 8.1 percent for UL strings and 2.8 percent on KL strings. These re-

sults, although better than either of the individual feature vectors, are still inferior to the results obtained from the combined feature vectors, again pointing out the importance of retaining both instantaneous and transitional spectral information in the observation vector.

F. Error Analysis for SI Runs

An analysis of the errors for the speaker independent testing run (using DBTI data) showed the following.

1) 66 digit insertions—exactly half (33) of these involved inserting an "oh" after the digit zero. This type of error leads to a semantically incorrect string and could easily be eliminated in the digit grammar. The digits 6 and 2 were inserted 8 and 7 times, respectively. All other digits were inserted 5 times or less.

2) 61 digit deletions—almost half of these (29) involved a deletion of the word "oh" in the context of 2 or more repetitions of "oh," e.g., "oh-oh" was recognized as "oh" or "oh-oh-oh" was recognized as "oh-oh." The digit "oh" was deleted 8 other times (i.e., not in the context of multiple "oh's"), and the digit 8 was deleted 19 times. No other digit was deleted more than 2 times.

3) 221 digit substitutions—about 40 percent of the digit substitutions (89) involved the word "oh." Most of the time an "oh" was substituted for the correct digit. The only other consistent digit substitution was a 9 for a 5, which occurred 23 times.

The above analysis shows that in about half the digit errors, the word "oh" was involved. This result is to be expected since "oh" can be spoken rather rapidly and therefore is a prime candidate for digit insertion, deletion, or substitution.

An analysis was also made of errors in the recognition of the training set, and trends very similar to those discussed above were found.

IV. Discussion

In this paper we have presented results that demonstrate major improvements in our ability to recognize relatively unconstrained strings of connected digits (i.e., strings up to 7 digits in length). We have shown that by incorporating information about the time derivatives of the cepstral coefficients, along with instantaneous cepstral coefficients, we can significantly enhance recognizer performance. A summary of the recognizer performance, in each of the 3 modes in which it was tested, is given in Table V. Overall string error rates of less than 3 percent for unknown string lengths and less than 2 percent for known string lengths were obtained on independent testing sets of data for both speaker independent and multispeaker modes. String error rates of less than 1 percent for unknown string lengths and less than 0.5 percent for known string lengths were obtained in the speaker trained case.

These results show that the transitional cepstral information made the recognizer relatively robust to talkers. In another paper, we have shown that the addition of the delta cepstrum analysis significantly improves performance with other vocabularies (e.g., the alphabet) in isolated word recognition tasks [21].

TABLE V
Summary of String Error Rates for the Three Recognition Modes

Recognition Mode	Database	Training Set		Testing Set	
		UL	KL	UL	KL
Speaker Trained	DB50	0.39	0.16	0.78	0.35
Multi-speaker (6 Models Per Digit)	DB50	1.74	0.98	2.85	1.65
Speaker Independent (4 Models Per Digit)	DBTI	1.24	0.36	2.94	1.75

To see how much progress has been made, it is worthwhile contrasting the results presented here with those of earlier studies. In earlier work, using the same databases and recognizer, but with a standard instantaneous cepstral analysis (i.e., without the transitional cepstral information), Rabiner *et al.* reported testing set string error rates of 1.83 percent (UL), and 0.81 percent (KL) in the speaker trained mode, and 6 percent (UL) and 3.4 percent (KL) in the multispeaker mode (using 10 models per digit as opposed to 6 models per digit here). The string error rates reported here are lower by a factor of 2 or more! Furthermore, in the speaker independent mode, the results [22] obtained for the testing set were string error rates of 7.9 percent (UL) and 5.2 percent (KL), again using 10 models per digit. Here the string error rates are lower by a factor of about 3 to 1, based on 4 models per digit. These comparisons strongly point out the advantages of the transitional cepstral information for recognition.

The only other comparison worth making is with the work of Bush and Kopec [5] who also used the TI database for their recognition tests. The best performance results on the testing set, obtained by Bush and Kopec, were 4 percent (UL) and 3 percent (KL) string error rates. The Bush and Kopec results were based on digit models derived from acoustic-phonetic knowledge, using wider bandwidth spectral analysis, with a network representation that handled some difficult cases (e.g., prepausal "oh" or eight), and with an explicit background silence model. The results given here were obtained *fully automatically*, using telephone bandwidth data, with no explicit silence model, and with no rules or corrections for difficult digit sequences.

V. Summary

In this paper we have shown that a very high performance connected digit recognition system can be implemented automatically based on our current understanding. The key to the improvement in performance over earlier implementations was the use of an analysis that included both instantaneous and transitional (time derivative) spectral information. The system was tested in three modes, namely, speaker trained, multispeaker, and speaker independent, and shown to be capable of recognizing digit strings with greater than 97 percent accuracy in all cases.

References

[1] H. Sakoe, "Two level DP-matching—A dynamic programming based pattern matching algorithm for connected word recognition," *IEEE Trans. Acoust., Speech, Signal Processing*, vol. ASSP-27, pp. 588–596, Dec. 1979.

[2] C. S. Myers and L. R. Rabiner, "Connected digit recognition using a level building DTW algorithm," *IEEE Trans. Acoust., Speech, Signal Processing*, vol. ASSP-29, pp. 351–363, June 1981.

[3] J. S. Bridle, M. D. Brown, and R. M. Chamberlain, "An algorithm for connected word recognition," *Automat. Speech Anal. Recognition*, J. P. Haton, Ed., pp. 191–204, 1982.

[4] H. Ney, "The use of a one-stage dynamic programming algorithm for connected word recognition," *IEEE Trans. Acoust., Speech, Signal Processing*, vol. ASSP-32, pp. 263–271, Apr. 1984.

[5] M. A. Bush and G. E. Kopec, "Network-based connected digit recognition," *IEEE Trans. Acoust., Speech, Signal Processing*, vol. ASSP-35, pp. 1401–1413, Oct. 1987.

[6] L. R. Rabiner, J. G. Wilpon, and B. H. Juang, "A segmental *k*-means training procedure for connected word recognition based on whole word reference patterns," *AT&T Tech. J.*, vol. 65, no. 3, pp. 21–31, May/June 1986.

[7] —, "A model-based connected-digit recognition system using either hidden Markov models or templates," *Comput. Speech Language*, vol. 1, no. 2, pp. 167–197, Dec. 1986.

[8] L. R. Rabiner, A. Bergh, and J. G. Wilpon, "An improved training procedure for connected digit recognition," *Bell Syst. Tech. J.*, vol. 61, no. 6, pp. 981–1001, July–Aug. 1982.

[9] L. R. Rabiner, J. G. Wilpon, A. M. Quinn, and S. G. Terrace, "On the application of embedded digit training to speaker independent, connected digit recognition," *IEEE Trans. Acoust., Speech, Signal Processing*, vol. ASSP-32, pp. 272–280, Apr. 1984.

[10] S. Furui, "Speaker independent isolated word recognition based on dynamics emphasized cepstrum," *Trans. IECE Japan*, vol. 69, no. 12, pp. 1310–1317, Dec. 1986.

[11] F. K. Soong and A. E. Rosenberg, "On the use of instantaneous and transitional spectral information in speaker recognition," in *Proc. ICASSP 1986*, Tokyo, Japan, Apr. 1986, pp. 877–880, Paper 17.5.1.

[12] Y. Tohkura, "A weighted cepstral distance measure for speech recognition," *IEEE Trans. Acoust., Speech, Signal Processing*, vol. ASSP-35, pp. 1414–1422, Oct. 1987.

[13] B. H. Juang, L. R. Rabiner, and J. G. Wilpon, "On the use of bandpass liftering in speech recognition," *IEEE Trans. Acoust., Speech, Signal Processing*, vol. ASSP-35, pp. 947–954, July 1987.

[14] S. E. Levinson, L. R. Rabiner, and M. M. Sondhi, "An introduction to the application of the theory of probabilistic functions of a Markov process to automatic speech recognition," *Bell Syst. Tech. J.*, vol. 12, no. 4, pp. 1035–1074, Apr. 1983.

[15] F. Jelinek, "Continuous speech recognition by statistical methods," *Proc. IEEE*, vol. 64, pp. 532–556, Apr. 1976.

[16] L. R. Rabiner, B. H. Juang, S. E. Levinson, and M. M. Sondhi, "Recognition of isolated digits using hidden Markov models with continuous mixture densities," *AT&T Tech. J.*, vol. 64, pp. 1211–1234, July–Aug. 1985.

[17] S. E. Levinson, "Continuously variable duration hidden Markov models for automatic speech recognition," *Comput. Speech Language*, vol. 1, no. 1, pp. 29–45, Mar. 1986.

[18] C. H. Lee and L. R. Rabiner, "A frame synchronous level building algorithm for connected word recognition," *IEEE Trans. Acoust., Speech, Signal Processing*, to appear.

[19] A. L. Gorin and D. B. Roe, "Parallel level building on a tree machine," in *Proc. ICASSP 88*, New York, Apr. 1988, pp. 295–298.

[20] R. G. Leonard, "A database for speaker-independent digit recognition," in *Proc. 1984 ICASSP*, Mar. 1984, pp. 42.11.1–4.

[21] L. R. Rabiner and J. G. Wilpon, "Some performance benchmarks for isolated word, speech recognition systems," *Comput. Speech Language*, vol. 2, pp. 343–357, Sept./Dec. 1987.

[22] L. R. Rabiner, J. G. Wilpon, and B. H. Juang, "A performance evaluation of a connected digit recognizer," in *Proc. ICASSP-87*, Dallas, TX, 1987, pp. 101–104, Paper 3.10.1.

Lawrence R. Rabiner (S'62–M'67–SM'75–F'76) was born in Brooklyn, NY, on September 28, 1943. He received the S.B. and S.M. degrees simultaneously in June 1964, and the Ph.D. degree in electrical engineering in June 1967, all from the Massachusetts Institute of Technology, Cambridge.

From 1962 through 1964 he participated in the cooperative plan in electrical engineering at Bell Laboratories, Whippany and Murray Hill, NJ. He worked on digital circuitry, military communications problems, and problems in binaural hearing. Presently he is engaged in research on speech recognition and digital signal processing techniques at Bell Laboratories, Murray Hill. He is coauthor of the books *Theory and Application of Digital Signal Processing* (Englewood Cliffs, NJ: Prentice-Hall, 1975), *Digital Processing of Speech Signals* (Englewood Cliffs, NJ: Prentice-Hall, 1978), and *Multirate Digital Signal Processing* (Englewood Cliffs, NJ: Prentice-Hall, 1983).

Dr. Rabiner is a member of Eta Kappa Nu, Sigma Xi, Tau Beta Pi, The National Academy of Engineering, and is a Fellow of the Acoustical Society of America.

Jay G. Wilpon (M'84–SM'87) was born in Newark, NJ, on February 28, 1955. He received the B.S. and A.B. degrees (cum laude) in mathematics and economics, respectively, from Lafayette College, Easton, PA, in 1977. He received the M.S. degree in electrical engineering/computer science from Stevens Institute of Technology, Hoboken, NJ, in 1982.

Since June 1977 he has been with the Speech Research Department at AT&T Bell Laboratories, Murray Hill, NJ, where he is a member of the Technical Staff. He has been engaged in speech communications research and is presently concentrating on problems in isolated and connected word speech recognition. He has published extensively in this field and has been awarded several patents. His current interests lie in training procedures for both speaker dependent and speaker independent recognition systems, speech detection algorithms, and determining the viability of implementing speech recognition systems for general usage over the telephone network.

Mr. Wilpon received the IEEE Acoustics, Speech, and Signal Processing Society's Paper Award in 1987 for his work on clustering algorithms for use in training automatic speech recognition systems.

Frank K. Soong (S'76–M'82) received the B.S., M.S., and Ph.D. degrees from the National Taiwan University, the University of Rhode Island, and Stanford University, respectively, all in electrical engineering.

Since 1982 he has been a member of the Technical Staff at AT&T Bell Labs, Murray Hill, NJ, first with the Acoustics Research Department and later with the Speech Research Department. His research work includes developing new coding algorithms at medium to low bit rates, investigating spectral distortion measures for speech processing, applying vector quantization to speaker recognition and normalization, and studying instantaneous and transitional spectral information of speech signals for speech and speaker recognition. He was an invited researcher at NTT-ECL, Japan, from 1987 to 1988. At NTT he has developed a phonetically labeled acoustic segment approach to speech processing and applied it to speech recognition, very low bit rate speech coding, and speech synthesis.

Speech recognition with continuous-parameter hidden Markov models

Lalit R. Bahl, Peter F. Brown, Peter V. de Souza and Robert L. Mercer

IBM Thomas J. Watson Research Center, Yorktown Heights, NY 10598, U.S.A.

Abstract

The acoustic modeling problem in automatic speech recognition is examined from an information-theoretic point of view. This problem is to design a speech-recognition system which can extract from the speech waveform as much information as possible about the corresponding word sequence. The information extraction process is broken down into two steps: a signal-processing step which converts a speech waveform into a sequence of information-bearing acoustic feature vectors, and a step which models such a sequence. We are primarily concerned with the use of hidden Markov models to model sequences of feature vectors which lie in a continuous space. We explore the trade-off between packing information into such sequences and being able to model them accurately. The difficulty of developing accurate models of continuous-parameter sequences is addressed by investigating a method of parameter estimation which is designed to cope with inaccurate modeling assumptions.

1. Introduction

A speech-recognition system is a device which translates a speech waveform, **z**, into the sequence of words, **w**, that was uttered by the speaker producing the waveform. Following Nadas (1983), a recognizer can be thought of as a decoding function f: $\mathbf{z} \rightarrow \mathbf{w}$. The probability that it will decode a word sequence correctly is $\Sigma_z \Pr(\mathbf{W}=f(\mathbf{z}),\mathbf{Z}=\mathbf{z})$. Since

$$\sum_{z} \Pr(\mathbf{W}=f(\mathbf{z}), \mathbf{Z}=\mathbf{z}) \leqslant \sum_{z} \max_{\mathbf{w}} \Pr(\mathbf{W}=\mathbf{w},\mathbf{Z}=\mathbf{z}), \tag{1}$$

an optimal recognizer will choose $f(\mathbf{z})$ such that

$$f(\mathbf{z}) = \operatorname*{argmax}_{\mathbf{w}} \Pr(\mathbf{W}=\mathbf{w},\mathbf{Z}=\mathbf{z}) \tag{2}$$

$$= \operatorname*{argmax}_{\mathbf{w}} \Pr(\mathbf{Z}=\mathbf{z}|\mathbf{W}=\mathbf{w})\Pr(\mathbf{W}=\mathbf{w}). \tag{3}$$

$\Pr(\mathbf{W}=\mathbf{w})$ is the prior probability of the word sequence **w**. $\Pr(\mathbf{Z}=\mathbf{z}|\mathbf{W}=\mathbf{w})$ is the conditional probability that the acoustic signal **z** will be produced given that **w** is spoken.

A real-life recognizer does not know these probabilities, but instead estimates $\Pr(\mathbf{W}=\mathbf{w})$ with a language model, ℓ, and estimates $\Pr(\mathbf{Z}=\mathbf{z}|\mathbf{W}=\mathbf{w})$ with a member of a family of acoustic models, $\mathcal{M}$. It will choose a word sequence $f(\mathbf{z})$ so that

$$f(\mathbf{z}) = \operatorname{argmax} \Pr_{\mathcal{M}}(\mathbf{Z}=\mathbf{z}|\mathbf{W}=\mathbf{w})\Pr_{\ell}(\mathbf{W}=\mathbf{w}). \tag{4}$$

Because it is difficult to model a speech waveform directly, a signal-processing operation is used to transform the acoustic signal **z** to a sequence **y**. We then pretend that all the information about the word sequence **w** that is contained in **z** is also contained in **y**. A measure of this information is the mutual information between **w** and **z**:

$$\mathrm{I}(\mathbf{w},\mathbf{z}) \triangleq \log \frac{\Pr(\mathbf{w},\mathbf{z})}{\Pr(\mathbf{w})\Pr(\mathbf{z})}. \tag{5}$$

We pretend that

$$\mathrm{I}(\mathbf{w},\mathbf{z}) = \mathrm{I}(\mathbf{w},\mathbf{y}). \tag{6}$$

Using this assumption, the recognizer's decoding function in (4) becomes

$$f(\mathbf{z}) = \operatorname*{argmax}_{\mathbf{w}} \Pr_{\mathcal{M}}(\mathbf{Y}=\mathbf{y}(\mathbf{z})|\mathbf{W}=\mathbf{w})\Pr_{\ell}(\mathbf{W}=\mathbf{w}). \tag{7}$$

In practice, when designing a signal-processing algorithm, we face a trade-off between preserving acoustic information in the output sequence **y**, and being able to model **y** accurately. Nearly all of today's systems both discard information and suffer from modeling inaccuracies.

Typically, the signal processor extracts vectors of acoustic parameters from the speech waveform at regular intervals. For example, every 10 milliseconds it might compute the energy in each of 20 spectral bands. In vector-quantizing recognizers, these acoustic parameter vectors are mapped into a finite alphabet (Gray, 1984; Makhoul, 1985). One reason for this mapping is that it is possible to model speech with nonparametric discrete output distributions. Vector quantization destroys information about the spoken word sequence. Because of this there have been a number of studies of recognizers which directly model the continuous-parameter vectors that are produced by the initial stage of the signal processor (Bahl, Bakis, Cohen, Cole, Jelinek, Lewis & Mercer, 1981; Juang & Rabiner, 1986; Poritz & Richter, 1986). In this paper, we investigate the problems of modeling such continuous-parameter sequences.

2. Hidden Markov models

A sequence of random variables $\mathbf{X} = X_1, X_2, \ldots$ is a *first-order* n-*state Markov chain* provided that for each t, X_t is defined over the integers 1 to n and

$$\Pr(X_{t+1}=x_{t+1}|\mathbf{X}_1^t=\mathbf{x}_1^t) = \Pr(X_{t+1}=x_{t+1}|X_t=x_t), \tag{8}$$

where the abbreviation $\mathbf{X}_i^j$ is used to represent the sequence $X_i, X_{i+1}, \ldots, X_j$. In a *stationary* Markov chain, $\Pr(X_{t+1}=x_{t+1}|X_t=x_t)$ is independent of t. The parameters of a stationary Markov chain are the *transition probabilities*

$$a_{ij}\stackrel{\triangle}{=}\Pr(X_{t+1}=j|X_t=i), \tag{9}$$

and the *initial-state probabilities*

$$c_i\stackrel{\triangle}{=}\Pr(X_1=i). \tag{10}$$

We say that a transition from state i to state j occurred at time t if the Markov chain was in state i at time t and in state j at time $t+1$.

In a *hidden Markov model* there is a sequence of random variables, **Y**, which is a probabilistic function of a stationary Markov chain **X**. **X** is a hidden Markov model for a sequence of discrete random variables, **Y**, provided that for each t, Y_t is defined over a discrete space, and

$$\Pr(Y_t=y_t|\mathbf{Y}_t^{t-1}=\mathbf{y}_t^{t-1},\mathbf{X}=\mathbf{x})=\Pr(Y_t=y_t|X_t=x_t,X_{t+1}=x_{t+1}). \tag{11}$$

X is a hidden Markov model for a sequence of continuous random variables, **Y**, provided that for each t, Y_t is defined over a continuous space, and

$$f(Y_t=y_t|\mathbf{Y}_1^{t-1}=\mathbf{y}_t^{t-1},\mathbf{X}=\mathbf{x})=f(Y_t=y_t|X_t=x_t,X_{t+1}=x_{t+1}), \tag{12}$$

where $f(Y_t=y_t)$ is the probability density at y_t. The probabilities in (11) and (12) are assumed to be independent of t. The sequence **y** is the observed output of the hidden Markov model. The state sequence **x** is not observed; it is hidden.

The parameters of a hidden Markov model are the initial-state probabilities, the transition probabilities, and the parameters of the output distributions. In the discrete case the output distributions in (11) are nonparametric and are determined by the output probabilities

$$b_{ij}(k)\stackrel{\triangle}{=}\Pr(Y_t=k|X_t=i,X_{t+1}=j). \tag{13}$$

In the continuous case, the output distributions in (12) are parameterized. In this paper we consider three different families of continuous parameter distributions: Gaussians, diagonal Gaussians, and Richter mixtures of Gaussians. In a diagonal Gaussian all the off-diagonal terms in the covariance matrix are zero. A Richter mixture of Gaussians is a mixture of Gaussians all of which have the same means and which have covariance matrices that are scalar multiples of one another. These mixtures were proposed by Alan Richter specifically to cope with the problems of outliers in speech data (Richter, 1986).

In order to avoid making every point twice, once for the discrete case and once for the continuous case, let us generalize the Pr notation to stand for both the probability of an event and for the probability density at a point. In the same way let us also use the term $b_{ij}(y_t)$ to refer to both a probability in the discrete case and a probability density in the continuous case:

$$b_{ij}(y_t)\stackrel{\triangle}{=}\begin{cases}\Pr(Y_t=y_t|X_t=i,X_{t+1}=j), & \text{in the discrete case;}\\ f(Y_t=y_t|X_t=i,X_{t+1}=j), & \text{in the continuous case.}\end{cases} \tag{14}$$

In both cases, we refer to $b_{ij}(y_t)$ as the *output* probability of y_t given the transition $i\rightarrow j$. The word *probability* will be used to refer to both a probability of a sample point from a discrete space and to the probability density at a sample point in a continuous space. Observations which are vectors of continuous parameters will be denoted by bold-face variables. Discrete observations will be denoted by light-face variables. Generic observations, which may be either from a discrete or a continuous space will also be denoted by light-face variables. Variables which denote whole sequences will always be in a bold-face type.

The probability that a hidden Markov model will generate a particular sequence $\mathbf{y}_1^T$ is

$$\Pr(\mathbf{Y}_1^T=\mathbf{y}_1^T)=\sum_{\mathbf{x}_1^{T+1}}\Pr(\mathbf{X}_1^{T+1}=\mathbf{x}_1^{T+1})\Pr(\mathbf{Y}_1^T=\mathbf{y}_1^T|\mathbf{X}_1^{T+1}=\mathbf{x}_1^{T+1}). \tag{15}$$

The computation of $\Pr(\mathbf{Y}_1^T)$ can be efficiently organized in the following manner. Let

$$a_i(t)\stackrel{\triangle}{=}\Pr(\mathbf{Y}_1^t=\mathbf{y}_1^t,X_{t+1}=i). \tag{16}$$

For all states, i,

$$a_i(0)=\Pr(X_1=i)=c_i, \tag{17}$$

and for $t>0$

$$a_i(t)=\sum_j a_j(t-1)a_{ji}b_{ji}(y_t). \tag{18}$$

Clearly

$$\Pr(\mathbf{Y}_1^T=\mathbf{y}_1^T)=\sum_i a_i(T). \tag{19}$$

Let us now consider a few simple modifications to the basic hidden Markov model.

Two transition probabilities are *tied* if they are constrained to be equal to one another. Let $\mathcal{T}_{ij}$ denote the set of all transitions which have transition probabilities that are tied to the transition probability on the transition $i\rightarrow j$. The distribution of transition probabilities at state i is tied to the distribution of transition probabilities at state j if there is a permutation, π, such that for all k, a_{ik} is tied to $a_{j\pi(k)}$. Let $\mathcal{S}_i$ denote the set of all states which have transition probability distributions that are tied to the transition probability distribution at state i. The output probability distributions on transitions $i\rightarrow j$ and $k\rightarrow l$ are tied if for all y_t, $\Pr(Y_t=y_t|X_t=i,X_{t+1}=j)$ is constrained to be equal to $\Pr(Y_t=y_t|X_t=k,X_{t+1}=l)$. Let $\mathcal{D}_{ij}$ denote the set of all transitions which have output probability distributions that are tied to the output probability distribution on the transition $i \to j$. Tying induces equivalence relations on transitions and states in the obvious ways.

The number of free parameters in a hidden Markov model can be reduced by fixing the values of some parameters. We may, for example, require that certain transition probabilities be zero. We say that a transition is *prohibited* if its probability is fixed at zero. We refer to a transition which has a transition probability that is fixed at zero as a *prohibited* transition. Similarly, by fixing certain initial-state probabilities at zero, we can ensure that all state sequences with non-zero probability begin in a set of *initial states*.

We will also want to insist that all state sequences end in a set of final states. The set of final states in a Markov model consists of those states from which all transitions are prohibited. The probability of a state sequence $\mathbf{x}_1^T$ is zero unless x_t is a final state. A Markov model with at least one reachable final state defines a probability distribution on state sequences.

In models with prohibited transitions we can often further reduce the number of allowed transitions required to adequately model an acoustic process by using *null transitions*, which allow the model to change state without producing any output (Bahl, Jelinek & Mercer, 1983).

Thus far, we have referred to a transition in a Markov model as a pair of states, an origin and a destination. If there are two different transitions with different output distributions between the states i and j then the output probability distribution given that a transition from i to j has occurred is a mixture of the distributions on the two transitions. We can thus implement output distributions which are mixtures in a straightforward manner by allowing multiple transitions between states.

These modifications to the basic hidden Markov model are important in the application of hidden Markov models to speech recognition. However, with the exception of tying, they are not crucial to the issues that are addressed in this paper. Furthermore, although it is straightforward to incorporate fixed probabilities, null transitions and multiple transitions between states into the models we will be discussing, it unnecessarily complicates many of the formulas. As a result, we will only amend our basic model by the inclusion of tied probabilities and tied distributions.

Automatic speech recognition can be performed by using a hidden Markov model for each word in the recognizer's vocabulary. A sequence of n models may be concatenated into a combined model by making the initial states of the first model the initial states of the combined model, by making the final states of the nth model the final states of the combined model and by creating null transitions from the final states of the ith model to the initial states of the $(i+1)$st model for $1 \leqslant i < n$. In this way, we can create a hidden Markov model m from any word sequence $\mathbf{w}$. Note that there will certainly be tied parameters in m if any word appears more than once in $\mathbf{w}$.

A set of hidden Markov models for words and sequences of words can be thought of as a family of models $\mathcal{M} = (m_1, m_2, \ldots)$ with parameter vector $\Theta = (\theta_1, \theta_2, \ldots)$, where θ_i is the parameter vector of m_i. The concept of tying is extended to include probabilities and probability distributions from different members of the family. Thus, we say that the transition probability on transition $i \to j$ in model m is tied to the transition probability $k \to l$ in model m', if a_{ij} is constrained to be equal to a'_{kl}. We extend the concept of tied transition probability distributions and tied output distributions in the same manner. In addition we say that the initial-state probability of state i in model m is tied to the initial-state probability of state j in model m' if c_i is constrained to be equal to c'_j. Because of tying or other constraints on Θ, it may be that any change to the parameter vector of one of the members of a family, say m', will necessitate a change to the parameter vector of some other member of the family, say m. When this is the case we say that m *entails* m'. A member, m, is *representative* of a family if it entails each member of the family. A family which has a representative member is said to be *close-knit* (Bahl, Brown, de Souza & Mercer, 1986).

The concept of a close-knit family is important when estimating the parameter vector of a family of hidden Markov models. This is because the parameters for all members of a close-knit family can be estimated from a sample which has been generated by a representative member. In speech recognition there is a family of hidden Markov models corresponding to the set of all word sequences—one model for each word sequence. The parameter vector for such a family can be estimated from a sample $(\mathbf{w},\mathbf{y})$ in which the training script, $\mathbf{w}$, corresponds to a model which is a representative member of the family.

3. Maximum likelihood estimation

Given the training data $\mathbf{w}$ and $\mathbf{y}$, in maximum likelihood estimation (MLE), we seek

$$\hat{\theta} = \underset{\theta}{\operatorname{argmax}} \Pr_\theta(\mathbf{W}=\mathbf{w}, \mathbf{Y}=\mathbf{y}), \tag{20}$$

where $\Pr_\theta(\mathbf{W}=\mathbf{w}, \mathbf{Y}=\mathbf{y})$ is the probability that the model parameterized by θ in the family of distributions under consideration will generate the sample $(\mathbf{w},\mathbf{y})$. We assume that θ is composed of a set of acoustic-model parameters, $\theta_{\mathcal{M}}$, and a set of language-model parameters, θ_ℓ, and that

$$\Pr_\theta = (\mathbf{W}=\mathbf{w}, \mathbf{Y}=\mathbf{y}) = \Pr_{\theta_{\mathcal{M}}}(\mathbf{Y}=\mathbf{y} \mid \mathbf{W}=\mathbf{w}) \Pr_{\theta_\ell}(\mathbf{W}=\mathbf{w}). \tag{21}$$

The acoustic-model parameters and language-model parameters can be estimated separately by choosing θ_ℓ to maximize $\Pr_{\theta_\ell}(\mathbf{W}=\mathbf{w})$, and by choosing $\theta_{\mathcal{M}}$ to maximize $\Pr_{\theta_{\mathcal{M}}}(\mathbf{Y}=\mathbf{y} \mid \mathbf{W}=\mathbf{w})$.

In Section 1 we saw that, if the true acoustic and language models were known, we could construct an optimal speech-recognition system. We might hypothesize that the closer the estimator is to the true parameter vector, the more nearly optimal will be the recognizer's performance. This hypothesis has been used by Nadas (1983) as the basis of an argument for MLE in pattern recognition. Suppose that there is a vector $\tilde{\theta}$ such that when the family of distributions assumed by the model is parameterized by $\tilde{\theta}$, it is equal to the true distribution of W and Y. The maximum likelihood estimator is consistent: it approaches $\tilde{\theta}$ as the size of the training sample becomes infinite. Furthermore, it has the smallest variance of all consistent estimators. With a large amount of training then, no estimator will, on average, provide a closer estimate of the true parameters than will the maximum likelihood estimator. If we assume that the performance of a system cannot get worse as its parameters get closer to the true parameters, then a system using MLE will, on average, perform as well as a system using any other form of estimation.

An estimate for the parameter vector of a hidden Markov model which locally maximizes the likelihood function can be obtained with an iterative procedure known as the *forward–backward* algorithm (Baum, 1972). Suppose we have training data $\mathbf{y} = \mathbf{y}_1^T$ and training script $\mathbf{w}$. Let m be a hidden Markov model for the word sequence $\mathbf{w}$. Let θ

be a vector of parameters for m. Each iteration the forward–backward algorithm derives a new parameter vector $\tilde{\theta}$ such that

$$\Pr_{\tilde{\theta}}(\mathbf{y}) \geqslant \Pr_{\theta}(\mathbf{y}). \tag{22}$$

Each iteration is a two-step procedure; on the first step, the parameter vector θ is used to compute the probability that each transition in the model is taken at each time, given that $\mathbf{y}$ is observed. On the second step, these probabilities are used to re-estimate $\tilde{\theta}$.

As in the previous section, let

$$a_i(t) \triangleq \Pr(\mathbf{Y}_1^t = \mathbf{y}_1^t, X_{t+1} = i). \tag{23}$$

Let

$$\beta_i(t) \triangleq (\mathbf{Y}_{t+1}^T = \mathbf{y}_{t+1}^T \mid X_{t+1} = i). \tag{24}$$

For all states, i, let

$$\beta_i(T) \triangleq \begin{cases} 1, & \text{if } i \text{ is a final state;} \\ 0, & \text{otherwise.} \end{cases} \tag{25}$$

Then for t, $0 \leqslant t < T$,

$$\beta_i(t) = \sum_j a_{ij} b_{ij}(y_{t+1}) \beta_j(t+1). \tag{26}$$

Then

$$\Pr(\mathbf{Y}_1^T = \mathbf{y}_1^T, X_t = i, X_{t+1} = j) = a_i(t-1) a_{ij} b_{ij}(y_t) \beta_j(t). \tag{27}$$

The probability that a transition $i \rightarrow j$ occurs at time t given that the model generates $\mathbf{y}_1^T$ is

$$\gamma_{ij}(t) \triangleq \Pr(X_t = i, X_{t+1} = j \mid \mathbf{Y}_1^T = \mathbf{y}_1^T) \tag{28}$$

$$= \frac{a_i(t-1) a_{ij} b_{ij}(y_t) \beta_j(t)}{\Sigma_k a_k(T)}.$$

Using the above recursions for the a's and β's, these probabilities can be computed in time which is linear in T (Baum, 1972).

Initial-state probabilities are re-estimated by setting each $\hat{c}_i$ to be proportional to the probability that a transition originating at i was taken at time 1:

$$\hat{c}_i = \frac{\Sigma_j \gamma_{ij}(1)}{\Sigma_{i,j} \gamma_{ij}(1)}. \tag{30}$$

Transition probabilities are re-estimated by setting each $\hat{a}_{ij}$ to be proportional to the expected number of times a transition in $\mathscr{T}_{ij}$ was taken while generating $\mathbf{y}$:

$$\hat{a}_{ij} = \frac{\Sigma_{k \rightarrow l \in \mathscr{T}_{ij}} \Sigma_{t=1}^T \gamma_{kl}(t)}{\Sigma_{k \in \mathscr{S}_i} \Sigma_l \Sigma_{t=1}^T \gamma_{kl}(t)}. \tag{31}$$

Let φ denote the vector of parameters of the output distribution associated with transitions that are tied to $i \rightarrow j$. φ is re-estimated so as to maximize

$$g(\varphi) \triangleq \sum_{k \rightarrow l \in \mathscr{L}_{ij}} \sum_{t=1}^{T} \gamma_{kl}(t) \log \Pr_{\varphi}(Y_t = y_t), \tag{32}$$

subject to whatever constraints may apply to φ. Re-estimation formulas for the output distributions that are discussed in this paper are presented by Brown (1987).

4. Maximum mutual information estimation

The argument for MLE presented in the previous section is based on an assumption that the true distribution of speech is a member of the family of distributions used by the recognizer. However, currently our understanding of speech is at such a primitive stage that if we are to use a model whose parameters can be reliably estimated, we will have to include some assumptions about speech which are simply false, thereby invaliding the rationale for MLE.

In this section we consider the acoustic parameter estimation problem from an information-theoretic point of view. Rather than attempting to find *true* parameters, we will be interested in finding parameters which minimize the recognizer's average uncertainty of what the correct word sequence is, given the output of the signal processor. This uncertainty is the conditional entropy of $\mathbf{W}$ given $\mathbf{Y}$:

$$\mathrm{H}_{\ell,\mathscr{M}}(\mathbf{W} \mid \mathbf{Y}) \triangleq -\sum_{\mathbf{w},\mathbf{y}} \Pr(\mathbf{W} = \mathbf{w}, \mathbf{Y} = \mathbf{y}) \log \Pr_{\ell,\mathscr{M}}(\mathbf{W} = \mathbf{w} \mid Y = \mathbf{y}), \tag{33}$$

where we assume that the recognizer uses language model ℓ, and the family of acoustic models $\mathscr{M}$. We have

$$\mathrm{H}_{\ell,\mathscr{M}}(\mathbf{W} \mid \mathbf{Y}) = \mathrm{H}_{\ell}(\mathbf{W}) - I_{\ell,\mathscr{M}}(\mathbf{W}; \mathbf{Y}), \tag{34}$$

in which

$$\mathrm{H}_{\ell}(\mathbf{W}) = -\sum_{\mathbf{w}} \Pr(\mathbf{W} = \mathbf{w}) \log \Pr_{\ell}(\mathbf{W} = \mathbf{w}), \tag{35}$$

and

$$I_{\ell,\mathcal{M}}(\mathbf{W};\mathbf{Y}) = \sum_{\mathbf{w},\mathbf{y}} \Pr(\mathbf{W}=\mathbf{w},\mathbf{Y}=\mathbf{y}) \log \frac{\Pr_{\ell,\mathcal{M}}(\mathbf{W}=\mathbf{w},\mathbf{Y}=\mathbf{y})}{\Pr_{\ell}(\mathbf{W}=\mathbf{w})\Pr_{\ell,\mathcal{M}}(\mathbf{Y}=\mathbf{y})}. \tag{36}$$

$H_\ell(\mathbf{W})$ is the entropy of the speaker's language as perceived by the recognizer. $I_{\ell,\mathcal{M}}(\mathbf{W};\mathbf{Y})$ is the average amount of information the recognizer can extract from an acoustic sequence $\mathbf{y}$ about a word sequence $\mathbf{w}$. Although in certain tasks it is possible to search for a model with the goal of minimizing $H_{\ell,\mathcal{M}}(\mathbf{W}|\mathbf{Y})$ directly (Hinton & Sejnowski, 1986), the problem of minimizing $H_{\ell,\mathcal{M}}(\mathbf{W}|\mathbf{Y})$ is normally divided into two separate steps: finding a language model which minimizes the first term $H_\ell(\mathbf{W})$, and then finding a family of acoustic models which maximizes $I_{\ell,\mathcal{M}}(\mathbf{W};\mathbf{Y})$.

Suppose that a language model, ℓ, is given. We would like to choose a vector of acoustic parameters, Θ, for $\mathcal{M}$ to maximize

$$I_{\ell,\mathcal{M}}(\mathbf{W};\mathbf{Y}) = \sum_{\mathbf{w},\mathbf{y}} \Pr(\mathbf{W}=\mathbf{w},\mathbf{y}=\mathbf{y}) \log \left(\frac{\Pr_{\ell,\Theta}(\mathbf{W}=\mathbf{w},Y=\mathbf{y})}{\Pr_{\ell}(\mathbf{W}=\mathbf{w})\Pr_{\ell,\Theta}(\mathbf{Y}=\mathbf{y})} \right). \tag{37}$$

Since we do not know $\Pr(\mathbf{W}=\mathbf{w},\mathbf{Y}=\mathbf{y})$, we assume that $(\mathbf{w},\mathbf{y})$ is a typical sample, and that the model for $\mathbf{w}$ is representative of the close-knit family of models corresponding to the set of all word sequences. We then choose Θ to maximize

$$I_{\ell,\Theta}(\mathbf{w};\mathbf{y}) = \log \frac{\Pr_{\ell,\Theta}(\mathbf{W}=\mathbf{w},\mathbf{Y}=\mathbf{y})}{\Pr_{\ell}(\mathbf{W}=\mathbf{w})\Pr_{\ell,\Theta}(\mathbf{Y}=\mathbf{y})} \tag{38}$$

$$= \log \Pr_{\Theta}(\mathbf{Y}=\mathbf{y}|\mathbf{W}=\mathbf{w}) - \log \Pr_{\ell,\Theta}(\mathbf{Y}=\mathbf{y}). \tag{39}$$

Choosing Θ to maximize the first term on the right is the same as finding the maximum likelihood estimate for the parameter vector of the model corresponding to the word sequence $\mathbf{w}$. The difference between MLE and maximum mutual information estimation (MMIE) is in the second term.

To understand the effect of this second term let us first expand it in terms of the language model, ℓ, and the acoustic parameter vector, Θ,

$$\Pr_{\ell,\Theta}(\mathbf{Y}=\mathbf{y}) = \sum_{\hat{\mathbf{w}}} \Pr_{\Theta}(\mathbf{Y}=\mathbf{y}|W=\hat{\mathbf{w}})\Pr_{\ell}(\mathbf{W}=\hat{\mathbf{w}}). \tag{40}$$

Letting

$$Q_i(\mathbf{y}|\mathbf{w}) \triangleq \frac{\partial \Pr_{\Theta}(\mathbf{Y}=\mathbf{y}|\mathbf{W}=\mathbf{w})}{\partial \Theta_i}, \tag{41}$$

consider the derivative of $I_{\ell,\Theta}(\mathbf{w};\mathbf{y})$ with respect to Θ_i

$$\frac{\partial I_{\ell,\Theta}(\mathbf{w};\mathbf{y})}{\partial \Theta_i} = \frac{Q_i(\mathbf{y}|\mathbf{w})}{\Pr_{\Theta}(\mathbf{Y}=\mathbf{y}|\mathbf{W}=\mathbf{w})} - \frac{\Sigma_{\hat{\mathbf{w}}} Q_i(\mathbf{y}|\hat{\mathbf{w}})\Pr_{\ell}(\mathbf{W}=\hat{\mathbf{w}})}{\Pr_{\ell,\Theta}(\mathbf{Y}=\mathbf{y})}$$

$$= Q_i(\mathbf{y}|\mathbf{w}) \left[\frac{1}{\Pr_{\Theta}(\mathbf{Y}=\mathbf{y}|\mathbf{W}=\mathbf{w})} - \frac{\Pr_{\ell}(\mathbf{W}=\mathbf{w})}{\Pr_{\ell,\Theta}(\mathbf{Y}=\mathbf{y})} \right] - \sum_{\hat{\mathbf{w}} \neq \mathbf{w}} \frac{Q_i(\mathbf{y}|\hat{\mathbf{w}})\Pr_{\ell}(\mathbf{W}=\hat{\mathbf{w}})}{\Pr_{\Theta}(\mathbf{Y}=\mathbf{y})}. \tag{42}$$

Compare this expression to the derivative of the objective function used in maximum likelihood estimation, $\Pr_{\Theta}(\mathbf{Y}=\mathbf{y}|\mathbf{W}=\mathbf{w})$,

$$\frac{\partial \Pr_{\Theta}(\mathbf{Y}=\mathbf{y}|\mathbf{W}=\mathbf{w})}{\partial \Theta_i} = Q_i(\mathbf{y}|\mathbf{w}). \tag{43}$$

The first term in the MMIE derivative is in the same direction as the MLE derivative. The role of the second term is to subtract a component in the direction of $Q_i(\mathbf{y}|\hat{\mathbf{w}})$ for each incorrect word sequence $\hat{\mathbf{w}} \neq \mathbf{w}$. In MLE, one tries to increase $\Pr_{\Theta}(\mathbf{Y}=\mathbf{y}|\mathbf{W}=\mathbf{w})$ for the correct word sequence $\mathbf{w}$. In MMIE, one similarly tries to increase $\Pr_{\Theta}(\mathbf{Y}=\mathbf{y}|\mathbf{W}=\mathbf{w})$, but also tries to decrease $\Pr_{\Theta}(\mathbf{Y}=\mathbf{y}|\mathbf{W}=\hat{\mathbf{w}})$ for every incorrect word sequence $\hat{\mathbf{w}} \neq \mathbf{w}$. This is a fundamental difference between MLE and MMIE; in MLE only the correct word sequence comes into play, in MMIE every word sequence is taken into account. Furthermore, the greater the prior probability, $\Pr_{\ell}(\mathbf{W}=\hat{\mathbf{w}})$ of a word sequence $\hat{\mathbf{w}}$, the more important it is in determining Θ. This is quite reasonable because the greater the probability that the system assigns to a sequence of words, $\hat{\mathbf{w}}$, *a priori*, the greater the chance the system will misrecognize $\mathbf{w}$ as $\hat{\mathbf{w}}$. In MLE a set of parameters is chosen to maximize the probability of generating the sample acoustic data given the corresponding sample word sequence. In MMIE a set of parameters is chosen with the explicit aim of discriminating between the correct word sequence and every other sequence.

Nadas (1983) points out that if the language model and the distribution family assumed in the acoustic models are correct, then both MLE and MMIE will be consistent estimators but that MMIE will have a greater variance. This implies that if the language model and the family of acoustic distributions are close to correct, then MLE will outperform MMIE. If, on the other hand, either is inaccurate, we might suspect that MMIE will outperform MLE since the argument for the use of MMIE does not presuppose model accuracy.

We now consider the problem of finding maximum mutual information estimates of hidden Markov model parameters. The forward–backward algorithm is a hill-climbing algorithm for maximum likelihood estimation. Its primary advantage over gradient descent is that it produces a direction and step size which are guaranteed to improve, or at least not to worsen, the likelihood function. Although Patterson (1986) has discovered a similar method for MMIE when applied to hidden Markov models of discrete sequences, no such method is known for sequences of continuous parameters, and we must therefore resort to the use of traditional maximation techniques.

To compute the derivative of $I_{\ell,\Theta}(\mathbf{w};\mathbf{y})$ as it is expressed in (42), we need to be able to compute the derivative of $\Pr_m(\mathbf{Y}=\mathbf{y})$, the probability that a model, m, will generate $\mathbf{y}$. If

Θ_i is a transition probability, and $\mathcal{T}_i$ is the set of all transitions with transition probabilities tied to Θ_i, then it can be shown (Brown, 1987) that

$$\frac{\partial \Pr_m(\mathbf{Y}_1^T = \mathbf{y}_1^T)}{\partial \Theta_i} = \sum_{t=1}^{T} \sum_{j \to k \in \mathcal{T}_i} a_j(t-1) b_{jk}(y_t) \beta_k(t). \tag{44}$$

If Θ_i is an initial-state probability, and $\mathcal{T}_i$ is the set of all initial-state probabilities tied to Θ_i then

$$\frac{\partial \Pr_m(\mathbf{Y}_1^T = \mathbf{y}_1^T)}{\partial \Theta_i} = \sum_{j \in \mathcal{T}_i} \beta_j(0). \tag{45}$$

If Θ_i is a parameter in an output probability distribution, and $\mathcal{D}_i$ is the set of all $j \to k$ that have that output distribution, then

$$\frac{\partial \Pr_m(\mathbf{Y}_1^T = \mathbf{y}_1^T)}{\partial \Theta_i} = \sum_{t=1}^{T} \sum_{j \to k \in \mathcal{D}_i} a_j(t-1) a_{jk} \left(\frac{\partial b_{jk}(y_t)}{\partial \Theta_i} \right) \beta_k(t). \tag{46}$$

The derivatives needed in (46) for the output distributions discussed in this paper are presented by Brown (1987). Using (42), (44), (45) and (46), we can compute the gradient of the mutual information between a word sequence, **w**, and an acoustic sequence **y**, and use it in a gradient-based hill-climbing algorithm.

5. Adjoining acoustic-parameter vectors

Certain acoustic events in speech are distinguished by phenomena that occur over time. Consider, for example, *labials*. The acoustic signatures of these phones can be very similar to those of other phones. It is, for example, often difficult to distinguish the labials *b*, *m* and *p* from the alveolars *d*, *n* and *t*. The formants of a sound preceding a labial tend to descend in frequency, and those of a sound following a labial tend to rise in frequency. An important clue, then, to the presence of a labial is found in information of how the acoustic spectrum is changing in time.

In many systems the parameters produced by the signal processor reflect some function of the energy in different frequency bands during a short interval of time. There is virtually no information in an individual parameter vector about how this short-term spectrum is changing in time. It is, however, a simple matter to include time-derivative information in the vectors. The original acoustic parameter sequence, $\mathbf{y}_1, y_2 \ldots, \mathbf{y}_T$, can be converted to the sequence $\mathbf{y}_1\mathbf{y}_2, \mathbf{y}_2\mathbf{y}_3, \ldots, \mathbf{y}_{T-1}\mathbf{y}_T$, by adjoining the spectra from adjacent frames. Time-derivative information can then be modeled directly with multivariate output distributions. Poritz & Richter (1986) have recently used this technique to improve the performance of an isolated word-recognition system. There are clearly all kinds of variations to this scheme. Poritz & Richter, for example, found that they maximized their performance by adjoining the current acoustic-parameter vectors with those that had been produced 8 centiseconds earlier. One might also consider adjoining three or more sets of parameters together.

This technique increases the dimension of the parameter vectors that must be modeled by the acoustic models, and hence increases the variances of the probability density estimates that are obtained from these models. Fortunately this is a problem for which there is an antidote; we can extract from these adjoined vectors of parameters a small number of information-bearing components by a technique similar to principal component analysis.

We extract linear combinations of parameters which vary a lot between phonetic classes relative to the amount that they vary within classes (Friedman, 1967). We refer to these components as *linear discriminants*. Suppose we have a sample of n p-dimensional vectors, with n_i vectors in class i. Assume that this sample has zero mean. Let T be the covariance matrix of the entire sample and W_i be the covariance matrix of vectors in the ith class. Let W be the average within-class covariance matrix:

$$W = \frac{1}{n} \sum_i n_i W_i. \tag{47}$$

The variance of the projection of the sample on to a vector $\mathbf{v}$ is $\mathbf{v}'T\mathbf{v}$. We would like to choose the ith discriminant, $\mathbf{v}_i$, to maximize

$$\frac{\mathbf{v}_i' T \mathbf{v}_i}{\mathbf{v}_i' W \mathbf{v}_i}, \tag{48}$$

subject to the constraint that it be uncorrelated with the first $i-1$ discriminants. It is easy to show that these components are simply the eigenvectors with the largest i eigenvalues (assuming they are distinct) of the equation

$$T\mathbf{v} = \lambda W \mathbf{v}. \tag{49}$$

The question of what is the best dimension to reduce the acoustic parameter vectors to must be addressed on a case-by-case basis. The answer depends on the number of output distributions, the type of output distributions, the amount of training data available.

6. Results on an *e*-set task

This section describes a series of experiments testing the ideas which have been discussed in the previous sections. It was important to find a small task for these experiments since MMIE with continuous-parameter hidden Markov models requires a large amount of computation. It was also important, however, that the task be difficult enough for there to be room for improvement. We chose isolated-word, multi-speaker recognition of the *e*-set, the letters *b*, *c*, *d*, *e*, *g*, *p*, *t*, *v* and *z*. The standard IBM system, which is described by Jelinek (1985), has a performance of 79% on this task.

One hundred male speakers were recorded, each speaking the nine letters twice, once for training data and once for test data. After discarding clear speaking errors there were 836 words of training data and 886 words of test data.

The recordings were made in offices and labs at the IBM Thomas J. Watson Research Center. The speech was recorded with a pressure-zone microphone which was mounted next to the screen of a PC-AT. It was digitized at 20 000 Hz. No effort was made to suppress the noise from the fans and disks on the PC or from other equipment in a speaker's work environment. An estimate of the signal-to-noise ratio for this data was made by assigning each 10-millisecond frame of speech to a phonetic category, including a noise category, and then computing the ratio of the average signal power of all frames which were mapped into a speech category to the average power of those which were mapped into the noise category. For the data used in these experiments, this signal-to-noise ratio was 16·4 decibels.

The speech was signal-processed as described by Cohen (1988), except that long-term adaptation was performed separately for each speaker. Every 10 milliseconds, a 20-dimensional vector of parameters is produced by this signal-processing algorithm. These parameters roughly correspond to the logarithms of the energies in each of 20 spectral bands. In discrete-parameter experiments, each 20-dimensional vector was vector quantized into one of 200 codebook entries (Nadas, 1981). In continuous-parameter experiments, parameter vectors that had not already been projected on to linear discriminants were rotated with principal components which were extracted from all the speech in the training sample. This was done to make the off-diagonal terms in the covariance matrices small, which is important when diagonal Gaussian distributions are used. It also affects the convergence rate of the gradient search methods used in MMIE.

We constructed hidden Markov models by concatenating hidden Markov models for individual phones. The phonetic spellings of the words as well as the phonetic models are described by Brown (1987).

We decoded test data using a language model with a uniform distribution over the nine words. Since each word occurred approximately 100 times in the test data, this language model was nearly perfect.

A list of the results is presented in Table 1. Richter-mixture output distributions were mixtures of four full-covariance Gaussians. When parameters were estimated with MLE, the covariance matrices of these Gaussians were constrained to be in the ratios 1 to 2, 4 and 8. During MMIE these ratios were allowed to vary.

TABLE I: *e*-set results

Experiment number	Output distribution	Estimation method	Single or adjoined frames	Parameter reduction	% correct
1	Discrete	MLE	Single	20→20	79·0
2	Discrete	MMIE	Single	20→20	77·9
3	Diagonal Gaussian	MLE	Single	20→20	65·1
4	Diagonal Gaussian	MMIE	Single	20→20	74·7
5	Full Gaussian	MLE	Single	20→20	76·9
6	Full Gaussian	MMIE	Single	20→20	83·4
7	Richter mixture	MLE	Single	20→20	79·8
8	Richter mixture	MMIE	Single	20→20	82·6
9	Diagonal Gaussian	MLE	Adjoined	40→40	59·8
10	Diagonal Gaussian	MMIE	Adjoined	40→40	86·6
11	Full Gaussian	MLE	Adjoined	40→40	64·4
12	Full Gaussian	MMIE	Adjoined	40→40	86·0
13	Richter mixture	MLE	Adjoined	40→40	82·5
14	Richter mixture	MMIE	Adjoined	40→40	85·8
15	Diagonal Gaussian	MLE	Adjoined	40→22	71·2
16	Diagonal Gaussian	MMIE	Adjoined	40→22	83·1
17	Full Gaussian	MLE	Adjoined	40→22	89·1
18	Full Gaussian	MMIE	Adjoined	40→22	91·0
19	Richter mixture	MLE	Adjoined	40→22	90·3
20	Richter mixture	MMIE	Adjoined	40→22	92·0

Experiment 1 is a benchmark to assess the performance of the system described by Jelinek (1985). The performance of this maximum-likelihood, discrete experiment was 79%. In Experiment 2 we replaced MLE by MMIE. The performance decreased by an insignificant amount to 77·9%. In Section 4 we noted that if the family of models used by the recognizer is accurate, we should expect MLE to perform as well as MMIE. Nonparametric output distributions make no assumptions that can be inaccurate, and evidently the inaccuracies in the word models and hidden Markov assumptions were not severe enough to allow MMIE to outperform MLE.

In Experiments 3 to 8 we modeled the 20-dimensional parameter vectors directly. With MLE, models which used either diagonal or full-covariance Gaussian output distributions performed worse than our original benchmark. With Richter mixtures, the performance improved slightly to 79·8%, indicating that there is a problem with outliers. With MMIE, the performance with each type of output distribution improved markedly. With full-covariance Gaussian output distributions, the performance became 83·4%. With Richter mixtures of full-covariance Gaussians, the performance became 82·6%. Both of these results are improvements over the discrete results. With MMIE, the system was able to overcome inaccuracies in the assumed families of the output distributions and make use of the additional information in the continuous-parameter observation sequences.

In Experiments 9 to 14 we concatenated the 20-dimensional vectors from adjacent frames to form 40-dimensional vectors. These 40-dimensional vectors were then projected on to 40 principal components. Using MLE, the diagonal and full-covariance Gaussian results deteriorated with the adjoined parameter vectors. With Richter mixtures, however, the performance improved to 82·5%. This reflects the fact that the outlier problem becomes more severe as the dimension of the feature vectors increases. Using MMIE, the diagonal Gaussian, full-covariance Gaussian and Richter-mixture performances improved to 86·6%, 86% and 85·8%, respectively. Evidently the outlier problem with Gaussian models has less of an effect on system performance when MMIE is used.

With single-frame 20-dimensional parameter vectors, the full-covariance output distributions performed significantly better than the diagonal Gaussian distributions. However, with MMIE and adjoined 40-dimensional parameter vectors, the diagonal distributions performed slightly better than the full-covariance Gaussians. We suspect that there was not enough training data to take advantage of the increased potential accuracy provided by the additional parameters in the full-covariance Gaussians.

In Section 5 we suggested that a possible antidote to this problem would be to project the 40-dimensional parameter vectors on to a smaller number of linear discriminants. Using MLE with Richter-mixture output distributions we conducted experiments with a number of different linear discriminants (4–30 in steps of two). As can be seen in Fig. 1, the best performance was obtained with 22-dimensional vectors. With too few parameters the performance suffers because too much acoustic information is discarded. With too many parameters, errors in density estimates prevent the recognizer from taking advantage of the additional acoustic information.

In Experiments 15 to 20 we evaluated the performance on these 22-dimensional vectors with MLE and MMIE using the different classes of output distributions we have

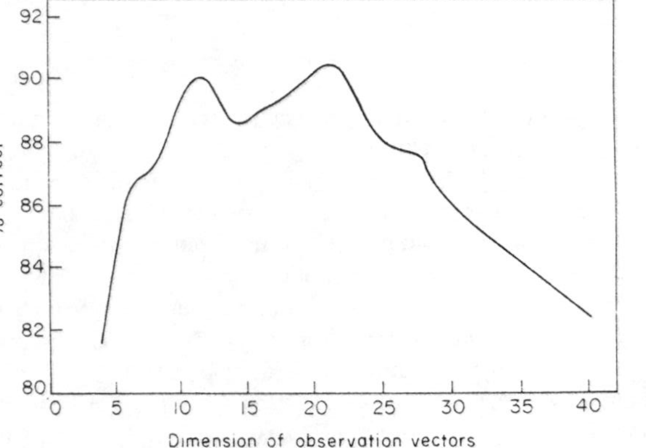

Figure 1. Parameter vector dimension *vs.* performance.

been considering. In each experiment the performance was significantly better than the corresponding performance using the original 40-dimensional vectors. The MMIE Richter-mixture performance of 92% is the best result obtained on this data.

Finally, 400 words were selected at random from the test data and listened to by four members of the IBM research staff. On average, they recognized 97·2% of the words correctly. When recognition decisions were made by a vote from the four listeners, and each tie was counted as half an error, the performance became 98%.

7. Conclusions

By removing the vector-quantization step from the signal-processing component of a speech recognizer, and directly modeling sequences of vectors of continuous parameters, it is possible to obtain a small performance improvement. However, to obtain this improvement it is important to model the parameter vectors with appropriate distributions. In agreement with the observations of Rabiner, Juang, Levinson & Sondhi (1985), we found that even after the parameter vectors were rotated with principal components, better results could be obtained with full-covariance Gaussians than with diagonal Gaussians. We also found that recognition accuracy can be increased by using distributions that are more robust to outliers than a single Gaussian distribution is. Because we cannot specify accurate models for continuous-parameter vectors, we found it useful to estimate statistics with a method that is specifically designed to cope with inaccurate modeling assumptions; in every continuous-parameter experiment better results were obtained with MMIE than with MLE. By modeling adjoined continuous-parameter vectors from adjacent frames with multivariate distributions, we were able to make use of information about how the acoustic spectrum changes in time. This technique increases the number of free parameters in the multivariate distributions, which increases the variances of density estimates. This problem was alleviated, however, by projecting these adjoined vectors on to a subspace of linear discriminants.

Although we have improved the machine performance on this *e*-set task from 79 to 92%, the human-listening result of 98% indicates that there is a long way to go.

Acknowledgements

We would like to thank Arthur Nadas, David Nahamoo and the other members of the Speech Recognition group at the IBM Research Center without whose contributions this work would not have been possible.

References

Bahl, L. R., Bakis, R., Cohen, P. S., Cole, A. G., Jelenik, F., Lewis, B. L. & Mercer, R. L. (1981) Continuous parameter acoustic processing for speech recognition of a natural speech corpus. In *Proceedings of the IEEE International Conference on Acoustics, Speech and Signal Processing*, pp. 1149–55, Atlanta, Georgia.

Bahl, L. R., Jelinek, F. & Mercer, R. L. (1983) A maximum likelihood approach to continuous speech recognition. *IEEE Transactions on Pattern Analysis and Machine Intelligence*, PAMI-5(**2**), 179–90.

Bahl, L. R., Brown, P. F., de Souza, P. V. & Mercer, R. L. (1986) Maximum mutual information estimation of hidden Markov model parameters for speech recognition. In *Proceedings of the IEEE International Conference on Acoustics, Speech and Signal Processing*, pp. 49–52, Tokyo, Japan.

Baum, L. E. (1972) An inequality and associated maximization technique in statistical estimation of probabilistic functions of a Markov process. *Inequalities*, **3**, 1–8.

Brown, P. F. (1987) *The Acoustic-Modeling Problem in Automatic Speech Recognition*. Ph.D. thesis, Carnegie-Mellon University. Also IBM Research Division Technical Report RC 12750.

Cohen, J. R. (1988) Application of an auditory model to speech recognition. *Journal of the Acoustic Society of America*, Forthcoming.

Friedman, H. P. & Rudin, J. (1967) On some invariant criteria for grouping data. *American Statistical Association Journal*, **00**, 1159–78.

Gray, R. M. (1984) Vector quantization. *IEEE ASSP Magazine*, **1**(2), 4–49.

Hinton, G. E. & Sejnowski, T. J. (1986) Learning and relearning in Boltzmann machines. In Rumelhart, D. E. & McClelland, J. L. (eds), *Parallel Distributed Processing*, Volume I: Foundations pp. 282–317, M.I.T. Press.

Jelinek, F. (1985) The development of an experimental discrete dictation recognizer. *Proceedings of the IEEE*, **73**(11), 1616–24.

Juang, B. H. & Rabiner, L. R. (1986) Mixture autoregressive hidden Markov models for speaker independent isolated word recognition. In *Proceedings of the IEEE International Conference on Acoustics, Speech and Signal Processing*, pp. 41–4, Tokyo, Japan.

Makhoul, J., Roucos, S. & Gish, H. (1985) Vector quantization in speech coding. *Proceedings of the IEEE*, **73**(11), 1551–88.

Nadas, A. (1983) A decision-theoretic formulation of a training problem in speech recognition and a comparison of training by unconditional versus conditional maximum likelihood. *IEEE Transactions on Acoustics, Speech and Signal Processing*, ASSP-31(**4**), 814–17.

Nadas, A., Mercer, R. L., Bahl, L. R., Bakis, R., Cohen, P. S., Cole, A. G., Jelinek, F. & Lewis, B. L. (1981) Continuous speech recognition with automatically selected prototypes obtained by either bootstrapping or clustering. In *Proceedings of the IEEE International Conference on Acoustics, Speech and Signal Processing*, pp. 1153–5, Atlanta, Georgia.

Patterson, N. (1986). Personal communication.

Poritz, A. B. & Richter, G. (1986) On hidden Markov models in isolated word recognition. In *Proceedings of the IEEE International Conference on Acoustics, Speech and Signal Processing*, pp. 705–8, Tokyo, Japan.

Rabiner, L. R., Juang, B. H., Levinson, S. E. & Sondhi, M. M. (1985) Recognition of isolated digits using hidden Markov models with continuous mixture densities. *Bell Systems Technical Journal*, **64**(6), 1211–34.

Richter, A. G. (1986) Modeling of continuous speech observations. Presented at the Advances in Speech Processing Conference at the IBM Europe Institute in Oberlech, Austria.

Semi-continuous hidden Markov models for speech signals

X. D. Huang* and M. A. Jack

Centre for Speech Technology Research, University of Edinburgh, 80 South Bridge, Edinburgh EH1 1HN, U.K.

Abstract

A semi-continuous hidden Markov model, which can be considered as a special form of continuous mixture hidden Markov model with the continuous output probability density functions sharing in a mixture Gaussian density codebook, is proposed in this paper. The semi-continuous output probability density function is represented by a combination of the discrete output probabilities of the model and the continuous Gaussian density functions of a mixture Gaussian density codebook. The amount of training data required, as well as the computational complexity of the semi-continuous hidden Markov model, can be significantly reduced in comparison with the continuous mixture hidden Markov model. Parameters of the vector quantization codebook and hidden Markov model can be mutually optimized to achieve an optimal model/codebook combination, which leads to a unified modelling approach to vector quantization and hidden Markov modelling of speech signals. Experimental results are included which show that the recognition accuracy of the semi-continuous hidden Markov model is measurably higher than both the discrete and the continuous hidden Markov model.

1. Introduction

Hidden Markov models (HMM), which can be based on either discrete output probability distributions (discrete HMM) or continuous output probability density functions (continuous HMM), have been shown to represent one of the most powerful statistical tools available for modelling speech signals (Jelinek, 1976, 1985; Levinson, Rabiner & Sondhi, 1983; Juang, 1985; Rabiner, Juang, Levinson & Sondhi, 1985; Levinson, 1986; Chow, Dunham, Kimball, Kranser, Kubala, Makhoul, Price, Roucos & Schwartz, 1987; Lee, 1988). In the continuous mixture HMM, parameter estimation of the model is usually based on maximum likelihood methods on the assumption that the observed signals have been generated by a mixture Gaussian process (Juang, 1985), or autoregressive process (Juang & Rabiner, 1985). Algorithms based on the Parzen estimator (Parzen, 1962) using some kernel function (Soudoplatoff, 1986) have also been used. The continuous mixture HMM usually offers more powerful modelling ability than the continuous HMM (single mixture) when sufficient training data exist. However, the continuous mixture HMM involves considerable computational complexity and is also very sensitive to initial estimates of several of the model parameters (Jung & Rabiner, 1985; Rabiner *et al.*, 1985). For the left-to-right HMM, a modified segmental k-means clustering procedure (Rabiner, Wilpon & Juang, 1986), similar to the vector quantization (VQ) procedure (Makhoul, Roucos & Gish, 1985) for the discrete HMM, has been developed to obtain reliable initial estimates. In the Parzen estimator, the key problem is how to choose the value of the radius, which has been determined from the sample data using a topological approach. In the estimation of probability density functions, the training data required for non-parametric methods, such as the Parzen estimator, are usually more than that for the parametric method, such as the Gaussian assumption, to achieve similar performance.

For the discrete HMM, VQ makes it possible to use a non-parametric, discrete output probability distribution to model the observed speech signals. The objective of VQ is to find the set of reproduction vectors, or *codebook*, that represents an information source with minimum expected *distortion*. By using VQ, the discrete HMM offers faster computation in comparison with the continuous HMM, since computing the discrete output probability of an observation reduces to a table-lookup operation. On the other hand, in the continuous HMM, many multiplication operations are required even when using the simplest single-mixture, multivariate Gaussian density with a diagonal covariance matrix. However, with the discrete HMM there may be some information lost in the VQ operations and the recognition accuracy for the discrete HMM can be considerably lower than for the continuous HMM (Rabiner *et al.*, 1985; Poritz & Richter, 1986), although other opposing results have been reported (Brown, 1987). As the discrete output probability generally contains more free parameters, the discrete HMM usually requires more training data in comparison with the continuous HMM. Various smoothing techniques have been proposed to eliminate the errors introduced by the conventional VQ (Nishimura & Toshioka, 1987; Tseng, Sabin & Lee, 1987; Lee, 1988).

In this paper, a semi-continuous hidden Markov model (SCHMM) is proposed, to extend the discrete HMM by replacing discrete output probabilities with a combination of the original discrete output probabilities and continuous probability density functions of a mixture Gaussian codebook that is modelled as a parametric family of mixture Gaussian densities. The EM algorithm (E for *expectation* and M for *maximization*) (Hasselblad, 1966; Dempster, Laird & Rubin, 1977) developed for estimation of mixture probability densities, works in a similar manner to the Baum–Welch algorithm (Baum, Petrie, Soules & Weiss, 1970). In the case of maximum likelihood estimation of HMM parameters using the Baum–Welch algorithm, the VQ codebook could in principle be adjusted together with the HMM parameters, in order to obtain the optimum maximum likelihood of the HMM, although this may not lead to optimal VQ distortion minimization. A unified modelling approach can therefore be applied to vector quantization and hidden Markov modelling of speech signals to achieve an optimum combination of HMM parameters and VQ codebook parameters. In the SCHMM, the continuous probability density functions of the codebook can be used either in the modified Viterbi decoding algorithm, or in estimation of the SCHMM parameters with the forward–backward algorithm to bridge between continuous observations and discrete parameters. From the continuous HMM point of view, the SCHMM can be considered as a special form of continuous mixture HMM with tied mixture continuous density functions. Because of the binding of the continuous density functions, in the

* Also Department of Computer Science and Technology, Tsinghua University, Beijing 100084, China.

0885–2308/89/030239 + 13 $03.00/0

SCHMM, the number of free parameters and the computational complexity are reduced in comparison with the continuous mixture HMM, while retaining the modelling powers of mixture HMM. From the discrete HMM point of view, the SCHMM can effectively minimize the errors involved in VQ operations. For speaker-dependent and speaker-independent isolated digit recognition, it has been shown that the SCHMM decoder based directly on discrete HMM parameters can offer improved recognition accuracy in comparison with the discrete HMM (Huang & Jack, 1988*a*,*b*).

This paper is organized as follows. In Section 2, the mathematical formulation of the HMM is reviewed and the concept of the SCHMM using parameter feedback to the VQ codebook is developed. In Section 3, the implementation of the SCHMM is discussed and experimental results for speaker-independent phoneme recognition are presented to permit comparison between the semi-continuous HMM, the discrete HMM, and the continuous HMM. Finally, Section 4 contains a summary and discussion of potential applications.

2. Semi-continuous hidden Markov models and codebook optimization

2.1. *Discrete HMM and continuous HMM*

An N-state Markov chain is considered with state transition matrix $A=[a_{ij}]$, $i,j=1,2,\ldots,N$, where a_{ij} denotes the transition probability from state i to state j; and a discrete output probability distribution, $b_j(O_k)$, or continuous output probability density function $b_j(\mathbf{x})$ associated with each state j of the unobservable Markov chain. Here O_k represents discrete observation symbols (usually VQ indexes), and $\mathbf{x}$ represents continuous observations (usually speech frame vectors) of K-dimensional random vectors.

With the discrete HMM, there are L discrete output symbols from an L-level VQ, and the output probability density function is modelled with discrete probability distributions of these discrete symbols. Let $\mathbf{O}$ be the observed sequence, $\mathbf{O}=O_{k_1},O_{k_2},\ldots,O_{k_T}$ observed over T samples. Here O_{k_i} denotes the VQ codeword k_i observed at time i. The observation probability of such an observed sequence, $\Pr(\mathbf{O}|\lambda)$, can be expressed as:

$$\Pr(\mathbf{O}|\lambda)=\sum_S \Pr(\mathbf{O},S|\lambda)=\sum_S \Pr(\mathbf{O}|S,\lambda)\Pr(S|\lambda)$$

$$=\sum_S \pi_{s_0}\prod_{t=1}^{T} a_{s_{t-1}s_t} b_{s_t}(\mathbf{O}_{k_t}) \tag{1}$$

where S is a particular state sequence, $S\in(s_0,s_1,\ldots,s_t)$, $s_t\in\{1,2,\ldots,N\}$, and the summation is taken over all of the possible state sequences, S, of the given model λ, which is represented by (π, A, B), where π is the initial state probability vector, A is the state transition matrix, and B is the output probability distribution matrix. In the discrete HMM, classification of O_{k_t} from $\mathbf{x}_t$ in the VQ may not be accurate, such as when an acoustic vector $\mathbf{x}_t$ is intermediate between two VQ indexes. The effects of VQ errors may cause the performance of the discrete HMM to be inferior to that of the continuous HMM (Rabiner *et al.*, 1985).

If the observation to be decoded is not vector quantized, then the probability density function, $f(\mathbf{X}|\lambda)$, of producing an observation of continuous vector sequences given the model λ, would be computed, instead of the probability of generating a discrete observation symbol, $\Pr(\mathbf{O}|\lambda)$. Here $\mathbf{X}$ is a sequence of continuous (acoustic) vectors $\mathbf{x}$, $\mathbf{X}=\mathbf{x}_1,\mathbf{x}_2,\ldots,\mathbf{x}_T$. The principle advantage of using the continuous HMM is the ability to model speech parameters directly without involving VQ. However, the continuous HMM requires considerably longer training and recognition times, especially when several mixture Gaussian distributions are used to represent the output probability. In the continuous HMM, Equation (1) can be rewritten as:

$$f(\mathbf{X}|\lambda)=\sum_S f(\mathbf{X}|S,\lambda)\Pr(S|\lambda)$$

$$=\sum_S \pi_{s_0}\prod_{t=1}^{T} a_{s_{t-1}s_t} b_{s_t}(\mathbf{x}_t) \tag{2}$$

where the output probability density function can be represented by the Gaussian probability density function. More generally, in the continuous Gaussian (M-component) mixture HMM (Juang, 1985), the output probability density of state j, $b_j(\mathbf{x})$, can be represented as

$$b_j(\mathbf{x})=\sum_{k=1}^{M} c_{jk}N(\mathbf{x},\mu_{jk},\Sigma_{jk}) \tag{3}$$

where $N(\mathbf{x},\mu,\Sigma)$ denotes a multi-dimensional Gaussian density function of mean vector μ and covariance matrix Σ. Here c_{jk} is a weighting coefficient for the kth Gaussian component.

2.2. *Semi-continuous hidden Markov models*

In the discrete HMM, the discrete probability distributions are sufficiently powerful to model any random events with mixture Gaussian density distributions. The major problem with the discrete output probability is that the VQ operation partitions the acoustic space into separate regions according to some distortion measure. This introduces errors, as the partition operations may destroy the original signal structure. The VQ codebook can be modelled as a family of Gaussian density functions such that the distributions are overlapped, rather than partitioned. Each codeword of the codebook can then be represented by one of the Gaussian probability density functions and may be used together with others to model the acoustic event. The use of a parametric family of finite mixture densities (a mixture density VQ) can be closely combined with the HMM methodology. From the continuous mixture HMM point of view, the output probability in the continuous mixture HMM can be shared among the Gaussian probability density functions of the VQ. This can reduce the number of free parameters to be estimated as well as the computational complexity. From the discrete HMM point of view, the partition of the VQ is unnecessary, and is replaced by the mixture density modelling with overlap, which can effectively minimize the VQ errors.

The problems of estimating the parameters which determine a mixture density has been the subject of a large diverse body of literature spanning some 90 years (Redner & Walker, 1984). The procedure, known as the EM algorithm (Dempster *et al.*, 1977), is a specialization to the mixture density context, of a general algorithm for obtaining maximum likelihood estimates for incomplete problems. Here the mixture density estimation problem is regarded as an estimation problem involving incomplete data by treating an unlabelled observation on the mixture as *missing* a label indicating its component population of origin. This has been defined early by Baum *et al.* (1970) in a similar way and has been widely used in HMM-based speech recognition methods. Thus, the VQ problems and HMM modelling problems can be unified under the same probabilistic framework to obtain an optimized VQ/HMM combination, which forms the foundation of the SCHMM.

Provided that each codeword of the VQ codebook is represented by a Gaussian density function, for a given state s_t of HMM, here assuming s_t and continuous observations, $\mathbf{x}$, are independent, the probability density function that s_t produces a vector $\mathbf{x}$ can then be written as:

$$b_{s_t}(\mathbf{x}) = f(\mathbf{x}|s_t) = \sum_{j=1}^{L} f(\mathbf{x}|O_{jt}, s_t)\Pr(O_{jt}|s_t)$$

$$= \sum_{j=1}^{L} f(\mathbf{x}|O_{jt})\Pr(O_{jt}|s_t) = \sum_{j=1}^{L} f(\mathbf{x}|O_{jt})b_{s_t}(O_{jt}) \tag{4}$$

where L denotes the VQ codebook level. Given the VQ codebook index O_{jt}, the probability density function $f(\mathbf{x}|O_{jt})$ can be estimated with the EM algorithm (Redner & Walker, 1984), or by maximum likelihood clustering (Huang & Jack, 1988*c*). It can also be obtained from the HMM parameter estimation directly as explained later. Using Equation (4) to represent the semi-continuous output probability density, it is possible to combine the codebook distortion characteristics with the parameters of the discrete HMM under a unified probabilistic framework. Here, each discrete output probability is weighted by the continuous conditional Gaussian probability density function derived from VQ. If these continuous VQ density functions are considered as the continuous output probability density function in the continuous mixture HMM, this also resembles the L-mixture continuous HMM with all the continuous output probability density functions shared with each other in the VQ codebook. The discrete output probability in state i, $b_i(O_{jt})$, becomes the weighting coefficients for the mixture components. In the decoding process, this results in an L-mixture continuous HMM with a computational complexity comparable to the continuous (single-mixture) HMM. In practice, Equation (4) can be replaced by finding the M most significant values of $f(\mathbf{x}|O_j)$ (in practice, some two to five values) over all possible codebook indices O_j, which can be easily obtained in the VQ procedure. This can significantly reduce the computational load for subsequent output probability computation, since M is of lower order than L. Experimental results show this to perform well in speech recognition as discussed in Section 3.

In the decoding process, the continuous probability density function of the VQ codebook can be used to bridge between the non-VQ observation sequence $\mathbf{X}$ and the discrete HMM parameters. The semi-continuous output probability density function defined in Equation (4) can be used directly in the Viterbi algorithm (Viterbi, 1967; Rabiner & Juang, 1986), which can find the single best path with the highest probability of the observation sequence.

2.3. *Mutual parameter re-estimation of the SCHMM and VQ codebook*

The SCHMM can be considered as a special form of continuous mixture HMM with tied mixture continuous density functions as discussed above. Because of the binding of the continuous density functions, in the SCHMM, the number of free parameters as well as computational complexity are reduced in comparison to the continuous mixture HMM while retaining the modelling powers of mixture HMM. Here, if the $b_i(O_{jt})$ are considered as the weighting coefficients of different mixture output probability density functions in the continuous mixture HMM, the re-estimation algorithm for the weighting coefficients can be extended to re-estimate $b_i(O_{jt})$ of the SCHMM (Juang, 1985). The re-estimation formulations can be more readily computed by defining a forward partial probability, $\boldsymbol{\alpha}_t(i)$, and a backward partial probability, $\boldsymbol{\beta}_t(i)$ for any time t and state i as:

$$\boldsymbol{\alpha}_t(i) = \Pr(\mathbf{x}_1, \mathbf{x}_2, \ldots, \mathbf{x}_t, s_t = i|\lambda)$$

$$\boldsymbol{\beta}_t(i) = \Pr(\mathbf{x}_{t+1}, \mathbf{x}_{t+2}, \ldots, \mathbf{x}_T|s_t = i, \lambda) \tag{5a}$$

The forward and backward probability can be computed recursively with $a_1(i) = \pi_i$ and $\beta_T(i) = 1$ as:

$$\boldsymbol{\alpha}_t(i) = \sum_{j=1}^{N} \boldsymbol{\alpha}_{t-1}(j)a_{ji}b_i(\mathbf{x}_t), \quad 2 \leqslant t \leqslant T;$$

$$\boldsymbol{\beta}_t(i) = \sum_{j=1}^{N} a_{ij}b_j(\mathbf{x}_{t+1})\boldsymbol{\beta}_{t+1}(j). \quad 1 \leqslant t \leqslant T-1. \tag{5b}$$

The intermediate probabilities, $\chi_t(i,j,k)$, $\gamma_t(i,j)$, $\gamma_t(i)$, $\zeta_t(i,j)$, and $\zeta_t(j)$ can be defined for efficient re-estimation of the model parameters. They are:

$$\chi_t(i,j,k) = \Pr(s_t = i, s_{t+1} = j, O_{k_{t+1}}|\mathbf{X}, \lambda)$$

$$= \frac{\boldsymbol{\alpha}_t(i)a_{ij}b_j(O_{k_{t+1}})f(\mathbf{x}_{t+1}|O_{k_{t+1}})\boldsymbol{\beta}_{t+1}(j)}{\Pr(\mathbf{X}|\lambda)}$$

$$\gamma_t(i,j) = \Pr(s_t = i, s_{t+1} = j|\mathbf{X}, \lambda)$$

$$\gamma_t(i) = \Pr(s_t = i|\mathbf{X}, \lambda)$$

$$\zeta_t(i,k) = \Pr(s_t = i, O_{k_t}|\mathbf{X}, \lambda)$$

$$\zeta_t(k) = \Pr(O_{k_t}|\mathbf{X}, \lambda) \tag{6a}$$

All these intermediate probability can be represented by $\chi_t(\,)$ with computational advantages as:

$$\gamma_t(i,j) = \sum_{k=1}^{L} \chi_t(i,j,k) \tag{6b}$$

$$\gamma_t(i) = \sum_{j=1}^{N} \gamma_t(i,j) \tag{6c}$$

$$\zeta_t(i,k)=\sum_{j=1}^{N}\chi_{t-1}(j,i,k) \tag{6d}$$

$$\zeta_t(k)=\sum_{i=1}^{N}\sum_{j=1}^{N}\chi_{t-1}(i,j,k) \tag{6e}$$

Using Equations (5) and (6), the re-estimation equations for π_i, a_{ij}, $b_i(O_j)$ can be written as:

$$\pi_i=\gamma_1(i), \quad 1\leq i\leq N; \tag{7}$$

$$\bar{a}_{ij}=\frac{\sum_{t=1}^{T-1}\gamma_t(i,j)}{\sum_{t=1}^{T-1}\gamma_t(i)}, \quad 1\leq i,j\leq N; \tag{8}$$

$$\bar{b}_i(O_j)=\frac{\sum_{t=1}^{T}\zeta_t(i,j)}{\sum_{t=1}^{T}\gamma_t(i)}, \quad 1\leq i\leq N;\ 1\leq j\leq L. \tag{9}$$

Equations (7) to (9) can be extended to the case of multiple training sequences (Juang & Rabiner, 1985).

The means and covariances of the Gaussian probability density functions can also be re-estimated to update the VQ codebook separately with Equations (5) and (6). The feedback from the HMM estimation results to the VQ codebook implies that the VQ codebook is optimized based on the HMM likelihood maximization rather than minimizing the total distortion errors from the set of training data. Although re-estimation of means and covariances of different models will involve interdependencies, the different density functions which are re-estimated are strongly correlated, so the new estimates can be expected to improve the discrimination ability of the VQ codebook. To re-estimate the parameters of the VQ codebook, i.e. the means, $\boldsymbol{\mu}_j$, and covariances matrices, Σ_j, of the codebook index j, it is not difficult to extend the continuous mixture HMM re-estimation algorithm. In general, it can be written as:

$$\bar{\boldsymbol{\mu}}_j=\frac{\sum_v\left[\sum_{t=1}^{T}\zeta_t(j)\mathbf{x}_t\right]}{\sum_v\left[\sum_{t=1}^{T}\zeta_t(j)\right]}, \quad 1\leq j\leq L; \tag{10}$$

and

$$\bar{\boldsymbol{\Sigma}}_j=\frac{\sum_v\left[\sum_{t=1}^{T}\zeta_t(j)(\mathbf{x}_t-\bar{\boldsymbol{\mu}}_j)(\mathbf{x}_t-\bar{\boldsymbol{\mu}}_j)^t\right]}{\sum_v\left[\sum_{t=1}^{T}\zeta_t(j)\right]}, \quad 1\leq j\leq L. \tag{11}$$

where v denotes the whole vocabulary size; and expressions in square brackets are variables of model v. In Equations (10) and (11), the re-estimation for the means and covariance matrices in the output probability density function of the SCHMM are tied up with all the HMM models. This is similar to the approach with tied transition probability inside the model (Jelinek & Mercer, 1980). From Equations (10) and (11), it can be observed that these are merely a special form of EM algorithm for parameter estimation of mixture density functions (Redner & Walker, 1984), and these are closely welded into the HMM re-estimation equations. Thus, a unified modelling approach to vector quantization and hidden Markov modelling of speech signals can be established for both of the VQ codebook and HMM parameter estimation.

2.4. Computational considerations

It should be noted that the computational complexity for decoding with this new SCHMM is less than that of continuous mixture HMM if the size of the VQ codebook is less than the number of output probability density functions in the continuous mixture HMM since $f(\mathbf{x}|O_j)$ need only be calculated for each codebook index as opposed to each state with several mixture density functions, and usually the total number of output probability density functions will be more than the codebook size for large vocabulary recognition. The memory requirements for the SCHMM are almost the same as the discrete HMM except that the memory for $f(\mathbf{x}|O_j)$ must be added for all the VQ codebook entries and observation sequences $\mathbf{X}$. In practice, if Equation (4) is simplified by using only the first three most significant values of $f(\mathbf{x}|O_j)$, the computational load of the SCHMM is comparable to that of the discrete HMM. For parameter re-estimation, the computational complexity is similar to the continuous HMM with three mixture. If simplified methods are used as explained in Section 3, the computational load can be reduced to that of the continuous HMM with single mixture.

3. Experimental evaluation

Experiments have been carried out to compare the performance of (a) discrete HMM; (b) SCHMM without re-estimation; (c) SCHMM with re-estimation; and (d) continuous HMM in a phoneme classification task as a useful exemplar domain to investigate the differences between SCHMM, continuous HMM, and discrete HMM algorithms. Other phoneme classification problems, such as coarticulation effects, speech modelling units, and model structure, are not discussed here.

3.1. Simplified SCHMM parameter re-estimation

For parameter re-estimation of the SCHMM, due to the extensive computation load of Equations (10) and (11), a simplified method is adopted here. The re-estimation procedure is divided into two stages. In the first stage, the discrete HMM re-estimation is run, and discrete HMM parameters are then used as initial parameters for the SCHMM. Only one mixture is used to represent the semi-continuous output probability density during parameter re-estimation, which is determined according to the most significant value of $b_i(O_j)$. The re-estimates (means and covariances) can be used either to replace the original means and covariances in the VQ codebook or to form an average with other re-estimates according to the preselected codeword index. This can be considered as a special technique of Equations (10) and (11) within an individual model v where the re-estimation of the means and covariance is constrained only to the most significant $b_i(O_j)$. These means and covariances are used as feedback to the VQ codebook for updating. This procedure can be re-estimated together with the transition probabilities. In the second stage, after re-estimation of the transition probabilities, along with the mean and the covariance matrices, the re-estimation algorithm for the weighting coefficients (Equation (9)) can be used again together with the transition probabilities on the updated codebook to obtain the final discrete output probability distributions for the SCHMM. With the simplified approach used here, the computational complexity of the SCHMM parameter re-estimation can be significantly reduced in comparison with Equations (10) and (11).

3.2. *Analysis conditions*

For both training and evaluation, the analysis conditions consisted of the following:

sampling rate: 16 kHz;
analysis method: 10 cepstrum coefficients derived from the 12th order autocorrelation LPC method (Rabiner *et al.*, 1985);
window type: Hamming window;
window length and shift: 20 ms and 10 ms;
pre-emphasis: $1–0·97z^{-1}$;
HMM structure: left-to-right model as shown in Fig. 1.

The database consists of two repetitions of the same continuous speech sentences from a male speaker. Each set has 98 sentences with 579 words. The sentences have been hand-labelled to the level of individual phonemes. Each of the 47 individual HMM are trained and decoded with hand-labelled phonemes, with the (unbalanced) number of phonemes used to derive individual models varying from 3 to 191.

The VQ codebook is generated using training data with a total of 20 000 frames by employing the LBG algorithm (Linde, Buzo & Gray, 1980). The first set of sentences is used to estimate HMM parameters with the forward–backward algorithm, and the second set of sentences is used in decoding by the Viterbi algorithm. The forward–backward algorithm is used iteratively three to six times and the final output probability is smoothed as suggested in Levinson *et al.* (1985).

3.3. *Experimental results*

The discrete HMM was first to be evaluated in the experiments as shown in Table I. When the VQ level varies from 128 to 256, the average phoneme recognition accuracy of the discrete HMM is 50·0% and 50·1% respectively for 47 phonemes. The fact that increasing the VQ level from 128 to 256 does not result in improved phoneme recognition accuracy is an indication that for the limited training data used here, a VQ level of 128 is adequate. Due to the limited training data, the covariance matrices used in continuous HMM and SCHMM are all assumed to be diagonal.

Using discrete HMM parameters, the recognition accuracy of SCHMM (without re-estimation) was tested. Varying the range of the most significant $f(\mathbf{x}|O_j)$ in Equation (4) from 1 to 5, the recognition accuracy of the SCHMM is shown in Fig. 2. Choice of the top three values is appropriate here and will be used in the following experiments. The recognition accuracy of SCHMM without re-estimation is 53·5%. When Equation (9) is used to re-estimate the output probability while keeping the VQ codebook unchanged, marginally higher accuracy is obtained for the SCHMM. However, when the continuous HMM is used, the measured accuracy improves to 55·2%, which is higher than both the

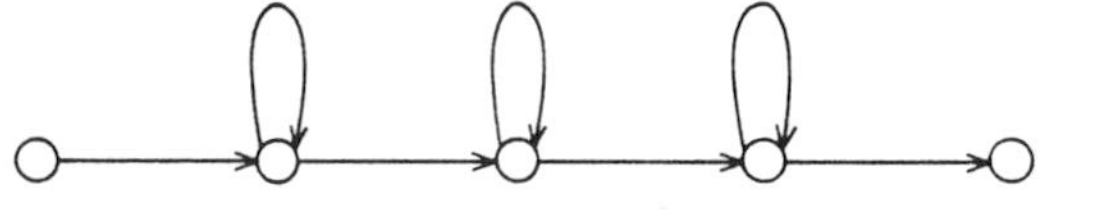

Figure 1. HMM structure.

TABLE I. Comparison of discrete HMM, continuous HMM, and semi-continuous HMM

Model	Average recognition (number of tests = 1748)	
	VQ level	Accuracy (correct recognized tests)
Discrete HMM	128	50·0% (874)
Discrete HMM	256	50·1% (875)
Continuous HMM	—	55·2% (966)
SCHMM without re-estimation	128	53·3% (923)
Discrete HMM with updated VQ	128	55·3% (968)
SCHMM with updated VQ	128	58·3% (1019)
Discrete HMM with new VQ	141	53·7% (940)
SCHMM with new VQ	141	58·5% (1023)

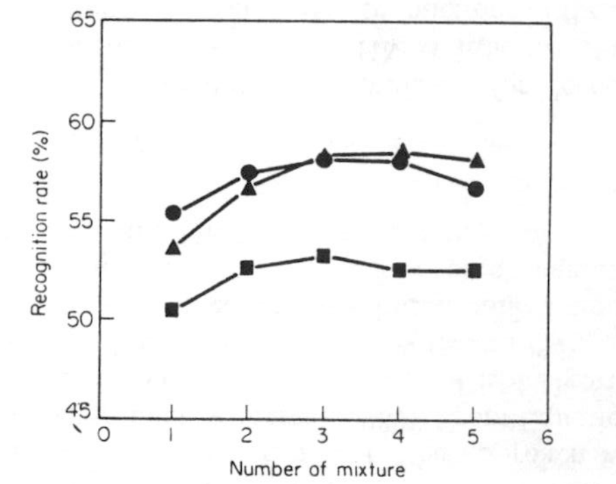

Figure 2. Performance comparison using different mixtures for decoding. ■: SCHMM without re-estimation; ●: SCHMM with updated VQ; ▲: SCHMM with VQ codebook obtained from the continuous HMM.

discrete HMM and the SCHMM without the re-estimated means and covariances. In the continuous HMM used here, parameters of the discrete HMM are used as initial parameters for the continuous HMM. The means and covariances corresponding to the maximum codeword in the discrete output probability are used as initial parameters for the continuous HMM and iterated thereafter with the forward–backward algorithm.

The simplified SCHMM parameter re-estimation technique is used for evaluation. The experimental results show that use of both the replacement or averaging techniques during the re-estimation produces similar recognition accuracy. This suggests strong correlation between re-estimated codewords. With re-estimated parameters and updated VQ codebook, the recognition accuracy of the SCHMM is 58·3%, which is measurably better than both the discrete HMM and the continuous HMM. Using the updated VQ codebook, it is interesting to note that the discrete HMM (55·3%) is comparable to the continuous HMM (55·2%). Here, the discrete output probability distribution is obtained from the SCHMM re-estimation formula Equation (9).

To avoid loss of information in the VQ codebook by the replacement of averaging operation described above, a novel approach is used here which involves using the means and covariances of the continuous HMM output probability density functions to form a new codebook. There are a total of 47 different phoneme models with three output probability density functions in each model. Therefore, a VQ codebook of 141 levels is constructed. Here again, Equation (9) is used to re-estimate the discrete output probability for the SCHMM. The recognition accuracy of the SCHMM with the new codebook is 58·5%, and the discrete HMM with the new codebook is 53·8%. From Table 1, it can be seen that re-estimated SCHMM with modified VQ codebook performs consistently better than both the continuous and discrete HMM. In addition, with the VQ codebook updated from the continuous HMM, or collected from the continuous HMM, the performance of the discrete HMM (55·3%) has improved towards that of the continuous HMM (55·2%). This strongly suggests that the unified modelling of vector quantization and HMM is necessary. To retain robustness, the continuous mixture HMM can also be applied with the same strategy, although this will result in a codebook of large level, an information–theoretic clustering can be easily extended to merge similar codewords.

4. Discussion and summary

The SCHMM takes the advantages of both the discrete HMM and continuous HMM, and results in a powerful tool for modelling time-varying signals sources. The distortion produced by VQ operations has been shown to be accommodated within the HMM methodology such that parameter estimation of the VQ codebook can be combined together with that of the HMM under the same probabilistic framework. The SCHMM technique described here can be considered as a method where a VQ codebook is updated with the HMM re-estimation algorithm and thus represents a special form of maximum likelihood vector quantization. Although the maximum likelihood VQ and the HMM forward–backward algorithms attempt to maximize the likelihood, the new SCHMM approach has some obvious advantages in that it maximizes the likelihood of each HMM using preclassified data, in contrast to other approaches which maximize the likelihood of VQ codebook with unclassified data. As a result, later estimates are more suitable for classification when the preclassified data and the HMM parameters are optimized together.

In summary, the SCHMM can be considered as a special form of continuous mixture hidden Markov model by merging the continuous output probability functions of the model into the VQ codebook. This can effectively reduce the amount of training data as well as computational complexity in comparison with the continuous mixture HMM. The VQ codebook obtained from maximizing the likelihood function of the HMM provides better discrimination powers than a conventional VQ codebook obtained from minimizing distortion errors. Vector quantization and hidden Markov modelling of speech signals are unified under the EM algorithm, which has been widely used in the context of mixture density estimation. Experimental results have demonstrated that the SCHMM algorithm proposed here offers improved phoneme recognition accuracy in comparison with both the discrete HMM and the continuous HMM with only limited computational complexity increases. We conclude that the SCHMM is a powerful new technique for modelling non-stationary stochastic processes with multi-model non-symmetric probabilistic functions of Markov chains.

The authors wish to thank Professor J. Laver, Dr Y. Ariki, and Dr F. McInnes, Centre for Speech Technology Research, Edinburgh University and Professor D. T. Fang, Computer Science and Technology Department, Tsinghua University for their support and contributions in the research work.

References

Baum, L. E., Petrie, T., Soules, G. & Weiss, N. (1979). A maximization technique occurring in the statistical analysis of probabilistic functions of Markov chains. *Annals of Mathematics and Statistics*, **41**, 164–171.

Brown, P. F. (1987). Acoustic–phonetic modelling problem in automatic speech recognition. Ph.D. Thesis, Department of Computer Science, Carnegie–Mellon University.

Chow, Y. L., Dunham, M. D., Kimball, O. A., Kranser, M. A., Kubala, G. F., Makhoul, J., Price, P. J., Roucos, S. & Schwartz, R. M. (1987). BYBLOS: The BBN continuous speech recognition system. *IEEE ICASSP 87*, Dallas, pp. 89–92.

Dempster, A. P., Laird, N. M. & Rubin, D. B. (1977). Maximum-likelihood from incomplete data via the EM algorithm. *Journal of the Royal Statistical Society, Series B (methodological)*, **39**, 1–38.

Hasselblad, V. (1966). Estimation of parameters for a mixture of normal distributions. *Technometrics*, **8**, 431–444.

Huang, X. D. & Jack, M. A. (1988*a*). Performance comparison between semi-continuous and discrete hidden Markov models. *IEE Electronics Letters*, **24**(3), 149–150.

Huang, X. D. & Jack, M. A. (1988*b*). On several problems of hidden Markov models. *Seventh FASE symposium, SPEECH 88*, Edinburgh, pp. 17–22.

Huang, X. D. & Jack, M. A. (1988*c*). Maximum likelihood clustering applied to semi-continuous hidden Markov models for speech recognition. *IEEE international symposium on information theory*, Kobe, Japan, p. 71.

Jelinek, F. (1976). Continuous speech recognition by statistical methods. *Proceedings of IEEE*, **64**, 532–556.

Jelinek, F. (1985). The development of an experimental discrete dictation recognizer. *Proceedings of IEEE*, **73**, 1616–1624.

Jelinek, F. & Mercer, R. L. (1980). Interpolated estimation of Markov source parameters from sparse data. *Proceedings of the workshop on pattern recognition in practice*. Amsterdam: North-Holland.

Juang, B. H. (1985). Maximum-likelihood estimation for mixture multivariate stochastic observations of Markov chain. *AT&T Technical Journal*, **64**, 1235–1249.

Juang, B. H. & Rabiner, L. R. (1985). Mixture autoregressive hidden Markov models for speech signals. *IEEE Transactions on Acoustics, Speech and Signal Processing*, **ASSP-33**, 1404–1413.

Lee, K. F. (1988). Large-vocabulary speaker-independent continuous speech recognition: The SPHINX system. Ph.D. Thesis, Department of Computer Science, Carnegie–Mellon University.

Levinson, S. E. (1986). Continuously variable duration hidden Markov models for automatic speech recognition. *Computer Speech and Language*, **1**, 29–45.

Levinson, S. E., Rabiner, L. R. & Sondhi, M. M. (1983). An introduction to the application of theory of probabilistic functions of a Markov process to automatic speech recognition. *Bell System Technical Journal*, **62**, 1035–1074.

Linde, Y., Buzo, A. & Gray, R. M. (1980). An algorithm for vector quantizer design. *IEEE Transactions and Communications*, **COM-28**, 84–95.

Makhoul, J., Roucos, S. & Gish, H. (1985). Vector quantisation in speech coding. *Proceedings of IEEE*, **73**, 1551–1588.

Nishimura, M. & Toshioka, K. (1987). HMM-based speech recognition using multi-dimensional multi-labeling. *IEEE ICASSP 87*, Dallas, pp. 1163–1166.

Parzen, E. (1962). On estimation of a probability density function and mode. *Annals of Mathematics and Statistics*, **33**, 000–000.

Poritz, A. B. & Richter, A. G. (1986). On hidden Markov models in isolated word recognition. *IEEE ICASSP 86*, Tokyo, Japan, pp. 705–708.

Rabiner, L. R. & Juang, B. H. (1986). An introduction to hidden Markov models. *IEEE ASSP Magazine*, January, 4–16.

Rabiner, L. R., Wilpon, J. G. & Juang, B. H. (1986). A segmental k-means training procedure for connected word recognition. *AT&T Technical Journal*, **65**, 21–31.

Rabiner, L. R., Juang, B. G., Levinson, S. E. & Sondhi, M. M. (1985). Recognition of isolated digits using hidden Markov models with continuous mixture densities. *AT&T Technical Journal*, **64**, 1211–1234.

Redner, R. A. & Walker, H. F. (1984). Mixture densities, maximum likelihood and the EM algorithm. *SIAM review*, **26**, 195–239.

Soudoplatoff, S. (1986). Markov modelling of continuous parameters in speech recognition. *IEEE ICASSP 86*, Tokyo, Japan, pp. 45–48.

Tseng, H. P., Sabin, M. & Lee, E. (1987). Fuzzy vector quantization applied to hidden Markov modelling. *IEEE ICASSP 87*, Dallas, pp. 641–644.

Viterbi, A. J. (1967). Error bounds for convolutional codes and an asymptotically optimum decoding algorithm. *IEEE Transactions on Information Theory*, **IT-13**, 260–269.

Context-Dependent Phonetic Hidden Markov Models for Speaker-Independent Continuous Speech Recognition[1]

Kai-Fu Lee

School of Computer Science
Carnegie Mellon University
Pittsburgh, Pennsylvania 15213

Abstract

The effectiveness of context-dependent phone modeling for speaker-dependent continuous speech recognition has recently been demonstrated [1]. In this study, we apply context-dependent phone models to speaker-independent continuous speech recognition, and show that they are equally effective in this domain. In addition to evaluating several previously proposed context-dependent models, we also introduce two new context-dependent phonetic units: (1) function-word-dependent phone models, which focus on the most difficult sub-vocabulary, and (2) generalized triphones, which combine similar triphones together based on an information-theoretic measure. The subword clustering procedure used for generalized triphones can find the optimal number of models given a fixed amount of training data. We demonstrate that context-dependent modeling reduces the error rate by as much as 60%.

1 Introduction

The most successful small-vocabulary speech recognition systems have been based on hidden Markov modeling (HMM) of *words* [2, 3]. However, as the vocabulary size increases, word modeling becomes more difficult, because it is unreasonable to expect the many repetitions of each word needed to train the word HMM. Instead, some *subword units* must be used. Two important criteria for good subword units are: (1) consistency — different instances of a unit have similar characteristics, and (2) trainability — sufficient training samples exist to create a robust model. In the seventies, researchers faced the dilemma of choosing larger subword units (syllables, demi-syllables, diphones) that are consistent but difficult to train, or choosing smaller units (phones, phonemes) that are trainable but inconsistent. The introduction of context-dependent phones [4, 5] opened a new chapter in subword modeling. Context-dependent phones are consistent units. Even though there may be a large number of context-dependent phones, because they are phone-like units, they can be interpolated with phones to achieve reasonable trainability and performance.

In this paper, we describe the application of context-dependent phone modeling to large-vocabulary speaker-independent continuous speech recognition. In addition to experiments with previously used subword models, we introduce two new types of context-dependent phonetic units: *function-word-dependent phones* and *generalized triphones*.

Function-word-dependent phone models explicitly model phones in function words, such as *in, a, the, and*. They focus on the most confusable sub-vocabulary, and can be well-trained because function words occur frequently. Function-word-dependent phone models can be interpolated with context-independent phone models to avoid insufficient training.

Generalized triphone models evolved from the *triphone* model [5, 6, 7]. A triphone is a phone that takes into consideration its left and right phonetic contexts, which cause the greatest variations in the realization of a phone.

[1]Appeared on the IEEE Trans. on Acoustics, Speech, and Signal Processing, April, 1990. This research was partly sponsored by a National Science Foundation Graduate Fellowship, and by Defense Advanced Research Projects Agency Contract N00039-85-C-0163. The views and conclusions contained in this document are those of the author and should not be interpreted as representing the official policies, either expressed or implied, of the National Science Foundation, the Defense Advanced Research Projects Agency, or the US Government.

Triphone models are typically poorly trained because there are many of them. Although interpolation with better trained models makes them usable, they are still under-trained and wasteful. In view of this, we introduce another new unit, generalized triphones. Generalized triphones exploit the fact that many phonetic contexts are very similar. Prior to training, triphones are clustered into generalized triphones using an information-theoretic measure. This not only results in substantially fewer context-dependent units, but also provides more training data for each model. This technique provides a way of finding the "right" number of models for any task. It can also be extended to clustering other types of phonetic models.

To combine detailed models (function-word-dependent phone models and generalized triphone models) with robust ones (context-independent phone models), we use deleted interpolation [8]. Deleted interpolation is an elegant EM (Estimate-Maximize) algorithm that estimates the weight of the models based on how well each model predicts unseen data.

These techniques were applied to the DARPA 997-word speaker-independent continuous speech resource management task [9]. With phonetic models, we attained word accuracies of 49.6%, 84.4%, and 90.6% for three different grammars. With function-word-dependent phone models and generalized triphone models, recognition rates improved to 70.6%, 93.7%, and 95.8%. This represents error rate reductions of 41%, 60%, and 55%, respectively.

The organization of this paper is as follows: section 2 provides a literature review of subword models. Section 3 describes the SPHINX speech recognition system, the resource management task and database. In Section 4, we describe our implementation and results of several previously proposed subword models. In Section 5 and 6, we introduce function-word-dependent phone modeling and generalized triphone models. Section 7 describes directions of future work. Finally, Section 8 contains the conclusions of this paper.

2 Literature Review

Good subword units should be *consistent* and *trainable*. Consistency means different instances of the same subword model have similar characteristics. Consistency is important because it improves the discrimination between different subword units, which governs the accuracy of speech recognition systems. Trainability means that each speech unit has been trained on sufficiently many examples. Trainability is important because our speech models require a considerable amount of training data. In this section, we will describe and evaluate a number of units using these two criteria.

2.1 Words

Words are the most natural units of speech because they are exactly what we want to recognize. Also, word models are able to capture within-word contextual effects. For example, the phone /t/ in *ten* is as expected, the phone /t/ in *thirty* is usually flapped, and the phone /t/ in *twenty* may be deleted. By modeling words as units, these phonological variations can be assimilated. Therefore, when there is sufficient data, word models will usually yield the best performance. This is demonstrated by the success of several recent small-vocabulary word-based recognizers [2, 3].

However, using word models in large-vocabulary recognition introduces several grave problems. Since training data cannot be shared between words, each word has to be trained individually. Thus, many examples of each word are needed for adequate training. But for a large-vocabulary task, this imposes too great a demand for training data. This problem is difficult for speaker-independent systems, and even more difficult for speaker-dependent ones. Another problem is that memory usage grows linearly with the number of words, since there is no sharing between words. Finally, for many tasks, it would be convenient to provide the user with the option of adding new words to the vocabulary. If word models are used, the user would have to produce many repetitions of each new word, which is extremely inconvenient. Therefore, while word models are natural and model contexts well, because of the lack of sharing across words, they are not practical for large-vocabulary speech recognition.

2.2 Phones

In order to allow sharing across words, some subword unit has to be used. The subword units most familiar to us are the phones of English. Since there are only about 50 phones in English, they can be sufficiently trained with just a few hundred sentences. Therefore, unlike word models, there is no training problem with phone models. However, phone models assume a phone in any context is equivalent to the same phone in any other context. Yet, this is far from the truth. Although we may try to say each word as a concatenated sequence of phones, these phones are not produced independently, because our articulators cannot move instantaneously from one position to another. Thus, the realization of a phone is strongly affected by its immediate neighboring phones. Figure 1 illustrates co-articulatory effects on the phone `/t/` in four different contexts.

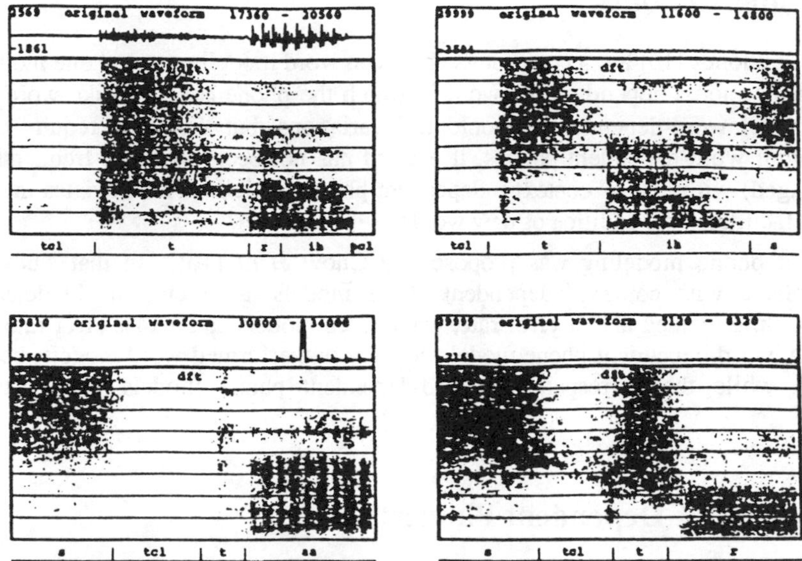

Figure 1: The waveforms and spectrograms for the phoneme `/t/` in four different contexts: part of `/t r/`, left of `/ih/`, part of `/s t/`, and part of `/s t r/`. It is clear that the realization of `/t/` is highly dependent on context, and that a context-independent `/t/` model is inadequate.

Another problem with using phone models is that phones in function words, such as *a*, *the*, *in*, and *me*, are often articulated poorly, and are not representative instances of the phones.

Bahl, *et. al*, [10] showed that word-based DTW performed significantly better than phone-based HMM for speaker-dependent recognition. Paul [7] also demonstrated that word-based HMMs resulted in 50% error rate reduction from phone-based HMMs. These results demonstrate that while word models lack generality, phone models over-generalize.

2.3 Multi-Phone Units

One way to model co-articulatory effects is to use larger units of speech. Examples of this include syllables [11], or demisyllables [12]. These units encompass the phone clusters that contain the most severe contextual effects. However, while the central portions of these units have no contextual dependencies, the beginning and ending portions are still susceptible to some contextual effects.

A more serious problem is the large number of these units. For example, there are over 20,000 syllables and over 1000 demisyllables in English. Although this may be a reduction from word models in a very large vocabulary, there are still too many parameters to reliably estimate when different units cannot share the same training data. Finally, experiments [12] showed that a demisyllable-based recognizer performed substantially worse than a word-based recognizer.

2.4 Explicit Transition Modeling

Since transitions in and out of phones are poorly modeled by phone models, one possible solution is to model these transitional regions explicitly. For example, diphones [13, 14] model pairs of phones without the use of stationary phones. Another approach is to use stationary phone models and insert transition models [15].

Transition modeling suffers from the same problem as multi-phone units. Instead of N phones, there are N^2 phone transitions. Like multi-phone units, these units cannot easily share training data. Therefore, transition models also result in too many parameters to estimate when there is no sharing.

2.5 Word-Dependent Phones

Word-dependent phones [16] are a compromise between word modeling and phone modeling. The parameters of a word-dependent phone model depend on the word in which the phone occurs. Like word models, word-dependent phone models can model word-dependent, phonological variations, but they also require considerable training and storage. However, with word-dependent phones, if a word has not been observed frequently, its parameters can be interpolated (or averaged) with that of context-independent phone models. This obviates the need of observing every word in training, and facilitates the addition of new words.

Word-dependent phone modeling was proposed by Chow *et al.* [16]. In that study, word-dependent phone models were interpolated with context-independent phone models using empirically determined weights. Word-dependent phone modeling yielded a 10% error rate, while word models had a 14% error rate, and phone models had a 24% error rate. Thus, word-dependent phone models actually outperformed word models, because some word models were poorly trained while the corresponding word-dependent phone models were reasonably trained through interpolation.

2.6 Triphones (Context-Dependent Phones)

Context-dependent phone models are similar to word-dependent phone models, except that instead of modeling phone-in-word, they model phone-in-context. A context usually refers to the immediate left and/or right neighboring phones. A *left-context dependent phone* is dependent on the left context, while a *right-context dependent phone* is dependent on the right context. A *triphone* model takes into consideration both the left and the right neighboring phones; if two phones have the same identity but different left or right context, they are considered different triphones. Triphone models are usually poorly trained because there are many triphones. But since triphone models are specific phone models, they can be interpolated with better-trained but less appropriate context-independent phone models.

Bahl *et al.* [4] first proposed context-dependent phonetic models. Schwartz *et al.* [5] at BBN were the first to publish comparative results of triphone modeling. In that study and later studies [1, 16], triphone models were interpolated with right-context-dependent models (phone models that are dependent on the right context), left-context-dependent models, and context-independent models. Each pdf in each model was given a different weight according to appropriateness (for example, left-context models have greater weights for leftmost pdf) and amount of training (for example, if a triphone has been observed many times, its weight will dominate). This weight matrix was tuned by hand. For both phone and word recognition, modeling phone-in-context reduced the error rate by about 50%.

Triphone modeling is powerful because it models the most important co-articulatory effect, and is much more consistent and detailed than phone modeling. However, triphone models have two problems. The first problem is memory wastage. When a triphone is observed once, a model is created for it, and with a large number of triphones, the memory used could be substantial. Also, many triphone models are poorly trained, and they do not take advantage of the fact that many triphones are similar.

2.7 Summary of Previous Units

In the preceding sections, we have evaluated several previously proposed units of speech. We emphasized two important properties for speech units, namely, consistency and trainability. If we have infinite training data, consistency is the only property of interest. But because our training data is not only finite, but often limited, trainability becomes an important issue. Trainability can be achieved either by using very general units (such as phones) at the cost of inconsistency, or by sharing among units.

Table 1 evaluates the appropriateness of the units we described for large-vocabulary recognition using these two criteria. Words are consistent units, but they are not easily trainable. Phones are not consistent, but are easily trainable. Multi-phone units and transition units are consistent, but are not easily trainable because there are no good means of sharing. Word-dependent phones and context-dependent phones are consistent, and can be trained because there exist means of sharing. Therefore, both are very appealing units. Our only criticism is that consistency is achieved with too fine a level of detail. More generalization can lead to fewer models and a higher level of trainability.

Unit	**Consistency**	**Trainability**
Word model	Yes	No
Phone model	No	Yes
Multi-phone model	Yes	Difficult
Transition model	Yes	Difficult
Word-dependent phone model	Yes	Through Sharing
Context-dependent phone model	Yes	Through Sharing

Table 1: Evaluation of previously proposed units of speech to large vocabulary recognition.

3 The SPHINX System

In this section, we describe the SPHINX speech recognition system, on which we experiment with various context-dependent phonetic models. We describe the speech processing, training, and recognition algorithms used in SPHINX. More details about the SPHINX System can be found in [17, 18].

3.1 Speech Processing

The speech is sampled at 16 KHz, and pre-emphasized using the transfer function $1 - 0.97z^{-1}$. A Hamming window with a width of 20 msec is applied every 10 msec. 14th-order LPC analysis is implemented using the autocorrelation method [19]. Next, a set of 12 LPC cepstral coefficients are computed from the LPC coefficients. Finally, these LPC cepstral coefficients are transformed to a mel-scale using a bilinear transform [20].

In addition to the LPC cepstral coefficients, we also compute differenced LPC cepstral coefficients, power, and differenced power for each frame. The temporal difference for frame t is the difference between frame t–2 and t+2, or a 40 msec difference. In speaker-independent recognition, the use of differential information and power information is extremely important [21, 22].

These coefficients are then vector quantized using three VQ codebooks, each with 256 prototype vectors, using:

1. 12 LPC cepstral coefficients.
2. 12 differenced LPC cepstral coefficients.
3. Power and differenced power.

We found that multiple codebooks reduce the VQ distortion by reducing the dimensions of the parameter space. Multiple codebooks were first used by Gupta, *et. al* [23].

3.2 Phonetic Hidden Markov Models

Hidden Markov models (HMM) [24, 25, 26] are parametric models particularly suitable for describing speech events. The success of HMMs is largely due to the forward-backward re-estimation algorithm [26], which is a special case of the EM algorithm [27]. Every iteration of the algorithm modifies the parameters to increase the probability of the training data until a local maximum has been reached.

Because our emphasis is on large-vocabulary recognition, we cannot train a model for each word. Thus, we have chosen to use phonetic HMMs, where each HMM represents a phone. A phonetic HMM is characterized by:

- $\{s\}$—A set of states including an initial state S_I and a final state S_F.
- $\{a_{ij}\}$—A set of transitions where a_{ij} is the probability of taking a transition from state i to state j.
- $\{b_{ij}(k)\}$—The output probability matrix: the probability of emitting symbol k when taking a transition from state i to state j. k corresponds to one of the 256 VQ codes.

We used an inventory of 48 phones (shown in Table 2) as subword units. In the initial version, each phone is modeled independent of context. The topology of our model is shown in Figure 2. The label of a transition designates the output pdf of that transition. The unlabeled lower transitions are assigned different output pdf's for different phones. This model is almost identical to that used by IBM [28].

Phone	Example	Phone	Example	Phone	Example
/iy/	*beat*	/l/	*led*	/t/	*tot*
/ih/	*bit*	/r/	*red*	/k/	*kick*
/eh/	*bet*	/y/	*yet*	/z/	*zoo*
/ae/	*bat*	/w/	*wet*	/v/	*very*
/ix/	*roses*	/er/	*bird*	/f/	*fief*
/ax/	*the*	/en/	*button*	/th/	*thief*
/ah/	*but*	/m/	*mom*	/s/	*sis*
/uw/	*boot*	/n/	*non*	/sh/	*shoe*
/uh/	*book*	/ng/	*sing*	/hh/	*hay*
/ao/	*bought*	/ch/	*church*	/sil/	(silence)
/aa/	*cot*	/jh/	*judge*	/dd/	*deleted*
/ey/	*bait*	/dh/	*they*	/pd/	*ship*
/ay/	*bite*	/b/	*bob*	/td/	*set*
/oy/	*boy*	/d/	*dad*	/kd/	*comic*
/aw/	*bough*	/g/	*gag*	/dx/	*butter*
/ow/	*boat*	/p/	*pop*	/ts/	*its*

Table 2: List of the set of phones used in SPHINX

Because we use three VQ codebooks, our discrete HMMs must produce three VQ codewords at each time frame. We assume that the three output pdf's are independent, which allows us to compute the output probability as the product of the probabilities of emitting the three VQ codewords.

3.3 HMM Training

The SPHINX training procedure operates in two stages. In the first stage, 48 context-independent phonetic models are trained. After initializing with HMMs trained for phone recognition [22], we run the forward-backward algorithm

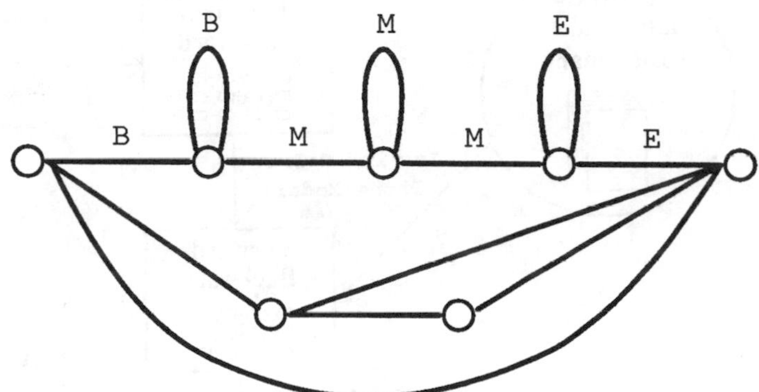

Figure 2: Phone model used in SPHINX. Upper transitions are labeled by the output distribution to which they are tied. B, M, E correspond to the beginning, middle, and end of a phone. Lower transitions are assigned different labels depending on the phone.

on a resource management database [9]. This database consists of 4200 sentences (105 speakers with 40 sentences each). For each sentence, a sentence model is created by concatenating the phone models that represent the words in the sentence, with optional silence models between words. Since the entire sentence model is trained, there is no need for hand segmentation or labeling. After two iterations of the forward-backward training, the parameters of the 48 phone models are trained.

These context-independent phone models could be directly used in recognition, or they could be used to initialize the training of the context-dependent phone models. In the second stage of context-dependent training, the same forward-backward algorithm is used. The only difference is that there are more context-dependent models, and that a context-dependent dictionary is used. For example, a context-independent dictionary expands *ship* into `/sh ih p/`, while a context-dependent dictionary might expand it into `/sh(5) ih(9) p(2)/`, where `/sh(5)/` is one of many units for `/sh/`. The context-dependent models are trained with two more iterations of the forward-backward algorithm.

Since there are usually a large number of context-dependent models, many trained probabilities may be zeroes. In order to estimate the probabilities of the unobserved and rare symbols, we interpolate the context-dependent model parameters with the corresponding context-independent ones. We use *deleted interpolation* [8] to derive appropriate weights in the interpolation. Deleted interpolation weighs each distribution according to its ability to predict unseen data. These weights can be estimated using the forward-backward, by viewing the weights as transition probabilities. (See [8] and [17] for more details.)

The SPHINX training procedure is shown in Figure 3.

3.4 Recognition

Our recognition search is a time-synchronous Viterbi beam search [16] for the optimal state sequence. A beam threshold is determined *a priori*, and at a particular time, all states worse than the best state by more than that threshold are pruned. We also enhanced the Viterbi beam search with a word duration model when no grammar is used. The word duration model provides a word duration probability when the word is exited in the Viterbi beam search. This duration probability is combined with the acoustic probability.

Currently, SPHINX can recognize speech with

- no language model—each word HMM (concatenated from phone HMM's) can transition into all other words. It has a perplexity of 997.
- a word pair language model—A word can only transition to words that can legally follow it; every pair of adjacent words must be legal in the grammar. All successors are considered equally likely. This language model has a perplexity of 60.
- a bigram language model—Similar to word-pair, except a probability for each successor is estimated from the underlying finite state grammar. The bigram language model has a perplexity of 20.

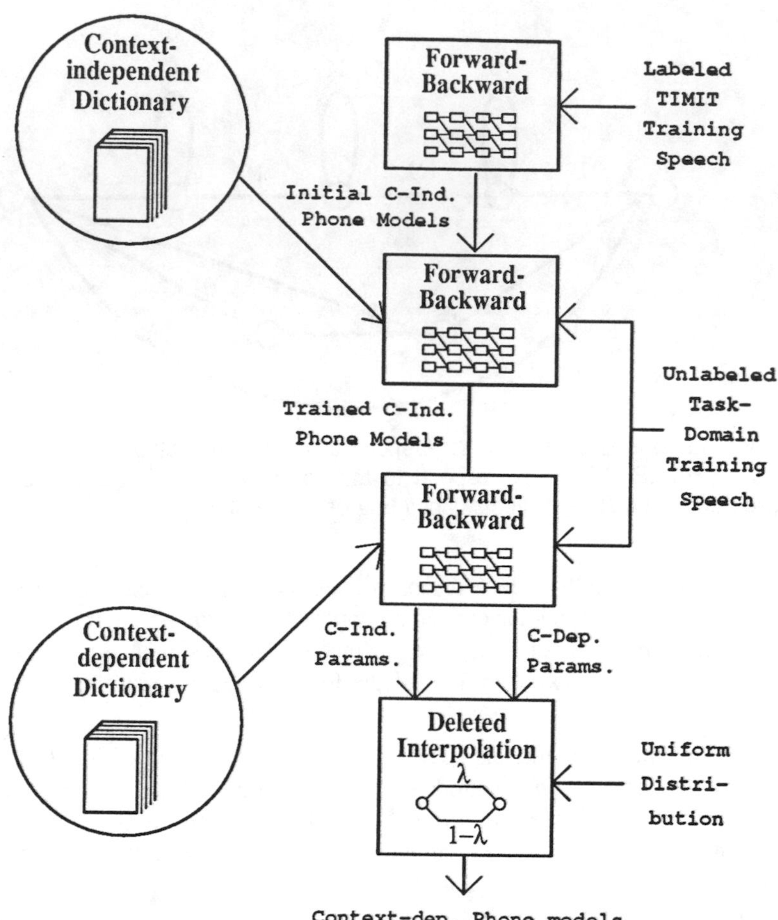

Figure 3: The SPHINX training procedure.

4 Results of Previously Proposed Subword Units

We applied various versions of SPHINX to the 997-word resource management task designated by DARPA [9]. All three grammars described in the previous sections were used. To determine the recognition accuracy, we first align the recognized word string against the correct word string using a string match algorithm supplied by the National Institute of Standards and Technology [29]. This alignment determines *WordsCorrect*, *Substitutions*, *Deletions*, *Insertions*. Finally, *WordAccuracy* is computed by:

$$Word\ Accuracy = 100 \cdot \frac{Correct\ Length - Subs - Dels - Ins}{Correct\ Length} \tag{1}$$

where *Correct Length* is the number of words in the correct sentence. Confusions between homonyms (such as *ship's* and *ships*, or *two* and *too*) are not counted for no language model, and are counted for the word pair and the bigram language model.

We used the 1987 DARPA speaker-independent test data for evaluation. This test data consists of 150 sentences, with 10 sentences spoken by each of 15 test speakers, who are not part of the training set. The same test set is used for all the results described in this paper.

The results with various context-dependent phonetic units are shown in Table 3. Left-context modeling of a phone considers two phones with the same identity to be different if their left-contexts are different. Left-context dependent phone parameters are interpolated with context-independent phone parameters and a uniform distribution. Right-context modeling is the same, except right contexts are used. The recognition rate improved substantially with the addition of left or right context, at the expense of 16 times as many models. Triphone context considers two phones with the same identity to be different when either the left or the right context is different. Similar to BBN's approach [1], triphone models are interpolated with left-context phone models, right-context phone models, context-independent models, and a uniform distribution. Triphone models led to significantly better results than left or right context models, which illustrates the importance of *both* left and right contexts.

Version	Models	No grammar	Word pair	Bigram
Context-independent	48	49.6%	84.4%	90.6%
Left-context	787	61.6%	89.0%	93.8%
Right-context	786	62.1%	89.3%	94.0%
Triphone-context	2381	69.9%	92.2%	95.1%

Table 3: Word accuracy results with context-independent and context-dependent phone modeling.

One difference between our approach and BBN's is that we use deleted interpolation to train the interpolation weights. Similar to other studies on triphones [1, 7], we have only considered intra-word triphones, and a special word-boundary marker is used as the context for the boundary phones. Inter-word triphones will be explored in the future.

5 Function-Word-Dependent Phone Models

Function words, such as *the, a, in, with,* are typically articles, prepositions, conjunctions, pronouns, and short verbs. These words are particularly problematic in continuous speech recognition. Waibel [30] found that in continuous speech only 14% of the function words are stressed, while 93% of the content words are stressed. These unstressed syllables are much harder to recognize [31, 32]. While function words are spoken clearly in isolated-word speech, they are articulated extremely poorly in continuous speech. The phones in function words are distorted in many ways. They may be shortened, omitted, or seriously affected by neighboring contexts. For example, Table 4 enumerates 50 phonetic transcription labels assigned by expert spectrogram readers for the word *the*. Many other function words have a large number of pronunciations. Since these effects are specific to the individual function words, explicit modeling of phones in these function words should lead to a much better representation.

/dh ax/	/dh ix/	/- dh ax/	/- dh ix/	/dh iy/
/ax/	/- dh iy/	/dh ah/	/ix/	/th ax/
/dh ih/	/- d ix/	/iy/	/th ix/	/- dh ah/
/th iy/	/- d ax/	/- d ih/	/- d iy/	/- dh ih/
/dh/	/- dh eh/	/d ix/	/dh ao/	/dh uh/
/dx ax/	/ih/	/- d ah/	/- dh ao/	/- dh uh/
/- t ah/	/- t ih/	/- th iy/	/ah/	/d ih/
/d iy/	/dh ax q/	/dh er/	/dh iy ih/	/dh iy n/
/dh m/	/dx ah/	/dx ih/	/dx ix/	/eh/
/nx ah/	/nx ey/	/nx ix/	/th eh/	/ux/

Table 4: 50 different ways *the* was pronounced, according to spectrogram readers.

Function words have caused considerable problems in SPHINX. Among the 684 errors in our system when no grammar was used, 334 were function word errors. Function words take up only 4% of the vocabulary, or about 30% if weighed by frequency, yet they are accountable for almost 50% of the errors.

In view of the above analysis, we propose a new speech unit: *function-word-dependent phones*. Function-word-dependent phones are the same as word-dependent phones, except they are used only for function words. This improves the modeling of the most difficult subset of words. Unlike word-dependent phones, function-word-dependent phones are easily trainable because function words occur frequently in any task. Finally, function-word-dependent phones can absorb multiple pronunciations, which are not explicitly modeled in SPHINX.

We selected a set of 42 function words, for which we felt there was significant word-dependent co-articulatory effects, as well as adequate training data. A few of these words are not usually considered function words, but are appropriate for this task. These function words are shown in Table 5.

A	ALL	AND	ANY	ARE	AT	BE
BEEN	BY	DID	FIND	FOR	FROM	GET
GIVE	HAS	HAVE	HOW	IN	IS	IT
LIST	MANY	MORE	OF	ON	ONE	OR
SHOW	THAN	THAT	THE	THEIR	TO	USE
WAS	WERE	WHAT	WHY	WILL	WITH	WOULD

Table 5: The list of 42 function words that SPHINX models separately.

Although function words are frequent, some distributions may still be under-trained, and some probabilities may have very small values. As with other context-dependent units, we use deleted interpolation to combine the function-word-dependent parameters with context-independent ones. Table 6 shows the phones in *are* and *be*, the counts for the distributions of each phone, and the λs for the function-word-dependent model parameters, phone model parameters, and uniform distribution. It can be seen that distributions (such as the last distribution of `/b/` and the first distribution of `/iy/` in *be*) are much more dependent on word context than their counts would have indicated.

Word	Phone	Dist.	Count	λ_{wdep}	λ_{indep}	$\lambda_{uniform}$
ARE	/aa/	Begin	2333	0.788	0.173	0.039
		Middle	2025	0.706	0.284	0.010
		End	1266	0.830	0.127	0.043
	/r/	Begin	1513	0.890	0.084	0.026
		Middle	1794	0.904	0.092	0.004
		End	2016	0.814	0.173	0.013
BE	/b/	Begin	176	0.207	0.786	0.007
		Middle	249	0.263	0.732	0.005
		End	243	0.705	0.295	0.000
	/iy/	Begin	222	0.636	0.358	0.006
		Middle	571	0.348	0.651	0.000
		End	329	0.337	0.659	0.004

Table 6: λs trained for phones in function words *be* and *are*. λ_{wdep} is the weight for the function-word-dependent distribution, λ_{indep} is the weight for the context-independent distribution, and $\lambda_{uniform}$ is the weight for uniform distribution.

Next, function-word-dependent phone models were used in conjunction with each of the context-dependent phone models. The results with and without function-word-dependent phone modeling are shown in Table 7. In each of the four cases, modeling function-word-dependent phones led to improvements. The improvement was the smallest for triphone contexts, because about half of the phones in function words have unique triphone contexts, which means triphone modeling was already doing function-word-dependent phone modeling for some of the function words. We expect that function-word-dependent phone models will significantly improve systems that do not have very detailed phone models, or systems with very large vocabularies, where phones in function words would not be uniquely specified by triphones.

Table 8 gives the number of errors (substitutions + deletions + insertions) made by SPHINX (context-independent models, no grammar) with and without the use of function-word-dependent phone models. With function-word-dependent phone modeling, function word errors are cut by 27%, which accounts for almost all of the improvement from 49.6% to 57.0% accuracy.

Version	Models	No grammar	Word pair	Bigram
Context-ind.	48	49.6%	84.4%	90.6%
CI+fnwd-dep.	153	57.0%	87.9%	93.0%
Left-context	787	61.6%	89.0%	93.8%
LC+fnwd-dep.	892	66.6%	91.1%	94.7%
Right-context	786	62.1%	89.3%	94.0%
RC+fnwd-dep.	891	67.2%	91.5%	94.7%
Triphone-context	2381	69.9%	92.2%	95.1%
TC+fnwd-dep	2447	69.9%	92.4%	95.2%

Table 7: Improvement from function-word-dependent phone modeling. Results shown are word-accuracy.

Model Type	Function Word Errors	Other Errors
Context-ind.	357	350
CI+fnwd-dep.	261	334

Table 8: Number of function word errors and non-function-word errors with and without function-word-dependent phone modeling. Context-independent models were used without grammar.

6 Generalized Triphones

In our evaluation of triphones, we argued that some phones have the same effect on neighboring phones. For example, the place of articulation has an important effect on the neighboring vowels. `/b/` and `/f/` have similar effects on the right-neighboring vowel, while `/r/` and `/w/` have similar effects on the right-neighboring vowel. Figure 4 illustrates this phenomenon. If we could identify these similar contexts, and merge them, we would have a much more manageable number of models, as well as much more training for each model.

One approach is to merge perceptually similar contexts together using human knowledge [33, 34]. This guarantees that the merged contexts are sensible ones; however, if we were to consider all triphones, this would be a complicated process. Moreover, while the example we gave is clear, there are many where there may be no consensus even among the experts. Therefore, we believe it is desirable to automate this process of context generalization.

We propose a context merging procedure to find and combine similar contexts:

1. Generate an HMM for every triphone context.
2. Create clusters of triphones, with each cluster consisting of one triphone initially.
3. Find the *most similar* pair of clusters that represents the same phone, and merge them together.
4. For each pair of clusters, consider moving every element from one to the other.
    1. Move the element if the resulting configuration is an improvement.
    2. Repeat until no such moves are left.
5. Until some convergence criterion is met, go to step 2.

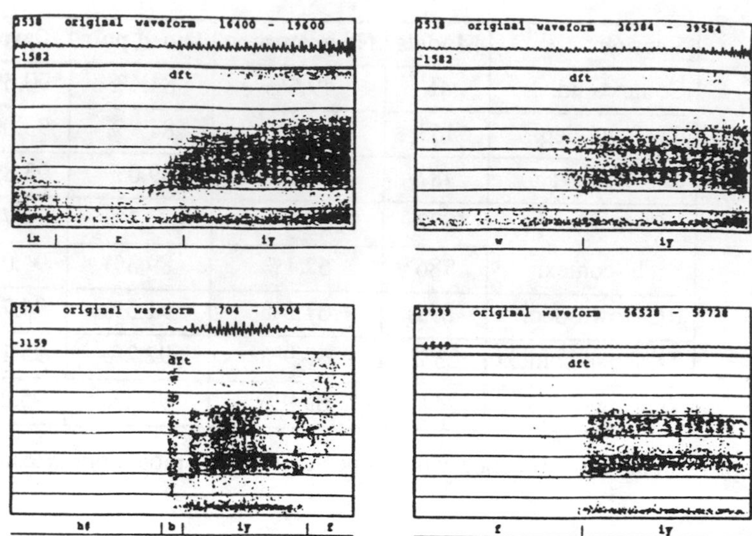

Figure 4: The waveforms and spectrograms for the phoneme /iy/ with four different *left-contexts* are illustrated. Note that /r/ and /w/ have similar effects on /iy/, while /b/ and /f/ have similar effects on /iy/. This illustrates that different left-contexts may have similar effects on a phone.

Without step 4, this is simply an agglomerate clustering procedure [35], where every merge cannot be undone. Step 4 is a heuristic optimization that attempts to improve the clustering by allowing elements to be moved from one cluster to another. Although it appears expensive, if we remember which clusters have changed, and which cluster-pairs need not be compared, step 4 only triples the total computation for our task.

Many criteria could be used to determine the similarity between two HMMs. Juang and Rabiner [36] proposed several similarity measures using cross entropy, divergence, and discrimination information. Paul and Martin [7] investigated merging of continuous HMMs using a chi-square measure. Finally, D'Orta *et al.* [37] proposed several measures, including output string/symbol probability, and maximum mutual information.

In this study, we use an information theoretic measure that determines the similarity between two HMMs based on the amount of information lost when the two models are merged. We use entropy of the original and merged HMMs to measure the information lost, and forward-backward counts to weigh the information lost. Entropy clustering has been used by Lucassen and Mercer [38] to derive word baseforms from spelling, and by Brown [28] to merge similar VQ codewords.

In order to minimize the amount of computation, we define the entropy of an HMM as the bits of information in the output pdf's. Let:

$N_{a,d}(i)$ be the count for codeword i in distribution d of context a of a phone as determined by the forward-backward algorithm.

$$N_{a,d} = \sum_i N_{a,d}(i) \tag{2}$$

These counts can be normalized into output probabilities:

$$P_{a,d}(i) = \frac{N_{a,d}(i)}{N_{a,d}} \tag{3}$$

The entropy of an output pdf for distribution d for some phone in context a is defined as:

$$H_{a,d} = -\sum_i P_{a,d}(i) \cdot \log\left(P_{a,d}(i)\right) \tag{4}$$

If we want to merge distribution d of two models that represent the same phone in context a and b into a merged model in context m, the new counts for distribution d in context m are simply:

$$N_{m,d}(i)=N_{a,d}(i)+N_{b,d}(i) \tag{5}$$

We can compute $H_{b,d}$ and $H_{m,d}$ as we computed $H_{a,d}$. The information lost when a distribution d for context a and b are merged into m, weighted by counts, is:

$$L_d(a,b) = N_{m,d}\, H_{m,d} - N_{a,d}\, H_{a,d} - N_{b,d}\, H_{b,d} \tag{6}$$

Finally, the information lost when two HMMs for context a and b are merged, weighted by counts, is:

$$L(a,b) = \sum_{d'} L_{d'}(a,b) \tag{7}$$

Equation 7 is the distance metric used in our triphone clustering algorithm. This distance metric weighs the difference between models according to the frequency of the models. By preferring to merge models that do not appear frequently, each generalized model will be more trainable.

For an alternate view of the distance metric, we transform Equation 6 into:

$$L_d(a,b) = N_{m,d}\, H_{m,d} - N_{a,d}\, H_{a,d} - N_{b,d}\, H_{b,d}$$

$$= -N_{m,d} \sum_i P_{m,d}(i) \cdot \log P_{m,d}(i) + N_{a,d} \sum_i P_{a,d}(i) \cdot \log P_{a,d}(i) + N_{b,d} \sum_i P_{b,d}(i) \cdot \log P_{b,d}(i)$$

$$= -\sum_i N_{m,d}(i) \cdot \log P_{m,d}(i) + \sum_i N_{a,d}(i) \cdot \log P_{a,d}(i) + \sum_i N_{b,d}(i) \cdot \log P_{b,d}(i)$$

$$= -\log\left(\prod_i (P_{m,d}(i))^{N_{m,d}(i)}\right) + \log\left(\prod_i (P_{a,d}(i))^{N_{a,d}(i)}\right) + \log\left(\prod_i (P_{b,d}(i))^{N_{b,d}(i)}\right)$$

$$= \log\left(\frac{\left(\prod_i (P_{a,d}(i))^{N_{a,d}(i)}\right) \cdot \left(\prod_i (P_{b,d}(i))^{N_{b,d}(i)}\right)}{\prod_i (P_{m,d}(i))^{N_{m,d}(i)}}\right) \tag{8}$$

Equation 8 shows that the "weighted loss of information" measure is equivalent to the logarithm of the ratio between the probability that the individual distributions generated the training data and the probability that the combined distribution generated the training data. Thus, this ratio maximizes the objective function:

$$\prod_{\forall d} \prod_i (P_{m,d}(i))^{N_{m,d}(i)} \tag{9}$$

which is consistent with the maximum-likelihood criterion used in the forward-backward algorithm.

This context generalization algorithm provides a means for finding the equilibrium between trainability and specificity. Armed with this technique, we could empirically find the "right" number of models for any given amount of training data.

Table 9 shows the 19 clusters created for the phone /ae/ when the clustering process has reduced 2381 triphones to 500 triphone clusters. Most clusters consist of triphones that are easily identified as similar contexts.

Results for generalized triphone modeling are shown in Table 10. We ran the information-theoretic agglomerate clustering algorithm from 2381 triphones, and saved the clusters for every 100 merges. We then trained and tested on 10 different sets of generalized triphones, with 100, 200, 300, 400, 500, 600, 800, 1000, 1200, and 1400 models. We also included results with 48 HMMs (phone models, complete generalization), and 2381 HMMs (triphone models, no generalization). In each case, the performance is superior to earlier context-dependent results that employed a comparable number of models. For example, with only 100-200 models generalized triphones performed as well as 700-800 left or right context dependent phones. Generalized triphone models also outperformed full triphone models, in spite of the fact that full triphone models were interpolated with three other types of models, while generalized triphone models were only interpolated with one. These results demonstrate the importance of modeling the left *and* right contexts. They also demonstrate that generalized triphones can improve the accuracy, while substantially reducing the memory requirements.

Table 10 illustrates that the performance of the system improved with more models until there were too many

```
[ 1] (dh,td)
[ 2] (hh,v) (hh,td)
[ 3] (hh,z) (p,s)
[ 4] (k,l) (g,l) (#,p)
[ 5] (k,sh) (k,dx)
[ 6] (l,n) (l,m)
[ 7] (l,ch) (l,sh) (l,ts) (l,td) (l,dx) (l,s)
[ 8] (m,k) (m,kd) (s,k)
[ 9] (p,kd) (p,k) (t,k)
[10] (k,n) (k,m) (k,r) (z,m) (ch,n) (s,m)
[11] (r,th) (r,s) (r,f) (r,kd) (r,k)
[12] (#,dx) (#,dd) (hh,dd) (b,jh) (b,dd)
[13] (#,l) (#,f) (#,b) (b,sh) (m,dx) (n,sh) (hh,f)
[14] (#,ae) (ay,m) (jh,n) (iy,kd) (y,ng) (d,g) (jh,k) (r,dd)
[15] (#,td) (#,s)
[16] (#,v) (#,r)
[17] (v,l)
[18] (s,dx) (d,dx) (f,s) (b,s) (k,td) (ch,dx) (s,s) (t,s)
 (k,z) (sh,s) (g,s) (k,s) (k,t) (k,th)
[19] (z,n) (s,n) (v,n) (#,ng) (b,ng) (m,n) (f,n) (p,n)
 (r,n) (r,m) (er,m)
```

Table 9: 19 clusters created for the (left, right) contexts for phone /ae/; # represents word-boundary context.

Number of gen. models	No grammar	Word pair	Bigram
48	49.6%	84.4%	90.6%
100	60.9%	89.1%	94.0%
200	66.4%	91.0%	94.2%
300	66.2%	91.1%	94.1%
400	67.9%	91.8%	94.3%
500	69.6%	92.0%	95.1%
600	70.0%	92.4%	95.1%
800	70.3%	92.9%	95.1%
1000	70.3%	93.3%	95.4%
1200	70.0%	93.0%	95.3%
1400	69.7%	92.7%	95.2%
2381	69.9%	92.2%	95.1%

Table 10: Results of generalized triphone modeling without function word modeling. Results shown are word accuracy.

models to train adequately. At 1000 models, an equilibrium between trainability and specificity was reached, given the amount of training. We believe the performance can be improved with more models and more training.

We performed an experiment where we reduced the number of speakers used in the training, and observed the effect of that on the optimal number of generalized triphones. Figure 5 illustrates that as we reduced the amount of training, the best number of generalized triphones decreased, because fewer models can be adequately trained. This further justified the use of generalization to find an equilibrium between trainability and specificity.

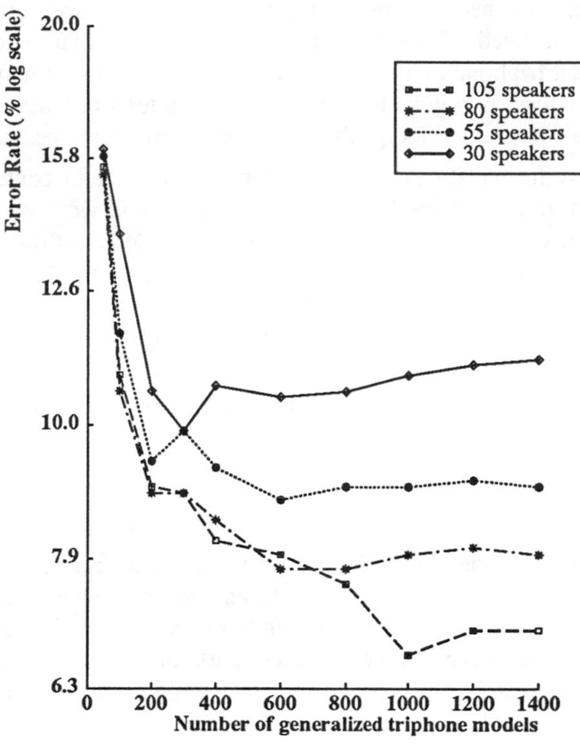

Figure 5: Results with the word-pair grammar as a function of the number of generalized triphone models and the number of training speakers.

Finally, we added function-word-dependent phone modeling to triphone clustering, and ran an experiment with 1000 generalized triphone models plus 153 function-word-dependent phone models. Since some of the function-word-dependent phones are uniquely specified by the generalized triphones, there are a total of 1076 models. The results with these 1076 models are shown in Table 11.

Version	Models	No grammar	Word pair	Bigram
Gen. Triphones	1000	70.3%	93.3%	95.4%
Gen. Triphones +fnwd-dep.	1076	70.6%	93.7%	95.8%

Table 11: Results with generalized triphone modeling plus function word modeling. Results shown are word-accuracy.

7 Future Work

There are many interesting areas of continuing research in context-dependent phone modeling. We believe that these research areas will improve our results considerably.

The triphone-based models used in SPHINX and other systems stop at word boundaries. In other words, the leftmost phone of each word has no known left context, and the rightmost phone of each word has no known right context. Yet, phonetic context beyond the word boundary clearly affects the realization of these word-boundary triphones. This suggests that modeling inter-word triphones should lead to superior results. We have recently implemented between-word triphone models, and preliminary results indicate that the error rate can be further reduced by about 20%. Details of this work will appear in [39, 40].

Another research area is the extension from *generalized triphones* to *generalized allophones*. The use of generalization from specific units need not be limited to triphones. As we obtain more training data, triphone models will be trainable without the need of generalization. However, at that time we believe it will be unwise to be complacent with well-trained triphone models. Instead, we should consider additional sources for phonetic variability, such as syllable position, stress, non-neighboring phones, or inter-word triphones [41]. The context generalization technique we described could be used to merge these more detailed allophones into generalized allophones.

Finally, we would like to investigate the vocabulary-dependence of context-dependent models. In other words, how well context-dependent models trained from one vocabulary will work on another vocabulary. Our initial results indicate serious performance degradation from training on a considerably different vocabulary. We believe that this is due to inadequate test set triphone coverage in the training set. Our approach to dealing with this problem is to train context-dependent models from a large database of "general English", and then apply them to specific tasks. We are currently collecting such a database for this experiment. We hope that the availability of a large database and more detailed generalized allophone models can compensate for the lack of vocabulary-specific training. If successful, this would enable speaker-independent speech recognition *without vocabulary-specific training*.

8 Conclusion

Speech production is a complex process, where the acoustic realization of different parts of a sentence are correlated and inter-dependent. Thus, the only way to ensure preservation of all the information is to model every possible sentence. Since there are an astronomical number of sentences, it is necessary to use concatenated words as sentences. Similarly, the acoustic realization of different parts of a word are highly inter-dependent, and there are still too many words to train adequately with the current technology and databases. Therefore, it is necessary to use concatenated subword units as words.

Because most inter-dependencies are local, using larger units would capture most of the important effects; however, as the units grow in size, they also grow in number, which causes trainability problems. Using smaller units, on the other hand, sacrifices important information by combining many different effects into one representation.

Context-dependent phonetic units are a compromise between specificity and trainability. By modeling context-dependent effects at the phone level, these units achieve the specificity needed to make fine phonetic distinctions. Yet, because they are phonetic units, they can be interpolated with context-independent phones for trainability. The most popular forms of context-dependent phone modeling have been triphones, which take into consideration the immediate left and right contexts of a phone.

In this work, we have shown the feasibility of context-dependent phone modeling to speaker-*independent* recognition. We have also proposed two new context-dependent units. The first unit is the function-word-dependent phone, which explicitly models phonetic events in the poorly articulated but frequent function words. This improves the discriminability of these function words. The other unit is the generalized triphone, which combines similar triphones together to improve trainability of the models. An information theoretic distance metric was used to cluster the models. This metric was shown to be consistent with the maximum likelihood criterion. Thus, this technique enables us to find a set of models that is as consistent and trainable as possible, given a fixed amount of training data.

Both function-word-dependent phone modeling and generalized triphone modeling improved recognition accuracy substantially from context-independent phone modeling. In particular, function-word-dependent phone modeling recovered a large number of function word errors. Generalized triphone models also led to higher recognition accuracies than triphone models, while saving 60% memory. We believe context-dependent phonetic modeling have potential for further improvements. Our future work will involve extending context-dependent phonetic models for between-word coarticulation modeling, generalized allophone modeling, and vocabulary-independent modeling.

Acknowledgments

The author wishes to thank Hsiao-Wuen Hon, Mei-Yuh Hwang, Raj Reddy, Peter Brown, and Richard Schwartz for their help and discussions.

References

1. Schwartz, R., Chow, Y., Kimball, O., Roucos, S., Krasner, M., Makhoul, J., "Context-Dependent Modeling for Acoustic-Phonetic Recognition of Continuous Speech", *IEEE International Conference on Acoustics, Speech, and Signal Processing*, April 1985.

2. Lippmann, R.P., Martin, E.A., Paul, D.P., "Multi-Style Training for Robust Isolated-Word Speech Recognition", *IEEE International Conference on Acoustics, Speech, and Signal Processing*, April 1987, pp. 705-8.

3. Rabiner, L.R., Wilpon, J.G., Soong, F.K., "High Performance Connected Digit Recognition Using Hidden Markov Models", *IEEE International Conference on Acoustics, Speech, and Signal Processing*, April 1988.

4. Bahl, L. R., Bakis, R., Cohen, P. S., Cole, A. G., Jelinek, F., Lewis, B. L., Mercer, R. L., "Further Results on the Recognition of a Continuously Read Natural Corpus", *IEEE International Conference on Acoustics, Speech, and Signal Processing*, April 1980.

5. Schwartz, R. M., Chow, Y. L., Roucos, S., Krasner, M., Makhoul, J., "Improved Hidden Markov Modeling of Phonemes for Continuous Speech Recognition", *IEEE International Conference on Acoustics, Speech, and Signal Processing*, April 1984.

6. Lee, K.F., Hon, H.W., "Large-Vocabulary Speaker-Independent Continuous Speech Recognition", *IEEE International Conference on Acoustics, Speech, and Signal Processing*, April 1988.

7. Paul, D.B., Martin, E.A., "Speaker Stress-Resistant Continuous Speech Recognition", *IEEE International Conference on Acoustics, Speech, and Signal Processing*, April 1988.

8. Jelinek, F., Mercer, R.L., "Interpolated Estimation of Markov Source Parameters from Sparse Data", in *Pattern Recognition in Practice*, E.S. Gelsema and L.N. Kanal, ed., North-Holland Publishing Company, Amsterdam, the Netherlands, 1980, pp. 381-397.

9. Price, P.J., Fisher, W., Bernstein, J., Pallett, D., "A Database for Continuous Speech Recognition in a 1000-Word Domain", *IEEE International Conference on Acoustics, Speech, and Signal Processing*, April 1988.

10. Bahl. L.R., Brown, P.F., De Souza, P.V., Mercer, R.L., "Acoustic Markov Models Used in the Tangora Speech Recognition System", *IEEE International Conference on Acoustics, Speech, and Signal Processing*, April 1988.

11. Hunt, M. J., Lennig, M., Mermelstein, P., "Experiments in Syllable-Based Recognition of Continuous Speech", *IEEE International Conference on Acoustics, Speech, and Signal Processing*, April 1980, pp. 880-883.

12. Rosenberg, A. E., Rabiner, L. R., Wilpon, J., Kahn, D., "Demisyllable-Based Isolated Word Recognition System", *IEEE Transactions on Acoustics, Speech, and Signal Processing*, Vol. ASSP-31, No. 3, June 1983, pp. 713-726.

13. Schwartz, R., Klovstad, J., Makhoul, J., Sorensen, J., "A Preliminary Design of a Phonetic Vocoder Based on a Diphone Model", *IEEE International Conference on Acoustics, Speech, and Signal Processing*, April 1980, pp. 32-35.

14. Klatt, D., "Problem of Variability in Speech Recognition and in Models of Speech Perception", in *Variability and Invariance in Speech Processes*, J.S. Perkell and D.M. Klatt, ed., Lawrence Erlbaum Assoc, Hillsdale, N.J., 1986, pp. 300-320.

15. Cravero, M, Pieraccini, R., Raineri, F., "Definition and Evaluation of Phonetic Units for Speech Recognition by Hidden Markov Models", *IEEE International Conference on Acoustics, Speech, and Signal Processing*, April 1986.

16. Chow, Y. L., Schwartz, R., Roucos, S., Kimball, O., Price, P., Kubala, F., Dunham, M., Krasner, M., Makhoul, J., "The Role of Word-Dependent Coarticulatory Effects in a Phoneme-Based Speech Recognition System", *IEEE International Conference on Acoustics, Speech, and Signal Processing*, April 1986.

17. Lee, K.F., *Large-Vocabulary Speaker-Independent Continuous Speech Recognition: The SPHINX System*, PhD dissertation, Computer Science Department, Carnegie Mellon University, April 1988.

18. Lee, K.F., *Automatic Speech Recognition: The Development of the SPHINX System*, Kluwer Academic Publishers, Boston, 1989.

19. Markel, J. D., Gray, A. H., *Linear Prediction of Speech*, Springer-Verlag, Berlin, 1976.

20. Shikano, K, "Evaluation of LPC Spectral Matching Measures for Phonetic Unit Recognition", Tech. report, Computer Science Department, Carnegie Mellon University, May 1985.

21. Furui, S., "Speaker-Independent Isolated Word Recognition Using Dynamic Features of Speech Spectrum", *IEEE Transactions on Acoustics, Speech, and Signal Processing*, Vol. ASSP-34, No. 1, February 1986, pp. 52-59.

22. Lee, K.F., Hon, H.W., "Speaker-Independent Phoneme Recognition Using Hidden Markov Models", Tech. report CMU-CS-88-121, Computer Science Department, Carnegie Mellon University, April 1988.

23. Gupta, V.N., Lennig, M., Mermelstein, P., "Integration of Acoustic Information in a Large Vocabulary Word Recognizer", *IEEE International Conference on Acoustics, Speech, and Signal Processing*, April 1987, pp. 697-700.

24. Baker, J. K., "The DRAGON System -- An Overview", *IEEE Transactions on Acoustics, Speech, and Signal Processing*, Vol. ASSP-23, No. 1, February 1975, pp. 24-29.

25. Jelinek, F., "Continuous Speech Recognition by Statistical Methods", *Proceedings of the IEEE*, Vol. 64, No. 4, April 1976, pp. 532-556.

26. Bahl, L. R., Jelinek, F., Mercer, R., "A Maximum Likelihood Approach to Continuous Speech Recognition", *IEEE Transactions on Pattern Analysis and Machine Intelligence*, Vol. PAMI-5, No. 2, March 1983, pp. 179-190.

27. Baum, L. E., "An Inequality and Associated Maximization Technique in Statistical Estimation of Probabilistic Functions of Markov Processes", *Inequalities*, Vol. 3, 1972, pp. 1-8.

28. Brown, P., *The Acoustic-Modeling Problem in Automatic Speech Recognition*, PhD dissertation, Computer Science Department, Carnegie Mellon University, May 1987.

29. Pallett, D., "Test Procedures for the March 1987 DARPA Benchmark Tests", *DARPA Speech Recognition Workshop*, March 1987, pp. 75-78.

30. Waibel, A. H., *Prosody and Speech Recognition*, PhD dissertation, Computer Science Department, Carnegie Mellon University, October 1986.

31. Klatt, D.H., Stevens, K.N., "Sentence Recognition from Visual Examination of Spectrograms and Machine-Aided Lexical Searching", *Proceedings 1972 Conference on Speech Communication and Processing*, IEEE and AFCRL, 1972, pp. 315-318.

32. Lea, W.A., *Trends in Speech Recognition*, Prentice-Hall, Englewood Cliffs, NJ, 1980.

33. Derouault, A.-M., "Context-Dependent Phonetic Markov Models for Large Vocabulary Speech Recognition", *IEEE International Conference on Acoustics, Speech, and Signal Processing*, April 1987, pp. 360-3.

34. Deng, L, Lennig, M., Gupta, V.N., Mermelstein, P., "Modeling Acoustic-Phonetic Detail in an HMM-based Large Vocabulary Speech Recognizer", *IEEE International Conference on Acoustics, Speech, and Signal Processing*, April 1988, pp. 509-512.

35. Duda, R. O., Hart, P. E., *Pattern Classification and Scene Analysis*, John Wiley & Sons, New York, N.Y., 1973.

36. Juang, B.H., Rabiner, L.R., "A Probabilistic Distance Measure for Hidden Markov Models", *The Bell System Technical Journal*, Vol. 64, No. 2, February 1985, pp. 391-408.

37. D'Orta, P, Ferretti, M., Scarci, S., "Phoneme Classification for Real Time Speech Recognition of Italian", *IEEE International Conference on Acoustics, Speech, and Signal Processing*, April 1987, pp. 81-84.

38. Lucassen, J.M., Mercer, R.L., "An Information Theoretic Approach to the Automatic Determination of Phonemic Baseforms", *IEEE International Conference on Acoustics, Speech, and Signal Processing*, 1984.

39. Hwang, M.Y., Hon, H.W., Lee, K.F., "Between-Word Coarticulation Modeling for Continuous Speech Recognition", Technical Report, Carnegie Mellon University, April 1989.

40. Hwang, M.Y., Hon, H.W., Lee, K.F., "Modeling Between-Word Coarticulation in Continuous Speech Recognition", *Proceedings of Eurospeech*, September 1989.

41. Chen, F., Stern, P.E., ''Contextual Variability in Speech Classification'', *IEEE Workshop on Speech Recognition*, June 1988.

A Stochastic Segment Model for Phoneme-Based Continuous Speech Recognition

S. Roucos and M. O. Dunham

BBN Laboratories Incorporated
Cambridge, MA 02238

Abstract -- Developing accurate and robust phonetic models for the different speech sounds is a major challenge for high performance continuous speech recognition. In this paper, we introduce a new approach, called the stochastic segment model, for modelling a variable-length phonetic segment X, an L-long sequence of feature vectors. The stochastic segment model consists of 1) time-warping the variable-length segment X into a fixed-length segment Y called a resampled segment, and 2) a joint density function of the parameters of the resampled segment Y, which in this work is assumed Gaussian. In this paper, we describe the stochastic segment model, the recognition algorithm, and the iterative training algorithm for estimating segment models from continuous speech. For speaker-dependent continuous speech recognition, the segment model reduces the word error rate by one third over a hidden Markov phonetic model.

1. Introduction

In large vocabulary speech recognition, a word is frequently modelled as a network of phonetic models. That is, the word is modelled acoustically by concatenating phonetic acoustic models according to a pronunciation network stored in a dictionary of phonetic spellings. In phoneme-based speech recognition systems, it is not necessary for the speaker to train all words in the vocabulary; only the phonetic models are trained. Assuming the above structure for a speech recognition system, the goal of this work is to look for an improved approach to phonetic modelling.

Hidden Markov modelling (HMM) is one method for probabilistic modelling of the acoustic realization of a phoneme. Although the HMM approach has been used successfully [1, 2, 3], its recognition performance is not sufficiently accurate for large vocabulary continuous speech recognition. We propose an alternative and novel approach, called a stochastic segment model, with the goal of improving phonetic modelling. The motivation for looking at speech on a segmental level, rather than on a frame-by-frame basis as in HMM or dynamic time warping (DTW), is that we can better capture the spectral/temporal relationship over the duration of a phoneme. Evidence of the importance of spectral correlation over the duration of a segment can be found in the success of segment-based vocoding systems [4].

A speech "segment" is a variable-length sequence of feature vectors, where the features might be, for example, cepstral coefficients. The stochastic segment model is defined on a fixed-length representation of the observed segment, which is obtained by a time-warping (or resampling) transformation. The stochastic segment model is a multivariate Gaussian density function for the resampled representation of a segment. The recognition algorithm chooses the phoneme sequence that maximizes a match score on the resampled segments. The training algorithm iterates between two steps: first, the maximum probability phonetic segmentation of the input speech is obtained, then maximum likelihood density estimates of the segment models are derived.

The paper is organized as follows. Section 2 introduces the segment model. Section 3 describes the segment-based recognition algorithm, and Section 4 describes the training algorithm. Section 5 presents experimental results for phoneme and word recognition, comparing the results to HMM recognition results for the same tasks. Finally, Section 6 contains a brief summary.

2. Stochastic Segment Model

In this section, we define the stochastic segment model for an observed sequence of speech frames $X = [x_1\, x_2 \ldots x_L]$, where x_i is a k-dimensional feature vector. We can think of this observation as a variable-length realization of an underlying fixed-length spectral trajectory $Y = [y_1\, y_2 \ldots y_m]$ where the duration of X is variable due to variation in speaking rate. Given X, we define the fixed-length representation $Y = XT_L$ where the L x m matrix T_L, called the resampling transformation, represents a time-warping. The segment Y, called a *resampled* segment, is an m-long sequence of k-dimensional vectors (or a k x m matrix). The stochastic segment model for each phoneme α is based on the resampled segment Y and is a conditional probability density function $p(Y|\alpha)$. The density $p(Y|\alpha)$ is assumed to be multivariate Gaussian which is a km-dimensional model for the entire fixed-length segment Y.

Resampling Transformations

The resampling transformation T_L is an L x m matrix used to transform an L-length observed segment X into an m-length resampled segment Y. We considered several different variable- to fixed-length transformations, concentrating on transformations which had previously been evaluated in the segment vocoder [4]. The best recognition results are obtained using linear time sampling without interpolation. Linear time sampling involves choosing m uniformly spaced times at which

CH2396-0/87/0000-0073 $1.00

to sample the segment trajectory. Sampling without interpolation refers to choosing the nearest observation in time to the sample point, rather than interpolating to find a value at the sample point.

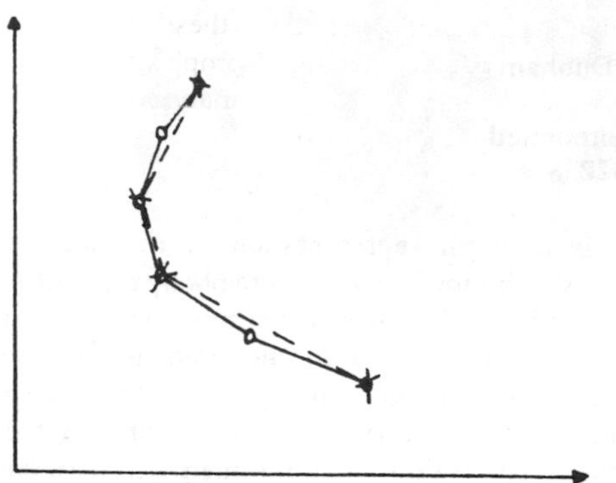

Figure 1: Input segment (o) and corresponding resampled segment (x). The two axes correspond to two cepstral coefficients.

Figure 1 shows an input segment with duration six in two-dimensional space and the corresponding resampled Y (with m = 4) using linear time warping without interpolation. The resampling transformation in this case is:

$$T = \begin{bmatrix} 1 & 0 & 0 & 0 \\ 0 & 0 & 0 & 0 \\ 0 & 1 & 0 & 0 \\ 0 & 0 & 1 & 0 \\ 0 & 0 & 0 & 0 \\ 0 & 0 & 0 & 1 \end{bmatrix}$$

Probabilistic Model

As already mentioned, the segment model is a multivariate Gaussian based on the resampled segment **Y**, $p(\mathbf{Y}|\alpha)$. Recall that resampled segments are *km*-dimensional, where *k* is the number of spectral features per sample and *m* is the number of samples. In this work, typically *k*=14 and *m*=10. Consequently, the segment model has 140 dimensions. Because of insufficient training, we cannot estimate the full phoneme-dependent covariance matrix, so we must make some simplifying assumptions about the structure of the problem. For the experiments reported here, we assume that the *m* samples of the resampled segment are independent of each other, which gives a block diagonal covariance structure for **Y**, where each block in the segment covariance matrix corresponds to the *k x k* covariance of a sample. The log of the conditional probability of a segment **Y** given phoneme α can then be expressed as

$$ln[p(\mathbf{Y}|\alpha)] = \sum_{j=1}^{m} ln[p_j(y_j|\alpha)], \qquad (1)$$

where $p_j(y_j|\alpha)$ is a k-dimensional multivariate Gaussian model for the j-th sample in the segment. The block-diagonal structure saves a factor of *m* in storage and a factor of m^2 in computation. The disadvantage of this approach is that the assumption of independence is not valid, particularly if resampling does not use interpolation where adjacent samples may be identical. In the future, with more training data, we hope to relax this assumption. It is likely that more detailed probabilistic models, such as Gaussian mixture models [5] and context-dependent (conditional) models [2, 3], will yield better recognition results than the simple Gaussian model. However, due to larger training requirements we did not pursue these models in this work.

Properties of the Segment Model

There are several aspects of the stochastic segment model which are useful properties for a speech recognition system. First, the transformation T_L, which maps the variable-length observation to a fixed-length segment, can be designed to constrain the temporal structure of a phoneme model so that all portions of the model are used in the recognition. We conjecture that the fixed transformation will provide a better model of phoneme temporal/spectral structure than either HMM or DTW. Second, the segment model is a joint representation of the phoneme, so the model can capture correlation structure on a segmental level. In HMM, frames are assumed independent given the state sequence. In the segment model, no assumptions of independence are *necessary*, though the model of Y given by Equation 1 is based on the assumption of sample independence because of limited training data in this study. The model is potentially more general than the special case of (1). Lastly, by using a segment model we can compute segment level features for phoneme recognition. In other words, the segment model provides a good structure for incorporating acoustic-phonetic features in a statistical (rather than rule-based) recognition system. For example, one might want to measure and incorporate formant frequency or energy differences over a segment. Section 5 includes results where sample duration is used as a feature, which can only be computed given the length of the entire segment.

3. Recognition Algorithm

In this section, we describe the recognition algorithm. First, we describeconsider the case when the input is phonetically hand-segmented. Then, we generalize to automatic recognition, that is, joint segmentation and recognition of continuous speech.

When the segmentation of the input is known, we consider a single segment X independently of neighboring segments. The input segment X is resampled as segment Y. The recognition algorithm is then to find the phoneme $\hat{\alpha}$ that maximizes $p(\mathbf{Y}|\alpha)$:

$$\hat{\alpha} = arg \max_{\alpha} ln[p(\mathbf{Y}|\alpha)p(\alpha)] \qquad (2)$$

where $\ln[p(\mathbf{Y}|\alpha)]$ is given by Equation 1. This decision rule is equivalent to a maximum a-posteriori rule.

In an automatic recognition system, it is necessary to find the segmentation as well as to recognize the phonemes. In this case, we hypothesize all possible segmentations of the input, and for each hypothesized segmentation $\underline{s}$ of the input into n segments, we choose the sequence of phonemes $\underline{\hat{\alpha}}$ that maximizes:

$$J(\underline{s}) = \sum_{i=1}^{n} \{ L(i)\, ln[p(Y_i|\hat{\alpha}_i)p(\hat{\alpha}_i] + C \} \quad (3)$$

where L(i) is the duration of the i-th segment, Y_i is the resampled segment corresponding to the i-th segment in $\underline{s}$, and $\hat{\alpha}_i$ is the phoneme that maximizes $p(Y_i|\alpha)p(\alpha)$. The cost C is adjusted to control the segment rate. An efficient solution to joint segmentation and recognition is implemented using a dynamic programming algorithm. Note that for joint segmentation and recognition, it is necessary to weight the segment probability by the duration of the segment, so that longer segments contribute proportionately higher scores to the match score J(.) of the whole sequence.

4. Training Algorithm

In this section, we present the training algorithm for estimating the segment models from continuous speech. We assume that the phonetic transcription of the training data is known and that we have an initial Gaussian model, $p_0(Y|\alpha)$ for all phonemes. (Phonetic transcriptions can be generated automatically from the word sequence that corresponds to the speech by using a word pronunciation dictionary.) We assume that the phonetic sequence $\underline{\alpha}$ has length n. The algorithm comprises two steps: automatic segmentation and parameter estimation. The algorithm maximizes the log likelihood of the optimal segmentation for the phonetic transcription, where the log likelihood of a segmentation $\underline{s}$ is given by:

$$l(\underline{s}) = \sum_{i=1}^{N} ln[p(Y_i|\alpha_i)p(\alpha_i)] \quad (4)$$

where Y_i is the resampled segment that corresponds to the i-th segment in the segmentation $\underline{s}$ and α_i is the i-th phoneme in the sequence $\underline{\alpha}$. With t = 0, the iterative algorithm is given by:

1. Find the segmentation $\underline{s}_t$ of the training data that maximizes $l(\underline{s}_t)$ for the given transcription and the current probability densities $\{p_t(Y|\alpha)\}$.
2. Find the maximum likelihood estimate for the densities $\{p_{t+1}(Y|\alpha)\}$ of all phonemes, using the segmentation $\underline{s}_t$.
3. t <- t + 1 and go to Step 1

Both steps of the algorithm are guaranteed to increase $l(\underline{s}_t)$ with t. If there are at least two *different* observations of every phoneme, then the probability of the sequence is bounded. Hence, the iterative training algorithm converges to a local optimum. Step 1 is implemented as a dynamic programming search whose complexity is linear with the number of phonetic models N. Step 2 is the usual sample mean and sample covariance maximum likelihood estimates for Gaussian densities.

5. Experimental Results

In this section we will present results for a phoneme recognition task, as well as word recognition results for a segment-based recognition system and an HMM-based system. All experiments use $m = 10$ samples per segment and $k = 14$ mel-frequency cepstral coefficients per sample. These values are based on work in segment quantization [6], and limited experimentation confirmed that these values represent a reasonable compromise between complexity and performance. Speech is sampled at 20 kHz, and analyzed every 10 ms with a 20 ms Hamming window.

Phoneme Recognition

The database used for phoneme recognition is approximately five minutes of continuous speech from a single speaker. The test set contains 270 phonemes. Both the test set and the training set are hand-labelled and segmented, using a 61 symbol phonetic alphabet. In counting errors, an 'AX' (schwa) recognized as 'IX' (fronted schwa) is considered acceptably correct, as is an 'URT' (unreleased T) recognized as a 'T'. All recognition rates presented represent "acceptably correct" recognition rates. The acceptable recognition rate is typically 6% to 8% higher than the strictly correct recognition rate.

Phoneme recognition results for three different cases are given in Table 1. The results illustrate a small degradation in performance due to moving from recognition based on manually segmented data to automatic recognition. Using automatic training does not degrade performance any further.

We also experimented with using an additional segmental feature to the cepstral parameters: sample duration which requires knowledge of the hypothesized duration of the segment. Using joint segmentation and recognition with hand-segmented training data, performance improved from 74.4% to 75.9% as a result of using the duration feature.

Training Segmentation	Test Segmentation	% Recognition	% Insertion
Manual	Manual	78.5	0.0
Manual	Automatic	74.4	10.0
Automatic	Automatic	73.7	7.8

Table 1: Recognition results using manually segmented speech and automatically segmented speech.

For reference, a discrete hidden Markov model with 3 states/phoneme and using a codebook with 256 entries has 62% phonetic recognition rate with 12% insertions. The HMM recognition performance on this database is higher when phoneme models are conditioned on left context, 75% correct with 12% insertions [2]. In the latter case, 600 left-context phonetic models are used in the HMM system while 61 phonetic models are used in the stochastic segment model.

Word Recognition

The segment-based word recognition system consists of a dictionary of phoneme pronunciation networks and a collection of segment phoneme models. A word model is built by concatenating phoneme models according to the pronunciation network. The recognition algorithm is simply a dynamic programming search (Viterbi decoding) of all possible word sequences. For the results in this paper, we assume that words are independent and equally probable; there is no grammar (statistical or deterministic) associated with recognition. Within each word, we find the best phoneme segmentation for that word, where the phoneme sequence is constrained by the word pronunciation network.

For continuous speech word recognition, we used a 350 word vocabulary, speaker-dependent database based on an electronic mail task. We present results for three different male speakers. Fifteen minutes of speech was used for training the 61 phoneme models for each speaker, from which the word models were then built. An additional 30 sentences (187 words) are used for recognition. Analysis parameters are the same as for the previous database. Again, "acceptable" error rates are reported here, where in this case, homophones such as "two" and "to" are considered acceptable errors. Since we do not use a grammar, homophones are indistinguishable.

The initial segment models are obtained on training from segmentations given by a discrete hidden Markov model recognition system. The results after one pass of training of the segment model for the three speakers are summarized in Table 2. The HMM recognition results are also given for comparison. For the HMM results, five passes of the forward-backward training algorithm are performed. The segment phoneme system outperforms the phoneme-based HMM system, reducing the error rate by one third (including insertions). However, the segment phoneme system does not quite match the HMM context model system. This suggests that context-dependent segment models might be useful. Note that in the earlier phoneme results, the segment system matched the performance of HMM models conditioned on left context only. Here we give results for HMM models conditioned on both left and right context. The HMM system with context models conditioned on both left and right context uses 2000 models, or thirty times the number used by the segment system.

Speaker	Segment-PH	HMM-PH	HMM-PH-LE-RI
RS	87/5.3	85/10.2	90/1.1
FK	83/2.1	75/ 5.4	88/2.7
AW	78/3.7	68/ 7.5	86/3.7
Average	83/3.7	76/ 7.7	88/2.5

Table 2: Word recognition/insertion rates for three speakers for the segment phoneme system and for two HMM systems: phoneme models and phoneme models conditioned on the left and right context.

6. Conclusion

To summarize, we feel that the segment model offers the potential for large improvements in speaker-dependent acoustic modelling of phonemes in continuous speech. Our initial results demonstrate the potential of the approach. Of course, a practical system requires automatic training and recognition, which we demonstrated to perform close to the hand-segmented case at the cost of a few insertions. For comparison, the automatic segment system reduces the word error rate by one third over an HMM system on a 350-word continuous speech recognition task.

Acknowledgements

This research was supported by the Advanced Research Projects Agency of the Department of the Defense and was monitored by ONR under Contract No. N00014-85-C-0279.

References

1. L.R. Bahl, F. Jelinek, and R.L. Mercer, "A Maximum Likelihood Approach to Continuous Speech Recognition", *IEEE Trans. Pattern Analysis and Machine Intelligence*, Vol. PAMI-5, No. 2, March 1983, pp. 179-190.

2. R.M. Schwartz, Y.L. Chow, O.A. Kimball, S. Roucos, M. Krasner, and J. Makhoul, "Context-Dependent Modeling for Acoustic-Phonetic Recognition of Continuous Speech", *IEEE Int. Conf. Acoust., Speech, Signal Processing*, Tampa, FL, March 1985, pp. 1205-1208, Paper No. 31.3.

3. Y.L. Chow, R.M. Schwartz, S. Roucos, O.A. Kimball, P.J. Price, G.F. Kubala, M.O. Dunham, M.A. Krasner, and J. Makhoul, "The Role of Word-Dependent Coarticulatory Effects in a Phoneme-Based Speech Recognition System", *IEEE Int. Conf. Acoust., Speech, Signal Processing*, Tokyo, Japan, April 1986, pp. 1593-1596, Paper No. 30.9.1.

4. S. Roucos, R. Schwartz, and J. Makhoul, "Segment Quantization for Very-Low-Rate Speech Coding", *IEEE Int. Conf. Acoust., Speech, Signal Processing*, Paris, France, May 1982, pp. 1565-1569.

5. B. -H. Juang and L.R. Rabiner, "Mixture Autoregressive Hidden Markov Models for Speech Signals", *IEEE Trans. Acoust., Speech and Signal Proc.*, Vol. ASSP-33, No. 6, December 1985, pp. 1404-1413.

6. S. Roucos, R. Schwartz, and J. Makhoul, "A Segment Vocoder at 150 B/S", *IEEE Int. Conf. Acoust., Speech, Signal Processing*, Boston, MA, April 1983, pp. 61-64.

Chapter 7

Connectionist Approaches

Introduction

Connectionist modeling of speech is the youngest development in speech recognition and still the subject of much controversy. In connectionist models, knowledge or constraints are not encoded in individual units, rules, or procedures, but distributed across many simple computing units. Uncertainty is modeled not as likelihoods or probability density functions of a single unit, but by the pattern of activity in many units. The computing units are simple in nature, and knowledge is not programmed into any individual unit's function; rather, it lies in the connections and interactions between linked processing elements. Because the style of computation that can be performed by networks of such units bears some resemblance to the the style of computation in the nervous system, connectionist models are frequently also referred to as "neural networks" or "artificial neural networks." Similarly, "parallel distributed processing" (PDP), or "massively distributed processing" are terms used to describe these models.

Not unlike stochastic models, connectionist models rely critically on the availability of good training or learning strategies. Connectionist learning seeks to optimize or organize a network of processing elements. However, connectionist models need not make assumptions about the underlying probability distributions. Multilayer neural networks can be trained to generate rather complex nonlinear classifiers or mapping functions. The simplicity and uniformity of the underlying processing element makes connectionist models attractive for hardware implementions, which enables the operation of a net to be simulated efficiently. On the other hand, training often requires many iterations over large amounts of training data and can, in some cases, be prohibitively expensive. While connectionism appears to hold great promise as plausible model of cognition, many questions relating to the concrete realization of practical connectionist recognition techniques still remain to be resolved. How should one represent the dynamic nature of speech, or model time-shift invariance and sequential constraints within connectionist models? Should connectionist models be merged with existing maturer techniques and if so, how? How do connectionist models scale, and how can they be interfaced within a larger system design?

The papers in this chapter describe several important recent ideas and models that represent the state of the field. We begin with *Review of Research on Neural Nets for Speech*, an overview by Lippmann that summarizes early advances in connectionist speech recognition.

The second paper, *Phoneme Recognition by Time-Delay Neural Networks* by Waibel et al. represents one of the earliest demonstrations that excellent performance can be achieved for phoneme-discrimination tasks. While many of the earlier connectionist attempts at phoneme classification require precise positioning (segmentation) of an input token with respect to the network, this paper assumes that networks scan input tokens and that relevant features must be detected independent of position in time. The network makes use of time-delayed connections, and is trained using an architecture that enforces time-shift invariance. The backpropagation learning procedure was used for training. The problem of scaling in Time-Delay Neural Networks is then addressed by modular incremental training techniques in the companion paper *Consonant and Phoneme Recognition by Modular Construction of Large Phonemic Time-Delay Neural Networks* by Waibel et al.[1]

An approach based on recurrent multilayer networks is described in *Learned Phonetic Discrimination Using Connectionist Networks* by Watrous et al. The paper describes the temporal flow model, a network model that employs units with recurrent connections—connections between a unit's outputs and its inputs. The paper shows that time-shift invariance and high recognition performance can be achieved on a phonetic discrimination task.

Shift-Tolerant LVQ and Hybrid LVQ-HMM for Phoneme Recognition by McDermott and Katagiri describes phoneme-recognition models based on Kohonen's LVQ2 learning strategy. This method does not develop internal hidden abstractions (no hidden units) of the task, and generally requires more resources (memory and computation) during recognition than multilayer networks. On the other hand, it generally trains faster, while also producing high-performing nonlinear classifiers. The paper also introduces techniques that allow for a hybrid design between LVQ2-based phoneme classification and hidden Markov models (see Chapter 6 on stochastic models) that provide for extensions to word recognition.

Based on good acoustic-level recognition performance, a variety of models now attempt to assemble phoneme models into words. The *'Neural' Phonetic Typewriter* by Kohonen combines phonetic classification in the form of phonotopic maps into word recognition.

Speaker-Independent Word Recognition Using Dynamic Programming Neural Networks by Sakoe et al. is a hybrid solution between multilayer feedforward nets and Dynamic Programming (DP) word models (see chapter on Template Matching). Here, the feedforward nets produce local distance measures rather than classification and the DP-procedure performs time alignment into words. The DP alignment and the networks' weights are optimized jointly with good success. Not unlike many template-based systems, the system was limited to a small vocabulary. Other hybrid models that have been extended to large vocabularies and continuous speech include combinations between TDNNs and DTW [Sawai 90], between multilayer networks and hidden Markov models [Bourlard 88], and the use of connectionist Viterbi training [Franzini 90].

In place of classification or distance calculation, "neural nets" can also be used to compute nonlinear mapping functions [Tamura 88] and nonlinear predictors [Lapedes 87] of speech. This property can also be exploited for speech recognition. *Speaker-Independent Word Recognition Using a Neural Prediction Model* by Iso and Watanabe describes an elegant technique by which a series of such neural-net-based predictors are chained together to represent a word. Recognition is carried out by identifying the sequence of predictors that best models the actually observed speech. Other variants and extensions of this approach are described elsewhere [Tebelskis 90; Levin 90].

References

[Bourlard 88] Bourlard, H., Wellekens, C.J. Links between Markov Models and Multilayer Perceptrons. In *Advances in Neural Network Information Processing Systems.* Morgan Kaufmann, 1988.

[Franzini 90] Franzini, M.A., Lee, K.F., Waibel, A.H. Connectionist Viterbi Training for Continuous Speech Recognition. In *IEEE International Conference on Acoustics, Speech, and Signal Processing.* April, 1990.

[Lapedes 87] Lapedes A., Farber R. *Nonlinear Signal Processing Using Neural Networks; Prediction and System Modeling.* Technical Report LA-UR-87-2662, Los Alamos National Laboratory, 1987.

[Levin 90] Levin, E. Speech Recognition Using Hidden Control Neural Network Architecture. In *Proceedings of the International Conference on Acoustics, Speech and Signal Processing.* IEEE, April, 1990.

[Sawai 90] Miyatake, M., Sawai, H., Shikano, K. Integrated Training for Spotting Japanese Phonemes Using Large Phonemic Time-Delay Neural Networks. In *IEEE International Conference on Acoustics,*

1. A more detailed version appeared in [Waibel 89].

Speech, and Signal Processing. May, 1990.

[Tamura 88] Tamura, S., Waibel A. Noise Reduction Using Connectionist Models. In *IEEE International Conference on Acoustics, Speech, and Signal Processing,* pp S12.7. April, 1988.

[Tebelskis 90] Tebelskis, J., Waibel, A. Large Vocabulary Recognition Using Linked Predictive Neural Networks. In *IEEE International Conference on Acoustics, Speech, and Signal Processing.* IEEE, April, 1990.

[Waibel 89] Waibel, A., Sawai, H., Shikano, K. Modularity and Scaling in Large Phonemic Neural Networks. In *IEEE Transactions on Acoustics, Speech, Signal Processing,* December, 1989.

Review of Neural Networks for Speech Recognition

Richard P. Lippmann*
MIT Lincoln Laboratory, Lexington, MA 02173, USA

The performance of current speech recognition systems is far below that of humans. Neural nets offer the potential of providing massive parallelism, adaptation, and new algorithmic approaches to problems in speech recognition. Initial studies have demonstrated that multi-layer networks with time delays can provide excellent discrimination between small sets of pre-segmented difficult-to-discriminate words, consonants, and vowels. Performance for these small vocabularies has often exceeded that of more conventional approaches. Physiological front ends have provided improved recognition accuracy in noise and a cochlea filter-bank that could be used in these front ends has been implemented using micro-power analog VLSI techniques. Techniques have been developed to scale networks up in size to handle larger vocabularies, to reduce training time, and to train nets with recurrent connections. Multilayer perceptron classifiers are being integrated into conventional continuous-speech recognizers. Neural net architectures have been developed to perform the computations required by vector quantizers, static pattern classifiers, and the Viterbi decoding algorithm. Further work is necessary for large-vocabulary continuous-speech problems, to develop training algorithms that progressively build internal word models, and to develop compact VLSI neural net hardware.

1 State of the Art for Speech Recognition

Speech is the most natural form of human communication. Compact implementations of accurate, real-time speech recognizers would find widespread use in many applications including automatic transcription, simplified man-machine communication, and aids for the hearing impaired and physically disabled. Unfortunately, current speech recognizers perform poorly on talker-independent continuous-speech recognition tasks that people perform without apparent difficulty. Although children learn to understand speech with little explicit supervision and adults take speech recognition ability for granted, it has proved to be a difficult task to duplicate with machines. As noted by Klatt (1986), this is due to variability and overlap of information in the acoustic signal, to the need for high computation rates (a human-like system must match inputs to 50,000 words in real time), to the multiplicity of analyses that must be performed (phonetic, phonemic, syntactic, semantic, and pragmatic), and to the lack of any comprehensive theory of speech recognition.

The best existing speech recognizers perform well only in artificially constrained tasks. Performance is generally better when training data is provided for each talker, when words are spoken in isolation, when the vocabulary size is small, and when restrictive language models are used to constrain allowable word sequences. For example, talker-dependent isolated-word recognizers can be trained to recognize 105 words with 99% accuracy (Paul 1987). Large-vocabulary talker-dependent word recognition accuracy with sentence context can be as high as 95% for 20,000 words from sentences in office memos spoken with pauses between words (Averbuch et al. 1987).

Accuracy for a difficult 997-word talker-independent continuous-speech task using a strong language model (an average of only 20 different words possible after any other word) can be as high as 96% (Lee and Hon 1988). This word accuracy score translates to an unacceptable sentence accuracy of roughly 50%. In addition, the word accuracy of this high-performance recognizer when tested with no grammar model is typically below 70% correct. Results such as these illustrate the poor low-level acoustic-phonetic matching provided by current recognizers. These recognizers depend heavily on constraining grammars to achieve good performance. Humans do not suffer from this problem. We can recognize clearly spoken but contextually inappropriate words in anomalous sentences such as "John drank the guitar" almost perfectly (Marslen-Wilson 1987).

The current best performing speech recognition algorithms use Hidden Markov Model (HMM) techniques. Good introductions to these techniques and to digital signal processing of speech are available in (Lee and Hon 1988; Parsons 1986; Rabiner and Juang 1986; Rabiner and Schafer 1978). The HMM approach provides a framework which includes an efficient decoding algorithm for use in recognition (the Viterbi algorithm) and an automatic supervised training algorithm (the forward-backward algorithm). New neural-net approaches to speech recognition must have the potential to overcome the limitations of current HMM systems. These limitations include poor low-level and poor high-level modeling. Poor low-level acoustic-phonetic modeling leads to confusions between acoustically similar words while poor high-level speech understanding or semantic modeling restricts applications to simple situations where finite state or probabilistic grammars are acceptable. In addition, the first-order Markov assumption makes it difficult to model coarticulation directly and HMM training algorithms can not currently learn the topological structure of word and sub-word models. Finally, HMM theory does not

*This work was sponsored by the Department of the Air Force. The views expressed are those of the author and do not reflect the official policy or position of the U.S. Government.

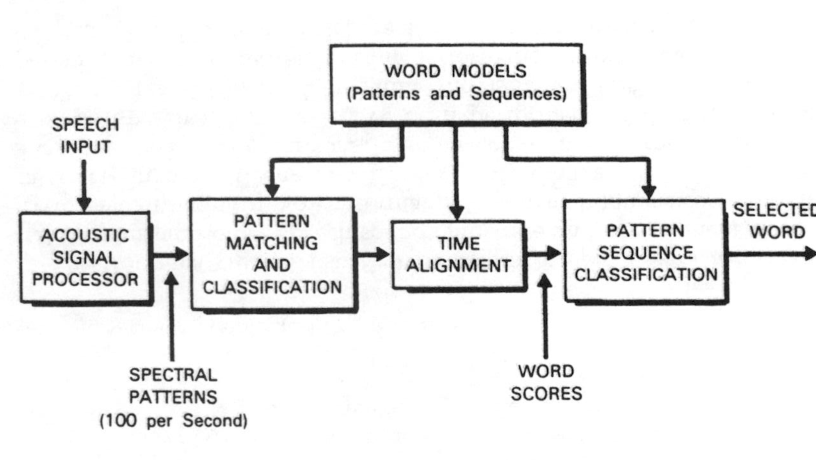

Figure 1: Block diagram of an isolated word recognizer.

specify the structure of implementation hardware. It is likely that high computation and memory requirements of current algorithms will require new approaches to parallel hardware design to produce compact, large-vocabulary, continuous-speech recognizers.

2 The Potential of Neural Nets

Neural nets for speech recognition have been explored as part of the recent resurgence of interest in this area. Research has focused on evaluating new neural net pattern classification and training algorithms using real speech data and on determining whether parallel neural net architectures can be designed which perform the computations required by important speech recognition algorithms. Most work has focused on isolated-word recognition.

A block diagram of a simple isolated word recognizer is shown in figure 1. Speech is input to this recognizer and a word classification decision is output on the right. Three major operations are required. First, a preprocessor must extract important information from the speech waveform. In most recognizers, an input pattern containing spectral information from a frame of speech is extracted every 10 msec using Fast Fourier Transform (FFT) or Linear Predictive Coding (LPC) (Parsons 1986; Rabiner and Schafer 1978) techniques. Second, input patterns from the preprocessor must be compared to stored exemplar patterns in word models to compute local frame-to-frame distances. Local distances are used in a third step to time align input pattern sequences to stored exemplar pattern sequences that form word models and arrive at whole-word matching scores. Time alignment compensates for variations in talking rate and pronunciation. Once these operations have been performed, the selected word to output is that word with the highest whole-word matching score.

This paper reviews research on complete neural net recognizers and on neural nets that perform the above three operations. Auditory preprocessors that attempt to mimic cochlea and auditory nerve processing are first reviewed. Neural net structures that can compute local distance scores are then described. Classification results obtained using static speech patterns as inputs are then followed by results obtained with dynamic nets that allow continuous-time inputs. Techniques to integrate neural net and conventional approaches are then described followed by a brief review of psychological and physiological models of temporal pattern sequence recognition. The paper ends with a summary and suggestions for future research. Emphasis throughout is placed on studies that used large public-domain speech data bases or that first presented new approaches.

3 Auditory Preprocessors

A preprocessor extracts important parameters from the speech waveform to compress the amount of data that must be processed at higher levels and provide some invariance to changes in noise, talkers, and the acoustic environment. Most conventional preprocessors are only loosely modeled on the cochlea and perform simple types of filtering and data compression motivated by Fourier analysis and information theory. Recent physiological studies of cochlea and auditory nerve responses to complex stimuli have led to more complex physiological preprocessors designed to closely mimic many aspects of auditory nerve response characteristics. Five of these preprocessors and the VLSI cochlea filter listed in table 1 are reviewed in this section. Good reviews of many of these preprocessors and of response properties of the cochlea and auditory nerve can be found in (Greenberg 1988a; 1988b).

The five preprocessors in table 1 rely on periodicity or synchrony information in filter-bank outputs. Synchrony information is related to the short-term phase of a speech signal and can be obtained from the arrival times of nerve spikes on the auditory nerve. It could increase recognition performance by supplementing the spectral magnitude information used in current recognizers. Synchrony information is typically obtained by filtering the speech input using sharp bandpass filters with characteristics similar to those of the mechanical filters in the cochlea. The resulting filtered waveforms are then processed using various types of time domain analyses that could be performed using analog neural net circuitry.

Study	Processing	Comments
Deng and Geisler (1987)	Cross-Channel Correlation of Neural Outputs	Physiologically Plausible (Untested for Speech Recognition)
Ghitza (1988)	Create Histogram of Time Intervals Between Threshold Crossings of Filter Outputs	Improved Speech Recognition In Noise
Hunt and Lefèbvre (1988)	Periodicity and Onset Detection	Improved Speech Recognition In Noise and with Spectral Tilt
Lyon and Mead (1988)	Tapped Transmission Line Filter with 49 Outputs	Implemented Using Micropower VLSI Techniques
Seneff (1988)	Provides Periodicity and Spectral Magnitude Outputs	Synchrony Spectrograms Provide Enhanced Spectral Resolution (Untested for Speech Recognition)
Shamma (1988)	Lateral Inhibition Across Cochlea Filter Outputs	Physiologically Plausible (Untested for Speech Recognition)

Table 1: Recent Physiological Preprocessors.

Spectrograms created using physiological preprocessors for steady state vowels and other speech sounds illustrate an improvement in ability to visually identify vowel formants (resonant frequencies of the vocal tract) in noise (Deng and Geisler 1987; Ghitza 1988; Seneff 1988; Shamma 1988). Comparisons to more conventional front ends using existing speech recognizers have been performed by Beet (Beet et al. 1988), Ghitza (1988), and by Hunt and Lefèbvre (1988). These comparisons demonstrated significant performance improvements in noise (Ghitza 1988; Hunt and Lefèbvre 1988) and with filtering that tilts the input spectrum up at high frequencies (Hunt and Lefèbvre 1988). Extensive comparisons have not, however, been made between physiological preprocessors and conventional preprocessors when the conventional preprocessors incorporate current noise and stress compensation techniques. Positive results from such comparisons and more detailed theoretical analyses would do much to foster the acceptance of these new and computationally intensive front ends.

Lyon and Mead (1988) describe a filter bank that could be used in a physiological preprocessor. This filter bank was carefully modeled after the cochlea, provides 49 analog outputs, and has been implemented using micropower analog VLSI CMOS processing. Extra circuitry would be required to provide synchrony or spectral magnitude information for a speech recognizer. This recent work demonstrates how preprocessors can be miniaturized using analog VLSI techniques. The success of this approach is beginning to demonstrate that ease of implementation using VLSI techniques may be more important when comparing alternative neural net approaches than computational requirements on serial Von Neuman machines.

4 Computing Local Distance Scores

Conventional speech recognizers compute local frame-to-frame distances by comparing each new input pattern (vector of parameters) provided by a preprocessor to stored reference patterns. Neural net architectures can compute local frame-to-frame distances using fine-grain parallelism for both continuous-observation and discrete-observation recognizers. New neural net algorithms can also perform vector quantization and reduce the dimensionality of input patterns.

Local distances for continuous-observation recognizers are functions related to log likelihoods of probability distributions. Simple log likelihood functions such as those required for independent Gaussian or binomial distributions can be calculated directly without training using single-layer nets with threshold-logic nonlinearities (Lippmann 1987; Lippmann et al. 1987). More complex likelihood functions can be computed using multilayer perceptrons (Cybenko 1988; Lapedes and Farber 1988; Lippmann et al. 1987), hierarchical nets that compute kernel functions (Albus 1981; Broomhead and Lowe 1988; Hanson and Burr 1987; Huang and Lippmann 1988; Moody 1988; Moody and Darken 1988), or high-order nets (Lee et al. 1986; Rumelhart et al. 1986a). Training to produce these complex functions is typically longest with multilayer perceptrons. These nets, however, often provide architectures with fewer nodes, simpler nodal processing elements, and fewer weights. They also may develop internal hidden abstractions in hidden layers that can be related to meaningful acoustic-phonetic speech characteristics such as formant transitions and that also could be applied to many different speech recognition tasks.

Discrete-observation recognizers first perform vector quantization and label each input with one particular symbol. Symbols are used to calculate local distances via look-up tables that contain symbol probabilities for each reference pattern. The look-up table calculation can be performed by simple single-layer perceptrons. The perceptron for any reference pattern must have as many inputs as there are symbols. Weights must equal symbol probabilities and all inputs must be equal to zero except for that corresponding to the current input symbol. Alternatively, a multilayer perceptron could be used to store probabilities for symbols that have been seen and interpolate between these probabilities for unseen symbols. The vector quantization operation can be performed using an architecture similar to that used by Kohonen's feature-map net (Kohonen 1984). Inputs to the feature-map net feed an array of codebook nodes containing one node for each symbol. Components of the Euclidean distance between the input and the reference pattern represented by weights to each node are computed in each node. The codebook node with the smallest Euclidean distance to the input is selected using lateral inhibition or other maximum-picking techniques (Lippmann et al. 1987). This process guarantees that only one node with the minimum Euclidean distance to the input has a unity output as required. Weights used in this architecture can be calculated using the feature-map algorithm or any other standard vector quantization algorithm based on Euclidean distances such as k-means clustering (Duda and Hart 1973).

Kohonen's feature-map vector quantizer is an alternative sequentially-trained neural net algorithm. It has been tested successfully in an experimental speech recognizer (Kohonen 1988; Kohonen et al. 1984) but not evaluated with a large public speech data base. A version with a small number of nodes but including training logic has been implemented in VLSI (Mann et al. 1988). Experiments with a discrete-observation HMM recognizer (Mann et al. 1988) and with a template-based recognizer (Naylor and Li 1988) demonstrated that this algorithm provides performance similar to that provided by conventional clustering procedures such as k-means clustering (Duda and Hart 1973). The feature-map algorithm incrementally trains weights to a two-dimensional grid of nodes such that after training, nodes that are physically close in the grid correspond to input patterns that are close in Euclidean distance. One advantage of this topological organization is that averaging outputs of nodes that are physically close using nodes at higher levels corresponds to a probability smoothing technique often used in speech recognizers called Parzen smoothing (Duda and Hart 1973). This averaging can be performed by nodes with limited fan-in and short connections.

The auto-associative multilayer perceptron (Elman and Zipser 1987; Hinton 1987) is a neural net algorithm that reduces the dimensionality of continuous-valued inputs. It is a multilayer perceptron with the same number of input and output nodes and one or more layers of hidden nodes. This net is trained to reproduce the input at the output nodes through a small layer of hidden nodes. Outputs of hidden nodes after training can be used as reduced dimensional inputs for speech processing as described in (Elman and Zipser 1987; Fallside et al. 1988). Recent theoretical analyses have demonstrated that auto-associative networks are closedly related to a standard statistical technique called principal components analysis (Baldi and Hornik 1989; Bourlard and Kamp 1988). Auto-associative nets are thus not a new analytical tool but instead a technique to perform the processing required by principal components analysis.

5 Static Classification of Speech Segments

Many neural net classifiers have been applied to the problem of classifying static input patterns formed from a spectral analysis of pre-segmented words, phonemes, and vowels. Table 2 summarizes results of some representative studies. Introductions to many of the classifiers listed in this table and to neural net training algorithms are available in (Cowan and Sharp 1988; Hinton 1987; Lippmann et al. 1987). Unless otherwise noted, error rates in this and other tables refer to talker-dependent training and testing, multilayer perceptrons were trained using back-propagation (Rumelhart et al. 1986a), and systems were trained and tested on different data sets. The number of tokens in this and other tables refers to the total number of speech samples available for both training and testing and the label "multi-talker" refers to results obtained by testing and training using data from the same group of talkers. The label "talker-independent" refers to results obtained by training using one group of talkers and testing using a separate group with no common members.

Input patterns for studies in table 2 were applied at once as one whole static spectrographic (frequency versus time) pattern. Neural nets were static and didn't include internal delays or recurrent connections that could take advantage of the temporal nature of the input for real-time processing. This approach might be difficult to incorporate in real-time speech recognizers because it would require long delays to perform segmentation and form the input patterns in an input storage buffer. It would also require accurate pre-segmentation of both testing and training data for good performance. This pre-segmentation was performed by hand in many studies.

Multilayer perceptrons and hierarchical nets such as the feature-map classifier and Kohonen's learning vector quantizer (LVQ) have been used to classify static patterns. Excellent talker-dependent recognition accuracy near that of experimental HMM and commercial recognizers has been provided by multilayer perceptrons using small sets of words and digits. Hierarchical nets have provided performance similar to that of

Study	Network	Speech Materials	Error Rate
Elman and Zipser (1987)	Multilayer Perceptron (MLP) 16 × 20 Inputs	1 Talker, CV's /b,d,g/ /i,a,u/ 505 Tokens	Cons. - 5% Vowels - 0.5%
Huang and Lippmann, (1988)	MLP, Feature Map Classifier (FMC) 2 Inputs	67 Talkers 10 Vowels 671 Tokens	Gaussian, FMC, MLP ≈ 20% FMC Trains Fastest
Kammerer and Kupper (1988)	MLP 16 × 16 Inputs	11 Talkers 20 Words 5720 Tokens	Talker Dep. - 0.4% Talker Indep. - 2.7%
Kohonen (1988)	Learning Vector Quantizer (LVQ) 15 Inputs	Labeled Finish Speech 3010 Tokens	Gaussian - 12.9% kNN - 12.0% LVQ - 10.9%
Lippmann and Gold (1987)	MLP 11 × 2 Inputs	16 Talkers 7 Digits 2,912 Tokens	Gaussian - 8.7% kNN - 6% MLP - 7.6%
Peeling and Moore (1987)	MLP 19 × 60 Inputs	40 Talkers 10 Digits 16,000 Tokens	Talker Dep. - 0.3% Multi Talker - 1.9%

Table 2: Recognition of Speech Patterns Using Static Neural Nets.

multilayer perceptrons but with greatly reduced training times and typically more connection weights and nodes.

5.1 Multilayer Perceptrons. Multilayer perceptron classifiers have been applied to speech problems more often than any other neural net classifier. A simple example from Huang and Lippmann (1988) presented in figure 2 illustrates how these nets can form complex decision regions with speech data. Input data obtained by Peterson and Barney (1952) consisted of the first two formants from vowels spoken by men, women, and children. Decision regions shown in the right side of figure 2 were formed by the two-layer perceptron with 50 hidden nodes trained using back-propagation shown on the left. Training required more than 50,000 trials. Decision region boundaries are near those that are typically drawn by hand to separate vowel regions and the performance of this net is near that provided by commonly used conventional k-nearest neighbor (kNN) and Gaussian classifiers (Duda and Hart 1973).

A more complex experiment was performed by Elman and Zipser (1987) using spectrographic-like inputs. Input patterns formed from 16 filter-bank outputs sampled 20 times over a time window of 64 msec were fed to nets with one hidden layer and 2 to 6 hidden nodes. The analysis time window was centered by hand on the consonant voicing onset. Networks were trained to recognize consonants or vowels in consonant-vowel (CV) syllables composed of the consonants /b,d,g/ and the vowels /i,a,u/. Error rates were roughly 5% for consonant recognition and 0.5% for vowel recognition. An analysis indicated that hidden nodes often become feature detectors and differentiate between important subsets of sound types such as consonants versus vowels. This study demonstrated the importance of choosing a good data representation for speech and of normalizing speech inputs. It also raised the important question of training time because many experiments on this small data base required more than 100,000 training trials.

Lippmann and Gold (1987) performed another early study to compare multilayer perceptrons and conventional classifiers on a digit classification task. This study was motivated by single-talker results obtained

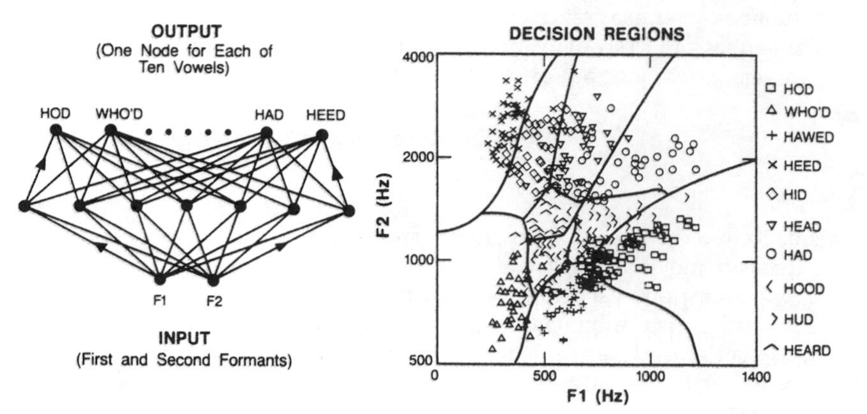

Figure 2: Decision regions formed by a 2-layer perceptron using back-propagation training and vowel formant data.

by Burr (1988a). Inputs were 22 cepstral parameters from two speech frames located automatically by finding the maximum-energy frame for each digit. One- to three-layer nets with from 16 to 256 nodes in each hidden layer were evaluated using digits from the Texas Instruments (TI) 20-Word Speech Data Base (Doddington and Schalk 1981). Multilayer perceptron classifiers outperformed a Gaussian but not a kNN classifier. Hidden layers were required for good performance. A single-layer perceptron provided poor performance, much longer training times, and sometimes never converged during training. Most rapid training (less than 1000 trials) was provided by all three-layer perceptrons. These results demonstrate that the simple hyperplane decision regions provided by single-layer perceptrons are sometimes not sufficient and that rapid training and good performance can be obtained by tailoring the size of a net for a specific problem. The digit data used in these experiments was also used to test a multilayer perceptron chip implemented in VLSI (Raffel et al. 1987). This chip performed as well as computer simulations when down-loaded with weights from those simulations.

Kammerer and Kupper obtained surprisingly good recognition results for words from the TI 20-word data base (Kammerer and Kupper 1988). A single-layer perceptron with spectrogram-like input patterns performed slightly better than a DTW template-based recognizer. Words were first time normalized to provide 16 input frames with 16 2-bit spectral coefficients per frame. Expanding the training corpus by temporally distorting training tokens reduced the error slightly and best performance was provided by single and not multilayer perceptrons. Talker-dependent error rates were 0.4% (14/3520) for the single-layer perceptron and 0.7% (25/3520) for the DTW recognizer. These error rates are better than all but one of the commercial recognizers evaluated in (Doddington and Schalk 1981) and demonstrate good performance for a single-layer perceptron without hidden nodes. Talker-independent performance was evaluated by leaving out the training data for each talker, one at a time, and testing using that talker's test data. Average talker-independent error rates were 2.7% (155/5720) for the single-layer perceptron and 2.5% (145/5720) for the DTW recognizer. Training time was 6 to 25 minutes per talker on an array processor for the talker-dependent studies and 5 to 9 hours for the talker-independent studies.

Peeling and Moore (1987) obtained extremely good recognition results for digit classification. A multilayer perceptron with one hidden layer and 50 hidden nodes provided best performance. Its talker-dependent performance was low and near that provided by an advanced HMM recognizer. Spectrogram-like input patterns were generated using a 19-channel filter-bank analyzer with 20 msec frames. Nets could accommodate 60 input frames (1.2 seconds) which was enough for the longest duration word. Shorter words were padded with zeros and positioned randomly in the 60 frame input buffer. Nets were trained using different numbers of layers and hidden units and speech data from the RSRE 40-speaker digit data base. Multi-talker experiments explored performance when recognizers were tested and trained using data from all talkers. Error rates were near zero for talker-dependent experiments 0.25% (5/2000) and low for multi-talker experiments 1.9% (78/4000). Error rates on an advanced HMM recognizer under the same conditions were 0.2% (4/2000) and 0.6% (25/4000) respectively. The computation required for recognition using multilayer perceptrons was typically more than five times less than that required for the HMM recognizer.

The good small-vocabulary word recognition results obtained by both Kammerer and Kupper (1988) and Peeling and Moore (1987) suggest that back-propagation can develop internal feature detectors to extract important invariant acoustic events. These results must be compared to those of other experiments which attempted to classify digits without time alignment. Burton, Shore, and Buck (Burton et al. 1985; Shore and Burton 1983) demonstrated that talker-dependent error rates using the TI 20-Word Data Base can be as low as 0.3% (8/2560) for digits and 0.8% (40/5120) for all words using simple vector-quantization recognizers that do not perform time alignment. These results suggest that digit recognition is a relatively simple task where dynamic time alignment is not necessary and talker-dependent accuracy remains high even when temporal information is discarded. The good performance of multilayer perceptrons is thus not surprising. These studies and the multilayer perceptron studies do, however, suggest designs for implementing computationally-efficient real-time digit and small-vocabulary recognizers using analog neural-net VLSI processing.

5.2 Hierarchical Neural Nets that Compute Kernel Functions. Hierarchical neural net classifiers which use hidden nodes that compute kernel functions have also been used to classify speech patterns. These nets have the advantage of rapid training and the ability to use combined supervised/unsupervised training data.

Huang and Lippmann (1988) described a net called a feature-map classifier and evaluated the performance of this net on the vowel data plotted in figure 2 and on difficult artificial problems. A block diagram of the feature-map classifier is shown in figure. 3. Intermediate codebook nodes in this net compute kernel functions related to the Euclidean distance between the input and cluster centers represented by these nodes. The lower feature map net is first trained without supervision to form a vector quantizer and the upper perceptron-like layer is then trained with supervision using a modified version of the LMS algorithm. This classifier was compared to the multilayer perceptron shown in figure 2 and to a kNN classifier. All classifiers provided an error rate of roughly 20%. The 2-layer perceptron, however, required more than 50,000 supervised training trials for convergence. The feature map classifier reduced the amount of supervised training required by three orders of magni-

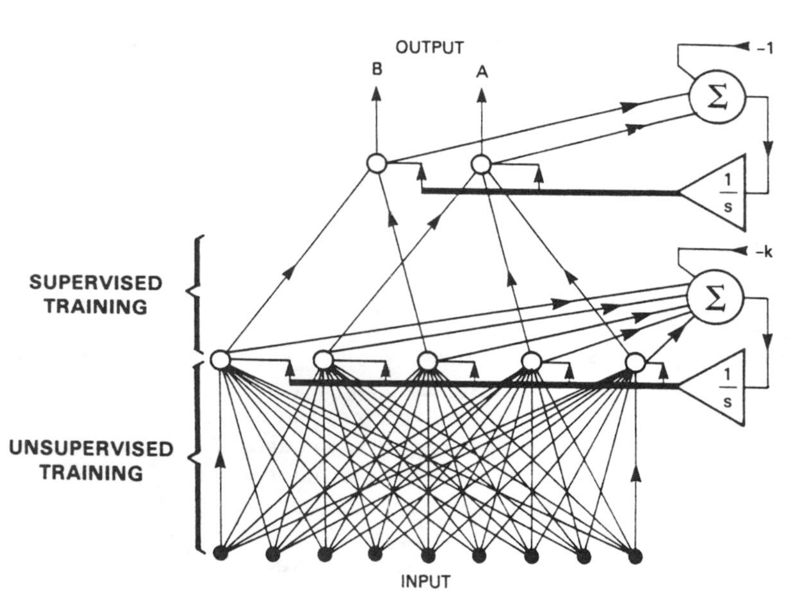

Figure 3: Block diagram of the hierarchical feature-map classifier.

tude to fewer than 50 trials. Similar results were obtained with artificial problems.

Kohonen and co-workers (Kohonen et al. 1988) compared a neural-net classifier called a learning vector quantizer (LVQ) to Bayesian and kNN classifiers. The structure of the learning vector quantizer is similar to that of the feature-map classifier shown in figure 3. Training differs from that used with the feature-map classifier in that a third stage of supervised training is added which adjusts weights to intermediate codebook nodes when a classification error occurs. Adjustments alter decision region boundaries slightly but maintain the same number of codebook nodes.

Bayesian, kNN and LVQ classifiers were used to classify 15-channel speech spectra manually extracted from stationary regions of Finnish speech waveforms. All classifiers were tested and trained with separate sets of 1550 single-frame patterns that were divided into 18 phoneme classes (Kohonen et al. 1988). A version of the LVQ classifier with 117 codebook nodes provided the lowest error rate of 10.9% averaging over results where training and testing data sets are interchanged. The Bayesian classifier and kNN classifiers had slightly higher error rates of 12.9% and 12.0% respectively. Training time for the LVQ classifier was roughly 10 minutes on an IBM PC/AT. These results and those of Huang and Lippmann (1988) demonstrate that neural nets that use kernel functions can provide excellent performance on speech tasks using practical amounts of training time. Other experiments on artificial problems described in (Kohonen et al. 1988) illustrate trade-offs in training time. Boltzmann machines provided near optimal performance on these problems followed by the LVQ classifier and multilayer perceptrons. Training times were 5 hours on an array processor for the Boltzmann machine, 1 hour on a Masscomp MC 5600 for the multilayer perceptron, and roughly 20 minutes on the Masscomp for the LVQ classifier.

Two recent studies (Niranjan and Fallside 1988; Bridle 1988) have begun to explore a hierarchical net where nodes in a hidden layer compute kernel functions called radial basis functions (Broomhead and Lowe 1988). These nets are similar to previous classifiers that use the method of potential functions (Duda and Hart 1973). They have an advantage over multilayer perceptrons in that once the locations of the kernel functions are established, weights to the output nodes are determined uniquely by solving a least squares problem using matrix-based approaches. Initial results with small amounts of speech data consisting of vowels (Niranjan and Fallside 1988) and words (Bridle 1988) have been encouraging. Further work must explore techniques to assign the locations of kernel functions and adjust scale factors that determine the range of influence of each kernel function.

6 Dynamic Classification of Speech Segments

New dynamic neural net classifiers that incorporate short delays, temporal integration, or recurrent connections have been developed specifically for speech recognition. Spectral inputs for these classifiers are applied to input nodes sequentially, one frame at a time. These classifiers could thus be integrated into real time speech recognizers more easily than static nets because accurate pre-segmentation is typically not required for good performance and only short delays are used.

Both multilayer nets with delays and nets with recurrent connections have been used to classify acoustically similar words, consonants, and vowels. Excellent performance has been obtained using time delay nets in many studies including those by Lang and Hinton (1988) and by Waibel et al. (1987; 1988). Performance for small vocabularies often slightly exceeded that provided by high-performance experimental HMM recognizers. Techniques have also been developed to scale nets up for larger vocabularies and to speed up training times both for feed-forward and recurrent nets. Rapid training has been demonstrated using a hierarchical learning vector quantizer with delays and good performance but extremely long training times has been provided by Boltzmann machines.

6.1 Time-Delay Multilayer Perceptrons. Some of the most promising neural-net recognition results have been obtained using multilayer perceptrons with delays and some form of temporal integration in output nodes (Lang and Hinton 1988; Waibel et al. 1987; Waibel et al. 1988). Table 3 summarizes results of six representative studies.

Early results on consonant and vowel recognition were obtained by Waibel and co-workers (Waibel et al. 1987) using the multilayer perceptron with time delays shown in figure 4. The boxes labeled τ in this figure represent fixed delays. Spectral coefficients from 10 msec speech frames (16 per frame) are input on the lower left. The three boxes on the bottom thus represent an input buffer containing a context of three frames. Outputs of the nodes in these boxes (16×3 spectral coefficients) feed 8 hidden nodes in the first layer. Outputs from these nodes are buffered across the five boxes in the first hidden layer to form a context of five frames. Outputs from these boxes (8×5 node outputs) feed three hidden nodes in the second hidden layer. Outputs from these three nodes are integrated over time in a final output node.

In initial experiments (Waibel et al. 1987), the time-delay net from figure 4 was trained using back-propagation to recognize the voiced stops /b,d,g/. Separate testing and training sets of 2000 voiced stops spoken by three talkers were excised manually from a corpus of 5260 Japanese words. Excised portions sampled the consonants in varying phonetic contexts and contained 15 frames (150 msec) centered by hand around the vowel onset. The neural net classifier provided an error rate of 1.5% compared to an error rate 6.5% provided by a simple discrete-observation HMM recognizer. Training the time-delay net took several days on a four-processor Alliant computer. More recent work (Waibel et al. 1988) has led to techniques that merge smaller nets designed to recognize small sets of

Study	Network	Speech Materials	Error Rate
Lang and Hinton (1988)	Time Delay MLP 16 Inputs	100 Talkers "B,D,E,V" 768 Tokens	Multi Talker - 7.8%
Unnikrishnan, Hopfield, and Tank (1988)	Time Concentration Net 32 Inputs	1 Talker Digits 432 Tokens	0.7%
Waibel et al. (1987)	Time Delay MLP 16 Inputs	3 Japanese Talkers, /b,d,g/, Many Contexts > 4,000 Tokens	/b,d,g/ - 1.5%
Waibel, Sawai, and Shikano (1988)	Time Delay MLP 16 Inputs	1 Japanese Talker, 18 Cons., 5 Vowels > 10,000 Tokens	/b,d,g,p,t,k/ - 1.4% 18 Cons. - 4.1% 5 Vowels - 1.4%
Watrous (1988)	Temporal Flow Structured MLP 16 Inputs	1 Talker Phonemes, Words > 2,000 Tokens	/b,d,g/ - 0.8% rapid/rabid - 0.8% /i,a,u/ - 0.0%
McDermott and Katagiri (1988)	Time Delay LVQ 16 Inputs	3 Japanese Talkers, /b,d,g/ > 4,000 Tokens	/b,d,g/ - 1.7%

Table 3: Recognition of Speech Using Time-Delay Neural Nets.

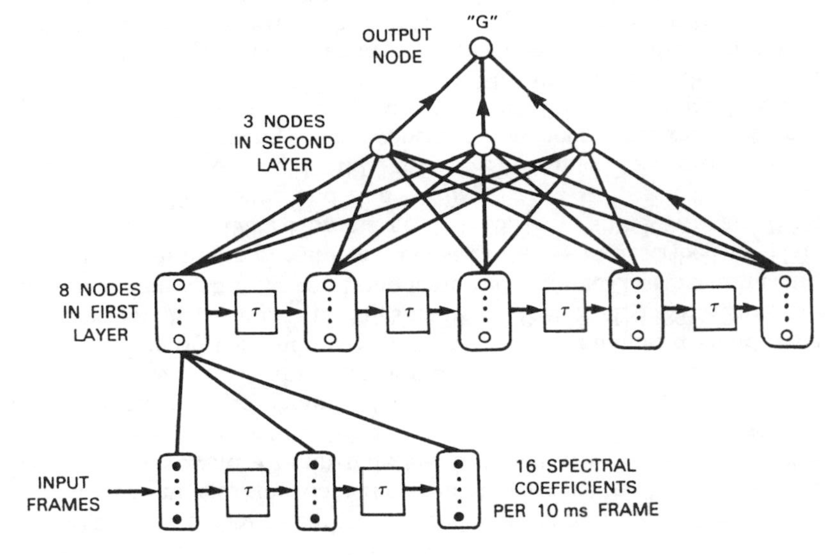

Figure 4: A time-delay multilayer perceptron.

consonants and vowels into large nets which can recognize all consonants at once. These techniques greatly reduce training time, improve performance and are a practical approach to the scaling problem. Experiments resulted in low error rates of 1.4% for the consonants /b,d,g,p,t,k/ and 1.4% for the vowels /i,a,u,e,o/. The largest net designed from smaller subnets provided a talker-dependent error rate for one talker of 4.1% for 18 consonants. An advanced discrete-observation HMM recognizer provided an error rate of 7.3% on this task. These two studies demonstrate that good performance can be provided by time-delay nets when the network structure is tailored to a specific problem. They also demonstrate how small nets can be scaled up to solve large classification problems without scaling up training times substantially.

Lang and Hinton (1988) describe an extensive series of experiments that led to a similar high-performance time-delay net. This net was designed to classify four acoustically similar isolated words "B", "D", "E", and "V" that are the most confusable subset from the spoken alphabet. A multi-talker recognizer for 100 male talkers was first trained and tested using pre-segmented 144 msec speech samples taken from around the vowel onset in these words. A technique called multi-resolution training was developed to shorten training time. This involved training nets with smaller numbers of hidden nodes, splitting weight values to hidden nodes to create larger desired nets, and then re-training the larger nets. A multiresolution trained net provided an error rate of 8.6%. This result, however, required careful pre-segmentation of each word. Pre-segmentation was not required by another net which allowed continuous speech input and classified the input as that word corresponding to the output node whose output value reached the highest level. Training used simple automatic energy-based segmentation techniques to extract 216 msecs of speech from around the vowel onset in each word. This resulted in an error rate of 9.5%. Outputs were then trained to be high and correct for the 216 msec speech segments as before, but also low for counter-example inputs selected randomly from the left-over background noise and vowel segments. Inclusion of counter-examples reduced the error rate to 7.8%. This performance compares favorably with the 11% error rate estimated for an enhanced HMM recognizer on this data base and based on performance with the complete E-set (Bahl et al. 1988; Lang and Hinton 1988).

Watrous (1988) also explored multilayer perceptron classifiers with time delays that extended earlier exploratory work on nets with recurrent connections (Watrous and Shastri 1987). These multilayer nets differed from those described above in that recurrent connections were provided on output nodes, target outputs were Gaussian-shaped pulses, and delays and the network structure were carefully adjusted by hand to extract important speech features for each classification task. Networks were tested using hand-segmented speech and isolated words from one talker. Good discrimination was obtained for many different recognition tasks. For example, the error rate was 0.8% for the consonants /b,d,g/, 0.8% for the word pair "rapid/rabid," and 0.0% for the vowels /i,a,u/. Watrous has also explored the use of gradient methods of nonlinear optimization to decrease training time (Watrous 1986).

Rossen et al. (1988) recently described another time delay classifier. It uses more complex input data representations than the time-delay nets described above and a brain-state-in-a-box neural net classifier to integrate information over time from lower-level networks. Good classification performance was obtained for six stop consonants and three vowels. Notable features of this work are training to reject noise inputs as in (Lang and Hinton 1988) and the use of modular techniques to build large nets from smaller trained modules as in (Waibel et al. 1988). Other recent work demonstrating good phoneme and syllable classification using structured multilayer perceptron nets with delays is described in (Harrison and Fallside 1988; Homma et al. 1988; Irino and Kawahara 1988; Kamm et al. 1988; Leung and Zue 1988).

Unnikrishnan, Hopfield, and Tank (1988) obtained low error rates on digit classification using a time-concentration neural net that does not use only simple delays. This net, described in (Tank and Hopfield 1987), uses variable length delay lines designed to disperse impulsive inputs such that longer delays result in more dispersion. Impulsive inputs to these delay lines are formed by enhancing spectral peaks in the outputs of 32 bandpass filters. Outputs of delay lines are multiplied by weights and summed to form separate matched filters for each word. These matched filters concentrate energy in time and produce a large output pulse at the end of the correct word. Limited evaluations reported in (Unnikrishnan et al. 1988) for digit strings from one talker demonstrated good performance using a modified form of back-propagation training. A prototype version of this recognizer using discrete analog electronic devices was also constructed (Tank and Hopfield 1987). Tests performed by Gold with a large speech data base and a hierarchical version of the time concentration net that included both allophone and word models yielded performance that was no better than that of an existing HMM recognizer (Gold 1988).

6.2 Hierarchical Nets that Compute Kernel Functions. McDermott and Katagiri (1988) used Kohonen's LVQ classifier on the same /b,d,g/ speech data base used by Waibel et al. (1987). They were able to obtain an error rate of 1.7% which is not statistically different from the 1.5% error rate obtained by Waibel et al. using the time-delay net shown in figure 4 (Waibel et al. 1987). Inputs for the LVQ classifier consisted of a 7-frame window of 16 filterbank outputs. The nearest of 150 codebook nodes were determined as the 15-frame speech samples were passed through this 7-frame window. The normalized distances between nearest nodes and 112-element input patterns were integrated over time and used to classify speech inputs. The error rate without the final stage of LVQ training was high (7.3%). It dropped to 1.7% after LVQ training was complete. This result demonstrates that nets with kernel functions and delays can perform as well as multilayer perceptrons with delays. These nets train faster but require more computation and memory during use. In this application, for example, the LVQ classifier required 17,000 weights which was more than 30 times as many required for the time-delay net used in (Waibel et al. 1987). If memory is not an important limitation, rapid search techniques such as hashing and k-d trees described in (Omohundro 1987) can be applied to the LVQ classifier to greatly reduce the time required to find nearest-neighbors. This would make the differences in computation time between these alternative approaches small on existing serial Von Neuman computers.

6.3 Nets with Recurrent Connections. Nets with recurrent connections have not been used as extensively for speech recognition problems as feed-forward nets because they are more difficult to train, analyze, and design. Table 4 summarizes results of three representative studies. Initial work explored the use of recurrent Boltzmann machines. These nets typically provided good performance on small problems but required extremely long training times. More recent studies have focused on modified back-propagation training algorithms described in (Almeida 1987; Jordan 1986; Pineda 1987; Rohwer and Forrest 1987; Rumelhart et al. 1986a; Watrous 1988) that can be used with recurrent nets and time varying inputs.

Study	Network	Speech Materials	Error Rate
Anderson, Merrill, and Port (1988)	Recurrent Net 36 Inputs	20 Talkers, CV's /b,d,g,p,t,k/, /a/ 561 Tokens	Talker Indep. - 13.1%
Prager, Harrison, and Fallside (1986)	Boltzmann Machine 2048 Inputs	6 Talkers 11 Vowels 264 Tokens	Multi Talker - 15%
Robinson and Fallside (1988b)	Recurrent Net 20 Inputs	7 Talkers 27 Phonemes 558 Sentences	Multi Talker - 30.8% Talker Dep. - 22.7%

Table 4: Recognition of Speech Using Recurrent Neural Nets.

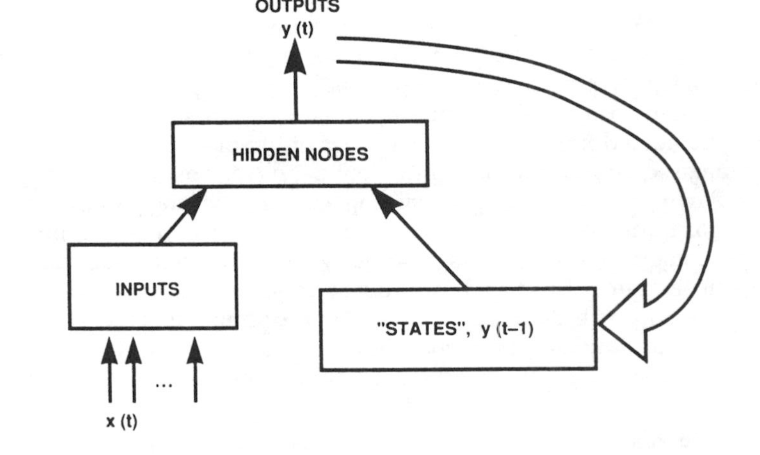

Figure 5: A recurrent neural net classifier.

Prager, Harrison, and Fallside (Prager et al. 1986) performed one of the first experiments to evaluate the use of Boltzmann machines for speech recognition. At the time this study was performed, the Boltzmann machine training algorithm described in (Ackley et al. 1985) was the only well-known technique that could be used to train nets with recurrent connections. This training algorithm is computationally intensive because simulated annealing procedures (Kirkpatrick et al. 1983) are used to perform a probabilistic search of connection weights. Binary input and output data representations were developed to apply Boltzmann machines to an 11-vowel recognition task. One successful net used 2048 input bits to represent 128 spectral values and 8 output bits to specify the vowel. Nets typically contained 40 hidden nodes and 7320 links. Training used 264 tokens from 6 talkers and required 6 to 15 hours of processing on a high-speed array processor. The resulting multi-talker error rate was 15%.

Prager, Harrison, and Fallside (Prager et al. 1986) also explored the use of a Boltzmann machine recognizer inspired by single-order Markov Model approaches to speech recognition. A block diagram of this recurrent net is presented in figure 5. The output of this net is delayed and fed back to the input to "carry" nodes that provide information about the prior state. This net was trained to identify words in two sentences spoken by one talker. Training time required 4 to 5 days of processing on a VAX 11/750 computer and performance was nearly perfect on the training sentences. Other recent work on Boltzmann machines (Bengio and De Mori 1988; Kohonen et al. 1988; Prager and Fallside 1987) demonstrates that good performance can be provided at the expense of excessive training time. Preliminary work on analog VLSI implementations of the training algorithm required by Boltzmann machines has demonstrated practical learning times for small hardware networks (Alspector and Allen 1987).

Many types of recurrent nets have been proposed that can be trained with modified forms of back-propagation. Jordan (1986) appears to have been the first to study nets with recurrent connections from output to input nodes as in figure 5. He used these nets to produce pattern sequences. Bourlard and Wellekens (1988) recently proved that such nets could be used to calculate local probabilities required in HMM recognizers and Robinson and Fallside (1988a) pointed out the relationship between these nets and state space equations used in classical control theory. Nets with recurrent self-looping connections on hidden and output nodes were studied by Watrous and Shastri (1987) for a speech recognition application. Nets with recurrent connections from hidden nodes to input nodes were studied by Elman (1988) and by Servan-Schreiber, Cleeremans, and McClelland (1988) for natural language applications.

Two recent studies have explored recurrent nets similar to the net shown in figure 5 when trained with modified forms of back-propagation. Robinson and Fallside (1988b) used such a net to label speech frames with one of 27 phoneme labels using hand-marked testing and training data. Training used an algorithm suggested by Rumelhart et al. (1986a) that, in effect, replicates the net at every time step during training. Talker-dependent error rates were 22.7% for the recurrent net and 26.0% for a simple feed-forward net with delays between input nodes to provide input context. Multi-talker error rates were 30.8% for the recurrent net and 40.8% for the feed-forward net. A 64 processor array of transputers provided practical training times in these experiments.

Anderson, Merrill, and Port (1988) also explored recurrent nets similar to the net in figure 5. Stimuli were CV syllables formed from six stop consonants and the vowel /a/ that were hand segmented to contain 120 msecs of speech around the vowel onset. Nets were trained on data from 10 talkers, tested on data from 10 other talkers, and contained from one to two hidden layers with different numbers of hidden nodes. Best performance (an error rate of 13.1%) was provided by a net with two hidden layers.

7 Integrating Neural Net and Conventional Approaches

Researchers are beginning to combine conventional HMM and DTW speech recognition algorithms with neural net classification algorithms and also to design neural net architectures that perform computations required by important speech recognition algorithms. This may lead to improved recognition accuracy and also to new designs for compact real-time hardware. Combining the good discrimination of neural net classifiers with the automatic scoring and training algorithms used in HMM recognizers could lead to rapid advances by building on existing high-performance recognizers. Studies that have combined neural net and conventional approaches to speech recognition are listed in table 5. Many (Bourlard and Wellekens 1987; Burr 1988b; Huang et al. 1988; Sakoe and Iso 1987) integrate multilayer perceptron classifiers with conventional DTW and HMM recognizers and one (Lippmann and Gold 1987) provides a neural-net architecture that could be used to implement an HMM Viterbi decoder. One study (Bourlard and Wellekens 1987) demonstrated how a multilayer perceptron could be integrated into a DTW continuous-speech recognizer to improve recognition performance.

Study	Approach	Comments
Bourlard and Wellekens (1987)	MLP Provides Allophone Distance Scores for DTW Recognizer	Good Performance on 918-Word, Talker-Dependent, Continuous-Speech Task
Burr (1988a)	MLP Classifier After Energy-Based DTW	Tested on Single-Talker E-Set
Huang and Lippmann (1988)	Second-Stage MLP Discrimination After HMM Recognizer	Improved Performance for "B,D,G" from TI Alpha-Digit Data Base
Lippmann and Gold (1987)	"Viterbi-Net" Neural Net Architecture for HMM Viterbi Decoder	Same Good Performance on Large Data Base as Robust HMM Recognizer
Sakoe and Iso (1987)	MLP Provides Distance Scores for DTW Recognizer	No Hand Labeling Required, Untested

Table 5: Studies Combining Neural Net and Conventional Approaches.

7.1 Integrating Multilayer Perceptron Classifiers with DTW and HMM Recognizers. At least three groups have proposed recognizers where multilayer perceptrons compute distance scores used in DTW or HMM recognizers (Bourlard and Wellekens 1987; Burr 1988a; Sakoe and Iso 1987). Bourlard and Wellekens (1987) demonstrated how the multilayer perceptron shown in figure 6 could be used to calculate allophone distance scores required for phoneme and word recognition in a DTW discrete-observation recognizer. One net had inputs from 15 frames of speech centered on the current frame, 50 hidden nodes, and 26 output nodes. Outputs corresponded to allophones in a 10-digit German vocabulary. Inputs were from 60 binary variables per frame. One input bit was on in each frame to specify the codebook entry that represented that frame. The multilayer perceptron was trained using hand-labeled training data to provide a high output only for that output node corresponding to the current input allophone. Recognition then used dynamic time warping with local distances equal to values from output nodes. This provides good discrimination from the neural net and integration over time from the DTW algorithm. Perfect recognition performance was provided for recognition of 100 tokens from one talker.

Bourlard and Wellekens (1987) also used a multilayer perceptron with contextual input and DTW to recognize words from a more difficult 919-word talker-dependent continuous-speech task. The net covered an input context of 9 frames, used one of 132 vectors to quantize each frame, had 50 or 200 hidden nodes, and had 50 output nodes corresponding to 50 German phonemes. This net was trained using 100 hand-segmented sentences and tested on 188 other sentences containing roughly 7300 phonemes. The phoneme error rate was 41.6% with 50 hidden nodes and 37% with 200 hidden nodes. These error rates were both lower than the 47.5% error rate provided by a simple discrete-observation HMM recognizer with duration modeling and one probability histogram per phoneme. Bourlard and Wellekens suggested that performance could be improved and the need for hand-segmented training data could be eliminated by embedding multilayer perceptron back-propagation training in an iterative Viterbi-like training loop. This loop could progressively improve segmentation for DTW or HMM recognizers. Iterative Viterbi training was not performed because the simpler single-pass training required roughly 200 hours on a SUN-3 workstation. As noted above, Bourlard and Wellekens (1988) also recently proved that recurrent neural nets could calculate local probabilities required in HMM recognizers.

Sakoe and Iso (1987) suggested a recognition structure similar to that of Bourlard and Wellekens (1987) where a multilayer perceptron with delays between input nodes computes local distance scores. They, however, do not require output nodes of the multilayer perceptron to represent sub-word units such as phonemes. Instead, a training algorithm is described that is similar to the iterative Viterbi-like training loop suggested by Bourlard and Wellekens (1987) but for continuous input parameters. No results were presented for this approach.

Burr (1988a) gave results for a recognizer where words were first aligned based on energy information to provide a fixed 20 input frames of spectral information. These inputs were fed to nine outputs representing members of the E-set ("B,C,D,E,G,P,T,V,Z"). This recognizer was trained and tested using 180 tokens from one talker. Results were nearly perfect when the initial parts of these words were oversampled.

Huang and Lippmann demonstrated how a second-stage of analysis using a multilayer perceptron could decrease the error rate of an HMM recognizer (Huang and Lippmann 1988). The Viterbi backtraces from an HMM recognizer were used to segment input speech frames and average HMM log probability scores for segments were provided as inputs to single- and multilayer perceptrons. Performance was evaluated using the letters "B,D,G" spoken by the 16 talkers in the TI alpha-digit data base. Ten training tokens per letter were used to train the HMM and neural net recognizer for each talker and the 16 other tokens were used for testing. Best performance was provided by a single-layer perceptron which almost halved the error rate. The error rate dropped from 7.2% errors with the HMM recognizer alone to 3.8% errors with the neural net postprocessor.

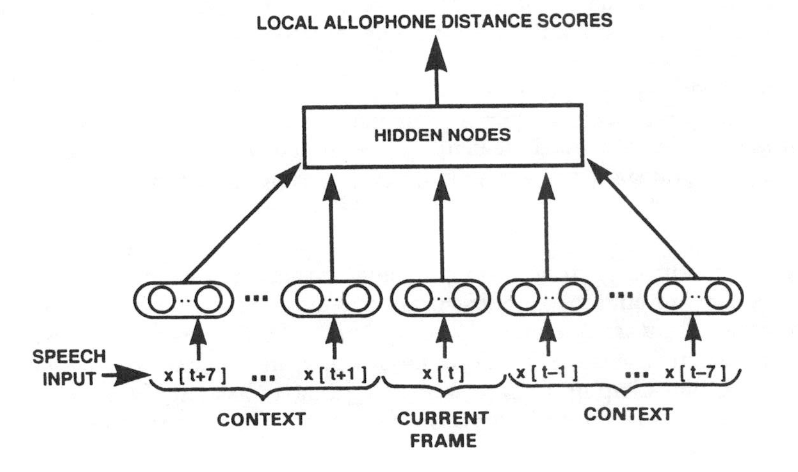

Figure 6: A feed-forward multilayer perceptron that was used to compute allophone distance scores for a DTW recognizer.

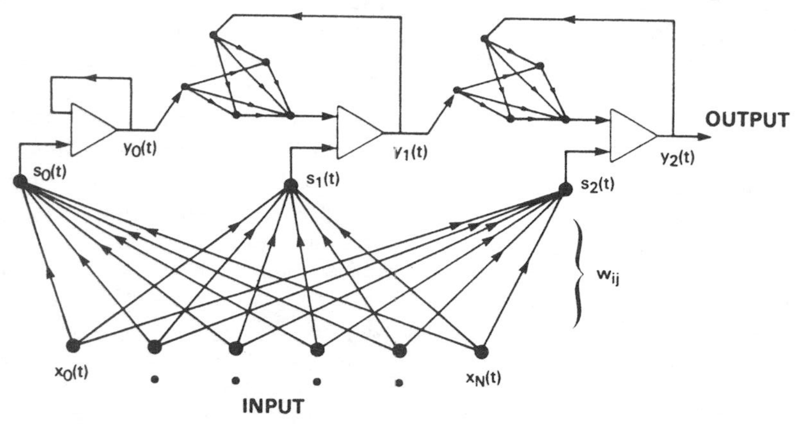

Figure 7: A recurrent neural net called a Viterbi net that performs the calculations required in an HMM Viterbi decoder.

7.2 A Neural Net Architecture to Implement a Viterbi Decoder. Lippmann and Gold (1987) described a neural-net architecture called a Viterbi net that could be used to implement the Viterbi decoder used in many continuous observation HMM recognizers using analog VLSI techniques. This net is shown in figure 7. Nodes represented by open triangles correspond to nodes in a left-to-right HMM word model. Each of these triangles represents a threshold-logic node followed by a fixed delay. Small subnets in the upper part of the figure select the maximum of two inputs as described in (Lippmann et al. 1987) and subnets in the lower part sum all inputs. A temporal sequence of input vectors is presented at the input and the output is proportional to the log probability calculated by a Viterbi decoder. The structure of the Viterbi net illustrates how neural net components can be integrated to design a complex net which performs the calculations required by an important conventional algorithm.

The Viterbi net differs from the Viterbi decoding algorithm normally implemented in software and was thus evaluated using 4000 word tokens from the 9-talker 35-word Lincoln Stress-Style speech data base. Connection strengths in Viterbi nets with 15 internal nodes (one node per HMM model state) were adjusted based on parameter estimates obtained from the forward-backward algorithm. Inputs consisted of 12 mel cepstra and 13 differential mel cepstra that were updated every 10 msec. Performance was good and almost identical to that of current Robust HMM isolated-word recognizers (Lippmann and Gold 1987). The error rate was 0.56% or only 23 out of 4095 tokens wrong. One advantage an analog implementation of this net would have over digital approaches is that the frame rate could be increased to provide improved temporal resolution without requiring higher clock rates.

8 Other Nets for Pattern Sequence Recognition

In addition to the neural net models described above, other nets motivated primarily by psychological and physiological findings and by past work on associative memories have been proposed for speech recognition and pattern sequence recognition. Although some of these nets represent new approaches to the problem of pattern sequence recognition, few have been integrated into speech recognizers and none have been evaluated using large speech data bases.

8.1 Psychological Neural Net Models of Speech Perception. Three neural net models have been proposed which are primarily psychological models of speech perception (Elman and McClelland 1986; MacKay 1987; Marslen-Wilson 1987; Rumelhart et al. 1986b). The COHORT model developed by Marslen-Wilson (1987) assumes a left-to-right real-time acoustic phonetic analysis of speech as in current recognizers. It accounts for many psychophysical results in speech recognition such as the existence of a time when a word becomes unambiguously recognized (recognition point), the word frequency effect, and recognition of contextually inappropriate words. This model, however, is descriptive and is not expressed as a computational model.

Hand crafted versions of the TRACE and Interactive Activation models developed by Elman, McClelland, Rumelhart, and co-workers were tested with small speech data bases (Elman and McClelland 1986; Rumelhart et al. 1986b). These models are based on neuron-like nodes, include both feed-forward and feed-back connections, use nodes with multiplicative operations, and emphasizes the benefits that can be obtained by using co-articulation information to aid in word recognition. These models are impractical because the problems of time alignment and training are not addressed and the entire network must be copied on every new time step. The Node Structure Theory developed by MacKay (1987) is a qualitative neural theory of speech recognition and production. It is similar in many ways to the above models, but considers problems related to talking rate, stuttering, internal speech, and rhythm.

8.2 Physiological Models For Temporal Pattern Recognition. Neural net approaches motivated primarily by physiological and behavioral results have also been proposed to perform some component of the time alignment task (Cohen et al. 1987; Dehaene et al. 1987; Wong and Chen 1986). Wong and Chen (1986) and Dehaene et al. (1987) describe similar models that have been tested with a small amount of speech data. These models include neurons with shunting or multiplicative nodes similar to those that have been proposed in the retina to compute direction of motion (Poggio and Koch 1987). Three neurons can be grouped to form a "synaptic triad" that can be used to recognize two component pattern sequences. This triad will have a strong output only if the modulator input goes "high" and then, a short time later, the primary input goes "high."

Synaptic triads can be arranged in sequences and in hierarchies to recognize features, allophones and words (Wong and Chen 1986). In limited tests, hand crafted networks could recognize a small set of words spoken by one talker (Wong and Chen 1986). More interesting is a proposed technique for training such networks without supervision (Dehaene et al. 1987). If effective, this could make use of the large amount of unlabeled speech data that is available and lead to automatic creation of sub-word models. Further elaboration is necessary to describe how networks with synaptic triads could be trained and used in a recognizer.

Cohen and Grossberg proposed a network called a masking field that has not yet been tested with speech input (Cohen and Grossberg 1987).

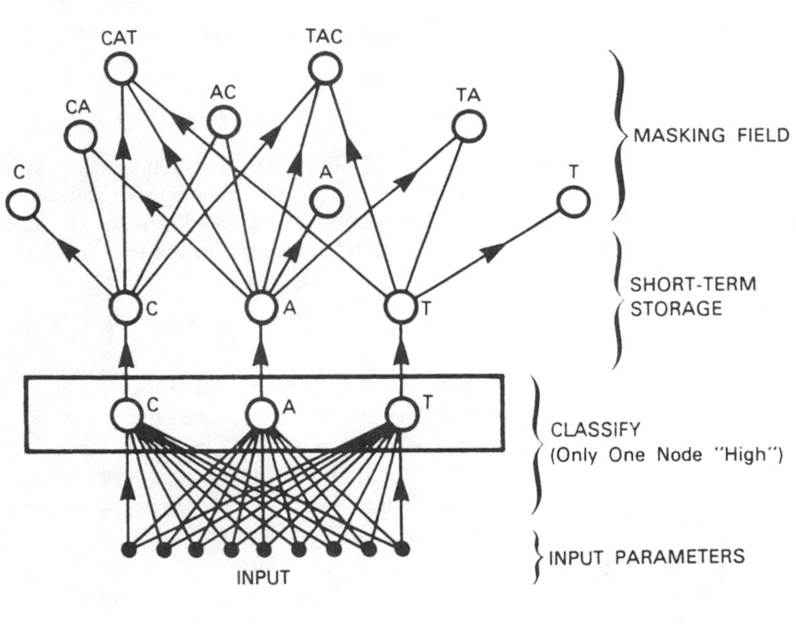

Figure 8: A model called a masking field that can be used to detect pattern sequences.

This network is shown in figure 8. Inputs are applied to the bottom subnet which is similar to a feature map net (Kohonen et al. 1984). Typically, only one node in this subnet has a "high" output at any time. Subnet node outputs feed short-term storage nodes whose outputs decay slowly over time. Different input pattern sequences thus lead to different amplitude patterns in short term storage. For example the input C-A-T sampled at the end of the word will yield an intensity pattern in short-term storage with node C low, node A intermediate, and node T high. The input T-A-C will yield a pattern with node C high, node A intermediate, and node T low. These intensity patterns are weighted and fed to nodes in a masking field with weights adjusted to detect different patterns. The masking field is designed such that all nodes compete to be active and nodes representing longer patterns inhibit nodes representing shorter patterns. This approach can recognize short isolated pattern sequences but has difficulty recognizing patterns with repeated sub-sequences because nodes in short-term storage corresponding to those sub-sequences can become saturated. Further elaboration is necessary to describe how masking fields should be integrated into a full recognizer. Other recent studies (Jordan 1986; Stornetta et al. 1988; Tattersall et al. 1988) have also proposed using slowly-decaying nodes as short-term storage to provide history useful for pattern recognition and pattern sequence generation.

8.3 Sequential Associative Memories. A final approach to pattern sequence recognition is to build a sequential associative memory for pattern sequences as described in (Amit 1988; Buhmann and Schulten 1988; Hecht-Nielsen 1987; Kleinfield 1986; Sompolinsky and Kanter 1986). These nets extend past work on associative memories by Hopfield and Little (Hopfield 1982; Little 1974) to the case where pattern sequences instead of static patterns can be restored. Recognition in this approach corresponds to the net settling into a desired sequence of stable states, one after the other, when driven by an input temporal pattern sequence.

Dynamic associative memory models developed by Amit, Kleinfield, Sompolinsky, and Kanter (Amit 1988; Kleinfield 1986; Sompolinsky and Kanter 1986) use long and short delays on links to generate and recognize pattern sequences. Links with short delays mutually excite a small set of nodes to produce stable states. Links with long delays excite nodes in the next expected stable state. Transitions between states thus occur at predetermined times that depend on the delays in the links. A net developed by Buhmann and Schulten (1988) uses probabilistic nodes to produce sequencing behavior similar to that produced by a Markov chain. Transitions in this net occur stochastically but at some average rate. A final net described by Hecht-Nielsen (1987) is a modified version of Grossberg's avalanche net (Grossberg 1988). The input to this net is similar in structure to Kohonen's feature map. It differs in that nodes have different rise and fall time constants and overall network activity is controlled such that only the outputs of a few nodes are "high" at any time.

A few relatively small simulations have been performed to explore the behavior of the sequential associative memories. Simulations have demonstrated that these nets can complete pattern sequences given the first element of a sequence (Buhmann and Schulten 1988) and also perform such functions as counting the number of input patterns presented to a net (Amit 1988). Although this approach is theoretically very interesting and may be a good model of some neural processing, no tests have been performed with speech data. In addition, further work is necessary to develop training procedures and useful decoding strategies that could be applied in a complete speech recognizer.

9 Summary of Past Research

The performance of current speech recognizers is far below that of humans. Neural nets offer the potential of providing massive parallelism, adaptation, and new algorithmic approaches to speech recognition problems. Researchers are investigating:

1. New physiological-based front ends,
2. Neural net classifiers for static speech input patterns,
3. Neural nets designed specifically to classify temporal pattern sequences,
4. Combined recognizers that integrate neural net and conventional recognition approaches,
5. Neural net architectures that implement conventional algorithms, and
6. VLSI hardware neural nets that implement both neural net and conventional algorithms.

Physiological front ends have provided improved recognition accuracy in noise (Ghitza 1988; Hunt and Lefèbvre 1988) and a cochlea filterbank that could be used in these front ends has been implemented using micro-power VLSI techniques (Lyon and Mead 1988). Many nets can compute the complex likelihood functions required by continuous-distribution recognizers and perform the vector quantization required by discrete-observation recognizers. Kohonen's feature map algorithm (Kohonen et al. 1984) has been used successfully to vector quantize speech and preliminary VLSI hardware versions of this net have been built (Mann et al. 1988).

Multilayer perceptron networks with delays have provided excellent discrimination between small sets of difficult-to-discriminate speech inputs (Kammerer and Kupper 1988; Lang and Hinton 1988; Peeling and Moore 1987; Waibel et al. 1987; Waibel et al. 1988; Watrous 1988). Good discrimination was provided for a set of 18 consonants in varying phonetic contexts (Waibel et al. 1988), similar E-set words such as "B,D,E,V" (Lang and Hinton 1988), and digits and words from small-vocabularies (Kammerer and Kupper 1988; Peeling and Moore 1987; Watrous 1988). In some cases performance was similar to or slightly better than that provided by a more conventional HMM or DTW recognizer (Kammerer and Kupper 1988; Lang and Hinton 1988; Peeling and Moore 1987; Waibel et al. 1987; 1988). In almost all cases, a neural net approach performed as well as or slightly better than conventional approaches but provided a parallel architecture that could be used for implementation and a computationally simple and incremental training algorithm.

Approaches to the problem of scaling a network up in size to discriminate between members of a large set have been proposed and demonstrated (Waibel et al. 1988). For example, a net that classifies 18 consonants accurately was constructed from subnets trained to discriminate between smaller subsets of these consonants. Algorithms that use combined unsupervised/supervised training and provide high performance and extremely rapid training have also been demonstrated (Huang and Lippmann 1988; Kohonen et al. 1988). New training algorithms are under development (Almeida 1987; Jordan 1986; Pineda 1987; Rohwer and Forrest 1987; Watrous 1988) that can be used with recurrent networks.

Preliminary studies have explored recognizers that combine conventional and neural net approaches. Promising continuous-speech recognition results have been obtained by integrating multilayer perceptrons into a DTW recognizer (Bourlard and Wellekens 1987) and a multilayer perceptron post processor has improved the performance of an isolated-word HMM recognizer (Huang et al. 1988). Neural net architectures have also been designed for important conventional algorithms. For example, recurrent neural net architectures have been developed to implement the Viterbi decoding algorithm used in many HMM speech recognizers (Lippmann and Gold 1987) and also to compute local probabilities required in discrete-observation HMM recognizers (Bourlard and Wellekens 1988).

Many new neural net models have been proposed for recognizing temporal pattern sequences. Some are based on physiological data and attempt to model the behavior of biological nets (Dehaene et al. 1987; Cohen et al. 1987; Wong and Chen 1986) while others attempt to extend existing auto-associative networks to temporal problems (Amit 1988; Buhmann and Schulten 1988; Kleinfield 1986; Sompolinsky and Kanter 1986). New learning algorithms and net architectures will, however, be required to provide the real-time response and automatic learning of internal word and phrase models required for high-performance continuous speech recognition. This is still a major unsolved important problem in the field of neural nets.

10 Suggestions for Future Work

Further work should emphasize networks that provide rapid response and could be used with real-time speech input. They must include internal mechanisms to distinguish speech from background noise and to determine when a word has been presented. They also must operate with continuous acoustic input and not require hand marking of test speech data, long internal delays, or duplication of the network for new inputs.

Short-term research should focus on a task that current recognizers perform poorly on such as accurate recognition of difficult sets of isolated words. Such a task wouldn't require excessive computation resources or extremely large data bases. A potential initial problem is talker-independent recognition of difficult E-set words or phonemes as in (Lang and Hinton 1988; Waibel et al. 1988). Techniques developed using small difficult vocabularies should be extended to larger vocabularies and continuous speech as soon as feasible. Efforts should focus on: developing training algorithms to construct sub-word and word models automatically without excessive supervision, developing better front-end acoustic-phonetic feature extraction, improving low-level acoustic/phonetic discrimination, integrating temporal sequence information over time, and developing more rapid training techniques. Researchers should continue integrating neural net approaches to classification with conventional approaches to training and scoring. Longer-term research on continuous-speech recognition must address the problems of developing high-level speech-understanding systems that can learn and use internal models of the world. These systems must be able to learn and use syntactic, semantic, and pragmatic constraints.

Efforts on building neural net VLSI hardware for speech recognition should also continue. The development of compact real-time speech recognizers is a major goal of neural net research. Parallel neural-net architectures should be designed to perform the computations required by successful algorithms and then these architectures should be implemented and tested. Recent developments in analog VLSI neural nets suggest that this approach has the potential to provide the high computation rates required for both front-end acoustic analysis and high-level pattern matching.

All future work should take advantage of the many speech data bases that currently exist and use results obtained with experimental HMM and DTW recognizers with these data bases as benchmarks. Descriptions of some common data bases and comments on their availability are in (Pallett 1986; Price et al. 1988). Detailed evaluations using large speech data bases are necessary to guide research and permit comparisons between alternative approaches. Results obtained on a few locally-recorded speech samples are often misleading and are not informative to other researchers.

Research should also build on the current state of knowledge in neural networks, pattern classification theory, statistics, and conventional HMM and DTW approaches to speech recognition. Researchers should become familiar with these areas and not duplicate existing work. Introductions to current HMM and DTW approaches are available in (Dixon and Martin 1979; Lee and Hon 1988; Parsons 1986; Rabiner and Juang 1986; Rabiner et al. 1978) and introductions to statistics and pattern classification are available in many books including (Duda and Hart 1973; Fukunaga 1972; Nilsson 1965).

Acknowledgments

I would like to thank members of Royal Signals and Radar Establishment including John Bridle and Roger Moore for discussions regarding the material in this paper. I would also like to thank Bill Huang and Ben Gold for interesting discussions and Carolyn for her patience.

References

Ackley, D.H., G.E. Hinton, and T.J. Sejnowski. 1985. A Learning Algorithm for Boltzmann Machines. *Cognitive Science* **9**, 147–160.

Albus, J.S. 1981. *Brain, Behavior, and Robotics*. BYTE Books.

Almeida, L.B. 1987. A Learning Rule for Asynchronous Perceptrons with Feedback in a Combinatorial Environment. *In:* 1st International Conference on Neural Networks. IEEE, II–609.

Alspector, J. and R.B. Allen. 1987. A Neuromorphic VLSI Learning System. *In:* Advanced Research in VLSI: Proceedings of the 1987 Stanford Conference, ed. P Losleben, 313–349. Cambridge: MIT Press.

Amit, D.J. 1988. Neural Networks for Counting Chimes. *Proceedings National Academy of Science, USA* **85**, 2141–2145.

Anderson, S., J. Merrill, and R. Port. 1988. *Dynamic Speech Categorization With Recurrent Networks*. Technical Report 258, Department of Linguistics and Department of Computer Science, Indiana University.

Averbuch, A., L. Bahl, and R. Bakis. 1987. Experiments with the Tangora 20,000 Word Speech Recognizer. *In:* Proceedings IEEE International Conference on Acoustics Speech and Signal Processing, Dallax, TX, 701–704.

Bahl, L.R., P.F. Brown, P.V. De Souza, and R.L. Mercer. 1988. Modeling Acoustic Sequences of Continuous Parameters. *In:* Proceedings IEEE International Conference on Acoustics, Speech and Signal Processing, New York, NY, 40–43.

Baldi, P. and K. Hornik. 1988. Neural Networks and Principal Component Analysis: Learning from Examples Without Local Minima. *Neural Networks* **2**, 53–58.

Beet, S.W., H.E.G. Powrie, R.K. Moore, and M.J. Tomlinson. 1988. Improved Speech Recognition Using a Reduced Auditory Representation. *In:* Proceedings IEEE International Conference on Acoustics, Speech and Signal Processing, New York, NY, 75–78.

Bengio, Y. and R. De Mori. 1988. Use of Neural Networks for the Recognition of Place of Articulation. *In:* Proceedings IEEE International Conference on Acoustics, Speech and Signal Processing, New York, NY, 103–106.

Bourlard, H. and Y. Kamp. 1988. Auto-Association by Multilayer Perceptrons and Singular Value Decomposition. *Biological Cybernetics* **59**, 291–294.

Bourlard, H. and C.J. Wellekens. 1988. *Links Between Markov Models and Multilayer Perceptrons.* Technical Report Manuscript M-263, Phillips Research Laboratory, Brussels, Belgium.

———. 1987. *Speech Pattern Discrimination and Multilayer Perceptrons.* Technical Report Manuscript M-211, Phillips Research Laboratory, Brussels, Belgium. Scheduled to appear in the December issue of *Computer, Speech and Language.*

Bridle, J. 1988. Neural Network Experience at the RSRE Speech Research Unit. ATR Workshop on Neural Networks and Parallel Distributed Processing, Osaka, Japan.

Broomhead, D.S. and D. Lowe. 1988. *Radial Basis Functions, multi-variable functional interpolation and adaptive networks.* Technical Report RSRE Memorandum No. 4148, Royal Speech and Radar Establishment, Malvern, Worcester, Great Britain.

Buhmann, J. and K. Schulten. 1988. Noise-Driven Temporal Association in Neural Networks. *Europhysics Letters* **4**, 1205–1209.

Burr, D.J. 1988a. Experiments on Neural Net Recognition of Spoken and Written Text. *In:* IEEE Transactions on Acoustics, Speech and Signal Processing, **36**, 1162–1168.

———. 1988b. Speech Recognition Experiments with Perceptrons. *In:* Neural Information Processing Systems, ed. D. Anderson, 144–153. New York: American Institute of Physics.

Burton, D.K., J.E. Shore, and J.T. Buck. 1985. Isolated-Word Speech Recognition Using Multisection Vector Quantization Codebooks. *In:* IEEE Transactions on Acoustics, Speech and Signal Processing, **ASSP-33**, 837–849.

Cohen, M. and S. Grossberg. 1987. Masking fields: A Massively Parallel Neural Architecture for learning, recognizing, and predicting multiple groupings of patterned data. *Applied Optics* **26**, 1866–1891.

Cohen, M.A., S. Grossberg, and D. Stork. 1987. Recent Developments in a Neural Model of Real-Time Speech Analysis and Synthesis. *In:* 1st International Conference on Neural Networks, IEEE.

Cowan, J.D. and D.H. Sharp. 1988. Neural Nets and Artificial Intelligence. *Daedalus* **117**, 85–121.

Cybenko, G. 1988. *Continuous Valued Neural Networks with Two Hidden Layers are Sufficient.* Technical Report, Department of Computer Science, Tufts University.

Dehaene, S., J. Changeux, and J. Nadal. 1987. Neural Networks that Learn Temporal Sequences by Selection. *Proceedings National Academy Science, USA, Biophysics* **84**, 2727–2713.

Deng, Li and C. Daniel Geisler. 1987. A Composite Auditory Model for Processing Speech Sounds. *Journal of the Acoustical Society of America* **82:6**, 2001–2012.

Dixon, N.R. and T.B. Martin. 1979. *Automatic Speech and Speaker Recognition.* New York: IEEE Press.

Doddington, G.R. and T.B. Schalk. 1981. Speech Recognition: Turning Theory into Practice. *IEEE Spectrum,* 26–32.

Duda, R.O. and P.E. Hart. 1973. Pattern Classification and Scene Analysis. New York: John-Wiley & Sons.

Elman, J.L. 1988. *Finding Structure in Time.* CRL Technical Report 8801, University of California, San Diego, CA.

Elman, J.L. and J.L. McClelland. 1986. Exploiting Lawful Variability in the Speech Wave. *In:* Invariance and Variability in Speech Processes, eds. J.S. Perkell and D.H. Klatt. New Jersey: Lawrence Erlbaum.

Elman, J.L. and D. Zipser. 1987. *Learning the Hidden Structure of Speech.* ICS Report 8701, Institute for Cognitive Science, University of California, San Diego, La Jolla, CA.

Fallside, F., T.D. Harrison, R.W. Prager, and A.J.R. Robinson. 1988. A Comparison of Three Connectionist Models for Phoneme Recognition in Continuous Speech. ATR Workshop on Neural Networks and Parallel Distributed Processing, Osaka, Japan.

Fukunaga, K. 1972. *Introduction to Statistical Pattern Recognition.* New York: Academic Press.

Ghitza, O. 1988. Auditory Neural Feedback as a Basis for Speech Processing. *In:* Proceedings IEEE International Conference on Acoustics Speech and Signal Processing, New York, NY, 91–94.

Gold, B. 1988. A Neural Network for Isolated Word Recognition. *In:* Proceedings IEEE International Conference on Acoustics Speech and Signal Processing, New York, NY, 44–47.

Greenberg, S. 1988a. The Ear as a Speech Analyzer. *Journal of Phonetics* **16**, 139–149.

———. 1988b. Special Issue on "Representation of Speech in the Auditory Periphery." *Journal of Phonetics* **16**.

Grossberg, S. 1988. Nonlinear Neural Networks: Principles, Mechanisms, and Architectures. *Neural Networks* **1**, 17–61.

Hanson, S.J. and D.J. Burr. 1987. *Knowledge Representation in Connectionist Networks.* Technical Report, Bell Communications Research, Morristown, New Jersey.

Harrison, T.D. and F. Fallside. 1988. *A Connectionist Structure for Phoneme Recognition.* Technical Report CUED/F-INFENG/TR.15, Cambridge University Engineering Department.

Hecht-Nielsen, R. 1987. Nearest Matched Filter Classification of Spatiotemporal Patterns. *Applied Optics* **26**, 1892–1899.

Hinton, G.E. 1987. *Connectionist Learning Procedures.* Technical Report CMU-CS-87-115, Carnegie Mellon University, Computer Science Department.

Homma, T., L.E. Atlas, and R.J. Marks. 1988. An Artificial Neural Network for Spatio-Temporal Bipolar Patterns: Application to Phoneme Classification. *In:* Neural Information Processing Systems, ed. D. Anderson, 31–40. New York: American Institute of Physics.

Hopfield, J.J. 1982. Neural Networks and Physical Systems with Emergent Collective Computational Abilities. *Proceedings of the National Academy of Sciences, USA* **79**, 2554–2558.

Huang, W.M. and R.P. Lippmann. 1988. Neural Net and Traditional Classifiers. *In:* Neural Information Processing Systems, ed. D. Anderson, 387–396. New York: American Institute of Physics.

Huang, W.M., R.P. Lippmann, T. Nguyen. 1988. Neural Nets for Speech Recognition. *In:* Conference of the Acoustical Society of America, Seattle WA.

Hunt, M.J. and C. Lefèbvre. 1988. Speaker Dependent and Independent Speech Recognition Experiments With an Auditory Model. *In:* Proceedings IEEE International Conference on Acoustics, Speech and Signal Processing **1**, New York, 215–218.

Irino, T. and H. Kawahara. 1988. A Study on the Speaker Independent Feature Extraction of Japanese Vowels by Neural Networks. ATR Workshop on Neural Networks and Parallel Distributed Processing, Osaka, Japan.

Jordan, M.I. 1986. *Serial Order: A Parallel Distributed Processing Approach.* Institute for Cognitive Science Report 8604, University of California, San Diego.

Kamm, C., T. Landauer, and S. Singhal. 1988. Training an Adaptive Network to Spot Demisyllables in Continuous Speech. ATR Workshop on Neural Networks and Parallel Distributed Processing, Osaka, Japan.

Kammerer, B. and W. Kupper. 1988. Experiments for Isolated-Word Recognition with Single and Multi-Layer Perceptrons, Abstracts of 1st Annual INNS Meeting, Boston. *Neural Networks* **1**, 302.

Kirkpatrick, S., C.D. Gelatt, and M.P. Vecchi. 1983. Optimization by Simulated Annealing. *Science* **229**, 671–679.

Klatt, K.H. 1986. The Problem of Variability In Speech Recognition and Models of Speech Perception. *In:* Invariance and Variability in Speech Processes, eds. J.S. Perkell and D.H. Klatt, 300-324. New Jersey: Lawrence Erlbaum.

Kleinfield, D. 1986. Sequential State Generation by Model Neural Networks. *Proceedings National Academy Science, USA, Biophysics* **83**, 9469–9473.

Kohonen, T. 1988. An Introduction to Neural Computing. *Neural Networks* **1**, 3–16.

Kohonen, T. 1984. *Self-Organization and Associative Memory.* Berlin: Springer-Verlag.

Kohonen, T., G. Barna, and R. Chrisley. 1988. Statistical Pattern Recognition with Neural Networks: Benchmarking Studies. *In:* IEEE Annual International Conference on Neural Networks, San Diego, July.

Kohonen, T., K. Makisara, and T. Saramaki. 1984. Phonotopic Maps — Insightful Representation of Phonological Features for Speech Recognition. *In:* IEEE Proceedings of the 7th International Conference on Pattern Recognition.

Lang, K.J. and G.E. Hinton. 1988. *The Development of the Time-Delay Neural Network Architecture for Speech Recognition.* Technical Report CMU-CS-88-152, Carnegie-Mellon University.

Lapedes, A. and R. Farber. 1988. How Neural Nets Work. *In:* Neural Information Processing Systems, ed. D. Anderson, 442–456. New York: American Institute of Physics.

Lee, Kai-Fu and Hsiao-Wuen Hon. 1988. Large-Vocabulary Speaker-Independent Continuous Speech Recognition Using HMM. *In:* Proceedings IEEE International Conference on Acoustics, Speech and Signal Processing **1**, 123–126.

Lee, Y.C., G. Doolen, H.H. Chen, G.Z. Sun, T. Maxwell, H.Y. Lee, C.L. Giles. 1986. Machine Learning Using a Higher Order Correlation Network. *Physica D*, 276–306.

Leung, H.C. and V.W. Zue. 1988. Some Phonetic Recognition Experiments Using Artificial Neural Nets. *In:* Proceedings IEEE International Conference on Acoustics, Speech and Signal Processing **1**.

Lippmann, R.P., B. Gold, and M.L. Malpass. 1987. *A Comparison of Hamming and Hopfield Neural Nets for Pattern Classification.* Technical Report TR-769, MIT Lincoln Lab.

Lippmann, R.P. 1987. An Introduction to Computing with Neural Nets. *IEEE ASSP Magazine* **4:2**, 4–22.

Lippmann, R.P. and Ben Gold. 1987. Neural Classifiers Useful for Speech Recognition. *In:* 1st International Conference on Neural Networks, IEEE, IV–417.

Little, W.A. 1974. The Existence of Persistent States in the Brain. *Mathematical Biosciences* **19**, 101–120.

Lyon, R.F. and C. Mead. 1988. An Analog Electronic Cochlea. *IEEE Transactions on Acoustics, Speech and Signal Processing* **36**, 1119–1134.

MacKay, D.G. 1987. *The Organization of Perception and Action*, New York: Springer Verlag.

Mann, J., J. Raffel, R. Lippmann, and B. Berger. 1988. A Self-Organizing Neural Net Chip. Neural Networks for Computing Conference, Snowbird, Utah.

Marslen-Wilson, W.D. 1987. Functional Parallelism in Spoken Word-Recognition. *In:* Spoken Word Recognition, eds. U.H. Frauenfelder and L.K. Tyler. Cambridge, MA: MIT Press.

McDermott, E. and S. Katagiri. 1988. Phoneme Recognition Using Kohonen's Learning Vector Quantization. ATR Workshop on Neural Networks and Parallel Distributed Processing, Osaka, Japan.

Moody, J. 1988. Speedy Alternatives to Back Propagation. Neural Networks for Computing Conference, Snowbird, Utah.

Moody, J. and C. Darken. 1988. *Learning with Localized Receptive Fields.* Technical Report YALEU/DCS/RR-649, Yale Computer Science Department, New Haven, CT.

Naylor, J. and K.P. Li. 1988. Analysis of a Neural Network Algorithm for Vector Quantization of Speech Parameters, Abstracts of 1st Annual INNS Meeting, Boston. *Neural Networks* **1**, 310.

Nilsson, Nils J. 1965. *Learning Machines.* New York: McGraw Hill.

Niranjan, M. and F. Fallside. 1988. *Neural Networks and Radial Basis Functions in Classifying Static Speech Patterns.* Technical Report CUED/F-INFENG/TR 22, Cambridge University Engineering Department.

Omohundro, S.M. 1987. Efficient Algorithms with Neural Network Behavior. *Complex Systems* **1**, 273–347.

Pallett, D.S. 1986. A PCM/VCR Speech Database Exchange Format. *In:* Proceedings IEEE International Conference on Acoustics, Speech and Signal Processing, Tokyo, Japan, 317–320.

Parsons, T. 1986. *Voice and Speech Processing*. New York: McGraw-Hill.

Paul, D.B. 1987. A Speaker-Stress Resistant HMM Isolated Word Recognizer. *ICASSP 87*, 713–716.

Peeling, S.M. and R.K. Moore. 1987. *Experiments in Isolated Digit Recognition Using the Multi-Layer Perceptron*. Technical Report 4073, Royal Speech and Radar Establishment, Malvern, Worcester, Great Britain.

Peterson, Gordon E. and Harold L. Barney. 1952. Control Methods Used in a Study of Vowels. *The Journal of the Acoustical Society of America* **24:2**, 175–84.

Pineda, F.J. 1987. Generalization of Back-Propagation to Recurrent Neural Networks. *Physical Review Letters* **59**, 2229–2232.

Poggio, T. and C. Koch. 1987. Synapses that Compute Motion. *Scientific American* **256**, 46–52.

Prager, R.W. and F. Fallside. 1987. A Comparison of the Boltzmann Machine and the Back Propagation Network as Recognizers of Static Speech Patterns. *Computer Speech and Language* **2**, 179–183.

Prager, R.W., T.D. Harrison, and F. Fallside. 1986. Boltzmann Machines for Speech Recognition. *Computer Speech and Language* **1**, 2–27.

Price, P., W.M. Fisher, J. Bernstein, D.S. Pallett. 1988. The DARPA 1000-Word Resource Management Database for Continuous Speech Recognition. *In:* Proceedings IEEE International Conference on Acoustics, Speech and Signal Processing, New York **1**, 651–654.

Rabiner, L.R. and B.H. Juang. 1986. An Introduction to Hidden Markov Models. *IEEE ASSP Magazine* **3:1**, 4–16.

Rabiner, Lawrence R. and Ronald W. Schafer. 1978. *Digital Processing of Speech*. New Jersey: Prentice-Hall.

Raffel, J., J. Mann, R. Berger, A. Soares, and S. Gilbert. 1987. A Generic Architecture for Wafer-Scale Neuromorphic Systems. *In:* 1st International Conference on Neural Networks, IEEE.

Robinson, A.J. and F. Fallside. 1988a. A Dynamic Connectionist Model for Phoneme Recognition. *nEuro '88*, Paris, France.

———. 1988b. Static and Dynamic Error Propagation Networks with Application to Speech Coding. *In:* Neural Information Processing Systems, ed. D. Anderson, 632–641. New York: American Institute of Physics.

Rohwer, R. and B. Forrest. 1987. Training Time-Dependencies in Neural Networks. *In:* 1st International Conference on Neural Networks, IEEE, II–701.

Rossen, M.L., L.T. Niles, G.N. Tajchman, M.A. Bush, J.A. Anderson, and S.E. Blumstein. 1988. A Connectionist Model for Consonant-vowel Syllable Recognition. *In:* Proceedings IEEE International Conference on Acoustics, Speech and Signal Processing, New York, NY, 59–66.

Rumelhart, D.E., G.E. Hinton, and R.J. Williams. 1986a. Interactive Processes in Speech Perception: The TRACE Model. *In:* Parallel Distributed Processing: Vol. 2, Psychological and Biological Models, eds. D.E. Rumelhart and J.L. McClelland. Cambridge, MA: MIT Press.

———. 1986b. Learning Internal Representations by Error Propagation. *In:* Parallel Distributed Processing: Vol. 1, Foundations. Cambridge, MA: MIT Press.

Sakoe, H. and K. Iso. 1987. *Dynamic Neural Network — A New Speech Recognition Model Based on Dynamic Programming and Neural Network.* IEICE Technical Report 87, NEC Corporation.

Seneff, S. 1988. A Joint Synchrony/Mean-Rate Model of Auditory Speech Processing. *Journal of Phonetics* **16**, 55–76.

Servan-Schreiber, D., A. Cleeremans, and J.L. McClellan. 1988. *Encoding Sequential Structure in Simple Recurrent Networks.* Technical Report CMU-CS-88-183, Carnegie Mellon University.

Shamma, S. 1988. The Acoustic Features of Speech Sounds in a Model of Auditory Processing: Vowels and Voiceless Fricatives. *Journal of Phonetics* **16**, 77–91.

Shore, J.E. and D.K. Burton. 1983. Discrete Utterance Speech Recognition Without Time Alignment. *IEEE Transactions on Information Theory* **IT-29**, 473–491.

Sompolinsky, H. and I. Kanter. 1986. Temporal Association in Asymmetrical Neural Networks. *Physical Review Letters* **57**, 2861–2864.

Stornetta, W.S., T. Hogg, and B.A. Huberman. 1988. A Dynamical Approach to Temporal Pattern Processing. *In:* Neural Information Processing Systems, ed. D. Anderson, 750–759. New York: American Institute of Physics.

Tank, D. and J.J. Hopfield. 1987. Concentrating Information in Time: Analog Neural Networks with Applications to Speech Recognition Problems. *In:* 1st International Conference on Neural Networks, IEEE.

Tattersall, G.D., P.W. Linford, and R. Linggard. 1988. Neural Arrays for Speech Recognition. *British Telecommunications Technology Journal* **6**, 140–163.

Unnikrishnan, K.P., J.J. Hopfield, and D.W. Tank. 1988. Learning Time-delayed Connections in a Speech Recognition Circuit. Neural Networks for Computing Conference, Snowbird, Utah.

Waibel, Alex, T. Hanazawa, G. Hinton, K. Shikano, and K. Lang. 1987. *Phoneme Recognition Using Time-Delay Neural Networks.* Technical Report TR-1-006, ATR Interpreting Telephony Research Laboratories, Japan. Scheduled to appear in March 1989 issue of *IEEE Transactions on Acoustics Speech and Signal Processing*.

Waibel, Alex, H. Sawai, and K. Shikano. 1988. *Modularity and Scaling in Large Phonemic Neural Nets.* Technical Report TR-I-0034, ATR Interpreting Telephony Research Laboratories, Japan.

Watrous, R.L. 1988. *Speech Recognition Using Connectionist Networks.* Ph.D thesis, University of Pennsylvania.

———. 1986. *Learning Algorithms for Connectionist Networks: Applied Gradient Methods of Nonlinear Optimization.* Technical Report MS-CIS-87-51, Linc Lab 72, University of Pennsylvania.

Watrous, R.L. and Lokendra Shastri. 1987. Learning Phonetic Features using Connectionist Networks: An Experiment in Speech Recognition. *In:* 1st International Conference on Neural Networks, IEEE, IV–381.

Wong, M.K. and H.W. Chen. 1986. Toward a Massively Parallel System for Word Recognition. *In:* Proceedings IEEE International Conference on Acoustics Speech and Signal Processing, 37.4.1–37.4.4.

Received 10 November; accepted 14 November 1988.

Phoneme Recognition Using Time-Delay Neural Networks

ALEXANDER WAIBEL, MEMBER, IEEE, TOSHIYUKI HANAZAWA, GEOFFREY HINTON, KIYOHIRO SHIKANO, MEMBER, IEEE, AND KEVIN J. LANG

Abstract—In this paper we present a Time-Delay Neural Network (TDNN) approach to phoneme recognition which is characterized by two important properties. 1) Using a 3 layer arrangement of simple computing units, a hierarchy can be constructed that allows for the formation of arbitrary nonlinear decision surfaces. The TDNN learns these decision surfaces automatically using error backpropagation [1]. 2) The time-delay arrangement enables the network to discover acoustic-phonetic features and the temporal relationships between them independent of position in time and hence not blurred by temporal shifts in the input.

As a recognition task, the speaker-dependent recognition of the phonemes "B," "D," and "G" in varying phonetic contexts was chosen. For comparison, several discrete Hidden Markov Models (HMM) were trained to perform the same task. Performance evaluation over 1946 testing tokens from three speakers showed that the TDNN achieves a recognition rate of 98.5 percent correct while the rate obtained by the best of our HMM's was only 93.7 percent. Closer inspection reveals that the network "invented" well-known acoustic-phonetic features (e.g., F2-rise, F2-fall, vowel-onset) as useful abstractions. It also developed alternate internal representations to link different acoustic realizations to the same concept.

I. Introduction

In recent years, the advent of new learning procedures and the availability of high speed parallel supercomputers have given rise to a renewed interest in connectionist models of intelligence [1]. Sometimes also referred to as artificial neural networks or parallel distributed processing models, these models are particularly interesting for cognitive tasks that require massive constraint satisfaction, i.e., the parallel evaluation of many clues and facts and their interpretation in the light of numerous interrelated constraints. Cognitive tasks, such as vision, speech, language processing, and motor control, are also characterized by a high degree of uncertainty and variability and it has proved difficult to achieve good performance for these tasks using standard serial programming methods. Complex networks composed of simple computing units are attractive for these tasks not only because of their "brain-like" appeal[1] but because they offer ways for automatically designing systems that can make use of multiple interacting constraints. In general, such constraints are too complex to be easily programmed and require the use of automatic learning strategies. Such learning algorithms now exist (for an excellent review, see Lippman [2]) and have been demonstrated to discover interesting internal abstractions in their attempts to solve a given problem [1], [3]–[5]. Learning is most effective, however, when used in an architecture that is appropriate for the task. Indeed, applying one's prior knowledge of a task domain and its properties to the design of a suitable neural network model might well prove to be a key element in the successful development of connectionist systems.

Naturally, these techniques will have far-reaching implications for the design of automatic speech recognition systems, if proven successful in comparison to already-existing techniques. Lippmann [6] has compared several kinds of neural networks to other classifiers and evaluated their ability to create complex decision surfaces. Other studies have investigated actual speech recognition tasks and compared them to psychological evidence in speech perception [7] or to existing speech recognition techniques [8], [9]. Speech recognition experiments using neural nets have so far mostly been aimed at isolated word recognition (mostly the digit recognition task) [10]–[13] or phonetic recognition with predefined constant [14], [15] or variable phonetic contexts [16], [14], [17].

A number of these studies report very encouraging recognition performance [16], but only few comparisons to existing recognition methods exist. Some of these comparisons found performance similar to existing methods [9], [11], but others found that networks perform worse than other techniques [8]. One might argue that this state of affairs is encouraging considering the amount of fine-tuning that has gone into optimizing the more popular, established techniques. Nevertheless, better comparative performance figures are needed before neural networks can be considered as a viable alternative for speech recognition systems.

Manuscript received November 3, 1987; revised January 3, 1988.

A. Waibel is with the Computer Science Department, Carnegie-Mellon University, Pittsburgh, PA 15213.

T. Hanazawa and K. Shikano are with ATR Interpreting Telephony Research Laboratories, Osaka, Japan.

G. Hinton is with the Department of Computer Science and the Department of Psychology, University of Toronto, Toronto, Ont., Canada, and the Canadian Institute for Advanced Research.

K. J. Lang is with Carnegie-Mellon University, Pittsburgh, PA 15213.

IEEE Log Number 8825654.

[1]The uninitiated reader should be cautioned not to overinterpret the now-popular term "neural network." Although these networks appear to mimic certain properties of neural cells, no claim can be made that present exploratory attempts simulate the complexities of the human brain.

One possible explanation for the mixed performance results obtained so far may be limitations in computing resources leading to shortcuts that limit performance. Another more serious limitation, however, is the inability of most neural network architectures to deal properly with the dynamic nature of speech. Two important aspects of this are for a network to represent temporal relationships between acoustic events, while at the same time providing for invariance under translation in time. The specific movement of a formant in time, for example, is an important cue to determining the identity of a voiced stop, but it is irrelevant whether the same set of events occurs a little sooner or later in the course of time. Without translation invariance, a neural net requires precise segmentation to align the input pattern properly. Since this is not always possible in practice, learned features tend to get blurred (in order to accommodate slight misalignments) and their performance deteriorates. In general, shift invariance has been recognized as a critically important property for connectionist systems and a number of promising models have been proposed for speech and other domains [18]–[21], [14], [17], [22].

In the present paper, we describe a Time-Delay Neural Network (TDNN) which addresses both of these aspects of speech and demonstrate through extensive performance evaluation that superior recognition results can be achieved using this approach. In the following section, we begin by introducing the architecture and learning strategy of a TDNN aimed at phoneme recognition. Next, we compare the performance of our TDNN's to one of the more popular current recognition techniques: Hidden Markov Models (HMM). In Section III, we start by describing an HMM, under development at ATR [23], [24]. Both techniques, the TDNN and the HMM, are then evaluated over a testing database and we report the results. We show that substantially higher recognition performance is achieved by the TDNN than by the best of our HMM's. In Section IV, we then take a closer look at the internal representation that the TDNN learns for this task. It discovers a number of interesting linguistic abstractions which we show by way of examples. The implications of these results are then discussed and summarized in the final section of this paper.

II. Time-Delay Neural Networks (TDNN)

To be useful for speech recognition, a layered feedforward neural network must have a number of properties. First, it should have multiple layers and sufficient interconnections between units in each of these layers. This is to ensure that the network will have the ability to learn complex nonlinear decision surfaces [2], [6]. Second, the network should have the ability to represent relationships between events in time. These events could be spectral coefficients, but might also be the output of higher level feature detectors. Third, the actual features or abstractions learned by the network should be invariant under translation in time. Fourth, the learning procedure should not require precise temporal alignment of the labels that are to be learned. Fifth, the number of weights in the network should be sufficiently small compared to the amount of training data so that the network is forced to encode the training data by extracting regularity. In the following, we describe a TDNN architecture that satisfies all of these criteria and is designed explicitly for the recognition of phonemes, in particular, the voiced stops "B," "D," and "G."

A. A TDNN Architecture for Phoneme Recognition

The basic unit used in many neural networks computes the weighted sum of its inputs and then passes this sum through a nonlinear function, most commonly a threshold or sigmoid function [2], [1]. In our TDNN, this basic unit is modified by introducing delays D_1 through D_N as shown in Fig. 1. The J inputs of such a unit now will be multiplied by several weights, one for each delay and one for the undelayed input. For $N = 2$, and $J = 16$, for example, 48 weights will be needed to compute the weighted sum of the 16 inputs, with each input now measured at three different points in time. In this way, a TDNN unit has the ability to relate and compare current input to the past history of events. The sigmoid function was chosen as the nonlinear output function F due to its convenient mathematical properties [18], [5].

For the recognition of phonemes, a three layer net is constructed.[2] Its overall architecture and a typical set of activities in the units are shown in Fig. 2.

At the lowest level, 16 normalized melscale spectral coefficients serve as input to the network. Input speech, sampled at 12 kHz, was Hamming windowed and a 256-point FFT computed every 5 ms. Melscale coefficients were computed from the power spectrum by computing log energies in each melscale energy band [25], where adjacent coefficients in frequency overlap by one spectral sample and are smoothed by reducing the shared sample by 50 percent [25].[3] Adjacent coefficients in time were collapsed for further data reduction resulting in an overall 10 ms frame rate. All coefficients of an input token (in this case, 15 frames of speech centered around the hand-labeled vowel onset) were then normalized. This was accomplished by subtracting from each coefficient the average coefficient energy computed over all 15 frames of an input token and then normalizing each coefficient to lie between -1 and $+1$. All tokens in our database were preprocessed in the same fashion. Fig. 2 shows the resulting coefficients for the speech token "BA" as input to the

[2] Lippmann [2], [6] demonstrated recently that three layers can encode arbitrary pattern recognition decision surfaces. We believe that complex nonlinear decision surfaces are necessary to properly perform classification in the light of considerable acoustic variability as reported in the experiments below.

[3] Naturally, a number of alternative signal representations could be used as input, but have not been tried in this study. Filterbank coefficients were chosen as they are simple to compute and readily interpretable in the light of acoustic-phonetics. The melscale is a physiologically motivated frequency scale that provides better relative frequency resolution for lower frequency bands. Our implementation resulted in coefficients with a bandwidth of approximately 190 Hz up to 1400 Hz, and with increasing bandwidths thereafter.

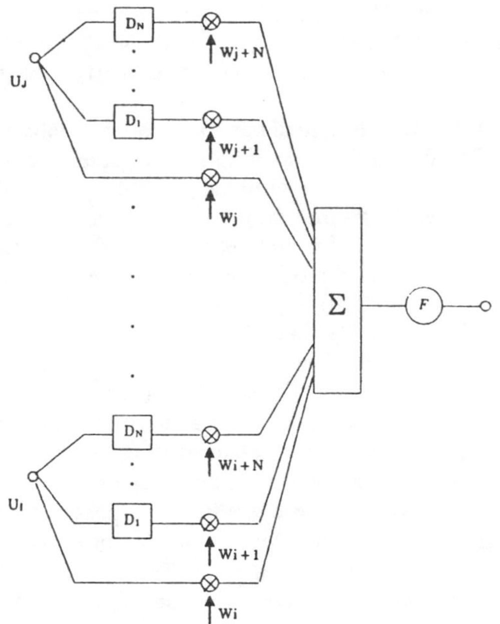

Fig. 1. A Time-Delay Neural Network (TDNN) unit.

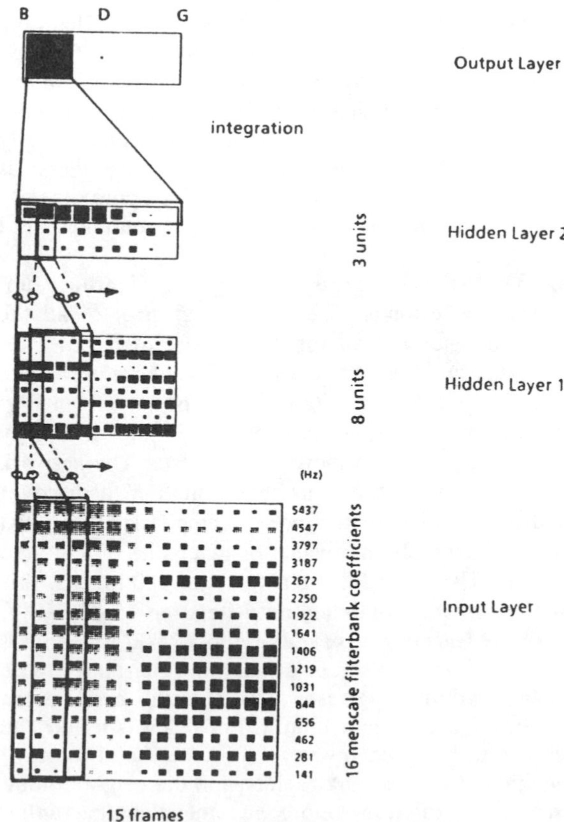

Fig. 2. The architecture of the TDNN.

network, where positive values are shown as black squares and negative values as gray squares.

This input layer is then fully interconnected to a layer of 8 time-delay hidden units, where $J = 16$ and $N = 2$ (i.e., 16 coefficients over 3 frames with time delay 0, 1, and 2). An alternative way of seeing this is depicted in Fig. 2. It shows the inputs to these time-delay units expanded out spatially into a 3 frame window, which is passed over the input spectrogram. Each unit in the first hidden layer now receives input (via 48 weighted connections) from the coefficients in the 3 frame window. The particular choice of 3 frames (30 ms) was motivated by earlier studies [26]-[29] that suggest that a 30 ms window might be sufficient to represent low level acoustic-phonetic events for stop consonant recognition. It was also the optimal choice among a number of alternative designs evaluated by Lang [21] on a similar task.

In the second hidden layer, each of 3 TDNN units looks at a 5 frame window of activity levels in hidden layer 1 (i.e., $J = 8$, $N = 4$). The choice of a larger 5 frame window in this layer was motivated by the intuition that higher level units should learn to make decisions over a wider range in time based on more local abstractions at lower levels.

Finally, the output is obtained by integrating (summing) the evidence from each of the 3 units in hidden layer 2 over time and connecting it to its pertinent output unit (shown in Fig. 2 over 9 frames for the "B" output unit). In practice, this summation is implemented simply as another nonlinear (sigmoid function is applied here as well) TDNN unit which has fixed equal weights to a row of unit firings over time in hidden layer 2.[4]

When the TDNN has learned its internal representation, it performs recognition by passing input speech over the TDNN units. In terms of the illustration of Fig. 2, this is equivalent to passing the time-delay windows over the lower level units' firing patterns.[5] At the lowest level, these firing patterns simply consist of the sensory input, i.e., the spectral coefficients.

Each TDNN unit outlined in this section has the ability to encode temporal relationships within the range of the N delays. Higher layers can attend to larger time spans, so local short duration features will be formed at the lower layer and more complex longer duration features at the higher layer. The learning procedure ensures that each of the units in each layer has its weights adjusted in a way that improves the network's overall performance.

B. Learning in a TDNN

Several learning techniques exist for optimization of neural networks [1], [2], [30]. For the present network, we adopt the Backpropagation Learning Procedure [18],

[4]Note, however, that as for all units in this network (except the input units), the output units are also connected to a permanently active threshold unit. In this way, both an output unit's one shared connection to a row in hidden layer 2 and its dc-bias are learned and can be adjusted for optimal classification.

[5]Thus, 13 frames of activations in hidden layer 1 are generated when scanning the 15 frames of input speech with a 3 frame time delay window. Similarly, 9 frames are produced in hidden layer 2 from the 13 frames of activation in the layer below.

[5]. Mathematically, backpropagation is gradient descent of the mean-squared error as a function of the weights. The procedure performs two passes through the network. During the forward pass, an input pattern is applied to the network with its current connection strengths (initially small random weights). The outputs of all the units at each level are computed starting at the input layer and working forward to the output layer. The output is then compared to the desired output and its error calculated. During the backward pass, the derivative of this error is then propagated back through the network, and all the weights are adjusted so as to decrease the error [18], [5]. This is repeated many times for all the training tokens until the network converges to producing the desired output.

In the previous section, we described a method of expressing temporal structure in a TDNN and contrasted this method to training a network on a static input pattern (spectrogram), which results in shift sensitive networks (i.e., poor performance for slightly misaligned input patterns) as well as less crisp decision making in the units of the network (caused by misaligned tokens during training).

To achieve the desired learning behavior, we need to ensure that the network is exposed to *sequences* of patterns and that it is allowed (or encouraged) to learn about the most powerful cues and sequences of cues among them. Conceptually, the backpropagation procedure is applied to speech patterns that are stepped through in time. An equivalent way of achieving this result is to use a spatially expanded input pattern, i.e., a spectrogram plus some constraints on the weights. Each collection of TDNN units described above is duplicated for each one frame shift in time. In this way, the whole history of activities is available at once. Since the shifted copies of the TDNN units are mere duplicates and are to look for the same acoustic event, the weights of the corresponding connections in the time shifted copies must be constrained to be the same. To implement this, we first apply the regular backpropagation forward and backward pass to all time-shifted copies as if they were separate events. This yields different error derivatives for corresponding (time shifted) connections. Rather than changing the weights on time-shifted connections separately, however, we actually update each weight on corresponding connections by the same value, namely by *the average* of all corresponding time-delayed weight changes.[6] Fig. 2 illustrates this by showing in each layer only two connections that are linked to (constrained to have the same value as) their time-shifted neighbors. Of course, this applies to all connections and all time shifts. In this way, the network is forced to discover useful acoustic-phonetic features in the input, regardless of when in time they actually occurred. This is an important property, as it makes the network independent of error-prone preprocessing algorithms that otherwise would be needed for time alignment and/or segmentation. In Section IV-C, we will show examples of grossly misaligned patterns that are properly recognized due to this property.

The procedure described here is computationally rather expensive, due to the many iterations necessary for learning a complex multidimensional weight space and the number of learning samples. In our case, about 800 learning samples were used, and between 20 000 and 50 000 iterations of the backpropagation loop were run over all training samples. Two steps were taken to perform learning within reasonable time. First, we have implemented our learning procedure in C and Fortran on a 4 processor Alliant supercomputer. The speed of learning can be improved considerably by computing the forward and backward sweeps for several different training samples in parallel on different processors. Further improvements can be gained by vectorizing operations and possibly assembly coding the innermost loop. Our present implementation achieves about a factor of 9 speedup over a VAX 8600, but still leaves room for further improvements (Lang [21], for example, reports a speedup of a factor of 120 over a VAX11/780 for an implementation running on a Convex supercomputer). The second step taken toward improving learning time is given by a staged learning strategy. In this approach, we start optimizing the network based on 3 prototypical training tokens only.[7] In this case, convergence is achieved rapidly, but the network will have learned a representation that generalizes poorly to new and different patterns. Once convergence is achieved, the network is presented with approximately twice the number of tokens and learning continues until convergence.

Fig. 3 shows the progress during a typical learning run. The measured error is 1/2 the squared error of all the output units, normalized for the number of training tokens. In this run, the number of training tokens used were 3, 6, 9, 24, 99, 249, and 780. As can be seen from Fig. 3, the error briefly jumps up every time more variability is introduced by way of more training data. The network is then forced to improve its representation to discover clues that generalize better and to deemphasize those that turn out to be merely irrelevant idiosyncracies of a limited sample set. Using the full training set of 780 tokens, this particular run was continued until iteration 35 000 (Fig. 3 shows the learning curve only up to 15 000 iterations). With this full training set, small learning steps have to be taken and learning progresses slowly. In this case, a step size of 0.002 and a momentum [5] of 0.1 was used. The staged learning approach was found to be useful to move the weights of the network rapidly into the neighborhood of a reasonable solution, before the rather slow fine tuning over all training tokens begins.

Despite these speedups, learning runs still take in the

[6]Note that in the experiments reported below, these weight changes were actually carried out each time the error derivatives from all training samples had been computed [5].

[7]Note that for optimal learning, the training data are presented by always alternating tokens for each class. Hence, we start the network off by presenting 3 tokens, one for each class.

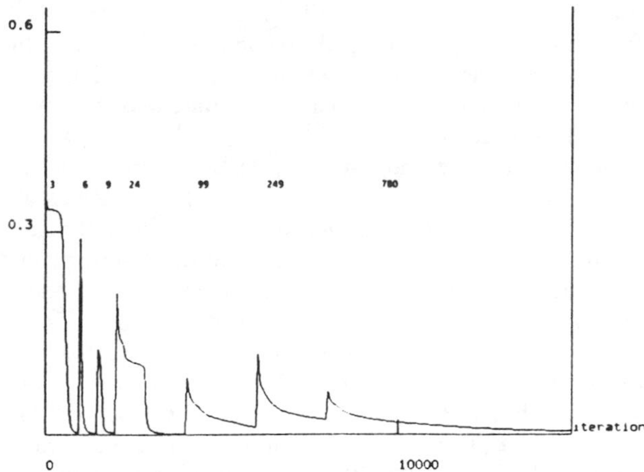

Fig. 3. TDNN output error versus number of learning iterations (increasing training set size).

order of several days. A number of programming tricks [21] as well as modifications to the learning procedure [31] are not implemented yet and could yield another factor of 10 or more in learning time reduction. It is important to note, however, that the amount of computation considered here is necessary *only for learning* of a TDNN and *not for recognition.* Recognition can easily be performed in better than real time on a workstation or personal computer. The simple structure makes TDNN's also well suited for standardized VLSI implementation. The detailed knowledge could be learned "off-line" using substantial computing power and then downloaded in the form of weights onto a real-time production network.

III. Recognition Experiments

We now turn to an experimental evaluation of the TDNN's recognition performance. In particular, we would like to compare the TDNN's performance to the performance of the currently most popular recognition method: Hidden Markov Models (HMM). For the performance evaluation reported here, we have chosen the best of a number of HMM's developed in our laboratory. Several other HMM-based variations and models have been tried in an effort to optimize our HMM, but we make no claim that an exhaustive evaluation of all HMM-based techniques was accomplished. We should also point out that the experiments reported here were aimed at evaluating two different *recognition philosophies.* Each recognition method was therefore implemented and optimized using its preferred representation of the speech signal, i.e., a representation that is well suited and most commonly used for the method evaluated. Evaluation of both methods was of course carried out using the same speech input data, but we caution the reader that due to the differences in representation, the exact contribution to overall performance of the recognition strategy as opposed to its signal representation is not known. It is conceivable that improved front end processing might lead to further performance improvements for either technique. In the following sections, we will start by introducing the best of our Hidden Markov Models. We then describe the experimental conditions and the database used for performance evaluation and conclude with the performance results achieved by our TDNN and HMM.

A. A Hidden Markov Model (HMM) for Phoneme Recognition

HMM's are currently the most successful and promising approach [32]–[34] in speech recognition as they have been successfully applied to the whole range of recognition tasks. Excellent performance was achieved at all levels from the phonemic level [35]–[38] to word recognition [39], [34] and to continuous speech recognition [40]. The success of HMM's is partially due to their ability to cope with the variability in speech by means of stochastic modeling. In this section, we describe an HMM developed in our laboratory that was aimed at phoneme recognition, more specifically the voiced stops "B," "D," and "G." The model described was the best of a number of alternate designs developed in our laboratory [23], [24].

The acoustic front end for Hidden Markov Modeling is typically a vector quantizer that classifies sequences of short-time spectra. Such a representation was chosen as it is highly effective for HMM-based recognizers [40].

Input speech was sampled at 12 kHz, preemphasized by $(1 - 0.97 z^{-1})$, and windowed using a 256-point Hamming window every 3 ms. Then a 12-order LPC analysis was carried out. A codebook of 256 LPC spectrum envelopes was generated from 216 phonetically balanced words. The Weighted Likelihood Ratio [41], [42] augmented with power values (PWLR) [43], [42] was used as LPC distance measure for vector quantization.

A fairly standard HMM was adopted in this paper as shown in Fig. 4. It has four states and six transitions and was found to be the best of a series of alternate models tried in our laboratory. These included models with two, three, four, and five states and with tied arcs and null arcs [23], [24].

The HMM probability values were trained using vector sequences of phonemes according to the forward–backward algorithm [32]. The vector sequences for "B," "D," and "G" include a consonant part and five frames of the following vowel. This is to model important transient information, such as formant movement, and has lead to improvements over context insensitive models [23], [24]. Again, variations on these parameters have been tried for the discrimination of these three voiced stop consonants. In particular, we have used 10 and 15 frames (i.e., 30 and 45 ms) of the following vowel in a 5 state HMM, but no performance improvements over the model described were obtained.

The HMM was trained using about 250 phoneme tokens of vector sequences per speaker and phoneme (see details of the training database below). Fig. 5 shows for a typical training run the average log probability normalized by the number of frames. Training was continued

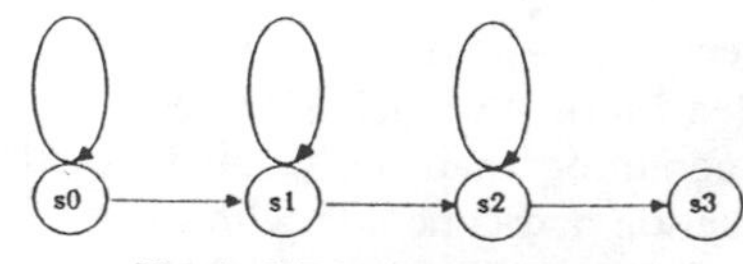

Fig. 4. Hidden Markov Model.

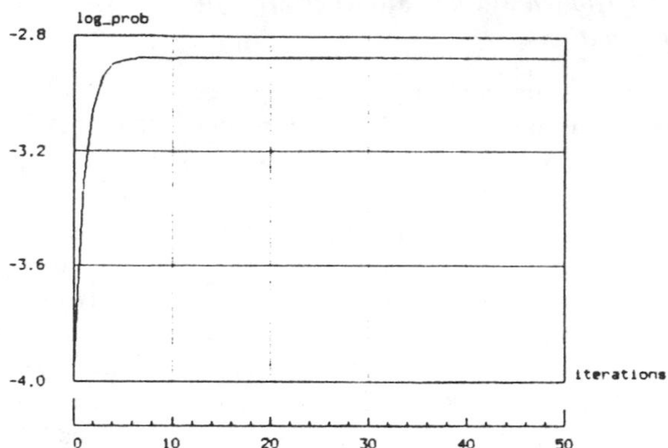

Fig. 5. Learning in the Hidden Markov Model.

until the increase of the average log probability between iterations became less than $2 * 10^{-3}$.

Typically, about 10–20 learning iterations are required for 256 tokens. A training run takes about 1 h on a VAX 8700. Floor values[8] were set on the output probabilities to avoid errors caused by zero probabilities. We have experimented with composite models, which were trained using a combination of context-independent and context-dependent probability values as suggested by Schwartz *et al.* [35], [36]. In our case, no significant improvements were attained.

B. Experimental Conditions

For performance evaluation, we have used a large vocabulary database of 5240 common Japanese words [44]. These words were uttered in isolation by three male native Japanese speakers (MAU, MHT, and MNM, all professional announcers) in the order they appear in a Japanese dictionary. All utterances were recorded in a sound-proof booth and digitized at a 12 kHz sampling rate. The database was then split into a training set (the even numbered files as derived from the recording order) and a testing set (the odd numbered files). A given speaker's training and testing data, therefore, consisted of 2620 utterances each, from which the actual phonetic tokens were extracted.

The phoneme recognition task chosen for this experiment was the recognition of the voiced stops, i.e., the phonemes "B," "D," and "G." The actual tokens were extracted from the utterances using manually selected acoustic-phonetic labels provided with the database [44]. For speaker MAU, for example, a total of 219 "B's," 203 "D's," and 260 "G's" were extracted from the training and 227 "B's," 179 "D's," and 252 "G's," from the testing data. Both recognition schemes, the TDNN's and the HMM's, were trained and tested speaker dependently. Thus, in both cases, separate networks were trained for each speaker.

In our database, no preselection of tokens was performed. All tokens labeled as one of the three voiced stops were included. It is important to note that since the consonant tokens were extracted from entire utterances and *not* read in isolation, a significant amount of phonetic variability exists. Foremost, there is the variability introduced by the phonetic context out of which a token is extracted. The actual signal of a "BA" will therefore look significantly different from a "BI" and so on. Second, the position of a phonemic token within the utterance introduces additional variability. In Japanese, for example, a "G" is nasalized, when it occurs embedded in an utterance, but not in utterance initial position. Both of our recognition algorithms are only given the phonemic identity of a token and must find their own ways of representing the fine variations of speech.

C. Results

Table I shows the results from the recognition experiments described above as obtained from the *testing data.* As can be seen, for all three speakers, the TDNN yields considerably higher performance than our HMM. Averaged over all three speakers, the error rate is reduced from 6.3 to 1.5 percent—a more than fourfold reduction in error.

While it is particularly important here to base performance evaluation on testing data,[9] a few observations can be made from recognition runs over the training data. For the training data set, recognition error rates were: 99.6 percent (MAU), 99.7 percent (MHT), and 99.7 percent (MNM) for the TDNN, and 96.9 percent (MAU), 99.1 percent (MHT), and 95.7 percent (MNM) for the HMM. Comparison of these results to those from the testing data in Table I indicates that both methods achieved good generalization from the training set to unknown data. The data also suggest that better classification rather than better generalization might be the cause of the TDNN's better performance shown in Table I.

Figs. 6–11 show scatter plots of the recognition outcome for the test data for speaker MAU, using the HMM and the TDNN. For the HMM (see Figs. 6–8), the log probability of the next best matching *incorrect* token is plotted against the log probability[10] of the correct token, e.g., "B," "D," and "G." In Figs. 9–11, the activation levels from the TDNN's output units are plotted in the same fashion. Note that these plots are not easily comparable, as the two recognition methods have been trained in quite different ways. They do, however, represent the

[8]Here, once again, the optimal value out of a number of alternative choices was selected.

[9]If the training data are insufficient, neural networks can in principle learn to *memorize* training patterns rather than finding generalization of speech.

[10]Normalized by number of frames.

TABLE I
RECOGNITION RESULTS FOR THREE SPEAKERS OVER TEST DATA USING TDNN AND HMM

speaker	number of tokens	number of errors	recognition rate	TDNN	number of errors	recognition rate	HMM
MAU	b(227)	4	98.2	98.8	18	92.1	92.9
	d(179)	3	98.3		6	96.7	
	g(252)	1	99.6		23	90.9	
MHT	b(208)	2	99.0	99.1	8	96.2	97.2
	d(170)	0	100		3	98.2	
	g(254)	4	98.4		7	97.2	
MNM	b(216)	11	94.9	97.5	27	87.5	90.9
	d(178)	1	99.4		13	92.7	
	g(256)	4	98.4		19	92.6	

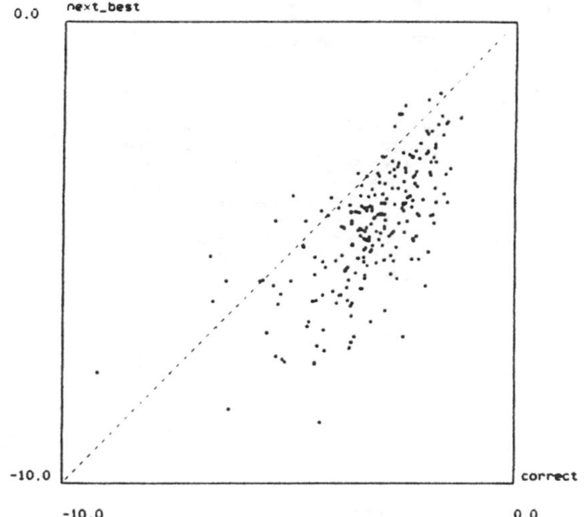

Fig. 6. Scatter plot showing log probabilities for the best matching incorrect case versus the correctly recognized "B's" using an HMM.

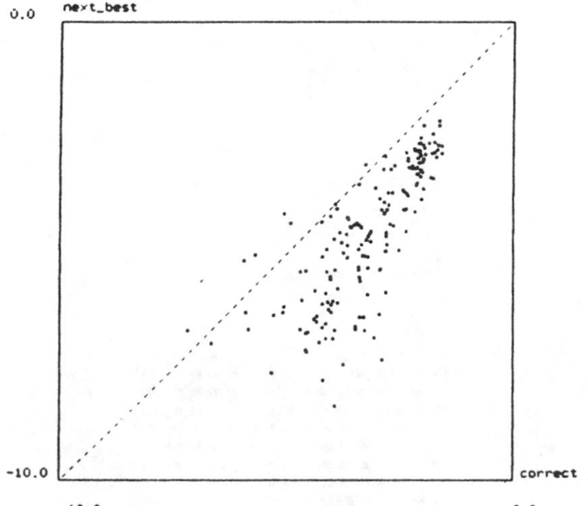

Fig. 7. Scatter plot showing log probabilities for the best matching incorrect case versus the correctly recognized "D's" using an HMM.

numerical values that each method's decision rule uses to determine the recognition outcome. We present these plots here to show some interesting properties of the two techniques. The most striking observation that can be made from these plots is that the output units of a TDNN have a tendency to fire with high confidence as can be seen

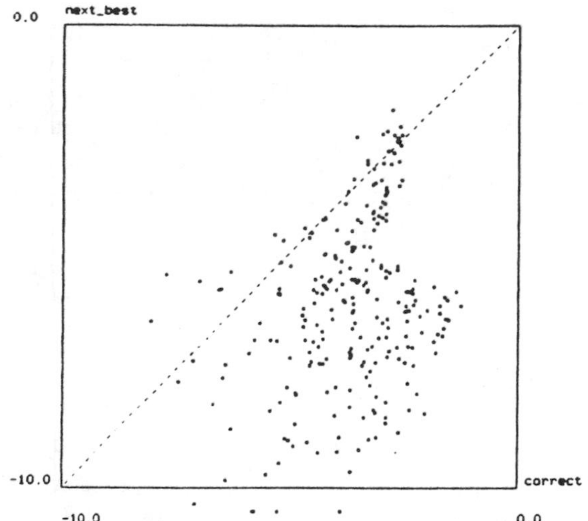

Fig. 8. Scatter plot showing log probabilities for the best matching incorrect case versus the correctly recognized "G's" using an HMM.

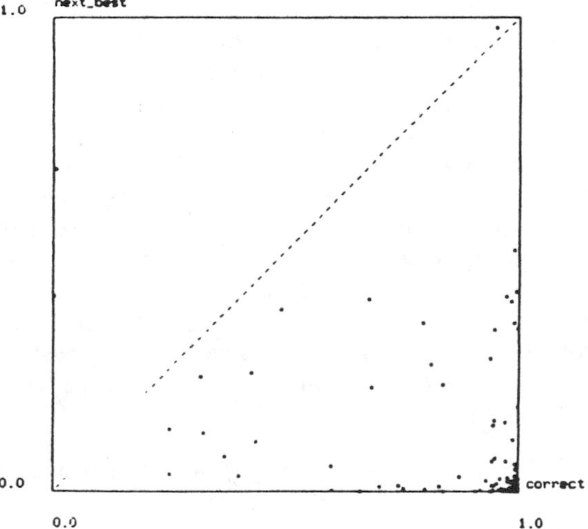

Fig. 9. Scatter plot showing activation levels for the best matching incorrect case versus the correctly recognized "B's" using a TDNN.

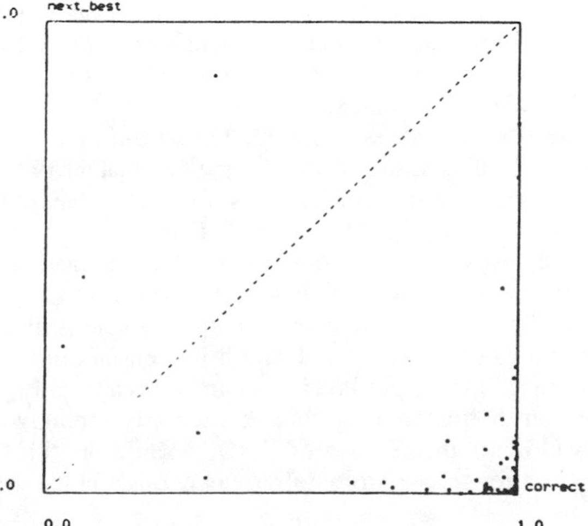

Fig. 10. Scatter plot showing activation levels for the best matching incorrect case versus the correctly recognized "D's" using a TDNN.

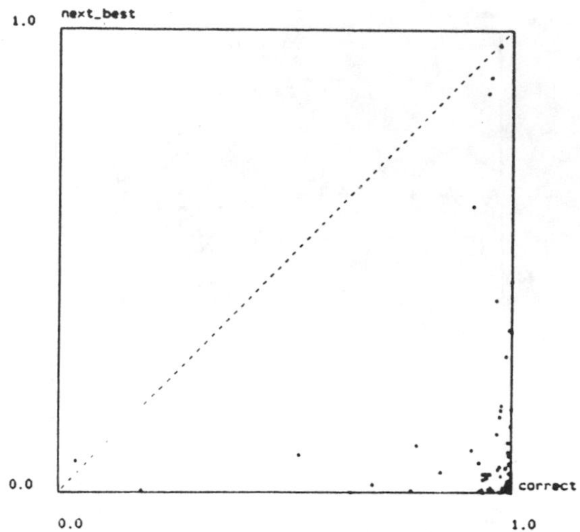

Fig. 11. Scatter plot showing activation levels for the best matching incorrect case versus the correctly recognized "G's" using a TDNN.

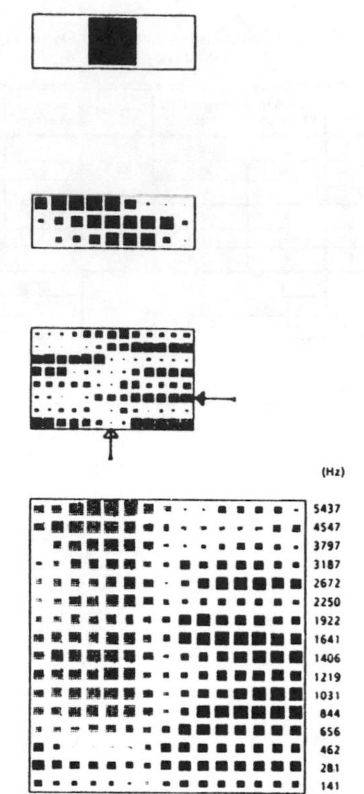

Fig. 12. TDNN activation patterns for "DA."

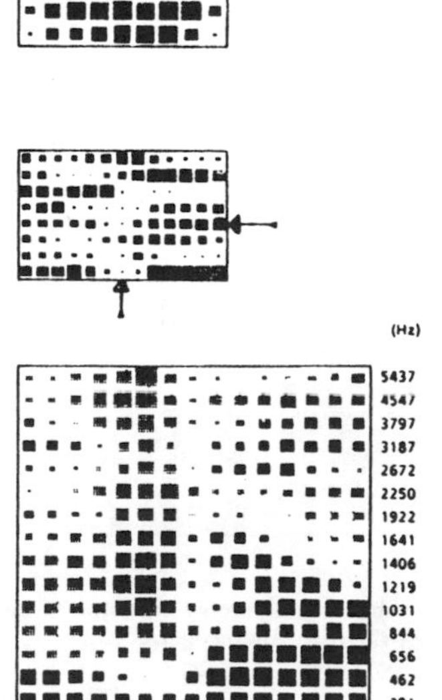

Fig. 13. TDNN activation patterns for "DO."

from the cluster of dots in the lower right-hand corner of the scatter plots. Most output units tend to fire strongly for the correct phonemic class and not at all for any other, a property that is encouraged by the learning procedure. One possible consequence of this is that rejection thresholds could be introduced to improve recognition performance. If one were to eliminate among speaker MAU's tokens all those whose highest activation level is less than 0.5 and those which result in two or more closely competing activations (i.e., are near the diagonal in the scatter plots), 2.6 percent of all tokens would be rejected, while the remaining substitution error rate would be less than 0.46 percent.

IV. The Learned Internal Representations of a TDNN

Given the encouraging performance of our TDNN's, a closer look at the learned internal representation of the network is warranted. What are the properties or abstractions that the network has learned that appear to yield a very powerful description of voiced stops? Figs. 12 and 13 show two typical instances of a "D" out of two different phonetic contexts ("DA" and "DO," respectively). In both cases, only the correct unit, the "D-output unit," fires strongly, despite the fact that the two input spectrograms differ considerably from each other. If we study the internal firings in these two cases, we can see that the network has learned to use alternate internal representations to link variations in the sensory input to the same higher level concepts. A good example is given by the firings of the third and fourth hidden unit in the first layer above the input layer. As can be seen from Fig. 13, the fourth hidden unit fires particularly strongly after vowel onset in the case of "DO," while the third unit shows stronger activation after vowel onset in the case of "DA."

Fig. 14 shows the significance of these different firing patterns. Here the connection strengths for the eight moving TDNN units are shown, where white and black blobs represent positive and negative weights, respectively, and the magnitude of a weight is indicated by the size of the

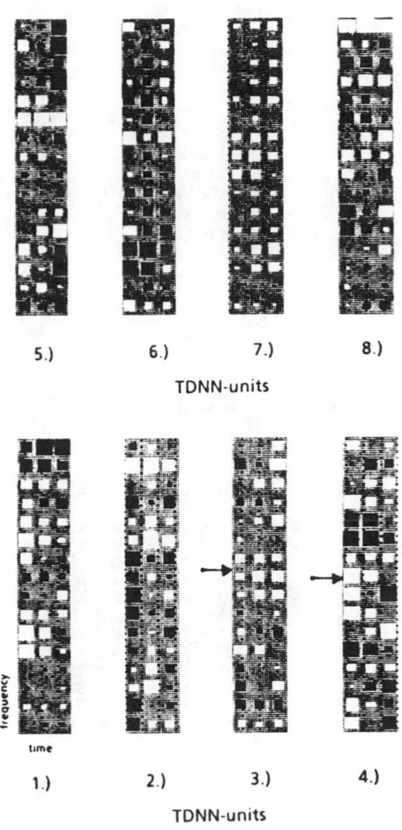

Fig. 14. Weights on connections from 16 coefficients over 3 time frames to each of the 8 hidden units in the first layer.

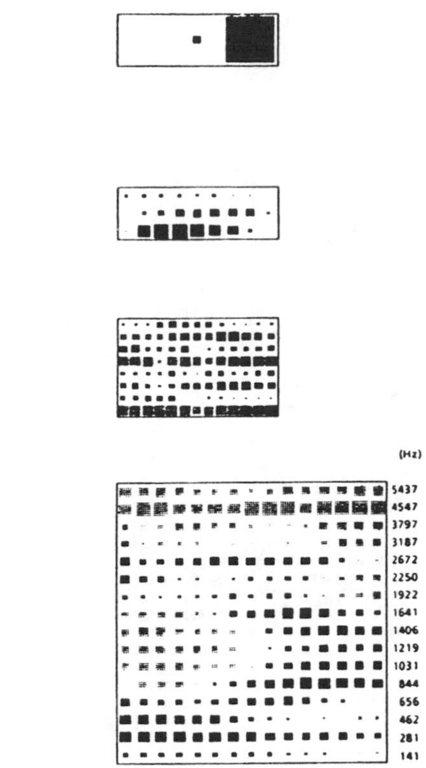

Fig. 15. TDNN activation patterns for "GA" embedded in an utterance.

blob. In this figure, the time delays are displayed spatially as a 3 frame window of 16 spectral coefficients. Conceptually, the weights in this window form a moving acoustic-phonetic feature detector that fires when the pattern for which it is specialized is encountered in the input speech. In our example, we can see that hidden unit number 4 (which was activated for "DO") has learned to fire when a falling (or rising) second formant starting at around 1600 Hz is found in the input (see filled arrow in Fig. 14). As can be seen in Fig. 13, this is the case for "DO" and hence the firing of hidden unit 4 after voicing onset (see row pointed to by the filled arrow in Fig. 13). In the case of "DA" (see Fig. 12), in turn, the second formant does not fall significantly, and hidden unit 3 (pointed to by the filled arrow) fires instead. From Fig. 14 we can verify that TDNN unit 3 has learned to look for a steady (or only slightly falling) second formant starting at about 1800 Hz. The connections in the second and third layer then link the different firing patterns observed in the first hidden layer into one and the same decision.

Another interesting feature can be seen in the bottom hidden unit in hidden layer number 1 (see Figs. 12 and 13, and compare them to the weights of hidden unit 1 displayed in Fig. 14). This unit has learned to take on the role of finding the segment boundary of the voiced stop. It does so in reverse polarity, i.e., it is always on *except* when the vowel onset of the voiced stop is encountered (see unfilled arrow in Figs. 13 and 12). Indeed, the higher layer TDNN units subsequently use this "segmenter" to base the final decision on the occurrence of the right lower features at the right point in time.

In the previous example, we have seen that the TDNN can account for variations in phonetic context. Figs. 15 and 16 show examples of variability caused by the relative position of a phoneme within a word. In Japanese, a "G" embedded in a word tends to be nasalized as seen in the spectrum of a "GA" in Fig. 15. Fig. 16 shows a word initial "GA." Despite the striking differences between these two input spectrograms, the network's internal alternate representations manage to produce in both cases crisp output firings for the right category.

Figs. 17 and 18, finally, demonstrate the shift invariance of the network. They show the same token "DO" of Fig. 13, misaligned by +30 ms and −30 ms, respectively. Despite the gross misalignment (note that significant transitional information is lost by the misalignment in Fig. 18), the correct result was obtained reliably. A close look at the internal activation patterns reveals that the hidden units' feature detectors do indeed fire according to the events in the input speech, and are not negatively affected by the relative shift with respect to the input units. Naturally, error rates will gradually increase when the tokens are artificially shifted to an extent that important features begin to fall outside the 15 frame data window considered here. We have observed, for example, a 2.6 percent increase in error rate when all tokens from

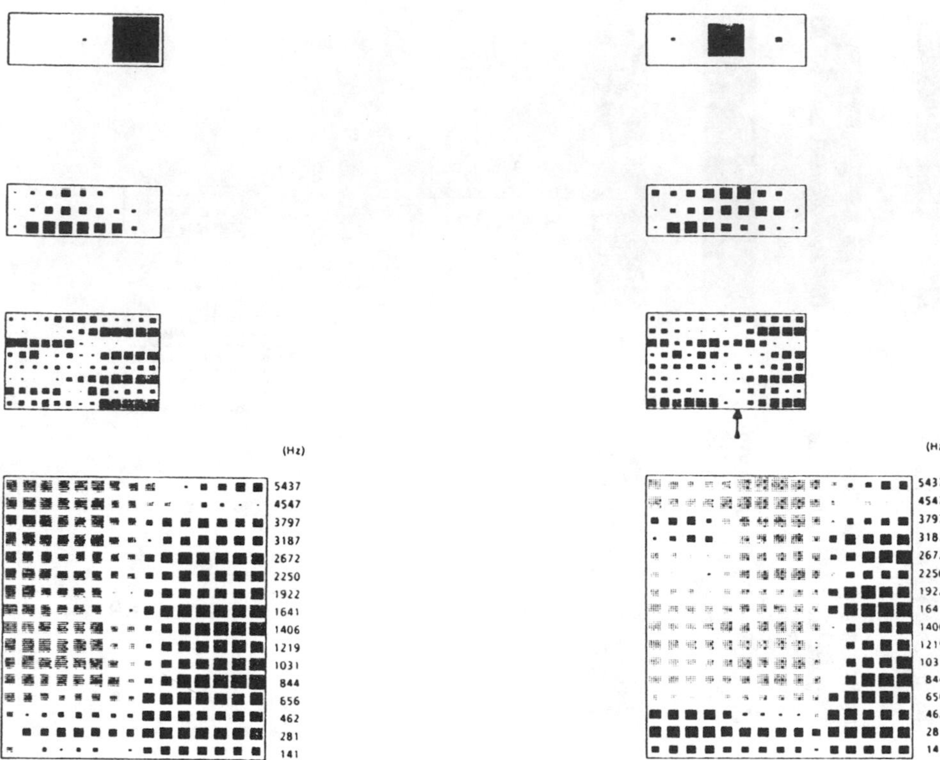

Fig. 16. TDNN activation patterns for "GA" in utterance initial position.

Fig. 18. TDNN activation patterns for "DO" misaligned by −30 ms.

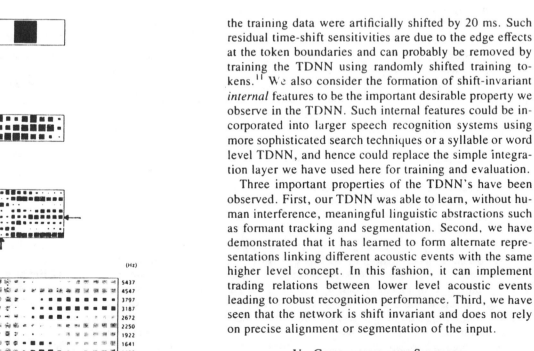

Fig. 17. TDNN activation patterns for "DO" misaligned by +30 ms.

the training data were artificially shifted by 20 ms. Such residual time-shift sensitivities are due to the edge effects at the token boundaries and can probably be removed by training the TDNN using randomly shifted training tokens.[11] We also consider the formation of shift-invariant *internal* features to be the important desirable property we observe in the TDNN. Such internal features could be incorporated into larger speech recognition systems using more sophisticated search techniques or a syllable or word level TDNN, and hence could replace the simple integration layer we have used here for training and evaluation.

Three important properties of the TDNN's have been observed. First, our TDNN was able to learn, without human interference, meaningful linguistic abstractions such as formant tracking and segmentation. Second, we have demonstrated that it has learned to form alternate representations linking different acoustic events with the same higher level concept. In this fashion, it can implement trading relations between lower level acoustic events leading to robust recognition performance. Third, we have seen that the network is shift invariant and does not rely on precise alignment or segmentation of the input.

V. Conclusion and Summary

In this paper we have presented a Time-Delay Neural Network (TDNN) approach to phoneme recognition. We

[11] We gratefully acknowledge one of the reviewers for suggesting this idea.

have shown that this TDNN has two desirable properties related to the dynamic structure of speech. First, it can learn the temporal structure of acoustic events and the temporal relationships between such events. Second, it is translation invariant, that is, the features learned by the network are insensitive to shifts in time. Examples demonstrate that the network was indeed able to learn acoustic-phonetic features, such as formant movements and segmentation, and use them effectively as internal abstractions of speech.

The TDNN presented here has two hidden layers and has the ability to learn complex nonlinear decision surfaces. This could be seen from the network's ability to use alternate internal representations and trading relations among lower level acoustic-phonetic features, in order to arrive robustly at the correct final decision. Such alternate representations have been particularly useful for representing tokens that vary considerably from each other due to their different phonetic environment or their position within the original speech utterance.

Finally, we have evaluated the TDNN on the recognition of three acoustically similar phonemes, the voiced stops "B," "D," and "G." In extensive performance evaluation over testing data from three speakers, the TDNN achieved an average recognition score of 98.5 percent. For comparison, we have applied various Hidden Markov Models to the same task and only been able to recognize 93.7 percent of the tokens correctly. We would like to note that many variations of HMM's have been attempted, and many more variations of both HMM's and TDNN's are conceivable. Some of these variations could potentially lead to significant improvements over the results reported in this study. Our goal here is to present TDNN's as a new and successful approach for speech recognition. Their power lies in their ability to develop shift-invariant internal abstractions of speech and to use them in trading relations for making optimal decisions. This holds significant promise for speech recognition in general, as it could help overcome the representational weaknesses of speech recognition systems faced with the uncertainty and variability in real-life signals.

Acknowledgment

The authors would like to express their gratitude to Dr. A. Kurematsu, President of ATR Interpreting Telephony Research Laboratories, for his enthusiastic encouragement and support which made this research possible. We are also indebted to the members of the Speech Processing Department at ATR and Mr. Fukuda at Apollo Computer, Tokyo, Japan, for programming assistance in the various stages of this research.

References

[1] D. E. Rumelhart and J. L. McClelland, *Parallel Distributed Processing; Explorations in the Microstructure of Cognition*, Vol. I and II. Cambridge, MA: M.I.T. Press, 1986.

[2] R. P. Lippmann, "An introduction to computing with neural nets," *IEEE ASSP Mag.*, vol. 4, Apr. 1987.

[3] D. C. Plaut, S. J. Nowlan, and G. E. Hinton, "Experiments on learning by back propagation," Tech. Rep. CMU-CS-86-126, Carnegie-Mellon Univ., June 1986.

[4] T. J. Sejnowski and C. R. Rosenberg, "NETtalk: A parallel network that learns to read aloud," Tech. Rep. JHU/EECS-86/01, Johns Hopkins Univ., June 1986.

[5] D. E. Rumelhart, G.E. Hinton, and R. J. Williams, "Learning representations by back-propagating errors," *Nature*, vol. 323, pp. 533-536, Oct. 1986.

[6] W. Y. Huang and R. P. Lippmann, "Comparison between neural net and conventional classifiers," in *Proc. IEEE Int. Conf. Neural Networks*, June 1987.

[7] J. L. McClelland and J. L. Elman, *Interactive Processes in Speech Perception: The TRACE Model*. Cambridge, MA: M.I.T. Press, 1986, ch. 15, pp. 58-121.

[8] S. M. Peeling, R. K. Moore, and M. J. Tomlinson, "The multi-layer perceptron as a tool for speech pattern processing research," in *Proc. IoA Autumn Conf. Speech Hearing*, 1986.

[9] H. Bourlard and C. J. Wellekens, "Multilayer perceptrons and automatic speech recognition," in *Proc. IEEE Int. Conf. Neural Networks*, June 1987.

[10] B. Gold, R. P. Lippmann, and M. L. Malpass, "Some neural net recognition results on isolated words," in *Proc. IEEE Int. Conf. Neural Networks*, June 1987.

[11] R. P. Lippmann and B. Gold, "Neural-net classifiers useful for speech recognition," in *Proc. IEEE Int. Conf. Neural Networks*, June 1987.

[12] D. J. Burr, "A neural network digit recognizer," in *Proc. IEEE Int. Conf. Syst., Man, Cybern.*, Oct. 1986.

[13] D. Lubensky, "Learning spectral-temporal dependencies using connectionist networks," in *Proc. IEEE Int. Conf. Acoust., Speech, Signal Processing*, Apr. 1988.

[14] R. L. Watrous and L. Shastri, "Learning phonetic features using connectionist networks: An experiment in speech recognition," in *Proc. IEEE Int. Conf. Neural Networks*, June 1987.

[15] R. W. Prager, T. D. Harrison, and F. Fallside, "Boltzmann machines for speech recognition," *Comput., Speech, Language*, vol. 3, no. 27, Mar. 1986.

[16] J. L. Elman and D. Zipser, "Learning the hidden structure of speech," Tech. Rep., Univ. Calif., San Diego, Feb. 1987.

[17] R. L. Watrous, L. Shastri, and A. H. Waibel, "Learned phonetic discrimination using connectionist networks," in *Proc. Euro. Conf. Speech Technol.*, Edinburgh, Sept. 1987, pp. 377-380.

[18] D. E. Rumelhart, G. E. Hinton, and R. J. Williams, *Learning Internal Representations by Error Propagation*. Cambridge, MA: M.I.T. Press, 1986, ch. 8, pp. 318-362.

[19] J. S. Bridle and R. K. Moore, "Boltzmann machines for speech pattern processing," in *Proc. Inst. Acoust. 1984*, 1984, 315-322.

[20] D. W. Tank and J. J. Hopfield, "Neural computation by concentrating information in time," in *Proc. Nat. Academy Sci.*, Apr. 1987, pp. 1896-1900.

[21] K. Lang, "Connectionist speech recognition," Ph.D. dissertation proposal, Carnegie-Mellon Univ., Pittsburgh, PA.

[22] K. Fukushima, S. Miyake, and T. Ito, "Neocognitron: A neural network model for a mechanism of visual pattern recognition," *IEEE Trans. Syst., Man, Cybern.*, vol. SMC-13, pp. 826-834, Sept./Oct. 1983.

[23] T. Hanazawa, T. Kawabata, and K. Shikano, "Discrimination of Japanese voiced stops using Hidden Markov Model," in *Proc. Conf. Acoust. Soc. Japan*, Oct. 1987, pp. 19-20 (in Japanese).

[24] ——, "Recognition of Japanese voiced stops using Hidden Markov Models," IEICE Tech. Rep., Dec. 1987 (in Japanese).

[25] A. Waibel and B. Yegnanarayana, "Comparative study of nonlinear time warping techniques in isolated word speech recognition systems," Tech. Rep., Carnegie-Mellon Univ., June 1981.

[26] S. Makino and K. Kido, "Phoneme recognition using time spectrum pattern," *Speech Commun.*, pp. 225-237, June 1986.

[27] S. E. Blumstein and K. N. Stevens, "Acoustic invariance in speech production: Evidence from measurements of the spectral characteristics of stop consonants," *J. Acoust. Soc. Amer.*, vol. 66, pp. 1001-1017, 1979.

[28] ——, "Perceptual invariance and onset spectra for stop consonants in different vowel environments," *J. Acoust. Soc. Amer.*, vol. 67, pp. 648-662, 1980.

[29] D. Kewley-Port, "Time varying features as correlates of place of articulation in stop consonants," *J. Acoust. Soc. Amer.*, vol. 73, pp. 322-335, 1983.

[30] G. E. Hinton, "Connectionist learning procedures," *Artificial Intelligence*, 1987.

[31] M. A. Franzini, "Speech recognition with back propagation," in *Proc. 9th Annu. Conf. IEEE/Eng. Med. Biol. Soc.*, Nov. 1987.

[32] F. Jelinek, "Continuous speech recognition by statistical methods," *Proc. IEEE*, vol. 64, pp. 532-556, Apr. 1976.

[33] J. K. Baker, "Stochastic modeling as a means of automatic speech recognition," Ph.D. dissertation, Carnegie-Mellon Univ., Apr. 1975.

[34] L. R. Bahl, S. K. Das, P. V. de Souza, F. Jelinek, S. Katz, R. L. Mercer, and M. A. Picheny, "Some experiments with large-vocabulary isolated-word sentence recognition," in *Proc. IEEE Int. Conf. Acoust., Speech, Signal Processing*, Apr. 1984.

[35] R. Schwartz, Y. Chow, O. Kimball, S. Roucos, M. Krasner, and J. Makhoul, "Context-dependent modeling for acoustic-phonetic recognition of continuous speech," in *Proc. IEEE Int. Conf. Acoust., Speech, Signal Processing*, Apr. 1985.

[36] A.-M. Derouault, "Context-dependent phonetic Markov models for large vocabulary speech recognition," in *Proc. IEEE Int. Conf. Acoust., Speech, Signal Processing*, Apr. 1987, pp. 360-363.

[37] K. F. Lee and H. W. Hon, "Speaker-independent phoneme recognition using hidden Markov models," Tech. Rep. CMU-CS-88-121, Carnegie-Mellon Univ., Pittsburgh, PA, Mar. 1988.

[38] P. Brown, "The acoustic-modeling problem in automatic speech recognition," Ph.D. dissertation, Carnegie-Mellon Univ., May 1987.

[39] L. R. Rabiner, B. H. Juang, S. E. Levinson, and M. M. Sondhi, "Recognition of isolated digits using hidden Markov models with continuous mixture densities," *AT&T Tech. J.*, vol. 64, no. 6, pp. 1211-1233, July-Aug. 1985.

[40] Y. L. Chow, M. O. Dunham, O. A. Kimball, M. A. Krasner, G. F. Kubala, J. Makhoul, S. Roucos, and R. M. Schwartz, "BYBLOS: The BBN continuous speech recognition system," in *Proc. IEEE Int. Conf. Acoust., Speech, Signal Processing*, Apr. 1987, pp. 89-92.

[41] M. Sugiyama and K. Shikano, "LPC peak weighted spectral matching measures," Inst. Elec. Commun. Eng. Japan, vol. 64-A, no. 5, pp. 409-416, 1981 (in Japanese).

[42] K. Shikano, "Evaluation of LPC spectral matching measures for phonetic unit recognition," Tech. Rep., Carnegie-Mellon Univ., May 1985.

[43] K. Aikawa and K. Shikano, "Spoken word recognition using vector quantization in power-spectrum vector space," Inst. Elec. Commun. Eng. Japan, vol. 68-D, no. 3, Mar. 1985 (in Japanese).

[44] Y. Sagisaka, K. Takeda, S. Katagiri, and H. Kuwabara, "Japanese speech database with fine acoustic-phonetic transcriptions," Tech. Rep., ATR Interpreting Telephony Res. Lab., May 1987.

Alexander Waibel (S'79-M'86) was born in Heidelberg, West Germany, on May 2, 1956. He received the B.S., M.S., and Ph.D. degrees in electrical engineering and computer science in 1979, 1980, and 1986 from the Massachusetts Institute of Technology, Cambridge, and from Carnegie-Mellon University, Pittsburgh, respectively.

From 1980 to 1985 he was a member of the Computer Science Research Staff at Carnegie-Mellon University. In 1986 he joined the Faculty of the Computer Science Department as Research Associate and is now a Research Computer Scientist with joined responsibilities in the Center for Machine Translation at Carnegie-Mellon and at the ATR Interpreting Telephony Research Laboratories in Osaka, Japan. From May 1987 to July 1988, he worked as Invited Research Scientist at the ATR Interpreting Telephony Research Laboratories in Osaka, Japan. He has published and lectured extensively on speech recognition and related areas. His current research interests include speech recognition and synthesis, neurocomputing, machine learning, and machine translation.

Dr. Waibel is a member of the IEEE Acoustics, Speech, and Signal Processing Society, the IEEE Computer Society, the Acoustical Society of America, the Association for Computational Linguistics, and the International Neural Network Society.

Toshiyuki Hanazawa was born in Japan on March 25, 1962. He received the B.S. degree in physics from Tokyo Metropolitan University, Tokyo, Japan, in 1985.

In 1985 he joined the Information Systems and Electronics Development Laboratory, Mitsubishi Electric Corporation, Kamakura, Japan, where he was engaged in speech recognition research. Since 1987 he has been with the ATR Interpreting Telephony Research Laboratories, Osaka, Japan, where he is currently engaged in speech recognition research.

Geoffrey Hinton received the B.A. degree in psychology from the University of Cambridge in 1970 and the Ph.D. degree in artificial intelligence from the University of Edinburgh in 1978.

He is a Professor in the Departments of Computer Science and Psychology at the University of Toronto, and a Fellow of the Canadian Institute for Advanced Research. His research interests include methods of using connectionist networks for learning, memory, perception, symbol processing, and motor control.

Kiyohiro Shikano (M'84) was born in Japan on October 12, 1947. He received the B.E., M.E., and the Ph.D. degrees in electrical engineering from Nagoya University, Nagoya, Japan, in 1970, 1972, and 1980, respectively.

From 1972 to 1986 he worked at the Electrical Communication Laboratories, Nippon Telegraph and Telephone Corporation, Tokyo, Japan, where he was engaged in speech recognition research. During 1984-1986, he was a Visiting Scientist in the Computer Science Department at Carnegie-Mellon University, Pittsburgh, PA, and was working on speech recognition. Since 1986 he has been with the ATR Interpreting Telephony Research Laboratories, Osaka, Japan, where he is currently Head of the Speech Processing Department.

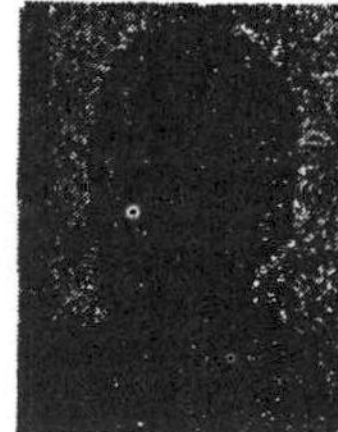

Kevin J. Lang received the B.A. degree in mathematics from Grinnell College.

He is presently a Ph.D. candidate at Carnegie-Mellon University. His research interests include programming language design and connectionist architectures for perception.

Consonant Recognition by Modular Construction of Large Phonemic Time-Delay Neural Networks

Alex Waibel Hidefumi Sawai Kiyohiro Shikano

Computer Science Department
Carnegie-Mellon University
Pittsburgh, PA 15213

ATR Interpreting Telephony Research Laboratories
Twin 21 MID Tower, 2-1-61 Shiromi, Higashi-ku,
Osaka, 540, Japan

Abstract

In this paper we show that neural networks for speech recognition can be constructed in a modular fashion by exploiting the hidden structure of previously trained phonetic subcategory networks. The performance of resulting larger phonetic nets was found to be as good as the performance of the subcomponent nets by themselves. This approach avoids the excessive learning times that would be necessary to train larger networks and allows for incremental learning. Large time-delay neural networks constructed incrementally by applying these modular training techniques achieved a recognition performance of 96.0% for all consonants and 94.7% for all phonemes.

1. Introduction

Recently we have demonstrated that connectionist architectures capable of capturing some critical aspects of the dynamic nature of speech, can achieve superior recognition performance for difficult but small phonemic discrimination tasks such as discrimination of the voiced consonants B,D and G [1, 2]. Encouraged by these results we wanted to explore the question, how we might expand on these models to make them useful for the design of speech recognition systems. A problem that emerges as we attempt to apply neural network models to the full speech recognition problem is the problem of scaling. Simply extending neural networks to ever larger structures and retraining them as one monolithic net quickly exceeds the capabilities of the fastest and largest supercomputers. The search complexity of finding a good solutions in a huge space of possible network configurations also soon assumes unmanageable proportions. Moreover, having to decide on all possible classes for recognition ahead of time as well as collecting sufficient data to train such a large monolithic network is impractical to say the least. In an effort to extend our models from small recognition tasks to large scale speech recognition systems, we must therefore explore modularity and incremental learning as design strategies to break up a large learning task into smaller subtasks. Breaking up a large task into subtasks to be tackled by individual black boxes interconnected in ad hoc arrangements, on the other hand, would mean to abandon one of the most attractive aspects of connectionism: the ability to perform complex constraint satisfaction in a massively parallel and interconnected fashion, in view of an overall optimal performance goal. In this paper we demonstrate based on a set of experiments aimed at phoneme recognition that it is indeed possible to construct large neural networks incrementally by exploiting the hidden structure of smaller pretrained subcomponent networks.

2. Small Phonemic Classes by Time-Delay Neural Networks

In our previous work, we have proposed a Time-Delay Neural Network architecture (as shown on the left of Fig.1 for B,D,G) as an approach to phoneme discrimination that achieves very high recognition scores [1, 2]. Its multilayer architecture, its shift-invariance and the time delayed connections of its units all contributed to its performance by allowing the net to develop complex, non-linear decision surfaces and insensitivity to misalignments and by incorporating contextual information into decision making (see [1, 2] for detailed analysis and discussion). It is trained by the back-propagation procedure [3] using shared weights for different time shifted positions of the net [1, 2]. In spirit it has similarities to other models recently proposed [4, 5]. This network, however, had only been trained for the voiced stops B,D,G and we began our extensions by training similar networks for the other phonemic classes in our database.

All phoneme tokens in our experiments were extracted using phonetic handlabels from a large vocabulary database of 5240 common Japanese words. Each word in the database was spoken in isolation by one male native Japanese speaker. All utterances were recorded in a sound proof booth and digitized at a 12 kHz sampling rate. The database was then split into a training set and a testing set of 2620 utterances each. A 150 msec range around a phoneme boundary was excised for each phoneme token and 16

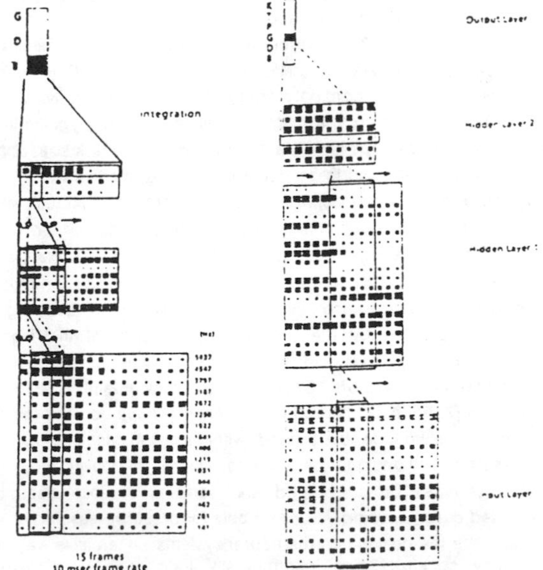

Figure 1. The TDNN architecture: BDG-net (left), BDGPTK-net (right)

mel scale filterbank coefficients computed every 10 msec [1, 2]. The preprocessed training and testing data was then used to train or to evaluate our TDNNs' performance for various phoneme classes. For each class, TDNNs with an architecture similar to the BDG-net in Fig.1 were trained. A total of seven nets aimed at the major coarse phonetic classes in Japanese were trained, including voiced stops B, D, G, voiceless stops P,T,K, the nasals M, N and syllabic nasals, fricatives S, SH, H and Z, affricates CH, TS, liquids and glides R, W, Y and finally the set of vowels A, I, U, E and O. Each of these nets was given between two and five phonemes to distinguish and the pertinent input data was presented for learning. Note, that each net was trained only within each respective coarse class and has no notion of phonemes from other classes yet. Evaluation of each net on test data within each of these subcategories revealed that an average rate of 98.8% can be achieved (see [6] for a more detailed tabulation of results).

3. Scaling TDNNs to Larger Phonemic Classes

We have seen that TDNNs achieve superior recognition performance on difficult but small recognition tasks. To train these networks substantial computational resources were needed. This raises the question of how our networks could be extended to encompass *all* phonemes or handle speech recognition in general. To shed light on this question of scaling, we consider first the problem of extending our networks from the task of voiced stop consonant recognition (hence the BDG-task) to the task of distinguishing among *all* stop consonants (the BDGPTK-task).

For a network aimed at the discrimination of the voiced stops (a BDG-net), approximately 6000 connections had to be trained over about 800 training tokens. An identical net (also with approximately 6000 connections[1]) can achieve discrimination among the voiceless stops ("P", "T" and "K"). To extend our networks to the recognition of *all* stops, i.e., the voiced *and* the unvoiced stops (B,D,G,P,T,K), a larger net is required. We have trained such a network for experimental purposes. To allow for the necessary number of features to develop we have given this net 20 units in the first hidden layer, 6 units in hidden layer 2 and 6 output units. On the right of Fig.1 we show this net in actual operation with a "G" presented at its input. Eventually a high performance network was obtained that achieves 98.3% correct recognition over a 1613-token BDGPTK-test database, but it took inordinate amounts of learning to arrive at the trained net (18 days on a 4 processor Alliant!). Although going from voiced stops to all stops is only a modest increase in task size, about 18,000 connections had to be trained. To make matters worse, not only the number of connections should be increased with task size, but in general the amount of training data required for good generalization of a larger net has to be increased as well. Naturally, there are practical limits to the size of a training database, and more training data translates into even more learning time. Learning is further complicated by the increased complexity of the higher dimensional weightspace in large nets as well as the limited precision of our simulators. Despite progress towards faster learning algorithms [7, 8], it is clear that we cannot hope for one single monolithic network to be trained within reasonable time as we increase size to handle larger and larger tasks. Moreover, requiring that all classes be considered and samples of each class be presented during training, is undesirable for practical reasons as we contemplate the design of large neural systems. Alternative ways to modularly construct and incrementally train such large neural systems must therefore be explored.

3.1. Experiments with Modularity

Four experiments were performed to explore methodologies for constructing phonetic neural nets from smaller component subnets. As a task we used again stop consonant recognition (BDGPTK) although other tasks have recently been explored with similar success (BDG and MNsN) [9]. As in the previous section we used a large database of 5240 common Japanese words spoken in isolation from which the testing an training tokens for the voiced stops (the BDG-set) and for the voiceless stops (the PTK-set) was extracted.

Two separate TDNNs have been trained. On testing data the BDG-net used here performed 98.3% correct for the BDG-set and the PTK-net achieved 98.7% correct recognition for the PTK-set. As a first naive attempt we have now simply run a speech token from either set (i.e., B,D,G,P,T or K) through both a BDG-net and a PTK-net and selected the class with the *highest activation* from either net as the recognition result. As might have been expected (the component nets had only been trained for their respective classes), poor recognition performance (60.5%) resulted from the 6 class experiment. This is partially due to the inhibitory property of the TDNN that we have observed elsewhere [1]. To combine the two networks more effectively, therefore, portions of the net had to be retrained.

We start by assuming that the first hidden layer in either net already contains all the lower level acoustic phonetic features we need for proper identification of the stops and freeze the connections from the input layer (the speech data) to the first hidden layer's 8 units in the BDG-net and the 8 units in the PTK-net. Back-propagation learning is then performed only on the connections between these 16 (= 2 X 8) units in hidden layer 1 and hidden layer 2 and between hidden layer 2 and the combined BDGPTK-net's output. This network is shown in Fig.2 with a "G" token presented as input. Only the higher layer connections had to be retrained (for about one day) in this case and the resulting network achieved a recognition performance of 98.1% over the testing data. Combination of the two subnets has therefore yielded a good net although a slight performance degradation compared to the subnets was observed. This degradation could be explained by the increased complexity of the task, but also by the inability of this net to develop lower level acoustic-phonetic features in hidden layer 1. Such features may in fact be needed for discrimination *between* the two stop classes, in addition to the within-class features.

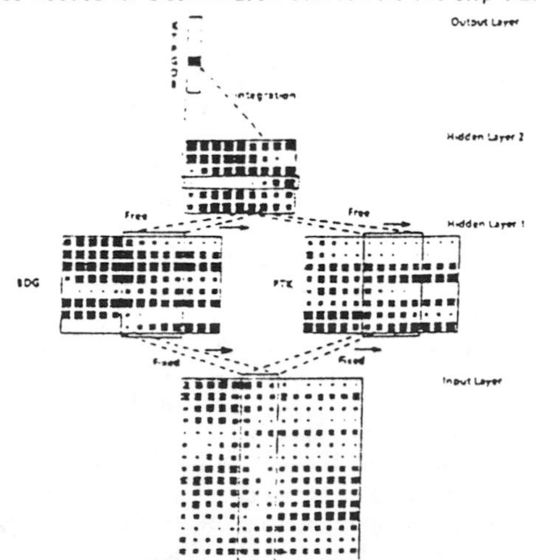

Figure 2. BDGPTK-net trained from hidden units from a BDG- and a PTK-net.

In a third experiment, we therefore first train a separate TDNN to perform the voiced/unvoiced (V/UV) distinction between the BDG- and the PTK-task. The network has a very similar structure as the BDG-net, except that only four hidden units were used in hidden layer 1 and two in hidden layer 2 and at the output. This V/UV-net achieved better than 99% voiced/unvoiced classification on the test data and its hidden units developed in the process are now used as

[1] Note, that these are connections over which a back-propagation pass is performed during each iteration. Since many of them share the same weights, only a small fraction (about 500) of them are actually free parameters.

additional features for the BDGPTK-task. The connections from the input to the first hidden layer of the BDG-, the PTK- and the V/UV nets are frozen and only the connections that combine the 20 units in hidden layer 1 to the higher layers are retrained. Training of the V/UV-net and subsequent combination training took between one and two days. The resulting net was evaluated as before on our testing database and achieved a recognition score of 98.4% correct.

In the previous experiment, good results could be obtained by adding units that we *believed* to be the useful class distinctive features that were missing in our second experiment. In a fourth experiment, we have now examined an approach that allows for the network to be free to discover *any* additional features that might be useful to merge the two component networks. In stead of previously training a class distinctive network, we now add four units to hidden layer 1, whose

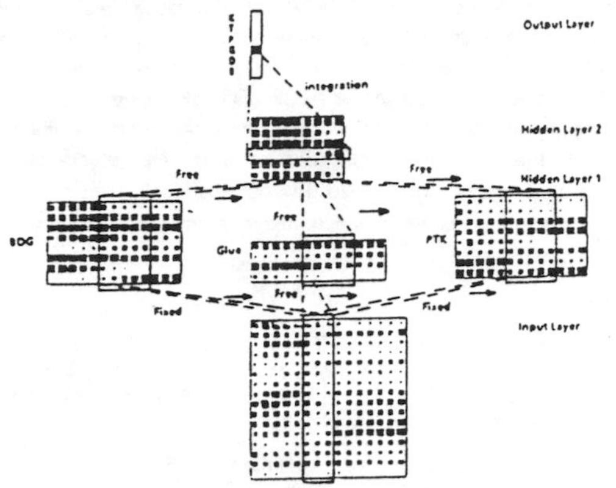

Figure 3. Combination of a BDG-net and a PTK-net using 4 additional units in hidden layer 1 as free "Connectionist Glue".

connections to the input are free to learn any missing discriminatory features to supplement the 16 frozen BDG and PTK features. We call these units the "*connectionist glue*" that we apply to merge two distinct networks into a new combined net. This network is shown in Fig.3. The hidden units of hidden layer 1 from the BDG-net are shown on the left and those from the PTK-net on the right. The connections from the moving input window to these units have been trained individually on BDG- and PTK-data, respectively, and -as before- remain fixed during combination learning. In the middle on hidden layer 1 we show the 4 free "Glue" units. Combination learning now searches for an optimal combination of the existing BDG- and PTK-features and also supplements these by learning additional interclass discriminatory features. Combination retraining with "glue" required a two day training run. Performance evaluation of this network over the BDGPTK test database yielded a recognition rate of 98.4%.

In addition to the techniques described so far, it may be useful to free *all* connections in a large modularly constructed network for an additional small amount of fine tuning. This has been done for the BDGPTK-net shown in Fig.3 yielding some additional performance improvements. Each iteration of the full network is indeed very slow, but convergence is reached after only few additional tuning iterations. The resulting network finally achieved (over testing data) a recognition score of 98.6%.

3.2. Steps for the Design of Large Scale Neural Nets

Table 3-1 summarizes the major results from our experiments. In the first row it shows the recognition performance of the two initial TDNNs trained individually to perform the BDG- and the PTK-tasks, respectively. Underneath, we show the results from the various experiments described in the previous section. The results indicate,

Method	bdg	ptk	bdgptk
Individual TDNNs	98.3 %	98.7 %	
TDNN:Max. Activation			60.5 %
Retrain BDGPTK			98.3 %
Retrain Combined Higher Layers			98.1 %
Retrain with V/UV-units			98.4 %
Retrain with Glue			98.4 %
All-Net Fine Tuning			98.6 %

Table 3-1: From BDG to BDGPTK; Modular Scaling Methods.

that larger TDNNs can indeed be trained *incrementally*, without requiring excessive amounts of training and without loss in performance. The total incremental training time was between one third and one half of a full monolithically trained net and the resulting networks appear to perform slightly better. Even more astonishingly, they appear to achieve performance as high as the subcomponent BDG- and PTK-nets alone. As a strategy for the efficient construction of larger networks we have found the following concepts to be extremely effective: *modular,incremental learning, class distinctive learning, connectionist glue, partial and selective learning and all-net fine tuning.*

4. Recognition of all Consonants and all Phonemes

The incremental learning techniques explored so far can now be applied to the design of networks capable of recognizing all consonant and all phonemes.

4.1. Network Architecture

Our consonant TDNN (shown in Fig.4.1) was constructed modularly from networks aimed at the consonant subcategories, i.e., the BDG-, PTK-, MNsN-, SShHZ-, TsCh- and the RWY-tasks. Each of these

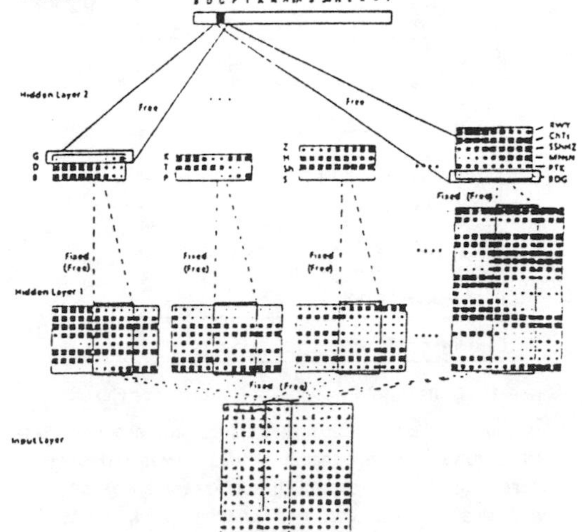

Figure 4. Modular Construction of an All Consonant Network

nets had been trained before to discriminate between the consonants *within* each class. Hidden layers 1 and 2 were then extracted from these nets, i.e. their weights copied and frozen in a new combined consonant TDNN. In addition, an interclass discrimination net was trained that distinguishes *between* the consonant subclasses and thus hopefully provides missing featural information for interclass discrimination much like the V/UV network described in the previous section. The structure of this network was very similar to other subcategory TDNNs, except that we have allowed for 20 units in hidden layer 1 and 6 hidden units (one for each coarse consonant class) in hidden layer 2. The weights leading into hidden layers 1 and 2 were then also copied from this interclass discrimination net into the consonant network and frozen. Three connections were then established to each of the 18 consonant output categories (B,D,G,P,T,K,M,N,sN,S, Sh,H,Z,Ch,Ts,R,W and Y): one to connect an output unit with the appropriate *interclass* discrimination unit in hidden layer 2, one with the appropriate *intraclass* discrimination unit from hidden layer 2 of the corresponding subcategory net and one with the always activated threshold unit (not shown in Fig.4.1) The overall network architecture is shown in Fig.4.1 for the case of an incoming test token (e.g., a "G"). For simplicity, Fig.4.1 shows only the hidden layers from the BDG-,PTK,SShHZ- and the inter-class discrimination nets. At the output, only the two connections leading to the correctly activated "G"-output unit are shown. Units and connections pertaining to the other subcategories as well as connections leading to the 17 other output units are omitted for clarity in Fig.4.1. All free weights were initialized with small random weights and then trained.

Another network (not shown here) was also trained that combines the consonant net described above with a vowel discrimination network. The vowel network by itself achieves a recognition performance of 98.6% correct on vowel testing data. It was combined with the consonantal subcategory networks and the consonant inter-class discrimination net in a joint hidden layer 3. The activations of each of the 23 hidden units in this layer were then integrated over time to activate one of the 23 Japanese phonemes.

4.2. Results

Consonants

Task	Recognition Rate (%)
bdg	98.6
ptk	98.7
mnN	96.6
sshhz	99.3
chts	100.0
rwy	99.9
cons. class	96.7
All consonant TDNN	95.0
All-Net Fine Tuning	95.9

Table 4-1: Consonant Recognition Performance Results.

Table 4.2 summarizes our results for the consonant recognition task. In the first 6 rows the recognition results (measured over the available test data in their respective sublasses) are given. The entry "cons.class" shows the performance of the interclass discrimination net in identifying the coarse phonemic subclass of an unknown token. 96.7% of all tokens were correctly categorized into one of the six consonant subclasses. After completion of combination learning the entire net was evaluated over 3061 consonant test tokens, and achieved a 95.0% recognition accuracy. All-net fine tuning was then performed by freeing up *all* connections in the network to allow for small additional adjustments in the interest of better overall performance. After completion of all-net fine tuning, the performance of the network then improved to 96.0% correct. To put these recognition results into perspective, we have compared these results with several other competing recognition techniques and found that our incrementally trained net compares favorably [6]. The incrementally trained all-phoneme network, finally, achieved a recognition score of 94.7%.

5. Conclusion

The serious problems associated with scaling smaller phonemic subcomponent networks to larger phonemic tasks are overcome by careful modular design. Modular design is achieved by several important strategies: *selective and incremental learning* of subcomponent tasks, *exploitation of previously learned hidden structure*, the application of *connectionist glue* or *class distinctive features* to allow for separate networks to "grow" together, *partial training* of portions of a larger net and finally, *all-net fine tuning* for making small additional adjustments in a large net. Our findings suggest, that judicious application of a number of connectionist design techniques could lead to the successful design of high performance large scale connectionist speech recognition systems.

References

1. Waibel, A., Hanazawa, T., Hinton, G., Shikano, K. and Lang K., "Phoneme Recognition Using Time-Delay Neural Networks", *IEEE, Transactions on Acoustics, Speech and Signal Processing*, March 1989.

2. Waibel, A., Hanazawa, T., Hinton, G., Shikano, K. and Lang K., "Phoneme Recognition: Neural Networks vs. Hidden Markov Models", *IEEE International Conference on Acoustics, Speech, and Signal Processing*, April 1988, pp. 8.S3.3.

3. Rumelhart, D.E., Hinton, G.E. and Williams, R.J., "Learning Internal Representations by Error Propagation", in *Parallel Distributed Processing; Explorations in the Microstructure of Cognition*, McClelland, J.L. and Rumelhart, D.E., ed., MIT Press, Cambridge, MA, 1986, pp. 318-362, ch. 8.

4. Watrous, R., *Speech Recognition Using Connectionist Networks*, PhD dissertation, University of Pennsylvania, October 1988.

5. Tank, D.W. and Hopfield, J.J., "Neural Computation by Concentrating Information in Time", *Proceedings National Academy of Sciences*, April 1987, pp. 1896-1900.

6. Waibel, A., Sawai, H. and Shikano, K., "Modularity and Scaling in Large Phonemic Neural Networks", Tech. report TR-I-0034, ATR Interpreting Telephony Research Laboratories, July 1988.

7. Haffner, P., Waibel, A. and Shikano, K., "Fast Back-Propagation Learning Methods for Neural Networks in Speech", *Proceedings of the Fall Meeting of the Acoustical Society of Japan*, October 1988.

8. Fahlman, S.E., "An Empirical Study of Learning Speed in Back-Propagation Networks", Tech. report CMU-CS-88-162, Carnegie-Mellon University, June 1988.

9. Waibel, A., "Connectionist Glue: Modular Design of Neural Speech Systems", *Proceedings of the 1988 Connectionist Models Summer School*, Morgan Kaufmann, 1988.

LEARNED PHONETIC DISCRIMINATION USING CONNECTIONIST NETWORKS

R.L.Watrous[1 2], L.Shastri[3], A.H.Waibel[4].

Abstract

A method for learning phonetic features from speech data using a *temporal flow model* is described, in which sampled speech data flows through a connectionist network from input to output units. The network uses hidden units with recurrent links to capture spectral/temporal characteristics of phonetic features. A simple experiment to discriminate the consonants [b,d,g] in the context of [i,a,u] using CV words is described. A supervised learning algorithm is used which performs gradient descent using a coarse approximation of the desired output as an target function. Context-dependent internal representations (features) were formed in the process of learning the discrimination task. A second experiment demonstrating learned vowel discrimination in various consonant environments is also presented. Both discrimination tasks were performed successfully without segmentation of the input, and *without a direct comparison of the training items.*

INTRODUCTION

The connectionist network approach to speech recognition is attractive because it offers a computational model which is well matched to the biological architecture that has served as their paradigm. Their learning capabilities, robust behavior, noise tolerance and graceful degradation are all capabilities which are becoming increasingly well understood and documented.

The networks consist of simple processing elements which integrate their inputs and broadcast the results to the units to which they are connected. Thus, the network response to input is the aggregate response of many interconnected units. It is the mutual interaction of many simple components that is the basis for robustness.

The perception of speech depends on the correct analysis of dynamic temporal/spectral relationships. The problem of designing connectionist networks which can learn these dynamic spectral/temporal characteristics has not yet been widely studied. Learning to associate static input/output pairs can be accomplished with layered connectionist networks with feedforward links alone. But recurrent, or feedback, links are required to provide the network with state sequence information, in order to capture sequential behavior.

A previous experiment showed that a simple network with recurrent links could be trained on a single instance of the word pair "no" and "go", and correctly discriminate 98% of 25 other tokens of each word for the same speaker [3]. The experiment was repeated for a second speaker and resulted in 100% discrimination performance.

An experiment is reported here which shows that connectionist networks can be optimized to discriminate the voiced stop consonants, [b,d,g], in various vowel contexts. A second experiment demonstrates the discrimination of the vowels [i,a,u] in the environment of various stop consonants. The results of these experiments show that connectionist networks can be designed and trained to successfully discriminate similar word pairs by learning context-dependent acoustic-phonetic features.

EXPERIMENT

The first experiment was designed to learn stop consonant discrimination in different vowel contexts, using CV words. The experiment used the voiced stops, [b,d,g] in three vowel contexts, [i,a,u]. A second experiment was designed to learn vowel discrimination in different consonant environments, using the same CV data.

For these experiments, a three-layer temporal flow model was implemented, as shown in Figure 1, with three output units, a variable number of hidden units, and 16 input units. The hidden and output units had self-recurrent links. The functions which define the unit behavior were chosen to approximate the computational properties of neural cells, and have convenient mathematical properties for the learning algorithm used in this experiment [2]. The unit output is a sigmoid function of the unit potential, which is the weighted sum of the outputs of the afferent units.

[1]Siemens Corp. Research, 105 College Road East, Princeton,NJ 08540
[2]Univ. of Pennsylvania, Computer and Information Sciences, Phila., PA 19104
[3]Univ. of Pennsylvania, Computer and Information Sciences
[4]ATR International Higashi-ku Osaka 540,Japan

Originally appeared in *European Conference on Speech Technology*, pp 377–380, Edinburgh (1987).

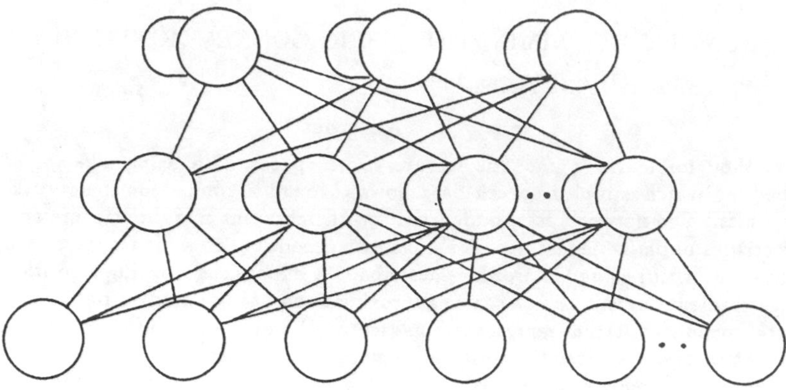

Figure 1: "Temporal Flow Model showing input, hidden and output layers"

The speech data used for these experiments consisted of isolated consonant-vowel (CV) utterances for a single speaker (RW) consisting of the stop consonants [b,d,g] in combination with the vowels [i,a,u]. Five repetitions of each CV word for a total of forty-five utterances were spoken into a commercial speech recognition device (Siemens CSE 1200), where it was passed through a 16-channel filter bank, full-wave rectified, log compressed and sampled every 2.5 milliseconds.

The data files were segmented by hand to extract the transition portion of the CV word. The initial segmentation boundary was set at a point of silence at least 50 ms prior to the consonant release and the final segment boundary in the center of the vowel nucleus. This segmentation was done to decrease the computational load on the optimization algorithm and did not involve an attempt to identify the consonant-vowel boundary. It is certain that sufficient if not complete discriminatory information remained in the segmented data.

For these experiments, the Broyden-Fletcher-Goldfarb-Shanno optimization algorithm (BFGS) was used [1]. This algorithm combines a linear search along a minimizing vector with an approximation of the second-derivative of the objective function f. In this way, knowledge about the structure of the error surface is used to select optimal search directions and achieve much more rapid convergence, especially in the neighborhood of the function minima. The algorithm was used to modify the unit connection weights in order to minimize the mean squared error between the actual and desired output values [3].

The target function for the output units consisted of a simple Gaussian function, with a variable center point and sharpness parameter. This represented the intuition that evidence for a particular phonetic category reaches a peak near some critical point in time. For the consonant experiment, the release of the stop closure was the critical event, which occurred roughly in the center of the data buffer. For this reason the target function center value was chosen as 0.5. For the vowel experiment, the Gaussian was shifted so that the maximum was at the end of the buffer (0.9). This corresponded to the intuition that the vowel discrimination reached a maximum toward the vowel center.

The computation of the gradient vector was accomplished by an extended form of the back-propagation learning algorithm for networks with recurrent links [2,4].

A randomly initialized network with 16 hidden units was optimized for consonant discrimination. The squared error decreased from 2934 to 121 after approximately 500 iterations. The response of the output units for the optimized network can be seen in Figure 2. The output units respond in equal and opposite ways to the input stimuli; in addition, their time response roughly approximates a Gaussian. Since the learned response closely fits the training function, the network shows very good discrimination between the items of the training set. The response of the network to the other items is analogous to that shown in the figure.

The response of the hidden units to the training data was also evaluated. An example can be seen in Figure 3, where it will be noticed that the hidden unit response is decidedly context specific.

A similarly initialized network, with 10 hidden units, was optimized for vowel discrimination. The

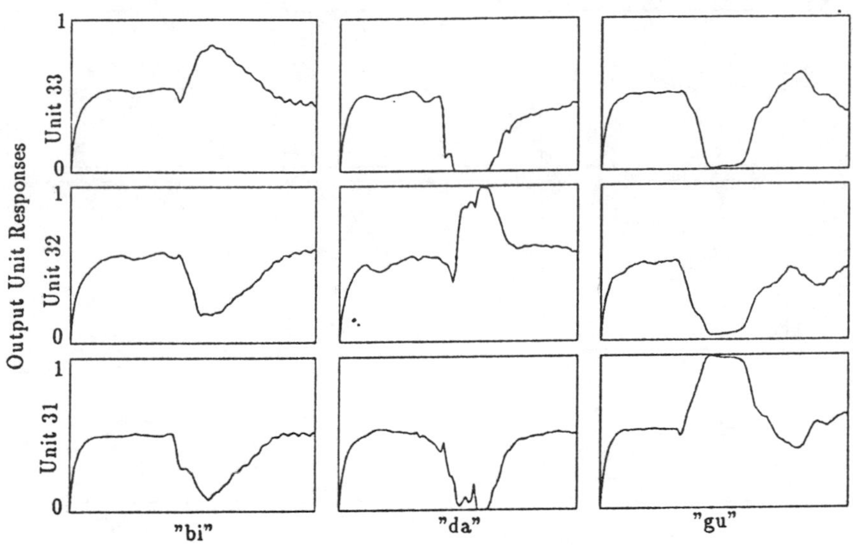

Figure 2: "Consonant Unit Responses to [bi,da,gu]"

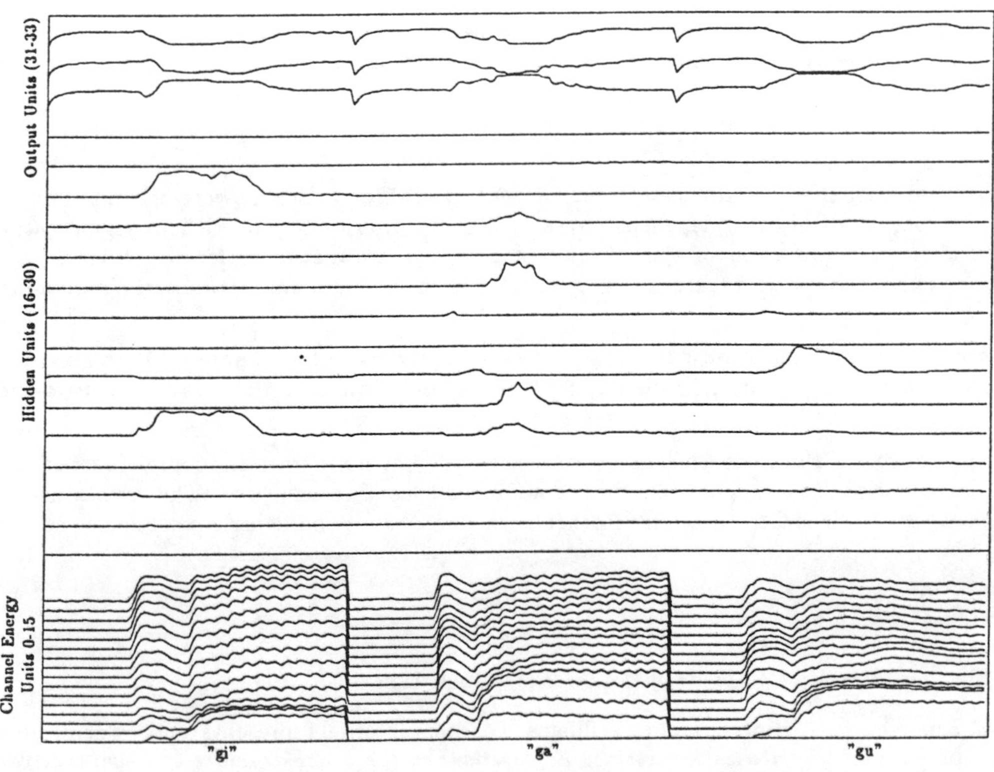

Figure 3: "Hidden Unit Responses to [gi,ga,gu]"

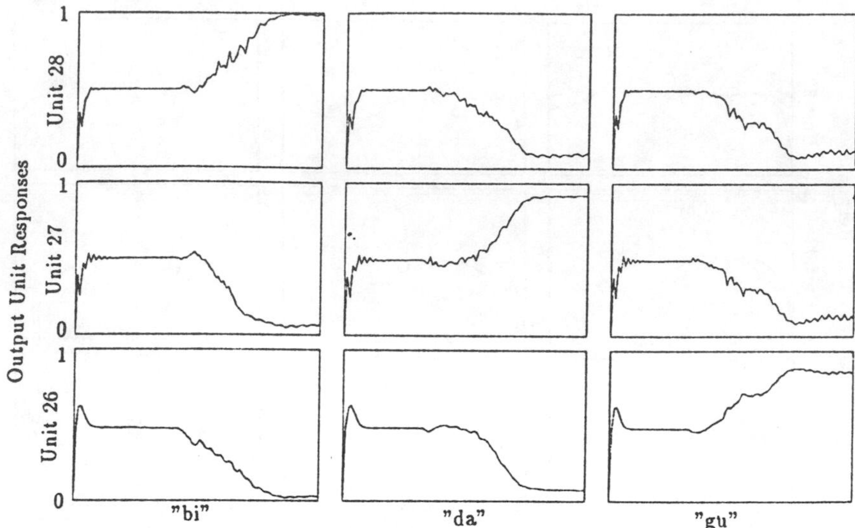

Figure 4: "Vowel Unit Responses to [bi,da,gu]"

squared error decreased from 2995 to 38.2 after approximately 140 iterations. The response of the output units for the optimized network can be seen in Figure 4. The output units show very good discrimination between the items of the training set. The response of both networks to the other items in the training set is analogous to that shown in the figures.

The analysis of the hidden unit activation in response to the training data showed little or no context dependence. The features responded similarly to the appropriate vowel across consonant contexts.

DISCUSSION

The significance of these results should not be overlooked. The networks were optimized on a small data set to perform context-independent vowel/consonant discrimination, without segmentation and without a direct comparison of the tokens. In doing so, the networks formed dynamic context-dependent temporal/spectral features, using an approximation of an unknown discrimination function **as a target.**

In conclusion, it has been shown that a connectionist network with a temporal data flow architecture with recurrent links can infer directly from real speech data a mechanism for acoustic-phonetic discrimination.

The long term goal of this research is to structure networks which can learn the complete set of phonetic class discriminations, to support real-time, continuous speech recognition. The results from these experiments are sufficient to encourage further work toward that end using connectionist networks.

References

[1] R. Fletcher. *Practical Methods of Optimization.* John Wiley, NY, 1980.

[2] D. E. Rumelhart, G. Hinton, and R. Williams. Learning internal representations by error propagation. In *Parallel Distributed Processing: Explorations in the Microstructure of Cognition: Volume I Foundations*, MIT Press, 1986.

[3] R. L. Watrous and L. Shastri. Learning acoustic features from speech data using connectionist networks. In *Proc. Cog. Sci. Conference*, July 1987.

[4] R. L. Watrous and L. Shastri. *Learning Phonetic Features Using Connectionist Networks: An Experiment in Speech Recognition.* Technical Report MS-CIS-86-78, Univ. of Penna., Oct. 1986.

The "Neural" Phonetic Typewriter

Teuvo Kohonen
Helsinki University of Technology

Based on a neural network processor for the recognition of phonetic units of speech, this speaker-adaptive system transcribes dictation using an unlimited vocabulary.

In 1930 a Hungarian scientist, Tihamér Nemes, filed a patent application in Germany for the principle of making an optoelectrical system automatically transcribe speech. His idea was to use the optical sound track on a movie film as a grating to produce diffraction patterns (corresponding to speech spectra), which then could be identified and typed out. The application was turned down as "unrealistic." Since then the problem of automatic speech recognition has occupied the minds of scientists and engineers, both amateur and professional.

Research on speech recognition principles has been pursued in many laboratories around the world, academic as well as industrial, with various objectives in mind.[1] One ambitious goal is to implement automated query systems that could be accessed through public telephone lines, because some telephone companies have observed that telephone operators spend most of their time answering queries. An even more ambitious plan, adopted in 1986 by the Japanese national ATR (Advanced Telecommunication Research) project, is to receive speech in one language and to synthesize it in another, on line. The dream of a phonetic typewriter that can produce text from arbitrary dictation is an old one; it was envisioned by Nemes and is still being pursued today. Several dozen devices, even special microcircuits, that can recognize isolated words from limited vocabularies with varying accuracy are now on the market. These devices have important applications, such as the operation of machines by voice, various dispatching services that employ voice-activated devices, and aids for seriously handicapped people. But in spite of big investments and the work of experts, the original goals have not been reached. High-level speech recognition has existed so far only in science fiction.

Recently, researchers have placed great hopes on artificial neural networks to perform such "natural" tasks as speech recognition. This was indeed one motivation for us to start research in this area many years ago at Helsinki University of Technology. This article describes the result of that research—a complete "neural" speech recognition system, which recognizes phonetic units, called *phonemes*, from a continuous speech signal. Although motivated by neural network principles, the choices in its design must be regarded as a compromise of many technical aspects of those principles. As our system is a genuine "phonetic typewriter" intended to transcribe orthographically edited text from an unlimited vocabulary, it cannot be directly compared with any more conventional, word-based system that applies classical concepts such as dynamic time warping[1] and hidden Markov models.[2]

Why is speech recognition difficult?

Automatic recognition of speech belongs to the broader category of pattern recognition tasks,[3] for which, during the past 30 years or so, many heuristic and even sophisticated methods have been tried. It may seem strange that while progress in many other fields of technology has

0018-9162/88/0300-0011$01.00 © 1988 IEEE

been astoundingly rapid, research investments in these "natural" tasks have not yet yielded adequate dividends. After initial optimism, the researchers in this area have gradually become aware of the many difficulties to be surmounted.

Human beings' recognition of speech consists of many tasks, ranging from the detection of phonemes from speech waveforms to the high-level understanding of messages. We do not actually hear all speech elements; we realize this easily when we try to decipher foreign or uncommon utterances. Instead, we continuously relate fragmentary sensory stimuli to contexts familiar from various experiences, and we unconsciously test and reiterate our perceptions at different levels of abstraction. In other words, what we believe we *hear*, we in fact *reconstruct* in our minds from pieces of received information.

Even in clear speech from the same speaker, distributions of the spectral samples of different phonemes overlap. Their statistical density functions are not Gaussian, so they cannot be approximated analytically. The same phonemes spoken by different persons can be confused too; for example, the /ɛ/ of one speaker might sound like the /n/ of another. For this reason, absolutely speaker-independent detection of phonemes is possible only with relatively low accuracy.

Some phonemes are spectrally clearer and stabler than others. For speech recognition purposes, we distinguish three acoustically different categories:

(1) Vocal (voiced, nonturbulent) phonemes, including the vowels, semivowels (/j/, /v/), nasals (/m/, /n/, /ŋ/), and liquids (/l/, /r/)

(2) Fricatives (/s/, /š/, /z/, etc.)

(3) Plosives (/k/, /p/, /t/, /b/, /d/,/g/, etc.)

The phonemes of the first two categories have rather well-defined, stationary spectra, whereas the plosives are identifiable only on the basis of their transient properties. For instance, for /k,p,t/ there is a silence followed by a short, faint burst of voice characteristic of each plosive, depending on its point of articulation (lips, tongue, palate). The transition of the speech signal to the next phoneme also varies among the plosives.

A high-level automatic speech recognition system also should interpret the semantic content of utterances so that it can maintain selective attention to particular portions of speech. This ability would call for higher thinking processes, not only imitation of the operation of the preattentive sensory system. The first large experimental speech-understanding systems followed this line of thought (see the report of the ARPA project,[4] which was completed around 1976), but for commercial application such solutions were too expensive. Machine interpretation of the meaning of complete sentences is a very difficult task; it has been accomplished only when the syntax has been artificially limited. Such "party tricks" may have led the public to believe that practical speech recognition has reached a more advanced level than it has. Despite decades of intensive research, no machine has yet been able to recognize general, continuous speech produced by an arbitrary speaker, when no speech samples have been supplied.

Machine interpretation of complete sentences has been accomplished only with artificially limited syntax.

Recognition of the speech of arbitrary speakers is much more difficult than generally believed. Existing commercial speaker-independent systems are restricted to isolated words from vocabularies not exceeding 40 words. Reddy and Zue estimated in 1983 that for speaker-independent recognition of connected speech, based on a 20,000-word vocabulary, a computing power of 100,000 MIPS, corresponding to 100 supercomputers, would be necessary.[5] Moreover, the detailed programs to perform these operations have not been devised. The difficulties would be even greater if the vocabularies were unlimited, if the utterances were loaded with emotions, or if speech were produced under noisy or stressful conditions.

We must, of course, be aware of these difficulties. On the other hand, we would never complete any practical speech recognizer if we had to attack all the problems simultaneously. Engineering solutions are therefore often restricted to particular tasks. For instance, we might wish to recognize isolated commands from a limited vocabulary, or to type text from dictation automatically. Many satisfactory techniques for speaker-specific, isolated-word recognition have already been developed. Systems that type English text from clear dictation with short pauses between the words have been demonstrated.[6] Typing unlimited dictation in English is another intriguing objective. Systems designed for English recognize words as complete units, and various grammatical forms such as plural, possessive, and so forth can be stored in the vocabulary as separate word tokens. This is not possible in many other languages—Finnish and Japanese, for example—in which the grammar is implemented by inflections and there may be dozens of different forms of the same root word. For inflectional languages the system must construct the text from recognized phonetic units, taking into account the transformations of these units due to coarticulation effects (i.e., a phoneme's acoustic spectrum varies in the context of different phonemes).

Especially in image analysis, but in speech recognition too, many newer methods concentrate on structural and syntactic relationships between the pattern elements, and special grammars for their analysis have been developed. It seems, however, that the first step, preanalysis and detection of primary features such as acoustic spectra, is still often based on rather coarse principles, without careful consideration of the very special statistical properties of the natural signals and their clustering. Therefore, when new, highly parallel and adaptive methods such as artificial neural networks are introduced, we assume that their capacities can best be utilized if the networks are made to adapt to the real data, finding relevant features in the signals. This was in fact one of the central assumptions in our research.

To recapitulate, speech is a very difficult stochastic process, and its elements are not unique at all. The distributions of the different phonemic classes overlap seriously, and to minimize misclassification errors, careful statistical as well as structural analyses are needed.

The promise of neural computers

Because the brain has already implemented the speech recognition function (and many others), some researchers have reached the straightforward conclusion that artificial neural networks should be able to do the same, regarding these networks as a panacea for such "natural" problems. Many of these people believe that the only bottleneck is computing power, and some even expect that all the remaining problems will be solved when, say, optical neural computers, with a vast computing capacity, become feasible. What these people fail to realize is that *we may not yet have discovered what biological neurons and neural systems are like.* Maybe the machines we call neural networks and neural computers are too simple. Before we can utilize such computing capacities, we must know *what* and *how* to compute.

It is true that intriguing simulations of new information-processing functions, based on artificial neural networks, have been made, but most of these demonstrations have been performed with artificial data that are separable into disjoint classes. Difficulties multiply when natural, stochastic data are applied. In my own experience the quality of a neural network must be tested in an on-line connection with a natural environment. One of the most difficult problems is dealing with input data whose statistical density functions overlap, have awkward forms in high-dimensional signal spaces, and are not even stationary. Furthermore, in practical applications the number of samples of input data used for training cannot be large; for instance, we cannot expect that every user has the patience to dictate a sufficient number of speech samples to guarantee ultimate accuracy.

On the other hand, since digital computing principles are already in existence, they should be used wherever they are superior to biological circuits, as in the syntactic analysis of symbolic expressions and even in the spectral analysis of speech waveforms. The discrete Fourier transform has very effective digital implementations.

Our choice was to try neural networks in a task in which the most demanding statistical analyses are performed—namely, in the optimal detection of the phonemes. In this task we could test some new learning methods that had been shown to yield a recognition accuracy comparable to the decision-theoretic maximum, while at the same time performing the computations by simple elements, using a minimal amount of sample data for training.

In practical neural-network applications, the number of input samples used for training cannot be large.

Acoustic preprocessing

Physiological research on hearing has revealed many details that may or may not be significant to artificial speech recognition. The main operation carried out in human hearing is a frequency analysis based on the resonances of the basilar membrane of the inner ear. The spectral decomposition of the speech signal is transmitted to the brain through the auditory nerves. Especially at lower frequencies, however, each peak of the pressure wave gives rise to separate bursts of neural impulses; thus, some kind of time-domain information also is transmitted by the ear. On the other hand, a certain degree of synchronization of neural impulses to the acoustic signals seems to occur at all frequencies, thus conveying phase information. One therefore might stipulate that the artificial ear contain detectors that mimic the operation of the sensory receptors as fully as possible.

Biological neural networks are able to enhance signal transients in a nonlinear fashion. This property has been simulated in physical models that describe the mechanical properties of the inner ear and chemical transmission in its neural cells.[7,8] Nonetheless, we decided to apply conventional frequency analysis techniques, as such, to the preprocessing of speech. The main motivations for this approach were that the digital Fourier analysis is both accurate and fast and the fundamentals of digital filtering are well understood. Standard digital signal processing has been considered sufficient in acoustic engineering and telecommunication. Our decision was thus a typical engineering choice. We also believed the self-organizing neural network described here would accept many alternative kinds of preprocessing and compensate for modest imperfections, as long as they occur consistently. Our final results confirmed this belief; at least there were no large differences in recognition accuracies between stationary and transient phonemes.

Briefly, the complete acoustic preprocessor of our system consists of the following stages:

(1) Noise-canceling microphone

(2) Preamplifier with a switched-capacitor, 5.3-kHz low-pass filter

(3) 12-bit analog-to-digital converter with 13.02-kHz sampling rate

(4) 256-point fast Fourier transform, computed every 9.83 ms using a 256-point Hamming window

(5) Logarithmization and filtering of spectral powers by fourth-order elliptic low-pass filters

(6) Grouping of spectral channels into a 15-component real-pattern vector

(7) Subtraction of the average from all components

(8) Normalization of the resulting vector into constant length

Operations 3 through 8 are computed by the signal processor chip TMS 32010 (our design is four years old; much faster processors are now available).

In many speech recognition systems acoustic preprocessing encodes the speech signal into so-called LPC (linear predictive coding) coefficients,[1] which contain approximately the same information as the spectral decomposition. We preferred the FFT because, as will be shown, one of the main operations of the neural network that recognizes the phonemes is to perform metric clustering of the phonemic samples. The FFT, a transform of the signal, reflects its clustering properties better than a parametric code.

We had the option of applying the overall root-mean-square value of the speech signal as the extra sixteenth component in the pattern vector; in this way we expected to obtain more information on the transient signals. The recognition accuracy remained the same, however, within one percent. We believe that the acoustic processor can analyze many other speech features in addition to the spectral ones. Another trick that improved accuracy on the order of two percent was to make the true pattern vector out of two spectra 30 ms apart in the time scale. Since the two samples represent two different states of the signal, dynamic information is added

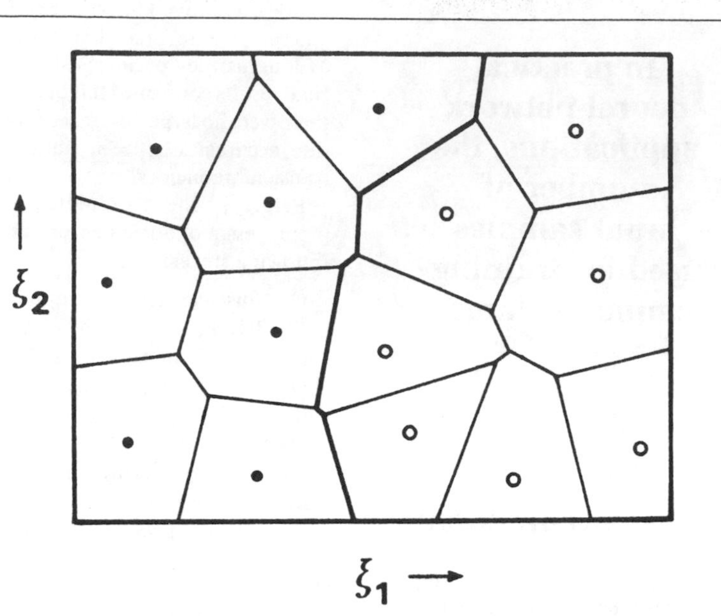

Figure 1. Voronoi tessellation partitions a two-dimensional (ξ_1, ξ_2) "pattern space" into regions around reference vectors, shown as points in this coordinate system. All vectors (ξ_1, ξ_2) in the same partition have the same reference vector as their nearest neighbor and are classified according to it. The solid and open circles, respectively, represent reference vectors of two classes, and the discrimination "surface" between them is drawn in bold.

to the preanalysis.

Because the plosives must be distinguished on the basis of the fast, transient parts of the speech waveform, we selected the spectral samples of the plosives from the transient regions of the signal, on the basis of the constancy of the waveform. On the other hand, there is evidence that the biological auditory system is sensitive not only to the spectral representations of speech but to their particular transient features too, and apparently it uses the nonlinear adaptive properties of the inner ear, especially its hair cells, the different transmission delays in the neural fibers, and many kinds of neural gating in the auditory nuclei (processing stations between the ear and the brain). For the time being, these nonlinear, dynamic neural functions are not understood well enough to warrant the design of standard electronic analogies for them.

Vector quantization

The instantaneous spectral power values on the 15 channels formed from the FFT can be regarded as a 15-dimensional real vector in a Euclidean space. We might think that the spectra of the different phonemes of speech occupy different regions of this space, so that they could be detected by some kind of multidimensional discrimination method. In reality, several problems arise. One of them, as already stated, is that the distributions of the spectra of different phonemic classes overlap, so that it is not possible to distinguish the phonemes by any discrimination method with 100 percent certainty. The best we can do is to divide the space with optimal discrimination borders, relative to which, on the average, the rate of misclassifications is minimized. It turns out that analytical definition of such (nonlinear) borders is far from trivial, whereas neural networks can define them very effectively. Another problem is presented by the coarticulation effects discussed later.

A concept useful for the illustration of these so-called vector space methods for pattern recognition and neural networks is called *Voronoi tessellation*. For simplicity, consider that the dissimilarity of two or more spectra can be expressed in terms of their vectorial difference (actually the norm of this difference) in an n-dimensional Euclidean space. Figure 1 exemplifies a two-dimensional space in which a finite number of *reference vectors* are shown as points, corresponding to their coordinates. This space is partitioned into regions, bordered by lines (in general, hyperplanes) such that each partition contains a reference vector that is the nearest neighbor to any vector within the same partition. These lines, or the midplanes of the neighboring reference vectors, constitute the Voronoi tessellation, which defines a set of *discrimination* or *decision surfaces*. This tessellation represents one kind of *vector quantization*, which generally means quantization of the vector space into discrete regions.

One or more neighboring reference vectors can be made to define a category in the vector space as the union of their respective partitions. Determination of such reference vectors was the main problem on which we concentrated in our neural network research. There are, of course, many classical mathematical approaches to this problem.[3] In very simple and straightforward pattern recognition, samples, or prototypes, of earlier observed vectors are used as such for the reference vectors. For the new or unknown vector, a small number of its nearest prototypes are sought; then majority voting is applied to them to determine classification. A drawback of this method is that for good statistical accuracy an appreciable number of reference vectors are needed. Consequently, the comparison computations during classification, expecially if they are made serially, become time-consuming; the unknown vector must be compared with all the reference vectors. Therefore, our aim was to describe the samples by a much smaller representative set of reference vectors without loss of accuracy.

Imagine now that a fixed number of discrete neurons is in parallel, looking at the speech spectrum, or the set of input signals. Imagine that each neuron has a template, a reference spectrum with respect to which the degree of matching with the input spectrum can be defined. Imagine further that the different neurons compete, the neuron with the highest matching score being regarded as the "winner." The input spectrum would then be assigned to the winner in the same way that an arbitrary vector is assigned to the closest reference vector and classified according to it in the above Voronoi tessellation.

There are neural networks in which such templates are formed adaptively, and which perform this comparison in parallel, so that the neuron whose template matches best with the input automatically gives an active response to it. Indeed, the self-organizing process described below defines reference vectors for the neurons such that their Voronoi tessellation sets near-optimal decision borders between the classes—i.e., the fraction of input vectors falling on the wrong side of the borders is minimized. In classical decision theory, theoretical minimization of the probability for misclassification is a standard procedure, and the mathematical setting for it is the Bayes theory of probability. In what follows, we shall thus point out that the vector quantization and nearest neighbor classification resulting in the neural network defines the reference vectors in such a way that their Voronoi tessellation very closely approximates the theoretical Bayesian decision surfaces.

The neural network

Detailed biophysical analysis of the phenomena taking place at the cell membrane of biological neurons leads to systems of nonlinear differential equations with dozens of state variables for each neuron; this would be untenable in a computational application. Obviously it is necessary to simplify the mathematics, while retaining some essentials of the real dynamic behavior. The approximations made here, while reasonably simple, are still rather "neural" and have been influential in many intriguing applications.

Figure 2 depicts one model neuron and defines its signal and state variables. The input signals are connected to the neuron with different, variable "transmittances" corresponding to the coupling strengths of the neural junctions called *synapses*. The latter are denoted by μ_{ij} (here i is the index of the neuron and j that of its input). Correspondingly, ξ_{ij} is the signal value (signal activity, actually the frequency of the neural impulses) at the jth input of the ith neuron.

Each neuron is thought to act as a pulse-frequency modulator, producing an output activity η_i (actually a train of neural impulses with this repetition frequency), which is obtained by integrating the input signals according to the following differential equation. (The biological neurons have an active membrane with a capacitance that integrates input currents and triggers a volley of impulses when a critical level of depolarization is achieved.)

$$d\eta_i/dt = \sum_{j=1}^{n} \mu_{ij}\xi_{ij} - \gamma(\eta_i) \tag{1}$$

The first term on the right corresponds to the coupling of input signals to the neuron through the different transmittances; a linear, superpositive effect was assumed for simplicity. The last term, $-\gamma(\eta_i)$, stands for a nonlinear leakage effect that describes all nonideal properties, such as saturation, leakage, and shunting effects of the neuron, in a simple way. It is assumed to be a stronger than linear function of η_i. It is further assumed that the inverse function γ^{-1} exists. Then if the ξ_{ij} are held stationary, or they are changing slowly, we can consider the case $d\eta_i/dt \sim 0$, whereby the output will follow the integrated input as in a nonlinear, saturating amplifier according to

$$\eta_i = \sigma[\sum_{j=1}^{n} \mu_{ij}\xi_{ij}] \tag{2}$$

Here $\sigma[.]$ is the inverse function of γ, and it usually has a typical sigmoidal form, with low and high saturation limits and a proportionality range between.

The settling of activity according to Equation 1 proceeds very quickly; in biological circuits it occurs in tens of milliseconds. Next we consider an adaptive process in which the transmittances μ_{ij} are assumed to change too. This is the effect regarded as "learning" in neural circuits, and its time constants are much longer. In biological circuits this process corresponds to changes in proteins and neural structures that typically take weeks. A simple, natural adaptation law that already has suggested many applications is the following: First, we must stipulate that parametric changes occur very selectively; thus dependence on the signals must be nonlinear. The classical choice made by most modelers is to assume that changes are proportional to the *product* of input and output activities (the so-called law of Hebb). However, this choice, as such, would be unnatural because the parameters would change in one direction only (notice that the signals are positive). Therefore it is necessary to modify this law—for example, by including some kind of nonlinear "forgetting" term. Thus we can write

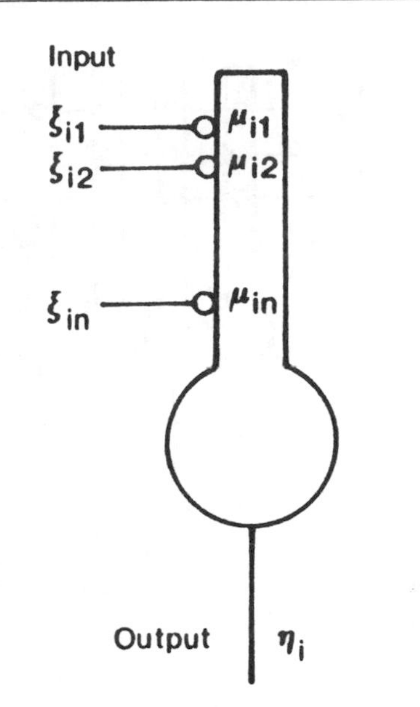

Figure 2. Symbol of a theoretical neuron and the signal and system variables relating to it. The small circles correspond to the input connections, the synapses.

$$d\mu_{ij}/dt = \alpha\eta_i\xi_{ij} - \beta(\eta_i)\mu_{ij} \tag{3}$$

where α is a positive constant, the first term is the "Hebbian" term, and the last term represents the nonlinear "forgetting" effect, which depends on the activity η_i; forgetting is thus "active." As will be pointed out later, the first term defines changes in the μ_{ij} in such a direction that the neuron tends to become more and more sensitive and selective to the particular combination of signals ξ_{ij} presented at the input. This is the basic adaptive effect.

On the other hand, to stabilize the output activity to a proper range, it seems very profitable for $\beta(\eta_i)$ to be a scalar function with a Taylor expansion in which the constant term is zero. Careful analyses have shown that this kind of neuron becomes selective to the so-called *largest principal component* of input.[9] For many choices of the functional form, it can further be shown that the μ_{ij} will automatically become normalized such that the vector formed from the μ_{ij} during the process tends to a constant length (norm) indepen-

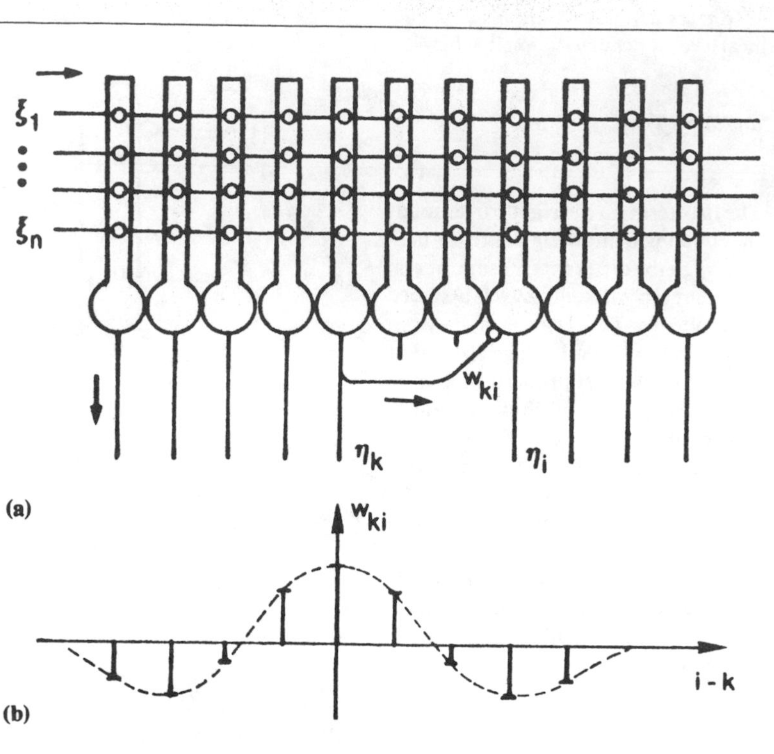

Figure 3. (a) Neural network underlying the formation of the phonotopic maps used in speech recognition. (b) The strengths of lateral interaction as a function of distance (the "Mexican hat" function).

dent of the signal values that occur in the process.[9] We shall employ this effect a bit later in a further simplification of the model.

One cannot understand the essentials of neural circuits unless one considers their behavior as a *collective* system. An example occurs in the "self-organizing feature maps" in our speech recognition application. Consider Figure 3a, where a set of neurons forms a layer, and each neuron is connected to its neighbors in the lateral direction. We have drawn the network one-dimensionally for clarity, although in all practical applications it has been two-dimensional. The external inputs, in the simplest model used for pattern recognition, are connected in parallel to all the neurons of this network so that each neuron can simultaneously "look" at the same input. (Certain interesting but much more complex effects result if the input connections are made to different portions of the network and the activation is propagated through it in a sequence.)

The feedback connections are coupled to the neurons in the same way as the external inputs. However, for simplicity, only the latter are assumed to have adaptive synapses. If the feedbacks were adaptive, too, this network would exhibit other more complex effects.[9] It should also be emphasized that the biological synaptic circuits of the feedbacks are different from those of the external inputs. The time-invariant coupling coefficient of the feedback connections, as a function of distance, has roughly the "Mexican hat" form depicted in Figure 3b, as in real neural networks. For negative coupling, signal-inverting elements are necessary; in biological circuits inversion is made by a special kind of inhibitory interneuron. If the external input is denoted

$$I_i = \sum_{j=1}^{n} \mu_{ij}\xi_{ij} \tag{4}$$

then the system equation for the network activities η_i, denoting the feedback coupling from neuron k to neuron i by w_{ki}, can be written

$$d\eta_i/dt = I_i + \sum_{k \in S_i} w_{ki}\eta_k - \gamma(\eta_i) \tag{5}$$

where k runs over the subset S_i of those neurons that have connections with neuron i. A characteristic phenomenon, due to the lateral feedback interconnections, will be observed first: The initial activity distribution in the network may be more or less random, but over time the activity develops into clusters or "bubbles" of a certain dimension, as shown in Figures 4 and 5. If the interaction range is not much less than the diameter of the network, the network activity seems to develop into a single bubble, located around the maximum of the (smoothed) initial activity.

Consider now that there is no external source of activation other than that provided by the input signal connections, which extend in parallel over the whole network. According to Equations 1 and 2, the strength of the initial activation of a neuron is proportional to the dot product $m_i^T x$ where m_i is the vector of the μ_{ij}, x is the vector of the ξ_{ij}, and T is the transpose of a vector. (We use here concepts of matrix algebra whereby m_i and x are column vectors.) Therefore, the bubble is formed around those units at which $m_i^T x$ is maximum.

The saturation limits of $\sigma[.]$ defined by Equation 2 stabilize the activities η_i to either a low or a high value. Similarly, $\beta(\eta_i)$ takes on either of two values. Without loss of generality, it is possible to rescale the variables ξ_{ij} and μ_{ij} to make $\eta_i \in \{0,1\}$, $\beta(\eta_i) \in \{0,\alpha\}$, whereby Equation 3 will be further simplified and split in two equations:

$$d\mu_{ij}/dt = \alpha(\xi_{ij} - \mu_{ij}) \tag{6a}$$

if $\eta_i = 1$ and $\beta = \alpha$ (inside the bubble)

$$d\mu_{ij}/dt = 0 \tag{6b}$$

for $\eta_i = \beta = 0$ (outside the bubble)

It is evident from Equation 6 that the transmittances μ_{ij} then adaptively tend to follow up the input signals ξ_{ij}. In other words, these neurons start to become selectively sensitized to the prevailing input pattern. But this occurs only when the bubble lies over the particular neuron. For another input, the bubble lies over other neurons, which then become sensitized to that input. In this way different parts of the network are automatically "tuned" to different inputs.

The network will indeed be tuned to different inputs in an ordered fashion, as if a continuous map of the signal space were formed over the network. The continuity of this mapping follows from the simple fact that the vectors m_i of contiguous units (within the bubbles) are modified in the same direction, so that during the course of the process the neighboring values become smoothed. The ordering of these values, however, is a very subtle phenomenon, the proof or complete explanation of which is mathematically very sophisticated[9] and cannot be given here. The effect is difficult to visualize without, say, an animation film. A concrete example of this kind of ordering is the phonotopic map described later in this article.

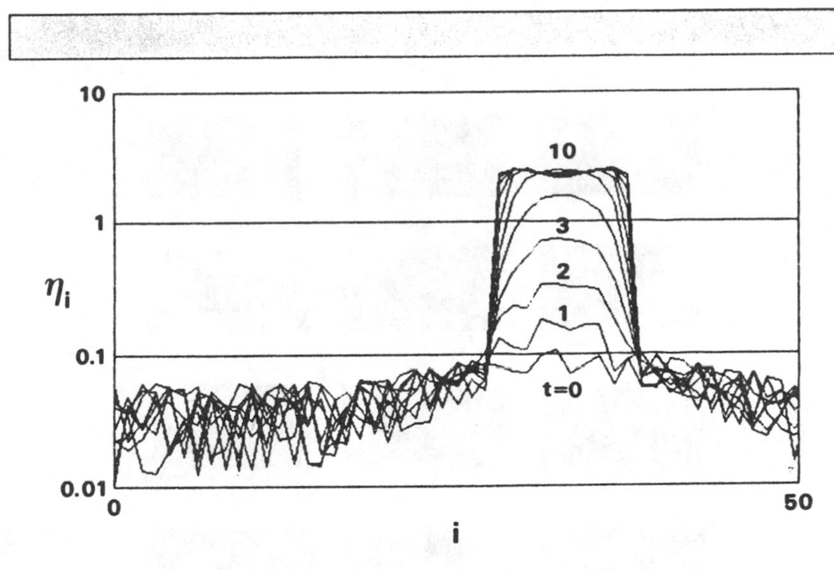

Figure 4. Development of the distribution of activity over time (t) into a stable "bubble" in a laterally interconnected neural network (cf. Figure 3). The activities of the individual neurons (η_i) are shown in the logarithmic scale.

Shortcut learning algorithm

In the time-continuous process just described, the weight vectors attain asymptotic values, which then define a vector quantization of the input signal space, and thus a classification of all its vectors. In practice, the same vector quantization can be computed much more quickly from a numerically simpler algorithm. The bubble is equivalent to a neighborhood set N_c of all those network units that lie within a certain radius from a certain unit c. It can be shown that the size of the bubble depends on the interaction parameters, and so we can reason that the radius of the bubble is controllable, eventually being definable as some function of time. For good self-organizing results, it has been found empirically that the radius indeed should decrease in time monotonically. Similarly $\alpha = \alpha(t)$ ought to be a monotonically decreasing function of time. Simple but effective choices for these functions have been determined in a series of practical experiments.[9]

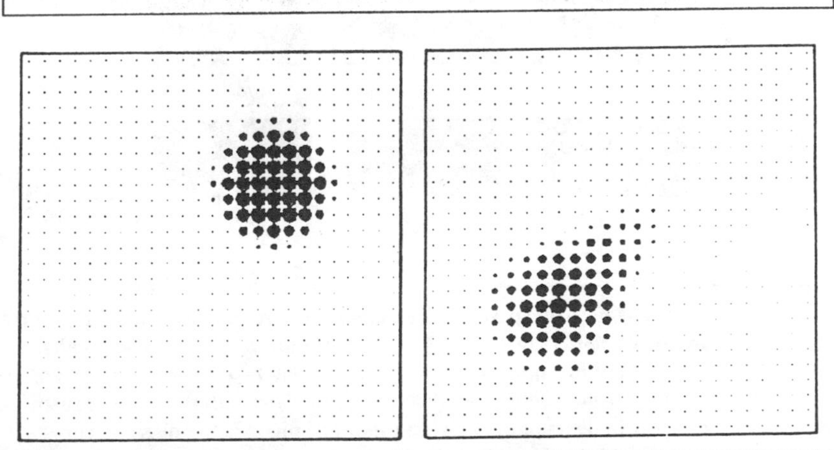

Figure 5. "Bubbles" formed in a two-dimensional network viewed from the top. The dots correspond to neurons, and their sizes correspond to their activity. In the picture on the right, the input was changing slowly, and the motion of the bubble is indicated by its "tail."

As stated earlier, the process defined by Equation 1 normalizes the weight vectors m_i to the same length. Since the bubble is formed around those units at which $m_i^T x$ is maximum, its center also coincides with that unit for which the norm of the vectorial difference $x - m_i$ is minimum.

Combining all the above results, we obtain the following shortcut algorithm. Let us start with random initial values $m_i = m_i(0)$. For $t = 0, 1, 2, \ldots$, compute:

(1) *Center of the bubble (c)*:

$$\|x(t) - m_c(t)\| = \min_i \{\|x(t) - m_i(t)\|\} \quad (7a)$$

(2) *Updated weight vectors*:

$$m_i(t+1) = m_i(t) + \alpha(t)\,(x(t) - m_i(t)) \quad \text{for } i \in N_c$$

$$m_i(t+1) = m_i(t) \quad \text{for all other indices } i \quad (7b)$$

As stated above, $\alpha = \alpha(t)$ and $N_c = N_c(t)$ are empirical functions of time. The asymptotic values of the m_i define the vector quantization. Notice, too, that Equation 7a defines the classification of input according to the closest weight vector to x.

We must point out that if N_c contained the index i only, Equations 7a and 7b

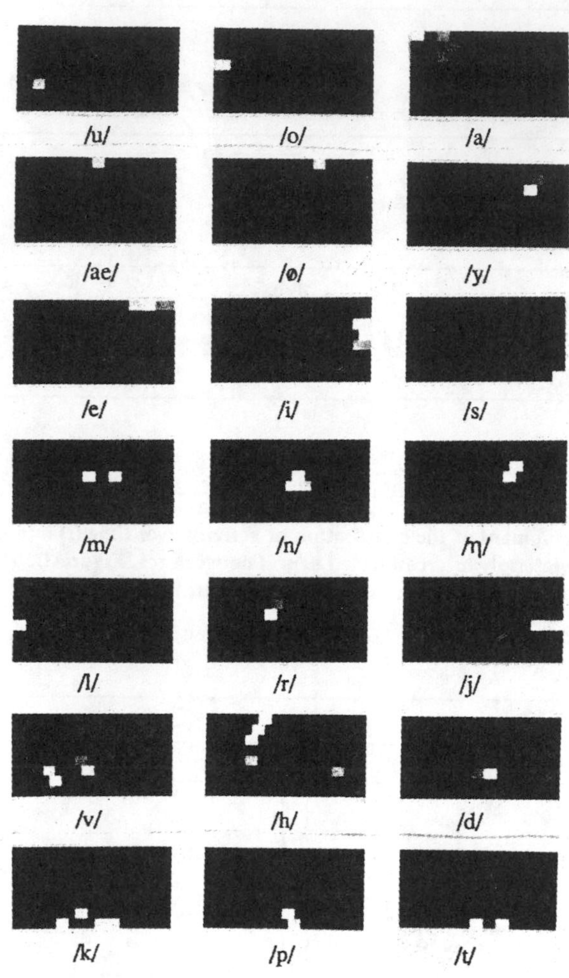

Figure 6. The signal of natural speech is preanalyzed and represented on 15 spectral channels ranging from 200 Hz to 5 kHz. The spectral powers of the different channel outputs are presented as input to an artificial neural network. The neurons are tuned automatically, without any supervision or extra information, to the acoustic units of speech identifiable as phonemes. In this set of pictures the neurons correspond to the small rectangular subareas. Calibration of the map was made with 50 samples of each test phoneme. The shaded areas correspond to histograms of responses from the map to certain phonemes (white: maximum).

would superficially resemble the classical vector quantization method called *k-means clustering*.[10] The present method, however, is more general because the corrections are made over a wider, dynamically defined neighborhood set, or bubble N_c, so that an *ordered* mapping is obtained. Together with some fine adjustments of the m_i vectors,[9] spectral recognition accuracy is improved significantly.

Phonotopic maps

For this discussion we assume that a lattice of hexagonally arranged neurons forms a two-dimensional neural network of the type depicted in Figure 3. As already described, the microphone signal is first converted into a spectral representation, grouped into 15 channels. These channels together constitute the 15-component stochastic input vector x, a function of time, to the network. The self-organizing process has been used to create a "topographic," two-dimensional map of speech elements onto the network.

Superficially this network seems to have only one layer of neurons; due to the lateral interactions in the network, however, its topology is in effect even more complicated than that of the famous multilayered Boltzmann machines or backpropagation networks.[11] Any neuron in our network is also able to create an internal representation of input information in the same way as the "hidden units" in the backpropagation networks eventually do. Several projects have recently been launched to apply Boltzmann machines to speech recognition. We should learn in the near future how they compete with the design described here.

The input vectors x, representing short-time spectra of the speech waveform, are computed in our system every 9.83 milliseconds. These samples are applied in Equations 7a and 7b as input data in their natural order, and the self-organizing process then defines the m_i, or the weight vectors of the neurons. One striking result is that the various neurons of the network become sensitized to spectra of different phonemes and their variations in a two-dimensional order, although teaching was not done by the phonemes; only spectral samples of input were applied. The reason is that the input spectra are clustered around phonemes, and the process finds these clusters. The maps can be calibrated using spectra of known phonemes. If then a new or unknown spectrum is presented at the inputs, the neuron with the closest transmittance vector m_i gives the response, and so the classification occurs in accordance with the Voronoi tessellation in which the m_i act as reference vectors. The values of these vectors very closely reflect the actual speech signal statistics.[11] Figure 6 shows the calibration result for different phonemic samples as a gray-level histogram of such responses, and Figure 7 shows the map when its neurons are labeled according to the majority voting for a number of different responses.

The speech signal is a continuous waveform that makes transitions between various states, corresponding to the phonemes. On the other hand, as stated earlier, the plosives are detectable only as transient states of the speech waveform. For that reason their labeling in Figure 7 is not reliable. Recently we solved the problem of more accurate detection of plosives and certain other phonemic categories by using special, auxiliary maps in which only a certain category of phonemes was represented, and which were trained by a subset of samples. For this purpose we first detect the presence of such phonemes (as a group) from the waveform, and then we use this information to activate the corresponding map. For instance, the occurrence of /k,p,t/ is indicated by low signal energy, and the corresponding spectral samples are picked from the transient regions following silence. The nasals as a group are detectable by responses obtained from the middle area of the main map.

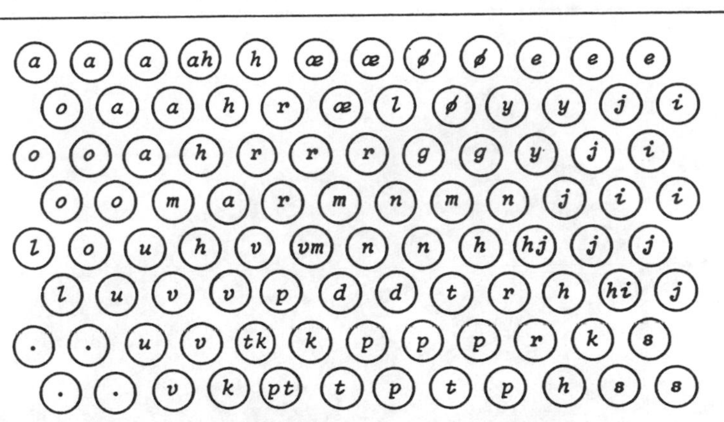

Figure 7. The neurons, shown as circles, are labeled with the symbols of the phonemes to which they "learned" to give best responses. Most neurons give a unique answer; the double labels here show neurons that respond to two phonemes. Distinction of /k,p,t/ from this map is not reliable and needs the analysis of the transient spectra of these phonemes by an auxiliary map. In the Japanese version there are auxiliary maps for /k,p,t/, /b,d,g/, and /m,n,η/ for more accurate analysis.

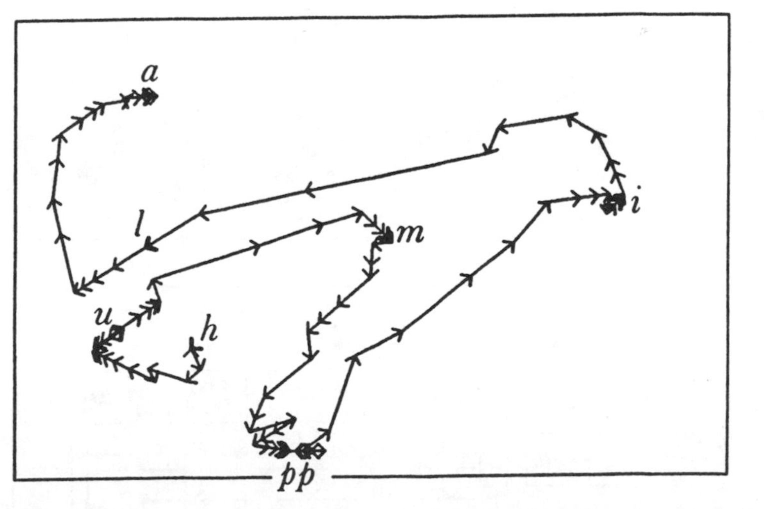

Figure 8. Sequence of the responses obtained from the phonotopic map when the Finnish word *humppila* was uttered. The arrows correspond to intervals of 9.83 milliseconds, at which the speech waveform was analyzed spectrally.

Another problem is *segmentation* of the responses from the map into a standard phonemic transcription. Consider that the spectral samples are taken at regular intervals every 9.83 milliseconds, and they are first labeled in accordance with the corresponding phonemic spectra. These labeled samples are called *quasiphonemes*; in contrast, the duration of a true phoneme is variable, say, from 40 to 400 milliseconds. We have used several alternative rules for the segmentation of quasiphoneme sequences into true phonemes. One of them is based on the degree of stability of the waveform; most phonemes, let alone plosives, have a unique stationary state. Another, more heuristic method is to decide that if m out of n successive quasiphonemes are the same, they correspond to a single phoneme; e.g., $m=4$ and $n=7$ are typical values.

The sequences of quasiphonemes can also be visualized as trajectories over the main map, as shown in Figure 8. Each arrowhead represents one spectral sample. For clarity, the sequence of coordinates shown by arrows has been slightly smoothed to make the curves more continuous. It is clearly discernible that convergence points of the speech waveform seem to correspond to certain (stationary) phonemes.

This kind of graph provides a new means, in addition to some earlier ones, for the visualization of the phonemes of speech, which may be useful for speech training and therapy. Profoundly deaf people may find it advantageous to have an immediate visual feedback from their speech.

It may be necessary to point out that the phonotopic map is not the same thing as the so-called formant maps used in phonetics. The latter display the speech signal in coordinates that correspond to the two lowest formants, or resonant frequencies of the vocal tract. Neither is this map any kind of principal component graph for phonemes. The phonotopic map displays the images of the complete spectra as points on a plane, the distances of which approximately correspond to the *vectorial differences* between the original spectra; so this map should rather be regarded as a *similarity graph*, the coordinates of which have no explicit interpretation.

Figure 9. The coprocessor board for the neural network and the postprocessing functions.

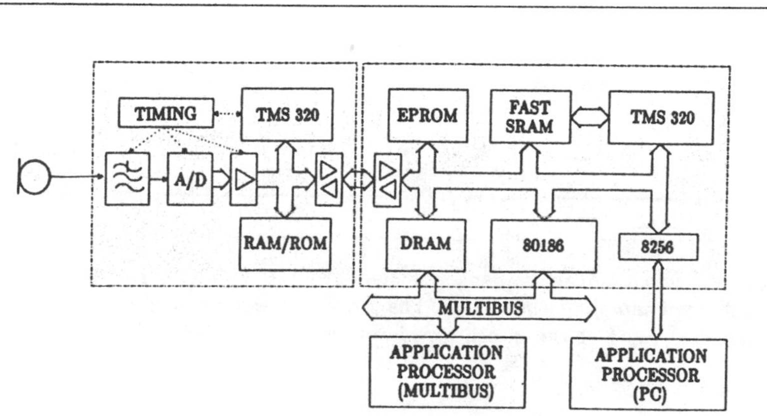

Figure 10. Block diagram of the coprocessor board. A/D: analog-to-digital converter. TMS320: Texas Instruments 32010 signal processor chip. RAM/ROM: 4K-word random-access memory, 256-word programmable read-only memory. EPROM: 64K-byte electrically erasable read-only memory. DRAM: 512K-byte dual-port random-access memory. SRAM: 96K-byte paged dual-port random-access memory. 80186: Intel microprocessor CPU. 8256: parallel interface.

Actually, the phoneme recognition accuracy can still be improved by three or four percent if the templates m_i are fine-tuned: small corrections to the responding neurons can be made automatically by turning their template vectors toward x if a tentative classification was correct, and away from x if the result was wrong.

Postprocessing in symbolic form

Even if the classification of speech spectra were error-free, the phonemes would not be identifiable from them with 100-percent reliability. This is because there are *coarticulation effects* in speech: the phonemes are influenced by neighboring phonemes. One might imagine it possible to list and take into account all such variations. But there may be many hundreds of different *frames* or *contexts* of neighboring phonemes in which a particular phoneme may occur. Even this, however, is an optimistic figure since the neighbors too may be transformed by other coarticulation effects and errors. Thus, the correction of such transformed phonemes should be made by reference to some kind of *context-sensitive stochastic grammar*, the rules of which are derived from real examples. I have developed a program code that automatically constructs the grammatical transformation rules on the basis of speech samples and their correct reference transcriptions.[12] A typical error grammar may contain 15,000 to 20,000 rules (productions), and these rules can be encoded as a data structure or stored in an associative memory. The optimal amount of context is determined automatically for each rule separately. No special hardware is needed; the search of the matching rules and their application can be made in real time by efficient and fast software methods, based on so-called hash coding, without slowing down the recognition operation.

The two-stage speech recognition system described in this article is a genuine phonetic typewriter, since it outputs orthographic transcriptions for unrestricted utterances, the forms of which only approximately obey certain morphological rules or regularities of a particular language. We have implemented this system for both Finnish and (romanized) Japanese. Both of these languages, like Latin, are characterized by the fact that their orthography is almost identical to their phonemic transcription.

As a complete speech recognition device, our system can be made to operate in either of two modes: (1) transcribing dictation of *unlimited* text, whereby the words (at least in some common idioms) can be connected, since similar rules are applicable for the editing of spaces between the words (at present short pauses are needed to insert spaces); and (2) isolated-word recognition from a large vocabulary.

In isolated-word recognition we first use the phonotopic map and its segmentation algorithm to produce a raw phonemic transcription of the uttered word. Then this transcription is compared with reference transcriptions earlier collected from a great many words. Comparison of partly erroneous symbolic expressions (strings) can be related to many standard similarity criteria. Rapid prescreening and spotting of the closest candidates can again be performed by associative or hash-coding methods; we have introduced a very effective error-tolerant searching scheme called *redundant hash addressing*, by which a small number of the best candidates, selected from vocabularies of thousands of items, can be located in a few hundred milliseconds (on a personal computer). After that, the more accurate final comparison between the much smaller number of candidates can be made by the best statistical methods.

Hardware implementations and performance

The system's neural network could, in principle, be built up of parallel hardware components that behave according to Equations 5 and 6. For the time being, no such components have been developed. On the other hand, for many applications the equivalent functions from Equations 7a and 7b are readily computable by fast digital signal processor chips; in that case the various neurons only exist *virtually*, as the signal processors are able to solve their equations by a timesharing principle. Even this operation, however, can be performed in real time, especially in speech processing.

The most central neural hardware of our system is contained on the coprocessor board shown in Figure 9. Its block diagram is shown in Figure 10. Only two signal processors have been necessary: one for the acoustic preprocessor that produces the input pattern vectors x, and another for timeshared computation of the responses from the neural network. For the time being, the self-organized computation of the templates m_i, or "learning," is made in an IBM PC AT-compatible host processor, and the transmittance parameters (synaptic transmittances) are loaded onto the coprocessor board. Newer designs are intended to operate as stand-alone systems. A standard microprocessor CPU chip on our board takes care of overall control and data routing and performs some preprocessing operations after FFT (such as logarithmization and normalization), as well as segmenting the quasiphoneme strings and deciding whether the auxiliary transient maps are to be used. Although the 80186 is a not-so-effective CPU, it still has extra capacity for postprocessing operations: it can be programmed to apply the context-sensitive grammar for unlimited text or to perform the isolated-word recognition operations.

The personal computer has been used during experimentation for all postprocessing operations. Nonetheless, the overall recognition operations take place in near real time. In the intended mode of operation the speech recognizer will only assist the keyboard operations and communicate with the CPU through the same channel.

One of the most serious problems with this system, as well as with any existing speech recognizer, is recognition accuracy, especially for an arbitrary speaker. After postprocessing, the present transcription accuracy varies between 92 and 97 percent, depending on speaker and difficulty of text. We performed most of the experiments reported here with half a dozen male speakers, using office text, names, and the most frequent words of the language. The number of tests performed over the years is inestimable. Typically, thousands of words have been involved in a particular series of tests. Enrollment of a new speaker requires dictation of 100 words, and the learning processes can proceed concurrently with dictation. The total learning time on the PC is less than 10 minutes. During learning, the template vectors of the phonotopic map are tuned to the new samples.

Isolated-word recognition from a 1000-word vocabulary is possible with an accuracy of 96 to 98 percent. Since the recognition system forms an intermediate symbolic transcription that can be compared with any standard reference transcriptions, the vocabulary or its active subsets can be defined in written form and changed dynamically during use, without the need of speaking any samples of these words.

All output, for unlimited text as well as for isolated words, is produced in near real time: the mean delay is on the order of 250 milliseconds per word. It should be noticed that contemporary microprocessors already have much higher speeds (typically five times higher) than the chips used in our design.

To the best of our knowledge, this system is the only existing complete speech recognizer that employs neural computing principles and has been brought to a commercial stage, verified by extensive tests. Of course, it still falls somewhat short of expectations; obviously some kind of linguistic postprocessing model would improve its performance. On the other hand, our principal aim was to demonstrate the highly adaptive properties of neural networks, which allow a very accurate, nonlinear statistical analysis of real signals. These properties ought to be a goal of all practical "neurocomputers."□

References

1. W.A. Lea, ed., *Trends in Speech Recognition*, Prentice-Hall, Englewood Cliffs, N.J., 1980.
2. S.E. Levinson, L.R. Rabiner, and M.M. Sondhi, "An Introduction to the Application of the Theory of Probabilistic Functions of a Markov Process to Automatic Speech Recognition," *Bell Syst. Tech. J.*, Apr. 1983, pp. 1035-1073.
3. P.A. Devijver and J. Kittler, *Pattern Recognition: A Statistical Approach*, Prentice-Hall, London, 1982.
4. D.H. Klatt, "Review of the ARPA Speech Understanding Project," *J. Acoust. Soc. Amer.*, Dec. 1977, pp. 1345-1366.
5. R. Reddy and V. Zue, "Recognizing Continuous Speech Remains an Elusive Goal," *IEEE Spectrum*, Nov. 1983, pp. 84-87.
6. P. Petre, "Speak, Master: Typewriters That Take Dictation," *Fortune*, Jan. 7, 1985, pp. 56-60.
7. M.R. Schroeder and J.L. Hall, "Model for Mechanical to Neural Transduction in the Auditory Receptor," *J. Acoust. Soc. Am.*, May 1974, pp. 1055-1060.
8. R. Meddis, "Simulation of Mechanical to Neural Transduction in the Auditory Receptor," *J. Acoust. Soc. Am.*, Mar. 1986, pp. 703-711.

9. T. Kohonen, *Self-Organization and Associative Memory*, Series in Information Sciences, Vol. 8, Springer-Verlag, Berlin-Heidelberg-New York-Tokyo, 1984; 2nd ed. 1988.
10. J. Makhoul, S. Roucos, and H. Gish, "Vector Quantization in Speech Coding," *Proc. IEEE*, Nov. 1985, pp. 1551-1588.
11. D.E. Rumelhart, G.E. Hinton, and R.J. Williams, "Learning Internal Representations by Error Propagation," in *Parallel Distributed Processing, Explorations in the Microstructure of Cognition, Volume 1: Foundations*, ed. by David E. Rumelhart, James L. McClelland, and the PDP Research Group, MIT Press, Cambridge, Mass., 1986, pp. 318-362.
12. T. Kohonen, "Dynamically Expanding Context, with Application to the Correction of Symbol Strings in the Recognition of Continuous Speech," *Proc. Eighth Int'l Conf. Pattern Recognition*, IEEE Computer Society, Washington, D.C., 1986, pp. 1148-1151.

Teuvo Kohonen is a professor on the Faculty of Information Sciences of Helsinki University of Technology, Finland. He is also a research professor of the Academy of Finland, a member of the Finnish Academy of Sciences, and a member of the Finnish Academy of Engineering Sciences. He received his D.Eng. degree in physics from Helsinki University of Technology in 1962. His scientific interests are neural computers and pattern recognition.

Kohonen has written four textbooks, of which *Content-Addressable Memories* (Springer, 1987) and *Self-Organization and Associative Memory* (Springer, 1988) are best known. He was the first vice chairman of the International Neural Network Society. Kohonen is a senior member of the IEEE. He was awarded the Eemil Aaltonen Honorary Prize in 1983 and the Cultural Prize of Finnish Commercial Television in 1984.

Kohonen's address is Helsinki University of Technology, Laboratory of Computer and Information Science, Rakentajanaukio 2 C, SF-02150 Espoo, Finland.

Shift-Tolerant LVQ and Hybrid LVQ-HMM for Phoneme Recognition

Erik McDermott, Hitoshi Iwamida, Shigeru Katagiri and Yoh'ichi Tohkura

ATR Auditory & Visual Perception Research Laboratories,
Sanpeidani, Inuidani, Seika-cho, Soraku-gun,
Kyoto 619-02, Japan

Abstract

An ongoing area of research concerns the application of neural network models to tasks in speech recognition. The neural network algorithm focused on here, called LVQ (Learning Vector Quantization) [Kohonen, 1986, 1988], is designed to pay close attention to approximating Bayes decision boundaries in pattern discrimination tasks. This endows the model with high discriminant power. Hidden Markov Models (HMMs), on the other hand, provide a good model of the sequential nature of speech. The work described here aims to combine the advantages inherent in each algorithm. We first illustrate the discriminant power of the LVQ algorithm by describing a high performance, Shift-Tolerant LVQ model for phoneme recognition. We then describe a hybrid LVQ-HMM phoneme recognition model, where the HMM uses an LVQ generated codebook instead of the conventional K-means codebook. This provides the HMM with high discriminant power at the phoneme recognition level while preserving the flexibility HMMs have in extending phone models to longer utterance models.

Concerning the Shift-Tolerant LVQ architecture, recognition performances in the 98-99% correct range were obtained for LVQ networks aimed at speaker-dependent recognition of phonemes in small but ambiguous Japanese phonemic classes. A correct recognition rate of 98% was achieved by a large LVQ network covering all Japanese consonants. These recognition results are as good as those obtained in the Time Delay Neural Network system developed by Alex Waibel et al. (1988). Concerning the hybrid LVQ-HMM architecture, single speaker phoneme recognition experiments showed that using LVQ-generated reference vectors as the HMM codebook results in an error rate that is 2 or 3 times lower than that of HMMs using conventional K-means generated codebooks of similar size. Furthermore, the LVQ-HMM recognition rates are as high as those of the Shift-Tolerant LVQ architecture and of TDNN.

Our results here demonstrate the high discriminant ability of LVQ for tasks in phoneme recognition, and show that by using LVQ instead of K-means to generate HMM codebooks, this discriminant ability can be integrated into an HMM architecture easily extendible to longer utterance models, such as word or sentence models.

1. Introduction

To achieve the end goal of large vocabulary, speaker-independent, continuous speech recognition, a useful first step is to achieve high-performance phoneme recognition. For a system to yield this high performance, it must be endowed with high classification power and invariance under translation in time. The Time Delay Neural Network architecture recently developed by Alex Waibel et. al. [3] and the Back-propagation algorithm used therein possess these properties, and high recognition results were attained using this system. However there are other algorithms with these capabilities. Recent work by Kohonen [2], suggests that Learning Vector Quantization (LVQ) is as powerful a classifier as Back-propagation and the Boltzmann Machine, and furthermore that LVQ requires significantly less learning time than either Back-propagation or the Boltzmann Machine. Thus LVQ seems like a viable candidate for tasks that involve a large training set size, such as speech recognition. We here present a Shift-Tolerant, LVQ-based phoneme recognition system which is capable of attaining recognition rates that are as high as those obtained for the TDNN system, and which requires little training time.

Given this highly discriminant phoneme recognition architecture, the question is how we might extend it to models for the recognition of words, phrases or sentences, in continuous speech. There have been a number of recent proposals, and some encouraging results, as to how one might extend this kind of highly discriminant neural net model to longer utterance models [21,22,23,24]. This is an ongoing area of research.

On the other hand, Hidden Markov models (HMMs) have been successfully applied to many speech recognition tasks, ranging from phoneme recognition tasks to large vocabulary speaker-independent continuous speech recognition systems [15]. An advantage of HMMs is that it is easy to extend phone models to long utterance models such as word or sentence models. However, HMMs are somewhat lacking in discriminant power [3].

There have been a number of recent studies concerning the links between neural nets and HMMs, and many suggestions for improving the discriminant ability of HMMs [14,17,19,20]. In the case of LVQ, a very straightforward possibility for integration into a discrete HMM framework easily extendible to word or sentence models is simply to use LVQ to generate a discriminant HMM codebook. The purpose of such a codebook will be to classify phonemes accurately, rather than, as in the conventional LBG or K-means clustering algorithms, to minimize distortion. By integrating HMMs and LVQ in this way, we hope to combine the advantages inherent in each of these algorithms. We here present phoneme recognition results for this hybrid system which show that the high discriminant power of LVQ can be used in an HMM framework extendible to word or sentence recognition of continuous speech.

Here we will first describe the LVQ algorithm. Then a Shift-Tolerant, LVQ-based phoneme recognition architecture will be described and tested. Two main comparisons will be presented: first, between LVQ and the conventional K-means clustering algorithm; second, between LVQ and TDNN. These comparisons will highlight the high-discriminant power of LVQ as applied in our Shift-Tolerant recognition architecture. Then we will turn to the LVQ-HMM hybrid system, which will be compared to both the Shift-Tolerant LVQ phoneme recognition system, and to TDNN. The utility of LVQ versus K-means in creating the HMM codebook will also be demonstrated. Although the tasks used to test the LVQ-HMM hybrid are here confined to phoneme recognition tasks, the fact that high recognition results can be obtained within an HMM framework suggests that the hybrid model combines the high discriminant power of LVQ with the HMM facility to extend phoneme models to longer utterance models.

2. Description of the Learning Vector Quantization Algorithm

Kohonen presents two versions of LVQ [2]; here our focus is on the second version, LVQ2. In both versions, each category to be learned is assigned a number of reference vectors, each of which has the same number of dimensions as the input vectors of the categories. In the recognition stage, an unknown input vector will be categorized by finding the reference vector that is closest to that input vector. The category that the reference vector belongs to will be given as the categorization of the unknown input vector. This classification scheme means partitioning the vector space into regions, or cells, defined by individual reference vectors. LVQ assumes a good initial configuration; this can be obtained by using the traditional K-means clustering procedure [8]. This initial configuration will place the reference vectors in the right general position. LVQ training then tries to adjust these positions so that each input vector has a reference vector of the right category as its closest reference vector. We now describe the algorithm in detail.

Kohonen, in his formulation of the LVQ2 algorithm, is particularly concerned with the problem of approximating decision lines corresponding to the Bayes decision rule. Given a vector x, a set of classes $\{C_i, i=1,2,....,K\}$, the a priori class probability $p(C_i)$ for a class C_i, the conditional probability density $p(x \mid C_i)$ for observing the vector x in a class C_i, and the joint probability density function $g_i(x) = p(x \mid C_i)p(C_i)$ of a class C_i, the Bayes decision rule is as follows:

$$x \text{ is assigned to } C_i \text{ iff } g_i(x) > g_j(x) \text{ for all } j \neq i$$

This rule will minimize the number of misclassifications [2, 12]. This becomes particularly relevant when the class joint density functions overlap. If there is overlap, it is impossible to separate the classes perfectly; the task becomes that of finding the decision line which minimizes the number of misclassifications. This will be achieved by a decision line at the place where the class joint density functions cross. Ideally, a neural network should generate decision lines that approximate this optimal line. This is the motivation for LVQ2.

Figure 1 helps to illustrate vector adaptation in LVQ2, for a simple one-dimensional situation. For a given training vector x, three conditions must be met for learning to occur: 1) the nearest class must be incorrect; 2) the next-nearest class (found by searching the reference vectors in the remaining classes) must be correct; 3) the training vector must fall inside a small, symmetric window defined around the midpoint of the reference vectors m_i and m_j-- this midpoint (in higher dimensions, "mid-hyperplane") being the decision boundary effected by the two vectors. If these conditions are met, the incorrect reference vector is moved further away from the input, while the correct reference vector is moved closer, according to:

$$m_i(t+1) = m_i(t) - \alpha(t)\,(x(t) - m_i(t))$$
$$m_j(t+1) = m_j(t) + \alpha(t)\,(x(t) - m_j(t))$$

where x is a training vector belonging to class j, m_i is the reference vector for the incorrect category, m_j is the reference vector for the correct category, and $\alpha(t)$ is a monotonically decreasing function of time.

These requirements, taken together, assure that the decision line between the two vectors will eventually approximate the Bayes decision boundary, at the place where the joint density functions cross.

The intuition here is that LVQ2 is making use of a local difference in the joint densities to move the boundary in the right direction. This local difference in joint density is measured indirectly by measuring a difference in the number of misclassifications on either side of the LVQ2 window. Figure 1 may help explain the overall, stochastic effect. A difference in the joint densities at the position of the actual boundary in the pattern space is taken to indicate that the actual boundary is not optimal, i.e., not at the position of the Bayes boundary. This is the case in Figure 1, where at the position of the actual boundary, the joint density of class j is greater than that of class i. In this scenario, there will be more misclassifications of j's on the left side of the window than misclassifications of i's on the right side of the window. Now note that every misclassification of a j token on the left side of the window satisfies the LVQ2 conditions. LVQ2 will then push the closest but incorrect m_i reference vector away from those j's, while pulling the m_j reference vector closer. Precisely the opposite vector motions will occur for misclassifications of i's on the right side of the window. In the Figure 1 scenario, there will then be more misclassified j's pushing the actual boundary to the left than misclassified i's pushing the boundary to the right. The net effect, then, will be to move the actual boundary to the left, i.e. closer to the Bayes boundary. This will continue until the number of j misclassifications on the left side of the window is equal to the number of i misclassifications on the right side of the window; for a small window, this position will be close to the optimal Bayes boundary.

Figure 1 also helps to illustrate the difference in goals between LVQ and K-means clustering. The reference vector configuration presented in Figure 1 more or less corresponds to what the result of K-means clustering might be, given the class joint densities shown. One can see, however, that the decision line realized by these two reference vectors is quite different from the optimal Bayes decision boundary, which is the target of LVQ learning.

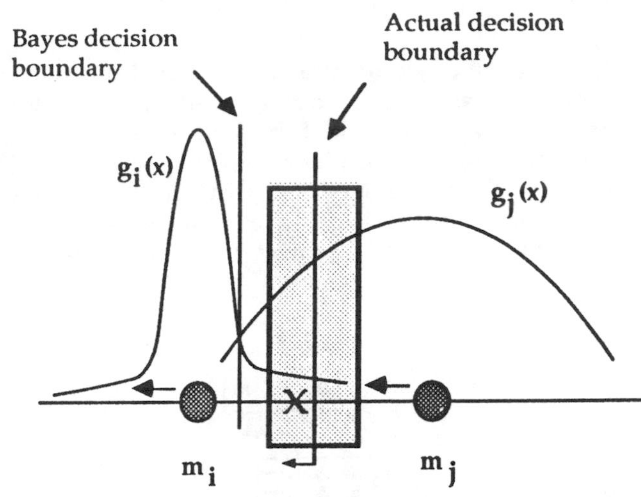

x: training vector of category j
m_i, m_j: reference vectors
$g_i(x)$, $g_j(x)$: category joint probability densities.

Figure 1. LVQ2 adaptation, one dimensional case.

3. System Architecture

This phoneme recognition system was previously described in [5], [6] and [7]. Figure 2 shows the architecture of the recognition system used for the /b/, /d/, /g/ task. Each category is assigned a number of reference vectors. The LVQ training procedure is then applied to speech patterns that are stepped through in time, thus providing the system with a measure of shift-tolerance. To achieve this effect, we defined a 7 frame window[1] which is shifted, one frame at a time, over the 15 frame speech token. Each window position yields an input vector of 112 dimensions (7 frames x 16 channels). Given this input vector, LVQ1 or LVQ2 is applied as described above.

This moving window scheme requires a slightly different recognition procedure than simply finding the closest vector, as there are now several closest vectors, one for each window position. For each window position we calculate the distances between the input vector and the closest reference vector within each category. From this distance measure, each category is assigned an activation value that is high for small distances, low for large distances:

[1] The choice of 7 frames here is somewhat arbitrary; widths ranging from 6 to 9 frames gave very similar performances.

$$A(c, t) = 1 - \frac{d(c)}{d(0) + d(1) + d(2)}$$

After the window has been shifted over all 15 frames, the activations obtained at each window position are summed, for each category. The category with the highest overall activation is chosen as the recognized category. Note that these activation calculations are not done using additional layers of connections: our system is essentially a one layer system.

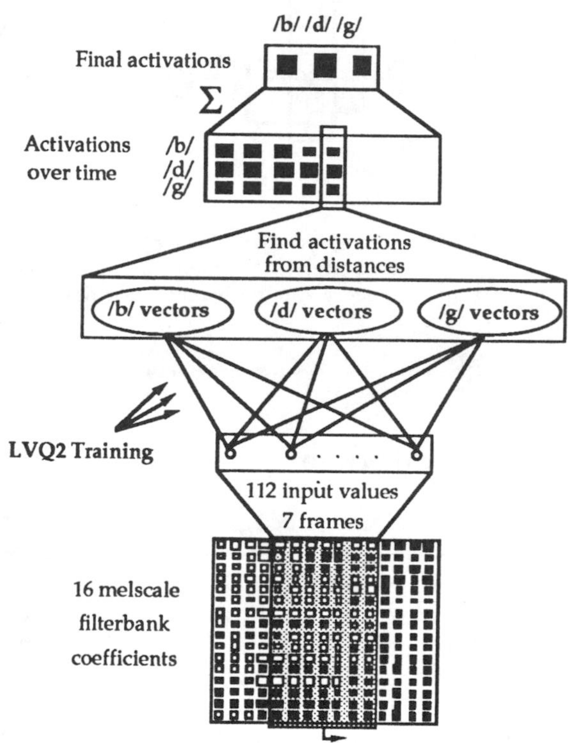

Figure 2. System architecture, /b/, /d/, /g/ task

4. Shift-Tolerant LVQ-based Phoneme Recognition Experiments

4.1. Speech Data Representation and Database

To be consistent in our comparison with the TDNN system, we used exactly the same data representation as that used in TDNN . One phoneme token consisted of 15 time frames of 16 melscale spectrum channels, with a frame rate of 10 msec. Input speech was sampled at 12 kHz, hamming windowed (using a window size of 20 msec), and a 256-point FFT computed every 5 msec. Melscale coefficients were generated from the power spectrum and coefficients adjacent in time were collapsed, yielding an overall frame rate of 10 msec. The coefficients were then normalized between 1.0 and -1.0 with the average at 0.0. Figure 2 displays these coefficients as black or white squares of varying sizes, size representing magnitude, black for positive values, white for negative values.

These tokens were drawn from a database of 5240 common Japanese words, uttered in a sound-proof booth by a male professional announcer. This is the same database as used in the TDNN experiments. The database was split into a training set and a testing set of 2620 utterances each, from which the phoneme tokens were then extracted using manually selected acoustic-phonetic labels. For consonant tokens, the center frame was set at the border between the consonant and the following vowel. For vowels, the center frame of each token was set at the center position of the vowel. This extraction procedure is identical to that used in the TDNN experiments. In effect, the tokens we used for both training and testing of the system were identical to those used in TDNN.

4.2. Network Initialization and Training Conditions

Before turning to the phoneme recognition tasks, we here describe some of our findings regarding initialization methods and training conditions. We here briefly address questions as to appropriate initialization of reference vectors, the setting of the learning rate $\alpha(t)$, and the method of token presentation during training.

One of the reasons LVQ2 requires few training epochs is that the initial conditions start out fairly well. Whereas Back-propagation networks are typically initialized by setting the weights to small random values, the reference vectors in LVQ2 can be initialized by performing K-means clustering, as mentioned above. The method most in line with LVQ theory, and recommended by Kohonen [1], would be to perform K-means clustering on the training tokens for all categories, and then assign category labels to the resulting reference vectors. A faster and simpler method is simply to perform K-means clustering on the training tokens for just one category at a time. This method, hereafter referred to as "phoneme dependent K-means," was found by Yokota et al.[9] to provide a system performance, both before and after training, that is better than that resulting from a variety of initialization methods, including the first method described here.

The learning rate $\alpha(t)$, mentioned above, is decremented linearly using a function such as:

$$\alpha(t) = \alpha(0)\,(1 - t/M),$$

where M is the maximum number of iterations, after which learning is halted. As such a function will force convergence, we need to estimate the number of iterations before training begins. Lacking a theory for this, we determined this number experimentally, using recognition rates on test data as the criterion for good learning. One way of estimating $\alpha(0)$ is to choose it as high as possible without it giving rise to an unstable system. In our system, a typical value of $\alpha(0)$ is 0.1; a typical value of M is 10 times the number of training tokens. We usually performed several training runs on the same set of reference vectors, progressively lowering the value of $\alpha(0)$.

To allow for the approximation of the Bayes boundary, it is important that the training tokens be presented in proportion to the overall probabilities (i.e. P(c)'s) of their classes. The training procedure, for each trial, is then to select a training token at random from the whole training set. Tokens from seldomly occuring categories are not duplicated; this would artificially raise the a priori class probabilities, and prevent the system from approximating the Bayes boundaries.

4.3. Recognition of /b/, /d/, /g/

As a first step in the evaluation of LVQ2, we applied our system to the /b/, /d/, /g/ task. For this task, training the system on 682 tokens from one speaker, we were able to obtain an overall recognition rate of 99.2% for 658 testing tokens (open test) of the same speaker.

We implemented our system on an 8-processor Alliant super mini-computer. The simple vector operations that constitute the core of LVQ allowed for very easy parallelization and thus high learning speed. Furthermore, the initial conditions start out well, so the required number of trials is not particularly large. Thus, for LVQ2 on the /b/, /d/, /g/ task, a recognition rate of 98 ~ 99% can be attained in about one minute of CPU time, corresponding to 5 epochs of training (one epoch = one full presentation of the training set).

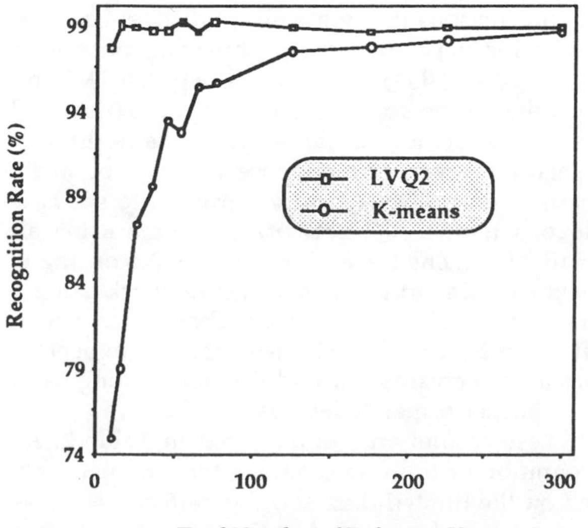

Figure 3. Performance vs. number of reference vectors, bdg task.

4.3.1. Evaluation of K-means and LVQ2 on the /b/, /d/, /g/ task

K-means clustering is a powerful method for vector quantization, and it provides an effective way of initializing LVQ reference vectors. However, the goal of K-means is not to reduce the number of misclassifications in a discrimination task, but to reduce the average distortion of a vector quantizer. The two goals may overlap, but are not identical; achieving one of these goals may well be at the expense of the other. To investigate this issue, we considered the difference in classification performance between LVQ and K-means clustering, on the /b/, /d/, /g/ task, for different numbers of reference vectors ranging from 15 to 300. Here each category was allotted reference vectors in proportion to the number of training samples available for that category. For each point in the plot, K-means was run on four different sets of initial reference vectors (sampled at random from the training set). Using the best of these four runs as the starting configuration, both versions of LVQ learning were performed. For a given initial configuration, LVQ2 was performed just four times, with exactly the same parameter settings, the only difference thus being the order of presentation of training tokens. Figure 3 shows, for each choice of total number of reference vectors, the test data performance for the best of the four K-means runs, and for the best of the LVQ2 training runs. This figure illustrates the asymptotic behavior of both LVQ and K-means as the number of reference vectors is increased. We also see that LVQ2 always does better than K-means, and that the difference in performance is accentuated for small numbers of reference vectors. To achieve a performance of around 98%, 9 reference vectors are sufficient for LVQ2, while about 175 are necessary for K-means.

task	LVQ2			k-means	TDNN
	#errors/ #tokens	%correct	total %	total %	total %
b	2/227	99.1	99.2	78.7	99.0
d	0/179	100			
g	3/252	98.8			
p	6/15	60.0	98.9	95.7	98.7
t	0/440	100			
k	5/500	99.0			
m	4/481	99.2	98.8	83.7	96.6
n	7/265	97.4			
N	4/488	99.2			
s	4/538	99.3	99.4	98.8	99.3
sh	0/316	100			
h	0/207	100			
z	3/115	97.4			
ch	0/123	100	100	100	100
ts	0/177	100			
r	0/722	100	99.6	99.2	99.9
w	1/78	98.7			
y	3/174	98.3			
a	0/600	100	99.1	96.7	98.6
i	2/600	99.7			
u	14/600	97.7			
e	6/600	99.0			
o	4/600	99.3			

Table 1. Test data recognition rates for small consonant clusters.

4.4 Recognition of Phonemes in 7 Consonant Clusters Using LVQ2.

Encouraged by these results for /b/, /d/ and /g/, we then applied our LVQ2 architecture to additional consonant clusters: the unvoiced stops, /p/, /t/, /k/; the nasals /m/, /n/, and syllabic nasals; the fricatives /s/, /sh/, /h/, /z/; the affricates /ch/ and /ts/; the liquids and glides /r/, /w/, /y/; and the vowels /a/, /i/, /u/, /e/, /o/. Together, these constitute nearly the entire phoneme set for Japanese. The training set size for each of these classes was roughly the same size as the test set size, shown in Table 1.

LVQ2 networks for each of these consonant clusters were initialized using K-means clustering and then trained in the manner described above.

The test data recognition results for these consonant clusters are shown in Table 1. Here we are comparing our results with those of the TDNN system [3], [4]. Note that each network here is only trained to discriminate phonemes within one consonant cluster, and thus does not know about phonemes from other clusters.

As can be seen, we obtained recognition results that are at least as good as those obtained in the TDNN system. Furthermore, all of these tasks required relatively little training time in the LVQ2 system. We do have a problem with the phoneme /p/: due to the very infrequent occurence of /p/'s in Japanese, our training data is not sufficient to produce good generalization.

Most of these networks did not achieve perfect recognition of the training data. The training data performance was typically in the high 99% range.

4.5 Recognition of All Japanese Consonants Using LVQ2

We next built an LVQ2 network that can discriminate among all Japanese consonants, not just within small consonant clusters. This network, illustrated in Figure 4, has the very same architecture as the small networks above, but with more categories. As before, the network is initialized using phoneme dependent K-means clustering, and then trained using LVQ2.

First, to compare this LVQ2 network with its TDNN counterpart [4, 10], we used the very same training and testing sets used in TDNN. The training set consisted of 5,063 tokens; the testing set consisted of 3061 tokens. For these data sets, our system architecture, initialized using K-means, recognizes 92.4% of the test data correctly; after LVQ2 training, the overall performance is 97.1%. This is compared with the best TDNN result for the all-consonant task, 96.7%.

Next, we trained and evaluated the all-consonant LVQ2 network using larger data sets. In TDNN, for reasons that we will not discuss here, the data sets for very frequently occurring phonemes were limited to 500 or 600 tokens (e.g. for /k/ and the vowels). To be consistent in our comparison, all the results presented so far used the same limited data sets. However, our purpose here is not solely comparison with TDNN, and we wanted to see how an all-consonant LVQ2 network performs using all the available tokens for each phoneme. Accordingly, our next step was to train an LVQ2 network using a full training set of 5,973 tokens, and evaluate it with a full testing set of 5,960 tokens. As expected, performance increases with additional training data. The overall performance here is 97.7%.

These results are summarized in Table 2. As to recognition of training data, for the first network, trained on the limited data set, the performance was 99.3%, while for the network trained on the full data set, the performance was 99.4%.

Training each network here required about 10 ~ 30 epochs in all, resulting in about 2 or 3 hours of CPU time: substantially more than for the small networks but still reasonable.

For the all-consonant results presented here, each category was assigned 25 reference vectors. Our experience suggests a picture similar to that detailed above for the /b/, /d/, /g/ network: above a certain total number of reference vectors, performance ceases to improve.

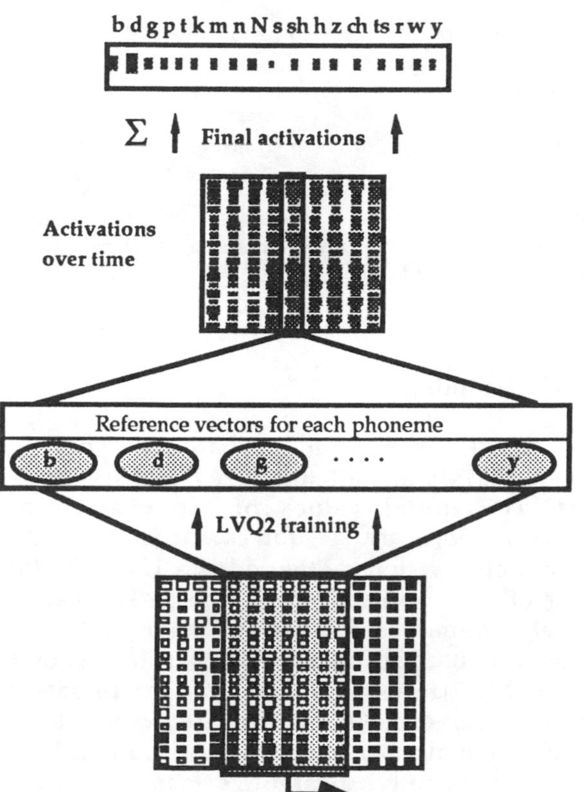

Figure 4. System architecture, all consonant task

Data Set	LVQ2	K-means	TDNN
Limited	97.1%	92.4%	96.7%
Full	97.7%	91.5%	-

Table 2. Recognition rates for all-consonant networks.

5. Hybrid LVQ-HMM

Having described and tested the above Shift-Tolerant LVQ-based phoneme recognition system, we now turn to the hybrid LVQ-HMM architecture. From the above results, it is clear that LVQ is endowed with high discriminant power. The task we address now is that of integrating this discriminant power into an HMM architecture extendible to longer utterance models.

5.1. LVQ-HMM System Architecture

Figure 8 shows a block diagram of a conventional discrete HMM. In this model, the codebook is generated by a distortion-minimizing clustering algorithm, such as K-means clustering. We will refer to this model as VQ-HMM. On the other hand, Figure 9 shows the new model we are proposing here. In this model, the codebook consists of highly discriminant reference vectors generated by LVQ training. We will refer to this model as LVQ-HMM.

Figure 10 shows a block diagram of phoneme recognition using LVQ-HMM. In initializing the codebook, we first use phoneme dependent K-means clustering to cluster all the feature vectors of the training samples, and generate a predetermined number of reference vectors. Next this codebook is trained using LVQ2 in order to provide the codebook with high classification ability. The training is done in the same way as for Shift-Tolerant LVQ, described above. As in the usual HMM method, this codebook is used to convert all the training samples into a code sequence which is then used to estimate the parameters of each HMM. To evaluate the resulting phoneme models on unknown data, test samples were also converted to a sequence of codes.

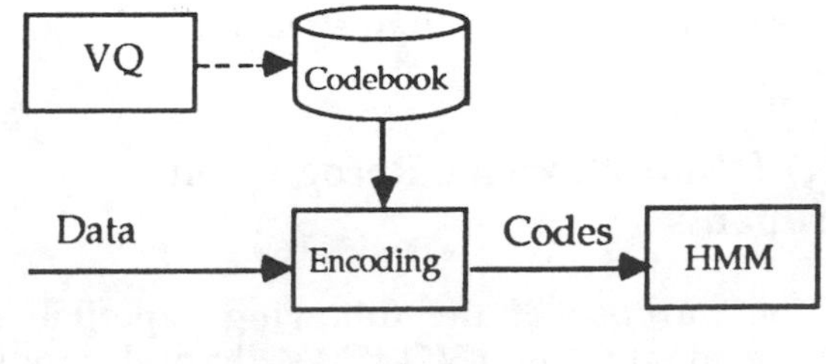

Fig.8 The concept of VQ-HMM.

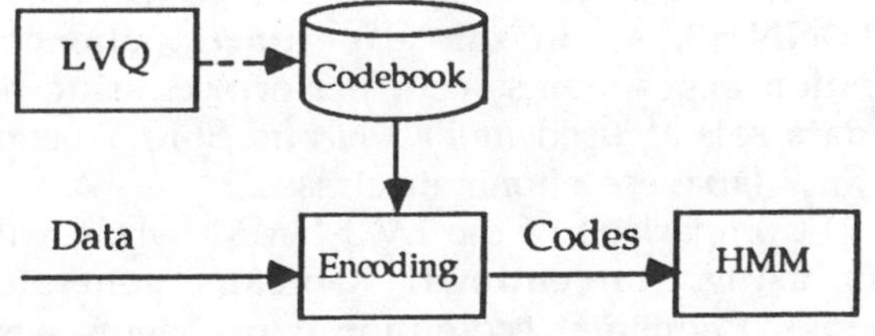

Fig.9 The concept of LVQ-HMM.

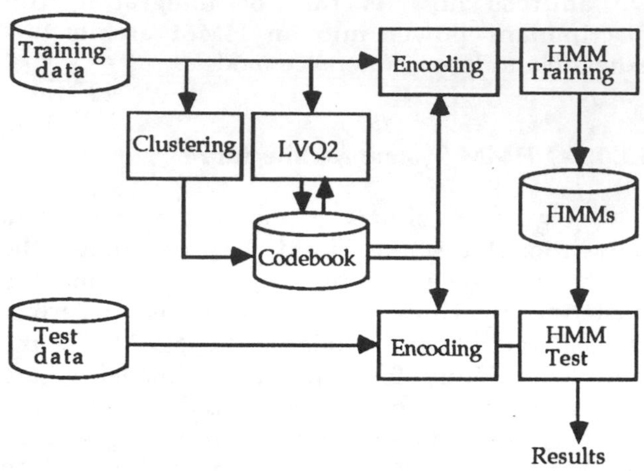

Fig.10 Block diagram of phoneme recognition using LVQ-HMM

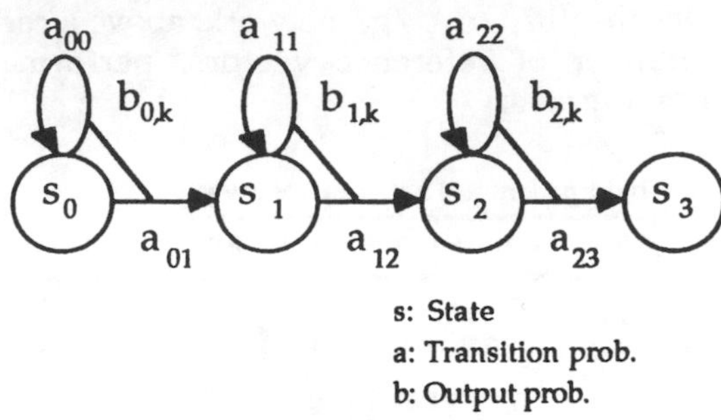

Fig.11 Phoneme model structure. A phoneme model consists of a left-to-right four state HMM.

5.4 Phone Models

There have been numerous studies, for instance [18], concerning the architecture that should be used for phone models. Here we summarize some conclusions.

1) There should be at least 3 states with loops per model.
2) The last state should not have a loop.
3) There is usually little difference in recognition rates between models that use tied arcs and models that don't.

Taking these considerations into account, we used the phone model structure shown in Fig. 11. In this figure, aij is the transition probability from state i to state j; and bik is the output probability of code k when there is a transition from state i.

6. LVQ-HMM Phoneme Recognition Experiments

The purpose of the following experiments was to evaluate the LVQ-HMM hybrid model proposed here. We performed two main comparisons:

1) Comparison of the hybrid algorithm with Shift-Tolerant LVQ (as described and tested above) and TDNN [3, 4]. In this experiment, phoneme recognition experiments were performed using the same data sets as used in TDNN and Shift Tolerant LVQ, for 7 Japanese phonemic classes.

2) Comparison of the LVQ-HMM hybrid with HMMs using conventional K-means generated codebooks. Phoneme recognition experiments were performed using phoneme tokens for 25 phoneme categories. Instead of using a fixed frame length for the data tokens, as in comparison (1) above, we here used tokens with a variable frame length that depended on the duration of each phoneme sample in the database.

6.1. HMM Training

The a_{ij} transition probabilities of the phoneme HMMs are all initialized to have equal values. The initial values of the observation probabilities b_{ik} are set, for each code k, at the number of observations of the code k, divided by the number of observations of all codes. The Baum-Welch algorithm, based upon maximum likelihood estimation, is used to train the HMMs. It is known that in this parameter estimation for phoneme models, convergence is attained after 5 iterations [18]; we set the number of iterations at 7. In order to prevent the output probabilities from becoming zero, should the number of training samples be too small, smoothing was performed to keep the parameters larger than 10^{-6}.

6.2. Speech Data

The tokens we used in the LVQ-HMM experiments are drawn from the same database as used above. Two data sets were used. The first is identical to the one used above. The second data set is very similar to the first one, with the main difference being that here we used tokens with a variable frame length that depended on the duration of each phoneme sample in the database. Coefficients adjacent in time were not collapsed as in the first data set, and were normalized so that the average lay at 0.0 (without limiting coefficient values between -1.0 and 1.0). This normalization was performed during LVQ training, with the LVQ time window length determining the duration over which the normalization was performed. The second data set also differs from the first in that it includes tokens from 2 additional phoneme classes, /f/ and /j/, as well as tokens from some phoneme contexts that had been excluded from the first data set. Thus the second data set includes a greater variety of phonemic expression.

The second set too was split into a training set and a test set, of roughly equal sizes.

6.3. Preliminary Experiments on the /b/, /d/, /g/ task

In order to guide the two comparisons mentioned above, we first ran some preliminary experiments on the task of recognizing /b/, /d/, and /g/, for tokens taken from the first data set. Specifically, the target of these preliminary investigations was to understand the effectiveness of LVQ compared to K-means as the generator of the HMM codebook, for two different codebook sizes and for two methods of K-means clustering.

In these preliminary experiments, we also examined codebook distortion vs. classification rate. Whereas conventional HMM theory assumes that the codebook should minimize distortion, the LVQ-HMM hybrid we are proposing here suggests that a codebook should instead minimize the number of phoneme classification errors. This is an important point, which will be illustrated in these preliminary /b/, /d/, /g/ experiments.

The training set here consisted of a total of 682 samples (219 for /b/, 203 for /d/, and 260 for /g/), while the test set consisted of 658 samples in all (227 for /b/, 179 for /d/, and 252 for /g/).

6.3.1 HMM Codebook Design: Phoneme Dependent K-means vs. Phoneme Independent K-means

The two K-means clustering procedures we used were as follows. The first is the above-mentioned "Phoneme Dependent K-means," consisting in performing K-means on the training vectors of just one category at a time. This is a very fast process, yielding several codebooks-- one per category-- which are then grouped together into a single codebook. This contrasts with the more common method, here referred to as "Phoneme Independent K-means," where the training vectors of all categories are considered at the same time.

To test these two methods for K-means clustering, we looked at two codebooks, each consisting of a total of 255 reference vectors, generated from phoneme speech segments that are stepped through in time, as described above. One of these codebooks was generated using phoneme dependent K-means (85 reference vectors per category), the other using phoneme independent K-means. Each of these codebooks was then used as the codebook for a /b/, /d/, /g/ HMM, which was then trained with the method described above.

Table 3 shows the classification rates on test data for these two HMMs. As shown in this table, the HMM with the phoneme dependent K-means codebook gives better classification performance here, with less than half the error rate of the HMM using the phoneme independent K-means codebook. These results suggest that phoneme dependent K-means is better suited to the goal of maximizing classification performance. This is in line with the results of similar investigations of these two methods of K-means clustering, reported in [9].

Codebook Design	Codebook Size	% correct	VQ distn.
P.I. K-means	255	95.3	1.959
P.D. K-means	255 (85/cat.)	97.9	2.004
P.D. K-means	30 (10/cat.)	82.1	3.839
P.D. K-means --> LVQ	30 (10/cat.)	98.6	6.727

Table 3 Recognition results on test tokens for a /b/, /d/, /g/ HMM system, for four different codebooks. P.I. (Phoneme Independent) K-means refers to K-means performed on all categories at the same time; P.D. (Phoneme Dependent) K-means refers to K-means performed on one category at a time.

6.3.2 HMM Codebook Design: LVQ vs. Phoneme Dependent K-means

Next, we investigated the efficiency of an HMM using an LVQ codebook compared to that of an HMM using a phoneme dependent K-means clustered codebook. Here the codebook size was much smaller than above, consisting of 10 reference vectors per category (for a total of 30 vectors in the /b/, /d/, /g/ task). This number was deemed sufficient since Shift-Tolerant LVQ applied to the /b/, /d/, /g/ task can achieve very high performance using this number of reference vectors, as seen above.

The procedure here is first to create the phoneme dependent K-means codebook, and assign it to the first HMM. The LVQ codebook is then created by using the same phoneme dependent K-means codebook to initialize the LVQ reference vectors, and then training those reference vectors using LVQ2, as described above. Training is performed so as to get as high a recognition rate as possible using the Shift-Tolerant LVQ recognition architecture. The resultant codebook is then used in the second HMM. Both HMMs are then trained in the manner described above.

The results on test data for these two HMMs are shown in Table 3. As can be seen, the HMM using the LVQ codebook has an error rate ten times smaller than that of the HMM with the K-means codebook.

6.3.3 VQ Distortion vs. Classification Rate

The distortions for the 4 codebooks examined in the two preceding sections are shown in Table 3. The definition of distortion here is the usual mean-square error, using the same test samples as used to calculate recognition rates. As can be seen from Table 3, the correlation between distortion and classification rate is tenuous. In fact, the codebook with the highest performance, that generated using LVQ2, has the highest distortion. Furthermore, in the comparison between phoneme dependent K-means and phoneme independent K-means, the higher performing phoneme dependent K-means yields a codebook with a greater distortion than that produced by phoneme independent K-means.

6.4. LVQ-HMM, Shift Tolerant LVQ and TDNN: Recognition Within 7 Consonant Clusters

Encouraged by these results for /b/, /d/ and /g/, we turned to the same consonant clusters examined above, still using the first data set.

Here we compared the performances of three systems: (1) HMMs using an LVQ trained codebook, (2) Shift-Tolerant LVQ, and (3) TDNN. Note that the reference vectors in (1) and (2) are identical, the result of the same Shift-Tolerant LVQ training. In the case of (1), the LVQ reference vectors are used as the HMM codebook, trained as above; in the case of (2), the reference vectors are used for the very simple generation and summation of activations in the Shift-Tolerant recognition architecture, described above. The number of reference vectors varied with each phonemic class examined, from 10 to 30 reference vectors per class. (3) Refers to the TDNN system described and evaluated in [4].

The recognition rates for these three systems are shown in Table 4. As can be seen, the LVQ-HMM hybrid attained a recognition performance as high as that of Shift-Tolerant LVQ and TDNN.

6.5. LVQ-HMM and Shift Tolerant LVQ: Recognition of All Consonants

We next turned to the more difficult task of recognizing all the above consonants taken together, not just within small consonant clusters. Here we are only comparing the LVQ-HMM hybrid with Shift-Tolerant LVQ. The data set here is still the first data set, of fixed length tokens. Twenty five reference vectors were assigned to each category, and LVQ training was performed as above. As above, the resulting reference vectors were used in an HMM framework for training and recognition; the same reference vectors were also used in the Shift-Tolerant LVQ recognition architecture. The performances on test data of these two systems are shown in Table 5. Once again, it can be seen that the LVQ-HMM hybrid performs as highly as Shift-Tolerant LVQ.

task	LVQ + HMM			LVQ	TDNN
	#errors/ #tokens	%correct	total	total	total
b	3/227	98.7	98.6	99.2	99.0
d	0/179	100.			
g	6/252	97.6			
p	7/ 15	53.3	98.4	98.9	98.7
t	2/440	99.5			
k	6/500	98.8			
m	7/481	98.5	98.5	98.8	96.6
n	6/265	97.7			
N	5/488	99.0			
s	5/538	99.1	99.3	99.4	99.3
sh	0/316	100.			
h	0/207	100.			
z	3/115	97.4			
ch	0/123	100.	100.	100.	100.
ts	0/177	100.			
r	0/722	100.	99.9	99.6	99.9
w	0/ 78	100.			
y	1/174	99.4			
a	0/600	100.	98.9	99.1	98.6
i	2/600	99.7			
u	21/600	96.5			
e	7/600	98.8			
o	2/600	99.7			

Table 4. Recognition results for 7 phonemic classes

6.6. VQ-HMM, LVQ-HMM and Shift-Tolerant LVQ: Phoneme Recognition Using Tokens of Variable Length

We now turn to the second data set described above. The phoneme tokens in this data set are taken from a greater variety of phonemic contexts than in the first data set; in addition the second data set contains tokens from two additional phonemes, /f/ and /j/, giving a total of 25 phonemes.

It was very simple to modify the Shift-Tolerant LVQ architecture to deal with the variable token length. At the first level, where LVQ2 training is performed (using reference vectors initialized by phoneme dependent K-means), the 7-frame time window was simply shifted over the length of the whole token, no longer limited at 15 frames. LVQ2 training was performed for each position of this time window over the token, as in the fixed frame length architecture. At the second level of the architecture, where activations are calculated and summed, the history of activations was simply extended or shortened depending on the token length. The calculation of final activations was obtained from the same process of summation as before.

task	LVQ + HMM			LVQ
	#errors/ #tokens	%correct	total	total
b	2/227	99.1	97.4	97.7
d	2/179	98.9		
g	14/252	94.4		
p	7/15	53.3		
t	9/440	98.0		
k	18/1163	98.5		
m	7/481	98.5		
n	7/265	97.4		
N	14/488	97.1		
s	16/538	97.0		
sh	3/316	99.1		
h	6/207	97.1		
z	6/115	94.8		
ch	6/123	95.1		
ts	10/177	94.4		
r	14/722	98.1		
w	6/ 78	92.3		
y	6/174	96.6		

Table 5: Recognition results for 18 consonants.

The HMMs we examined here are trained and tested as above, with the exception that the tokens used for training are of variable length.

Here too we performed a number of experiments. We examined two codebook sizes: 250 reference vectors in all (10 per category for phoneme dependent K-means) and 625 reference vectors in all (25 per category for phoneme dependent K-means). Our focus here was to compare VQ-HMM, LVQ-HMM, and Shift-Tolerant LVQ, for these two codebook sizes. In addition, for VQ-HMM, we compared phoneme dependent K-means and phoneme independent K-means.

Table 6 shows the results for these systems. These results confirm the finding of the preliminary investigations of section 3.2, that phoneme dependent K-means provides the HMMs with better discriminant ability than phoneme independent K-means. We also see that Shift-Tolerant LVQ by itself performs better than VQ-HMM, and that the LVQ-HMM hybrid performs significantly better than the VQ-HMM. For the large codebook, the hybrid model's error rate is 1.5 ~ 2 times lower than that of VQ-HMM; for the small codebook, 2 ~ 3 times lower.

Recognition System	K-means Procedure	Codebook Size	
		250	625
VQ-HMM	Phon. Ind.	92.8	96.1
VQ-HMM	Phon. Dep.	94.7	96.9
LVQ-HMM	Phon. Dep.	97.2	98.0
Shift Tolerant LVQ	Phon. Dep.	95.3	97.5

Table 6 Recognition results for 25 phonemes where the tokens are of variable length. Phon. Ind. (Phoneme Independent) K-means refers to K-means performed on all categories at the same time; Phon. Dep. (phoneme dependent) K-means refers to K-means performed on one category at a time.

7. Discussion

7.1 Shift-Tolerant LVQ

Our results for the Shift-Tolerant LVQ-based architecture presented above suggest that LVQ2 is a powerful classifier, comparable in ability to Back-propagation.

Clearly, *from the viewpoint of classifier performance*, LVQ2 is more powerful than K-means clustering. As suggested above, this is due to a difference in goals between LVQ and K-means clustering. K-means does not attempt to generate optimal Bayes decision lines in a categorization task; similarly, LVQ is not meant to minimize distortion. As our interest here is phoneme recognition accuracy, within the framework of the recognition system presented here, the LVQ algorithm is more appropriate than K-means clustering.

We saw above that with large numbers of reference vectors, LVQ and K-means have about the same performance. However, the fact that LVQ can achieve high performance even with small numbers of reference vectors is quite significant. The goal of vector quantization is to reduce data from a large number of training vectors to a small number of reference vectors. For the purposes of our phoneme recognition system, LVQ achieves this goal more fully. Furthermore, even for large numbers of reference vectors, LVQ performs slightly better than K-means.

We have throughout mentioned that LVQ is a very fast algorithm, mainly due to the good initial conditions obtained using K-means clustering. At the time of the TDNN implementation in [3], it took 4 days for TDNN to learn /b/, /d/, /g/. Thus the minute or so required for LVQ2, on the same computer, compared quite favorably. Recently, however, Haffner et al. [10] have achieved speed-ups of several orders of magnitude for TDNN, such that we can no longer claim speed as a decisive advantage over TDNN. However, it still seems fair to say that LVQ, in its basic form, is faster than Back-propagation in its basic form.

We should mention that our LVQ networks are significantly bigger than their corresponding TDNNs, by a factor ranging from about 4 to about 13. Since LVQ training does not require many training iterations (from 5 to 30 presentations of the whole training set), the large network size poses few problems of training time. Of course, in the recognition phase, it will take longer to recognize a single token using the Shift Tolerant LVQ architecture presented here than using TDNN. Nonetheless, our system implementation still recognizes tokens in real time. We should note that the architecture we present here is undoubtedly not the best LVQ architecture for phoneme recognition, and other architectures we are now considering may well allow for significantly smaller networks. Another point is that as a vector quantizer, LVQ is open to the many existing techniques for editing out unnecessary vectors, as well as for finding the closest vector in logarithmic time [13].

We find the simplicity of the learning rule quite appealing. It involves no calculations of sigmoid functions or derivatives, the main calculation being that for finding the Euclidean distance between two vectors, which is very easy to implement and parallelize.

The shifting window scheme described here means that it is not essential that the center frame of the phoneme be perfectly aligned with the center frame of the input layer for it to be correctly recognized. This is quite an important property, as we cannot reasonably expect databases to be so accurately labelled. Another advantage of the shifting window scheme is that training on shifted segments in a way results in an expansion of the training data, which might be beneficial.

7.2 Hybrid LVQ-HMM

Concerning the hybrid LVQ-HMM system, our results suggest a rather different approach to codebook design, concerned not so much with reducing spectral distortion, but rather with providing information as to the phonemic identity of the speech segments under consideration. Table 3 illustrates this point. For codebooks of the same size, we see that there is in fact an inverse relationship between distortion and the HMM's recognition rate. It makes sense that phoneme independent K-means would be better at reducing distortion than phoneme dependent K-means, as it takes the whole data set into account. It is not so clear why phoneme dependent K-means yields a configuration better suited to reducing the number of misclassifications. It could be that phoneme dependent K-means is better at describing the probability distribution of each category, especially at the category boundaries. This explanation is consistent with the motivation for LVQ, which is to pay very close attention to the category boundaries, for the purpose of obtaining high classification performance. When comparing the LVQ codebook with the K-means codebooks, the inverse relationship between distortion and recognition rate is readily understood. LVQ starts from a K-means configuration, where distortion is minimal, and adjusts that configuration for the purpose of reducing the number of misclassifications. Clearly the resulting configuration will no longer minimize distortion, but the classification rate will be better than that of the original configuration.

In Table 3, we see that using an LVQ codebook can provide an HMM with a better recognition rate than a K-means codebook that is 10 times larger. Thus, in this case, LVQ yields an improvement in performance as well as a ten-fold reduction in computation time-- the search for the nearest reference vector can be done in less time as there are fewer reference vectors in all. In the hybrid LVQ-HMM system at hand, there is the additional advantage of making HMM parameter estimation easier. The number of observation probabilities to be estimated is decreased, and this in turn reduces the quantity of training data necessary to estimate these parameters. In effect, the overall size of the HMM recognition system, including both codebook and parameters, is very significantly reduced. Thus a small LVQ codebook, compared to a much larger K-means codebook, can provide an HMM with substantial gains in memory size, speed and performance.

From Tables 4, 5 and 6, we see that the phoneme recognition performance for LVQ-HMM is as high as that of Shift-Tolerant LVQ. The advantage of the hybrid LVQ-HMM system proposed here is that it can very easily be extended to models for longer utterances, such as words, phrases and sentences. Thus, even though the results we present here only concern phoneme recognition, the fact that the LVQ-HMM hybrid performs phoneme recognition in an HMM framework establishes the crucial link between the high discriminant power of the Shift-Tolerant LVQ system and the ability HMMs have to concatenate small utterance models into long utterance models.

The hybrid presented here is just one of several possibilities for using LVQ in combination with HMMs. In addition, LVQ is also open to integration with other speech recognition techniques, such as DTW.

8. Conclusion

The first part of our study was designed to investigate the phoneme recognition ability of the LVQ algorithm. Compared to K-means clustering, LVQ allows for higher recognition accuracy, especially for small numbers of reference vectors. Our Shift-Tolerant LVQ based system achieved recognition rates in the 98%-99% correct range for 7 Japanese phonemic classes, and a recognition rate of nearly 98% for all Japanese consonants. These results are as high as those obtained in the TDNN system developed by Waibel et al.[3].

In the second part of our study our goal was to integrate the high discriminant power of the LVQ classifier into an HMM framework extendible to long utterance models. Our findings for the LVQ-HMM system parallel those for the Shift-Tolerant LVQ-based recognition system described and tested in the first part. Compared to K-means clustering, LVQ provides the HMM with much better discriminant power-- thereby suggesting that codebook distortion is not a good index of HMM classification performance. Applying the LVQ-HMM hybrid system to a variety of phonemic recognition tasks yielded results that were as high as those for the Shift-Tolerant LVQ system and TDNN.

Thus we have shown here 1) the high discriminant ability of LVQ, as applied to phoneme recognition tasks and 2) a new approach to discrete HMM speech recognition, using a codebook whose purpose is to classify phonemes correctly rather than to minimize spectral distortion.

Acknowledgments

The authors would like to acknowledge the considerable contribution that Manami Yokota made to this study. This study also owes a lot to both Alex Waibel and Patrick Haffner for providing valuable advice and engaging in friendly scientific competition with us. The authors also wish to thank Toshiyuki Hanazawa in the ATR Interpreting Telephony Research Laboratories for helping us with HMM software. Thanks are also due to Dr. Kiyohiro Shikano, also in the ATR Interpreting Telephony Research Laboratories, for his valuable advice.

References

[1] T. Kohonen, *Self-organization and Associative Memory* (2nd Ed.), pp. 199-202, Springer, Berlin-Heidelberg-New York-Tokyo, 1988.

[2] T. Kohonen, G. Barna and R. Chrisley, "Statistical Pattern Recognition with Neural Networks: Benchmarking Studies," *IEEE, Proc. of ICNN*, Vol. I, pp. 61-68, July 1988.

[3] A. Waibel, T. Hanazawa, G. Hinton, K. Shikano, and K.J. Lang, "Phoneme Recognition Using Time-Delay Neural Networks," in IEEE Trans. Acoust. Speech, Signal Processing, vol. ASSP-37, pp. 328-339, 1989.

[4] A. Waibel, H. Sawai, K. Shikano, "Consonant Recognition by Modular Construction of Large Phonemic Time-Delay Neural Networks," in Proc. Int. Conf. Acoust., Speech, Signal Processing, Glasgow, U.K., 1989, pp. 112-115..

[5] E. McDermott, S. Katagiri, "Shift-Invariant, Multi-Category Phoneme Recognition using Kohonen's LVQ2," in Proc. Int. Conf. Acoust., Speech, Signal Processing, Glasgow, U.K., 1989, pp. 81-84.

[6] E. McDermott, S. Katagiri, "Phoneme Recognition Using Kohonen Networks," *Proc. of ATR Neural Net Workshop*, July 1988.

[7] E. McDermott, S. Katagiri, "Shift-invariant Phoneme Recognition Using Kohonen Networks," *Proc. of Acoustical Society of Japan*, October 1988.

[8] J. Makhoul, S. Roucos, and H. Gish, (1985), "Vector Quantization in Speech Coding," *Proc IEEE 73*, No. 11, 1551-88.

[9] M. Yokota, S. Katagiri and E. McDermott; "Learning in an LVQ Based Phoneme Recognition System," *IEICE Technical Report*, SP88-104, pp. 65-72, December 1988

[10] P. Haffner, A. Waibel, K. Shikano; "Fast Back-Propagation Learning Methods for Neural Networks in Speech," Technical Report TR-I-0058, ATR Interpreting Telephony Research Laboratories, November 1988.

[11] D.E. Rumelhart, Learning and Generalization: The Role of Minimal Networks, *Proc. of the ATR Workshop on Neural Networks and PDP*, July 1988, Osaka.

[12] Duda, R.O., Hart, P.E.: *Pattern Classification and Scene Analysis* , Chapter 2, Wiley, New York, 1973.

[13] Omohundro, S.M.; "Efficient Algorithms with Neural Network Behavior," *Complex Systems*, 1:273-347, 1987.

[14] H. Bourlard and C.J. Wellekens, "Links between Markov Models and Multilayer Perceptrons," in Proc. NIPS Conference, Denver, CO, 1988.

[15] K-F. Lee and H-W. Hon; "Large-Vocabulary Speaker Independent Continuous Speech Recognition Using HMM," in Proc. Int. Conf. Acoust., Speech, Signal Processing, New York, NY, 1988, pp. 123-126.

[16] P. Brown., "The Acoustic-Modeling Problem in Automatic Speech Recognition," PhD dissertation, Computer Science Department, Carnegie Mellon University, 1987.

[17] L.R. Bahl, P.F. Brown, P.V. de Souza, and K.L. Mercer, "Maximum Mutual Information Estimation of Hidden Markov Parameters for Speech Recognition," in Proc. Int. Conf. Acoust., Speech, Signal Processing, Tokyo, Japan, 1986, pp. 49-52.

[18] T. Hanazawa, T. Kawabata, K. Shikano, "Recognition of Japanese voiced stops using Hidden Markov Models," Inst. Elec. Inf. Com. Eng. of Jpn. IEICE Technical Report, SP87-98, pp. 7-12, 1987. (in Japanese)

[19] G. Doddington, "Phonetically Sensitive Discriminants for Improved Speech Recognition," in Proc. Int. Conf. Acoust., Speech, Signal Processing, Glasgow, U.K., 1989, pp.556-559.

[20] L.R. Bahl, et. al., "Large Vocabulary Natural Language Continuous Speech Recognition," in Proc. Int. Conf. Acoust., Speech, Signal Processing, Glasgow, U.K., 1989, pp.465-467

[21] D.J. Burr, "Speech Recognition Experiments with Perceptrons", in Neural Information Processing Systems (E. Anderson Ed.), pp. 144-153, American Institute of Physics

[22] R.P. Lippmann and B. Gold, "Neural Net Classifiers Useful for Speech Recognition," Proc. of International Conference on Neural Networks, IEEE, San Diego, June 1987.

[23] H. Sakoe, R. Isotani and K. Iso, "Speaker-Independent Word Recognition Using Dynamic Programming Neural Networks," in Proc. Int. Conf. Acoust., Speech, Signal Processing, Glasgow, U.K., 1989, pp. 29-32.

[24] L-Y. Bottou, "Reconnaissance de la Parole par Reseaux multi-couches." Proc. of Neuro-Nimes 88, Novermber 1988.

SPEAKER-INDEPENDENT WORD RECOGNITION USING DYNAMIC PROGRAMMING NEURAL NETWORKS

Hiroaki Sakoe, Ryosuke Isotani, Kazunaga Yoshida, Ken-ichi Iso, and Takao Watanabe
C&C Information Technology Research Laboratories
NEC Corporation
4-1-1 Miyazaki, Miyamae-ku, Kawasaki, 213 JAPAN

ABSTRACT

This paper describes speaker-independent word recognition based on a new neural network model (Dynamic programming Neural Network; DNN), which can treat time-sequence patterns. The proposed model, DNN, is based on the integration of multi-layer neural network and dynamic programming based matching. Speaker-independent isolated Japanese digit recognition experiments were carried out using data uttered by 107 speakers (50 speakers for training and 57 speakers for testing). As a result, 99.3% recognition accuracy was obtained. This suggests that the proposed model can be effective for speech recognition.

INTRODUCTION

In most speech recognition systems, speech is dealt with as a time sequence of feature parameters. Major problems there have been time axis distortion and spectral pattern variation. The former has been mathematically well modeled and solved by use of dynamic programming (DP) matching[1],[2]. On the other hand, the spectral pattern variation, which is caused by a complex mixture of several effects, is hard to treat.

The neural network[3],[4] is quite a general pattern recognition mechanism which, by being fed training samples of given categories, can learn to achieve a function to discriminate between the categories. Therefore, the neural network is suitably applicable to pattern recognition problems where an analytical approach is inapplicable. This, in turn, implies the usefulness of the neural network model in solving spectral pattern variation problems.

The Dynamic Programming Neural Network (DNN), proposed in this paper, is a new speech recognition model based on the integration of DP and multi-layer neural networks. Lower layers (near the input) are time-sequence structured, meaning that neural units in those layers are arranged in a block structure frame along the time axis. The input pattern is optimally time aligned with this lower layer structure by DP, so that an output unit gives maximum output (similarity measure).

This new recognition model possesses both DP and neural network features. They are time alignment function, expandability to continuous speech recognition, and high tolerance to the spectral pattern variation.

In the following sections, the proposed neural network structure is described first, followed by the recognition and learning algorithm. Then the experimental results are presented.

TIME-SEQUENCE-STRUCTURED NEURAL NETWORK

A. Proposed Neural Network Structure

Basically, the neural network considered here is a multi-layered network[4]. In typical organization, a neural network has several output units, each of which stands for one of the given categories. In the other organization, a neural network has only one output unit. In this case, a neural network works as a discriminator which decides whether the input pattern belongs to the given category or not. It can be considered, therefore, that the output from the neural network, or the signal from the output unit, gives a similarity between the given input pattern and the category the neural network stands for. In the following discussions, the latter model is quoted for notation simplicity.

Figure 1 shows the proposed time-sequence-structured neural network organized in three layer structure. The input layer and the hidden layer are organized in frame structure with time axis j. Each input frame contains K input units (j,k), while each hidden frame contains L hidden units (j,l). To each hidden frame (j), τ (two, for example) time-delayed input frames are connected. This set of input frames constitutes an input block (j).

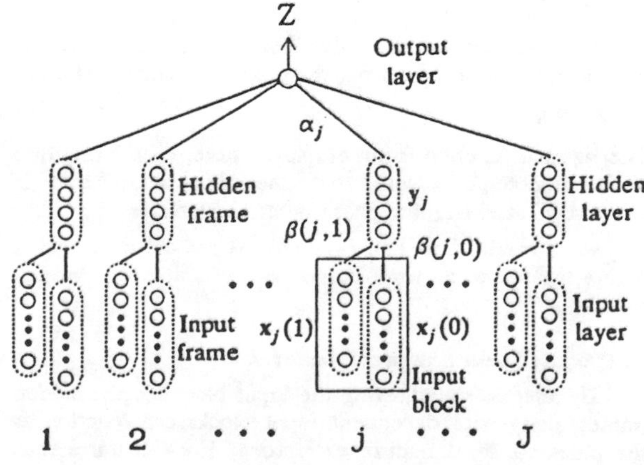

Figure 1. Time-Sequence-Structured Neural Network.

The input layer receives input signal

$$X=X(1)X(2).....X(j)......X(J). \quad (1)$$

Each input block (j) receives input signal fragment

$$X(j)=\mathbf{x}_j(0)\mathbf{x}_j(1).....\mathbf{x}_j(t)......\mathbf{x}_j(\tau-1)$$

where

$$\mathbf{x}_j(t)=[x_{j1}(t),x_{j2}(t),...,x_{jk}(t),...,x_{jK}(t)]'$$

is a t-delayed input frame vector. A t-delayed input unit (j,k), upon receiving $x_{jk}(t)$, outputs the input value to hidden units without any operation.

The hidden unit (j,l) calculates a weighted summation of the signals from input units in the accompanying input block (j),

$$net(j,l)=\sum_t\sum_k \beta_{lk}(j,t)x_{jk}(t), \quad (2)$$

where $\beta_{lk}(j,t)$ is the weighting coefficient for the connection from the t-delayed input unit (j,k). The output signal for this hidden unit (j,l) is given by

$$y(j,l)=f(net(j,l)) \quad (3)$$

where $f(\cdot)$ is a sigmoid function. There is another parameter used to shift the value (net) to an optimum operating point, which is omitted here for notation simplicity.

Output signals $y(j,l)$ from a hidden frame (j) form a hidden frame output vector

$$\mathbf{y}_j=[y_{j1}...y_{jl}...y_{jL}]'. \quad (4)$$

The above function, for deriving vector $\mathbf{y}_j$ from input frame vectors $\mathbf{x}_j(t)$, is formally denoted by

$$\mathbf{y}_j=f(\sum_t \beta(j,t)\mathbf{x}_j(t)) \quad (5)$$

where $\beta(j,t)=[\beta_{lk}(j,t)]$ is a coefficient matrix.

For each connection to an output unit from a hidden unit (j,l), a weighting coefficient $\alpha(j,l)$ is given. Consider a coefficient vector

$$\alpha_j=[\alpha(j,1)...\alpha(j,l)...\alpha(j,L)]. \quad (6)$$

Then, the input to the output unit is given by

$$Net=\sum_j \alpha_j\cdot\mathbf{y}_j$$

$$=\sum_j \alpha_j\cdot f(\sum_t \beta(j,t)\mathbf{x}_j(t)) \quad (7)$$

which gives the output value for the output unit, or, equivalently, the output from the proposed neural network.

$$Z=Net \quad (8)$$

The sigmoid function is not employed here, considering that it is monotonic. Note that the sigmoid function is employed in the learning phase described later.

As a result, Eqs. (5), (7), and (8) are obtained, which define the neural network output as a function of input signal X.

B. Proposed neural network features

By adequately adjusting the input block length, hidden frames along with dependent input blocks can function as the phoneme level feature extractors. Local features thus extracted are integrated at the output unit, yielding an output signal Z, which gives the similarity measure for given input pattern X to the conceptual reference pattern the network has in the form of weighting coefficients.

The most marked features are:

(1) The summation form in Eq.(7) implies that a DP based time alignment operation can be put into this time-sequence-structured network.

(2) The network intrinsically has a learning capability. The block structure in the input layer is suitable to solve the parameter level pattern variation problem.

Other than these merits, it should be noted that, with the time-sequence structure, connections between the input layer and the hidden layer are considerably reduced, compared with a general neural network. This significantly simplifies the computation problems, both in the learning phase and in the recognition phase.

DYNAMIC PROGRAMMING NEURAL NETWORK (DNN)

In the following discussion, input block length τ is fixed at 2 for simplicity. In the previous section, the input-to-output relation (7) was derived. The summation form of the equation strongly implies the DP based time alignment technique applicability.

Let

$$A=\mathbf{a}_1\cdots\mathbf{a}_i\cdots\mathbf{a}_I \quad (9)$$

be an input pattern to neural network B. Figure 2 shows a time alignment scheme. Consider a warping function $i=i(j)$ between input pattern time i and neural network block j. Consider that, by this warping function, a hidden frame (j) and the dependent input block (j) are warped as if they were a single rigid unit. This means

$$\text{if } \mathbf{x}_j(0)=\mathbf{a}_{i(j)}, \text{ then } \mathbf{x}_j(1)=\mathbf{a}_{i(j)-1}.$$

According to Eqs. (7) and (8), the output from the neural network is

$$Z=\sum_j \alpha_j\cdot f(\beta(j,0)\mathbf{a}_i+\beta(j,1)\mathbf{a}_{i-1}). \quad (10)$$

Let

$$r(i,j)=\alpha_j\cdot f(\beta(j,0)\mathbf{a}_i+\beta(j,1)\mathbf{a}_{i-1}). \quad (11)$$

The time alignment problem is now formulated as

$$Z(A,B)=\max_{i=i(j)}\left[\sum_j r(i,j)\right]. \quad (12)$$

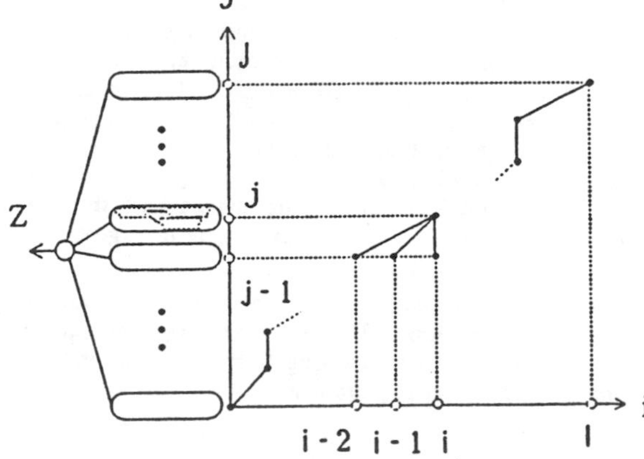

Figure 2. Dynamic Programming for the Neural Network.

This maximization problem is solved by the following very familiar dynamic programming algorithm[1].

[Initial condition]

$g(1,1)=r(1,1)$

[DP-equation]

$$g(i,j)=r(i,j)+\max\begin{bmatrix} g(i,j-1) \\ g(i-1,j-1) \\ g(i-2,j-1) \end{bmatrix} \quad (13)$$

[Network output]

$Z(A,B)=g(I,J)$

This model, as described above, is called a dynamic programming neural network (DNN), after dynamic programming. More strictly, this is called an $i(j)$-type DNN, considering that the time alignment is achieved by a single valued function $i=i(j)$. In this category, $r(i,j)$ accumulation proceeds along the j increment. Analogously, a $j(i)$-category DNN can be defined, where $r(i,j)$ accumulation proceeds along with the i increment.

As in ordinary DP-matching[1], various conditions other than the slope constraint condition (DP equation described above) can be introduced. For example, the adjustment window condition, which restricts the region where the matching path can go through in the i-j plane (see Figure 2), can be used to avoid too excessive time axis normalization.

LEARNING

The well-known back propagation method[4] is applied to the present DNN. It should be noted, however, that DNN itself has sufficient time alignment ability. It is, therefore, unnecessary to learn all the time distortion patterns.

A. Fixed time alignment learning procedure

Consider two pattern categories, n and $\bar{n}$. As a training sample set, $\{A_m\}$ is prepared.

$$A_m=\mathbf{a}_{m1}\cdots\mathbf{a}_{mi}\cdots\mathbf{a}_{mI(m)},$$

where $A_m \in n$, or $A_m \in \bar{n}$. Determine a scale reference pattern $A=\mathbf{a}_1\cdots\mathbf{a}_j\cdots\mathbf{a}_J$ for category n. (A may be a centroid of the subset $\{A_m \in n\}$.) Time-align all A_m patterns to the scale reference time base by DP, generating a database $\{AA_m\}$. Using these data, conduct the standard back propagation training[4], with the following target:

$$f(Z)=1, \text{ when } AA_m \in n, \quad (14)$$

$$f(Z)=0, \text{ when } AA_m \in \bar{n}.$$

In the above learning procedure, time alignment is first conducted and then fixed. Effective training patterns $\{AA_m\}$ are invariant during back propagation iterations. So, this learning procedure is called fixed time alignment.

B. Adaptive time alignment learning procedure

Another learning procedure can be considered. Differing from the above fixed time alignment method, time alignment operation for training patterns $\{A_m \in \bar{n}\}$ is made with DNN, so that current DNN gives maximum output value Z (or equivalently $f(Z)$). This time alignment is repeated every time training pattern $A_m \in \bar{n}$ appears in training iterations. This means that each training pattern $A_m \in \bar{n}$ is adaptively warped, yielding a pattern AA_m most unseparable by current DNN. Giving the most unseparable training pattern is considered desirable for learning efficiency.

Note that the time alignment for training patterns $\{A_m \in n\}$ is not adaptive. Rather, it is fixed, quite the same as in the fixed time alignment learning procedure. This is to retain the learning stability.

C. Fixed time alignment vs. adaptive time alignment

From the computational economy viewpoint, fixed time alignment is by far superior to adaptive time alignment. Next, the learning quality aspect is discussed. Consider, for each training pattern A_m, a set of patterns derived from it by warping time axis i, and name it $\tilde{A}_m$. In the fixed time alignment, only the patterns nearest to the time base pattern are selected among $\tilde{A}_m$ by DP and used for learning. Therefore, DNN's discriminating function achieved by this learning procedure is not greater than separating these fixed warped patterns. When the same pattern, as that which appeared in the training set, is submitted to recognition, it is warped so as to maximize the output value. It may produce a greater value than in the learning phase, and, as a result, may be misclassified to the category n. In the adaptive time alignment learning, time warpings for $A_m \in \bar{n}$ are made with DNN directly. Patterns which give the larger value among $\tilde{A}_m \in \bar{n}$ appear in the course of learning iteration. Hence, after the convergence, all patterns in $\tilde{A}_m \in \bar{n}$ are proved to be classified to $\bar{n}$. This qualitative discussion means that higher recognition accuracy can be expected by applying adaptive time alignment than by applying fixed time alignment.

EXPERIMENTS

As preliminary experiments to examine the proposed model effectiveness, speaker-independent isolated Japanese digit word recognition experiments were carried out using data uttered by 107 speakers (62 male speakers and 45 female speakers). Each speaker uttered each vocabulary word once via a telephone, where the telephone output was directly connected with the AD converter. The utterances were sampled at an 8.0 kHz sampling rate, and analyzed by a 16 msec frame period. As a feature parameter set for each time frame, 10 mel-scaled cepstral parameters (excluding 0-th order) and a changing ratio parameter for amplitude were calculated from FFT based spectrum with 0.3 - 3.4 kHz band limitation. An $i(j)$-type DNN with 11 input units per frame (10 units when using only cepstral parameters) was prepared for each vocabulary word. The samples were divided into two sets. 50 speakers' samples were used for training, and 57 speakers' samples were used for recognition test. An adjustment window with 9 frames width (±4 input frames from linear time alignment) was used.

First, the correct recognition rate was examined as a function of the number of hidden units. Only cepstral parameters were used as input parameters, and the adjustment window was not used. Learning was implemented using adaptive time alignment procedure. The results are shown in Table 1. In this case, the optimum number of hidden units was 4 per frame.

Next, the time alignment effectiveness in recognition was investigated. As in fixed time alignment learning, fixed time alignment in the recognition phase can be considered. Input patterns are time-aligned to the scale reference time base by DP. Neural networks, having the same structure as DNN, receive them without any further time alignment operation. Learning is accomplished using fixed time alignment with the same scale reference time base. The performance obtained by this method was compared with that for DNN. Two learning procedures for DNN were also compared. Only cepstral parameters were used as input parameters, and the adjustment window described above was adopted. Four hidden units per frame were prepared. The results are shown in Table 2. This result indicates that the dynamic programming based time alignment function in DNN works effectively. The adaptive time alignment learning superiority to fixed time alignment learning was also confirmed, which coincides with analytical discussion results. Figure 3 shows the learning curve for the DNN trained by adaptive time alignment learning.

Table 3 shows recognition experiments results reached while changing the conditions of input parameters and adjustment window. The number of hidden units per frame was fixed at 4, and learning was carried out using adaptive time alignment procedure. The results obtained by ordinary DP-matching, using the same training and test data, are also presented. Using the adjustment window and changing ratio parameter for amplitude improved the performance. When both were used, 99.3% recognition accuracy was achieved, which exceeded the value obtained by ordinary DP-matching. This value indicates a high potential applicability for the proposed DNN to speech recognition.

Table 1. Correct Recognition Rate as Function of the Number of Hidden Units

Number of hidden units per frame	2	4	8
Correct recognition rate	97.5%	98.2%	97.5%

Table 2. Time Alignment Comparison (correct recognition rate)

Learning	Recognition	Accuracy
fixed	fixed	97.4%
fixed	DNN(adaptive)	97.5%
adaptive	DNN(adaptive)	98.8%

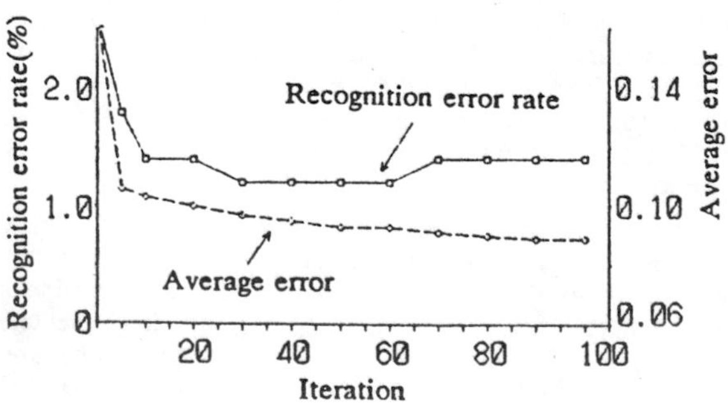

Figure 3. Learning Curve.

Table 3. Correct Recognition Rate for Various Input Parameters and Adjustment Window Conditions

Input parameter	Cepstral parameters only (10 parameters)	With amplitude changing ratio (11 parameters)
Without adjustment window	98.2%	99.1%
With adjustment window	98.8%	99.3%
DP-matching	98.4%	98.9%

CONCLUSION

A new speech recognition model, called Dynamic Programming Neural Network (DNN), was presented, where a time-sequence-structure was used for a neural network. Dynamic programming based time alignment was incorporated into the model. DNN thus derived has valuable features of both DP-matching and neural network. They are excellent time normalization ability and flexible learning facility. An efficient training strategy was also investigated. In the preliminary experiment, speaker-independent isolated Japanese digit words were recognized. A recognition accuracy as high as 99.3% was obtained. This shows a high potential applicability for the proposed DNN to speech recognition problems.

ACKNOWLEDGEMENT

The authors wish to thank Dr. Yasuo Kato, Dr. Kazumoto Iinuma, and Dr. Masahiro Yamamoto for their support and encouragement. They also thank members of the Media Technology Research Laboratory for invaluable discussions.

REFERENCES

[1] H.Sakoe and S.Chiba, "Dynamic Programming Algorithm Optimization for Spoken Word Recognition", *IEEE Trans. on Acoustics, Speech, and Signal Processing*, vol.ASSP-26, no.1, pp.43-49, 1978.

[2] J.Bridle, M.Brown and R.Chamberlain, "An Algorithm for Connected Word Recognition", *Proc. ICASSP-82*, pp.899-902, 1982.

[3] S.Amari, "A Mathematical Approach to Neural Systems", in *Systems Neuroscience*, pp.67-117, Academic press, 1977.

[4] D.Rumelhart and J.McClelland, "Parallel Distributed Processing", MIT Press, 1986.

[5] W.Y.Huang, R.P.Lippmann, and B.Gold, "A Neural Net Approach to Speech Recognition", *Proc. ICASSP-88*, pp.99-102, 1988.

[6] D.J.Burr, "Speech Recognition Experiments with Perceptrons", in *AIP Conference Proceedings*, Neural Information Processing Systems, 1987.

SPEAKER-INDEPENDENT WORD RECOGNITION USING A NEURAL PREDICTION MODEL

Ken-ichi Iso and Takao Watanabe
C & C Information Technology Research Laboratories
NEC Corporation
4-1-1 Miyazaki, Miyamae-ku, Kawasaki 213, JAPAN

ABSTRACT

A new speech recognition model, Neural Prediction Model (NPM), is proposed. The model uses a sequence of Multilayer Perceptrons (MLP) as a separate nonlinear predictor for each class. It is designed to represent temporal structures of speech patterns as recognition cues. In particular, temporal correlation in successive feature vectors of a speech pattern is represented in the mappings formed as MLP input-output relations. Contrary to this, temporal distortion of speech is efficiently normalized by dynamic-programming technique. Recognition and training algorithms are presented based on the combination of dynamic-programming and back-propagation techniques.

Evaluation experiments were conducted, using 10 digit vocabulary samples uttered by 107 speakers. A 99.8 % recognition accuracy was obtained. This suggests that the proposed model is effective for speaker-independent speech recognition.

1. INTRODUCTION

Artificial neural networks, and more particularly Multilayer Perceptrons (MLP), have recently been recognized as attractive tools for information processing. One of their main advantages lies in the existence of the effective training algorithm, called back-propagation [1]. Another important MLP characteristic is their capability to approximate a very wide range of continuous mappings between input and output vector spaces [2].

In speech recognition, MLPs are usually employed as speech pattern discriminators, where output-layer units represent class names. In case of a small number of classes, higher performances than achievable by conventional methods are reported [3, 4]. At present, however, there are practical problems in applying MLPs as discriminators to large vocabulary, continuous speech recognition. First, the MLP discriminators require a very large training data set to learn complex discrimination hyperplanes for a large number of classes. Second, if new recognition classes are added, discriminators in the system must be retrained using a training data set for all classes. Finally, it is difficult to absorb temporal distortion of speech patterns and to handle continuous speech. Many attempts to overcome these difficulties involved in using MLP discriminators are now under investigation [5, 6, 7, 8, 9].

The approach taken in this paper is different. This paper proposes a new speech recognition model, Neural Prediction Model (NPM), where MLPs are used as pattern predictors instead of pattern discriminators. Hence, problems inherent in the nature of discriminators are avoided. The model uses an MLP sequence as a separate nonlinear predictor for each class. It is designed to represent temporal structures for speech patterns and to consider these features as recognition cues. In particular, temporal correlation between successive feature vectors in a speech pattern is focused, since it is considered to include cues in speech recognition. Contrary to this, temporal distortion of speech is efficiently normalized by dynamic-programming technique. Features of the model are summarized in the following.

- Temporal correlations in speech patterns are used as cues in the recognition.
- Temporal distortion of speech is normalized by dynamic-programming technique.
- Optimal training algorithm for the model is given, based on dynamic-programming and back-propagation techniques.
- Required training data amount is rather small.
- The model is applicable to continuous speech recognition.
- It is easy to add new recognition classes.

The paper is organized as follows. In Section 2, the prediction by MLP is described first, followed by the proposed recognition and training algorithms. Experimental results on speaker-independent isolated word recognition are presented in Section 3.

2. NEURAL PREDICTION MODEL

2.1. Prediction by Multilayer Perceptrons

Figure 1 shows a speech pattern MLP predictor. It outputs a predicted feature vector $\hat{\mathbf{a}}_t$ using the preceding input speech feature vectors $\mathbf{a}_{t-\tau}, \ldots, \mathbf{a}_{t-1}$ as inputs. The subscripts represent frame numbers of speech feature vectors. The symbol τ indicates the number of input speech feature vectors used for prediction.

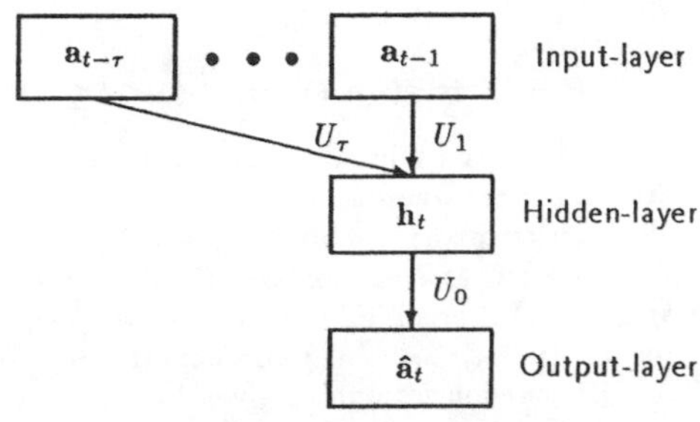

Figure 1: Speech pattern MLP predictor

Originally appeared in *IEEE International Conference on Acoustics, Speech, and Signal Processing*, IEEE, April, 1990.

The input-output relation for the MLP predictor is given by the following vector equations.

$$\mathbf{h}_t = \mathbf{f}(\sum_{s=1}^{\tau} U_s \mathbf{a}_{t-s}), \quad (1)$$
$$\hat{\mathbf{a}}_t = U_0 \mathbf{h}_t, \quad (2)$$

where $U_0, U_1, \ldots, U_\tau$ are weight matrices, $\mathbf{h}_t$ is an output vector for hidden units, and the vector function $\mathbf{f}(\mathbf{x})$ gives a vector obtained by applying a sigmoid function to each component of the argument vector $\mathbf{x}$. For notation simplicity, threshold values for hidden and output units are omitted.

The predicted feature vector, $\hat{\mathbf{a}}_t$, can be compared with the input speech feature vector, $\mathbf{a}_t$. Their squared Euclidian distance, $||\hat{\mathbf{a}}_t - \mathbf{a}_t||^2$, gives a measure of the prediction residual.

2.2. Recognition Algorithm

This section presents the recognition algorithm for the NPM. For simplicity, the following discussion is focused on isolated word recognition. Its application to continuous speech recognition is discussed later.

A word model in NPM is a sequence of MLP predictors. Figure 2 shows a graph representation for word w NPM, where each node has an MLP predictor and its total number is denoted by N_w.

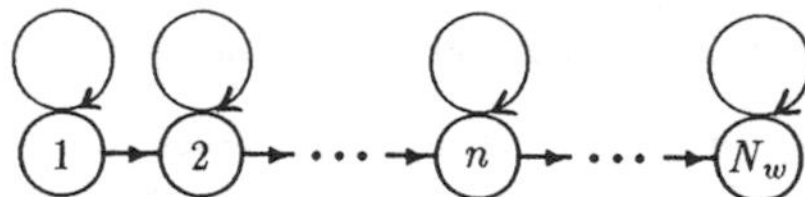

Figure 2: Neural Prediction Model for word w

In the prediction by word w NPM, input speech is divided into N_w segments and the n-th MLP predictor makes a prediction for the n-th segment ($1 \leq n \leq N_w$). The optimal segmentation of the input speech is determined by minimizing the accumulated prediction residual

$$D(w) = \min_{\{n(t)\}} \sum_{t=1}^{T} ||\hat{\mathbf{a}}_t(w, n(t)) - \mathbf{a}_t||^2, \quad (3)$$

where $||\cdot||$ is an Euclidian norm of a vector and $\hat{\mathbf{a}}_t(w, n)$ represents a feature vector, predicted by the n-th MLP predictor for word w. Here, $n(t)$ determines which MLP predictor is assigned to the prediction at frame t. It must satisfy the following constraints,

$$n(1) = 1, \quad (4)$$
$$n(T) = N_w, \quad (5)$$
$$n(t) = n(t-1) \; or \; n(t-1)+1, \quad (1 < t \leq T). \quad (6)$$

Under these constraints, the minimization can be accomplished by the use of dynamic-programming (DP).

Figure 3 illustrates a plane visualizing the DP computation, where horizontal and vertical axes represent the time direction for input speech and the MLP predictor sequence for word w, respectively. The sequence $\{n(1), \ldots, n(T)\}$ represents the trajectory on the plane. The DP recursion formula is given by

$$g_w(t, n) = d_w(t, n) + \min\{g_w(t-1, n), g_w(t-1, n-1)\}, \quad (7)$$

where the local distance measure $d_w(t, n)$ is defined as follows:

$$d_w(t, n) = ||\hat{\mathbf{a}}_t(w, n) - \mathbf{a}_t||^2. \quad (8)$$

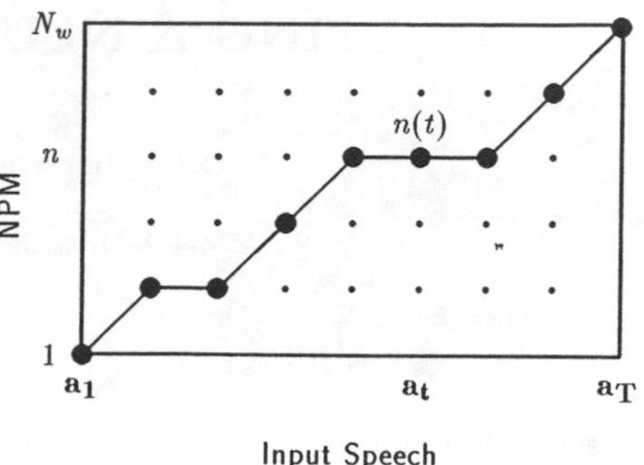

Figure 3: Prediction residual minimization by DP

At the end of recursive application of Eq.(7), it is possible to obtain $D(w) = g_w(T, N_w)$. The backtracking for the optimal trajectory $\{n^*(t)\}$ provides the input speech segmentation.

The accumulated prediction residual $D(w)$ can be regarded as the global distance between input speech and word w. Therefore, the word giving the minimum residual value should be selected as a recognition result.

The algorithm described above can be extended in a straightforward manner for continuous speech recognition, because it is the same as the conventional DP matching based algorithms, except for the representation of the reference patterns [10].

2.3. Training Algorithm

This section presents a training algorithm for estimating word NPM from isolated training utterances. Its extension for continuous speech is discussed later. The training goal is to find a set of MLP predictor weights, which minimizes the accumulated prediction residuals for a training data set. The objective function for the minimization is defined as the average value for accumulated prediction residuals for all training utterances for word w:

$$\bar{D}(w) = \frac{1}{M_w} \sum_{m=1}^{M_w} D(w, m), \quad (9)$$

where M_w is the number of training utterances of word w and $D(w, m)$ is the accumulated prediction residual for the m-th training utterance. The optimization can be made by an iterative procedure, combining dynamic-programming (DP) and back-propagation (BP) techniques. The algorithm is given as follows:

1. Initialize all MLP predictor weights.
2. Repeat the following procedures for all training utterances ($1 \leq m \leq M_w$).
3. Compute the accumulated prediction residual $D(w, m)$ using DP and determine the optimal trajectory $\{n^*(t)\}$, using its backtracking.
4. Correct weights for each MLP predictor by BP along the optimal trajectory $\{n^*(t)\}$, where desired output $\mathbf{a}_t$ is assigned to the actual output $\hat{\mathbf{a}}_t(w, n^*(t))$ for the $n^*(t)$-th MLP predictor (see below).

The weight correction criterion is to decrease the accumulated prediction residual $D(w, m)$ along the optimal trajectory $\{n^*(t)\}$ on the DP plane (see Figure 3). At each location $(t, n^*(t))$ along the optimal trajectory, local distance measure $||\hat{\mathbf{a}}_t(w, n^*(t)) - \mathbf{a}_t||^2$ can be regarded as the BP error function. Therefore, weight correction can be accomplished by BP, where desired output $\mathbf{a}_t$, corresponding to the actual output $\hat{\mathbf{a}}_t(w, n^*(t))$ for the $n^*(t)$-th MLP predictor, is determined.

For MLP discriminators, convergence proofs for the training procedure based on successive DP and BP processes have already been given independently [5, 11]. The proof given below is their application to MLP predictors. Let $\bar{D}_k(w)$ be the score of the objective function at the k-th iteration:

$$\bar{D}_k(w) = \frac{1}{M_w} \sum_{m=1}^{M_w} D_k(w, m), \qquad (10)$$

$$D_k(w, m) = \min_{\{n(t)\}} \sum_{t=1}^{T_m} ||\hat{\mathbf{a}}_t(w, n(t), m, k) - \mathbf{a}_t(m)||^2. \qquad (11)$$

where $\hat{\mathbf{a}}_t(w, n(t), m, k)$ is the $n(t)$-th MLP predictor output for the m-th training utterance of class w at the k-th iteration. At the k-th iteration, the weight correction by BP is accomplished along the optimal trajectory $\{n^*(t)\}$, where the desired output $\mathbf{a}_t(m)$ is assigned to the actual output $\hat{\mathbf{a}}_t(w, n^*(t), m, k)$ for the $n^*(t)$-th MLP predictor. The resultant score along the same trajectory, $\bar{D}_{k,BP}(w)$, is decreased, because BP works as the gradient descent method for the score $\bar{D}_k(w)$:

$$\bar{D}_{k,BP}(w) \leq \bar{D}_k(w). \qquad (12)$$

After the weight correction by BP, the trajectory optimality is lost. Thus, the DP at $k+1$-th iteration finds an optimal trajectory giving the minimum score for the corrected weights, $\bar{D}_{k+1}(w)$.

$$\bar{D}_{k+1}(w) \leq \bar{D}_{k,BP}(w). \qquad (13)$$

Combining Eqs.(12) and (13), a decreasing relation is obtained between successive scores for the iterations.

$$\bar{D}_{k+1}(w) \leq \bar{D}_k(w). \qquad (14)$$

This relation insures the proposed training algorithm convergence.

Using the concatenation of word models, the training algorithm presented above can be easily extended for continuous speech, where an accumulated prediction residual is computed by DP between the concatenation of word models and a training utterance. Weight correction by BP is carried out along the optimal trajectory that gives the word boundaries and the segment boundaries in a word.

3. EXPERIMENTS

3.1. Speech Data and Model Configuration

In order to examine the validity of the proposed model, speaker-independent isolated Japanese digit word recognition experiments were carried out, using data uttered by 107 speakers (62 male speakers and 45 female speakers). Each speaker uttered each vocabulary word once via a telephone, where the telephone output was directly connected with the AD converter. The utterances were sampled at an 8.0kHz sampling rate, and analyzed by a 16 msec frame period. As a feature vector for each time frame, 10 mel-scaled cepstral parameters (excluding 0-th order) and a changing ratio parameter for amplitude were calculated from FFT based spectrum with 0.3-3.4kHz band limitation. The samples were divided into two sets. 50 speakers' samples were used for training, and 57 speakers' samples were used for recognition test.

The NPM, composed of N_w MLP predictors, was prepared for each vocabulary word w (Table 1). The N_w value was determined as half the average training sample durations (in frames). Every MLP predictor has 9 hidden units and 11 output units, corresponding to the feature vector dimensions. The number of input speech feature vectors, denoted by τ in Figure 1, is 2. Thus, the input layer for the MLP predictor receives 11×2 inputs.

Table 1: Number of MLP predictors N_w for each vocabulary word w

w	1	2	3	4	5	6	7	8	9	0
N_w	12	9	12	10	9	13	12	14	10	11

All MLP weights are randomly initialized before training. During the first 100 iterations in the training, the adjustment window constraint is applied to the DP computation. It restricts the region, where the trajectories can go through in the DP plane (see Figure 3). This can be used to avoid too excessive temporal normalization in the initial stage of the training process, starting from randomly initialized models.

3.2. Training Data Amount Evaluation

Table 2 shows performances for the models trained by different amounts of training data. One was trained by 50 speakers' utterances (Case A). Another was trained by 10 speakers' utterances (Case B). As a result, only 0.2 % performance degradation was observed for Case B, trained by 20 % amount of training data for Case A.

Table 2: Recognition error rate vs. training data amount M_w

	Training data amount, M_w	Recognition error rate (%)
A	50	0.2
B	10	0.4

In Figure 4, recognition error rates for Case A are plotted for the number of iterations through the training set. The dashed line at 100 iterations indicates the point where the adjustment window constraint was released.

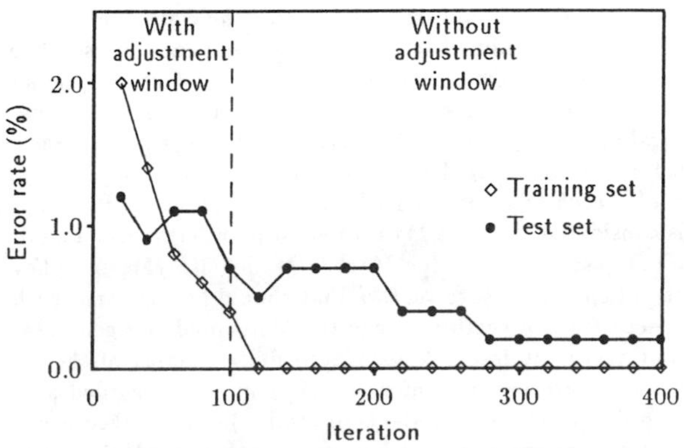

Figure 4: Recognition error rate vs. training iterations

3.3. Comparison with Linear Prediction

In the proposed model, MLPs were used as predictors, because it was considered that temporal correlation in speech patterns was quite complex and that MLPs have the capability to approximate complex nonlinear mappings between input and output vector spaces. However, the necessity for nonlinearity in the prediction mapping should be experimentally investigated. The proposed recognition and training algorithms are exactly applicable to models using linear predictors, instead of nonlinear predictors. Therefore, an experimental comparison between their performances was carried out. Table 3 shows the results, where 50 speakers' utterances were used for training. By combining the results with the results indicated in Table 2, it is shown that MLP predictors work better than linear predictors, even under the limited training data condition. This confirms the necessity for nonlinearity in prediction mapping.

Table 3: Recognition error rate vs. predictor category

Predictor category	Recognition error rate (%)
Nonlinear(MLP)	0.2
Linear	0.9

3.4. Comparison with Other Methods

Experiments with other methods, using the same training and test data set, were carried out for a comparison. One is the conventional DP matching, where the multiple template technique was used. Another is the Dynamic Programming Neural Networks (DNN), which uses MLPs as discriminators [4]. Table 4 shows the results, which suggest the advantages of the proposed model.

Table 4: Comparison with other methods

Method	Recognition error rate (%)
DP	1.1
DNN	0.7
NPM	0.2

3.5. Discussion

The proposed model is constructed as a set of separate predictors for each class, which has been trained without using training data from other classes. Thus, the model does not learn the discrimination between classes like MLP discriminators, but it learns temporal correlation in speech patterns for the class. The model independence is considered to be important in practical use. The experimental results are encouraging, due to the fact that higher performances were obtained in comparison with the discriminative neural networks (DNN). Furthermore, the high performance, observed under the limited training data condition, suggests the validity of speech modeling, based on prediction by MLPs.

It is considered that the MLP predictors in NPM play a similar role to the states in Hidden Markov Model (HMM) [12]. They both output speech feature vectors that should be compared with input speech feature vectors. Since the MLP predictor generates its output vector at frame t, using the finite number of the input speech feature vectors before t, NPM may be regarded as a multiple-order Markovian model (not hidden). Hence, theoretical and experimental comparisons between NPM and HMM will be interesting.

4. CONCLUSION

This paper presents a new speech recognition model, Neural Prediction Model (NPM), which uses Multilayer Perceptrons (MLP) as pattern predictors instead of pattern discriminators. In the model, reference patterns to be compared with input speech are generated through the prediction by MLPs. The authors proposed optimal recognition and training algorithms, based on dynamic-programming and back-propagation techniques. Speaker-independent Japanese isolated digit word recognition experiments were conducted. In comparison with conventional methods, higher recognition accuracy (99.8 %) was obtained. Furthermore, it was confirmed that the proposed model works fairly well under the limited training-data condition.

ACKNOWLEDGEMENTS

The authors wish to thank Prof. Hiroaki Sakoe for his valuable discussions and suggestions. They also thank members of the Media Technology Research Laboratory for their continuous support.

REFERENCES

[1] R.P.Lippmann, "An Introduction to Computing with Neural Nets," *IEEE ASSP Magazine*, **3**, pp.4-22, 1987.

[2] K.Funahashi, "On the Approximate Realization of Continuous Mappings by Neural Networks," *Neural Networks*, **2**, pp.183-192, 1989.

[3] A.Waibel, T.Hanazawa, G.Hinton, K.Shikano and K.Lang, "Phoneme Recognition Using Time-Delay Neural Networks," *Proc. ICASSP-88*, pp.107-110, New York, 1988.

[4] H.Sakoe, R.Isotani, K.Yoshida, K.Iso and T.Watanabe, "Speaker-Independent Word Recognition Using Dynamic Programming Neural Networks," *Proc. ICASSP-89*, pp.29-32, Glasgow, 1989.

[5] H.Bourlard and C.J.Wellekens, "Speech Pattern Discrimination and Multilayer Perceptrons," *Computer Speech and Language*, **3**, pp.1-19, 1989.

[6] H.Bourlard and C.J.Wellekens, "Speech Dynamics and Recurrent Neural Networks," *Proc. ICASSP-89*, pp.33-36, Glasgow, 1989.

[7] A.Waibel, H.Sawai and K.Shikano, "Consonant Recognition by Modular Construction of Large Phonemic Time-Delay Neural Networks," *Proc. ICASSP-89*, pp.112-115, Glasgow, 1989.

[8] H.Sawai, A.Waibel, M.Miyatake and K.Shikano, "Spotting Japanese CV-Syllables and Phonemes Using Time-Delay Neural Networks," *Proc. ICASSP-89*, pp.25-28, Glasgow, 1989.

[9] M.A.Franzini, M.J.Witbrock and Kai-Fu Lee, "A Connectionist Approach to Continuous Speech Recognition," *Proc. ICASSP-89*, pp.425-428, Glasgow, 1989.

[10] J.Bridle, M.Brown and R.Chamberlain, "An Algorithm for Connected Word Recognition," *Proc. ICASSP-82*, pp.899-902, 1982.

[11] T.Watanabe, "Combined Learning of Neural Network and Time Axis Normalization for Speech Recognition," in *Conference of the Acoustical Society of Japan*, pp.283-284, March 1989.(in Japanese).

[12] S.E.Levinson, "Structural Methods in Automatic Speech Recognition," *Proc. IEEE*, **73**, no.11, pp.1625-1650, 1985.

Chapter 8

Language Processing for Speech Recognition

Introduction

In the previous chapters, we have concentrated on the problems of acoustic representation and modeling, which are the usual foci of speech-recognition research. However, acoustic-modeling research alone will not reach human-like performance for large-vocabulary tasks. The reason is that humans make use of many nonacoustic sources of information, including syntax, semantics, pragmatics, dialogue, and knowledge of the speaker. These sources of information are collectively termed language processing, and modeling of these sources is *language modeling*. This chapter is concerned with language models for speech recognition and understanding.

One approach of language modeling is the statistical approach. Here, the goal is to estimate $P(\underline{W})$, or the probability of any word sequence. Once determined, this probability can be combined with the acoustic probability, $P(\underline{Y} \mid \underline{W})$, to determine most likely sentence given acoustics, or $P(\underline{W} \mid \underline{Y})$[1], using Bayes rule.

Estimating $P(\underline{W})$ for all sentences is clearly impossible. But if we make the assumption that the probability of each word depends only on the previous N words, and that the probability of different words are independent, it becomes possible to estimate parameters, for small Ns (typically 1 or 2). This type of N-gram modeling is described in the first paper, *Self-Organized Language Modeling for Speech Recognition* by Fred Jelinek. This paper covers the mathematical basis of N-gram models, techniques for smoothing the sparse distributions, as well as an alternative technique for automatically discovering word categories. Although the paper is dated 1990, the work described has been ongoing since 1970s at IBM. This paper provides the technical information of the very successful *trigram* language model used in IBM's TANGORA System (see Paper 9.3).

One might argue that to predict the next word, more context than the two previous words is needed. However, the N-gram models requires V^N parameters, which becomes too large very quickly. In order to overcome this problem, Bahl, et al., proposed a different approach in *A Tree-Based Statistical Language Model for Natural Language Speech Recognition*, using decision trees to selectively ask questions about the previous 20 words to determine the probabilities of the next word. This approach requires a very time-consuming tree-building process, but results in a more powerful language model than trigrams.

These two statistical approaches are powerful in perplexity[2] reduction, which makes them very useful for tasks like *dictation*, where the goal is to transcribe the words spoken. However, they do not directly contribute to speech *understanding*. In

1. The goal of most speech recognizers is to find $\underline{W}$ for which $P(\underline{W} \mid \underline{Y})$ is maximized.

2. Roughly the average number of words that can occur at any decision point, see the paper in this chapter by Jelinek for a precise definition.

order to achieve speech understanding, models of syntax, semantics, pragmatics, and beyond, must be generated. To date, most research has focused on syntax and semantics, which are more tangible than other knowledge sources.

A syntactic model typically defines a set of (possibly infinite) sentences that are acceptable. Only these sentences will be accepted by the recognizer; any uttered sentence will be recognized as one of the acceptable sentences (ideally the one that provides the best acoustic match). This set of acceptable sentences can be specified in terms of a finite-state grammar [Lowerre 80], a context-free grammar [Ney 87], or a unification grammar [Hemphill 89]. The selected grammar is then integrated into the recognizer so that only legal sequences and partial sequences are hypothesized and evaluated.

Finite-state grammars are a class of Markov models, and can be easily and efficiently implemented in either HMM or DTW-based recognition systems. The other grammars require considerable recursion, and many more hypotheses must be generated. The major problem with these grammars is efficiency. The next two papers in this chapter present different efficient algorithms. Paeseler's *Modification of Earley's Algorithm for Speech Understanding*, describes one efficient implementation of a recognizer based on context-free grammar. Paeseler's work extended Early's chart-parsing algorithm [Early 70] to speech recognition. Further, it was empirically shown that using beam-search pruning, the parsing time no longer increased exponentially with input length. Another approach that combines LR parsing with HMMs is reported by Kita [Kita 89]. Paper 9.6 in this volume describes a system based on this approach.

The previous attempts to integrate linguistic information into speech recognizers involved left-to-right parsing from a grammar. An alternative control strategy is used in the HWIM system, as described by Woods in *Language Processing for Speech Understanding*. Instead of a left-to-right grammar, HWIM used an *island-driven* strategy, which involves an initial scan of an utterance to find the most confident islands (of phonemes, words, or phrases), and then growing them until an entire sentence is hypothesized. The island-driven algorithm in HWIM uses an ATN grammars, which are similar to context-free grammars. An important attribute of ATN grammars is that common parts of the grammar are merged, thereby reducing the parse time required. HWIM integrated an ATN grammar with an island-driven searching using a novel *middle-out* algorithm. Island-driven search is attractive as a possible mechanism to better deal with random perturbations in ill-formed natural spontaneous speech. However, the detection of reliable islands in an utterance is an unsolved problem in itself. Consequently, present systems are dominated by left-to-right parsing systems, due to their greater efficiency and simplicity.

Prosodic Knowledge Sources for Word Hypothesization in a Continuous Speech Recognition System by Waibel summarizes the operation and application of several knowledge sources that were designed as modules to use prosodic cues explicitly to constrain word hypothesization for large-vocabulary continous-speech-recognition systems. Prosodic cues (pitch, loudness, rhythm, stress) are known to be critically important for human speech perception. By contrast, current speech-recognition systems generally rely on phonetic cues and ignore or eliminate prosodic parameters during processing. The paper demonstrates that prosodic cues alone can identify characteristic properties of words and help significantly in preselecting, constraining or identifying legal word hypotheses in continuous speech. Moreover, other work [Lea 80] has also shown that prosody could also constrain syntactic hypotheses or lead to anchor points for an island-driven search strategy. Although prosody is also known to correlate with the pragmatic and semantic intent of an utterance and the emotional state of the speaker, no attempt has yet been made to incorporate this information in speech-understanding systems.

Semantics, or the meaning a sentence, is very difficult to embed in a recognizer. In fact, there is no general agreement on the very definition of "meaning." Certainly, some semantic information is contained in some syntactic parsers, as well as in statistical-language models. However, most speech recognizers determine the meaning of an input using some simple mechanisms that are not generalizable. One exception is the paper, *High Level Knowledge Sources in Usable Speech Recognition Systems* by Young, et al. This paper describes the MINDS System, which integrates higher level knowledge predictively by compiling a different grammar for each sentence (rather than using the same grammar for all sentences). Knowledge used includes semantics, pragmatics, dialogue information, and user modeling. Since predictions may fail, a fail-soft mechanism, *layered predictions*, is used so that when a tight prediction fails, the constraints can be relaxed. This work shows that for a given domain, the use of higher-level knowledge sources can reduce the error rate of a system by an order of magnitude. It remains to be shown that the intensive task-dependent tuning can be automated.

References

[Early 70] Early, J. An Efficient Context-Free Parsing Algorithm. In *CACM,* pp 94–102. February, 1970.

[Hemphill 89] Hemphill, C., Picone, J. Robust Speech Recognition in a Unification Grammar Framework. In *IEEE International Conference on Acoustics, Speech, and Signal Processing.* May, 1989.

[Kita 89] Kita, K., Kawabata, T., Saito, H. HMM Continuous Speech Recognition Using Predictive LR Parsing. In *IEEE International Conference on Acoustics, Speech, and Signal Processing.* May, 1989.

[Lea 80] Lea, W.A. Prosodic Aids to Speech Recognition. *Trends in Speech Recognition.* Speech Science Publications, Apple Valley, Minn. (1986).

[Lowerre 80] Lowerre, B.T., Reddy, D.R. The HARPY Speech Understanding System. *Trends in Speech Recognition.* Speech Science Publications, Apple Valley, Minn. (1980).

[Ney 87] Ney, H. Dynamic Programming Speech Recognition Using a Context-Free Grammar. In *IEEE International Conference on Acoustics, Speech, and Signal Processing,* pp 3.2.1–3.2.4. IEEE ASSP, April, 1987.

SELF-ORGANIZED LANGUAGE MODELING FOR SPEECH RECOGNITION

by

F. Jelinek
Continuous Speech Recognition Group
IBM T.J.Watson Research Center
Yorktown Heights, N.Y. 10598

1. INTRODUCTION

The purpose of this article is to discuss intuitively the problems of language modeling for speech recognition, and to suggest some lines of possible solution related to self-organized statistical information extraction from large stored texts. The aim is to show to linguists the power of probabilistic approaches in order to elicit from them contributions they are specially capable of making. The paper concentrates on the simplest schemes; it is not comprehensive. Mathematics is kept at a minimum in the main body. Its presentation is relegated to appendices that attempt to survey, on a fundamental level, some of the methods that have been found useful in automatic language model derivation.

A speech recognizer is a device which automatically transcribes speech into text. It can be thought of as a voice actuated "typewriter" in which the transcription is carried out by a computer program and the transcribed text appears on a workstation display. The recognizer is usually based on some finite vocabulary that restricts the words that can be "printed" out. For the purposes of this article, the designation *word* denotes a *word form* defined by its spelling. Two differently spelled inflections or derivations of the same stem are considered different words.. Homographs having different parts of speech or meanings constitute the same word.

A language model assigns a probability value to every string of words $w_1, w_2, \ldots w_n$ taken from the prescribed vocabulary. In speech recognition, this value is interpreted as the a priori probability that the speaker will say that string. These probabilities guide the search of the recognizer among various (partial) text hypotheses and are a contributing factor in determining the final transcription. More precisely, the recognizer operates as follows. Let

$$W = w_1, w_2, \ldots w_n \tag{1}$$

denote a string of n words, and let A denote the acoustic evidence (data) on the basis of which the recognizer will make its final decision about which words were spoken: If $P(W|A)$ denotes the probability that the words W were spoken, given that the evidence A was observed,[1] then the recognizer should decide in favor of a word string $\hat{W}$ satisfying

$$P(\hat{W}|A) = \max_{W} P(W|A) \tag{2}$$

That is, the recognizer will pick the most likely word string given the observed acoustic evidence.

The well known Bayes' formula allows us to re-write the right hand side probability of (2) as

$$P(W|A) = \frac{P(W)\, P(A \mid W)}{P(A)} \tag{3}$$

where $P(W)$ is the probability that the word string W will be uttered, $P(A \mid W)$ is the probability that when the speaker says W the acoustic evidence A will be observed, and $P(A)$ is the average probability that A will be observed. That is,

$$P(A) = \sum_{W} P(W')\, P(A \mid W') \tag{4}$$

Since the maximization in (2) is carried out with the variable A fixed, it follows from (2) and (3) that the aim of the recognizer is to find the word string $\hat{W}$ that maximizes the product $P(W)\, P(A \mid W)$, i.e. satisfies

$$P(\hat{W})\, P(A \mid \hat{W}) = \max_{W} P(W)\, P(A \mid W) \tag{5}$$

The a priori probabilities $P(W)$ whose values are given by the language model are thus central to the speech recognition process.

[1] Throughout this paper the vertical bar | will denote conditioning. Thus, for instance, $P(A \mid B)$ is the probability of the event A conditioned on the occurrence of the event B.

This article is not concerned with the development of an acoustic model that would provide the probabilities $P(A \mid W)$. The next section describes in some detail what a statistical language model is. Section 3 shows one of the simple language models used in IBM recognizers, and introduces a measure of language model quality (a fuller discussion of the measure, called perplexity, can be found in Appendix A). Sections 4 and 5 are devoted to problems of language model construction from word n -grams extracted from relatively sparse text data bases. Section 6 concerns attempts to incorporate into the language model information contained in longer segments of preceding text. In Section 7 we face the problem of selecting the recognizer's vocabulary and tailoring it to particular users. Finally, Section 8 discusses the construction of language models that adjust to changes of the vocabulary or the discourse domain.

The mathematical appendices of this paper are organized as follows. Based on results of Information Theory, Appendix A provides a statistical measure of language model quality called perplexity, and describes the Shannon Game that can be used to estimate the intrinsic difficulty of texts. Appendix B introduces the Hidden Markov Chain concept that is useful in the formulation and optimization of language models. Appendix C applies the concepts to language modeling. It describes automatic part of speech annotation of texts and discovery of statistically significant word classes. In Appendix D the same discovery is accomplished on the basis of concepts of Information Theory. Appendix E outlines a special method of combining frequencies of word n -grams to obtain estimates of corresponding probabilities. Finally, Appendix F deals with a possible approach to prediction of lexical content of words from relatively long preceding text.

2. PRACTICAL ASPECTS OF LANGUAGE MODELING

It is obviously desirable that words be displayed by a speech recognizer soon after they are spoken. Even though some later changes are permissible as context develops, the bulk of the text should be correct and stay fixed from the time of its first appearance on the display screen. Thus intermediate decision criteria must be developed in addition to and in harmony with the final decision criterion (5). A sentence by sentence approach (involving too much delay in any case) might at first glance allow the language model to consist of a conventional parser. The latter would assign $P(W) = 0$ to all ungrammatical sentences W. But what probability should be given to the remaining grammatical sentences? Unmodified parsers can at best serve as final filters accepting or rejecting word strings that were arrived at with the help of a more appropriate language model. Moreover, since speakers' performance varies, a recognizer that would reject ungrammatical sequences out of hand may turn out to be unacceptable. Nevertheless, we will see below that language models can be based on grammar, if it is used in a way facilitating practical estimation of probabilities of word strings.

Using elementary rules of probability theory, the language model's probability $P(W)$ can be formally decomposed as

$$P(W) = \prod_{i=1}^{n} P(w_i \mid w_1,...,w_{i-1}) \tag{6}$$

where $P(w_i \mid w_1,...w_{i-1})$ is the probability that w_i will be spoken given that words $w_1,...w_{i-1}$ were said previously. Formula (6) simply states that the probability of uttering a word string W is given by the probability of uttering the first word, times the probability of uttering the second word given that the first word was uttered, etc., times the probability of uttering the last word of the string given that all of the previous ones were uttered. Hence in general, the choice of w_i is modeled to depend on the entire past history of the dictation.

The sequential decomposition (6) is an appropriate one for speech recognition because it leads to the development of natural intermediate decision criteria allowing a minimal delay in the response of the recognizer to the progressing dictation. In reality, of course, the probabilities $P(w_i \mid w_1,...,w_{i-1})$ would be impossible to estimate for even moderate values of i, since most histories $w_1,...,w_{i-1}$ would be unique or would have occurred only a very few times. Indeed, for a vocabulary of size L there are L^{i-1} different histories, and so to specify $P(w_i \mid w_1,...,w_{i-1})$ completely, L^i values would have to be estimated. This is an astronomically large number for practical values of L (for L =5000 and i =3, L^i is equal to 125 billion!), and thus the probabilities $P(w_i \mid w_1,...,w_{i-1})$ could neither be stored nor retrieved when needed by the recognizer.

It follows that the various possible conditioning histories $w_1,...,w_{i-1}$ must be distinguished as belonging to some manageable number M of different equivalence classes. Indeed, from a linguistic point of view, it is intuitively obvious that thinking of many of the histories as equivalent will not appreciably weaken the ability to predict the next word w_i. In fact, for practical vocabulary sizes and i>3, most of the N^i word strings $w_1,...,w_i$ will never occur in English.

Let S be a (many to one) mapping of histories into some (perhaps large) number of equivalence classes. If $S[w_1,...,w_{i-1}]$ denotes the equivalence class of the string $w_1,...,w_{i-1}$, then the probability $P(W)$ may be approximated by

$$P(W) = \prod_{i=1}^{n} P(w_i \mid S[w_1,...,w_{i-1}]) \tag{7}$$

One way the classifier S might function is on the basis of a finite state grammar. At time $i - 1$, the grammar is in state S_{i-1}, and the next word forces a change to state S_i. Then (7) can be re-written as

$$P(W) = \prod_{i=1}^{n} P(w_i \mid S_{i-1}) \tag{8}$$

For this relatively simple situation, how can the probabilities $P(w_i \mid S_{i-1})$ be estimated for dictation of office correspondence? One could acquire some large corpus of office text, run its word sequences through the finite state grammar, and accumulate counts $C(w, J)$ of the number of times the word w was fed to the grammar immediately after the grammar was in state J. If $C(J)$ denotes the number of times the grammar reached state J,

$$C(J) = \sum_{w} C(w, J) \tag{9}$$

the first order estimate of the desired probability would be

$$P(w_i \mid S_i = J) = C(w_i, J)/C(J) \tag{10}$$

There is no requirement that the histories be classified deterministically (unambiguously): a statistical distribution over the possible class values would be entirely adequate. In that case, the probability of uttering w_i would be computed as the probability that w_i was uttered given the classification of the past history, averaged over all the possible classifications of that history, i.e., the terms in the product of (7) would be replaced by their averages

$$\left\{ \sum_{J=1}^{M} P(w_i \mid S_{i-1} = J) P(S[w_1,\ldots,w_{i-1}] = J) \right\} \tag{11}$$

The classification may be carried out by a context free or any other available parser. The averaging formula (11) allows for possible parsing ambiguities that will be produced by even the best parsers arising when the history does not end on a sentence boundary (i.e. when w_{i-1} is not a sentence terminal symbol). Intuitively, a grammatical classification of a history $w_1,\ldots,w_{i-1}$ may be something like

> " w_{i-1} was ' *the* '; it is a part of a VP with head
> ' *blows* '; the previous phrase was an NP with head
> ' *exhaust* '. "

The selected classification scheme S will of necessity be a compromise between two requirements: (a) The classification must be sufficiently refined to provide adequate information about the history so it can serve as a basis for prediction. (b) When applied to histories of the given training corpus, it must yield its M possible classes frequently enough so that the probabilities $P(w \mid S = J)$ can be reliably estimated (not necessarily by the crude relative frequency approach (10)).

The purpose of a language model for speech recognition is not an exact analysis for meaning extraction, but an apportionment of probability among alternative futures. This provides an opportunity for creative use of appropriate grammatical principles that are on the whole accurate, even if open to counter-examples.

3. THE INTERPOLATED LANGUAGE MODEL AND ITS QUALITY

The language model of the current speech recognizer of the IBM Yorktown research group is based on a very simple equivalence classification: histories are equivalent if they end in the same two words. Thus

$$P(W) = \prod_{i=1}^{n} P(w_i \mid w_{i-2}, w_{i-1}) \tag{12}$$

Originally we tried to estimate the basic trigram probabilities by the simple relative frequency approach

$$P(w_3 \mid w_1, w_2) = f(w_3 \mid w_1, w_2) = \frac{C(w_1, w_2, w_3)}{C(w_1, w_2)} \tag{13}$$

where the function C counts the number of strings in its argument. We found early on that (13) was an inadequate formula, since many possible English word trigrams w_1, w_2, w_3 never actually take place even in very large corpora of training text. A language model based on (13) would assert the impossibility of such trigrams, assign $P(W) = 0$ to strings W containing them, and would thus force a large number of word errors in a recognizer operating under the statistical decision criterion

$$P(\hat{W})P(A \mid \hat{W}) = \max_{W} P(W)P(A \mid W) \tag{5}$$

In fact, when we divided a corpus of patent descriptions into test and training subsets (of size 300,000 and 1,500,000 words, respectively), we found that 23% of the trigrams appearing in the test subset never took place in the training subset! It is therefore necessary to "smooth" the trigram frequencies. This can be done most simply by interpolating trigram, bigram, and unigram relative frequencies,

$$P(w_3 \mid w_1, w_2) = q_3 f(w_3 \mid w_1, w_2) + q_2 f(w_3 \mid w_2) + q_1 f(w_3) \tag{14}$$

where the nonnegative weights satisfy $q_1 + q_2 + q_3 = 1$. Since $f(w_3 \mid w_1, w_2)$ approximates $P(w_3 \mid w_1, w_2)$ better if it is based on a larger count $C(w_1, w_2)$, the weights are chosen to depend on the conditioning counts $C(w_1, w_2)$ and $C(w_2)$. Given these restrictions, the values q_i are chosen to satisfy the maximum-likelihood criterion[2] and are in that sense optimal.

An intuitive feeling for the quality of the language model (14) may be gleaned from Figure 1. The language model is used to predict in their order the words of the sentence *We need to resolve all the important issues within the next two days*. The figure displays all the words that are predicted to be more likely than the actual word, given the language model's perfect knowledge of the past (at the beginning of the sentence nothing but the fact that it begins is known). Thus, knowing the two preceding words *all,the* the language model estimates that the most likely next word is *necessary*, and that the words *data* ,..., *shop* are all more likely than the actual word *important* which is estimated as the 641-th likeliest, given that particular past. We can observe that the language model (14) is quite good at predicting most function words (e.g.,' *we* ', ' ', ' *the* ', ' *next* ', etc.), but that it is uncertain about some content words (e.g., ' *resolve* ' and ' *important* ') just as human beings might be (no claim is made here that they wouldn't do better; just that they too might have trouble).

Of course, one example proves nothing. We would like to have an objective measure of language model quality. It should be based on results from Information Theory which concerns itself with sources of information. In simplest terms, a source is a device which puts out symbols chosen from some finite set V that is known to the user. Underlying the source operations is a statistical law which governs the choice of output symbols. When putting out a symbol, a source provides information by removing the user's uncertainty about the identity of that symbol. Thus the source contains more information if its outputs are more uncertain.

---

[2] That is, the weights are adjusted so that the probability $P(W)$ of some "typical" large new text W is maximal when formula (14) is substituted into (12). Appendix C contains additional discussion of the maximum likelihood approach.

Language can be thought of as an information source whose outputs are words w_i. Let $w_1, w_2, \ldots, w_n$ denote the words of some text to be recognized, and let $\hat{P}(w_1, w_2, \ldots, w_n)$ be the estimate of the probability of the text provided by the language model. Then it can be argued (see Appendix A) that the "perplexity"

$$PP = \hat{P}(w_1, w_2, \ldots, w_n)^{(-1/n)} \tag{15}$$

is the correctly computed average size of the set of words between which the recognizer must decide when transcribing a word of the spoken text. Thus the text perplexity PP measures the recognition difficulty of the text relative to the given language model. Note that for a given vocabulary V, (15) is maximized if the words of the text are chosen independently of each other with uniform probability, i.e., if

$$\hat{P}(w_1, w_2, \ldots, w_n) = L^{-n} \tag{16}$$

in which case $PP = L$.

All other things being equal, we therefore seek a language model with the least perplexity.

4. PROBLEMS WITH TRIGRAM MODEL PROBABILITY ESTIMATION

The interpolation formula

$$P(w_3 \mid w_1, w_2) = q_3 f(w_3 \mid w_1, w_2) + q_2 f(w_3 \mid w_2) + q_1 f(w_3) \tag{14}$$

which estimates $P(w_3 \mid w_1, w_2)$ has many problems. If the dictation contains a trigram w_1, w_2, w_3 which never took place in the training text, then w_3 must be estimated from bigrams and unigrams. If the training text didn't even contain w_2, w_3, then the language model (14) will fall back on the unigram relative frequency $f(w_3)$. The difficulty is that $f(w_3)$ puts most weight on the most frequent words in the vocabulary, such as ' *the* ', ' *a* ', etc. But since there must be a good linguistic reason why the sequence w_2, ' *the* ' never occurred in training, then the language model should actually assign a lower probability to the sequence w_2, ' *the* ' than to sequences w_2, w_3 where w_3 is some low frequency word (of course, this argument applies to all high frequency words w_3, not just to ' *the* ')!

Thus formula (14) should be improved. w_1, w_2. One possibility is smoothing on the basis of parts of speech (POS). Let $g(w_i) = g_i$ denote the classification of the word

w_i reflecting its part-of-speech use in the text (for many words the classifications depend on context, e.g. *'light'* can be a noun, verb, adjective, or adverb). Then the interpolation

$$P(w_3 \mid w_1, w_2) =$$

$$q_3 f(w_3 \mid w_1, w_2) + q_2 f(w_3 \mid g(w_1), w_2) + q_1 f(w_3 / g(w_1) g(w_2)) + q_0 f(w_3) \quad (17)$$

is possible. Formula (17) involves tracking of the POS functions of the words w_i in the recognized text and therefore it complicates the language modeling task. Tracking can be accomplished by a purely statistical approach (see the concluding paragraph of Appendix C) so that no conventional grammatical analysis is needed. We have based our POS classification on that used by the 1972 Harvard Predictive Analyzer. We obtained 29 parts of speech, and added 11 additional ones related to semantics, such as DATE, NUMBER, NAME, COMPANY, etc. Use of formula (17) resulted in a 5 % decrease in the perplexity. Since we did not deem this improvement adequate to justify the additional language model complexity, we are not using (17) in our recognizer.

Another possibility is to predict the word w_3 in two steps: first a class and then a choice from the class. For example, if w_1, w_2 was never followed in the training text by a determiner, then any particular determiner should be predicted only with a small probability. Using a POS classification, the estimate in question would be based on the formula

$$\sum_{g_3} k(w_3 \mid g_3)\ h(g_3 \mid g(w_1),\ g(w_2)) \quad (18)$$

which could be added as a fourth interpolation component to (14) or as a fifth one to (17). Note that if the weights q_i are chosen optimally (as we are doing) then adding a component can never make the language model worse. If a component is worthless compared to the other ones, then it will simply get a very low weight q.

The probabilities k and h used in (18) can be estimated automatically by a statistical procedure described in Appendix C. In particular, k can be derived by annotating (again automatically, see Appendix C) the words in the training text by their parts of speech g and then computing the relative frequency of word w occurring in text positions annotated by g. By this method we can directly obtain the relative frequencies $k(w_3 \mid g_3, w_2)$ and $k(w_3 \mid g_3, w_1, w_2)$ which are related to $f(w_3 \mid w_2)$ and $f(w_3 \mid w_1, w_2)$ as $k(w_3 \mid g_3)$ is to $f(w_3)$. In that case (18) can be refined to yield

$$\sum_{g_3} k^*(w_3 \mid g_3, w_1, w_2)\ h(g_3 \mid g(w_1),\ g(w_2)) \quad (19a)$$

where

$$k^{*}(w_3 \mid g_3, w_1, w_2) = r_3\, k(w_3 \mid g_3, w_1, w_2) + r_2\, k(w_3 \mid g_3, w_2) + r_1\, k(w_3 \mid g_3) \qquad (19b)$$

and r_i are weights adding to 1.

Both approaches (18) and (19) yield language model improvements, but suffer from the fact that the POS classification is too crude and not necessarily suited to language modeling. The parts of speech used by us have only one verb category (i.e. do not distinguish between transitive, intransitive, or any other verbs) and nouns are divided only into plurals and singulars. It might be useful to further split small but frequent categories such as prepositions: ' *in* 'and ' *on* ' might turn out to predict different noun phrases as their objects. In any case, the approach using conventional parts of speech leads to classes of grossly unequal frequency and yields an equivalence classification S that is a bad compromise between requirements (a) and (b) of the last paragraph of Section 2.

In Appendices C and D we show two methods of deriving automatically a prescribed number M of *nuclear* parts of speech (NPOS) which provide a more suitable equivalence classification than the natural ones. The first method (which gives rise to the term *nuclear*) starts out by taking the M most frequent words of the vocabulary and assigning them to different NPOS classes. Each of the remaining $L - M$ non-nuclear words are originally allowed to belong to any of the M classes. Through a self-organized "clustering" process the words gradually shed most of their class memberships, until all words take on a maximum of about 4 NPOS classes each. Most words actually end up falling into the class of that nuclear word to which they are most similar in their semantic/syntactic behavior. The clustering process is based directly on the formula

$$\sum_{g_3} k(w_3 \mid g_3)\, h(g_3 \mid g(w_1), g(w_2)) \qquad (18)$$

i.e. on the language model component that will make use of the resulting NPOS classification. The NPOS approach when applied to the predictor (19) yields a 15% improvement in language model perplexity (Peter deSouza carried out this particular experiment based on classes that he derived by the method of Appendix D), and we do plan to incorporate it into the next generation recognizer.

5. CONCLUDING REMARKS ON N-GRAM MODELING

The problems discussed in the previous section are related to the estimation of $P(w_3 \mid w_1 w_2)$ based on "smoothing" of the relative frequencies $f(w_3 \mid w_1, w_2)$ to compensate for the sparseness of data on which they are based. A direct way to achieve an improvement in language model quality is to derive it from a much larger training text. But this approach leads to further questions:

A. Where would one get a sufficiently large corpus (e.g. 1 billion words)?

B. If the matrix $f(w_3 \mid w_1, w_2)$ were not sparse, how would one store and retrieve the information?

C. The resulting language model would still be bound to the area of discourse from which it was extracted. How about language models for other areas?

D. If a resulting trigram model turned out to be a good one, why not use an n-gram model with $n > 3$? For the language model to incorporate extraction of information which humans accomplish very simply, doesn't n have to be extremely large?

The above considerations show that the smoothing and equivalence classification problem remains an important one regardless of the size of the training corpus.

There are other ways than formula (14) to use bigrams and unigrams to smooth out trigram estimates. One, outlined in Appendix E is due to S. Katz <7> and is being used in the language model of the current IBM recognizer. It "backs off" from a trigram to a bigram to a unigram estimate, rather than interpolating the three. The idea is incorporated in the approximate formula

$$P(w_3 \mid w_1,w_2) = \begin{cases} s_3\, f(w_3 \mid w_1,w_2) & \text{if } C(w_1,w_2,w_3) > 0 \\ s_2\, f(w_3 \mid w_2) & \text{if } C(w_1,w_2,w_3) = 0 \\ & \text{and } C(w_2,w_3) > 0 \\ s_1\, f(w_3) & \text{otherwise} \end{cases} \tag{20}$$

where s_i are factors that depend on the counts C and assure that the probability P when summed over all words w_3 adds up to 1.

Another method of obtaining unigram probabilities, based on parametric empirical Bayes' estimation, was originated by A. Nadas <8>. This, as well as the two previous methods, results in comparable language model perplexity values.

The trigram model is, of course, too rigid. Since strings of different lengths are never put into the same equivalence class, advantage cannot be taken of the probably similar predictive power of phrases with the same heads (e.g. '*big machine*', '*light machine*', '*machine*'). At least some skipping of words would surely be in order. For instance, since determiners might have strong predictive qualities when they immediately precede the word w_i to be predicted, but weak ones when there is at least one word between them and w_i, then a better equivalence classification of the history $w_1,\ldots,w_{i-1}$ would probably be

$$P(w_i \mid w_1,\ldots,w_{i-1}) = \begin{cases} P(w_i \mid w_{i-3},w_{i-1}) & \text{if } w_{i-2} = \text{determiner} \\ P(w_i \mid w_{i-2},w_{i-1}) & \text{otherwise} \end{cases} \quad (21)$$

A word is a rather arbitrary building block for a language model. It can surely be argued that '*Puddleby on the Marsh*' or '*nuclear magnetic resonance*' should be basic elements of the vocabulary V, rather than composites taking up all three positions of the trigram (and more), and considerably weakening the coupling between the past and the future. An automatic way of deciding which phrases should be included in the vocabulary was suggested by R.L. Mercer. It is based on an iterative use of the concept of mutual information (see Appendix A) between adjacent words

$$J(w_1,w_2) = \log \frac{C(w_1,w_2)\, n}{C(w_1)\, C(w_2)} \quad (22)$$

In (22), C denotes the count function and n is the size of the training corpus over which the counts were collected.

Since a large value of $J(w_1,w_2)$ indicates that the words w_1 and w_2 occur as a sequence much more frequently than can be expected from pure chance (namely, that $n\, C(w_1,w_2) > C(w_1)\, C(w_2)$) , $J(w_1,w_2)$ can be used as a measure of desirability of including w_1,w_2 as a unit into the vocabulary. We therefore establish two thresholds, TJ and TC, and start out by augmenting the basic vocabulary V_0 by all phrases w_1,w_2 for which simultaneously

$$J(w_1,w_2) > TJ \quad \text{and} \quad C(w_1,w_2) > TC \quad (23)$$

In this way a new vocabulary V_1 is established. The second threshold is needed to make sure that the first comparison of (23) is reliably based on sufficient data.

The counts are next adjusted to reflect their new base vocabulary V_1. That is, for every new element $w^* = w_1,w_2$ of V_1 , the old counts $C(w_1)$ and $C(w_2)$ are decremented by $C(w_1,w_2)$. The process (23) then resumes with V_1 as its basis, leading to a new vocabulary V_2. The augmentation terminates when no new phrases over the current vocabulary can be found satisfying (23). It is obvious that, in principle, the final vocabulary may include phrases of unlimited length.

None of the suggested approaches are capable of relating to one another the various derivations or inflections of the same word stems. In the preceding statistical formulation, the designations w_i are abstract quantities. They simply identify the corresponding word as a particular member of the vocabulary list V. So ' *lead* ' is the same word, whether it refers to a heavy metal, a piece of wire, or the action of showing the way. We have not incorporated any mechanism capable of taking advantage of the connection between words such as ' *was* ' and ' *is* ', or ' *advice* ' and ' *advise* '. In fact, some inflections of words may belong to V, while others may be missing. Certain word relations may be established through the POS or NPOS approach, but it might be better to base a language model on stems and suffixes rather than on word forms.

As before, let w denote a word form, and let x denote a word stem and y a suffix. Then with & denoting the process of adding suffixes, we can say abstractly that $w = x \,\&\, y$. If $x(w)$ and $y(w)$ are the stem and suffix of the word w, a trigram stem language model can operate on the basis of the generation formula

$$P(w_i \mid w_{i-2},w_{i-1}) =$$

$$\sum_{g_i} k(w_i \mid x_i,g_i)\; h(g_i \mid g(w_{i-2}),g(w_{i-1}))\; t(x_i \mid x(w_{i-2}),x(w_{i-1})) \qquad (24)$$

where the word form conditioned probability $k(w_i \mid x_i,g_i)$ is derived from the joint probability

$$P(w_i,x_i,g_i) = f(w_i)\; P(g_i \mid y(w_i)) \quad \text{where} \quad w_i = x_i \,\&\, y(w_i) \qquad (25)$$

The probability $P(g_i \mid y(w_i))$, of course, reflects the co-ocurrence in the training text of the part of speech g_i with the suffix $y(w_i)$.

The stem language model (24) is based on the belief, manifested through the probability t, that stems predict stems. The trigram form of the model can be easily adapted to more general equivalence classifications.

Good arguments can obviously be made for many expedients, but they cannot all be evaluated. The difficult-to-realize aim of language modeling should be to set up a general model structure capable of self-organizing itself to an efficient (best is too much to hope for) solution on the basis of a training corpus.

6. INCORPORATING PAST INFORMATION INTO THE LANGUAGE MODEL

When predicting words from past text, human beings use information contained in words that considerably precede the last two. The introspections of players of the Shannon Game (It is described in Appendix A. In the game, humans predict unknown words from known past history.) confirm this conclusion. Players are very much aware of the topic, the general situation, the phrase structure, etc. They expect the rare words seen in the past to be repeated, they enforce tense and number agreement, and easily guess word suffixes. To come close to human performance (and it is not known what precise considerations account for it) the equivalence classes of histories would have to be based on sophisticated syntactic and semantic analysis. It will be difficult to make the correct choice that yields reliable statistics extractable from available training text.

As a first compromise intended to extract additional semantic information from the past, Eva Muckstein used her Controlled Partitioned Grammar parser to analyze text into phrases and extract their heads. Let $H^*_{i,1}$ and $H^*_{i,2}$ be the headwords of the two phrases immediately preceding the word w_{i-1}. Her language model operated on the basis of the probability

$$P(w_i \mid w_{i-1}, w_{i-2}, H^*_{i,1}, H^*_{i,2}) \qquad (26)$$

that was estimated from the parsed training corpus. Since the number of parameters in the argument of (26) is too large for direct relative frequency estimation, a sophisticated interpolation formula was used. The parser had at its disposal complete sentences of the training text, a situation not available during recognition. In that phase, the identity of the headwords was estimated statistically. As a result, for each word string recognition hypothesis $w_1, \ldots, w_i$ the decoder must carry several headword assignment hypotheses (Of course, thresholds were used to eliminate low probability hypotheses from further consideration. It was gratifying to observe that the most probable surviving headword assignment attached to the actually spoken sentence was invariably the correct one.).

The headword language model (26) reduced by 10% the perplexity of the recognition task that it was designed for (reading of laser patent descriptions). The main objection to its use was that the parser took several years to develop and was specific to the discourse domain and its vocabulary. We did not deem it worthwhile to transfer it to the current task. We are, however, developing a self-organized phrase parsing and headword extraction grammar, and we do plan to experiment with it.

A simple approach based on collocation may be used to extract semantic information from a more distant past. Let the vocabulary words be assigned to (possibly overlapping) lexical content categories, denoted by c. With g denoting, as before, a grammatical class, we can use the basic probability decomposition formula to write

$$P(w_i \mid w_1,\dots w_{i-1}) = \sum_{c_i,g_i} P(w_i,c_i,g_i \mid w_1,\dots w_{i-1})$$

$$= \sum_{c_i,g_i} k(w_i \mid c_i,g_i)\, h(g_i \mid w_1,\dots,w_{i-1})\, t(c_i \mid g_i,w_1,\dots,w_{i-1}) \tag{27}$$

The second equality in (27) is only an approximation, based on the intuitive notion that if the lexical and syntactic categories of w_i are known, then the history $w_1,\dots,w_{i-1}$ provides little additional information.

We have found experimentally that formula

$$\sum_{g_3} k(w_3 \mid g_3)\, h(g_3 \mid g(w_1),\ g(w_2)) \tag{18}$$

is an adequate basis for tracking the part of speech classification of words. In fact, let $G = g_1,g_2,\dots,g_n$ be some POS sequence. Then for a given text $W = w_1,w_2,\dots,w_n$,

$$P(W,G) = \prod_{i=1}^{n} k(w_i \mid g(w_i))\ \ h(g(w_i) \mid g(w_{i-2}), g(w_{i-2})) \tag{18'}$$

is the probability that the text W is generated and its words have the parts of speech G. It turns out that the assignment $\hat{G}$ which maximizes (18′) for a fixed text W (i.e., the most probable POS assignment) agrees to within 3% with the POS assignment that humans would give to the words of the same text (an algorithm finding the maximizing assignment $\hat{G}$ is discussed in Appendix C).

The above result indicates that the h probability in (27) may be sufficiently approximated by $h(g_i \mid g(w_{i-2}), g(w_{i-1}))$, so that we have the model

$$P(w_i \mid w_1,...w_{i-1}) =$$

$$= \sum_{c_i, g_i} \{k(w_i \mid c_i, g_i)\ h(g_i \mid g(w_{i-2}),\ g(w_{i-1}))\ t(c_i \mid g_i, w_1, ..., w_{i-1})\} \tag{28}$$

It then remains to simplify the probability t. Let $H^*_{i,j}$ denote the headword of the jth phrase preceding w_{i-1}, and let $c^*_{i,j} = c(H^*_{i,j})$ denote the lexical category of the headword $H^*_{i,j}$. Then we show in Appendix F that a reasonable approximation of the probability t is given by

$$t(c_i \mid g_i, w_1, ..., w_{i-1}) =$$

$$NORM\ \ P(c_i, g_i)\ \ P(w_{i-1} \mid c^*_{i,1}, c_i, g_i)\ [\ \prod_{j=1}^{m-1} P(c^*_{i,j} \mid c^*_{i,j+1}, c_i)\ ] \tag{29}$$

where NORM is a normalizing factor that assures that the right-hand side of (29) adds up to 1 when summed over all possible values of c_i (as a probability must) and m is the number of phrases preceding w_i. The number of factors m is chosen so that the product in (29) includes terms corresponding to headwords whose lexical category may be expected to influence the category c_i of the word being predicted. Note that the probabilities $P(c^*_{i,j} \mid c^*_{i,j+1}, c_i)$ represent the collocational influence of the headwords $H^*_{i,j}$ and $H^*_{i,j+1}$ on the word w_i.

To identify the headwords $H^*_{i,j}$, a parser is required that may work either on grammatical principles or on self-organizing statistical ones.

The remaining unsolved problem is the content categorization c. It is, of course, desirable to accomplish it in a self-organized manner. A possible approach aimed at making the grammatical and lexical classifications "orthogonal" is described in Appendix F.

It is obvious that lexical information contained in the past is incorporated only weakly in the model defined by (28) and (29). Furthermore, as stated at the start of this section, no information about agreement or word choice is provided. Many other important implications of histories about the future are also completely absent.

7. VOCABULARY SELECTION AND PERSONALIZATION FROM TEXT DATA BASES

Every speech recognizer is based upon a vocabulary V of finite size L whose words are the only ones that can appear in the transcribed text. As a consequence any attempt to recognize a word not belonging to V will result in an error. Such an error will force the language model into a bad state, increasing the probability of an error in the next word. Since the difficulty of constructing a language model and its complexity grow with the vocabulary size, it is desirable that the vocabulary be as small as possible. Therefore, it must be chosen carefully so that the expected coverage of the dictated text (the percentage of words in the running Text that belong to V) is maximized.

Since the IBM recognizer is intended for dictation of office correspondence, its 5000 word vocabulary is based on three collections of business memoranda and letters concerned with computer manufacture and usage. The first collection, OC1, has about 1 million words of text and is a mixture of letters from IBM customers from 6 different industry segments, and of IBM inter-office memoranda concerning administrative matters such as personnel, requests for financial support, scheduling of visits, etc. The second collection, OC2, is of size 1.5 million and consists of correspondence of the Communications Systems Division of IBM located in Sterling Forest, N.Y. Finally, the third is a collection of 22 million word 6-grams extracted (to preserve privacy) from memoranda and reports (administrative, technical, financial, etc) produced in the Data Systems Division (manufacturing) of IBM in Poughkeepsie, N.Y.

The vocabulary was determined by R. L. Mercer in two steps. First a basic subvocabulary of size M was constructed, consisting of words whose availability was thought necessary, such as recognizer control words, numbers (e.g. *'thousand'*, *'million'*, etc), dates (e.g. *'Monday'*, *'November'*, etc), and the first and last names of some of our colleagues at IBM Research. Then the remaining 5000 - M words were chosen to be those that have the highest maximal order in the vocabularies of our three data bases (OC1, OC2, and OC3) and do not belong to the subvocabulary. In fact, list the words of the data base vocabularies in accordance with their frequency of occurance, with the most frequent word in position 1, the next most frequent word in position 2, etc. Let $L_1(w)$, $L_2(w)$, and $L_3(w)$ be the positions of the word w in the vocabularies, sorted by frequency, of data bases OC1, OC2, and OC3 (the value of $L_i(w)$ is defined to be infinity for any word w that does not occur in the data base OC_i). Define the maximal order

$$L_m(w) = \max\{L_1(w), L_2(w), L_3(w)\} \tag{30}$$

and create a new list by arranging all words that are not in the basic sub-vocabulary according to the value of the maximal order L_m. Then the chosen vocabulary will consist of the basic sub-vocabulary plus the top 5000 - M words in the new list.

Basing the selection method on the maximal order (30) results in the omission from the vocabulary of words that have little universal use and are peculiar to a particular data base.

We are in possession of three additional business data bases. The first, PDB, consists of 2 million words of correspondence by a single colleague at the T.J. Watson Research Center. The second, MNG1, contains written memoranda from one of us, from the director of research, and from the chairman of the IBM Corporation. The third data base, MNG2, was created from transcribed spontaneous dictation of memoranda by four Research staff members. Our 5000 word vocabulary covered about 93% of words in each of the three text collections.

Our final three corpora have a more general character. The 30 million word data base APHB is a collection of books and articles originally intended for transcription to Braille. The 90 million word corpus DEP consists of legal depositions made in connection with the recent anti-trust suit brought by the Justice Department against IBM. Finally, we have available the CPC corpus consisting of 120 million words from the proceedings of the Canadian Parliament in Ottawa (we hold both English and French versions).

It is clearly desirable to cover more than 93% of the words in memos dictated to a recognizer. A greater coverage can be achieved by both increasing the vocabulary size and by personalizing the vocabulary to the users of the system. Inspection of the American Heritage Word Frequency Book <1> clearly indicates that simply increasing the vocabulary size will not be enough. In fact, quite familiar words such as '*admonition*' and '*deluded*' are not among the 86000 most frequent words. Furthermore, the Word Frequency Book does not even contain technical words particular to an individual user's field! On the other hand, there are only 19000 distinct words in the corpus OC1 that is made up of 1 million words, and H. Kucera observes that there are only 29000 distinct words in all of Shakespeare's works. Therefore, the problem of finding a moderate size vocabulary that is appropriate to a known user is not a hopeless one.

Using a slight modification of the vocabulary selection method described above, R. L. Mercer of IBM Research constructed vocabularies of varying sizes. Table 1 shows their coverage of the PDB corpus when names and acronyms occurring in it have been disregarded.

VOCABULARY SIZE	TEXT COVERAGE
5000	92.5%
10000	95.9%
15000	97.0%
20000	97.6%

TABLE 1

Our method of fixed vocabulary construction may be satisfactory if the intended user belongs to some easily identifiable category (e.g. an employee of the data processing industry) for which text data bases are available. Still, it is hardly acceptable that before making a purchase a customer would have to identify the recognizer's use so it could be equipped with an appropriate language model. The only way out seems to be either a more practical method of personalization or an extraordinarily large fixed vocabulary. To keep its complexity down, the corresponding language model would have to be based on a more economical set of building blocks (perhaps on stems or morphemes) from which word inflections and derivations could be constructed. Henry Kucera estimates that vocabulary compression by a factor of 6 to 10 may be attainable in this way.

A crude method of personalization is achieved by maintaining during dictation a dynamically varying vocabulary consisting at any given moment of the last L different words used. The coverage is then defined as the asymptotic probability that the word spoken next already belongs to the vocabulary. Table 2 gives the result for the PDB data base. The second column is the good news : 99% coverage is achieved by a 15 thousand word vocabulary. The third column is the bad: it takes 640 thousand words of text before a set of 15 thousand different words is assembled. This then is not a practical way of vocabulary personalization, except for the most prolific of writers. It may, however, result in a satisfactory vocabulary for an entire recognizer installation site, if it is extracted from a single pool of texts produced by all the resident users.

VOCABULARY SIZE	TEXT COVERAGE	TEXT SIZE NEEDED TO REACH COVERAGE
5000	95.5%	56000
10000	98.2%	240000
15000	99.0%	640000
20000	99.5%	1300000

TABLE 2

For direct personalization it would be desirable if a request for a low frequency word would automatically bring into the vocabulary other words that collocate with it. Perhaps a very large "dormant" vocabulary could be classified into overlapping sets of words, and the use of a certain number of such words belonging to the same set would trigger the activation of the rest of the set, with consequent deactivation of unused sets. At the start of the process, the recognizer would be provided with an active vocabulary consisting of a permanent core subset of the most frequent English words (derived from general data bases such as APHB), and an initial replaceable subset of words used in one of a small number of specified business fields.

There are at least four different aspects in which a vocabulary is particular to a speaker and his task. First, his choice of words reflects the speaker's habits of expression that are related, for example, to his level of education. His usage is also conditioned by the general domain of discourse (e.g., data processing, musicology, medical reports, etc.) that calls for a variety of technical terms, cliches, and such. Furthermore, the speaker should have available those names, addresses, and other expressions that are peculiar to his current interests. Finally, he may require words that are special to the topic of the present document. A large, fixed vocabulary can at most provide for the speaker's habitual usage and for the discourse domain, but a completely satisfactory coverage can be attained only through his active, though limited participation. In particular, while he could be asked to indicate whether a proper noun is a personal or company name, location, etc., and even to annotate technical terms, he cannot be expected to provide any feature classification of ordinary English words. Information about the latter should either be contained in some large stored source lexicon, or, better still, should be extracted from the actual syntactic / semantic function that these words play in the previously transcribed text.

8. LANGUAGE MODELS FOR VARYING DISCOURSE DOMAINS

The IBM trigram language model (see Section 3) was constructed from the combined text data bases OC1, OC2, and OC3. The extracted trigrams, made up of words in the chosen vocabulary covered 84% of correspondingly restricted trigrams found in the test data bases PDB and MNG1, while the coverage of PDB and MNG1 by trigrams collected solely from the 1 million word data base OC1 was only 55%. These percentages are indicative of the need for bigram and unigram smoothing in formula

$$P(w_3 \mid w_1, w_2) = q_3 f(w_3 \mid w_1, w_2) + q_2 f(w_3 \mid w_2) + q_1 f(w_3) \tag{14}$$

introduced in Section 3.

For a dynamically changing active (personalized) vocabulary, a straight trigram language model (14) cannot be constructed solely from the text created by the user. He will never dictate enough. The only conceivable way is to extract the model from an already stored trigram collection appropriate to a large vocabulary that includes the active subset. It is obvious that the more the active vocabulary of size L differs from the L most frequent words of the fixed training corpus, the less will the trigrams in the dictated text be covered by trigrams collected from the training text. Therefore a truly gigantic corpus would have to be used as a basis for a satisfactory model.

A more powerful method of language model construction is required not only to accommodate dynamic vocabularies, but also to limit the need to produce a large number of very different models for the many discourse domains. In fact, it is hard to list the latter, and for some important domains it will be impossible to find corresponding data bases.

One partial solution might be as follows. Assume that a basic discourse domain is identified which is believed to be representative of English. Let it have a vocabulary V^* of size L^* whose words are denoted by x. Let a "source" language model be constructed for the representative domain, on whatever equivalence principles, estimating in some particular way the probabilities $P^*(x_i \mid x_1,\ldots,x_{i-1})$. For every word w of the "target" vocabulary V of size L find that word x from V^* that is most similar to w in its grammatical behavior. We will denote this unique mapping of w by $x(w)$. Then we can obtain a target language model by the relation

$$P(w_i \mid w_1,\ldots,w_{i-1}) = k(w_i \mid x(w_i)) \quad P^*(x(w_i) \mid x(w_1),\ldots,x(w_{i-1})) \tag{31}$$

Intuitively, the hypothesized history $w_1,\ldots,w_{i-1}$ is being mapped into its image $x_1,\ldots,x_{i-1}$ in the source domain. The source language model P^* is then used to predict the next word x_i from the image history. Finally, the target word is selected by the probability k from all words in the target vocabulary V having the mapping x_i.

As the target domains change, the language model (31) can be constructed simply by finding the appropriate word classification scheme $x(w)$ and estimating the relative frequency function $k(w \mid x)$.

A language model for changing vocabularies can perhaps be constructed on the basis of the predictor

$$P(w_i \mid w_1,...w_{i-1}) =$$

$$= \sum_{c_i, g_i} \{ k(w_i \mid c_i, g_i)\, h(g_i \mid g(w_{i-2}), g(w_{i-1}))\, t(c_i \mid g_i, w_1, ..., w_{i-1}) \} \quad (28)$$

derived in Section 6, where

$$t(c_i \mid g_i, w_1, ..., w_{i-1}) =$$

$$NORM\ P(c_i, g_i)\quad P(w_{i-1} \mid \dot{c}_{i,1}, c_i, g_i)\ [\prod_{j=1}^{m-1} P(\dot{c}_{i,j} \mid \dot{c}_{i,j+1}, c_i)\ ] \quad (29)$$

The grammatical part $h(g_i \mid g_{i-2}, g_{i-1})$ of (28) can be derived once and for all, since it is independent of discourse domain. One might also hope (although with less conviction) that a judicious choice of lexical categories would allow universal estimation of their collocations $P(\dot{c}_{i,j} \mid \dot{c}_{i,j+1}, c_i)$ (the categories used in a particular discourse domain would possibly be a subset of the universal categories). Thus personalization or change of domain would involve only the syntactic and lexical classification of the target vocabulary, followed by estimation of the probabilities $k(w \mid g, c)$.

It is clear in any case that a desirable language model would be one containing only a relatively small number of parameters whose adjustment would result in needed specialization to any given discourse domain. Ideally, no declaration by the user should be needed for a switch of operation from one discourse domain to another. Continuous tracking of the changing domains should be carried out simply by observing the changing histories $w_1, ..., w_{i-1}$.

APPENDIX A

ENTROPY, PERPLEXITY, MUTUAL INFORMATION, AND THE SHANNON GAME

In this appendix we will derive an objective measure of language model quality. We will base it on results of Information Theory which concerns itself with sources of information. In simplest terms, a source is a device which puts out symbols chosen from some finite set V that is known to the user. Underlying the source operations is a statistical law which governs the choice of output symbols. When putting out a symbol a source provides information by removing the user's uncertainty about the identity of that symbol. Thus a source contains more information if the uncertainty about the next output is greater. For a given size L of the set V, uncertainty and therefore information is maximal if each of the possible symbols is chosen with equal probability and independently of previously chosen symbols. The information content of such a source is

$$I = \log L \qquad (A.1)$$

The correctness of the logarithmic measure in (A.1) can be appreciated by noting that putting out two symbols from the source is equivalent to putting out one symbol from a corresponding uniform source of set size $L' = L^2$ and that this latter act should provide twice as much information. But

$$I' = \log L' = \log L^2 = 2 \log L = 2I \qquad (A.2)$$

so (A.1) agrees with our intuition.

Let x denote a symbol put out by the source with probability $P(x)$. Then it can be shown in general that the proper measure of information is entropy H (in thermodynamics it measures disorder), which for sources that choose their symbols independently of each other is given by

$$H = -\left[\sum_{x=1}^{L} P(x) \log P(x) \right] \qquad (A.3)$$

Note that if the source is uniform, i.e. $P(x) = 1/L$, then (A.3) reduces to (A.1).

The logarithms in (A.3) are usually taken to the base 2, in which case the information is measured in units of binary symbols (0 or 1) called "bits" (for $L = 2$, formula

(A.1) yields $I = 1$). In fact, the fundamental coding theorem of Information Theory states that on the average it takes H bits to represent a symbol put out by a source of entropy H (the idea is to encode source output sequences into binary sequences from which the original symbol sequences can be fully recovered).

It follows from (A.3) and (A.1) that a source of entropy H can be thought of as one that has as much information content as a source which chooses symbols equiprobably from an alphabet of size

$$L' = 2^H \tag{A.4}$$

By direct extension of (A.3) it follows that if x_i is the i th symbol put out, then for general sources

$$H = -\lim_{n \to \infty} (1/n) \left[\sum P(x_1,\ldots,x_n) \log P(x_1,\ldots,x_n) \right] \tag{A.5}$$

where the sum is over all sequences $x_1,\ldots x_n$. It is easily checked that when the source is independent, i.e.,

$$P(x_1,\ldots,x_n) = P(x_1)\, P(x_2) \ldots P(x_n)$$

then (A.5) reduces to (A.3).

If the source is "well behaved" so that sufficiently long sequences of symbols are typical of it and can be used to deduce its statistical structure (this property is technically known as ergodicity), then it can be shown that (A.5) is equivalent to

$$H = -\lim_{n \to \infty} (1/n) \left[\log P(x_1, x_2,\ldots,x_n) \right] \tag{A.6}$$

Thus entropy can be directly estimated from long sequences of source symbols.

We can now apply the above theory to language models. Language can be thought of as an information source whose outputs are words w_i. The amount of information per word in some corpus can then be estimated by

$$H = -(1/n) \left[\log P(w_1,w_2,\ldots,w_n) \right] \tag{A.7}$$

where n is the size of the corpus (of course, the larger the text size n, the better the estimate). Because the information content is equal to the average number of bits it takes to specify a word (as pointed out in the paragraph following (A.3)), (A.7) is also an estimate of the recognition difficulty of speech generated by the same "mechanism" as gave rise to the corpus. In fact, it is exactly H bits of information that the recognizer must extract on the average from the acoustic data in order to determine a spoken word.

In order to determine (A.7), one would need to know the actual probabilities $P(w_1,w_2,...,w_n)$ of strings of the language. These probabilities are in practice unknowable. At best we can have their estimates $\hat{P}(w_1,w_2,...,w_n)$ which the language model provides to the recognizer. Thus from the point of view of the recognizer, the difficulty of the recognition of speech generated by the same mechanism as a given (large) sample text is measured by its logprob

$$LP = -(1/n)\,[\,\log \hat{P}(w_1,w_2,...,w_n)\,] \qquad (A.7')$$

It is easy to show that $LP \geq H$, assuming properly ergodic behavior of the text generating source. In the case of the trigram language model,

$$LP = -(1/n)\,[\,\sum_{i=1}^{n} \log P(w_i \mid w_{i-1},w_{i-2})\,] \qquad (A.8)$$

It is intuitively more satisfying to measure the difficulty of a recognition task relative to a given language model by the value of its perplexity PP defined by (compare this with (A.4))

$$PP = 2^{LP} = \hat{P}(w_1,w_2,..., w_n)^{(-1/n)} \qquad (A.9)$$

Thus to the first order of approximation (which disregards the acoustic distances between particular words) the task can be thought to be as difficult as would the recognition of a language with PP equally likely words. Perplexity is therefore a measure of the average "branching" of the text when presented to the language model.

In practice, any estimation of perplexity depends on the sample text whose length n is finite. The perplexity of our trigram language model is 70 when measured on the data base OC1 (see Section 7) of documents obtained from the same establishment that generated the data base used to construct that model. When the basis of measurement is a collection of memos MNG2 (see Section 7) generated spontaneously by managers of the IBM Research Division, the perplexity rises to 128. A model constructed on different principles (using another equivalence classification) or from a different data base will approximate $P(w_1,w_2,...,w_n)$ in a different way and will lead to a lower perplexity if the model is better.

It is very useful to have a measure of information provided by output symbols y of one source about outputs x of a related source. Intuitively, this information should be equal to the difference between the uncertainties about the outputs of Source 2 before and after the output of Source 1 was observed.

Let $P(x \mid y)$ be the probability that the symbol x will be put out by Source 2 given that y was observed as the output of Source 1. Then it follows from (A.3) that the uncertainty about what x is going to be is

$$H(X \mid y) = -\sum_{x=1}^{L} P(x \mid y) \log P(x \mid y) \qquad (A.10)$$

Thus on the average, after the output of Source 1 has been observed, the remaining uncertainty about Source 2 is

$$H(X \mid Y) = \sum_{y=1}^{L'} P(y) H(X \mid y) =$$

$$= -\sum_{y=1}^{L'} \sum_{x=1}^{L} P(y)\, P(x \mid y) \log P(x \mid y) \qquad (A.11)$$

where L' is the size of the output alphabet of Source 1 and $P(y)$ is the probability that it will put out the symbol y. Consequently, the information that Source 1 provides about Source 2 is

$$I(X;Y) = H(X) - H(X \mid Y) =$$

$$= \sum_{y=1}^{L'} \sum_{x=1}^{L} P(y)\, P(x \mid y) \log \frac{P(x \mid y)}{P(x)}$$

$$= \sum_{y=1}^{L'} \sum_{x=1}^{L} P(x,y) \log \frac{P(x,y)}{P(x)P(y)} \qquad (A.12)$$

where $H(X)$ denotes the entropy of Source 1 given by (A.3) and the last equality follows directly from (A.3) and (A.11) and straightforward algebraic manipulation. $I(X;Y)$ is called the *average mutual information* between Sources 1 and 2 and is a symmetrical function of the variables X and Y.

Let us now return to the discussion of the quality of language models. The entropy measures the intrinsic difficulty of the recognition task, the logprob its difficulty relative to the language model used. The difference between logprob and entropy, if it were known, would indicate the scope of potential language model improvement. Folklore has it that in a famous paper <2> Shannon estimated the entropy of English to be 1 bit per letter, i.e., assuming the average word length (including the delimiting space) to be 5.5 letters, about 5.5 bits per word, which is equivalent to a perplexity of 45. Actually, based on a sample text, Shannon provided bounds on the logprob of natural language models intrinsic to human subjects. His bounds place the logprob between 0.6 and 1.3 bits per letter, and thus the perplexity between 10 and 142. We will outline below his method which depends on guessing a text. His results would be valid only if the text they were based on was representative and large enough for his statistical estimates to converge. Representativity of English can never be established, and the test passage Shannon chose was much too short. But given enough perseverance by human subjects, valid results for the narrow genre of office correspondence could be obtained. Also, introspection during guessing may provide clues to the construction of more effective language models.

In the Shannon method, the human subject is asked to guess the text, letter by letter (including the space marker between words, punctuation, etc.). He is advised about the correctness of each guess. When he finds the first letter, he starts guessing the second, then the third, etc. . Let r_i be the number of tries it takes to guess the i th letter. Then assuming that given the same state of his knowledge the subject would always guess in the same order, the text can be completely recovered by him from the guess order sequence $r_1, r_2, \ldots, r_i, \ldots$. The sequence is thus a perfect encoding of the text. Hence the subject's logprob of $r_1, r_2, \ldots, r_i, \ldots$ is the same as his logprob of the text. Let $Q(j)$ be the relative frequency with which the number j appears in the order sequence. Then it is easy to show that

$$H^{+} = -\sum_{j} [\, Q(j) \log Q(j) \,] \tag{A.13}$$

is an upper bound on the logprob of the code $r_1, r_2, \ldots, r_i, \ldots$ and therefore on the logprob of the text. If m is the average number of letters per word in the text, then 2^{mH^+} is an upper bound on the perplexity of the text. Shannon also derived a lower bound formula on the text logprob. Cover and King later obtained a direct estimate of the text logprob by replacing the guesses in Shannon's procedure by bets <3>.

Stephen and Vincent Della Pietra have automated the Shannon procedure <2> on a computer. The resulting Shannon Game has several additional features. The text is chosen at random from a data base. It is possible to have the estimate converge faster by having part of the text revealed from the start. The information contained in n -grams (sequences of n words) can be measured by selecting at random the word to be guessed and revealing to the subject exactly n preceding words. The subject is also provided with two aids. Consistent with the letters guessed so far, the possible words of the vocabulary are shown together with their probabilities as computed by the trigram language model (given the preceding two words of the text). Another display panel shows the probabilities of the next letter, as computed by the language model consistent with the revealed past. If the subject guesses the wrong letter, it is removed from the allowed set and the probabilities for the remaining letters are recomputed and displayed. The computer keeps the running H^{+} score and compares it to the score that would have been incurred had the subject been guided strictly by the language model.

In playing the Shannon Game it is not our sole aim to estimate the human perplexity of office correspondence. We also wish to discover what manner of information is used by humans in word prediction. We hope that this will help us design the structure of future language models. Even keeping in mind that H^{+} is only an upper bound, it is already clear that the trigram language model can be substantially improved. In the Shannon Game humans beat the trigram model by factors of 3 or more in perplexity. The advantage that humans have seems mostly based on their ability to use relevant information found contained in a text passage that often precedes by many words the word they are currently guessing.

APPENDIX B

HIDDEN MARKOV CHAINS: A BASIS FOR LANGUAGE MODELING

This appendix is devoted to the discussion of the probabilistic concept of Hidden Markov Chains that is the basis for most of our methods of language modeling. In particular, the concept can be used (a) to determine the interpolation weights q_i used in the trigram probability estimation

$$P(w_3 \mid w_1,w_2) = q_3 f(w_3 \mid w_1,w_2) + q_2 f(w_3 \mid w_2) + q_1 f(w_3) \tag{14}$$

(see Section 3), (b) to annotate text automatically by parts of speech (see Section 4), (c) to estimate the probabilities k and h in the word prediction formula

$$\sum_{g_3} k(w_3 \mid g_3)\, h(g_3 \mid g(w_1), g(w_2)) \tag{15}$$

that involves part of speech classification of words $g(w)$ (see Sections 4.6, and 5), and (d) to discover nuclear part of speech classes (see Section 4). These applications are discussed in Appendix C.

The simplest statistical generation of word strings is one based on independent selection of words from a given vocabulary V. Under this regime, the probability $P(W)$ of generating the string

$$W = w_1, w_2, \ldots, w_n \tag{1}$$

is given by

$$P(W) = P(w_1)\, P(w_2) \ldots P(w_n) \tag{B.1}$$

where $P(w)$ is the probability of using the word w, and

$$\sum_{w \in V} P(w) = 1 \tag{B.2}$$

The sum in (B.2) is over all words of the vocabulary V.

Obviously, (B.1) is a very bad estimate of the probability with which actual word strings are generated. In real text, successive words are not independent of each other! A more realistic description of generation is one based on k -gram dependence, where

$$P(W) = \prod_{i=1}^{n} P(w_i \mid w_{i-k}, \ldots, w_{i-1}) \tag{B.3}$$

In (B.3) the selection of any word depends on the identity of the previous k words (for purposes of the formula, the words $w_{-k+1}, \ldots, w_0$ that precede the first word w_1 may be though of as identical to some conventional "beginning of text word"). In the trigram model (12) described in Section 3, $k = 2$.

Assuming that it were possible to estimate the probabilities $P(w_i \mid w_{i-k}, \ldots, w_{i-1})$, the model (B.3) could be made arbitrarily accurate by choosing a sufficiently large memory size k. Unfortunately, the resulting complexity would be prohibitive. In fact, for a vocabulary of size L, the model would be based on $L^{(k+1)}$ parameters. We need a statistical description that is more parsimonious in its use of parameters! We have argued in Section 3 that to reduce complexity we should put the histories $w_{i-k}, \ldots, w_{i-1}$ into equivalence classes. The following approach is essentially identical.

The history $w_{i-k}, \ldots, w_{i-1}$ can be thought of as the state S_{i-1} which the word generator reached at time i-1. The state at time i is then specified by

$$S_i = w_{i-k+1}, \ldots, w_i \tag{B.4}$$

and the word generation process is based on the state succession sequence $S_1, S_2, \ldots, S_n$ whose identity is statistically determined by the rule

$$P(S_1, S_2, \ldots, S_n) = \prod_{i=1}^{n} P(S_i \mid S_{i-1}) \tag{B.5}$$

In (B.5) the starting state S_0 consists of k copies of the "beginning of text word". The generation of the words w_i put out when state S_i is reached can be thought of as carried out by a deterministic output function F imposed on the states,

$$w_i = F(S_i) \tag{B.6}$$

As pointed out in Section 2,

$$P(S_1, S_2, \ldots, S_n) = \prod_{i=1}^{n} P(S_i \mid S_1, \ldots, S_{i-1}) \tag{B.7}$$

states the general product decomposition rule for the probability of sequences $S_1, S_2, \ldots, S_n$. A statistical process that is governed by the much simpler formula (B.5) is known as a Markov Chain (The concept is due to A.A. Markov who actually used it to model sequences of vowels and consonants in Pushkin's poem "Eugen Onegin". The reason for the terminology "chain" will become apparent below.). It is determined by probabilities $P(S' \mid S)$ of one step state - to - state transitions $S \rightarrow S'$, and therefore possesses a single symbol memory

$$P(S_i \mid S_1, \ldots, S_{i-1}) = P(S_i \mid S_{i-1}) \tag{B.8}$$

The word generating Markov chain introduced above is special because (B.4) prohibits transitions between most of the states. In fact, if $S = w_1, \ldots, w_k$ and $S' = w'_1, \ldots, w'_k$ then

$$P(S' \mid S) = 0 \qquad \text{unless } w'_i = w_{i+1} \qquad \text{for } i = 1, \ldots, k-1 \tag{B.9}$$

This Markov chain can be criticized as wasting state space. A subtler, more efficient approach might accomplish comparable statistical modeling precision while based on considerably fewer parameters. The formulation of Hidden Markov Chains decouples the strict relationship (B.4) and (B.6) between states and generated words w_i. Underlying states S are defined abstractly, transitions between all of them are in principle allowed, and words that are generated are not deterministically specified by the state S (as in (B.6)), but are selected randomly with probability $q(w \mid S \rightarrow S')$ that w is generated when the transition $S \rightarrow S'$ takes place. The reason for the term *hidden* is that it is generally impossible to deduce the state sequence $S_1, S_2, \ldots, S_n$ from the observed output sequence $w_1, w_2, \ldots, w_n$.

Hidden Markov Chains have been found to have many interesting properties. In order to discuss some of them, it will be useful to abstract their formulation from the setting of word generation.

A Markov chain is defined by the set of its states S^* and by the transition probabilities $P(S' \mid S)$ between them. Without loss of generality, one state may be designated as initial. All transitions $S \to S'$ such that $P(S' \mid S) > 0$ are said to be allowed, the rest are prohibited. An intuitive feeling about a given Markov chain may be gained by diagramming the allowed transitions between states. Figure B.1 is an example of such a diagram for a 4 state chain (its appearance suggests the terminology) which does not allow all the possible transitions (e.g., transitions from state 2 to states 1 and 4 are prohibited). Note that self-transitions are possible, such as those of states 2 and 3 to themselves. The numbers attached to the arrows specify the probability with which a transition is taken once its initial state is reached. A chain can be viewed as a mechanism that, starting operation in the initial state, changes its state at discrete time intervals along some allowed transition. A state sequence $S_0, S_1, S_2, \ldots$ has positive probability if and only if it can be traced in the diagram as a path leading out of the designated initial state S_0. Transition diagrams, although impractical for large state sets, define the chain fully.

To make a hidden out of an ordinary Markov chain, all one needs to do is to decide on the output alphabet A^* (the set of outputs x that can be generated) and to attach an output probability distribution $q(x \mid S \to S')$ to each allowed transition $S \to S'$. Of course, distributions q must satisfy

$$\sum_{x \in A^*} q(x \mid S \to S') = 1 \qquad \text{for all allowed} \qquad S \to S' \tag{B.10}$$

A completely equivalent, second formulation yields a useful visualization of hidden Markov chains, at least for small state and alphabet set sizes. Let $a_1, a_2, \ldots, a_k$ be the set of letters x which can be generated when some particular transition $S \to S'$ is taken (i.e., for the remaining letters x of A^*, $q(x \mid S \to S') = 0$). We will replace the transition $S \to S'$ in the chain diagram by exactly k transitions from S to S', with the i th transition labeled by the letter a_i. When such replacement is carried out for all allowed transition pairs $S \to S'$, and the probabilities

$$P(S \to S', a_i) = q(a_i \mid S \to S')\, P(S' \mid S) \tag{B.11}$$

are attached to the transitions labeled a_i, then the resulting diagram will completely define the hidden Markov chain.

Figure B.2 is an example of a 3 state hidden Markov chain generating letters from the binary alphabet {0,1}. For greater clarity, values of the transition probabilities have been omitted from the diagram; only output labels were retained. Note that once the state $S = 3$ is reached, it is impossible to generate the output 0 next, while output 1 can be generated in two ways: going to state $S = 1$, or to $S = 2$. It follows that even if the starting state should be known, the output sequence $x_1, x_2, \ldots$ would not in general specify the underlying state sequence. Indeed, the infinite sequence 0,0,...,0 can be generated in one way only, while there are many ways to generate the sequence 1,1,...,1.

A hidden Markov chain can then be defined by an output alphabet A^*, by a set S^* of states S (one of which is designated as initial), and by a set T^* of transitions t to each of which are attached a probability $q(t)$ and a letter $a(t)$ from A^*. The probabilities $q(t)$ when summed over all the transitions t leaving any state S must add to 1. The operation of a chain results in a transition path $T = t_1, t_2, \ldots, t_n$ between the states, generating the output sequence $a(t_1), a(t_2), \ldots, a(t_n)$ consisting of the letters attached to the transitions. The probability $P(T)$ of this event is given by

$$P(T) = \prod_{i=1}^{n} q(t_i) \qquad (B.12)$$

The probability that a given output sequence $X = x_1, x_2, \ldots, x_n$ will be generated is

$$P(X) = \sum \left[\prod_{i=1}^{n} q(t_i)\right] \qquad (B.13)$$

where the sum is over all sequences T generating X, i.e., sequences such that $a(t_i) = x_i$ for all $i = 1, 2, \ldots, n$. Since there are potentially K^n such sequences (where K is the size of the state space S^*), formula (B.13) seems prohibitively hard to compute. Fortunately, it is possible to derive an algorithm for computing (B.13) (see reference <4>) whose complexity grows only linearly with n, by taking advantage of the limited memory of Markov chains. The basic characteristic used is the fact that the probability that the tail $x_{k+1}, \ldots, x_n$ will be generated depends on the head $x_1, \ldots, x_k$ only through the probability distribution of the states S_k at time k. That is,

$$P(x_{k+1}, \ldots, x_n \mid x_1, \ldots, x_k) =$$

$$= \sum_{S_k = 1}^{K} P(x_{k+1}, \ldots, x_n \mid S_k) \; P(S_k \mid x_k, \ldots, x_n) \qquad (B.14)$$

An additional degree of freedom for modeling of observed sequence generation may be gained by augmenting the output alphabet A by the invisible letter ϕ. Transitions t to which ϕ is attached are called null transitions since they result in no output at all.

In hidden Markov chain diagrams null transitions are depicted as an interrupted arc (see Figure B.3). If a sequence $t_1,t_2,...,t_n$ contains k null transitions then it results in an output sequence $x_1,x_2,...,x_{n-k}$ that is shorter by k letters. Using the chain of Figure B.3, the sequence 1,1,1 may be generated by taking a minimum of 3 and a maximum of 11 transitions.

Finally, let us observe that the transition probabilities of the underlying Markov chain are given by

$$P(S' \mid S) = \sum q(t) \qquad (B.15)$$

where the sum is over all transitions t from S to S'. The correspondence to the first formulation of hidden Markov chains is demonstrated by noting that the output distributions of the latter are specified by

$$q(x = a(t) \mid S \rightarrow S') = q(t)/P(S' \mid S) \qquad (B.16)$$

APPENDIX C

LANGUAGE MODELING BY HIDDEN MARKOV CHAINS

A hidden Markov chain is a possible language model if its output alphabet A is equal to the vocabulary V augmented by the invisible word ϕ. In this appendix we will use hidden Markov chain models (a) to determine the interpolation weights q_i used in the trigram probability estimation

$$P(w_3 \mid w_1,w_2) = q_3\, f(w_3 \mid w_1,w_2) + q_2\, f(w_3 \mid w_2) + q_1\, f(w_3) \qquad (14)$$

(see Section 3), (b) to annotate text automatically by parts of speech (see Section 4), (c) to estimate the probabilities k and h in the word prediction formula

$$\sum_{g_3} k(w_3 \mid g_3)\, h(g_3 \mid g(w_1),\ g(w_2)) \qquad (18)$$

that involves part of speech classification of words $g(w)$ (see Sections 4,6, and 8), and (d) to discover nuclear part of speech classes (see Section 4).

The interpolated language model (14) is a hidden Markov chain that has for each word pair $[w_1,w_2]$ a maximum of 4 states, denoted by $S_0[w_1,w_2]$, $S_1[w_1,w_2]$, $S_2[w_1,w_2]$, and $S_3[w_1,w_2]$. A section of the transition diagram is shown in Figure C.1. The null transitions $S_0 \rightarrow S_1$, $S_0 \rightarrow S_2$, and $S_0 \rightarrow S_3$ take place with probabilities q_1, q_2, and q_3, respectively. From each state $S_i[w_1,w_2]$, there emanate transitions into L (equal to the size of the vocabulary) states $S_0[w_2,w]$, one for each word w of the vocabulary. The transition from $S_1[w_1,w_2]$ to $S_0[w_2,w]$ takes place with probability $f(w)$, that from $S_2[w_1,w_2]$ with probability $f(w \mid w_2)$, and that from $S_3[w_1,w_2]$, with probability $f(w \mid w_1,w_2)$.

As pointed out in Section 3, the relative frequencies f in (14) are obtained by counting trigrams, bigrams, and unigrams in some training text:

$$f(w_3 \mid w_1,w_2) = \frac{C(w_1, w_2, w_3)}{C(w_1,w_2)}$$

$$f(w_3 \mid w_2) = \frac{C(w_2, w_3)}{C(w_2)}$$

$$f(w_3) = \frac{C(w_3)}{C} \qquad (13)$$

The question is how to determine the weights q_i. One way to approach the problem is from the Maximum Likelihood point of view, that is, to adjust the free parameters of the probability function so as to make the observed data most probable after the adjustment. In our case, this means to take some text W, different from the one used to compute the relative frequencies (13), and to attempt to adjust the weights q_i so as to maximize the probability of W

$$P(W) = \prod_{i=1}^{n} P(w_i \mid w_{i-2},w_{i-1}) \qquad (12)$$

when the terms in the product are based on formula (14). It can be shown that the following intuitively satisfying method arrives at the desired maximization.

Suppose the text W was actually generated by the hidden Markov chain of Figure C.1 with weights q_i set to some value. If it were possible to observe the operation of the chain, one could count the number of times, $C(S_0)$, the state S_0 was reached, and the number of times, $C(S_0 \rightarrow S_1)$, $C(S_0 \rightarrow S_2)$, and $C(S_0 \rightarrow S_3)$, with which the corresponding transitions were taken, and then estimate q_i by the relative frequencies

$$q_1 = C(S_0 \rightarrow S_1)/C(S_0)$$

$$q_2 = C(S_0 \rightarrow S_2)/C(S_0)$$

$$q_3 = C(S_0 \rightarrow S_3)/C(S_0) \quad (C.1)$$

Unfortunately, the Markov chain is a hidden one and so it is impossible to observe which of the three transitions $S_0 \rightarrow S_i$ was taken in any given instance. However, if we knew the value of the weights q_i, then for any position in the text W in which the bigram w_1,w_2 appears followed by some word w, we could compute the probability $p_i(w)$ that the transition $S_0 \rightarrow S_i$ took place just before w was generated. In fact,

$$p_1(w) = q_1 f(w)/P(w \mid w_1,w_2)$$

$$p_2(w) = q_2 f(w \mid w_2)/P(w \mid w_1,w_2)$$

$$p_3(w) = q_3 f(w \mid w_1,w_2)/P(w \mid w_1,w_2) \quad (C.2)$$

where $P(w \mid w_1,w_2)$ is given by (14).

Since $p_1(w) + p_2(w) + p_3(w) = 1$, then the probabilities $p_i(w)$ can be thought of as the fraction of time the transition $S_0 \rightarrow S_i$ will be taken in many trials (occasioned by instances in the text W where w_1,w_2 takes place followed by w). Define the function $I(w', w'')$ to be equal to 1 when $w' = w_1$ and $w'' = w_2$ and equal to 0 otherwise. We call $I(w', w')$ an *indicator function* of w_1,w_2 because it marks occurrences of w_1,w_2 in the text W. In fact,

$$C(S_0) = \sum_{i=1}^{n} I(w_{i-2},w_{i-1}) \quad (C.3)$$

is number of times w_1,w_2 appear in W followed by some word w. Furthermore,

$$C^*(S_0 \rightarrow S_1) = \sum_{i=1}^{n} I(w_{i-2},w_{i-1})\, p_1(w_i)$$

$$C^*(S_0 \rightarrow S_2) = \sum_{i=1}^{n} I(w_{i-2},w_{i-1})\, p_2(w_i)$$

$$C^*(S_0 \rightarrow S_3) = \sum_{i=1}^{n} I(w_{i-2},w_{i-1})\, p_3(w_i) \quad (C.4)$$

are estimates of the number of times the transitions $S_0 \rightarrow S_i$ take place in W. Because of the fractional interpretation of the probabilities p_i, it is reasonable to expect (and can be proven) that for a sufficiently large text size n, the values of the actual counts $C(S_0 \rightarrow S_i)$ and their estimates $C^*(S_0 \rightarrow S_i)$ will be nearly equal.

Even though the text W was not in fact generated by the hidden Markov chain, we still wish to estimate the weights q_i so as to best model the generation process. Let us then guess at the values of q_i, and use (C.2) through (C.4) to compute the pseudo-counts C^*. In analogy with (C.1) we can then obtain new re-estimated weights

$$q_1^* = C^*(S_0 \rightarrow S_1)/C^*(S_0)$$

$$q^*2 = C^*(S_0 \rightarrow S_2)/C^*(S_0)$$

$$q^*_3 = C^*(S_0 \rightarrow S_3)/C^*(S_0) \qquad (C.5)$$

The weights q^*_i should lead to a better modeling of the generation of text than the original, arbitrary weights q_i, since the former reflect through (C.3) and (C.4) the actual data W. It can, in fact, be proven that when the values q_i^* are used in (14), the probability $P(W)$ computed in (17) will be larger than the one based on the original q_i (unless $q_i^* = q_i$, in which case q_i are the maximizing weights). Thus iterating this process (i.e. computing the probabilities $p_i(w)$ on the basis of the new weights q^*_i, using the former to get new fractional weights C^* and thereby getting a fresh set of values q^*_i in (C.5)) will make $P(W)$ increase further. It can then be shown that when the limit of this process is reached (i.e., when $P(W)$ does not increase any more), the final re-estimated weights q^*_i will have the values that maximize $P(W)$.

The general modeling problem is to find the values of transition probabilities of a hidden Markov chain of a given structure that would result in maximizing the probability $P(W)$ that some given text W was generated by the chain. This can be accomplished by the so called Forward - Backward (F-B) algorithm (it is explained in Section VII of reference <5> with speech recognition applications in mind) that is a direct generalization of the re-estimation process outlined above. One starts with guessed transition probability values and improves them iteratively by computing expected transition counts that would take place if the given data W were generated by the chain governed by the guessed probabilities. Of course, the process converges faster if the original guesses are better. For more complex chains than the one of Figure C.1, the convergence is to a local rather than a global maximum.

As the second example of text generation modeling, consider the hidden Markov chain whose states S_{i-1} at time $i-1$ are the parts of speech g_{i-2}, g_{i-1} of the words w_{i-2}, w_{i-1}. A transition to a state

$$S_i = g_{i-1}, g_i \tag{C.6}$$

takes place (i.e., the part of speech g_i of the next word is selected) and as a result the next word w_i is generated, dependent only on its part of speech g_i. Using the terminology of the second hidden Markov chain formulation associated with (B.11), the probability of transition $S \rightarrow S'$ with attached output w is given by (compare with (B.11))

$$P(S \rightarrow S', w) = \begin{cases} k(w \mid g'_2)\, h(g'_2 \mid g_1, g_2) & \text{if } g'_1 = g_2 \\ 0 & \text{otherwise} \end{cases} \tag{C.7}$$

where $S = g_1, g_2$ and $S' = g_1', g_2'$. This model leads to the word prediction formula

$$\sum_{g_3} k(w_3 \mid g_3)\, h(g_3 \mid g(w_1), g(w_2)) \tag{18}$$

discussed in Section 4.

How would one go about estimating the probabilities k and h underlying the model? The straightforward approach would be to annotate some large text by parts of speech and base the estimates on counts

$$h(g_3 \mid g_1, g_2) = \frac{C(g_1, g_2, g_3)}{C(g_2, g_3)}$$

$$k(w \mid g) = \frac{C(w, g)}{C(g)} \tag{C.8}$$

where $C(w,g)$ is the number of times the word w was annotated with part of speech g.

The problem of this counting approach is that in order to be accurate, the estimates (C.8) would have to be based on a lot of text in which the parts of speech were first determined either automatically (see below) or by experts. However, since the probabilities k and h underly a hidden Markov chain, it is possible to use the F - B algorithm to estimate them directly. The crucial step is the choice of the initial values of k and h that starts the re-estimation process. For our model we used 40 part of speech classes (see Section 4) and chose h to be uniform,

$$h(g_3 \mid g_1, g_2) = 1/40 \tag{C.9}$$

For each word w of the vocabulary, we then specified the set $G(w)$ of parts of speech that w could assume (take on). We set the probability that w functions as a part of speech g to the same value for all g in the allowed set $G(w)$ and to 0 otherwise. Denoting the size of $G(w)$ by $M(w)$, the initial k was therefore chosen to be

$$k(w \mid g) = \begin{cases} K(g)C(w)/M(w) & \text{if } g \text{ is in } G(w) \\ 0 & \text{otherwise} \end{cases} \qquad (C.10)$$

where $C(w)$ is the number of occurrences of w in the training text W, and $K(g)$ is a normalizing constant that assures that summing $k(w \mid g)$ over all words w of the vocabulary adds up to 1.

Using the initial choices (C.9) and (C.10), we applied the F-B algorithm to the problem and obtained certain probabilities k and h. We then wished to judge the degree to which the resulting state space organization was related to the ordinary parts of speech we were familiar with. The way to tell was to use the extracted k and h values to annotate automatically some text W, and then have experts inspect the resulting annotation.

Suppose it were possible to find the most probable state sequence $S_0, S_1, S_2, \ldots, S_n$ that the chain went through when generating W, i.e., the sequence maximizing the product

$$P(S_0 \rightarrow S_1, w_1)\, P(S_1 \rightarrow S_2, w_2) \ldots P(S_{n-1} \rightarrow S_n, w_n) \qquad (C.11)$$

Because of state definition (C.6), the sequence $S_1, S_2, \ldots, S_n$ implies a part of speech sequence $g_1 g_2, \ldots, g_n$ which is then the most probable one. The latter sequence constitutes a text annotation. The most likely state sequence for data generated by a hidden Markov chain can be determined by the Viterbi algorithm (it is explained in Section V of reference <5> with speech recognition applications in mind).

Based on the k and h values derived by the F - B algorithm, we used the Viterbi algorithm to determine the most likely part of speech sequence corresponding to the training text W. We found that in 97% of the cases the automatic annotation agreed with the one provided by experts.

A very interesting application of hidden Markov models to English text is contained in a paper by Cave and Neuwirth <6> who are able to discover automatically classes of letters (such as vowels and consonants) and other intuitively satisfying letter sequence relations.

In Section 4 we mentioned that the part of speech model is hampered by the fact that it is based on content classes (nouns, verbs, adjectives, and adverbs) which provide too crude an equivalence classification. The Nuclear Part of Speech approach is based on the assumption that a relatively small number N of identified words constitute examples of significantly different grammatical behavior. If one were then to classify all words into N classes (many of the words belonging to several classes), with the identified words forming their nuclei, the resulting classification might overcome the shortcomings of the natural POS model. The identification of the nuclear set is a problem which we approached heuristically by first augmenting the set of the M most frequent words by 200 - M words that had important grammatical characteristics that were missing from the set of the M frequent words. Each member of the resulting set N^* of 200 *nuclear* words was then assigned its own part of speech, and the remaining words of the vocabulary were initially allowed to belong to all 200 classes. The hidden Markov chain (C.7) that would best model the given training data W was then determined by running the F-B algorithm to estimate the probabilities h and k. The initial choice

$$h(g_3 \mid g_1, g_2) = 1/200 \tag{C.12}$$

and

$$k(w \mid g) = \begin{cases} K(g)C(w) & \text{if } w \text{ is in } N^* \text{ and } g \text{ is the designated class of } w \\ 0 & \text{if } w \text{ is in } N^* \text{ and } g \text{ is not the designated class of } w \\ K(g)C(w)/200 & \text{if } w \text{ is not in } N^* \end{cases} \tag{C.13}$$

assures that words in N^* will belong to their own class only. In (C.13), the normalizing factor $K(g)$ is chosen to make $k(w \mid g)$ add up to 1 when summed over all words w.

The resulting model is too complex since, after training, many of the words belong to a large number of classes, albeit with small probability. The simplification achieved by restricting class membership of words to the 3 most probable classes and running several additional iterations of the F-B algorithm does not degrade the model noticeably. In fact, when the derived predictor is added as a fourth component to the trigram model (14), the perplexity of the resulting augmented trigram model

$$P(w_3 \mid w_1, w_2) = q_3 f(w_3 \mid w_1, w_2) + q_2 f(w_3 \mid w_2) + q_1 f(w_3)$$

$$+ q_4 \sum_{g_3} k(w_3 \mid g_3)\, h(g_3 \mid g(w_1),\ g(w_2)) \tag{C.14}$$

is 20% lower than before augmentation.

The membership of the self-organized nuclear classes that we determined by the above method is intuitively satisfying. All numbers form one class, first names another, months yet another (with '*may*' belonging also to a class populated by auxiliaries), etc. First names share membership with '*Mr.*', '*Mrs.*', and '*Ms.*'. Plurals are not mixed with singulars, or intransitive verbs with clearly transitive ones. It is truly remarkable that this spontaneous classification of all words that do not belong to the nuclear set N^* is solely due to the initial choice of N^*, the probability assignment (C.13), and the technique of hidden Markov chain modeling!

We conclude this appendix by considering the increase in language model complexity that results when words are allowed multiple class membership. In that case the Markov chain state S_i at time i,

$$S_i = g_{i-1}g_i \qquad (C.6)$$

is not determined by the words w_{i-1}, w_i, but can take on all values allowed by the bigram. In fact, the history $w_1, \ldots, w_i$ induces a probability distribution

$$P_i(g_{i-1}g_i) = P(g_{i-1}g_i \mid w_1, \ldots, w_i) \qquad (C.15)$$

over the possible states, which is then used by the language model in the actual predictor

$$\sum_{g_{i+1}} k(w_{i+1} \mid g_{i+1}) \left[\sum_{g_{i-1}, g_i} h(g_{i+1} \mid g_{i-1}g_i)\, P_i(g_{i-1}g_i) \right] \qquad (C.16)$$

that replaces the component (18) in (C.14) when words have multiple classes. Fortunately, the probabilities P_i (defined in (C.15)) that must be stored by the language model can be obtained by a simple recursion

$$P_i(g_{i-1}g_i) = K_i \left[\sum_{g_{i-2}} k(w_i \mid g_i)\, h(g_i \mid g_{i-2}g_{i-1})\, P_{i-1}(g_{i-2}g_{i-1}) \right] \qquad (C.17)$$

from previously computed probabilities P_{i-1}. In (C.17), K_i is a normalizing constant that assures that P_i adds to 1 when summed over all states $g_{i-1}g_i$ permissible by the class membership of the bigram w_{i-1}, w_i. The computation (C.17) of the probability distributions of the Markov chain states at time i is referred to as language model tracking of the class assignment.

APPENDIX D

WORD EQUIVALENCE CLASSIFICATION BASED ON MUTUAL INFORMATION

In Section 4 we discussed the desirability of discovering word classes that might prove a better basis of language modeling than conventional parts of speech. The aim is to provide the component

$$\sum_{g_3} k(w_3 \mid g_3)\ h(g_3 \mid g(w_1),\ g(w_2)) \tag{18}$$

for an augmented trigram language model (C.14). In the last paragraphs of Appendix C we have discussed a self-organized hidden Markov chain approach to class discovery. Here we will outline an alternate method based on the mutual information function introduced in Appendix A. It will enable us to determine the function $g(w)$ (see (18)) that assigns each word w of a vocabulary to one of M classes. A generalization to multiple class assignment while possible, will not be pursued.

We take the point of view that a good assignment is one in which the class $g(w_i)$ was a good predictor of the next word w_{i+1}. The heuristic reasoning of Appendix A, which is supported by many mathematical theorems, indicated to R. L. Mercer that it would make sense to select the classes so as to maximize the average mutual information $I\,(g(w_i)\ ;\ w_{i+1})$ between the classes $g(w_i)$ and the words w_{i+1}. Substituting into the formula

$$I\,(X;Y) = H(X) - H(X \mid Y) =$$

$$= \sum_{y=1}^{L'} \sum_{x=1}^{L} P(x,y)\ \log \frac{P(x,y)}{P(x)\ P(y)} \tag{A.12}$$

that applies to general related events x and y, we get

$$I(\,g\,(w_i)\ ;\ w_{i+1}) =$$

$$= \sum_{w_{i+1}=1}^{L}\ \sum_{g(w_i)=1}^{M}\ P(g(w_i),w_{i+1})\ \log \frac{P(\,g\,(w_i),w_{i+1})}{P(\,g\,(w_i))\ P(w_{i+1})} \tag{D.1}$$

where L is the vocabulary size and M is the number of classes.

The mathematical problem before us is to find that assignment of words into M classes that would maximize the value of (D.1). The way to proceed is to substitute counts of bigrams w_1,w_2 occurring in a training text W for the probabilities of (D.1). If $n + 1$ is the total length of the text W, then it has n bigrams in it. Let C denote the count function introduced in Section 3, and let us approximate probabilities by relative frequencies

$$f(w_3 \mid w_1,w_2) = \frac{C(w_1,w_2,w_3)}{C(w_1,w_2)}$$

$$f(w_3 \mid w_2) = \frac{C(w_2,w_3)}{C(w_2)}$$

$$f(w_3) = \frac{C(w_3)}{n} \tag{13}$$

Then the relevant mutual information may be computed by

$$I(g(w_1);w_2) =$$

$$= (1/n)\left[\sum_{w_2=1}^{L}\sum_{g_1=1}^{M} C(g_1,w_2)\log\frac{C(g_1,w_2)n}{C(g_1)C(w_2)}\right] \tag{D.2}$$

where the notation

$$C(g_1,w_2) = \sum_{w_1 \in g_1} C(w_1,w_2)$$

$$C(g_1) = \sum_{w_1 \in g_1} C(w_1) \tag{D.3}$$

is used.

Realizing that class assignment does not influence the value of n or of $C(w_2)$, it follows from (D.2) that our task is to find that assignment of words into M classes that would maximize

$$\hat{I} = \sum_{w_2=1}^{L}\sum_{g_1=1}^{M} C(g_1, w_2)\log\frac{C(g_1,w_2)}{C(g_1)} \tag{D.4}$$

One simple, but non-optimal way to proceed is to assign each word to a different class and arrive at the M class solution by successively merging pairs of classes. At the beginning of this process, the criterion function (D.4) has the value

$$\hat{I}_1 = \sum_{w_2=1}^{L} \sum_{w_1=1}^{L} C(w_1,w_2) \log \frac{C(w_1,w_2)}{C(w_1)} \qquad (D.5)$$

If a new class should be formed by merger of the classes containing the single members w_1' and w_1'', then $\hat{I}$ of (D.4) would have the new value

$$\hat{I}_2 = \hat{I}_1 - C(w_1',w_2) \log \frac{C(w_1',w_2)}{C(w_1')} - C(w_1'',w_2) \log \frac{C(w_1'',w_2)}{C(w_1'')}$$

$$+ (C(w_1',w_2) + C(w_1'',w_2)) \log \frac{C(w_1',w_2) + C(w_1'',w_2)}{C(w_1') + C(w_1'')} \qquad (D.6)$$

Clearly those words w' and w'' should be merged into a single class for which (D.6) would be largest. Once they are found, their merger into one class will reduce the number of classes from L to $L - 1$. We will denote the corresponding value of (D.6) by $\hat{I}_2$. In general, the $i - 1$ th merger will result in a value $\hat{I}_i$ and $L - i + 1$ classes will exist. We will then be looking for those currently existing classes g_1' and g_1'' for which

$$\hat{I}_{i+1} =$$

$$\hat{I}_i - C(g_1',w_2) \log \frac{C(g_1',w_2)}{C(g_1')} - C(g_1'',w_2) \log \frac{C(g_1'',w_2)}{C(g_1'')}$$

$$+ (C(g_1',w_2) + C(g_1'',w_2)) \log \frac{C(g_1',w_2) + C(g_1'',w_2)}{C(g_1') + C(g_1'')} \qquad (D.7)$$

is maximal and merge the maximizing g_1' and g_1'' once we found them.

While the above procedure is sub-optimal, because once the merger is made it cannot be unmade, it does result in a classification leading to a language model (18) whose quality is comparable to the one based on nuclear part of speech classes arrived at by self-organization of the hidden Markov chain (see Appendix C).

The above development was somewhat simplified because it did not take directly into account that the desired classification was to be used in the language model component

$$\sum_{g_3} k(w_3 \mid g_3)\ h(g_3 \mid g(w_1),\ g(w_2)) \tag{18}$$

which predicts w_{i+1} by first predicting its class $g(w_{i+1})$ and then choosing w_{i+1} from the latter. We will now appropriately modify the above development.

The probability $P(g(w_i) \mid w_{i+1})$ underlying (D.1) should be restricted to have the form

$$P(g(w_i) \mid w_{i+1}) = k(w_{i+1} \mid g(w_{i+1}))\ P(g(w_i), g(w_{i+1})) \,/\, P(w_{i+1}) \qquad (D.8)$$

Formula (D.8) holds because of our assumption that each word belongs to a unique class.

As a consequence, we will rewrite (D.1) as

$$I(g(w_i)\ ;\ w_{i+1}) =$$

$$= \sum_{w_{i+1}=1}^{L} \sum_{g(w_i)=1}^{M} [\, k(w_{i+1} \mid g(w_{i+1}))\ P(g(w_i), g(w_{i+1}))$$

$$\log \frac{k(w_{i+1} \mid g(w_{i+1}))\ P(g(w_i), g(w_{i+1}))}{P(w_{i+1})\ P(g(w_i))} \,] \qquad (D.9)$$

Approximating probabilities by relative frequencies, the argument leading to (D.4) would then establish the new criterion function

$$I^* = \sum_{w_2=1}^{L} \sum_{g_1=1}^{M} k(w_2 \mid g(w_2)) \; C(g_1, g(w_2)) \; \log \frac{k(w_2 \mid g(w_2)) \; C(g_1, g(w_2))}{C(g_1)} \tag{D.10}$$

But

$$k(w_2 \mid g(w_2)) = C(w_2)/C(g(w_2)) \tag{D.11}$$

so we can rewrite (D.10) as

$$I^* = \sum_{w_2=1}^{L} \sum_{g_1=1}^{M} (C(w_2) \; C(g_1, g) \; / \; C(g)) \;\; \log \frac{C(w_2) \; C(g_1, g)}{C(g_1) \; C(g)}$$

$$= \sum_{g=1}^{M} \sum_{w_2 \in g} \sum_{g_1=1}^{M} (C(w_2) \; C(g_1, g) \; / \; C(g)) \;\; \log \frac{C(w_2) \; C(g_1, g)}{C(g_1) \; C(g)}$$

$$= \sum_{g=1}^{M} \sum_{w_2 \in g} \sum_{g_1=1}^{M} (C(w_2) \; C(g_1, g) \; / \; C(g)) \; \log \frac{C(g_1, g)}{C(g_1) \; C(g)} \; +$$

$$+ \sum_{g=1}^{M} \sum_{w_2 \in g} \sum_{g_1=1}^{M} (C(w_2) \; C(g_1, g) \; / \; C(g)) \;\; \log C(w_2) \tag{D.12}$$

Since the sum of $C(g_1, g)$ over all g_1 is equal to $C(g)$, then

$$\sum_{g=1}^{M} \sum_{w_2 \in g} \sum_{g_1=1}^{M} (C(w_2) C(g_1, g)/C(g)) \log C(w_2) =$$

$$= \sum_{g=1}^{M} \sum_{w_2 \in g} (C(w_2) C(g)/C(g)) \log C(w_2) =$$

$$= \sum_{g=1}^{M} \sum_{w_2 \in g} C(w_2) \log C(w_2) \tag{D.13}$$

Since (D.13) is independent of class assignment $g(w)$, the second term on the right hand side of (D.12), which is equal to (D.13), can be omitted from the criterion function. Since summing $C(w_2)$ over all words in g results in $C(g)$, then

$$\sum_{g=1}^{M} \sum_{w_2 \in g} \sum_{g_1=1}^{M} (C(w_2)\, C(g_1,g) \,/\, C(g)) \log \frac{C(g_1,g)}{C(g_1)\, C(g)} =$$

$$= \sum_{g=1}^{M} \sum_{g_1=1}^{M} (C(g)\, C(g_1,g) \,/\, C(g)) \log C \frac{(g_1,g)}{C(g_1)\, C(g)} \qquad (D.14)$$

Thus the remaining first term on the right hand side of (D.12) becomes

$$IS = \sum_{g_2=1}^{M} \sum_{g_1=1}^{M} C(g_1,g_2) \log \frac{C(g_1,g_2)}{C(g_1)C(g_2)} \qquad (D.15)$$

and is the appropriate criterion upon which to base the merger procedure resulting in the final word class assignment.

APPENDIX E

THE BACK-OFF METHOD OF SMOOTHING OF N-GRAM PROBABILITIES

In Section 5 we mentioned that to estimate trigram probabilities, it is possible to smooth relative frequencies differently than is done in the formula

$$P(w_3 \mid w_1,w_2) = q_3 f(w_3 \mid w_1,w_2) + q_2 f(w_3 \mid w_2) + q_1 f(w_3) \qquad (14)$$

In fact, it is reasonable to argue that as long as the trigram count $C(w_1,w_2,w_3)$ is sufficiently large, then

$$P(w_3 \mid w_1,w_2) = f(w_3 \mid w_1,w_2) = \frac{C(w_1,w_2,w_3)}{C(w_1,w_2)} \qquad (13)$$

is a better estimate of the probability $P(w_3 \mid w_1,w_2)$ than formula (14). The smoothing approach of S.Katz <7>, which is based on an argument by Turing, satisfies (13).

We will outline the method in a way that will exhibit the main idea. We will first develop an estimate of probabilities $P(w_2 \mid w_1)$ and then use it to compute $P(w_3 \mid w_1,w_2)$.

Consider two samples of text, W_1 and W_2, generated by the same source. Let $C_1(w_1,w_2)$ be the number of times the words w_1,w_2 occur adjacent to each other in W_1, and let $C_1(w_1)$ be the number of occurrences of w_1 in W_1. Finally, let r_1 be the number of different bigrams w_1,w_2 that occur exactly once in W_1 (i.e. such that $C_1(w_1,w_2) = 1$) and let N_1 be the size of W_1. Turing asserts that r_1 / N_1 is a good estimate of the probability that in the text W_2 a randomly located bigram w_i,w_{i+1} will be one that has never occurred in the text W_1 (i.e., $C_1(w_i,w_{i+1}) = 0$). Thus $P_2(w_1,w_2)$, the probability of finding a bigram w_1,w_2 in the text W_2, should be chosen so that it satisfies

$$\sum_{W_1} P_2(w_1,w_2) = 1 - (r_1/N_1) \qquad (E.1)$$

where the sum is over all bigrams occurring in W_1.

Now the usual estimate of the probability $P_2(w_1,w_2)$ would be the relative frequency $C_1(w_1,w_2)/N_1$ extracted from the text W_1, and its sum over all bigrams in W_1 would equal to 1. To satisfy (E.1), it would thus be reasonable to choose

$$P_2(w_1,w_2) = dC_1 \frac{C_1(w_1,w_2)}{N_1} \quad \text{for} \quad C_1(w_1,w_2) > 0 \qquad (E.2)$$

where dC_1 is some positive factor less than 1 determined so as to satisfy (E.1). In fact, since

$$P_2(w_1,w_2) = P_2(w_1', w_2') \quad \text{whenever} \quad C_1(w_1,w_2) = C_1(w_1', w_2') \qquad (E.3)$$

should surely hold, then dC_1 should depend on the count $C_1(w_1,w_2)$, as the notation indicates. Furthermore, since relative frequency is for large counts $C_1(w_1,w_2)$ a good estimate of probability, dC_1 should be a monotonically increasing function of the count C_1 that is equal to 1 for $C_1 > C^*$ (S.Katz found experimentally that $C^* = 5$ is a good choice for this threshold).

Now consider $P_2(w_2 \mid w_1)$, the probability that in the text W_2 a randomly located word w_1 will be followed by the word w_2, and $P_2(w_1)$, the probability that the word w_1 will be found at a random location in W_2. Estimating the latter probability by relative frequency $C_1(w_1)/N_1$, we get the relation

$$P_2(w_1,w_2) = P_2(w_2 \mid w_1) \frac{C_1(w_1)}{N_1} \tag{E.4}$$

It therefore follows from (E.2) and (E.4) that a good estimate for the conditioned probability is

$$P_2(w_2 \mid w_1) = dC_1 \frac{C_1(w_1,w_2)}{C_1(w_1)} \qquad \text{if} \quad C_1(w_1,w_2) > 0 \tag{E.5}$$

where the assumption $C_1(w_1) > 0$ is justified if W_1 is large enough so that every word has been seen in it.

It remains to estimate $P(w_2 \mid w_1)$ for words w_2 that never followed w_1 in W_1 (i.e. w_2 for which $C_1(w_1,w_2) = 0$). If w_2 and w_2' are two such words, then it is reasonable to set their probabilities in proportion to their counts, i.e.,

$$\frac{P_2(w_2' \mid w_1)}{P_2(w_2 \mid w_1)} = \frac{C_1(w_2')}{C_1(w_2)} \tag{E.6}$$

Furthermore, the total probability allocated to such words should be the probability $Q_.(w_1)$ left over from the allocation (E.5) to words that have followed w_1 in W_1,

$$Q_1(w_1) = 1 - \sum_{W_1} P_2(w_2 \mid w_1) =$$

$$= 1 - \frac{1}{C_1(w_1)} \sum_{w_2} dC_1 \; C_1(w_1,w_2) \tag{E.7}$$

where the first sum is over all words w_2 such that $C_1(w_1,w_2) > 0$.

It thus follows from (E.6) and (E.7) that if $t_1(w_1)$ denotes the normalizing factor equal to the sum of $C_1(w)$ over all words w for which $C_1(w_1,w) = 0$, then the proper estimate is

$$P(w_2 \mid w_1) = Q_1(w_1) \frac{C_1(w_2)}{t_1(w_1)} \qquad \text{if} \quad C_1(w_1,w_2) = 0 \tag{E.8}$$

Putting all the above reasoning together, we get the overall formula

$$P_2(w_2 \mid w_1) = \begin{cases} \dfrac{C_1(w_1,w_2)}{C_1(w_1)} & \text{if } C_1(w_1,w_2) \geq 6 \\[2ex] dC_1 \dfrac{C_1(w_1,w_2)}{C_1(w_1)} & \text{if } 6 > C_1(w_1,w_2) > 0 \\[2ex] Q_1(w_1) \dfrac{C_1(w_2)}{t_1(w_1)} & \text{if } C_1(w_1,w_2) = 0 \end{cases} \qquad (E.9)$$

where the *discounts* dC_1 are chosen to satisfy (E.1). In reference <7> Katz determines dC_1 by a formula based on the original reasoning of Turing. However, the discounts could also be estimated by a direct calculation maximizing the probability of the bigrams in W_2 assuming they were generated by the rule (E.2).

The above method of estimating the probabilities of occurrence of words in unseen text is referred to as one of "backing off" from bigram to unigram estimation when bigram data is not available.

We are now ready to estimate trigram probabilities. For histories w_1,w_2 such that $C_1(w_1,w_2) > 0$, the straightforward application of the above reasoning leads to the overall formula

$$P_2(w_3 \mid w_1,w_2) = \begin{cases} \dfrac{C_1(w_1,w_2,w_3)}{N_1 P_2(w_1,w_2)} & \text{if } C_1(w_1,w_2,w_3) \geq 6 \\[2ex] eC_1 \dfrac{C_1(w_1,w_2,w_3)}{N_1 P_2(w_1,w_2)} & \text{if } 6 > C_1(w_1,w_2,w_3) > 0 \\[2ex] Q_1(w_1,w_2) \dfrac{P_2(w_3 \mid w_2)}{t_1(w_1,w_2)} & \text{if } C_1(w_1,w_2,w_3) = 0 \end{cases} \qquad (E.10)$$

In (E.10), eC_1 are discounts whose value depends on $C_1(w_1,w_2,w_3)$ and assures that

$$\sum_{w_1} eC_1 \frac{C_1(w_1,w_2,w_3)}{N_1} = 1 - \frac{s_1}{N_1} \qquad (E.11)$$

where s_1 is the number of different trigrams w_1,w_2,w_3 that occurred exactly once in W_1 (i.e., such that $C_1(w_1,w_2,w_3) = 1$.) The exact specifications of eC_1 can be found in reference <7>. $P_2(w_1,w_2)$ are probabilities given by (E.2). Analogously to (E.7), $Q_1(w_1,w_2)$ is the left over probability allocation given by

$$Q_1(w_1,w_2) = 1 - \sum_{W_1} P_2(w_3 \mid w_1,w_2) \qquad (E.12)$$

where the sum is over all w_3 such that $C_1(w_1,w_2,w_3) > 0$, and finally the normalizing factor is

$$t_1(w_1,w_2) = \sum_{W_1} P_2(w_3 \mid w_2) \qquad (E.13)$$

where the sum is over all w_3 such that $C_1(w_1,w_2,w_3) = 0$.

Of course, when $C_1(w_1,w_2) = 0$ then $P_2(w_3 \mid w_1,w_2)$ is simply set equal to $P_2(w_3 \mid w_1)$.

In (E.10) we have a formula for estimating trigram probabilities based on trigram, bigram, and unigram counts collected over some available training text. Obviously, the same reasoning would allow us to estimate fourgram probabilities on the basis of trigram probabilities, just as (E.10) was based on (E.9). Therefore, the above method can be used to calculate n -gram probabilities.

APPENDIX F

PREDICTION OF LEXICAL CONTENT FROM LONG HISTORY

In this appendix we consider estimates of the probability $t(c_i \mid g_i, w_1, \ldots, w_{i-1})$ which is the factor in formula

$$P(w_i \mid w_1,\ldots, w_{i-1}) =$$

$$= \sum_{c_i,g_i} [\, k(w_i/c_i, g_i)\; h(g_i/g(w_{i-2}), g(w_{i-1}))\; t(c_i/g_i, w_1,\ldots, w_{i-1})\,] \qquad (28)$$

of Section 6 that predicts from a relatively long past history the content class c_i of the next word w_i. We will also discuss here a possible self-organized method of discovery of lexical content classes appropriate to a discourse domain.

The first problem is to construct an estimate of $t(c_i \mid g_i, w_1, \ldots, w_{i-1})$ from components whose value can be extracted from a training text of reasonable size. We proceed as follows.

Let $wc_{i,1}, wc_{i,2}, \ldots, wc_{i,n}$ be the content words in the history $w_1, w_2, \ldots, w_{i-2}$, and let $wf_{i,1}, wf_{i,2}, \ldots, wf_{i,m}$ be the remaining function words (we assume that a decision about the functional character of a word is a straightforward one). We can now write

$$P(w_1, w_2, \ldots, w_{i-1}, c_i, g_i) =$$

$$[\, P(c_i, g_i)\, P(wc_{i,1} \mid c_i, g_i)\, P(wc_{i,2} \mid wc_{i,1}, c_i, g_i) \ldots P(wc_{i,n} \mid wc_{i,1}, \ldots, wc_{i,n-1}, c_i, g_i)$$

$$P(w_{i-1} \mid wc_{i,1}, \ldots, wc_{i,n}, c_i, g_i)\, P(wf_{i,1}, \ldots, wf_{i,m} \mid wc_{i,1}, \ldots wc_{i,n}, w_{i-1}, c_i, g_i)\,] \qquad (F.1)$$

In (F.1) we have used the standard chain rule to decompose the probability by first developing the content word dependence, and then the rest. The complexity of the factors of (F.1) must now be reduced.

Since the generation of a word at a time j depends on the identity of the word at time $j-l$ more than on earlier words, we will make the approximation that it is completely independent of them. Also, content words $wc_{i,j}$ that precede w_i by more than one position are influenced very little by the syntactic category g_i of w_i, once the content word $wc_{i,j-1}$ preceding them is known. Finally, if w_{i-1} is given, the function words $wf_{i,1}, \ldots, wf_{i,m}$ are uninfluenced by the content category c_i of the word w_i. These considerations simplify (F.1) as follows:

$$P(w_1, w_2, \ldots, w_{i-1}, c_i, g_i) =$$

$$[\, P(c_i, g_i)\, P(wc_{i,1} \mid c_i)\, P(wc_{i,2} \mid wc_{i,1}, c_i) \ldots P(wc_{i,n} \mid wc_{i,n-1}, c_i)\, P(w_{i-1} \mid wc_{i,n}, c_i, g_i)$$

$$P(wf_{i,1}, \ldots, wf_{i,m} \mid wc_{i,1}, \ldots, wc_{i,n}, w_{i-1}, g_i)\,] \qquad (F.2)$$

Substituting (F.2) into the numerator and denominator of the standard conditioned probability formula

$$t(c_i \mid g_i, w_1, \ldots, w_{i-1}) = \frac{P(w_1, w_2, \ldots, w_{i-1}, c_i, g_i)}{\sum_{c_i'} P(w_1, w_2, \ldots, w_{i-1}, c_i', g_i)} \qquad (F.3)$$

we observe that the term $P(wf_{i,1}, \ldots, wf_{i,m} \mid wc_{i,1}, \ldots, wc_{i,n}, w_{i-1}, g_i)$ cancels, since it is not a function of c_i. Furthermore, if the difference between the time i and the time at which $wc_{i,j}$ takes place is sufficiently large, then the probability $P(wc_{i,j} \mid wc_{i,j-1}, c_i)$ depends on the content class c_i only weakly, so we will cancel such terms as well. Therefore, defining the probability

$$Q(wc_{i,n-k+1},\ldots,wc_{i,n},w_{i-1}, c_i, g_i \mid wc_{i,n-1}) = [\, P(wc_{i,n-k+1} \mid wc_{i,n-k}, c_i)$$

$$\ldots P(wc_{i,n} \mid wc_{i,n-1}, c_i)\, P(w_{i-1} \mid wc_{i,n}, c_i, g_i)\, P(c_i, g_i)\,] \tag{F.4}$$

we end up with the final estimate

$$t(c_i \mid g_i, w_1, \ldots, w_{i-1}) = \frac{Q(wc_{i,n-k+1},\ldots,wc_{i,n}, w_{i-1}, c_i, g_i \mid wc_{i,n-k})}{\sum_{c_i'} Q(wc_{i,n-k+1}\ldots wc_{i,n}, w_{i-1}, c_i', g_i \mid wc_{i,n-k})} \tag{F.5}$$

that is based on terms that involve only the $k + 1$ most recent content words of the history $w_1, w_2, \ldots, w_{i-2}$. Unfortunately, even if k is moderate, unless some precomputation is done, it will be difficult to carry out the summation in (F.5) during recognition, and even more so the summation in (28).

The number of terms in (F.5) can be further reduced by basing the probability $t(c_i \mid g_i, w_1, \ldots, w_{i-1})$ on headwords $H^*_{i,j}$ of phrases ($H^*_{i,j}$ denotes the j th headword preceding w_{i-1}) instead of on content words $wc_{i,j}$. That approach, which may require a parser, may pay off in the long run. Another simplification is possible if we impose a lexical classification on the headwords $H^*_{i,j}$ and thus replace them by their classes $c^*_{i,j}$. Choosing the number of headwords, m, that will be involved in the prediction formula, we then end up with the estimate

$$t(c_i / g_i, w_1, \ldots, w_{i-1}) =$$

$$NORM\; P(c_i g_i)\; P(w_{i-1} \mid c^*_{i,1}, c_i g_i) \prod_{j=1}^{m-1} P(c^*_{i,j} \mid c^*_{i,j+1}, c_i) \tag{29}$$

where NORM is a normalizing factor, corresponding to the inverse of the sum in the denominator of (F.5), which assures that the righthand side of (29) adds up to 1 when summed over all possible values of c_i (as a probability must).

The estimation of the individual terms $P(c^*_{i,j} \mid c^*_{i,j+1}, c_i)$ involves the marking of content words in the text, and then collecting counts $C(c^*_{i,j}, c^*_{i,j+1}, c_i)$. In the face of insufficient data, the estimation may be made more robust by combining counts over a window of size k. For $k = 3$ the probability would be based on the pseudo-count $\hat{C}$ given by

$$\hat{C}(c^*_{i,j}, c^*_{i,j+1}, c_i) =$$

$$C(c^{\bullet}_{i,j-1}, c^{\bullet}_{i,j}, c_i) + C(c^{\bullet}_{i,j}, c^{\bullet}_{i,j+1}, c_i) + C(c^{\bullet}_{i,j+1}, c^{\bullet}_{i+2,j}, c_i) \tag{F.6}$$

The remaining unsolved problem is the content categorization c. It is, of course, desirable to discover it in a self-organized manner, directly from text. A possible approach aimed at making the syntactic and lexical classification "orthogonal" is as follows.

Annotate the words w_i of the text by their parts of speech g_i. Let J_i denote a fixed window of words surrounding w_i, say the words $w_{i-m},...,w_{i-1},w_{i+1},...,w_{i+m}$ (the use of a window around w_i was suggested by Prof. J. Sinclair). Basing the prediction of w_i on words whose position is randomly chosen from a window J_i of moderate size (e.g., $m = 4$) should compensate for possible sparseness of data while destroying the potential syntactic component of the prediction which depends on position in the word sequence. Thus if $E_i(c)$ denotes the event that a word chosen at random from the window J_i belongs to class c, then we will wish to find that partition of the vocabulary V into L classes which maximizes the average information provided by events $E_i(c)$ about the class $c(w_i)$ of the word w_i, given its POS annotation g_i. The nontechnical reader should interpret the above statement intuitively. Results of Information Theory summarized in Appendix A show that

$$I(\, c(w_i)\,;\, E_i(c)\mid g_i) = \sum_{c',\,c,\,g} [\, P(\, c(w_i) = c',\; E_i(c), g_i = g) \log \frac{P(\, c(w_i) = c',\; E_i(c) \mid g_i = g)}{P(c(w_i) = c' \mid g_i = g) P(E_i(c) \mid g_i = g)} \,] \tag{F.7}$$

has the required mathematical properties, and is therefore the criterion to be maximized. The iterative method of Appendix D can be easily modified to find the requisite (suboptimal) classification.

ACKNOWLEDGEMENT

The author gratefully acknowledges the many helpful suggestions made by his colleague Peter Brown, concerning both the content and the form of this article. The ideas discussed here are the result of extended cooperation on language modeling with L.R. Bahl, J.K. Baker, E. Black, P. Brown, P. deSouza, S.M. Katz, R.L. Mercer,

E. Muckstein, and A. Nadas. Irene Halpin prepared the numerous revisions of the current manuscript.

REFERENCES

<1> J.B. Carroll, P. Davies, and B. Richman, Word Frequency Book, New York: American Heritage , 1971.

<2> C.E. Shannon, "Prediction and Entropy of Printed English." Bell Syst. Tech. Jr., Vol 30, pp 50 - 64, 1951.

<3> T.M. Cover and R.C. King, "A Convergent Gambling Estimate of the Entropy of English," IEEE Trans. on Information Theory, Vol IT-24, No-4, pp. 413 - 420, July 1978.

<4> L.R. Bahl and F. Jelinek, "Decoding for Channels with Insertions, Deletions, and Substitutions with Applications to Speech Recognition." IEEE Trans. on Information Theory, Vol IT-21, No 4, pp 404 - 411, July 1975.

<5> L.R. Bahl, F. Jelinek , and R.L. Mercer, "A Maximum Likelihood Approach to Continuous Speech Recognition," IEEE Trans. on Pattern Analysis and Machine Intelligence, Vol PAMI-5, No 2, pp. 179 - 190, March 1983.

<6> R.L. Cave and L.P. Neuwirth: "Hidden Markov Models for English," in J.D. Ferguson, ed., *Hidden Markov Models for Speech,* Princeton: IDA - CRD, pp. 8 - 15, October 1980.

<7> S.M. Katz, "Recursive m-gram Language Model via a Smoothing of Turing's Formula", a forthcoming paper and patent.

<8> A. Nadas, "Estimation of Probabilities in the Language Model of the IBM Speech Recognition System, " IEEE Transactions ASSP, Volume ASSP-32, Number 4, pp. 859-861, August 1984.

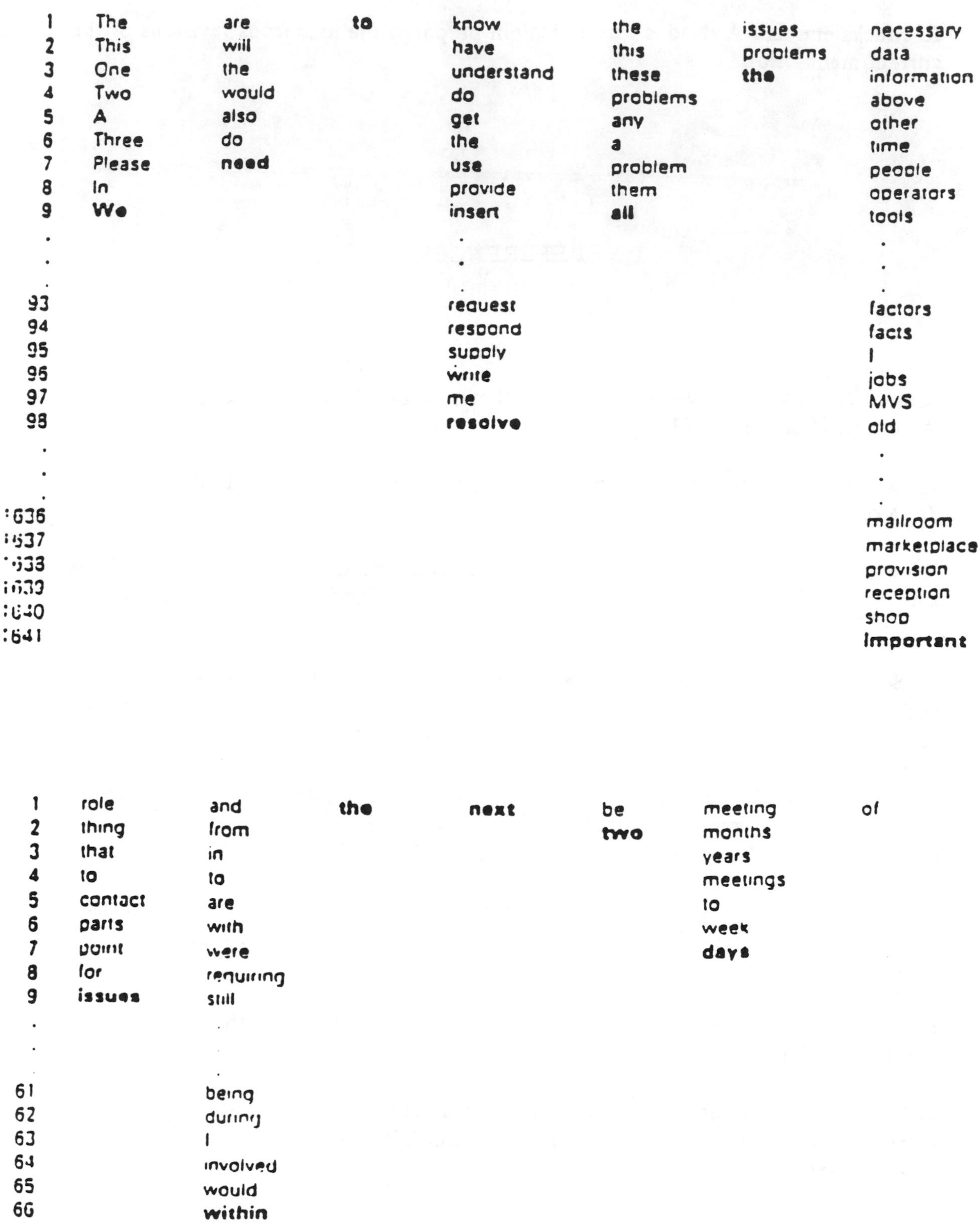
1 The are to know the issues necessary
2 This will have this problems data
3 One the understand these the information
4 Two would do problems above
5 A also get any other
6 Three do the a time
7 Please need use problem people
8 In provide them operators
9 We insert all tools
.
.
.
93 request factors
94 respond facts
95 supply I
96 write jobs
97 me MVS
98 resolve old
.
.
.
1636 mailroom
1637 marketplace
1638 provision
1639 reception
1640 shop
1641 important
1 role and the next be meeting of
2 thing from two months
3 that in years
4 to to meetings
5 contact are to
6 parts with week
7 point were days
8 for requiring
9 issues still
.
.
.
61 being
62 during
63 I
64 involved
65 would
66 within

FIGURE 1

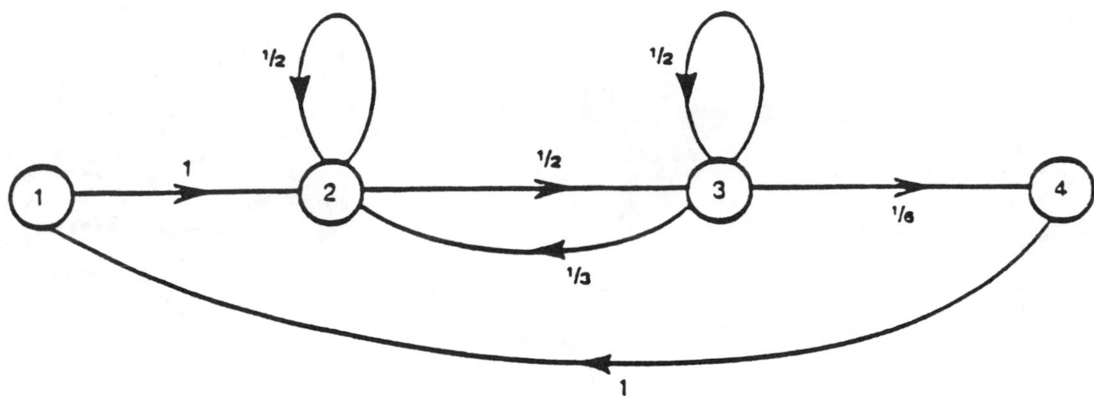

Figure B.1

A four state Markov chain transition diagram

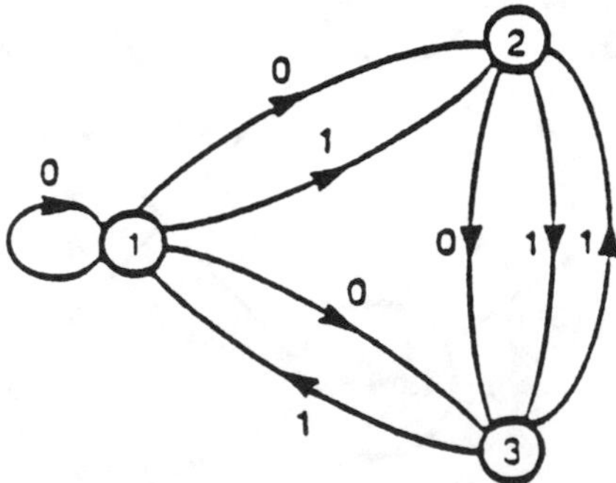

Figure B.2

A three state hidden Markov chain with a binary output alphabet {0,1}. Values of transition probabilities are not indicated.

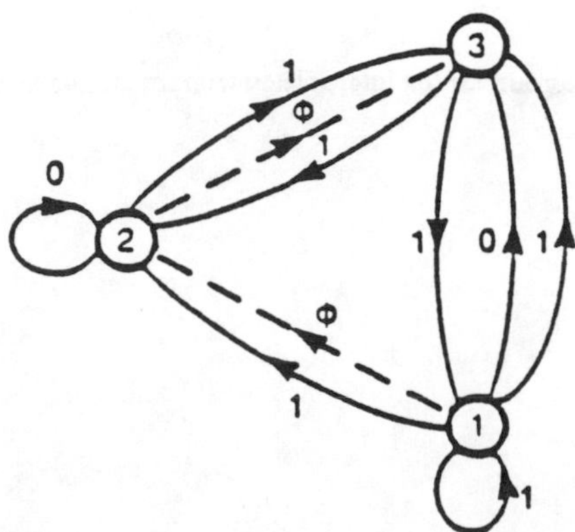

Figure B.3

A three state hidden Markov chain with null transitions and binary outputs. Values of transition probabilities are not indicated.

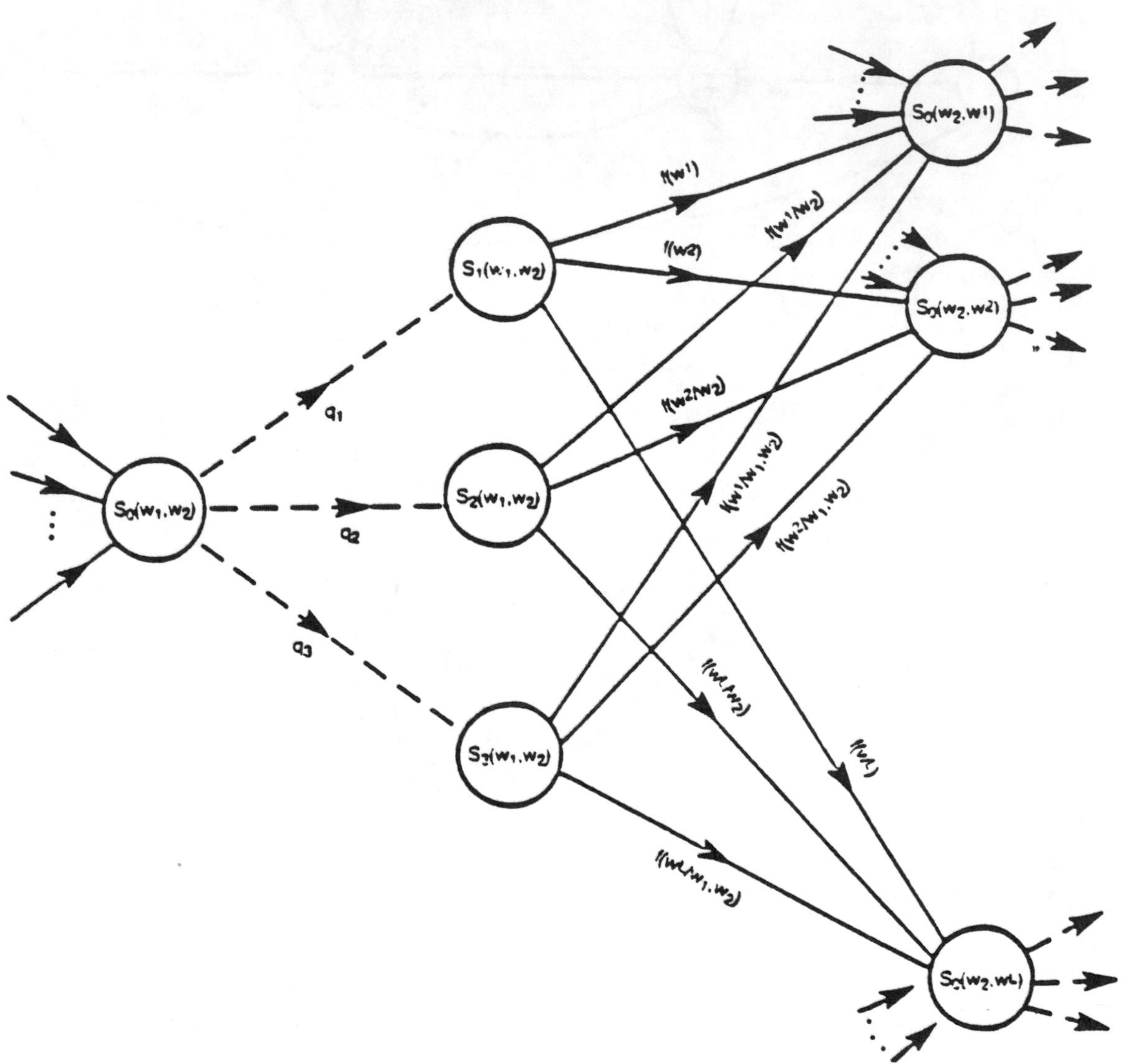

Figure C.1

Section of hidden Markov transition diagram for the interpolated trigram language model. The vocabulary consists of words $\{w^1, w^2, \ldots, w^L\}$.

A Tree-Based Statistical Language Model for Natural Language Speech Recognition

LALIT R. BAHL, MEMBER, IEEE, PETER F. BROWN, PETER V. DE SOUZA, AND ROBERT L. MERCER, MEMBER, IEEE

Abstract—This paper is concerned with the problem of "predicting" the next word a speaker will say, given the words already spoken; specifically, the problem is to estimate the probability that a given word will be the next word uttered. Algorithms are presented for automatically constructing a binary decision tree designed to estimate these probabilities. At each node of the tree there is a yes/no question relating to the words already spoken, and at each leaf there is a probability distribution over the allowable vocabulary. Ideally, these nodal questions can take the form of arbitrarily complex Boolean expressions, but computationally cheaper alternatives are also discussed. The paper includes some results obtained on a 5000-word vocabulary with a tree designed to predict the next word spoken from the preceding 20 words. The tree is compared to an equivalent trigram model and shown to be superior.

I. Introduction

Given some acoustic evidence A derived from a spoken word sequence W, the problem in automatic speech recognition is to determine W. In one approach [1], [5], an estimate $\hat{W}$ of W is obtained as

$$\hat{W} = \underset{W}{\text{argmax}} \Pr\{W|A\}. \quad (1)$$

By Bayes' rule, this can be rewritten as

$$\hat{W} = \underset{W}{\text{argmax}} \frac{\Pr\{A|W\} \cdot \Pr\{W\}}{\Pr\{A\}}. \quad (2)$$

The denominator in (2) is independent of W and can be ignored in the search for $\hat{W}$. The first term in the numerator is the probability of observing the acoustic evidence A when the speaker says W. It is the job of an acoustic model to estimate this probability. The second term in the numerator is the probability that the speaker will say W. This is called the *prior* probability of W. The purpose of a language model is to estimate the prior probabilities.

The prior probability of a word sequence $W = w_1, w_2, \cdots, w_n$ can be written as

$$\Pr\{W\} = \prod_{i=1}^{n} \Pr\{w_i|w_1, w_2, \cdots, w_{i-1}\}, \quad (3)$$

so the task of language modeling can be reduced to the problem of estimating terms like $\Pr\{w_i|w_1, w_2, \cdots, w_{i-1}\}$: the probability that w_i will be said after $w_1, w_2, \cdots, w_{i-1}$. The number of parameters of a language model is the number of variables that must be known in advance in order to compute $\Pr\{w_i|w_1, w_2, \cdots, w_{i-1}\}$ for any word sequence $w_1, w_2, \cdots, w_i$.

Manuscript received November 24, 1987; revised September 23, 1988.
The authors are with the Speech Recognition Group, IBM Thomas J. Watson Research Center, P.O. Box 218, Yorktown Heights, NY 10598.
IEEE Log Number 8928123.

In any practical natural-language system with even a moderate vocabulary size, it is clear that the language model probabilities $\Pr\{w_i|w_1, w_2, \cdots, w_{i-1}\}$ cannot be stored for each possible sequence $w_1, w_2, \cdots, w_i$. Even if the sequences were limited to one or two sentences in length, the number of distinct sequences would be so large that a complete set of probabilities could not be computed, never mind stored or retrieved. To be practicable, then, a language model must have many fewer parameters than the total number of possible sequences $w_1, w_2, \cdots, w_i$. An obvious way to limit the number of parameters is to partition the various possible word histories $w_1, w_2, \cdots, w_{i-1}$ into a manageable number of equivalence classes.

A simple-minded, but surprisingly effective, definition of equivalence classes can be found in the N-gram language model [5], [10]. In this model, word sequences are treated as equivalent if and only if they end with the same $N - 1$ words. Typically $N = 3$, in which case the model is referred to as a 3-gram or trigram model. The trigram model is based upon the approximation

$$\Pr\{w_i|w_1, w_2, \cdots, w_{i-1}\} = \Pr\{w_i|w_{i-2}, w_{i-1}\}, \quad (4)$$

which is clearly inexact, but apparently quite useful. Maximum-likelihood estimates of N-gram probabilities can be obtained from their relative frequencies in a large body of training text. But since many legitimate N-grams are likely to be missing from the training text, it is necessary to "smooth" the maximum-likelihood estimates so as to avoid probabilities of zero. The trigram model can be smoothed in a natural way using the bigram and unigram relative frequencies as described in [6].

The trigram language model has the following advantages: the equivalence classes are easy to determine, the relative frequencies can all be precomputed with very little computation, and the probabilities can be smoothed "on the fly" quickly and efficiently. The main disadvantage of the trigram model lies in its naive definition of

0096-3518/89/0700-1001$01.00

equivalence classes. All words prior to the most recent two are ignored, and useful information is lost. Additionally, word sequences ending in different pairs of words should not necessarily be considered distinct; they may be functionally equivalent from a language model point of view. Separating equivalent histories into different classes, as the trigram model does, fragments the training data unnecessarily and reduces the accuracy of the resulting probability estimates.

In Section II we describe a tree-based language model which avoids both of the above weaknesses in the trigram model. Although the tree-based model is as convenient to apply as the trigram model, it requires a massive increase in computation to construct. Some results are presented in Section III.

II. Constructing a Tree-Based Language Model

Let us now consider the construction of binary decision trees and their application to the language modeling problem. An example of a binary decision tree is shown in Fig. 1.

At each nonterminal node of the tree, there is a question requiring a yes/no answer, and corresponding to each possible answer there is a branch leading to the next question. Associated with each terminal node, i.e., leaf, is some advice or information which takes into account all the questions and answers which lead to that leaf. The application of binary decision trees is much like playing the venerable TV game "What's My Line?" where contestants try to deduce the occupation of a guest by asking a series of yes/no questions. In the context of language modeling, the questions relate to the words already spoken; for example: "Is the preceding word a verb?". And the information at each leaf takes the form of a probability distribution indicating which words are likely to be spoken next. The leaves of the tree represent language model equivalence classes. The classes are defined implicitly by the questions and answers leading to the leaves.

Notice that an N-gram language model is just a special case of a binary-tree model. With enough questions of the form "Is the last word w_i?" or "Is the second to last word w_j?" the N-gram language model can be represented in the form of a tree. Thus, an optimally constructed tree language model is guaranteed to be at least as good as an optimally constructed N-gram model, and is likely to be much better, given the weaknesses in N-gram models already discussed.

The object of a decision tree is to reduce the uncertainty of the event being decided upon, be it an occupation in a game show, a diagnosis, or the next word a speaker will utter. In language modeling, this uncertainty is measured by the entropy of the probability distributions at the leaves. We seek a decision tree which minimizes the average entropy of the leaf distributions. Let $\{l_1, l_2, \cdots, l_L\}$ denote the leaves of a decision tree, and let Y denote

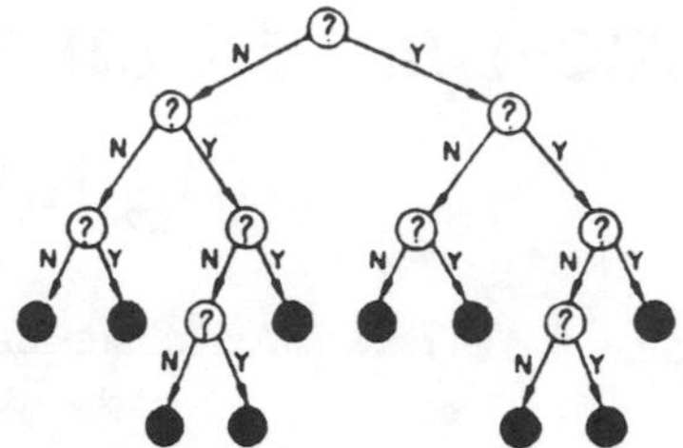

Fig. 1. Example of a binary decision tree.

the event being decided upon—the next word spoken. The average entropy of the leaf distributions is

$$\bar{H}(Y) = \sum_{i=1}^{L} H_i(Y) \cdot \Pr\{l_i\}, \tag{5}$$

where $H_i(Y)$ is the entropy of the distribution associated with leaf l_i, and $\Pr\{l_i\}$ is the prior probability of visiting leaf l_i. The entropy at leaf l_i, measured in bits, is

$$H_i(Y) = -\sum_{j=1}^{V} \Pr\{w_j | l_i\} \cdot \log_2 \Pr\{w_j | l_i\}. \tag{6}$$

where V is the size of the vocabulary, and $\Pr\{w_j | l_i\}$ is the probability that word w_j will be the next word spoken given that the immediate word history leads to leaf l_i.

Notice that the average entropy is defined in terms of the *true* leaf distributions, and not the relative frequencies as obtained from a sample of data. The sample entropy, i.e., the entropy on training data, can always be made arbitrarily small by increasing the number of leaves so as to make the leaf sample sizes arbitrarily small. The entropy on test data, however, cannot usually be made arbitrarily small. Typically, trees which perform extremely well on training data achieve their success by modeling idiosyncrasies of the training data themselves rather than by capturing generalizations about the process which gave rise to the data. In the algorithm described below, in order to avoid making such deceptively good trees, we divide the data into two independent halves. Improvements suggested by one half are verified against the other half. If they do not perform well there, they are rejected.

Although we would like to construct the tree with minimum entropy for test data, there is no way of doing so. The best hope is for a "good" tree, having low entropy on test data. Searching for a tree which is good is essentially a problem in heuristics, and many procedures are possible. These procedures include manual tree construction by linguistic experts, as well as automatic tree-growing algorithms. Automatic methods have some important advantages over manual construction: they are not generally language-dependent and may therefore be applied to any language, any domain, and any vocabulary of interest. In many cases, expert linguistic knowledge may not even exist.

In this paper we shall describe only one automatic method: a greedy algorithm, with restrictions on the form of the questions. The algorithm is greedy in the sense that at any node in the tree the question selected is the one giving the greatest reduction in entropy at that node, without regard to subsequent nodes. Thus, the algorithm aims to construct a tree which is locally optimal, but very likely not globally optimal; the hope being that a locally optimal tree will be globally "good." This tree-construction paradigm has been advocated before [4], and has been used successfully in other applications [3], [8]. A dynamic programming algorithm for the determination of a truly optimal tree is described in [9], but is only suitable in restricted applications with relatively few variables; it is inappropriate for the present application. A treatise on the art and science of tree growing can be found in [2].

Because the search space of possible questions is enormous, we will place restrictions on the form of the questions. Initially, we shall only allow "elementary" questions of the form "$X \in S$?" where X denotes a discrete random variable with a finite number of possible values, and S is a subset of the values taken by X. For example, if X denotes the preceding word, and S is the set of all verbs in the permitted vocabulary, then "$X \in S$?" represents the question "Is the preceding word a verb?". Similarly, if X denotes the head of the most recent noun phrase, and S is the set of all plural nouns in the vocabulary, then "$X \in S$?" represents the question "Does the head of the most recent noun phrase have the attribute *plural*?". Later we shall discuss the possibility of relaxing these restrictions by allowing composite questions comprising several elementary questions.

Let $X_1, X_2, \cdots, X_m$ be the discrete random variables whose values may be questioned. We shall call these the *predictor* variables. Clearly the power of the decision tree depends on the number and choice of predictor variables. The trigram model makes use of only two predictors: the preceding word, X_1, and the word before that, X_2. But, obviously, the list of predictor variables need not be limited to those two; it can easily be extended to include the last N words spoken, $N > 2$, without encountering the difficulty of combinatorial explosion that besets the general N-gram model. Furthermore, if a parser that can handle partial sentences is available, then the list of predictors can also include information from the parser, like the head of the most recent noun phrase. As far as tree construction is concerned, it makes no difference how the predictors are defined; the construction algorithm only uses their values and the value of the next word, Y. As far as the number of equivalence classes is concerned, it makes no difference how many predictor variables there are; increasing the number of predictors does not, in itself, increase the number of equivalence classes. However, the amount of computation involved in tree construction will increase as the number of predictors increases, and therefore, the choice of predictors should be limited to those variables which provide significant information about the word being predicted.

The tree-growing algorithm can be summarized as follows.

1) Let c be the current node of the tree. Initially c is the root.

2) For each predictor variable X_i ($i = 1, 2, \cdots, m$), find the set S_i^c which minimizes the average conditional entropy at node c

$$\begin{aligned}\overline{H}_c(Y|\text{``}X_i \in S_i^c\text{?''}) &= -\Pr\{X_i \in S_i^c|c\} \sum_{j=1}^{V} \Pr\{w_j|c, X_i \in S_i^c\} \\ &\quad \cdot \log_2 \Pr\{w_j|c, X_i \in S_i^c\} \\ &\quad - \Pr\{X_i \notin S_i^c|c\} \sum_{j=1}^{V} \Pr\{w_j|c, X_i \notin S_i^c\} \\ &\quad \cdot \log_2 \Pr\{w_j|c, X_i \notin S_i^c\}. \qquad (7)\end{aligned}$$

3) Determine which of the m questions derived in Step 2 leads to the lowest entropy. Let this be question k, i.e.,

$$k = \operatorname*{argmin}_i \overline{H}_c(Y|\text{``}X_i \in S_i^c\text{?''}). \qquad (8)$$

4) The reduction in entropy at node c due to question k is

$$R_c(k) = H_c(Y) - \overline{H}_c(Y|\text{``}X_k \in S_k^c\text{?''}), \qquad (9)$$

where

$$H_c(Y) = -\sum_{j=1}^{V} \Pr\{w_j|c\} \cdot \log_2 \Pr\{w_j|c\}.$$

If this reduction is "significant," store question k, create two descendant nodes, c_1 and c_2, corresponding to the conditions $X_k \in S_k^c$ and $X_k \notin S_k^c$, and repeat Steps 2–4 for each of the new nodes separately.

The reduction in entropy in Step 4 is the mutual information between Y and question k at node c. Thus, seeking questions which minimize entropy is just another way of saying that questions are sought which are maximally informative about the event being predicted—an eminently reasonable criterion.

The true probabilities in Step 2 are generally unknown. In practice, they can be replaced by estimates obtained from relative frequencies in a sample of training text. This means, of course, that the algorithm must be conducted using estimates $\hat{\overline{H}}$, $\hat{H}$, and $\hat{R}$, instead of the true values $\overline{H}$, H, and R, respectively.

If the distribution of $\hat{R}$ were known, its statistical significance could be determined in Step 4 when assessing the utility of the selected question. In our case, however, we were unable to determine the distribution of $\hat{R}$ and resorted to an empirical test of significance instead. Using independent (held-out) training data, we computed the reduction in entropy due to the selected question, and retained the question if the reduction exceeded a threshold.

The threshold allows the arborist to state what is considered to be *practically* significant, as opposed to *statistically* significant. The definition of "significant" in Step 4 determines whether or not a node is subdivided into two subnodes, and is responsible, therefore, for the ultimate size of the tree, and the amount of computation required to construct it.

The only remaining issue to be addressed in the above tree-growing algorithm is the determination of the set S_i^c in Step 2. This amounts to partitioning the values taken by X_i into two groups: those in S_i^c and those not in S_i^c. Again, there is no known practical way of achieving a certifiably optimal partition, especially in applications like language modeling where X_i can take a large number of different values. As before, the best realistic hope is to find a "good" set S_i^c via some kind of heuristic search. Possible search strategies range from relatively simple greedy algorithms to the computationally expensive techniques of simulated annealing [7].

Let $\mathbf{X}$ denote the set of values taken by the variable X. In our case, $\mathbf{X}$ is the entire vocabulary. The following algorithm determines a set S in a greedy fashion.

1) Let S be empty.

2) Insert into S the $x \in \mathbf{X}$ which leads to the greatest reduction in the average conditional entropy (7). If no $x \in \mathbf{X}$ leads to a reduction, make no insertion.

3) Delete from S any member x, if so doing leads to a reduction in the average conditional entropy.

4) If any insertions or deletions were made to S, return to Step 2.

Using this set-construction algorithm and the earlier tree-growing algorithm, a language-model decision tree could certainly be constructed, but because of the restrictive form of the questions it would be somewhat inefficient. For example, suppose that the best question to place at some node of the tree is actually a composite question of the form: "Is ($X_i \in S_i^c$) OR ($X_j \in S_j^c$)?". This is still a binary question, but with the existing restrictions on the form of the questions, it can only be implemented as two separate questions in such a way that the data are split into three subgroups rather than two. The data for which the answer is "yes" are unavoidably fragmented across two nodes. This is inefficient in the sense that these two nodes may be equivalent from a language model point of view. Splitting data unnecessarily across two nodes leads to duplicated branches, unnecessary computation, reduced sample sizes, and less accurate probability estimates.

To avoid this inefficiency, the elementary questions at each node of the tree must be replaced by composite binary questions. We would like the structure of the composite questions to permit Boolean expressions of arbitrary complexity, containing any number of elementary conditions of the form $X \in S$ and any number of AND, OR, and NOT operators, in any combination. This can be achieved if the questions are themselves represented by binary trees, but with the leaves tied in such a way that

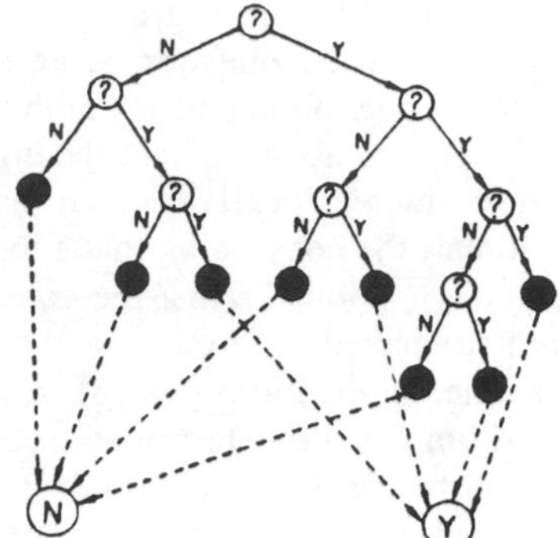

Fig. 2. Example of the topology of an unrestricted composite binary question.

there are only two outcomes. Fig. 2 shows an example of such a structure.

The tree in Fig. 2 has eight leaves which are tied as shown by the dotted lines. The four leaves attached to no-branches are tied; they lead to the same final N-state. And the four leaves attached to yes-branches are tied similarly. Thus, the structure is still that of a binary question; there are only two possible final states. There are many different routes to each of the final states, each route representing a different series of conditions. Thus, the composite condition leading to either one of the final states can only be described with multiple OR operators: one for each distinct route. Similarly, the description of any particular route requires the use of multiple AND operators: one for each node on the route. Since there need be no limits on the number of leaves or the depth of a binary tree, it can be seen that any composite binary question, however complex, can be represented by a binary tree with tied leaves similar to that shown in Fig. 2. Note that NOT operators are superfluous here. The condition "NOT ($X \in T$)" can be rewritten in elementary form "$X \in S$" by defining S to be the complement of T.

Since composite questions are essentially just binary trees with elementary questions at each node, they can be constructed using the greedy tree-growing and set-construction algorithms already described. The entropies, however, must be computed from relative frequencies obtained after pooling all tied data.

Constructing a tree-based language model with composite questions involves a lot of computation. There are trees within trees: at each node of the global binary tree there is a local binary tree. If the computation appears to be excessive, it may be necessary to compromise on some form of question that is more general than an elementary question, but less general than a fully fledged binary tree. One compromise is provided by the pylon shown in Fig. 3.

The pylon has two states, N and Y. Starting at the top (level 1), all the data are placed in the N-state. An elementary question is then sought which splits the data in the N-state into two subgroups; the data answering "yes" being assigned to the Y-state, and the rest remaining in

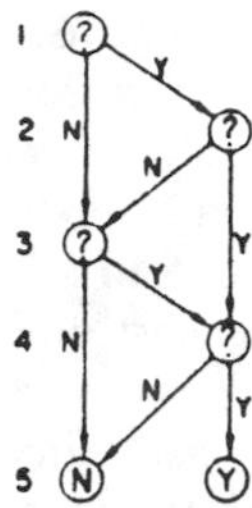

Fig. 3. Example of a pylon: a restricted form of composite binary question.

the N-state. At level 2, a refinement is applied to the data in the Y-state; an elementary question is sought which splits the data into two subgroups: the data answering "no" being returned to the N-state to rejoin the data already there, and the rest remaining in the Y-state. The procedure continues in this fashion, level by level, swapping data from one state to the other, until no further swaps can be found which lower the entropy.

The pylon is equivalent to a restricted binary tree which is constructed by determining a single question to apply simultaneously to all terminal nodes attached to no-branches, followed by a single question to apply simultaneously to all terminal nodes attached to yes-branches, and so on. Thus, the questions attached to several different no-branches are constrained to be identical, as are the questions attached to several different yes-branches.

The pylon has no memory: there are many different routes to most pylonic nodes, but no distinction is made between those different routes when the data are processed. The unconstrained binary tree has memory: different routes lead to different nodes, and since different nodes are subjected to different questions, a distinction is made between the different routes when the data are processed. Hence, the questions in the tree can be tailored to the questions already asked; in the pylon they cannot.

Although most composite questions cannot be represented in pylonic form, many useful composite questions can. For example, "Is the preceding word an adjective AND the one before that an article?". Or, "Is there any computer jargon in the last fifteen words?". The latter question requires a pylon 30 levels deep. As can be seen from these examples, the pylon can express certain types of semantic questions as well as grammatical questions. Both are important in determining what word will be spoken next.

Having constructed a tree, with whatever question topology can be afforded, there remains one important issue: the estimation of the probability distributions at the leaves of the decision tree. With a relatively small tree of 10 000 leaves, and a modest vocabulary of 10 000 words, there are one-hundred-million probabilities to estimate. Even with a reasonably generous one-billion words of training data, there would still be insufficient data to estimate the probabilities accurately. Thus, the probability distributions cannot simply be estimated from the relative frequencies in the training data, which are biased in any case. Just as the trigram probabilities are smoothed with lower order bigram and unigram distributions to ameliorate problems due to sparse data, so too can each leaf distribution be smoothed with the lower order nodal distributions between the root and the leaf.

Let $\{n_1, n_2, \cdots, n_r\}$ denote the set of nodes between the root, n_1, and a given leaf, n_r. Let $q_i(w)$ denote the relative frequency of word w at node n_i as obtained from the tree-growing training text, and let q_i denote the distribution of relative frequencies at node n_i. Further, let q_0 denote the uniform distribution over the vocabulary. A smoothed leaf probability distribution may be obtained as

$$q_r = \sum_{i=0}^{r} \lambda_i q_i, \qquad (10)$$

where the λ's are chosen to maximize the probability of some additional independent (held-out) training data, subject to the constraints that

$$\sum_{i=0}^{r} \lambda_i = 1 \qquad (11)$$

and $\lambda_i \geq 0$, $(0 \leq i \leq r)$. The λ values may be determined from independent training data using the forward–backward parameter estimation algorithm, as described in [1].

It should be clear from the above prescription that tree-growing involves a great deal of computation; the vast majority being devoted to set construction. Certainly it involves a lot more work than the creation of a trigram model. It is also clear, however, that at any given node of the decision tree, the best question to ask is completely independent of the data and questions at any other node. This means that the nodes can be processed independently in any convenient order. Given enough parallel processors, tree growing need not take an excessive amount of time.

III. Results

We tested the foregoing ideas on tree-based language models in a pilot experiment involving a 5000-word vocabulary. The vocabulary consisted of the 5000 most frequent words in a database of IBM office correspondence.

The training and test data were drawn from 550 books and magazines which ranged from intellectually stimulating romantic novels to silly issues of *Datamation*. The books and magazines were divided randomly into four parts as follows:

1) training data for tree construction: approximately 10-million words;

2) data for testing the significance of a reduction in entropy: approximately 10-million words;

3) data for computing the smoothed leaf probability distributions: approximately 9-million words; and

4) test data; approximately 1-million words.

No book or magazine was split between more than one of the above categories. Words not in the vocabulary were treated as a single generic "unknown" word.

The purpose of the experiment was to predict the 21st word of a 21-gram, given the first 20 words. This is equivalent to predicting the next word a speaker will say given the last 20 words spoken. Thus, Y was a discrete random variable taking 5000 values. There were 20 predictor variables $X_1, X_2, \cdots, X_{20}$, each of which represented one of the preceding 20 words, and was, therefore, a discrete random variable taking 5000 values. Note that some of the preceding 20 words may be from earlier sentences or even earlier paragraphs or chapters.

We constructed a tree with pylonic questions using the tree-growing and set-construction algorithms of Section II, with two minor changes. First, instead of adding one word at a time to the set S in Step 2 of set construction, we added one group of words at a time. The groups were predefined to represent grammatical classes such as days of the week, months, nouns, verbs, etc. The classes were of differing coarseness and overlapped; many words belonged to several classes. For example, "July" belonged to the class of months, the class of nouns, as well as its own class, the class of "July," which contained only that one word. Adding groups of words simultaneously allows set construction to proceed more rapidly. Since individual words may be discarded from the set, little harm is done by inserting words several at a time.

Second, since this was only a pilot experiment, we limited the tree to 10 000 leaves. To ensure even growth, the nodes were processed in order of size.

The adequacy of a language model may be assessed by its ability to predict unseen test data. This ability is measured by the perplexity of the data given the model [1]. Put simply, a script with a perplexity of p with respect to some model has the same entropy as a language having p equally likely choices in all contexts. Clearly, the lower the perplexity, the better the model.

Ignoring those 21-grams in the test data which ended in the generic "unknown" word, the perplexity of the test data with respect to the tree was 90.7. This compares to a perplexity of 94.9 with respect to an equivalent trigram language model. Although the tree was by no means fully grown, it still outperformed the trigram model. The difference in perplexity, however, is not great.

A bigger difference is evident in the numbers of very bad predictions. Speech recognition errors are more likely to occur in words given a very low probability by the language model. Using the trigram model, 3.87 percent of the words in the test data were given a probability of less than 2^{-15}. (It is convenient to work in powers of 2 when performing perplexity and entropy calculations.) In the case of the tree, only 2.81 percent of the test words had such a low probability. Thus, the number of words with a probability of less than 2^{-15} was reduced by 27 percent, which could have a significant impact on the error rate of a speech recognizer.

The improvement of the tree over the trigram model was obtained despite the fact that the tree was incomplete and comprised substantially fewer distinct probability distributions than the trigram model. The tree has one distribution per leaf—10 015 in all. The trigram model, on the other hand, has at least one distribution per unique bigram in the training text, and there were 796 000 of them. Apparently, the vastly greater resolution of the trigram model is insufficient to compensate for its other weaknesses vis-à-vis the tree-based model.

Although the tree has 10 015 distributions as compared to 796 000 for the trigram model, the storage necessary for them is about the same. Many of the trigram distributions have very few nonzero entries, which is not true for the tree distributions.

We also created a language model which combined the tree and the trigram. The combined probabilities were obtained as

$$\Pr\{w_{21} | w_1, w_2, \cdots, w_{20}\} = \tilde{\lambda}_r \tilde{q}_r(w_{21}) + (1 - \tilde{\lambda}_r) \Pr\{w_{21} | w_{19}, w_{20}\} \quad (12)$$

with $\tilde{\lambda}_r$ determined from independent training data as discussed in [1]. Here r denotes the leaf corresponding to the sequence $w_1, w_2, \cdots, w_{20}$; $\tilde{q}_r(w_{21})$ and $\Pr\{w_{21} | w_{19}, w_{20}\}$ denote the tree and trigram probability estimates, respectively. The weight $\tilde{\lambda}_r$ was a function of the leaf only, and lay between 0 and 1 as always.

The perplexity of the test data with respect to the combined model was 82.5—13 percent lower than the trigram perplexity and 9 percent lower than the tree perplexity. Additionally, 2.73 percent of the correct words had a probability of less than 2^{-15}. Thus, the number of words with a probability of less than 2^{-15} was only slightly less than with the tree alone, but was almost 30 percent less than obtained with the trigram model on its own.

For interest, we tabulated the depths of the 10 014 pylons in the tree. The results are shown in Fig. 4. It can be seen from Fig. 4 that roughly one-half of the pylons represented a single elementary question, while the other half represented composite questions of varying complexity. This supports the argument for composite questions at the nodes.

We also tabulated how often each predictor was the subject of a question. The 10 014 pylons contained 22 160 questions in total; their subjects are tabulated in Fig. 5. As would be expected, most of the questions are directed toward the more recent words; these being more useful for determining the likely part of speech of the next word to be uttered. Earlier words have not been ignored, although they have been interrogated somewhat less; they are useful for determining the likely semantic category of the forthcoming word. Certainly, it is not the case that all questions are directed toward the two most recent words w_{19} and w_{20}; this underlines the limitations of the trigram model, and the potentially useful information it discards.

Depth	Number Of Pylons
1	5052
2	2267
3	1197
4	568
5	337
6	197
7	126
8	90
9	60
10	29
11	22
12	21
13	11
14	4
>14	33

Fig. 4. Histogram of the depths of 10 014 pylons.

Subject	Number Of Questions
w_{20}	3793
w_{19}	6451
w_{18}	5147
w_{17}	2501
w_{16}	1208
w_{15}	615
w_{14}	370
w_{13}	284
w_{12}	234
w_{11}	188
w_{10}	184
w_9	181
w_8	160
w_7	138
$w_1 - w_6$	706

Fig. 5. Histogram of the question subjects.

In summary, the tree-based language model provided a lower perplexity and fewer very bad probabilities than an equivalent trigram model. However, the combined trigram-tree model had appreciably lower perplexity than either model on its own. Thus, the most effective use of a tree-based model may be as an adjunct to a trigram model, rather than a replacement for it.

IV. Epilogue

A good language model ought to have the property that the probability assigned to real text is high, and the probability of nonsensical text is low. With this in mind, we probed the properties of the trigram and tree-based models by generating some text using the models. Words following quotation marks or a period were selected at random in accordance with their probabilities. In all other contexts, the most probable word was selected. The generic "unknown" word was excluded from the allowable vocabulary. The initial word history was selected at random from real text.

The excerpts below are included mainly for the reader's amusement, and are not claimed to be typical. The generated text reflects the language models' heritage in romantic novels. The punctuation has been left exactly as it was generated. Each punctuation symbol is considered to be a word and has a probability of being the next "word" spoken like any other word.

The following paragraph was obtained with the trigram model.

If you don't have to be a good deal of the world."
"I said.
She was a good deal of the world. But the fact that the only one of the world. When the first time in the world.

Less monotonous are the following paragraphs obtained with the tree-based model.

"What do you mean?"
"I don't know. You know," said the man.
"Is it?" he asked.
"You know," said the man.
"They are not not to be a good idea. The first time I was a good idea." She was a good idea.

"Certainly," I said.
"What's the matter?"
"May I be able to get the money."
"Well," said the man. Scott was a good idea.

"Mrs. King," Nick said. "I don't know what I mean."
"Take a look at the door. He was a good idea. I don't know what I mean. Didn't you know," he said.

It is the collective unbiased opinion of the authors that these paragraphs are at least as stimulating as the average romantic novel.

The trigram sentences consist of very reasonable 3-grams, but the limited memory of the trigram model results in stilted 4-grams, 5-grams, etc., and hence leads to meaningless sentences. Quotation marks are unmatched because there is no mechanism to remember the number of unmatched quotes.

The tree-generated sentences exemplify the effects of the longer 20-word memory. Punctuation is vastly improved, and repetition is much reduced. Some of the component 3-grams, however, are not as reasonable as before. "Are not not" and "not not to" are pretty unusual constructions, but trigrams like those are not not to be found in scientific journals.

Acknowledgment

We would like to thank the other members of the Speech Recognition Group at the IBM Research Center for their help and encouragement. We are also indebted to the

American Printing House for the Blind who provided the books and magazines used in the experiments.

References

[1] L. R. Bahl, F. Jelinek, and R. L. Mercer, "A maximum likelihood approach to continuous speech recognition," *IEEE Trans. Pattern Anal. Machine Intell.*, vol. PAMI-5, pp. 179-190, Mar. 1983.
[2] L. Breiman, J. H. Friedman, R. A. Olshen, and C. J. Stone, *Classification and Regression Trees.* Monterey, CA: Wadsworth, 1984.
[3] R. G. Casey and G. Nagy, "Decision tree design using a probabilistic model," *IEEE Trans. Inform. Theory*," vol. IT-30, pp. 93-99, Jan. 1984.
[4] C. R. P. Hartmann, P. K. Varshney, K. G. Mehrotra, and C. L. Gerberich, "Application of information theory to the construction of efficient decision trees," *IEEE Trans. Inform. Theory*, vol. IT-28, pp. 565-577, July 1982.
[5] F. Jelinek, "Continuous speech recognition by statistical methods," *Proc. IEEE*, vol. 64, pp. 532-556, Apr. 1976.
[6] ——, "The development of an experimental discrete dictation recognizer," *Proc. IEEE*, vol. 73, pp. 1616-1624, Nov. 1985.
[7] S. Kirkpatrick, C. D. Gelatt, Jr., and M. P. Vecchi, "Optimization by simulated annealing," *Science*, vol. 220, pp. 671-680, May 1983.
[8] J. M. Lucassen and R. L. Mercer, "An information theoretic approach to the automatic determination of phonemic baseforms," in *Proc. 1984 IEEE Int. Conf. Acoust., Speech, Signal Processing*, San Diego, CA, Mar. 1984, pp. 42.5.1-42.5.4.
[9] H. J. Payne and W. S. Meisel, "An algorithm for constructing optimal binary decision trees," *IEEE Trans. Comput.*, vol. C-26, pp. 905-916, Sept. 1977.
[10] C. E. Shannon, "Prediction and entropy of printed English," *Bell Syst. Tech. J.*, vol. 30, pp. 50-64, Jan. 1951.

Lalit R. Bahl (S'66-M'68) is an ex-coding theorist who works for IBM on acoustic and language models for speech recognition.

Peter F. Brown is an ex-speech recognition researcher who works for IBM on automatic language translation.

Peter V. de Souza is an ex-biostatistician who works for IBM on acoustic and language models for speech recognition.

Robert L. Mercer (M'83) is an ex-physicist who works for IBM on acoustic and language models for speech recognition.

MODIFICATION OF EARLEY'S ALGORITHM FOR SPEECH RECOGNITION

Annedore Paeseler

Philips GmbH Forschungslaboratorium Hamburg,
Vogt-Koelln-Str. 30, D-2000 Hamburg 54, FRG

Abstract: This paper describes an adaptation of Earley's algorithm for the recognition of spoken sentences. Earley's algorithm is one of the most efficient parsing algorithms for written sentences. The modifications and extensions of Earley's algorithm required by the variability and ambiguity of the speech signal concern the scoring of word and sentence hypotheses and the application of a beam search or pruning technique.

1. INTRODUCTION

The main problems of continuous-speech recognition are due to the unreliable recognition of both the word boundaries and the spoken words. To improve the recognition rate of a speech recogniton system, it is useful to define a grammar which is used to restrict the search for the best matching sequence of words for a spoken sentence to those that are grammatically correct.

Earley's algorithm /Ear 70/ is one of the most efficient parsing algorithms for general context-free grammars. It was one of the first parsing methods that used a central data structure, usually called chart, for storing all intermediate results during the parsing process of a sentence. Subsequently chart parsers were widely used in natural language systems for written input. Moreover Earley's algorithm was extended for error-correcting parsing /Lyo 74/, /Fu 82/ and spoken sentence recognition /Nak 87/. In /Ney 87/ a similar method is described that uses a context-free grammar for speech recognition, which is based on the Cocke-Younger-Kasami algorithm /Hop 79/.

NATO ASI Series, Vol. F46
Recent Advances in Speech Understanding and Dialog Systems
Edited by H. Niemann et al.

2. THE MODIFIED ALGORITHM

The modified algorithm for speech recognition has to determine the grammatically correct sequence of words that yielded the best score. Scores can be computed by probabilistic methods or as geometric distance between acoustic vectors.

The modified algorithm comprises two levels. At the 'acoustic' level, the reference patterns of hypothesized words are compared with the string of input symbols into which the speech signal is converted by an acoustic analysis module (e.g. acoustic vectors or phoneme symbols). Scores for the hypothesized words are computed by dynamic programming /Ney 82/ which provides an optimal nonlinear time alignment of reference pattern and spoken sentence. Each time the end of a word reference-pattern is reached, a 'scanner' operation gives the corresponding word and the score to the 'grammar' level.

At the grammar level, recognized words and their scores are used by the 'completer' to extend already found sequences of words or, more precisely, to extend partial derivations. According to the grammar rules those words are determined by a 'predictor' and given to the acoustic level, which can follow the found word sequences.

As in the original version of Earley's algorithm we use item lists or state sets to store the intermediate results while processing the string of input symbols from left to right. All possible derivations of grammar rules are expanded simultaneously. Item list j contains all partial derivations and for each of them the best matching sequence of words that has been found while processing the input symbols along the time axis 1 to j.

Let $G = \{S, N, T, R\}$ be a context-free grammar where $S \in N$ is the start symbol, N a set of nonterminal symbols, T a set of terminal symbols and R a set of context-free rules $A \rightarrow w$. The following notation is used:

A, B, C	: $\in N$;	a, b, c	: $\in T$;
u, w, x, y, z:	$\in (N \cup T)^*$;	g, h	: $\in T^*$;
i, j, k :	: number of item lists;	Ø	: the empty string.
U, V, W, X	: scores;		

An item represents the 'state' of the application of a grammar rule. An item [A, x, y, i, j, U, V, abc] has the following interpretation (cf. Fig. 1): in R exists a rule A --> u. The right-hand side of this rule is split into two parts x and y. x has already been compared to the input string, whereas y has still to be considered. i and j are positions within the string of input symbols. i points back to that input symbol after which the application of this rule was started. j indicates the position at which x has been completed and after which the verification of y begins. j also serves as the identifier of the item list in which this item is stored. abc is that specific sequence of terminal symbols (i. e. words of the vocabulary) of all sequences of terminal symbols derivable from x, that yielded the minimal score in the comparison between the input symbols from i+1 until j and their reference patterns. In other words abc is the 'best explanation' for that sequence of input symbols. V is the 'initialisation score' (IS), i.e. the minimal score value of all derivations that span the input symbols 1 to i and request the application of rule A → u for finding a grammatically correct continuation. The 'accumulated score' (AS) U is the sum of V and the minimal score for the words that have already been derived and compared to the input symbols (in the example: the score for abc).

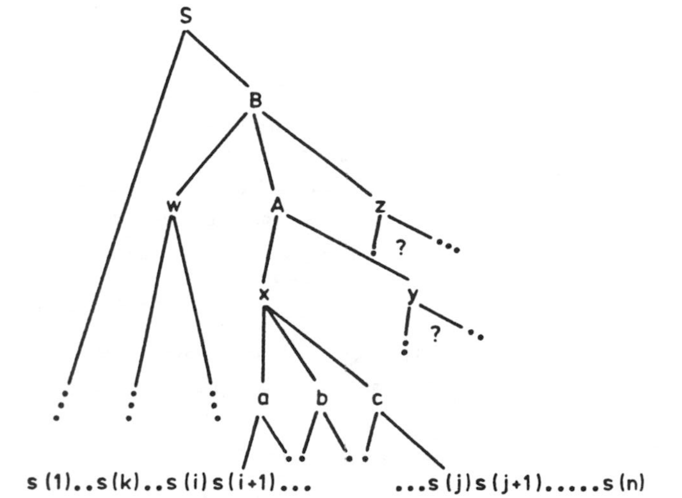

Fig. 1: Partial derivation tree after processing input symbols s(1)..s(j).

2.1 Scoring of Hypotheses

Using the two scores IS and AS is essential, if a beam search or pruning strategy shall be applied, because this requires normalized and thus comparable scores for all hypotheses. The AS of an item I in list j is the best score that can be achieved applying the grammar rule I stands for by taking into account (as IS) the best score of all rules that started the application of this rule and that are still waiting for its completion. It is a characteristic feature of Earley's algorithm that (in using the predictor operation) it is guaranteed that for each item such a predecessor exists /Gra 76/ and has already been matched to the beginning of the input string.

The IS V of an item I = [A, x, y, i, j, U, V, g] is the minimal AS of all items in list i, which have A as next expandable symbol:

$$IS(I) = \min \{ W \mid [B, w, Az, k, i, W, X, h], k \le i \}.$$

The AS is defined as:

$$AS([S, \emptyset, x, 0, 0, 0, 0, \emptyset]) = 0,$$

$$AS(I) = INI(I) + CS(x, i, j).$$

CS (x, i, j) is the best score of the acoustic match of the input symbols i+1 to j and the reference patterns of the words derived from the already processed part of the right hand side of the rule:

$$CS(x, i, i) = 0,$$

$$CS(a, i, j) = \text{Score for matching the reference pattern of word a to the input symbols i+1 until j.}$$

$$CS(A, i, j) = \min_{I} (AS(I) - INI(I)), \quad \text{where } I = [A, w, \emptyset, i, j, U, V, g],$$

$$CS(yz, i, j) = \min_{k} (CS(y, i, k) + CS(z, k, j)), \quad \text{with } i \le k \le j.$$

2.2 Formal Description

As in the original algorithm each item list is defined as a set of items, i.e. duplicates of items are not allowed. Two items [A, y, x, k, l, U, V, g] and [B, w, z, i, j, W, X, h] are identical, if A = B, y = w, x = z, k = i and l = j. If an operation tries to create an item I2 that is identical to an already existing item I1, depending on which one has the lower accumulated score either I1 or I2 is retained. This dynamic programming minimization is correct, since I1 and I2 represent the same state of the application of one rule and cover the same portion of the input string.

The modified algorithm works the following way:

1) Initialisation:
Create [S, Ø, S, 0, 0, 0, 0, Ø], set j := 0.

2) Modification of item-list I(j):
Repeat step 2.1 and 2.2 until no new items can be created.

2.1) Predictor: for all [A, y, Bz, i, j, U, V, g] and rules B -> x create
[B, Ø, x, j, j, U, U, Ø].

2.2) Completer: for all [B, x, Ø, i, j, U, V, g] and
[A, y, Bz, k, i, W, X, h] create
[A, yB, z, k, j, W + U - V, X, hg].

3) Hypo-Words: for all [A, x, ay, i, j, U, V, g] give a, U and j to the acoustic level, where a new entry in the 'active-word-list' is created. If a is the next symbol of more than one item, take the minimal accumulative score U. U is the initial score to which the local distances between the reference pattern for word a and the input symbols are added.

4) Modification of the active-word-list:
Set j:= j+1. Carry out the comparison between the reference patterns of the words in the active-word-list and the j-th input symbol. Apply a dynamic programming method for nonlinear time-alignment, which computes for each word the minimal cumulative score. If the end of the reference pattern for a word a is reached, which was hypothesized from item-list k and has Score W (difference between the initial and accumulated score of a), do step 5.

5) Scanner: for all [A, x, ay, i, k, U, V, g] create
[A, xa, y, i, j, U + W, V, ga].

If j = n, i.e. the end of the input is reached, look for the item [S, y, Ø, 0, n, U, 0, g] with minimal U and give out g. If j < n, then if list j is empty go to step 4, else go to step 2.

For the space and time complexity the same considerations are valid as in the original version of the algorithm. The length of the i-th item list is proportional to i, which restricts the space complexity for the grammar level to n^2, if n is the length of the input string.

The scanner executes at most $|T|*i$ for the i-th item list, if each word a ∊ T is hypothesized at each position of the input string and no length restrictions for the reference patterns are given. The number of predictor operations for each item list is proportional to the list length. The completer has to do i^2 operations for the i-th list, since in the worst case it has to process for each item I in list i all items of the list k, to which I points back. Therefore the number of operations for processing the whole sentence has a cubic dependence on the number of input symbols.

The pruning of unlikely hypotheses was not explicitly mentioned in the formal description of the algorithm. It is easily implemented by first determining the best score after the processing of all words in the active-word-list for one input symbol. Then the sum of this best score and a certain value gives a threshold for pruning. All words that have a higher score than the threshold are removed from the list. In the same way no item is put into an item list that has an accumulated score higher than the threshold.

3. EXPERIMENTAL RESULTS

Recognition tests were performed on continuously spoken commands for a text editor. The context-free grammar consists of 84 rules. The vocabulary comprises 84 words. An acoustic preprocessor converted the input speech signal into a sequence of phonemes, which were the input to the recognition module. Since the phoneme recognition rate was rather high, word recognition errors occured only in 6 of 80 sentences.

In these experiments a drastic reduction of the number of operations was achieved by pruning. Instead of a cubic a linear dependence on the number of input symbols was observed. Tab. 1 reflects the influence of the beam search strategy on the number of operations.

Table 1:

Computational steps of scanner, completer, and predictor operations for a full search and beam search.

Length of input	No. of operations full search	beam search
10	21599	208
15	76248	374
25	327004	1389
59	2500894	3676

4. CONCLUSIONS

An algorithm based on Earley's method was developed that allows the use of a general context-free grammar for guiding the search for the best matching sequence of words for a spoken sentence. It preserves the cubic dependence of the number of operations on the number of symbols in the input string. Since for spoken sentences this number is much higher than for written sentences, a reduction of the number of operations has to be achieved. Therefore a scoring method is used that allows direct comparison of different hypotheses and thus is appropriate for a beam search strategy. In recognition experiments based on phoneme strings, on the average a linear dependence of the number of operations on the number of input symbols was achieved.

ACKNOWLEDGMENT

The work described was carried out in a joint Siemens-Philips-IPO (Eindhoven) project ('SPICOS') and sponsored by the German Federal Ministery for Research and Technology (BMFT) under grant No. 413-5839-ITM 8401. Only the author is responsible for the contents of this publication.

The author would like to thank Dominique Snyers of Philips Research Laboratories Brussels for supplying her with the data base and grammar rules for the text-editor task.

REFERENCES

/Ear 70/ : J. Earley, 'An Efficient Context-Free Parsing Algorithm', Comm. of the ACM, Vol. 13, No. 2, Feb. 1970, pp. 94-102.

/Fu 82/ : K. S. Fu, 'Syntactic Pattern Recognition and Applications', Prentice-Hall, Englewood Cliffs, 1982.

/Gra 76/ : S. L. Graham, M. A. Harrison, W. L. Ruzzo: 'On-Line Context-Free Language Recognition in less than Cubic Time', Proc. of the 8. Annual ACM Symposium on Theory of Computing, 1976.

/Lyo 74/ : G. Lyon, 'Syntax-Directed Least-Error Analysis for Context-Free Languages: A Practical Approach', Comm. of the ACM, Vol. 17, No. 1, Jan. 1974, pp. 3-14.

/Nak 87/ : S. Nakagawa, 'Spoken Sentence Recognition by Time-Synchronous Parsing Algorithm of Context-Free Grammar', Proc. of the Int. Conf. on Acoustics, Speech, and Signal Processing, Dallas, TX, April 1987, pp. 20.9.1-4.

/Ney 82/ : H. Ney, 'Dynamic Programming as a Technique for Pattern Recognition', Proc. 6th Int. Conf. on Pattern Recognition, Muenchen, S. 1119 - 1125, 1982.

/Ney 87/ : H. Ney, 'Dynamic Programming Speech Recognition using a Context-Free Grammar', Proc. of the Int. Conf. on Acoustics, Speech, and Signal Processing, Dallas, TX, 1987, pp. 3.2.1-4.

12. LANGUAGE PROCESSING FOR SPEECH UNDERSTANDING

W.A. Woods

Applied Expert Systems Inc.,
Cambridge, Mass 02142, USA.

12.1 THE PROBLEM OF SPEECH UNDERSTANDING

A fundamental characteristic of the speech understanding task, above and beyond the difficulty of acoustic phonetic recognition, is that there is generally not enough information in the acoustic signal alone to determine the phonetic content of the message. Acoustic cues are sufficient to constrain the possible identities of a given sound but frequently not sufficient to determine its identity uniquely. For example, it may be possible to determine that a given sound is a weak fricative but not whether it is an "f" or "th". The subtle acoustic cues which distinguish these sounds may be unreliable or unavailable either due to noise or distortion in the communication channel or to errors in pronunciation or lack of careful articulation on the part of the speaker.

There is ample evidence from human perceptual experiments that this inability is not just a limitation of mechanical signal analysis and computerized acoustic-phonetic analysis, but rather a fundamental characteristic of human speech. The human listener is highly skilled at using his "common sense" knowledge of the vocabulary and syntax of his language and his expectations for what his speaker might say to compensate for small errors in pronunciation, and possibly for this reason, people generally do not speak any more distinctly than is necessary to make themselves understood.

Thus, one cannot expect to achieve continuous speech understanding without making use of the higher level constraints imposed on an utterance by the vocabulary and syntax of the language and the knowledge of what makes sense. In this chapter I will consider language understanding techniques and control strategies that can be applied to provide higher level support from these sources to aid in the understanding of spoken utterances.

The discussion will be illustrated with concepts and examples from the BBN speech understanding system, HWIM (which stands for "Hear What I Mean") [10, 8]. The HWIM system was conceived as an assistant to a travel budget manager, a system that would store information about planned and taken trips, travel budgets and their status, plane fares and *per diems*, and other information important to planning. This task was chosen as a small and easily comprehensible version of a generalized management problem. The system was able to respond to commands and answer questions spoken into a microphone and was able to synthesize spoken responses as output.

HWIM was a prototype system used to drive speech understanding research, and during the life of the project reached a level of performance where it could understand approximately 50% of a set of new test utterances, using a phonetic-based approach, with no speaker training, and a relatively unconstraining English grammar. Although the system was never fully debugged and tuned and its acoustic phonetic knowledge was incomplete, the success rate for complete understanding of (52%) of a 400 word system (branching ratio 67) fell only 8 percentage points (to 44%) when tested with no further tuning on a 1000 word vocabulary (branching ratio 196). This indicates a substantial robustness in the method.

12.1.1 Knowledge components for speech understanding

One can identify the following conceptually distinct sources of knowledge as important in determining the interpretation of a spoken utterance:

1. Segmentation and Labelling

   A process of detecting acoustic-phonetic events in the speech signal and characterizing the nature of the individual segments of the signal.

2. Lexical Retrieval

   A process of retrieving candidate words from the lexicon that are acoustically similar to the labelled segments.

3. Word Matching

   A process of determining some measure of the goodness of a word hypothesis at a given point in the speech signal.

4. Syntax

   The ability to determine if a given sequence of words is a possible subpart of a grammatical sentence and to predict possible continuations for such sentence fragments.

5. Semantics

   The ability to determine if a given hypothesized sentence is meaningful or nonsensical (in addition to being grammatical).

Originally appeared in *Computer Speech Processing*, Prentice-Hall International, Englewood Cliffs, N.J. (1983).

6. Pragmatics

The ability to determine if a sentence is appropriate to the context in which it is uttered, given knowledge of the particular speaker, the task he is trying to accomplish, and what has been said previously in the discourse.

7. Prosodics

The ability to use cues such as intonation and rhythm to predict the possible syntactic structure of an utterance or to confirm or reject a proposed syntactic structure.

In addition to these sources of knowledge, there is a major issue of control, i.e. the framework and algorithms for making decisions about which possible fragmentary hypotheses to rule out, which ones to pursue further by trying to find compatible interpretations of adjacent portions of the utterance, when to return to a previously rejected hypothesis in light of new information, etc.

12.1.2 Putting it all together

It is one thing to say that all of the above processes and sources of knowledge must interact in the understanding of continuous speech. It is another thing to know how to do it. A variety of different approaches have been explored. Generally, they fall into two classes - top-down, or syntax driven, and bottom-up, or lexically driven. Some systems attempt to take a grammar of possible things to say and use it to predict possible words which the system then attempts to verify against the input. Other systems attempt to recognize words either at the phoneme or syllable level and then use dictionary entries for these words to drive a syntactic component. In both cases, one component is used as a generator of possible hypotheses and the other as a filter.

In general, the syntax driven approaches are successful only for highly constrained applications where the system has a good chance of predicting a small number of choices for the next word at each point in the input. For less restricted situations, only lexically driven approaches have been moderately successful, although this requires some clever lexical retrieval techniques to avoid having to match every possible vocabulary item against the input.

A major problem is how to integrate the different sources of knowledge in such a way as to exploit their interaction. For example, the HWIM system, for lack of any more suitable integrative framework, combined syntactic, semantic, and pragmatic information into a single "pragmatic" ATN grammar, while keeping separate components for the phonetic and lexical levels. The CMU HARPY system [6] achieved integration by compiling a finite state grammar together with lexical and phonetic information into a single network of possible phoneme sequences, each path through which corresponded to a possible sentence. Hearsay-II [5], on the other hand, created a blackboard structure to attempt to coordinate a diverse collection of multiple knowledge sources.

In what follows, I will attempt to set forth a framework in which to view the interaction of such knowledge sources and discuss some general algorithms and techniques for using higher level knowledge for speech understanding.

12.2. CONTROL STRATEGIES FOR SPEECH PERCEPTION

Speech understanding is a special case of a general class of perceptual processes. Perception can be viewed as the process of forming a believable coherent hypothesis which can account for some or all of one's sensory stimuli. Although this process is generally subconscious and one is not aware of any substeps, it can be thought of computationally as a derivation of a comprehensive hypothesis that is arrived at by successive refinement and extension of partial hypothesis until a best complete hypothesis is found. I will refer to this successive refinement as incremental perception.

In general, a perceptual system must incorporate some basic epistemological assumptions about the things which it can perceive and the rules governing their assembly. That is, the object perceived is generally a compound object, constructed from members of a finite set of elementary constituents according to well-formedness rules. The well-formedness rules can be used to reject impossible interpretations of the input stimuli, and may also be used to predict other constituents that could be present if a given partial hypothesis is correct. The elementary constituents, as well as the relationships among them that are invoked in the well-formedness rules, must be directly perceptible. In the case of speech understanding, the directly perceptible elements are the basic speech phonemes (or more correctly their features), and the well-formedness rules are the rules governing their formation into words, phrases, sentences, and coherent discourse.

In this section, we will be concerned with strategies governing the formation and refinement of partial hypotheses about the identity of a speech utterance. We assume a system that contains the following components:

(a) A Lexical Retrieval component that can find the k best matching words in any region of an utterance, subject to certain constraints, and can be recalled to continue enumerating word matches in decreasing order of goodness (where possible constraints include anchoring the left or right end of the word to particular points in the utterance or to particular adjacent word matches). We assume that this component is interfaced to appropriate signal processing, acoustic-phonetic, and phonological analysis components, as in HWIM, and that it assigns a "quality" score to each word match reflecting the goodness of the match.

(b) A Linguistic component that, given any sequence of words, can determine whether that sequence can be parsed as a possible initial, final, or internal subsequence of a syntactically correct and semantically and pragmatically appropriate utterance, and can propose compatible classes of words at each end of such a sequence.

A control strategy for such a system must answer questions such as:

(a) At which points in the utterance to call the Lexical Retrieval component, and when,

(b) What number of words to ask for,

(c) When to give subsequences of the results to the Linguistic component, and

(d) When to recall the Lexical Retrieval component to continue enumerating words at a given point.

The goal of the control strategy is to discover the best scoring sequence of words that covers the entire utterance and is acceptable to the Linguistic component. We will consider here a particular class of control strategies which we refer to as "island-driven".

12.2.1 Island-driven strategies

In an island-driven control strategy, partial hypotheses about the possible identity of the utterance are formed around initial "seed" words somewhere in the utterance and are grown into larger and larger "island" hypotheses by the addition of words to one or the other end of the island. Occasionally, two islands may "collide" by proposing and discovering the same word in the gap between them and may then be combined into a single larger island.

Each island hypothesis is evaluated by the Lexical Retrieval component to determine its degree of match with the acoustic evidence and is checked for syntactic, semantic, and pragmatic consistency by the Linguistic component. We will refer to a partial hypothesis that has been so evaluated and checked for consistency as a "theory". The strategies that we will consider operate by successively processing "events" on an event queue, where events correspond to suspended or dormant processes that may result in the creation of theories.

The general algorithm operates as follows:

(1) An initial scan of the utterance is performed by the Lexical Retrieval component to discover the n best matching words anywhere in the utterance according to some criterion of "best" and for some value n. An initial seed event is created for each such word and placed on the event queue. In addition, one or more continuation events, which can be processed to continue the enumeration of successively lower scoring words (regardless of position in the utterance), is created and placed on the queue. Each seed event is assigned a priority score (derived, in one of several ways to be described shortly, from the quality score that the Lexical Retrieval component gave it). Each continuation event is assigned a priority score that can be guaranteed to bound the priority score of any word that can be generated by that event (e.g. derived from the score of the last word enumerated prior to the continuation). The events are ordered on the event queue by their priority scores and are processed in order of priority.

(2) The highest priority event is selected for processing. This consists of (i) creating the corresponding theory (a one-word theory in the case of a seed event), (ii) calling the Linguistic component to check the consistency of the theory and to make predictions for words and/or word classes that can occur adjacent to it at each end of the theory, (iii) calling the Lexical Retrieval component to enumerate the k best matching words satisfying these predictions at each end of the theory, and (iv) generating a "word" event for each such word found. A word event is an event that will add one word to a theory to create a larger theory. Continuation events are also created that will continue the enumeration of successively lower scoring words adjacent to the theory. If island-collision is permitted as an operation (island collision is a feature that can be permitted or not), then each word event generated is checked against an island table to see if the same word (at the same position in the input) has been proposed and found in the other direction by some theory. If so, an "island-collision event" is created that will combine the new word and the two theories on either side of it. Both word and island-collision events are assigned priority scores derived from the quality scores of words that they contain and are inserted into the event queue according to their priorities.

(3) Step 2 is repeated until a theory is discovered that spans the entire utterance and is syntactically, semantically, and pragmatically acceptable as a complete sentence.

Although the basic island-driven strategy is presented here as involving an initial scan of the entire utterance before beginning the processing of events, there is nothing to prevent an implementation from dovetailing this initial scan with the event processing so that, for example, event processing on the early portions of an utterance could begin before the entire utterance had been heard.

12.2.2 Priority scoring

The score assigned to a theory by the summation of lexical retrieval scores we refer to as the quality score of the theory. One can distinguish this from a possibly separate score called the priority score, which is used to rank order events on the event queue to determine the order in which they are to be done. A desirable property for a priority score is a guarantee that the first complete theory found will be the best scoring one that can be found. Using the quality scores directly as priority scores does not ordinarily provide such a guarantee. That is, a straightforward "best-first" search strategy does not guarantee discovery of the best overall hypothesis.

An algorithm that is guaranteed in this way to find the best entity in some search space is said to be admissible. For speech understanding applications, admissibility is a desirable property, but not necessarily essential if the cost of its attainment is too great. In this section we will discuss several priority scores, derived from but not identical with the quality score, that result in admissible algorithms. The first measures the difference between the quality score for a theory and an upperbound on the possible quality for any theory covering the same portion of the utterance. This is called the shortfall score. Two other priority scores are obtained by dividing either the quality score or the shortfall score by the time duration of the island to give quality density scoring and shortfall density scoring, respectively.

12.2.3 Shortfall scoring

Shortfall scoring measures the amount by which the score of a theory falls below an upper bound on the possible score that could be achieved on the same region by any theory. When shortfall scoring is being used, a MAXSEG profile is constructed, having the property that the score of a word match between boundaries i and j will be less than or equal to the area under the MAXSEG profile from i to j (call this latter the MAXSCORE for the region from i to j). The shortfall score for a theory is then computed as the sum over all the word matches in the theory of the difference between the score of the word match and the MAXSCORE for the same region. The relationship of the MAXSEG profile to the actual score of a theory is illustrated in Fig. 12.1.

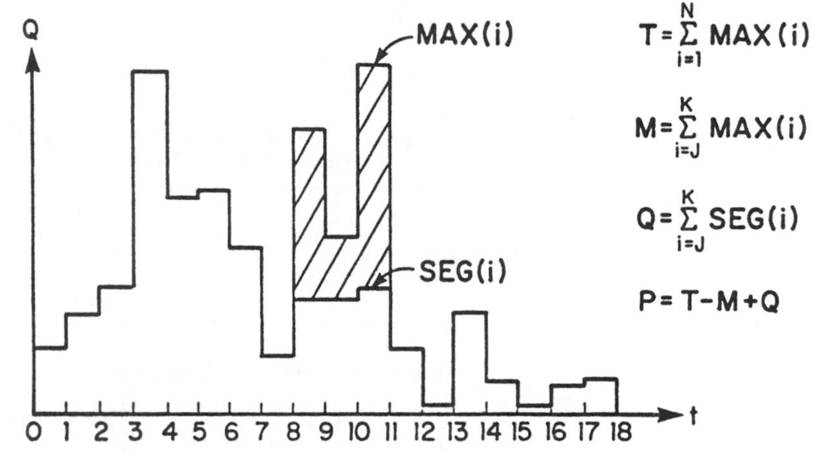

Fig. 12.1 Measuring Shortfall from a MAXSEG Profile

The theoretical characteristics of the shortfall scoring algorithm are that if the words are returned by the Lexical Retrieval component in shortfall order and events are processed in order of increasing magnitude of shortfall (plus a few other assumptions, documented in [14]), then the first complete spanning interpretation found will be the best scoring interpretation that can be found by any strategy (modulo ties). For any quality metric that is additive, shortfall scoring is admissible without searching the entire space of possible word sequences. The proof of admissibility depends only on the fact that when the first complete spanning theory is found, all other events on the queue will already have fallen below the ideal maximum score by at least as much. Thus the result does not depend on the scores being likelihood ratios, nor does it make any assumption about the nature of the grammar (e.g. that it be a finite state Markov process), provided a parser exists that can make the necessary judgements. The admissibility of the basic shortfall method also does not depend on the order of scanning the utterance - it is true both for middle-out and for left-to-right strategies.

12.2.4 Density scoring

Another type of priority scoring is density scoring. Here the score used to order the event queue is some basic score divided by the duration of the event. Conceptually, we can think of this scoring metric as predicting the potential score for the region not covered by a theory to be an extrapolation of the same score density already achieved. (In these terms, the shortfall strategy can be thought of as predicting that the potential score for the uncovered region will achieve the upper bound.) Unlike the shortfall scores, density scores can get worse and then get better again as new words are added to a theory. Hence the density score is not guaranteed to be an upper bound of the expected eventual score. However, it has another interesting property: in exactly those cases where it does not upperbound the eventual score, there is a word to be added somewhere else that has a better score density and whose score density does upperbound the eventual score. This arises from the property of densities that the density of two regions combined will lie between the densities that they each have. It turns out that this alone is not sufficient to guarantee admissibility, since it is still possible for the density score starting from the best correct seed to fall below that of some other less-than-optimal spanning theory before it can be extended to a complete theory itself. However, with the addition of a facility for island collisions, the density scoring strategy, working middle-out from multiple seeds, has been shown to be admissible. Density scoring does not depend on any assumptions about the basic scores to which it is being applied other than that they be additive (and capable of division). Hence the density method can be applied to either the original quality score or to a shortfall score.

12.2.5 Shortfall density scoring

The shortfall density method of scoring partial hypotheses is a combination of the shortfall and density methods. Experimental comparison of the algorithms [14] suggests that the shortfall density method is superior to quality density, which is in turn superior to the shortfall method alone. The superiority of the density methods over the shortfall method can be accounted for by the excessive conservatism (over-optimistic scoring of alternative hypotheses) of the shortfall method. The superiority of the combined shortfall density method can be attributed to an improved "focus of attention" strategy as follows.

12.2.6 Focus of attention by a MAXSEG profile

A major effect of prioritizing events by the shortfall from a MAXSEG profile is that the score differences in different parts of the utterance are effectively levelled out, so that events in a region of the utterance where the best word matches are not very good can hold their own against alternative interpretations in regions where there are high quality words. This promotes the refocusing of attention from a region where there may happen to be high quality accidental word matches only slightly worse than the best, to other regions whose best word match quality may not be as great. If this were not done, then many secondary matches in the high scoring region could be considered before any theories worked their way across the low scoring regions. Thus, an apparently satisfactory and intuitively reasonable strategy for focusing attention emerges from the same method that guarantees admissibility.

Notice that in the shortfall density method, the MAXSEG profile is no longer serving the role of guaranteeing admissibility that it did in the shortfall method. In this case, the admissibility is guaranteed by the nature of densities and island collisions. Rather, in this method the MAXSEG profile is used only to provide this levelling of effort over portions of the utterance to promote the refocusing of attention. In fact, it is no longer necessary that the MAXSEG profile be an upper bound (although there are undesirable effects when the shortfall density goes negative).

12.2.7 Admissible versus inadmissible strategies

The admissible strategies discussed above are only some of the control strategy options implemented in the HWIM speech understanding system. In addition there are a large number of strategy variations that result in deliberately inadmissible strategies, including strictly left-to-right density strategies and "hybrid" strategies that start near the left end of an utterance and work left to the end and then left-to-right across the rest of the utterance. For reasons of time and resource limitations, the final test run of the HWIM system was made using one of the inadmissible hybrid left-to-right strategies. Subsequently, a much smaller experiment was run to compare various control strategies on a set of ten utterances chosen at random from the larger set. Although this sample is much too small to be relied on, the results are nevertheless suggestive. For two comparable experiments using the best left-to-right method (left-hybrid shortfall density) and the best nearly admissible method (shortfall density with ghosts, island collisions, and direction preference), both with a resource limitation of 100 theories, the inadmissible left-hybrid strategy found the best (and in these cases the correct) interpretation within the resource limitation in 6 of the 10 cases and misinterpreted two additional utterances with no indication to distinguish them from the other 6. The shortfall density strategy found 5 correct interpretations (not a significant difference for this size sample) and rejected the others.

If this left-hybrid strategy were used in an actual application with comparable degrees of acoustic degradation (e.g. due to a noisy environment), the system would claim to understand most of its utterances, but would actually misunderstand a significant fraction of those due to failure to find the best interpretation. The shortfall density strategy, on the other hand, would only misunderstand an utterance if its correct interpretation actually had a lower score than the one it found (hopefully a negligible fraction of the cases).

The middle-out shortfall density algorithm in the above experiments expanded only 50% more theories (and incidentally used only 30% more cpu time) than did the left-hybrid strategy. Although as we said before, this test set is much too small to draw firm conclusions, the success rate of the two methods are not much different, except that the middle-out method is clearly less likely to make an incorrect interpretation. If one considers proposals to improve the performance of inadmissible strategies by having them continue to search for additional interpretations after the first one is found, the time difference shown above could easily be reversed and there would still be no guarantee that the interpretation found would be the best one.

12.3 ATN GRAMMARS

Having considered the issue of control strategies for using higher level knowledge in speech understanding, let us now turn to the problem of representing and using that knowledge to make the judgements required. The principal device that I will present for this purpose is the concept of an Augmented Transition Network (ATN) grammar. ATN grammars, as presented in [9], are a form of pushdown store automata, augmented to carry a set of register contents in addition to state and stack information and to permit arbitrary computational tests and actions associated with the state transitions. Conceptually, an ATN consists of a network of states representing partial states of knowledge that arise in the course of parsing a sentence. States are connected by arcs indicating kinds of constituents that can cause transitions from one state to another. The states in the network can be conceptually divided into "levels" corresponding to the different constituents that can be recognized. Each such level has a start state and one or more final states, and behaves as a recognition automaton for its particular kind of constituent.

Transitions between states are of three basic types, indicated by three different types of arc. A WRD (or CAT) transition corresponds to the consumption of a single element from the input string, a JUMP transition corresponds to a transition from one state to another without consuming any of the input string, and a PUSH transition

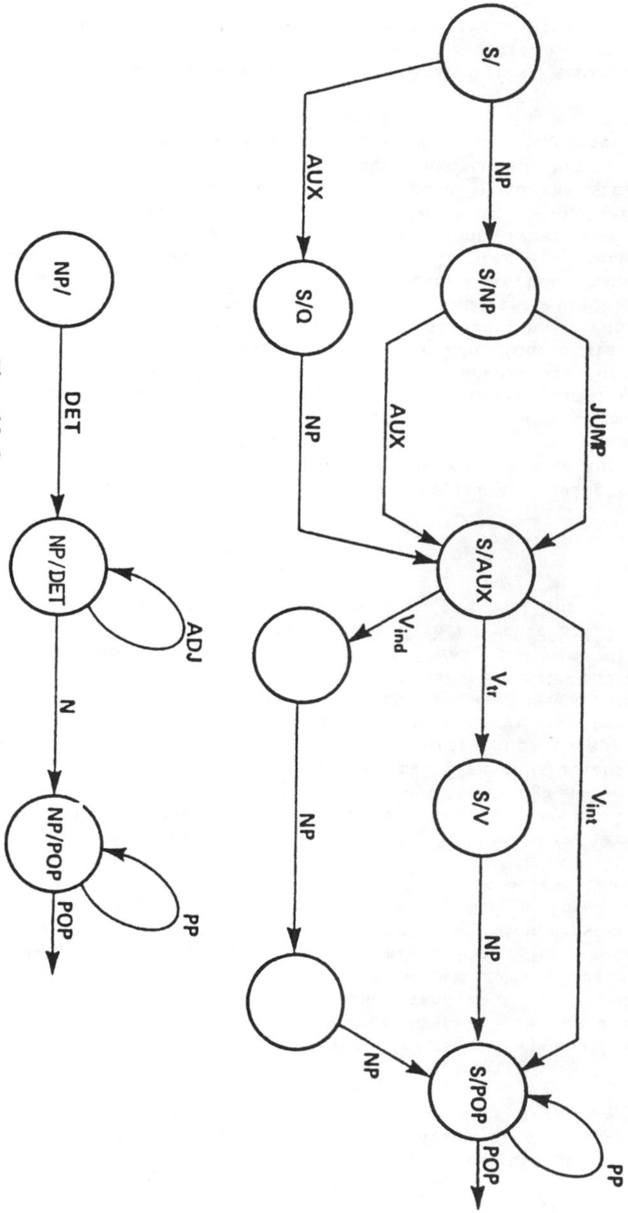

Fig. 12.2 An Example of an ATN Grammar

corresponds to the consumption of a phrase parsed by a subordinate invocation of some level of the network to recognize a constituent.

ATN's have the advantage of being a class of automata into which ordinary context-free phrase structure and "augmented" phrase structure grammars have a straighforward embedding, but which permit various transformations to be performed to produce grammars that can be more efficient than the original. Such transformations can reduce the number of states or arcs in the grammar or can reduce the number of alternative hypotheses that need to be explicitly considered during parsing. Both kinds of efficiency result from a principle that I have called "factoring", which amounts to merging common parts of alternative paths in order to reduce the number of alternative combinations explicitly enumerated. <u>Conceptual factoring</u> results from merging common parts of the grammar to make the grammar as compact as possible, while <u>hypothesis factoring</u> results from arranging the grammar so as to merge common parts of hypotheses that will be enumerated at parse time (see [9] for further discussion).

Fig. 12.2 illustrates a small fragment of an ATN for recognizing basic sentences of English. This grammar compactly represents the information that would be specified by the following infinite set of context-free grammar rules:

```
S -> NP Vint
S -> NP Vtr NP
S -> Vind NP NP
S -> NP AUX Vint
S -> NP AUX Vtr NP
S -> AUX Vind NP NP
S -> AUX NP Vint
S -> AUX Vtr NP
S -> AUX NP Vind NP NP
S -> NP Vint PP
S -> NP Vtr NP NP
S -> NP Vind NP NP NP
        .
        .
        .
S -> NP Vint PP PP
        .
        .
        .
S -> NP Vint PP PP PP
        .
        .
        .
```

(where NP stands for Noun Phrase, PP for Prepositional Phrase, Vint for an intransitive verb, Vtr for a transitive verb, Vind for a verb that takes indirect objects, and AUX for an auxilliary verb such as "is" or "does").

ATN grammars are very effective for specifying complex grammars of natural language as well as for a variety of other structured entities. One can think of them as a class of abstract perceptual automata for recognizing structured sequences of elements.

A state in an ATN can be thought of dually as a concise representation of a set of alternative possible sequences of elements leading to it from the left or as a concise prediction of a set of possible sequences of elements to be found to the right. Alternatively, it can be thought of in a right-to-left mode as a concise representation of a set of possible sequences of elements found to the right and a prediction of possible sequences to be found to the left. The reification of these states as concrete entities that can be used to represent partial states of knowledge and prediction during parsing is one of the major contributions of ATN grammars to the theory and practice of natural language understanding. They are even more important in representing states of partial knowledge in the course of speech understanding.

In addition to concisely specifying alternative sequences of constituents, ATN grammars serve as a conceptual map of possible sentence structures and a framework on which to hang information about constraints that apply between separate constituents of a phrase and the output structure that the grammar would like to assign to a phrase. This is done through conditions and structure-building actions associated with the arcs of the ATN. These conditions and actions operate on the constituent being accepted and a set of registers that can hold arbitrary information picked up elsewhere in the parse. Although in the original ATN formulation, these were presented as arbitrary LISP procedures to be executed in the context of a left-to-right parse of a sentence, they can be viewed as general constraints to be applied and generalized specifications of intended structure assignments.

12.3.1 HWIM's ATN grammar notation

The ATN grammars used by HWIM use five different arc types: PUSH, POP, WRD, CAT, and JUMP.

A PUSH arc essentially "consumes" a phrase of a specified type (e.g. a noun phrase) by causing an invocation of a subordinate transition network corresponding to the desired type of phrase. If the lower level transition network can successfully accept the next segment of the input string, it is exited by a POP arc, and processing will continue in the transition network containing the invoking PUSH arc. Each final state in a transition network will contain a POP arc that signifies successful completion of its level of the network and indicates what structure is to be returned for use by its calling network.

WRD and CAT arcs are the only terminal-consuming (i.e. word consuming) arcs in the grammar. That is, they are the only arcs that advance the "input pointer" that marks the current position in the input string. (This pointer may move during a PUSH arc, but only as a result of WRD and CAT arcs taken in the lower network.) WRD and CAT arcs differ only in the way they express the set of terminals they can consume. A WRD arc specifies its terminals explicitly and exhaustively, while a CAT arc specifies them implicitly via the syntactic-semantic category to which they must belong.

A JUMP arc causes a transition between states, but does not consume a terminal in doing so and hence does not advance the input pointer.

Fig. 12.3 shows the notation used for describing a HWIM ATN grammar; it is similar to most other ATN formalism, except that conditions on arcs are expressed in terms of an action (VERIFY <condition>) and actions can be embedded in SCOPE statements to indicate left context dependencies (see Section 12.3.2).

```
<ATN> -> (<state> <state>*)
<state> -> (<state-name><arc><arc>*)
<arc> -> <W> | <B> | <C> | <J>

<W> -> (CAT <category-name> <action>* (TO <state-name>))
       (WRD <terminal "word"> <action>* (TO <state-name>))

<B> -> (PUSH <state-name> <action>* (TO <state-name>))
<C> -> (POP <form> <action>*)
<J> -> (JUMP <state-name> <action>*)

<action> -> <action1> |
            (SCOPE <scope-spec> <action1> <action1>*)

<action1> -> (VERIFY <action1>) |
             <register-setting-action> |
             <structure-building-action> |
             <testing-action>

<scope-spec> -> (<state-name> <state-name>*) |
               NIL | T
```

Fig. 12.3 A BNF Specification of HWIM's ATN Grammar Notation

12.3.2 A middle-out view of an ATN grammar

HWIM's island-driven control strategy requires a parser that can begin in the middle of an utterance and extend an island in either direction. This entails an ability to parse right-to-left as well as left-to-right and to do so with an incomplete context in the other direction. Since ATN grammars are normally conceived as parsing automata that proceed in a left left-to-right manner from the beginning of a sentence, setting and testing registers as they go, it is not immediately obvious that they could be used by such a parser. In this section we will discuss how this can be done.

In one view of ATN grammars, a state is viewed merely as a bundle of arcs, and an arc is merely a component of its begin-state. While this conceptualization is adequate for left-to-right parsing, for HWIM's parser, it is more useful to think of an arc as a connection between two states that can be traversed in either direction. An arc, then, is associated with a left state, a right state, a type (WRD, CAT, etc.), a label (NP, AUX, Vint, etc.), a set of context free actions that can be done when the arc is first encountered regardless of the direction or context, and a set of context sensitive actions, which will be deferred, if necessary, until adequate left context is available. A state, then, has two associated collections of arcs, one set leading to the left and the other leading to the right.

The major difficulty in using an ATN grammar for middle-out parsing stems from the way that conditions and actions on the arcs use registers. During normal left-to-right processing in a standard ATN parser, actions call for both accessing and changing the contents of registers that have been set by arcs to their left in the grammar. We will say that an arc action in the grammar has a <u>left dependency</u> when it either requires the value of a register that is set somewhere to the left or changes the value of a register that is used somewhere to the left. If such an action is executed on an arc in the middle of a sentence without having processed a suitable left context, problems will arise. In the first case, executing the action without the left context could not produce the correct effect, while in the second case, executing it prematurely in a right-to-left parsing would cause the later execution of the arc action to the left to get the wrong value. Such arc actions are referred to as <u>context sensitive</u>. Fortunately, fewer than half of the actions in the HWIM ATN grammars turn out to have such dependencies.

This problem is solved in HWIM's grammars by providing all context sensitive actions with a <u>scope specification</u> that indicates what left context is necessary before the action can be executed. By analysis of the paths through the grammar, it is possible to determine, for each context sensitive arc action, a set of states having the property that the action can be safely done if its execution in a right-to-left parse is delayed until the parse has passed through one of those states. We refer to this set of states as the <u>scope</u> of the action, an indication of how far left in the grammar its left-to-right dependency extends. The HWIM parser interprets scope specifications on arc actions by saving the action with its local context until its scope is satisfied (if it is not already satisfied when the action is first considered).

This scoping mechanism allows a grammar that was created from a left-to-right viewpoint to be used in middle-out parsing with very little modification. It is only necessary to add appropriate scope specifications to the context-sensitive conditions and actions. To the grammar writer, the ATN can remain basically a left-to-right machine; its arc actions can be written almost as if the parser were operating only left to right. The grammar has actions on arcs where they should be executed if the entire appropriate left context were set. As in standard left-to-right grammars, in no case is it ever necessary to worry about the right context. This is not necessarily the best way to represent bidirectional ATN grammars, but it works. It would be possible to construct an algorithm to compute the scopes automatically if the dependencies of the arc actions were explicitly marked, but for reasons of expediency no such facility was implemented in HWIM. Rather, the scope annotations were created by hand.

The format of a scope statement is given in Fig. 12.3. The scope-spec is either a list of state names, T, or NIL. If the scope spec is a list of state names, then the action(s) can be executed when the parse begins at or has passed through any state in that list. If the scope-spec is T, the action is not to be executed until the parse has hypothesized the left end for that level of the grammar.

The following example from one of HWIM's grammars illustrates the notation for expressing scoping:

```
(S/WHAT-IS-IN-BUDGET
   (JUMP S/WHAT-IS-BUDGETED)
   (JUMP S/POP
      (SCOPE (S/WHAT-DO S/WHAT-HAVE)
             (VERIFY (GETR LEFT))
             (SETR SUBJ (NPBUILD)))))
```

From this state in HWIM's grammar, it is possible to jump to S/POP to end the utterance only if we have a question such as "WHAT IS LEFT IN THE BUDGET." In these cases the register LEFT will have been set earlier. If we are parsing right to left, we must know how far left we must carry the parse before making this test. The JUMP arc to S/POP indicates in the scope of the VERIFY action that the parse must have passed through either S/WHAT-DO or S/WHAT-HAVE.

12.3.3 <u>Cascaded ATN's</u>

One of the long standing problems in natural language understanding has been dealing with the interaction of syntactic and semantic information. Ways of achieving close interaction between syntax and semantics have traditionally involved writing semantic interpretation rules in one to one correspondence with phrase structure rules (e.g. Thompson [7]), writing "semantic grammars" that integrate syntactic and semantic constraints in a single grammar (e.g. Burton [3]), or writing ad hoc programs that combine such information in unformalized ways. The first approach requires as many syntactic rules as semantic rules, and hence is not really much different from the semantic grammar approach (this is the conventional way of defining semantics of programming languages). The third approach, of course, may yield some level of operational system, but does not usually shed any light on how such interaction should be organized, and is difficult to extend.

The semantic grammar approach, while effective, tends to miss generalizations and its results do not extend well to new domains. It misses syntactic generalizations, for example, by having to duplicate the syntactic information necessary to characterize the determiner structures of noun phrases for each of the different semantic kinds of noun phrase that can be accepted. Likewise, it tends to miss semantic generalizations by repeating the same semantic tests in various places in the grammar where a given semantic constituent can occur. HWIM's "pragmatic" grammar is an instance of the semantic grammar approach carried one more level, and thus gains its integration at the expense of modularity, transportability, and brevity.

Rusty Bobrow's RUS parser [1] is the first parser to my knowledge to make a clean separation between syntactic and semantic specification while gaining the benefit of early and incremental semantic filtering and maintaining the factoring advantages of an ATN. Its operation can be characterized by a generalization of ATN grammars that I have called cascaded ATN's (CATN's). A cascade of ATN's provides a way to reduce having to say the same thing multiple times or in multiple places, while providing efficiency comparable to a semantic grammar and at the same time maintaining a clean separation between syntactic and semantic levels of description. It is essentially a mechanism for permitting decomposition of an ATN grammar into an assembly of cooperating ATN's, each with its own characteristic domain of responsibility.

A CATN is essentially a sequence of ATN transducers with each successive machine taking input from the output of the previous one. Specifically, a CATN is a sequence of ordinary ATN's that include among the actions on their arcs an operation TRANSMIT, which transmits an element to the next machine in the sequence. The first machine in the cascade takes its input from the input sequence, and subsequent machines take their input from the TRANSMIT commands of the previous ones. The output of the final machine in the cascade is the output of the machine as a whole. The only feedback from later stages to earlier ones is a filtering function that causes paths of the nondeterministic computation to die if a later stage cannot accept the output of an earlier one.

The conception of cascaded ATN's actually arose from observing the interaction between the lexical retrieval component and the linguistic component of the HWIM speech understanding system. HWIM's lexical retrieval component made use of a network that consumed successive phonemes from the output of an acoustic phonetic recognizer and grouped them into words. Because of phonological effects across word boundaries, this network could consume several phonemes that were part of the transition into the next word before determining that a given word was possibly present. At certain points, it would return a found word together with a node in the network at which matching should begin to find the next word (essentially a state remembering how much of the next word has already been consumed due to the phonological word boundary effect). This can be viewed as an ATN that consumes phonemes and transmits words as soon as it has enough evidence that the word is there.

The lexical retrieval component of HWIM can thus be viewed as an ATN whose output drives another ATN. This leads to the conception of a complete speech understanding system as a cascade of ATN's, one for acoustic phonetic recognition, one for lexical retrieval (word recognition), one for syntax, one for semantics, and one for subsequent discourse tracking and other pragmatic constraints.

12.3.4 Lexical retrieval as an ATN

One of the difficult aspects of constructing a lexically driven speech understanding system is providing a mechanism to determine efficiently what words in the lexicon match the input. At least for conventional serial machines, it is not acceptable to compare each word in a large vocabulary against the input string. However, by viewing the lexicon as an ATN grammar of acceptable phoneme sequences, one can factor together the common parts of words that begin the same, so that the grammar begins from a single state with arcs for each phoneme that can begin a word leading to states that compactly represent the sequence of phonemes recognized so far and the set of phonemes that can follow them. This much structure, which is illustrated in Fig. 12.4, is the same as a classical decision tree, and is effectively the same structure used by the CMU HARPY system [6] to organize its entire recognition system. However, by viewing it as an ATN, it is possible to account for some more subtle phenomena.

Specifically, by viewing the lexical component as a stage of an ATN cascade that accepts a sequence of phonemes and generates a sequence of words, it is possible to model the behaviour of Klovstad's lexical retrieval component in the HWIM system [11], whereby cross-word-boundary phonological rules are efficiently handled. Klovstad's technique consisted of wrapping such a lexical decision tree around on itself by allowing jump transitions from its leaves to its root, so that viewed as an ATN it accepted sequences of words rather than simply single words. Klovstad then matched cross-word-boundary phonological rules across these special jump transitions and spliced in the resulting changes in cross-word-boundary pronunciations from the point in the word where the change began to the point in the decision tree where the remainder of the next word would begin.

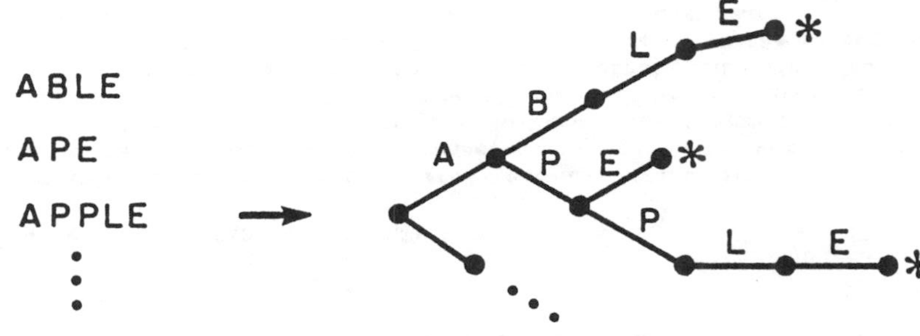

Fig. 12.4 A Lexical Decision Tree

Klovstad was then able to merge common inter-word coarticulation patterns by remembering the word involved on the left (as if in an ATN register) before entering the portion of the network that was shared by different words, and he was able to confirm that word if he found the appropriate coarticulation pattern (at which point he would already have consumed an initial portion of the next word and be positioned at the right point in the discrimination net to continue recognizing whatever word it was). We can view this as transmitting the recognized word slightly out of synchrony with the consumption of input phonemes. The lexical retriever can often identify what word is expected before it gets all the evidence necessary to confirm its presence. When it has confirmed the presence of a word, it will sometimes have already begun to accumulate evidence for the next one. (This complexity of the word boundary phenomenon is one of the major difficulties that sets speech understanding apart from text understanding, where the boundaries between words are clearly marked by spaces and punctuation.)

12.3.5 Benefits of CATN's

The decomposition of a natural language analyzer into a cascade of ATN's gains a "factoring" advantage similar to that which ATN's themselves provide with respect to ordinary phrase structure grammars. Specifically, the cascading allows alternative configurations in the later stages of the cascade to share common processing in the earlier stages that would otherwise have to be done independently. That is, if several semantic hypotheses can use a certain kind of constituent at a given place, there need be only one syntactic process to recognize it.

Cascades also provide a simpler overall description of the acceptable input sequences than a single monolithic ATN combining all of the information into a single network would give. That is, if any semantic level process can use a certain kind of constituent at a given place, then there need be only one place in the syntactic stage ATN that will recognize it. Conversely, if there are several syntactic contexts in which a constituent filling a given semantic role can be found, there need be only one place in the semantic ATN to receive that role. (A single network covering the same facts would be expected to have a number of states on the order of the product, rather than the sum, of the numbers of states in the individual stages of the cascade.)

One might note here as an aside that an additional advantage provided by the factoring aspects of a cascade, for future systems that will learn much of their behaviour, is the localization of activities in a single place where a given linguistic fact is to be learned. Without such factoring, essentially the same syntactic fact might have to be learned separately in different semantic contexts, and a given semantic fact might have to be learned separately in different syntactic contexts. Moreover, the separation of the stages of the cascade provides a decomposition of the overall problem into individually learnable skills. These facts may be of significance not only for theories of human language development and use, but also for computer systems that can be easily debugged or can contribute to their own acquisition of improved language skill. The above facts suggest that the traditional characterization of natural language in terms of the levels of phonemes, syllables, words, phrases, sentences, and higher level pragmatic constructs may be more than just a convenient way to present the subject.

12.4 MIDDLE-OUT PARSING WITH ATN'S

HWIM's control strategy requires that the syntactic component be able to take any island (i.e. consecutive sequence of word matches) and determine if it can be parsed as an acceptable fragment of a sentence. If so, the syntactic component must be able to return a list of words and categories that would form acceptable extensions to the fragment at either end. The constraints this places on the parser are that it must be able to start at any point in the grammar and at any point in the input and work in either direction. Moreover, it must be able to process islands that may partially or fully traverse several different levels of the grammar. In this section we will describe a middle-out parsing system for ATN grammars that supports the island-driven control strategies of HWIM.

Whereas the state of a parse for a conventional left-to-right ATN can be represented by the current state, the register contents, and a stack of unfinished configurations at higher levels, the representation of a configuration for a middle-out parser is considerably more complex. Since in general one needs to represent the parsing of an island that contains incomplete constituents at each end, a representation is required that can deal with fragments such as "man saw the girl in" as in "The man saw the girl in the park". This in general requires a collection of partial analyses of segments at different levels whose overall structure is in the shape of a "stile" (a set of steps that goes over a fence). That is, there is some topmost fragment with (in general) an incomplete partial analysis at a lower level at both its left and its right, which can in turn have partial analyses at still lower levels adjacent to them, etc. The prototypical structure is illustrated in Fig. 12.5.

The horizontal lines in Fig. 12.5 correspond to transitions from one state to another annotated with the word in the input that enabled the transition. Sequences of such transitions at a single level will be called segment configurations (or SCONFIGS) and a collection of SCONFIGS covering an island (forming one or more stiles) will be called an island configuration (or ICONFIG). In general, an SCONFIG in an ICONFIG may be adjacent to several other SCONFIGS at other levels, and thus participate in several different stiles covering the island, corresponding to different ways to parse it. We will refer to each sequence of compatible SCONFIGS forming a stile covering the island as a path through the island. The parser will at various points need to trace paths through the island in order to determine which SCONFIGs at one end of the island are compatible with which SCONFIGs at the other.

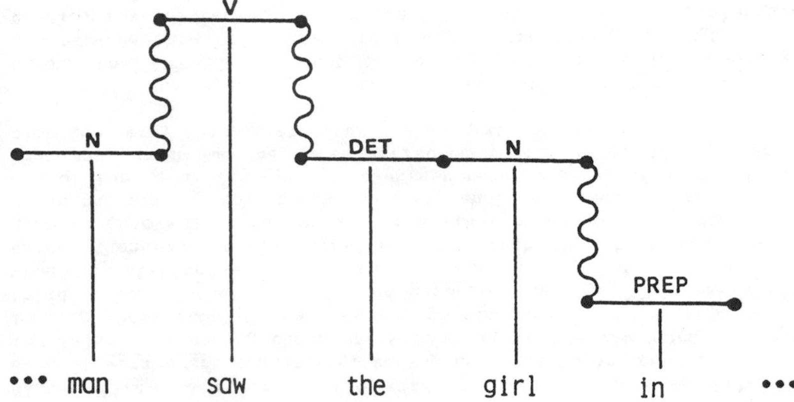

Fig. 12.5 A Prototypical Island Configuration is Shaped Like a Stile

The wavy vertical lines in Fig. 12.5 correspond to relations of indirect pushing and popping in the ATN grammar. It is important that the relationships be indirect, so that the representation can be nonexplicit about the number of possible intervening levels of structure that might occur in connecting one such SCONFIG to another. This use of indirect pushing and popping relations is similar to the technique used in Earley's algorithm [4] to avoid the combinatorics associated with explicitly enumerating alternative stacks and has similar advantages here.

12.4.1 <u>State relations used in the HWIM parser</u>

The HWIM parser makes use of a variety of indices constructed from its ATN grammar in order to perform its analyses efficiently. One of these is an index by word and syntactic category to all of the WRD and CAT arcs in the grammar, so that given a word, it can efficiently identify all of the arcs that can use that word. Another operation that it needs to perform efficiently is to identify whether an arc can be joined to an SCONFIG by a sequence of nonconsuming transitions (i.e. jumps, pushes, and pops). To support this it makes use of indices based on a set of relations between states that is in some sense a generalization of the "left closure" relationship used in Earley's algorithm, LR-k grammars and selective top-down and selective bottom-to-top-parsing algorithms.

Let us define the relation B (for "begin") to hold between two states x and y if there is a push arc leaving state x that pushes to state y. Similarly we will define the relation C (for "complete") to hold between states x and y if state x can pop a constituent that is consumed by a push arc whose destination is state y. That is, the relation B holds between states bridging the left boundary of a constituent and C holds between states bridging a right boundary. We will define the relation J to hold between x and y if there is a jump arc from state x to state y.

The relations B, C, and J cover all of the ways that an ATN can make transitions between states without consuming any input. Some generalized closure relations derived from these relations (and their converses, which we will call UB, UC, and LJ, for "unbegin", "uncomplete", and "left jump") play an important role in the HWIM parser. We use the Kleene star (*) to indicate 0 or more occurrences of a relation and the symbol + to represent the disjunctive union of two relations. For example, the relation (x J* y) is true if x is the same state as y or if there exists some sequence of jump arcs leading from x to y. The relation (x (J + P) y) is true if there is either a jump arc from x to y or a push arc leaving state x that pushes to y. We can also concatenate these basic relationships to describe a sequence of transitions. For example, the relation (x J*BJ* y) is true if there are intermediate states z and w such that the relations (x J* z), (z B w), and (w J* y) are all true.

Using this notation we can now name some additional relations that are important to the HWIM parser. These are:

```
 B! = B (J* B)*
 C! = C (J* C)* (J* B)*
UB! = UB (LJ* UB)* (LJ* UC)*
UC! = UC (LJ* UC)*
```

The relation B! corresponds to indirect pushing from the left, while C! corresponds to going up and over a stile of nonconsuming arcs by completing some phrases and then beginning some new ones. UB! corresponds to going over a stile from right to left, while UC! is the transition from higher to lower levels coming from the right (the left-hand version of a push). Even more useful than these relations are the relations J*B!J*, J*C!J*, LJ*UB!LJ*, and LJ*UC!LJ*. These can be intuitively described in English as the paths that will reach all possible states on other levels of the grammar that can be reached using only non-consuming arcs. The utility of these indices is fairly clear; if there is a segment configuration ending in state x, and a new word is to be added to the island that can be consumed by an arc that begins at state y, then there can be a path that will connect the island to the new word only if the relation (x (J* + J*B!J* + J*C!J*) y) is true.

12.4.2 <u>Paths</u>

Two adjacent SCONFIGS in an ICONFIG will be said to be <u>compatible</u> if the left one stands in the (J*B!J* + J*C!J*) relation to the right one (i.e. the right state of the left one stands in that relation to the left state of the right one). That is, two adjacent segments are compatible if the left one either pushes or pops, perhaps indirectly, to the right one. A sequence of compatible adjacent segments will be called a <u>path</u> provided that it contains no sequence of three segments such that the first stands in the J*B!J* relation to the second, which in turn stands in the J*C!J* relation to the third. (Whenever such a compatible sequence of three segments exists, the middle one can be completed and consumed by a PUSH arc that incorporates it into either the left or right segment or perhaps combines all three into a single segment.)

Associated with each path is an indication of which segment is at a higher level in the grammar than any other. Note that it is possible to have two paths that are identical except for which segment is chosen as the top. Marking the top segment of a path divides the remaining ones into two groups, which must then be at successively lower levels as they get further away from the top.

Paths are used by the HWIM parser for making predictions adjacent to an island. In order to add a new word to an island, it may be necessary to complete one of the SCONFIGS at that end and pop its constituent to one of the internal SCONFIGs, which will then reach the end of the island and connect to the new word. The internal SCONFIGs that need to be considered are on the paths leading from the SCONFIG being completed. Also, when a new word is added to one end of an island, it may be incompatible with some of the SCONFIGs at that end. These incompatible SCONFIGs are purged from the representation of the resulting new island. However, their removal may leave other internal SCONFIGs "disconnected" in that they do not now participate in any paths through the island. All such SCONFIGs are purged from the representation. Ultimately this may result in the removal of SCONFIGs at the other end of the island. In this way, words added at one end of an island can result in tightening the predictions of compatible words at the other end.

12.4.3 The parser

The HWIM parser has four basic actions, corresponding to different tasks it is called upon to perform by the Control component. The first, seed event processing, creates a new one-word island and a representation for every path covering that word that the grammar allows (i.e. each arc in the grammar that can consume it). The second, word event processing, adds a new word to one end of an existing island, extending those paths that allow the new word and eliminating those SCONFIGs that do not participate in any such path. The third action of the parser is end event processing. This takes place when an existing island has reached one end of the utterance. The parser then extends the paths that can reach the start state of the grammar (for a left end event) or a final state of the grammar (for a right end event) without consuming any additional words. If the other end of the island is open, the parser returns a set of predictions at that end, which may be more restricted than before; if that end is also complete, the parser returns a complete parse.

The fourth type of action, island collision event processing allows the Control component to combine two islands with a one-word gap between them and a new word filling that gap. Although one can develop special techniques for combining the parses of two islands, it is sufficient simply to perform new word events until one island has incorporated all the words of the other. This is how island collision events were implemented in the HWIM parser, for reasons of expediency.

12.4.4 The principal parser functions

In the remainder of this section we will describe the main functions in the HWIM parser and their operation. The presentation is intended to reveal some of the complexities of the middle-out parsing algorithm. It is not intended to give enough detail to guide an implementation, although with diligent study of the section that might be possible. However, the discussion is pretty demanding, so the casual reader may well want to skim it or skip to the next section.

The functions described here are all suffixed -RIGHT to indicate that they are used when adding a new word to the right of an existing island. There is a set of similar functions (suffixed -LEFT), which work on adding words to the left. The differences between the left-to-right and right-to-left functions are small, brought on by the fact that a new level is begun at one particular state on the left (the label of the PUSH arc) but can pop from any of a number of accepting states (states with POP arcs) on the right. These differences usually involve only an extra loop to be executed a bounded number of times.

12.4.5 Starting an island

To begin a one-word island, the parser finds all arcs in the grammar that can consume the new word match, using an index of pointers from each word and category to the arcs that consume them. It processes those arcs, creating a segment configuration (SCONGFIG) for each one. These are collected into an island configuration (ICONFIG), which is then processed to find the proposals to return to Control.

12.4.6 Processing an arc

The basic transition function in the parser, DOARC, takes an old SCONFIG, an adjacent arc, and, if it is a consuming arc, a word or constituent to be consumed. The result is a new SCONFIG representing the state of the computation after the new arc and input have been incorporated. DOARC is applied to a list of SCONFIGS to be processed for a given arc and direction. The result is a new list of SCONFIGs. Its operation is as follows:

For each SCONFIG:

1. Verify that the arc is adjacent to the old SCONFIG;
2. Do the context free actions on the arc;
3. For each context sensitive action on the arc: - if the context is not yet complete, create an undone scoped action to be added to the new SCONFIG - otherwise evaluate the action.

4. If the direction is to the left, see if the scope of any saved actions in the old SCONFIG has now been satisfied. If so, evaluate those actions.

5. Construct the new SCONFIG by: - setting the new boundaries and end states - saving the registers and undone scoped actions - adding the left state of the arc to the list of states that the computation has passed through (if the direction is to the left).

12.4.7 Connecting a new word to an island

In extending a segment at the end of an old island to meet a new word to be added, the sequence of intervening non-consuming arcs that make the connection can be all at the same level of the network (the J* case); they can change to a lower level (the J*B!J* case); or they can change levels in a way equivalent to one or more POPs followed by zero or more PUSHes (the J*C!J* case). The function CONNECT-RIGHT takes groups of SCONFIGs that terminate at the right boundary of an existing island and joins them to sets of arcs that can consume the new word to be added. We will call these arcs that can consume the new word that CONNECT-RIGHT is trying to connect to the island the destination arcs. CONNECT-RIGHT calls a function EXTEND-PATHS-RIGHT to do most of the work.

EXTEND-PATHS-RIGHT follows jump transitions to states that either 1) begin a destination arc, 2) push for a constituent that can begin with a destination arc, or 3) pop from the current constituent to a higher level that can begin with (or can then push for) a destination arc. EXTEND-PATHS-RIGHT begins from an SCONFIG group whose members share the same right boundary and completes the JUMP paths on that level that are required to reach the states mentioned above.

EXTEND-PATHS-RIGHT is used in several contexts in CONNECT-RIGHT, so it must have a way of deciding which of the above cases are relevant. To do this it must be supplied with an argument (TRYDIRS) indicating how many of the above three ways to look for a connection it should try. The operation of EXTEND-PATHS-RIGHT can be described as follows:

Let J*TOSTATES be the set of states that can J* to one of the destination arcs. Let J*FROMSTATES be the union of the J* sets of the right end states of the input SCONFIGs.

If the value of TRYDIRS is 1 or more (i.e. always), EXTEND-PATHS-RIGHT considers states on the same level as the input SCONFIGs (i.e. the states in J*FROMSTATES). All possible jump paths that reach one of the destination arcs are processed by DOARC. The resulting SCONFIGs are connected into groups according to their rightmost state and extended to include the destination arcs to which they attach.

In addition, if the value of TRYDIRS is 2 or more, then EXTEND-PATHS-RIGHT considers paths that lead to a lower level constituent, as well as ones on the same level as the input SCONFIGs. Each of the states x in J*FROMSTATES is also tested to see if it can reach a state y in J*TOSTATES via a B! transition. If so, then all jump paths are completed from the input SCONFIGs to state x, and new SCONFIGs starting in state y are created and given EXTEND-PATHS-RIGHT with TRYDIRS = 1.

In addition, if the number of directions (TRYDIRS) is 3, EXTEND-PATHS-RIGHT also considers paths that complete segments of the input SCONFIGs and return to a higher level. These higher levels may contain one of the destination arcs or may then push for new constituents that contain a destination arc. Note that these paths are just the C! set. For each state x in J*FROMSTATES that can reach a state in J*TOSTATES via a C! transition, all jump paths from the input SCONFIGs to x are created, and the resulting group of SCONFIGs is placed in a completion queue C!Q.

12.4.8 Processing the completion queue

The C!Q queue contains all SCONFIGs that have reached an accepting state. However, there is a major difference between those of its segments which are now complete at both ends and those which are still incomplete at the other end. In the first case, the appropriate constituent must be created and the process resumed at the higher level (COMPLETE-RIGHT). In the second case, all states in the C! set of the right state of the segment must still be considered for extension, since the segment has no left context.

SPLITC!Q checks the left boundary of each SCONFIG in the C!Q. If it is the left boundary of the island, then the segment is considered open and is put in the C!OPENLEFTQ. If it is within the island, then SPLITC!Q picks up RSTATES, the list of right end states, from the list of segments whose right end coincides with the left end of the segment being considered. This is done by keeping an index of segments in the island by right boundary. If there is an intersection between RSTATES and the UB! set of the left end state of the SCONFIG being considered, then the SCONFIG could have been pushed for from one of those segments, so the SCONFIG is put in the C!COMPLETEQ. If there is an intersection between RSTATES and the UC! set of the left end states of the SCONFIG, then it is possible for the SCONFIG to belong to a path in which it is the highest level SCONFIG. It is therefore put in the C!OPENLEFTQ. It is possible for an SCONFIG to be in both queues as a result of different possible paths.

At the end of this process, C!OPENLEFTQ is given to EXTEND-PATHS-RIGHT with TRYDIR = 2, and C!COMPLETEQ is given to a function COMPLETE-RIGHT.

12.4.9 Completing a constituent

The function COMPLETE-RIGHT is called to build a constituent for a segment that can connect to a destination arc by popping and which is pushed for (perhaps indirectly) by an SCONFIG to the left in the island. COMPLETE-RIGHT creates the new constituent to be popped, joining it to the island in one of two ways. It may add it to an existing segment at the next higher level, or if such a segment does not exist, it will create a new intermediate segment for each arc that can use the completed constituent and is compatible with some SCONFIG on the left.

When completing a segment and creating a new constituent, COMPLETE-RIGHT causes all undone scoped actions to be executed and creates the new constituent from the label of the POP arc. COMPLETE-RIGHT then looks to see if any existing segment immediately to the left of the new constituent could have pushed for it. If so, its PUSH arc is executed to include the new constituent. COMPLETE-RIGHT also looks to see if any segment to the left of the new constituent can push for it indirectly and still reach a destination arc. For each of these cases, COMPLETE-RIGHT must create a new segment, extend it from its beginning state to the state that pushes for the new constituent, and execute that push arc to create a new segment that is complete on the left and that includes the new constituent on the right.

After a segment has been extended to include the new constituent, it is placed back in the TODOQ because it may need to be further extended. CONNECT-RIGHT will deal with this correctly since the new segment behaves very much like the segments that were in the old island.

12.4.10 Making predictions

PREDICT-RIGHT is a function that creates a list of all terminal-consuming arcs that can be reached by any path of non-consuming arcs from the right end of an island. The word and category predictions made by the Syntactic component are collected from this list and a corresponding one for the left end of the island.

It is not sufficient for PREDICT-RIGHT merely to list all arcs that can be reached from states that can end the island; these predictions must be restricted by segment configurations within the island that are at a higher level than segments on the right. To make the list of predicted arcs, PREDICT-RIGHT groups the SCONFIGs by end states and boundaries so that ambiguous parses of one level are together. For each SCONFIG group at the right boundary, PREDICT-RIGHT checks to see if it can reach the left end of the island without passing through a higher level segment. If so, then all consuming arcs in all states reachable by (J* + J*B!J* + J*C!J*) are predicted. If not, PREDICT-RIGHT divides the predictions into two cases. First, all terminal consuming arcs in states reachable from the SCONFIG by (J* + J*B!J*) are predicted. Secondly, if the SCONFIG has a nonempty J*C! set, then for each SCONFIG to its left that can push for it, PREDICT-RIGHT repeats the prediction process on the higher level SCONFIG as if its right end state were the right state of the PUSH arc that pushes for the segment at the right boundary. As a result of this process, all predictions on the right that are compatible with possible paths across the island are generated.

12.5 MIDDLE-OUT PARSING WITH CATN'S

[13] presents a discussion of parsing with CATN's in a conventional left-to-right mode. For our purposes, however, it is interesting to consider the problem of a middle-out algorithm. Since the breakdown that HWIM imposes between the lexical retrieval component and the linguistic consultant is exactly the boundary between two stages of an ATN cascade when viewed appropriately, the island-driven control strategy coupled with the middle-out ATN parser described above can be viewed as an instance of a CATN parser.

This view of the HWIM system as a middle-out parser for an ATN cascade suggests an approach to a minor problem that was present in the HWIM implementation. HWIM's lexical retrieval component used two dictionary trees, one going left-to-right and one going right-to-left, in order to support growing an island in either direction. This technique did not really deal adequately with seed words, which were handled by grouping both left-to-right and right-to-left matches of the same word into a single "fuzzy word match" (see [14]). Left-to-right seeds could handle inter-word coarticulation on the right, and right-to-left seeds could handle such coarticulation on the left, but there was no mechanism for forming seeds with coarticulation effects at both ends. The best one could do in such cases was a fuzzy word match with some of its elements faithfully representing the left end effects and some representing the right end effects. Neither of these would have an ideal score because of their failure to model the coarticulation effect at their other end.

If one used the same approach in the lexical ATN that is used in the middle out parsing of the linguistic component, then one could begin word match hypotheses from highly reliable seed hypotheses such as vowels and sonorants in stressed syllables and then extend such hypotheses in both directions. This would in fact be considerably simpler than for the syntactic parser, since the lexical ATN contains no pushing and popping. An ICONFIG for the lexical ATN would consist of merely a single SCONFIG recording the left and right end states in the lexical ATN, the score of the match, and possibly a register remembering the word to be transmitted or an undone scoped action to set such a register when a suitable left state is encountered. This approach would eliminate the need for two separate dictionary trees, and would create possibilities for somewhat different factoring of the common parts of the dictionary. (Whereas the HWIM dictionary tree merges common initial portions of word pronunciations, this approach would permit merging designed to capture commonalities on both left and right.)

Perhaps more interestingly, one could introduce a separate stage of the cascade for a syllable level analysis, with seed events starting at syllable nuclei and moving outward in both directions until they encounter adjacent syllables via island collision. This would have the advantage of moving from reliable acoustic phonetic evidence into less reliable regions in exactly the way that a theoretical analysis of the shortfall density algorithm shows to be effective.

Another application of cascades would be to replace HWIM's pragmatic grammar with a cascade of separate ATN's for syntax, semantics, and pragmatics. This would provide a cleaner separation between the different sources of knowledge and an overall reduction in the size of the grammar needed to capture a comprehensive range of interactions between syntactic, semantic, and pragmatic phenomena. Further developments along these lines would include cascades of generalized transition networks [12] and the use of sophisticated knowledge representation systems such as KL-ONE [2,15].

12.6 ACKNOWLEDGEMENTS

The speech understanding system HWIM is the result of a large group effort. Participants in the project included Madeleine Bates, Geoffrey Brown, Bertram Bruce, Craig Cook, Laura Gould, Gregory Harris, Dennis Klatt, Jack Klovstad, John Makhoul, Bonnie Webber, Richard Schwartz, and Victor Zue. The middle-out parser described here was implemented by Geoffrey Brown. The initial speech research was supported by the Advanced Research Projects Agency of the Department of Defence and was monitored by ONR under contract N00014-75-C-0053. Subsequent theoretical work and the writing of this chapter was supported in part by ONR under contract N00014-77-C-0371.

12.7 REFERENCES

[1] Bobrow, R.J., The RUS System, BBN Report 3878, Bolt Beranek & Newman Inc., 1978.

[2] Brachman, R.J. & Schmolze, J., 'An Overview of the KL-ONE Knowledge Representation System', Cognitive Science, forthcoming.

[3] Burton, R.R., Semantic Grammar: An Engineering Technique for Constructing Natural Language Understanding Systems, BBN Report 3453, Bolt Beranek & Newman Inc., December 1976.

[4] Earley, J., An Efficient Context-Free Parsing Algorithm, Ph.D. Dissertation, Computer Science Dept., Carnegie-Mellon University, August 1968.

[5] Lesser, V.R., Fennell, R.D., Erman, L.D. and Reddy, D.R., 'Organization of the Hearsay II Speech Understanding System', IEEE Trans. Acoustics, Speech, and Signal Processing, ASSP-23"(1),11-24, 1975.

[6] Lowerre, B.T., The HARPY Speech Recognition System, Technical Report, Computer Science Dept., Carnegie-Mellon University, Pittsburgh, PA, 1976.

[7] Thompson, F.B., The Semantic Interface in Man-Machine Communication, Technical Report RM 63TMP-35, General Electric Co., Santa Barbara, September 1963.

[8] Wolf, J.J. and Woods, W.A., 'The HWIM Speech Understanding System', in Wayne A. Lea (ed), Trends in Speech Recognition, pp.1-24, Prentice-Hall, Inc., Englewood Cliffs, NJ, 1980.

[9] Woods, W.A., 'Transition Network Grammars for Natural Language Analysis', CACM 13 (10), 591-606, October 1970.

[10] Woods, W.A., Bates, M., Brown, G., Bruce, B., Cook, C., Klovstad, J., Makhoul, J., Nash-Webber, B., Schwartz, R., Wolf, J. and Zue, V., Speech Understanding Systems, Final Technical Progress Report, Volumes I-V, Technical Report 3848, BBN, 1976.

[11] Woods, W.A., Bates, M., Brown, G., Bruce, B., Cook, C., Klovstad, J., Makhoul, J., Nash-Webber, B., Schwartz, R., Wolf, J. and Zue, V. Volume III, Lexicon, Lexical Retrieval and Control, Speech Understanding Systems, Final Technical Progress Report, 30 October 1974 to 29 October 1976, Technical Report, BBN, 1976. This volume may be obtained through NTIS by specifying AD No. A035277.

[12] Woods, W.A., Research in Natural Language Understanding, Quarterly Progress Report No.4: Generalizations of ATN Grammars, Technical Report, 3963, BBN, August 1978.

[13] Woods, W.A., 'Cascaded ATN Grammars', Amer. J. Computational Linguistics, 6 (1), 1-15, Jan-Mar 1980.

[14] Woods, W.A., 'Optimal Search Strategies for Speech Understanding Control', in Webber, B. & Nilsson N. (eds), Readings in Artificial Intelligence, pp.30-68, Tioga Publishing Co., Palo Alto, CA, 1981.

[15] Woods, W.A., 'What's Important About Knowledge Representation', IEEE Computer Magazine, Special Issue on Knowledge Representation, October 1983.

Prosodic Knowledge Sources for Word Hypothesization in a Continuous Speech Recognition System

Alex Waibel

Computer Science Department
Carnegie Mellon University
Pittsburgh, PA 15213

Abstract

Previously we have reported on the extraction of prosodic cues (such as stress, pitch, duration) from continuous speech [1] and have reported on possible uses of some prosodic information (e.g., temporal cues [2]) in large vocabulary word recognition systems. In this paper we extend these previous findings to a speaker-independent continuous speech recognition system. Speaker-independent knowledge sources (KS) were implemented that attempt to hypothesize words based on only prosodic cues found in the signal. The prosodic cues exploited were temporal cues (syllable durations, ratios of unvoiced segment durations to syllable durations, voiced segment durations), intensity profiles and likelihoods of stressedness. Each KS extracts the appropriate prosodic cue and searches its knowledge base for words whose prosodic patterns satisfy the constraints found in the signal. Usign a multispeaker continuous speechdatabase for evaluation, each prosodic KS is shown to hypothesize the correct word substantially better than chance. All prosodic KSs were then combined and compared with a speaker-independent acoustic-phonetic word hypothesizer. After applying the prosodic KSs, the correct word ranked on average 25th (out of 252 words). The acoustic-phonetic KS alone yielded an average rank of 40 (out of 252) without the addition of prosodic information. After prosodic and phonetic KSs were combined the average rank was reduced to 15 out of 252. The results indicate that prosodic information indeed adds complementary information that substantially improves word hypothesization in speaker-independent continuous speech recognition systems.

1. Introduction

To this day, the prosodic cues in the speech signal, duration, rhythm, intensity, pitch, and stress, are frequently being ignored in the implementation of speech recognition systems. In systems aimed at small vocabulary sizes, most research has centered around suitable representations of spectral information and around optimal search procedures used to align the unknown pattern with reference word template. In large vocabulary continuous speech recognition systems, atomic units of speech smaller than the word are usually chosen and recognition is performed by detecting and assembling phonemic or phone like units into strings of hypothesized words. Several attempts at using prosodic cues in speech recognition systems have mostly been limited to aiding syntactic analysis by hypothesizing phrase or clause boundaries (from pitch excursions) and/or hypothesizing phonemically reliable parts of the utterance ("islands of reliability") from the amount of stress found in the signal [3]. Only a few studies have attempted to use these cues to aid in the hypothesization or verification of words in English, despite the known strong contributions of prosodic cues to human word perception (see [4, 5] for a review). For isolated large vocabulary word recognition it has been shown [2, 6] that temporal cues can indeed be used effectively to hypothesize words, even in the absence of phonetic information. Moreover, these prosodic cues are shown to be predictable such that all necessary reference information for particular word candidates could be synthesized from text [2, 5]. These results, however, were limited to speaker dependent isolated word recognition and used only the temporal information in the signal.

This research was sponsored in part by the National Science Foundation, Grant MCS-7825824 and in part by the Defense Advanced Research Projects Agency (DOD), ARPA Order No. 3597, monitored by the Air Force Avionics Laboratory under Contract F33615-78-C-1551.

The views and conclusions contained in this document are those of the authors and should not be interpreted as representing the official policies, either expressed or implied, of the Defense Advanced Research Projects Agency or the US Government.

In this paper we expand on these encouraging findings along several dimensions. First, we explore three separate prosodic parameters. In addition to temporal cues, we will use intensity and stress patterns as descriptors of the word. Second, we will be using two continuous speech databases. The former, a training and development database, consists of 50 Harvard sentences [7] and was recorded and hand-labelled at CMU. The latter, the testing database, consists of two sets of these 50 Harvard sentences, read by different speakers at MIT. The third dimension, finally is the speaker dimension. All development and testing will be performed using multiple speakers for our results to measure *speaker independent* performance. Each ten sentences in the training and testing databases were therefore read by a different speaker.

The sections of this paper are organized according to prosodic cues. For each cue, a KS was developed that using only this cue attempts to hypothesize word candidates that are most likely to satisfy the detected prosodic pattern. We will report below the operation and performance of each of these KSs. We will then compare all prosodic KSs with each other and combine them into and statistically optimal combined prosodic KS. The performance of these prosodic KSs will then also be compared with a speaker-independent phonetic word hypothesizer developed at CMU. We will show that the performance of the prosodic KSs compares favorably with the performance of the phonetic KS and that the combination of the two results in dramatic overall improvements.

2. Prosodic Knowledge Sources

Conceptually, each KS described below consists of three major components: a prosodic parameter extraction algorithm, a knowledge base, and a matcher to search for suitable word candidates. The parameter extraction algorithm performs the appropriate measurements on the acoustic signal to obtain the relevant prosodic cues. The knowledge base contains for each word candidate one or more (to allow for alternates) entries. Each entry consists of parametric descriptions of the word in terms of the KS-specific prosodic cue. To allow for such a knowledge base to be expanded to larger vocabularies, it is also desirable that the prosodic representation of each word be valid across different speakers or that it can be automatically predicted from text without user training. The matcher, finally, uses the prosodic cue measured by the extraction algorithm and searches the knowledge base for similar tokens. This search is typically done by assigning a score to each word candidate based on the similarity of its prosodic pattern to the pattern found in the unknown signal. The list of word candidates is then ranked according to their scores. At the absence of begin/end points in continuous speech, this analysis was performed by each KS repeatedly for each possible word anchor point, given by each hypothesized syllable boundary. Using the hand-labelled speech databases described above, the ability of each KS to hypothesize words based only on prosodic cues was then evaluated. The evaluations reported below will show the rates at which the correct word candidate will be found among the N top ranking candidates.

2.1. Duration and Rhythm

Three measures of duration were explored in three KSs: the syllable durations in a word, the ratios of the duration of the unvoiced segments in a syllable to the syllable duration, and the duration of vocalic segments. A syllable boundary was defined to lie at the onset of a rise in vocalic energy. The syllable boundaries and the unvoiced/voiced segment boundaries needed for measurement of the relevant duration patterns were detected by a set of segmentation and syllabification algorithms described in detail elsewhere [2, 5]. Two knowledge bases were evaluated. The first used duration measurements obtained from the training database, i.e., the CMU-Harvard database. For the second, all durations were synthetically generated using a knowledge compiler developed earlier [2, 6].

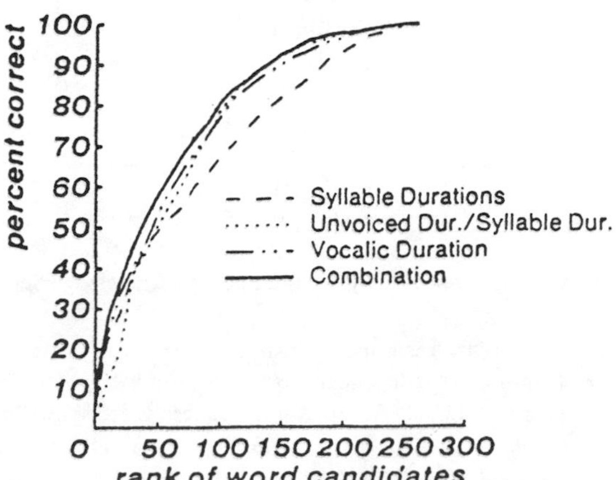

Figure 1. Percent Correct for Given Rank and for Different Durational Knowledge Sources; Testing Data.

Fig. 1 shows the results obtained by the three durational KSs. For this evaluation the testing data (100 MIT-Harvard sentences) was used. The knowledge base consisted of measured durations. All three durational measurements yield comparable performance with the syllable duration measure lagging behind somewhat. Fig. 2 shows performance results

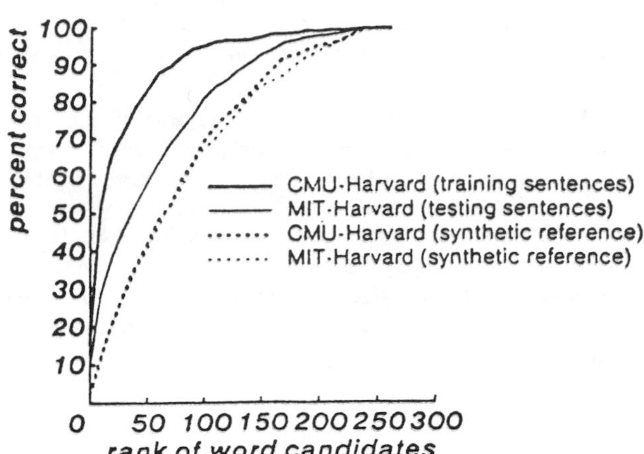

Figure 2. Percent Correct for Given Rank in Training and Testing Data; Knowledge Bases of Measured and Synthetic Durations.

for the combination of the three durational KSs using a simple geometric mean of each KS's rank orderings. Here the effect of measured vs. synthetic knowledge base was evaluated. Also both evaluation runs were performed for both the testing and the training database. The performance degradation due to segmentation/syllabification errors can be inferred in this figure from the less than perfect performance obtained when the training data was used for both the knowledge base and as evaluation data. The inherent variability of durational cues is reflected by the additional decrement in performance when evaluation was performed using different, e.g., the testing data. Further degradation can be observed when measured durations were replaced by the synthetically generated durations. Despite these performance degrading factors, however, it is clear from this evaluation that better-than-random word hypothesization can be performed based on durational cues only.

2.2. Stress

Similar in spirit to the previous subsection, a KS based on stress patterns was implemented and tested. The KS uses stress probabilities

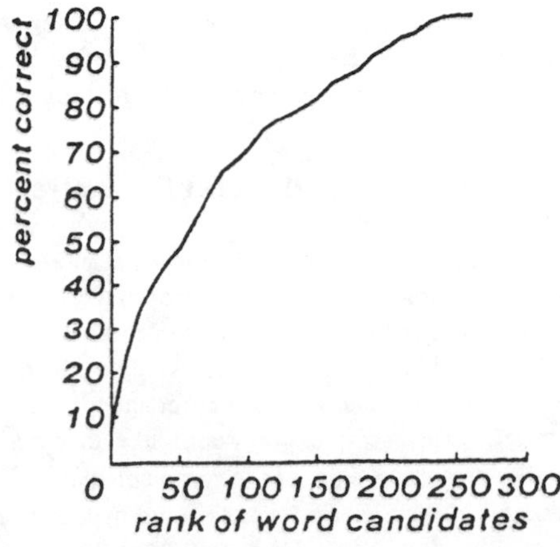

Figure 3. Percent Correct for Given Rank Using a Stress Based Knowledge Source; Testing Data.

obtained from a probabilistic stress detector [1, 5]. Thus stress *probabilities* rather than discrete stress assignments were used. This provided a finer grain and hence a continuum of similarities between tokens.

The knowledge base therefore contained stress probability as measured in the training data. Fig. 3 shows the performance obtained when this KS was evaluated over the 100 MIT-Harvard test sentences. Although word hypothesization can be better than random, these performance results are inferior to those obtained by the durational KSs. This is due to the great variability in stressedness that is indeed found in continuous speech. Considerable disagreement about the levels of stressedness was found in this data even for groups of human subjects [5].

2.3. Intensity

An intensity based KS was also implemented and evaluated. The peak-to-peak amplitude of the signal waveform was chosen as a measure of intensity. The knowledge base contained coarse amplitude patterns for the words in the vocabulary. Matching was done by measuring the similarity between the incoming patterns and the patterns in the knowledge base. Allowance was made for slight misalignments of corresponding patterns.

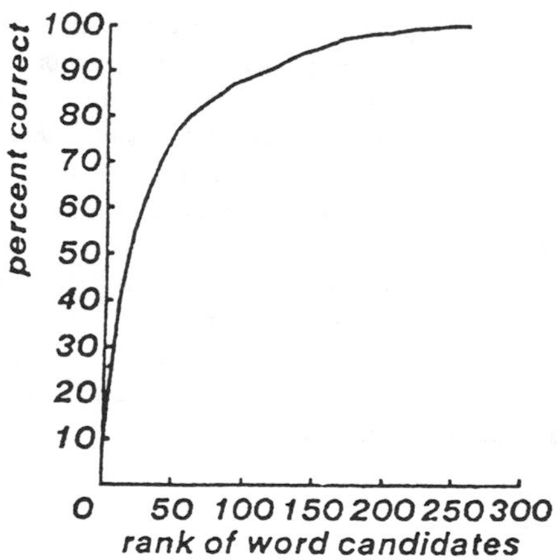

Figure 4. Percent Correct for Given Rank Using an Intensity Based Knowledge Source; Testing Data.

Fig. 4 shows the results from an evaluation run using the testing database. It can be seen that word hypothesization performance considerably better than random can be obtained from this KS.

3. Combination of Prosodic and Phonetic Knowledge Sources

In the preceding section we have demonstrated that prosodic cues can indeed be used at the word level to rank appropriate word hypotheses better than chance and speaker independently in continuous speech. In this section we would like to combine and evaluate all prosodic KSs and compare their performance with a speaker independent phonetic word hypothesizer. Furthermore, we would like to experimentally determine whether prosodic KS do lead to complementary information, that would be useful *in addition* to a phonetic word hypothesizer.

We start with the combination of prosodic KSs. To obtain a statistically optimal combination of the all five KSs described in the previous sections, we have collected variances and covariances of the scores obtained from each KS. The resulting covariance matrix was then used to compute a Mahalanobis distance as a combined prosodic similarity measure. In this fashion the contributions from each KS were weighted according to their relative merit in the light of the performance of the other competing KSs. The resulting performance graph (using the test-database) is shown in Fig. 5. Note, that the intensity KS appears to be yielding near optimal performance.

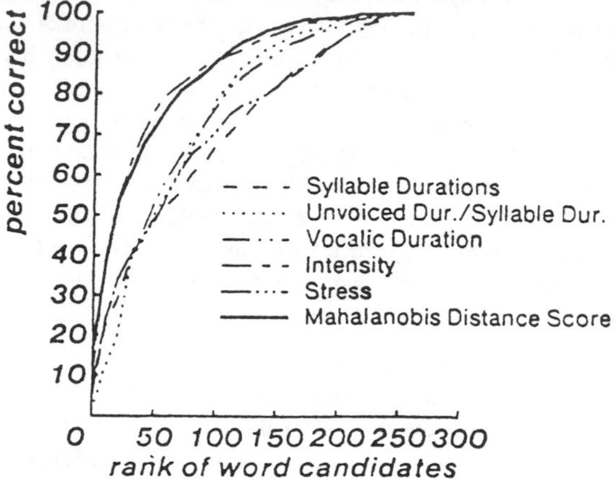

Figure 5. Combination of Prosodic Knowledge Sources

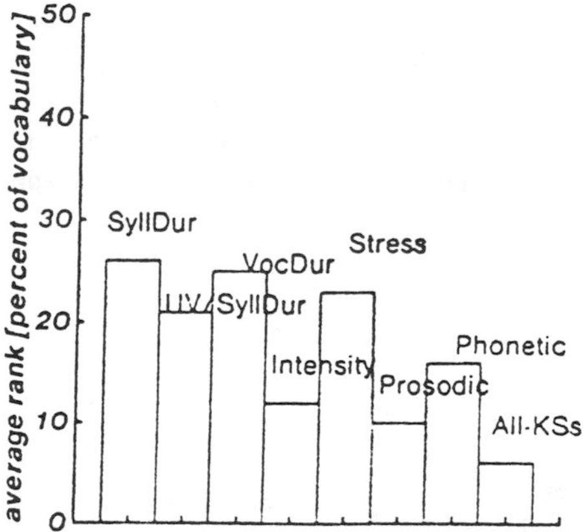

Figure 6. Comparison of Prosodic and Phonetic Knowledge Sources

Using ten test sentences a more detailed evaluation of these prosodic KSs and a speaker-independent phonetic word hypothesizer was subsequently carried out. The performance results are shown in Fig 6 in the form of a bar graph. For each KS the *average rank* of the correct word in the list of word candidate is given as a percentage of vocabulary size. Thus, for example, an average rank of 68 (for the syllable duration KS) is given as 26%, based on a vocabulary size of 252 words. From Fig. 6 we can see again that intensity patterns were the most useful prosodic cue for word identification (lowest rank). This can in part be explained by the comparatively robust prosodic parameter extraction in this case. Following the five bars representing each prosodic KS, Fig. 6 then shows the combination of all five prosodic KSs as discussed before. It is worth noting that not only was the average rank of the combined prosodic KSs better than each individual KS by itself, but that the standard deviation of the combination (not shown in this graph) was found to be considerably lower. More robust performance can therefore be expected from the exploitation of *all* cues. This combined prosodic performance measure was then compared with a speaker-independent word hypothesizer developed at CMU. It should be mentionned, that this word hypothesizer was only a preliminary version of a more advanced word hypothesizer that is currently under development. Fig. 6 shows that the rank of the combined prosodic KSs is actually lower than the phonetic word hypothesizer. Finally, combination of prosodic *and* phonetic KSs leads to substantially reduced hypothesization rank. It can be seen that adding prosodic information to the phonetic word hypothesizer reduced the average rank of the correct word hypothesis to about 1/3.

4. Conclusion

In this paper we have demonstrated that the prosodic cues of duration, intensity, and stress can be effectively used in word hypothesization. Using prosodic cues only, performance comparable or better than a speaker-independent phonetic word hypothesizer was obtained. Moreover, the combination of prosodic *and* phonetic KSs leads to dramatic improvements over phonetic word hypothesization alone. This result clearly demonstrates, that prosodic cues yield complementary information. Speech recognition systems can therefore benefit considerably from the exploitation of these cues. This paper has shown only one strategy towards achieving effective integration of prosodic analysis. Alternate strategies, such as top down verification of confusable word hypotheses are conceivable and work along these lines is in progress.

1. A. Waibel, "Recognition of Lexical Stress in a Continuous Speech Understanding System - A Pattern Recognition Approach", *ICASSP '86 Proceedings*, IEEE, 1986, pp. 2287-2290.

2. A. Waibel, "Suprasegmentals in Very Large Vocabulary Isolated Word Recognition", *ICASSP '84 Proceedings*, IEEE, 1984, pp. 26.3.1-26.3.4.

3. W.A. Lea, *Prosodic Aids to Speech Recognition*, Prentice-Hall, Englewood Cliffs, NJ, 1980, ch. 8.

4. I. Lehiste, *Suprasegmentals*, MIT-Press, Cambridge, MA, 1970.

5. A. Waibel, *Prosody and Speech Recognition*, PhD dissertation, Computer Science Department, Carnegie Mellon University, 1986.

6. A. Waibel, *Suprasegmentals in Very Large Vocabulary Word Recognition*, In: Pattern Recognition by Humans and Machines, E.C. Schwab and H.C. Nusbaum, editors, Academic Press, Orlando, Florida 32887, 1986, ch. 5.

7. IEEE, "IEEE Recommended Practice for Speech Quality Measurements", *IEEE Transactions on Audio and Electroacoustics*, Vol. AU-17, No. 3, September 1969, pp. 225-246, Standards Publication No. 297, available from IEEE

HIGH LEVEL KNOWLEDGE SOURCES IN USABLE SPEECH RECOGNITION SYSTEMS

The authors detail an integrated system which combines natural language processing with speech understanding in the context of a problem solving dialogue. The MINDS system uses a variety of pragmatic knowledge sources to dynamically generate expectations of what a user is likely to say.

SHERYL R. YOUNG, ALEXANDER G. HAUPTMANN, WAYNE H. WARD, EDWARD T. SMITH, and PHILIP WERNER

Understanding speech is a difficult problem. The ultimate goal of all speech recognition research is to create an intelligent assistant, who listens to what a user tells it and then carries out the instructions. An apparently simpler goal is the *listening typewriter*, a device which merely transcribes whatever it hears with only a few seconds delay. The listening typewriter seems simple, but in reality the process of transcription requires almost complete understanding as well. Today, we are still quite far from these ultimate goals. But progress is being made.

One of the major problems in computer speech recognition and understanding is coping with large search spaces. The search space for speech recognition contains all the acoustic associated with words in the lexicon as well as all the legal word sequences. Today, the most widely used recognition systems are based on hidden Markov models (HMM) [2]. In these systems, typically, each word is represented as a sequence of phonemes, and each phoneme is associated with a sequence of phonemes, and each phoneme is associated with a sequence of states. In general, the search space size increases as the size of the network of states increases. As search space size increases, speech recognition performance decreases. Knowledge can be used to constrain the exponential growth of a search space and hence increase processing speed and recognition accuracy [9, 17]. Currently, the most common approach to constraining search space is to use a grammar. The grammars used for speech recognition constrain legal word sequences. Normally they are used in a strict left to right fashion and embody syntactic and semantic constraints on individual sentences. These constraints are represented in some form of probabilistic or semantic network which does not change from utterance to utterance [16–18].

As we move toward habitable systems and spontaneous speech, the search space problem is greatly magnified. Habitable systems permit users to speak naturally. Grammars for naturally spoken sentences are significantly larger than the small grammars typically used by speech recognition systems. When one considers interjections, restarts and additional natural speech phenomena, the search space problem is further compounded. These problems point to the need for using knowledge sources beyond syntax and semantics to constrain the speech recognition process.

There are many other knowledge sources besides syntax and semantics. Typically, these are clustered into the category of pragmatic knowledge. Pragmatic knowledge includes inferring and tracking plans, using context across clausal and sentence boundaries, determining local and global constraints on utterances and dealing with definite and pronominal reference. Work in the natural language community has shown that pragmatic knowledge sources are important for understanding language. People communicate to accomplish goals, and the structure of the plans to accomplish them are well understood [9, 24, 26, 32, 33]. When speech is used in a structured task such as problem solving, prag-

This research was sponsored by the Defense Advance Research Projects Agency (DOD), ARPA Order No. 5167, monitored by the Air Force Avionics Laboratory under contract N00039-85-C-0163. The views and conclusions contained in this document are those of the authors and should not be interpreted as representing the official policies, either expressed or implied, of the Defense Advanced Research Projects Agency or the US Government.

matic knowledge sources are available for constraining search spaces.

In the past, pragmatic dialogue level knowledge sources were used in speech to either correct speech recognition errors [4, 10] or to disambiguate spoken input and perform inferences required for understanding [20, 21, 30, 35]. In these systems, pragmatic knowledge was applied to the output of the recognizer.

In this article we describe an approach for flexibly using contextual constraints to dynamically circumscribe the search space for words in a speech signal. We use pragmatic knowledge to derive constraints about what the user is likely to say next. Then we loosen the constraints in a principled manner. We generate layered sets of predictions which range from very specific to very general. To enable the speech system to give priority to recognizing what a user is most likely to say, each prediction set dynamically generates a grammar which is used by the speech recognizer. The prediction sets are tried in order of most specific first, until an acceptable parse is found. This allows optimum performance when users behave predictably, and displays graceful degradation when they do not. The implemented system (MINDS) uses these layered constraints to guide the search for words in our speech recognizer. For our recognizer, we use a modified version of the SPHINX [19] large vocabulary, speaker independent, continuous speech recognition system. The MINDS spoken language dialogue system developed at Carnegie-Mellon University applies pragmatic knowledge-based constraints as early as possible in the speech recognition process to eliminate incorrect recognition choices and drastically reduce the speech system error rate.

The main problem in speech recognition is the enormous complexity involved in analyzing speech input. Variations in pronunciation, accent, speaker physiology, emphasis and characteristics of the acoustic environment typically produce hundreds of different possible phoneme classifications for each sound. In turn, the many phoneme classifications can result in many possible word hypotheses at each point in the utterance. All of these word choices can then be combined to yield hundreds of sentence candidates for each utterance. The resulting search space is huge. Yet a speech system is required to filter out all incorrect candidates and correctly recognize an utterance in real time. Different approaches have been used in the past to limit the exponential explosion of the search space and trim the computational complexity to a more manageable level.

In an attempt to reduce complexity, the speech recognition problem has been simplified along different dimensions. The first speech recognition systems [18] were tailored to specific speakers only. This reduced much of the speech signal variation due to speaker characteristics such as sex, age, accent and physiological characteristics. The early systems also only recognized very few words. This reduction in vocabulary eliminated much confusion during recognition, especially if the words were all acoustically distinct. To avoid the problem of slurred and coarticulated words, the early systems required that each word be pronounced separately and that the speaker pause slightly between words. A final simplification of the speech problem was to artificially limit the number of different words that could be used at any one point. Similar to the choices available in a series of menus, the speaker could only use one of a few words at any place in the utterance. This technique depends on the previously uttered sentential context to reduce the so-called branching factor. The effective vocabulary at each point is made much smaller than the overall vocabulary available to the system.

Speech technology has made great strides in the recent past. We are now in a position where we can progress beyond systems that merely type out a sentence which was read to it for demonstration purposes. The speech recognition research focus has shifted toward integrated spoken language systems, which can be used by people trying to accomplish a task. For the rest of this article we will only be concerned with speaker independent, large vocabulary, connected speech recognition systems.

THE NEED TO INTEGRATE SPEECH AND NATURAL LANGUAGE

Speech recognition techniques at the word level are inadequate. Error rates are fairly high even for the best currently available systems. The Carnegie-Mellon SPHINX system [19] is considered to be the best speaker independent connected speech recognition system today. But even the Sphinx system has an error rate of 29.4 percent for speaker independent, 1,000 word connected speech recognition, when recognizing individual words in sentences without using knowledge about syntax or semantics. Clearly we need some forms of higher level knowledge to understand speech better. This is the kind of knowledge that has been used for years by researchers concerned with natural language understanding of typed input.

Just using the modules developed by the typed natural language understanding community is not as simple as it may seem. There are a number of very specific demands to a speech system interface which differ from a typed system interface. Many of the techniques for parsing typed natural language do not adapt well to speech specific problems. The following points highlight some of the unique speech problems not found in typed natural language.

Probability Measures. There is nothing uncertain about what a person has typed.

The ASCII characters are transmitted unambiguously to the program. The speech system has to deal with many uncertainties during recognition. At each level of processing, the uncertainties compound. The result of each processing step is usually expressed in terms of some probability or likelihood estimate. Any techniques developed for typed natural language systems need to be adapted to account for different alternatives with different probabilities.

Identifying Words. The speech system usually has many words hypothesized for each word actually spoken. The word identification problem has several components, some of those include:

- Uncertainty of the location of a word in the input. For almost every acoustic event in the utterance, there are words hypothesized that start and end at this event. Many of these words overlap and are mutually exclusive.
- Multiple alternatives at every word location. Even at the correct word location, the system is never certain of what word is actual input. A list of word candidates is usually hypothesized with different probabilities.
- Word boundary and juncture identification. Often words are coarticulated such that their boundaries became merged and unrecognizable. *Some milk* is a classic example of a phrase where the two words overlap without a clear boundary.

Phonetic Ambiguity of Words. Many words sound completely alike and the orthographic representation can only be distinguished from larger context. This is the case for *ice cream* and *I scream.*

Syllable Omissions. Spoken language tends to be terse. Because people are so good at disambiguating the speech signal, speakers unconsciously omit syllables. An example of this is frequently found in the pronunciation of *United States* which is reduced to sound like *unite states* in everyday speech.

Missing Information. The speech system will occasionally fail to recognize the correct word completely. Even though the speaker may have said the word correctly, it cannot be hypothesized from the acoustic evidence. There will be too many other word candidates that receive a better score and the correct word will be left out.

Ungrammatical Input. If miss-typing is the kind of phenomenon a standard natural language system has to deal with, speech systems encounter miss-spoken words and filled pauses like *ah* and *uhm* which further complicate recognition [15]. Natural human speech is also more likely to be ungrammatical [6].

The effect of all these differences requires speech recognition systems to deal with many more alternatives and a much larger search space than typed natural language systems. Therefore all techniques that have been developed by the natural language processing community must be restructured if they are to be adapted for the speech specific problems. They especially must be adapted to deal with the huge search spaces that result from the magnitude of the problem if these knowledge sources are to be used to assist in actual speech recognition.

Uses of Knowledge in Speech Recognition Systems

In the past, speech systems have used a variety of different kinds of knowledge sources to reduce the magnitude of the search space. The following list describes the major information sources used by different speech systems. We restrict ourselves to enumerating the knowledge sources above the level of complete words as they apply to sentences, dialogues, user goals and user focus.

- *Word Transition Probabilities.* If one wants to use knowledge of more than one word, the obvious solution is to use two words. By analyzing a large set of training sentences, a matrix of word pairs is constructed. The sentences are analyzed individually, without regard to dialogue structure, focus of attention or user goals. The resulting word pair matrix indicates which words can follow an already recognized word. A further extension of this method uses likelihoods of transitions encoded in the matrix instead of just binary values. Not only do we know which word pairs are legal, but we also have an indication of how likely they are. Empirically derived trigrams of words have also been used. Here a matrix is computed which, when given a sequence of the two preceding words, indicates which words can immediately follow at this point. Variations on the word transition probability estimates using Markov modeling techniques have been used by [2]. A minor modification of this approach uses word categories instead of words. Word categories are independent of the actual vocabulary size and require less training data to establish the transition probability matrix. While this approach does well to reduce the amount of search that is required, there is still much information missing in the triplets of allowable words [28, 31].
- *Syntactic Grammars.* A syntactic grammar first divides all words into different syntactic categories. Instead of using transition probabilities between word pairs or triplets, a syntactic grammar specifies all possible sequences of syntax word categories for a sentence [34]. Network grammars seem to be the most efficient representation for this type of constraint, since fast processing times are crucial in a speech system. Other grammar parsing representations are not as efficient when faced with the large numbers of candidates in a speech recognition situation. While the grammar may be written in a different notation, it can usually be compiled down to a network for the actual speech processing. The big drawback of these grammars is that they are difficult to construct by hand. They also assume the speaker will produce an utterance which is recognizable by the grammar.
- *Semantic Grammars.* Semantic grammars have been the most popular form of sentential information encoded in speech recognition systems. The grammar rules are similar to those of syntactic grammars, but words are categorized by a combination of syntactic class and semantic function. Only sentences that are both syntactically well formed as well as meaningful in the context of the application will be recognized

by a semantic grammar. Semantic grammars express stronger constraints than syntactic grammars, but also require more rules. These grammars are also easily representable as networks. Compared to the syntactic-grammars above, they are even more difficult to construct by hand. Nevertheless, most speech systems which use higher level knowledge have chosen to use semantic grammars as their main sentential knowledge source [5, 17, 18, 21, 36].

Some speech recognition systems emphasized semantic structure while minimizing syntactic dependencies [12, 16]. This approach results in a large number of choices due to the lack of appropriate constraints. The recognition performance therefore suffers due to the increased ambiguities. None of these systems proposed to use any knowledge beyond the constraints within single sentences.

• *Thematic Memory.* Barnett [3] describes a speech recognition system which uses a notion of history for the last sentences. The system keeps track of previously recognized content words and predicts that they are likely to reoccur. The possibility of using a dialogue structure is mentioned by Barnett, but no results or implementation details are reported. The *thematic memory* idea was picked up again by Tomabechi and Tomita [29], who demonstrated an actual implementation in a sophisticated frame-based system. Both speech recognition systems use an utterance to activate a context. This context is then transformed into word expectations which prime the speech recognition system for the next utterance.

• *History-based Models.* Fink, Biermann and others [4, 10] implemented a system that used a dialogue feature to correct errors made by a small vocabulary, commercial speech recognition system. Their module was strictly history-based. It remembered previously recognized meanings (i.e., semantic structures) of sentences as a finite state dialogue network. If the currently analyzed utterance was semantically similar to one of the stored sentence meanings and the system was at a similar state of the dialogue at that time, the stored meaning can be used to correct the recognition of the new utterance. Significant improvements were found in both sentence and word error rates when a prediction from a previous utterance could be applied. However, the history-based expectation was only applied after a word recognition module had processed the speech, in an attempt to correct recognition errors.

• *Strategy Knowledge.* Strategy knowledge was applied as a constraint in the voice chess application of Hearsay-I [25]. The task domain was defined by the rules of chess. The "situational semantics of the conversation" were given by the current board position. Depending on these, a list of legal moves could be formulated which represented plausible hypotheses of what a user might say next. In addition, a user model was defined to order the moves in terms of the goodness of a move. From these different knowledge sources, an exhaustive list of all sentences possible was derived. This list of sentences was then used to constrain the acoustic-phonetic speech recognition. Hearsay-I went too far in the restriction of constraints. A classic anecdote tells of the door slamming during a demonstration and the system *recognizing* the sentence: "*Pawn to Queen 4*". Hearsay-I applied its constraints in an extremely limited domain and overly restricted what could be said. Nevertheless, the principles of using a user model, task semantics and situational semantics are valid.

• *Natural Language Back-Ends.* Several speech recognition systems claim to have dialogue, discourse or pragmatic components [20, 21, 30, 35]. However, most of these systems only use this knowledge just like any typed natural language understanding system would. The speech input is processed by a speech recognition module which uses all its constraints up through the level of semantic grammars to arrive at a single best sentence candidate. This sentence is then transformed into the appropriate database query, anaphoric references are resolved, elliptic utterances are completed and the discourse model is updated. All these higher level procedures are applied *after* the sentence is completely recognized by the speech front-end. There is no interaction between the natural language processing modules and the speech recognizer.

Natural Language Research

There has been much research on discourse, focus, planning, inference and problem solving strategies in the natural language processing community. Some of the research was not directly carried out in the context of natural language systems, but describes methods for representation and analysis of these issues. We will briefly review the key principles which influenced the design of the MINDS spoken language dialogue system.

Plans. The utility of tracking plans and goals in a story has been well established. A number of researchers [1, 22] have described the utility of identifying a speaker's goals to disambiguate natural language sentences and to provide helpful system responses. Similarly, Cohen and Perrault [8] have developed a plan-based dialogue model for understanding indirect speech acts. A program called *PAM* [32] showed how an understanding of a person's goal can explain an action of the person. The goal and subsequent actions can also be used to infer the particular plan which the person is using to achieve this goal. Additionally, Wilensky [33] developed methods for dealing with competing goals and partial goal failures. The ways in which a plan can be broken down into a hierarchical set of goals and subgoals was originally demonstrated by Sacerdoti [26].

Problem Solving. Newell and Simon [24] were key influences in the study of human problem solving. Among other things, they showed how people constantly break goals into subgoals when solving problems. Their findings, as well as much of the other research done in this area [22] illustrate the function of user goals represented as goal trees, and traversal procedures for goal trees.

Focus. Focus determines a set of relevant concepts for a particular situation. Grosz [13] found that natural language communication is highly structured at the level of dialogues and problem solving. She showed how the notion of a user focus in problem solving dialogues is related to a partitioning of the semantic space. Focus can also provide an indication how to disambiguate certain input. Additional work by Sidner [27] confirmed the use of focus as a powerful notion in natural language understanding. Sidner successfully used a focus mechanism to restrict the possibilities of referent determination in pronominal anaphora.

Ellipsis. Elliptical utterances are incomplete sentences which rely on previous context to become meaningful. Methods for interpreting elliptical utterances were studied in depth by Frederking [11]. He used a chart-based representation to remember fragments of preceding sentences which were suitable complements for elliptic phrases.

User Domain Knowledge. Chin [7] showed how the knowledge of the user about the domain can influence the expectations and behavior of a system. In addition, he described ways in which the user expertise could be inferred by the system.

THE MINDS SYSTEM

The main problem in speech recognition is the enormous complexity involved in analyzing speech input. As search space size increases recognition performance decreases and processing speed increases. The value of a reduced search space and stronger constraints is well known in the speech recognition community [9, 17, 23]. Reducing the search to only the most promising word candidates by pruning often erroneously eliminates the correct path. By applying knowledge-based constraints as early as possible, one can trim the exponential explosion of the search space to a more manageable size without eliminating correct choices. Previously we delimited the key knowledge sources incorporated into the MINDS system to provide constraint. Now we briefly overview the entire MINDS system and enumerate the primary innovations of this new approach. The approach employs knowledge based constraints to reduce the exponential growth of the search space the speech recognizer must analyze.

To demonstrate our new approach in speech recognition, we have built MINDS, a *M*ulti-modal, *IN*teractive *D*ialog *S*ystem [14, 38]. It allows a user to speak, type and point during a problem solving session with the system. The system outputs information in a variety of media. It produces a natural language answer to the user's question as well as displaying relevant information on multiple raster display screens. These screens display the current information in various contexts emphasizing different aspects of the dialogue history and the current world situation. The MINDS system operates in real time.

MINDS works in a resource management domain, featuring information obtained from a database of facts about ships in the United States Navy. The basic problem scenario involves a damaged ship performing a particular task. The system user must determine the impact of the damage on the mission and then determine whether the damaged ship should continue in degraded condition or should be replaced by a different ship. If a replacement ship is being considered, the user must locate one with similar capabilities and a ship which will have minimal impact on other mission operations. An excerpt from a sample interaction transcript can be found in Figure 1.

For the purposes of this article, MINDS can be viewed as a speaker-independent continuous speech recognition system that uses dialogue knowledge, user goals, plans and focus to understand what was said in its naval logistics problem solving domain. The system uses this higher level knowledge of dialogues in addition to a representation of user's domain knowledge to predict what the current user will talk about next. The predictions drastically reduce the search space before the sentence and word detection modules even begin to analyze the speech input.

In very general terms, we can describe the main operations of the MINDS system as a continuous loop. First, the system generates a set of predictions based on the last user query, the database response and the state of the dialogue. Then, the predictions are translated

```
List the casualty reports for ships in the
Persian Gulf?
```
Gridley is in the Persian Gulf. Harpoon missile is disabled.
```
What's its mission?
```
Gridleys mission is escort.
```
Show me Gridley's required capabilities.
```
Harpoon missile, Phalanx gun, SPS-10 radar are required capabilities
```
Let me see all Leahy-class cruisers in the
Persian Gulf.
```
England is a Leahy-class ship. It is a cruiser. It is in the Persian Gulf.
Gridley is a Leahy-class ship. It is a cruiser. It is in the Persian Gulf.
```
What is the mission for England?
```
Englands mission is transport.
```
Priority?
```
Englands mission importance is 1.
```
What are her capabilities?
```
It has Harpoon missile.
It has Phalanx gun.
It has SPS-10 radar.
It has torpedo tubes.
It has SM-2 missile.
```
Does England have any CASREPS?
```
Nothing found in the database.

FIGURE 1. An Excerpt of a Typical Dialogue with the MINDS System

into a semantic grammar. The active lexicon is restricted to only cover words which are part of the predictions. The next user query is parsed using the dynamically created grammar and lexicon, and the user's question is displayed for verification. The database response to user request is then presented in output modalities.

Innovations of the MINDS System

The MINDS system represents a radical departure from the principles of most other speech recognition systems. The key innovations of the MINDS system include the following:

1. Use of a combination of knowledge sources including discourse and dialogue knowledge, problem solving knowledge, pragmatics, user domain knowledge goal representation, as well as task semantics and syntax in an integrated system.
2. All the knowledge is used predictively. Instead of applying the knowledge to correct an error or resolve ambiguities after they occur, the knowledge is applied in a predictive way to constrain all possibilities as they are generated.
3. The constraints generated by the system are immediately applied to the low-level speech processing to reduce the search space. We use the predictive constraints to eliminate large portions of the search space for the earliest acoustic-phonetic analysis.
4. In case the predictions fail, the system provides a principled way of recovery when constraints are violated. If the constraints are satisfied, recognition is more accurate and faster. However, if some of our predictions are violated the system does not break—it degrades gracefully.
5. In addition to speech input, the MINDS system allows pointing and clicking as well as typed modes of interaction. The user may use the mouse to select objects displayed graphically on the screen. For those users who are uncomfortable speaking to a computer, anything that could be spoken can also be typed on a keyboard.

MINDS exploits knowledge about users' domain knowledge problem solving strategy, their goals and focus as well as the general structure of a dialogue to constrain speech recognition down to the signal processing level. Pragmatic knowledge sources are used predictively to circumscribe the search space for words in the speech signal [14, 37]. In contrast to other systems, we do not correct misrecognition errors after they happen, but apply our constraints as early as possible during the analysis of an utterance. Our approach uses predictions derived from the problem-solving dialogue situation to limit the search space at the lower levels of speech processing. At each point in the dialogue, we predict a set of concepts that may be used in the next utterance. This list of concepts is combined with a set of syntactic networks for possible sentence structures. The result is a dynamically constructed semantic network grammar, which reflects all the constraints derived from all our knowledge sources. To avoid getting trapped by predictions which are not fulfilled, we generate them at different level of specificity. When the parser then analyzes the spoken utterance, the dynamic network allows only a very restricted set of word choices at each point. This reduces the amount of search necessary and cuts down on the possibility of recognition errors due to ambiguity and confusion between words. The bottom line is that the MINDS system uses as much knowledge as possible to achieve accurate speech recognition and help the user complete his task efficiently.

The Predictive Use of Knowledge

Predictions are derived from what we know about the current state of the dialogue. This knowledge is then refined to constrain what we expect the user will actually say. In some sense predictions cover everything we expect to happen, and exclude events which are unlikely to happen. To be able to create predictions, we have three very important data structures in the system:

A knowledge base of domain concepts. In this data structure we represent all objects and their attributes in the domain. The representation uses a standard frame language which provides the capability to express inheritance and multiple relations between frames. The domain concepts also represent everything that can be expressed by the user. Each possible utterance will map into a combination of domain concepts which constitute the meaning of that utterance. This representation of meaning is also used to generate the database queries from the utterance.

Hierarchical goal trees. The goal trees represent a hierarchy of all possible abstract goals as user may have during the dialogue. The goal trees are composed of individual goal nodes, structured as AND-OR trees. Each goal node is characterized by the possible subgoals it can be decomposed into and a set of domain concepts involved in trying to achieve this goal. The concepts associated with a goal tend to be restricted from previous dialog context. These restrictions on concept expansions are dynamically computed for each concept. The computation is based upon principles for inheriting and propagating constraints based upon their embedding and are often referred to as local and global focus in the natural language literature. The goal tree not only defines the goals, subgoals and domain concepts, but also the traversal options available to the user. A goal node's associated concepts can be optional or required, single use or multiple use. If a concept is optional, it is possible but not necessary for a user to apply this concept in the current problem-solving step. If a concept is defined as multi-usable, then a user could refer to it several times in different utterances during the current problem solving step.

A User Model. A user model represents domain concepts and the relations between domain concepts which a user knows about. These models are represented as control structures which are associated with goals in the goal tree. The control structures express which goals may be exclusive because the user can infer the information in one goal once the other, exclusive goal has been completed. Other goals may be optional because the user is unfamiliar with the domain concept or its potential importance in deriving a solution to the current problem. Additionally, the control structures contain probabilistic orderings for conjunctive subgoals. Hence, the user model provides the system with potential traversal options which are more restrictive than the traversal options provided by the other knowledge sources.

These three complex data structures are currently only constructible by hand—based on a detailed and careful analysis of the problem-solving task itself.

We will now try to explain how the knowledge is used by the MINDS system to track the progress of a user during a problem-solving session. We will also show how predictions in the form of domain concepts are generated during a dialogue.

When an input utterance and its database response have been processed, we first try to determine which goal states were targeted by the present interaction. Determination of activated goal states is by no means unambiguous. During one interaction cycle, several goal states may be completed and many new goal states may be initiated. Similarly, it is possible that an assumed goal state is not being pursued by the user. To deal with these ambiguities, we use a number of algorithms. Goals that have just been completed by this interaction and that are consistent with previous plan steps are preferred. Based on the information we have available, we select the most likely plan step to be executed next. If the current goal is not complete, then our most likely plan step will attempt to complete the current goal. If the current goal is satisfied, we identify the next goal states to which a user could transit. The result of tracking the goal states is a list of potential goals and subgoals which a user will try to complete in the current utterance. Additionally, since there are always many active goals which may or may not be hierarchically embedded, we also maintain a list of all active goals. Hence, the procedures described above are used for determining the best, most likely goal state a user will transit to. To generate our most restrictive predictions, we then restrict the most likely goal state further by taking the constraints from the user model. The next prediction layer ignores the user model and is derived only from the best, most likely next goal. Finally, additional less restrictive sets of predictions are derived from currently active goals which are at higher levels of the goal tree. This procedure continues until all active goals are incorporated into a prediction set. The goals all have an associated list of concepts in the task domain. These are the concepts a user will refer to when trying to satisfy the current goal.

For example, in a goal state directed at assessing a ship's damage, we expect the ship's name to appear frequently in both user queries and system statements. We also expect the user to refer to the ship's capabilities. The predicted sentence structures should allow questions about the features of a ship like "Does its sonar still work?" Display the status of all radars for the Spark" and "*What is Badger's current speed*?"

Some domain concepts which are active at a goal tree node during a particular dialogue phase have been partially restricted by previous goal states. The representation of the domain concepts associated with goal nodes provides a mechanism to specify what prior goal can restrict the current concept. These restrictions may come either from the user's utterances or from the system responses. Thus each goal state not only has a list of active domain concepts, but also a set of concepts whose values were partially determined by an earlier goal state.

In our example, once we know which ship was damaged, we can be sure all statements in the damage assessment phase will refer to the name of that ship or its hull number only. In addition to the knowledge mentioned earlier, we also restrict what kinds of anaphoric referents are available at each goal node. The possible anaphoric referents are determined by user focus. From the current goal or subgoal state, focus identifies previously mentioned dialogue concepts and answers which are relevant at this point. These concepts are expectations of the referential content of anaphora in the next utterance.

Continuing our example, it does not make sense to refer to a ship as "it" before the ship's name has been mentioned at least once. We also do not expect the use of anaphoric "it" if we are currently talking about a group of several potential replacement ships.

Elliptic utterances are predicted when we expect the user to ask about several concepts of the same type after having seen a query for the first concept.

If the users have just asked about the damage to the sonar equipment of a ship, and we expect them to query about damage to the radar equipment, we must include the expectation for an elliptic utterance about radar in our predictions.

Expanding Predictions into Networks

After the dialogue tracking module has identified the set of concepts which could be referred to in the next utterance, we need to expand these into possible sentence fragments. Since these *predicted concepts* are abstract representations, they must be translated into word sequences which signify that appropriate conceptual meaning. For each concept, we have precompiled a set of possible surface forms, which can be used in an actual utterance. In effect, we reverse the classic understanding process by un-parsing the conceptual representation into all possible word strings which can denote the concept. A predicted concept can be quickly un-parsed into all its possible semantic network grammar subnets.

In addition to the individual concepts, which usually expand into noun phrases, we also have a complete semantic network grammar that has been partitioned into subnets. Each subnet expresses a complete sentence. A subnet defines allowable syntactic surface forms to express a particular semantic content. For example, all ways of asking for the capabilities of ships are grouped together into subnets. The semantic network is further partitioned into separate subnets for elliptical utterances, and subnets for anaphora. The semantic grammar subnets are precompiled to allow direct access for processing efficiency. The terminal nodes in the networks are word categories instead of words themselves, so no recompilation is necessary as new lexical items in existing categories are added to or removed from the lexicon.

The final expansion of predictions brings together the partitioned semantic networks and the predicted concepts which were translated into their surface forms. Through a set of cross-indices, we intersect all predicted concept expressions with all the predicted semantic networks. This operation generates dynamically one combined semantic network grammar which embodies all the dialogue level and sentence level constraints. This dynamically created network grammar is used by the parser to process an input utterance.

To illustrate this point, let us assume that the frigate "Spark" has somehow been disabled. We expect the user to ask for its capabilities next. The dialogue tracking module predicts the "shipname" concept restricted to the value "Spark" and any of the "ship-capabilities" concepts. Single anaphoric reference to the ship is also expected, but ellipsis is not meaningful at this point. The current damage assessment dialogue phase allows queries about features of a single ship.

During the expansion of the predicted concepts, we find the word nets such as "the ship," "this ship," "the ship's," "this ship's," "it," "its," "Spark" and "Spark's." We also find the word nets for the capabilities such as "all capabilities," "radar," "sonar," "Harpoon," "Phalanx," etc. We then intersect these with the sentential forms allowed during this dialogue phase. Thus we obtain the nets for phrases like "Does {it, Spark, this_ship, the_ship} have {phalanx, harpoon, radar, sonar}," "What {capabilities, radar, sonar} does {the_ship, this_ship, it, Spark} have," and many more. This semantic network now represents a maximally constrained grammar at this particular point in the dialogue.

Recognizing Speech Using Dynamic Networks

We use the SPHINX system [19] as the basis for our recognizer. SPHINX samples input speech in centisecond frames. Based on the LPC cepstrum coefficients, each frame is then mapped into one of 256 prototype vectors. Vector-quantized speech is also used to train Hidden Markov Models (HMMs) for phonemes. HMMs are trained from a corpus of approximately 4200 sample utterances. Each word is represented in the dictionary as a single sequence of phonemes. The models for words are pre-compiled by concatenating the HMMs for each phoneme in a word. During recognition, SPHINX performs a time-synchronous beam search known as the Viterbi algorithm, matching word models against the input.

In the MINDS system, we use the active set of semantic networks to control word transitions instead of the word-pair constraints normally used by the SPHINX system. The search begins at the set of initial words for all active subnets. This set includes only currently active words from the dynamically created lexicon for this utterance. As the search matches a word from the input utterance, it transits along the arc in the grammar represented by that word. A score is assigned to each path in the beam, indicating how well the input is matching the HMMs in the path. Paths falling below a threshold score are pruned. The dynamically created semantic network is used to allow only *legal* word transitions. The network does not affect the score of a path but simply restricts words which can continue a particular path. If no string of words is found which matches the HMMs better than a certain threshold score, a different grammar and lexicon from a more general set of predictions must be used to re-process the utterance. After the spoken input has been processed, the word string with the best score is passed back to the system for parsing.

When Predictions Fail

There are a number of assumptions built into the use of predictions. If a user conforms to our model of a problem-solving dialogue, the advantages are clear. However, we must consider the case when some assumptions are violated. There are two points to consider when predictions fail: We must first be able to identify the situation of failed predictions and then find a way to recover.

In the MINDS system, the first point is accomplished without extra work. When the user speaks an utterance which was not predicted, the speech recognition component usually fails to produce a complete parse. The spoken words do not match the predicted words and receive low probability scores. This may not always be as easy in other recognition systems.

As a mechanism for recovery from failed predictions, the MINDS system always produces several sets of predictions for each utterance. These sets of predictions range from very specific to very general. For the most specific predictions, the system uses all the possible constraints. Each successive set of predictions then becomes more general. The number of levels of constraint relaxation depends on the goal tree structure at that point. Predictions are made more general by assuming additional goal nodes are active. Eventually we reach a level of prediction constraints which is identical to the constraints provided by the full semantic grammar with all possible words. We now can parse any syntactically

As a mechanism for recovery from failed predictions, the MINDS system always produces several sets of predictions for each utterance.

and semantically legal utterance, disregarding all dialogue considerations. Beyond that we can only relax the constraints to a point where any word can be followed by any other word. This would be necessary if a user spoke an utterance that was not covered by the grammar. In this case, we must rely on heuristics during the semantic interpretation of the utterance to provide a correct meaning and database query. Details of this procedure are described in [38].

When the speech recognition module fails to parse at a particular level of constraints, the next set of predictions is used to reparse the same utterance until a successful parse is obtained. If the user is cooperative and within our predictions, recognition accuracy will be high and response time immediate. As the system backs up over several levels of constraints, the search space of the recognition module becomes larger and processing time increases while accuracy drops. However, the system never experiences a complete loss of continuity when predictions are violated.

EVALUATION OF PROGRESS

Many systems developed by researchers in the artificial intelligence community lack a rigorous evaluation. While the individual systems may incorporate brilliant ideas, it is rarely shown that they are in some way better than other systems based on a different approach. If the research in a field wants to make progress, that progress must be made visible and measurable.

In the field of speech understanding one clear measure of success is recognition accuracy. Recognition accuracy can be measured in terms of word accuracy, sentence accuracy as well as semantic accuracy. Word accuracy is defined here as the number of words that were recognized correctly divided by the number of words that were spoken. In addition to the number of correct words, we also record the number of insertions of extra words by the recognizer. This number is otherwise not reflected in the percentage of correct words. Recognition accuracy thus takes into account deleted words and word substitutions (i.e., "its" was spoken but "his" was recognized.) On the other hand, error rate reflects insertions, deletions, and subtitutions. If the speech recognizer makes minor errors in recognizing an utterance, but the underlying meaning of the utterance is preserved, the utterance is considered to be recognized *semantically accurate* even though some words were incorrect. Semantic accuracy therefore is the percentage of sentences with correct meaning. In our system, a sentence is considered semantically correct if the recognition produces the correct database query.

To test the ability of the MINDS system to reduce search space and improve speech recognition performance, we performed two experiments. The first experiment assessed search space reduction caused by predictive use of all pragmatic knowledge sources. The second experiment measured improvement in recognition accuracy rates resulting from the use of layered predictions. Both studies used a test set of data which was independent from the training data used to develop the system. This means that the utterances and dialogues processed by the system to obtain the experimental results had not been seen previously by the system or the developers.

Our test data consisted of 10 problem solving scenarios. These were adapted versions of three actual transcripts of naval personnel solving problems caused by a disabled vessel. The personnel must determine whether to delay a mission, find a replacement vessel or schedule a repair for a later date. They use a database to find necessary problem solving information. In addition, we created seven additional scenarios by paraphrasing the original three. The test scenarios contained an average of nine sentences with an average of eight words each. An excerpt of a dialogue sequence is given in Figure 1.

The training data had consisted of five different problem solving scenarios from transcripts of naval personnel performing the same basic task. The training scenarios were used for developing the user models. Dialogue phases, goals and problem solving plans were derived from an abstract description of the stages and options available to a problem solver. The abstract plan descriptions had been provided by the Navy.

Since our database was different from the one used in gathering the original transcripts, we were forced to adapt all scenarios. Lexical items which were unknown to our system were substituted with known words. Shipnames, locations, capabilities, mission requirements, etc. were changed to be consistent with our database. We feel these adaptations had minimal impact on the integrity of the data and did not alter the problem solving structure of the task. The lexicon for this domain contained 1,000 words.

Reduction of Search Space and Perplexity

Since the magnitude of the search space is such a critical factor in speech recognition, one measure of success is the reduction in search space provided by a system. To measure the constraint imposed by the knowledge sources we use two measures: perplexity and search space reduction. Perplexity is an information theoretic measure that is widely used in speech systems to characterize the constraint provided by a grammar. Perplexity consists of the geometric mean of the number of nodes which are visited during the processing of an utterance. In our case, we use the semantic network grammars to calculate the number of word alternatives which the system has to consider. Test set perplexity is computed specifically for actual utterances. After we compute the alternatives for a word in the utterance, we assume the system recognizes this word correctly and continues by only computing the alternatives which directly follow this word in the grammar. A more detailed justification of this measure is given in [17]. The size of the search space is calculated by raising the sentence perplexity value to the number of words in the sentence.

Our first experiment was designed to test the perplexity and search space reduction resulting from applying pragmatic constraints. To measure the reduction in perplexity and search space we collected test set perplexity measurements for each of the parsed sentences in two conditions. The first condition represented the constraints provided by the complete semantic grammar networks with the full vocabulary available. The second condition measured perplexity for the most specific set of predictions that could be applied. The estimate for the second condition is the perplexity obtained by merging the successful prediction level with all of the more specific but unsuccessful levels of constraints. Otherwise, the results would be misleading whenever the predictions were not fulfilled.

As seen in Table I, by applying our best constraints, test set perplexity was reduced by an order of magnitude, from 279.2 to 17.8 while search spaces decreased by roughly 10 orders of magnitude.

TABLE I. Reduction in Branching Factor and Search Space

	Complete Grammar	Best Predictions
Test Set Perplexity	279.2	17.8
Search Space	3.81×10^{19}	1.01×10^{9}

Improvements in Recognition Accuracy

To evaluate the effectiveness of using predictions on recognition performance we used 10 speakers (8 male, 2 female) who had never before spoken to the system. To assure a controlled environment for these evaluations, each speaker read 20 sentences from the adapted test scenarios provided by the Navy transcripts. Each of these utterances was recorded. The speech recordings were then analyzed by the MINDS system in two conditions. The first condition ignored all constraints except those provided by the complete semantic grammar. In other words, all possible meaningful sentences were acceptable at all times. The second condition used the MINDS system with the most specific set of predictions appropriate for the utterance.

To prevent confounding of the experiment due to misrecognized words, the system did not use its normal speech recognition result to change state. Instead, after producing the speech recognition result, the system read the correct recognition from a file which contained the correct set of utterances. Thus, the system always changed state according to a correct analysis of the utterance.

The results can be found in Table II. The system performed significantly better with the predictions. Error rate decreased from 17.9 percent to 3.5 percent. Perhaps just as important is the nature of the individual errors. In the condition with the most specific successful predictions, almost all of the errors (insertions and deletions) were made on the word "the." Another large proportion of errors consisted of substituting the word "his" for the word "its." Furthermore, none of the errors in the "with predictions" condition resulted in an incorrect database query. Hence, semantic accuracy was 100 percent on this sample of 200 spoken sentences.

TABLE II. Recognition Performance

	Complete Grammar	Best Predictions
Test Set Perplexity	242.4	18.3
Word Accuracy	82.1%	97.0%
Insertions	0.0%	0.5%
Semantic Accuracy	85%	100%
Deletions	8.5%	1.6%
Substitutions	9.4%	1.4%
Error Rate	17.9%	3.5%

CONCLUSIONS

It is obvious that the MINDS system represents only a beginning in the integration of speech recognition with natural language processing. We have shown how one can apply various forms of dialogue level knowledge to reduce the complexity of a speech recognition task. Our experiments demonstrated the effectiveness of the added constraints on the recognition accuracy of the speech system. We have also demonstrated that specific predictions can fail and the system will recover gracefully using our mechanism for gradually relaxing constraints.

For this domain, we hand-coded all the goal trees and grammars into the knowledge sources of the system. For larger domains and vocabularies it would be desirable to automate the process of deriving the goal trees and grammars during interactions with the initial users. There is much more work needed on automatic modeling of human problem solving processes based on empirical observation.

We do not claim that these exact results should be obtainable in any domain or any task. Rather it was our intent to demonstrate the usefulness of dialogue level knowledge for speech recognition. Future spoken language systems dealing with larger domains and very large vocabularies will be well advised to consider incorporating the kinds of mechanisms described in this article.

Acknowledgements. We are indebted to Raj Reddy, who chaperoned this research effort.

REFERENCES

1. Allen, J.F., and Perrault, C.R. Analyzing intention in utterances. *Art. Intel. 15*, 3 (1980), 143–178.
2. Bahl, L.R., Jelinek, F., and Mercer, R.L. A maximum likelihood approach to continuous speech recognition. *IEEE Trans. Patt. Anal. and Mach. Intell. 5*, 2 (1983), 179–190.
3. Barnett, J. A vocal data management system. *IEEE Trans. Audio and Electroacoustics AU-21*, 3 (June 1973), 185–186.
4. Biermann, A., Rodman R., Ballard, B., Betancourt, T., Bilbro, G., Deas, H., Fineman, L., Fink, P., Gilbert, K., Gregory, D., and Heidlage, F. Interactive natural language problem solving: A pragmatic approach. In *Proceedings of the Conference on Applied Natural Language Processing* (Santa Monica, Calif., Feb. 1–3, 1983), pp. 180–191.
5. Borghesi, L., and Favareto, C. Flexible parsing of discretely uttered sentences. *COLING-82*, Association for Computational Linguistics, (Prague, July, 1982), pp. 37–48.
6. Chapanis, A. Interactive human communication: Some lessons learned from laboratory experiments. In Shackel, B., Ed., *Man-Computer Interaction: Human Factors Aspects of Computers and People*, Sijthoff and Noordhoff, Rockville, Md., 1981, pp. 65–114.
7. Chin, D.N. *Intelligent Agents as a Basis for Natural Language Interfaces*. Ph.D. dissertation, Computer Science Division (EECS), University of California (Berkeley), 1988. Report No. UCB/CSD 88-396.
8. Cohen, P.R., and Perrault, C.R. Elements of a plan-based theory of speech acts. *Cog. Sci. 3* (1979), 177–212.
9. Ermen, L.D., and Lesser, V.R. The Hearsay-II speech understanding system: A tutorial. In W.A. Lea (Ed.) *Trends in Speech Recognition*. Prentice-Hall, Englewood Cliffs, N.J., 1980.
10. Fink, P.E., and Biermann, A.W. The correction of ill-formed input using history-based expectation with applications to speech understanding. *Comput. Ling. 12*, 1 (1986), 13–36.
11. Frederking, R.E. *Natural Language Dialogue in an Integrated Computational Model*. Ph.D. dissertation, Department of Computer Science, Carnegie-Mellon University, Pittsburgh, PA, 1986. Tech Rep. CMU-CS-86-178.
12. Gatward, R.A., Johnson, S.R., and Conolly, J.H. A natural language processing system based on functional grammar. Speech Input/Output; Techniques and Applications, Institute for Electrical Engineers, 1986, pp. 125–128.
13. Grosz, B.J. The representation and use of focus in dialogue understanding. SRI Stanford Research Institute, Stanford, CA, 1977.
14. Hauptmann, A.G., Young, S.R., and Ward, W.H. Using dialog-level knowledge sources to improve speech recognition. In *Proceedings of AAAI-88, The 7th National Conference on Artificial Intelligence*, American Association for Artificial Intelligence, 1988, pp. 729–733. Saint Paul, MN.
15. Hauptmann, A.G., and Rudnicky, A.I. Talking to computers: An empirical investigation. *International J. Man-Machine Studies* (*in press*) (1988).
16. Hayes, P.J., Hauptmann, A.G., Carbonell, J.G., and Tomita, M. Parsing spoken language; A semantic caseframe approach. In *Proceedings of COLING-86*, Association for Computational Linguistics, Bonn, Germany, August, 1986.
17. Kimball, O., Price, P., Roucos, S., Schwartz, R., Kubala, F., Chow, Y.-L., Haas, A., Krasner, M. and Makhoul, J. Recognition performance and grammatical constraints. In *Proceedings of the DARPA Speech Recognition Workshop*, Science Applications International Corporation Report Number SAIC-86/1546, 1986, pp. 53–59.
18. Lea, W.A. (Ed.). *Trends in Speech Recognition*. Prentice-Hall, Englewood Cliffs, N.J., 1980.
19. Lee, K-F. *Large-Vocabulary Speaker-Independent Continuous Speech Recognition: The Sphinx System*. Ph.D. dissertation, Department of Computer Science, Carnegie-Mellon University, Pittsburgh, PA, 1988. Tech Rep. CMU-CS-88-148.
20. Levinson, S.E., and Rabiner, L.R. A task-oriented conversational mode speech understanding system. *Bibliotheca Phonetica 12* (1985), 149–196.
21. Levinson, S.E., and Shipley, K.L. A conversational-mode airline information and reservation system using speech input and output. *The Bell Systems Technical Journal 59* (1980), 119–137.
22. Litman, D.J., and Allen, J.F. A plan recognition model for subdialogues in conversation. *Cog. Sci. 11*, 2 (1987), 163–200.
23. Lowerre, B. and Reddy, R. The Hearsay Speech Understanding System. In *Trends in Speech Recognition*, W.A. Lea (Ed.). Prentice-Hall, Englewood Cliffs, N.J., 1980.
24. Newell, A. and Simon, H.A. *Human Problem Solving*. Prentice-Hall, Englewood Cliffs, N.J., 1972.
25. Reddy, R., and Newell, A. Knowledge and its representation in a speech understanding system. In *Knowledge and Cognition*, Gregg L.W., Ed. L. Erlbaum Associates, Potomac, Md., 1974, pp. 256–282.
26. Sacerdoti, E.D. Planning in a hierarchy of abstraction spaces. *Artif. Intell. 5*, 2 (1974), 115–135.
27. Sidner, C.L. Focusing for interpretation of pronouns. *Amer. J. Comput. Ling. 7*, 4 (Oct.–Dec. 1981), 217–231.
28. Stern, R.M., Ward, W.H., Hauptmann, A.G., and Leon, J. Sentence parsing with weak grammatical constraints. ICASSP-87, 1987, pp. 380–383.
29. Tomabechi, H., and Tomita, M. The integration of unification-based syntax/semantics and memory-based pragmatics for real-time understanding of noisy continuous speech input. In *Proceedings of AAAI-88, The 7th National Conference on Artificial Intelligence*, American Association for Artificial Intelligence, 1988, pp. 724–728. Saint Paul, MN.
30. Walker, D.E. SRI research on speech recognition. In W.A. Lea (Ed.) *Trends in Speech Recognition*. Prentice-Hall, Englewood Cliffs, N.J., 1980.
31. Ward, W.H., Hauptmann, A.G., Stern, R.M., and Chanak, T. Parsing spoken phrases despite missing words. ICASSP-88, 1988.
32. Wilensky, R. *Understanding goal-based stories*. Ph.D. dissertation, Yale University, Sept. 1978.
33. Wilensky, R., *Planning and Understanding*. Addison Wesley, Reading, Mass., 1983.
34. Winograd, T. *Language as a Cognitive Process, Volume I: Syntax*. Addison Wesley, Reading, Mass., 1982.
35. Wolf, J.J. and Woods, W.A. The HW1H Speech Understanding Systems. In W.A. Lea (Ed.) *Trends in Speech Recognition*. Prentice-Hall, Englewood Cliffs, N.J., 1980.
36. Woods, W.A., Bates, M., Brown, G., Bruce, B., Cook, C., Klovstad, J., Makhoul, J., Nash-Webber, B., Schwartz, R., Wolf, J., and Zue, V. Speech understanding systems—Final technical report. Tech. Rep. 3438, Bolt, Beranek, and Newman, Inc., Cambridge, Mass., 1976.
37. Young, S.R., Hauptmann, A.G., and Ward, W.H. An integrated speech and natural language dialog system: Using dialog knowledge in speech recognition. Department of Computer Science, CMU-CS-88-128, Carnegie-Mellon University, April, 1988.
38. Young, S.R., and Ward, W.H. Towards habitable systems: Use of world knowledge to dynamically constrain speech recognition. *2d Symposium on Advanced Man-Machine Interfaces through Spoken Language*, Hawaii. Nov., 1988. (submitted).

ABOUT THE AUTHORS:

SHERYL R. YOUNG is a research faculty member of the Computer Science Department at Carnegie Mellon University. She has a B.A. in math and psychology from the University of Michigan and a Ph.D. in cognitive science/psychology from the University of Colorado.

ALEXANDER G. HAUPTMANN is working toward a Ph.D. in computer science at CMU. He has a B.A. and M.A. in psychology from Johns Hopkins University and a Diploma (M.A.) in computer science from the Technische Universitaet Berlin in West Germany.

WAYNE H. WARD is a research associate in the CMU Computer Science Department. He has a B.A. in mathematical science from Rice University and a Ph.D. in psychology from the University of Colorado. Authors' present address: Young, Hauptmann and Ward, Computer Science Department, Carnegie Mellon University, Pittsburgh, PA 15213.

EDWARD T. SMITH is president of Greenfield Educational Software, 1014 Flemington St., Pittsburgh, PA 15217. His research interests include small educational simulations for grade and high school students.

PHILIP WERNER is a software developer for MAD Intelligent Systems in Cambridge, Massachusetts. He has an M.Sc. in cognitive science from the University of Edinburgh and held a research assistantship while attending CMU as a graduate student.

Chapter 9

Systems

Introduction

This chapter focuses on several seminal speech-recognition systems. These systems have made strong impacts on the field for various reasons, such as high accuracy, real-time performance, or understanding capability. We hope the presentation of a variety of systems demonstrates the progress in speech recognition, and provides an overview of the state of the art.

An early attempt to build continuous speech recognizers was initiated by the Defense Advanced Research Projects Agency (ARPA, now DARPA) in 1971. An ambitious goal of continuous-speech recognition with a 1000-word vocabulary and an artificially constrained grammar was set. A number of institutions undertook this project. Klatt's paper, *Review of the ARPA Speech Understanding Project* gives a good summary of these efforts. The most notable of these efforts are Carnegie Mellon's HEARSAY system (Paper 5.4), HARPY system (Paper 9.2), and BBN's HWIM system (Paper 8.4). These three systems had vastly different motivations and approaches. HEARSAY was based on the blackboard architecture, which permitted complex interaction among all the knowledge sources that contribute to the recognition of a sentence. HARPY was a pragmatic system that combined features of the HEARSAY and DRAGON systems into a highly optimized and compiled network for efficient and accurate recognition. Finally, the HWIM system relied on more sophisticated parametric analysis, segmentation, phonological rules, and lexical access. Of the three systems, HARPY was the only one that exceeded the ambitious DARPA goals. However, it did so by using a highly constrained grammar and an efficient search strategy. Klatt's paper also reviews the other systems and projects under the ARPA project. Although the ARPA Speech Understanding project was terminated in 1976, it provided many key concepts that have reshaped the field and enhanced our understanding.

The second paper in this chapter, *The Harpy Speech Understanding System* by Lowerre and Reddy, provides a more detailed treatment of the most successful system in the ARPA Speech Understanding project. The HARPY System combined important concepts from DRAGON (integrated network) and HEARSAY (segmented input, juncture rules). It also used a new search strategy, called beam search, to probe the finite-state network of possible sentences. HARPY demonstrated that efficiently compiled high-level constraints can yield high accuracy, in spite of simplistic acoustic modeling. This does not imply that simplistic models are superior, but that higher-level constraints are powerful and can compensate for inadequte acoustic modeling.

Jelinek's paper, *The Development of an Experimental Discrete Dictation Recognizer*, describes perhaps the longest ongoing research system. The IBM speech group began to work on large vocabulary continuous speech recognition in 1972. As mentioned in Chapter 6, IBM was the pioneer of the hidden Markov model (HMM). Using HMMs, they demonstrated performances substantially better than HARPY [Bahl 83] on constrained, speaker-dependent, continuous tasks. Around 1980, the IBM group began to concentrate on the problem of "natural language dictation," which led to the 5000-word system described in this paper.

This system is based on hidden Markov models and trigram language models (see Paper 8.1). This system had a word error rate of 2% on recorded, read speech. More detailed treatments of this system can be found in [Bahl 88a], which describes the acoustic models used, and in [Bahl 88b], which describes the fast match used to prune candidates. After 1985, IBM has extended this system to 20,000-word isolated-word dictation (TANGORA) [Averbuch 87], as well as a 5,000-word continuous-speech recognizer [Bahl 89]. Each of these IBM systems has been ambitious undertaking that has advanced the state of the art.

The next two papers are representative of the systems that evolved from the more recent DARPA continuous speech recognition project. Unlike the first ARPA project, there were many more contractors, most of whom demonstrated systems by 1988. The first paper, by Chow, et al. describes the first high-performance DARPA system, BBN's BYBLOS. BYBLOS pioneered the concept of context-dependent phonetic HMMs (see Paper 6.7), and produced highly accurate speaker-dependent continuous-speech recognition from a 1000-word task. Unlike HARPY's task, however, this "resource management" task [Price 88] has a much more difficult grammar, with a 13-fold increase in perplexity (or geometric average of word branches in the grammar; see Chapter 8). Another system, Carnegie Mellon's SPHINX, used multiple codebooks, generalized triphones, and function-word HMMs to yield high accuracy for *speaker-independent* recognition of the same task. In addition to BYBLOS and SPHINX, many other successful systems were developed under the DARPA project, including Lincoln Laboratories [Paul 89], SRI [Bernstein 89], and MIT [Zue 90].

Motivated by a considerably larger character set, Japanese laboratories have contributed significantly to speech recognition for many years. Several Japanese papers from NTT, NEC, and ATR have appeared in the previous chapters. A large-scale system developed at ATR Interpreting Telephony Research Laboratories is described in *ATR HMM-LR Continuous Speech Recognition System* by Hanazawa, et al. This system used predictive LR parsing to drive an HMM-based phonetic verifier. The HMM technology uses multiple codebooks and duration control. The system has been successfully applied to continuous phrase recognition in both speaker dependent and adaptive modes.

The final paper is *A Word Hypothesizer for a Large Vocabulary Continuous Speech Understanding System* by Fissore, et al. It describes a modular system that first uses a fast algorithm to produce a tree of possible acoustic matches. Then, only words that form paths in the tree are verified to produce a word lattice, which is parsed by the syntax/semantic module. The system was successfully applied to a 1000-word continuous-speech-recognition task. This approach differs from conventional integrated approaches used by the systems above. Although more modular, it also faces problems associated with bottom-up approaches, namely it is difficult for a higher level to recover from errors made at the lower level, and that it is difficult for lower levels to apply higher-level constraints. With the formation of the Common Market, a new scientific inititative called Esprit was organized in Europe, whose efforts include European collaborative projects in the field of speech recognition. The final paper is one of its major results.

References

[Averbuch 87] Averbuch, et al. Experiments with the TANGORA 20,000 Word Speech Recognizer. In *IEEE International Conference on Acoustics, Speech, and Signal Processing.* April, 1987.

[Bahl 83] Bahl, L. R., Jelinek, F., Mercer, R. A Maximum Likelihood Approach to Continuous Speech Recognition. *IEEE Transactions on Pattern Analysis and Machine Intelligence* PAMI-5(2):179-190, March, 1983.

[Bahl 88a] Bahl. L.R., Brown, P.F., De Souza, P.V., Mercer, R.L. Acoustic Markov Models Used in the TANGORA Speech Recognition System. In *IEEE International Conference on Acoustics, Speech, and Signal Processing.* April, 1988.

[Bahl 88b] Bahl, L.R., Brown, P.F., De Souza, P.V., Mercer, R.L. Obtaining Candidate Words by Polling in a Large Vocabulary Speech Recognition System. In *IEEE International Conference on Acoustics, Speech, and Signal Processing.* April, 1988.

[Bahl 89] Bahl, L.R., et al. Large Vocabulary Natural Language Continuous Speech Recognition. In *IEEE International Conference on Acoustics, Speech, and Signal Processing.* May, 1989.

[Bernstein 89] Bernstein, J., Cohen, M., Murveit, H., Weintraub, M. Linguistic Constraints in Hidden Markov Model Based Speech Recognition. In *IEEE International Conference on Acoustics, Speech, and Signal Processing.* May, 1989.

[Paul 89] Paul, D.B. The Lincoln Robust Continuous Speech Recognizer. In *IEEE International Conference on Acoustics, Speech, and Signal Processing,* pages 449–452. May, 1989.

[Price 88] Price, P.J., Fisher, W., Bernstein, J., Pallett, D. A Database for Continuous Speech Recognition in a 1000-Word Domain. In *IEEE International Conference on Acoustics, Speech, and Signal Processing.* April, 1988.

[Zue 90] Zue, V., Glass, M., Phillips, M., Seneff, S. The Summit Speech Recognition System: Phonological Modelling and Lexical Access. In *IEEE International Conference on Acoustics, Speech, and Signal Processing.* April, 1990.

Review of the ARPA Speech Understanding Project

Dennis H. Klatt

Massachusetts Institute of Technology, Cambridge, Massachusetts 02139

(Received 10 May 1977; revised 1 September 1977)

In September of 1976, four speech understanding systems were demonstrated, signifying the end of a five-year program of research and development sponsored by the Advanced Research Projects Agency (ARPA). The best performance was displayed by the Harpy system developed at Carnegie-Mellon University. Harpy satisfied a set of design goals that were specified at the beginning of the program, including the goal of understanding over 90% of a set of naturally spoken sentences composed from a 1000-word lexicon. After defining the nature of the speech understanding problem, the four systems are described and critically evaluated. Based on this review, a structure for a next-generation speech understanding system is proposed and parts of it are considered as a possible model of the early stages of speech perception. The perceptual model addresses the issue of lexical access and includes a decoding network composed of expected spectral sequences for all word strings of English.

PACS numbers: 43.10.Ln, 43.70.Sc, 43.70.Dn

INTRODUCTION

In November of 1971, the Information Processing Technology Office of the Advanced Research Projects Agency of the Department of Defense (ARPA) initiated a five-year research and development program with the objective of obtaining a breakthrough in speech understanding capability that could then be used toward the development of practical man—machine communication systems (Newell *et al.*, 1973). The specific goals set forth by an ARPA study group[1] are outlined in Table I. The objectives were to develop several speech understanding systems that accept continuous speech from many cooperative speakers of a General American dialect. Recordings were to be made in a quiet room using a good-quality microphone. Slight tuning of the system would be allowed to handle new speakers, but the users could be required to make only natural adaptations to the system. The language definition should include a slightly selected vocabulary of at least 1000 words and an artificial syntax appropriate to the limited task situation (e.g., a data management task). Less than 10% semantic error would be tolerated and the system would have to run in a few times real time using the next generation of computers [(i.e., machines capable of executing 100 million machine instructions per second (MIPS)]. These goals were to be achieved by November 1976.

Significantly (and deliberately) absent from the specifications were requirements that the demonstration tasks be relevant to real-world problems, that the languages be habitable, and that the systems be cost effective. These omissions helped to get the project focused on scientific and computational issues, but they have resulted in questions concerning the work remaining to develop future practical systems.

The study group emphasized the concept of speech understanding as opposed to speech recognition. They believed that the hope for the program lay in analyzing speech within the context of specific tasks that employed strong grammatical constraints, as well as strong semantic and dialogue constraints, so that many sources of knowledge could be brought to bear to attain successful understanding of what was said or intended by the speaker. Accuracy was to be measured by the correctness of the response and not by whether all of the words were correctly recognized.

There were two possible ways to meet the ARPA goals: (1) simplify the general speech recognition problem by finding ways to apply syntactic and semantic constraints and (2) improve upon previous speech recognition capabilities. As noted above, the steering committee emphasized the first alternative and recommended that funding be given to research groups that were composed mainly of computer scientists, not speech scientists. It turned out that the various research groups tried different combinations of the two strategies, but the only clearly successful speech understanding system, Harpy, relied heavily on the first technique. In fact, if the ARPA project were to be judged on its contributions to speech recognition and the speech sciences, rather than judging it against its stated goals, a more negative appraisal might have to be given.

The second column of Table I characterizes the performance of the Harpy speech understanding system, which was developed at Carnegie—Mellon University (Lowerre, 1976; Reddy *et al.*, 1977). Harpy essentially meets or exceeds each of the specifications. Given this set of criteria, Harpy performed the best of all the systems that were demonstrated at the end of the project.

A general overview of what has been accomplished during the past five years has been published by the

TABLE I. The ARPA five-year goals are compared with the performance of Harpy.

GOAL (Nov., 1971)	Harpy (Nov., 1976)
ACCEPT CONNECTED SPEECH	YES
FROM MANY	5 (3 MALE, 2 FEMALE)
COOPERATIVE SPEAKERS	YES
IN A QUIET ROOM	COMPUTER TERMINAL ROOM
USING A GOOD MICROPHONE	CLOSE-TALKING MICROPHONE
WITH SLIGHT TUNING/SPEAKER	20 TRAINING SENTENCES/TALKER
ACCEPTING 1000 WORDS	1011
USING AN ARTIFICIAL SYNTAX	AVG. BRANCHING FACTOR = 33
IN A CONSTRAINING TASK	DOCUMENT RETRIEVAL
YIELDING < 10% SEMANTIC ERROR	5%
IN A FEW TIMES REAL TIME	80 TIMES REAL TIME
ON A 100 MIPS MACHINE	ON A .4 MIPS PDP-KA10
	USING 256K OF 36-BIT WORDS AND
	COSTING $5 PER SENTENCE PROCESSED

ARPA steering committee (Medress *et al.*, 1977). The primary concern of this review is to compare and evaluate the structures and components of four speech understanding systems that were developed.[2] Only brief mention will be made of other activities that were carried out in support of the system development efforts. The remainder of the paper is divided into an initial section that sets forth the scientific problems to be solved, a section describing the four speech understanding systems, and a section concerned with an overall scientific evaluation of the program, a proposal for a second-generation speech understanding system, and a discussion of the implications of this research for models of the speech perception process.

The ARPA project, while large in funding terms, is only one of many past and present efforts to recognize spoken utterances. The reader is referred to other sources for a more complete picture. For example, there are reviews such as have been published by Lindgren (1965), Pierce (1969), Fant (1970), Hyde (1972), Wolf (1976), and especially Reddy (1976); conference proceedings such as have been edited by Erman (1974), Reddy (1975), Fant (1975), Teacher (1976), and Silverman (1977); and descriptions of other recent speech understanding systems such as have been published by Bahl *et al.* (1976), Jelenek (1976), De Mori *et al.* (1975), Sakai and Nakagawa (1975), Haton and Pierrel (1976), and Medress *et al.* (1977).

I. THE PROBLEM

At the beginning of the ARPA project, isolated word recognition by pattern matching techniques was enjoying some initial success. However, it was realized that many words appearing in sentence contexts varied dramatically in acoustic characteristics depending on the surrounding phonetic environment and depending on certain phonological processes of English (Stevens and Klatt, 1973; Oshika *et al.*, 1975), so a simple-minded pattern-matching word identification strategy could not be applied to the sentence understanding problem. Therefore it seemed necessary to follow a more traditional approach, the first step of which was to process the acoustic input to recover a phonetic transcription of what had been said. A phonetic transcription is a discrete representation of articulatory activity in terms of a sequence of configurational goals or states called phonetic segments.

The second step in the hypothetical understanding strategy would be to take the (probably errorful) phonetic transcription of an unknown utterance and try to find candidate words and word sequences that might be present. Consider the phonetic transcription:

[d ɪ ǰ ə h ɪ ɾ ɪ t ə t a m] (1)

No word boundaries are indicated in (1) because acoustic cues to word boundary locations are rarely present. The lexical search problem [to find the sequence of words corresponding to (1)] is extremely difficult because of the combinatorics of possible word boundary locations, because the phonetic transcription may contain substitution errors, omissions, and extra segments, and because the talker uses a system of phonological rules to modify and simplify the pronunciation of individual words in some sentence environments. For example, the normal way to say "Did you" is [d ɪ ǰ ə], i.e., "Dija" but "you" is pronounced differently in "are you." The "t" in "hit" usually is realized as a very brief tongue flap [ɾ] in "hit it," but not in "hit some." The two adjacent "t"s of "it to" reduce to a single [t], resulting in (1) as the normal way to pronounce "Did you hit it to Tom?"

Each of the simplifications in (1) can be described by general phonological rules that presuppose an underlying basic representation for the word (called the phonemic representation). The phonemic string that would be stored in the lexicon for "you" might be /yu/. A phonological rule [d # y]→[ǰ] transforms the /y/ into [ǰ] if the previous word ends in a [d]. The application of inverse phonological rules for sentence decoding is complicated by the fact that there is no unique inverse rule in most cases. A [ǰ] that is observed could be the first or last sound of a word like "judge," or it could be the surface manifestation of /d/—/y/ in a word pair like "did you." Similarly an observed flap [ɾ] may indicate a word containing a /t/, a /d/, or possibly even an /n/. Almost any segment could be simultaneously the manifestation of the last phoneme of one word and the first phoneme of the next word.

All of these phonological phenomena result in lexical ambiguity so that even the best lexical hypothesis routines will propose many words that are not in the original sentence, simply due to fortuitous matches. The third step in the process would therefore be to use syntactic–semantic modules to weed out the false lexical hypotheses and put together a word string that represents what was spoken.

The block diagram shown in Fig. 1 summarizes what we have just said. Speech understanding systems may be thought to consist of two main components, a "bottom end" that converts acoustic data into lexical hypotheses and a "top end" that accepts lexical hypotheses and tries to find the most likely sentence that could have been spoken.

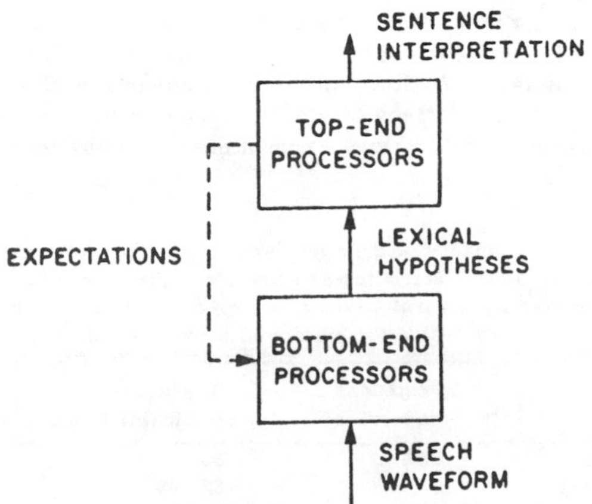

FIG. 1. Simplified overview of the speech understanding problem.

An important point to make concerning Fig. 1 is that the top end can provide the bottom end processor with constraints concerning what might be expected next. The relative success of the four speech understanding systems to be described is more highly correlated with the type of constraint provided by the top end than with any other variable. The most successful system, Harpy, exhaustively lists those and only those acoustic segment sequences that form acceptable input sentences, and the Harpy grammar severely constrains the acoustic alternatives much of the time. The advantage of applying strong constraints at the acoustic level is that one can avoid having to perform generalized phonetic recognition or generalized lexical hypothesization that would otherwise generate a large number of spurious hypotheses that have to be rejected later by the top end (a computationally costly and often difficult undertaking).

When the ARPA program began, it was believed that the scientific problems associated with top end design would be concerned with how to combine lexical hypotheses into larger and larger sentence fragments that are (1) syntactically acceptable, (2) semantically acceptable, (3) and plausible given what the user has said previously and some notion of what he/she wants to do. Syntactic analyzers used earlier in text processing applications would have to be modified to function in the face of errorful input, to consider and score multiple alternatives, and to include semantic knowledge before sufficient constraints could be applied effectively in the speech understanding context. The algorithms would have to be fast enough to permit evaluation of many word combinations and they would have to include sophisticated scoring algorithms to select among those alternatives that are grammatically acceptable. Progress in each of these areas is summarized in Sec. III.

The scientific problems associated with bottom end design when the ARPA program began included (1) selecting an acoustic representation, (2) improving segmentation and phonetic labeling strategies that had been developed previously, and (3) recognizing words that have undergone phonetic modifications at word boundaries and/or phonological recoding. Unanswered questions were: What kinds of improvements could be made to existing phonetic recognition strategies? How good does phonetic recognition have to be? Does one have to normalize for speaking rate? Can routines be made to work for any talker? How can one take advantage of prosodic cues (the pattern of voicing fundamental frequency, segmental durations, and intensity fluctuations),

TABLE II. Performance of the speech understanding systems as of November 1976. Statistics are based on more than 100 sentences spoken by several talkers, except for CMU Hearsay-II whose preliminary evaluation employed a smaller data set.

System	Sentences understood	Average branching factor
CMU Harpy	95%	33
CMU Hearsay-2	91, 74	33, 46
BBN Hwim	44	195
SDC	24	105

TABLE III. Task domains of the four systems and an example of an acceptable input sentence.

Group	Task	Sample sentence
SDC	FACTS ABOUT SHIPS	"How fast is the Theodore Roosevelt?"
BBN Hwim	TRAVEL BUDGET MANAGEMENT	"What is the plane fare to Ottawa?"
CMU Harpy	DOCUMENT RETRIEVAL	"How many articles on psychology are there?"
Hearsay-II	DOCUMENT RETRIEVAL	"How many articles on psychology are there?"

which indicate syllable stress and the syntactic structure of a spoken sentence? Progress in these areas and an interesting change in viewpoint are discussed in Sec. III.

The block diagram of Fig. 1 describes a *system*. Some issues of speech understanding system design are obscured if one simply discusses component performance requirements. The system design problems extant at the onset of the ARPA program included (1) how to coordinate the effort to bring up and debug effectively a very large system, (2) how to define communication links between system components, (3) how to schedule activity among components, and (4) how to combine conflicting scores from different knowledge sources.

II. THE SPEECH UNDERSTANDING SYSTEMS

The performance of the final four speech understanding systems, when processing sentences composed from a 1000 word lexicon, is summarized in Table II. Also presented is one measure of the constraint provided by the syntactic and semantic knowledge. The average branching factor is defined here to be the average number of words that would have to be considered at each point along the correct left-to-right path through the syntactic production rules during the processing of a typical utterance. Branching factor has been shown to be a better measure of task difficulty than vocabulary size *per se*, although other aspects of the grammar and inherent confusibility of lexical items contribute to task complexity. Some systems do not process an utterance in a strictly left-to-right manner, but the estimated branching factors are roughly comparable.

Taking account of the range of task difficulties implied in part by the different branching factors, it is unclear whether there are large differences in ability among the top three systems. However, only Carnegie–Mellon University (CMU) was able to meet the ARPA goals. In judging the performance figures given in Table II, it should also be noted that System Development Corporation (SDC) was handicapped by the loss of one of their computers, which prevented them from making use of components being developed jointly with Stanford Research Institute.

The tasks employed by the three system builders are summarized in Table III. Also included is an example of a sentence accepted by each grammar. Each task involves data management of one sort or another. While only questions are given as examples in Table III, each

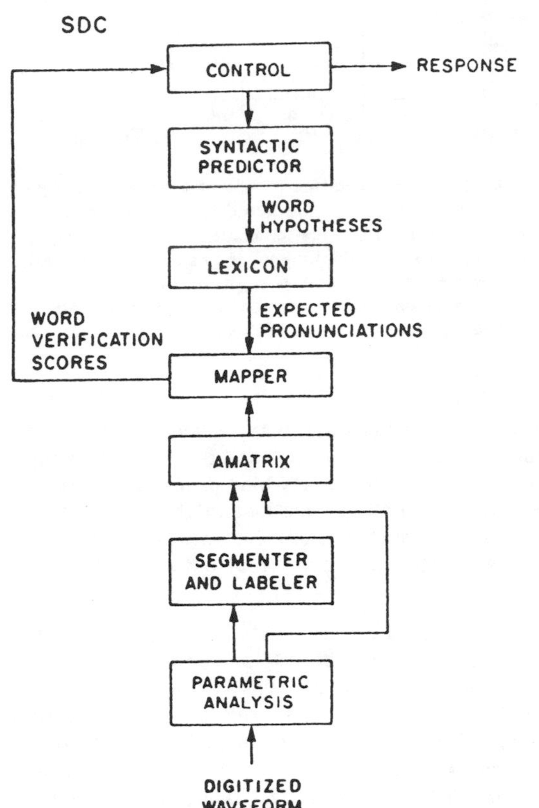

FIG. 2. Block diagram of the SDC system organization.

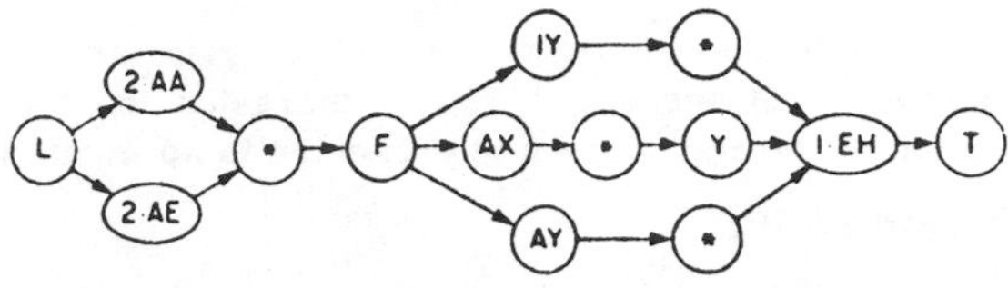

FIG. 3. Lexical representation in the SDC system for the word "Lafayette." Branches in the string indicate acceptable alternative pronunciations. The "•" is a syllable boundary symbol, and the "1" and "2" indicate relative lexical stress levels. Other phonemic symbols have the obvious interpretation. The advantages of a network representation for alternative phonetic pronunciations of words include compactness of form and efficiency of search compared with a simple list of alternatives.

of the systems was also capable of understanding commands and statements of various types.

A. Systems development corporation

The structure of the final SDC speech understanding system is shown in Fig. 2 (Ritea, 1975; Bernstein, 1976). Formant frequencies and other parameters are first extracted from the input waveform. A phonetic transcription is obtained, including several alternative labels for each phonetic segment, and all of this information is placed in a data array called the A-matrix for later examination by top-end routines.

The utterance is processed from left to right by first generating a list of all possible sentence-initial words. The control box then retrieves an abstract phonemic representation from the lexicon for each lexical hypothesis and computes expected phonetic variants, resulting in a phonetic graph representation such as is shown in Fig. 3. The phonetic graphs are sent, one at a time, to the mapper to see how good an acoustic match is obtained with the current position in the unknown utterance. The mapper is organized according to the syllable structure of a word and it examines the A-matrix in order to determine if the expected vowels and proper allophones of adjacent consonants are present. Since an exact match is unlikely, the mapper includes techniques for estimating the probability that the expected word is present given the phonetic and acoustic data. Performance of the mapper is indicated in Table IV.

On the basis of mapper scores, the control box decides which word or partial sentence hypothesis to pursue next, and generates a list of all words that can follow this sentence fragment. A similar "best-first" control strategy was used earlier in the Hearsay I speech understanding system (Reddy, Erman, and Neely, 1973)

TABLE IV. Performance statistics for three work verification components—the SDC mapper, the BBN verifier, and the CMU Hearsay-II verifier. The last row indicates that the SDC verifier is presented with lexical hypotheses from a syntactic module, whereas the BBN and CMU verifiers are preceded by lexical hypothesizers that screen out all but the best acoustic candidates.

	VERIFICATION DECISION					
	SDC		BBN		CMU	
LEXICAL PROPOSAL	ACCEPT	REJECT	ACCEPT	REJECT	ACCEPT	REJECT
CORRECT WORD	65	6	101	19	312	20
PERCENT	92%	8%	84%	16%	94%	6%
INCORRECT WORD	372	11,253	367	713	6462	6591
PERCENT	3%	97%	34%	66%	49%	51%
WORDS HYPOTH. CORRECT WORD	165		10		40	
ACOUST. SIMILARITY	RANDOM		BEST 5%		BEST 14%	

and in a system developed at Lincoln Laboratories (Klovstad and Mondshein, 1975). A more detailed description of the SDC system is presented in Appendix A.

Discussion of SDC

The mapper constitutes a verification strategy based on syllables, which is a theoretically attractive design for embedding context-dependent rules for expected manifestations of phonetic segments. The mapper is capable of rejecting a large fraction of the word hypotheses not in the sentence, but at a cost of rejecting about 10% of the words actually present. Fatal absolute rejections of correct words occurred either because the mapper lost track of which syllable was being processed or because a phonetic confusion occurred that had not been seen during a prior statistics-gathering run.

Unfortunately, the mapper performance is not good enough for a top-end system organization in which there is no mechanism for recovering from a single bad lexical matching score. It is unfortunate that SDC had so little time to design a more powerful top end after being prevented from using an SRI module, because a system can only perform as well as its weakest link.

The main criticism that can be made of the SDC effort is that their system failed its objectives in such a way that it is difficult to say what more restricted goals could be met by a modified system design. Is it simply a matter of shaking the bugs out of the system, or must one place further restrictions on the vocabulary and/or syntax? Or is it that the simple control strategy employed is essentially incapable of performing at an acceptable understanding rate in any moderate sized task because of the nature of speech and the inherent inaccuracies to be expected in any kind of mapper? Answers to these and other questions might have come from a year of system performance evaluation that was planned by the steering committee, but not funded by ARPA.

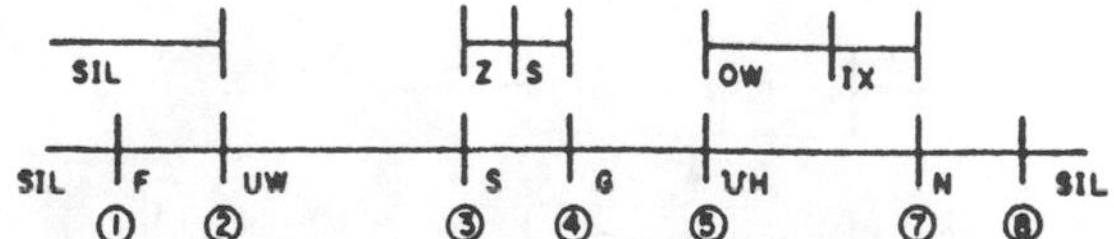

FIG. 5. A BBN segment lattice for the utterance "Who's going?" Alternative segmentations are displaced vertically, while each label represents the top choice among a set of 71 phonetic categories. Similarity scores are computed for all possible labels at each alternative segmentation point. For example, the segment starting at boundary (1) is labeled "F," but the correct phonetic segment "H" was the fourth best label choice.

An interesting aspect of the SDC system emerged in comparing its performance with an earlier version that did better on an easier task. The earlier system understood 65% of a set of test sentences formed from a 200-word lexicon and a more rigid syntax that was devoid of function words. Function words are usually acoustically reduced and difficult to identify. One might speculate that one reason for the poor performance of the more ambitious system was the dependence on function word recognition. Creation of a syntax that perhaps allowed some function words, but in no way depended on their identification to choose a path in the grammar, might be a better strategy for the realization of limited systems. (It is interesting to note that the Harpy grammar is essentially of this form.)

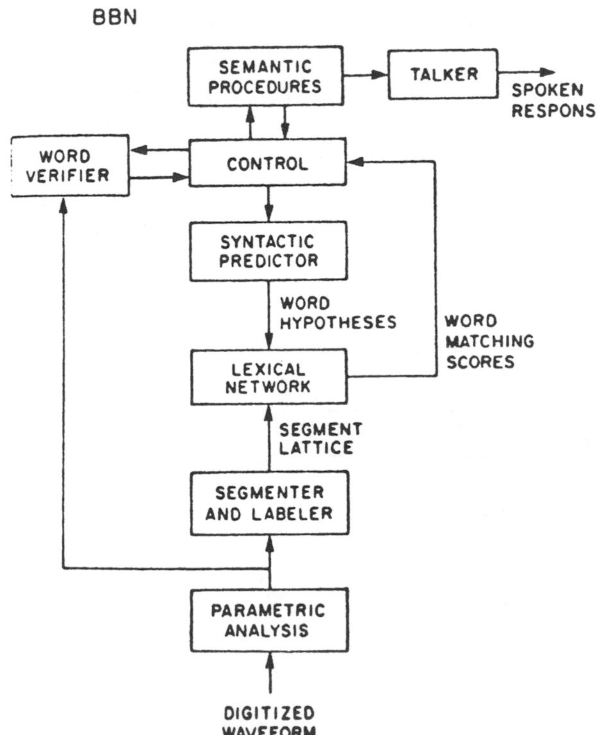

FIG. 4. Block diagram of the BBN Hwim system organization.

B. Bolt Beranek and Newman Inc. Hwim

The general organization of the BBN Hwim (Hear what I mean) system is shown in Fig. 4 (Woods *et al.*, 1976). As a first step in the processing of an unknown utterance, formant frequencies and other parameters are extracted from the digitized waveform. This information is used to derive a set of phonetic transcription alternatives that are arranged in a "segment lattice," as shown in Fig. 5. The advantage claimed for the lattice structure is that it can represent segmentation ambiguity in those cases where decisions are most difficult.

The identification process begins by searching through the segmental representation of the utterance for good matching words (anywhere in the utterance) that can be used as "seeds" for building up longer partial sentence hyptheses. The best-scoring initial word match is sent to a word verification component which returns to the parametric data to get a quasi-independent measure of the quality of the match. The method of verification is analysis by synthesis (Klatt, 1975).[3] The verification score is combined with the lexical matching score, and if the combined score is high, the word hypothesis is then sent to a syntactic predictor component which pro-

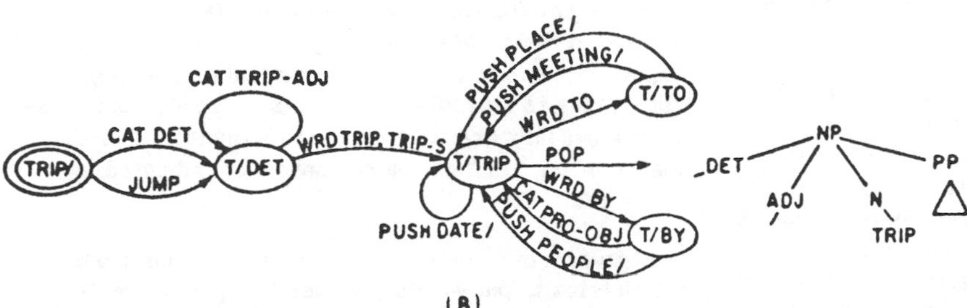

FIG. 6. A portion of the augmented transition network grammar. The network of part (a) defines acceptable noun phrases as consisting of the categories determiner, optional adjective string, noun, and optional prepositional phrases. A way to embed semantic constraints on the relations between words of an acceptable noun phrase is shown in part (b). Only one type of noun phrase concerning a trip is accepted by this fragment of the ATN grammar.

poses words that can appear to the left and to the right of the seed word, given the grammatical constraints. An augmented transition network grammar (Woods, 1970) is used to characterize syntactic and semantic constraints, in a manner that is illustrated in Fig. 6.

Matching scores are obtained for all of these word proposals, using a lexical decoding network (Klovstad, 1977). The lexical decoding network contains a representation of the expected phonetic realizations of each word in all possible phonetic contexts. To derive this network, a set of phonological rules (Woods and Zue, 1976) first transforms a phonemic lexicon into phonetic alternatives arranged in a tree structure, as shown in Fig. 7(a). Then a second set of word-boundary phonological rules attaches terminal nodes back to selected initial nodes of the tree, creating a network of permissible phonetic strings for all possible word sequences from the 1000-word lexicon. For example, the word "list" may be pronounced as [lis] in "list some" due to an optional word boundary phonological rule OPT {ST#S} → {S}, and this fact is captured in the network structure of Fig. 7(b). However, if "list" is to be recognized without the {t}, a word beginning with [s] must follow.

Each word receiving a good score from the lexical decoding network is combined with the seed word to produce a two-word hypothesis, a verification score is derived for the new two-word hypothesis and the hypothesis is then placed in an "event queue." The best scoring partial sentence hypothesis is always extended next. When a complete sentence is found, a deep structure representation of the word string can be sent to the semantic procedures component in order to compute an appropriate response. The response is spoken over a loudspeaker, using a speech synthesis by rule program. A more detailed description of the system is given in Appendix B.

Discussion of BBN

The BBN speech understanding system has a task domain with a more general syntax than the other systems, so it is difficult to judge how much better or worse the system design and individual components are. The same criticism applies to BBN that was leveled at SDC: The way in which the demonstration system failed to meet the ARPA goals makes it impossible to determine what more

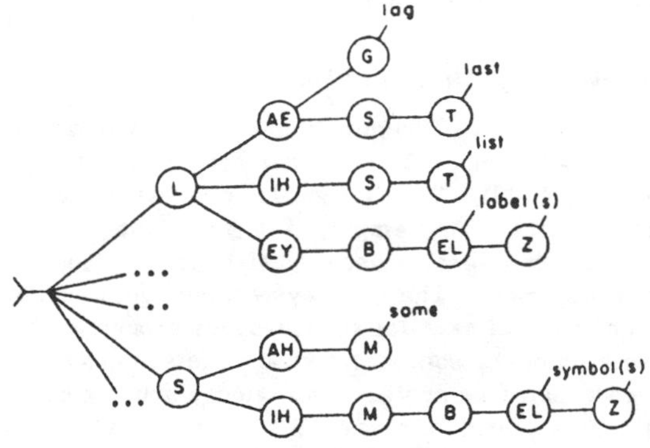

(B) FINAL DECODING NETWORK

FIG. 7. The partial lexical tree for the phonetic representation of several English words shown in part (a) is transformed into a lexical decoding network for the recognition of sequences of words by application of a set of word-boundary phonological rules (Klovstad, 1977).

limited task domain might have resulted in acceptable *performance*. It would be interesting to know, for *example*, how much of an improvement in certain critical components is needed to achieve acceptable performance, or how much improvement would be gained by restricting the language definition in various ways.

The most interesting ideas to come out of the BBN project were a lexical decoding network incorporating sophisticated phonological rules, the technique of representing segmentation ambiguity by a lattice of alternatives, and the concept of word verification at the parametric level. However the performance of these components individually and as a total system did not seem to live up to their theoretical potential. Because of the slowness of the system, there was apparently not enough effort devoted to debugging and optimizing individual components in a system context. Specific problems that were never resolved were (1) how to ensure that the segment lattice was in fact providing more information than a linear string of best guesses, (2) how to normalize for talker differences, (3) whether sufficient data were analyzed to rely on the probability estimates of various phonetic confusions, extra segments, and missing segments, and (4) whether the system would perform significantly better if it were fast enough to evaluate many more partial sentence fragments.

C. Carnegie-Mellon University Hearsay-II

The CMU Hearsay-II system organization is shown in Fig. 8 (Lesser *et al.*, 1975; Lesser and Erman, 1977; Reddy *et al.*, 1977). The recognition process is similar in some respects to that employed in BBN Hwim, although the block diagrams and organizational philosophies are disparate. The CMU system configuration consists of a set of parallel asynchronous processes that simulate each of the component knowledge sources of a speech understanding system. Knowledge sources communicate via a global "blackboard" data base. When activated by the appearance of certain types of new information on the blackboard, a knowledge source tries to extend the analysis.

The information on the blackboard is divided into several major categories: sequences of segment labels, syllables, lexical items proposed, accepted words, and partial phrase theories. A knowledge source accepts information at one level and attempts to provide new information at a higher level (bottom-up analysis) or lower level (top-down prediction and verification).

Initially, amplitude and zero-crossing parameters are used to divide an utterance into segments that are categorized by manner-of-articulation features (Goldberg and Reddy, 1976). Good performance is obtained by avoiding the more difficult place-of-articulation decisions in the preliminary analysis.

A word hypothesizer lists all words having a syllable structure compatible with the partial phonetic representation. For example, there might be ten lexical items that are consistent with a fricative–stop–vowel–stop pattern, three items consistent with a fricative–stop–vowel subpattern, and five more items consistent with a stop–vowel subpattern. The performance of the lexical hypothesizer is such that only 70 percent of the correct words are detected (Smith, 1976), but others are found by top-down prediction at a later stage.

A word verification component scores each lexical hypothesis by comparing an expected sequence of spectra with observed linear-prediction spectra. The lexicon used for verification is adapted from Harpy and thus is defined in terms of expected spectral patterns instead of expected phonetic patterns. Coarticulation across word boundaries is a problem using this approach, but some word-boundary acoustic rules are included. Performance of the verification component is indicated in Table IV.

High-scoring words activate a syntactic component which tries to put words together into partial sentence theories. Grammatically acceptable adjacent words are also predicted since the word hypothesizer is not expected to get all of the words of the sentence. The control strategy is similar to that used by BBN in that best-scoring words or sentence-fragment pieces are sought anywhere in the utterance and extended to the left and/or to the right. CMU obtained significantly better performance with an island-driven strategy than BBN, but it is argued below that the Harpy left-to-right control strategy has advantages over any middle-out strategy. Once a complete sentence has been found, a response could be computed by accessing a data base. A more detailed description of the system is presented in Appendix C.

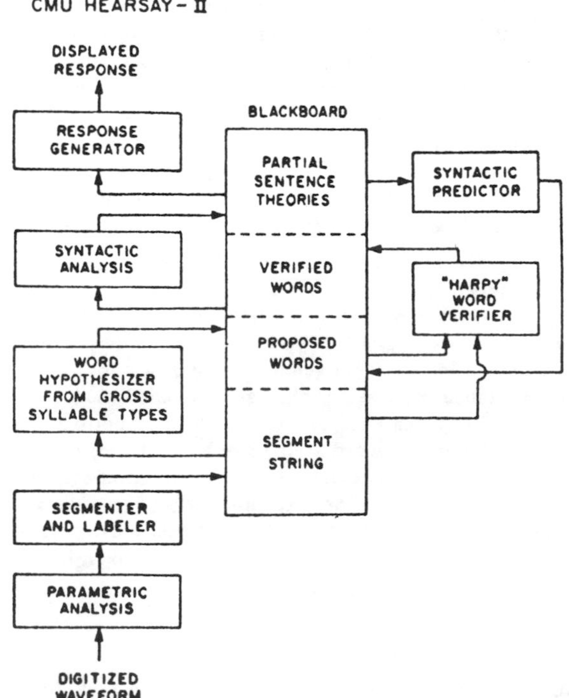

FIG. 8. A block diagram of the CMU Hearsay-II system organization.

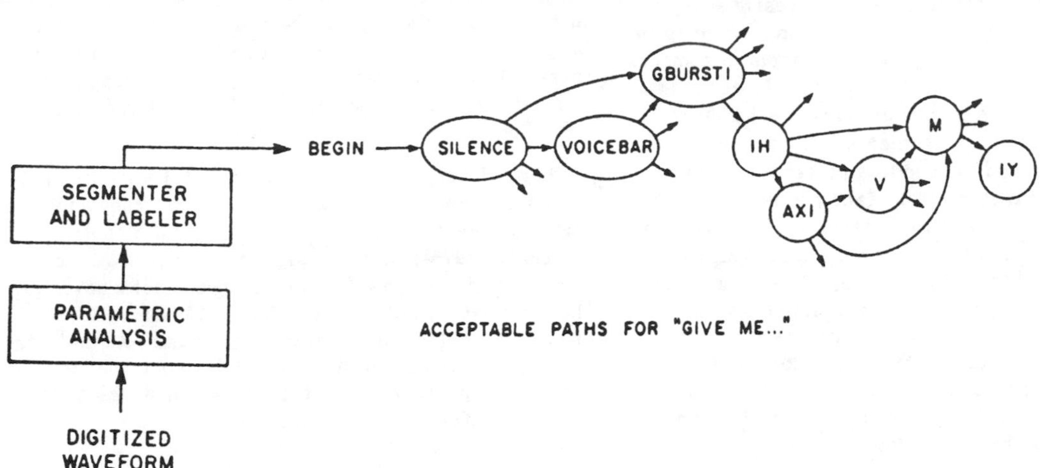

FIG. 9. A block diagram of the CMU Harpy system organization. Shown is a small (hypothetical) fragment of the Harpy state transition network, including paths accepted for sentences beginning with "Give me." Each node is named by the expected linear-prediction spectrum pattern. In general, many paths leave each node, corresponding to other possible sentence-initial words. A finite set of about 10**8 sentences (of length up to 8 words drawn from a 1011 word lexicon) can be recognized by the 15 000 state Harpy network.

Discussion of CMU Hearsay-II

Hearsay-II exhibited the best performance of the systems other than Harpy. Since it is not at all clear that Hearsay-II used components having better absolute performance, it is of interest to speculate on those aspects of the overall system design that account for its superior behavior. There are three essential reasons in my view: (1) as in the BBN system, absolute decisions (e.g., to reject a word hypothesis) were avoided by assigning graded scores so that component errors were not necessarily fatal, (2) computational efficiency issues were always of primary concern so that more alternatives could be considered, and (3) syntactic complexity (i.e., the average number of words to be considered to the right of any correct word) was directly controlled and reduced to a point where the system performance was acceptable. The use of strong syntactic and semantic constraints was encouraged by the ARPA goal structure, and should be utilized in future practical systems to improve performance.

D. Carnegie-Mellon University Harpy

The Harpy system, as implemented by Lowerre (1976), is shown in Fig. 9. The system includes a network of 15 000 states. Embedded in the state transition network are (1) all possible paths through the finite state grammar (i.e., a graph representation of all possible sentences), (2) alternate representations of all lexical items in terms of acoustic segments, and (3) a set of rules describing expected changes to acoustic segment sequences across word boundaries. The set of word-boundary rules, lexical representations, and grammar equations are automatically compiled into the efficient network representation shown in the figure.

The input utterance is divided into brief roughly stationary acoustic segments. Each segment is compared with 98 talker-specific linear-prediction spectral templates to obtain a set of 98 spectral distances, using the minimum residual error metric (Itakura, 1975). Template selection for a new talker is automatic, but requires that the user read about 20 selected sentences.

Each state in the network has an associated spectral template. The decoding strategy is to try to find the best scoring path through the state transition network by comparing the distance between the observed spectra and template sequences given in the network. Generally a state can accept a sequence of several sufficiently similar input segments, although some states are constrained so as to grab a specified minimum or maximum duration of the input.

Harpy is an extension of a Markov model of sentence decoding originally employed by Baker (1974) in a sentence recognition system called Dragon. In Dragon, a "breadth-first" dynamic programming strategy was used to find the optimal path through a network, but in the Harpy implementation a "beam-search" technique is used in which a restricted beam of near-miss alternatives around the best-scoring path are considered, thus reducing the search time significantly. Dragon also *used a priori* probabilities in choosing the most likely path through the network, while Harpy considers only spectral distance. A more detailed description of the CMU Harpy system is presented in Appendix D.

Discussion of CMU Harpy

Harpy and its predecessor Dragon represent a significant breakthrough in the application of simple structured models to speech recognition. It might seem to someone versed in the intricacies of phonology and the acoustic–phonetic characteristics of speech that a search of a graph of expected acoustic segments is a naive and foolish technique to use to decode a sentence. In fact such a graph and search strategy (and probably a number of other simple models) can be constructed and made to work very well indeed if the proper acoustic–phonetic details are embodied in the structure. The keys to success seem to me to be (1) the way that important structural aspects of language and speech can be folded into an initial network structure, (2) the possibility of optimizing of the network and the spectral templates using a very large body of training utterances, and (3) imposition of strong syntactic constraints.

Harpy is essentially a verification strategy. All alternative sentences are specified by the network, and the task is to verify which sequence of spectral states (path through the network) corresponds to the input sequence of spectra. It has been argued elsewhere (Klatt and Stevens, 1973) that verification of expected acoustic patterns for words is an easier task than phonetic analysis due to the inherent ambiguity of acoustic–phonetic decoding rules. To the extent that phonologists are better able to write generative than analytic rules to describe speech, the advantages of verification strategies will remain.

Due to syntactic constraints, the Harpy network is not particularly dense, so that minimal acoustic–phonetic distinctions are rarely required to distinguish between utterances. The present spectral sequence network may be capable of distinguishing minimal pairs of words quite well, but there is no direct evidence that it can, and some reason to doubt its detailed phonetic abilities given only 98 templates and limited word-boundary acoustic–phonetic rules. Even when syntactic constraints have been applied and the correct sentence has been identified, only 40% of the time does the top-scoring template match the expected template for each state in the best-scoring path through the network. If the templates were analogous to phonetic segments (which is roughly true for consonants in the current implementation, but not as true for vowels) this statistic would imply a less than 40% phonetic transcription performance in the absence of syntactic constraints, which is worse than in any of the other systems. However, there seems to me to be no fundamental limit to the ultimate transcription performance ability of Harpy-like networks if the lexical representations and word-boundary rules are sufficiently detailed.

The grammar on which Harpy and Hearsay-II were demonstrated was actually a member of a set of related grammars manifesting different branching factors and thus a range of task difficulties. One of the reasons for CMU's success was the ability to manipulate branching factor and observe changes to performance. This was a significant achievement given the ARPA objectives. Unfortunately, within the set of branching factors investigated, excellent performance was achieved only by using a rather low branching factor grammar, i.e., one that constrained acceptable sentences so that just two large syntactic classes were allowed: topics, and authors. Test sentences were always constrained so that at least one of these two classes appeared in each test sentence.

There clearly exist tasks for which a Harpy-like network would appear to be applicable [e.g., connected digit recognition or even perhaps air traffic control (Connolly, 1975)], but the languages for such applications will have to be fairly artificial and not a so-called "habitable subset of English" (Watt, 1968). Still the job of creating a Harpy system for a new task domain is not simple; it took careful analysis of 747 sentences to achieve the present level of Harpy performance on this particular 1000-word lexicon.

E. Other ARPA-funded speech understanding research

The ARPA project included a number of supporting efforts that were important to the task of creating the four large speech understanding systems just described. In this review, we have emphasized the systems, but a brief mention of the activities of the other contractors is provided in the paragraphs below.

1. Lincoln Laboratory

Researchers at MIT Lincoln Laboratory spent considerable effort on the development of phonetic recognition strategies (Weinstein *et al.*, 1975). Techniques included formant tracking and the use of formant transition information for stop place-of-articulation categorization. The performance and documentation of these strategies was probably the best of the initial system builders at the time when funds were re-allocated from five to the three research groups showing promise of putting together the best total systems. Lincoln staff also developed a lexical network representation (Klovstad and Mondshein, 1975) that later evolved into the BBN lexical decoding network.

2. Stanford Research Institute

When a planned joint SDC/SRI system development program was no longer possible, Stanford Research Institute staff were forced to carry out their development and testing of system components and strategies using a simple simulation of the behavior of a SDC mapper for word verification. Simulation proved to be a valuable technique for optimizing several system design choices concerning speed/accuracy tradeoffs, without the added run-time cost of using the actual mapper (Paxton, 1976; 1977). The results of the simulations were used, for example, to specify the performance required from the mapper for a given vocabulary size in order to obtain 90% sentence understanding, using a language definition that allows fairly general syntactic constructions, an independent semantic component, and capabilities for anaphoric references and ellipsis in processing sequential items in a dialogue (Walker, 1976).

3. Special contractors

As part of the overall research and development plan, funds were allocated to several research groups to provide support in the area of acoustic–phonetic analysis. The research contributions of the special smaller contractors[3] have not been discussed in this review. However, significant work was performed toward the development of phonological/phonetic rules for the description of spoken English sentences (Oshika *et al.*, 1975), prosodic decoding rules (Lea *et al.*, 1975), acoustic–phonetic recognition strategies (Mermelstein, 1975a; 1975b), and evaluation of the complexity of the grammars employed in the four systems (O'Malley, unpublished).

III. DISCUSSION AND CONCLUSIONS

Is there a need for speech understanding systems? Ochsman and Chapanis (1974) present evidence that man–man communication via speech is more natural and efficient than other modes of communication such as typing. This would presumably also be true of man–machine communication, especially for unskilled persons interacting with a system for either data input or information retrieval (Lea, 1968). It seems that the need for speech understanding systems is already present, and this need will grow as our dependence on computerized stores of information increases.

One answer to the demand for automated man–machine communication by voice might be a system that recognizes sentences formed by speaking a series of words separated by pauses (Herscher and Cox, 1976). It has been claimed that users can readily learn to insert short pauses between words, transforming the sentence recognition problem into an easier isolated word recognition problem. Coarticulation between words is minimized in this way and word identification by pattern matching is possible. Syntactic and semantic constraints can be applied to limit the set of acceptable words at each sentence location, and thus perform with a recognition rate significantly better than *P-to-the-N*th, where P is the probability of single word recognition, and N is the number of words in the pseudosentence.

Isolated word concatenation appears to have practical applications in many limited task domains (Martin, 1976). However, it is no more that a compromise solution to the attainment of fast natural communication with computers. The procedures have yet to be generalized to handle large vocabulary tasks, and it has not been shown that users are able to stay in the "pause-between-words" mode in a more complex task environment. There was and is a pressing practical need to study and develop procedures for simulating normal sentence understanding.

Given the demand for speech understanding by computers, was the ARPA project a good thing? The list of scientific achievements in the next section indicates that significant advances have been made in the speech understanding field. Yet if one spends three million dollars a year for five years and the best system turns out to be a one-man-year Ph.D. thesis, not all is well. The other projects sought to build more powerful general systems, but all failed to meet the ARPA goals.

It was potentially beneficial to shake-up the field with a large funding effort, and much good can still come from the ARPA project. On the other hand, it is disruptive to send funding oscillations through the basic research community and to subject science to fads and anti-fads. The danger now is that funds will be less available for the basic science that must be done in the speech analysis area before real further progress is made.

A. Scientific achievements of the ARPA program

The following paragraphs list a number of good ideas drawn from the four speech understanding systems and elsewhere.[4] In addition to identifying several scientific achievements of the ARPA program, this section is intended to summarize the state of the art and to suggest guidelines for the development of future speech understanding systems.

1. System organization

The structures of Harpy and Dragon represent a significant improvement in the realization of sentence verification procedures. System organization is immensely simplified by precompiling disparate knowledge into a uniform network representation at the spectrum level. A second new organizational concept comes from Hearsay-II and involves creation of a set of parallel asynchronous processes that communicate via a blackboard. As a conceptual model, the approach may be applicable in other problem solving domains.

2. Grammar design

The ability to manipulate grammatical complexity and observe changes to system performance as the task is simplified was an important factor in the success of CMU. The shift of attention from size of the lexicon to effective grammatical branching factor is an important advance in the quantification of task difficulty from the original ARPA goal of a 1000-word lexicon. It means that a difficult problem can be made easier by reducing the apparent size of the lexicon. What is needed now are techniques to reduce grammatical complexity while maintaining task objectives and retaining language habitability.

3. Control strategy

Control strategies that work from the middle out, starting with a good-matching content word utilize less syntactic constraint and have been found to cost a great deal more in complexity and computation time than strategies based on strict left-to-right processing through an utterance. If phonological rules handle function word variability well, then a strict left-to-right strategy with a breadth-of-search capability, as in Harpy, seems to be the best choice.

4. Semantics and context

Most semantic constraints employed by these systems are realized within the syntactic production rules. BBN Hwim contained a separate semantics module, but it was not used very much during sentence recognition. None of the four systems were able to use prior discourse information to reject a sentence such as "What is their registration fee?" because there was no assignable referent for "their." However, earlier, Hearsay-I (Reddy *et al.*, 1973) contained a chess-playing program that checked requested moves for plausibility.

5. Syntax

It is likely that almost any parser structure will do for simple speech understanding tasks in which all that is required is an enumeration of the possible lexical items following a given sentence fragment. In fact, the best solution for a finite grammar is very likely to precompile a list of the permissible word sequences into a network, as is done in Harpy.

The speech understanding project has benefitted from prior work on the automatic parsing (syntactic analysis) of written sentences. Powerful mechanisms such as an augmented transition network grammar and parser (Woods, 1970) have already been developed for processing word strings from left to right. While many grammar formulations could be considered, the augmented transition network grammar has the advantages of permitting semantic constraints to be written into the grammar and allowing many alternative parses to be computed efficiently in parallel (Woods, 1970). The grammar also includes simple methods of searching most-likely structures first and can produce structural representations that are ideal input for semantic processing routines involved in response generation.

6. Word identification/verification

Each word or morpheme of the lexicon has been specified at a fairly abstract phonemic level in several of the systems. This makes lexical development and augmentation much easier than if all possible detailed phonetic or acoustic forms must be listed. Phonological rules that operate within words and/or across word boundaries are used to expand the lexicon into multiple representations. Phonology seems to have come of age over the past few years in that formal rules of considerable predictive power have been developed. As a starting point the morphological expansions and phonological rules of Zue (Woods *et al.*, 1976, Vol. 3, pp. 57–72) might be used. Additional more general rules are to be found in the work of Cohen and Mercer (1975) and Oshika *et al.* (1975).

The potential role of the syllable in lexical verification was elaborated by SDC, who suggested that allophonic variations can be predicted in a relatively straightforward way if one begins verification at a syllable peak and then looks for acoustic evidence of adjacent consonants that are expected. The advantages of the syllable as a recognition unit are less clear. It might be argued that the dyad (Peterson, Wang, and Sivertsen, 1958), an interval from the middle of one phonetic segment to the middle of the next segment, is a unit having about the same theoretical advantages. There are far fewer dyad types than syllable types in English. Silverman and Dixon (1976) have employed the dyad as a recognition unit with good success for a single talker. The diad has been termed a "diphone" when used as a building block for speech synthesis (Dixon and Maxey, 1968).

Word identification in sentence contexts is possible only if the effects of phonetic/phonological recoding at word boundaries can be decoded. This requires that the phonological encoding rules be known, and that computational procedures be available for applying the inverse rules rapidly and selectively. To take the example of the rule [s t # s] → [s] as in "list some," it would be costly to test every [s] in an utterance for a possible underlying [s t # s], especially considering the number of word-boundary rules that would have to be treated in this way. The solution that comes from the BBN system is to incorporate word boundary phonology into the stored lexical representations by first constructing a lexical tree of expected phonetic sequences, and then transforming the tree into a phonetic-sequence network of the type shown in Fig. 7.

7. Acoustic-phonetic processing

An advance in the area of acoustic–phonetic processing has been the realization that *phonetic* segmentation and labeling is not necessary to word identification in connected speech. The Harpy philosophy of representing words by sequences of spectral templates in a network that takes into account word boundary phonology shows great promise.

The actual spectral representation (linear prediction spectral analysis) used in Harpy and the spectral distance measure (the minimum residual error) used are computationally very efficient, but probably not optimal and not related very closely to perceptual distance. For example, the metric does not incorporate overall spectral intensity and may therefore confuse a silence spectrum with some speech sound having a similar spectral shape. Also Harpy used only 98 templates to represent the entire inventory of spectral variations in speech. The excellent performance of Harpy may mean that the details of spectral representations and distance measures are not critical. On the other hand, perhaps even better performance in harder task domains is possible within the Harpy framework by using improved metrics.

Comparison of the general performance of the phonetic analysis components of the SDC, BBN, and CMU Hearsay-II systems in phonetic labeling with for example, Silverman and Dixon (1976), Weinstein *et al.*, 1975, and earlier work suggests that the contribution of the ARPA project to improved phonetic recognition strategies is not in proportion to the level of effort expended. Schwartz and Cook (1977) have recently attained 67%

correct phonetic transcription capabilities using 71 phonetic categories in a phonetic vocoder application, but their system is not well documented. There is a clear need for continued work in this area.

Shockey and Reddy (1975) discovered that linguists are actually not very consistent at phonetic transcription if the language is unfamiliar. From their data, they speculate that machines should not be expected to do better than 60%–70% correct phonetic transcription performance. We believe that their results may be a reasonable test of the current status of a universal phonetic theory, but they do not measure transcription abilities of listeners who are permitted to make use of the phonetic and phonological constraints of English. Recent experiments by Mark Liberman and Lloyd Nakatani (personal communication) suggest that listeners can transcribe English nonsense names embedded in sentences (and obeying the phonological constraints of English) with better than 90% phonemic accuracy. It is likely that machine performance must approach this figure before very powerful speech understanding systems are realized. Alternatively, perhaps the best bet is not to do phonetic labeling at all, as in Harpy.

Prosodic cues (fundamental frequency, segmental duration, and the intensity contour) suggest a stress pattern for the incoming syllable string, and thus could assist in lexical hypothesization. Prosodic cues also indicate clause boundaries, phrase boundaries, and, to a minor extent, word boundaries. While relatively little use was made of prosodic information in the four speech understanding systems, some ideas for prosodic analysis were proposed (Lea, Medress, and Skinner, 1975).

8. Use of statistics

Jelenek (1976) argues for the use of decision strategies that are based on the collection of an appropriate set of probabilities determined experimentally. Several of the speech understanding systems used estimates of the probability of a phonetic or lexical decision given the acoustic data in scoring the goodness of a theory, and each seems to have gotten into trouble by so doing. The problem is to analyze enough data to be sure of the probability of infrequent confusions. This is nearly impossible if one wants to take into consideration factors such as phonetic environment.

9. Acoustic analysis

It is now known that the important information-bearing elements of the speech code are contained in the magnitude spectrum of speech, i.e., in a sequence of well-chosen short-term spectra. Linear prediction spectra have proven to be a robust spectral representation having the additional advantages of being a pleasing visual idealization of speech, of having an existing simple metric for spectral comparisons, and of permitting the estimation of formant frequencies. On the other hand, it appears that filter banks designed carefully to take into account critical bands and other psychophysical constraints are equally useful as spectral representations (Klatt, 1976b).

10. Talker normalization

A surprisingly powerful method of talker normalization is incorporated in the Harpy system. About twenty known sentences are processed to derive talker-specific spectral templates automatically. These templates are capable of capturing a wide range of talker characteristics including important differences between men and women. Other talker differences such as differences in dialect are best overcome for the present by restricting system usage to talkers of a single fairly uniform dialect.

11. Response generation

The BBN Hwim system and CMU Hearsay-II included a data base and response generator (although these components were not usually connected during a recognition demonstration). In this sense, a distinction between speech understanding (is the response correct?) and speech recognition (are all of the words correct?) was realized. Cases where a correct response would be generated in spite of lexical identification errors were fairly frequent in Hearsay-II. To that extent, the systems described here represent the beginnings of true machine understanding of spoken language.

To generate a proper response, one must solve an information retrieval problem, choose an appropriate frame sentence for a response, and synthesize an audio output. Some progress in general solutions to these problems was achieved at BBN (Woods *et al.*, 1976; Klatt, 1976a).

12. Contributions to speech science

Many of the scientific achievements listed above impact on the speech sciences. One might have expected more in the way of detailed algorithms for the recognition of phonetic categories or descriptions of acoustic–phonetic details of sentences spoken by different talkers, but speech scientists should be made aware of advances such as the observations that (1) linear prediction spectra are a useful representation of speech for spectral analysis or formant frequency analysis (2) progress has been made in describing the steps involved in predicting the phonetic characteristics of words in sentences from a phonemic representation, (3) strategies exist for automatic phonetic transcription with performance of about 60%–70% correct, (4) talker normalization by acquisition of talker-specific spectral templates works surprisingly well, (5) lexical hypothesization need not include a step in which a phonetic transcription is derived, and (6) some of the computational structures suggested for a speech understanding system may in fact constitute a good model of sentence perception.

13. A proposed future system

A possible structure for a future speech understanding system that incorporates many of these ideas is shown in Fig. 10. An acoustic-segment lexical decoding network is generated off-line from a phonemically organized task-specific lexicon. A set of phonological rules, a diphone dictionary, and a set of word-boundary phono-

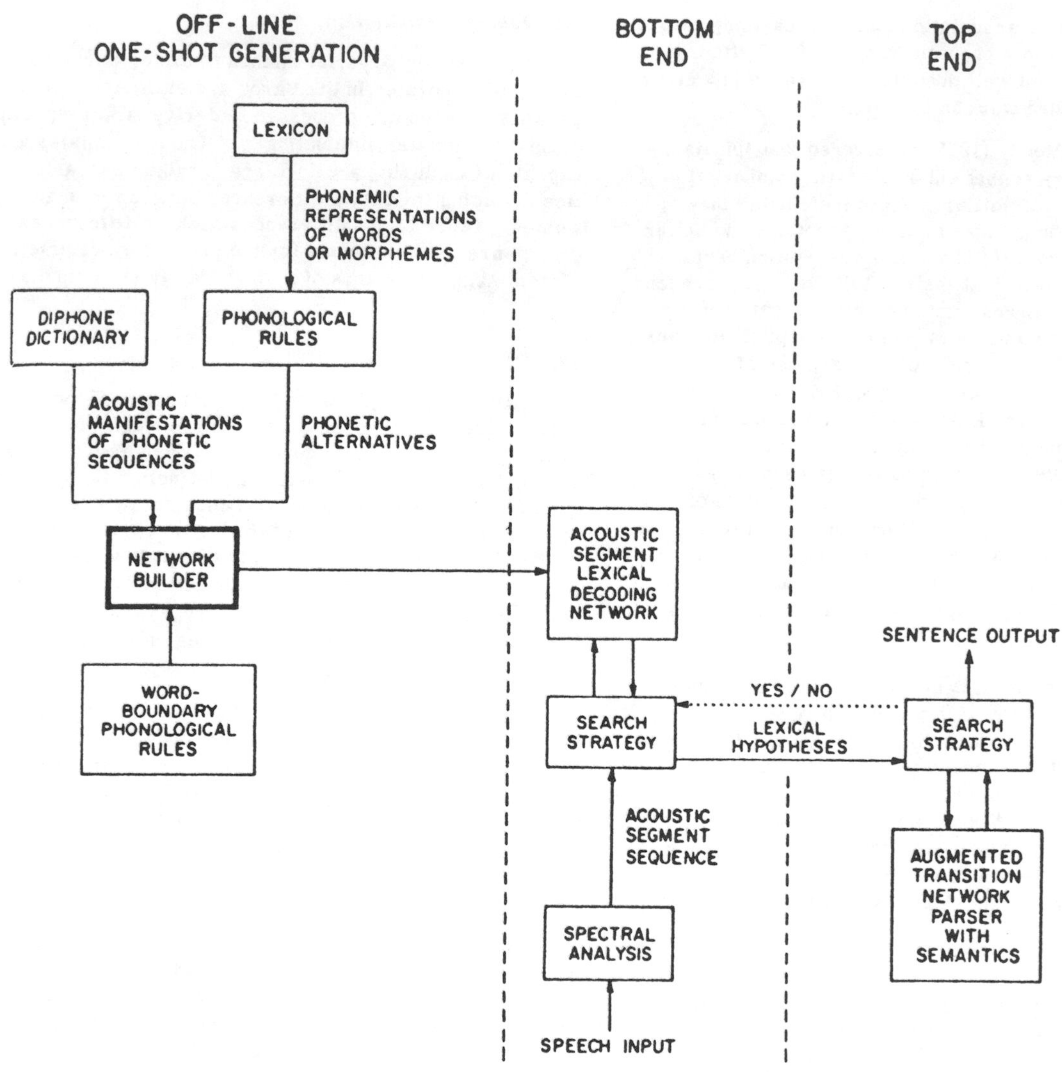

FIG. 10. **Proposed structure for a future speech understanding or sentence recognition system.**

logical rules convert the lexical representations into a network of expected acoustic segment sequences for all possible word sequences composed from the vocabulary. Each state of the network is represented by one of a moderate set of spectral templates.

A spectral template is envisioned to be something like a short-time spectrum, but the representation is refined to take into account critical bands, masking, loudness, and other limitations imposed by the peripheral auditory system. The comparison of spectral templates with input spectra is assumed to include sophisticated calculations depending on the types of spectra being compared. The decoding network includes a specification of duration limits for each template and an ability to normalize these durational constraints on the basis of estimates of local speaking rate or stress.

The bottom end is patterned after that of Harpy[1]. An input sequence of acoustic segments is processed from left to right, always seeking the best path through the lexical decoding network. The resulting partial string of words is sent to the top end to see if the sequence is permitted by the grammar or if the next-best path through the network should be pursued instead. The Harpy talker normalization procedure of adaptive acquisition of talker-specific templates is assumed, although more than 98 spectral templates will probably be required to achieve optimum phonetic and lexical discrimination. There is no phonetic or phonemic level of representation at any stage in the bottom end recognition process, although important use is made of these linguistic concepts during network generation.

The top end uses an augmented transition network parser to monitor the word sequence proposed by the bottom end and to terminate immediately ungrammatical hypotheses. The first acceptable sentence that spans the input is sent to a semantics/response generation module (not shown) or is simply typed out if the system is being run in sentence recognition mode.

The keys to success of this proposed approach are the selection of a good set of spectral templates, development of a diphone dictionary that captures the acoustic characteristics of English phone sequences, and a set of phonological rules that can generate all possible phonetic manifestations of word sequences. Stated in this way, the task ahead is still formidable, but it is an interesting and well-defined challenge. The missing pieces must come from speech science: the computer sciences have done the job of providing a structure in which to embed speech knowledge for recognition purposes.

B. Relations to psychological models of speech perception

Previous psychological models of phonetic analysis include the motor theory of speech perception (Liberman *et al.*, 1962; 1967), analysis by synthesis (Halle and Stevens, 1962; Stevens, 1972b), multistage feature-based models (Pisoni, 1977), and quantal invariance models (Stevens, 1972a; Cole and Scott, 1974). An alternative psychological model of early stages in the speech perception process might be based on the organization shown in Fig. 10. This model makes four novel claims which, in terms of speech perception, must be looked upon as conjectures:

Conjecture 1: lexical decoding is usually direct, with no analysis-by-synthesis or other mechanism for rich information feedback from higher linguistic levels.

Conjecture 2: generative rules are used to precompile acoustic–phonetic and phonological knowledge into an appropriate decoding structure because analytic rules are too ambiguous and thus computationally inefficient.

Conjecture 3: there is no use made of a phonetic level of representation during sentence processing.

Conjecture 4: syntactic analysis is direct, using a precompiled network to characterize permitted sentence structures rather than a set of generative rules and an analysis-by-synthesis strategy.

These are independent claims. It is possible that any or all of them are true. The first claim has some support in the recent experimental work of Garrett (1977). The second claim is a theoretical argument that would be invalidated if, e.g., processing time for "list some" were greater than for "list one" due to the extra processing required to overcome [t] deletion in the one case. The third claim is superficially contradicted by numerous experiments concerned with the properties of phonetic feature detectors (see Studdert-Kennedy, 1975, for a review). However, if one looks carefully at these experiments, one can argue that none of them have invalidated the kind of template theory that we have in mind because the concept of phonetic similarity, as measured by the number of phonetic features that are shared, can be replaced directly by a concept of spectral similarity. The fourth claim already has its proponents (Wanner and Maratsos, 1978).

Research is needed to (1) investigate how pieces of the model might evolve during language acquisition, (2) determine how prosodic analysis is performed in such a model, (3) see how unfamiliar words are added to the lexicon, (4) determine how noise-corrupted speech is processed, and (5) make predictions that would distinguish the model from phonetic feature based models.

The model of Fig. 10 is probably too simple to be true. It is more likely that the central nervous system can make use of many strategies, including phonetic analysis and analysis-by-synthesis, in which case the conjecture made here is that, under normal circumstances, the primary way of initiating sentence analysis is indicated by the block diagram of Fig. 10.

C. Future research

The key to improved bottom-end performance (lexical hypothesization) in future speech understanding systems, it seems to me, is the transformation of a phonetic identification problem into a spectral state verification problem, as was done in Harpy. Phonetic representations for words of the lexicon are replaced by sequences of expected spectra and some durational constraints. This translation problem is nontrivial and required many trial-and-error iterations during Harpy development. The availability of a list of expected template sequences for all possible phonetic strings of English would considerably aid in bringing up new lexicons. The main objective of future research in this area should therefore be the accumulation of more detailed linguistic and acoustic–phonetic facts about English sentences.

Future research on top-end design might focus on the imposition of realistic semantic and task constraints and on computational efficiencies that will ultimately permit the use of more general grammars. Another worthwhile pursuit might be to interface a Harpy-like lexical recognition network to a top end with a nonfinite grammar, as in Fig. 10.

Additional research will be required to build a practical speech understanding system that has a complete human-engineered interactive capability. Problem areas in need of further work include the design of habitable languages, how to monitor the input to know when a signal is present (Rabiner and Sambur, 1975), including rejecting "umm's" and breath noise (Martin, 1975), how to know when an utterance is complete, whether it will be necessary for a user to see a display of the request and give a "yes"–"no" response, etc.

The steering committee prepared a follow-on research plan (Newell *et al.*, 1975) that took up a number of these issues and also proposed that the four speech understanding systems not be allowed to die. They argued that the systems required substantial additional debugging and tuning before reaching their full potential and that experiments were needed to better understand their capabilities and limitations. The committee proposed that the systems ought to be preserved as a resource for use by a wider community because considerable scientific insight might be gained from widespread experimentation with these systems. Based on the current funding picture, it appears that none of these recommendations will come to pass.

As a final note, we may ask "How hard is the sentence understanding problem in the limited contexts investigated during the ARPA project?" In 1970, when compared with isolated word recognition, the problems seemed immense. After the limited success of Harpy, one becomes more optimistic about the abilities of future systems. Still, the nature of the problem is elusive. Even the dimensions of task difficulty have yet to be adequately defined. Limited experience suggests that significant increases in difficulty are associated with increased grammar branching factor (caused by increased lexical size or increased syntactic freedom), the inherent acoustic ambiguity of words that must be distinguished, and the importance of unstressed function word recognition to sentence decoding. If these factors can be controlled in a particular task domain, speech understanding by machines is now a practical goal.

ACKNOWLEDGMENT

Preparation of this review was supported by the Advanced Research Projects Agency of the Department of Defense under Contract N00014-75-C-0533. I wish to thank everyone associated with the ARPA Speech Understanding Project who spent many hours helping me to understand these complex systems. Special thanks go to W. A. Lea, A. Newell, J. E. Shoup, D. R. Reddy, J. J. Wolf, and W. A. Woods for correcting some of my errors of judgment.

APPENDIX A. DETAILED DESCRIPTION OF THE SDC SYSTEM

A. Acoustic analysis

The speech waveform is digitized at 20000 samples/sec with no prior frequency-domain preemphasis. The waveform is divided into 10-ms chunks, and the energy is computed for each chunk. Other parameters that are computed every 10 ms include zero crossing counts and the fundamental frequency contour. Fundamental frequency is extracted with a down-sampled center-clipped autocorrelation technique (Gillmann, 1975). A linear prediction spectral analysis is performed every 10 ms, using 24 coefficients and a 25.6-ms Hamming window. A formant tracker estimates which of the linear prediction poles are the four lowest formant frequencies over voiced intervals.

These parameters are used to apply gross phonetic labels to relatively stationary sequences of 10-ms spectra. Special routines then characterize vowel-like segments (Kameny, 1975; 1976) and frication spectra (Molho, 1976) in terms of phonetic labels with associated scores for the three best alternatives. A post-analysis pass smooths the label names through local continuity constraints. The resulting analysis is placed in an array called the A-matrix. Segmental identification is based on acoustic-phonetic recognition strategies having a good theoretical basis—formants for vowels, gross spectral shapes for fricatives and plosive burst onsets. However, the performance (first choice label correct about 50 percent of the time for 40 phonetic categories) suggests that there are not enough detailed facts about expected influences of coarticulation with adjacent phones in the algorithms.

B. Lexical representations

The format used to represent the word "Lafayette" in the lexicon was shown in Fig. 3. The pronunciation variants for this lexical item were generated automatically from a set of phonological rules (Barnett, 1974) and then stored in the form shown in Fig. 3 so as not to have to execute the rules each time a word is hypothesized by the top end. Similar lexical networks have been used in other speech understanding systems (Tappert, Dixon, and Rabinowitz, 1973; Tappert, 1975; Cohen and Mercer, 1975; Baker, 1975; Woods and Zue, 1976).

C. Word verification

The mapper forms the interface between the top end and the A-matrix. Each time a word is hypothesized, the mapper calls "phoneme sniffer" subroutines that give matching scores for each expected phoneme. The mapper is organized in terms of syllables, attempting to match a vowel nucleus first, then working outward to verify expected adjacent consonants. The best-scoring alternative of a lexical spelling lattice is found, and phoneme scores are combined by taking the geometric mean to get a total word score. Use of the geometric mean penalizes a single bad phonemic match. The control program converts this score into an estimate of the probability of correct verification (on the basis of a prior data collection experiment) and accepts the best word from a syntactic class if it exceeds a threshold. Other words from this syntactic class that exceed the threshold may be used later to form other sentence fragment hypotheses if the best word fails to generate an acceptable total sentence. Frequently there are unexplained temporal gaps and overlaps between the starting and ending times of adjacent words of a sentence hypothesis, so the control box also sends word pairs to the mapper for evaluation of word adjacency plausibility.

The phoneme sniffers first consult the list of phoneme labels in the A-matrix in their search for a match (Weeks, 1974). If there is not a direct match with the phoneme being sought, other parameters of the A-matrix may be examined. In other cases, a matching score is obtained by consulting a phoneme confusion probability matrix in which entries reflect the probability that phoneme x will be confused with phoneme y, as estimated from a limited data sample. Phonetic context, such as the fact that [t] and [k] are more likely to be confused before [i] than before other vowels, is not considered when using the confusion matrix.

One of the more difficult problems in structuring the mapper has been to keep track of the time position within the A matrix, and not to miss a syllable or detect extra syllables. Errors of this type are fatal if they reject a correct word, since the top end cannot overcome such a decision. Fatal errors (often of this type) occurred in 40% of the large set of utterances tested, indicating that the present mapper/A-matrix combination must be improved, or the exclusively top-down system strategy must be changed.

The mapper has been evaluated by making over 11 000 verification requests using the 1000-word lexicon in the course of attempting to recognize several sentences. Relevant performance statistics are given in Table IV. Of 71 correct words hypothesized, 65 were verified and 6 were (fatally) rejected. Of 11 000 decoy word proposals, all but 372 were correctly rejected. However, the 372 false "yes" answers mean that for each of the 65 correct responses by the mapper, there are on the average 6 false words accepted that must be rejected by syntactic constraints imposed by the top end as attempts are made to extend these false partial sentence theories.

APPENDIX B. DETAILED DESCRIPTION OF THE BBN HWIM SYSTEM

A. Acoustic analysis

The speech waveform is digitized at 20 000 samples/sec and the first difference is computed to remove the dc component and tilt the spectrum up somewhat. A 13-pole selective linear prediction analysis (Makhoul, 1975) is performed over the 0–5-kHz range every 10-ms using a 20-ms Hamming window. (Essentially no use was ever made of the 5–10-kHz information.) Formant frequencies are estimated as the lowest bandwidth poles in the linear prediction analysis during voiced intervals. Other parameters used for segmentation and labeling include the energy as a function of time in several different frequency passbands, a zero-crossing count, and fundamental frequency.

Segmentation and phonetic labeling is accomplished in several passes across the data, with each new pass refining the decisions made on an earlier pass. Segmentation ambiguity is represented by a lattice of alternatives, as shown in Fig. 5. For each segment of the lattice, all possible phonetic labels are given a rating score based on acoustic similarity and/or experimentally determined confusion probability. As in the SDC system, probability matrix entries were computed independent of phonetic context.

The performance of the segmenter has been evaluated for 124 sentences read by three talkers, using the dictionary spelling for the words of an utterance as the correct answer. For 2850 dictionary segments, the segmenter found 5127 segments arranged in a lattice such that, if one followed the most-correct path through the lattice, only 1.6% of the expected segmentation points were missed, and only 1.8% of the time did the best path contain an extra segment (Woods *et al.*, 1976, Vol. 2, pp. 9–39).

The labeling performance of the system was evaluated by considering the best path through the lattice, as defined above. With 71 possible phonetic labels, the rank-order distribution of the correct label ranges from 52% correct first choice to being within the top five label choices 83% of the time. This performance might appear to be somewhat better than that of the other systems, but it is not certain that the lexical matcher will find the best path through the lattice. Some high-scoring false word matches may be generated by using the alternative incorrect paths. A measure of information content would be needed to compare objectively the segment labelers used in the three systems.

The lexicon contains phonemic spellings for each word or morpheme. A set of phonological rules are applied to generate alternative pronunciations (Woods and Zue, 1976). On the average, a word begins with a single phonemic spelling and ends up with about two acceptable phonetic realizations after application of a modest set of phonological rules. Additional rules of the BBN phonological rule expansion system optionally delete or change some segment labels that are frequently missed by the acoustic–phonetic labeler. For example, a rule optionally deletes the /n/ in poststressed /nt/ clusters. If possible, it would have been better to make improvements to the labeler so that it could detect nasalization in these cases, but it is nevertheless very important for the lexicon to predict what is actually observed by the acoustic processing routines, and these special rules are one possible way of achieving this goal.

The entire lexicon of alternative pronunciations is folded into a single state transition network that incorporates word-boundary phonological rules and that can be searched very efficiently for lexical matches (Klovstad, 1977; Klovstad and Mondshein, 1975; Woods *et al.*, 1976, Vol. 3, pp. 12–27). The lexical decoding network is of sufficient theoretical interest for the design of future speech understanding systems that its general character will be described in some detail here. The first step in the creation of a lexical decoding network is to combine the expected phonetic spellings for all lexical items into a tree structure, as shown in Fig. 7a. Initial parts of words are combined with other words having the same beginning phonetic segments. The termination of each word is identified by one or more nodes in the tree, and these word-terminal nodes are unique insofar as the words of the lexicon have disjoint phonetic representations.

The tree shown in Fig. 7(a) is transformed into a network by application of a set of word-boundary pronunciation rules. Consider the word "list" in the tree. The pronunciation of "list" may be [l IH s] in the environment "list some," so the derived network representation of "list" shown in Fig. 7(b) has a path going from the [s] node of "list" directly to the second phone of all words starting with [s], and a path from the [t] node of "list" to the first phone of all words. This network structure captures a general word-boundary phonological rule stating that words ending in [s t] can be pronounced (optionally) without the [t], but that this can only happen if the following word begins with [s]. The rule is stated in a natural notation: OPT{S T # S}−{S} before being compiled into various modifications to the lexical tree. In this example, it is possible to accept the word "list" without seeing a [t], but only words starting with [s] can be matched thereafter.

It is possible to embed within this network structure any of the types of rules in the literature on word boundary phonology. The advantages of a lexical decoding network go beyond its being a concise statement of allowable phonetic strings corresponding to all word sequences of connected-word utterances. The network also allows computational (search) and storage efficiencies that can become significant as vocabulary size increases. Klovstad has developed scoring procedures for input phonetic strings having a missing segment or an extra segment by referring to experimentally determined probabilities of these phenomena. In my opinion, this is an attractive structure for representing lexical information in a generalized speech understanding system, although there are problems in accumulating sufficient statistics to score missing/extra segments properly.

B. Word verification by parametric synthesis

A word verification component is included in the BBN system to overcome the inherent inaccuracies in performance of the segmentation and labeling scheme by returning to the parametric level. One can be more certain about what acoustic data to expect if a word and, if possible, its phonetic context are given (Klatt and Stevens, 1973). The strategy is of some theoretical interest since it is a concrete example of an analysis-by-synthesis model of speech perception (Halle and Stevens, 1962).

Verification of a word begins by sending the phonemic representation, obtained from the lexicon, and adjacent phonemes, if known, to a speech synthesis-by-rule program (Klatt, 1976a), which was modified to predict spectra instead of generating waveforms (Woods *et al.*, 1976, Vol. 2, pp. 40–57). Verification scores are obtained by comparing 10-ms frames of synthesized spectra with selected spectral frames of the unknown utterance, using a dynamic programming algorithm to find the best possible alignment (Woods *et al.*, 1976, Vol. 2, pp. 58–68).

The performance of the verification component has been tested during operation of the speech understanding system. The distribution of verification scores for words that the lexical matcher thought were good word candidates during sentence recognition can be compared with an arbitrary threshold to obtain the performance figures shown in Table IV (Cook and Schwartz, 1977), although the system used graded scores rather than an absolute accept/reject threshold of the type implied by the contents of Table IV. The performance evaluation included three talkers, and a few changes were made (by hand) to the synthesis rules for each talker. Superficially, performance may seem poorer than for the SDC verifier, but the lexical matcher has removed nearly 95% of the worst matching words from consideration by the BBN verification component, while the SDC verifier processes all words permitted by the syntax.

Analysis by synthesis has been a popular model of the perceptual process. However, considering the computational cost of analysis-by-synthesis techniques and the problems of normalization for different talkers, it is the author's opinion that a more promising verification alternative for a computer system is the spectral-sequence verification strategy implicit in the Harpy speech understanding system.

C. Syntactic/semantic component

The syntactic component consists of an augmented transition network (ATN) parser; a portion of the ATN grammar is shown in Fig. 6 (Woods, 1970). The network indicates several possible paths that can be taken after a determiner has been found. The label PP is an abbreviation for a sub-network that recognizes prepositional phrases. The network is augmented with registers that are used to develop a quantified predicate calculus "deep-structure" representation for the sentence, i.e., the surface effects of certain grammatical transformations are undone to arrive at a standard syntactic representation appropriate for semantic interpretation. For example, there is a subject register, a "negative-particle-found" register, etc. The contents of the registers are modified as the parser discovers e.g., that the sentence is in the passive mode. This type of parser is considered by some psycholinguists to be the best current model of how a listener decodes the underlying structure of a spoken sentence (Wanner and Maratsos, 1977).

Semantic constraints are applied in the BBN system by adding them to the parsing grammar (although a separate semantic network was used for response generation). As an example of how semantic constraints are added, the general noun phrase subnetwork shown in Fig. 6(a) is expanded into a number of specialized noun phrase recognition networks, one of which is shown in Fig. 6(b).

Augmented transition net parsers were originally designed to process a sentence from left-to-right. However, the BBN parser has been modified to work in either direction or middle-out for the speech understanding application (Woods *et al.*, 1976, Vol. 4; Bates, 1975). Since the grammar is fairly general and complex, computational efficiencies are achieved by precomputing the answers to certain frequently asked questions concerning what can appear to the left and right of word hypotheses belonging to selected syntactic categories.

D. Control strategies

A speech understanding system can be divided into a set of quasi-independent components (this is especially true of the Hearsay-II system), each of which provides some information toward the ultimate decoding of the utterance. The problem of combining information from the segment lattice, the lexical decoding network, and the verifier is handled in the BBN system by a philosophy of transforming all scores into log likelihood ratios that can be added to form an overall score for a sentence fragment hypothesis. The idea is that scores can be more easily combined if each is based on the probability of being correct, as estimated from prior performance analysis for each component.

A number of control strategies were investigated at BBN as means to find the correct sentence without considering too many alternatives. Quick convergence is needed because, as currently implemented, the system is very slow. One strategy estimated the best possible matching score as a function of position within an utterance (using the lexical matcher to compare all lexical items with all possible segment starting positions). Partial sentence theories were then scored with respect to how far they fell short of reaching this maximum possible score. If a best-first search both to the left and right of a partial sentence theory were always pursued, BBN showed that the first sentence found had to be the best possible interpretation of the utterance. This optimal search theorem assumed that the initial scan gave an accurate estimate of the best possible score at any position in the utterance (not necessarily a good assumption since word boundary phonology was ignored in the initial scan).

Experience showed this strategy to be computationally costly whenever the segment lattice contained a phonetic error of a type not seen before in the probability-gathering stage. The system did not have time to recover from the resulting poor matching score for a correct word, so BBN modified the control strategy to work mostly from left to right, but to retain the theoretical advantage of initially jumping over the first few (less distinctly articulated) segments to find a seed word. The system then worked backward to find the word(s) to the left, and then worked strictly left-to-right. Strictly left-to-right sentence analysis is to be preferred in most speech understanding applications (and humans probably also process essentially left-to-right) because there are fewer local syntactic constraints that can be applied to a sentence fragment in the middle of an utterance.

The BBN system runs in about 1000 times real time on a PDP-KA10, which has a speed of about 0.4 MIPS (million instructions per second). This was a serious problem for system development and knowledge source debugging because it took a long time to accumulate performance data. BBN argued that a good deal can be learned about control issues by careful observation of system traces for only a few sentences. They claimed that it would be possible to implement the speech understanding system in real time on a large 100-MIPS machine by converting some of the code from INTERLISP to assembly language.

E. Response generation

The BBN system included a set of semantic procedures for accessing a data base to compute the response to an input utterance. An appropriate syntactic frame was selected to verbalize the response, and phonemic representations for the words of the response were sent to a speech synthesis by rule program (Klatt, 1976 a). The fully automatic generation of a spoken response to a correctly recognized sentence was demonstrated in February 1976.

APPENDIX C. DETAILED DESCRIPTION OF THE CMU HEARSAY-II SYSTEM

A. Acoustic analysis

The speech waveform is low-pass filtered to 5 kHz, digitized at 10 000 samples/sec, and filtered using a first difference to remove dc and tilt the spectrum up somewhat. The resulting waveform and a second waveform obtained from it using a low-pass smoothing filter are then divided into 10-ms chunks and characterized by a peak-to-peak amplitude and a zero-crossing measure. The two amplitude and zero-crossing functions are used to segment the utterance into intervals of relatively little acoustic change. Then each interval is assigned to one of several broad manner-of-articulation classes using a decision tree of logical threshold tests on the four parametric functions. The performance of the segmenter was compared with that of a hand segmentation. It was found that the segmenter missed 2% of the segments, hypothesized 20% extra segments, and gave a correct manner classification 90% of the time (Goldberg and Reddy, 1976).

A label was assigned to each quasi-phonetic segment (or several labels if they received about the same score) based on the distance between the linear prediction spectrum of the middle 10-ms frame of the segment and a set of 98 templates. The performance of the labeler was also evaluated. It was found that the correct label was the first choice 42% of the time and it was one of the five top choices 75% of the time, using 98 templates to represent 98 phonetic segment types and the minimum prediction residual distance measure to rank-order phonetic choices.

B. Word hypothesization

A word hypothesizer component takes as input the segment label string and tries to find word matches anywhere within the string, using the lexicon of stored representations for words. The hypothesizer is organized around the syllable structure of a word. All lexical items having the same syllable structure as a portion of the input (e.g., fricative—vowel followed by plosive—vowel) are proposed by the lexical hypothesizer. The technique is based on the assumption that manner-of-articulation decisions are more reliable than place-of-articulation decisions.

Performance evaluation of the word hypothesis component indicates that for a typical sentence, 50 words out of the 1000-word lexicon are hypothesized per word position, and the correct word is among the 50 about 70% of the time. Words can also be hypothesized top-down, using a syntactic predictor, so correct words missed by the word hypothesizer need not cause a fatal error in overall system performance.

C. Word verification

A word verification component is used to reduce the number of lexical hypotheses to be considered by the higher-level modules, and to rank order the merits of each accepted hypothesis. This component has the same structure as the Harpy system described below, i.e., a network consisting of sequences of expected spectral template alternatives for each word. Performance evaluation of the word verification component (Table IV) shows that, depending on the threshold employed, up to half the hypothesized words can be rejected while falsely rejecting only 6% of the correct words. The ratings of *the verification* component are such as to place the correct word in about fourth position, on the average, of the 50 or so words hypothesized to start at that position. This type of verification structure has great potential, but the Hearsay-II implementation does not presently account for very many phonetic and phonological interactions at word boundaries.

The observed scoring behavior of the verification component is not good enough to be used as an absolute ranking criterion when deciding, for example, whether to pursue one of two non-overlapping sentence fragments. Instead, scores at each position in a sentence are normalized with respect to the best matching word observed so far at that position (a strategy similar to that employed at BBN).

A second type of verification procedure is used to see if two words proposed to be adjacent are acoustically compatible with the segment label string. A special set of rules is employed to consider only the critical time interval, taking into account phonological processes occurring across word boundaries. During one run of sentence understanding, 7100 two-word hypotheses were processed by this component. One hundred and ninety five (i.e., 95% of the correct word pairs) were correctly accepted and 59% of the many decoy word pairs were correctly rejected.

D. Syntax, semantics, and control strategies

The syntax and semantics module uses the Cocke algorithm (Aho and Ullman, 1972) to list all possible words to the left or right of a high-scoring seed word. Verification scores are obtained for some or all of these word hypotheses, and the best-scoring word hypothesis is combined with the seed word to form a partial phrase. Many partial phrase theories are considered in parallel, and the parser is capable of saying whether adjacent partial phrases can be combined syntactically. All semantic knowledge contained in the system is presently embedded in the syntactic rules.

The control strategy is to expand larger sentence fragments first (depth first) because such fragments are not expected to occur randomly. However, since the correct word rarely has the best verification score, it is necessary to pursue many paths before a complete sentence is obtained. The first sentence found is not necessarily the best scoring possible sentence, so the recognition process continues until all remaining sentence fragments have a lower score.

The Hearsay-II system design with its blackboard concept permits a good deal of potential parallelism. For example, the components of the system might be implemented on a set of smaller computers connected in parallel (Bell *et al.*, 1973). Also, since each knowledge source is independent, taking its input from the blackboard and placing its output on the blackboard, knowledge sources can be changed fairly easily. The demonstrated advantage of this system design approach is that six months before the end of the project, the performance of Hearsay-II was such that an intensive effort was made to redesign nearly every component in the system, and even eliminate some of the components that provided little help. This resulted in a significant improvement in performance.

The Hearsay-II system ran in about 250 times real time on a PDP-KA10 (0.4 MIPS) computer. The final performance of Hearsay-II (Table II) is encouraging, although the evaluation was restricted to a small number of sentences from a single talker. Of interest is the fact that only 77% of the sentences were correctly *recognized* (all words correct) while 91% were *understood* correctly. It appears that the CMU grammar contains some desirable characteristics for the realization of computer understanding.

APPENDIX D. DETAILED DESCRIPTION OF THE CMU HARPY SYSTEM

A. Acoustic analysis

The preliminary acoustic analysis performed in Harpy is of interest because it obviates the need for sophisticated acoustic-phonetic decoding rules. A speech waveform is low-pass filtered at 5 kHz, digitized at 10 000 samples per second, and 14 linear prediction coefficients are computed every 10 msec. 10-ms frames are then grouped together into "acoustic segments" if sufficiently similar. Working from left to right, the control component takes the parametric representation for a frame and compares it with the first frame and the middle frame of the current segment. A new segment is proposed if either distance exceeds a threshold.

The linear prediction coefficients used to represent the combined segment are obtained from the sum of the autocorrelation coefficients of all the frames in the segment. On the average, segments consist of about three 10-ms frames, and there are thus two to three acoustic segments for every phonetic segment in a word. The process of grouping together 10-ms frames reduces the number of matches with the network, decreases the recognition time, and is intended to smooth out potential noise in the label sequences that are obtained from the linear prediction spectra. Each segment is characterized by a 14-pole spectrum, and the distances between this spectrum and a set of 98 spectral templates are computed using a minimum residual error measure (Itakura, 1975).

The system is sensitive to missing segments (being constrained not to skip a state in the network), but redundant sequences of labels are easily handled by including an implicit output path that returns to the same state for each state in the network. Therefore the segmenter is biased to produce extra segments rather than to miss an expected segment. The advantage of this simple strategy is that time normalization of the input stream is not required in the template matching process. Little phonetic constraint seems to be lost by allowing each state to grab as many acoustic segments as it can (subject to certain minimum and maximum times for remaining in particular states).

B. Template selection

The spectral template inventory was developed by starting with a single template for each phoneme (two for plosives, affricates, and diphthongs) and expanding the number of templates for cases where this simple approximation lead to recognition errors. Experimenter judgment was required to decide when to change a lexical representation using other available templates, when to add a word boundary rule, and when it was absolutely necessary to add to the template inventory. After processing over 700 sentences from a single talker, the number of templates reached 98, of which almost all of the additions helped describe voiced portions of consonant-vowel transitions.

C. Network generation

The Harpy grammar consists of a set of BNF statements that generate a finite list of acceptable sentences, where most sentences contain a word from a large class of "authors" and/or a large class of "topics." The lexical representation for each word consists of a state transition network of expected alternative sequences of spectral states, with duration limits given in parentheses for some of the states. A modest number of word-boundary rewrite rules are specified, but the coarticulatory phenomena covered are surprisingly few in number, and the restricted notation could not handle, for example, the {S T # S} phonological deletion example given earlier (unless the [s t] spectral sequence were replaced by a special dummy symbol). All this information is transformed into a 15 000 state network by a set of procedures that collapse common representations where possible, while assuring an ability to backtrack through the network once a terminal node is reached in order to determine what word sequence was spoken.

D. System tuning and talker normalization

The templates used in the segment labeler are tuned to each new talker, but the lexical representations stay the same for all talkers of a common dialect (it is acknowledged that a few phonetic alternatives may have to be added to improve performance for some individuals). Templates for a new talker are obtained by attempting to recognize a set of about 20 training sentences using someone else's template patterns. The system automatically generates a new set of template patterns from the label sequences used in a forced correct path through the network. For a 1000 word lexicon, it takes about a half hour to record and process the training sentences. This is perhaps more than intended by the ARPA steering committee specifications, but there is no doubt that the procedure contributes significantly to the very good performance of the system. Recent changes permit the system to adapt to a new talker dynamically by starting with a talker-independent set of templates and modifying their properties based on correctly understood input utterances (Lowerre, 1977) in a manner similar to that used in Hearsay I (Reddy, Erman, and Neely, 1973).

The Harpy system uses about 30 MIPSS (millions of instructions executed per second of speech). This is less than the computing time in the other systems, but it is far from real-time operation on the computer used (0.4 MIPS PDP-KA10). However, it is well within the target specifications of real-time response on a 100-MIPS future machine. Harpy also requires a large program space to store and manipulate its 15 000 state network representation of speech knowledge. The present program barely fits into 200K of 36-bit words, and it would probably not fit if the average branching factor of the grammar were increased.

[1]Members of the ARPA steering committee were F. S. Cooper, J. W. Forgie, C. C. Green, D. H. Klatt, J. C. R. Licklider (Ex-chairman), M. F. Medress (Acting Chairman), E. P. Newburg, A. Newell (ex-chairman), M. H. O'Malley, D. R. Reddy, B. Ritea, J. E. Shoup, D. E. Walker, and W. A. Woods.

[2]The original 5 system builders were a group at Bolt Beranek and Newman Inc. (BBN) headed by W. A. Woods, a group at Carnegie-Mellon University (CMU) headed by D. R. Reddy, a group at Lincoln Laboratories (LL) headed by J. Forgie, a group at Stanford Research Institute (SRI) headed by D. Walker, and a group at System Development Corporation (SDC) headed by B. Ritea. After two years, funding was concentrated on three main system builders. Smaller supporting research efforts were funded at Haskins Laboratories (F. S. Cooper), at Speech Communications Research Laboratory (J. E. Shoup), at Univac (M. F. Medress), and at Univ. California at Berkeley (M. H. O'Malley).

[3]In addition to serving on the ARPA advisory steering committee, the author also worked as a consultant during the development of the BBN system.

[4]No claim is made for the strict originality of these techniques. Even in the context of speech understanding systems, some of the ideas were preceded by or developed in parallel with research taking place elsewhere. For example, a major speech recognition effort was initiated at IBM about the same time as the ARPA project began (Bahl *et al.*, 1976; Jelenek, 1976). See Reddy (1976) for an excellent comparative review of progress in the field up to early 1976.

Aho, A. V., and Ullman, J. D. (1972). *Theory of Parsing, Translation and Compiling* (Prentice-Hall, Englewood Cliffs, NJ).

Bahl, L., Baker, J., Cohen, P., Dixon, N., Jelenek, F., Mercer, R., and Silverman, H. (1976). "Preliminary results on the Performance of a System for the Automatic Recognition of Continuous Speech," pp. 425–429 in Teacher (1976).

Baker, J. (1975). "The Dragon System—An Overview," IEEE Trans. Acoust. Speech Signal Process. ASSP-23, 24–29.

Barnett, J. A. (1974). "A Phonological Rule Compiler," pp. 188–192 in Erman (1974).

Bates, M. (1975). "The Use of Syntax in a Speech Understanding System," IEEE Trans. Acoust. Speech Signal Process. ASSP-23, 112–117.

Bell, C., Chen, R., Fuller, S., Grason, J., Rege, S., and Siewiorek, D. (1973). "The Architecture and Application of Computer Modules: A Set of Components for Digital Systems Design," Compcon 73, San Francisco, CA, pp. 177–180.

Bernstein, M. I. (1976). "Interactive Systems Research: Final Report to the Director, Advanced Research Projects Agency," System Development Corporation, Santa Monica, CA, Report No. TM-5243/006/00.

Chomsky, N., and Halle, M. (1968). *The Sound Pattern of English* (Harper and Row, New York).

Cohen, P. S., and Mercer, R. L. (1975). "The Phonological Component of an Automatic Speech Recognition System," pp. 275–320 in Reddy (1975).

Cole, R. A., and Scott, B. (1974). "Toward a Theory of Speech Perception," Psychol. Rev. 81, 348–374.

Connolly, D. (1975). "Minutes of the Speech Understanding Workshop," 81–82, Science Applications Inc., Arlington, VA.

Cook, C. C., and Schwartz, R. M. (1977). "Advanced Acoustic Techniques in Automatic Speech Understanding," pp. 663–666 in Silverman (1977).

De Mori, R., Rivoira, S., and Serra, A. (1975). "A Speech Understanding System with Learning Capability," in *Proceedings of the 4th International Joint Conference on Artificial Intelligence* (Tbilisi, USSR).

Dixon, N. R., and Maxey, H. D. (1968). "Terminal Analog Speech Synthesis of Continuous Speech Using the Diphone Method of Segment Assembly," IEEE Trans. Aud. Electroacoust. AU-16, 40–50.

Erman, L. D., Ed. (1974). *Contributed Papers of the IEEE Symposium on Speech Recognition* (IEEE Catalog No. 74CH0878-9 AE).

Fant, G. (1970). "Automatic Recognition and Speech Research," Q. Prog. and Status Rep. QPSR-1, Speech Transmission Laboratories, KTH, Stockholm, Sweden, 16–31.

Fant, G., Ed. (1975). *Proceedings of the Stockholm Speech Communications Seminar* (Almqvist and Wiksell, Stockholm, and Wiley, New York).

Forgie, J. W., *et al.* (1974). *Speech Understanding Systems—Semiannual Technical Summary Report* (MIT Lincoln Laboratories, Lexington, MA).

Garrett, M. F. (1977). "Word and Sentence Processing," in *Handbook of Sensory Physiology, Volume 8: Perception*, edited by R. Held and X. Leibowitz (Springer-Verlag, Heidelberg).

Gillmann, R. A. (1975). "A Fast Frequency-Domain Pitch Algorithm," J. Acoust. Soc. Am. 58, S63(A).

Goldberg, H. G., and Reddy, R. (1976). "Feature Extraction, Segmentation and Labeling in the Harpy and Hearsay-II Systems," J. Acoust. Soc. Am. 60, S11(A).

Halle, M., and Stevens, K. N. (1962). "Speech Recognition: A Model and a Program for Research," IRE Trans. Inf. Theory IT-8, 155–159.

Haton, J.-P., and Pierrel, J.-M. (1976). "Organization and Operation of a Connected Speech Understanding System at Lexical, Syntactic and Semantic Levels," pp. 430–433 in Teacher (1976).

Hayes-Roth, F., and Lesser, V. R. (1976). "Focus of Attention in a Distributed-Logic Speech Understanding System," pp. 416–420 in Teacher (1976).

Herscher, M. B., and Cox, R. B. (1976). "Source Entry Using Voice Input," pp. 190–193 in Teacher (1976).

Hyde, S. R. (1972). "Automatic Speech Recognition: A Critical Survey and Discussion of the Literature," in *Human Communication: A Unified View*, edited by E. E. David and P. B. Denes (McGraw-Hill, New York).

Itakura, F. (1975). "Minimum Prediction Residual Principle Applied to Speech Recognition," IEEE Trans. Acoust. Speech Signal Process. ASSP-23, 67–72.

Jelenek, F. (1976). "Continuous Speech Recognition by Statistical Methods," Proc. IEEE 64, 532–556.

Kameny, I. (1975). "Comparison of Formant Spaces of Retroflexed and Nonretroflexed Vowels," IEEE Trans. Acoust. Speech Signal Process. ASSP-23, 38–49.

Kameny, I. (1976). "Automatic Acoustic-Phonetic Analysis of Vowels and Sonorants," pp. 166–169 in Teacher (1976).

Klatt, D. H. (1975). "Word Verification in a Speech Understanding System," pp. 321–341 in Reddy (1975).

Klatt, D. H. (1976a). "Structure of a Phonological Rule Component for a Synthesis-by-Rule Program," IEEE Trans. Acoust. Speech Signal Process. ASSP-24, 391–398.

Klatt, D. H. (1976b). "A Digital Filter Bank for Spectral Matching," pp. 537–540 in Teacher (1976).

Klatt, D. H. (1978). "Speech Perception: A Spectral-Sequence Decoding Network as a Model of Lexical Access" (in preparation).

Klatt, D. H., and Stevens, K. N. (1973). "On the Automatic Recognition of Continuous Speech: Implications of a Spectrogram-Reading Experiment," IEEE Trans. Audio Electroacoust AU-21, 210–217.

Klovstad, J. W. (1977). "Computer-Automated Speech Perception System," Ph.D. thesis (MIT).

Klovstad, J. W., and Mondshein, L. F. (1975). "The CASPERS Linguistic Analysis System," IEEE Trans. Acoust. Speech Signal Process. ASSP-23, 18–123.

Lea, W. A. (1968). "Establishing the Value of Voice Communication with Computers," IEEE Trans. Audio Electroacoust. AU-16, 184–197.

Lea, W. A., Medress, M. F., and Skinner, T. E. (1975). "A Prosodically Guided Speech Understanding System," IEEE Trans. Acoust. Speech Signal Process. ASSP-23, 30–38.

Lesser, V. R., Fennell, R. D., Erman, L. D., and Reddy, D. R. (1975). "Organization of the Hearsay-II Speech Understanding System," IEEE Trans. Acoust. Speech Signal Process. ASSP-23, 11–23.

Lesser, V. R., and Erman, L. D. (1977). "A Retrospective View of the Hearsay-II Architecture," IJCAI-77 (in press).

Liberman, A. M., Cooper, F. S., Harris, K. S., and MacNeilage, P. F. (1962). "A Motor Theory of Speech Perception," *Proceedings of the Speech Communication Seminar*, (Royal Institute of Technology, Stockholm), Paper D3.

Liberman, A. M., Cooper, F. S., Shankweiler, D. S., and Studdert-Kennedy, M. (1967). "Perception of the Speech Code," Psychol. Rev. 74, 431–461.

Lindgren, N. (1965). "Machine Recognition of Human Language," IEEE Spectrum 2, March, April, May.

Lowerre, B. T. (1976). "The Harpy Speech Recognition System," Ph.D. thesis (Department of Computer Science, Carnegie-Mellon University, Pittsburgh, PA.)

Lowerre, B. T. (1977). "Dynamic Speaker Adaptation in the Harpy Speech Recognition System," pp. 788–790 in Silverman (1977).

Martin, T. B. (1975). "Applications of Limited Vocabulary Recognition Systems," pp. 55–71 in Reddy (1975).

Martin, T. B. (1976). "Practical Applications of Voice Input to Machines," Proc. IEFE 64, 487–500.

Makhoul, J. (1975). "Linear Prediction: A Tutorial Review," Proc. IEEE 63, 561–480.

Medress, M. F., Cooper, F. S., Forgie, J. W., Green, C. C., Klatt, D. H., O'Malley, M. H., Newburg, E. P., Newell, A., Reddy, D. R., Ritia, B., Shoup-Hummel, J. E., Walker, D. E., and Woods, W. A. (1977). "Speech Understanding Systems: Report of a Steering Committee," Sigart Newsletter 62, 4–7 (April 1977); IEEE Trans. Prof. Commun. (1977) (in press).

Medress, M. F., Skinner, T. E., Kloker, D. R., Diller, T. C., and Lea, W. A. (1977). "A System for Recognition of Spoken Connected Word Sequences," pp. 468–473 in Silverman (1977).

Mermelstein, P. (1975a). "A Phonetic-Context Controlled Strategy for Segmentation and Phonetic Labeling of Speech," IEEE Trans. Acoust. Speech Signal Process. ASSP-23, 79–82.

Mermelstein, P. (1975b). "Automatic Segmentation of Speech into Syllable Units," J. Acoust. Soc. Am. 58, 880–883.

Molho, L. M. (1976). "Automatic Acoustic-Phonetic Analysis of Fricatives and Plosives," pp. 182–185 in Teacher (1976).

Newell, A., Barnett, J., Forgie, J. W., Green, C. C., Klatt, D. H., Licklider, J. C. R., Munson, J., Reddy, D. R., and Woods, W. A. (1973). *Speech Understanding Systems: Final Report of a Study Group* (North-Holland/American Elsevier, Amsterdam).

Newell, A., Cooper, F. S., Forgie, J. W., Green, C. C., Klatt, D. H., Medress, M. F., Newburg, E. P., O'Malley, M. H., Reddy, D. R., Ritea, B., Shoup-Hummel, J. E., Walker, D. E., and Woods, W. A. (1975). *Considerations for a Follow-on ARPA Research Program for Speech Understanding Systems* (August 1975). Available from Computer Science Department, Carnegie-Mellon University, Pittsburgh, PA 15213.

O'Malley, M. H. (1975). "The Children of Lunar: An Exercise in Comparative Grammar" (unpublished).

Ochsman, R. B., and Chapanis, A. (1974). "The Effects of

10 Communication Modes in the Behavior of Teams during Cooperative Problem Solving," Int. J. Man-Machine Stud. **6**, 579–619.

Oshika, B., Zue, V. W., Weeks, R. V., Nue, H., and Aurbach, J. (1975). "The Role of Phonological Rules in Speech Understanding Research," IEEE Trans. Acoust. Speech Signal Process. ASSP-**23**, 104–112.

Paxton, W. H. (1977). *A Framework for Speech Understanding*, Ph.D. dissertation (Stanford University).

Paxton, W. H. (1976). "Experiments in Speech Understanding System Control," Artificial Intelligence Center Technical Note 134, Stanford Research Institute Project 4762, Menlo Park, CA.

Peterson, G., Wang, W., and Silvertsen, E. (1958). "Segmentation Techniques in Speech Synthesis," J. Acoust. Soc. Am. **30**, 739–742.

Pierce, J. R. (1969). "Whither Speech Recognition," J. Acoust. Soc. Am. **46**, 1049–1051.

Pisoni, D. (1977). "Speech Perception," *Handbook of Learning and Cognitive Processes, Vol.* 5, edited by W. K. Estes (Erlbaum, New Jersey).

Rabiner, L. R., and Sambur, M. R. (1975). "An Algorithm for Determining the Endpoints of Isolated Utterances," Bell Syst. Tech. J. **54**, 297–315.

Reddy, D. R. (1975). *Speech Recognition: Invited Papers Presented at the* 1974 *IEEE Symposium* (Academic, New York).

Reddy, D. R. (1976). "Speech Recognition by Machine: A Review," Proc. IEEE **64**, 501–531.

Reddy, D. R., Erman, L. D., and Neely, R. B. (1973). "A Model and a System for Machine Recognition of Speech," IEEE Trans. AU-**21**, 229–238.

Reddy, D. R., *et al.* (1977). *Speech Understanding Systems Final Report* (Computer Science Department, Carnegie-Mellon University).

Ritea, B. (1975). "Automatic Speech Understanding Systems," *Proceedings of the 11th IEEE Computer Society Conference*, Washington, DC, pp. 319–322.

Sakai, T., and Nakagawa, S. (1975). "Continuous Speech Understanding System LITHAN," Technical Report, Department of Information Science, Kyoto University, Kyoto, Japan.

Schwartz, R. M., and Cook, C. C. (1977). "Advanced Acoustic Techniques in Automatic Speech Understanding," (IEEE Catalog No. 663.666).

Shockey, L., and Reddy, D. R. (1975). "Quantitative Analysis of Speech Perception," in Fant (1975).

Silverman, H. F. (Chairman) (1977). "Conference Record of the 1977 IEEE International Conference on Acoustics, Speech and Signal Processing," Hartford, 9–11 May (IEEE Catalog No. 77CH1197-3 ASSP).

Silverman, H. F., and Dixon, N. R. (1976). "The 1976 Modular Acoustic Processor (MAP): Diadic Segment Classification and Final Phoneme String Estimation," pp. 15–20 in Teacher (1976).

Smith, A. R. (1976). "Word Hypothesization in the Hearsay-II Speech Understanding System," pp. 549–552 in Teacher (1976).

Stevens, K. N. (1972a). "The Quantal Nature of Speech: Evidence from Articulatory-Acoustic Data," in *Human Communication: A Unified View*, edited by E. E. David and P. B. Denes.

Stevens, K. N. (1972b). "Segments, Features, and Analysis by Synthesis," in *Language by Eye and by Ear*, edited by J. F. Kavenaugh and I. G. Mattingly (MIT, Cambridge, MA), pp. 47–52.

Studdert-Kennedy, M. (1975). "Speech Perception," in *Contempory Issues in Experimental Phonetics*, edited by N. J. Lass.

Tappert, C. C. (1975). "Experiments with a Tree-Search Method for Converting Noisy Phonetic Representation into Standard Orthography," IEEE Trans. Acoust. Speech Signal Process. ASSP-**23**, 129–135.

Tappert, C. C., Dixon, N. R., and Rabinowitz, A. S. (1973). "Application of Sequential Decoding for Converting Phonetic to Graphic Representation in Automatic Speech Recognition of Continuous Speech (ARCS)," IEEE Trans. Audio Electroacoust. AU-**21**, 225–228.

Teacher, C. (Chairman) (1976). *Conference Record of the* 1976 *IEEE International Conference on Acoustics Speech and Signal Processing*, Philadelphia, PA, 12–14 April (IEEE Catalog No. 76CH1067-8 ASSP).

Walker, D. E. (1975). "The SRI Speech Understanding System," IEEE Transl. Acoust. Speech Signal Process. ASSP-**23**, 397–416.

Walker, D. E. (Ed.) (1976). "Speech Understanding Research: Final Technical Report," Stanford Research Institute, Menlo Park, CA.

Wanner, E., and Maratsos, M. (1977). "An ATN Approach to Comprehension," in *Linguistic Theory and Psychological Reality*, edited by J. Bresnan and M. Halle (MIT, Cambridge, MA).

Watt, W. C. (1968). "Habitability," Am. Doc. **19**, 338–351.

Weeks, R. V. (1974). "Predictive Syllable Mapping in a Continuous Speech Understanding System," pp. 154–158 in Erman (1974).

Weinstein, C. J., McCandless, S. S., Mondshein, L. F., and Zue, V. W. (1975). "A System for Acoustic-Phonetic Analysis of Continuous Speech," IEEE Trans. Acoust. Speech Signal Process. ASSP-**23**, 54–67.

Weisen, R. A., and Forgie, J. W. (1974). "An Evaluation of the Lincoln Laboratory Speech Recognition System," J. Acoust. Soc. Am. **56**, S27(A).

Wolf, J. J. (1976). "Speech Recognition and Understanding," in *Digital Pattern Recognition*, edited by K. S. Fu (Springer-Verlag, Berlin).

Woods, W. A. (1970). "Transition Network Grammars for Natural Language Analysis," Commun. Assoc. Comput. Mach. **13**, 591–602.

Woods, W. A., and Zue, V. (1976). "Dictionary Expansion via Phonological Rules for a Speech Understanding System," 561–564 in Teacher (1976).

Woods, W., Bates, M., Brown, G., Bruce, B., Cook, C., Klovstad, J., Makhoul, J., Nash-Webber, B., Schwartz, R., Wolf, J., and Zue, V. (1976). "Speech Understanding Systems: Final Technical Progress Report," Bolt Beranek and Newman, Inc. Report No. 3438, Cambridge, MA (in 5 volumes).

THE HARPY SPEECH UNDERSTANDING SYSTEM

Bruce Lowerre
Raj Reddy
Carnegie-Mellon University
Pittsburgh, PA 15213

15-1. ABSTRACT

Harpy is one of the first systems to demonstrate that high performance, large vocabulary connected speech recognition systems can in fact be realized economically for task-oriented (restricted) languages. In this chapter we present, using simple examples, the principles of organization of the Harpy system. We will illustrate how knowledge sources (KSs) are specified, how the knowledge compiler integrates the KSs into a unified directional graph representation, and how this knowledge is utilized. In conclusion, we will discuss many of the limitations of the present system and how these can be eliminated or reduced in future systems.

15-2. INTRODUCTION

Harpy is one of the systems developed as part of the five year ARPA speech understanding research effort. A study group headed by Allen Newell proposed a set of specific performance goals in 1971 to be achieved within a five year period (Newell, et al., 1971). Figure 15-1 presents the original stated goals and the performance of the Harpy system. It is interesting to note that Harpy not only met all the specifications but exceeded several of the stated objectives. In particular, the system ran an order of magnitude faster with only about half the error rate, in a noisy environment using a poor frequency-response close speaking microphone.

A comprehensive review of the recent speech recognition research including the ARPA speech program is given in Reddy (1976), Klatt (1977), and Lea (this volume). Here, we will briefly mention some of the prior research which directly contributed to the success of the Harpy System.

The parametric representation and the distance metric used in the Harpy system are based on LPC coefficients (Atal, 1971; Itakura, 1968; and Markel, 1972) using minimum distance residual metric (Itakura, 1975). The segmentation and labeling are extensions of techniques used in Hearsay II (Erman, this volume), Hearsay I (Reddy, et al., 1973), and earlier work of our group (Reddy, 1967). Other significant early work in this area is by Tappert et al. (1970) using the transeme approach. The juncture rules were all empirically derived but were influenced by the work of Oshika, et al., (1975) and Cohen & Mercer, (1975). The integrated network representation of knowledge is based on the Dragon system developed by Jim Baker at Carnegie-Mellon University. The best-few beam search technique is an extension of the best-first technique used in the Hearsay I system. Of all these, the single most important intellectual legacy upon which Harpy is based is the representation and delayed-decision techniques first used effectively in the Dragon system (Baker, 1975). It is also important to note the intellectual ferment created

Targets (from 1971)	HARPY Performance (1976)
Accept connected speech	Yes
from many	5 (3 male, 2 female)
cooperative speakers of the General American Dialect	Yes
in a quiet room	Computer terminal room
using a good quality microphone	Ordinary microphone
with slight tuning/speaker	Substantial tuning (20-30 utterances/speaker)
requiring only natural adaptation by the user	No adaptation required
permitting a slightly selected vocabulary of 1000 words	1011 words, no post-selection
with a highly artificial syntax and highly constrained task	Combined syntactic and semantic constraints → Avg. branching factor of 10
providing graceful interaction	modest interaction capabilities
tolerating < 10% semantic error	9% sentence error -- 5% semantic
in a few times real-time* [on a 100 MIPS machine]	80 times real-time on a* .35 MIPS PDP-KA10 Using 256K of 36-bit words With a simple program organization Costing about $5 per sentence
and be demonstrable in 1976 with a moderate chance of success.	Operational 13 August 1976

* A few times real-time on 100 MIPS processor is anywhere from 200 to 500 MIPSS (Millions of Instructions executed Per Second of Speech). The actual performance of Harpy was about 28 MIPSS, i.e., 80 times real-time on a .35 MIPS processor.

Figure 15-1.
Performance of the Harpy system.

Originally appeared in *Trends in Speech Recognition*, Speech Science Publications, Apple Valley, Minn. (1986).

by the large ARPA effort and continued interactions with several other groups actively pursuing similar research objectives.

15-3. KNOWLEDGE SOURCES

An important tenet that distinguishes speech understanding systems from recognition systems is the assumption that the speech signal does not have all the necessary information to uniquely decode the message and that one must use linguistic and context dependent knowledge sources to infer (or deduce) the intent of the message. However, this distinction appears to be getting fuzzy as time progresses and systems use not all the available sources of knowledge, but only a few of the knowledge sources, e.g., phonological, prosodic, lexical, and syntactic knowledge. Harpy belongs to this class of systems. Although we have implemented two tasks (chess and abstract retrieval) for which we have included task and context specific knowledge, most tasks implemented on Harpy do not include this knowledge. However, the structure and implementation of the Harpy system do not preclude the use of such knowledge.

In this section we will illustrate, by means of a simple example, typical knowledge sources used in a task and their specification and modification by the user. Figure 15-2 contains all the knowledge sources for a Mini-Query-Language (MQL). This is the usual form in which a user specifies various knowledge sources. Figure 15-3 illustrates some of these knowledge sources as directed graph representations. If an interactive graphics display terminal is available, knowledge sources can be specified directly in this network form by the user. This is the more natural form of specification as the knowledge compiler (Sec. 15-4) operates on the directed graph representation.

15-3.1 Syntactic Knowledge.

The syntax of the language is given in Fig. 15-2a as a set of four syntax equations. This is a special form for representing a class of phrase structure languages and is often called in computer science literature Backus Normal Form (BNF). Sentences "Please help me." or "Please show us everything." are legal in this language. The first equation states that a sentence in this language consists of a begin symbol ([) followed by phrase <SS> (in the second equation) followed by an ending symbol (]). The second equation states that the symbol <SS> may be defined in terms of two alternative phrase structures: please followed by help followed by any phrase defined by symbol <M> or please followed by show followed by <M> followed by phrase <Q>. Equation 3 states the phrase <Q> can be either everything or something. Equation 4 states that the phrase <M> can be either me or us. Figure 15-3a shows how these equations would be specified in directed graph representation.

Specifying the grammar for a new task is the role of a language design expert. He needs to have a deep understanding of the implications of each of the design decisions. The language must permit as much flexibility and graceful interaction as possible without sacrificing the recognizability and accuracy. Controlling the branching factor and the vocabulary ambiguity are two basic techniques available to the language designer. Goodman (1976) provides a formal model combining both of these aspects. Some of the language design tools developed by Goodman were instrumental in the development of a family of languages for the Harpy system which led to the successful demonstration in 1976. Although time pressures made it difficult to fine-tune these languages, it is clear that constrained and yet habitable languages can

```
<SENT> ::=   [ <SS> ]
<SS> ::=     please help <M>
             please show <M> <Q>
<Q> ::=      everything
             something
<M> ::=      me
             us
```

Figure 15-2(a). Grammar of MQL.

```
everything   (-,0) (EH,EH2) V R IY2 TH IH3 NX
help         (-,0) HH AA3 EL3 (← (-,0), -) P
me           (-,0) M IY
please       (← (-,0), -) (P (L,L2), PL (L,0)) IY (Z{4}, (Z,0) S)
show         (-,0) SH AA5 (OW,0)
something    (-,0) S AA M TH IH3 NX
us           (-,0) IH6 S (HH,0)
[            -
]            -
```

Figure 15-2(b). Pronunciation dictionary for MQL.

```
#,-↑-{,100}
-,#↑.-{,100}
-,-↑-{1,40}
0,-↑.< -{1,40}
Z,HH}
[Z,S],SH{
P,M{
OW,IH6↑(.< (>,0), >)
IY,[EH,EH2]↑(.< (>,0), >)
0,<{
```

Figure 15-2(c). Word juncture rules for MQL.

-	1	5	HH	3	6	AA	4	10
←	1	8	M	3	6	AA3	6	12
P	3	8	NX	5	12	AA5	3	8
PL	4	10	R	2	5	OW	2	20
V	3	6	L	2	4	IH3	3	7
Z	2	10	L2	2	5	IH6	2	6
TH	3	8	EL3	8	14	IY	4	20
S	4	12	EH	6	14	IY2	4	8
SH	4	12	EH2	2	7			

Figure 15-2(d). Phone templates for MQL.

Figure 15-2. Knowledge source for a Mini-Query-Language (MQL).

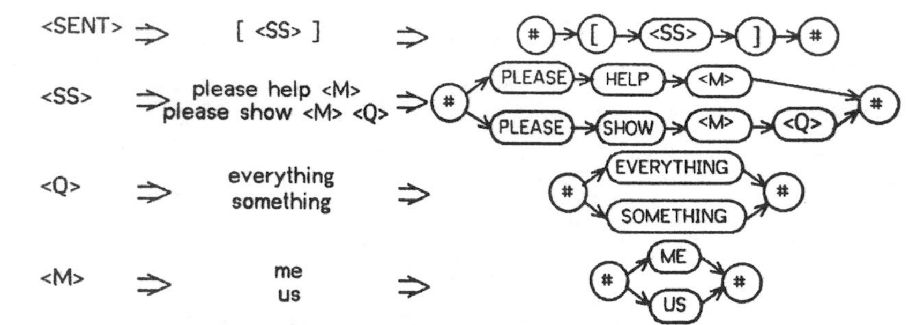

Figure 15-3(a). Representation of the grammar in Fig. 15-2(a).

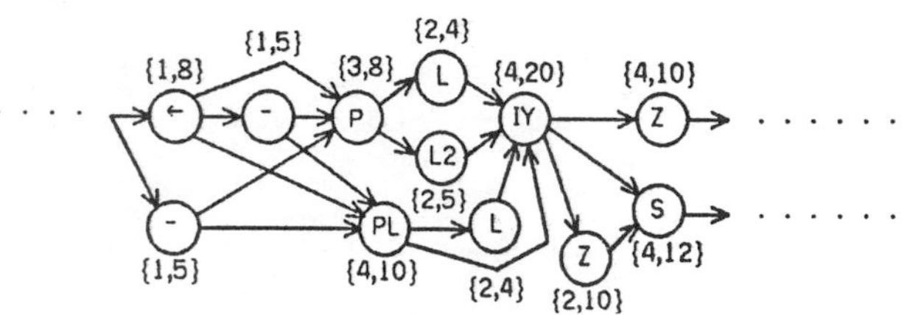

Figure 15-3(b). Representation of the word "please".

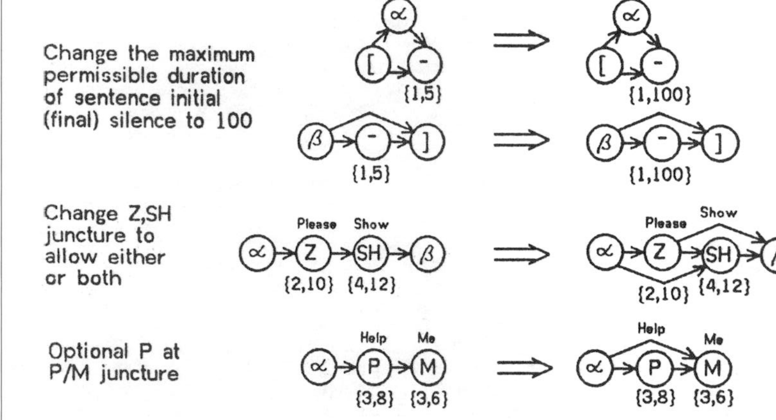

Figure 15-3(c). Representation of some of the juncture rules.

Figure 15-3. Directed graph representation of some of the knowledge given in Fig. 15-2.

be designed for use in specific task domains.

15-3.2 Lexical Knowledge.

Figure 15-2b gives the pronunciation dictionary for the MQL. Alternative pronunciations of each word are represented in a special notation (Lowerre, 1976, pg. 41). This is a string representation of the pronunciation graph. Figure 15-3b gives the graph representation for the word please. In the string notation, parentheses are used to indicate alternative choices and commas separate the alternatives. "0" is used to indicate null choice. Curly brackets are used to specify duration in centi-seconds, if the expected duration differs from the normal range of durations given as part of phone specification.

Note that the pronunciation graph in Fig. 15-3b is significantly more complex than what would normally appear as a baseform in a pronunciation dictionary. This is because the Harpy dictionary attempts to capture all the intra-word phonological phenomena as part of pronunciation. In the example given in Fig. 15-3b we see several such phenomena: /l/ in please may be partly or wholly devoiced and /z/ may be voiced, devoiced, or mixed. For each of these alternative phones, spectral patterns expected may be different for different allophones and require distinct symbolic notation.

Making up pronunciation dictionaries for a new vocabulary is perhaps the most time consuming task at present. Our initial attempts to derive all the intra-word phenomena from a set of pre-defined phonological rules operating on a baseform proved to be a failure. It appears that numerous subtle and complex processes have to be modeled very carefully before we can derive the pronunciation graph at the level of detail required by the Harpy system. Our present plan is to develop automatic and/or interactive knowledge acquisition techniques for learning the word structure directly from examples without the use of any predefined model.

15-3.3 Juncture Rules.

Another aspect of speech knowledge that is important for the successful operation of Harpy relates to the phenomena that occur at word boundaries. Unlike written text, where word boundaries are clearly defined, in spoken language word boundaries tend to overlap making it difficult to detect the end of one word and the beginning of the next. Knowledge about such phenomena is represented in Harpy in the form of Juncture Rules.

Figure 15-2c gives a set of word juncture rules for MQL. In general juncture rules contain examples of insertion, deletion, and change of phones occuring at word junctures. For this simple task, only a few juncture rules are required. Lowerre (1976, pg. 42) gives the notation used for specifying juncture rules. The exact details are unimportant here. What is interesting to observe is that many of these rules can be rewritten in the form of graph-rewriting rules (as illustrated in Fig. 15-3c) and many of the known phonological phenomena can be represented in this form. Figure 15-3c contains an example of duration change at sentence initial and final positions, an example of feature assimilation, and an example of phone deletion at word boundaries.

The approach taken in the design of Harpy is to manually tailor the juncture rules to the task at hand. This is a time consuming process. In the long run a complete set of rules capturing a wide variety of juncture phenoma has to be collected, revised, and refined. Phonological rules available in the literature do not provide the necessary level of detail to be used directly in Harpy-like systems. This is a case where automatic knowledge acquisition from examples is likely to be very helpful.

15-3.4 Phonemic Knowledge.

Figure 15-2d shows the list of phones used in MQL and the range of durations permissible for each phone, in centi-seconds. The durations are determined empirically. Missing in the figure are the phone templates which are represented as a transformation of linear prediction coefficients.

In general, the phone list for a given task consists of all the allophones (with distinct spectral characteristics) necessary to uniquely represent the expected spectral sequences in the word list. Each distinct allophone of a given phoneme is identified by adding a digit at the end of the phoneme symbol.

The generation of the spectral templates for various allophones is one of the significant innovations within the Harpy system. Lowerre (1977) describes this process in detail. There are three sources of variability that affect the phone template characteristics: environmental noise, transducer characteristics, and speaker characteristics.

In the Harpy system a single composite template is generated automatically for each allophone, capturing all three sources of variability. A speaker is asked to repeat 20 or so predefined sentences in the environment using the microphone. The Harpy system analyzes these sentences using a speaker independent set of templates to identify the location of each word and each phone within the word (more on the recognition process in Sec. 15-5). All instances of a given allophone in the 20 or so training sentences are averaged to generate a speaker specific, microphone specific, and environment specific template. Note that the template generation process is entirely automatic. Since any number of instances of an allophone can be averaged to generate the template, the same technique can be used to generate speaker independent or microphone independent templates by averaging over an appropriate set.

15-4. KNOWLEDGE COMPILER

An interesting aspect that distinguishes the speech problem from many other knowledge intensive systems in AI is the diversity of the knowledge sources (KSs). Each deals with a different aspect of the problem, and each "speaks a different language." Yet the KSs must cooperate somehow in decoding an unknown utterance. The Hearsay II System (Erman, in this volume) provides one interesting solution to the problem. The so-called "blackboard" model is used to effect communication and cooperation. The Harpy system attempts to structure all knowledge into a unified directed graph representation. Some KSs syntax are easily represented as a graph. But many other aspects: juncture rules, pronunciation variability, and duration effects, are not as easily represented as a graph and often require considerable ingenuity. Much of the Harpy's success is the result of solving the difficult technical problems associated with forcing all the diverse KSs into a unified framework.

As we saw in Sec. 15-3, the KSs are specified by the user as independent units, each with its own notation (Fig. 15-2). Translating KSs represented in different notations into a single unified graph requires using a knowledge compiler. This process is not unlike translating programs specified in a higher level language into machine code using a language compiler. Figure 15-4 gives a flowchart of knowledge compiling process in the Harpy system. This is by far the most computer-intensive process of the Harpy system. It took over 13 hours of DEC System/10 (KL) time to compile the 1011 word vocabulary document retrieval task into a 15,000 state network.

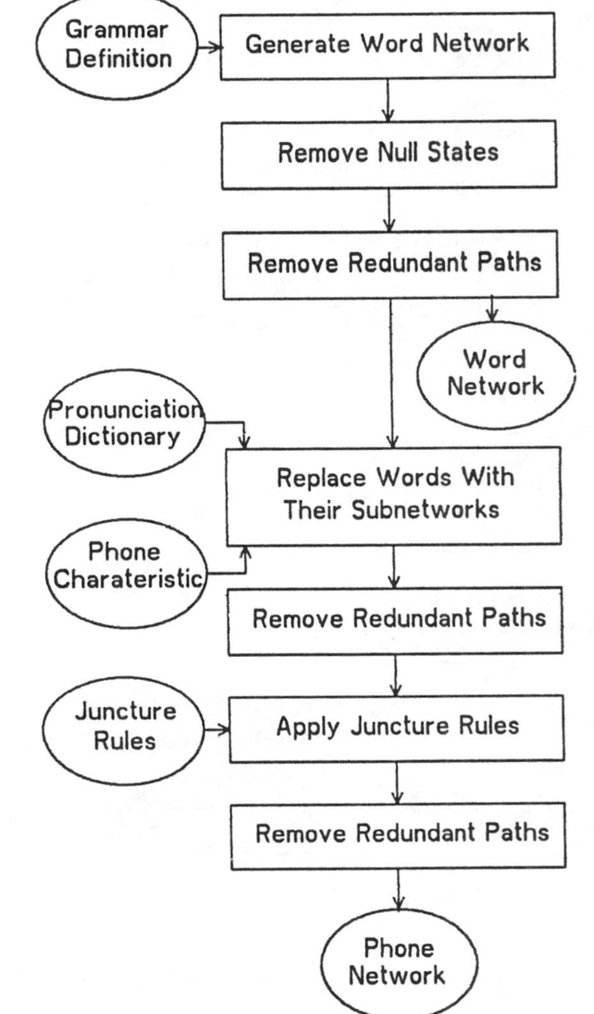

Figure 15-4. Flowchart of the knowledge compiler.

The first step in the compiling process is to generate a word network from the BNF specification of the type given in Fig. 15-2a. The goal is to replace all occurrences of non-terminal symbols (ones that require further specification; enclosed within <...>) by terminal symbols (words of the language). In the top equation <SENT> is redefined repetitively until all the paths in the directed graph contain only terminal symbols. The Harpy system uses two different techniques to achieve this transformation: substitution and pointer replacement. In the substitution technique every occurrence of a non-terminal is replaced by its definition. In the pointer replacement technique all occurrences of a non-terminal are changed so that they point to the definition of that non-terminal. In cases where each non-terminal occurs only once on the righthand side of the equation, both these techniques yield identical graphs. Otherwise the pointer replacement technique results in a more compact but less constrained grammar than the original grammar. If one wants an exactly equivalent syntax then one uses the substitution rather than the pointer replacement. We do not illustrate it here because of lack of space.

Figure 15-5 illustrates this process along with null state elimination and redundant path removal. We start with the basic definition of <SENT> as shown at the top of Fig. 15-3a. We modify the pointers so that pointers to <SS> are altered to point to the definition of <SS>. This process is repeated for each non-terminal encountered in the equations as seen in Fig. 15-5a. Figure 15-5b shows a topological equivalent graph to Fig. 15-5a resulting from pointer replacement technique.

Two important facts are worth noting in the graph in Fig. 15-5b. Note that it permits some sentences that were not legal in the original grammar, e.g., "please show me" and "please help me everything". Secondly the graph has a large number of null nodes (#) which serve no function at this stage.

Lowerre (1976, pp. 44-51) gives details of techniques for state space reduction by removing null states and redundant states. Figure 15-5c shows the graph after the null states are removed. The null state removal reduces the number of states but usually increases the number of pointers. Figure 15-5d shows the word network after the removing of redundant states. Two states A and B in the graph are redundant if: 1) each has the same terminal lexical symbol and the same set of prior states or following states. Using this definition we find that the two occurrences of the word please in Fig. 15-5c can be replaced by a single state as shown in Fig. 15-5d. The pronunciation network please shown in Fig. 15-3b is a further specification of please appearing in Fig. 15-5d. Thus, we can replace the word please in Fig. 15-5d with its pronunciation network. Likewise, replacing every node in the word network in Fig. 15-5d with its pronunciation network generates a new finite state graph, where each path is a pronunciation of an acceptable sentence. Figure 15-6 shows part of the phone network for our MQL example. We remove redundant states in the phone network using the same techniques as in the word network. Applying the graph rewriting juncture rules, the examples given in Fig. 15-3c, adding an optional silence before the final state and again removing redundant states we get part of the final compiled knowledge network for our Mini-Query-Language as shown in Fig. 15-7.

In its final compiled form each state in the network contains the following information: word lexicon number, phone lexicon number, word id number, minimum phone duration, maximum phone duration, transition count, intersection state marker, and a list of its following states. The word lexicon number is calculated from a sequential numbering of the dictionary words. This serves as an internal lexical pointer to the actual word name (string) for recognition. The phone number is likewise calculated from a sequential numbering of the phones and serves as a pointer to the phone name.

The word id is used to uniquely identify every occurrence of a terminal

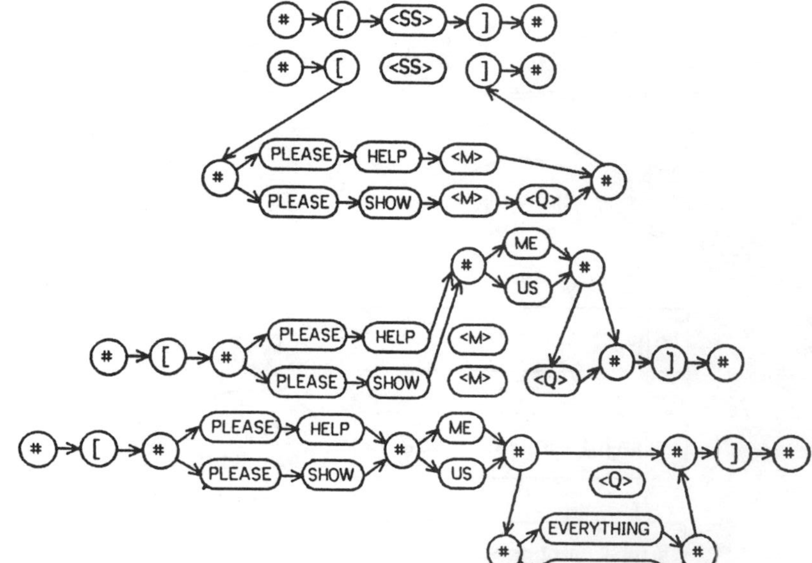

Figure 15-5(a).

Generation of the word network from the grammar specifications.

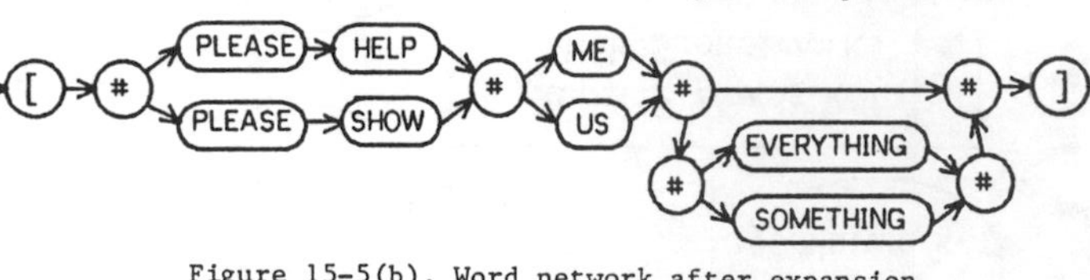

Figure 15-5(b). Word network after expansion.

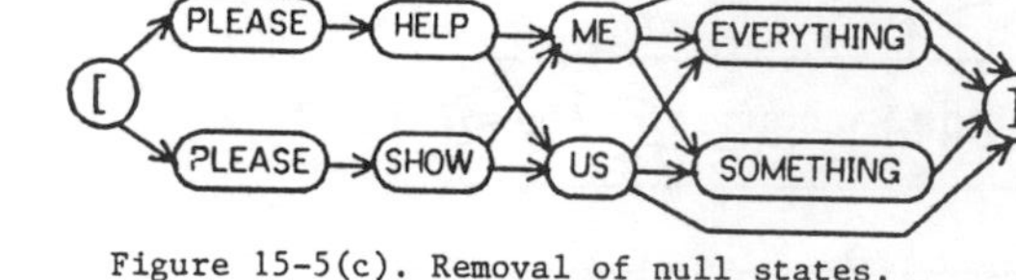

Figure 15-5(c). Removal of null states.

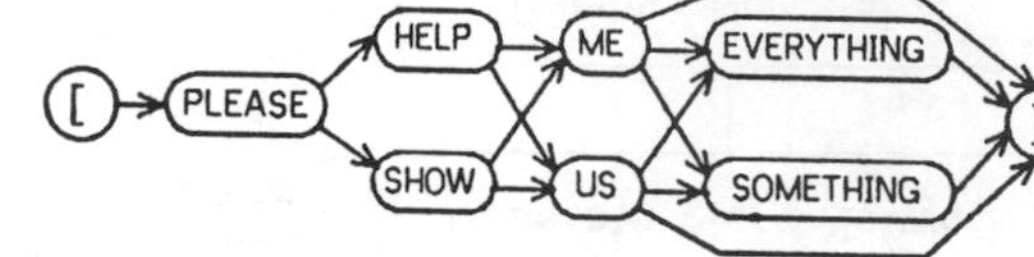

Figure 15-5(d). Removal of redundant states.

Figure 15-5. Generation of word network.

symbol (word) in the BNF grammar. Some words may occur more than once in the grammar. However, each will be given a unique id number. This is necessary for the recognition process to recognize that a transition has been made from one word to the next. This problem is especially prevalent in cases where the same word can occur two or more times in a row, such as in a series of digits. In this case, the BNF grammar must be constructed so that there are two lists of digits where the first list is linked to the second and the second is linked back to the first. This will generate connected network states with the same word lexical number but with different word id numbers.

The minimum duration is the minimum expected phone duration in centi-seconds. This is used by the recognition process in calculating transition probabilities. An inter-state transition which does not allow minimum duration in the exited state will be penalized. Similarly an intra-state transition which causes the maximum duration to be exceeded will be penalized.

The transition count is the minimum number of inter-state transitions needed to reach the final state. This is used by the recognition process to prune "dead-end" paths. For example, if state J has a transition count of N, and at a point in the recognition the number of segments left to go is less than N, then state J is pruned from consideration since its path cannot reach the final state before the end of the utterance. A side effect of this pruning is that on the last segment, the only state being considered is the final state (with transition count of 0).

Discussion. There are several other technical aspects of the knowledge compiler such as subsumption, intersection states, determination of transition count, and other details that are omitted for lack of space. Many of these tend to be efficiency issues in space and time. We have omitted discussion on how semantic, pragmatic, and prosodic knowledge would be incorporated into the network. We have been able to formulate solutions to these problems in several cases and do not anticipate any major difficulties in using these classes of knowledge within the Harpy framework.

15-5. THE RECOGNITION PROCESS

In this section we will describe how knowledge is used in the recognition of an unknown utterance. Figure 15-8 gives the complete graphical trace of an utterance recognition. The unknown sentence is digitized, segmented, matched with phone templates, and compared with the sentences in the language using the knowledge network. The utterance with the best score is chosen as the sentence and displayed at the bottom of the waveform. In the rest of this section we will briefly described each of these steps in the recognition process using the example in Fig. 15-8.

15-5.1 Digitization

All the experiments using the Harpy system were conducted in a computer terminal room environment (approx. 65 dbA) using an Electrovoice head-mounted close speaking microphone (model no. RE51). The signal was low pass filtered at 4.5 KHz using a Kronhite (model no. 3750R) and sampled at 10 KHz sampling rate. The time sharing operating system was modified to accept high data rate signal without any data loss. Utterance begining and end detection was done using amplitude and zero-crossing measurements of the signal (Gill, et al. 1978). The digitized waveform is displayed as in Fig. 15-8. Note that the second line of the waveform is a continuation of the first and the third is a continuation of the second.

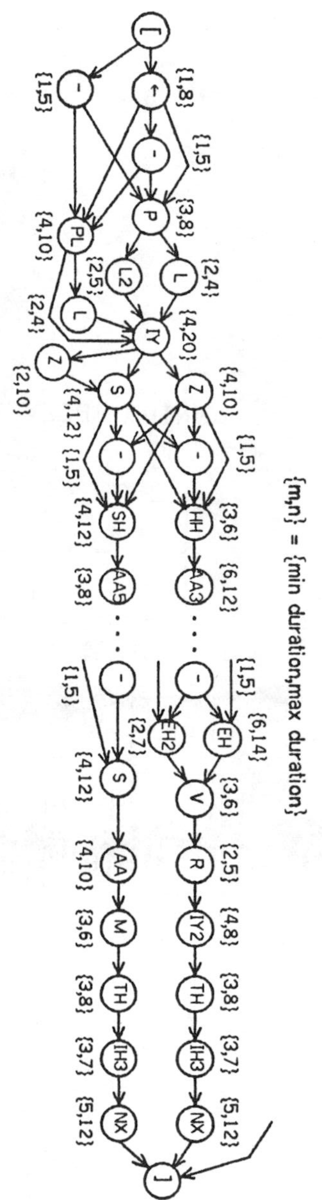

Figure 15-6. Network after replacing all words with phone subnetworks (part of network not shown).

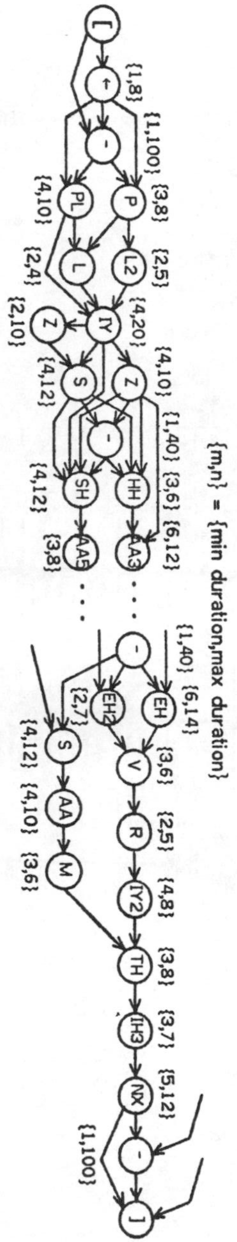

Figure 15-7. Network after removal of redundant paths, application of juncture rules and addition of optional silence before final state (part of network not shown).

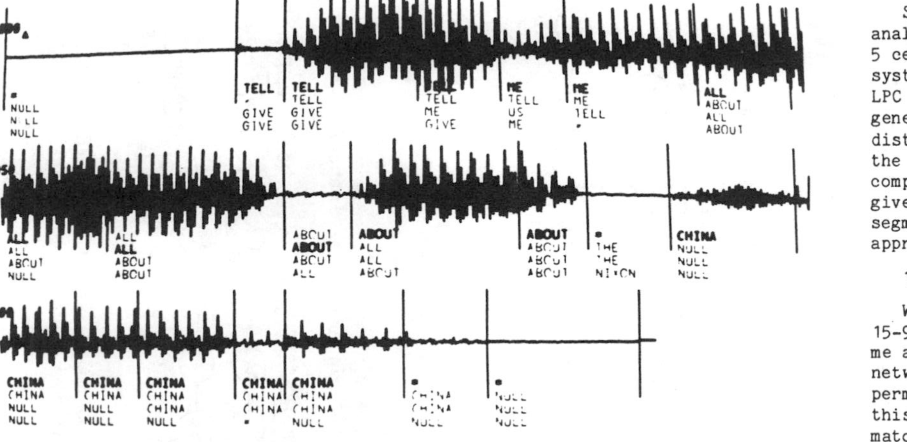
I heard "TELL ME ALL ABOUT CHINA"

Figure 15-8. A graphical trace of the recognition process.

15-5.2 Segmentation

The continuous speech signal is segmented into discrete components using ZAPDASH (zerocrossings and peaks in smoothed and differenced waveforms) parameters. The segmentation process is described in detail by Gill et al., (1978). A recursive top down segmentation procedure is used to identify segments based on features such as silence, voicing, frication, peak detection and dip detection. Figure 15-8 shows a typical segmentation achieved by the system. Note that segmentation boundaries are marked by vertical bars. Note that vowels are usually divided into two or more segments. There is one missing segment boundary at the juncture of the words all and about. The l-schwa boundary is missing. But given the constraints of the language the system recovers from this error.

15-5.3 Phone Template Matching

Spectral characteristics of each segment are determined by using LPC analysis at the midpoint of the segment. The average segment length is about 5 centi-seconds, resulting in a factor 5 improvement in signal analysis over systems which perform LPC analysis each centi-second. For each segment the LPC coefficients of the segments are matched with speaker dependent templates generated using the procedure described in Sec. 15-4.4. The LPC minimum distance residual metric is based on Itakura (1975). In certain versions of the Harpy system only templates which are permissable in that context are computed. Note that implicit within this discussion is the assumption that given enough allophone templates it is reasonable to attempt labeling of segments using pattern matching techniques. This was by no means an accepted approach to phone labeling until recently.

15-5.4 Recognition and Match

We will illustrate the steps in matching and search process using Fig. 15-9. Figure 15-9a is part of a knowledge network in which the sentence "Tell me all about China." is legal. Only the first few states of the knowledge network are shown. Note that given this network, only four phone labels are permissible in the sentence initial position, namely IH2, G, -, and T. Given this information, the phone template matching procedure only performs these matches. The values of the acoustic match distance are given on the right side of the boxes in Fig. 15-9b. Note that the silence phone /-/ has the smallest distance of 0.23 for the first segment, /T/ has distance of 1.46, /g/ a distance of 1.57, and /IH2/ has a distance of 2.26. Since these are the only legal phones for this position, none of the other phone distances are evaluated.

As the acoustic matches are generated, Harpy begins the recognition process. The goal of the recognition task is to find an optimal sequence of phones satisfying two criteria. The sequence must represent a legal path through the knowledge network and should consist of phones with high acoustic match probabilities (the actual calculation produces "- log probability").

The beam search technique used by the Harpy system is a heuristic search technique which locates a near-optimal sequence of phones that is consistent with the network. Beam search is a technique in which a group of near-miss alternatives around the best path are examined. By searching many alternatives simultaneously, this method avoids the need for backtracking. The search is executed by creating and examining a tree structure of phones whose connections are consistent with transitions in the knowledge net. Each ply (or column) in the recognition tree, given in Fig. 15-9b, represents the matching associated with one segment of the digitized utterance.

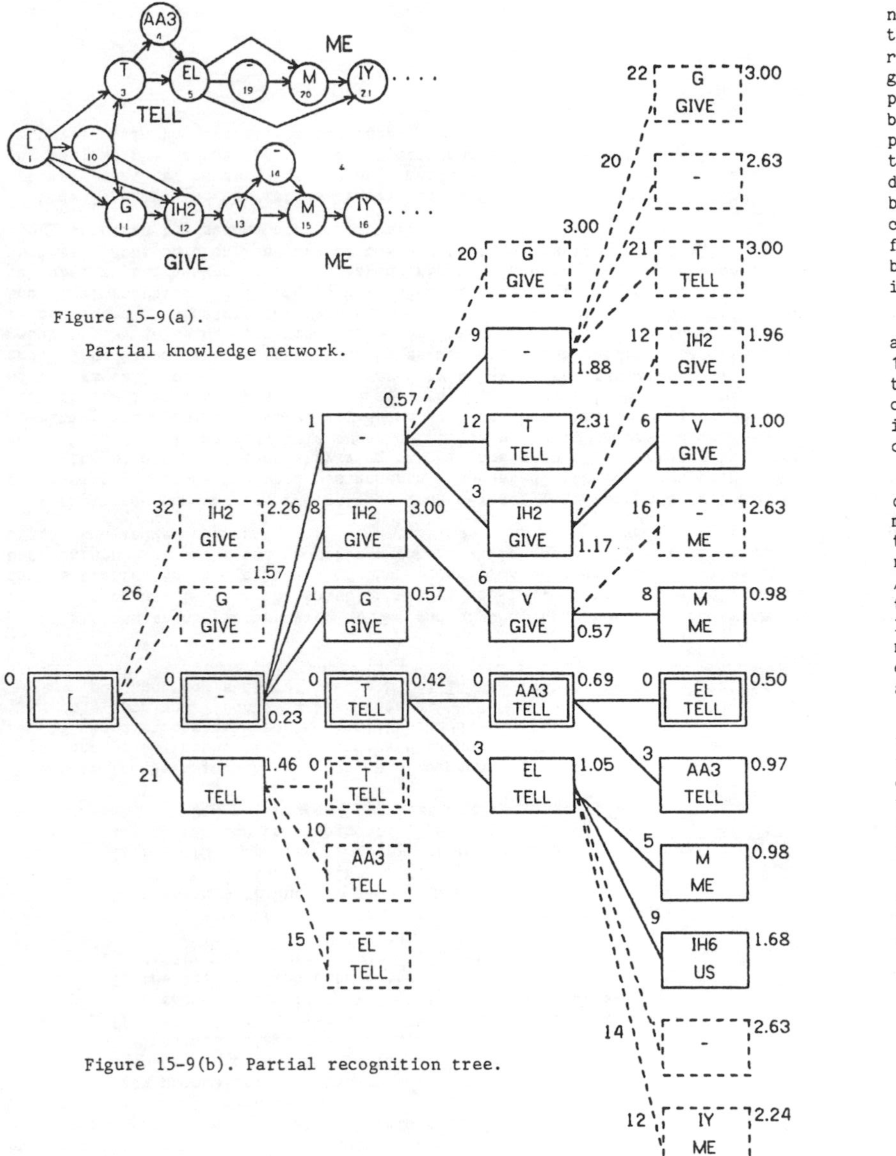

Figure 15-9(a).

Partial knowledge network.

Figure 15-9(b). Partial recognition tree.

Figure 15-9. Recognition process using beam search.

The root node of the tree is the sentence beginning state "[" of the network in Fig. 15-9a. Harpy begins the search by taking all the legal phones that can follow from the sentence initial state and entering them in the recognition tree. Refering to Fig. 15-9b, each box in the second ply (column) gives phone and the word associated with candidate state. Next, a path probability is calculated for each candidate. This is a cumulative value based on the path probability of the previous node and the acoustic match probability of the current node. The path probability value is indicated on the left side of each box. The path with the best probability (boxes with double lines in Fig. 15-9b) is determined. In this case the "-" state has the best value. All the remaining candidates are then compared with it. Those candidates that fall below a threshold of acceptability are pruned from further searching. In Fig. 15-9b the pruned states are indicated by dotted boxes. The successors of each surviving candidate are expanded, based on the information in the knowledge network.

As can be seen from Fig. 15-9a, there are four successors to the /-/ state and three successors to the /t/ state. Note that, although not shown in Fig. 15-9a as a specific pointer, each state can transition to itself. This permits two or more segments to be matched to the same state. Thus, the segmentation can introduce extra segment markers without significant penalty while a missing segment causes problems. Therefore, potential missing states must be created as optional states during the network creation time.

When the successor states are copied onto the recognition tree as candidates for match with the next segment in the segment list, two or more states may generate the same successor. Instead of retaining two independent paths through the same node, we can collapse them into a common path, avoiding redundant computation. In Fig. 15-9b both the /-/ and the /t/ states generate /t/ as a successor. Only the path with the highest prior value is relevant at this point. The deleted path is indicated by a double broken-line box. Thus, lesser-valued paths can be discarded because their path probabilities can never exceed the one with the highest value. The path probabilities are calculated as before, the best path is established and unpromising alternatives are pruned.

The forward search continues, expanding the recognition tree and saving those connections that satisfy the threshold, until we reach the end of the utterance. It was not possible to show the entire tree. Figure 15-9b shows only a portion of the recognition tree, i.e., up to the fourth segment of the waveform shown in Fig. 15-8. Returning to Figure 15-8, we see under each segment the words associated with the best four states in the candidate list for that segment.

So far we have explained the beam search technique informally by means of an example. The following algorithmic description of the search process provides a more formal and precise definition of the search and matching process.

```
Start:
Put the initial state in the list of previous states:
Repeat the following for each segment:
  For each state A in the list of previous states:
      Take A out of the list
      For each successor B of state A:
          Compute the cumulative loglikelihood P of
              transitioning from A to B as:
          P(A →B) = P associated with A + acoustic match between the
               phoneme associated with B and the current segment
          If the list of candidate paths contains a path X→ B
             If P(A→B) is greater than P(X→B)
                replace X→ B and P(X→B) with A→B
                   and P(A →B) in the list of candidate paths
          Else store A →B and P(A →B) in the list of
                 candidate paths
          If P(A →B) is better than any other loglikelihood computed
              so far for this segment:
                 P(A →B) becomes the best loglikelihood P(best)

  Compute the beamwidth E as function of segment duration
  For each path in the list of candidate paths:
    If the distance between the loglikelihood associated with
      the path and P(best) is less than E:
        put the "to" state of the path (B) in the list of previous states.
```

Of all the paths that survive at the end of the utterance, the one with the best path probability is the solution we are seeking. This is the only path that satisfies the two criteria of the recognition process. It provides the best interpretation of the acoustic matches, while satisfying the constraint of the knowledge network.

A backtrace through the recognition tree reveals the desired solution indicating the phone and word assignments associated with the best path. Since the pointers for each surviving path in the beam of the recognition tree are retained till the end, this turns out to be a straight forward look-up operation and does not involve any search. Note that what appears to be the best choice for each segment in the forward search may not, in fact, be part of the globally best sequence discovered by delaying the decision till the end. Thus, local errors introduced by segmentation and acoustic matches are recovered by delaying commitment to a particular path until the forward search is completed. Therefore the forward search may be errorful without affecting the final solution. Refering to Fig. 15-8 again, the final word choice selected by the backtrace is indicated brighter than the rest of the candidate choices. Note that on line two of the waveform the assignment of <u>all</u> and <u>about</u> involves the second best choices.

Occasionally, the heuristics associated with the beam search miss the optimal path, but because the acoustic matches are less than perfect, attempting to find the optimal path at great cost and effort leads to little or no improvement in the overall performance.

15-6. PERFORMANCE

In this section we will present a summary of the Harpy system performance for several tasks. A more detailed description of these results is given in Reddy et al., (1976). Table 15-1 summarizes some of the interesting results from these experiments. The first four tasks essentially have no syntactic or other higher level knowledge. The rest of the tasks use some form of syntactic and other task-dependent information.

Table 15-1 contains several relevant dimensions for each task. Each task was tested with several speakers, as shown in column 2. The pair of numbers in parentheses indicates the number of male and female speakers in each group. Column 3, 4, and 5 are indicative of the measure of complexity of each task. Size of the vocabulary is usually quoted as a measure of complexity. This is usually acceptable for languages which do not use syntactic or other task dependent constraints. The average branching factor is a measure of lexical fanout (Reddy, et al., 1977 pg. 41) allowed by the grammar. The branching factor based on entropy (2 ↑ entropy) of the language has been used by Cohen and Mercer (1975) and Goodman (1976). The IBM group uses the term "perplexity" to refer to this measure. The last two columns give performance of the Harpy system on these tasks: word error rate and millions of instructions executed per second of speech.

<u>Effect of telephone</u>: We conducted an experiment to evaluate the effect of telephone input on Harpy performance. We note from Table 15-1 (task 2) that using telephone speech increases the word error rate by a factor of 3 to 4.

<u>Effect of speaker</u>: Task 3 in Table 15-1 shows the effect of using speaker independent phone templates. Again, we see that there is a significant increase in error rate. Rabiner and Sambur (Rabiner, 1976) state that they get about 4% word error using a speaker independent recognition system. The IBM group (Bahl, 1978) reports less than 1% word error rate using speaker dependent training in a quiet environment.

<u>Effect of vocabulary</u>: The principal effect of the vocabulary size appears to be to increase the space required. It appears to have very little effect on the accuracy or speed of the system.

<u>Effect of branching factor</u>: Clearly, increase in branching factor increases the error rate and processing required. Different groups seem to prefer different measures. The IBM group (Bahl, 1978) claims that the performance of their system correlates highly with the entropy based perplexity measure. The Harpy system does not exhibit any such clear correlation. Both the digits task (perplexity 10) and the 1011 word abstract retrieval task (perplexity 5) both have the same error rate. Further, the retrieval task with a perplexity of 5, is 8 times slower than the digits task with higher "perplexity". Further, Harpy has a better error rate of only 12% with the spelling task (perplexity 26) while the IBM group reports an error rate of 30% using a task with a perplexity of 20. Independent of what measure is best to use, Harpy clearly demonstrates that it is possible to have high performance connected speech input for task-oriented constrained languages.

	No of Speakers	Vocab. Size	Average Branching Factor	Entropy based B.F., "Perplexity"	Word* Error rate (%)	MIPS* required to process a second of speech
Connected digits -Speaker dependent	10 (7+3)	10	10	10	2	3.5
Connected digits -Telephone	4 (3+1)	10	10	10	7	3.5
Connected digits -Speaker independent templates	20 (14+6)	10	10	10	7	3.5
Alphabet -Spelling task	2 (2+0)	26	26	26	12	5.2
Abstract retrieval	5 (3+2)	1001	33	5	2	28

Table 15-1

*Results as of September 1976

15-7. DISCUSSION

There are several important factors that contributed to the success the Harpy system. Foremost among them are the representation of knowledge and the beam search technique. Several speech related decisions that led to improved performance were: use of large number of allophone templates, dynamic adaptation of template characteristics for a new speaker, the decision to encode intra-word phonological phenomeme into the pronunciation dictionary, lpc analysis, Itakura metric, and so on. Several questions arise about the generality and extendability of Harpy-like systems. We will raise some of these and present our current views on these topics.

1. Doesn't finite state grammar restriction make Harpy useless for use with natural language? From a computational point of view the answer appears to be "No". If one is willing to place a restriction on the length of sentence then the language can be modeled using finite state graph (FSG) representation. A simple FSG where any word can follow any other word, would accept all legal sentences but would permit many more illegal sentences as well. However, one need not take such a drastic step. As we observed in Sec. 15-5, if one is willing to accept some loss of constraints, the language can be represented by a suitable FSG which covers the language.

2. Doesn't FSG representation require a large amount of memory for complex tasks? The answer is "Yes" but given the advances in computer technology it doesn't matter. A graph structure that attempts to capture every possible variation requires a great deal of memory. Our current estimate is that a complex language may require a few million states (the 1011 word task has about 15,000) and that semiconductor memories capable of holding such state information would be available for a few hundred dollars. We have also been studying issues of paging knowledge networks from secondary memory and the possibility of using multi-level networks rather than a single integrated network. Multi-level networks require a greater degree of dynamic interpretation during execution. Both of these appear technically feasible. It will be purely a question of space-time-cost trade-off in system organization.

3. How can Harpy handle sentences that are not part of its grammar? In general it cannot, but neither can any other system or human. To be able to handle new words and new sentence constructs that are not part of one's vocabulary and language one needs a knowledge acquisition facility. We have been developing concepts that would permit Harpy-like systems to acquire new words and new constructs. This requires an ability for the system to recognize that the unknown utterance is inconsistent with its internal knowledge and activate partial matching and word spotting type networks which are substantially less constrained. If all the words are known but they are ungrammtical (as in "sleep roses dangerously young colorless"), the sentence construct, if desired, can be assimilated into the word network. If one or more words are unknown then one needs a "speak and spell" program to learn the new words or variations of existing words.

In conclusion, we see that there are many possible avenues for evolving Harpy-like systems. It appears that many of the present limitations of the system can be removed without losing the high performance aspects of the system. However, these changes are likely to take many years to come given the limited research activity in the area.

15-8. ACKNOWLEDGEMENTS

The research reported here was supported by the Defense Advanced Research Projects Agency and monitored by the Airforce Office of Scientific Research under contract number F44620-73-C-0074.

We would like to thank Gary Goodman and Ron Cole for their helpful comments on this manuscript and John Zsarnay for his help in generating the illustrations.

15-9. REFERENCES

Atal, B.S., & S.L. Hanauer, "Speech analysis & synthesis by linear prediction of the speech wave", J. Acoust. Soc. Amer. vol 50, no 2, 1971.

Bahl, et al., "Automatic recognition of continuously spoken sentences from a finite state grammar", in Proc. IEEE-ICASSP Conf. 1978, Tulsa, Okla.

Baker, J.K., "The DRAGON system - An overview", IEEE Trans. ASSP, vol 23, 1975.

Baker, J.K., "Stochastic modeling for automatic speech understanding", in Speech Recognition: Invited Papers of the IEEE Symp., D.R. Reddy (ed.), 1975.

Cohen, P.S., & R.L. Mercer, "The Phonological component of an automatic speech recognition system", in Speech Recognition: Invited Papers of the IEEE Symp., D.R. Reddy(ed.), 1975.

Erman, L.D. & V.R. Lesser, "A multi-level organization for problem solving using many, diverse cooperating sources of knowledge", in Proc. 4th IJCAI, 1975, Tbilisi, USSR.

Erman, L.D., "The Hearsay-II speech understanding system", ch.16 this volume.

Gill, G.S. et al., "A recursive segmentation procedure for continuous speech", tech. rep., Computer Science Dept., Carnegie-Mellon U., 1978.

Goodman, G., "Analysis of Languages for man-machine voice communication", tech. rep., Computer Science Dept., Carnegie-Mellon U., 1976.

Itakura F., & S. Saito, "Analysis synthesis telephony based on the maximum likelihood method", Proc. 6th Int. Congr. Acoustics, 1968.

Itakura, F., "Minimum prediction residual principle applied to speech recognition", IEEE Trans. ASSP, vol 23, 1975.

Klatt, D.H., "Review of the ARPA Speech Understanding Project", .J. Acoust. Soc. Amer. vol 62, no 6, 1977.

Lea, W.A., "Speech Recognition: Past, Present, Future", ch. 4 this volume.

Lowerre, B., "The Harpy speech recognition systems", Ph.D. dissertation, Computer Science Dept., Carnegie-Mellon U., 1977.

Markel, J.D., "Digital inverse filtering - A new tool for formant trajectory estimation", IEEE Trans. Audio Electroacoust., vol AU-20, 1972.

Newell, A. et al., Speech Understanding Systems: Final Report of a Study Group, 1971. (Reprinted by North-Holland/American Elsevier, Amsterdam, Netherlands, 1973).

Oshika, B.T. et al., "The role of phonological rules in speech understanding research", IEEE Trans. ASSP, vol 23, 1975.

Rabiner, L.R., "Preliminary results in recognition of connected digits", IEEE Trans. Acoust., Speech, Signal Processing, April 1976.

Reddy, D.R., "Computer recognition of connected speech", J. Acoust. Soc. Amer. vol 42, 1967.

Reddy. D.R., et al., "The Hearsay speech understanding system: an example of the recognition process", Proc. IJCAI-73, 1973, Stanford, CA.

Reddy, D.R., "Speech recognition by machine: A review", Proc. of the IEEE (Apr. 1976).

Reddy, D.R., et al., "Speech Understanding Systems: summary of results of the five-year research effort at CMU", Computer Science Dept., Carnegie-Mellon U., 1977.

Tappert, C.C., et al., "The use of dynamic segments in the automatic recognition of continuous speech", tech. rep., RADC-TR-70-22, IBM, Systems Development Div. Research, Triangle Park, N.C., 1970.

The Development of an Experimental Discrete Dictation Recognizer

FREDERICK JELINEK, FELLOW, IEEE

Invited Paper

This paper describes an experimental real-time recognizer of isolated word dictation implemented at the IBM Thomas J. Watson Research Center, on a system of commercially available computers and array processors. The recognizer's intended use is creation of office memoranda. It is based on a 5000-word vocabulary. A specially designed workstation enables the user to correct and edit the transcribed speech.

The paper outlines the self-organized, statistical approach underlying the basic algorithms of the recognizer. Results of several recognition experiments are then presented. The rest of the paper considers important issues in the future development of dictation recognizers, such as vocabulary selection, language model creation, and human factors.

I. Introduction

Since 1972 the Continuous Speech Recognition Group of IBM has been working on large-vocabulary speech recognition [1], [2]. In 1981 we decided to develop a real-time recognizer capable of handling dictation of office correspondence. The algorithms known to us at that time could not provide for real-time recognition of continuous speech on any feasible combination of commercially available processors, and it seemed prudent not to rely on self-implemented hardware. Thus we limited the proposed system to isolated word input. Preliminary simulation experiments [3], [4] suggested that discrete dictation with immediate text display would be a more productive text-creation mode than either handwriting or dictation on a standard recording machine, and that users preferred discrete input with large vocabularies to continuous input with small vocabularies. We expected that experience with the recognizer would provide valuable information about human factors of speech recognition.

In June 1984 we completed a real-time discrete dictation recognizer with a workstation that allows speech or keyboard editing of text (e.g., correction, insertion, etc.) which appears on a screen. The recognizer uses only algorithms also applicable to continuous speech recognition.

Our recognizer runs on the Speech Development System, consisting of an IBM 4341 host machine and three Floating Point Systems 190L array processors, to which a workstation based on an Apollo DN-400 computer is attached. The speech signal is picked up by a Crown PZM-6S pressure-zone microphone placed freely on the desk. A mouse is used for pointing. The system is diagrammed in Fig. 1. Fig. 2 depicts the workstation, the microphone is above the mouse on the right.

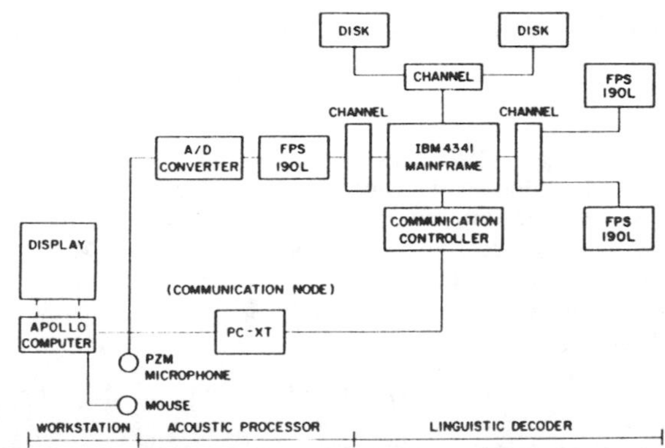

Fig. 1. Schematic of the hardware components of the Speech Development System.

Fig. 2. The Speech Development System workstation. The microphone is on the right of the screen.

Manuscript received March 6, 1985; revised April 1, 1985.

The author is with the Continuous Speech Recognition Group, IBM Thomas J. Watson Research Center, Yorktown Heights, NY 10598, USA.

0018-9219/85/1100-1616$01.00 ©1985 IEEE

The vocabulary is limited to 5000 words and a spelling mode facilitates input of the complete text by speech. The system operates in a quiet office environment. A speech training sample 20 min long is required to adjust the recognizer to a new user. It is capable of keeping up with an average discrete speech rate of 90 words a minute, but a variable delay of about 3 words exists between the time a word is spoken and displayed on the screen, allowing the use of bidirectional context by the recognizer.

The next section is devoted to an overview of our approach to speech recognition. A more precise formulation was given elsewhere [1], [2]. In Section III we give results of experiments with our system. Section IV addresses the problems of vocabulary selection and personalization. Section V deals with achievement of better language models and measurement of their quality. Section VI concludes the paper with a discussion of desirable characteristics of practical recognizers for text creation and of our plans to achieve them.

II. A Statistical Approach to Speech Recognition

We will now outline our approach to speech recognition. Let

$$W = w_1, w_2, \cdots, w_n \tag{2.1}$$

denote a string of n words, and let A denote the acoustic evidence (data) on the basis of which the recognizer will make its decision about which words were spoken. If $P(W/A)$ denotes the probability that the words W were spoken given that the evidence A was observed, our recognizer is designed to decide in favor of a word string $\hat{W}$ satisfying

$$P(\hat{W}/A) = \max_{W} P(W/A). \tag{2.2}$$

Decision criterion (2.2) is natural and generally acceptable. For a language whose spelling system is roughly phonetic, a dictation recognizer based on (2.2) will tend to minimize the number of corrections necessary to obtain the spoken text.

Application of Bayes' formula

$$P(W/A) = \frac{P(W)P(A/W)}{P(A)} \tag{2.3}$$

to the criterion (2.2) reveals the different research areas of speech recognition.

We must first determine the nature of the acoustic evidence A on which the recognizer's decision will be based. The transformation of the speech signal into the evidence A is called *acoustic processing*. In our recognizer (see Fig. 3), the acoustic signal is synchronously transformed by the

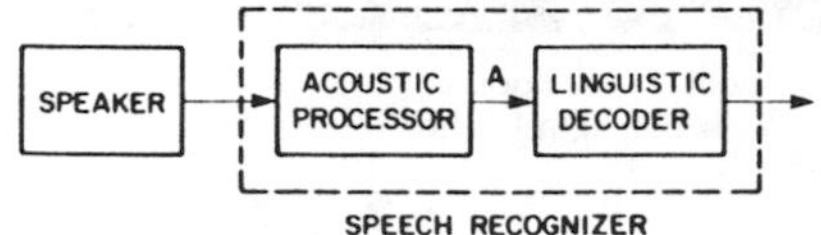

Fig. 3. The speech recognition system.

Acoustic Processor into a sequence of labels $A = a_1, a_2, \cdots$ from an alphabet $\mathcal{A}$ of size 200. Fig. 4 shows the acoustic processor schematically. Every 10 ms, the signal processor extracts a vector of 20 parameters from a 20-ms window of the speech input. This vector is compared to a set of 200 pre-stored prototype vectors and the label of the prototype that is closest to the parameter vector is put out [1], [2]. The design of our signal processor is based on current knowledge of the performance of the human ear [5]. The 200 prototypes are selected essentially by the method of vector quantization [6], [7]. The signal processor output parameter vectors corresponding to a 5-min long speech training sample are collected. Considered as points in a 20-dimensional space, they are partitioned into 200 clusters. The cluster centers become the stored prototypes which in our system are specific to each speaker.

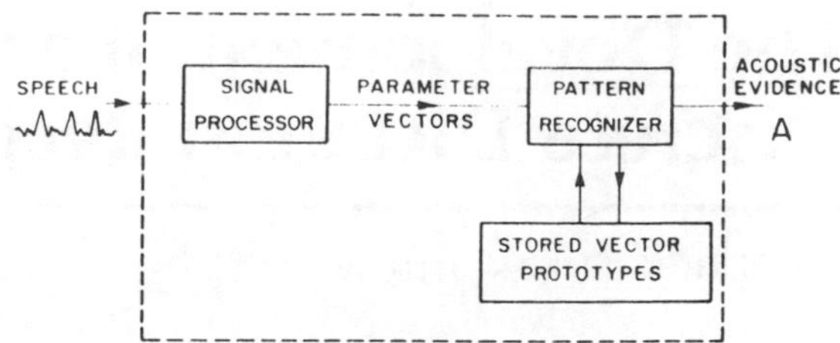

Fig. 4. The acoustic processor.

Returning to (2.3), it is next necessary to create an *acoustic model* describing statistically the interaction between the speaker and the acoustic processor. The acoustic model allows us to compute the probability $P(A/W)$ that the acoustic processor will put out the label string A if the speaker says the word sequence W. In our system, the acoustic model is built up out of models of pronunciation of phonetic symbols. In brief, the model for a word string W consists of a concatenation of models of the individual words w_i, and these in turn are made up of a concatenation of models of the phonetic symbols defining the basic word pronunciations.

To each word w of the vocabulary $\mathcal{W}$ there corresponds a baseform $B(w) = b_1, \cdots, b_k$ consisting of a string of symbols b_i from a phonetic alphabet $\mathcal{B}$. The baseform models the basic pronunciation of the word w.[1] To each symbol b of $\mathcal{B}$ there corresponds a Markov source (hidden Markov chain) [1], [2], [8] which is an abstract model of the response of the acoustic processor to the act of "pronouncing" the phonetic symbol b. The transitions between states are labeled by letters of the alphabet $\mathcal{A}$ (Fig. 5). As the source changes state, it outputs the label attached to the transition it takes. The acoustic model of any word w of the vocabulary $\mathcal{W}$ is obtained by concatenating the Markov sources corresponding to the symbols of the baseform $B(w)$ of the

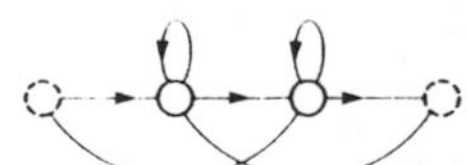

Fig. 5. Structure of a Markov model of acoustic label generation resulting from "pronunciation" of phonetic symbols. Each solid arc represents 200 labeled transitions, one for each letter of the output alphabet $\mathcal{A}$. The transition probabilities are estimated during the training process and differ for different phonetic symbols.

[1] The phonetic alphabet $\mathcal{B}$ contains several symbols corresponding to various modes of silence and so in isolated word dictation the baseforms both start and end with substrings of these silence symbols.

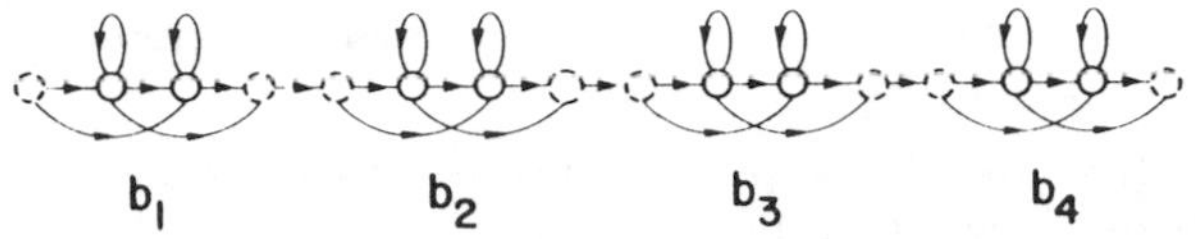

b1 b2 b3 b4

Fig. 6. Markov model of a word whose baseform is b_1, b_2, b_3, b_4.

word (see Fig. 6). The probability $P(A/W)$ is then computed as follows: A composite Markov source for the string W is obtained by concatenating the Markov sources corresponding to the n words of $W = w_1, \cdots, w_n$. $P(A/W)$ is the probability that the composite source will produce the string A when it is placed in its initial state and left running until it reaches the final state.[2]

The various Markov sources (Fig. 5) corresponding to the phonetic symbols b of the alphabet $\mathcal{B}$ are characterized by the different probabilities with which these sources take various transitions labeled by the letters a of the alphabet $\mathcal{A}$. While the baseforms $B(w)$ used by our recognizer are speaker independent (although intended for the standard American dialect), the transition probabilities of sources are specific to the speaker. They are estimated by the Forward–Backward algorithm [1], [2], [9] from data A generated by the speaker's reading a prescribed text of 100 sentences, resulting in a 20-min speech sample.

Next, in order to use (2.3) it is necessary to construct a *language model* computing the probability $P(W)$ that the speaker will wish to say the word string W. Now

$$P(W) = \prod_{i=1}^{n} P(w_i/w_{i-1}, \cdots, w_1). \tag{2.4}$$

But the probability values $P(w_i/w_{i-1}, \cdots, w_1)$ cannot in reality depend on the full apparent set of i parameters, since the number of these values N^i for even a moderate vocabulary size N would be too large to be estimated, stored, or retrieved. Hence the various possible conditioning histories $w_1, \cdots, w_{i-1}$ must be partitioned into a manageable number of equivalence classes. The classification would most fruitfully be based on syntactic and semantic information. The selection of the exact classification scheme, and its use in determining the probability values from a large amount of text, is an unsolved problem that will claim increasing attention of researchers.

In our system, all histories ending in the same two words w_{i-2}, w_{i-1} are considered equivalent, so that the factors $P(w_i/w_{i-1}, \cdots, w_1)$ of (2.4) are defined equal to $P(w_i/w_{i-1}, w_{i-2})$. Unfortunately, these probabilities cannot be approximated directly by relative frequencies obtained by counting trigrams occurring in some large text, since the vast majority of possible English word trigrams will not take place even in very large databases. In fact, the number of different trigrams of a 5000-word vocabulary is 1.25×10^{11}, which is far bigger than any conceivable database.

Our current method of estimating the required probabilities was worked out by S. Katz [10], based on Good's elaboration [11] of an argument by Turing. We present here a rudimentary version that contains the main idea. We first develop an estimate of probabilities $P(w_2/w_1)$ and then use it to compute $P(w_3/w_2, w_1)$.

[2]A computationally efficient algorithm for computing $P(A/W)$ was given by Bahl and Jelinek [28].

Consider two samples of text generated by the same source. Referring to the first sample, let N be the total number of bigrams, let $N(w_1, w_2)$ be the number of times the words w_1, w_2 occur adjacent to each other, and let $N(w_1)$ be the number of times w_1 takes place. Finally, let r be the number of different pairs that occur exactly once (i.e., such that $N(w_1, w_2) = 1$). Turing argues that r/N is a good estimate of the probability that a random pair of words selected from the second sample will be one never seen in the first. Then it is reasonable to estimate the required conditional probability by the formula

$$P(w_2/w_1) = \begin{cases} \left(1 - \dfrac{r}{N}\right) \times \dfrac{N(w_1, w_2)}{N(w_1)}, & \text{if } N(w_1, w_2) > 0 \\ \left(\dfrac{r}{N}\right) \times \dfrac{N(w_2)}{K_2(w_1)}, & \text{otherwise} \end{cases} \tag{2.5a}$$

where $K_2(w_1)$ is a normalizing factor that assures that the probabilities estimated by (2.5a) add up to 1 when summed over all the words w_2. The method is referred to as one of "backing off" from bigram to unigram estimation when bigram data are not available.

Let s be the number of trigrams w_1, w_2, w_3 occurring exactly once in the training text. Then application of backing off approach leads straightforwardly to the formula

$$P(w_3/w_2, w_1) = \begin{cases} \left(1 - \dfrac{s}{N}\right) \times \dfrac{N(w_1, w_2, w_3)}{N(w_1, w_2)}, & \text{if } N(w_1, w_2, w_3) > 0 \\ \left(\dfrac{s}{N}\right) \times \dfrac{P(w_3/w_2)}{K_3(w_2)}, & \text{otherwise} \end{cases} \tag{2.5b}$$

where $P(w_3/w_2)$ is computed by (2.5a) and $K_3(w_1, w_2)$ is a normalizing factor.

The backing off formulas of Katz [10] are more subtle than those of (2.5), but they too depend on the frequencies of word trigrams, bigrams, and unigrams, computed from a very large (25 million words) office correspondence text. Section V examines additional aspects of language modeling.

Our system actually uses two language models. In addition to the one described above, another smaller one exists to support spelling recognition. It has the form (2.5), but its "words" belong to a vocabulary of size 76 consisting of letters, digits, punctuation marks, and nine control words. Its basic relative frequencies were estimated from a sample of 5 million characters of office text.

So far, the discussion of the recognizer components has taken care of the numerator of (2.3). Since the denominator is not a function of W, it need not be evaluated to find the maximizing sequence $\hat{W}$ satisfying (2.2). So the remaining problem is that of *hypothesis search* for $\hat{W}$. From the combinatorics involved, it is clear that this search cannot be exhaustive even for a very moderate vocabulary size N and sequence length n. It is necessary to severely limit the search to only a very small fraction of the N^n possible word strings W.

A method that is successful is an adaptation of stack sequential decoding studied extensively by Information Theory [12]. We have described it elsewhere [1], [2]; here we just outline it. The hypothesis tree appropriate to the search has a root node from which stem N branches, one for each word in the vocabulary. From each branch there stem N more branches, etc. The problem of speech recognition can be thought of as one of finding a complete tree path (that corresponds to one definite string of words W) that is most probable given the acoustic evidence A (see (2.2)). The idea is to conduct a left to right search of the acoustic evidence A, comparing it to various subpaths (of different length) of the word hypothesis tree. The search is efficient if relatively few paths are examined.

Let $L(W)$ be an evaluation function of the path corresponding to the word string W that depends appropriately on $P(W)$ and $P(A/W)$. Assume that L has the property that if $L(W) > L(W')$ then W is more likely than W' to be the beginning of the spoken word sequence resulting in A, regardless of the relative lengths of W and W'. Such a function is described in a previous paper [2]. A good search strategy is as follows:

1) Arrange words w of the vocabulary $\mathscr{W}$ in decreasing order of $L(w)$, creating a stack.

2) Let W^* be the path on top. Remove it and insert into the stack its extensions $W' = [W^*, w]$ for all vocabulary words w, keeping the stack ordered by the values $L(W)$.

3) If the last word of the path W^* on top of the stack corresponds to an end of sentence marker, and if W^* accounts for the complete evidence A, decide that W^* was the sentence spoken. Else go to step 2).

The algorithm above can serve as a basis for a practical search procedure because the function L has the property that the value $L(W')$ is a simple update of $L(W^*)$ that depends essentially only on w and on that portion of acoustics A corresponding to w.

As it stands in step 2), the algorithm requires the evaluation of L, called *the detailed match*, for N different extensions W' of W^*. For large vocabularies this represents too much work. Thus the list of extensions of W^* must be reduced further. One way to do that is to split the acoustics A into the front part A^* accounted for by W^*, and the remaining tail part $\mathcal{A}'$, and then to confine the detailed match to a small subset of words w that could possibly account for the beginning of the tail $\mathcal{A}'$. The determination of the subset is called *the fast match*, and many techniques are possible.

In one method of fast match the vocabulary is pre-clustered into subsets of acoustically similar words [13]. Each subset is associated with a word "centroid." During recognition the data tail $\mathcal{A}'$ is matched against the centroids. The word extension list for W^* is made up of subsets having centroids whose match exceeds a pre-determined threshold.

Another option is to first carry out the match $P(\mathcal{A}'/w)$ over all words w of the vocabulary, but in an approximate, fast manner [14]. The extension list is then made up only of those words whose approximate match exceeds a threshold.

The processor configuration of the recognition system of Fig. 1 mirrors the research categories discussed in this section. The array processor on the left (connected to the microphone) is devoted to acoustic processing, the remaining two array processors carry out the detailed and fast matches, and the host IBM 4341 system computes the language model probabilities, conducts the hypothesis search, and communicates the recognition results to the workstation.

III. The Performance of the Yorktown Dictation Recognizer [15]

The experiments described here tested the recognizer under three conditions:

1) prerecorded speech
2) speech read in real time
3) speech produced spontaneously in real time.

A total of five speakers, including one female, were represented.

Each speaker trained the system by reading 100 sentences containing 1107 words (about 20 min of speech). Next, in the same recording session, the speaker read 50 test sentences containing roughly 591 words, which we call the "prerecorded speech." Both training and test sentences were chosen from our database of office correspondence (the test sentences, however, were kept separate from the data used to estimate language model parameters).

The speech read in real time and the spontaneous speech were collected over the course of 2 months in half-hour dictation sessions. Within each session, the first 20 test sentences (of the 50 mentioned above) were read; this constituted the "read speech." The "spontaneous speech" consisted of actual memos dictated by the speakers, and averaged 150 words per memo. Each time a new topic was chosen by the speaker.

In the next section we discuss how the 5000 words of the system's vocabulary were chosen. The recognition results on words of this vocabulary are shown in Table 1 (words not in the vocabulary have been omitted from the data). As can be seen, performance on prerecorded speech is better than on live speech, and performance on read speech is better than that on spontaneous speech. The performance on prerecorded speech is high because the test and training data were collected during the same session. Performance on spontaneous speech may be lower than that on read speech for a number of reasons. First, the error rate on spontaneous speech reflects not only dictated sentences but also efforts by the speaker to experiment with the system. For example, a speaker might try to correct a recognition error by redictating portions of the memo and the same error is likely to recur. Second, the language model may be doing a poorer job of predicting words in spontaneous speech than for "normal" office correspondence, and, in fact, the perplexity[3] of text dictated spontaneously by our subjects is higher than that of the test data. Also, any word not in the vocabulary places the language

Table 1 Word Error Rate of the Real-Time Recognizer

Speaker	Prerecorded Speech (%)	Read Speech (%)	Spontaneous Speech (%)
JC	2.7	3.1	7.8
BF[1]	3.0	4.3	6.7
MP	1.4	3.3	3.7
SD	2.0	3.8	6.2
LB	1.0	1.0	4.1
Average	2.0	3.1	5.7

[1]Female speaker.

[3]Perplexity is a basic measure of complexity of text relative to the language model used [16], [17]. It is further discussed in Section V.

model automatically in a wrong state for prediction of the next word. Finally, our training method does not reflect the change in speaker acoustic style from read to spontaneous speech.

The system has also been tested on a number of speakers with foreign accents (British English, Persian, Russian, Czech); on average, there were again half as many word errors.

IV. Selection of a Recognition Vocabulary and its Personalization

We define a word by its spelling. Thus two differently spelled inflections of the same stem constitute different words. Different meanings or parts of speech of the same spelling (homographs) constitute the same word. The 5000 words of our vocabulary were selected in two steps. First a basic subvocabulary of size M was constructed, consisting of words whose availability was thought necessary, such as recognizer control words, numbers (e.g. "thousand," "million," etc.), dates (e.g., "Monday," "November," etc.), and the first and last names of some of our colleagues at IBM Research. The remaining $5000 - M$ words of the vocabulary were chosen to be those that have the highest minimal count in three databases (OC1, OC2, and OC3) and do not belong to the subvocabulary. This selection method left out words that have little universal use and are peculiar to a particular database.

We are in possession of three additional databases. The first, PDB, consists of 2 million words of correspondence by a single colleague at the T. J. Watson Research Center. The second, MNG1, contains written memoranda from one of us, from the director of research, and from the chairman of the corporation. The third database MNG2 was created from transcribed spontaneous dictation of memoranda by four Research staff members. Our 5000-word vocabulary covered about 93 percent of words in all three of these text collections. That is, with probability 0.07 a random word selected from any of the texts does not belong to the vocabulary. As a consequence, if no words are spelled, the error rate of our recognizer will exceed 7 percent regardless of how good it is otherwise. Moreover, when a word outside the vocabulary is spoken, the resulting recognition error forces the language model into a wrong state, increasing the probability of an error in the next word.

A substantially better text coverage by the vocabulary is clearly desirable. It must be achieved by a combination of vocabulary size increase and personalization. Inspection of standard references on frequencies of English words [18], [19] clearly indicates that a large fixed size alone will not do the job. In fact, quite familiar words such as "admonition" or "deluded" occupy a position higher than 86 000 in the American Heritage list [19]. And this does not even take into account technical words particular to the individual user's field! On the other hand, it turns out that the total vocabulary of all works of Shakespeare is only 29 000 [20], and the vocabulary of a 1 million-word large varied office text by many authors (database OC1) is 19 000, so the problem is not a hopeless one.

Using the previously described method, R. L. Mercer [21] constructed vocabularies of varying larger sizes. Table 2 shows the PDB coverage when names and acronyms occurring in it have been disregarded. The selection rule for the

Table 2 Static Coverage of the Personal Database PDB as a Function of Vocabulary Size

Vocabulary Size	Text Coverage (%)
5000	92.5
10 000	95.9
15 000	97.0
20 000	97.6

20 000 word vocabulary had to be modified because the OC database contains fewer than that many different words.

Our method of fixed vocabulary construction may be satisfactory if the intended user belongs to some easily identifiable category (e.g., employee of the data processing industry) for which text databases are available. Still, it is hardly acceptable that the recognizer's use would have to be identified before the system could be adequately equipped. The only way out seems to be some more practical method of personalization or a fixed vocabulary of really gigantic size. The latter would have to be synthetic, consisting of inflections and derivations based on a substantially smaller set of building blocks (stems? morphemes?). Henry Kucera estimates that vocabulary compression by a factor of 6 to 10 may be attainable in this way [20].

A crude method of personalization is achieved by maintaining during dictation a dynamically varying vocabulary consisting at any given moment of the last N different words used. The coverage is then defined as the asymptotic probability that the word spoken next already belongs to the vocabulary. Table 3 gives the result for the PDB database [21] when names and abbreviations have been excluded. The second column is the good news (99-percent coverage by a 15 thousand-word vocabulary), while the third is the bad: It takes 613 thousand words of text before a set of 15 thousand different words is assembled. This then is not a practical way of vocabulary personalization, except for the most prolific of writers. It may, however, result in a satisfactory vocabulary for an entire installation site if the text produced by all the resident users is pooled.

Table 3 Dynamic Coverage of the Personal Database PDB as a Function of Vocabulary Size (The last column indicates the amount of text processed before the number of different words contained in it is equal to the vocabulary size.)

Vocabulary Size	Text Coverage (%)	Text Size to Reach Coverage
5000	95.5	56 000
10 000	98.2	240 000
15 000	99.0	640 000
20 000	99.5	1 300 000

There are at least four different ways in which a vocabulary is particular to a speaker. First is the peculiar active vocabulary reflecting his habits of expression, possibly related to his level of education. Next is the general domain of his discourse (e.g., data processing, musicology, medical reports, etc.) containing technical expressions, cliches, and such. Then, there are the names, addresses, and other information that reflects the user's needs. Finally, there is the vocabulary needed for the document at hand. A large, fixed vocabulary can take care of the first category and conceivably of some part of the second as well. The rest must be obtained through active participation by the user.

In the discussion above we have not considered the problem of language modeling. We constructed our trigram language model (see Section III and [1], [2]) using the 25 million word text database OC3. The trigrams from OC3 made up of words in our vocabulary covered 84 percent of correspondingly restricted trigrams in the test databases PDB and MNG1, while the coverage of the same texts by trigrams from the 1 million word database OC1 was only 55 percent.

A trigram language model for a personalized vocabulary cannot be constructed solely from the text created by the user. He will never dictate enough. The only conceivable way is to extract the model from an already stored trigram collection appropriate to a large vocabulary that includes the personalized one. It is obvious that the more the personalized vocabulary of size N differs from the N most frequent words of the training corpus, the less will the trigrams in the dictated text be covered by trigrams collected from the training text. Therefore, a truly gigantic training corpus would have to be used as a basis for a satisfactory dynamic (personalized) language model.[4]

The need for a more general method of language model construction is thus clear. It seems that the trigram idea can be preserved only if it is based on equivalence between words whose statistical properties are similar. For instance, one could envision having 5000 categories g, one for each word in the basic vocabulary for which a trigram model $P(g_3/g_2, g_1)$ was constructed based on a training corpus representative of English. Every word w of the total potential vocabulary would then be classified as belonging to one of the 5000 categories. The probabilities of use of words w in category g, $P(w/g)$, could be estimated. The actual language model for a large or personalized vocabulary would then function using the trigram formula

$$P(w_3/w_2, w_1) = P(w_3/g_3) \times P(g_3/g_2, g_1) \quad (4.1)$$

where g_i, $i = 1, 2, 3$, are the categories to which the words w_i belong.

V. Language Model Perplexity and the Shannon Game

There is, of course, nothing to recommend the trigram language model except its simplicity and ease of construction from training text. Just how good is it? Information theory measures the information content of sources by their *entropy* H [22]. Since in speech recognition the source can be thought of as generating word sequences, then by definition

$$H = -\lim_{N\to\infty} \left(\frac{1}{N}\right) \times \log_2 P(w_1, w_2, \cdots, w_N) \quad (5.1)$$

where N is the size of the sample text generated by the source.

We see from (5.1) that to compute the entropy H one would need to know the actual probabilities $P(w_1, w_2, \cdots, w_N)$ of strings of the language. These probabilities are, in practice, unknowable. At best we can have their estimates $\hat{P}(w_1, w_2, \cdots, w_N)$ which the language model provides to the recognizer. Thus from the point of view of the recognizer, the difficulty of recognition of a given text is measured by its *logprob* (LP)

$$\text{LP} = -\lim_{N\to\infty} \left(\frac{1}{N}\right) \times \log_2 \hat{P}(w_1, w_2, \cdots, w_N). \quad (5.2)$$

It is easy to show [22] that $\text{LP} \geqslant H$, assuming properly ergodic behavior of the text generating source. In the case of the trigram language model

$$\text{LP} = -\lim_{N\to\infty} \left(\frac{1}{N}\right) \times \sum_{i=1}^{N} \log_2 P(w_i/w_{i-1}, w_{i-2}). \quad (5.3)$$

It is intuitively more satisfying to measure the difficulty of a recognition task relative to a given language model by the value of its *perplexity* (PP) defined by [16], [17]

$$\text{PP} = 2^{\text{LP}} \quad (5.4)$$

A basic argument of Information Theory shows that to the first order of approximation (which disregards the acoustic distances between particular words) the task can be thought to be as difficult as would the recognition of a language with PP equally likely words. Thus perplexity gives the correctly computed "branching factor" of the language model.

In practice, any estimation of the perplexity depends on the sample text whose length N is finite. The perplexity of our trigram model when applied to the databases OC1 and MNG2 is 70 and 128, respectively. A different model will approximate $P(w_1, w_2, \cdots, w_N)$ in a different way and will thus lead to a different perplexity that will be lower if the model is better.

Entropy measures the intrinsic difficulty of the task, logprob its difficulty relative to the language model used. The difference between logprob and entropy, if it were known, would indicate the scope of potential language model improvement. Folklore has it that in a famous paper [23] Shannon estimated the entropy of English to be 1 bit per letter, i.e., assuming the average word length to be 5.5 letters, about 5.5 bits per word. Actually, based on a sample text, Shannon provided bounds on logprob of natural language models intrinsic to human subjects. His bounds place logprob between 0.6 and 1.3 bits, and thus perplexity between 10 and 142. We will outline below his method that depends on guessing a text. His results would be valid only if the text they were based on was representative and large enough for his statistical estimates to converge. Representativity of English can never be established, and the test passage Shannon chose was much too short. But given enough perseverance by human subjects, valid results for the narrow genre of office correspondence could be obtained. Also, introspection during guessing may provide clues to the construction of more effective language models.

In the Shannon method, the subject is asked to guess the text, letter by letter (including the space marker between words, punctuation, etc.). He is advised about the correctness of each guess. When he finds the first letter, he starts guessing the second, then the third, etc.... Let r_i be

[4] If we think of the personalized vocabulary as consisting of a common core together with a personal set, the words in the latter will on average be longer and thus acoustically more distinguishable. This may compensate for weak prediction by the language model of words outside the core.

the number of tries it takes to guess the ith letter. Then assuming that given the same state of knowledge the subject would always guess in the same order, the text can be perfectly recovered by the subject from the guess order sequence $r_1, r_2, \cdots, r_i, \cdots$. The sequence is thus a perfect encoding of the text. Hence the logprob of $r_1, r_2, \cdots, r_i, \cdots$ is the same as the logprob of the text. Let $Q(n)$ be the relative frequency with which the number n appears in the order sequence. Then it is easy to show [22] that

$$H^+ = -\sum_n [Q(n) \times \log Q(n)] \quad (5.5)$$

is an upper bound on the logprob of the encoding $r_1, r_2, \cdots, r_i, \cdots$ and therefore on the logprob of the text. If m is the average number of letters per word in the text, then 2^{mH^+} is an upper bound on its perplexity. Shannon also derived a lower bound formula on text logprob. Cover and King later obtained a direct estimate of text logprob by replacing the guesses in Shannon's procedure by bets [24].

Stephen and Vincent Della Pietra have automated the Shannon procedure [23] on a computer [25]. The resulting Shannon game has several additional features. The text is chosen at random from a database. It is possible to have the estimate converge faster by having part of the text revealed from the start. The information contained in n-grams can be measured by selecting at random the word to be guessed and revealing to the subject exactly n preceding words. The subject is also provided with two aids. Consistent with the letters guessed so far, the possible words of the vocabulary are shown together with their probabilities as computed by the trigram language model (given the preceding two words of the text). Another display panel shows the letter probabilities of the guess to be made next, as computed by the language model consistent with the revealed past and the guesses already made for the current letter position. The computer keeps the running H^+ score and compares it to the score that would have been incurred had the subject been guided strictly by the language model.

As already pointed out, our aim in playing the Shannon game is not to estimate the human perplexity of office correspondence, but to discover what manner of information is used by humans in word prediction. We hope that this will help us design the structure of future language models. Even keeping in mind that H^+ is only an upper bound, it is already clear that the trigram language model can be substantially improved. In the Shannon game humans beat the trigram model by factors of 3 or more in perplexity (2^{mH^+}). The advantage of humans seems mostly based on their ability to use relevant information found contained in a text passage that often considerably precedes the currently guessed letters.

VI. Future Aspects of Text Creation by Voice

Gould and Boies [26] "*observed that handwriting was the main method by which principals composed. (They) had the intuitive belief that dictation was potentially a superior method of composition. Dictation is potentially five times faster than writing, on the basis of estimates of maximum writing and speaking rates when composition is not required (see [27]). Dictation may also be qualitatively superior: potentially faster transfer of ideas from limited capacity human working memory to a permanent record may reduce forgetting attributable to interference or decay.*"

Those who could pay for it have been creating text by voice for a long time. Originally by direct dictation to a secretary, later also by using conventional dictating (recording) equipment. This method of text creation is linear and does not allow for easy review and immediate modification of what has been said. Insertion, change of phrasing, or text reorganization while dictating are not possible. The job cannot be completed in one sitting, there are delays, and the convenience, work load, office hours, and various habits of the typist must be taken into account.

Word processing via computer terminals or personal computers gives more control over the process to the user, but the natural human inclination to communicate by voice rather than keyboard is sacrificed. We hope that automatic dictation recognition will solve the problem. Two conditions must be fulfilled: the speech recognizer must be reliable, and the man–machine interface must be a convenient one.

The interface problem, shared with word processing, is not a trivial one. Perhaps due to early childhood experiences (I believe the cause is deeper), hands-on editing with paper and pencil seems preferable. It is easy to direct the typist to rearrange text by circling it, or to indicate text insertion, correction, deletion, or indentation. Pointing by a mouse or a touch-sensitive screen, or text movement via marking the beginning and end of a section followed by cursor specification of the place of insertion, are not as convenient. To get a really good interface, it may prove necessary to use writing tablets and achieve automatic recognition of hand-produced diacritical marks and possibly of handwriting as well. Clearly, the recognizer must be an integral part of the total office support system that includes facilities such as electronic mail or database access. The machine should not take up extra space or be otherwise intrusive. Thus most of the feedback it gives should be visual and not acoustic.

To gain reliability, accuracy, and ease of use, the IBM project will attempt to enhance four facets of recognition: vocabulary text coverage, noise immunity, speaker independence, and continuous speech. The first problem was discussed in Section IV. The remaining three will now be addressed.

Our pressure-zone microphone picks up all sounds in its vicinity and the recognizer interprets them as part of the dictation. We consider this a worthwhile price to pay for eliminating the head mounted microphone that usually inconveniences users of speech recognizers. Nevertheless, the appearance of extraneous text on the screen is extremely annoying, as is the somewhat increased error rate due to background noise. It should be possible to adjust our signal processing to filter out speech by others than the dictator, as well as noise bursts such as telephone ringing, dropped books, rustling of paper, or door slams. Tracking of the speaker's position by a microphone array may prove part of the answer. Improved recognition algorithms should take care of higher ambient noise levels.

Our training procedure currently consists of reading of 100 sentences of average length of 12 words. Thus about 20 min of speech is needed. The sentences were selected at random from our office text and somewhat adjusted with the aim of covering all basic sound combinations. We do not expect to change this approach when we increase the vocabulary. The current training text contains only 700 different words. The necessary statistical parameters of the speaker's personal acoustic model are estimated off-line using the Forward–Backward algorithm [1], [2], [9], as are the 200 prototype vectors. It takes a day or so of elapsed time to sign a new speaker onto the recognizer. This delay will be drastically cut when we implement the training algorithm on our real-time system, but the sign-on will still be time consuming. It is clearly desirable to create a system capable of recognizing without any training any standard American speaker with tolerable accuracy. The performance should improve as the recognizer is used until the best achievable speaker accuracy rate is reached.

As the results of Section III indicate, we have encountered only moderate problems in recognizing spontaneous (as opposed to read) speech. However, with rare exceptions, to achieve satisfactory results, speakers whose native tongue is not English must pronounce the entire vocabulary several times during training. Even then the recognition performance is slightly worse. This we think is due mainly to the inconsistency and occasional self-consciousness of the accented speech. For instance, F. Jelinek occasionally (both during training and recognition) remembers to voice the final "s" in plurals, pronounces the word "of" as 'ov' (rather than his usual 'of'), or attempts to adjust his 'th' sound to make it conform to what he imagines is its correct pronunciation. At other times he tries to remember how he pronounced particular words during training. Such efforts lead mostly to trouble. We do not know yet how to handle these difficulties. It is unfortunately possible that the first commercial dictation recognizers will not perform adequately for some nonnative speakers.

We believe that isolated word dictation will be acceptable for text creation, but the desirability of recognizing continuous speech is self-evident. This is how people speak. Our algorithms do not make any explicit use of the pauses between words and are therefore not limited to isolated word recognition. Unfortunately, even assuming that our methods prove sufficient to overcome problems such as co-articulation, an increase of 6 to 10 times in computing speed will be required to achieve real-time recognition of continuous speech. Our current Speech Development System is not powerful enough. Wanting real-time recognition as we do, we will need to use a new generation of array processors or reluctantly base the development of algorithms on special-purpose hardware. In any case, much progress in work station human factors, noise immunity, vocabulary text coverage, and speaker independence will be necessary before text creation by natural speech becomes everyday reality.

Acknowledgment

The work reported here was carried out individually and collectively by present and past members of the Continuous Speech Recognition Group of the IBM T. J. Watson Research Center. Very significant contributions were made by J. Cocke. All the ideas presented that are of any value resulted from exceptionally effective collaboration by these colleagues.

The present Group members are A. Averbuch, L. Bahl, R. Bakis, P. Brown, A. Cole, G. Daggett, S. Das, K. Davies, S. De Gennaro, P. de Souza, E. Epstein, D. Fraleigh, I. Halpin, F. Jelinek, S. Katz, B. Lewis, H. Meleis, R. Mercer, A. Nadas, D. Nahamoo, M. Picheny, G. Shichman, and P. Spinelli.

The past group members are T. Ancheta, J. K. Baker, J. M. Baker, S. Chang, J. Cohen, P. Cohen, N. R. Dixon, M. Fitzgerald, G. Freeman, R. Freitas, M. Garrett, G. Hatfield, G. Heidorn, C. Junker, P. Loewner, L. Loh, F. Mintzer, J. Mommens, E. M. Mueckstein, L. Mullin, J. Raviv, R. Riekert, J. Robinson, J. Rosenfeld, R. Sadr, H. Silverman, C. Tappert, D. Teaney, and A. Wadia.

We have all benefited from the help given us by our visitors F. Adler, R. Ambrosio, E. Black, S. Bozic, L. Braida, G. Brown, M. Brown, D. Bustamante, L. Butler, W. Chang, P. Chen, P. Corsi, S. Della Pietra, V. Della Pietra, A. M. Derouault, I. Feerst, R. Findlay, T. Fine, D. Francis, L. Fridman, A. Fronistas, E. Goldwasser, S. Haltsonen, S-S. Huang, T. Im, T. Kaneko, V. Khazatsky, S. Kuo, D. Lee, B. Lotto, J. Lucassen, A. Martelli, M. Morf, A. Nobel, M. Okhochi, A. Pickholtz, J. Pitrelli, S. Pombra, L. Powers, N. C. Rabin, S. Rao, M. Rentmeesters, C. Richardson, M. Roberts, S. Scarci, M. Scott, S. Soudoplatoff, E. Strum, K. Toshioka, and L. Wilcox.

References

[1] F. Jelinek, "Continuous speech recognition by statistical methods," *Proc. IEEE*, vol. 64, no. 4, pp. 532–556, Apr. 1976.

[2] L. R. Bahl, F. Jelinek, and R. L. Mercer, "A maximum likelihood approach to continuous speech recognition," *IEEE Trans. Pattern Anal. Machine Intell.*, vol. PAMI-5, no. 2, pp. 179–190, Mar. 1983.

[3] J. D. Gould, J. Conti, and T. Hovanyecz, "Composing letters with a simulated listening typewriter," *Commun. ACM*, vol. 26, no. 4, pp. 295–308, Apr. 1983.

[4] E. Goldwasser, an unpublished memorandum, 1980.

[5] J. R. Cohen, "Application of a sensor—Neural model to speech recognition," to be published.

[6] H. Abut, R. M. Gray, and G. Rebolledo, "Vector quantization of speech and speech-like waveforms," *IEEE Trans. Acoust., Speech, Signal Processing*, vol. ASSP-30, no. 3, pp. 423–435, June 1982.

[7] A. Nadas, R. L. Mercer, L. R. Bahl, R. Bakis, P. S. Cohen, A. G. Cole, F. Jelinek, and B. L. Lewis, "Continuous speech recognition with automatically selected acoustic prototypes obtained by either bootstrapping or clustering," in *Proc. Int. Conf. on Acoustics, Speech, and Signal Processing* (Atlanta, GA, Apr. 1981), pp. 1153–1155.

[8] J. D. Ferguson, "Hidden Markov analysis: An introduction," in J. D. Ferguson, Ed., *Hidden Markov Models for Speech*. Princeton, NJ: IDA-CRD, Oct. 1980, pp. 8–15.

[9] L. E. Baum, "An inequality and associated maximization technique in statistical estimation of probabilistic functions of Markov processes," *Inequalities*, vol. 3, no. 1, pp. 1–8, 1972.

[10] S. Katz, "Recursive M-Gram language model via a smoothing of Turing's formula," a forthcoming paper.

[11] I. J. Good, *The Estimation of Probabilities. An Essay on Modern Bayesian Methods.* Cambridge, MA: MIT Press, Mar. 1965.

[12] F. Jelinek, "A fast sequential decoding algorithm using a stack," *IBM J. Res. Devel.*, vol. 13, pp. 675–685, Nov. 1969.

[13] D. P. Huttenlocher and V. W. Zue, "A model of lexical access from partial phonetic information," in *Proc. ICAASP 84*, vol. 2, pp. 26.4.1–26.4.4, Mar. 1984.

[14] T. Kaneko and N. R. Dixon, "A hierarchical decision approach to large vocabulary discrete utterance recognition," *IEEE Trans. Accoust., Speech, Signal Processing*, vol. ASSP-31, no. 5, pp. 1061–1066, Oct. 1983.

[15] A. Averbuch *et al.*, "A real-time, isolated-word, speech recognition system for dictation transcription," in *Proc. Int. Conf. on Acoustics, Speech, and Signal Processing* (Tampa, FL, Mar. 1985).

[16] F. Jelinek, R. L. Mercer, L. R. Bahl, and J. K. Baker, "Perplexity —A measure of difficulty of speech recognition tasks," presented at the 94th Meet. Acoustical Society of America, Miami Beach, FL, Dec. 15, 1977.

[17] M. M. Sondhi and S. E. Levinson, "Computing relative redundancy to measure grammatical constraint in speech recognition tasks," in *Proc. Int. Conf. on Acoustics, Speech, and Signal Processing* (Tulsa, OK, Apr. 1978), pp. 409–412.

[18] W. N. Francis and H. Kucera, *Frequency Analysis of English Usage*. Boston, MA: Houghton-Mifflin, 1982.

[19] J. B. Carroll, P. Davies, and B. Richman, *Word Frequency Book*. New York, NY: American Heritage, 1971.

[20] H. Kucera, personal communication.

[21] R. L. Mercer, personal communication.

[22] F. Jelinek, *Probabilistic Information Theory*. New York, NY: McGraw-Hill, 1968.

[23] C. E. Shannon, "Prediction and entropy of printed English," *Bell Syst. Tech. J.*, vol. 30, pp. 50–64, 1951.

[24] T. M. Cover and R. C. King, "A convergent gambling estimate of the entropy of English," *IEEE Trans. Informat. Theory*, vol. IT-24, no. 4, pp. 413–420, July 1978.

[25] S. Della Pietra and V. Della Pietra, personal communication.

[26] J. D. Gould and S. J. Boies, "Human factors challenges in creating a principal support office system—The speech filing system approach," *ACM Trans. Office Inform. Syst.*, vol. 1, no. 4, pp. 273–298, Oct. 1983.

[27] _____, "Writing, dictating, and speaking letters," *Science*, vol. 201, pp. 1145–1147, 1978.

[28] L. R. Bahl and F. Jelinek, "Decoding for channels with insertions, deletions, and substitutions with applications to speech recognition," *IEEE Trans. Informat. Theory*, vol. IT-21, no. 4, pp. 404–411, July 1975.

BYBLOS: The BBN Continuous Speech Recognition System

Y.L. Chow, M.O. Dunham, O.A. Kimball, M.A. Krasner, G.F. Kubala, J. Makhoul, P.J. Price, S. Roucos, and R.M. Schwartz

BBN Laboratories Incorporated
10 Moulton Street
Cambridge, MA 02239

Abstract

In this paper, we describe BYBLOS, the BBN continuous speech recognition system. The system, designed for large vocabulary applications, integrates acoustic, phonetic, lexical, and linguistic knowledge sources to achieve high recognition performance. The basic approach, as described in previous papers [1, 2], makes extensive use of robust context-dependent models of phonetic coarticulation using Hidden Markov Models (HMM). We describe the components of the BYBLOS system, including: signal processing frontend, dictionary, phonetic model training system, word model generator, grammar and decoder. In recognition experiments, we demonstrate consistently high word recognition performance on continuous speech across: speakers, task domains, and grammars of varying complexity. In speaker-dependent mode, where 15 minutes of speech is required for training to a speaker, 98.5% word accuracy has been achieved in continuous speech for a 350-word task, using grammars with perplexity ranging from 30 to 60. With only 15 seconds of training speech we demonstrate performance of 97% using a grammar.

1. Introduction

Speech is a natural and convenient form of communication between man and machine. The speech signal, however, is inherently variable and highly encoded. Vast differences occur in the realizations of speech units related to context, style of speech, dialect, talker. This makes the task of large vocabulary continuous speech recognition (CSR) by machine a very difficult one. Fortunately, speech is also structured and redundant: information about the linguistic content in the speech signal is often present at the various linguistic levels. To achieve acceptable performance, the recognition system must be able to exploit the redundancy inherent in the speech signal by bringing multiple sources of knowledge to bear. In general, these can include: acoustic-phonetic, phonological, lexical, syntactic, semantic and pragmatic knowledge sources (KS). In addition to designing representations for these KSs, methodologies must be developed for interfacing them and combining them into a uniform structure. An effective and coherent search strategy can then be applied based on global decision criteria. Practical issues that need to be resolved include computation and memory requirements, and how they could be traded off to obtain the desired combination of speed and performance.

In BYBLOS, we have explored many issues that arise in designing a large and complex system for continuous speech recognition. This paper is organized as follows. Section 2 gives an overview of the BYBLOS system. Section 3 describes our signal processing frontend. Section 4 describes the trainer system used for phonetic model knowledge acquisition. Section 5 describes the word model generator module that compiles word HMMs for each lexical item. Section 6 describes the syntactic/grammatical knowledge source that operates on a set of context-free rules describing the task domain to produce an equivalent finite state automaton used in the recognizer. Section 7 describes the BYBLOS recognition decoder using combined multiple sources of knowledge. Finally, Section 8 presents some figures and discussions on BYBLOS recognition performance.

2. Byblos System Overview

Figure 1 is a block diagram of the BYBLOS continuous speech recognition system. We show the different modules and knowledge sources that comprise the complete system, the arrows indicating the flow of module/KS interactions. The modules are represented by rectangular boxes. They are, starting from the top: Trainer, Word Model Generator, and Decoder. Also shown are the knowledge sources, which are represented by the ellipses. They include: Acoustic-Phonetic, Lexical, and Grammatic knowledge sources. We will describe briefly the various modules and how they interact with the various KSs.

Acoustic-Phonetic KS

The Trainer module is used for the acquisition of the acoustic-phonetic knowledge source. It takes as input a dictionary and training speech and text, and produces a database of context-dependent HMMs of phonemes.

Lexical KS

The Word Model Generator module takes as input the phonetic models database, and compiles word models phonetic models. It uses the dictionary - the lexical KS, in which phonological rules of English are used to represent each lexical item in terms of their most likely phonetic spellings. The lexical KS imposes phonotactic contraints by allowing only legal sequences of phonemes to be hypothesized in the recognizer, reducing the search space and improves performance. The output of the Word Model Generator is a database of word models used in the recognizer.

Grammatical KS

More recently, we have been working on representation and integration of higher levels of knowledge sources into BYBLOS, including both syntactic and semantic KSs. By incorporating both of these KSs into BYBLOS in the form of a grammar into our recognizer, we demonstrate improved recognition performance. In Section 6, we describe the Grammatical KS in more detail.

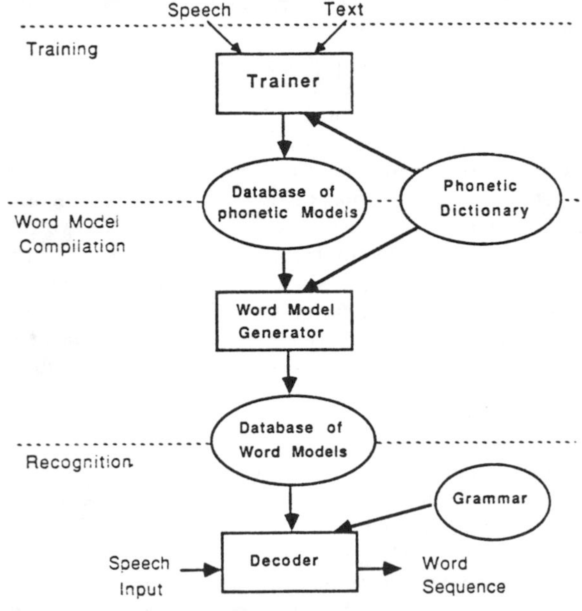

Figure 1: BYBLOS System Diagram.

3. Signal Processing and Analysis Component

The BYBLOS signal processing frontend performs feature extraction for the acoustic models used in recognition. Sentences are read directly into a close talking microphone in a natural but deliberate style in a normal office environment. The input speech is lowpass filtered at 10 kHz and sampled at 20 kHz. Fourteen Mel-frequency cepstral coefficients (MFCC) are computed from short-term spectra every 10 ms using a 20 ms analysis window. This MFCC feature vector is then vector quantized to an 8-bit (256 bins) representation. The vector quantization (VQ) codebook is computed using the k-means clustering algorithm with about 5 minutes of speech. We perform a variable-frame-rate (VFR) compression in which strings of up to 3 identical vector codes are compressed to a single observation code. We found this VFR procedure speeds up computation with no loss in performance.

4. Training/Acquisition Of Phonetic Coarticulation Models

The training system in BYBLOS acquires and estimates the phonetic coarticulation models used in recognition. Given that we model speech parameters as probabilistic functions of a hidden Markov chain, we make use of the Baum-Welch (also known as the Forward-Backward) algorithm [3] to estimate the parameters of the HMMs automatically from spoken speech and corresponding text transcription. For each training utterance, the training system takes speech and text, and builds a network of phonemes using the dictionary. It first builds the phonetic network for the word by using the phonetic transcription provided by the dictionary. The phonetic network is expanded into a triphone network so that each arc completely defines a phonetic context up to the triphone. These triphone networks of the word are then concatenated to form a single network for the sentence, which in general can take into account within word as well as across-word phonological effects. The training system then compiles a set of phonetic context models for each triphone arc in the network. It then runs the forward-backward algorithm to estimate the parameters of the phonetic context models. The Trainer operates in two modes: speaker-dependent and speaker-adapted. Associated with these two modes are two distinct methods for training the parameters of the hidden Markov models described below.

Speaker-Dependent

This is the algorithm used to find the parameters of the HMMs that maximizes the probability of the observed data given the model. This method produces HMMs that are finely tuned to a particular speaker, therefore in general would work well only for this speaker. Typically about 15 minutes of speech from a speaker is required for speaker-dependent training.

Speaker-Adapted

This is a new method of training that transforms HMM models of one speaker to model the speech of a second speaker [4]. This procedure estimates a probabilistic spectral mapping from a well-trained prototype speaker to a new speaker. Using this method it is possible for a new speaker to used the system with as little as 15 seconds of speech.

5. Word Model Generator

Prior to recognition, word HMMs are computed for each word in the vocabulary. The word model generator takes as input two objects: a database of phonetic HMMs as obtained in training, and a dictionary that contains phonetic spellings for each word. For each phoneme in each word of the lexicon, it first finds in the phonetic HMM database all the context models that are relevant to this phoneme in its particular phonetic environment. It then combines this set of phonetic models with appropriate weights to produce a single HMM for each phoneme in the word. This combination process saves computation by precompiling the many levels of phonetic context models that can occur for a given phonetic context into a single representation. The output of the word model generator is a database of word HMMs serving as the input to the decoder.

6. Grammatical Knowledge Source

To solve the CSR problem requires major advances in two areas: acoustic modeling and language modeling. A good acoustic model is essential in making fine phonetic distinctions when needed. However, it is not sufficient by itself to solve the CSR problem. In a complex task with large vocabulary where the number of hypothesized word candidates is large, the probability for acoustic confusability can be high, and the recognizer could make errors. A conceptually simple yet effective way to restrict the number of words that are allowed to be hypothesized, and therefore decrease probability of acoustic similarity, is to incorporate a grammar into the recognizer. It is well known that recognition performance improves as vocabulary size decreases. Similarly, when syntactical information is used to reduce the number of words that can legally follow a given sequence of words, a recognizer is expected to make fewer errors. The purpose for using a grammar then, is to improve recognition performance, with an added benefit of reducedcomputation.

Grammar Design and Implementation

We approach the implementation of a grammar in BYBLOS in two stages. First, we create a description of the task domain language using a modified context-free notation. Typically this description is based on a representative set of sentences that characterizes the task domain, and is designed to capture generalizations of the linguistic phenomena found in them. Second, we use a tool that transforms this description into structures in our recognizer that provide the corresponding grammatical constraints. This tool provides us with a general facility for capturing in BYBLOS an approximation of any language expressible in context-free grammars (CFG) expressed as context-free rules. We elected to implement the grammatical constraints in the form of a finite state automaton (FA) similar to those described in [5].

At the first stage in generating a grammar, we use a context-free notation augumented with variables in order to simplify the process of describing a language. For example, this notation would allow a rule that says a noun phrase of any number can be replaced by an article and a noun of the same number; ordinary context-free notation would require two rules that are identical except that one would be for singular number and the other for plural.

Our system first translates the augmented notation into ordinary CFGs and then constructs a FA based on these rules. Because context-free grammars can accept recursive languages and a FA cannot, recursion is approximated in the FA by limiting the number of levels of recursion. Such an approximation is reasonable for most task languages, since spoken sentences do not ordinarily use more than a few levels of recursion.

7. Recognition Search Strategy

Once the FA is compiled from the context-free description of the task domain, it is ready to be used in the decoder. An important characteristic of a recognizer is the search strategy that is used to find the word sequence that best matches the input speech. We believe that an optimum search strategy avoids making local decisions; the search decision should be made globally, based on scores from all the KSs. One such search paradigm is the one used in BYBLOS: the search is made top down, linguistically driven, with tightly coupled KSs.

The FA is convenient for deploying such a search strategy. It is used as follows in our recognizer. We associate with each transition in the FA a hidden Markov model for the word. This model is used to compute the probability of the acoustic event (sequence of VQ spectra) given the occurrence of the word at that place in the grammar. Before the start of recognition, the initial state of the FA where a legal sequence of words can begin is initialized to unity, and all the other states are initialized to zero. For each 10 ms frame of the input speech, the scores for the states in all the words in the FA network are updated using modified Baum-Welch algorithm [2]. In addition to state updates within a word, a word can have a score propagated to its initial state from its best scoring predecessor word. This simple state update operation is repeated every 10 ms for each FA transition until the end of the utterance is reached. The decoder output is then computed by tracing back through the FA network to find the highest scoring sequence of words that end in the terminal state of the FA.

One potential problem associated with using a FA grammar for recognition is that computation is expected to be proportional to the number of transitions in the FA. This number can be quite large for complex languages. However, in our experience with different grammars in our recognizer, we find that a beam search effectively reduces the computation to a very manageable level while maintaining the same performance as that of an exhaustive search.

8. Byblos Recognition Performance

In [2], we presented word recognition results for a 334-word electronic mail task. In speaker-dependent mode, we demonstrated performance of 90% across several speakers without the use of a grammar (i.e., branching factor of 334). Since then, we have tested the system along many dimensions: two task domains, FA grammars with varying perplexities, varying amounts of adaptation speech, and different speaker types. The results are tabulated in Figure 2. Below we describe the different conditions in more detail.

Task Domains

The two task domains tested are: Electronic Mail (EMAIL) and Naval Database Retrieval (FCCBMP). Both tasks have vocabulary sizes of approximately 350 word (334 for EMAIL, 354 for FCCBMP). A description of the task domain language was created using CFG. The CFGs were designed to capture generalizations of linguistic phenomena found in example task domain sentences.

Grammars

Two finite state grammars were generated for each task domain: Command and Sentence. The Command Grammar in each case was designed to cover only the command subset of

Grammar/Perplexity \ Training Time	EMAIL		FCCBMP	
	Command (20)	Sentence (30)	Command (22)	Sentence (30)
15 minute	98.4	98.8	99.6	99.5
2 minute	97.9	94.9	96.6	96.2

Figure 2: BYBLOS Recognition Results. Two task domains (EMAIL and FCCBMP), two grammars for each task (Command and Sentence), and varying amounts of training speech (2 minutes and 15 minutes). Also shown are maximum perplexity measures for the grammars.

the language; the Sentence Grammar was designed to cover all of the language, which included both command and question type constructs. The maximum perplexity measures of the grammars, as proposed in [6], are shown in Figure 2. In both tasks, the sentence grammars have a higher perplexity than their command counterparts.

Adaptation Time

As described in Section 2, The BYBLOS operate in two modes, speaker-dependent and speaker-adapted. In speaker-dependent mode, 15 minutes of training speech is required for a speaker. This mode in general will give word accuracy in the 98.5+ range. In the speaker-adaptive mode, anywhere from 2 minutes down to 15 seconds of speech from a new speaker is needed to "adapt" the HMM parameters to the new speaker. The performance in this case is 97%.

Speaker Type

We have tested BYBLOS on several speakers with different dialects, including a female speaker, a non-native speaker, and 3 naive (uncoached) speakers. The recognition results for these speakers showed little deviation typical male speakers of standard American dialects.

9. Summary

We have presented BYBLOS, a system for large vocabulary continuous speech recognition. We showed how we integrate multiple sources of knowledge to achieve high recognition performance. In recognition experiments, we demonstrated consistent performances across task domains, grammars, adaptation time, and speaker type.

We are currently working to improve various aspects of the system, including: a real time implementation of the recognizer, search strategy, acoustic modeling, and language modeling. In the future, we plan to work on integration of speech and natural language for speech understanding applications.

Acknowledgement

This work was supported by the Defense Advanced Research Projects Agency and was monitored by the Space and Naval Warfare Systems Command under Contract No. N00039-85-C-0423.

References

1. R.M. Schwartz, Y.L. Chow, O.A. Kimball, S. Roucos, M. Krasner, and J. Makhoul, "Context-Dependent Modeling for Acoustic-Phonetic Recognition of Continuous Speech", *IEEE Int. Conf. Acoust., Speech, Signal Processing*, Tampa, FL, March 1985, pp. 1205-1208, Paper No. 31.3.

2. Y.L. Chow, R.M. Schwartz, S. Roucos, O.A. Kimball, P.J. Price, G.F. Kubala, M.O. Dunham, M.A. Krasner, and J. Makhoul, "The Role of Word-Dependent Coarticulatory Effects in a Phoneme-Based Speech Recognition System", *IEEE Int. Conf. Acoust., Speech, Signal Processing*, Tokyo, Japan, April 1986, pp. 1593-1596, Paper No. 30.9.1.

3. L.R. Bahl, F. Jelinek, and R.L. Mercer, "A Maximum Likelihood Approach to Continuous Speech Recognition", *IEEE Trans. Pattern Analysis and Machine Intelligence*, Vol. PAMI-5, No. 2, March 1983, pp. 179-190.

4. R.M. Schwartz, Y.L. Chow, G.F. Kubala, "Rapid Speaker Adaptation using a Probabilistic Spectral Mapping", *IEEE Int. Conf. Acoust., Speech, Signal Processing*, Dallas, TX, April 1987, Elsewhere in these proceedings

5. R.G. Goodman, *Analysis of Languages for Man-Machine Communication*, PhD dissertation, Carnegie-Mellon University, May 1976.

6. M.M. Sondhi and S.E. Levinson, "Computing Relative Redundancy to Measure Grammatical Constraint in Speech Recognition Tasks", *IEEE Int. Conf. Acoust., Speech, Signal Processing*, Tulsa, OK, April 1978, pp. 409-412.

An Overview of the SPHINX Speech Recognition System

KAI-FU LEE, MEMBER, IEEE, HSIAO-WUEN HON, AND RAJ REDDY, FELLOW, IEEE

Abstract—Speaker independence, continuous speech, and large vocabularies pose three of the greatest challenges in automatic speech recognition. Previously, accurate speech recognizers avoided dealing simultaneously with all three problems. This paper describes SPHINX, a system that demonstrates the feasibility of accurate, large-vocabulary speaker-independent, continuous speech recognition.

SPHINX is based on discrete hidden Markov models (HMM's) with LPC-derived parameters. To provide speaker independence, we added knowledge to these HMM's in several ways: multiple codebooks of fixed-width parameters, and an enhanced recognizer with carefully designed models and word duration modeling. To deal with coarticulation in continuous speech, yet still adequately represent a large vocabulary, we introduce two new subword speech units—function-word-dependent phone models and generalized triphone models. With grammars of perplexity 997, 60, and 20, SPHINX attained word accuracies of 71, 94, and 96 percent on a 997-word task.

I. Introduction

CONSIDERABLE progress has been made in speech recognition in the past 15 years. Many successful systems [1]-[7] have emerged. Each of these systems has attained very impressive accuracy. However, they owe their success to one or more of the constraints they impose. This paper describe SPHINX, a system that tries to overcome three of these constraints: 1) speaker dependence, 2) isolated words, and 3) small vocabulary.[1]

Speaker independence has been viewed as the most difficult constraint to overcome. This is because most parametric representations of speech are highly speaker dependent, and a set of reference patterns suitable for one speaker may perform poorly for another speaker. Researchers have found that errors increased by 300-500 percent when a speaker-dependent system is trained and tested in speaker-independent mode [8], [9]. Because of these difficulties, most speech recognition systems are speaker dependent. In other words, they require a speaker to "train" the system before reasonable performance can be expected. This training phase typically requires several hundred sentences. While speaker-trained systems are useful for some applications, they are inconvenient, less robust, more wasteful, and simply unusable for some applications. Speaker-independent systems must train on less appropriate training data. However, many more data can be acquired, which may compensate for the less appropriate training material.

Continuous speech recognition is significantly more difficult than isolated word recognition. Its complexity is a result of three innate properties of continuous speech. First, word boundaries are difficult to locate. Second, *coarticulatory effects* are much stronger in continuous speech, causing the same sound to appear differently in various contexts. Third, *content words* (nouns, verbs, adjectives, etc.) are often emphasized, while *function words* (articles, prepositions, pronouns, short verbs, etc.) are poorly articulated. Error rates increase drastically from isolated-word to continuous speech. For example, Bahl *et al.* [10] reported a 280 percent error rate increase from isolated-word to continuous speech recognition. However, in spite of these problems and degradations, we believe that it is important to work on continuous speech research. Only with continuous speech can we achieve the desired speed and naturalness of man-machine communications.

Large vocabulary typically implies a vocabulary of about 1000 words or more. As vocabulary size increases, so does the number of confusable words. Also, larger vocabularies require the use of *subword models*, because it is difficult to train whole word models. Unfortunately, subword units usually lead to degraded performance because they cannot capture coarticulatory (interunit) effects as well as word models can. Error rate increased by 200-1000 percent in several studies [11]-[13]. In spite of these problems, large vocabulary systems are still needed for many versatile applications, such as dictation, dialog systems, and speech translation systems.

In this paper, we describe SPHINX, a large-vocabulary speaker-independent, continuous speech recognition system. SPHINX employs discrete hidden Markov models (HMM's) with LPC-derived parameters. To deal with speaker independence, we added knowledge to these HMM's in several ways. We represented additional knowledge through the use of multiple vector quantized codebooks. We also enhanced the recognizer with carefully designed models and word duration modeling. To

Manuscript received July 5, 1988; revised March 22, 1989. This work was supported in part by a National Science Foundation Graduate Fellowship, and by Defense Advanced Research Projects Agency Contract N00039-85-C-0163. The views and conclusions contained herein are those of the authors and should not be interpreted as representing the official policies, either expressed or implied, of the National Science Foundation, the Defense Advanced Research Projects Agency, or the U.S. Government.

The authors are with the School of Computer Science, Carnegie Mellon University, Pittsburgh, PA 15213.

IEEE Log Number 8931685.

[1]There are many other constraints that SPHINX does impose: simple language model, benign environment, cooperative speakers, etc.

0096-3518/90/0100-0035$01.00 © 1990 IEEE

deal with coarticulation in continuous speech, yet adequately represent a large vocabulary, we introduced two new speech units—function-word-dependent phone models and generalized triphone models. With these techniques, SPHINX achieved speaker-independent word recognition accuracies of 71, 94, and 96 percent on the 997-word DARPA resource management task [14] with grammars of perplexity 997, 60, and 20.

In this paper, we first describe the task and database used for evaluating SPHINX in the following section. Section III then describes a baseline implementation of SPHINX. Enhancements to SPHINX using additional human knowledge and improved subword models are described in Sections IV and V. Section VI summarizes the results with SPHINX, and Section VII concludes with some final remarks. A full description of the SPHINX System can be found in [15] and [16].

II. Task and Database

A. The Resource Management Task

SPHINX was evaluated on the DARPA *resource management* task [14]. This task, containing a vocabulary of 997 words, was designed for database query of naval resources. As such, there are a large number of long words, such as *Apalachicola*, *Chattahoochee*, and *ECG041*. These words are relatively easy to recognize. On the other hand, it also contains many confusable pairs, such as *what/what's*, *what/was*, *the/a*, *four/fourth*, *are/were*, *any/many*, etc. Also, there are many function words (such as *a*, *and*, *of*, *the*, *to*), which are articulated very poorly and are hard to recognize or even locate. In particular, *the* and *a* are the most frequent words, but are optional according to the grammar.

The original grammar designed for the resource management task was a finite state grammar. This grammar had a perplexity of only about 9, which was too simple. Instead, we used three more difficult grammars with SPHINX: 1) null grammar (perplexity 997), where any word can follow any other word, 2) word-pair grammar (perplexity 60), a simple grammar that specifies a list of words that can legally follow any given word, and 3) bigram grammar (perplexity 20), a word-pair grammar that uses word-category transitions probabilities estimated from the grammar. It should be noted that the training and testing sentences were generated from the finite state grammar, which may reduce acoustic confusability [17].

B. The TIRM Database

Texas Instruments supplied Carnegie Mellon with a large speech database for the resource management task described in the previous section. The TIRM database contains 80 "training" speakers, 40 "development test" speakers, and 40 "evaluation speakers." At the time of this writing, only the 80 training speakers and the 40 development test speakers are available. Of these speakers, 85 are male and 35 are female, with each speaker reading 40 sentences generated by the sentence pattern grammar.

These sentences were recorded using a Sennheiser HMD-414-6, close-talking noise-cancelling headset-boom microphone in a sound-treated room. All speakers were untrained and instructed to read a list of sentences in a natural continuous fashion. The speech was sampled at 20 kHz at TI, downsampled to 16 kHz at the National Institute of Standards and Technology and saved on magnetic tapes.

In this study, all 80 training speakers, as well as 25 of the development test speakers, were used as training material. This gave us a total of 4200 training sentences. The remaining 15 development test speakers were set aside as testing speakers. Ten sentences were taken from each speaker, for a total of 150 test sentences.

III. The Baseline SPHINX System

To establish a performance benchmark using standard HMM techniques on the resource management task, we began with a baseline HMM system. This system uses standard HMM techniques employed by many other systems [18]-[20]. We will show that, using these techniques alone, we can already attain reasonable, albeit mediocre, accuracies.

A. Speech Processing

The speech is sampled at 16 kHz, and preemphasized with a filter whose transform function is $1-0.97z^{-1}$. The waveform is then blocked into frames. Each frame spans 20 ms, or 320 speech samples. Consecutive frames overlap by 10 ms, or 160 speech samples. Each frame is multiplied by a Hamming window with a width of 20 ms and applied every 10 ms.

From these smoothed speech samples, we computed the LPC coefficients using the autocorrelation method [21]. LPC analysis was performed with order 14. Finally, a set of 12 LPC-derived cepstral coefficients was computed from the LPC coefficients. This representation is very similar to that used by Shikano *et al.* [22] and Rabiner *et al.* [23].

The 12 LPC cepstrum coefficients for each frame were then vector quantized into one of 256 prototype vectors. These vectors were generated by a variant of the Linde-Buzo-Gray algorithm [24], [22] using Euclidean distance. We used 150 00 frames of nonoverlapped 20-ms coefficients extracted from 4000 sentences to generate the 256-vector codebook.

B. Phonetic Hidden Markov Models

Hidden Markov Models (HMM) were first described by Baum [25]. Shortly afterwards, they were independently extended to automatic speech recognition by Baker [26] and Jelinek [27]. However, only in the past few years have HMM's become the predominant approach to speech recognition.

HMM's are parametric models particularly suitable for describing speech events. The success of HMM's is largely due to the forward-backward reestimation algorithm [19], which is a special case of the EM algorithm [25]. Every iteration of the algorithm modifies the parameters to increase the probability of the training data until a local maximum has been reached.

Because the resource management task is a large-vocabulary one, we cannot adequately train a model for each word. Thus, we have chosen to use phonetic HMM's, where each HMM represents a phone. There are a total of 45 phones, each characterized by

- $\{s\}$—a set of states including an initial state S_I and a final state S_F.
- $\{a_{ij}\}$—a set of transitions where a_{ij} is the probability of taking a transition from state i to state j.
- $\{b_{ij}(k)\}$-the output probability matrix: the probability of emitting symbol k when taking a transition from state i to state j, k corresponds to one of the 256 VQ codes.

Each phonetic HMM has the topology shown in Fig. 1. The three self-loops model three parts of a phone, and the lower transitions explicitly model durations of one, two, or three frames. Instead of assigning a unique output pdf to each transition, each phone is assigned three distributions, representing the beginning, middle, and end of the phone. Each of these three distributions is shared by several transitions. This model is almost identical to that used by IBM [28].

C. Training

To initialize our phone model parameters, we used hand-segmented and hand-labeled segments from 2240 TIMIT [29] sentences. We ran one iteration of forward-backward on these hand-labeled phone segments, and produced a model for each phone. This set of 45 phone models was used to initialize the parameters in the actual training.

After this initialization, we ran the forward-backward algorithm on the resource management (TIRM) training sentences. For each of the 4200 sentences, we created a sentence model from word models, which were in turn concatenated from phone models. To determine the phonetic spelling of a word, we used a pronunciation dictionary adopted from the baseform of the ANGEL System [30], where each word is mapped to a single linear sequence of phones. Then, to create a sentence model from word models, we accounted for possible between-word silences by inserting a mandatory silence model at the beginning and at the end of the sentence. Between-word silences were also allowed, but were optional. This sentence model represents the *expected pronunciation* of the sentence. It was trained against the actual input speech using the forward-backward algorithm [19].

Two iterations of forward-backward training were then run. Most other HMM systems run more iterations, but we found that with our appropriate initialization, two iterations were sufficient. The trained transition probabilities were used directly in recognition. The output probabilities, however, were smoothed with a uniform distribution to avoid probabilities that were too small.

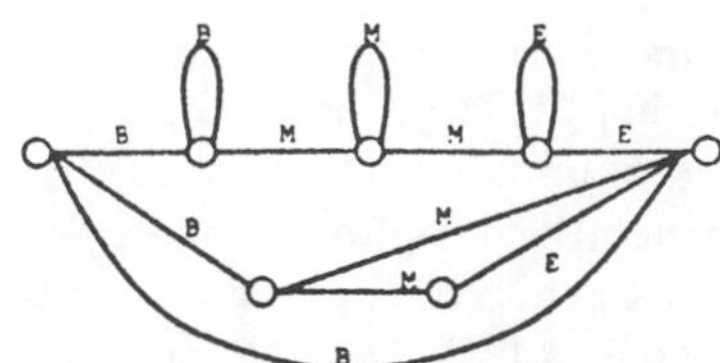

Fig. 1. The phone HMM used in baseline SPHINX. The label on a transition represents the output pdf to which the transition is tied.

The SPHINX recognition search is a standard time-synchronous Viterbi beam search [19], [20]. The search processes input speech time synchronously, completely updating all accessible states for a time frame $t - 1$ before moving on to frame t. The update for time t consists of two stages. First, for each within-word transition between states s_{from} and S_{to}, if $P(s_{from}, t - 1) \cdot P(transition) \cdot P(output)$ is greater than $P(s_{to}, t)$, then $P(s_{to}, t)$ is updated. Second, for the final state of every word, all legal word successors are tried, using $P(transition)$ derived from the language model.

In the Viterbi beam search, a hypothesis is pruned if its log probability is less than that of the best hypothesis by more than a preset threshold. We found it is possible to prune 80-90 percent of the hypotheses without any loss in accuracy. After the search is completed, a backtrace is performed to recover the best path.

D. Results

The results with the baseline SPHINX system, using 15 new speakers with 10 sentences each for evaluation, are shown in Table I. To determine the recognition accuracy, we first align the recognized word string against the correct word string using a string match algorithm supplied by the National Institute of Standards and Technology [31]. This alignment determines *WordsCorrect*, *Substitutions*, *Deletions*, *Insertions*. Finally, *PercentCorrect* and *WordAccuracy* are computed by

$$\text{Percent Correct} = 100 \cdot \frac{\text{Words Correct}}{\text{Correct Length}} \quad (1)$$

$$\text{Word Accuracy} = 100 \cdot \frac{\text{Correct Length—Subs—Dels—Ins}}{\text{Correct Length}}. \quad (2)$$

Confusions between homonyms (such as *ship's* and *ships*, or *two* and *too*) are not counted for the null language model, and are counted for the word pair and the bigram language model.

The results of this system are mediocre at best. Since

TABLE I
BASELINE SPHINX RESULTS, EVALUATED ON 150 SENTENCES FROM 15 SPEAKERS

Grammar	Perplexity	Percent Correct	Word Accuracy
None	997	31.1%	25.8%
Word-Pair	60	61.8%	58.1%
Bigram	20	76.1%	74.8%

the bigram grammar already imposes tight constraints, we concluded that our baseline system was inadequate for any realistic large-vocabulary applications. In the subsequent sections, we describe our steps to improve the baseline SPHINX by incorporating knowledge and contextual modeling.

IV. Adding Knowledge to SPHINX

A. Fixed-Width Speech Parameters

The easiest way to add knowledge to HMM's is to introduce additional fixed-width parameters, or parameters than can be computed for every fixed-size frame. All we have to do is to devise a way of incorporating these parameters into the output pdf of the HMM's. In this section, we consider several types of frame-based parameters, and discuss possible ways of integrating them.

1) Bilinear Transform on the Cepstrum Coefficients: The human ear's ability to discriminate between frequencies is approximated by a logarithmic function of the frequency, or a *bark scale* [32]. Furthermore, Davis and Mermelstein [33] have shown these logarithmically scaled coefficients yield superior recognition accuracy compared to linearly scaled ones. Therefore, there is strong motivation for transforming the LPC cepstrum coefficients into a mel-frequency scale.

Shikano [34] reported significant improvement from using a *bilinear transform* [35] on the LPC cepstral coefficients. Bilinear transform is a technique that transforms a linear frequency axis into a warped one using the all-pass filter

$$z_{new}^{-1} = \frac{(z^{-1} - a)}{(1 - az^{-1})}, \; (-1 < a < 1) \tag{3}$$

$$\omega_{new} = \omega + 2 \tan^{-1}\left(\frac{a \sin \omega}{1 - a \cos \omega}\right) \tag{4}$$

where ω is the sampling frequency expressed by the normalized angular frequency, ω_{new} is the converted frequency, and a is a frequency warping parameter. A positive a converts the frequency axis into a low-frequency weighted one. When a takes on values between 0.4 and 0.8, the frequency warping by a bilinear transform is comparable to that of the mel or Bark scales. In this work, we use a value of 0.6 for a.

2) Differenced Cepstrum Coefficients: Temporal changes in the spectra play an important role in human perception [36]. This is particularly true for speaker-independent recognition, where formant slopes are more reliable than absolute formant locations. Thus, it would be desirable to incorporate "slope" measurements into recognizers. Moreover, since HMM's assume each frame is independent of the past, it would be desirable to broaden the scope of a frame.

We use a simple slope measure, *differenced LPC cepstrum coefficients* [34]. The difference coefficients for frame n are the difference between the coefficients of frame $n + \delta$ and $n - \delta$. In our current implementation, a differenced coefficient is computed every frame, with $\delta = 2$ frames, giving a 40 ms difference. In a preliminary experiment, we found this measure to be as good as the *regression coefficients* used in [37] and [7].

3) Power and Differenced Power: Although LPC-based parameters perform well in speech recognition, they do not contain sufficient information about power. For example, coefficients in silence or noise regions are not very meaningful. Therefore, it is desirable to incorporate power into our recognizer. Rabiner *et al.* [23] obtained significant improvement by adding power into the distance metric in vector quantization, and Shikano [34] reported similar results. Finally, in a detailed study of prosody in speech recognition, Waibel [38] found power to be the most important prosodic cue.

Since raw power may vary widely from speaker to speaker, we normalized power by subtracting the maximum power value in the sentence from each power value in the sentence. In our real-time system, we used an automatic gain control algorithm with a 250-ms look-ahead to predict the maximum power in a sentence.

Another important source of information is *differenced power*, which is computed the same way as *differenced LPC cepstrum coefficients*. Differenced power provides information about relative changes in amplitude or loudness. Indeed, our preliminary experiments indicated that differenced power is more useful than power.

4) Integrating Fixed-Width Parameters in Multiple Codebooks: There are many ways to integrate the above coefficients into the framework of a discrete HMM recognizer. We considered several possibilities [15], and decided to use *multiple-codebook integration* [39]. Using this technique, coefficients are divided into sets, and each set is quantized into a separate codebook. We created three codebooks, each with 256 codes. These codebooks were generated from 1) bilinear-transformed LPC cepstrum coefficients, 2) differenced bilinear-transformed LPC cepstrum coefficients, and 3) a weighted combination of power and differenced power.

For each frame of speech, not one but several VQ codes are used to replace the input vector. Since each input frame is no longer a single symbol, but rather a vector of symbols, the discrete HMM algorithms must be modified to produce multiple symbols at each time frame. By assuming that the multiple output observations are independent, the output probability of emitting multiple symbols can then be computed as the product of the probability of producing each symbol.

The multiple-codebook approach has a distinct advantage over single-codebook approaches—namely, reduced quantization error. If too many features are used in VQ, the distortion will be very large, which means the observed vectors will match their corresponding prototype vectors poorly. Multiple codebooks reduce the distortion by partitioning the feature space into several smaller subspaces. Table II clearly illustrates this point with the comparison of one-codebook distortion and three-codebook distortion.

Another advantage of multiple codebooks is the large increase in the dynamic range and precision of the resulting parameters. With three codebooks, there are 256^3 possible parameter combinations using just 256 × 3 parameters. With such an increase in precision comes the ability to make finer distinctions.

However, the independence assumption with multiple codebooks is inaccurate. Also, more memory and time are needed with multiple codebooks. But we felt that these disadvantages were well compensated by the advantages.

TABLE II
Quantization Error of a Single Codebook Versus the Total Quantization Error in Three Codebooks

Codebook Size	1-codebook distortion	3-codebook distortion
2	2.42	1.86
4	1.94	1.12
8	1.45	0.81
16	1.19	0.61
32	1.00	0.48
64	0.83	0.39
128	0.72	0.31
256	0.61	0.25

B. *Lexical/Phonological Improvements*

Our next set of improvements involved the modification of the set of phones and the pronunciation dictionary. These changes lead to more accurate assumptions about how words are articulated, without changing our assumption that each word has a single pronunciation.

The first step we took was to replace the baseform pronunciation with the most likely pronunciation. For example, the first vowel of the word *delete* will appear as /iy/ in most dictionaries, but it is actually pronounced as /ih/ most of the time. This correction process modified about 40 percent of all the baseforms.

With our linear representation of pronunciation, it is difficult to model the deletions of phonetic events. For example, the first /d/ of the word *did* is always released, while the last /d/ may be unreleased. Also, closures before stops are optional. We model these two types of deletions implicitly in the HMM parameters. We created separate models for the released stops and optional stops. We also merged closure-stop pairs as a single phone. These changes enabled the modeling of deletions within linear HMM's.

Although the English phonemes are well defined, there are actually many frequently used sounds that are not phonemic. For example, stop-fricative pairs such as /ks/, /ps/, /ts/, /bz/, /dz/, or /gz/ are actually quite different from the concatenated phoneme pairs. They appear more like different affricates. Thus, it is sensible to model them as special phones. In this study, we only model /ts/ in this fashion due to the lack of training data for the other nonphonemic affricates.

In order to improve the appropriateness of the word pronunciation dictionary, a small set of rules was created to 1) modify closure-stop pairs into optional compound phones when appropriate, 2) modify /t/'s and /d/'s into /dx/ when appropriate, 3) reduce nasal /t/'s when appropriate, and 4) perform other mappings such as /t s/ to /ts/.

Finally, there is the issue of what HMM topology is optimal for phones in general, and what topology is optimal for each phone. We found that although the choice of model was not critical for continuous speech recognition, the model shown in Fig. 1 led to the best results. In addition, we experimented with different ways of labeling the transitions, i.e., which output pdf should be tied to each transition. Each phone was assigned an appropriate set of tied transitions.

The improvements in this section led to the set of phones enumerated in Table III. These improvements have increased the number of phones from 45 to 48. Table IV shows a section of our final phonetic pronunciation dictionary.

C. *Word Duration Modeling*

HMM's model duration of events with transition probabilities, which lead to a geometric distribution for the duration of state residence, for states with self-loops:

$$P_i(d) = (1 - a_{ii})\, a_{ii}^d \tag{5}$$

where $P_i(d)$ is the probability of taking the self-loop at state i for exactly d times. Several researchers have argued that this is an inadequate distribution for speech events, and proposed alternatives for duration modeling [40], [41], [7].

We incorporated word duration into SPHINX as a part of the Viterbi search. The duration of a word is modeled by a univariate Gaussian distribution, with the mean and variance estimated from a supervised Viterbi segmentation of the training set. By precomputing the duration score for various durations, this duration model has essentially no overhead.

D. *Results*

We have presented various strategies for adding knowledge to SPHINX. The results of these strategies are shown in Table V. The version abbreviations are defined in Table VI.

Consistent with earlier results [33], [34], we found that bilinear transformed coefficients improved the recognition rates. An even greater improvement came from the use of differential coefficients, power, and differenced power in three separate codebooks. Next, we enhanced the dictionary and the phone set—a step that led to an appreciable improvement.

TABLE III

LIST OF THE IMPROVED SET OF PHONES IN SPHINX

Phone	Example	Phone	Example	Phone	Example
/iy/	beat	/l/	led	/t/	tot
/ih/	bit	/r/	red	/k/	kick
/eh/	bet	/y/	yet	/z/	zoo
/ae/	bat	/w/	wet	/v/	very
/ix/	roses	/er/	bird	/f/	fief
/ax/	the	/en/	button	/th/	thief
/ah/	but	/m/	mom	/s/	sis
/uw/	boot	/n/	non	/sh/	shoe
/uh/	book	/ng/	sing	/hh/	hay
/ao/	bought	/ch/	church	/sil/	(silence)
/aa/	cot	/jh/	judge	/dd/	deleted
/ey/	bait	/dh/	they	/pd/	ship
/ay/	bite	/b/	bob	/td/	set
/oy/	boy	/d/	dad	/kd/	comic
/aw/	bough	/g/	gag	/dx/	butter
/ow/	boat	/p/	pop	/ts/	its

TABLE IV

A SECTION OF THE SPHINX DICTIONARY WITH WORD, ORIGINAL BASEFORM, AND THE PRONUNCIATION AFTER RULE APPLICATION

Word	Baseform	After rules
ADDED	/ae d ix d/	/ae dx ix dd/
ADDING	/ae d ix ng/	/ae dx ix ng/
AFFECT	/ax f eh k t/	/ax f eh k td/
AFTER	/ae f t er/	/ae f t er/
AGAIN	/ax g eh n/	/ax g eh n/
AJAX	/ey jh ae k s/	/ey jh ae k s/
ALASKA	/ax l ae s k ax/	/ax l ae s k ax/
ALERT	/ax l er t/	/ax l er td/
ALERTS	/ax l er t s/	/ax l er ts/

TABLE V

THE SPHINX RESULTS WITH KNOWLEDGE ENHANCEMENTS. RESULTS SHOWN ARE PERCENT-CORRECT (WORD-ACCURACY)

Version	No grammar	Word Pair	Bigram
Baseline	31.1% (25.8%)	61.8% (58.1%)	76.1% (74.8%)
Bilinear Trans.	34.2% (28.6%)	63.1% (59.4%)	78.5% (76.0%)
4F3C	45.6% (40.1%)	83.3% (81.1%)	88.8% (87.9%)
Phonology	50.0% (45.3%)	86.8% (84.4%)	91.2% (90.6%)
Duration	55.1% (49.6%)	85.7% (83.8%)	91.4% (90.6%)

TABLE VI

THE DEFINITION OF THE VERSION ABBREVIATIONS USED IN TABLE V

Version	Description
Baseline	The version in Table I.
Bilinear Trans.	After adding bilinear transform.
4F3C	After adding four feature sets and three codebooks.
Phonology	After all the dictionary and phonological improvements, plus implicit insertion/deletion modeling.
Duration	After integration of word duration probabilities into the Viterbi Search.

Finally, the addition of durational information significantly improved SPHINX's accuracy when no grammar was used, but was not helpful with a grammar. With no grammar, the recognizer must consider many word hypotheses, and word duration modeling can filter out many hypotheses with implausible word durations. On the other hand, when a grammar is used, much more constraint is applied, sharply decreasing the utility of duration. Therefore, in subsequent versions, duration modeling is used only without grammar.

V. CONTEXT MODELING IN SPHINX

Given that we will use hidden Markov models to model speech, one important question is: what unit of speech should an HMM represent? In the previous sections, we have used phones as the fundamental unit of speech. An even more natural unit is words. In this section, we will discuss the strengths and weaknesses of word and phone models, as well as a number of other units proposed by earlier work. Then, we shall propose two new units that will substantially improve the performance of speaker-independent continuous speech recognizers. Finally, we will present comparative results of different variations of these units.

A. *Previously Proposed Units of Speech*

Words are the most natural units of speech because they are exactly what we want to recognize. Word models are able to capture within-word contextual effects, so by modeling words as units, phonological variations can be assimilated. Therefore, when there are sufficient data, word models will usually yield the best performance. However, using word models in large-vocabulary recognition introduces several grave problems. Since training data cannot be shared between words, each word has to be trained individually. For a large-vocabulary task, this imposes too great a demand for training data and memory. Also, for many tasks, it would be convenient to provide the user with the option of adding new words to the vocabulary. If word models were used, the user would have to produce many repetitions of the word, which would be extremely inconvenient. Therefore, while word models are natural and model contexts well, because of the lack of sharing across words, they are not practical for large-vocabulary speech recognition.

In order to improve trainability, some subword unit has to be used. The most commonly used subword units are the phones of English. The implementation of SPHINX we have described thus far is based on phone models. With only about 50 phones in the English language, they can be sufficiently trained with just a few hundred sentences. We have seen that the earlier implementations of SPHINX yielded reasonably accurate results. However, studies [42], [13] have shown that well-trained word models outperform well-trained phone models. This is because phone models assume a phone in any context is equivalent to the same phone in any other context. However, phones are not produced independently, because our articulators cannot move instantaneously from one position to another. Thus, the realization of a phone is strongly affected by its immediate neighboring phones. Another problem with using phone models is that phones in function words, such as *a*, *the*, *in*, *me*, are often articulated poorly, and are not representative instances of the phones. Thus, while word models lack generality, phone models overgeneralize.

Word-dependent phones [12] are a compromise between word modeling and phone modeling. The parameters of a word-dependent phone model depend on the word in which the phone occurs. Like word models, word-dependent phone models can model word-dependent, phonological variations, but they also require considerable training and storage. However, with word-dependent phones, if a word has not been observed frequently, its parameters can be interpolated (or averaged) with those of context-independent phone models. This obviates the need of observing every word in training, and facilitates the addition of new words.

Another alternative—context-dependent phones [20], [12]—is similar to word-dependent phones; instead of modeling phone-in-word, they model phone-in-context. The most commonly used context-dependent model is the triphone model. A *triphone* model is a phone-size model that takes into consideration the left and the right neighboring phones. Triphone modeling is powerful because it models the most important coarticulatory effects, and is much more sensitive than phone modeling. However, the large number of triphones causes them to be poorly trained, in spite of some robustness provided by interpolating with phones. Moreover, some phonetic contexts are quite similar, and triphones cannot take advantage of that.

B. Function-Word Dependent Phones

Function words are typically prepositions, conjunctions, pronouns, articles, and short verbs, such as *the*, *a*, *in*, *are*. Function words are particularly problematic in continuous speech recognition because they are typically unstressed. Moreover, the phones in function words are distorted in many ways. They may be shortened, omitted, or seriously affected by neighboring contexts. Since these effects are specific to the individual function words, explicit modeling of phones in these function words should lead to a much better representation. Function words have caused considerable problems in SPHINX. Function words take up only 4 percent of the vocabulary, or about 30 percent if weighed by frequency, yet they are accountable for almost 50 percent of the errors.

In view of the above analysis, we propose a new speech unit: *function-word-dependent phones*. Function-word-dependent phones are the same as word-dependent phones, except they are only used for function words. This strategy improves the modeling of the most difficult subset of words. Because function words occur frequently in any large-vocabulary task, function-word-dependent phones are readily trainable.

We selected a set of 42 function words (shown in Table VII), for which we felt there were significant word-dependent coarticulatory effects, as well as adequate training data. A few of these words are not usually considered function words, but were appropriate for this task.

TABLE VII
THE LIST OF 42 FUNCTION WORDS THAT SPHINX MODELS SEPARATELY

A	ALL	AND	ANY	ARE	AT	BE
BEEN	BY	DID	FIND	FOR	FROM	GET
GIVE	HAS	HAVE	HOW	IN	IS	IT
LIST	MANY	MORE	OF	ON	ONE	OR
SHOW	THAN	THAT	THE	THEIR	TO	USE
WAS	WERE	WHAT	WHY	WILL	WITH	WOULD

C. Generalized Triphones

Although triphones model the most important coarticulatory effects, they are sparsely trained and consume substantial memory. We now describe a technique to deal with these problems by combining similar triphones. This approach is justified by the fact that some phones have the same effect on neighboring phones [15]. By merging similar triphones, we both improve the trainability and reduce the memory usage.

We created *generalized triphones* by merging contexts with an agglomerative clustering procedure [43].

1) Generate an HMM for every triphone context.
2) Create clusters of triphones, with each cluster consisting of one triphone initially.
3) Find the *most similar* pair of clusters that represents the same phone, and merge them together.
4) For each pair of clusters, consider moving every element from one to the other.
   i) Move the element if the resulting configuration is an improvement.
   ii) Repeat until no such moves are left.
5) Until some convergence criterion is met, go to step 2.

To determine the similarity between two models, we use the following distance metric:

$$D(a, b) = \frac{\left(\prod_i (P_a(i))^{N_a(i)}\right) \cdot \left(\prod_i (P_b(i))^{N_b(i)}\right)}{\prod_i (P_m(i))^{N_m(i)}} \tag{6}$$

where $D(a, b)$ is the distance between two models of the same phone in context a and b. $P_a(i)$ is the output probability of codeword i in model a, and $N_a(i)$ is the forward-backward count of codeword i in model a. m is the merged model obtained by adding N_a and N_b. In measuring the distance between the two models, we only consider the output probabilities and ignore the transition probabilities, which are of secondary importance.

Equation (6) measures the ratio between the probability that the individual distributions generated the training data and the probability that the combined distribution generated the training data. This ratio is consistent with the maximum-likelihood criterion used in the forward-backward algorithm. This distance metric is equivalent to, and was motivated by, entropy clustering used by [44] and [28].

This context generalization algorithm provides the ideal means for finding the equilibrium between trainability and sensitivity. Given a fixed amount of training data, it is possible to find the largest number of trainable detailed models. Armed with this technique, we could attack any problem and find the "right" number of models that are as sensitive and trainable as possible.

D. Smoothing Detailed Models

While the detailed models introduced in the previous sections are more accurate models of acoustics-phonetics, they are less robust because many output probabilities will be zeros, which can be disastrous to recognition. We could intelligently replace the zeros with nonzero probabilities by combining these detailed models with other more robust ones. For example, we could combine the function-word-dependent phone models or the generalized triphone models with the robust context-independent phone models.

An ideal solution for weighting different estimates of the same event is *deleted interpolated estimation* [45]. Deleted interpolation weighs each distribution according to its ability to predict unseen data. By equating these weights to transition probabilities on parallel transitions, the interpolation problem is transformed into an HMM problem, and the weights are learned by the forward-backward algorithm.

In our implementation for training detailed (function-word-dependent and generalized triphone) models, we first initialized the detailed models with the general (context-independent) models. Two iterations of the normal forward-backward algorithm were run using detailed modeling. During the last iteration, we divided the data into two blocks, and maintained separate output and transition counts for each block. After the end of the last iteration, 100 iterations of deleted interpolation were run to combine:

- a detailed model (function-word-dependent or generalized triphone),
- a general model (context-independent phone models—the counts for a general model are the sum of the counts in all the detailed models that correspond to the general model),
- a uniform distribution.

Thus, this procedure not only combined detailed (but less robust) models with robust (but less detailed) models, but also smoothed the distribution using the uniform distribution. The summary of the entire training procedure is illustrated in Fig. 2.

E. Results

Table VIII shows that the direct modeling of phones in function words substantially reduced errors. Table IX gives the number of errors (substitutions + deletions + insertions) made by SPHINX (context-independent models, no grammar) with and without the use of function-word-dependent phone models. With function-word-dependent phone modeling, function word errors are cut by 27 percent, which accounts for almost all of the improvement from 45.3 to 53.4 percent accuracy.

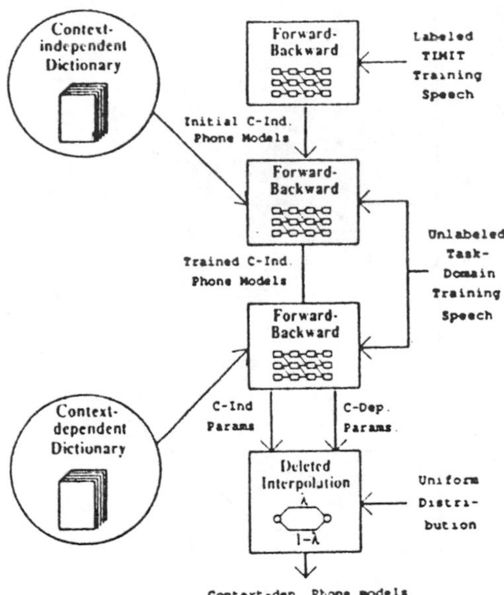

Fig. 2. The training procedure in SPHINX.

TABLE VIII
IMPROVEMENT FROM FUNCTION-WORD-DEPENDENT PHONE MODELING AND GENERALIZED TRIPHONE MODELING. RESULTS SHOWN ARE PERCENT-CORRECT (WORD-ACCURACY)

Version	Models	No grammar	Word pair	Bigram
Context-ind.	48	55.1% (49.6%)	86.8% (84.4%)	91.2% (90.6%)
+Fnwd-dep.	153	62.9% (57.0%)	90.6% (87.9%)	93.8% (93.0%)
+Gen. Triphones	1076	74.2% (70.6%)	94.7% (93.7%)	96.2% (95.8%)

TABLE IX
NUMBER OF FUNCTION WORD ERRORS AND NONFUNCTION-WORD ERRORS WITH AND WITHOUT FUNCTION-WORD-DEPENDENT PHONE MODELING. CONTEXT-INDEPENDENT MODELS WERE USED WITHOUT GRAMMAR

Model Type	Function Word Errors	Other Errors
Context-ind.	357	350
CI+fnwd-dep.	261	334

As indicated in Table VIII, generalized triphone modeling led to another substantial improvement. We ran the agglomerative clustering algorithm to reduce 2381 triphones to 1000 generalized triphones. Combined with function-word-dependent phones, there were a total of 1076 models.

More detailed descriptions and results on contextual modeling can be found in [15] and [46].

VI. SUMMARY OF RESULTS

Fig. 3 shows improvements from all versions of SPHINX described in this paper. The six versions in Fig. 3 correspond to the following descriptions with incremental improvements:

1) the baseline system, which uses only LPC cepstral parameters in one codebook;

2) the addition of differenced LPC cepstral coefficients, power, and differenced power in one codebook;

3) all four feature sets were used in three separate

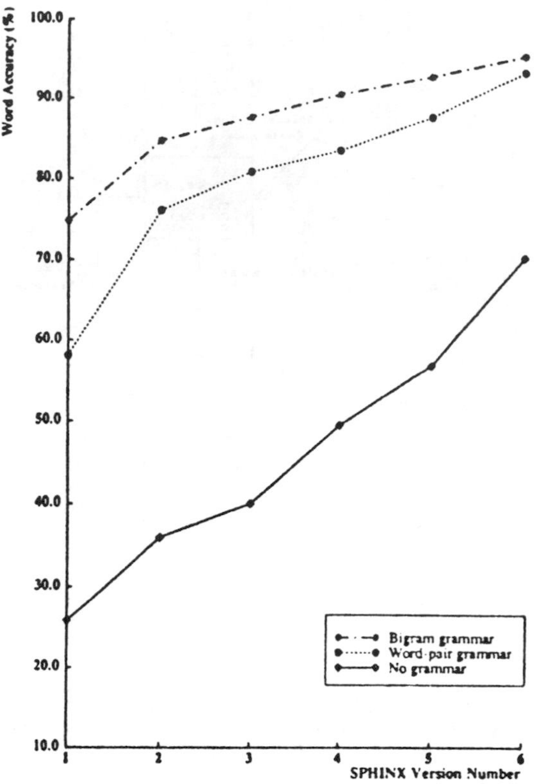

Fig. 3. Results of five versions of SPHINX.

codebooks (this version was reported in [47], the first description of the SPHINX System;

4) tuning of phone models and the pronunciation dictionary, and the use of word duration modeling;

5) function word dependent phone modeling (this version was reported in [48]); and

6) generalized triphone modeling (this version was reported in [15] and [49].

Table X shows the word accuracy, gender, and geographical distribution of the 15 testing speakers. Although the performance appears to vary from speaker to speaker, this variability is not predictable from the speaker's gender or dialect.

VII. Conclusion

We have described SPHINX—a hidden Markov model-based system for large-vocabulary speaker-independent continuous speech recognition. On the one hand, HMM's perform better with detailed models. On the other hand, HMM's need considerable training. This need is accentuated in large-vocabulary speaker-independence, and discrete HMM's. However, given a fixed amount of training, model specificity and model trainability pose two incompatible goals. More specificity usually reduces trainability, and increased trainability usually results in over generality.

Thus, our work can be viewed as finding an equilibrium between specificity and trainability. To improve trainability, we used one of the largest speaker-independent speech databases. To facilitate sharing between models, we used deleted interpolation to combine robust models with detailed ones. By combining poorly trained (context-dependent, generalized context, function-word-dependent speaker-dependent) models with well-trained (context-independent speaker-independent, uniform) models, we improved trainability through sharing.

TABLE X
SPHINX Word Accuracy by Speakers. "Moved" Means that the Speaker Grew Up in More than One Region. Results Shown are Word Accuracy

Initials	Gender	Dialect	No Grammar	Word Pair	Bigram
bcg	F	Moved	61.7%	91.9%	97.7%
sah	F	New Eng.	61.4%	91.0%	94.4%
ljd	F	North Mid.	67.3%	93.7%	98.2%
lmk	F	South	71.3%	96.6%	96.6%
awf	F	South	73.9%	94.4%	95.5%
dpk	M	New Eng.	65.5%	90.2%	93.9%
dab	M	New Eng.	71.3%	95.5%	98.5%
dlc	M	North Mid.	92.6%	100.0%	100.0%
gwt	M	Northern	83.2%	96.4%	97.6%
ctm	M	Northern	72.7%	89.3%	92.9%
jfc	M	NYC	61.2%	93.4%	88.9%
sjk	M	NYC	80.3%	95.1%	96.3%
ctt	M	South	73.6%	94.3%	98.9%
bth	M	Western	69.8%	97.7%	96.6%
jfr	M	Western	62.0%	88.1%	92.4%

To improve specificity, we used multiple codebooks of various LPC-derived features, and integrated external knowledge sources into the system. We also improved the phone set to include multiple representations of some phones, and introduced the use of function-word-dependent phone modeling and generalized triphone modeling.

Through these techniques we have demonstrated that large-vocabulary speaker-independent continuous speech recognition is feasible. We believe that with a powerful learning paradigm, the performance of a system can always be improved with more training data, subject to our ability to make the models more sophisticated. The sophisticated modeling techniques introduced in this paper reduced the error rate of our baseline system by as much as 85 percent, resulting in accuracies of 71, 94, and 96 percent for a 997-word vocabulary with grammars of perplexity 997, 60, and 20.

Acknowledgment

The authors wish to thank the members of the Carnegie Mellon Speech Group. In particular, we would like to acknowledge Hwang, R. Bisiani, and J. Polifroni. We would also like to thank P. Brown and R. Schwartz for helpful discussions, suggestions, and critique. Finally, we thank R. Taylor for reading drafts of this paper.

References

[1] B. T. Lowerre, "The HARPY speech recognition system," Ph.D. dissertation, Comput. Sci. Dep., Carnegie Mellon Univ., Apr. 1976.

[2] J. G. Wilpon, L. R. Rabiner, and A. Bergh, "Speaker-independent isolated word recognition using a 129-word airline vocabulary," *J. Acoust. Soc. Amer.* vol. 72, no. 2, pp. 390-396, Aug. 1982.

[3] R. A. Cole, R. M. Stern, M. S. Phillips, S. M. Brill, P. Specker, and A. P. Pilant, "Feature-based speaker independent recognition of English letters," presented at the IEEE Int. Conf. Acoust., Speech, Signal Processing, Oct. 1983.

[4] F. Jelinek *et al.*, "A real-time, isolated-word, speech recognition system for dictation transcription," in *Proc. IEEE Int. Conf. Acoust., Speech, Signal Processing*, Mar. 1985.

[5] D. B. Paul, R. P. Lippmann, Y. Chen, and C. Weinstein, "Robust HMM-based techniques for recognition of speech produced under stress and in noise," *Speech Tech.*, Apr. 1986.

[6] Y. L. Chow, M. O. Dunham, O. A. Kimball, M. A. Krasner, G. F. Kubala, J. Makhoul, S. Roucos, and R. M. Schwartz, "BYBLOS: The BBN continuous speech recognition system," in *Proc. IEEE Int. Conf. Acoust., Speech, Signal Processing*, Apr. 1987, pp. 89-92.

[7] L. R. Rabiner, J. G. Wilpon, and F. K. Soong, "High performance connected digit recognition using hidden Markov models," presented at the IEEE Int. Conf. Acoust., Speech, Signal Processing, Apr. 1988.

[8] S. E. Levinson, A. E. Rosenberg, and J. L. Flanagan, "Evaluation of a word recognition system using syntax analysis," presented at the IEEE Int. Conf. Acoust., Speech, Signal Processing, Apr. 1977.

[9] B. T. Lowerre, "Dynamic speaker adaptation in the Harpy speech recognition system," presented at the IEEE Int. Conf. Acoust., Speech, Signal Processing, Apr. 1977.

[10] L. R. Bahl, R. Bakis, P. S. Cohen, A. G. Cole, F. Jelinek, B. L. Lewis, and R. L. Mercer, "Speech recognition of a natural text read as isolated words," presented at the IEEE Int. Conf. Acoust., Speech, Signal Processing, Apr. 1981.

[11] A. E. Rosenberg, L. R. Rabiner, J. Wilpon, and D. Kahn, "Demisyllable-based isolated word recognition system," *IEEE Trans. Acoust., Speech, Signal Processing*, vol. ASSP-31, pp. 713-726, June 1983.

[12] Y. L. Chow, R. Schwartz, S. Roucos, O. Kimball, P. Price, F. Kubala, M. Dunham, M. Krasner, and J. Makhoul, "The role of word-dependent coarticulatory effects in a phoneme-based speech recognition system," presented at the IEEE Int. Conf. Acoust., Speech, Signal Processing, Apr. 1986.

[13] D. B. Paul and E. A. Martin, "Speaker stress-resistant continuous speech recognition," presented at the IEEE Int. Conf. Acoust., Speech, Signal Processing, Apr. 1988.

[14] P. J. Price, W. Fisher, J. Bernstein, and D. Pallett, "A database for continuous speech recognition in a 1000-word domain," presented at the IEEE Int. Conf. Acoust., Speech, Signal Processing, Apr. 1988.

[15] K. F. Lee, "Large-vocabulary speaker-independent continuous speech recognition: The SPHINX system," Ph.D. dissertation, Comput. Sci. Dep., Carnegie Mellon Univ., Apr. 1988.

[16] ——, *Automatic Speech Recognition: The Development of the SPHINX System*. Boston, MA: Kluwer Academic, 1989.

[17] L. R. Bahl, R. Bakis, P. S. Cohen, A. G. Cole, F. Jelinek, B. L. Lewis, and R. L. Mercer, "Recognition results with several experimental acoustic processors," presented at the IEEE Int. Conf. Acoust., Speech, Signal Processing, Apr. 1979.

[18] L. R. Rabiner, S. E. Levinson, and M. M. Sondhi, "On the application of vector quantization and hidden Markov models to speaker-independent, isolated word recognition," *Bell Syst. Tech. J.*, vol. 62, no. 4, pp. 1075-1105, Apr. 1983.

[19] L. R. Bahl, F. Jelinek, and R. Mercer, "A maximum likelihood approach to continuous speech recognition," *IEEE Trans. Pattern Anal. Machine Intell.*, vol. PAMI-5, pp. 179-190, Mar. 1983.

[20] R. Schwartz, Y. Chow, O. Kimball, S. Roucos, M. Krasner, and J. Makhoul, "Context-dependent modeling for acoustic-phonetic recognition of continuous speech," presented at the IEEE Int. Conf. Acoust., Speech, Signal Processing, Apr. 1985.

[21] J. D. Markel, and A. H. Gray, *Linear Prediction of Speech*. Berlin: Springer-Verlag, 1976.

[22] K. Shikano, K. Lee, and D. R. Reddy, "Speaker adaptation through vector quantization," presented at the IEEE Int. Conf. Acoust., Speech, Signal Processing, Apr. 1986.

[23] L. R. Rabiner, K. C. Pan, F. K. Soong, "On the performance of isolated word speech recognizers using vector quantization and temporal energy contours," *AT&T Bell Lab. Tech. J.*, vol. 63, no. 7, pp. 1245-1260, Sept. 1984.

[24] Y. Linde, A. Buzo, and R. M. Gray, "An algorithm for vector quantizer design," *IEEE Trans. Commun.*, vol COM-28, pp. 84-95, Jan. 1980.

[25] L. E. Baum, "An inequality and associated maximization technique in statistical estimation of probabilistic functions of Markov processes," *Inequalities*, vol. 3, pp. 1-8, 1972.

[26] J. K. Baker, "The DRAGON system—An overview," *IEEE Trans. Acoust., Speech, Signal Processing*, vol. ASSP-23, pp. 24-29, Feb. 1975.

[27] F. Jelinek, "Continuous speech recognition by statistical methods," *Proc. IEEE*, vol. 64, pp. 532-556, Apr. 1976.

[28] P. Brown, "The acoustic-modeling problem in automatic speech recognition," Ph.D. dissertation, Comput. Sci. Dep., Carnegie Mellon Univ., May 1987.

[29] W. M. Fisher, V. Zue, J. Bernstein, and D. Pallett, "An acoustic-phonetic data base," presented at the 113th Meet. Acoust. Soc. Amer., May 1987.

[30] A. Rudnicky, L. Baumeister, K. DeGraaf, and E. Lehmann, "The lexical access component of the CMU continuous speech recognition system," presented at the IEEE Int. Conf. Acoust., Speech, Signal Processing, Apr. 1987.

[31] D. Pallett, "Test procedures for the March 1987 DARPA benchmark tests," in *Proc. DARPA Speech Recog. Workshop*, Mar. 1987, pp. 75-78.

[32] E. Zwicker, "Subdivision of the audible frequency range into critical bands (Frequenzgruppen)," *J. Acoust. Soc. Amer.*, vol. 33, p. 248, Feb. 1961.

[33] S. B. Davis and P. Mermelstein, "Comparison of parametric representations of monosyllabic word recognition in continuously spoken sentences," *IEEE Trans. Acoust., Speech, Signal Processing*, vol. ASSP-28, pp. 357-366, Aug. 1980.

[34] K. Shikano, "Evaluation of LPC spectral matching measures for phonetic unit recognition," Tech. Rep., Comput. Sci. Dep., Carnegie Mellon Univ., May 1985.

[35] A. V. Oppenheim and D. H. Johnson, "Discrete representation of signals," *Proc. IEEE*, vol. 60, pp 681-691, June 1972.

[36] G. Ruske, "Auditory perception and its application to computer analysis of speech," in *Computer Analysis and Perception*, Auditory Signals, Vol. II, C. Y. Suen and R. De Mori, Eds. Boca Raton, FL: CRC Press, 1982.

[37] S. Furui, "Speaker-independent isolated word recognition using dynamic features of speech spectrum," *IEEE Trans. Acoust., Speech, Signal Processing*, vol. ASSP-34, pp. 52-59, Feb. 1986.

[38] A. H. Waibel, "Prosody and speech recognition," Ph.D. dissertation, Comput. Sci. Dep., Carnegie Mellon Univ., Oct. 1986.

[39] V. N. Gupta, M. Lennig, and P. Mermelstein, "Integration of acoustic information in a large vocabulary word recognizer," in *Proc. IEEE Int. Conf. Acoust., Speech, Signal Processing*, Apr. 1987, pp. 697-700.

[40] M. J. Russel and R. K. Moore, "Explicit modeling of state occupancy in hidden Markov models for automatic speech recognition," in *Proc. IEEE Int. Conf. Acoust., Speech, Signal Processing*, Apr. 1985, pp. 5-8.

[41] S. E. Levinson, "Continuously variable duration hidden Markov models for automatic speech recognition," *Comput. Speech Language*, pp. 29-45, 1986.

[42] L. R. Bahl, P. F. Brown, P. V. De Souza, and R. L. Mercer, "Acoustic Markov models used in the Tangora speech recognition system," presented at the IEEE Int. Conf. Acoust., Speech, Signal Processing, Apr. 1988.

[43] R. O. Duda and P. E. Hart, *Pattern Classification and Scene Analysis*. New York: Wiley, 1973.

[44] J. M. Lucassen and R. L. Mercer, "An information theoretic approach to the automatic determination of Phonemic baseforms," in *Proc. IEEE Int. Conf. Acoust., Speech, Signal Processing*, 1984.

[45] F. Jelinek and R. L. Mercer, "Interpolated estimation of Markov source parameters from sparse data," in *Pattern Recognition in Practice*, E. S. Gelsema and L. N. Kanal, Eds. Amsterdam, The Netherlands: North-Holland, 1980, pp. 381-397.

[46] K. F. Lee, "Context-dependent phonetic hidden Markov models for continuous speech recognition," submitted to the *IEEE Trans. Acoust., Speech, Signal Processing*.

[47] "Towards speaker-independent continuous speech recognition," presented at the 1987 NATO ASI Speech Recogn. Dialog Understanding, July 1987.

[48] K. F. Lee and H. W. Hon, "Large-vocabulary speaker-independent continuous speech recognition," in *Proc. IEEE Int. Conf. Acoust., Speech, Signal Processing*, Apr. 1988.

[49] K. F. Lee, "On large-vocabulary speaker-independent fcontinuous speech recognition," *J. Euro. Assoc. Signal Processing (Speech Communications)*, no. 7, pp. 375-379, Dec. 1988.

Kai-Fu Lee (S'85-M'88) was born in Taipei, Taiwan, in 1961. He received the A.B. degree (summa cum laude) in computer science from Columbia University, New York, NY, in 1983, and the Ph.D. degree in computer science from Carnegie Mellon University, Pittsburgh, PA, in 1988.

Since May 1988 he has been a Research Computer Scientist at Carnegie Mellon, where he currently directs the speech recognition effort within the speech group. His current research interests include automatic speech recognition, spoken language systems, artificial intelligence, and neural networks.

Dr. Lee is a member of Phi Beta Kappa, Sigma Xi, the Acoustical Society of America, and the American Association of Artificial Intelligence.

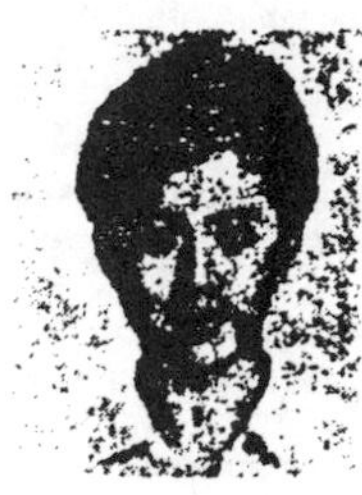

Hsiao-Wuen Hon was born on May 31, 1963. He received the B.S. degree in electrical engineering from National Taiwan University in 1985.

Since 1986 he has been a Ph.D. student in the Computer Science Department, Carnegie-Mellon University, Pittsburgh, PA, where he is involved in speech research. From 1985 to 1986 he was a full-time Teaching Assistant at the Department of Computer Science and Information Engineering, National Taiwan University. His research interests include speech recognition, artificial intelligence, neural networks, pattern recognition, stochastical modeling, and signal processing.

Raj Reddy (F'83) is University Professor of Computer Science and Robotics, and Director of the Robotics Institute at Carnegie Mellon University. His current research activities involve the study of artificial intelligence, including speech, vision, and robotics; man/machine communication; applications specific computer architectures; and rapid prototyping. Prior to joining Carnegie Mellon's Department of Computer Science in 1969, he was an Assistant Professor of Computer Science at Stanford University. He also served as an Applied Science Representative for International Business Machines Corporation (IBM) in Sydney, Australia. Currently he is the Chairman for the DARPA Information Science and Technology (ISAT) Study Group; and a member of the Academic Advisory Panel for the Technology Transfer Intelligence Committee (TTIC) and the Computer Science and Technology Board of the National Research Council.

Dr. Reddy is a Fellow of the Acoustical Society of America; member of the National Academy of Engineering; and President of the American Association for Artificial Intelligence (1987-1989). He was presented the Legion of Honor, France's highest honor, by President Mitterrand of France in 1984.

ATR HMM-LR CONTINUOUS SPEECH RECOGNITION SYSTEM

Toshiyuki HANAZAWA, Kenji KITA, Satoshi NAKAMURA†,
Takeshi KAWABATA and Kiyohiro SHIKANO

ATR Interpreting Telephony Research Laboratories
Seika-chou, Souraku-gun, Kyoto 619-02, JAPAN

ABSTRACT

This paper describes an improvement of the HMM-LR continuous speech recognizer using multiple codebooks, HMM state duration control and fuzzy vector quantization. The system recognizes Japanese phrases (Bunsetsu) according to a context-free grammar including 1,035 words. In speaker dependent condition, a phrase recognition rate of 88.4 % (99.0 % for the top five candidates) was attained. The system was also tested with speaker adaptation based on a codebook mapping algorithm[8]. An average speaker adapted phrase recognition rate of 81.6 % (98.0 % for the top five candidates) was attained.

1. INTRODUCTION

HMM (Hidden Markov Model) is a powerful stochastic model to cope with acoustical variations of speech. It has been developed for continuous speech recognition[1][2][3][4]. In particular, phone-based HMM approaches are widely applied to large vocabulary continuous speech recognition systems.

The ATR continuous speech recognition system, HMM-LR[5], is based on HMM phone modeling and generalized LR parsing[6]. Generalized LR parsing is an extension of LR parsing used for handling arbitrary context-free grammars. Hereafter, this Generalized LR parser is referred to as LR parser for short. In this system, the LR parsing mechanism is used to quickly predict phones according to a context-free grammar. HMM phone verifiers are driven directly by the LR parser to verify predicted phones. For accurate phone recognition, HMM state duration control and multiple codebooks[7] are used. A speaker adaptation algorithm[8] based on fuzzy VQ codebook mapping is also used.

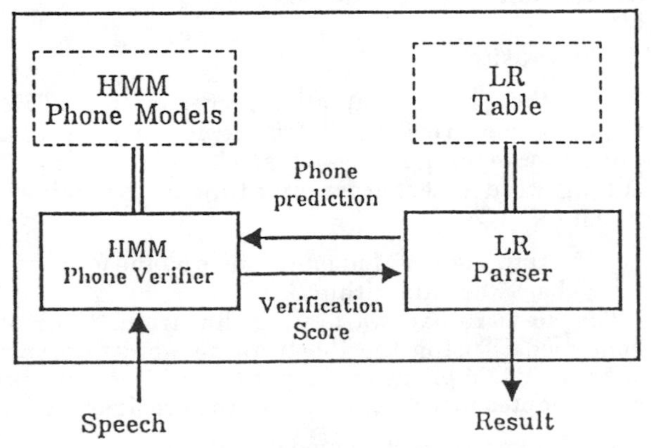

Fig.1 HMM-LR continuous speech recognition system

†Central Research Laboratories, SHARP Corporation

2. HMM-LR CONTINUOUS SPEECH RECOGNITION SYSTEM

2.1 System overview

The schematic diagram of the HMM-LR continuous speech recognition system is shown in Fig 1. The system consists of a predictive LR parser, and HMM phone verifiers. The predictive LR parser is based on the generalized LR parser reported in [6], and is used for phone prediction. The parser is guided by an LR table which is precompiled from context-free grammar rules. In the predictive LR parsing mechanism, the LR table is used to predict the next phone quickly.

The actual recognition process is as follows. First, the parser picks up all phones predicted by the initial state of the LR table. Next, the system invokes the HMM models of these predicted phones to verify their existence. The parser then proceeds to the next state in the LR table. During this process, all possible parsing branches are executed in parallel, and partial parsing branches are pruned by HMM likelihood score.

High recognition performance is attained by driving the HMM phone verifiers directly without any intervening structure such as a phone lattice. A more detailed algorithm of the system is presented in [5].

2.2 HMM phone model

HMM phone models based on discrete HMM are used as phone verifiers. A three-loop model for consonants and a one-loop model for vowels are trained using each phone data extracted from the ATR isolated word database[9].

2.2.1 Multiple codebooks[7]

To represent phone models with smaller distortion, multiple codebooks are used, where the following parameters are vector-quantized separately.

Originally appeared in *IEEE International Conference on Acoustics, Speech, and Signal Processing*, IEEE, April, 1990.

1) Spectrum(WLR[10]),
2) LPC cepstral difference,
3) power.

With multiple codebooks, multiple speech features can be quantized without increasing VQ distortion.

2.2.2 Duration control

HMMs are effective in expressing speech data statistically, but phone duration information from speech data is not modeled statistically in the HMM phone models. In order to make a statistical duration model, an HMM state duration control algorithm is introduced as follows,

(step 1) Calculate HMM state duration distribution.
After the HMM training, HMM state duration distribution is determined using the Viterbi alignment for training data. The distribution of HMM state duration is approximated by a Gaussian distribution.

(step 2) Control HMM state duration.
In the recognition phase, state duration control is carried out by adding a state duration penalty. The forward probability controlled by the state duration is computed as follows:

$$\alpha^{(s)}(j,t) = \sum_i \sum_\tau \alpha^{(s)}(i, t-\tau-1) a_{ij} b_{ijv_{t-\tau}}$$

$$\cdot \left(\prod_{k=t-\tau+1}^{t} a_{jj} b_{jjv_k} \right) \cdot \left(d^{(s)}(j,\tau) \right)^{w_2} \qquad (1)$$

, where
$\alpha^{(s)}(i,t)$: forward probability,
a_{ij} : transition probability,
b_{ijv} : output probability,
$d^{(s)}(i,t)$: HMM state duration distribution,
w_2 : constant.

3. HMM speaker adaptation

Two speaker adaptation algorithms are implemented in this system. One is based on fuzzy VQ codebook mapping and the other is based on composite modeling of an adapted model and a speaker dependent model.

3.1 Fuzzy vector quantization[11]

Fuzzy Vector Quantization (fuzzy VQ) represents an input vector as a weighted combination of the code-vectors. Fuzzy VQ is realized as follows:

$$x \rightarrow \sum_{i=1}^{M} m_i v_i \qquad (2)$$

$$m_i = (1/d_i)^{(1/F-1)} / \sum_{k=1}^{M} (1/d_k)^{(1/F-1)} \qquad (3)$$

, where
x : input vector,
m_i : membership function,
v_i : code-vector,
d_i : distance between x and v_i,
M : constant ($\leqq$ codebook size),
F : constant (fuzziness < 1).

Fuzzy VQ is effective not only in codebook mapping for speaker adaptation, but also in HMM parameter smoothing[11] , by representing an input vector as a weighted combination of the code-vectors.

3.2 Speaker adaptation based on codebook mapping[8]

A speaker adaptation algorithm based on fuzzy VQ codebook mapping is realized as follows,

(step 1) Generate VQ codebooks for both speakers.
New speaker A and standard speaker B utter the same words (adaptation training words). Multiple VQ codebooks for spectrum(WLR), LPC cepstral difference and power are generated using the training word utterances from each speaker.

(step 2) Match and make a correspondence histogram.
The new speaker's training word utterances are quantized using fuzzy VQ. The optimal correspondence path between the same word utterances from a new speaker and a standard speaker are determined using the dynamic time warping. A correspondence histogram is made by accumulating the correspondences for fuzzy sets of code-vectors.

(step 3) Alter HMM output probabilities.
Using the correspondence histogram, HMM output probabilities for the standard speaker are changed in order to adapt the standard speaker's code-vectors to the new speaker's code-vectors according to the following equation.

$$b_i^{(a)} = \sum_{j=1}^{K} h_{ij} b_j \qquad (4)$$

, where
$b^{(a)}_i$: HMM output probability for the new speaker,
b_j : HMM output probability for the standard speaker,
h_{ij} : VQ code-vector correspondence histogram,
K : constant ($\leqq$ codebook size).

3.3 Composite model

After the speaker adaptation procedure in 3.2, HMM phone models are trained by the forward-backward algorithm to make a composite model, using the training word utterances according to the following procedure,

(step 1) Train the HMM phone models by the forward-backward algorithm.
The forward-backward algorithm trains the HMM phone models using the the training word utterances, where the HMM phone model parameters are initialized by the adapted models obtained in the previous section.

(step 2) Make a composite model.
A composite model is obtained by mixing the HMM phone model and the adapted phone model as shown in Equation (5).

$$b^{(c)} = w b^{(a)} + (1-w) b^{(d)} \qquad (5)$$

, where $b^{(c)}$ is a composite model parameter, $b^{(a)}$, $b^{(d)}$ are adapted model and dependent model parameters, respectively.

4. Recognition Experiments

The HMM-LR speech recognition system was tested for speaker dependent and speaker adapted conditions.

4.1 Conditions

4.1.1 Speech data

Short Japanese phrases (Bunsetsu) and isolated words from the ATR phonetically labeled speech database[9], uttered by four speakers (three male, one female) were used for recognition experiments and evaluation. This data was used for training and testing as described below,

[HMM training data]
Phones extracted from the 5,240 Important Japanese Word database, and 216 Phonetically Balanced Word database were used for HMM training.

[Speaker adaptation data]
25 or 100 words were extracted from the 216 Word database for speaker adaptation by the fuzzy codebook mapping.

[Test data]
279 Japanese phrases from the database referred to as "The International Conference Secretary Service" were used for testing. The data is uttered phrase by phrase. Examples of phrase-wise utterances are shown in Table 1.

As descried above, HMM phone models were trained using a large vocabulary word database, because the models should be independent of the particular continuous speech task domain.

The data is sampled at 12 kHz, pre-emphasized by $(1 - 0.97z^{-1})$, and windowed using a 256-point Hamming window every 9 msec. Then, 12-order LPC analysis is carried out. Spectrum(WLR[10]), difference cepstrum coefficients, and power are computed. Multiple VQ codebooks for each feature were generated using 216 phonetically balanced words. Hard Vector quantization without the fuzzy VQ was performed for HMM training. Fuzzy vector quantization (*fuzziness = 1.6*) was used for test data.

4.1.2 Grammar

A context-free grammar for Japanese phrases is used in the experiments. The complexity of the grammar is measured by "task entropy" and "phone perplexity"[13]. Task entropy is defined as the logarithm of the number of phrases the grammar can generate. The phone perplexity is defined as the average number of phones predicted at each step. The complexity of the grammar is summarized in Table 2.

The grammar includes 1,035 words and the phone perplexity is 5.9. Assuming that the average word length in phones is three, the word perplexity becomes more than 100.

4.1.3 Modification of HMM duration parameters[14]

As descried in 4.1.1, HMM phone models were trained using the word utterances, whereas the phrase recognition experiments are carried out using continuous speech. Therefore, the speaking rates of the training data and testing data are different. To realize accurate duration control, HMM duration parameters were modified according to the speaking rates of word and phrase utterances.

Table 1. Examples of Japanese phrases (Bunsetsu)
(from the International Conference Secretary Service database)

/daiikkai/ /tsuuyaku/ /deNwa/ /kokusai/
/kaigini/ /saNkano/ /tourokuo/ /gokibousareru/
/katawa/ /shoteino/ /moushikomi/ /youshini/

(You can make a registration for the first international conference on interpreting telephony --------)

Table 2 Grammar complexity

Vocabulary	1,035 words
Task Entropy	17.0
Phone Perplexity	5.9
Estimated Word Perplexity	more than 100

4.2 Speaker dependent experiments

A phrase recognition experiment for the speaker dependent condition was carried out. The result is shown in the top curve of Fig 2. Average phrase recognition rates of 88.4 % for the top candidate and 99.0 % for the top five candidates were attained using the multiple codebooks and the duration control.

Without duration control, the recognition rates are 78.3 % for the top candidate and 94.9 % for the top five candidates (not shown in Fig 2). This result proves that duration control is necessary for accurate continuous speech recognition.

A phone recognition experiment based on phonetic labels was also carried out, resulting in a phone recognition rate of 85.9 % for the top candidate, and 98.9 % for the top five candidates.

4.3 Speaker adapted experiments

A speaker adapted phrase recognition experiment was carried out. One male speaker is selected as a standard speaker and the others (two male and one female) were used for testing speakers. A twenty five-word set and a one hundred-word set extracted from the 216 Phonetically Balanced Word set were used for speaker adaptation training. HMM phone model adaptation was based on the fuzzy VQ code-vector mapping described in 3.2.

The results are shown in Fig 2. Using the 100-word set for adaptation, the average phrase recognition rates are 78.6 % for the top candidate and 97.3 % for the top five candidates. Phone recognition rates are 76.9 % for the top candidate and 97.3 % for the top five candidates. Without speaker adaptation, the average phrase recognition rates were 59.6 % and 84.2 %, respectively.

Moreover, using composite models generated from the adapted models and HMM concatenation trained models, in the case of the 100-word set, the average phrase recognition rates improved to 81.6 % for the top candidate and 98.0 % for the top five candidates.

5. Summary

This paper described the ATR HMM-LR continuous speech recognition system performance. The system can recognize short Japanese phrases (Bunsetsu) using a generalized LR parser and discrete HMM Phone verifiers. For accurate phone recognition, HMM state duration control, multiple codebooks and fuzzy vector quantization were introduced. A speaker adaptation algorithm based on the fuzzy codebook mapping was also incorporated in the system.

Recognition experiments were carried out using Japanese phrases uttered by four speakers (three male and one female). HMM phone models were trained using the ATR isolated word database (5,456 words) for each speaker. A context-free grammar including 1,035 words was adopted for the experiments.

In the speaker dependent mode, average phrase recognition rates of 88.4 % for the top candidate and 99.0 % for the top five candidates were attained. The experiment result proves that the HMM-LR can attain high recognition performance. Without duration control, the phrase recognition rate degraded to 78.3% for the top choice. This shows that duration control is necessary for accurate continuous speech recognition.

In the speaker adaptation mode, the average recognition rates were 81.6 % for the top candidate and 98.0 % for the top 5 candidates. These results, using fuzzy codebook mapping, show that the HMM-LR can attain high recognition performance in a speaker adaptation mode.

Acknowledgment

The authors would like to thank Dr. Akira Kurematsu, president of ATR Interpreting Telephony Research Laboratories for his continuous support of this work. We are also indebted to the members of the Speech Processing Department at ATR Interpreting Telephony Research Laboratories.

References

1) F. Jelinek, : "Continuous Speech Recognition by Statistical Methods", Proc. IEEE, Vol. 64., pp532-556 (1976-4)
2) Y. L. Chow, M. O. Dunham, O. A. Kimball, M. A. Krasner, G. F. Kubala, J. Makhoul, P. J. Price and S. Roucos, : "BYBLOS: The BBN Continuous Speech Recognition System", ICASSP87 pp 89-92, (1987)
3) K-F. Lee, H-W. Hon, M-Y. Hwang, S. Mahajan and R. Reddy, : "The SPHINX Speech Recognition System", ICASSP89, pp445-448 (1989)
4) A. Paeseler and H. Ney, : "Continuous-Speech Recognition Using a Stochastic Language Model", ICASSP89, pp719-722 (1989)
5) K. Kita, T. Kawabata, H. Saito, : "HMM Continuous Speech Recognition Using Predictive LR Parsing", ICASSP89, pp703-706 (1989)
6) M. Tomita, : "A Efficient Augmented-Context-Free Parsing Algorithm", Computational Linguistics, Vol. 13, No. 1-2, January-June, pp31-46, (1987)
7) V.N. Gupta, M. Lennig and P. Mermelstein, : "Integration of Acoustic Information in a Large Vocabulary Word Recognizer", ICASSP87, pp697-700, (1987)
8) S. Nakamura, K. Shikano, : "Speaker Adaptation Applied to HMM and Neural Networks", ICASSP89, pp89-92 (1989)
9) H. Kuwabara, K. Takeda, Y. Sagisaka, S. Katagiri, S. Morikawa, T.Watanabe, : "Construction of a Large-Scale Japanese Speech Database and its Management System", ICASSP89, pp560-563 (1989)
10) M. Sugiyama, K. Shikano, : "LPC Peak Weighted Spectral Matching Measure", Trans., IECEJ., J64-A, No.5.,pp409-416, (1981)
11) H.P. Tseng, M.J. Sabin and E.A. Lee, : "Fuzzy Vector Quantization Applied to Hidden Markov Modeling", ICASSP87, pp 641-644, (1987)
12) R. Schwartz, Y. Chow, S. Roucos M. Krasner and J.Makhoul, : "Improved Hidden Markov Modeling of Phonemes for Continuous Speech Recognition", ICASSP84 ,pp35.6.1-35.6.4
13) T. Kawabata, K. Shikano and K. Kita, : "Task Entropy and Phone Perplexity", The Acoustic Society of Japan Spring Meeting Proc., 3-6-12 pp93-94 (1989)
14) T. Kawabata and K. Shikano, : "Island-Driven Continuous Speech Recognizer Using Phone-Based HMM Word Spotting", ICASSP89 pp461-464 (1989)

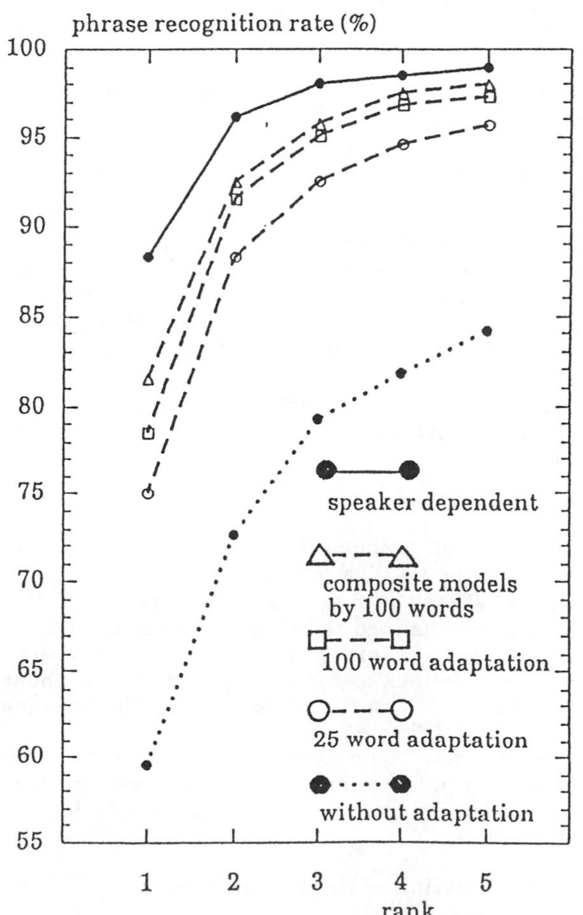

Fig.2 Phrase recognition performance by the HMM-LR continuous speech recognition system

A Word Hypothesizer for a Large Vocabulary Continuous Speech Understanding System

L. Fissore ◇ P. Laface ⋆ G. Micca ◇ R. Pieraccini ◇

◇ CSELT- Centro Studi e Laboratori Telecomunicazioni
Via G. Reiss Romoli 274 - 10148 Torino, Italy
⋆ Dipartimento di Informatica ed Applicazioni
Universitá di Salerno, 84018 Baronissi (Salerno), Italy

Abstract

In the framework of the European ESPRIT project P26 "Advanced algorithms and architectures for signal processing", a continuous speech recognition and understanding system for a thousand word vocabulary has been designed and implemented. It is able to answer to queries put to a geographical data-base in natural Italian language.
This paper presents the recognition component of the system. It can produce a word lattice that is then processed by a syntactic-semantic component. In addition, a linguistic decoder exploiting word-pair constraints has also been experimented. Its results have been compared with those obtained by similar approaches reported in the literature. As a second goal it can produce simpler lattices. The system relies on word preselection through lexical access by means of broad phonetic classes and on Hidden Markov Modeling of sub-word units. Here, the improvements to the basic approach are presented and the system performance is given as a result of the new tests.
The average word accuracy and correct sentence recognition obtained for speaker dependent tests performed by 2 speakers pronouncing 214 sentences are 94.5% and 89.3% respectively. The perplexity of the word-pair language model is 25.

1 Introduction

The basic approach and preliminary results of a continuous speech recognition and understanding system for a thousand word vocabulary have been described in previous papers of the last year ICASSP [4,5]. A functional block diagram of the word recognition subsystem is shown in Fig. 1. A lattice of word hypotheses is produced, where each word has associated its score and time boundaries. The lattice is processed by a score driven syntactic-semantic parser whose computational complexity and performance are, obviously, affected by the score accuracy of the lexical hypotheses and by the correctness of their time alignment [3]. Alternatively, the acoustic-phonetic decoding is integrated with the linguistic decoding by exploiting word-pair constraints to recognise a sentence as the best scored sequence of words. Both approaches, therefore, take advantage of better acoustic-phonetic decoding.

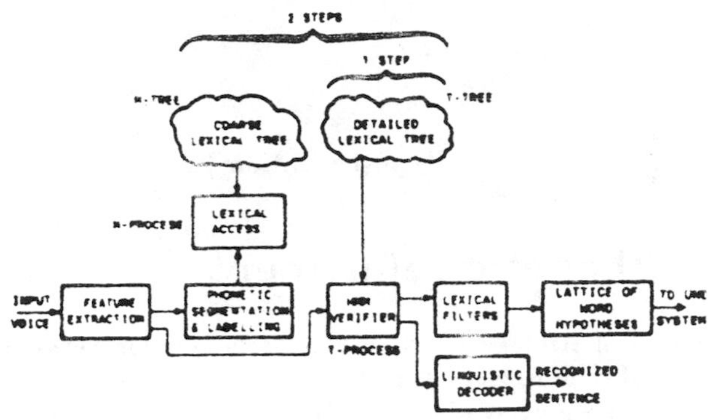

Figure 1: Functional block diagram

An integrated hypothesise and test strategy is used that allows words to be preselected on the basis of their coarse phonetic description and detailed matching to be performed on this reduced set of candidates only.

The **Feature Extraction** module computes a feature vector of 17 Mel-based cepstral coefficients every 10ms. The **Phonetic Classifier and Segmenter** estimates the likelihood that a feature vector belongs to one of 6 broad phonetic classes and produces a small lattice of phonetic segments. This lattice is matched by the **Lexical Access** module against the phonetic transcription of each word of the application vocabulary to constrain the detailed verification which is then performed by the **HMM Verifier**, a decoding process based on HMMs of sub-word units. **Lexical Filters** leave out unlikely word hypotheses.
Section 2 is devoted to the description of an improved system control strategy, in Section 3 a set of features is presented that have been added to the system to obtain better performance, they include different codebooks, new acoustic models and training procedures. Section 4 deals with the linguistic decoder.

CH2673-2/89/0000-0453 $1.00 © 1989 IEEE

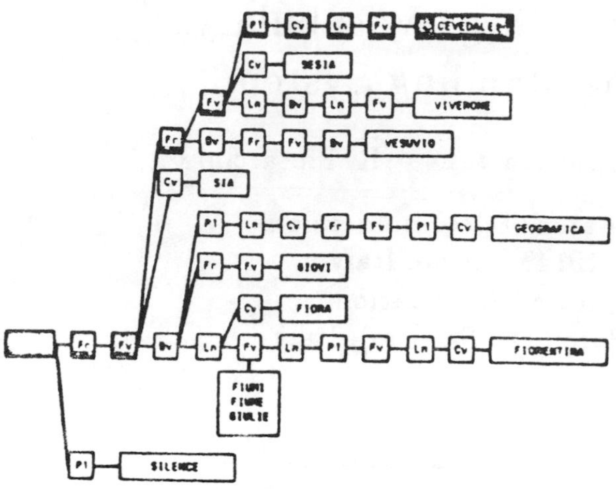

Figure 2: Hypothesisation tree

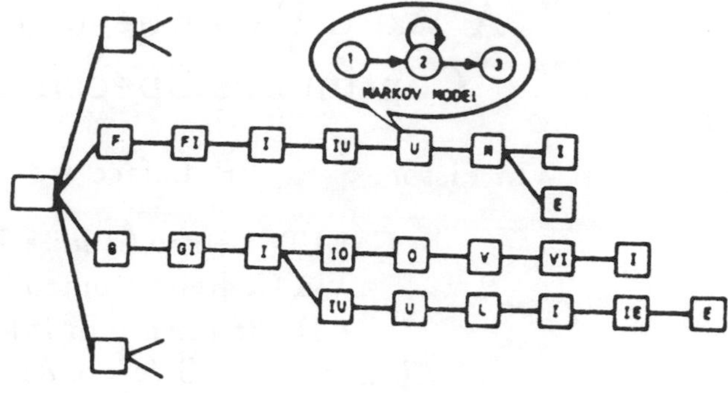

Figure 3: Test tree

2 Phonetic refinement

The control strategy relies on a tight integration between two parallel processes: the Hypothesisation process (Hp) and the Test process (Tp) that dynamically constrain each other.
Both processes have their lexical knowledge represented by a tree. The nodes of the hypothesisation tree (Ht) represent phonemes described in terms of 6 broad phonetic classes, namely plosive (pl), fricative (fr), liquid/nasal (ln), front vowel (fv), central vowel (cv) and back vowel (bv). The nodes of the verification tree (Tt), instead, are the states of HMMs representing detailed phonetic recognition units. A hypothesisation tree and part of the corresponding verification tree are shown in Fig. 2 and in Fig. 3 respectively. The tree search is performed through a beam search strategy. If syntactic constraints are not used, a word can be followed by every word of the vocabulary. Hence, whenever a node in the Ht (as well as in the Tt) has to expand beyond a 'terminal' node - a node associated to a word -, the word is hypothesised and the root node is considered again as a possible expansion.

The control strategy, sketched in Fig. 4, can be summarised as follows:
The input to the Hp process is a lattice of phonetic segments. Each segment can be associated with one or two labels belonging to 6 coarse phonetic classes. A Dynamic Programming algorithm finds the best sequence of segments in the lattice that matches the description of a word in terms of coarse classes, allowing substitution, insertion and deletion errors (SID model).
For a given input segment, the paths corresponding to active Ht nodes are expanded according to the constraints given by the SID model. Node expansion, controlled by a beam search threshold, generates a list of active nodes.
After a segment has been processed by the Hp, the current Ht active nodes constrain the Tp node expansion. To that purpose a mapping between the Ht and the Tt has been established. The Tp expands a Tt node only if its corresponding node in the Ht is active at that particular time frame.
Similarly, after the last frame of the segment has been processed by the Tp, the current Tt active nodes constrain the Hp node expansion. The expansion of an active Ht node, in fact, is not allowed if its pointers refer to Tt nodes that have been deactivated by the beam search strategy.
The Dp receives as input all active Tt terminal nodes for each processed frame. The corresponding word hypotheses are then compared with the list of those already collected at previous frames. If no hypotheses exist in the list having the same word identifier and the same beginning frame, the new hypothesis is inserted, otherwise the new one updates the old one only if it has a better score.

3 Acoustic modeling

This Section describes the results of the experiments referring to new features that have been added to the system in order to obtain better performance.
The effect of several parameters and experimental conditions has been taken into account, in particular:
- use of composite codebooks;
- definition of a new set of sub-word units;
- training of the SID models and of the HMM of the units by using sentences rather than isolated words;
- normalisation of the likelihood of the words;

3.1 Composite codebooks

A composite codebook has been obtained by separately processing voice and silence frames. Voice-silence discrimination is simply obtained by means of a threshold on the energy of each frame. A 7-bit codebook for voice frames and a 4-bit codebook for silence frames have been merged to form a codebook of 144 codewords.

Given a phoneme alphabet $P = (p_1, p_2, \ldots, p_{N_p})$ and a codeword alphabet $C = (c_1, c_2, \ldots, c_{N_c})$, an "efficiency"

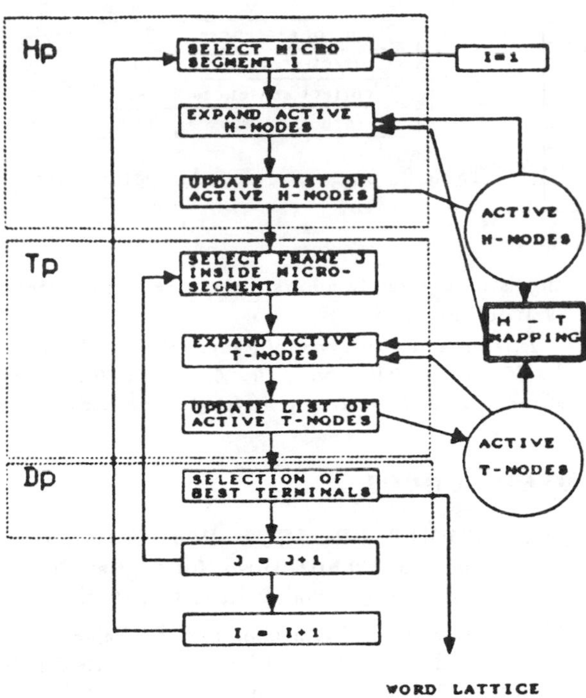

Figure 4: Hypothesize and Test integration

measure of a codebook can be defined as

$$e = (H(P) - H(P|C))/H(P)$$

where $H(P) = \sum_{k=1}^{N_p} prob(p_k) \cdot \log prob(p_k)$ is the entropy of the phonemes (with respect to a given speech training database) and $H(P|C)$ is the entropy of the phoneme alphabet given the codebook.

Codebook efficiency is 0 if $H(P|C) = H(P)$, that is if each codeword carries no information about a phoneme, while it reaches the value of 1 when each codeword identifies a phoneme. For the database used in our experiments to obtain the codebooks, the efficiency of a Single Codebook (SC) of 128 codewords and of a 144 codeword Composite Codebook (CC) is 0.672 and 0.683 respectively. Strong correlation has been observed between the efficiency of a codebook and the recognition rate of the system using that codebook, as can it be verified in Table 1.

3.2 Sub-word units

The inventory of sub-word units used for the detailed verification was defined accounting for a tradeoff between their descriptive capability and the statistical significance of the training database [2]. A new set of units has been defined that is reduced in size (23 stationary and 55 transition units), but it better accounts for coarticulation effects that arise in continuous speech mostly at word junctions.

From the orthographic form of a sentence, through a set of transformation rules, a graph is produced that represents the most frequent coarticulation phenomena. The rules basically account for diphthongs and hiatuses, vowel clusters and function words, diphone deletion, dialectal pronunciations, possible pauses between words. Multiple descriptions of words are also allowed. The Forward-Backward algorithm has been adapted to train the HMM units using the graph representation of the training sentences. HMM models using both discrete and by Gaussian probability density functions have been experimented and compared. The results of these experiments are shown in Table 1. 144 vector quantisation symbols were used in the discrete case, while a multivariate Gaussian with diagonal covariance matrix approximates the actual densities of the cepstral coefficient vector features. Markov models with continuous densities were successfully applied to other recognition tasks [7].

Even for lexical access a graph of broad phonetic descriptions is produced and the SID model is trained by an extension of the Dynamic Programming procedure described in [6]. The training database is composed of the pronunciation of 128 phonetically balanced sentences.

3.3 Probability normalisation

The score of a word hypothesis is computed by subtracting the score of the tree path at the root node to the score attained by the path at the terminal node. We are interested in the probability

$$\max_i P(M_i|\mathbf{O}_{t_1,t_2}) = P(\mathbf{O}_{t_1,t_2}|M_i) \cdot P(M_i)/P(\mathbf{O}_{t_1,t_2})$$

that is the model which gets the highest probability of explaining the observation subsequence $\mathbf{O}_{t_1,t_2}$, from the frame t_1 to the frame t_2. $P(\mathbf{O}_{t_1,t_2}|M_i)$ is computed by the Forward algorithm, while the $P(M_i)$ probabilities, in the present implementation, are uniformly distributed. Finally $P(\mathbf{O}_{t_1,t_2})$ can be derived by the computation of the Forward probabilities by using the scaling coefficients introduced in [9]: $P(\mathbf{O}_{t_1,t_2}) = 1/\Pi_{j=t_1}^{t_2} csk_j$ where csk_j is the scaling coefficient related to frame j. Therefore, the following score

$$P(M_i|\mathbf{O}_{t_1,t_2}) = P(\mathbf{O}_{t_1,t_2}|M_i) \cdot \Pi_{j=t_1}^{t_2} csk_j$$

can be computed in the Tp, by using the forward probability estimation within a word model, while the Viterbi decoding selects the best terminal node for the path expansion to the tree root. This normalisation has the advantage that word scoring becomes less dependent from the acoustic quality of a given observation interval. As a consequence, word hypotheses are more accurate both in their score and in their time boundaries.

3.4 Experimental results

Two different measures, g_1 and g_2, have been defined to assess the quality of lattices [5]. Both are based on the concept of rank r_k of the $k-th$ word of a sentence: g_1 is the average number of words in the lattice corresponding to the correct $k-th$ one that have a better score. g_2 is the average number of words which, in the whole lattice, have a better score than the $k-th$ correct one. In Table 1 these quality measures are given along with the number of missing words

Training	Isolated words			Sentences		
pdf	Discrete		Gaussian	Discrete		Gaussian
codebook	SC	CC		SC	CC	
Missing words	19	18	13	4	3	1
g1	0.59	0.60	0.66	0.66	0.67	0.72
g2	0.36	0.36	0.41	0.41	0.40	0.43
N. of Hyp per lattice	371	343	319	452	423	212

Table 1: Word hypothesiser performance

and the average number of words per lattices. "Isolated words" refers to a training performed by using a database of phonetically balanced pronunciations of isolated words, while "Sentences" refers to a database of 128 continuous speech sentences. The discrete and Gaussian *pdf* have been described in Section 3.2, "SC" and "CC" refer to single and composite codebook respectively. The tests have been performed on a database of 214 sentences, the total number of words in these sentences is 1624. The average number of the Tt tree nodes expanded per frame is 1542, the average number of the Ht tree nodes expanded per frame reduces from 443 to 244 by using the phonetic refinement approach.

4 Linguistic constraints

Let L_{wp} denote a word-pair language model that has been obtained from a set of sentences of the one thousand word geographical database query task. As it is strictly dependent on the sample sentences, another language model, L_{cp}, has been defined, where a set of geographic semantic classes C_k are taken into account. For instance, the set of proper nouns of mountains belongs to the same class. Words that do not belong to any of these semantic classes (i.e. verbs, adjectives, etc.) are modelled according to the L_{wp} language model. If a word-pair $w_a w_b$ exists in L_{wp}, where word w_a (w_b) is a member of the semantic class C_k, the L_{cp} model generalises this pair by including also the set of pairs $w_i w_b$ ($w_a w_i$), where w_i is a member of the class C_k. The perplexity of this language model is 25. The recognition results are given in terms of Word Accuracy computed according to [8]. Preliminary results giving the linguistic decoder performance are summarised in Table 2. These results are obtained by training the new units with continuous sentences, but with discrete *pdf* of the model states. In these experiments the Hp process has been excluded.

5 Conclusions

A set of new features has been described that improve the performance a speech recognition and understanding system. The results show that the use of a reduced set of well trained acoustic models gives good performance in a thousand word vocabulary task. Furthermore, the use of linguistic constraints allows a sentence to be recognized in 89.3% of the cases.

Num. of sentences	214
Correct sentences	191
% correct sentences	89.3
Word accuracy	94.5

Table 2: Linguistic decoder performance

This work has been partially supported by ESPRIT project No.26. The contribution of Dr. A. Jarre to the optimisation of the new set of units is gratefully acknowledged

References

[1] . ESPRIT PROJECT P26, **Advanced Algorithms and Architectures for Signal Processing, Final Report**. Technical Report, , 1988.

[2] M. Cravero, R. Pieraccini, and F. Raineri. **Definition and Evaluation of Phonetic Units for Speech Recognition by Hidden Markov Models** . In *Proc. of the ICASSP*, 1986. sect. 42.3.

[3] M. De Mattia and E. Giachin. **Experimental results on large vocabulary continuous speech understanding**. In *This Conference*, 1989.

[4] L. Fissore, E. Giachin, P. Laface, G. Micca, R. Pieraccini, and C. Rullent. **Experimental results on large vocabulary continuous speech recognition and understanding**. In *Proc. of the ICASSP*, pages 414-417, 1988. sect. S10.2.

[5] L. Fissore, P. Laface, G. Micca, and R. Pieraccini. **Interaction between fast lexical access and word verification in large vocabulary continuous speech recognition**. In *Proc. of the ICASSP*, pages 279-282, 1988. sect. S7.4.

[6] L. Fissore, P. Laface, G. Micca, and R. Pieraccini. **Lexical Access to Very Large Vocabularies**. *IEEE Trans. Acoust., Speech and Signal Processing*, August Issue:, 1989.

[7] L. Fissore and G. Pirani. **Markov Models with continuous densities: computational aspects and results**. In *Proc. of EUSIPCO*, pages 345-348, The Hague, Holland, 1986.

[8] K.F. Lee and H.W. Hon. **Large Vocabulary Speaker Independent Continuous Speech Recognition Using HMM** . In *Proc. of the ICASSP*, pages 123-126, 1988. sect. S3.7.

[9] S.E. Levinson, L.R. Rabiner, and M.M. Sondhi. **Introduction to the Application of the Theory of Probabilistic Functions of a Markov Process to Automatic Speech Recognition**. *Bell System Technical Journal*, 62(4):1035-1074, 1983.

Index

C

D

Credits

The editors would like to thank the publishers and authors for permission to reprint copyrighted material in this volume.

Bahl, L.R., F. Jelinek, and R. Mercer, "A Maximum Likelihood Approach to Continuous Speech Recognition," © 1983, IEEE. Reprinted with permission of the publisher and authors from *IEEE Transactions on Pattern Analysis and Machine Intelligence* PAMI-5(2):179-190, March, 1983.

Bahl, L.R., P.F. Brown, P.V. Souza, and R.L. Mercer, "Speech Recognition with Continuous-Parameter Hidden Markov Models," © 1987. Reprinted with permission of the publisher and authors from *Computer Speech and Language* 2(3/4), September/December, 1987.

Bahl, L.R., P.F. Brown, P.V. de Souze, and R.L. Mercer, "A Tree-Based Statistical Language Model for Natural Language Speech Recognition," © 1989, IEEE. Reprinted with permission of the publisher and authors from *IEEE Transactions on Acoustics, Speech, and Signal Processing* ASSP-37(7):1001-1008, July, 1989.

Baker, J.K., "Stochastic Modeling for Automatic Speech Understanding," © 1975. Reprinted with permission of the publisher and author from *Speech Recognition*, pp 521-541, Academic Press, New York, N.Y., 1975.

Chow, Y.L., M.O. Dunham, O.A. Kimball, M.A. Krasner, G.F. Kubala, J. Makhoul, S. Roucos, and R.M. Schwartz, "BYBLOS: The BBN Continuous Speech Recognition System," © 1987, IEEE. Reprinted with permission of the publisher and authors from *IEEE International Conference on Acoustics, Speech, and Signal Processing*, pp 89-92, April 1987.

Cole, R.A., R.M. Stern, and M.J. Lasry, "Performing Fine Phonetic Distinctions: Templates versus Features," © 1986. Reprinted with permission of the publisher and authors from J.S. Perkitt and D.M. Klatt (eds) *Variability and Invariance in Speech Processes*. Lawrence Erlbaum Assoc., Hillsdale, N.J. 1986.

Davis, S.B. and P. Mermelstein, "Comparison of Parametric Representations of Monosyllabic Word Recognition in Continuously Spoken Sentences," © 1980, IEEE. Reprinted with permission of publisher and authors from *IEEE Transactions on Acoustics, Speech, and Signal Processing* ASSP-28(4):357-366, August, 1980.

DeMori, R., L. Lam, and M. Gilloux, "Learning and Plan Refinement in a Knowledge-Based System for Automatic Speech Recognition," © 1987, IEEE. Reprinted with permission of the publisher and author from *IEEE Transactions on Pattern Analysis and Machine Intelligence* PAMI-9(2):289-305, February, 1987.

Erman, L.D., and V.R. Lesser, "The Hearsay-II Speech Understanding System: A Tutorial," © 1980. Reprinted with permission of publisher and author from *Trends in Speech Recognition*, pp 361–381 chapter 16, Prentice Hall, 1980; Speech Science Publications, 1980. *Trends in Speech Recognition* is currently in print, and available form Speech Science Publications, P.O. Box 24428, Apple Valley, MN.

Fissore, L., P. Laface, G. Micca, and R. Pieraccini, "A Word Hypothesizer for a Large Vocabulary Continuous Speech Understanding System," © 1989, IEEE. Reprinted with permission of the publisher and author from *IEEE International Conference on Acoustics, Speech and Signal Processing*, April 1989.

Gray, R.M., "Vector Quantization," © 1984, IEEE. Reprinted with permission of the publisher and author from *IEEE ASSP Magazine* 1(2):4-29, April 1984.

Hanazawa, T., K. Kita, S. Nakamura, T. Kawabata, and K. Shikano, "ATR HMM-LR Continuous Speech Recognition System," © 1990, IEEE. Reprinted with permission of the publisher and authors from *IEEE International Conference on Acoustics, Speech, and Signal Processing*, April, 1990.

Huang, X.D., and M.A. Jack, "Semi-Continuous Hidden Markov Models for Speech Recognition," © 1989. Reprinted with permission of the publisher and authors from *Computer Speech and Language* 3(3):239–252, July, 1989.

Iso, K. and T. Watanabe, "Speaker-Independent Word Recognition Using a Neural Prediction Model," © 1990, IEEE. Reprinted with permission of the publisher and authors from *IEEE International Conference on Acoustics, Speech and Signal Processing*, April, 1990.

Itakura, F., "Minimum Prediction Residual Principle Applied to Speech Recognition," © 1975, IEEE. Reprinted with permission of the publisher and author from *IEEE Transactions on Acoustics, Speech and Signal Processing* ASSP-23(1):67-72, February, 1975.

Jelinek, F., "The Development of an Experimental Discrete Dictation Recognizer," © 1985, IEEE. Reprinted with permission of the publisher and author from *Proceedings of the IEEE* 73(11):1616-1624, November, 1985.

Jelinek, F., "Self-Organized Language Modeling for Speech Recognition," © 1990. Reprinted with permission of the author.

Klatt, D.H., "Review of the ARPA Speech Understanding Project" © 1977. Reprinted with permission of the publisher from *The Journal of the Acoustical Society of America* 62(6):1324-1366, December, 1977.

Kohonen, T., "The 'Neural' Phonetic Typewriter," © 1988, IEEE. Reprinted with permission of the publisher and author from *IEEE Computer*:11-22, March, 1988.

Lea, W.A., "The Value of Speech Recognition Systems," © 1986. Reprinted with permission of publisher and author from *Trends in Speech Recognition*, chapter 1, Prentice Hall, 1980; Speech Science Publications, 1986. *Trends in Speech Recognition* is currently in print, and available form Speech Science Publications, P.O. Box 24428, Apple Valley, MN.

Lee, K.F., "Context Dependent Phonetic Hidden Markov Models for Continuous Speech Recognition," © 1990, IEEE. Reprinted with permission of the publisher and author from *IEEE Transactions on Acoustics, Speech and Signal Processing*, April 1990.

Lee, K., H.W. Hon, and R. Reddy, "An Overview of the SPHINX Speech Recognition System," © 1990, IEEE. Reprinted with permission of the publisher and authors from *IEEE Transactions on Acoustics, Speech, and Signal Processing*, January, 1990.

Lippman, R.P., "Review of Research on Neural Nets for Speech," c 1989. Reprinted with permission of the publisher (Lincoln Laboratory, Massachusetts Institute of Technology, Lexington, Massachusetts) and author from Neural Computation 1(1), March, 1989.

Lowerre, B.T., and D.R. Reddy, "The Harpy Speech Understanding System," © 1980. Reprinted with permission of publisher and author from *Trends in Speech Recognition*, Prentice-Hall, 1980; Speech Science Publications, 1986. *Trends in Speech Recognition* is currently in print, and available form Speech Science Publications, P.O. Box 24428, Apple Valley, MN.

McDermott, E., H. Iwamida, S. Katagiri, and Y. Tohkura, "Shift-Tolerant LVQ and Hybrid LVQ-HMM for Phoneme Recognition," © 1990, IEEE. Reprinted with permission of the publisher and authors from Readings in Speech Recognition, Morgan Kaufmann Publishers, San Mateo, California, 1990.

Mercier, G. D. Bigorgne, L. Miclet, L. Le Guennec and M. Querre, © 1989. Reprinted with permission of the publisher and authors in IEE Proceedings 136(2):145-154, April, 1989.

Ney, H., "The Use of a One-Stage Dynamic Programming Algorithm for Connected Word Recognition," © 1984, IEEE. Reprinted with permission of publisher and author from *IEEE Transactions on Acoustics, Speech and Signal Processing* ASSP-32(2):263-271, April, 1984.

Paeseler, A., "Modification of Earley's Algorithm for Speech Understanding," © 1987. Reprinted with permission of the publisher and author from *Recent Advances in Speech Understanding and Dialog Systems*. Springer-Verlag, berlin, 1987.

Rabiner, L.R., "A Tutorial on Hidden Markov Models and Selected Applications in Speech Recognition," © 1989, IEEE. Reprinted with permission of the publisher and author from *Proceedings of the IEEE*, 1989.

Rabiner, L.R., S.E. Levinson, A.E. Rosenberg, and J.G. Wilpon, "Speaker-Independent Recognition of Isolated Words using Clustering Techniques," © 1979. Reprinted with permission of publisher and authors from IEEE Transactions on Acoustics, Speech, and Signal Processing ASSP-27(4): 336-349, August, 1979.

Rabiner, L., J.G. Wilpon, and F.K. Soong, "High Performance Connected Digit Recognition Using Hidden Markov Models," © 1989, IEEE. Reprinted with permission of the publisher and authors from *IEEE Transactions on Acoustics, Speech and Signal Processing* 37(8):1214-1225, August, 1989.

Rabiner, L.R. and Levinson, S.E., "Isolated and Connected Word Recognition–Theory and Selected Applications," © 1981, IEEE. Reprinted with permission of the publisher and authors from *The IEEE Transactions on Communications* COM-29(5):621-659, May, 1981.

Reddy, D. R., "Speech Recognition by Machine: A Review," © 1976, IEEE. Reprinted, with permission of publisher and authors, from *Proceedings of the IEEE* 64(4): 502-503, April, 1976.

Roucos, S. and M.O. Dunham, "A Stochastic Segment Model for Phoneme-Based Continuous Speech Recognition, © 1987, IEEE. Reprinted with permission of the publisher and authors from *IEEE International Conference on Acoustics, Speech, and Signal Processing*, pp 73-76. April, 1987.

Sakoe, H., "Two-Level DP-MAtching–A Dynamic Programming-Based Pattern Matching Algorithm for Connected Word Recognition," © 1979, IEEE. Reprinted with permission of the publisher and author from *IEEE Transactions on Acoustics, Speech, and Signal Processing* ASSP-27(6):588-595, December, 1979.

Sakoe, H., and S. Chiba, "Dynamic Programming Algorithm Optimization for Spoken Word Recognition," © 1978, IEEE. Reprinted with permission of the publisher and authors from *IEEE Transactions on Acoustics, Speech, and Signal Processing* ASSP-26(1):43-49, February, 1978.

Sakoe, H., R. Isotani, K. Yoshida, Ki. Iso, and T. Watanabe, "Speaker-Indepedent Word Recognition Using Dynamic Programming Neural Networks," © 1989, IEEE. Reprinted with permission of the publisher and authors from *IEEE Internatinal Conference on Acoustics, Speech, and Signal Processing*, pp 29-32. May, 1989.

Schafer, R.W., and L.R. Rabiner, "Digital Representations of Speech Signals," © 1975, IEEE. Reprinted with permission of publisher and authors from *Proceedings of the IEEE* 63(4):662-667, April, 1975.

Seneff, S. "A Joint Synchrony/Mean-Rate Model of Auditory Speech Processing," © 1988. Reprinted with permission of the publisher and author from *Journal of Phonetics* 16(1):55-76, January, 1988.

Waibel, A., "Prosodic Knowledge Sources for Word Hypothesization in a Continuous Speech Recognition System," © 1987, IEEE. Reprinted with permission of the publisher and author from *ICASSP '87 Proceedings*, pp 20.16.1-20.16.4. IEEE, 1987.

Waibel, A. , T. Hanazawa, G. Hinton, K. Shikano, and K. Lang, "Phoneme Recognition Using Time-Delay Neural Networks," © 1989, IEEE. Reprinted with permission of the publisher and authors from *IEEE International Conference on Acoustics, Speech and Signal Processing*, May, 1989.

Waibel, A., H. Sawai, and K. Shikano, "Consonant and Phoneme Recognition by Modular Constructions of Large Phonemic Time-Delay Neural Networks," © 1989, IEEE. Reprinted with permission of the publisher and authors from *IEEE International Conference on Acoustics, Speech and Signal Processing*, May, 1989.

Watrous, R.L., L. Shastri, and A.H. Waibel, "Learned Phonetic Discrimination Using Connectionist Networks," © 1987. Reprinted with permission of the publisher and authors from European Conference on Speech Technology, pp 377-380. Edinburgh, September, 1987.

Woods, W.A. "Language Processing for Speech Understanding," © 1983. Reprinted with permission of the publisher and author from Computer Speech Processing, Prentice-Hall International, Hemel Hempstead, England, 1983.

Young, S.R., A.G. Hauptmann, W.H. Ward, E.T. Smith, and P. Werner, "High Level Knowledge Sources in Usable Speech Recognition Systems," © 1989. Reprinted with permission of the publisher and author from *Communications of the ACM* 32(2), 1989.

Zue, V.W., "The Use of Speech Knowledge in Automatic Speech Recognition," © 1985, IEEE. Reprinted with permisson of the publisher and author from *Proceedings of the IEEE* 73(11):1602-1615, November, 1985.